Zoran Majkić

Intensional First-Order Logic

Also of Interest

Knowledge Engineering for Modern Information Systems
Methods, Models and Tools
Sharma, Kautish, Agrawal, Madaan, Gupta, Nanda (Eds.), 2022
ISBN 978-3-11-071316-9, e-ISBN 978-3-11-071363-3

Noise Filtering for Big Data Analytics
Bhattacharyya, Ghosh (Eds.), 2022
ISBN 978-3-11-069709-4, e-ISBN 978-3-11-069721-6

Big Data Analytics Methods
Analytics Techniques in Data Mining, Deep Learning and Natural Language Processing
Ghavami, 2019
ISBN 978-1-5474-1795-7, e-ISBN 978-1-5474-0156-7

Big Data Management
Data Governance Principles for Big Data Analytics
Ghavami, 2020
ISBN 978-3-11-066291-7, e-ISBN 978-3-11-066406-5

Advanced Data Management
For SQL, NoSQL, Cloud and Distributed Databases
Wiese, 2015
ISBN 978-3-11-044140-6, e-ISBN 978-3-11-044141-3

Zoran Majkić

Intensional First-Order Logic

From AI to New SQL Big Data

DE GRUYTER

Author
Zoran Majkić
Via Palestro 13
00185 Rome
Italy
majk.1234@yahoo.com

ISBN 978-3-11-099494-0
e-ISBN (PDF) 978-3-11-098143-8
e-ISBN (EPUB) 978-3-11-098146-9

Library of Congress Control Number: 2022940161

Bibliographic information published by the Deutsche Nationalbibliothek
The Deutsche Nationalbibliothek lists this publication in the Deutsche Nationalbibliografie; detailed bibliographic data are available on the Internet at http://dnb.dnb.de.

Cover image: dem10 / E+ / Getty Images
Typesetting: VTeX UAB, Lithuania
Printing and binding: CPI books GmbH, Leck

www.degruyter.com

Dedicated to my daughters
Viviana and Sofia

Calypso, the beautiful goddess, was the first to speak, and said: “Son of Laertes, sprung from Zeus, Odysseus of many devices, would’st thou then fare now forthwith home to thy dear native land! Yet, even so fare thee well. Howbeit if in thy heart thou knewest all the measure of woe it is thy fate to fulfil before thou comest to thy native land thou wouldest abide here and keep this house with me, and wouldest be immortal, for all thy desire to see thy wife for whom thou longest day by day. Surely not inferior to her do I declare myself to be either in form or stature, for in no wise is it seemly that mortal women should vie with immortals in form or comeliness.”
Then Odysseus of many wiles answered her, and said: “Mighty goddess, be not wroth with me for this. I know full well of myself that wise Penelope is meaner to look upon than thou in comeliness and in stature, for she is a mortal, while thou art immortal and ageless. But even so I wish and long day by day to reach my home, and to see the day of my return. And if again some god shall smite me on the wine-dark sea, I will endure it, having in my breast a heart that endures affliction. For ere this I have suffered much and toiled much amid the waves and in war; let this also be added unto that.”
So he spoke, and the sun set and darkness came on.

The Odyssey, book 5, by Homer.

Preface

In "Über Sinn und Bedeutung," Frege concentrated mostly on the senses of names, holding that all names have a sense (meaning). It is natural to hold that the same considerations apply to any expression that has an extension. But two general terms can have the same extension and different cognitive significance. So, general terms, predicates, and sentences all have senses as well as extensions. The same goes for any expression that has an extension, or is a candidate for extension.

The significant aspect of an expression's meaning is its extension. We can stipulate that the extension of a sentence is its truth-value, and that the extension of a singular term is its referent. The extension of other expressions can be seen as associated entities that contribute to the truth-value of a sentence in a manner broadly analogous to the way in which the referent of a singular term contributes to the truth-value of a sentence. In many cases, the extension of an expression will be what we intuitively think of as its referent, although this need not hold in all cases. While Frege himself is often interpreted as holding that a sentence's referent is its truth-value, this claim is counterintuitive and widely disputed. We can avoid that issue in the present framework by using the technical term "extension." In this context, the claim that the extension of a sentence is its truth-value is a stipulation.

"Extensional" is most definitely a technical term. Say that the extension of a name is its denotation, the extension of a predicate is the set of things it applies to, and the extension of a sentence is its truth value. A logic is extensional if coextensional expressions can be substituted one for another in any sentence of the logic "salva veritate," that is, without a change in truth value. The intuitive idea behind this principle is that in an extensional logic the only logically significant notion of meaning that attaches to an expression is its extension. An intensional logics is exactly one in which substitutivity salva veritate fails for some of the sentences of the logic.

The first conception of intensional entities (or concepts) is built into the *possible-worlds* treatment of Properties, Relations and Propositions (PRP)s. This conception is commonly attributed to Leibniz, and underlies Alonzo Church's alternative formulation of Frege's theory of senses ("A formulation of the Logic of Sense and Denotation" in Henle, Kallen and Langer, 3–24, and "Outline of a Revised Formulation of the Logic of Sense and Denotation" in two parts, Nous, VII (1973), 24–33, and VIII, (1974), 135–156). This conception of PRPs is ideally suited for treating the *modalities* (necessity, possibility, etc.) and to Montague's definition of intension of a given virtual predicate $\phi(x_1, \ldots, x_k)$ (a FOL open sentence with the tuple of free variables $(x_1, \ldots x_k)$), as a mapping from possible worlds into extensions of this virtual predicate. Among the possible worlds, we distinguish the *actual* possible world. For example, if we consider a set of predicates, of a given database, and their extensions in different time-instances, then the actual possible world is identified by the current instance of the time.

https://doi.org/10.1515/9783110981438-201

The second conception of intensional entities is to be found in Russell's doctrine of logical atomism. In this doctrine, it is required that all complete definitions of intensional entities be finite as well as unique and noncircular: it offers an *algebraic* way for definition of complex intensional entities from simple (atomic) entities (i. e., algebra of concepts), conception also evident in Leibniz's remarks. In a predicate logics, predicates and open-sentences (with free variables) expresses classes (properties and relations), and sentences express propositions. Note that classes (intensional entities) are *reified*, i. e., they belong to the same domain as individual objects (particulars). This endows the intensional logics with a great deal of uniformity, making it possible to manipulate classes and individual objects in the same language. In particular, when viewed as an individual object, a class can be a member of another class.

The distinction between intensions and extensions is important (as in lexicography [1]), considering that extensions can be notoriously difficult to handle in an efficient manner. The extensional equality theory of predicates and functions under higher-order semantics (e. g., for two predicates with the same set of attributes $p = q$ is true iff these symbols are interpreted by the same relation), i. e., the strong equational theory of intensions, is not decidable, in general. For example, the second-order predicate calculus and Church's simple theory of types, both under the standard semantics, are not even semidecidable. Thus, separating intensions from extensions makes it possible to have an equational theory over predicate and function names (intensions) that is separate from the extensional equality of relations and functions.

Relevant recent work about the intension, and its relationship with FOL, has been presented in [2] in the consideration of rigid and *nonrigid* objects, w. r. t. the possible worlds, where the rigid objects, like "George Washington," and are the same things from possible world to possible world. Nonrigid objects, like "the Secretary-General of United Nations," are varying from circumstance to circumstance and can be modeled semantically by functions from possible worlds to the domain of rigid objects, like intensional entities.

Another approach used in intensional logic programming is a new form of logic programming based on intensional logic and possible worlds semantics, and is a well-defined practice in using the intensional semantics [3]. Intensional logic allows us to use logic programming to specify nonterminating computations and to capture the dynamic aspects of certain problems in a natural and problem-oriented style. The meanings of formulas of an intensional first-order language are given according to intensional interpretations and to elements of a set of possible worlds. Neighborhood semantics is employed as an abstract formulation of the denotations of intensional operators. The model-theoretic and fixed-point semantics of intensional logic programs are developed in terms of least (minimum) intensional Herbrand models. Intensional logic programs with intensional operator definitions are regarded as metatheories.

Some of the important questions about intensional First-order Logic (FOL) was enounced by Melvin Fitting in his 2003 preprint [2]:

> *"What is first-order modal logic for? Since this is obviously not a simple question; perhaps we should begin by asking, what is propositional modal logic for? Here we are on well-explored ground. With propositional modal logic, and its relational semantics, we want to explicate various constructs from natural language, and explore nuances of certain concepts arising in philosophical investigations. We want to model knowledge, at least in an ideal sense. We want to reason about action. And there is another purpose as well, one that has become clearer over the years. In studying propositional modal logics, – primarily those characterized by classes of frames, – we are also studying fragments of classical first-order (and higher-order) logic. This is known as correspondence theory. For this purpose axiomatizability (or not) is a central issue. In addition, axiom systems allow the construction of canonical models, which provides a metamathematical methodology that is uniform across many logics. Details matter a great deal, of course, but the broad outlines of propositional modal logics have been standardized for some time.*
> *But the original question above was, what is first-order modal logic for? What do quantifiers add to the mix?"*

But in his approach, differently from this one, Fitting changes also the syntax of the FOL, by introducing an "extension of" the operator, $\downarrow$, in order to distinguish the intensional entity "*gross domestic product of Denmark,*" and its use in "*the gross domestic product of Denmark is currently greater than gross domestic product of Finland.*" In his approach, if x is an intensional variable, $\downarrow x$ is extensional, while $\downarrow$ is not applicable to extensional variables, different from ours, where each variable (concept) has both intensional and extension. Moreover, in his approach the problem arises because the action of letting x designate, i. e., evaluating $\downarrow x$, and the action of passing to an alternative possible world, that is of interpreting the existential modal operator $\diamond$, are not actions that commute. To disambiguate this, one more piece of machinery is needed as well, which substantially and ad hoc changes the syntax and semantics of FOL, introduces the higher-order modal logics, and is not a conservative extension of Tarski's semantics. In the most recent work in [4, 5] is given an intensional version of first-order *hybrid* logic, which is also a hybridized version of Fitting's intensional FOL, by a kind of generalized models; thus, is different from our approach to a conservative extension of Tarski's semantics to intensional FOL.

Another recent relevant work is presented by I-logic in [6], which combines both approaches to semantics of intensional objects of Montague and Fitting.

In his approach, Fitting followed the Montague tradition, different from my wider approach provided in this book that uses both Montague tradition and algebraic Bealer's approach, and enriched them by a more detailed investigation of modal logics of FOL, and by the way introduced naturally the intensional semantics into traditional extensional FOL with Tarski's semantics and, moreover, how to introduce in such minimal intensional FOL and the "higher level" modal operators. Most relevant for my personal research has been two significant approaches to intensional FOL:

1. Montague's approach based on possible world representation [7, 8, 9, 10, 11], the *intension* of a proposition is a *function* from possible worlds $\mathcal{W}$ to truth-values, and properties and functions from $\mathcal{W}$ to sets of possible (usually not actual) objects.

2. Bealer's approach in [12] to the intensional logic the fundamental entities are *intensional abstracts* or so-called, "that-clauses" and his introduction of intensional algebras.

These two approaches are unified in my approach, with providing a conservative extension of Tarski's semantics to intensional FOL as well.

Quo vadis logic-based AI?

Why this title? I will try to explain it by my relevant research history from 2003 to 2020. At "La Sapienza," Roma, Italy, we had a number of good professors and researches in logic-based AI, and especially in the research group of my PhD advisor, Professor M. Lenzerini (from 94 to 98), who in that period was chief of the PhD programs and research in knowledge basis and AI. In that period, the book [13] of the logic based approach to AI was a reference for my introduction to this field, and my book in some way is a continuation of that approach. I returned again to his department in 2002, 4 years after I finished my PhD thesis, to work for the European interuniversity project of Semantic Web, called SEWASIE project IST-2001-34825. I have written, with initial help of Lenzerini, three or four research papers for this European research program. In that period, Lenzerini was the chief research leader in data integration and it was also the very beginning of the P2P data integration systems, based on the first-order logic and its second-order extensions for the interdatabase mappings. Thus, the whole framework was just in standard extensional logics, which demonstrated a lot of theoretical problems about mutually inconsistent information coming from different sources.

Of course, all my work in this project was just in this working logic framework, but I tried to consider many-valued logics to overcome these problems about the inconsistences and to find a more robust data integration P2P system, trying to overcome the strong (extensional) mapping between databases. When I organized a first short paper with these new ideas, Lenzerini accepted to join with me to write the final version, but from the fact that he published papers with his working group of other professors and researches, he asked me to wait on the decision of this group if they would accept me as new member of this group, and hence authorized to publish the research papers for journals or conferences together.

Unfortunately for me, somebody in his group did not like my participation and Lenzerini was sorry, but promised that if my papers were accepted for the conferences or journals, that department would support all expenses (traveling, participation costs, etc.) for presentations. Their decision explains why, during the 3 years working with his research group for this European project, I have no any publication with them in journals or conferences, and why all such work was done by me only. With economical support by the department of Lenzerini, I published a dozen papers by myself, and I developed clear ideas about new intensional logic to use as a good solution for intensional weak semantic mappings between peer databases.

However, no one in the department followed my ideas, and after the invitation of Director V. S. Subrahmaninan of UMIACS Laboratory of Computer Science at College Park University (Washington, D. C.) in January 2005, I stopped this research for 1 year to dedicate time for mathematical problems about algebra for the generation of aggregates in temporal-probabilistic (TP) databases. We published two papers [14, 15], and I finished this work by a fundamental revision of the erroneous Subrahmaninan's fixed-point semantics of TP-logic programs [16].

In that period, Jack Minker was an Emeritus Professor at the University of Maryland, Department of Computer Science, and I visited him, from the fact that I worked just in his main research AI field where he was a leading authority, to hear what his opinion was regarding current problems in logic-based AI and their applications. Professor Minker was the editor of the book [17] in logic-based AI in 2001, so it was just a good moment to exchange at least the short opinions with him. My intension was to improve the standard database technology of RDB management systems (based on the extensional FOL) with a more general intensional logic framework, with conservative extension of classical RDB in order to support all previously developed RDB applications and be able to support the AI applications. From the fact that various logic-based development frameworks as Prolog, Datalog, Golog, HiLog, etc., has been separated from the mainstream database applications based on RDB, I wanted also to know if there was another analog approach for a wide introduction of logic-based AI into a conservative extension of RDB technology. I understood that there was not any such a large project because AI fields worked differently with very specialized groups of researches to resolve some ad hoc problems. A basic wide approach, with a big business impact and with ambition to improve industrially dominant RDB technology, did not get initiated.

With this impression in mind, from a leading authority at the end of his carrier, after 2006 when I finished my post-PhD experience at UMIACS, I continued to work in this direction alone, toward a new intensional FOL, by integrating Montague's and algebraic Bealer's [12] approaches. The basic result was the publication of the conservative extension of Tarski's semantics to intensional FOL [18], and two-step intensional semantics [19], which guaranteed a conservative extension of current RDB, but with more than 50-year-old technology, toward new IRDB (Intensional RDB). Indeed, in my next Manifesto of IRDB [20], I hoped to find interested research groups and funds to begin the realization of IRDB as a new platform (compatible with all previously developed RDB applications), and also able to support NewSQL for big data, and ready for other AI improvements.

I returned again to Italy and tried to find a venture capital for a new start-up software company, but without success. So, waiting for some opportunity, I dedicated my free time to develop some new ideas on the completion of quantum mechanics (based on some Einstein's ideas) and unification with classical mechanics and general relativity. When I finished this enormous work, published in three books,[1] I returned to the still open problem about "quo vadis logic-based AI," and realized that after all it seems like that now AI is reduced only to the development of algorithms[2]: pattern matching, machine learning, visual recognitions, statistical "intelligent" mining, predictive statistical analysis, etc. It is enough to research in Google about "books in AI," and it seems that everything is about algorithms, and that logic-based AI remains as it was 20 years ago. Within specialized and dedicated conferences and workshops, it appears that logic-based AI has no any significant role in business life and in the development of new software products.

No more logics??

Semantic Web (W3C) continues with ad hoc languages, and database systems still use RDB with some extension to integration with data-federation (extensional integration) and is deeply analyzed in my book [21] in 2014. From such a situation, comes my motivation to write this new book, after the previous theoretical book on *extensional* database integration [21], but now this one is about new intensional FOL for a conservative extension of extensional RDBs, and able to support the intensional DB integration, many-valued AI applications, and a new SQL and vectorial big data management. Moreover, my aim is not only a complete development of the new logic-based theory, but to provide different and fundamental examples for perspective industrial applications as well.

Knowledge representation, strongly connected to the problem if knowledge processing, reasoning and "drawing inferences," is one of the main topics in AI. By reviewing the knowledge representation techniques that have been used by humans, we will be aware of the *importance of language*. The predominant part of the IT industry and user's applications is based on some sublanguage of the standard (extensional) FOL with Tarski's semantics based (only) on the truth; my effort is to pass to a more *powerful evolution of the FOL* able to support the meaning of knowledge as well, by replacing the standard FOL and its DB theory and practice in the IT business. Twenty years after Minker's book (that consists of 24 refereed papers presented at the workshop), it is time for a new book in logic-based AI that is able to substitute old RDB technology in a conservative way to protect the enormous amount of previously developed business applications.

---

1 Soft Computing Applications in Industry, B. Prasad, Z. Majkic (Eds), 2008. ISBN 978-3-540-77464-8, e-ISBN 978-3-540-77465-5; Big Data Integration Theory: Theory and Methods of Database Mappings, Programming Languages and Semantics, Zoran Majkic, 2014. ISBN 978-3-319-04155-1, e-ISBN 978-3-319-04156-8.

2 https://www.guru99.com/ai-machine-learning-books.html,
https://builtin.com/artificial-intelligence/ai-books,
https://link.springer.com/search/page/3?facet-discipline="Computer+Science"&query=Artificial+intelligence+2020 etc.

This book is not a collection of different research papers of different authors but a result of unifying, coherent and complete development of a new Intensional FOL (IFOL) as a result of my personal research in last 15 years with more than 70 % unpublished. Conservative migration from the standard extensional FOL into more powerful IFOL is able to express not only the logic truth but also the sense (meaning) of concepts and is a basic promotion of the formal theory and applications in this new book. Particular attention is given to the *new mathematical concepts of symmetry*, both in logic semantics (predicate compression and ontological encapsulation transformations) and intensional abstract transformations with categorial symmetry. This approach to AI by symmetries, which render *invariant knowledge* during transformations, is as far I know an innovative method in AI (as it was in the development of the laws of physics).

The principal Chapter 1 of this book analyzes the minimal intensional semantic enrichment of the syntax of the FOL language, by unification of different views: Tarskian extensional semantics of the FOL, modal interpretation of quantifiers and a derivation of the Tarskian theory of truth from unified semantic framework based on a recursive compositional theory of meaning. We show that not all modal predicate logics are intensional, and that an equivalent modal of Kripke's interpretation of logic quantifiers in FOL results in a particular pure extensional modal predicate logic (as is the standard Tarskian semantics of the FOL). This minimal intensional enrichment is obtained by adopting the theory of properties, relations and propositions (PRP) as the universe or domain of the FOL, composed by particulars and universals (or concepts), with the two-step interpretation [18] of the FOL that eliminates the weak points of the Montague's intensional semantics. Different from the Bealer's intensional FOL, we show that the introduction of the intensional abstraction in order to obtain the intensional properties of the FOL is not necessary.

The final result of this chapter is represented by the commutative homomorphic diagram that holds in each given possible world of this new intensional FOL, from the free algebra of the FOL syntax, toward its intensional algebra of concepts, and successively, to the new extensional relational algebra. Particular attention is given to the reification intensional properties by the development of a new kind of intensional abstract operator that transforms the FOL formulae into abstracted terms. A significant number of applications of these operators are provided in all of the other chapters, from Nilson's probabilistic logic, constraint databases, semantic web, new intensional RDBs with multivalued attributes, etc.

Acknowledgments

This work required a lot of time to conclude because of the necessary motivation to provide a significant evolution of the first-order logic that is interesting not only from the theoretical point of view, but also for the important industrial advancement of current IT technology in the area of knowledge and database systems in a conservative way that preserves most of today's IT applications. Thanks to all of the people who helped me to begin my research activity, to learn new topics and to improve my ideas and confront our different points of view and experiences, and finally to finish this effort.

I wanted to offer my help directly to young PhD students and post-PhD researches, as a best way to transfer to them all what I have received previously from my academic fathers, and from 2005 to 2015 (also after my successful book in big data integration theory) to take the Assistant Professor position in the USA, by responding to a big number of internet calls. I left this academic position at 1981 and believed that my publishing activity and participation to a dozen international conferences would be sufficient for taking such an initial position, but in today's academic situation, it seems that there are more important and strong recommendation letters (necessary for young people still without a high number of publications). So, I hope that PhD students will receive from this book all that what I could not transfer personally to them. I was surprised as well, at the end of writing this book, of how I really worked together in mathematics, category theory, lambda calculus and quasi all kinds of logics and databases, so that this monograph is also a testament for new generations, before my retirement from academic life.

Roma 2022 Zoran Majkić

https://doi.org/10.1515/9783110981438-202

Dependencies between the chapters

This book is divided into two parts: the first one, from Chapter 1 to Chapter 4, is dedicated to the conservative Tarskian extension of standard FOL into Intensional FOL (IFOL), where Chapter 1 is theoretical and the other three chapters provide significant applications of this new theory, with the most important work in Chapter 4 dedicated to the big data extension of a standard Relational Data Base (RDB) into new Intensional RDB (IRDB) with multivalued attributes as well. With this work, we propose an evolution from FOL to IFOL, conservative in sense that this evolution preserves software applications actually in practice, by offering new advanced features. It is a fundamental advance w. r. t. the current database and P2P systems and semantic web applications.

PART II, instead, from Chapter 5 to Appendix A, is a conservative generalization of the Chapter 1 to many-valued IFOL able to support AI applications based on many-valued, relevant and paraconsistent logics in a unique intensional FOL framework. Chapter 5 is the theoretical development of many-valued FOL, with additional material provided in Appendix A, with a number of applications presented in Chapter 6.

The readers interested more in theoretical issues after Chapter 1 can directly continue to Chapter 5, with the help of Appendix A. The reader interested in the semantic web, P2P systems and newSQL and Big Data extensions of standard RDB, after Chapter 1 can choose any other thematic chapter after it. The reader interested in nonclassical logics (many-valued, relevant and paraconsistent logics will find Chapters 6 and Appendix A interesting, with a number of new developments of nonstandard logics. They are given as examples of how different kinds of nonclassical logics can be embedded into this general intensional FOL framework.

Detailed Plan

Chapter 1: After introduction to FOL, modal and intensional logics (of Montague's and Bealer's approaches) in Section 1.2 is presented with the PRP theory and the two-step intensional semantics for modal predicate logics, with the unique intensional interpretation I, which maps the logic formulae into the concepts (intensional entities), and the set of extensionalization functions, which determine the extension of any given concept in different possible worlds. After that, we define an extensional algebra of relations for the FOL, different from standard cylindric algebras and the homomorphisms I_T^* (derived from Tarski's FOL interpretation) from the syntax FOL algebra $\mathcal{A}_{\mathrm{FOL}}$ into the extensional algebra $\mathcal{A}_{\mathfrak{R}}$ of relations for the FOL, different from standard cylindric algebras.

In Section 1.2.1, we consider the FOL syntax with the modal Kripke's semantics for each particular application of quantifiers $(\exists x)$, and we obtain a multimodal predicate logic $\mathrm{FOL}_{\mathcal{K}}$, equivalent to the standard FOL with Tarski's interpretation. Moreover, we

https://doi.org/10.1515/9783110981438-203

define the generalized Kripke semantics for modal predicate logics, and we show their diagram of fundamental reductions, based on the restrictions over possible worlds. In Section 1.2.2, we consider the intensionality of modal logics, and we show that not all modal logics are intensional as supposed: in fact, the modal translation of the FOL syntax results in a multimodal predicate logic $\mathrm{FOL}_{\mathcal{K}}$ that is pure extensional as it is the standard Tarskian FOL. Then we define the full intensional enrichment for multimodal predicate logics.

In Section 1.3, we consider the minimal intensional enrichment of the FOL (which does not change the syntax of the FOL), by defining $\mathrm{FOL}_{\mathcal{I}}(\Gamma)$ intensional logic with the set of explicit possible worlds equal to the set of Tarski's interpretations of the standard extensional FOL. We show that its intensionality corresponds to the Montague's point of view. Then we define the intensional algebra of concepts for this intensional $\mathrm{FOL}_{\mathcal{I}}(\Gamma)$, and the homomorphic correspondence of the two-step intensional semantics with the Tarskian semantics of the FOL [18], valid in every possible world of $\mathrm{FOL}_{\mathcal{I}}(\Gamma)$. Finally, we obtain the commutative diagram of Frege/Russel semantics with intermediate intensional algebra $\mathcal{A}_{\mathrm{int}}$ and equality between Tarski's interpretation I_T^* of the FOL syntax and composed mapping $h \circ I$ where I is a fixed intensional interpretation of FOL into intensional algebra and h the extensionalization mapping from it into extensional algebra. In Section 1.3.1, we provide a new (different from Bealer's semantics) intensional abstraction operator theory, while in Section 1.3.2 new methods in Computer Science are introduced based on mathematical (categorial) *symmetries* for the invariant transformations of the logic knowledge.

Chapter 2 is dedicated to three examples of application of an intensional abstract operator for reification of logic formulae, and hence to be used as terms inside other predicates, without generation the second-order logic (for another special important example we dedicate the next chapter to intensional RDBs with multivalued attributes). In Section 2.1, dedicated to the theory of predicate compression theory (by introduction of hidden-quantifiers) with an application for constraint databases, we use the nonground abstracted terms of a special unary predicate with the meaning "*it is abstracted that $\phi(x)$ by hiding variables in α*," for a number of examples where $\phi(x)$ defines the 3-dimensional geometric objects.

The next application, given in Section 2.2, for Nilson's probability theory, by transforming it into a many-valued logic and introduction of a binary predicate that express the value of probability of a given sentence, transformed into an abstracted ground term of intensional FOL. So, by using such reification of sentences we are able to "*reason about probabilities of the sentences*" by syntax and semantics of interval-based probabilistic logic programs and TP databases.

The last application for web semantics (RDF and Web Ontology Language (OWL)) is presented in Section 2.3. We show the intensional properties of the Patrick Hayes RDF model theory (RDFS support reflection on its own syntax that violates principles of extensional set theory), and how it can be implemented inside intensional FOL by using the intensional abstracted terms for the reification/nesting (natural-language property) of RDF triples. The last subsection is an application of this RDF embedding in intensional FOL for P2P view-based data integration applications that use the logic programs for the semantic web with RDF ontologies.

Chapter 3: The notion of ontology has become widespread in the semantic web. The meaning of concepts and views defined over some database ontology can be considered as intensional objects, which have a particular extension in some possible world: for instance, in the *actual* world. This chapter is also a continuation of the semantic web application in Chapter 2 with the unique difference that instead of RDF triples for the definition of ontologies, here we are using standard RDB structures. The intensional property of IFOL is used to define a new kind of interschema mappings between peer databases based on *intensionally equivalent* views.

The P2P database systems are formally defined in Section 3.2. Thus, a noninvasive mapping between completely independent peer databases in a P2P system can be naturally specified by the set of couples of intensionally equivalent views, which have the same mining (intension), over two different peers. Such a kind of mapping has very different semantics from the standard view-based mappings based on the material implication commonly used for data integration. We show that the extension of a P2P database intensional FOL in the actual world can be modeled by a particular multimodal logic, where each peer database is an epistemic logic system with its own modal operator "*Peer knows that...*," while a global query answering, which depends on a sound P2P query rewriting algorithm, corresponds to the extension of an existential modal query formula.

The complete logical embedding of P2P systems into intensional FOL is provided in Section 3.3, with the logical reasoning based on the bridge rules of local contextual deduction and with the resulting kind of nonomniscient weak intensional inference.

For a query answering, we consider nonomniscient query agents and we define an object-oriented class for them, which implements the method for the query rewriting algorithm. Finally, in Section 3.4 we show that this query answering algorithm is sound and complete w. r. t. the weak deduction of the P2P intensional logic. Then, in Section 3.5 we provide denotational coalgebraic semantics of query answering for P2P systems defined in intensional FOL.

Chapter 4 is developed as a continuation of big data integration theory [21] (developed for standard (extensional) RDBs) to more powerful intensional RDB (IRDB), as it was announced [20] by "IRDB Manifesto" in 2014. It is the most (also for IT industry) important application of intensional FOL because there is a deep and potentially large impact for a new DB platform in the future. Although the intensional FOL has a very large possibility to be applied in AI and higher ontology-based applications, the passage from standard RDBs to IRDBs has a horizontal impact in the entire IT business. Beacause of such an impact, the theory of IRDBs is a conservative w. r. t. traditional RDB technology and preserves the software developed for current RDB models, but offers new features as vector big data relations with NewSQL and multivalued attributes of DB relations. This largest chapter is divided in three thematic parts:

After a short introduction in Section 4.1, in the next Section 4.2, is defined a new IRDB, based on data integration theory where the ER model of the user's application is a global DB schema with empty relations, used as a user's and software-application interface and source DB has a big data architecture based on vector relations. Thus, standard SQL written by users is rewritten by IRDBMS over such materialized big vector relations. Then canonical models are defined for such a data integration system and an implementation of NewSQL by query-rewriting methodology. Finally, the features of such new database IRD systems with an example of application to big data interoperability systems are analyzed.

The strict conservative extension of classic RDBs into new IRDBs, described previously, is extended in Section 4.3 by the introduction of multivalued attributes as intensional unary concepts of IFOL, by using the reification of them inside the source vectorial database. The NewSQL is enriched by a new syntax in order to use the multivalued attributes as well. We provide the definition of canonical models for IRDB with multivalued attributes and query-rewriting method for them as well. We specify the migration from RDBs to IRDBS with multivalued attributes and also the inverse migration by using a new relational table containing the values of multivalued attributes, so that extensional RDBs can use the standard joined with this new relation in order to also manage this new information.

In last Section 4.4, we provide formal denotational (algebraic) semantics for the IRDBs with multivalued attributes. These semantics are an extension of the denotational functorial semantics for data integration systems developed previously for standard RDBs in [21], and hence based on the **DB** category for databases and functional mappings between them, that is in the categorial Kleisli semantics with an introduction of saturated morphisms for the multivalued attributes.

Chapter 5: The first section is not only an introduction to MV-logics but also a development of an alternative nonmatrix based model theory of MV-logics with a new representation theorem based on the truth-preserving entailment. This new model of semantics of MV-logics is founded on the new Kripke canonical autoreferential representation of MV-logics by set-based complex algebras. The set of possible worlds in this Kripke semantics is the set of join-irreducible truth elements of the complete distributive lattice of truth values of a given MV-logic. Then we provide the important application of this new theory to Belnap's bilattice, used in a number of applications in this book, from the fact that it permits the management of incomplete and inconsistent knowledge as well, that often appear in practice, especially in the semantic web, data integration and P2P systems.

In Section 5.2, we present a generalization of the intensional FOL (developed in Chapter 1) to MV-logics, again in conservative way similar to ontological encapsulation introduced in Section A.4, but without changing the syntax of predicates: the logic values are presented only in the extensions (relations) of formulae with free variables. Thus, we obtain a general model of intensional FOL, in which each concrete MV-logic can be embedded. That is, in which are represented by all MV-logics in an unified framework, with conservative extension of Tarski's semantics to intensional FOL as in Chapter 1. We introduce also the two many-valued, mutually independent, quantifiers: existential and universal as in FOL. Finally, in the last section we provide the resolution of the liar formula in this many-valued intensional FOL.

Chapter 6: It is dedicated to show a number of applications for the MV-intensional FOL developed in Chapter 5. We provide three original examples of MV-logics: in Section 6.1, we develop a relevant logic by weakening the fusion and fission logic connectives of the infinitary Lukasiewicz–Tarski logic with complete distributive lattice of truth values represented by fuzzy interval of reals $[0, 1]$.

In Section 6.2, we present the new paraconsistent relevant mZ-logic obtained by da Costa weakening of logic negation. It is shown that obtained logic is weakened intuitionistic logic, and as examples are provided the weakened Kleene's 3-valued logic, Belnap's 4-valued logic, fuzzy logic and the Gödel–Dummett logic.

The third example for MV-intensional FOL, developed in Chapter 5, is presented in the last Section 6.3. Here, we propose Belnap's 4-valued logic for management of P2P data integration with incomplete and inconsistent data as well. Then we show that the process of filtering of query preanswers is, from a logical point of view, represented equivalently by modal query language applied over databases with a particular "quality-based" partial order.

Appendix A: In this chapter, we present only some basic technical notions for algebras, MV-logics, database theory and and category theory that is used in previous chapters of this book. These are very short introductions and more advanced notions can be found in given references. This presentation is not fully self-contained; it needs a good background in relational database theory, relational algebra and first-order logic. This very short introduction is enough for the logic and database readers.

Two special sections, indicated as support for the many-valued intensional FOL developed in Chapter 5, are Section A.3 dedicated to new autoreferential semantics for many-valued modal logics based on complete latices of truth values, and Section A.4 with concepts of semantic reflection and ontological encapsulation of many-valued into two-valued logics. They provide some fundamental methods used for definition of intensional many-valued logic in Chapter 5.

Notation conventions

The symbol $=_{\text{def}}$ will be used for the explicit definition of the mathematical concepts, while the symbol "=" (also it will be used sometimes for the same fact when it is clear from the context) for the usual meaning of the equivalence of the left- and right-hand sides in the equations.

The symbol $\equiv$ denotes standard logical equivalence, while $\doteq$ for the binary identity predicate in the first-order logic. We denote by $R_{\doteq}$ the Tarski's interpretation of $\doteq$. So, for the equality we will use the standard symbol =, while for different equivalence relations we will employ the symbols $\simeq, \approx, \asymp$, etc. The term "iff" is used for "if and only if."

We use logical symbols both in our formal languages and in the metalanguage. The notation slightly differs: in classical propositional and FOL, we use $\wedge, \vee, \Rightarrow, \neg$ (and $\exists, \forall$ for the FOL quantifiers). As the metasymbol for conjunction, the symbol "&" will be used.

In our terminology, we distinguish functions (graphs of functions) and maps. A (graph of) *function* from X to Y is a binary relation $F \subseteq X \times Y$ (subset of the Cartesian product of the sets X and Y) with domain A satisfying the functionality condition $(x, y) \in F \& (x, z) \in F$ implies $y = z$, and the triple $\langle f, X, Y\rangle$ is then called a *map* (or morphism in a category) from A to B, denoted by $f : X \to Y$ as well. The composition of functions is denoted by $g \cdot f$, so that $(g \cdot f)(x) = g(f(x))$, while the composition of mappings (in a given category) by $g \circ f$. $\mathcal{N}$ denotes the set of natural numbers. Here are some other set-theoretic notation:

- The symbol $\mathbb{N}$ is used for the set of natural numbers, while $\emptyset$ denotes the empty set;
- $\mathcal{P}(X)$ denotes the power set of a set X, and $X^n =_{\text{def}} \overbrace{X \times \cdots \times X}^{n}$ the n-ary Cartesian product, and Y^X denotes the set of all functions from X to Y;
- We use $\subseteq$ for inclusion, $\subset$ for proper inclusion (we use $\leq, \preceq, \sqsubseteq$ for partial orders), and $X \subseteq_\omega Y$ denotes that X is a *finite* subset of an infinite set Y. By $X \backslash Y$ or $X - Y$, we denote the set difference between the set X and set Y;
- R^{-1} is the converse of a binary relation $R \subseteq X \times Y$ and $\overline{R}$ is the complement of R (equal to $(X \times Y) \backslash R$);
- id_X is the identity map on a set X. $|X|$ denotes the cardinality of a set (or list) X;
- For a set of elements $x_1, \ldots, x_n \in X$, we denote by $\mathbf{x}$ the sequence (or *tuple*) $(x_1, \ldots, x_n)$, and if $n = 1$ simply by x_1, while for $n = 0$ the empty tuple $\langle\,\rangle$. An n-ary relation R, with $n = ar(R) \geq 1$, is a set (also empty) of tuples $\mathbf{x}_i$ with $|\mathbf{x}_i| = n$, with $\langle\,\rangle \in R$ (the empty tuple is a tuple of every relation);
- By $\pi_{\mathbf{K}}(R)$, where $\mathbf{K} = [i_1, \ldots, i_n]$ is a sequence of indexes with $n = |\mathbf{K}| \geq 1$, we denote the projection of R with columns defined by ordering in $\mathbf{K}$. If $|\mathbf{K}| = 1$, we write simply $\pi_i(R)$;

https://doi.org/10.1515/9783110981438-204

- Given two sequences $\mathbf{x}$ and $\mathbf{y}$, we write $\mathbf{x} \subseteq \mathbf{y}$ if every element in the list $\mathbf{x}$ is an element in $\mathbf{y}$ (not necessarily in the same position) as well, and by $\mathbf{x}\&\mathbf{y}$ their concatenation; $(\mathbf{x}, \mathbf{y})$ denotes a tuple $\mathbf{x}\&\mathbf{y}$ composed by variables in $\mathbf{x}$ and $\mathbf{y}$, while $\langle \mathbf{x}, \mathbf{y} \rangle$ is a tuple of two tuples $\mathbf{x}$ and $\mathbf{y}$. The set of elements of a list $\mathbf{x}$ is denoted by $\overline{\mathbf{x}}$;
- By f, t, we denote empty set $\emptyset$ and singleton set $\{\langle\ \rangle\}$, respectively (with the empty tuple $\langle\ \rangle$, i. e., the unique tuple of 0-ary relation), which may be thought of as falsity f and truth t, as those used in the relational algebra. For a given domain of intensional logics $\mathcal{D}$, we define that $\mathcal{D}^0$ is a singleton set $\{\langle\ \rangle\}$, so that $\{f, t\} = \mathcal{P}(\mathcal{D}^0)$, where $\mathcal{P}$ is the powerset operator.

A *relational symbol* (a predicate letter in FOL) r and its extension (relation table) R will be often called shortly as "relation" where it is clear from the context. If R is the extension of a relational symbol r, we write $R = \|r\|$.

Contents

1 Theory of new intensional first-order logic

1.1 Introduction

Contemporary use of the term “intension” is derived from the traditional logical Frege–Russell’s doctrine that an idea (logic formula) has both an extension and an intension. Although there is divergence in formulation, it is accepted that the extension of an idea consists of the subjects to which the idea applies, and the intension consists of the attributes implied by the idea. From Montague’s point of view, the meaning of an idea can be considered as particular extensions in different possible worlds. The simplest aspect of an expression’s meaning is its extension. We can stipulate that the extension of a sentence is its truth value, and that the extension of a singular term is its referent. The extension of other expressions can be seen as associated entities that contribute to the truth value of a sentence in a manner broadly analogous to the way in which the referent of a singular term contributes to the truth value of a sentence.

“Extensional” is most definitely a technical term. Say that the extension of a name is its denotation, the extension of a predicate is the set of things it applies to, and the extension of a sentence is its truth value. A logic is extensional if coextensional expressions can be substituted one for another in any sentence of the logic “salva veritate,” i. e., without a change in truth value. In “Über Sinn und Bedeutung,” Frege concentrated mostly on the senses of names, holding that all names have a sense. It is natural to hold that the same considerations apply to any expression that has an extension. Two general terms can have the same extension and different cognitive significance; two predicates can have the same extension and different cognitive significance; two sentences can have the same extension and different cognitive significance. So general terms, predicates and sentences all have senses as well as extensions. The same goes for any expression that has an extension, or is a candidate for extension.

The distinction between intensions and extensions is important, considering that extensions can be notoriously difficult to handle in an efficient manner. The extensional equality theory of predicates and functions under higher-order semantics (e. g., for two predicates with the same set of attributes $p = q$ is true iff these symbols are interpreted by the same relation), i. e., the strong equational theory of intensions, is not decidable, in general. For example, in the second-order predicate calculus and Church’s simple theory of types, both under the standard semantics, is not even semidecidable. Thus, separating intensions from extensions make it possible to have an equational theory over predicate and function names (intensions) that is separate from the extensional equality of relations and functions.

The first conception of intensional entities (or concepts) is built into the *possible-worlds* treatment of Properties, Relations and Propositions (PRP)s. This conception is commonly attributed to Leibniz, and underlies Alonzo Church’s alternative formulation of Frege’s theory of senses (“*A formulation of the Logic of Sense and Denotation*” in Henle, Kallen and Langer, 3–24, and “*Outline of a Revised Formulation of the*

https://doi.org/10.1515/9783110981438-001

Logic of Sense and Denotation" in two parts, Nous, VII (1973), 24–33, and VIII, (1974), 135–156). This conception of PRPs is ideally suited for treating the *modalities* (necessity, possibility, etc.) and to Montague's definition of intension of a given virtual predicate $\phi(x_1,\dots,x_k)$ (a FOL open sentence with the tuple of free variables $(x_1,\dots x_k)$) as a mapping from possible worlds into extensions of this virtual predicate. Among the possible worlds, we distinguish the *actual* possible world. For example, if we consider a set of predicates of a given database and their extensions in different time instances, the actual possible world is identified by the current instance of the time.

The second conception of intensional entities is to be found in Russell's doctrine of logical atomism. On this doctrine, it is required that all complete definitions of intensional entities be finite as well as unique and noncircular: it offers an *algebraic* way for definition of complex intensional entities from simple (atomic) entities (i. e., algebra of concepts), conception also evident in Leibniz's remarks. In a predicate logics, predicates and open-sentences (with free variables) expresses classes (properties and relations), and sentences express propositions. Note that classes (intensional entities) are *reified*, i. e., they belong to the same domain as individual objects (particulars). This endows the intensional logics with a great deal of uniformity, making it possible to manipulate classes and individual objects in the same language. In particular, when viewed as an individual object, a class can be a member of another class.

The standard semantics of First-order Logic (FOL) are Tarski-style models, which are extensional. In this respect, FOL is extensional. But the open question is if it is possible to obtain also an intensional semantics of FOL such that the Tarski's extensions of its expressions are equal to extensions of concepts (intensional entities) of the same FOL expressions in the actual possible world.

1.1.1 Introduction to first-order logic

We will shortly introduce the syntax of the first-order logic (FOL) language $\mathcal{L}$, and its extensional semantics based on Tarski's interpretations, as follows.

Definition 1. The syntax of the first-order logic language $\mathcal{L}$ is as follows: Logic operators $(\wedge, \neg, \exists)$ over bounded lattice of truth values $\mathbf{2} = \{f, t\}$, f for falsity and t for truth; Predicate letters $p_1^{k_1}, p_2^{k_2}, \dots$ with a given arity $k_i \geq 1$, $i = 1, 2, \dots$, and special built-in identity binary predicate "$\doteq$," in P; Functional letters $f_1^{k_1}, f_2^{k_2}, \dots$ with a given arity $k_i \geq 1$ in F (language constants $c, d, \dots$ are considered as particular case of nullary functional letters); Variables $x, y, z, \dots$ in $\mathcal{V}$, and punctuation symbols (comma, parenthesis).

With the following simultaneous inductive definition of *term* and *formula*:

1. All variables and constants are terms.
2. If $t_1, \dots, t_k$ are terms and $f_i^k \in F$ is a k-ary functional symbol, then $f_i^k(t_1, \dots, t_k)$ is a term, while $p_i^k(t_1, \dots, t_k)$ is a formula for a k-ary predicate letter $p_i^k \in P$.
3. If ϕ and ψ are formulae, then $(\phi \wedge \psi)$, $\neg\phi$, and $(\exists x_i)\phi$ for $x_i \in \mathcal{V}$ are formulae.

An interpretation (Tarski) I_T consists in a nonempty domain $\mathcal{D}$ and a mapping that assigns to any predicate letter $p_i^k \in P$ a relation $R = I_T(p_i^k) \subseteq \mathcal{D}^k$, to any functional letter $f_i^k \in F$ a function $I_T(f_i^k) : \mathcal{D}^k \to \mathcal{D}$, or equivalently, its graph relation $R = I_T(f_i^k) \subseteq \mathcal{D}^{k+1}$ where the $k+1$-th column is the resulting function's value, and to each individual constant $c \in F$ one given element $I_T(c) \in \mathcal{D}$.

A predicate logic $\mathcal{L}_P$ is a subset of the FOL without the quantifier $\exists$.

Remark. The *propositional* logic can be considered as a particular case of predicate logic when all symbols in P are nullary, that is a set of propositional symbols, while F, $\mathcal{D}$ and $\mathcal{V}$ are empty sets. By considering that $\mathcal{D}^0 = \{\langle\,\rangle\}$ is a singleton set composed by empty tuple $\langle\,\rangle$, then for any $p_i \in P$, $I_T(p_i) \subseteq \mathcal{D}^0$, i. e., $I_T(p_i) = f$ (empty set) or $I_T(p_i) = t$ (singleton set $\{\langle\,\rangle\}$). That is, I_T becomes an interpretation $I_T : P \to \mathbf{2}$ of this logic, which can be homomorphically extended to all formulae in the unique standard way. □

In a formula $(\exists x)\phi$, the formula ϕ is called "action field" for the quantifier $(\exists x)$. A variable y in a formula ψ is called bounded variable iff it is the variable of a quantifier $(\exists y)$ in ψ, or it is in the action field of a quantifier $(\exists y)$ in the formula ψ. A variable x is free in ψ if it is not bounded.

The universal quantifier is defined by $\forall = \neg\exists\neg$. Disjunction and implication are expressed by $\phi \vee \psi = \neg(\neg\phi \wedge \neg\psi)$, and $\phi \Rightarrow \psi = \neg\phi \vee \psi$. In the FOL with the identity $\doteq$, the formula $(\exists_1 x)\phi(x)$ denotes the formula $(\exists x)\phi(x) \wedge (\forall x)(\forall y)(\phi(x) \wedge \phi(y) \Rightarrow (x \doteq y))$.

We can introduce the sorts in order to be able to assign each variable x_i to a sort $S_i \subseteq \mathcal{D}$ where $\mathcal{D}$ is a given domain for the FOL (e. g., for natural numbers, for reals, for dates, etc. as used for some attributes in database relations). An assignment $g : \mathcal{V} \to \mathcal{D}$ for variables in $\mathcal{V}$ is applied only to free variables in terms and formulae. If we use sorts for variables, then for each sorted variable $x_i \in \mathcal{V}$ an assignment g must satisfy the auxiliary condition $g(x_i) \in S_i$.

Such an assignment $g \in \mathcal{D}^{\mathcal{V}}$ can be recursively uniquely extended into the assignment $g^* : \mathcal{T} \to \mathcal{D}$, where $\mathcal{T}$ denotes the set of all terms, by:

1. $g^*(t_i) = g(x) \in \mathcal{D}$ if the term t_i is a variable $x \in \mathcal{V}$.
2. $g^*(t_i) = I_T(c) \in \mathcal{D}$ if the term t_i is a constant $c \in F$.
3. If a term t_i is $f_i^k(t_1, \dots, t_k)$, where $f_i^k \in F$ is a k-ary functional symbol and $t_1, \dots, t_k$ are terms, then $g^*(f_i^k(t_1, \dots, t_k)) = I_T(f_i^k)(g^*(t_1), \dots, g^*(t_k))$ or, equivalently, in the graph interpretation of the function, $g^*(f_i^k(t_1, \dots, t_k)) = u$ such that $(g^*(t_1), \dots, g^*(t_k), u) \in I_T(f_i^k) \subseteq \mathcal{D}^{k+1}$.

In what follows, we will use the graph interpretation for functions in FOL like its interpretation in intensional logics. We denote by t_i/g (or ϕ/g) the ground term (or formula) without free variables, obtained by assignment g from a term t_i (or a formula ϕ), and by $\phi[x/t_i]$ the formula obtained by uniformly replacing x by a term t_i in ϕ. A *sentence* is a formula having no free variables.

A Herbrand base of a logic $\mathcal{L}$ is defined by

$$H = \{p_i^k(t_1, \dots, t_k) \mid p_i^k \in P \text{ and } t_1, \dots, t_k \text{ are ground terms}\}.$$

A *FOL interpretation* $\mathfrak{I}$ is a triple $(\mathcal{D}, g, I_T)$, where $\mathcal{D}$ is domain of interpretation, $g \in \mathcal{D}^{\mathcal{V}}$ an assignment and I_T is a function (called *valuation* v as well) that maps constants of FOL (nullary functions) into domain $\mathcal{D}$, the k-ary predicate into relation $\mathcal{D}^k$ and k-ary function into relation $\mathcal{D}^{k+1}$ as explained above in reason of intensional FOL.

Tarski defined the satisfaction for the logic formulae in $\mathcal{L}$ and a given assignment $g : \mathcal{V} \to \mathcal{D}$ inductively (recursively), as follows.

If a formula ϕ is an atomic formula $p_i^k(t_1, \dots, t_k)$, then this assignment g satisfies ϕ iff $(g^*(t_1), \dots, g^*(t_k)) \in I_T(p_i^k)$; g satisfies $\neg\phi$ iff it does not satisfy ϕ; g satisfies $\phi \wedge \psi$ iff g satisfies ϕ and g satisfies ψ; g satisfies $(\exists x_i)\phi$ iff exists an assignment $g' \in \mathcal{D}^{\mathcal{V}}$ that may differ from g only for the variable $x_i \in \mathcal{V}$, and g' satisfies ϕ.

A model is $\mathcal{M} = (\mathcal{D}, I_T)$, so that for $g \in \mathcal{D}^{\mathcal{V}}$ and a formula ϕ we use the notation

$$\mathcal{M} \vDash_g \phi \quad \text{or} \quad I_T^*(\phi/g) = t \in \mathbf{2}, \tag{1.1}$$

which means "*the formula ϕ is true in the model $\mathcal{M} = (\mathcal{D}, I_T)$, for assignment g.*"

Remark. In what follows, instead of notation $\mathcal{M} \vDash_g \phi$, we prefer to use the *nonstandard* functional notation $I_T^*(\phi/g)$, because in intensional FOL the new symbol I_T^* will denote a *homomorphism* between the syntax algebra of FOL and extensional algebra of relations (of *extensional logic* which allows evaluation of the truth value of a sentence, in Corollary 1, Section 1.2). So, for ground atoms I_T^* is equal to Herbrand interpretation, instead, for atoms with variables only it is equal to original Tarski's mapping I_T. That is, for any atom $p_j^k(\mathbf{x})$ with variables $\mathbf{x} = (x_1, \dots, x_k)$,

$$I_T(p_j^k) = I_T^*(p_j^k(\mathbf{x})) = \{(g(x_1), \dots, g(x_k)) \mid g \in \mathcal{D}^{\mathcal{V}}, \text{ and } I_T^*(p_j^k(\mathbf{x})/g) = t\} \tag{1.2}$$

□

A formula ϕ is `true` for a given interpretation I_T iff ϕ is satisfied by every assignment $g \in \mathcal{D}^{\mathcal{V}}$. A formula ϕ is `valid` (i. e., tautology) iff ϕ is true for every Tarski's interpretation $I_T \in \mathfrak{I}_T$. An interpretation I_T is a `model` of a set of formulae Γ iff every formula $\phi \in \Gamma$ is true in this interpretation. By FOL(Γ), we denote the FOL with a set of assumptions Γ, and by $\mathfrak{I}_T(\Gamma)$ the subset of Tarski's interpretations that are models of Γ, with $\mathfrak{I}_T(\emptyset) = \mathfrak{I}_T$. A formula ϕ is said to be a *logical consequence* of Γ, denoted by $\Gamma \Vdash \phi$, iff ϕ is true in all interpretations in $\mathfrak{I}_T(\Gamma)$.

Thus, $\Vdash \phi$ iff ϕ is a tautology.

The basic set of axioms of the FOL are that of the propositional logic with two additional axioms:

- (A1) $(\forall x)(\phi \Rightarrow \psi) \Rightarrow (\phi \Rightarrow (\forall x)\psi)$, ($x$ does not occur in ϕ and it is not bound in ψ).

- (A2) $(\forall x)\phi \Rightarrow \phi[x/t_i]$, (neither x nor any variable in t_i occurs bound in ϕ).
- (A3) For the FOL with identity (the binary predicate $\doteq$), we need the *proper* axiom $x_1 \doteq x_2 \Rightarrow (x_1 \doteq x_3 \Rightarrow x_2 \doteq x_3)$.
  We denote by $R_=$ the Tarski's interpretation of $\doteq$.

The inference rules are modus ponens and generalization (G) "*if ϕ is a theorem and x is not bound in ϕ, then $(\forall x)\phi$ is a theorem.*"

Here, the FOL denotes this minimal first-order logic (consistent and complete), while FOL(Γ) denotes a logic extended by a new set of *proper* axioms in Γ and, generally (by the Gödel theorem), it is not complete.

In what follows, any open-sentence, a formula $\phi(\mathbf{x})$ with nonempty tuple of free variables $\mathbf{x} = (x_1, \dots, x_m)$, will be called a m-ary *virtual predicate*, denoted also by $\phi(x_1, \dots, x_m)$. This definition contains the precise method of establishing the *ordering* of variables in this tuple: such a method that will be adopted here is the ordering of appearance, from left to right, of free variables in ϕ, as explained in Definition 8 with important properties for the intensional concepts of the intensional logics.

The FOL is considered as an extensional logic because two open sentences with the same tuple of variables $\phi(x_1, \dots, x_m)$ and $\psi(x_1, \dots, x_m)$ are `equal` iff they have the *same extension* in a given interpretation I_T, i. e., iff $I_T^*(\phi(x_1, \dots, x_m)) = I_T^*(\psi(x_1, \dots, x_m))$, where I_T^* is the unique extension of I_T to all formulae, as follows:

1. For a (closed) sentence ϕ/g, we have that $I_T^*(\phi/g) = t$ iff g satisfies ϕ, as recursively defined above.
2. For an open sentence ϕ with the tuple of free variables $(x_1, \dots, x_m)$, we have that

$$I_T^*(\phi(x_1, \dots, x_m)) =_{\text{def}} \{(g(x_1), \dots, g(x_m)) \mid g \in \mathcal{D}^{\mathcal{V}} \text{ and } I_T^*(\phi/g) = t\}.$$

It is easy to verify that for a formula ϕ with the tuple of free variables $(x_1, \dots, x_m)$,

$$I_T^*(\phi(x_1, \dots, x_m)/g) = t \quad \text{iff} \quad (g(x_1), \dots, g(x_m)) \in I_T^*(\phi(x_1, \dots, x_m)).$$

This extensional *equality* of virtual predicates can be generalized to the extensional *equivalence* when both predicates ϕ, ψ has the same set of free variables but their ordering in the *tuples* of free variables are not identical: such two virtual predicates are equivalent if the extension of the first is equal to the proper permutation of columns of the extension of the second virtual predicate. It is easy to verify that such an extensional equivalence corresponds to the logical equivalence denoted by $\phi \equiv \psi$.

Let $\mathfrak{R} = \bigcup_{k \in \mathbb{N}} \mathcal{P}(\mathcal{D}^k) = \sum_{k \in \mathbb{N}} \mathcal{P}(D^k)$ be the set of all k-ary relations over a domain $\mathcal{D}$, where $k \in \mathbb{N} = \{0, 1, 2, \dots\}$. Then this extensional equivalence between two relations $R_1, R_2 \in \mathfrak{R}$ with the same arity will be denoted by $R_1 \approx R_2$, while the extensional identity will be denoted in the standard way by $R_1 = R_2$.

1.1.2 Introduction to multimodal logics

A multimodal logic is a standard predicate/propositional logic (see Definition 1) extended by a number of *existential modal* operators $\Diamond_i, i \geq 1$. In the standard Kripke semantics, each existential modal operator $\Diamond_i$ is defined by an accessibility binary relation $\mathcal{R}_i \subseteq \mathcal{W} \times \mathcal{W}$, for a given set of *possible worlds* $\mathcal{W}$. A more exhaustive and formal introduction to modal logics and their Kripke's interpretations can easily be found in the literature, e. g., in [22].

Here, only a short version will be given, in order to clarify the definitions used in the next paragraphs. We define $\mathcal{N} = \{0, 1, 2, \dots, n\} \subset \mathbb{N}$ where n is a maximal arity of symbols in the finite set $P \bigcup F$ of predicate and functional symbols, respectively.

In the case of the propositional logics, we have that $n = 0$, so that P is a set of propositional symbols (that are the nullary predicate symbols) and $F = \emptyset$ is the empty set. Here, we will present two definitions for modal logics, one for the propositional and other for predicate logics, as is used in current literature.

Definition 2 (Propositional multimodal logic). By $\mathcal{M} = (\mathcal{W}, \{\mathcal{R}_i\}, I_K)$, we denote a multimodal Kripke's interpretation with a set of possible worlds $\mathcal{W}$, the accessibility relations $\mathcal{R}_i \subseteq \mathcal{W} \times \mathcal{W}$, $i = 1, 2, \dots$, and a mapping $I_K : P \to \mathbf{2}^{\mathcal{W}}$, such that for any propositional letter $p_i \in P$, the function $I_K(p_i) : \mathcal{W} \to \mathbf{2}$ defines the truth of p_i in a world $w \in \mathcal{W}$.

For any formula φ, we define $\mathcal{M} \vDash_w \varphi$ iff φ is satisfied in a world $w \in \mathcal{W}$. For example, a given propositional letter p_i is true in w, i. e., $\mathcal{M} \vDash_w p_i$, iff $I_K(p_i)(w) = t$.

The Kripke semantics is extended to all formulae as follows:

$$\begin{aligned}
&\mathcal{M} \vDash_w \varphi \wedge \phi \quad \text{iff} \quad \mathcal{M} \vDash_w \varphi \text{ and } \mathcal{M} \vDash_w \phi,\\
&\mathcal{M} \vDash_w \neg\varphi \quad \text{iff} \quad \text{not } \mathcal{M} \vDash_w \varphi,\\
&\mathcal{M} \vDash_w \Diamond_i\varphi \quad \text{iff} \quad \text{exists } w' \in \mathcal{W} \text{ such that } (w, w') \in \mathcal{R}_i \text{ and } \mathcal{M} \vDash_{w'} \varphi.
\end{aligned}$$

The universal modal operator $\Box_i$ is equal to $\neg\Diamond_i\neg$. A formula φ is said to be *true in a Kripke's interpretation* $\mathcal{M}$ if for each possible world w, $\mathcal{M} \vDash_w \varphi$. A formula is said to be *valid* if it is true in each interpretation.

In a more general cases when $n \geq 1$, we have the multimodal predicate logics defined as follows.

Definition 3 (Predicate multimodal logic). By $\mathcal{M} = (\mathcal{W}, \{\mathcal{R}_i \mid 1 \leq i \leq k\}, \mathcal{D}, I_K)$, we denote a multimodal Kripke model with finite $k \geq 1$ modal operators with a set of possible worlds $\mathcal{W}$, the accessibility relations $\mathcal{R}_i \subseteq \mathcal{W} \times \mathcal{W}$, nonempty domain $\mathcal{D}$, and a mapping $I_K : \mathcal{W} \times (P \bigcup F) \to \bigcup_{n \in \mathcal{N}} (\mathbf{2} \bigcup \mathcal{D})^{\mathcal{D}^n}$, such that for any world $w \in \mathcal{W}$,

1. For any functional letter $f_i^k \in F$, $I_K(w, f_i^k) : \mathcal{D}^k \to \mathcal{D}$ is a function (interpretation of f_i^k in w).

2. For any predicate letter $p_i^k \in P$, the function $I_K(w, p_i^k) : \mathcal{D}^k \to \mathbf{2}$ defines the extension of p_i^k in a world w,

$$\|p_i^k(x_1, \dots, x_k)\|_{\mathcal{M},w} =_{\text{def}} \{(d_1, \dots, d_k) \in \mathcal{D}^k \mid I_K(w, p_i^k)(d_1, \dots, d_k) = t\}.$$

For any formula φ, we define $\mathcal{M} \vDash_{w,g} \varphi$ iff φ is satisfied in a world $w \in \mathcal{W}$ for a given assignment $g : \mathcal{V} \to \mathcal{D}$. For example, a given atom $p_i^k(x_1, \dots, x_k)$ is satisfied in w by assignment g, i. e., $\mathcal{M} \vDash_{w,g} p_i^k(x_1, \dots, x_k)$, iff $I_K(w, p_i^k)(g(x_1), \dots, g(x_k)) = t$.

The Kripke semantics is extended to all formulae as follows:

$$\begin{aligned} &\mathcal{M} \vDash_{w,g} \varphi \wedge \phi \quad \text{iff} \quad \mathcal{M} \vDash_{w,g} \varphi \text{ and } \mathcal{M} \vDash_{w,g} \phi, \\ &\mathcal{M} \vDash_{w,g} \neg\varphi \quad \text{iff} \quad \text{not } \mathcal{M} \vDash_{w,g} \varphi, \\ &\mathcal{M} \vDash_{w,g} \Diamond_i \varphi \quad \text{iff} \quad \text{exists } w' \in \mathcal{W} \text{ such that } (w, w') \in \mathcal{R}_i \text{ and } \mathcal{M} \vDash_{w',g} \varphi. \end{aligned}$$

A formula φ is said to be *true in a Kripke's interpretation* $\mathcal{M}$ if for each assignment function g and possible world w, $\mathcal{M} \vDash_{w,g} \varphi$. A formula is said to be *valid* if it is true in each interpretation.

Any virtual predicate $\phi(x_1, \dots, x_k)$ has different extensions $\|\phi(x_1, \dots, x_k)\|_{\mathcal{M},w} =_{\text{def}} \{(g(x_1), \dots, g(x_k)) \mid g \in \mathcal{D}^{\mathcal{V}} \text{ and } \mathcal{M} \vDash_{w,g} \phi\}$ for different possible worlds $w \in \mathcal{W}$. Thus, we cannot establish the simple extensional identity for two concepts as in FOL.

Remark. We can consider the following reductions and extensions of the modal predicate logics:

- The propositional modal logic can be considered as a particular case of a predicate modal logic when all symbols in P are nullary, that is a set of propositional symbols, while F, $\mathcal{D}$ and $\mathcal{V}$ are empty sets. So that I_K is reduced to a mapping $I_K : P \to \mathbf{2}^{\mathcal{W}}$, such that we do not use the assignments g, and for any propositional letter $p_i \in P$, the function $I_K(p_i) : \mathcal{W} \to \mathbf{2}$ defines the truth of p_i in a world $w \in \mathcal{W}$;
- However, as we will present in Definition 12 we can generalize this standard Kripke semantics of modal predicate logic by introducing generalized possible worlds $\mathbb{W} =_{\text{def}} \mathcal{W} \times \mathcal{D}^{\mathcal{V}}$, so that each generalized world $\mathbf{w} = (w, g) \in \mathbb{W}$ is a tuple of two different types of worlds, original (or *explicit*) worlds $w \in \mathcal{W}$ and the new kind of *intrinsic* worlds $g \in \mathcal{D}^{\mathcal{V}}$ (i. e., the assignments $g : \mathcal{V} \to \mathcal{D}$), and by introducing more powerful nonstandard Kripke interpretations $I_K : \mathbb{W} \times (P \bigcup F) \to \bigcup_{n \in \mathcal{N}} (\mathbf{2} \bigcup \mathcal{D})^{\mathcal{D}^n}$. In this case, we obtain the satisfaction relation of a formula φ can be given simply as in the case of the propositional modal logics, i. e., by $\mathcal{M} \vDash_{\mathbf{w}} \varphi$ iff φ is satisfied in a world $\mathbf{w} \in \mathbb{W}$. So, e. g., in the case of the standard predicate modal logic in Definition 3 above, we will have that

$$\mathcal{M} \vDash_{\mathbf{w}} p_i^k(x_1, \dots, x_k), \quad \text{iff} \quad I_K(w, p_i^k)(g(x_1), \dots, g(x_k)) = t.$$

We will see in next sections how we are able to enrich the FOL with intensional properties, by giving them a modal semantics (for the FOL quantifiers) and by providing the more sophisticated mappings I_K. □

It seams apparently that Tarski's interpretation for the FOL and the Kripke's interpretation for modal predicate logics are inconceivable. Currently, each modal logic is considered as a kind of intensional logic. The open question is what about the modality in the FOL, if it is intrinsic also in the FOL, i. e., if there is an equivalent multimodal transformation of the FOL where the Kripke's interpretation is equivalent to the original Tarski's interpretation for the FOL. The positive answer to these questions is one of the main contributions of this chapter.

1.1.3 Two significant approaches to intensional first-order logic

Intensional entities are such things as concepts, propositions and properties. What make them "intensional" is that they violate the principle of extensionality; the principle that extensional equivalence implies identity. All (or most) of these intensional entities have been classified at one time or another as kinds of universals [23]. In the next section, we will shortly consider two different approaches to intensions: Motague's and Bealer's approaches.

Montague's approach

In the Montague's possible worlds representation [7–11], the *intension* of a proposition is a *function* from possible worlds $\mathcal{W}$ to truth values, and properties and functions from $\mathcal{W}$ to sets of possible (usually not-actual) objects.

In what follows, we will use one simplified S5 modal logic framework (we will not consider the time as one independent parameter as in Montague's original work) with a model $\mathcal{M} = (\mathcal{W}, \mathcal{R}, \mathcal{D}, I_K)$, where $\mathcal{W}$ is the set of explicit possible worlds, $\mathcal{R}$ is a reflexive, symmetric and transitive accessibility relation between worlds ($\mathcal{R} = \mathcal{W} \times \mathcal{W}$), $\mathcal{D}$ is a non-empty domain of individuals, while I_K is a function defined in Definition 3.

Definition 4 (Montague's intension). For a given logical language $\mathcal{L}$, Montague defined the *intension* as a mapping

$$I_n : \mathcal{L} \to \mathfrak{R}^{\mathcal{W}}$$

where $\mathfrak{R} = \bigcup_{k \in \mathbb{N}} \mathcal{P}(\mathcal{D}^k)$ is the set of all k-ary relations, where $k \in \mathbb{N} = \{0, 1, 2, \dots\}$.

One thing that should be immediately clear is that intensions are more general that extensions: if the intension of an expression is given, one can determine its extension with respect to a particular world but not vice versa.

Remark. The problematic issue of the Montague's approach is that it is *not a constructive* approach to intensional logic. The intension of one concept is defined mathematically as the mapping from the (possibly infinite) set of possible worlds to the possible extension of this concepts in these worlds. But we have no always the knowledge in what is exactly this set of possible worlds, so that $\mathcal{W}$ can be a generally not well-defined set (the set is defined by its members and we do not know all these members), and especially, we do not know apriory what is exact extension for this concept in each of these possible worlds (*factual omniscience*[1]). Simply, we are not able to define the intension of any nonrigid[2] concept so that we cannot use practically any algebra over these intensional objects. Moreover, if we are not able to know all world, and hence the extensions of two concepts in them, we are not able to specify that these two concepts have the same mining (because can exists other unknown worlds in which they have no the same extension). Just because of that, I used Bealer's method for the generation of the intensional algebra of meanings, by defining the algebra $\mathcal{A}_{int}$, in which we can use directly the terms of the equality of two intensional concepts of the same type (as shown in Example 4 in Section 1.3).

In fact, we can consider that the extension of the same nonrigid concept in different possible worlds can be different, so that we cannot use the standard extensional, set-based logic for such concepts: but this extensional variability of the concept is the *result* only of the fact that they are intensional concepts. As we noted, the intensional concepts (or classes) are *conceptual processes* that examine real-world images, and give the one of the possible answers: "yes," "no," or "do not know" for the fact that this image is a member of this class. For example, let us consider as real-world image any one-page text written in English, and the text mining software developed to recognize if a text presented as its input describes some car (and we suppose that it is embedded into a black box; any attempt to access its code in order to analyze it would destroy it): in that case, the intension of the nonrigid concept "car" corresponds to the examination process implemented by this software. In any possible world (e. g., today, tomorrow, after tomorrow, etc.), we are able to present some number of documents to this software and obtain the answers: the set of documents with the answer "yes" from this software will correspond to the extension of the intensional concept 'car" in a given world. But we have no general set of all possible one-page documents in order to be able to establish all possible extensions in all possible worlds. Practically, we are not able to define the meaning of this software based only on the finite

1 If the speaker knows the composition of all the possible worlds, the actual included, then he knows the latter *ipso fact*. This conclusion, however, does not follow. What he is missing is the ability to tell the actual world from the other possible worlds, i. e., the ability to recognize the actual world as such.

2 Variables may be given world-independent meanings in models. Such meanings are said to be rigid. Historically, this was the first quantified modal semantics to be introduced, and technically it is the simplest approach.

number of its elaborations, i. e., the intension of the concept "car" in this case can not be constructively defined based on the extensions in possible worlds.

However, I decided to make the embedding of the Montague's semantics as well, because the syntactic rules of a natural language are formulated in his basic papers in terms of recursive definitions (recursive semantics thesis of Donald Davidson, based on Frege's *compositionality principle*,

> *"the meaning of a sentence is a function of the meaning of its parts and of their mode of combinations"*)

specifying how complex sentences are to be formed out of simpler ones. These syntactic rules constitute a *categorial grammar*. Researches of natural language tried previously to develop a notation to restrain natural language to an existing formal language such as predicate calculus. The spirit of Montague's contribution is exactly the opposite: it models logical calculations according to the syntax of natural language, with the aim of formalizing valid reasoning process, which resist being so restraint. This recursive method I implemented in the intensional algebra $\mathcal{A}_{\text{int}}$ in the way that by intensional interpretation of the FOL syntax we obtain complex intensional terms of this algebra.

Bealer's approach

In his approach [12] to the intensional logic the fundamental entities are *intensional abstracts* or the so-called, "that-clauses." We assume that they are singular terms; Intensional expressions like "mean, and "assert" are standard two-place predicates that take "that-clauses" as arguments. Expressions like "is interesting," "is nice," etc., can be considered as one-place predicates that take "that"-clauses as arguments. For example, in the "intensional sentence," it is nice "that ϕ," where ϕ is a proposition, the "that ϕ" is denoted by the $<\phi>$, where $< >$ is the intensional abstraction operator, which transforms a logic formula into a *term*. So that the sentence "it is nice that ϕ" is expressed by the logic atom $N(<\phi>)$, where N is the unary predicate "is nice."

In this way, we are able to avoid to have the higher-order syntax for our *intensional* logic language (predicates appear in variable places of other predicates), as for example, HiLog [24] where the *same* symbol may denote a predicate, a function or an atomic formula. In the FOL with intensional abstraction, we have more fine distinction between a sentence ϕ and its use as a *term* "that ϕ," denoted by $<\phi>$ and considered as intensional name, inside some other predicate and, e. g., to have the first-order formula $\neg\phi \wedge p_i^2(t, <\phi>)$ instead of the second-order HiLog formula $\neg\phi \wedge p_i^2(t, \phi)$.

Definition 5. The syntax of the first-order logic language with intensional abstraction $< >$, denoted by $\mathcal{L}$, is as follows:

Logic operators $(\wedge, \neg, \exists)$; predicate letters in P (functional letters are considered as particular case of predicate letters); variables $x, y, z, \dots$ in $\mathcal{V}$; abstraction $<\_>$ and punctuation symbols (comma, parenthesis). With the following simultaneous inductive definition of *term* and *formula*:

1. All variables and constants (0-ary functional letters in P) are terms.
2. If $t_1, \dots, t_k$ are terms, then $p_i^k(t_1, \dots, t_k)$ is a formula ($p_i^k \in P$ is a k-ary predicate letter).
3. If ϕ and ψ are formulae, then $(\phi \wedge \psi)$, $\neg\phi$, and $(\exists x)\phi$ are formulae.
4. If $\phi(\mathbf{x})$ is a formula and, from Definition 23 in Section 2.1.1, $\alpha \subseteq \overline{\mathbf{x}}$ is a possibly empty subset of *hidden* (compressed) variables, then $<\phi(\mathbf{x})>^{\beta}_{\alpha}$ is an abstracted term where β is remained subset of free visible variables in ϕ. So, the subtuples of hidden and visible variables (preserving the ordering of the tuple $\mathbf{x}$ are $\pi_{-\beta}\mathbf{x}$ and $\pi_{-\alpha}\mathbf{x}$, respectively). If α or β is empty sequence, then it can be omitted (e. g., if ϕ is closed formula, then this term is denoted by $<\phi>$). An occurrence of a variable x_i in a formula (or a term) is *bound* (*free*) iff it lies (does not lie) within a formula of the form $(\exists x_i)\phi$ (or a term of the form $<\phi(\mathbf{x})>^{\beta}_{\alpha}$ with $x_i \in \alpha$). A variable is free (bound) in a formula (or term) iff it has (does not have) a free occurrence in that formula (or term).

A *sentence* is a formula having no free variables. The logic operators $\forall, \vee, \Rightarrow$ are defined in terms of $(\wedge, \neg, \exists)$ in the usual way.

For example, "x tells that ϕ" is given by formula $p_k^2(x, <\phi>)$ (p_k^2 is a binary "tell" predicate), 'being a bachelor is the same thing as being an unmarried man" is given by the identity of terms $<p_k^2(x)>_x = <p_i^1(x) \wedge p_j^1(x)>_x$ (with p_k^2 for "bachelor," p_i^1 for "unmarried" and p_j^1 for "man," unary predicates).

Remark. The k-ary functional symbols, for $k \geq 1$, in standard (extensional) FOL are considered as $(k+1)$-ary predicate symbols p^{k+1}: the function $f : \mathcal{D}^k \to \mathcal{D}$ is considered as a relation obtained from its graph $R = \{(d_1, \dots, d_k, f(d_1, \dots, d_k)) \mid d_i \in \mathcal{D}\}$, represented by a predicate symbol p^{k+1}. □

1.2 Intensionality and intensional/extensional semantics

Contemporary use of the term "intension" derives from the traditional logical doctrine that an idea has both an extension and an intension. Although there is divergence in formulation, it is accepted that the extension of an idea consists of the subjects to which the idea applies, and the intension consists of the attributes implied by the idea. In contemporary philosophy, it is linguistic expressions (here it is a logic formula), rather than concepts, that are said to have intensions and extensions. The intension is the concept expressed by the expression, and the extension is the set of items to which the expression applies. This usage resembles use of Frege's use of "Bedeutung" and "Sinn" [25]. It is evident that two ideas could have the same extension but different intensions. The systematic study of intensional entities has been pursued largely in the context of intensional logic; that part of logic in which the principle of (extensional) substitutivity of equivalent expressions fails.

Intensional entities (or concepts) are such things as propositions, relations and properties. What make them "intensional" is that they violate the principle of extensionality; the principle that extensional equivalence implies identity. All (or most) of these intensional entities have been classified at one time or another as kinds of universals [23]. Accordingly, standard traditional views about the ontological status of universals carry over to intensional entities. Nominalists hold that they do not really exist. Conceptualists accept their existence but deem it to be mind-dependent. Realists hold that they are mind-independent. *Ante rem* realists hold that they exist independently of being true of anything; *in re* realists require that they be true of something [23]. In what follows, we adopt the *Ante rem* realism.

In a predicate logics, (virtual) predicates expresses classes (properties and relations), and sentences express propositions. Note that classes (intensional entities) are *reified*, i. e., they belong to the same domain as individual objects (particulars). This endows the intensional logics with a great deal of uniformity, making it possible to manipulate classes and individual objects in the same language. In particular, when viewed as an individual object, a class can be a member of another class.

The extensional reductions, such as propositional complexes and propositional functions, to intensional entities are inadequate, there are several technical difficulties [26], so that we adopt the nonreductionist approaches and we will show how it corresponds to the possible world semantics. We begin with the informal theory that universals (properties (unary relations), relations and propositions in PRP theory [27]) are genuine entities that bear fundamental logical relations to one another. To study properties, relations and propositions, one defines a family of set-theoretical structures, one defines the intensional algebra, a family of set-theoretical structures most of which are built up from arbitrary objects and fundamental logical operations (conjunction, negation, existential generalization, etc.) on them.

The value of both traditional conceptions of PRPs (the "possible worlds" and "algebraic" Russel's approaches) is evident, and in Bealer's work both conceptions are developed side by side [12]. But Bealer's approach to intensional logic locates the origin of intensionality a single underlying *intensional abstraction* operation, which transforms the logic formulae into terms, so that we are able to make reification of logic formulae without the necessity of the second-order logics. In fact, the *intensional abstracts* are the so-called "that-clauses," as explained in the Introduction (Section 1.1.3).

Definition 6 (Intensional logic PRP domain $\mathcal{D}$). In intensionl logic, the concepts (properties, relations and propositions) are denotations for open and closed logic sentences, thus elements of the structured domain $\mathcal{D} = D_{-1} + D_I$, (here $+$ is a disjoint union) where

- A subdomain D_{-1} is made of particulars (individuals).
- The rest $D_I = D_0 + D_1 \ldots + D_n \ldots$ is made of universals (*concepts*):[3] D_0 for propositions with a distinct concept Truth $\in D_0$, D_1 for properties (unary concepts) and D_n, $n \geq 2$, for the n-ary concept.

The concepts in $\mathcal{D}_I$ are denoted by $u, v, \ldots$, while the values (individuals) in D_{-1} by $a, b, \ldots$ The empty tuple $\langle\,\rangle$ of the nullary relation $r_\emptyset$ (i. e., the unique tuple of 0-ary relation) is an individual in D_{-1}, with $\mathcal{D}^0 =_{\text{def}} \{\langle\,\rangle\}$. Thus, we have that $\{f, t\} = \mathcal{P}(\mathcal{D}^0) \subseteq \mathcal{P}(D_{-1})$, where by f and t we denote the empty set $\emptyset$ and set $\{\langle\,\rangle\}$, respectively.

A sort S is a subset of a domain $\mathcal{D}$. For example, $[0, 1]$ is closed interval of reals sort, $\{0, 1, 2, 3, \ldots\} \subseteq D_{-1}$ is the sort of integers, etc. These sorts are used for sorted variables in many-sorted predicate logics so that the assigned values for each sorted variable must belong to its sort. The unsorted variables can be considered as variables with a top sort equal to $\mathcal{D}$.

The *intensional interpretation* is a mapping between the set $\mathcal{L}$ of formulae of the logic language and intensional entities in $\mathcal{D}$, $I : \mathcal{L} \to \mathcal{D}$ is a kind of "conceptualization," such that an open sentence (virtual predicate) $\phi(x_1, \ldots, x_k)$ with a tuple of all free variables $(x_1, \ldots, x_k)$ is mapped into a k-ary *concept*, i. e., an intensional entity $u = I(\phi(x_1, \ldots, x_k)) \in D_k$, and (closed) sentence ψ into a proposition (i. e., *logic* concept) $v = I(\psi) \in D_0$ with $I(\top) =$ Truth $\in D_0$ for the FOL tautology $\top \in \mathcal{L}$ (the falsity in the FOL is a logic formula $\neg\top \in \mathcal{L}$). A language constant c is mapped into a particular $a = I(c) \in D_{-1}$ if it is a proper name, otherwise in a correspondent concept in $\mathcal{D}$. Thus, in any application of intensional FOL, this intensional interpretation that determines the meaning (sense) of the knowledge expressed by logic formulae is *uniquely determined (prefixed)*.

However, the extensions of the concepts (with this prefixed meaning) vary from a context (possible world, expressed by an extensionalizzation function) to another context in a similar way as for different Tarski's interpretations of the FOL.

Definition 7 (Extensions and extensionalization functions). Let $\mathfrak{R} = \bigcup_{k\in\mathbb{N}} \mathcal{P}(\mathcal{D}^k) = \sum_{k\in\mathbb{N}} \mathcal{P}(D^k)$ be the set of all k-ary relations, where $k \in \mathbb{N} = \{0, 1, 2, \ldots\}$. Notice that $\{f, t\} = \mathcal{P}(\mathcal{D}^0) \subseteq \mathfrak{R}$, i. e., $f, t \in \mathfrak{R}$, and hence the truth values are extensions in $\mathfrak{R}$. We define the function $f_{\langle\,\rangle} : \mathfrak{R} \to \mathfrak{R}$, such that for any $R \in \mathfrak{R}$,

$$f_{\langle\,\rangle}(R) =_{\text{def}} \{\langle\,\rangle\} \quad \text{if } R \neq \emptyset; \quad \emptyset \text{ otherwise.} \tag{1.3}$$

The extensions of the intensional entities (concepts) are given by the set $\mathcal{E}$ of extensionalization functions $h : \mathcal{D} \to D_{-1} + \mathfrak{R}$, such that

---

3 In what follows, we will define also a language of concepts with intensional connectives defined as operators of the intensional algebra $\mathcal{A}_{\text{int}}$ in Definition 16, so that D_I is the set of terms of this intensional algebra.

$$h = h_{-1} + h_0 + \sum_{i\geq 1} h_i : \sum_{i\geq -1} D_i \longrightarrow D_{-1} + \{f,t\} + \sum_{i\geq 1} \mathcal{P}(D^i) \tag{1.4}$$

where $h_{-1} : D_{-1} \to D_{-1}$ for the particulars, while $h_0 : D_0 \to \{f,t\} = \mathcal{P}(\mathcal{D}^0)$ assigns the truth values in $\{f,t\}$ to all propositions with the constant assignment $h_0(\text{Truth}) = t = \{\langle\,\rangle\}$, and for each $i \geq 1$, $h_i : D_i \to \mathcal{P}(D^i)$ assigns a relation to each concept.

Consequently, intensions can be seen as `names` of atomic or composite concepts, while the extensions correspond to various rules that these concepts play in different worlds.

Thus, for any open sentence $\phi(x_1,\dots,x_k)$, we have that its extension, in a given world $w \in \mathcal{W}$ of the Kripke's interpretation $\mathcal{M} = (\mathcal{W}, \{\mathcal{R}_i \mid 1 \leq i \leq k\}, \mathcal{D}, I_K)$ for modal (intensional) logics in Definition 3, is equal to

$$\begin{aligned} h(I(\phi(x_1,\dots,x_k))) &= \|\phi(x_1,\dots,x_k)\|_{\mathcal{M},w} \\ &= \{(g(x_1),\dots,g(x_k)) \mid g \in \mathcal{D}^{\mathcal{V}} \text{ and } \mathcal{M} \vDash_{w,g} \phi\}. \end{aligned}$$

The intensional entities for the same logic formula, e. g., $x_2 + 3 = x_1^2 - 4$, which can be denoted by $\phi(x_2,x_1)$ or $\phi(x_1,x_2)$, from above we need to differentiate their concepts by $I(\phi(x_2,x_1)) \neq I(\phi(x_1,x_2))$ because otherwise we would obtain erroneously that $h(I(\phi(x_2,x_1))) = h(I(\phi(x_1,x_2)))$. Thus, in intensional logic the ordering in the tuple of variables $\mathbf{x}$ in a given open formula ϕ is very important, as follows.

Definition 8 (Virtual predicates). *The virtual predicate* obtained from an open formula $\phi \in \mathcal{L}$ is denoted by $\phi(x_1,\dots,x_m)$ where $(x_1,\dots,x_m)$ is a particular fixed sequence of the set of all free variables in ϕ. This definition contains the precise method of establishing the *ordering* of variables in this tuple: such an method that will be adopted here is the ordering of appearance, from left to right, of free variables in ϕ. This method of composing the tuple of free variables is unique and canonical way of definition of the virtual predicate from a given open formula.

The virtual predicates are useful also to replace the general FOL quantifier on variables $(\exists x)$ by specific quantifiers $\exists_i$ of the FOL syntax algebra $\mathcal{A}_{\text{FOL}}$, where $i \geq 1$ is the position of variable x inside a virtual predicate. For example, the standard FOL formula $(\exists x_k)\phi(x_i,x_j,x_k,x_l,x_m)$ will be mapped into intensional concept $\exists_3\phi(\mathbf{x}) \in \mathcal{A}_{\text{FOL}}$ where $\mathbf{x}$ is the list(tuple) of variables (x_i,x_j,x_k,x_l,x_m).

We will denote by $\phi(x_1,\dots,x_m)_\lambda$ the virtual predicate, obtained from the (canonical) virtual predicate $\phi(x_1,\dots,x_m)$, with ordering of variables determined by the given permutation $\lambda : \mathbb{N} \to \mathbb{N}$.

Remark. The *virtual predicates* are used in the syntax FOL algebra $\mathcal{A}_{\text{FOL}}$, in order to extend the intensional interpretation I into a homomorphism between $\mathcal{A}_{\text{FOL}}$ and intensional algebra $\mathcal{A}_{\text{int}}$. We will see that also for the intensional algebra of concepts $\mathcal{A}_{\text{int}}$ in Definition 16, we will use intensional unary operators exists$_k$ (corresponding to the logic quantifiers $\exists_k$), and hence we consider that each n-ary concept $u \in D_n$ implicitly has also the tuple $\mathbf{x}$ (with $n = |\mathbf{x}|$) of concepts variables. Having this in mind, we will never write $u(\mathbf{x}) \in D_n$, but simply $u \in \mathcal{D}_n$.

We recall that the concepts obtained by intensional mapping I of virtual predicates, will implicitly preserve the (ordered) tuple of variables of such virtual predicates. □

It is well known that we are able to make the extensional algebraization of the FOL by using the *cylindric* algebras [28] that are the extension of Boolean algebras with a set of binary operators for the FOL identity relations and a set of unary algebraic operators ("projections") for each case of FOL quantification ($\exists x$). In what follows, we will make an analog extensional algebraization over $\mathfrak{R}$ but by interpretation of the logic conjunction $\wedge$ by a set of *natural join* operators over relations introduced by Codd's relational algebra [29, 30] as a kind of a predicate calculus whose interpretations are tied to the database.

Definition 9. Let us define the extensional relational algebra for the FOL by

$$\mathcal{A}_{\mathfrak{R}} = (\mathfrak{R}, R_{=}, \{\langle\,\rangle\}, \{\bowtie_S\}_{S \in \mathcal{P}(\mathbb{N}^2)}, \sim, \{\pi_{-n}\}_{n \in \mathbb{N}}),$$

where $\{\langle\,\rangle\} \in \mathfrak{R}$ is the algebraic value correspondent to the logic truth, $R_{=}$ is the binary relation for extensionally equal elements, with the following operators:

1. Binary operator $\bowtie_S : \mathfrak{R} \times \mathfrak{R} \to \mathfrak{R}$, such that for any two relations $R_1, R_2 \in \mathfrak{R}$, the $R_1 \bowtie_S R_2$ is equal to the relation obtained by natural join of these two relations `if` S is a nonempty set of pairs of joined columns of respective relations (where the first argument is the column index of the relation R_1 while the second argument is the column index of the joined column of the relation R_2); `otherwise` it is equal to the Cartesian product $R_1 \times R_2$.
2. Unary operator $\sim : \mathfrak{R} \to \mathfrak{R}$, such that for any k-ary (with $k \geq 1$) relation $R \in \mathcal{P}(\mathcal{D}^k) \subset \mathfrak{R}$ we have that $\sim (R) = \mathcal{D}^k \backslash R \in \mathcal{P}(\mathcal{D}^k)$, where "\" is the substraction of relations. For $u \in \{f, t\} = \mathcal{P}(\mathcal{D}^0) \subseteq \mathfrak{R}$, $\sim (u) = \mathcal{D}^0 \backslash u$.
3. Unary operator $\pi_{-n} : \mathfrak{R} \to \mathfrak{R}$, such that for any k-ary (with $k \geq 1$) relation $R \in \mathcal{P}(\mathcal{D}^k) \subset \mathfrak{R}$ we have that $\pi_{-n}(R)$ is equal to the relation obtained by elimination of the n-th column of the relation R `if` $1 \leq n \leq k$ and $k \geq 2$; equal to, from (1.3), $f_{\langle\,\rangle}(R)$ `if` $n = k = 1$; `otherwise` it is equal to R.

We will use the symbol "=" for the extensional identity for relations in $\mathfrak{R}$.

Notice that $\mathfrak{R}$ is a poset with the bottom element $\emptyset$ and the top element $\{\langle\,\rangle\}$, and the partial ordering $\preceq$ defined as follows: for any two relations $R_1, R_2 \in \mathfrak{R}$,

$$R_1 \preceq R_2 \quad \text{iff} \quad \text{“for some operation } \bowtie_S \text{ it holds that } (R_1 \bowtie_S R_2) = R_1.\text{”}$$

It is easy to verify that for any $R \in \mathfrak{R}$ and operation $\bowtie_S$ it holds that $(\emptyset \bowtie_S R) = \emptyset$, and $(R \bowtie_S \{\langle\,\rangle\}) = R$. That is, $\emptyset \preceq R \preceq \{\langle\,\rangle\}$.

Let us define the FOL syntax algebra $\mathcal{A}_{\mathrm{FOL}}$. For example, the FOL formula $\phi(x_i, x_j, x_k, x_l, x_m) \wedge \psi(x_l, y_i, x_j, y_j)$ will be replaced by a specific *virtual predicate* $\phi(x_i, x_j, x_k, x_l, x_m) \wedge_S \psi(x_l, y_i, x_j, y_j)$, with $S = \{(4,1),(2,3)\}$, and then traduced by the algebraic expression $R_1 \bowtie_S R_2$ where $R_1 \in \mathcal{P}(\mathcal{D}^5), R_2 \in \mathcal{P}(\mathcal{D}^4)$ are the extensions for a given Tarski's interpretation I_T of the virtual predicate ϕ, ψ relatively. In this example, the resulting relation will have the following ordering of attributes: $(x_i, x_j, x_k, x_l, x_m, y_i, y_j)$. In the case when S is empty (i. e., its cardinality $|S| = 0$), then the resulting relation is the Cartesian product of R_1 and R_2. Consequently, we have that for any two formulae $\phi, \psi \in \mathcal{L}$ and a particular join operator $\bowtie_S$ uniquely determined by tuples of free variables in these two formulae,

$$I_T^*(\phi \wedge_S \psi) = I_T^*(\phi) \bowtie_S I_T^*(\psi).$$

For example, the logic formula (a virtual predicate) $\neg\phi(x_i, x_j, x_k, x_l, x_m)$ will be traduced by the algebraic expression $\mathcal{D}^5 \backslash R$ where R is the extensions for a given Tarski's interpretation I_T of the virtual predicate ϕ. Consequently, we have that for any formula $\phi \in \mathcal{L}$,

$$I_T^*(\neg\phi) =\sim (I_T^*(\phi)).$$

For example, the FOL formula $(\exists x_k)\phi(x_i, x_j, x_k, x_l, x_m)$ will be replaced in $\mathcal{A}_{\mathrm{FOL}}$ by a specific virtual predicate $(\exists_3)\phi(x_i, x_j, x_k, x_l, x_m)$ and then traduced by the algebraic expression $\pi_{-3}(R)$ where R is the extension for a given Tarski's interpretation I_T of the virtual predicate ϕ. The resulting relation will have the following ordering of attributes: (x_i, x_j, x_l, x_m). Consequently, we have that for any formula $\phi \in \mathcal{L}$ with a free variable x, where m is equal to the position of this variable x in the tuple of free variables in ϕ (or $m = 0$ otherwise, where π_{-0} is the identity function),

$$I_T^*((\exists_m)\phi) = \pi_{-m}(I_T^*(\phi)).$$

Based on the new set of logical connectives introduced above, where the standard FOL operators $\wedge$ and $\exists$ are substituted by a set of specialized operators $\{\wedge_S\}_{S\in\mathcal{P}(\mathbb{N}^2)}$ and $\{\exists n\}_{n\in\mathbb{N}}$ as explained above, we can define the following free syntax algebra for the FOL.

Corollary 1 (Extensional FOL semantics). *Let $\mathcal{A}_{\mathrm{FOL}} = (\mathcal{L}, \doteq, \top, \{\wedge_S\}_{S\in\mathcal{P}(\mathbb{N}^2)}, \neg, \{\exists n\}_{n\in\mathbb{N}})$ be an* extended *free syntax algebra for the first-order logic with identity $\doteq$, with the set $\mathcal{L}$ of first-order logic formulae with the set of variables in $\mathcal{V}$, with $\top$ denoting the tautology formula (the contradiction formula is denoted by $\bot \equiv \neg\top$).*

Then, for any Tarski's interpretation I_T its unique extension to all formulae $I_T^* : \mathcal{L} \to \mathfrak{R}$ is also the Tarski's homomorphism *$I_T^* : \mathcal{A}_{\mathrm{FOL}} \to \mathcal{A}_{\mathfrak{R}}$ from the free syntax FOL algebra into this extensional relational algebra.*

Proof. The proof is directly from the definition of the semantics of the operators in $\mathcal{A}_{\mathfrak{R}}$ in Definition 9 and previous examples. Let us take, e. g., the case of conjunction of logic formulae $\phi(x_i, x_j, x_k, x_l, x_m) \wedge \psi(x_l, y_i, x_j, y_j)$, for which $S = \{(4,1),(2,3)\}$ and:

$$\begin{aligned}
&I_T^*(\phi \wedge_S \psi)\\
&= I_T^*(\varphi) = \{(g(x_i), g(x_j), g(x_k), g(x_l), g(x_m), g(y_i), g(y_j)) \mid I_T^*(\varphi/g) = t\}\\
&= \{(g(x_i), g(x_j), g(x_k), g(x_l), g(x_m), g(y_i), g(y_j)) \mid I_T^*(\phi/g \wedge_S \psi/g) = t\}\\
&= \{(g(x_i), g(x_j), g(x_k), g(x_l), g(x_m), g(y_i), g(y_j)) \mid I_T^*(\phi/g) = t \text{ and } I_T^*(\phi/g) = t\}\\
&= \{(g(x_i), g(x_j), g(x_k), g(x_l), g(x_m), g(y_i), g(y_j)) \mid (g(x_i), g(x_j), g(x_k), g(x_l), g(x_m))\\
&\in I_T^*(\phi) \text{ and } (g(x_l), g(y_i), g(x_j), g(y_j)) \in I_T^*(\phi)\}\\
&= I_T^*(\phi) \bowtie_S I_T^*(\psi).
\end{aligned}$$

Thus, it is enough to show that it is also valid $I_T^*(\top) = \{\langle\,\rangle\}$, and $I_T^*(\neg\top) = \emptyset$. The first property comes from the fact that $\top$ is a tautology, thus satisfied by every assignment g, i. e., it is true, i. e., $I_T^*(\top) = t$ (and t is equal to the empty tuple $\{\langle\,\rangle\}$). The second property comes from the fact that $I_T^*(\neg\top) =\sim (I_T^*(\top)) =\sim (\{\langle\,\rangle\}) = \mathcal{D}^0 \backslash \{\langle\,\rangle\} = \{\langle\,\rangle\} \backslash \{\langle\,\rangle\} = \emptyset$. That is, the tautology and the contradiction have the true and false logic value, respectively, in $\mathfrak{R}$.

We have also that $I_T^*(\doteq(x,y)) = I_T(\doteq) = R_=$ for every interpretation I_T because $\doteq$ is the built-in binary predicate, i. e., with the same extension in every Tarski's interpretation.

So, the mapping $I_T^* : (\mathcal{L}, \doteq, \top, \{\wedge_S\}_{S\in\mathcal{P}(\mathbb{N}^2)}, \neg, \{\exists n\}_{n\in\mathbb{N}}) \to \mathcal{A}_{\mathfrak{R}}$ is a homomorphism that represents the extensional Tarskian semantics of the FOL. □

Notice that the ordering of attributes of resulting relations corresponds to the method used for generating the ordering of variables in the tuples of free variables adopted for virtual predicates.

From a logic point of view, two possible worlds w and w' are indistinguishable if all sentences have the same extensions in them, so that we can consider an extensionalization function h as a "possible world," similar to the semantics of a probabilistic logic, where possible worlds are Herbrand interpretations for given set of predicate letters P in a given logic. Thus, for a given modal logic we will have that there is a bijection $\mathcal{F} : \mathcal{W} \to \mathcal{E}$ between the set of possible worlds and the set of extensionalization functions.

Definition 10 (Two-step intensional semantics [19]). The intensional semantics of the logic language with the set of formulae $\mathcal{L}$ can be represented by the mapping

$$\mathcal{L} \longrightarrow_I \mathcal{D} \Longrightarrow_{h\in\mathcal{E}} \mathfrak{R},$$

where $\longrightarrow_I$ is a *fixed intensional* interpretation $I : \mathcal{L} \to \mathcal{D}$ with image $\mathrm{im}(I) \subset \mathcal{D}$, and $\Longrightarrow_{h\in\mathcal{E}}$ is *the set* of all extensionalization functions $h = \mathcal{F}(w) : \mathrm{im}(I) \to \mathfrak{R}$ in $\mathcal{E}$, where the mapping $\mathcal{F} : \mathcal{W} \to \mathcal{E}$ is the mapping from the set of possible worlds to the set of extensionalization functions.

We use the mapping $I_n : \mathcal{L}_{op} \to \mathfrak{R}^{\mathcal{W}}$ in Definition 4, where $\mathcal{L}_{op}$ is a subset of formulae with free variables (virtual predicates), such that for any virtual predicate $\phi(x_1, \dots, x_k) \in \mathcal{L}_{op}$ the mapping $I_n(\phi(x_1, \dots, x_k)) : \mathcal{W} \to \mathfrak{R}$ is the Montague's meaning (i. e., *intension*) of this virtual predicate [7–11], i. e., the mapping, which returns with the extension of this (virtual) predicate in every possible world in $\mathcal{W}$.

Note that the domain of $h \in \mathcal{E}$ is subset of $\mathcal{D}$ of intensional elements derived only from the set of formulae $\mathcal{L}$ used by a singular application, so $h_1 \neq h_2$ is determined only by elements in $\mathrm{im}(I)$ and so is determined also the set $\mathcal{E}$ of (different) extensionaliztion functions.

Example 1. Let us consider the following two past participles: "bought" and "sold" (with unary predicates $p_1^1(x)$, "x has been bought," and $p_2^1(x)$, "x has been sold"). These two different concepts in Montague's semantics would have not only the same extension but also their intension, from the fact that their extensions are identical in every possible world.

Within the two-steps formalism, we can avoid this problem by assigning two different concepts (meanings) $u = I(p_1^1(x))$ and $v = I(p_2^1(x))$ in $\in D_1$.

Note that the same problem we have in the Montague's semantics for two sentences with different meanings, which bear the same truth value across all possible worlds: in Montague's semantics, they will be forced to the *same* meaning.

Based on this definition, we can establish the direct relationship between Bealer's and Montague's intensionality.

Proposition 1 (Bealer–Montague relationship). *For any logic formula (a virtual predicate) $\phi(\mathbf{x})$, with a tuple of free variables $\mathbf{x}$, its extension in a possible world $w \in \mathcal{W}$ satisfies the following equation:*

$$\mathcal{F}(w)(I(\phi(\mathbf{x}))) = I_n(\phi(\mathbf{x}))(w) \tag{1.5}$$

Proof. The proof is directly from the definition of the identification of a possible world w of Montague's approach with the extensional function $h = \mathcal{F}(w) \in \mathcal{E}$ in the Bealer's approach, where $I_n(\phi(\mathbf{x}))(w)$ is the "functional" intension of Montague, and $\mathcal{F}(w)$ is the Bealer's extensionalization function corresponding to the Montague's world $w \in \mathcal{W}$. □

We adopted this two-step intensional semantics, instead of the well-known Montague's semantics (which lies in the construction of a compositional and recursive semantics that covers both intension and extension) because of a number of its weakness, as that in Example 1 above. But there is also another advantage of this two-step intensional semantics in Definition 10: here, we are able to define an intensional algebra $\mathcal{A}_{int}$ over intensional entities in $\mathcal{D}$, which is self-sufficient, different from Montague's semantics where the compositional and recursive semantics of intensions can be defined only by their extensional properties.

As we will see in Section 1.3, this intensional algebra is defined in the way that each extensional mapping $h = \mathcal{F}(w) : \mathcal{D} \to \mathfrak{R}$ is also a *homomorphism* between this intensional algebra $\mathcal{A}_{int}$ and the extensional relational algebra $\mathcal{A}_{\mathfrak{R}}$ that represents the compositional and recursive semantics of the extensions in Corollary 1.

In this way, the compositional and recursive semantics of the intensions in $\mathcal{A}_{int}$ coincides with the Montague's semantics, where, e. g., the mapping $I_n(\phi \wedge \psi) : \mathcal{W} \to \mathfrak{R}$, i. e., Montague's intension of the composite formula $\phi \wedge \psi$ is functionally dependent on the mappings $I_n(\phi) : \mathcal{W} \to \mathfrak{R}$ and $I_n(\psi) : \mathcal{W} \to \mathfrak{R}$ (i. e., dependent on the Montague's intensions of ϕ and ψ).

Remark. The mapping I_n can be extended also to all sentences (the formulae without free variables), such that for any sentence ϕ, $I_n(\phi) : \mathcal{W} \to \{f, t\} = \mathcal{P}(\mathcal{D}^0) \subseteq \mathfrak{R}$ is a mapping that defines the truth value (i. e., an extension in $\mathfrak{R}$ in Definition 7) of this sentence in each possible world $\mathcal{W}$. Equivalently to this, Montague's semantics for intensions of logic formulae, we can use the Carnap's semantics [31] of concepts in $\mathcal{D}$, i. e., $I_{n,c} : \mathcal{D} \to \mathfrak{R}^{\mathcal{W}}$ such that the intension of a *concept* $u \in \mathcal{D}$ is a mapping $I_{n,c}(u) : \mathcal{W} \to \mathfrak{R}$ from possible worlds to extensions. This Carnap's semantics of concepts is similar to the second mapping of the diagram $\mathcal{D} \Rightarrow_{w \in \mathcal{W}} \mathfrak{R}$ in the two-step intensional semantics. □

Tarski's FOL interpretation we represent by new single mapping $I_T^* : \mathcal{L} \to \mathfrak{R}$, as explained in the Introduction dedicated to FOL in (1.1) and (1.2). But also intensional semantics is given by $h \circ I : \mathcal{L} \to \mathfrak{R}$ where $\circ$ is a composition of functions. So, if there is a modal Kripke semantics with a set of possible worlds $\mathcal{W}$ (thus, an intensional semantics) for FOL, *equivalent* to the standard FOL semantics given by the Tarski's interpretation I_T, then we obtain correspondence $I_T^* = h \circ I$ for such FOL, such that for any $\phi \in \mathcal{L}$, $h(I(\phi)) = I_T^*(\phi)$. For any constant c of the FOL language, we assume that $I(c) = I_T(c) \in \mathcal{D}$.

Definition 11 (Tarski's constraints). This intensional semantics has to preserve standard Tarski's semantics of the FOL. That is, for any formula $\phi(\mathbf{x}) \in \mathcal{L}$ with a tuple of free variables $(x_1, \ldots, x_k)$, and $h \in \mathcal{E}$, the following conservative conditions for all assignments $g, g' \in \mathcal{D}^{\mathcal{V}}$ has to be satisfied:

$$(T) \quad h(I(\phi(\mathbf{x})/g)) = t \quad \text{iff} \quad (g(x_1), \ldots, g(x_k)) \in h(I(\phi(\mathbf{x}))) \tag{1.6}$$

and for each $(k-1)$-ary functional symbol f^{k-1} in standard FOL, $k \geq 2$, in *intensional* FOL we define ϕ to be a predicate letter p_i^k, such that

$$(TF) \quad h(I(p_i^k(\mathbf{x})/g)) = h(I(p_i^k(\mathbf{x})/g')) = t \quad \text{and} \quad \forall_{1 \leq i \leq k-1}(g'(x_i) = g(x_i))$$
$$\text{implies } g'(x_{k+1}) = g(x_{k+1}).$$

We consider that the domain $\mathcal{D}$ is equal in each possible world $w \in \mathcal{W}$. It is demonstrated that also in the case of different domains $\mathcal{D}_w$ in different possible worlds, we can always obtain the constant domain model (as in Definition 2.1 in [32]) $\mathcal{D} = \bigcup_{w\in\mathcal{W}} \mathcal{D}_w$ and by introducing a new built-in binary predicate $e(x,y)$ where x has as domain the set of possible worlds, so that $e(w,d)$ is true if $d \in \mathcal{D}_w$.

The particulars in $\mathcal{D}_{-1}$, which are *rigid objects* like the "Eiffel tower" or "George Washington," have equal extension (denotation) in each possible world: it holds from the fact that for every rigid object c, a possible world $w \in \mathcal{W}$, and a given intensional interpretation I we have that $d = I(c) \in \mathcal{D}_{-1}$ and its extension is $h(d) = \mathcal{F}(w)(d) = d$ constant independently from w.

The *nonrigid objects* and relative complications considered by Fitting in [2, 32, 33], as "the gross domestic product of Denmark" or "the Secretary General of the United Nations," here are constants c of the language that are mapped into particulars $d = I(c) \in \mathcal{D}_{-1}$ with extension $h(d) = \mathcal{F}(w)(d) = d$ that depends on the possible world $w \in \mathcal{W}$.

The previous considerations explain why in these two-step interpretations, intensional and extensional, we can work in an unified *general rigid* framework, and overcome the major difficulties for modal first-order logics, considered by Fitting in the number of his papers, by introducing new operations like "extension of" operators $\downarrow$ and "predicate abstracts," $\langle \lambda x_1,\dots,x_n.\phi\rangle$ that transforms the logic formula with a tuple of free variables $\phi(x_1,\dots,x_n)$ into new *atomic* formula $\langle \lambda x_1,\dots,x_n.\phi\rangle(t_1,\dots,t_n)$ for any given set of terms $t_i, i = 1,\dots,n$ (Definition 2.3 in [32]). Notice that different from this Fitting's approach, we do not consider a virtual predicate $\phi(x_1,\dots,x_n)$ as a new *atom*, but as a standard logic formula.

Another relevant question w. r. t. this two-step interpretations of an intensional semantics is how in it the extensional identity relation $\doteq$, binary predicate of the identity of the FOL is managed (we prefer to distinguish this *formal symbol* $\doteq \in P$ of the built-in identity binary predicate letter in the FOL from the standard mathematical symbol "=" used in all mathematical definitions).

Here, this extensional identity relation is mapped into the binary concept $\mathrm{Id} = I(\doteq(x,y)) \in D_2$, such that $(\forall w \in \mathcal{W})(\mathcal{F}(w)(\mathrm{Id}) = R_{=})$, where $\doteq (x,y)$ denotes an atom of the FOL of the binary predicate for identity in FOL, usually written by FOL formula $x \doteq y$. That is, for every possible world w and its correspondent extensionalization function $h = \mathcal{F}(w)$, the extensional identity relation in $\mathcal{D}$ is the extension of the binary concept $\mathrm{Id} \in D_2$, as defined by Bealer's approach to intensional FOL with intensional abstraction in [12].

1.2.1 First-order logic and modality

In propositional modal logics (see Definition 2), the possible worlds are entities where a given propositional symbol can be true or false. Thus, from *logical* point of view the *possible worlds* [34, 35] in Kripke's relational semantics are characterized by property to determine the truth of logic sentences. The important question relative to the syntax of the FOL is if there is a kind of basic set of possible worlds that have such properties.

The answer is affirmative. In fact, if we consider a k-ary predicate letter p_i^k as a new kind of "propositional letter," then an assignment $g : \mathcal{V} \to \mathcal{D}$ can be considered as an *intrinsic* (par excellence) possible world, where the truth of this "propositional letter" p_i^k is equal to the truth of the ground atom $p_i^k(g(x_1), \ldots, g(x_k))$. Consequently, in what follows we will denote by $\mathcal{W}$ the set of *explicit* possible worlds (defined explicitly for each particular case of modal logics), while the set $\mathcal{D}^{\mathcal{V}}$ will be considered as the set of *intrinsic* possible worlds (which is invariant and common for every *predicate* modal logic introduced in Definition 3). In the case when $\mathcal{V} = \emptyset$ is the empty set, we obtain the singleton set of intrinsic possible worlds $\mathcal{D}^{\mathcal{V}} = \{*\}$, with the empty function $* : \emptyset \to \mathcal{D}$.

By $\mathbb{W} \subseteq \{(w, g) \mid w \in \mathcal{W}, g \in \mathcal{D}^{\mathcal{V}}\}$, we denote the set of (generalized) possible worlds. In this way, as in the case of propositional modal logic, we obtain that a formula φ is *true* in a Kripke's interpretation $\mathcal{M}$ if for each (generalized) possible world $u = (w, g) \in \mathbb{W}$, $\mathcal{M} \models_u \varphi$. By $\|\phi\| = \{(w, g) \in \mathbb{W} \mid \mathcal{M} \models_{w,g} \phi\}$, we denote the set of all worlds where the formula ϕ is satisfied by interpretation $\mathcal{M}$. Thus, as in the case of the propositional modal logics, also in the case of predicate modal logics, we have that a formula ϕ is true iff it is satisfied in all (generalized) possible worlds, i. e., iff $\|\phi\| = \mathbb{W}$.

Different from the FOL with original Tarski's interpretation for the unique existential operator $\exists$, the modal point of view for the FOL with Kripke's interpretation replaces each $(\exists x)$, for a variable $x \in \mathcal{V}$, with a particular existential modal operator $\Diamond_x$ [36]. As usual, the universal modal operators defined for $(\forall x) = \neg(\exists x)\neg$ are $\Box_x = \neg\Diamond_x\neg$.

Consequently, the *same syntax* for the FOL, given by algebra $\mathcal{A}_{\mathrm{FOL}} = (\mathcal{L}, \doteq, \top, \{\wedge_S\}_{S \in \mathcal{P}(\mathbb{N}^2)}, \neg, \{\exists n\}_{n \in \mathbb{N}})$ in Corollary 1, of a formula $(\exists n)\phi$ can have *two* equivalent semantics: the original Tarski's interpretation that interprets the existential operators $(\exists n)$, and Kripke's relational interpretation where $(\exists n)$ are interpreted as existential modal operators $\Diamond_n$. This is valid approach based on the fact that, from the algebraic point of view, the syntax of $(\exists n)$ can be interpreted as an unary operation, which is *additive*, i. e., it holds that $(\exists n)(\phi \vee \psi) = (\exists n)(\phi) \vee (\exists n)(\psi)$, and *normal*, i. e., $(\exists n)(\bot) = \bot$ where $\bot$ denotes a contradiction sentence (the negation of the tautology $\top$). This property is common for all *existential modal* operators of the *normal* Kripke modal logics. In fact, the generalization inference rule (G) of FOL here becomes the rule of necessitation, and the axiom (A1) a particular case of Kripke axiom of normal modal logics.

With this new arrangement, we can reformulate the standard semantics for multimodal predicate logic in Definition 3 (π_1 and π_2 denote the first and the second projections).

Definition 12 (Generalized Kripke semantics for predicate modal logics). By $\mathcal{M} = (\mathbb{W}, \{\mathcal{R}_i\}, \mathcal{D}, I_K)$, we denote a Kripke's interpretation with a set of generalized possible worlds $\mathbb{W}$ (with a set of explicit possible worlds $\mathcal{W} = \pi_1(\mathbb{W})$ and $\mathcal{D}^{\mathcal{V}} = \pi_2(\mathbb{W})$), the accessibility relations $\mathcal{R}_i \subseteq \mathbb{W} \times \mathbb{W}$, $i \in \mathbb{N}$ for existential modal operators, domain $\mathcal{D}$ and a mapping $I_K : \mathbb{W} \times (P \bigcup F) \rightarrow \bigcup_{n \in \mathcal{N}} \mathbf{2}^{\mathcal{D}^n}$, such that for any $\mathbf{w} = (w, g) \in \mathbb{W}$:

1. For any predicate letter $p_i^k \in P$, the function $I_K(\mathbf{w}, p_i^k) : \mathcal{D}^K \rightarrow \mathbf{2}$ defines the extension of p_i^k in a world $\mathbf{w}$,

$$\|p_i^k(x_1, \ldots, x_k)\| =_{\text{def}} \{(d_1, \ldots, d_k) \in \mathcal{D}^k \mid I_K(\mathbf{w}, p_i^k)(d_1, \ldots, d_k) = t\}.$$

2. For any functional letter $f_i^k \in F$, here considered as a p_i^{k+1} predicate, $I_K(\mathbf{w}, f_i^k) : \mathcal{D}^{k+1} \rightarrow \mathbf{2}$ defines the graph of this function in a world $\mathbf{w}$ (as for a predicate above, with d_{k+1} equal to the result of this function).

For any formula φ, we define $\mathcal{M} \vDash_{\mathbf{w}} \varphi$ iff φ is satisfied in a world $\mathbf{w} = (w, g) \in \mathbb{W}$. So, a given letter p_i^k is true in $\mathbf{w} = (w, g)$, i. e., $\mathcal{M} \vDash_{\mathbf{w}} p_i^k(x_1, \ldots, x_k)$ iff $I_K(\mathbf{w}, p_i^k)(g(x_1), \ldots, g(x_k)) = t$.

The Kripke semantics is extended to all formulae as follows:

$$\mathcal{M} \vDash_{\mathbf{w}} \varphi \wedge \phi \quad \text{iff} \quad \mathcal{M} \vDash_{\mathbf{w}} \varphi \text{ and } \mathcal{M} \vDash_{\mathbf{w}} \phi,$$
$$\mathcal{M} \vDash_{\mathbf{w}} \neg\varphi \quad \text{iff not} \quad \mathcal{M} \vDash_{\mathbf{w}} \varphi,$$
$$\mathcal{M} \vDash_{\mathbf{w}} \Diamond_i \varphi \quad \text{iff} \quad \text{exists } \mathbf{w}' \in \mathbb{W} \text{ such that } (\mathbf{w}, \mathbf{w}') \in \mathcal{R}_i \text{ and } \mathcal{M} \vDash_{\mathbf{w}'} \varphi.$$

The universal modal operator $\Box_i$ is equal to $\neg\Diamond_i\neg$.

A formula φ is said to be *true in a Kripke's interpretation* $\mathcal{M}$ if for each possible world $\mathbf{w}$, $\mathcal{M} \vDash_{\mathbf{w}} \varphi$. A formula is said to be *valid* if it is true in each interpretation.

Note that for the modal predicate logics with *generalized* Kripke semantics in the definition above, the satisfaction relation $\vDash_{\mathbf{w}}$, while it conserves the same semantics, has the syntax equal to that used for the *propositional* modal logics.

Consequently, we have two particular "projections" of the generalized Kripke semantics for multimodal logics, defined above: the first one is an explicit-worlds projection resulting in the Kripke semantics of multimodal propositional logics (i. e., "PL $\mathcal{K}$-semantics"); the second one is an intrinsic-worlds projection resulting in the *Kripke semantics of FOL* (i. e., "FOL $\mathcal{K}$-semantics").

Proposition 2 (Explicit-worlds "projection" into PL $\mathcal{K}$-semantics). *The Kripke semantics of multimodal* `propositional` *logic in Definition* 2 *is a particular case of the Definition* 12 *when $\mathcal{D}, F$ and $\mathcal{V}$ are empty sets, and P has only nullary symbols, i. e., the propositional symbols.*

Proof. In this case, when $\mathcal{V} = \emptyset$ is the empty set, we have that $\mathcal{D}^{\mathcal{V}}$ is a singleton set, denoted by $\{*\}$, with unique element equal to the empty function $* : \mathcal{V} \rightarrow \mathcal{D}$ (i. e., the function with empty graph). Thus, $\mathbb{W} = \mathcal{W} \times \{*\}$ is equivalent to the set of explicit worlds $\mathcal{W}$, so that the original satisfaction relation $\mathcal{M} \vDash_{w,g}$, where $g = *$, $w \in \mathcal{W}$, of predicate modal logic in Definition 3 can be equivalently reduced to the satisfaction relation $\mathcal{M} \models_w$ for only explicit worlds of propositional logic in Definition 3.

While $I_K : \mathcal{W} \times P \to \bigcup_{n \in \mathcal{N}} \mathbf{2}^{\mathcal{D}^n}$ in this case $\mathcal{N} = \{0\}$ is reduced to $I_K : \mathcal{W} \times P \to \mathbf{2}^{\mathcal{D}^0}$, with a singleton set $\mathcal{D}^0 =_{\text{def}} \{\langle\,\rangle\}$, and hence $\mathbf{2}^{\mathcal{D}^0}$ is equivalent to $\mathbf{2}$. So, we obtain the reduction into the mapping $I_K : \mathcal{W} \times P \to \mathbf{2}$, and by currying (the λ abstraction), we obtain the mapping $I'_K : P \to \mathbf{2}^W$, such that for any $p_i \in P$ and $w \in \mathcal{W}$ we have that $I_K(w, p_i) = I'_K(p_i)(w) \in \mathbf{2}$ is the truth value of propositional letter (nullary predicate symbol in P) in the explicit possible world w. It is easy to verify that this obtained mapping I'_K is that of the *propositional* modal logic given in Definition 2. □

An interesting consequence of this explicit-world projection of the generalized Kripke semantics is the idea of the *extension* of a propositional nullary predicate symbol p_i^0, denoted here as a propositional symbol p_i, given by Definition 12 by

$$\begin{aligned}\|p_i\| = \|p_i^0\| &=_{\text{def}} \{(d_0) \in \mathcal{D}^0 \mid I_K(w, p_i^0)(d_0) = t\} \\ &= \{\langle\,\rangle \mid I_K(w, p_i^0) = t\} = \{\langle\,\rangle \mid I'_K(p_i)(w) = t\} = I'_K(p_i)(w).\end{aligned}$$

That is, it is equal to $t = \{\langle\,\rangle\}$ if p_i is true in the explicit world w, or equal to f (the empty set) if p_i is false in the explicit world w. It is analogous to the consideration of extensions of sentences defined in the intensional semantics, as defined in Section 1.2, where the *truth* is the extension of sentences, distinct from their *meaning*, i. e., their intension (from Montague's point of view, the intension of the propositional letter p_i used above would be the function $I'_K(p_i) : \mathcal{W} \to \mathbf{2}$).

It is well known for predicate logic and FOL (which is a predicate logic extended by logic quantifiers) that we have not any defined set of *explicit* possible worlds. Thus, trying to define the Kripke semantics (given by Definition 12) to FOL, we can assume that the generalized possible worlds coincide with the intrinsic possible worlds, i. e., $\mathbb{W} = \mathcal{D}^{\mathcal{V}}$.

In the case of the pure predicate logic (without quantifiers), we do not need the possible worlds: a ground atom in order to be true in such a Kripke's interpretation has to be true in *every* possible world (or, alternatively, it has to be false in every possible world). Consequently, in the predicate logics the truth of ground atoms and sentences is invariant w. r. t. the possible worlds, which renders the definition unuseful of possible worlds and Kripke's semantics for these logics. But in the case of the modal interpretation of the FOL, the FOL quantifiers have to be interpreted by modal operators and their accessibility relations: thus, the possible worlds are necessary in order to determine the truth of logic formulae with quantifiers. So, we have the following case of Definition 12 for the Kripke semantics of the FOL.

Definition 13 (Intrinsic-worlds "projection" into FOL $\mathcal{K}$-semantics). Kripke semantics of the FOL is a particular case of the Definition 12 when $\mathcal{M} = (\mathbb{W}, \{\mathcal{R}_n \mid n \in \mathbb{N}\}, \mathcal{D}, I_K)$ is a multimodal Kripke's interpretation of the FOL, with $\mathcal{W} = \{\hbar\}$, where $\hbar$ denotes the so-called actual explicit world. So, a set of (generalized) possible worlds reduces to $\mathbb{W} = \{\hbar\} \times \mathcal{D}^{\mathcal{V}}$ (i. e., to the set of intrinsic possible worlds (assignments)), the accessibility relation for each existential modal operator $\exists_n$ (corresponding in $\mathcal{A}_{\mathrm{FOL}}$ to FOL quantifier $(\exists x), x \in \mathcal{V}$),

$$\begin{aligned}\mathcal{R}_n &= \{(\mathbf{w}_1, \mathbf{w}_2) \mid \mathbf{w}_1 = (\hbar, g_1), \mathbf{w}_2 = (\hbar, g_2) \in \mathbb{W} \text{ for all } y \in \mathcal{V}\backslash\{x\}(g_1(y) = g_2(y))\} \\ &= \{(g_1, g_2) \mid g_1, g_2 \in \mathcal{D}^{\mathcal{V}} \text{ for all } y \in \mathcal{V}\backslash\{x\}(g_1(y) = g_2(y))\},\end{aligned}$$

with nonempty domain $\mathcal{D}$ and a mapping $I_K : \mathcal{W} \times (P \bigcup F) \to \bigcup_{n \in \mathcal{N}} \mathbf{2}^{\mathcal{D}^n}$, such that for the explicit actual world $\hbar \in \mathcal{W}$:

1. For any predicate letter $p_i^k \in P$, the function $I_K(\hbar, p_i^k) : \mathcal{D}^k \to \mathbf{2}$ defines the extension of p_i^k in the actual world $\hbar$.
2. For any functional letter $f_i^k \in F$, here considered as a p_i^{k+1} predicate, $I_K(\hbar, f_i^k) : \mathcal{D}^{k+1} \to \mathbf{2}$ defines the graph of this function in the actual world $\hbar$.

For a formula φ, we define $\mathcal{M} \vDash_{\mathbf{w}} \varphi$ iff φ is satisfied in a world $\mathbf{w} = (\hbar, g) \in \mathbb{W}$. So, a given letter p_i^k is true in $\mathbf{w} = (\hbar, g)$, i. e., $\mathcal{M} \vDash_{\mathbf{w}} p_i^k(x_1, \ldots, x_k)$ iff $I_K(\hbar, p_i^k)(g(x_1), \ldots, g(x_k)) = t$, and we denote by $\|\varphi\| =_{\mathrm{def}} \{\mathbf{w} = (\hbar, g) \in \mathbb{W} \mid \mathcal{M} \vDash_{\mathbf{w}} \varphi\}$ the set of worlds in which φ is true.

The Kripke semantics is extended to all formulae for each word $\mathbf{w} = (\hbar, g) \in \mathbb{W}$ by:

$$\begin{aligned}&\mathcal{M} \vDash_{\mathbf{w}} \varphi \wedge \phi \quad \text{iff} \quad \mathcal{M} \vDash_{\mathbf{w}} \varphi \text{ and } \mathcal{M} \vDash_{\mathbf{w}} \phi, \\ &\mathcal{M} \vDash_{\mathbf{w}} \neg\varphi \quad \text{iff} \quad \text{not } \mathcal{M} \vDash_{\mathbf{w}} \varphi, \\ &\mathcal{M} \vDash_{\mathbf{w}} \Diamond_i\varphi \quad \text{iff} \quad \text{exists } \mathbf{w}' = (\hbar, g') \in \mathbb{W} \text{ such that } (\mathbf{w}, \mathbf{w}') \in \mathcal{R}_i \text{ and } \mathcal{M} \vDash_{\mathbf{w}'} \varphi.\end{aligned}$$

A formula φ is said to be *true in a Kripke's interpretation* I_K if for each possible world $\mathbf{w} = (\hbar, g) \in \mathbb{W}$, we have that $\mathcal{M} \vDash_{\mathbf{w}} \varphi$. A formula is said to be *valid* if it is true in each interpretation I_K.

Remark. Notice that the satisfaction relation in the definition above, $\vDash_{\mathbf{w}}$ where $\mathbf{w} = (\hbar, g) \in \mathcal{W} \times \mathcal{D}^{\mathcal{V}}$, can be simplified by the syntax containing only the intrinsic worlds $\vDash_g$ with $g \in \mathcal{D}^{\mathcal{V}}$, because the set of explicit worlds $\mathcal{W}$ is a singleton composed by the actual world $\hbar$ only. We will denote by $\mathrm{FOL}_{\mathcal{K}}$ the FOL with these modal Kripke models. We recall that $\mathrm{FOL}_{\mathcal{K}}$ has *the same syntax* as $\mathcal{A}_{\mathrm{FOL}}$, i. e., the same set of formulae, and the same domain $\mathcal{D}$.[4]

4 Different from the standard embedding of the modal predicate logics into the FOL: this standard embedding introduces a new built-in predicate symbol for each binary accessibility relation $\mathcal{R}_i$, and enlarges the original domain $\mathcal{D}$ with the set of possible worlds, and enlarges the set of variables $\mathcal{V}$ by the new variables for these new built-in symbols.

The introduction of the Kripke semantics of the FOL, in Definition 13, is fundamental in order to obtain a bijective mapping between the set of Kripke interpretations I_K of these modal semantics of FOL and the set of standard Tarski's interpretation of the FOL, as it will be demonstrated in the next theorem. □

It is easy to verify that each accessibility binary relation $\mathcal{R}_n$ of the modal operator $\exists_n$ (corresponding to the FOL quantifier $(\exists x)$) is a reflexive, transitive and symmetric relation. Thus, each pair of modal operators $\diamond_n$ (here denoted by $\exists_n$) and $\forall_n =_{\text{def}} \neg\exists_n\neg$ is an example of existential and universal modal operators of the S5 modal logics, so that $\forall_n$ is "*it is known* for all values assigned to x that" modal operator, whose semantics is equivalent to standard FOL "for all values assigned to x" semantics.

It is analogous to monadic algebras of Halmos [37] and his algebraic study of quantifiers, where S5 modal logic is characterized by the class of all closure algebras in which each closed element is also open. In fact, the *complex algebra* (over the set of possible worlds) of this S5 multimodal logic $\text{FOL}_{\mathcal{K}}$ uses several S5 algebraic modal operators to provide a Boolean model features of FOL as indicated by Davis [38] in his doctoral thesis supervised by Garret Birkhoff. As far as I know, Definition 13 is the first attempt to give a relational Kripke semantics to the FOL, analogous to such an algebraic approach. As we can see from the definition of Kripke models of the FOL, every function and predicate are *rigid* in it, i. e., they have the same extension in every possible world $w \in \mathbb{W}$.

Theorem 1. *The modal Kripke semantics, with a model $\mathcal{M}$ in Definition 13, is an adequate semantics for the FOL. For each Tarski's interpretation I_T, there is a unique Kripke's interpretation I_K, and vice versa, such that for any $p_i^k \in P$, $f_i^k \in F$, $k \geq 1$, $(d_1, \ldots, d_k) \in \mathcal{D}^k$ and any intrinsic world (assignment) $g : \text{Var} \to \mathcal{D}$. It holds that:*

$$I_K(\hbar, p_i^k)(d_1, \ldots, d_k) = t \quad \textit{iff} \quad (d_1, \ldots, d_k) \in I_T(p_i^k) \quad \textit{and}$$
$$I_K(\hbar, f_i^k)(d_1, \ldots, d_k, d_{k+1}) = t \quad \textit{iff} \quad d_{k+1} = I_T(f_i^k)(d_1, \ldots, d_k).$$

We define $\mathfrak{I}_K(\Gamma) = \{I_K$ defined above from $I_T \mid I_T \in \mathfrak{I}_T(\Gamma)\}$ with the bijection $\flat : \mathfrak{I}_T(\Gamma) \simeq \mathfrak{I}_K(\Gamma)$, so that for any Tarski's interpretation we have its equivalent Kripke's interpretation $I_K = \flat(I_T)$, where Γ is a set of assumptions in this FOL. Moreover, there exists the following diagram of reductions from the predicate modal logics in Definition 12:

Predicate modal logics —— *Intrinsic-worlds "projection," $\mathcal{W} = \{\hbar\}$* ——→ $\mathit{FOL}_{\mathcal{K}}$

↓ *Explicit-worlds "projection"* (left); *Reduction $\mathcal{V} = \mathcal{D} = F = \emptyset$* ↓ (right)

Propositional modal logics —— *Actual world reduction, $\mathcal{W} = \{\hbar\}$* ——→ *Propositional logics*

Proof. Let $(d_1, \ldots, d_k) \in I_T(p_i^k)$, then from definition in this theorem $I_K(\hbar, p_i^k)(d_1, \ldots, d_k) = t$, and from Definition 13 we obtain that $|p_i^k(d_1, \ldots, d_k)| = \mathbb{W}$, i. e., the ground atom $p_i^k(d_1, \ldots, d_k)$ is true also in correspondent Kripke's modal semantics. Vice versa, if $(d_1, \ldots, d_k) \notin I_T(p_i^k)$, then $\|p_i^k(d_1, \ldots, d_k)\| = \emptyset$ is a empty set, i. e., the ground atom $p_i^k(d_1, \ldots, d_k)$ is false also in the correspondent Kripke's modal semantics.

Let us suppose that for any closed formula (without free variables) ϕ/g with n logic connectives, true w. r. t. Tarski's interpretation I_T, it holds that $\|\phi/g\| = \mathbb{W}$, i. e., it is true in the correspondent Kripke's interpretation $I_K = \flat(I_T)$. Let us show that it holds for any formula ψ with $n+1$ logic connectives, true w. r. t. Tarski's interpretation I_T. There are the following three cases:

1. $\psi = \phi_1 \wedge_S \phi_2$. Then $\|\psi\| = \|\phi_1\| \bigcap \|\phi_2\| = \mathbb{W}$, from the fact that both formulae ϕ_1, ϕ_2 must be true in Tarski's interpretation I_T and that have less than or equal to n logic connectives, and consequently (by inductive assumption), $\|\phi_i\| = \mathbb{W}$ for $i = 1, 2$. That is, ψ is true in the correspondent Kripke's interpretation $I_K = \flat(I_T)$.
2. $\psi = \neg\phi$. Then $\|\psi\| = \mathbb{W} \backslash \|\phi\| = \mathbb{W}$, from the fact that the formula ϕ must be false in Tarski's interpretation I_T and that has less than or equal to n logic connectives, and consequently (by inductive assumption), $\|\phi\| = \emptyset$. That is, ψ is true in the correspondent Kripke's interpretation $I_K = \flat(I_T)$.
3. $\psi = \exists_n \phi(x)$ where $\phi(x)$ denotes the formula ϕ with the unique free variable x quantified in FOL by $(\exists x)$. From the fact that $(\exists x)\phi(x)$ is true in Tarski's interpretation, we have that there is a value $u \in \mathcal{D}$ such that a sentence $\phi[x/u]$ (a formula ϕ where the variable x is substituted by the value $u \in \mathcal{D}$) is a true sentence. Then we obtain
$$\|\exists_n \phi(x)\| = \{(\hbar, g) \mid \text{exists } g' \text{ such that } (g, g') \in \mathcal{R}_n \text{ and } \mathcal{M} \vDash_{(\hbar, g')} \phi(x)\} = \mathbb{W},$$
because for any assignment $g \in \mathcal{D}^{\mathcal{V}}$ there is $g' \in \mathcal{D}^{\mathcal{V}}$ such that $g'(x) = u$ and for all $y \in (\mathcal{V} \backslash \{x\}) g'(y) = g(y)$, and consequently, $(g, g') \in \mathcal{R}_n$. It holds that $\mathcal{M} \vDash_{(\hbar, g')} \phi(x)$, i. e., $\phi(x)$ is satisfied for the assignment g', because $g'(x) = u$ and $\phi(g'(x))$ is equivalent to $\phi[x/u]$, which is a true sentence with (from the inductive hypothesis) $\|\phi[x/u]\| = \mathbb{W}$.

Consequently, any sentence, which is true in Tarski's interpretation, I_T is also true in the Kripke's interpretation $I_K = \flat(I_T)$. Vice versa, for any sentence true in Kripke's interpretation $I_K \in \mathfrak{I}_K(\Gamma)$, it can be analogously shown that it is also true in the Tarski's interpretation $I_T = \flat^{-1}(I_K)$, where $\flat^{-1}$ is inverse of the bijection $\flat$. Thus, the Kripke's semantics given in Definition 13 is an adequate semantics for the FOL.

Thus, both "projections" in the diagram above (the arrow *Intrinsic-worlds "projection"* described in Definition 13, and the arrow *Explicit-worlds "projection"* described in Proposition 2), where $\text{FOL}_{\mathcal{K}}$ denotes this adequate Kripke's version of the FOL (i. e., of the $\mathcal{A}_{\text{FOL}}$ where the quantifiers $\exists_n$ are interpreted as *modal* existential operators) are valid.

Let us show that also other two reductions (which are the arrows in the diagram of this theorem) into propositional logics are well defined, so that this diagram commutes. So, we consider the following arrows of the diagram:

1. *Actual world reduction, when* $\mathcal{W} = \{\hbar\}$, corresponding to the bottom horizontal arrow in the reduction diagram. Thus, for this unique explicit actual world $\hbar$ we have that we can have only one (nonempty) accessibility relation $\mathcal{R}_i = \{(\hbar, \hbar)\}$, so that unique possible existential modal operator $\diamond_i$, of this modal propositional logic obtained by this reduction, is an *identity* operation. That is, obtained reduction is a propositional logic without modal operators, i. e., it is a pure propositional logic. In fact, we have that for any propositional formula ϕ and the unique explicit actual world $\hbar \in \mathcal{W}$ (see Definition 12),

   $$\mathcal{M} \vDash_\hbar \diamond_i\phi \quad \text{iff} \quad \text{exists } w' \in \mathcal{W} \text{ such that } (\hbar, w') \in \mathcal{R}_i \text{ and } \mathcal{M} \vDash_{w'} \phi \text{ iff } \mathcal{M} \vDash_\hbar \phi.$$

   The Kripke's mapping $I_K : P \to \mathbf{2}^{\mathcal{W}}$, for the singleton set $\mathcal{W} = \{\hbar\}$ and the bijection $\mathbf{2}^{\{\hbar\}} \simeq \mathbf{2}$, becomes the propositional interpretation $I'_K : P \to \mathbf{2}$. Thus, we obtained a pure propositional logic in the actual world.
2. *Reduction* $\mathcal{V} = \mathcal{D} = F = \emptyset$, corresponding to the vertical arrow of the reduction diagram. So, $\mathcal{V}$ is the empty set of variables, and hence P is composed only by propositional symbols, and hence the obtained logic is without modal operators (i. e., without the FOL quantifier $\exists$). Thus, the obtained logic is a propositional logic with a unique generalized world equal to the empty function $* : \emptyset \to \mathcal{D}$, from the fact that $\mathbb{W} = \mathcal{D}^\emptyset = \{*\}$. The Kripke's mapping $I_K : \mathcal{W} \times P \to \bigcup_{n \in \mathcal{N}} \mathbf{2}^{\mathcal{D}^n}$ for $\text{FOL}_\mathcal{K}$ in this reduction becomes the mapping $I_K : \{*\} \times P \to \mathbf{2}^{\mathcal{D}^0}$ where $\mathcal{D}^0$ is the singleton set $\{\langle\,\rangle\}$, so that from bijections $\{*\} \times P \simeq P$ and $\mathbf{2}^{\{\langle\,\rangle\}} \simeq \mathbf{2} = \{f, t\}$, this mapping becomes the propositional interpretation $I'_K : P \to \mathbf{2}$. Hence, the unique generalized world $*$ is just the actual world $\hbar$, so that we obtain exactly the same propositional logics in the actual world, as in the case above.

There is a surprising result from this theorem and its commutative diagram: we obtained that a FOL (i. e., its modal interpretation of quantifiers in $\text{FOL}_\mathcal{K}$) is a particular *reduction* from the predicate modal logics with generalized Kripke semantics (Definition 12).

It is well known that the propositional modal logics can be, based on modal correspondence theory [39, 40], embedded into the FOL by transforming each propositional letter p_i into an unary predicate $p_i^1(x)$ (where x is a new variable with a domain of values equal to the set of possible worlds of the original propositional modal logic), and by introducing a binary predicate $\mathcal{R}(x, y)$ for the accessibility relation of the Kripke semantics for propositional modal operators. For example, the (T) axiom $\Box p_i \Rightarrow p_i$ of the propositional modal logic with the universal modal operator $\Box$ and with the associated binary accessibility relation $\mathcal{R}$ over the set of possible worlds, will be translated in the

FOL formula $(\forall x)((\forall y)(\mathcal{R}(x,y) \Rightarrow p_i^1(y)) \Rightarrow p_i^1(x))$. Analogously, the fact that a propositional letter p_i is satisfied in the possible world w in a given Kripke interpretation $\mathcal{M}$, denoted by $\mathcal{M} \vDash_w p_i$, is translated in the true ground FOL atom $p_i^1(w)$.

Let us show that the *standard* embedding of the modal predicate logic $\text{FOL}_\mathcal{K}$ into the FOL *is not* possible. It is possible for translation of satisfaction of the atoms of $\text{FOL}_\mathcal{K}$ in a possible world $\mathbf{w} = (\hbar, g)$, i. e., for $\mathcal{M} \vDash_\mathbf{w} p_i^k(x_1, \dots, x_k)$, into a ground FOL atom $p_i^k(g(x_1), \dots, g(x_k))$. But, for example, the translation of the satisfaction of the modal formula of $\text{FOL}_\mathcal{K}$, i. e., for $\mathcal{M} \vDash_\mathbf{w} \exists_m p_i^k(x_1, \dots, x_m, \dots, x_k)$ where $\exists_m$ is an existential modal operator corresponding to the FOL quantifier $(\exists x_m)$, will be the formula $(\exists g')(\mathcal{R}_m(g,g') \wedge p_i^k(g'(x_1), \dots, g'(x_m), \dots, g'(x_k)))$. But it is a *second-order* formula, because $(\exists g')$ is a quantification over functions (or equivalently over predicates that represent the graphs of the assignment functions in $\mathcal{D}^\mathcal{V}$).

As we will also see that the predicate modal logic $\text{FOL}_\mathcal{K}$ is an extensional logic as is the FOL (they are equivalent logics), notice that the general predicate modal logics in Definition 12 are more expressive than the FOL, because they can have also modal operators different from that used to translate FOL quantifiers. Hence, also without enriching logics with the intensionality, the modal predicate logics with generalized Kripke semantics are still more expressive then the FOL. □

1.2.2 Modal logics and intensionality

$\text{FOL}_\mathcal{K}$ represents the modal interpretation of the first-order logic, with Kripke relational semantics based on the set of possible worlds $\mathbb{W} = \{\hbar\} \times \mathcal{D}^\mathcal{V}$ with a *unique* explicit possible world, equal to the actual world $\hbar$. Consequently, based on considerations in Section 1.2, which demonstrate that each modal logic with a set of possible worlds can be considered as an intensional logic, we are invited to conclude that also FOL is intrinsically an intensional logic. That is, by introducing the particular structure of a domain $\mathcal{D}$ in Definition 6, based on PRPs, we are able to define the intensional interpretation I of the FOL and the set of extensionalization functions $h = \mathcal{F}(\mathbf{w}) \in \mathcal{E}$ for any possible world $\mathbf{w} = (\hbar, g) \in \mathbb{W}$ in the $\text{FOL}_\mathcal{K}$ Kripke semantics of the FOL. However, in the case of modal $\text{FOL}_\mathcal{K}$ we will see that the intensions of logic formulae are equivalent to their extensions, i. e., the original FOL also with Kripke semantics (equivalent to Tarski's semantics) is not able to support the intensionality separately from the extensionality.

Proposition 3. *The intension (sense) of any virtual predicate $\phi(x_1, \dots, x_k)$ in the $\text{FOL}_\mathcal{K}$, with a set of only intrinsic possible worlds $\mathbb{W} = \{\hbar\} \times \mathcal{D}^\mathcal{V}$, is equivalent to its extension in a given Tarski's interpretation of the FOL. That is, it is impossible to support the intensions in the standard FOL with Tarskian semantics.*

Proof. We have to show that the intension (see Definition 10) $I_n(\phi(x_1, \dots, x_k)) : \mathbb{W} \to \mathfrak{R}$ of any FOL formula $\phi(x_1, \dots, x_k)$ in a given Tarski's homomorphism $I_T^* : \mathcal{L} \to \mathfrak{R}$ is a constant function from the set of possible worlds $\mathbb{W} = \{\hbar\} \times \mathcal{D}^{\mathcal{V}}$ in $\mathrm{FOL}_{\mathcal{K}}$, such that for all $\mathbf{w} = (\hbar, g) \in \mathbb{W}$ we have that $I_n(\phi(x_1, \dots, x_k))(\mathbf{w}) = R$, where $R = I_T^*(\phi(x_1, \dots, x_k))$ is the extension of this formula in Tarski's interpretation. We can show it by the structural recursion:

Case 1: When $\phi(x_1, \dots, x_k)$ is a predicate letter $p_i^k \in P$, then

$$\begin{aligned} I_n(p_i^k(x_1, \dots, x_k))(\mathbf{w}) &= \|p_i^k(x_1, \dots, x_k)\| \\ &= \{(d_1, \dots, d_k) \in \mathcal{D}^k \mid \mathcal{M} \vDash_{\mathbf{w}} p_i^k(d_1, \dots, d_k)\} \\ &= \{(d_1, \dots, d_k) \mid I_K(\hbar, p_i^k)(d_1, \dots, d_k) = t\} \\ &= \{(d_1, \dots, d_k) \mid (d_1, \dots, d_k) \in I_T(p_i^k)\} = I_T(p_i^k). \end{aligned}$$

Case 2: When $\phi(x_1, \dots, x_k)$ is a virtual predicate, from Theorem 1 it holds that, for a world $\mathbf{w} = (\hbar, g) \in \mathbb{W}$, if for this assignment $g \in \mathcal{D}^{\mathcal{V}}$ a ground formula $\phi(x_1, \dots, x_k)/g$ is true in a given Tarski's interpretation I_T (i. e., when $I_T^*(\phi(x_1, \dots, x_k)/g) = t$), then $\|\phi(x_1, \dots, x_k)/g\| =$ mathbb W (it is true in the correspondent Kripke's interpretation), i. e., $\mathcal{M} \vDash_{\mathbf{w}} \phi(x_1, \dots, x_k)/g$ for *every* possible world $\mathbf{w} = (\hbar, g) \in \mathbb{W}$. Thus, we have that the intension of this virtual predicate is

$$\begin{aligned} & I_n(\phi(x_1, \dots, x_k))(\mathbf{w}) \\ &= \|\phi(x_1, \dots, x_k)\| \\ &= \{(g(x_1), \dots, g(x_k)) \in \mathcal{D}^k \mid g \in \mathcal{D}^{\mathcal{V}} \text{ and } \mathcal{M} \vDash_{\mathbf{w}} \phi(x_1, \dots, x_k)/g\} \\ &= \{(g(x_1), \dots, g(x_k)) \mid g \in \mathcal{D}^{\mathcal{V}} \text{ and } I_T^*(\phi(x_1, \dots, x_k)/g) = t\} \\ &= \{(g(x_1), \dots, g(x_k)) \mid g \in \mathcal{D}^{\mathcal{V}} \text{ and } (g(x_1), \dots, g(x_k)) \in I_T^*(\phi(x_1, \dots, x_k))\} \\ &= I_T^*(\phi(x_1, \dots, x_k)). \end{aligned}$$

Consequently, the function I_n is invariant w. r. t. the possible worlds $\mathbf{w} \in \mathbb{W}$, and returns with the extension, of a considered (virtual) predicate, determined by a given Tarski's interpretation. □

What does it mean? First of all, it means that not every modal logic with a given set of possible worlds $\mathbb{W}$ is an intensional logic, and that the quality of the intensionality, which can be expressed by a given modal logic depends on the set of possible worlds $\mathbb{W}$ and their capacity to model the possible extensions of logic formulae. For example, if $\mathbb{W}$ is a finite set with very small cardinality, it often would not be able to express the all possible extensions for logic formulae, and consequently, its intensional capability will be very limited.

But also if $\mathbb{W}$ is infinite, as in the case above when $\mathcal{D}$ is an infinite domain, we demonstrated that they are not able to express the intensionality (consider, e. g., Montague's semantics of the intensional meaning, in which we need a lot of explicit possible worlds so that the extension in each of these worlds of the same formula with free variables can be different in order to be able to define the intensional meaning (the "sense") of such a formula) for the $\mathrm{FOL}_{\mathcal{K}}$. The fundamental fact that $\mathrm{FOL}_{\mathcal{K}}$ (with its predicate modal semantics) is not an intensional logic is that the set of explicit possible worlds $\mathcal{W}$ is a singleton set composed by only actual world $\hbar$. Consequently, in order to be able to express the full intensionality in a given predicate modal logic, it is very important to choose the new *appropriate set* of possible worlds (by an extension of the explicit possible worlds $\mathcal{W}$), independently from the original set of possible worlds of the particular given modal logic.

In fact, from this point of view, the left arrow in the diagram in Theorem 1 represents the logics with (partial) intensionalities, while the right arrow of the same diagram represents two extremal reductions of the intensionality, by identifying it with the pure extensionality (the propositional logic can be seen as a modal logic with the unique actual possible worlds, so that the intensionality corresponds to the extensionality, as in the case of the $\mathrm{FOL}_{\mathcal{K}}$).

Remark. The natural choice for the set of explicit possible worlds for the fully intensional logic is the set of interpretations of its original logic (modal or not, determined by its set of axioms, inference relations and a predefined set Γ (possibly empty), for which these interpretations are models), because such a set of interpretations is able to express all logically possible extensions of the formulae of the original (not fully intensional) logic. In what follows, we will provide this intensional upgrade for the standard (not modal) FOL(Γ), but generally it can be done to every kind of logics, thus to any kind of modal logics, and hence also to the modal logic $\mathrm{FOL}_{\mathcal{K}}(\Gamma)$: in that case, we obtain the two-levels of modal logic (as in [41, 42]).

At the lower level, we will have original modal logics with their original set of possible worlds (the set $\mathcal{D}^{\mathcal{V}}$ of intrinsic worlds, with a unique explicit world $\hbar$, in the case of $\mathrm{FOL}_{\mathcal{K}}(\Gamma)$), while at the new upper level we have that each new explicit possible world corresponds to the particular Kripke's interpretation I_K of the original modal logics. This upper-level intensional logic has a kind of *rigid* semantics, where the domains and the extensions of built-in predicates/propositions of the "lower-level" modal logics are identical in every upper-level possible world. □

A k-ary functional symbol $f_i^k \in F$ in an intensional logic is considered as a new $k+1$-ary predicate symbol $f_i^{k+1} \in P$ (with (TF) constraint in Definition 11) whose extension is the graph of this function, such that cannot exists two tuples $(d_1, \ldots, d_k, u_1), (d_1, \ldots, d_k, u_2)$ in its extension with $u_1 \neq u_2$. Thus, in intensional FOL we will have only the set of predicate symbols P while F is empty set.

This two-level intensional modal logic with the old possible worlds of the original modal logic $\mathbb{W} = \mathcal{W} \times \mathcal{D}^{\mathcal{V}}$ is enriched by a new set of explicit possible worlds $\mathfrak{I}_K$ (the set of all Kripke interpretations $I_K \in \mathfrak{I}_K(\Gamma)$, of the original (nonintensional) modal logic, in which all assumptions in Γ (possibly empty set) are true), means that the obtained intensional modal logic has the set of explicit possible worlds equal to the cartesian product of old worlds $\mathcal{W}$ and new added worlds in $\mathfrak{I}_K(\Gamma)$, so that new generalized possible worlds are equal to the set $\widehat{\mathbb{W}} = \mathfrak{I}_K(\Gamma) \times \mathbb{W} = \mathfrak{I}_K(\Gamma) \times (\mathcal{W} \times \mathcal{D}^{\mathcal{V}})$. Consequently, the Kripke semantics of *fully intensional* modal logic, obtained as an enrichment of the original modal logic, can be given by the following definition.

Definition 14 (Intensional enrichment of multimodal logics). Let $\mathcal{M} = (\mathbb{W}, \{\mathcal{R}_i\}, \mathcal{D}, I_K)$ be a Kripke's model of a predicate multimodal logic with the set of possible worlds $\mathbb{W} = \mathcal{W} \times \mathcal{D}^{\mathcal{V}}$ and the set of existential modal "low-level" operators $\Diamond_i$ with accessibility relations $\mathcal{R}_i$ and the set of standard Kripke's interpretations $\mathfrak{I}_K(\Gamma)$.

Then we define a Kripke's interpretation of its intensional enrichment $\widehat{\mathcal{M}} = (\widehat{\mathbb{W}}, \{\mathcal{R}_i\}, \{\widehat{\mathcal{R}}_j\}, \mathcal{D}, \widehat{I}_K)$, with the set of possible worlds $\widehat{\mathbb{W}} = \mathfrak{I}_K(\Gamma) \times \mathbb{W}$, an optional set of new `intensional` modal operators $\widehat{\Diamond}_j$ with the accessibility relations $\widehat{\mathcal{R}}_j \subseteq \mathfrak{I}_K(\Gamma)^2$ and new mapping $\widehat{I}_K : (\mathfrak{I}_K(\Gamma) \times \mathcal{W}) \times P \to \bigcup_{n \in \mathcal{N}} \mathbf{2}^{\mathcal{D}^n}$, such that for any explicit world $(I_K, w) \in \mathfrak{I}_K(\Gamma) \times \mathcal{W}$ and $p_i^k \in P$ we have that $\widehat{I}_K(I_K, w, p_i^k) =_{\text{def}} I_K(w, p_i^k) : \mathcal{D}^k \to \mathbf{2}$. The satisfaction relation $\vDash_{I_k,w,g}$ for a given world $(I_k, w, g) \in \widehat{\mathbb{W}}$ is defined as follows:

1. $\widehat{\mathcal{M}} \vDash_{I_K,w,g} p_i^k(x_1, \ldots, x_k)$ iff $\widehat{I}_K(I_K, w, p_i^k)(g(x_1), \ldots, g(x_k)) = t$.
2. $\widehat{\mathcal{M}} \vDash_{I_K,w,g} \varphi \wedge \phi$ iff $\widehat{\mathcal{M}} \vDash_{I_k,w,g} \varphi$ and $\widehat{\mathcal{M}} \vDash_{I_K,w,g} \phi$,
3. $\widehat{\mathcal{M}} \vDash_{I_K,w,g} \neg\varphi$ iff not $\widehat{\mathcal{M}} \vDash_{I_K,w,g} \varphi$,
4. $\widehat{\mathcal{M}} \vDash_{I_K,w,g} \Diamond_i \varphi$ iff exists $(w', g') \in \mathbb{W}$ such that $((w, g), (w', g')) \in \mathcal{R}_i$ and $\widehat{\mathcal{M}} \vDash_{I_K,w',g'} \varphi$.
5. $\widehat{\mathcal{M}} \vDash_{I_K,w,g} \widehat{\Diamond}_j \varphi$ iff exists $I'_K \in \mathfrak{I}_K$ such that $(I_K, I'_K) \in \widehat{\mathcal{R}}_j$ and $\widehat{\mathcal{M}} \vDash_{I'_K,w,g} \varphi$.

Notice that this intensional enrichment is *maximal* one: in fact, we have taken *all* Kripke's interpretations of the original modal logics for the possible worlds of this new upgraded intensional logic. Moreover, from the points 4 and 5, it holds that this intensional enrichment Kripke's interpretation $\widehat{\mathcal{M}}$ *is not a standard* Kripke's interpretation with the "high-level" modal operators $\widehat{\Diamond}_j$.

We can obtain partial intensional enrichments if we take only a strict subset of $S \subset \mathfrak{I}_K(\Gamma)$ in order to define generalized possible worlds $\widehat{\mathbb{W}} = S \times \mathbb{W}$. In that case, we would introduce the nonmonotonic property for obtained intensional logic.

Example 2 (Intensional enrichment of the FOL). Let us consider the intensional enrichment of the multimodal logic $\text{FOL}_{\mathcal{K}}(\Gamma)$ given by Definition 13 with the Kripke's interpretation $\mathcal{M} = (\mathbb{W}, \{\mathcal{R}_i \mid i \in \mathbb{N}\}, \mathcal{D}, I_K)$ of the FOL(Γ), with a set of (generalized) possible worlds reduced only to the intrinsic worlds $\mathbb{W} = \{\hbar\} \times \mathcal{D}^{\mathcal{V}}$ (from the fact that $\mathcal{W}$ is a singleton set composed by only actual world $\hbar$) and the accessibility relation for each existential modal operator $\exists_i$ (corresponding in $\mathcal{A}_{\text{FOL}}$ to the FOL quantifier $(\exists x), x \in \mathcal{V}$), between intrinsic worlds $g_1, g_2 \in \mathcal{D}^{\mathcal{V}}$, $\mathcal{R}_i = \{(g_1, g_2) \in \mathbb{W}^2 \mid \text{for all } y \in \mathcal{V}\backslash\{x\}(g_1(y) = g_2(y))\}$ as was shown in Definition 13.

We denote by $\mathfrak{I}_K(\Gamma)$ the set of Kripke's interpretations of this modal translation of the FOL (bijective to the set of the Tarski's interpretations of the FOL, as demonstrated by Theorem 1). Then we define its intensional enrichment by a new Kripke's interpretation (the higher level w. r. t. the modal interpretation $\mathcal{M}$ of the FOL) $\widehat{\mathcal{M}} = (\widehat{\mathbb{W}}, \{\mathcal{R}_i\}, \{\widehat{\mathcal{R}}_j\}, \mathcal{D}, \widehat{I}_K)$, with:

- The set of generalized possible worlds $\widehat{\mathbb{W}} = \mathfrak{I}_K(\Gamma) \times \mathbb{W} = \mathfrak{I}_K(\Gamma) \times \{\hbar\} \times \mathcal{D}^{\mathcal{V}}$ (here the set of explicit worlds is $\mathcal{W}_e =_{\text{def}} \mathfrak{I}_K(\Gamma) \times \{\hbar\}$, while the set of intrinsic worlds remains equal to $\mathcal{D}^{\mathcal{V}}$);
- An optional set of new modal operators $\widehat{\Diamond}_j$ with the accessibility relations $\widehat{\mathcal{R}}_j$ over the worlds in $\mathfrak{I}_K(\Gamma)$,
- The new mapping $\widehat{I}_K : (\mathfrak{I}_K(\Gamma) \times \{\hbar\}) \times P \to \bigcup_{n \in \mathcal{N}} \mathbf{2}^{\mathcal{D}^n}$, such that for any explicit world $(I_K, \hbar) \in \mathfrak{I}_K(\Gamma) \times \{\hbar\}$ and $p_i^k \in P$ we have that $\widehat{I}_K(I_K, \hbar, p_i^k) =_{\text{def}} I_K(\hbar, p_i^k) : \mathcal{D}^k \to \mathbf{2}$. For each world $\mathbf{w} = (I_K, \hbar, g) \in \widehat{\mathbb{W}}$, we have that
  1. $\widehat{\mathcal{M}} \vDash_{I_K, \hbar, g} p_i^k(x_1, \ldots, x_k)$ iff $\widehat{I}_K(I_K, \hbar, p_i^k)(g(x_1), \ldots, g(x_k)) = t$.
  2. $\widehat{\mathcal{M}} \vDash_{I_K, \hbar, g} \varphi \wedge \phi$ iff $\widehat{\mathcal{M}} \vDash_{I_K, \hbar, g} \varphi$ and $\widehat{\mathcal{M}} \vDash_{I_K, \hbar, g} \phi$,
  3. $\widehat{\mathcal{M}} \vDash_{I_K, \hbar, g} \neg\varphi$ iff not $\widehat{\mathcal{M}} \vDash_{I_K, \hbar, g} \varphi$,
  4. $\widehat{\mathcal{M}} \vDash_{I_K, \hbar, g} \Diamond_i \varphi$ iff exists $g' \in \mathcal{D}^{\mathcal{V}}$ such that $(g, g') \in \mathcal{R}_i$ and $\widehat{\mathcal{M}} \vDash_{I_K, \hbar, g'} \varphi$,
  5. $\widehat{\mathcal{M}} \vDash_{I_K, \hbar, g} \widehat{\Diamond}_j \varphi$ iff exists $I'_K \in \mathfrak{I}_K(\Gamma)$ such that $(I_K, I'_K) \in \widehat{\mathcal{R}}_j$ and $\widehat{\mathcal{M}} \vDash_{I'_K, \hbar, g} \varphi$.

So, from Definition 10 for the intensional semantics, the mapping $I_n : \mathcal{L}_{\text{op}} \to \mathfrak{R}^{\mathfrak{I}_K(\Gamma)}$, where $\mathcal{L}_{\text{op}}$ is the subset of formulae with free variables (virtual predicates), such that for any virtual predicate $\phi(x_1, \ldots, x_k) \in \mathcal{L}_{\text{op}}$ the mapping $I_n(\phi(x_1, \ldots, x_k)) : \mathfrak{I}_K(\Gamma) \to \mathfrak{R}$ is Montague's meaning (*intension*) of this virtual predicate, i. e., mapping, which returns with the extension of this predicate in every possible world (i. e., Kripke's interpretation of $\text{FOL}_{\mathcal{K}}(\Gamma)$), $I_K \in \mathfrak{I}_K(\Gamma)$. That is, we have that

$$I_n(\phi(x_1, \ldots, x_k))(I_K) =_{\text{def}} \|\phi(x_1, \ldots, x_k)\| = \{(g(x_1), \ldots, g(x_k)) \in \mathcal{D}^k \mid g \in \mathcal{D}^{\mathcal{V}} \text{ and } \widehat{\mathcal{M}} \vDash_{I_K, \hbar, g} \phi(x_1, \ldots, x_k)\} \tag{1.7}$$

In what follows, the *minimal* (i. e., without new intensional modal operators $\widehat{\Diamond}_i$) intensional enrichment of the multimodal logic $\text{FOL}_{\mathcal{K}}$ we will denote by $\text{FOL}_{\mathcal{K}_{\mathcal{I}}}$.

This two-level intensional modal logic, described above, has the following correspondence property between the Kripke's interpretation $\mathcal{M}$ of the original modal logic and the Kripke's interpretation $\widehat{\mathcal{M}}$ of its intensional enrichment:

Proposition 4. *For any logic formulae ϕ of the original multimodal logic, with the set of (generalized) possible worlds $\mathbb{W} = \mathcal{W} \times \mathcal{D}^{\mathcal{V}}$ and the set of existential modal operators $\Diamond_i$ with accessibility relations $\mathcal{R}_i$ given by Definition 12, the following property holds:*

$$\widehat{\mathcal{M}} \vDash_{I_K, \mathbf{w}, g} \phi \quad \textit{iff} \quad \mathcal{M} \vDash_{\mathbf{w}, g} \phi \tag{1.8}$$

where $\mathcal{M} = (\mathbb{W}, \{\mathcal{R}_i\}, \mathcal{D}, I_K)$ is Kripke's interpretation of the original multimodal logic. That is, this intensional extension from the "low-level" into the intensional ("high-level") *predicate modal logic is conservative one: if for a given Kripke interpretation I_K of the "low-level" the formula ϕ is satisfied in the world (w, g) than in the "high-level" world (I_K, w, g) it is satisfied as well, and vice versa.*

Proof. Let us demonstrate it by structural induction on the length of logic formulae. For any atom $\phi = p_i^k(x_1, \dots, x_k)$, we have from Definition 14 that $\widehat{\mathcal{M}} \vDash_{I_K,w,g} p_i^k(x_1, \dots, x_k)$ iff $\widehat{I}_K(I_K, w, p_i^k)(g(x_1), \dots, g(x_k)) = I_K(w, p_i^k)(g(x_1), \dots, g(x_k)) = t$ iff $\mathcal{M} \vDash_{w,g} p_i^k(x_1, \dots, x_k)$. Let us suppose that such a property holds for every formula ϕ with less than n logic connectives of the original multimodal logic (thus without new intensional "high-level" existential modal operators $\widehat{\Diamond}_i$), and let us show that it holds also for any formula with n logic connectives. There are the following cases:

1. The case when $\phi = \neg\psi$ where ψ has $n - 1$ logic connectives. Then $\widehat{\mathcal{M}} \vDash_{I_K,w,g} \phi$ iff $\widehat{\mathcal{M}} \vDash_{I_K,w,g} \neg\psi$ iff not $\widehat{\mathcal{M}} \vDash_{I_K,w,g} \psi$ iff (by inductive hypothesis) not $\mathcal{M} \vDash_{w,g} \psi$ iff $\mathcal{M} \vDash_{w,g} \neg\psi$ iff $\mathcal{M} \vDash_{w,g} \phi$.
2. The case when $\phi = \psi_1 \wedge \psi_2$, where both ψ_1, ψ_2 have less than n logic connectives, is analogous to the case 1.
3. The case when $\phi = \Diamond_i\psi$ where ψ has $n - 1$ logic connectives. Then $\widehat{\mathcal{M}} \vDash_{I_K,w,g} \phi$ iff $\widehat{\mathcal{M}} \vDash_{I_K,w,g} \Diamond_i\psi$ iff exists w' such that $(w, w') \in \mathcal{R}_i$ and $\widehat{\mathcal{M}} \vDash_{I_K,w,g} \psi$ iff (by inductive hypothesis) exists w' such that $(w, w') \in \mathcal{R}_i$ and $\mathcal{M} \vDash_{w,g} \psi$ iff $\mathcal{M} \vDash_{w,g} \Diamond_i\psi$ iff $\mathcal{M} \vDash_{w,g} \phi$. □

Notice that the property verified by this proposition is a direct consequence of the definition of the new Kripke's mapping $\widehat{I}_K$ in Definition 14, such that the following diagram (where Λ is the currying operator from lambda calculus used in diagram A.10 in Section A.5 in the Appendix)

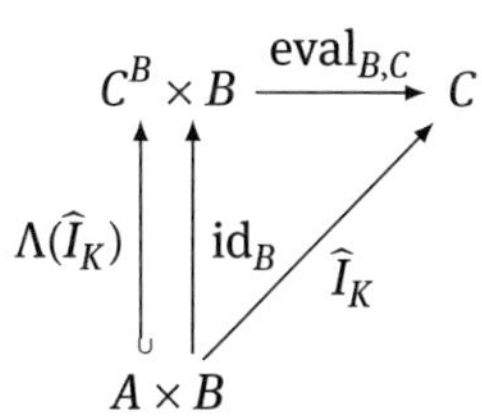

where $A = \mathfrak{I}_K(\Gamma)$, $B = \mathcal{W} \times P$ and $C = \bigcup_{n \in \mathcal{N}} \mathbf{2}^{\mathcal{D}^n}$, so that the curried function $\Lambda(\widehat{I}_K)$ *is an inclusion*. Consequently, for any "low-level" Kripke's interpretation $I_K \in A$, we obtain that $\Lambda(\widehat{I}_K)(I_K) = I_K : B \to C$, and hence for each $(w, p_i^k) \in B$, $\mathrm{eval}_{B,C}(I_K, (w, p_i^k)) = I_K(w, p_i^k)$, which from the commutativity of this diagram above is equal to $\widehat{I}_K(I_K, (w, p_i^k))$.

1.3 First-order logic and intensionality

Thus, from the previous section, in order to be able to provide the intensions of logic formulae, our modal Kripke semantics for the FOL(Γ) has to be enriched also by a set of explicit possible worlds. In this way, e. g., in any two different explicit worlds a given predicate can have *different* extensions (as required by Montague's intensional meaning of this predicate).

Such an *intensional semantics* of FOL(Γ) is strictly more expressive [36] than a single Tarski's semantics of FOL(Γ), as presented by Example 2 where the set of explicit worlds is $\mathcal{W}_e =_{\text{def}} \mathfrak{I}_K(\Gamma) \times \mathcal{W}$, i. e., from the bijection between Tarski's and Kripke's interpretations (see Theorem 1), $\flat : \mathfrak{I}_T(\Gamma) \simeq \mathfrak{I}_K(\Gamma)$, we can define $\mathcal{W}_e =_{\text{def}} \mathfrak{I}_T(\Gamma) \times \mathcal{W}$ and from fact that $\mathcal{W} = \{\hbar\}$ is a singleton set, we obtain the reduction of explicit worlds $\mathcal{W}_e = \mathfrak{I}_T(\Gamma)$ to the set of *all* Tarski's interpretations of the FOL(Γ), which are models of Γ. As we have seen in Section 1.2, the intensional semantics of FOL(Γ) with a set of logic formulae $\mathcal{L}$ (and with the bijection between Tarski's homomorphisms $\mathcal{W}_e = \mathfrak{I}_T(\Gamma)$ and the set of extensionalization functions of intensional logic, the bijection $\mathcal{F} : \mathcal{W}_e \simeq \mathcal{E}$) is given by the composed mapping $\mathcal{L} \longrightarrow_I \mathcal{D} \Longrightarrow_{h \in \mathcal{E}} \mathfrak{R}$ in Definition 10, where (for a fixed intensional interpretation I) for each extensionalization function $h \in \mathcal{E}$ we obtain a Tarski's interpretation I_T with the mapping $I_T^* = h \circ I : \mathcal{L} \to \mathfrak{R}$.

In fact, with a given standard Tarski's interpretation I_T of FOL(Γ) we are not able to express the *intensional equality* of two open formulae with the same tuple of free variables, $\phi(x_1, \dots x_n), \psi(x_1, \dots x_n)$, defined by $(\forall h)(h(I(\phi(x_1, \dots x_n))) = h(I(\psi(x_1, \dots x_n))))$. So, as presented in Example 4 at the end of this section, if we introduce the intensional equality, then it reduces the set of Tarski's interpretations of the FOL that cannot consider such intensional constraints. Consequently, the bijection $\flat : \mathfrak{I}_T(\Gamma) \simeq \mathfrak{I}_K(\Gamma)$ in Theorem 1 is not more valid, because it was derived for the pure embedding of standard (extensional) FOL into minimal intensional FOL (without added intensional features). So, we need a new definition of possible worlds $\mathcal{W}_e$ valid also for intensional extension of the FOL, for a given fixed intensional interpretation I:

$$\mathcal{W}_e =_{\text{def}} \{I_T^* = h \circ I : \mathcal{L} \to \mathfrak{R} \mid h : \text{im}(I) \to \mathfrak{R} \in \mathcal{E}\} \subseteq \mathfrak{I}_T(\Gamma) \tag{1.9}$$

So, $\mathcal{W}_e = \mathfrak{I}_T(\Gamma)$ *only* for minimal intensional FOL used only for embedding of standard (extensional) FOL, but not for proper extensions of intensional features.

Let us define this *minimal intensional* first-order logic $\text{FOL}_{\mathcal{I}}(\Gamma)$, which has the same syntax as standard FOL (hence without other "high-level" modal logic connectives $\widehat{\Diamond}_i$), by elimination of the singleton set $\mathcal{W} = \{\hbar\}$ in Definition 14 and Example 2, when (1.9) reduces to $\mathcal{W}_e = \mathfrak{I}_T(\Gamma)$:

Definition 15 (Minimal intensional first-order logic ($\text{FOL}_{\mathcal{I}}(\Gamma)$)). Let $\mathcal{M} = (\mathbb{W}, \{\mathcal{R}_i\}, \mathcal{D}, I_K)$ be Kripke's model of a predicate multimodal logic, obtained from FOL(Γ) with a set of its Tarski's interpretations $\mathfrak{I}_T(\Gamma)$, which are models of Γ, with the set of possible worlds $\mathbb{W} = \mathcal{D}^{\mathcal{V}}$ and the set of existential modal "low-level" operators $\Diamond_i$ for each existential modal operator $\exists_i$ in $\mathcal{A}_{\text{FOL}}$ (corresponding to FOL quantifier $(\exists x), x \in \mathcal{V}$) with the accessibility relation $\mathcal{R}_i = \{(g_1, g_2) \in (\mathcal{D}^{\mathcal{V}})^2 | \text{ for all } y \in \mathcal{V} \backslash \{x\}(g_1(y) = g_2(y))\}$ as was shown in Definition 13.

The mapping $I_K : P \to \bigcup_{n\in\mathcal{N}} \mathbf{2}^{\mathcal{D}^n}$ is a standard Kripke's interpretation such that, for a given Tarski's interpretation $I_T^* \in \mathfrak{I}_T(\Gamma)$ of FOL(Γ) and a predicate $p_i^k \in P$, $I_K(p_i^k)(d_1,\ldots,d_k) = I_T^*(p_i^k(d_1,\ldots,d_k))$, i.e., from Theorem 1, $I_K = \flat(I_T^*)$.

Then we define the Kripke's interpretation of the intensional logic $\mathrm{FOL}_{\mathcal{I}}(\Gamma)$ by $\mathcal{M}_{\mathrm{FOL}_{\mathcal{I}}(\Gamma)} = \widehat{\mathcal{M}} =_{\mathrm{def}} (\widehat{\mathbb{W}}, \{\mathcal{R}_i\}, \mathcal{D}, \widehat{I}_K)$ with a set of (generalized) possible worlds $\widehat{\mathbb{W}} = \mathfrak{I}_T(\Gamma)\times\mathcal{D}^{\mathcal{V}}$, where $\mathcal{W}_e = \mathfrak{I}_T(\Gamma)$ is the set of explicit possible worlds (the set of Tarski's interpretation of FOL(Γ)), nonempty domain $\mathcal{D}$, and the mapping $\widehat{I}_K : \mathcal{W}_e\times P \to \bigcup_{n\in\mathcal{N}} \mathbf{2}^{\mathcal{D}^n}$ such that for each $I_T^* \in \mathcal{W}_e$ and $p_i^k \in P$, $\widehat{I}_K(I_T^*, p_i^k)(d_1,\ldots,d_k) = I_K(p_i^k)(d_1,\ldots,d_k)$ where $I_K = \flat(I_T^*)$.

For each world $\mathbf{w} = (I_K, g) \in \widehat{\mathbb{W}}$, we have that:

1. $\widehat{\mathcal{M}} \vDash_{I_K,g} p_i^k(x_1,\ldots,x_k)$ iff $\widehat{I}_K(I_T, p_i^k)(g(x_1),\ldots,g(x_k)) = t$.
2. $\widehat{\mathcal{M}} \vDash_{I_K,g} \varphi\wedge\phi$ iff $\widehat{\mathcal{M}} \vDash_{I_k,g} \varphi$ and $\widehat{\mathcal{M}} \vDash_{I_K,g} \phi$,
3. $\widehat{\mathcal{M}} \vDash_{I_K,g} \neg\varphi$ iff not $\widehat{\mathcal{M}} \vDash_{I_K,g} \varphi$,
4. $\widehat{\mathcal{M}} \vDash_{I_K,g} \Diamond_i\varphi$ iff exists $g' \in \mathcal{D}^{\mathcal{V}}$ such that $(g,g') \in \mathcal{R}_i$ and $\widehat{\mathcal{M}} \vDash_{I_K,g'} \varphi$.

Notice that the intensional semantics above is given for the ordinary syntax of the first-order logic with the existential quantifier $\exists$ only, without other "high-level" modal logic connectives $\widehat{\Diamond}_i$, thus with the empty set of accessibility binary relations over the set of explicit possible worlds $\mathcal{W}_e = \pi_1(\widehat{\mathbb{W}}) = \mathfrak{I}_T(\Gamma)$: this is the reason to denominate it by "minimal."

Let us show that this unique intensional Kripke model $\mathcal{M}_{\mathrm{FOL}_{\mathcal{I}}(\Gamma)} = (\widehat{\mathbb{W}}, \{\mathcal{R}_i\}, \mathcal{D}, \widehat{I}_K)$ models the Tarskian *logical consequence* of the first-order logic with a set of assumptions in Γ, so that the added intensionality preserves the Tarskian semantics of the FOL.

Proposition 5 (Montague's intension and Tarski's interpretations). *Let* $\mathcal{M}_{\mathrm{FOL}_{\mathcal{I}}(\Gamma)} = (\widehat{\mathbb{W}}, \{\mathcal{R}_i\}, \mathcal{D}, \widehat{I}_K)$ *be the unique* `intensional` *Kripke model of the first-order logic with a set of assumptions in* Γ*, as specified in Definition* 15.

So, a formula ϕ *is a logical consequence of* Γ *in the Tarskian semantics for the FOL, i. e.,* $\Gamma \Vdash \phi$*, iff* ϕ *is true in this Kripke intensional model* $\mathcal{M}_{\mathrm{FOL}_{\mathcal{I}}(\Gamma)}$*, i. e., iff* $\|\phi\| = \widehat{\mathbb{W}} = \mathcal{W}_e\times\mathcal{D}^{\mathcal{V}}$ *with the set of Tarski's interpretations, which are models of* Γ *(explicit worlds)* $\mathcal{W}_e = \mathfrak{I}_T(\Gamma)$.

If $I_n : \mathcal{L}_{\mathrm{op}} \to \mathfrak{R}^{\mathcal{W}_e}$ *is the mapping given in Definition* 10*, then for any (virtual) predicate* $\phi(x_1,\ldots,x_k)$*, the mapping* $I_n(\phi(x_1,\ldots,x_k)) : \mathcal{W}_e \to \mathfrak{R}$ *represents Montague's meaning (intension) of this logic formula, such that for any Tarski's interpretation (an explicit possible world)* $I_T^* = w \in \mathcal{W}_e = \pi_1(\mathbb{W})$,

$$I_n(\phi(x_1,\ldots,x_k))(w) = w(\phi(x_1,\ldots,x_k)) = I_T^*(\phi(x_1,\ldots,x_k)) \tag{1.10}$$

Proof. Let us show that for any first-order formula ϕ, it holds that $\mathcal{M}_{\mathrm{FOL}_{\mathcal{I}}(\Gamma)} \vDash_{w,g} \phi$ iff $w(\phi/g) = t$, where w is the Tarski's interpretation $w = I_T^* \in \mathcal{W}_e = \mathfrak{I}_T(\Gamma)$. Let us demonstrate it by the structural induction on the length of logic formulae. For any atom $\phi = p_i^k(x_1,\dots,x_k)$, we have from Definition 15 that

$$\mathcal{M}_{\mathrm{FOL}_{\mathcal{I}}(\Gamma)} \models_{I_T^*,g} p_i^k(x_1,\dots,x_k) \quad \text{iff} \quad I_K(I_T^*, p_i^k)(g(x_1),\dots,g(x_k)) = t$$
$$\text{iff} \quad I_T^*(p_i^k(x_1,\dots,x_k)/g) = t.$$

Let us suppose that such a property holds for every formula ϕ with less than n logic connectives of the FOL, and let us show that it holds also for any formula with n logic connectives. There are the following cases:

1. The case when $\phi = \neg\psi$ where ψ has $n-1$ logic connectives. Then $\mathcal{M}_{\mathrm{FOL}_{\mathcal{I}}(\Gamma)} \models_{I_T^*,g} \phi$ iff $\mathcal{M}_{\mathrm{FOL}_{\mathcal{I}}(\Gamma)} \models_{I_T^*,g} \neg\psi$ iff not $\mathcal{M}_{\mathrm{FOL}_{\mathcal{I}}(\Gamma)} \models_{I_T^*,g} \psi$ iff (by inductive hypothesis) not $I_T^*(\psi/g) = t$ iff $I_T^*(\neg\psi/g) = t$ iff $I_T^*(\phi/g) = t$.
2. The case when $\phi = \psi_1 \wedge \psi_2$, where both ψ_1, ψ_2 have less than n logic connectives, is analogous to the case 1.
3. The case when $\phi = (\exists x)\psi$ where ψ has $n-1$ logic connectives. It is enough to consider the case when x is a free variable in ψ. Then $\mathcal{M}_{\mathrm{FOL}_{\mathcal{I}}(\Gamma)} \models_{I_T^*,g} \phi$ iff $\mathcal{M}_{\mathrm{FOL}_{\mathcal{I}}(\Gamma)} \models_{I_T^*,g} (\exists x)\psi$ iff exists $u \in \mathcal{D}$ such that $\mathcal{M}_{\mathrm{FOL}_{\mathcal{I}}(\Gamma)} \models_{I_T^*,g} \psi[x/u]$ iff (by inductive hypothesis) exists $u \in \mathcal{D}$ such that $I_T^*(\psi[x/u]/g) = t$ iff $I_T^*((\exists x)\psi/g) = t$ iff $I_T^*((\phi/g)) = t$.

It is easy to verify that the intension of predicates in the $\mathrm{FOL}_{\mathcal{I}}(\Gamma)$ defined above can be expressed by the mapping I_n such that for any $p_i^k \in P$ and $w = I_T^* \in \mathcal{W}_e$, $I_n(p_i^k(x_1,\dots,x_k))(w) = w(p_i^k(x_1,\dots,x_k)) = I_T(p_i^k(x_1,\dots,x_k))$ and, more general, for any virtual predicate $\phi(x_1,\dots,x_k)$,

$$\begin{aligned}
&I_n(\phi(x_1,\dots,x_k))(w)\\
&= \|\phi(x_1,\dots,x_k)\|\\
&= \{(g(x_1),\dots,g(x_k)) \in \mathcal{D}^k \mid g \in \mathcal{D}^{\mathcal{V}} \text{ and } \mathcal{M}_{\mathrm{FOL}_{\mathcal{I}}} \models_{w,g} \phi(x_1,\dots,x_k)\}\\
&= \{(g(x_1),\dots,g(x_k)) \mid g \in \mathcal{D}^{\mathcal{V}} \text{ and } w(\phi(x_1,\dots,x_k)/g) = t\}\\
&= \{(g(x_1),\dots,g(x_k)) \mid g \in \mathcal{D}^{\mathcal{V}} \text{ and } (g(x_1),\dots,g(x_k)) \in w(\phi(x_1,\dots,x_k))\}\\
&= w(\phi(x_1,\dots,x_k)) = I_T^*(\phi(x_1,\dots,x_k)),
\end{aligned}$$

where w is the Tarski's interpretation $w = I_T^* \in \mathcal{W}_e = \mathfrak{I}_T(\Gamma)$. Consequently, $I_n(\phi(x_1,\dots, x_k)) : \mathcal{W} \to \mathfrak{R}$ is t Montague's meaning (i. e., the intension) of the (virtual) predicate $\phi(x_1,\dots,x_k)$. □

Note that the this result in equation (1.10), valid also for general case (1.9) of non-minimal intensional FOLs, is analogous to the previous result in equation (1.7). It is clear that in Kripke semantics of this intensional first-order logic, denoted by $\mathrm{FOL}_{\mathcal{I}}(\Gamma)$, if the set of assumptions is empty ($\Gamma = \emptyset$), then a formula ϕ is true in the intensional

Kripke model $\mathcal{M}_{\mathrm{FOL}_{\mathcal{I}}(\Gamma)}$ iff it is *valid* in Tarskian semantics of the FOL, ie., iff $\Vdash \phi$ in the FOL.

The main difference between Tarskian semantics and this intensional semantics is that this unique intensional Kripke model $\mathcal{M}_{\mathrm{FOL}_{\mathcal{I}}(\Gamma)}$ encapsulates the set of all Tarski models of the first-order logic with a (possibly empty) set of assumptions Γ.

Corollary 2. *The intensionalities of two different minimal intensional enrichments of the first-order syntax, given by intensional logics* $\mathrm{FOL}_{\mathcal{I}}(\Gamma)$ *(in Definition 15) and* $\mathrm{FOL}_{\mathcal{K}_{\mathcal{I}}}(\Gamma)$ *(in Example 2), are equivalent and correspond to Montague's intensionality.*

Proof. Let us denote by $I_n^{\mathrm{FOL}_{\mathcal{I}}(\Gamma)}, I_n^{\mathrm{FOL}_{\mathcal{K}_{\mathcal{I}}}(\Gamma)} : \mathcal{L}_{op} \to \mathfrak{R}^{\mathcal{W}}$ the intensional mappings (from Definition 10 of the intensional semantics) for these two intensional enrichments of the FOL(Γ). Notice that the set of explicit possible worlds $\mathcal{W}$ in $\mathrm{FOL}_{\mathcal{I}}(\Gamma)$ is equal to $\mathfrak{I}_T(\Gamma)$ while in $\mathrm{FOL}_{\mathcal{K}_{\mathcal{I}}}(\Gamma)$ is equal to $\mathfrak{I}_K(\Gamma)$, with the bijection (from Theorem 1) $\flat : \mathfrak{I}_T(\Gamma) \simeq \mathfrak{I}_K(\Gamma)$. We have to show that for any formulae $\phi(x_1, \dots, x_n) \in \mathcal{L}_{op}$ its extension, in a given explicit world $I_T \in \mathfrak{I}_T(\Gamma)$ of the intensional logic $\mathrm{FOL}_{\mathcal{I}}(\Gamma)$, is equal to its extension in the correspondent explicit world $I_K = \flat(I_T^*) \in \mathfrak{I}_K(\Gamma)$ of the intensional logic $\mathrm{FOL}_{\mathcal{K}_{\mathcal{I}}}(\Gamma)$. In fact, we have that

$$\begin{aligned}
&I_n^{\mathrm{FOL}_{\mathcal{I}}(\Gamma)}(\phi(x_1,\dots,x_k))(I_T)\\
&\quad = \{(g(x_1),\dots,g(x_k)) \in \mathcal{D}^k \mid g \in \mathcal{D}^{\mathcal{V}} \text{ and } \mathcal{M}_{\mathrm{FOL}_{\mathcal{I}}(\Gamma)} \vDash_{I_T,g} \phi(x_1,\dots,x_k)\}\\
&\quad = \{(g(x_1),\dots,g(x_k)) \mid g \in \mathcal{D}^{\mathcal{V}} \text{ and } I_T^*(\phi(x_1,\dots,x_k)/g) = t\} \quad \text{(from Proposition 5)}\\
&\quad = \{(g(x_1),\dots,g(x_k)) \mid g \in \mathcal{D}^{\mathcal{V}} \text{ and } \mathcal{M} \vDash_g \phi(x_1,\dots,x_k)\}\\
&\quad\quad \text{(from Proposition 3 and Theorem 1 where } \mathcal{M} \text{ is the Kripke interpretation of}\\
&\quad\quad \mathrm{FOL}_{\mathcal{K}}(\Gamma) \text{ with } I_K = \flat(I_T^*))\\
&\quad = \{(g(x_1),\dots,g(x_k)) \mid g \in \mathcal{D}^{\mathcal{V}} \text{ and } \widehat{\mathcal{M}}_{\mathrm{FOL}_{\mathcal{K}}(\Gamma)} \vDash_{I_K,g} \phi(x_1,\dots,x_k)\}\\
&\quad\quad \text{(from Proposition 4)}\\
&\quad = I_n^{\mathrm{FOL}_{\mathcal{K}_{\mathcal{I}}}(\Gamma)}(\phi(x_1,\dots,x_k))(I_K).
\end{aligned}$$

□

Remark. Consequently, independently on how we interpret the quantifiers of the FOL, as in standard FOL or as modal operators in $\mathrm{FOL}_{\mathcal{K}}$, the intensionality of the FOL is obtained only by one adequate *semantic enrichment*, without modifying its syntax. Consequently, we have demonstrated that an intensional FOL does not need the other logic operators as required by Bealer [12], i. e., we do not need an intensional abstraction operator or another modal operator. Because of that, such an intensional FOL is denominated as the *minimal* intensional logic. □

Another IFOL without the intensional abstraction is given in the following example.

Example 3 (Enrichment of minimal intensional FOL by "high-level" modal operators). In order to be able to recognize the intensional *equivalence* (different from intensional identity) between (virtual) predicates, that may be used in intensional mapping between P2P databases [42–44], we need to extend this *minimal* intensional FOL also syntactically, by introducing the new modal existential operator $\widehat{\Diamond}$ (as the "high-level" modal operators with the semantics introduced in point 5 of Definition 14 and Example 2), so that $\phi(x_1, \dots x_n)$ and $\psi(x_1, \dots x_n)$ are *intensionally equivalent* iff the modal first-order formula $\widehat{\Diamond}\phi(x_1, \dots x_n) \equiv \widehat{\Diamond}\psi(x_1, \dots x_n)$ is true in this modal FOL.

The Kripke semantics for this extended modal first-order logic is a S5 modal FOL with the accessibility relation $\widehat{\mathcal{R}} = \mathcal{W}_e \times \mathcal{W}_e$.

Two intensional *equivalent* predicates does need to have equal extensions in each explicit possible world as it is required by intensional *equality* (equal meaning from Montague's point of view) when $\phi(x_1, \dots x_n) \equiv \psi(x_1, \dots x_n)$ is true, where "≡" is the standard logic equivalence connective.

Notice that if they are intensionally equal, it does not mean that they are equal concepts, i. e., that $I(\phi(x_1, \dots x_n)) = I(\phi(x_1, \dots x_n)) \in \mathcal{D}$, but only that they are necessarily equivalent. In fact, the two atoms $p_1^1(x)$, "x has been bought," and $p_2^1(x)$, "x has been sold," are necessarily equivalent, i. e., it holds that $p_1^1(x) \equiv p_2^1(x)$ but they are two different *concepts*, i. e., $I(p_1^1(x)) \neq I(p_2^1(x))$.

Remark. Such an distinction of equal concepts and of the intensional equality (i. e., the necessary equivalence) is not possible in Montague's semantics, and explains why we adopted the PRP theory and two-step intensional semantics in Definition 10 analogously to Bealer's approach. □

That is, if we denote by '≈' this new *intensional equivalence* and by '≡' the *intensional equality*, we can show the following intensional logic property.

Corollary 3. *Any two first-order open formulae, $\phi(x_1, \dots x_n)$ and $\psi(x_1, \dots x_n)$, are intensionally* equivalent *iff $\widehat{\Diamond}\phi(x_1, \dots x_n)$ and $\widehat{\Diamond}\psi(x_1, \dots x_n)$ are intensionally* equal, *i. e.,*

$$\phi(x_1, \dots x_n) \approx \psi(x_1, \dots x_n) \quad \textit{iff} \quad \widehat{\Diamond}\phi(x_1, \dots x_n) \equiv \widehat{\Diamond}\psi(x_1, \dots x_n) \tag{1.11}$$

Proof. We have that for any explicit possible world (Tarski's homomorphism) $w' = I_T^{*'} \in \mathcal{W}_e$ in (1.9):

$$\begin{aligned}
&I_n(\widehat{\Diamond}\phi(x_1, \dots, x_k))(w') \\
&= \{(g(x_1), \dots, g(x_k)) \in \mathcal{D}^k \mid g \in \mathcal{D}^{\mathcal{V}} \text{ and } \mathcal{M} \vDash_{w',g} \widehat{\Diamond}\phi(x_1, \dots, x_k)\} \\
&= \{(g(x_1), \dots, g(x_k)) \mid g \in \mathcal{D}^{\mathcal{V}} \text{ and exists } w = I_T^* \in \mathcal{W}_e \\
&\quad \text{such that } (w', w) \in \widehat{\mathcal{R}} = \mathcal{W}_e \times \mathcal{W}_e \text{ and } \mathcal{M} \vDash_{w,g} \phi(x_1, \dots, x_k)\} \\
&= \{(g(x_1), \dots, g(x_k)) \mid g \in \mathcal{D}^{\mathcal{V}} \text{ and exists } w = I_T^* \in \mathcal{W}_e \\
&\quad \text{such that } \mathcal{M} \vDash_{w,g} \phi(x_1, \dots, x_k)\}
\end{aligned}$$

$$= \bigcup_{w=I_T\in\mathcal{W}_e} I_n(\phi(x_1,\ldots,x_k))(w)$$
$$= \bigcup_{w\in\mathcal{W}} w(\phi(x_1,\ldots,x_k))$$
$$= \bigcup_{I_T\in\mathcal{W}} I_T^*(\phi(x_1,\ldots,x_k)).$$

That is, the intension of $\widehat{\Diamond\phi}(x_1,\ldots x_n)$ is a *constant* function (which does not depend on the explicit possible world $w \in \mathcal{W}_e$).

Thus, $\phi(x_1,\ldots x_n)$ and $\psi(x_1,\ldots x_n)$ are intensionally *equivalent* if

$$\bigcup_{w\in\mathcal{W}_e} I_n(\phi(x_1,\ldots,x_k))(w)$$
$$= \bigcup_{w\in\mathcal{W}_e} I_n(\psi(x_1,\ldots,x_k))(w), \text{ i. e.,}$$

if $I_n(\Diamond\phi(x_1,\ldots,x_k))(w) = I_n(\Diamond\phi(x_1,\ldots,x_k))(w)$ for every world $w \in \mathcal{W}$, i. e., if $\widehat{\Diamond\phi}(x_1,\ldots x_n)$ and $\widehat{\Diamond\psi}(x_1,\ldots x_n)$ are intensionally *equal*. □

Another extension of this minimal intensional FOL is of course the intensional FOL defined by Bealer in [12], if we use the bijective mapping $\mathcal{F} : \mathcal{W}_e \to \mathcal{E}$ from (1.9) as the Montague–Bealer's isomorphism (bijection) between explicit possible worlds and the set of extensionalization functions. Notice that both versions of intensional FOL are modal logics, and hence we can define two different logic inferences for them: the *local* inference relation '$\vdash_w$' and the *global* inference relation '$\vdash$', is as follows:

1. For a given set of logic formulae Γ, we tell that they locally infer the formula ϕ in a possible world $w \in \mathcal{W}_e$, i. e., $\Gamma \vdash_w \phi$ iff $(\forall$ models $\mathcal{M})(\forall g)((\forall\psi \in \Gamma).\mathcal{M} \vDash_{w,g} \psi$ implies $\mathcal{M} \vDash_{w,g} \phi)$.
2. For a given set of logic formulae Γ, we tell that they globally infer the formula ϕ, i. e., $\Gamma \vdash \phi$ iff $(\forall$ models $\mathcal{M})(\forall g)(\forall w \in \mathcal{W}_e)((\forall\psi \in \Gamma).\mathcal{M} \vDash_{w,g} \psi$ implies $\mathcal{M} \vDash_{w,g} \phi)$.

The intensional first-order logic $\mathrm{FOL}_{\mathcal{I}}(\Gamma)$ in Definition 15 has *one* unique Kripke model $\mathcal{M} = \mathcal{M}_{\mathrm{FOL}_{\mathcal{I}}(\Gamma)}$. Thus, we obtain that in this modal intensional logic $\mathrm{FOL}_{\mathcal{I}}(\Gamma)$:

1. $\Gamma \vdash_w \phi$ iff ϕ is true in the Kripke model $\mathcal{M}_{\mathrm{FOL}_{\mathcal{I}}(\Gamma)}$ in a given possible world $w \in \mathfrak{I}_T(\Gamma)$, i. e., if ϕ is true in the Tarski's model $I_T^* = w$ of Γ. Thus, this local inference $\vdash_w$ corresponds to the derivation of true formulae in a given Tarski model $I_T^* = w$ of Γ.
2. $\Gamma \vdash \phi$ iff ϕ is true in the Kripke model $\mathcal{M}_{\mathrm{FOL}_{\mathcal{I}}(\Gamma)}$, i. e., iff $\Gamma \Vdash \phi$, so that the global inference $\vdash$ corresponds to the Tarskian logical consequence $\Vdash$ in the standard first-order logic.

In the rest of this section, we will consider the full homomorphic (algebraic) extensions of intensional semantics defined in Definition 10.

The first step is to define the intensional algebra $\mathcal{A}_{\text{int}}$ of concepts, analogous to concept languages as, e. g., in the case of the Description Logic (DL).

Concept languages steam from semantic networks [45–47], which for a large group of graphical languages used in the 1970s to represent and reason with conceptual knowledge. But they did not have a rigorously defined statement as emphasized by Brachman and Levesque [48, 49]. After that, different versions of DL [50] with formal semantics appeared, as a family of knowledge representation formalisms that represent the knowledge of an application domain by first defining the relevant *concepts* and *roles* as a terminology (TBox) and then the *assertions* (ABox) about named individuals in terms of this terminology. The concepts denote sets of individuals, and roles denote binary relationships between individuals.

In our approach, we will use not only binary, but also general k-ary relationships between individuals, in order to manage not only unary (as in DL) but all k-ary concepts. This approach is similar to Bealer's intensional algebra, with the difference that our algebra is not an extension of intensional Boolean algebra as in the Bealer's work, where the intensional conjunction is extensionally interpreted by set intersection (here, instead, it is interpreted by the natural join operations, defined in the FOL extensional algebra $\mathcal{A}_{\mathfrak{R}}$ in Corollary 1).

So, we will define only the minimal intensional algebra (with a minimal number of operators) able to support the homomorphic extension of the intensional mapping $I : \mathcal{L} \to \mathcal{D}$.

Definition 16 (Basic intensional FOL algebra). Intensional FOL algebra is a structure

$$\mathcal{A}_{\text{int}} = (\mathcal{D}, \text{Id}, \text{Truth}, \{\text{conj}_S\}_{S \in \mathcal{P}(\mathbb{N}^2)}, \text{neg}, \{\text{exists}_n\}_{n \in \mathbb{N}}),$$

with binary operations $\text{conj}_S : D_I \times D_I \to D_I$, unary operation $\text{neg} : D_I \to D_I$ and unary operations $\text{exists}_n : D_I \to D_I$, such that for any extensionalization function $h \in \mathcal{E}$, and $u \in D_k, v \in D_j, k, j \geq 0$,

1. $h(\text{Id}) = R_=$ and $h(\text{Truth}) = \{\langle\,\rangle\}$, for $\text{Id} = I(\doteq (x,y))$ and $\text{Truth} = I(\top)$.
2. $h(\text{conj}_S(u,v)) = h(u) \bowtie_S h(v)$, where $\bowtie_S$ is the natural join operation defined in Definition 9 and $\text{conj}_S(u,v) \in D_m$ where $m = k + j - |S|$ if for every pair $(i_1, i_2) \in S$ it holds that $1 \leq i_1 \leq k$, $1 \leq i_2 \leq j$ (otherwise $\text{conj}_S(u,v) \in D_{k+j}$).
3. $h(\text{neg}(u)) =\sim (h(u)) = \mathcal{D}^k \backslash (h(u))$, if $k \geq 1$, where $\sim$ is the operation defined in Definition 9 and $\text{neg}(u) \in D_k$. For $u_0 \in \mathcal{D}_0$, $h(\text{neg}(u_0)) =\sim (h(u_0)) = \mathcal{D}^0 \backslash (h(u_0))$.
4. $h(\text{exists}_n(u)) = \pi_{-n}(h(u))$, where π_{-n} is the operation defined in Definition 9 and $\text{exists}_n(u) \in D_{k-1}$ if $1 \leq n \leq k$ (otherwise exists_n is the identity function).

Notice that for $u, v \in D_0$, so that $h(u), h(v) \in \{f, t\}$,

$$h(\text{neg}(u)) =\sim (h(u)) = \mathcal{D}^0 \backslash (h(u)) = \{\langle\,\rangle\} \backslash (h(u)) \in \{f, t\}, \quad \text{and}$$
$$h(\text{conj}_\emptyset(u,v)) = h(u) \bowtie_\emptyset h(v) \in \{f, t\}.$$

We define a derived operation union : $(\mathcal{P}(D_i)\backslash\emptyset) \to D_i$, $i \geq 0$, such that, for any $B = \{u_1, \ldots, u_n\} \in \mathcal{P}(D_i)$ and $S = \{(l, l) \mid 1 \leq l \leq i\}$ we have that

$$\text{union}(\{u_1, \ldots, u_n\}) =_{\text{def}} \begin{cases} u_1, & \text{if } n = 1 \\ \text{neg}(\text{conj}_S(\text{neg}(u_1), \text{conj}_S(\text{neg}(u_2), \ldots, \text{neg}(u_n)) \ldots), & \text{otherwise} \end{cases} \tag{1.12}$$

Then we obtain that for $n \geq 2$:

$$\begin{aligned} h(\text{union}(B)) &= h(\text{neg}(\text{conj}_S(\text{neg}(u_1), \text{conj}_S(\text{neg}(u_2), \ldots, \text{neg}(u_n)) \ldots) \\ &= \mathcal{D}^i\backslash((\mathcal{D}^i\backslash h(u_1)) \bowtie_S \cdots \bowtie_S (\mathcal{D}^i\backslash h(u_n))) \\ &= \mathcal{D}^i\backslash\Big((\mathcal{D}^i\backslash h(u_1)) \bigcap \cdots \bigcap (\mathcal{D}^i\backslash h(u_n))\Big) \\ &= \bigcup\{h(u_j) \mid 1 \leq j \leq n\}, \quad \text{i.e.,} \\ h(\text{union}(B)) &= \bigcup\{h(u) \mid u \in B\} \end{aligned} \tag{1.13}$$

Note that it is valid also for the propositions in $u_1, u_2 \in D_0$, so that $h(\text{union}(u_1, u_2)) = h(u_1) \bigcup h(n_2) \in \{f, t\}$ where f is empty set $\emptyset$ while t is a singleton set $\{\langle\,\rangle\}$ with empty tuple $\langle\,\rangle$, and hence the join $\{\langle\,\rangle\} \bowtie \emptyset = \emptyset$ and $\{\langle\,\rangle\} \bowtie \{\langle\,\rangle\} = \{\langle\,\rangle\}$.

We define the following homomorphic extension of the intensional interpretation $I : \mathcal{L} \to \mathcal{D}$ for the formulae in syntax algebra $\mathcal{A}_{\text{FOL}}$ from Corollary 1:

1. The logic formula $\phi(x_i, x_j, x_k, x_l, x_m) \wedge_S \psi(x_l, y_i, x_j, y_j)$ will be intensionally interpreted by the concept $u_1 \in D_7$, obtained by the algebraic expression $\text{conj}_S(u, v)$ where $u = I(\phi(x_i, x_j, x_k, x_l, x_m)) \in D_5, v = I(\psi(x_l, y_i, x_j, y_j)) \in D_4$ are the concepts of the virtual predicates ϕ, ψ, relatively, and $S = \{(4, 1), (2, 3)\}$. Consequently, we have that for any two formulae $\phi, \psi \in \mathcal{L}$ and a particular operator conj_S uniquely determined by tuples of free variables in these two formulae, $I(\phi \wedge_S \psi) = \text{conj}_S(I(\phi), I(\psi))$.
2. The logic formula $\neg\phi(x_i, x_j, x_k, x_l, x_m)$ will be intensionally interpreted by the concept $u_1 \in D_5$, obtained by the algebraic expression $\text{neg}(u)$ where $u = I(\phi(x_i, x_j, x_k, x_l, x_m)) \in D_5$ is the concept of the virtual predicate ϕ. Consequently, we have that for any formula $\phi \in \mathcal{L}$, $I(\neg\phi) = \text{neg}(I(\phi))$.
3. The logic formula $(\exists_3)\phi(x_i, x_j, x_k, x_l, x_m)$ will be intensionally interpreted by the concept $u_1 \in D_4$, obtained by the algebraic expression $\text{exists}_3(u)$ where $u = I(\phi(x_i, x_j, x_k, x_l, x_m)) \in D_5$ is the concept of the virtual predicate ϕ. Consequently, we have that for any formula $\phi \in \mathcal{L}$ and a particular operator exists_n uniquely determined by the position of the existentially quantified variable in the tuple of free variables in ϕ (otherwise $n = 0$ if this quantified variable is not a free variable in ϕ), $I((\exists_n)\phi) = \text{exists}_n(I(\phi))$.

Corollary 4 (Intensional/extensional FOL semantics). *For any of Tarski's interpretation I_T of the minimal intensional FOL in Definition* 15, *the following diagram of homomorphisms commutes* [18]*:*

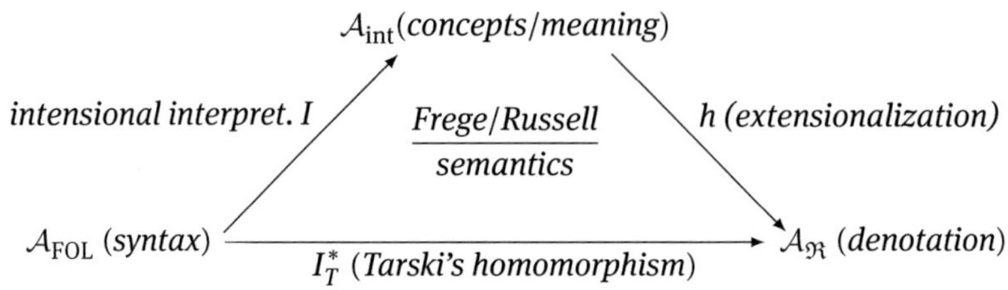

(1.14)

where $h = \mathcal{F}(w)$ is part of a two-step intensional semantics in Definition 10, *where $w = I_T^* \in \mathcal{W}_e = \mathfrak{I}_T(\Gamma)$ is the explicit possible world of the Kripke frame in Definition* 15.

Proof. The homomorphism of intensional mapping I is defined by the intensional interpretation above. Let us also show that the isomorphism (bijective mapping) $\mathcal{F} : \mathcal{W}_e \simeq \mathcal{E}$ between Tarski's homomorphism $I_T^* \in \mathcal{W}_e$ and the extensionalization mappings $h \in \mathcal{E}$ is uniquely determined in order to make the above diagram homomorphic and commutative. It can be done by inductive structural recursion on the length of FOL formulae in $\mathcal{L}$: for any atom $p_i^k(x_1, \dots, x_k) \in \mathcal{L}$, we define $\mathcal{F} : I_T^* \mapsto h$ by the requirement that $h(I(p_i^k(x_1, \dots, x_k))) = I_T(p_i^k)$. Let us suppose that for any formula ϕ with n logic connectives it holds that the mapping $\mathcal{F} : I_T^* \mapsto h$ satisfies requirement that $h(I(\phi)) = I_T^*(\phi)$. Let us show that it holds also for any logic formula ϕ with $n + 1$ logic connectives. It is enough to show it in the case when $\varphi = \phi \wedge_S \psi$ (the other two cases are analogous):

$$\begin{aligned} h(I(\varphi)) &= h(I(\phi \wedge_S \psi)) = h(\text{conj}_S(I(\phi), I(\psi))) \quad \text{(from the homomorphism of } I) \\ &=_{\text{def}} h(I(\phi)) \bowtie_S h(I(\psi)) \quad \text{(from Definition 16)} \\ &= I_T^*(\phi) \bowtie_S I_T^*(\psi) \quad \text{(by inductive hypothesis)} \\ &= I_T^*(\varphi), \end{aligned}$$

from the fact that the same conjunctive formula φ is mapped by I into conj_{S_1} and by I_T^* into $\bowtie_{S_2}$ where $S_1 = S_2$. □

This homomorphic diagram formally express the fusion of Frege's and Russell's semantics [25, 51, 52] of meaning and denotation of the FOL language, and renders mathematically correct the definition of what we call an "intuitive notion of intensionality," in terms of which a language is intensional if denotation is distinguished from sense: that is, if both a denotation and sense is ascribed to its expressions. This notion is simply adopted from Frege's contribution (without its infinite sense-hierarchy, avoided by Russell's approach where there is only one meaning relation, one fundamental relation between words and things, here represented by one fixed intensional interpretation I), where the sense contains a mode of presentation (here described algebraically as an algebra of concepts (intensions) $\mathcal{A}_{\text{int}}$), and where sense determines denotation for any given extensionalization function h (correspondent to a given Traski's interpretation I_T^*).

More about the relationships between Frege's and Russell's theories of meaning may be found in the Chapter 7, "Extensionality and meaning," in [12]. As noted by Gottlob Frege and Rudolf Carnap (he uses terms intension/extension in the place of Frege's terms sense/denotation [31]), the two logic formulae with the same denotation (i. e., the same extension for a given Tarski's interpretation I_T) need not have the same sense (intension), thus such codenotational expressions are not *substitutable* in general.

In fact, there is exactly *one* sense (meaning) of a given logic formula in $\mathcal{L}$, defined by the uniquely fixed intensional interpretation I, and *a set* of possible denotations (extensions) each determined by a given Tarski's interpretation of the FOL as follows from Definition 10:

$$\mathcal{L} \longrightarrow_I \mathcal{D} \Longrightarrow_{h \in \mathcal{E}} \mathfrak{R} \tag{1.15}$$

Often "intension" has been used exclusively in connection with possible worlds semantics, however, here we use (as in many others as Bealer, for example) "intension" in a more wide sense, i. e., as an *algebraic expression* in the intensional algebra of meanings (concepts) $\mathcal{A}_{\text{int}}$, which represents the structural composition of more complex concepts (meanings) from the given set of atomic meanings. Consequently, not only the denotation (extension) is compositional, but also the meaning (intension) is compositional.

Notice that this compositional property holds also for the generation of subconcepts: e. g., given a virtual predicate $\phi(x_1, \ldots x_n)$ with correspondent concept $I(\phi) \in D_n$, its subconcept is defined by $I(\phi[x_i/c]) = I(\phi(x_1, \ldots, x_{i-1}, [x_i/c], x_{i+1}, \ldots, x_n)) \in D_{n-1}$, where the i-th free variable of the original virtual predicate is substituted by a language constant c. The following compositional relationship exists between extensions of concepts and their subconcepts.

Proposition 6. *For any extensionalization function h and a virtual predicate ϕ with a tuple of free variables $(x_1, \ldots, x_{i-1}, x_i, x_{i+1}, \ldots, x_n)$, $n \geq i \geq 1$, it holds that*

$$h(I(\phi[x_i/c])) = \begin{cases} \pi_{-i}(\{(u_1, \ldots, u_{i-1}, u_i, u_{i+1}, \ldots, u_n) \in h(I(\phi)) \mid u_i = I(c)\}), & \textit{if } n \geq 2 \\ f_{\langle\,\rangle}(\{(u) \in h(I(\phi)) \mid u = I(c)\}), & \textit{if } i = n = 1 \end{cases} \tag{1.16}$$

where the function $f_{\langle\,\rangle} : \mathfrak{R} \to \mathfrak{R}$ is that introduced in (1.3). *For the sentences, we have that for any virtual predicate $\phi(x_1, \ldots, x_n)$ and an assignment g,*

$$h(I(\phi/g)) = t \quad \textit{iff} \quad (g(x_1), \ldots, g(x_n)) \in h(I(\phi)).$$

Proof. The proof is directly from the homomorphic diagram of Frege/Russell's intensional semantics in Corollary 4. Let us consider the first case when $n \geq 2$, then

$$\begin{aligned}
&h(I(\phi[x_i/c])) \\
&\quad = I_T^*(\phi[x_i/c]) \\
&\quad = \{(g(x_1),\ldots,g(x_{i-1}),g(x_{i+1}),\ldots,g(x_n)) \\
&\quad \in D_{n-1} \mid g \in \mathcal{D}^{\mathcal{V}} \text{ and } I_T^*(\phi(g(x_1),\ldots,g(x_{i-1}),I(c),g(x_{i+1}),\ldots,g(x_n))) = t\} \\
&\quad = \pi_{-i}(\{(g(x_1),\ldots,g(x_{i-1}),g(x_i),g(x_{i+1}),\ldots,g(x_n)) \in D_{n-1} \mid g \in \mathcal{D}^{\mathcal{V}} \text{ and } I_T^*(\phi/g) = t \\
&\qquad \text{and } g(x_i) = I(c)\}) \\
&\quad = \pi_{-i}(\{(g(x_1),\ldots,g(x_{i-1}),g(x_i),g(x_{i+1}),\ldots,g(x_n)) \in I_T^*(\phi) \mid g \in \mathcal{D}^{\mathcal{V}} \text{ and } g(x_i) = I(c)\}) \\
&\quad = \pi_{-i}(\{(u_1,\ldots,u_{i-1},u_i,u_{i+1},\ldots,u_n) \in I_T^*(\phi) \mid u_i = I(c)\}) \\
&\quad = \pi_{-i}(\{(u_1,\ldots,u_{i-1},u_i,u_{i+1},\ldots,u_n) \in h(I(\phi)) \mid u_i = I(c)\}).
\end{aligned}$$

The other cases are similar. □

From this proposition, it is clear that we are aware of the importance of the homomorphic extensions of the two-step intensional semantics in Definition 10. Without this homomorphic commutativity with the Tarski's interpretations, given by Corollary 4, we will not be able to specify the interdependence of extensions of correlated concepts in $\mathcal{D}$. Thus, the homomorphic extension of Frege/Russell's intensional semantics is not only a meaningful theoretical contribution but also a necessary issue to be able to define the correct intensional semantics for the FOL.

The commutative homomorphic diagram in (1.14) Corollary 4 explains in which way the Tarskian semantics neglects meaning, as if truth in language where autonomous. This diagram shows that such a Tarskian approach, quite useful in logic, is very approximate. In fact, the Tarskian fact "ϕ is a true sentence" (horizontal arrow in the diagram above with $I_T^*(\phi) = t$), is equivalent to "ϕ expresses a true proposition" (where the proposition is an intensional entity equal to $I(\phi)$, and its truth is obtained by extensionalization mapping $h(I(\phi)) = t = \{\langle\ \rangle\}$, i. e., the set with unique empty tuple $\langle\ \rangle$). That is, the diagram (1.14) considers also the theory of truth as a particular case of the theory of meaning, where we are dealing with propositions in $D_0 \subset \mathcal{D}$.

Remark. Notice that the commutative diagram (1.14) in Corollary 4 *between the algebras* (so that mappings are the homomorphisms) is not valid for the enrichment of minimal intensional FOL by "high-level" modal operators $\widehat{\Diamond} : \mathcal{A}_{\mathrm{FOL}} \to \mathcal{A}_{\mathrm{FOL}}$ presented in Example 3. In fact, for this S5 modal logic with its accessibility relation $\widehat{\mathcal{R}} = \mathcal{W}_e \times \mathcal{W}_e$, we have that for a given Tarski's homomorphism $I_T^* = w \in \mathcal{W}_e$,

$$I_T^*(\widehat{\Diamond}\phi(\mathbf{x})) =_{\mathrm{def}} \bigcup_{w' \in \mathcal{W}_e} w'(\phi(\mathbf{x})) \neq \widehat{\alpha}(I_T^*(\phi(\mathbf{x}))) \tag{1.17}$$

for each unary relational operator $\widehat{\alpha} : \mathfrak{R} \to \mathfrak{R}$, from the fact that $\widehat{\alpha}$ is a function such that for a given relation $R \in \mathfrak{R}$ gives a result that depends only on this value R and not on the union of another relations $w'(\phi(\mathbf{x})) \in \mathfrak{R}$. Consequently, we do not have a homomorphic property between algebras $\mathcal{A}_{\mathrm{FOL}}$ and $\mathcal{A}_{\mathfrak{R}}$ in the diagram above for the "high-level" modal operators $\widehat{\Diamond}$. □

Thus, the homomorphic diagram is valid for the minimal intensional FOL (just the strict embedding of the extensional FOL into this more powerful IFOL), and also in the case when the intensional algebra $\mathcal{A}_{\mathrm{int}}$ has a minimal requirement (structure) to obtain the homomorphism of the intensional interpretation $I : \mathcal{A}_{\mathrm{FOL}} \to \mathcal{A}_{\mathrm{int}}$. So, in such a minimal IFOL, it seems that intensionality of logic is completely representable by the extensionality represented by Tarski's homomorphism $I_T^* : \mathcal{A}_{\mathrm{FOL}} \to \mathcal{A}_{\mathfrak{R}}$ into the pure extensional algebra $\mathcal{A}_{\mathfrak{R}}$. But as we have shown by the remark above, by introducing "high-level" modal operators (which in the next section will be used to specify intensional equivalence relationship), or by the introduction of the intensional abstraction operator (in the next section), or by incrementing the expressive power of the intensional algebra $\mathcal{A}_{\mathrm{int}}$ as follows.

Example 4 (Intensional equality). Let us consider now the intensional algebra $\mathcal{A}_{\mathrm{int}}$ in Definition 16 enriched by the possibility to write the equations between intensional terms (expressions of this algebra) of the same type, i. e., the equations $u_1 = u_2$ such that $u_1, u_2 \in D_k \subset \mathcal{D}$ for any finite $k \geq -1$. This intensional algebraic identity is different from the binary identity predicate $\doteq$ introduced in Definition 1 in Section 1.1.1, and this difference can be shown by considering a ground logic atom $\doteq (c_1, c_2)$ for two given constants (nullary functions), c_1 and c_2, such that its intensional interpretation is given by

$$I(\doteq (c_1, c_2)) =_{\mathrm{def}} \mathrm{equal}(u_1, u_2) \in D_0 \quad \text{where } u_i = I(c_i) \in D_{-1},\ i = 1, 2 \tag{1.18}$$

such that denotation of this intensional term for every extensionalization function h, for any two $u_1, u_2 \in D_k$, $k \geq -1$, is defined by

$$h(\mathrm{equal}(u_1, u_2)) = t \quad \text{iff} \quad h(u_1) = h(u_2) \tag{1.19}$$

Take the case when $u_1 \in D_{-1}$ is the intensional term "Morning Star" and $u_2 \in D_{-1}$ is the intensional term "Evening Star."

Let "Morning Star" and "Evening Star" be two constants (nullary function symbols) of FOL, so that both Tarski's interpretation I_T and intensional interpretations are identities for them. However, while for standard FOL I_T("Evening Star") = "Evening Star" is a (simple) value in a domain $\mathcal{D}$, for IFOL instead $u = I$("Evening Star") = `Evening Star` $\in D_1 \subset \mathcal{D}$ is an intensional particular (name), for which the extension (denotation) is determined by the extensionalization function h, e. g., $h(u) = h(I(\text{"Evening Star"})) = h($`Evening Star`$) =$ "Venus." Let us now specify an *intensional equation* in the intensional algebra $\mathcal{A}_{\text{int}}$. Take the case when $u_1 \in D_{-1}$ is the intensional term $u_1 = I(\text{“Morning Star”}) = \texttt{Morning Star}$ and $u_2 \in D_{-1}$ is the intensional term `Evening Star`, and we define the equality (equation (1)) between these two intensional terms of equal intensional type (in D_{-1}) in $\mathcal{A}_{\text{int}}$:

$$(\text{Eq.}\,(1))\quad u_1 = u_2 \tag{1.20}$$

Let us now define a ground logic atom of the FOL bynary identity predicate $\doteq$, $\doteq$(“Morning Star,” “Evening Star”), so that for every Tarski's interpretation we have that $I_T^*(\doteq(\text{“Morning Star,” “Evening Star”})) = f$, because

$$(\text{“Morning Star,” “Evening Star”}) \notin I_T(\doteq).$$

That is, for each Tarskian interpretation this ground atom is false. For the intensional interpretation, instead we have from (1.19) that

$$\forall h \in \mathcal{E}.h(I(\doteq (\text{“Morning Star,” “Evening Star”}))) = t$$

in contrast with Tarskian interpretation, so that $I_T^* \neq h \circ I$, i. e., the diagram in (1.14) *is not commutative*. Moreover, in intensional FOL semantics, we have the two-step interpretation, and hence as we have seen, by using the extensionalization function h, we can express the fact that both `Morning Star` and `Evening Star` denote the planet Venus.

Because of that, the intensionality is a generalization of the Tarskian theory of truth that is useful in mathematical logic but inessential to the semantics for natural language. It explains why the modern intelligent information retrieval in Web P2P database systems requires the intensionality, and the application of the general theory of meaning in the place of the simpler Tarskian theory of truth.

1.3.1 Enrichment by intensional abstraction operator and its logic inverse

Semantics is the theory concerning the fundamental relations between words and things. In Tarskian semantics of the FOL, one defines what it takes for a sentence in a language to be true relative to a model. This puts one in a position to define what it takes for a sentence in a language to be valid. Tarskian semantics often prove quite useful in logic. Despite this, Tarskian semantics neglect meaning, as if truth in language were autonomous. Because of that the Tarskian theory of truth becomes inessential to the semantics for more expressive logics, or more “natural” languages, it is the starting point of my investigation in the previous sections about how to provide the necessary, or minimal, intensionality to the syntax of the FOL.

However, as it was shown, we are able to enrich the expressivity of such a minimal FOL intensionality by new modal operators, or in different way provided in what follows. As we have seen in the introduction to Bealer's intensional FOL, he introduced the intensional abstraction operator in point 4 of Definition 5, which will be considered in rest of this section, as a significant enrichment of the intensional FOL considered in the previous section.

In reflective languages, reification data is causally connected to the related reified aspect such that a modification to one of them affects the other. Therefore, the reification data is always a faithful representation of the related reified aspect. *Reification data* is often said to be made a *first class object*. In programming language design, a first-class citizen (also type, object, entity or value) in a given programming language is an entity, which supports all of the operations generally available to other entities. These operations typically include being passed as an argument, returned from a function, modified and assigned to a variable. The concept of first- and second-class objects was introduced by Christopher Strachey in the 1960s when he contrasted real numbers (first-class) and procedures (second-class) in ALGOL. In FOL, we have the variables as arguments inside the predicates and terms, which can be assigned to variables are first-class objects while the predicates are the second-class objects. When we transform a virtual predicate into a term, by using the intensional abstraction operator, we transform a logic formula into the first class object to be used inside another predicates as first-class objects. Thus, abstracted terms in the intensional FOL are just such abstracted terms as reification of logic formulae. For example, the sentence "Marco thinks *that Zoran runs*," expressed by thinks(*Marco*, <runs(*Zoran*)>) by using the binary predicate thinks and unary predicate runs where the ground atom runs(*Zoran*) is reified into the predicate thinks.

If $\phi(\mathbf{x})$ is a formula (virtual predicate) with a list (a tuple) of free variables in $\mathbf{x} = (x_1, \ldots, x_n)$ (with ordering from left-to-right of their appearance in ϕ), and α is its subset of *distinct* variables, then $<\phi(\mathbf{x})>^{\beta}_{\alpha}$ is a term, where β is the remaining set of free variables in $\mathbf{x}$. The externally quantifiable variables are the *free* variables not in α. When $n = 0$, $<\phi>$ is a term, which denotes a proposition, for $n \geq 1$ it denotes a n-ary concept.

We recall that we denote by t/g (or ϕ/g) the ground term (or formula) without free variables, obtained by assignment g from a term t (or a formula ϕ), and by $\phi[x/t]$ the formula obtained by uniformly replacing x by a term t in ϕ.

Definition 17 (Intensional abstraction convention). From the fact that we can use any permutation of the variables in a given virtual predicate, we introduce the convention that

$$<\phi(\mathbf{x})>^{\beta}_{\alpha} \quad \text{is a term obtained from virtual predicate } \phi(\mathbf{x}) \tag{1.21}$$

if α is *not empty* such that $\alpha \bigcup \beta$ is the set of all variables in the list (tuple of variables) $\mathbf{x} = (x_1, \ldots, x_n)$ of the virtual predicate (an open logic formula) ϕ, and $\alpha \bigcap \beta = \emptyset$, so that $|\alpha| + |\beta| = |\mathbf{x}| = n$. Only the variables in β (which are the only free variables of this term), can be quantified. If β is empty, then $<\phi(\mathbf{x})>_\alpha$ is a *ground term*. If ϕ is a sentence, and hence both α and β are empty, we write simply $<\phi>$ for this ground term.

An assignment $g : \mathcal{V} \to \mathcal{D}$ for variables in $\mathcal{V}$ is applied only to free variables in terms and formulae. Such an assignment $g \in \mathcal{D}^{\mathcal{V}}$ can be recursively uniquely extended into the assignment $g^* : \mathcal{T} \to \mathcal{D}$, where $\mathcal{T}$ denotes the set of all terms (here I is an intensional interpretation of this FOL, as explained in what follows), by:

1. $g^*(t) = g(x) \in \mathcal{D}$ if the term t is a variable $x \in \mathcal{V}$.
2. $g^*(t) = I(c) \in \mathcal{D}$ if the term t is a constant $c \in P$.
3. If t is an abstracted term obtained for an open formula ϕ_i, $<\phi_i(\mathbf{x}_i)>_{\alpha_i}^{\beta_i}$, then

$$g^*(<\phi_i(\mathbf{x}_i)>_{\alpha_i}^{\beta_i}) =_{\text{def}} \begin{cases} I(\phi_i(\mathbf{x}_i)) \in D_{|\alpha_i|}, & \text{if } \beta_i \text{ is empty} \\ I(\phi_i[\beta_i/g(\beta_i)]) \in D_{|\alpha_i|}, & \text{otherwise} \end{cases} \tag{1.22}$$

   where $g(\beta) = g(\{y_1, \dots, y_m\}) = \{g(y_1), \dots, g(y_m)\}$ and $[\beta/g(\beta)]$ is a uniform replacement of each i-th variable in the set β with the i-th constant in the set $g(\beta)$. Notice that α is the set of all free variables in the formula $\phi[\beta/g(\beta)]$.
4. $g^*(t) = I(\phi(\mathbf{x})/g) \in D_0 \subset \mathcal{D}$ if t is an intensional term $I(\phi(\mathbf{x})) \in D_{|\mathbf{x}|}$.[5]

The abstracted terms $<\phi>_\alpha^\beta$ can be used as terms in any predicate $p_j^k \in P$, e. g., for an atom $p_j^3(<\phi>_\alpha^\beta, y, z)$ with free variables y, z and that in β. Let $p_j^k(t_1, \dots, t_k)$ be an atom with at least one of abstract term $t_i = <\phi_i(\mathbf{x}_i)>_{\alpha_i}^{\beta_i}$ with β_i nonempty and let β denote the union of all β_i of the abstracted terms in this atom. We can consider this atom as a virtual predicate $\phi(\mathbf{x})$ with ordered tuple of free variables $\mathbf{x}$, and we denote by $\mathbf{y}$ its ordered subtuple without variables in β with $n = |\mathbf{y}| \leq k$. Then we have that for each assignment $g \in \mathcal{D}^\beta$, $p_j^k(t_1/g, \dots, t_k/g)$ is a standard atom (all abstracted terms $t_i/g = g^*(t_i)$ by using (1.22) are transformed to values in $\mathcal{D}$ and $I(p_j^k(t_1/g, \dots, t_k/g)) \in D_n \subset \mathcal{D}$), while for Tarskian interpretation we obtain the following set of tuples:

$$I_T^*(p_j^k(t_1/g, \dots, t_k/g)) =_{\text{def}} \{g_1(\mathbf{y}) \mid g_1 \in \mathcal{D}^{\overline{\mathbf{y}}} \text{ and } I_T^*(p_j^k(t_1/g, \dots, t_k/g)[\overline{\mathbf{y}}/g_1(\overline{\mathbf{y}})]) = t\} \tag{1.23}$$

where $I_T^*(p_j^k(t_1/g, \dots, t_k/g)[\overline{\mathbf{y}}/g_1(\overline{\mathbf{y}})]) = t$ iff $(t_1/g, \dots, t_k/g)[\overline{\mathbf{y}}/g_1(\overline{\mathbf{y}})] \in I_T(p_j^k)$, and we recall that $I_T^*(p_j^k(z_1, \dots, z_k)) =_{\text{def}} I_T(p_j^k)$ if all z_i, $1 \leq i \leq k$, are free variables.

So, general Tarski's and intensional interpretations are defined by

$$\begin{aligned} I_T^*(p_j^k(t_1, \dots, t_k)) &=_{\text{def}} \bigcup \{I_T^*(p_j^k(t_1/g, \dots, t_k/g)) \mid g \in \mathcal{D}^\beta\} \neq I_T(p_j^k) \subseteq \mathcal{D}^k \\ I(p_j^k(t_1, \dots, t_n)) &=_{\text{def}} \text{union}(\{I(p_j^k(t_1/g, \dots, t_k/g)) \mid g \in \mathcal{D}^\beta\}) \end{aligned} \tag{1.24}$$

where the derived operator "union" of intensional algebra is given by (1.12).

5 It happens when the abstracted term (1.22) is inside another predicate and we make the assignment for attributes of this predicate.

Let us consider the logic atoms of the predicates with multivalued attributes, as presented in Section 4.3.1, to correspond in the FOL to another predicate whose extension will have a number of tuples, each one corresponding to one particular value. So, such a many-valued attribute has to be transformed into an abstracted term in order to be an argument of the predicate with such multivalued attribute without generating a second-order logic.

Example 5 (Multivalued attributes for RDBs). We will consider the intensional RDBs, introduced in a dedicated chapter and specifically in Section 4.3.1. Let us introduce a multivalued attribute `hobies` for the relation `Contacts` representing the concept with a key (identifier) attribute with the name `contactID` of a person, his address and his hobbies:

$$\mathtt{Contacts(contactID, firstName, lastName, street, zipCode, hobbies)}.$$

Let this attribute `hobbies` be represented by a binary predicate $p_i^2(x_1, y)$ where the variable x_1 is used for the identifiers of contacts `contactID` and variable y for a number of different hobbies referred to this contact identifier. If we represent the relation with name `Contacts` by a 6-ary predicate letter p_j^6, then this relation in *intensional FOL* will be represented by the atom

$$p_j^6(x_1, x_2, x_3, x_4, x_5, \lessdot p_i^2(x_1, y)\gtrdot_{\alpha_i}^{\beta_i}) \tag{1.25}$$

with $\beta_i = \{x_1\}$ and hidden variables $\alpha_i = \{y\}$. So, having only one abstracted term $t_6 = \lessdot p_i^2(x_1, y)\gtrdot_{\alpha_i}^{\beta_i}$ (traduced by "that y is a hobby of x_1") in this logic atom, we have that $\beta = \beta_i = \{x_1\}$ and let us take an assignment $g \in \mathcal{D}^\beta = \mathcal{D}^{\{x_1\}}$, i. e., $g : \{x_1\} \to \mathcal{D}$, such that $g(x_1) = 123$ is a value of the attribute `contactID` and from (1.22),

$$u = g^*(t_6) = g^*(\lessdot p_i^2(x_1, y)\gtrdot_{\alpha_i}^{\beta_i}) = I(p_i^2(123, y)) \in D_1$$

for a given intensional interpretation I. So, for this assignment of variables in $\beta = \{x_1\}$, $g \in \mathcal{D}^\beta$, from atom (1.25) we obtain a *standard FOL* atom with variables:

$$p_j^6(x_1, x_2, x_3, x_4, x_5, \lessdot p_i^2(x_1, y)\gtrdot_{\alpha_i}^{\beta_i})/g = p_j^6(132, x_2, x_3, x_5, x_5, u) \tag{1.26}$$

This unary concept $u \in D_1 \subset \mathcal{D}$ (a property) in $\mathcal{D}$ can be represented, e. g., by the name `hobbies_of_123`, and hence the extension of this intensional unary concept $u = I(p_i^2(123, y))$, corresponding to free variable y, has to be equal to the set of hobbies of this `Contact` specified by its identifier `ContactID` = 123, i. e.,

$$\begin{aligned} h(u) &= h(I(p_i^2(123, y))) \\ &= I_T^*(p_i^2(123, y)) \quad \text{(from the commutativity } I_T^* = h \circ I) \\ &= \{g'(y) \in \mathcal{D} \mid g \in \mathcal{D}^{\{y\}} \text{ and } I_T^*(p_i^2(123, g'(y))) = t\} \end{aligned}$$

Let us consider now a total assignment $g_1 \in \mathcal{D}^{\mathcal{V}}$, such that $g_1(x_1) = g(x_1) = 123$ with the ground atom of the predicate p_j^6,

$$p_j^6(x_1, x_2, x_3, x_4, x_5, <p_i^2(x_1, y)>_{\alpha_i}^{\beta_i})/g_1 = p_j^6(132, \text{Zoran}, \text{Majkic}, \text{Appia}, 0187, u) \quad (1.27)$$

where, from the fact that $u \in D_1$ is a value (name) `hobbies_of_123` of a domain $\mathcal{D}$, we can see clearly how an obtained ground atom is a *standard FOL ground atom* (in which we have no more of the abstracted terms). The atom (1.25) has a hidden variable y and the tuple $\mathbf{x} = (x_1, x_2, x_3, x_4, x_5)$ of free variables, so that its ordered subtuple without variables in β is $\mathbf{y} = (x_2, x_3, x_4, x_5)$ with $n = |\mathbf{y}| = 4$. Hence, the Tarski's interpretation of the atom in (1.26) is obtained, from (1.23), for an assignment $g : \beta \to \mathcal{D}$, by

$$\begin{aligned} &I_T^*(p_j^6(x_1, x_2, x_3, x_4, x_5, <p_i^2(x_1, y)>_{\alpha_i}^{\beta_i})/g) \\ &= I_T^*(p_j^6(132, x_2, x_3, x_4, x_5, u)) \\ &= \{g'(x_2, x_3, x_4, x_5) \mid g' \in \mathcal{D}^{\overline{\mathbf{y}}} \text{ and } I_T^*(p_j^k(132, x_2, x_3, x_4, x_5, u)[\overline{\mathbf{y}}/g'(\overline{\mathbf{y}})]) = t\} \end{aligned}$$

where $\overline{\mathbf{y}} = \{x_2, x_3, x_4, x_5\}$ denotes the *set* of variables. So, from (1.27) we have that

$$(\text{Zoran}, \text{Majkic}, \text{Appia}, 0187) \in I_T^*(p_j^6(x_1, x_2, x_3, x_4, x_5, <p_i^2(x_1, y)>_{\alpha_i}^{\beta_i})/g).$$

However, in our case where the first attribute of p_j^6 is the KEY-attribute (identifier) and is fixed by assignment g by $g(x_1) = 132$, the Tarski's interpretation above will return exactly with one tuple:

$$I_T^*(p_j^6(x_1, x_2, x_3, x_4, x_5, <p_i^2(x_1, y)>_{\alpha_i}^{\beta_i})/g) = \{(\text{Zoran}, \text{Majkic}, \text{Appia}, 0187)\}.$$

Remark. The predicate p_i^2 dedicated to multivalued attribute needs to provide not only a variable y for this attribute but also the subset of attributes, which define the KEY of the relation that contains this multivalued variable. In our case, the KEY of the relation `Contact` is composed by its single attribute `contactID` represented by variable x_1.

In fact, if we eliminate these KEY attributes of the relation that contains this multivalued attribute, and propose a unary predicate for the multivalued attribute, $p_i^1(y)$, then a relation `Contact` is given by the atom $p_j^6(x_1, x_2, x_3, x_4, x_5, <p_i^1(y)>_y)$ with *ground term* $t_6 = <p_i^1(y)>_y$. Consequently, in this case, for *all* assignments $g \in \mathcal{D}^{\mathcal{V}}$, from (1.22), we would obtain *the same* $u = g^*(t_6) = I(p_i^1(y)) \in D_1$, and hence the extension of this unary concept for hobbies would have the set of hobbies used by all contacts in the relation `Contact`. So, we would not be able to obtain the hobbies of each single contact as that of (Zoran, Majkic, Appia, 0187) corresponding to value "132" of the KEY attribute `contactID`.

We introduce the special new "it is abstracted" unary predicate $A(\_)$, which composes well- defined atoms *only for abstracted terms* $A(<\phi(\mathbf{x})>_{\alpha}^{\beta}) \in \mathcal{L}_{\omega}$ with the prefixed meaning[6]

"it is abstracted that $\phi(\mathbf{x})$ by hiding variables in α"

The meaning of "hiding" variables in $\alpha \neq \emptyset$ is that these variables are not influenced in this predicate A by the assignments, so that $A(\lessdot\phi(\mathbf{x})\gtrdot_{\alpha}^{\beta})/g$ is equal to $A(\lessdot\phi[\beta/g(\beta)]\gtrdot_{\alpha})$ with remaining variables in α, and that for each variable $x \in \alpha$, the FOL formula $(\exists x)A(\lessdot\phi(\mathbf{x})\gtrdot_{\alpha}^{\beta})$ is not well-defined in L_{ω}. So, we obtain the particular intensional and Tarskian semantics for this predicate $A(\_)$ such that this predicate transfers the interpretation directly to the *reified formula* inside abstracted term.

Definition 18 (Semantics of "it is abstracted" unary predicate). Intensional interpretation of this unary predicate is defined by

$$I(A(\lessdot\phi(\mathbf{x})\gtrdot_{\alpha}^{\beta})) =_{\text{def}} \begin{cases} I(\phi(\mathbf{x})), & \text{if } \beta \text{ is empty} \\ \text{union}(\{I(\phi[\beta/g(\beta)]) \mid g \in \mathcal{D}^{\beta}\}), & \text{otherwise} \end{cases} \tag{1.28}$$

Consequently, for a Tarski's interpretation I_T, the atom $A(\lessdot\phi(\mathbf{x})\gtrdot_{\alpha}^{\beta})/g$ is considered as a virtual predicate $\phi[\beta/g(\beta)]$ with free variables in (nonempty) α, so that

$$I_T^*(A(\lessdot\phi(\mathbf{x})\gtrdot_{\alpha}^{\beta})/g) =_{\text{def}} \begin{cases} \pi_{-\beta}(I_T^*(\phi[\beta/g(\beta)])) \subseteq \mathcal{D}^{|\alpha|}, & \text{if } \beta \text{ is not empty} \\ I_T^*(\phi(\mathbf{x})), & \text{otherwise} \end{cases} \tag{1.29}$$

where

$$\begin{aligned} &I_T^*(\phi[\beta/g(\beta)]) \\ &\quad = \{g'(\mathbf{x}) \mid g' \in \mathcal{D}^{\mathcal{V}} \text{ such that } \forall x_j \in \beta.(g'(x_j) = g(x_j)) \text{ and } I_T(\phi(g'(\mathbf{x}))) = t\}, \end{aligned}$$

and, when β is not empty, in a general case:

$$I_T^*(A(\lessdot\phi(\mathbf{x})\gtrdot_{\alpha}^{\beta})) = \bigcup\{I_T^*(A(\lessdot\phi(\mathbf{x})\gtrdot_{\alpha}^{\beta})/g) \mid g \in \mathcal{D}^{\beta}\} \tag{1.30}$$

Once one has found a method for specifying the denotations of singular terms of $\mathcal{L}_{\omega}$ (taken into consideration the particularity of abstracted terms), the Tarski-style definitions of truth and validity for $\mathcal{L}_{\omega}$ may be given in the customary way.

An *intensional interpretation* [12] of this intensional FOL is a mapping between the set $\mathcal{L}$ of formulae of the logic language and intensional entities in $\mathcal{D}$, $I : \mathcal{L} \to \mathcal{D}$ is a kind

6 In this way, we avoid the introduction of hidden quantifiers $(\rotatebox[origin=c]{180}{$\exists$}x_i)_{\mathbf{x}}$ of predicate-compression theory provided in Definition 23, Section 2.1.1, where "it is abstracted" atom $A(\lessdot\phi(\mathbf{x})\gtrdot_{\alpha}^{\beta})$ is logically equivalent to the formula $\prod_{x_i \in \alpha}(\rotatebox[origin=c]{180}{$\exists$}x_i)_{\mathbf{x}})\phi(\mathbf{x})$. More about the embedding of hidden quantifiers by intensional abstract terms is provided in Section 2.1.3.

of compositional "conceptualization," as defined in Section 1.2, with the following extension to the special new "ground" atoms from (1.28) for a given assignment g,

$$I(A(<\phi(\mathbf{x})>_{\alpha}^{\beta})/g) =_{\text{def}} \begin{cases} I(\phi[\beta/g(\beta)]) \in D_{|\alpha|}, & \text{if } \beta \text{ is not empty} \\ I(\phi(\mathbf{x})), & \text{otherwise} \end{cases} \tag{1.31}$$

analog to that in (1.29) for Tarski's interpretations. The interpretation of a more complex abstract term $<\phi(\mathbf{x})>_{\alpha}^{\beta}$ is defined in terms of the interpretations of the relevant syntactically simpler expressions, because the interpretation of a more complex formulae is defined in terms of the interpretation of the relevant syntactically simpler formulae, based on the intensional algebra above. This is the recursive "composition of meaning." For example,

$$I(p_i^1(x) \wedge_{\{(1,1)\}} p_k^1(x)) = \text{conj}_{\{(1,1)\}}(I(p_i^1(x)), I(p_k^1(x))), \quad \text{and}$$
$$I(\neg\phi) = \text{neg}(I(\phi)), \text{ and } I(\exists x_i)\phi(x_i, x_j, x_i, x_k) = \text{exists}_3(I(\phi(x_i, x_j, x_i, x_k))).$$

What is being considered specifically is a method how we apply an assignment $g \in \mathcal{D}^{\mathcal{V}}$ to abstracted terms with free variables in β: so, from (1.22) we have that $g^*(<\phi(\mathbf{x})>_{\alpha}^{\beta}) = I(\phi[\beta/g(\beta)]) \in D_{|\alpha|}$ will denote an appropriate property or relation, depending on the value of $|\alpha| \geq 1$. We have seen in Example 5 how it can be used for multivalued attributes in intensional RDBs.

Notice that if $\beta = \emptyset$ is the empty set then, from (1.22), $g^*(<\phi(\mathbf{x})>_{\alpha}^{\beta}) = I(\phi(\mathbf{x})) \in D_{|\mathbf{x}|}$. In the case when ϕ is an atom $p_i^m(x_1, \ldots, x_m)$, then $g^*(<p_i^m(x_1, \ldots, x_m)>_{x_1,\ldots,x_m}) = I(p_i^m(x_1, \ldots, x_m)) \in D_m$. The application of an assignment to a more complex abstract $<\phi>_{\alpha}$ is defined in terms of the assignments of the relevant syntactically simpler abstract(s) [12]. For example, $g^*(<\phi(x) \wedge_S \psi(x)>_x) = I(\phi(x) \wedge_S \psi(x)) = \text{conj}_S(I(\phi(x)), I(\psi(x))) = \text{conj}_S(g^*(<\phi(x)>_x), g^*(<\phi(x)>_x)) \in D_1$, where "$\text{conj}_S$" with $S = (1,1)$, is the intensional operator in the intensional algebra $\mathcal{A}_{\text{int}}$ corresponding homorphically to the logic conjunction operator of the syntax algebra of the FOL logic (in the extension of intensional interpretation I into the homomorphism, as for example, in the commutative diagram (1.14) in Corollary 4, Section 1.3).

Consequently, based on the intensional algebra in Definition 16 and on intensional mapping in (1.24), which eliminates the abstracted terms from intensional algebra, it holds that the intensional interpretation of any formula in $\mathcal{L}$ will be reduced to an algebraic expression over interpretations of primitive atoms in $\mathcal{L}$. This obtained expression is finite for any finite formula, and represents the composed *meaning* of such finite formula.

The distinction between intensions and extensions is important especially because we are now able to have and *equational theory* over intensional entities (as $<\phi>$), that is predicate and function *names*, and is separate from the extensional equality of relations and functions. An *extensionalization function* h assigns to the intensional elements of $\mathcal{D}$ an appropriate extension as specified in Definition 7, Section 1.2,

$$h = h_{-1} + h_0 + \sum_{i\geq 1} h_i : \sum_{i\geq -1} D_i \longrightarrow D_{-1} + \{f,t\} + \sum_{i\geq 1} \mathcal{P}(D^i)$$

and we have the two-step intensionally semantics in Definition 10, Section 1.2.

From the fact that the abstract terms in intensional FOL algebra $\mathcal{A}_{\mathrm{FOL}}$ does not propagate to intensional concepts and intensional terms of intensional algebra $\mathcal{A}_{\mathrm{int}}$, for the extensionalization homomorphism $h : \mathcal{A}_{\mathrm{int}} \rightarrow \mathcal{A}_{\mathfrak{R}}$ all remains equal to the case when we do not use abstracted terms, so also Tarski's constraints in Definition 113 remains invariant.

Consequently, the *extension* of an abstracted term satisfy the following property.

Proposition 7. *The commutative diagram* (1.14) *of the Frege/Russell semantics of the* minimal *intensional FOL in Corollary* 4, *with* $I_T^* = h \circ I$, *is preserved also for the enrichment by the intensional abstract operators.*

Proof. Let us show that it holds in both cases: when abstracted terms are used inside the special unary predicate A (with particular semantics), and in a more general case when are used inside all other standard predicates:

1. Case of the special atoms $A(<\phi(\mathbf{x})>_\alpha^\beta)$:

$$\begin{aligned} I_T^*(A(<\phi(\mathbf{x})>_\alpha^\beta)/g) &= I_T^*(\phi[\beta/g(\beta)]) \quad \text{from (1.29)} \\ &= h(I(\phi[\beta/g(\beta)])) \quad \text{from Corollary 4} \\ &= h(I(A(<\phi(\mathbf{x})>_\alpha^\beta)/g)) \quad \text{from (1.31)} \end{aligned}$$

So, in a general case, we obtain

$$\begin{aligned} I_T^*(A(<\phi(\mathbf{x})>_\alpha^\beta)) &= \bigcup\{I_T^*(A(<\phi(\mathbf{x})>_\alpha^\beta)/g) \mid g \in \mathcal{D}^\beta\} \quad \text{from (1.30)} \\ &= \bigcup\{h(I(A(<\phi(\mathbf{x})>_\alpha^\beta)/g)) \mid g \in \mathcal{D}^\beta\} \quad \text{from above} \\ &= \bigcup\{h(I(\phi[\beta/g(\beta)])) \mid g \in \mathcal{D}^\beta\} \quad \text{from (1.31)} \\ &= h(\mathrm{union}(\{I(\phi[\beta/g(\beta)]) \mid g \in \mathcal{D}^\beta\})) \quad \text{from homomorphism of } h \\ &= h(I(A(<\phi(\mathbf{x})>_\alpha^\beta))) \quad \text{from (1.28).} \end{aligned}$$

2. Case of any atom $p_j^k(t_1,\ldots,t_k)$ with at least one of abstract term $t_i = <\phi_i(\mathbf{x}_i)>_{\alpha_i}^{\beta_i}$ with β_i nonempty and let β denotes the union of all β_i of the abstracted terms in this atom. We can consider this atom as a virtual predicate $\phi(\mathbf{x})$ with ordered tuple of free variables $\mathbf{x}$, and we denote by $\mathbf{y}$ its ordered subtuple without variables in β with $n = |\mathbf{y}| \leq k$. So, we have that for each assignment $g \in \mathcal{D}^\beta$, $p_j^k(t_1/g,\ldots,t_n/g)$ is a standard atom (all abstracted terms $t_i/g = g^*(t_i)$ by using (1.22) are transformed to values in $\mathcal{D}$ and $I(p_j^k(t_1/g,\ldots,t_k/g)) \in D_n \subset \mathcal{D}$). From the fact that in the atom $p_j^k(t_1/g,\ldots,t_n/g)$, we have no abstracted terms, it is valid for them the Frege/Russell semantics of the intensional FOL in Corollary 4, with $I_T^* = h \circ I$, i. e.,

$$(1)\quad I_T^*(p_j^k(t_1/g,\ldots,t_n/g)) = I_T^*(p_j^k(t_1,\ldots,t_n)/g) = h(I(p_j^k(t_1,\ldots,t_n)/g)).$$

Thus, in a general case, from (1.24), we have that

$$\begin{aligned} &I_T^*(p_j^k(t_1,\ldots,t_k)) \\ &\quad = \bigcup\{I_T^*(p_j^k(t_1/g,\ldots,t_k/g)) \mid g \in \mathcal{D}^\beta\} \\ &\quad = \bigcup\{h(I(p_j^k(t_1/g,\ldots,t_k/g))) \mid g \in \mathcal{D}^\beta\} \quad \text{from (1)} \\ &\quad = h(\text{union}(\{I(p_j^k(t_1/g,\ldots,t_k/g)) \mid g \in \mathcal{D}^\beta\})) \quad \text{from homomorphism of } h \\ &\quad = h(I(p_j^k(t_1,\ldots,t_k))) \quad \text{from (1.24).} \end{aligned}$$

Thus, $I_T^* = h \circ I$ also for the enrichment of the minimal intensional FOL (without intensional equations, shown in Example 4) by intensional abstract operators. □

Hence, from this proposition, for each Tarski's interpretation I_T of the intensional FOL with intensional abstraction operators and fixed intensional interpretation I, we have an extensionalization function h such that $I_T^* = h \circ I$, and hence the extension of the "ground" predicate $A(<\phi(\mathbf{x})>_\alpha^\beta)/g = A(<\phi(\mathbf{x})>_\alpha^\beta/g)$, is obtained by

$$\begin{aligned} &I_T^*(A(<\phi(\mathbf{x})>_\alpha^\beta/g)) = h(I(\phi[\beta/g(\beta)])) = I_T^*(\phi[\beta/g(\beta)]), \quad \text{i.e.,} \\ &I_T^*(A(<\phi(\mathbf{x})>_\alpha^\beta/g)) = \{g'(\pi_{-\beta}(\mathbf{x})) \mid g' \in \mathcal{D}^\alpha, I_T^*(\phi[\beta/g(\beta)][\alpha/g'(\alpha)]) = t\} \end{aligned} \tag{1.32}$$

where $\pi_{-\beta}(\mathbf{x})$ is the sublist of $\mathbf{x}$ from which are eliminated the variables in β.

Example 6 (Global compression of predicates). Let us consider for a fixed set α of $n = |\alpha|$ hidden variables, the following Herbrand base $H =_{\text{def}} \{A(<r_j^k(\mathbf{x})>_\alpha^\beta/g) \mid g \in \mathcal{D}^\mathcal{V}, r_j^k \in P, k \geq |\alpha|\}$, and flattened Herbrand base

$$H_F =_{\text{def}} \{r_j^k(\mathbf{x})[\beta/g(\beta)][\alpha/g'(\alpha)] \mid g' \in \mathcal{D}^\alpha, r_j^k \in P, k \geq |\alpha|\},$$

so that for $\mathcal{W} = \mathcal{D}^n$, we have the bijection is : $H_F \to H \times \mathcal{W}$, the higher part of diagram (A.3) in Section A.4 in the Appendix represent the following *global compression* represented by higher order Herbrand base H and its flattened (standard) version H_F,

Higher-order

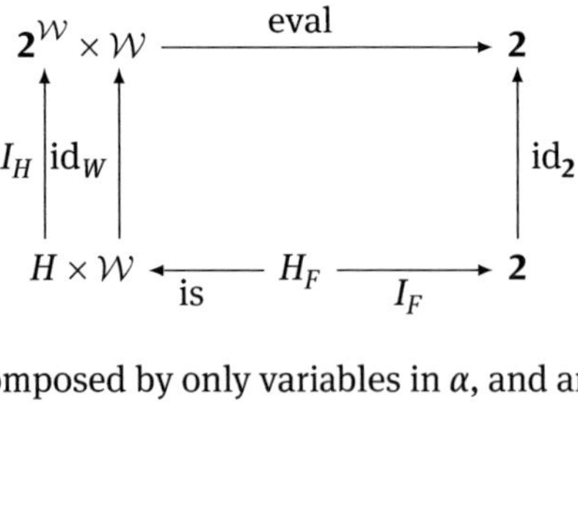

(1.33)

such that for $\mathbf{y}$ subtuple of $\mathbf{x}$ composed by only variables in α, and any $g' \in \mathcal{D}^\alpha$, tuple $\mathbf{d} = g'(\mathbf{y}) \in \mathcal{W}$, we have that

$$I_H(A(<r_j^k(\mathbf{x})>_\alpha^\beta/g))(\mathbf{d}) = I_F(r_j^k(\mathbf{x})[\beta/g(\beta)][\alpha/g'(\alpha)])$$

Now we are able to define the intensional equivalences, introduced previously in Example 3 and equation (1.11) in Corollary 3 for the minimal intensional FOL in Definition 15 enriched by the universal "high-level" modal operator $\widehat{\Box}$ and existential modal operator $\widehat{\Diamond} = \neg\widehat{\Box}\neg$ with accessibility relation $\mathcal{R} = \mathcal{W}_e \times \mathcal{W}_e$ (where $\mathcal{W}_e = \mathfrak{I}_T(\Gamma)$ is the set of all Tarski's interpretation of this intensional FOL), between the abstracted terms $<\phi(\mathbf{x})>_\alpha^{\beta_1}/g$ (i. e., $<\phi[\beta_1/g(\beta_1)]>_\alpha$) and $<\psi(\mathbf{y})>_\alpha^{\beta_2}/g$ (i. e., $<\psi[\beta_2/g(\beta_2)]>_\alpha$), where all free variables (not in α) are instantiated by $g \in \mathcal{D}^{\mathcal{V}}$ (we recall that $A \equiv B$ denotes the formula $(A \Rightarrow B) \wedge (B \Rightarrow A))$, i. e., the formula $\neg(A \wedge \neg B) \wedge \neg(\neg A \wedge B)$:

1. (Strong) intensional equivalence (or *equality*) "$\asymp$" is defined by

$$<\phi(\mathbf{x})>_\alpha^{\beta_1}/g \asymp <\psi(\mathbf{y})>_\alpha^{\beta_2}/g \quad \text{iff} \quad \widehat{\Box}(\phi[\beta_1/g(\beta_1)] \equiv \psi[\beta_2/g(\beta_2)]) \tag{1.34}$$

   with $\mathcal{M} \vDash_{w,g'} \widehat{\Box}\varphi[\beta_1/g(\beta_1)]$ iff for all $w' \in \mathcal{W}_e$, $(w, w') \in \mathcal{R}$ implies $\mathcal{M} \vDash_{w',g'} \varphi[\beta_1/g(\beta_1)]$.
   So, we have that $<p_1^1(x)>_x \asymp <p_2^1(x)>_x$, i. e., "$x$ has been bought" and "x has been sold" are intensionally equivalent, but they have not the same meaning (the concept $I(p_1^1(x)) \in D_1$ is different from $I(p_2^1(x)) \in D_1$).
2. Weak intensional equivalence "$\approx$" is defined by

$$<\phi(\mathbf{x})>_\alpha^{\beta_1}/g \approx <\psi(\mathbf{y})>_\alpha^{\beta_2}/g \quad \text{iff} \quad \widehat{\Diamond}\phi[\beta_1/g(\beta_1)] \equiv \widehat{\Diamond}\psi[\beta_2/g(\beta_2)] \tag{1.35}$$

   This weak equivalence is used for P2P database integration in a number of papers [42, 53–58].

Note that if we want to use the intensional equality in our language, then we need the correspondent operator "necess" in intensional algebra $\mathcal{A}_{\text{int}}$ for the universal operator "$\widehat{\Box}$" (modal necessity logic operator).

This semantics is equivalent to the algebraic semantics for $\mathcal{L}$ in [27] for the case of the conception where intensional entities are considered to be *equal* if and only if they are *necessarily equivalent*. Intensional equality is much stronger that the standard *extensional equality* in the actual world, just because requires the extensional equality in *all* possible worlds, in fact, if $<\phi(\mathbf{x})>_\alpha^{\beta_1}/g \asymp <\psi(\mathbf{y})>_\alpha^{\beta_1}/g$ then $h(I(A(<\phi(\mathbf{x})>_\alpha^{\beta_1}/g))) = h(I(A(<\psi(\mathbf{y})>_\alpha^{\beta_2}/g)))$ for all extensionalization functions $h \in \mathcal{E}$ (i. e., for possible worlds (Tarski's interpretations), $I_T^* = w = \text{is}^{-1}(h) \in \mathcal{W}_e = \mathfrak{I}_T(\Gamma)$). It is easy to verify that the intensional equality means that in every possible world $w \in \mathcal{W}_e$ (i. e., Tarski's interpretation) the intensional entities u_1 and u_2 have the same extensions.

Let the logic modal formula $\widehat{\Box}\phi[\beta_1/g(\beta_1)]$, where the assignment g is applied only to free variables in β_1 of a formula ϕ not in the set of variables in $\alpha = (x_1, \ldots, x_n)$, $n \geq 1$, represents a n-ary intensional concept such that $I(\widehat{\Box}\phi[\beta_1/g(\beta_1)]) \in D_n$ and, from (1.22), $I(\phi[\beta_1/g(\beta_1)]) = g^*(<\phi(\mathbf{x})>_\alpha^{\beta_1}) \in D_n$. Then the extension of this n-ary concept is equal to (here the mapping necess : $D_i \to D_i$ for each $i \geq 0$ is a new operation of the intensional algebra $\mathcal{A}_{\text{int}}$ in Definition 16):

$$\begin{aligned} h(I(\hat{\Box}\phi[\beta_1/g(\beta_1)])) &= h(\text{necess}(I(\phi[\beta_1/g(\beta_1)]))) \\ &= \{(g'(x_1),\ldots,g'(x_n)) \mid \mathcal{M} \vDash_{w,g'} \hat{\Box}\phi[\beta_1/g(\beta_1)] \text{ and } g' \in \mathcal{D}^{\mathcal{V}}\} \\ &= \{(g'(x_1),\ldots,g'(x_n)) \mid g' \in \mathcal{D}^{\mathcal{V}} \text{ and } \forall w_1((w,w_1) \in \mathcal{R} \text{ implies } \mathcal{M} \vDash_{w_1,g'} \phi[\beta_1/g(\beta_1)])\} \\ &= \bigcap_{h_1 \in \mathcal{E}} h_1(I(\phi[\beta_1/g(\beta_1)])). \end{aligned}$$

While,

$$\begin{aligned} h(I(\hat{\Diamond}\phi[\beta_1/g(\beta_1)])) &= h(I(\neg\hat{\Box}\neg\phi[\beta_1/g(\beta_1)])) \\ &= h(\text{neg}(\text{necess}(I(\neg\phi[\beta_1/g(\beta_1)])))) = \mathcal{D}^n \backslash h(\text{necess}(I(\neg\phi[\beta_1/g(\beta_1)]))) \\ &= \mathcal{D}^n \backslash \Big(\bigcap_{h_1 \in \mathcal{E}} h_1(I(\neg\phi[\beta_1/g(\beta_1)])) \Big) \\ &= \mathcal{D}^n \backslash \Big(\bigcap_{h_1 \in \mathcal{E}} h_1(\text{neg}(I(\phi[\beta_1/g(\beta_1)]))) \Big) \\ &= \mathcal{D}^n \backslash \Big(\bigcap_{h_1 \in \mathcal{E}} \mathcal{D}^n \backslash h_1(I(\phi[\beta_1/g(\beta_1)])) \Big) \\ &= \bigcup_{h_1 \in \mathcal{E}} h_1(I(\phi[\beta_1/g(\beta_1)])). \end{aligned}$$

Consequently, the modal formulae $\hat{\Box}\phi[\beta_1/g(\beta_1)]$ and $\hat{\Diamond}\phi[\beta_1/g(\beta_1)]$ are the *built-in* (or rigid) concept as well, whose extensions does not depend on possible worlds.

Thus, two concepts are intensionally *equal*, i. e., $<\phi(\mathbf{x})>_{\alpha}^{\beta_1}/g \asymp <\psi(\mathbf{y})>_{\alpha}^{\beta_2}/g$, iff $h(I(\phi[\beta_1/g(\beta_1)])) = h(I(\psi[\beta_2/g(\beta_2)]))$ for every h, i. e., iff $I_T^*(\phi[\beta_1/g(\beta_1)]) = I_T^*(\psi[\beta_2/g(\beta_2)])$ for every Tarski's homomorphism $I_T^* \in \mathcal{W}_e$.

Analogously, two concepts are *weakly* equivalent, i. e.,

$$\begin{aligned} &<\phi(\mathbf{x})>_{\alpha}^{\beta_1}/g \approx <\psi(\mathbf{y})>_{\alpha}^{\beta_2}/g, \\ &\text{iff} \quad h(I(\hat{\Diamond}\phi[\beta_1/g(\beta_1)])) = h(I(\hat{\Diamond}\psi[\beta_2/g(\beta_2)])), \quad \text{i. e.,} \\ &\text{iff} \quad I_T^*(\Diamond\phi[\beta_1/g(\beta_1)]) = I_T^*(\Diamond\psi[\beta_2/g(\beta_2)]) \\ &\text{for every Tarski's homomorphism } I_T^* \in \mathcal{W}_e. \end{aligned}$$

The weak equivalency will be used for the P2P database mappings, in the cases when $\beta_1 = \beta_2 = \emptyset$ are empty sets, and hence α is the set of all variables in the list (tuple) of variables $\mathbf{x}$, so that (1.35) is reduced to simpler form

$$\phi(\mathbf{x}) \approx \psi(\mathbf{x}) \quad \text{iff} \quad <\phi(\mathbf{x})>_\alpha \approx <\psi(\mathbf{x})>_\alpha \quad \text{iff} \quad \widehat{\Diamond}\phi(\mathbf{x}) \equiv \widehat{\Diamond}\psi(\mathbf{x}) \tag{1.36}$$

where $\phi(\mathbf{x})$ and $\psi(\mathbf{x})$ are two intensionally equivalent queries over peer databases in such a P2P database system, with $I_T'^*(\widehat{\Diamond}\phi(\mathbf{x})) = \bigcup_{I_T \in \mathcal{W}_e} I_T^*(\phi(\mathbf{x}))$, which does not depend on $I_T'^*$ and hence $\widehat{\Diamond}\phi(\mathbf{x})$ is rigid concept which Tarski's interpretation can be denoted by "least upper bound" $\text{lub}(\phi(\mathbf{x}))$, i. e.,

$$\text{lub}(\phi(\mathbf{x})) =_{\text{def}} \bigcup_{I_T \in \mathcal{W}_e} I_T^*(\phi(\mathbf{x})) \tag{1.37}$$

so that the intensional equivalence in (1.36) holds when

$$\text{lub}(\phi(\mathbf{x})) = \text{lub}(\psi(\mathbf{x})), \tag{1.38}$$

i. e., when $I_T^*(\widehat{\Diamond}\phi(\mathbf{x}) \equiv \widehat{\Diamond}\psi(\mathbf{x})) = \mathfrak{R}$, for each Tarski's homomorphism $I_T^* \in \mathcal{W}_e$.

The bound (hidden) variables of the special "it is abstracted" unary atom A with the argument given by an abstracted term $<\phi(\mathbf{x})>_\alpha^\beta$ with at least one bound variable, i. e., $|\alpha| \geq 1$, will be extensively used for the constraint databases in Section 2.1.3, where these bound variables are hidden (encapsulated in the compressed virtual predicate) and cannot be affected by the assignments and quantifiers. In order to give the possibility to observe also these attributes of abstracted virtual predicate, it is convenient to have also the inverse operator of the intensional abstraction, denoted by "$\lhd$," as follows.

Definition 19 (Inverse operator to abstraction). The unary logic operator inverse of the intensional abstraction operator for any given intensional FOL formula $\psi(\mathbf{y})$, which does not contain this operator "$\lhd$," is defined by a formula

$$\lhd\, \psi(\mathbf{y}) \quad \text{is equivalent to} \quad \begin{cases} \phi(\mathbf{x}), & \text{if } \psi(\mathbf{y}) \text{ is the atom } A(<\phi(\mathbf{x})>_\alpha^\beta) \text{ and } \mathbf{y} = \pi_{-\beta}\mathbf{x} \\ \psi(\mathbf{y}), & \text{otherwise} \end{cases} \tag{1.39}$$

so that it left invariant any formula different from "it is abstracted" unary atom A. Consequently, with introduction of this logic unitary operator, the Kripke semantics of intensional FOL in Definition 15 does not change, because from above, for this new operator we have

$$\widehat{\mathcal{M}} \models_{I_K,g} \lhd A(<\phi(\mathbf{x})>_\alpha^\beta) \quad \text{iff} \quad \widehat{\mathcal{M}} \models_{I_k,g} \phi(\mathbf{x})$$

where the right-hand side condition is already provided by Definition 15.

Remark. The definition of this unary logic operator "$\lhd$'' given by (1.39) extends to all formulae of intensional FOL by a standard way:

1. $\lhd (\neg\psi(\mathbf{x})) = \neg(\lhd \psi(\mathbf{x}))$;
2. $\lhd (\psi_1(\mathbf{x}) \odot \psi_2(\mathbf{y})) = (\lhd \psi_1(\mathbf{x})) \odot (\lhd \psi_2(\mathbf{y}))$, for each FOL binary logic connective $\odot$.
3. $\lhd ((\exists x_j)\psi(\mathbf{x})) = (\exists x_j) \lhd \psi(\mathbf{x})$, with constraint that if $\psi(\mathbf{x})$ correspond to $A(<\phi(\mathbf{x})>^{\beta}_{\alpha})$ atoms then x_j must be a visible variable in β.

The utility of this inverse operator for the observation of the hidden attributes of the geometrical objects used in constrained databases will be considered in Section 2.1.3. We will show how the truth of the sentence $\lhd A(<\phi(\mathbf{x})>^{\beta}_{\alpha})/g$ is a possible way to observe the values $g(\pi_{-\beta}\mathbf{x})$ of the hidden variables of the "ground" formula $A(<\phi(\mathbf{x})>^{\beta}_{\alpha})/g$.

1.3.2 Logics via symmetry: intensional abstraction and ontological encapsulation transformations

Most related philosophical questions deal with specific symmetries, objectivity, interpreting limits on physical theories, classification and laws of nature. The recent history of the philosophy of mathematics is largely focused on grasping and defining the nature and essence of mathematics and its objects. Attempts to do this include explicating versions of: mathematics is just logic, mathematics is just structure, mathematics is a meaningless game, mathematics is a creation of the mind, mathematics is a useful fiction, etc.

Symmetries play a fundamental role in physics because they are related to conservation laws. This is stated in Noether's theorem, which says that invariance of the action under a symmetry transformation implies the existence of a conserved quantity. For instance, the conservation of the momentum vector $\vec{\mathbf{p}}$ is associated with translation invariance of the Lagrangian, i. e., the Poincare transformation $\vec{\mathbf{r}} \to \vec{\mathbf{r}} + \vec{\mathbf{r}_0}$, where $\vec{\mathbf{r}_0}$ is a constant vector; while the conservation of energy comes from the invariance under time translations $t \to t + t_0$. Thus, in the field theory of physics, the Lagrangian density $\mathcal{L}_G$ is a function of independent variables q_j, for $j = 0, 1, 2, 3$ with q_0 time coordinate, and other three are three orthogonal space coordinates, and dependent variables v_j, complex field $\Psi(q_0, q_1, q_2, q_3) \in \mathbb{C}$, and their derivatives up to a fixed but arbitrary order, thus $\mathcal{L}_G(\Psi, \partial_j\Psi, q_j, v_j)$, and hence the Lagrangian L_G is defined by (we denote dV by d^3q and $dtdV$ by d^4q):

$$L_G = \int_{\mathbb{R}^3} d^3q\mathcal{L}_G(\Psi, \partial_j\Psi, q_j, v_j) \tag{1.40}$$

Thus, for any closed finite time-interval $[t_0, t_1]$ and time–space volume $\Omega = [t_0, t_1]\times\mathbb{R}^3$, the action of a field theory with Lagrangian density $\mathcal{L}_G$ is defined by

$$S[\Psi] = \int_{[t_0,t_1]} dtL_G = \int_{\Omega} d^4q\mathcal{L}_G(\Psi, \partial_j\Psi, q_j, v_j) \tag{1.41}$$

The action S is a functional of the field Ψ and we are looking for a field configuration Ψ that extremizes the action, from which the equation of motion can be derived by the *Hamiltonian principle of least action* (1.41).

Differently from physics, in logics, of a given predicate modal logic $\mathcal{L}$ with the set of sentences $F(\mathcal{L})$, the Herbrand base (ground atoms) $H \subseteq F(\mathcal{L})$, and a given lattice $(X, \leq)$ of logic truth values, we have no the continuous functions and their derivations. We also introduce the binary predicate p_M^2, not present in $\mathcal{L}$, with first argument for abstracted terms and second for logic truth values in X. So, let us consider the following analogy:

1. A discrete abstract *time–space* of points $\Omega = F(\mathcal{L}) \times X$, where "time" $F(\mathcal{L})$ is the set of *sentences* $\phi \in \mathcal{L}$ and X is the "space." Thus, the "integration" over "time–space" will be replaced by set union.
2. The concept of 2-valued scalar *field* $\Psi : \Omega \to \mathbf{2}$, such that at a point $(\phi, x) \in \Omega$, $\Psi(\phi, x) \in \mathbf{2}$ is the truth of the two-valued metasentence "*the truth value of sentence ϕ is equal to x*," denoted by the ground atom $p_M^2(<\phi>, x)$ representing logical *knowledge*.
3. The "*Lagrangian density*" $\mathcal{L}_G(\Psi, v)$ for the field Ψ and parameter $v \in X^H$ (which is a Herbrand valuation of this logic $\mathcal{L}$) can be defined by the logic inference relation $\mathcal{L} \vDash_v$ of $\mathcal{L}$, that is by "*the inference from $\mathcal{L}$ for its Herbrand valuation v*."
4. The "*Lagrangian*" at a time $\phi \in F(\mathcal{L})$, from (1.40), by

$$L_G(\phi) = \int_X dx \mathcal{L}_G(\Psi(\phi, x), v) =_{\text{def}} \{p_M^2(<\phi>, x) \mid x \in X, p_M^2(<\phi>, x) \text{ is true}\}, \quad \text{i. e.,}$$

$$L_G(\phi) = \int_X dx \mathcal{L}_G(\Psi(\phi, x), v) = \{p_M^2(<\phi>, v^*(\phi))\} \tag{1.42}$$

   where $v^*(\phi)$ denotes the inferred logic truth-value of ϕ (the "integration" over "space" X can produce only one truth-value (space-position), so we obtain a singleton set). That is, the "logic Lagrangian" L_G defines the truth value of each sentence of this logic.
5. Thus, the action (1.41) in Logics is obtained by

$$S[\Psi] = \int_{F(\mathcal{L})} d\phi L_G(\phi) =_{\text{def}} \bigcup_{\phi \in F(\mathcal{L})} L_G(\phi) = \{p_M^2(<\phi>, v^*(\phi)) \mid \phi \in F(\mathcal{L})\} \tag{1.43}$$

   which defines the *extended valuation* $v^* : F(\mathcal{L}) \to X$ of the "parameter" $v : H \to X$ in Lagrangian density $\mathcal{L}_G$. So, for this parameter, the action $S[\Psi]$ is complete logical knowledge of predicate modal logic $\mathcal{L}$.
6. Principle of minimal action: Let us consider a monotonic consequence binary relation $\vdash$ (see Section A.2 in Appendix), and consider in our case the metalogic based on the binary predicate p_M^2, with $\Gamma \triangleq \{p_M^2(<\phi>, v(\phi)) \mid \phi \in H\}$, which is the subset of the set of ground atoms $\mathcal{L}_0 \triangleq \{p_M^2(<\phi>, x) \mid \phi \in F(\mathcal{L})\}, x \in X\}$, so that $\Gamma \vdash$

$p_M^2(<\phi>,x)$ denotes that the sentence (ground atom) $p_M^2(<\phi>,x) \in \mathcal{L}_0$, is inferred from the set Γ. Thus, we obtain the consequence operation (see Section A.2), a mapping $C : \mathcal{P}(\mathcal{L}_0) \to \mathcal{P}(\mathcal{L}_0)$, where $\mathcal{P}(\mathcal{L}_0)$ denotes the set of *all* subsets of $\mathcal{L}_0$. Consequently, the Hamiltonian principle of minimal action in Logics is represented by

$$S[\Psi] = C(\Gamma) \triangleq \{p_M^2(<\phi>,x) \in \mathcal{L}_0 \mid \Gamma \vdash p_M^2(<\phi>,x)\}, \tag{1.44}$$

i. e., by the fact that the action (1.43) is exactly the *least fixed point of the consequence relation*. So, the Euler–Lagrange equation is the equation $C(C(\Gamma)) = C(\Gamma)$.

From the fact that $v \in X^H$ is a parameter of "Lagrangian density" $\mathcal{L} \models_v$, this least action is always well-defined. Note that this least action is the set of all facts (ground atoms) with their truth-value, and hence represent the logic *knowledge*. So, we are able now to represent the symmetry transformation $\Psi \mapsto \Psi'$ in physics with equal actions (1.41), $S[\Psi] = S[\Psi']$, by corresponding symmetry in logics.

Definition 20. The transformations of "field" $\Psi \mapsto \Psi'$ represent a logic symmetry if the following bijection of the least actions (1.44) is valid:

$$\mathrm{is}_S : S[\Psi] \simeq S[\Psi'] \tag{1.45}$$

Note that from this extension of the symmetries from physics to logics, this bijection is the isomorphism in the **Set** category, of the two sets that represent the logic **knowledge**. So, the Noether's invariant charge, in Logic corresponds to the logic knowledge: Symmetries are the transformations of a predicate modal logic $\mathcal{L}$ which preserve the logic knowledge. The previous correspondence of symmetries in physics and logics can be shortly represented in Table 1.1.

Table 1.1: Physics/Logics Correspondence.

	Physics	**Logics**
Coordinates	time–space $(q_0, q_1, q_2, q_3) \in \Omega = [t_0, t_1] \times \mathbb{R}^3$	sentence-truth $(\phi, x) \in \Omega = F(\mathcal{L}) \times X$
Field	complex function Ψ	metasentences truth $\Psi : \Omega \to \mathbf{2}$
Lagrangian density	$\mathcal{L}_G(\Psi, \partial_j \Psi, q_j, v_j)$	inference $\mathcal{L}_G(\Psi, v)$, i. e., $\mathcal{L} \models_v$
Transformations	$\Psi \mapsto \Psi'$	$\mathcal{L} \mapsto \mathcal{L}', X \mapsto X'$
Symmetry	least action equality $S[\psi] = S[\Psi']$	least action isomorphism $\mathrm{is}_S : S[\Psi] \simeq S[\Psi']$
Invariance	Noether's charges	knowledge

From the very beginning of my academic research, the symmetry was the center of my attention, and in fact my PhD thesis "Categories: Symmetry, n-dimensional levels and applications" [59] was just a development of a symmetry in abstract category theory. In Section A.5.1 in the Appendix is provided a short introduction to *internal* categorial symmetry, taken from my PhD thesis, and after a number of examples provided in [59], 16 years after it, in my "Big Data Integration Theory" book [59] I developed a **DB** category as a general denotational semantics model for RDB databases (seen as complex objects) and semantic mapping morphisms (derived from a kind of second-order logic sentences) between them with the categorial symmetry property: an algebraic representation of an ontology. In fact, the notion of ontology has become widespread in fields such as intelligent information integration, cooperative information systems, information retrieval, electronic commerce and knowledge management, and also in this book I presented a number of such examples.

Let us consider the following two kinds of logic transformations: First, one has categorial but not logic symmetry, while second has logic but not categorial symmetry:

Intensional abstraction transformations

The categories heaving internal symmetry property (see Section A.5.1 in the Appendix) are able to represent not only a particular theory but also the metatheories about this basic "initial" particular theory inside *the same* category. So, such categories are similar to the natural language properties, differently from, e. g., the standard (extensional) first-order logic with Tarskian truth semantics. Such properties become important in the area of semantic WEB, a proposal to build an infrastructure of machine-readable semantics for the data (ontology) on the world wide web. The enormous amount of data has made difficult to find, access, present and maintain the information required by users. This is because information content is presented primarily in natural language, and needs the formal language specification with natural language features, as, for example, reification. Section 2.3 is dedicated just to the embedding of the semantic web-languages RDF and Web Ontology Language (OWL) where the statements are also resources, so that statement can be applied recursively to statements, allowing their nesting (reification).

Now, if we consider such statements as the morphisms in a given category, the necessity to use such morphisms also as the objects of this category in order to make another statements about them (reification), then we need the categorial symmetry inside this category. Intensional abstraction is a kind of *language categories* transformation symmetry (of logic sentences into terms) different from *semantic symmetries*: of predicate compression transformations and of ontological encapsulation by semantic reflection transformations of many-valued logics. In fact, in this case we do not change the syntax of "reference" (standard) predicate logic but only an extension of its terms by new terms obtained from the sentences. While the reification, which uses these abstracted terms inside other predicates *changes* the logic knowledge of the "reference" predicate logic, the (only) intensional abstraction transformation of logic ground atoms into abstracted terms does not change this logic's knowledge. Thus, the *logic's knowledge remains invariant* by intensional abstraction transformations *only if we do not use abstracted terms* inside other predicates. This duality "sentences-terms" is an analogy to the duality "arrows-objects" in mathematical concept of category, and hence in this case we will generate a particular symmetry in the category for the Herbrand base, where the morphisms represent the ground atoms in Herbrand base and the objects are the terms.

So, the intensional abstraction of an atom into a term is just the transformation of a morphism into an object, used in definition of categorial symmetry in Section A.5.1.

Definition 21. Let us define the graph G_H of the Herbrand base H of the intensional FOL with abstraction operator.

Each atom $p_i^k(\mathbf{d}) \in H$ is represented as an arrow $l : \mathbf{d} \to x_X$ in G_H (left-hand side in diagram (1.49)) from domain $\mathbf{d} = (d_1, \ldots, d_k)$, tuple of values in $\mathcal{D}$, into the logic-variable x_X of the lattice $(X, \leq)$ of the truth values.

We denote by $\mathbf{Sch}(G_H)$ the sketch category derived from this graph G_H where to each object (node) $\mathbf{d}$ is associated the identity arrow equal to the ground atom $\doteq (\mathbf{d}, \mathbf{d})$, and to each object equal to abstracted term $<A>$ for some atom $A \in H$ is associated the identity arrow equal to the ground atom $\doteq (<A>, <A>)$, where "$\doteq$" is the binary identity predicate. The composition of morphisms (arrows) in $\mathbf{Sch}(G_H)$ is defined by logic conjunction $\wedge$, so that two arrows in it are equal if are logically equivalent.

Note that there is no arrow from object x_X (which *is not terminal*) toward other objects and all identity arrows in category $\mathbf{Sch}(G_H)$ are tautologies, and composition of arrows is logic conjunction, so we can omit the identity arrows from the compositions. The only nonidentity arrows in $\mathbf{Sch}(G_H)$ (see in left-hand side of Figure 1.49) are that obtained from the ground atoms in H.

If we extend the graph with the morphisms represented by sentences $\phi(\mathbf{x})/g : g(\mathbf{x}) \to x_X$, then we obtain the sketch category with categorial symmetry extended to all sentences of the logic language with objects (terms) $<\phi(\mathbf{x})/g>$ as well.

Corollary 5. *We have categorial symmetry of morphisms* Mor *and objects* Ob *in* $\mathbf{Sch}(G_H)$*. However,* $\mathbf{Sch}(G_H)$ *is not conceptually closed category.*

Proof. The function $B_T : \mathrm{Mor} \to \mathrm{Ob}$ in Definition 128 in Section A.5.1 in the Appendix, we define in the way that for each identity arrow in $\mathbf{Sch}(G_H)$ it is equal to the dom $\in \Sigma$, which returns with the domain object of this arrow; otherwise it is equal to abstraction operator $< >$, which transforms logic atoms into terms. So, $B_T(\mathrm{id}_B) = B \simeq B$, and hence is satisfied the representability principle.

From the fact that the operator $* : \mathrm{Ob}^2 \to \mathrm{Ob}$ is *partial* mapping, we can omit it completely because we have no composition of two arrows in $\mathbf{C} = \mathbf{Sch}(G_H)$ in which both of them are different from the identity arrow. From the fact that in $(\mathrm{Mor}, \circ)$, we can eliminate all identity arrows in composition only distinct, and we have no composition of two nonidentity arrows, in this case we can consider that there is no any composition of objects by the operator $*$. So, the Corollary 33 in Section A.5.1 in the Appendix is satisfied. □

Note that if we use the abstracted terms by reification inside other unary predicates (what is the reason to introduce the intensional abstraction transformation), then we obtain an enlarged Herbrand base with also reified atoms, and hence with this we change the logic knowledge, and hence *generally we do not obtain the logic symmetry*.

2. Ontological encapsulation transformations (from Section A.4.2 in the Appendix)
Sketches are called graph-based logic and provide very clear and intuitive specification of computational data and activities. For any small sketch $\mathbf{E}$, the category of models $Mod(\mathbf{E})$ is an accessible category by Lair's theorem and reflexive subcategory of $\mathbf{Set}^{\mathbf{E}}$ by the Ehresmann–Kennison theorem. In fact, in our case for a given Herbrand interpretation $v : H \to X$, the covariant functor $F = (F^0, F^1) : \mathbf{Sch}(G_H) \to \mathbf{Set}$ is a model of $\mathbf{Sch}(G_H)$ if it satisfies the following property.

Definition 22. For each Herbrand interpretation $v : H \to X$, we can define the following two functorial models of a given Herbrand base category $\mathbf{Sch}(G_H)$ in Definition 21:
1. The covariant functor $F(v) = (F^0, F^1) : \mathbf{Sch}(G_H) \to \mathbf{Set}$, such that for any object B in $\mathbf{Sch}(G_H)$, and a distinct constant $\flat$ not belonging to domain $\mathcal{D}$,

$$F^0(B) = \begin{cases} X\bigcup\{\flat\}, & \text{if } B = x_X \\ \{B, \flat\}, & \text{otherwise} \end{cases} \tag{1.46}$$

and for any nonidentity morphism (ground atom) $l = p_j^k(\mathbf{d}) : \mathbf{d} \to x_X$, the function $f_{p_j^k} = F^1(p_j^k(\mathbf{d})) : \{\mathbf{d}, \flat\} \to (X\bigcup\{\flat\})$ has to satisfy that

$$f_{p_j^k}(\mathbf{d}) = v(p_j^k(\mathbf{d})) \in X \quad \text{and} \quad f_{p_j^k}(\flat) = \flat \tag{1.47}$$

Obviously, it has to be satisfied also for the nested (reified) arrows $p_n^1(\lt A\gt) : \lt A\gt \to x_X$ with $A \in H$.
2. The contravariant functor $\overline{G}(v) = (\overline{G}^0, \overline{G}^1) : \mathbf{Sch}(G_H) \to \mathbf{Set}$, such that for the objects $\overline{G}^0 = F^0$ is equal to the covariant functor $F(v)$ above, while for any nonidentity morphism (ground atom) $l = p_j^k(\mathbf{d}) : \mathbf{d} \to x_X$, we obtain the function $f_{p_F^{k+1}} = \overline{G}^1(p_j^k(\mathbf{d})) : (X\bigcup\{\flat\}) \to \{\mathbf{d}, \flat\}$ (a reversed arrow), such that

$$f_{p_F^{k+1}}(a) = \begin{cases} \mathbf{d}, & \text{if } a = v(p_j^k(\mathbf{d})) \in X \\ \flat, & \text{otherwise} \end{cases} \tag{1.48}$$

Note that the *contravariant* functor $\overline{G}(v) = (\overline{G}^0, \overline{G}^1) : \mathbf{C} \to \mathbf{Set}$ in point 2 above, where the category $\mathbf{C} = \mathbf{Sch}(G_H)$, can be equivalently represented (see Section A.5

in the Appendix) by the *covariant* functor $G(v) = (G^0, G^1) : \mathbf{C}^{\mathrm{OP}} \to \mathbf{Set}$, such that $G^0 = \overline{G}^0$ while for the arrows $G^1(l^{\mathrm{OP}}) = \overline{G}^1(l)$, as represented by the following diagram corresponding to the ontological encapsulation syntax transformation (the symmetry), such that the opposite arrow of $l = p_j^k(\mathbf{d})$ in $\mathbf{C}$ is defined by 2-valued flattened atom $l^{\mathrm{OP}} = p_F^{k+1}(\mathbf{d}, x_X)$:

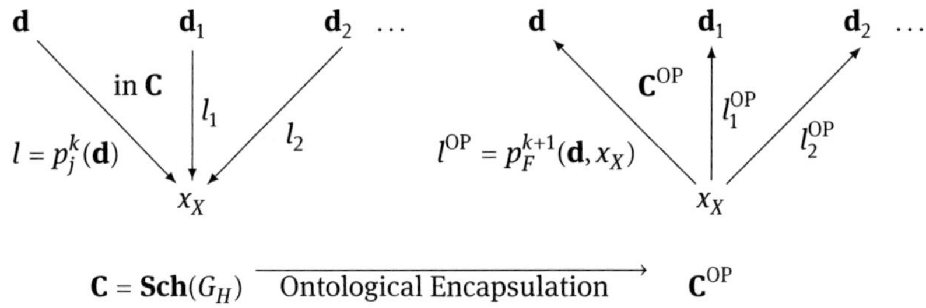

(1.49)

The knowledge invariance of the ontological encapsulation transformation based on the categorial duality principle (a general form of categorial symmetry) can be formalized by the following.

Corollary 6. *The knowledge* invariance *of the ontological encapsulation transformations based on categorial duality, for a given Herbrand interpretation $v : H \to X$, can be mathematically expressed by the natural transformation $\eta : F(v) \xrightarrow{\cdot} \overline{G}(v)$ from the covariant functor $F(v)$ into the contravariant functor $\overline{G}(v)$ specified by point 1 and 2 of Definition 22 relatively, such that the arrows in* **Set** *obtained by this natural transformation are the* identity arrows.

Proof. Let us consider the arrow $l = p_j^k(\mathbf{d}) : \mathbf{d} \to x_X$ in the category $\mathbf{C} = \mathbf{Sch}(G_H)$ (corresponding to the arrow $l^{\mathrm{OP}} = p_F^{k+1}(\mathbf{d}, x_X)$ in the dual category $\mathbf{C}^{\mathrm{OP}}$), which represent the encapsulation (flattening) of the ground atom $p_j^k(\mathbf{d})$ into flattened atom $p_F^{k+1}(\mathbf{d}, x_X)$ obtained by enlargement of the original atom by the truth-variable x_X. Let us show that the natural transformation η for the covariant functors $F(v), \overline{G}(v) : \mathbf{C} \to \mathbf{Set}$, applied to the arrow $l = p_j^k(\mathbf{d})$, generates the following natural transformation diagram in the **Set**:

$$\begin{array}{ccc} A = F^0(\mathbf{d}) = \{\mathbf{d}, \flat\} & \xrightarrow{\eta_A} & A = \overline{G}^0(\mathbf{d}) = \{\mathbf{d}, \flat\} \\ f_{p_j^k} = F^1(p_j^k(\mathbf{d})) \Big\downarrow & & \Big\uparrow f_{p_F^{k+1}} = \overline{G}^1(p_j^k(\mathbf{d})) \\ B = F^0(x_X) = X \bigcup \{\flat\} & \xrightarrow{\eta_B} & B = \overline{G}^0(x_X) = X \bigcup \{\flat\} \end{array} \tag{1.50}$$

where for η_A equal to identity arrow of the object A and η_B equal to identity arrow of the object B this diagram commutes (easy to verify from Definition 22). □

Note that we obtained the identity composition, $f_{p_F^{k+1}} \circ f_{p_j^k} = \mathrm{id}_A$, but $f_{p_j^k} \circ f_{p_F^{k+1}} \neq \mathrm{id}_B$, i. e., there is not the natural transformation from the contravariant functor $\overline{G}(v)$ into the covariant functor $F(v)$ (in fact, for $a \in X$ such that $a \neq v(p_j^k(\mathbf{d}))$, we obtain that $f_{p_F^{k+1}}(a) = \flat \notin X$, and hence $f_{p_j^k}(f_{p_F^{k+1}}(a)) = \flat \neq a$).

The knowledge in our case, represented with Herbrand base H, is specified by the truth of the facts expressed by ground atoms in H, i. e., this "logic knowledge" is just expressed by given Herbrand interpretation $v : H \to X$, which assigns the logic value in X to each atom in H. So, we need to verify that this ontological encapsulation transformations, expressed formally (mathematically) by the *categorial natural transformation* η in Corollary 6 preserves by the logic knowledge of the "reference" (original many-valued) logic. Note, that both functors $F(v)$ and $\overline{G}(v)$ generates the *models* for the reference logic and for the metalogic obtained by encapsulation, relatively, and hence this identity natural transformation η indeed represents the invariance ("identity") of logic knowledge.

This invariance of knowledge is represented for a given $v : H \to X$ and each assignment g to variables in $\mathbf{x}$, as explained by "semantic-reflection" in Definitions 117, 118 and 119 in Section A.4.2 in the Appendix, by: if an atom $p_j^k(\mathbf{x})/g$ has, a logic value $a = v(p_j^k(\mathbf{x})/g) \in X$, then the 2-valued flattened atom $p_F^{k+1}(\mathbf{x}, a)/g = \mathcal{E}(p_j^k(\mathbf{x})/g)$ is true. So, for transformed "field" action $S[\Psi'] \triangleq \{p_M^2(<\mathcal{E}(\phi/g)>, 1) \mid \mathcal{M} \vDash_{w,g} \mathcal{E}(\phi)$ for $w = v^*(\phi/g)$, the symmetry (1.45) is given by bijection $\mathrm{is}_S(p_M^2(<p_j^k(\mathbf{x})/g>, a)) = p_M^2(<(p_F^{k+1}(\mathbf{x}, a)/g>, 1)$, i. e., for any sentence $\phi/g \in F(\mathcal{L})$,

$$\mathrm{is}_S(p_M^2(<\phi/g>, v^*(\phi/g))) = p_M^2(<\mathcal{E}(\phi/g)>, 1)$$

2 Applications of the intensional abstraction operator

2.1 Predicate (de)compression transformations

It is well known that the prominent role that *symmetry* plays in the development of the laws of physics, e. g., the symmetries of the 9-D time-space Galilean group in quantum theory [60, 61]. Physicists have generalized the term "symmetry" from descriptions of objects to descriptions of the laws of nature. A law of nature exhibits a symmetry when it can be viewed from multiple perspectives and still remain the same. We say that such a law is "invariant" with respect to some change of perspective. Just as symmetry considerations have helped clarify many issues in the philosophy of science so, too, our work sheds light on familiar problems in the philosophy of mathematics. Mathematicians talk about numerous geometrical or topological theorems such as the Jordan curve theorem. This statement says that any nonself-intersecting (simple) closed continuous curve in the plane splits the plane into an "inside" and an "outside." So, for every closed continuous curve, there are two regions. Here, in the logic as domain of discourse, we will split the attributes of a predicate into "hidden" and "visible" attributes (variables), which is an invariant transformation w. r. t. the knowledge represented by this predicate (*knowledge conservation law* as a kind of categorial symmetry, shown in Section 1.3.2). From this perspective, one can see how variables are so central to the mathematical discourse and why mathematicians from Felix Klein to Tarski to Whitehead touted their import for mathematics.

Knowledge-based systems must typically deal with imperfection in knowledge in the form of incompleteness and uncertainty. Extensions to many-valued logic programming and deductive databases for handling incompleteness/uncertainty are numerous. They can broadly be characterized into nonprobabilistic and probabilistic formalisms. In Section A.4, we show how the higher types of Herbrand interpretations for logic programs, where it is not possible to associate a fixed logic value (a constant from a given domain of truth values) to a given ground atom of a Herbrand base, arise often in practice when we have to deal with uncertain information. In such cases, we associate some *degree of belief* to ground atoms, which can be simple probability, a probability interval or other more complex data structures, as for example, in Bayesian logic programs where for a different kind of atoms we may associate different (from probability) kind of *measures* also.

But we can see the approximate (uncertain) information as some kind of *relativization* of truth values for sentences also: Let H be a Herbrand base for a logic program, which handles the uncertain information, and $r(\mathbf{d})$ a ground atom in H, which logically defines some particular fact for which we have only an approximated information when it happened. Thus, this atom $r(\mathbf{d})$ is not longer *absolutely* true or false, but its truth depends on the approximate temporal information about this fact: in some

https://doi.org/10.1515/9783110981438-002

time points it can be true, in others, it can be false. If we consider such temporal approximation as a *context* for this ground fact $r(\mathbf{d}) \in H$, then we obtain that the truth of $r(\mathbf{d})$ is a function from the time to the ordinary set of truth values $\mathbf{2} = \{f, t\}$ (with f for false and t for true value, respectively). So that the truth values of ground atoms in this Herbrand base are the functions, i. e., they have a *higher-order type* (this term is taken from the typed lambda calculus) with respect to the set **2** of truth constants. Intuitively, the approximated information is relativized to its context, and such context further specifies the semantics for uncertain information. This intuitive way to introduce the higher-order Herbrand model types framework for uncertain information is not only an interesting point of view for such approximated information. Such analogies are provided in other logic theories also: for instance, in the possible-world semantics for a probabilistic logic programming [62–64]. All such context sensitive applications, with higher-order Herbrand models, can be transformed (i. e., *flattened*) to logic theories with basic (ordinary) Herbrand interpretations, by enlarging the original predicates with new attributes for the properties of the context: in this way, the context becomes a part of the language of the logic theory, i. e., it becomes *visible*.

The higher types of Herbrand interpretations arise also in the compression of databases, i. e., in a kind of database encapsulation where some number of attributes of its relations are hidden for users. More recently, other applications have required the use of database technology to manage not only finite data but also *infinite* ones. This phenomena is particularly important for the *constraint databases* [65]: Constraints are natural to describe temporal, spatial and geographic data. Since time and space are infinite, spatial and temporal objects are commonly expressed over rational or real variables using linear or polynomial inequalities. Starting from the observation that often infinite information can be finitely represented by using mathematical constraints, constraint databases have been proposed with the aim of inserting mathematical constraints both at the data and at the language level. At the data level, constraints allow the finite representation of infinite objects. At the language level, constraints increase the expressive power of specific query languages, by allowing mathematical computations. Thus, constraints are the logic formulae composed by the built-in predicates. For example, a rectangle with its center at point (x_0, y_0) can be described by the following constraint virtual predicate $\phi(x, y, x_0, y_0)$ defined by the following composition of the built-in binary predicate "$\leq$":

$$(x \leq x_0 + 5) \wedge (x_0 - 5 \leq x) \wedge (y \leq y_0 + 14) \wedge (y_0 - 14 \leq y).$$

By *compression* of the virtual predicate $\phi(x, y, x_0, y_0)$, we mean to hide (to compress) the variables x and y (with infinite possible values inside this rectangle) and to represent this rectangle by new compressed virtual predicate denoted by $\psi_\alpha(x, y, x_0, y_0)$ where $\alpha = \{x, y\}$ is the set of compressed (hidden) variables while the set of visible variables β is composed by two coordinates $\beta = \{x_0, y_0\}$ of the center of this rectangle. Thus, for this virtual predicate $\phi(x, y, x_0, y_0)$ of classic two-valued logic, we will denote by $\phi_\alpha(x, y, x_0, y_0)$ a compressed predicate, which does not belong to classical two-valued logic.

In fact, for any assignment $g \in \mathcal{D}^{\mathcal{V}}$, the original (flat) virtual predicate $\phi/g = \phi(g(x_0), g(y_0), g(x), g(y))$ can be only true or false (thus in classical two-valued FOL), while for the same assignment this compressed virtual predicate $\phi_\alpha(x, y, x_0, y_0)/g = \phi_\alpha[\beta/g(\beta)]$ fixes only the center of this rectangle $g(\beta) = \{g(x_0), g(y_0)\}$; other two hidden variables x and y in α remains free variables, so that the truth value of $\phi_\alpha[\beta/g(\beta)] = \phi_\alpha(x, y, g(x_0), g(y_0))$ (representing however this rectangle) is a function $f : \mathbb{R}^2 \to \{0, 1\}$, such that for any point $(a, b) \in \mathbb{R}^2$, $f(a, b) = 1$ iff this point is inside the rectangle. So, we obtained the higher-order Herbrand interpretation for compressed predicates: see Definition 109 in Section A.4 for the functional space T equal to $(\mathbf{2}^{W_2})^{W_1}$, where $W_1 = W_2 = \mathbb{R}$ and $\mathcal{W} = W_1 \times W_2 = \mathbb{R}^2$, with "truth value" $f \in T = \mathbf{2}^{\mathcal{W}}$ so that we obtain an infinitary many-valued logic.

Knowledge-conservative predicate compression

Let H be the Herbrand base of a database DB and P be the set of all predicate symbols used in this DB. The compression of a predicate $r(\mathbf{x})$, for the list of variables $\mathbf{x} = (x_1, \dots, x_n)$, generates the new *compressed* predicate $r_\alpha(\mathbf{x})$ in the relational schema of compressed database, i. e., $r_\alpha \in \mathrm{DB}_{\mathrm{com}}$, where $\alpha \subseteq (x_1, \dots, x_n)$ is the subset of compressed (hidden) attributes. Let $\mathcal{W}$ be the domain of the subset $\beta \subseteq (x_1, \dots, x_n)$ of visible attributes of the parameterized predicate $r(\mathbf{x})$, $r \in P$, and $I : H \to \mathbf{2}$ be a standard two-valued Herbrand interpretation for a database $\mathcal{DB}$. Then, given a knowledge invariant higher-order interpretation I_E, we will have that for any "ground" atom $r_\alpha[\beta/g(\beta)]$ with hidden variables in $\mathbf{y} = \pi_{-\beta}\mathbf{x}$, we obtain that $I_E(r_\alpha[\beta/g(\beta)]) : \mathcal{W} \to \mathbf{2}$ is a mapping such that for any tuple of values $g(\mathbf{y}) \in \mathcal{W}$ for a given assignment $g \in \mathcal{D}^{\mathcal{V}}$, holds that

$$I_E(r_\alpha[\beta/g(\beta)])(g(\mathbf{y})) = I(r(\mathbf{x})/g) \tag{2.1}$$

as a particular case of a general case, as shown in the next section in Proposition 9.

In order to avoid such side effect and to remain in the standard two-valued logic also when we are using the compressed predicates for the applications that use the constraint databases, we can use the two-valued intensional FOL as it will be shown in what follows. □

Remark. Notice that the *compressed* predicate $r_\alpha(\mathbf{x})$ *is not* a simple projection π_α of the original predicate for attributes in the set β, because it contains also all hidden attributes, and its interpretations are of higher-type: the logic values of its ground atoms are the *functions* instead of the set of classic logic values in $\mathbf{2} = \{f, t\}$; these functions encapsulate the semantics of the hidden attributes. Evidently, it *is not* the result of the existential quantification, i. e., $r_\alpha(\mathbf{x}) \neq \exists\alpha r(\mathbf{x})$, because the last remains an ordinary 2-valued formula, while the compressed predicate has the higher-order interpretations. Notice that it *has no* relationship with abstract interpretation of logic programs [66], not with abstract interpretation theory [67], which are approximate (generally finite) representations of computational objects to make the problem of program dataflow analysis tractable and where abstract interpretations define a nonstandard semantics, which can approximate the meaning or behavior of the program in a finite way. The functional analogy with the "currying," applicable to the functions (in a typed λ-calculus) is only apparent: here, we are dealing with compression of *predicates*, by the compression of its attributes, and consequently by modifying the Herbrand base of the original logic theory. □

There are numerous applications where we have to deal with the *data-base compression*, i. e., with a kind of database transformation where a number of attributes of its relations are *hidden* (compressed) but *not eliminated* as in the case of ordinary projections over relations: we still consider all inferential effects of all information contained in a database, but with respect to the reduced number of "visible" attributes.

For example, while the variables can be used for querying a database, the hidden attributes cannot appear in a query language formulae, but they still are present in a query-answering process (e. g., in join operations) so that the inference power of this transformed (compressed) database is equal to the inferential power of the original database.

As far as we know, there is no current literature for the definition for these concepts, but we needed them for the formal development of the logic theory with general imprecise, or context sensitive information, and to show that nonstandard logic models, often introduced ad hoc for such logic systems can be effectively reduced to canonical standard Herbrand models, as for example, by reducing the temporal-probabilistic logic programs into constraint logic programs [68].

2.1.1 Introduction of hidden-quantifiers for predicate logics

In what follows, we will denote by $\mathcal{D}$ the universe of constants for a given *predicate logic* language $\mathcal{L}_P$ (without quantifiers) with the set of predicate symbols in P, such that for any $p^n \in P$, with $n = ar(p)$ is the arity of this predicate, and $\{x_1, \dots x_m\}$ is a subset of variables in $\mathcal{V}$, used for predicate attributes. We assume that each attribute of each predicate in P has a unique variable name in $\mathcal{V}$. Each variable $x_i \in \mathcal{V}$ has a domain of constants, $\mathfrak{D}(x_i) \subseteq \mathcal{D}$, which can be assigned to this variable.

We denote by $\mathbf{x} = \langle x_1, \dots x_n \rangle$ the (ordered) *tuple* (list) of variables and by $\mathfrak{D}(\mathbf{x})$ the set of tuples of constants in $\mathcal{D}$ given by the Cartesian product $\mathfrak{D}(x_1) \times \cdots \times \mathfrak{D}(x_n)$ where $x_i \in \mathcal{V}, 1 \le i \le n$; when it is an empty tuple (list) $\mathbf{x} = \emptyset$, then we denote its domain by a particular empty-tuple singleton $\langle\,\rangle \in \mathcal{D}$, i. e., $\mathfrak{D}(\emptyset) = \{\langle\,\rangle\}$. By $\overline{\mathbf{x}} = \{x_1, \dots x_n\}$, we denote the *set* of variables in the tuple $\mathbf{x}$, and hence we have that $\mathfrak{D}(\mathbf{x}) = \{g(\mathbf{x}) = (g(x_1), \dots, g(x_n)) \mid g \in \mathcal{D}^X\}$, and we can define the basic principle of predicate compression.

Definition 23. Given a tuple of $n \geq 1$ variables $\mathbf{x}$, with its set of variables $\overline{\mathbf{x}}$, for any proposed set $Y \subseteq \mathcal{V}$ of variables that we desire to compress in the tuple $\mathbf{x}$, we define

$$\alpha =_{\text{def}} \overline{\mathbf{x}} \bigcap Y \quad \text{and} \quad \beta = \overline{\mathbf{x}} - \alpha \tag{2.2}$$

where $-$ is set substraction, so that $\alpha \bigcap \beta = \emptyset$ and $\alpha \bigcup \beta = \overline{\mathbf{x}}$, where:

1. α is called the set of really obtained hidden (compressed) variables in $\mathbf{x}$, while the order-preserving tuple of these hidden variable is given by $\mathbf{y} = \pi_{-\beta}\mathbf{x}$, so that $\alpha = \overline{\mathbf{y}}$.
2. β is called the set of visible variables in $\mathbf{x}$, while the order-preserving tuple of these visible variables is given by $\mathbf{y}_1 = \pi_{-\alpha}\mathbf{x}$, so that $\beta = \overline{\mathbf{y}_1}$.
3. In order to hide a free variable $x_i \in \mathcal{V}$ in a given tuple $\mathbf{x}$, i. e., when $x_i \in \overline{\mathbf{x}}$, we will use the hidden-quantifiers denoted by

   $(\exists x_i)_{\mathbf{x}}$ and traduced by "there exists *hidden* variable x_i in the tuple $\mathbf{x}$"

   different from the existential $(\exists x_i)$ and universal quantifier $(\forall x_i)$ used in FOL but with the common property that also these new quantifiers protect their variables from the assignments $g \in \mathcal{D}^{\mathcal{V}}$.
4. We define the bijective permutation-mapping[1] $is_{\mathbf{x}/\alpha} : \mathfrak{D}(\mathbf{x}) \to \mathfrak{D}(\mathbf{z}) \times \mathfrak{D}(\mathbf{y})$, such that it divides the tuples in $\mathfrak{D}(\mathbf{x}) =_{\text{def}} \{g(\mathbf{x}) \mid g \in \mathcal{D}^{\overline{\mathbf{x}}}\}$ into two order-preserving subtuples composed by visible attributes in $\mathbf{z} = \pi_{-\alpha}\mathbf{x}$ and by hidden attributes in $\mathbf{y} = \pi_{-\beta}\mathbf{x}$. Its inverse is^{-1} permutes the element of a tuple in $\mathfrak{D}(\mathbf{z}) \times \mathfrak{D}(\mathbf{y})$ in order to obtain the original tuple in $\mathfrak{D}(\mathbf{x})$.

For any assignment $g : \mathcal{V} \to \mathcal{D}$, and a tuple of variables $\mathbf{x}$ we will denote by $g(\mathbf{x})$ the reduction of assignment g to the subset $\overline{\mathbf{x}}$ of variables in $\mathbf{x}$, such that for any variable $x_i \in \overline{\mathbf{x}}$, $g(x_i) \in \mathfrak{D}(x_i) \subseteq \mathcal{D}$. Given a predicate logic language $\mathcal{L}_P$ with predicates in P and standard (classic) logic connectives $\neg, \wedge, \vee$ and $\Rightarrow$ (negation, conjunction, disjunction and implication, respectively), used to compose logic formulae, any assignment $g : \mathcal{V} \to \mathcal{D}$, can be extended to all formulae and terms in a standard way as explained in Section 1.1.1. A logic theory $\mathcal{L}$ is any subset of formulae in $\mathcal{L}_P$, i. e., any $\mathcal{L} \subseteq \mathcal{L}_P$.

We will define a Herbrand interpretation for a logic $\mathcal{L}_P$, a mapping $I_H : H \to \mathbf{2}$, where $\mathbf{2} = \{f, t\}$ is the set of classic logic values f (false) and t (true). Notice that these constants can be alternatively seen as constant functions $f_0, f_1 : \mathfrak{D}(\emptyset) \to \mathbf{2}$, such that $f_0(\langle\,\rangle) = f$ and $f_1(\langle\,\rangle) = t$.

Definition 24 (Extended syntax of predicate logic by hidden quantifiers). Let $\mathcal{L}$ be the predicate logic theory of a given predicate logic language $\mathcal{L}_P$, with P the set of its predicates and $\mathcal{V}$ the set of all variables of predicates in P. We define the extended logic

1 These mapping are based on the fact that each domain $\mathfrak{D}(\mathbf{v})$ is a ordered Cartesian product of domains of single variables in $\mathbf{v}$, so for the permutation of variables $\sigma : \mathbf{x} \to \mathbf{z} \times \mathbf{y}$ and its inverse permutation $\sigma^{-1} : \mathbf{z} \times \mathbf{y} \to \mathbf{x}$ we have that $\sigma \circ \sigma^{-1}$ and $\sigma^{-1} \circ \sigma$ are identities.

theory $\mathcal{L}_E$, such that $\mathcal{L} \subseteq \mathcal{L}_E$, by using the symbol of compression of variables by hidden-quantifiers $(\dashv x_i)_{\mathbf{x}}$, as follows:

1. We can introduce a new virtual predicate denoted shortly by $p_\alpha(\mathbf{x}) \in \mathcal{L}_E$, for a given atom $p(\mathbf{x}) \in \mathcal{L}$ with $\alpha \subseteq X = \overline{\mathbf{x}}$. We will call the attributes in α as HIDDEN attributes, while the rest, from (2.2), $\beta = X - \alpha$, by VISIBLE attributes. For the homogeneity, we can denote the original predicates $p(\mathbf{x}) \in P$ also by $p_\emptyset(\mathbf{x})$, where $\emptyset$ denotes empty set of hidden (compressed) variables.
2. This compression can be extended also to any composed formula $\phi(\mathbf{x}) \in \mathcal{L}$, so that $\phi_\alpha(\mathbf{x})$ denotes shortly a logic formula with the hidden variables in $\alpha \subseteq X$ and visible free variables in $\beta = X - \alpha$, where $-$ is set substraction.

So, in the theory $\mathcal{L}_E$ we can have only the formulae of $\mathcal{L}$ (without compression symbols) or the formulae $\phi_\alpha(\mathbf{x})$ with the set of hidden variables in $\alpha \subseteq \overline{\mathbf{x}}$. Thus, the extended logic theory $\mathcal{L}_E$ has also a set of unary hidden-quantifier operators $(\dashv x)_{\mathbf{x}}$ introduced in point 3 of Definition 23, so that the denoted virtual predicates with set α of hidden variables are not well-defined syntax logic forms in $\mathcal{L}_E$, but only denote the logic formulae using the hidden-quantifier operators. That is:

a. $p_\alpha(\mathbf{x})$ denotes the well-defined syntax $(\dashv x_i)_{\mathbf{x}} \dots (\dashv x_j)_{\mathbf{x}} p(\mathbf{x})$, where α is the set of all variables that appear in the hidden-quantifier operators in front of the predicate $p(\mathbf{x})$, and this formal syntax can be shortened by $(\prod_{x_i \in \alpha} (\dashv x_i)_{\mathbf{x}}) p(\mathbf{x})$;

b. $\phi_\alpha(\mathbf{x})$ denotes the well-defined syntax of a composed formula ϕ with the free variables in $\beta \subseteq \overline{\mathbf{x}}$ and with hidden-quantifiers $(\dashv x_i)_{\mathbf{x}}$ with $x_i \in \alpha$ (where α and β satisfy the requirements[2] in Definition 23) inside this formula ϕ. The Tarski's interpretation I_T^* of compressed predicates, for a given assignment $g \in \mathcal{D}^{\mathcal{V}}$, is given by

$$I_T^*\left(\left(\prod_{x_i \in \alpha} (\dashv x_i)_{\mathbf{x}}\right) p(\mathbf{x})/g\right)$$
$$= \{g'(\pi_{-\beta}\mathbf{x}) \mid g' \in \mathcal{D}^{\overline{\mathbf{x}}} \text{ such that } \forall x_i \in \beta.(g'(x_i) = g(x_i)) \text{ and } I_T^*(p(g'(\mathbf{x}))) = t\} \tag{2.3}$$

and, by extension to all compressed formulae (having inside it the hidden quantifiers) $\phi_\alpha(\mathbf{x}) \in \mathcal{L}_E$,

$$I_T^*(\phi_\alpha(\mathbf{x})/g)$$
$$= \{g'(\pi_{-\beta}\mathbf{x}) \mid g' \in \mathcal{D}^{\overline{\mathbf{x}}} \text{ such that } \forall x_i \in \beta.(g'(x_i) = g(x_i)) \text{ and } I_T^*(\psi(g'(\mathbf{x}))) = t\} \tag{2.4}$$

---

2 Hidden-quantifier $(\dashv x_i)_{\mathbf{x}}$ can be correctly applied only to a formula for which the ordered list (from left to right) of its free variables (visible and hidden) is equal to the tuple $\mathbf{x}$ of this quantifier. Otherwise, its application to a formula has no any effect as, e. g., if we apply the standard existential FOL quantifier $(\exists x_i)$ to a formula $\psi(\mathbf{y})$ such that $x_i \notin \overline{\mathbf{y}}$.

where the new formula $\psi(\mathbf{x}) \in \mathcal{L}$ is obtained from $\phi(\mathbf{x})$ by elimination all hidden quantifiers from it. We define also the functional space (P-space) $\mathcal{F}_P$ as follows:

- $\{f_0, f_1\} \subseteq \mathcal{F}_P$, where $f_0, f_1 : \mathfrak{D}(\emptyset) \to \mathbf{2}$, such that $f_0(\langle\,\rangle) = f$ and $f_1(\langle\,\rangle) = t$;
- For each $\overline{\mathbf{y}} \subseteq \mathcal{V}$, $\mathbf{2}^{\mathfrak{D}(\mathbf{y})} \subseteq \mathcal{F}_P$, where $\mathbf{2}^{\mathfrak{D}(\mathbf{y})}$ denotes the set of all functions from the set of tuples of constants in $\mathfrak{D}(\mathbf{y})$ to the set $\mathbf{2}$. The tuples $\mathbf{y}$ corresponds to hidden variables of compressed predicates.

For example, the assignment $g \in \mathcal{D}^{\mathcal{V}}$ applied to compressed predicate denoted by $p_\alpha(\mathbf{x})$, that is to $(\prod_{x_i \in \alpha}(\dashv x_i)_\mathbf{x})p(\mathbf{x})$, written as usual by $(\prod_{x_i \in \alpha}(\dashv x_i)_\mathbf{x})p(\mathbf{x})/g$, is equal to formula $(\prod_{x_i \in \alpha}(\dashv x_i)_\mathbf{x})p[\beta/g(\beta)]$ where β is the set of free variables in the logic formula $(\prod_{x_i \in \alpha}(\dashv x_i)_\mathbf{x})p(\mathbf{x})$.

Remark. We will use the words *compression* and *decompression* of a predicate $p(\mathbf{x})$ for the transformation of a visible predicate's variable into a hidden variable by using the hidden quantifiers $(\dashv x_i)_\mathbf{x}$, and for the transformation of a hidden variable into a visible variable by deleting the hidden quantifiers from the composed logic formulae that defines this virtual predicate. □

In what follows, we will present a simple example, in order to render more intuitive arguments.

Example 7 (*Constraint databases* and constraint logic programming). Let us consider, e. g., a logic theory with a concept of "class of spheres" given by a virtual predicate $\phi(\mathbf{x})$ with the tuple of free variables $\mathbf{x} = (x, x_0, y, y_0, z, z_0, v)$ where v represents the radius, $\{x_0, y_0, z_0\}$ coordinates of center and $\{x, y, z\}$ a point inside a sphere. This virtual predicate can be given by the built-in binary predicate $\leq ((x-x_0)^2+(y-y_0)^2+(z-z_0)^2, v^2)$, or with common mathematical expression, $(x-x_0)^2+(y-y_0)^2+(z-z_0)^2 \leq v^2$. Let us now consider a compressed virtual predicate $\phi_\alpha(\mathbf{x}) \in \mathcal{L}_E$, where the set of hidden (compressed) variables is $\alpha = \{x, y, z\}$ and the set of visible variables is $\beta = \{v, x_0, y_0, z_0\}$, with the order-preserving tuple of hidden variables $\mathbf{y} = \pi_{-\beta}\mathbf{x} = (x, y, z)$ and the order-preserving tuple of visible variables $\mathbf{z} = \pi_{-\alpha}\mathbf{x} = (x_0, y_0, z_0, v)$. The logic formula of this compressed virtual predicate, by using the hidden quantifiers, is given

$$(\dashv x)_\mathbf{x}(\dashv y)_\mathbf{x}(\dashv z)_\mathbf{x}\phi(\mathbf{x}),$$

i. e., by

$$(\dashv x)_\mathbf{x}(\dashv y)_\mathbf{x}(\dashv z)_\mathbf{x} \leq ((x - x_0)^2 + (y - y_0)^2 + (z - z_0)^2, v^2) \tag{2.5}$$

Then a *concrete* concept of sphere, fixed by an assignment $g \in \mathcal{D}^{\mathcal{V}}$, with a radius $d = g(v)$ and the center in $(a, b, c) = g(x_0, y_0, z_0)$, is given by the "ground" compressed virtual predicate $\phi_\alpha(\mathbf{x})/g$, i. e., by $\phi_\alpha[\beta/g(\beta)]$, logically equivalent to the ordinary predicate logic formula (without hidden quantifiers) $\phi(d, x, a, y, b, z, c)$ with the tuple of bound variables in $\mathbf{y} = \pi_{-\beta}\mathbf{x} = (x, y, z)$. However, in the last formula a given assignment can have effects on these variables, while in compressed virtual predicate cannot have the effects as shown above for $\phi_\alpha(\mathbf{x})/g$, and also these variables cannot be quantified by the existential and universal FOL quantifiers. So, the compressed virtual predicate is a really new kind of logic formulae underlined by the explicit use of new hidden quantifiers in (2.5).

Let us consider now the case in which we have only a 2-dimensional device for a visualization, so that we has to fix also the value for the coordinate z in the value $g(z)$ of this concrete sphere defined by compressed virtual predicate $\phi_\alpha(\mathbf{x})/g$. To do this, we need to decompress this compressed virtual predicate by reducing the hidden variables into the set $\alpha_1 = \{x, y\}$, i. e., into tuple $\mathbf{y}_1 = (x, y)$. Hence, in the visible set of variables $\beta_1 = \{x_0, y_0, z_0, v, z\}$ we have the coordinate z as well, with tuple $\mathbf{z}_1 = \pi_{-\alpha}\mathbf{x} = (x_0, y_0, z, z_0, v)$, and hence we obtain new compressed virtual predicate $\phi_{\alpha_1}(\mathbf{x})/g$ with formal synatx

$$(\dashv x)_{\mathbf{x}}(\dashv y)_{\mathbf{x}}\phi(\mathbf{x})/g$$

by elimination of the hidden quantifier $(\dashv z)_{\mathbf{x}}$. This new concrete concept $\phi_{\alpha_1}(\mathbf{x})/g$, i. e., $\phi_{\alpha_1}[\beta_1/g(\beta_1)]$ represents a circle obtained from the intersection of the sphere $\phi_\alpha(\mathbf{x})/g$ with the plane $z = g(z)$, from the fact that $g(\beta_1) = g(\beta) \bigcup \{g(z)\}$, rendering visible also the coordinate $g(z)$ of this plane. So, by compression and decompression we are able to express different geometrical objects (geometrical projections) derived from a given class-object $\phi(\mathbf{x})$.

The *meaning* (sense) of compressed virtual predicates is expressed by its hidden variables: in the case of $\phi_\alpha(\mathbf{x})/g$ its meaning is the set of all points inside a concrete sphere defined by assignment $g(\beta)$, while in the case of $\phi_{\alpha_1}(\mathbf{x})/g$ its meaning is the set of all points of the circle obtained as intersection of the previous sphere by the plane determined by $z = g(z)$, i. e., by assignment $g(\beta_1) = g(\beta) \bigcup \{g(z)\}$. Indeed, this fact will be usefully and naturally supported by the intensional FOL introduced in Chapter 1.

The visible variables in β can be fixed by an assignment $g \in \mathcal{D}^{\mathcal{V}}$, so that for a concrete sphere $\phi_\alpha(\mathbf{x})/g$, we obtain the visible tuple $g(\mathbf{y}) = (a, b, c, d)$ which in our *natural language* indeed represents a sphere with radius equal to $d = g(v)$ and with center in $(a, b, c) = (g(x_0), g(y_0), g(z_0))$, and hence just the visible variables are used to *specify* the geometrical objects.

The compressed virtual predicates cannot have an ordinary Herbrand interpretation because the assignment g has no effect on the hidden variables. To explain it, let us consider the constrained databases, without the hidden-quantifiers, so that for the sphere we need to define a particular predicate letter $p_j^7 \in P$, with the tuple of variables $\mathbf{x}$ equal to that used in the virtual predicate $\phi(\mathbf{x})$. In this case, a particular sphere $\phi_\alpha[\beta/g(\beta)]$ is a the simple atom $p_j^7(x, a, y, b, z, c, d)$ with the order-preserving tuple of free variables $\mathbf{y} = (x, y, z)$, and to define that this atom represents a particular sphere with radius d and center in point (a, b, c). In the constraint database, we will use the following constraint logic programs clause:

$$p_j^7(x, a, y, b, z, c, d) \leftarrow C(\mathbf{y}) \tag{2.6}$$

where x, y, z are free variables of the constraint $C(\mathbf{y})$ defined by the equation $(x-a)^2 + (y-b)^2 + (z-c)^2 \leq d^2$. The characteristic function of this constraint $f_C(\mathbf{y}) = f_C(x, y, z) : \mathfrak{D}(\mathbf{y}) \to \mathbf{2}$, satisfies that, for any tuple of constants $\mathbf{d} = (a_1, b_1, c_1) \in \mathfrak{D}(\mathbf{y}) = \mathbb{R}^3$, we have that $f_C(\mathbf{d}) = t$ iff $C(\mathbf{d})$ is true in a given Herbrand interpretation I_H.

Let $I_H : H \to \mathbf{2}$ be a Herbrand interpretation of this constraint database with such programming language clauses having the Herbrand base H (of its ground atoms), then the part of Herbrand base H determined by this atom $p_j^7(x, a, y, b, z, c, d)$ is given by

$$M_H = \{p_j^7(a_1, a, b_1, b, c_1, c, d) \mid a_1, b_1, c_1 \in \mathbb{R}, (a_1-a)^2 + (b_1-b)^2 + (c_1-c)^2 \leq d^2\},$$
$$\text{i.e.,}\quad I_H(p_j^7(a_1, a, b_1, b, c_1, c, d)) = t \quad \text{iff} \quad (a_1-a)^2 + (b_1-b)^2 + (c_1-c)^2 \leq d^2.$$

Hence, for this Herbrand interpretation I_H, if we want that the compressed virtual predicate $\phi_\alpha(\mathbf{x})/g$ with the hidden variables in $\mathbf{y}$ represents the same sphere defined by the Herbrand subset M_H, we need a new extended interpretation I_E for this compressed virtual predicate with variables in $\mathbf{y}$, such that $I_E(\phi_\alpha(\mathbf{x})/g) = f_C(\mathbf{y})$. So, from the fact that $f_C(\mathbf{y}) \in \mathbf{2}^{\mathfrak{D}(\mathbf{y})}$, it means that the new interpretation I_E of compressed predicates must be a *higher-order interpretation* and hence this fact will be analyzed in the next Example 8.

2.1.2 Formal theory of the semantics of predicate compression

In this section, we will develop the formal theory for predicate compression and decompression. While the ordinary (noncompressed) predicates will continue to have standard logic values in $(\mathbf{2}, \leq)$ with $f < t$, the compressed virtual predicates denoted by $p_\alpha(\mathbf{x})$ will have the higher-order logic values in $\mathcal{F}_P$.

For example, in this case, for a given assignment of free (visible) variables $g \in \mathcal{D}^\beta$, and a given Tarski's interpretation I_T^* of $\mathcal{L}$, we can assign to $p_\alpha(\mathbf{x})$ the higher-order truth value $f(\mathbf{y}) \in \mathcal{F}_P$, i.e., the function $f(\mathbf{y}) : \mathfrak{D}(\mathbf{y}) \to \mathbf{2}$, where $\mathbf{y} = \pi_{-\beta}\mathbf{x}$ is the tuple of *only hidden* variables, such that for any tuple of constants $\mathbf{d} \in \mathfrak{D}(\mathbf{y})$,

$$f(\mathbf{d}) = t \quad \text{iff} \quad \mathbf{d} \in I_T^*\Big(\Big(\prod_{x_i \in \alpha} (\dashv x_i)_{\mathbf{x}}\Big) p[\beta/g(\beta)]\Big) \tag{2.7}$$

From the fact that we can extend the compression (to hide the variables) to any composed formula $\phi(\mathbf{x}) \in \mathcal{L}_P$, we need to introduce into the functional space $\mathcal{F}_P$ not only the truth-preorder $\sqsubseteq$, but also the algebraic operators corresponding to standard logic operators in a given predicate logic theory $\mathcal{L}$ and to unary hidden-quantifiers, as follows.

Proposition 8. *Let us define the following preordering $\sqsubseteq$ in $\mathcal{F}_P$, based on the truth ordering in the lattice $(\mathbf{2}, \leq)$: For any $f_j : \mathfrak{D}(\mathbf{y}_j) \to \mathbf{2}, f_k : \mathfrak{D}(\mathbf{y}_k) \to \mathbf{2} \in \mathcal{F}_P$ with $\mathbf{y} = \mathbf{y}_j \times \mathbf{y}_k^*$, where $\mathbf{y}_k^*$ is the tuple of variables obtained from the tuple $\mathbf{y}_k$ by eliminating from it the variables which appear also in $\mathbf{y}_j$, we define the preorder:*

$$f_j \sqsubseteq f_k \quad \textit{iff} \quad \forall g \in \mathcal{D}^Y (f_j(g(\mathbf{y}_j)) \leq f_k(g(\mathbf{y}_k))).$$

We write $f_j \approx f_k$ iff $f_j \sqsubseteq f_k$ and $f_k \sqsubseteq f_j$ (when $\mathbf{y}_j = \mathbf{y}_k$ then the equivalence '$\approx$' is an identity '$=$'). So, we introduce the following operators:

1. *meet operator: $f_j \curlywedge f_k : \mathfrak{D}(\mathbf{y}) \to \mathbf{2}$ is a function such that $\forall g \in \mathcal{D}^Y ((f_j \curlywedge f_k)(g(\mathbf{y})) = f_j(g(\mathbf{y}_j)) \wedge f_k(g(\mathbf{y}_k)))$.*
2. *join operator: $f_j \curlyvee f_k : \mathfrak{D}(\mathbf{y}) \to \mathbf{2}$ is a function such that $\forall g \in \mathcal{D}^Y ((f_j \curlyvee f_k)(g(\mathbf{y})) = f_j(g(\mathbf{y}_j)) \vee f_k(g(\mathbf{y}_k)))$.*
3. *negation operator: $\sim f_j : \mathfrak{D}(\mathbf{y}_j) \to \mathbf{2}$ such that for any $g \in \mathcal{D}^{\mathcal{V}}$, $\sim f_j(g(\mathbf{y}_j)) = t$ iff $f_j(g(\mathbf{y}_j)) = f$ and vice versa $\sim f_j(g(\mathbf{y}_j)) = f$ iff $f_j(g(\mathbf{y}_j)) = t$; thus, $\sim: \mathcal{F}_P \to \mathcal{F}_P$ is antimonotonic.*
4. *$(f_j \Rrightarrow f_k) = (\sim f_j \curlyvee f_k)$ is a function with the Galois connection, $(f_m \curlywedge f_j) \sqsubseteq f_k$ iff $f_m \sqsubseteq (f_j \Rrightarrow f_k)$, so that $(f_j(\mathbf{y}_j) \Rrightarrow f_k(\mathbf{y}_k)) \approx \curlyvee\{f_m(\mathbf{y}) \mid f_m \curlywedge f_j \sqsubseteq f_k\}$, is a relative pseudo-complement.*
5. *hidden-quantifier: if $\mathbf{y}_1$ with $\overline{\mathbf{y}_1} = \overline{\mathbf{y}} \bigcup \{x_i\}$ preserve the variable's ordering in $\mathbf{x}$,*

$$\begin{aligned} \dashv_{x_i \in \mathbf{x}} f(\mathbf{y}) &= f_1 : \mathfrak{D}(\mathbf{y}_1) \to \mathbf{2} \quad \textit{if } x_i \notin \overline{\mathbf{y}} \subseteq \overline{\mathbf{x}}; \\ &= f(\mathbf{y}) \quad \textit{otherwise.} \end{aligned}$$

The resulting function $f_1(\mathbf{y}_1) \in \mathcal{F}_P$ is defined by: for every $g \in \mathcal{D}^{\mathcal{V}}$,

$$f_1(g(\mathbf{y}_1)) = f(g(\mathbf{y})), \tag{2.8}$$

and hence in both cases we obtain the equivalence "$\approx$"

$$\dashv_{x_i \in \mathbf{x}} f \approx f, \tag{2.9}$$

i. e., in the complete lattice $\mathcal{F}_P$, the function $\dashv_{x_i \in \mathbf{x}} : \mathcal{F}_P \to \mathcal{F}_P$ maps each element $f \in \mathcal{F}_P$ into itself.

Let $\mathfrak{D}(\mathbf{V})$ be the complete domain of all variables in $\mathcal{V}$. The constant functions, denoted by $1_f : \mathfrak{D}(\mathbf{V}) \to \{f\} \subseteq \mathbf{2}$ and $1_t : \mathfrak{D}(\mathbf{V}) \to \{t\} \subseteq \mathbf{2}$, are the bottom and top values in $\mathcal{F}_P$. So, in the p-space algebra,

$$\mathcal{A}_P = (\mathcal{F}_P, \sqsubseteq, 1_f, 1_t, \curlywedge, \curlyvee, \sim, \Rrightarrow, \{\exists_{x_i \in \mathbf{x}}\}) \tag{2.10}$$

hold De Morgan laws, $f_j \curlywedge f_k =\sim (\sim f_j \curlyvee \sim f_k)$ *and* $f_j \curlyvee f_k =\sim (\sim f_j \curlywedge \sim f_k)$.

Proof. We have that if $f_j \sqsubseteq f_k$ then $\sim f_j \sqsupseteq \sim f_k$, i. e., $\sim$ is antimonotonic, with $\sim 1_t = 1_f$ and $\sim 1_f = 1_t$. For any $f \in \mathcal{F}_P$, $(f \curlywedge \sim f) \approx 1_f$ and $(f \curlyvee \sim f) \approx 1_t$.

For any subset $S \subseteq \mathcal{F}_P$, the joins $\curlyvee S = f : \mathfrak{D}(\mathbf{y}) \to \mathbf{2}$, where $\overline{\mathbf{y}} =_{\text{def}} \bigcup \{\overline{\mathbf{y}}_i \mid f_i(\mathbf{y}_i) \in S\}$, such that for any assignment g, $f(g(\mathbf{y})) = \curlyvee\{f_i(g(\mathbf{y}_i)) \mid f_i \in S\}$. Thus, $\curlyvee S \in \mathcal{F}_P$, and $f_j \curlywedge f_k \approx f_j$ iff $f_j \curlyvee f_k \approx f_k$ iff $f_j \sqsubseteq f_k$, i. e., $\curlywedge, \curlyvee$ are meet and join operators.

It is well known that in Boolean algebras (i. e., complemented distributive lattices) each element can be expressed as joins of a subset of atoms. For each tuple of variables $\mathbf{y}$ with $n = |\mathbf{y}| \geq 1$, the set of n-ary atoms in $\mathcal{F}_P$ is defined by

$$\text{Att}(n) = \{f_{\mathbf{a}} : \mathfrak{D}(\mathbf{y}) \to \mathbf{2} \mid \mathbf{a} \in \mathfrak{D}(\mathbf{y}), \text{such that for any } \mathbf{b} \in \mathfrak{D}(\mathbf{y}), f_{\mathbf{a}}(\mathbf{b}) = t \text{ iff } \mathbf{a} = \mathbf{b}\}$$

So, any element $f_j(\mathbf{y})$, such that $f_j(g(\mathbf{y})) = t$ iff $g(\mathbf{y}) \in R_j \subseteq \mathfrak{D}(\mathbf{y})$, in the algebra $\mathcal{F}_P$ can be expressed in normal form as joins of atoms, $f_j(\mathbf{y}) \approx \curlyvee\{f_{\mathbf{a}}(\mathbf{y}) \mid \mathbf{a} \in R_j\}$, with $\sim f_j(\mathbf{y}) \approx \curlyvee\{f_{\mathbf{a}} \mid \mathbf{a} \in \mathfrak{D}(\mathbf{y})$ and $\mathbf{a} \notin R_j\}$.

Thus, $f_j(\mathbf{y}) \sqsubseteq f_k(\mathbf{y})$ iff $R_j \subseteq R_k$, $f_j(\mathbf{y}) \curlywedge f_k(\mathbf{y}) \approx \curlyvee\{f_{\mathbf{a}} \in \text{Att}(n) \mid \mathbf{a} \in R_j \bigcap R_k\}$, and $f_j(\mathbf{y}) \curlyvee f_k(\mathbf{y}) \approx \curlyvee\{f_{\mathbf{a}} \in \text{Att}(n) \mid \mathbf{a} \in R_j \bigcup R_k\}$.

Analogously, $(f_j(\mathbf{y}) \Rrightarrow f_k(\mathbf{y})) = (\sim f_j(\mathbf{y}) \curlyvee f_k(\mathbf{y})) \approx \curlyvee \{f_{\mathbf{a}} \in \text{Att}(n) \mid \mathbf{a} \in (\mathfrak{D}(\mathbf{y})/R_j) \bigcup R_k\} = \curlyvee \{f_{\mathbf{a} \in R} \mid (R \bigcap R_j) \subseteq R_k\}$, so that if we define $f_m(\mathbf{y}) = \curlyvee\{f_{\mathbf{a}} \in \text{Att}(n) \mid \mathbf{a} \in R\}$, the we obtain the relative pseudo-complement:

$$(f_j(\mathbf{y}) \Rrightarrow f_k(\mathbf{y})) \approx \curlyvee\{f_m(\mathbf{y}) \in \mathcal{F}_P \mid (f_m \curlywedge f_j) \sqsubseteq f_k\}.$$

Between operators $\Rrightarrow$ and $\curlywedge$ holds the Galois connection, i. e., from the fact that for any assignment g holds the Galois connection of the classical 2-valued logic, $f_m(g(\mathbf{y}_m)) \wedge f_j(g(\mathbf{y}_j)) \leq f_k(g(\mathbf{y}_k))$ iff $f_m(g(\mathbf{y}_m)) \leq f_j(g(\mathbf{y}_j)) \Rightarrow f_k(g(\mathbf{y}_k))$, we obtain that $f_m \curlywedge f_j \sqsubseteq f_k$ iff $f_m \sqsubseteq f_j \Rrightarrow f_k$.

The proof for the hidden quantifier, $f_1(\mathbf{y}_1) = \exists_{x_i \in \mathbf{x}} f(\mathbf{y})$ can be shown by the following commutative diagram. We define $\alpha = \overline{\mathbf{y}}$ (with $x_i \in \beta = \overline{\mathbf{x}} - \alpha$) and $\alpha_1 = \overline{\mathbf{y}}_1$ with $\mathbf{z} = \pi_{-\alpha}\mathbf{x}$ and $\mathbf{z}_1 = \pi_{-\alpha_1}\mathbf{x}$, while the bijections (permutations) $\text{is}_{\mathbf{x}/\alpha}$ and $\text{is}_{\mathbf{x}/\alpha_1}$ and their inversions are defined in point 4 of Definition 23, and derived bijection (permutation of variables) $\text{is}_0 = \text{is}_{\mathbf{x}/\alpha} \circ \text{is}^{-1}_{\mathbf{x}/\alpha_1}$.

Let $f(\mathbf{y}) \in \mathbf{2}^{\mathfrak{D}(\mathbf{y})}$ be a result of hiding the variables $\overline{\mathbf{y}}$ of a predicate $p(\mathbf{x})$ for a fixed Tarski's interpretation I_T^*. See the example in (2.7) with $f_0(\mathbf{x}) : \mathfrak{D}(\mathbf{x}) \to \mathbf{2}$ such that for any for any assignment $g \in \mathcal{D}^{\mathcal{V}}$, $f_0(g(\mathbf{x})) = I_T^*(p(\mathbf{x})/g)$. We denote by $f_{g(\beta)}(\mathbf{x})$ the reduction of the function $f_0(\mathbf{x})$ into its *subdomain* $\mathfrak{D}(\mathbf{x}[\beta/g(\beta)])$. So, $f(\mathbf{y}) = \Lambda(f_{g(\beta)} \circ \text{is}^{-1}_{\mathbf{x}/\alpha})(g(\mathbf{z}))$ where λ is the currying operator from lambda calculus in the commutative diagram (A.10) in the Appendix, and by hiding also the variable x_i of the same predicate $p(\mathbf{x})$, $f_1(\mathbf{y}_1) = \Lambda(f_{g(\beta)} \circ \text{is}^{-1}_{\mathbf{x}/\alpha_1})(g(\mathbf{z}_1))$, we obtain the following commutative diagram:

$$\begin{array}{ccccc}
\mathbf{2}^{\mathfrak{D}(\mathbf{y})} \times \mathfrak{D}(\mathbf{y}) & \xrightarrow{\exists_{x_i\in\mathbf{x}} \times i_n} & \mathbf{2}^{\mathfrak{D}(\mathbf{y}_1)} \times \mathfrak{D}(\mathbf{y}_1[x_i/g(x_i)]) & \xrightarrow{\text{eval}} & \mathbf{2} \\
\Big\uparrow \Lambda(f_{g(\beta)} \circ \mathrm{is}_{\mathbf{x}/\alpha}^{-1}) \times \mathrm{id}_{\mathfrak{D}(\mathbf{y})} & & \Big\uparrow \Lambda(f_{g(\beta)} \circ \mathrm{is}_{\mathbf{x}/\alpha_1}^{-1}) \times \mathrm{id}_{\mathfrak{D}(\mathbf{y}_1[x_i/g(x_i)])} & & \Big\uparrow f_{g(\beta)}(\mathbf{x}) \\
\{g(\mathbf{z})\} \times \mathfrak{D}(\mathbf{y}) & \xleftarrow{\mathrm{is}_0} & \{g(\mathbf{z}_1)\} \times \mathfrak{D}(\mathbf{y}_1[x_i/g(x_i)]) & \xrightarrow{\mathrm{is}_{\mathbf{x}/\alpha_1}^{-1}} & \mathfrak{D}(\mathbf{x}[\beta/g(\beta)]) \subset \mathfrak{D}(\mathbf{x}) \\
 & & & & \\
p_\alpha(\mathbf{x})/g & & (\exists x_i)_{\mathbf{x}} p_\alpha(\mathbf{x}) = p_{\alpha_1}(\mathbf{x})/g & & p(\mathbf{x}[\beta/g(\beta)])
\end{array} \tag{2.11}$$

where the right-hand side commutative diagram is an example of diagram (A.10) in the Appendix, where eval is the application of the first argument (function) over the second argument. The bijection $i_n : \mathfrak{D}(\mathbf{y}) \to \mathfrak{D}(\mathbf{y}_1[x_i/g(x_i)])$ is just an extension of the tuple in $\mathfrak{D}(\mathbf{y})$ by the value $g(x_i)$. So, from the commutativity of this diagram, we obtain (from the arrow above in the left) $f_1(\mathbf{y}_1) = \exists_{x_i\in\mathbf{x}}(f(\mathbf{y}))$, such that for each assignment $g' \in \mathcal{D}^V$,

$$f_1(g'(\mathbf{y}_1[x_i/g(x_i)])) = f(g'(\mathbf{y})) = f_{g(\beta)}(g'(\mathbf{x}[\beta/g(\beta)])).$$

So, from the fact that it holds for any g, and hence if $g = g'$, we obtain finally the definition of f_1 in (2.8), such that for each $g' \in \mathcal{D}^V$, $f_1(g'(\mathbf{y}_1)) = f(g'(\mathbf{y}))$, and hence the definition of $\exists_{x_i\in\mathbf{x}}(f(\mathbf{y}))$.

In the bottom row, we represented an example of logic formulae corresponding to vertical arrows of the commutative diagram above, such that the original classic 2-valued predicate $p(\mathbf{x}[\beta/g(\beta)])$ has $f_{g(\beta)} : \mathfrak{D}(\mathbf{x}[\beta/g(\beta)]) \to \mathbf{2}$ as a reduction of a 2-valued characteristic function for a fixed Tarski's interpretation I_T to the subdomain $\mathfrak{D}(\mathbf{x}[\beta/g(\beta)])$ of $\mathfrak{D}(\mathbf{x})$; the virtual predicate $p_\alpha(\mathbf{x})$ has the characteristic many-valued function $f(\mathbf{y}) = \Lambda(f_{g(\beta)} \circ \mathrm{is}_{\mathbf{x}/\alpha}^{-1})(g(\mathbf{z}))$, while the virtual predicate $p_{\alpha_1}(\mathbf{x}) = (\exists x_i)_{\mathbf{x}} p_\alpha(\mathbf{x})$ has the characteristic many-valued function $\exists_{x_i\in\mathbf{x}}(f(\mathbf{y})) = \Lambda(f_{g(\beta)} \circ \mathrm{is}_{\mathbf{x}/\alpha_1}^{-1})(g(\mathbf{z}_1))$. It explains the relationship between attribute compression for predicates in logic and *λ-abstraction* Λ that determines their characteristic functions, and the relationship between logic attribute hidden-quantifier operator $(\exists x_i)_{\mathbf{x}}$ and its algebraic corresponding operator $\exists_{x_i\in\mathbf{x}}$.

Notice that when $\beta = \{x_i\}$, and hence $\mathbf{y}_1 = \mathbf{x}$ with empty tuple $\mathbf{z}_1 = \langle\,\rangle$, we obtain for the central vertical arrow in the commutative diagram the reduction of the function $\Lambda(f_{g(\beta)} \circ \mathrm{is}_{\mathbf{x}/\alpha_1}^{-1}) : \{\langle\,\rangle\} \to \mathbf{2}^{\mathfrak{D}(\mathbf{x})}$ such that $\Lambda(f_{g(\beta)} \circ \mathrm{is}_{\mathbf{x}/\alpha_1}^{-1})(\langle\,\rangle) = f_{g(\beta)}$.

Let in_p represents the inclusion which maps the tuple of values $g(\mathbf{x})$ into the tuple $g(\mathbf{z}_1) \times g(\mathbf{y}_1)$ of $\mathfrak{D}(\mathbf{z}_1) \times \mathfrak{D}(\mathbf{y}_1)$. Then each assignment g (i. e., $\mathrm{in}_p \circ g$) is an EQUALIZER of the functions $(\exists_{x_i\in\mathbf{x}} \circ \Lambda(f_{g(\beta)} \circ \mathrm{is}_{\mathbf{x}/\alpha}^{-1}) \times i_n) \circ \mathrm{is}_0$ and $\Lambda(f_{g(\beta)} \circ \mathrm{is}_{\mathbf{x}/\alpha_1}^{-1}) \times \mathrm{id}_{\mathfrak{D}(\mathbf{y}_1)}$, graphically

$$\{\mathbf{x}\} \xrightarrow{\mathrm{in}_p \circ g} \mathfrak{D}(\mathbf{z}_1) \times \mathfrak{D}(\mathbf{y}_1) \underset{\Lambda(f_{g(\beta)} \circ \mathrm{is}^{-1}_{\mathbf{x}/\alpha_1}) \times \mathrm{id}_{\mathfrak{D}(\mathbf{y}_1)}}{\overset{(\dashv_{x_i \in \mathbf{x}} \circ \Lambda(f_{g(\beta)} \circ \mathrm{is}^{-1}_{\mathbf{x}/\alpha}) \times i_n) \circ \mathrm{is}_0}{\rightrightarrows}} \mathbf{2}^{\mathfrak{D}(\mathbf{y}_1)} \times \mathfrak{D}(\mathbf{y}_1)$$

It is easy show that it holds De Morgan laws. □

It is easy to verify that $\sqsubseteq$ is reflexive and transitive but not antisymmetric ($f_j \sqsubseteq f_k$ and $f_k \sqsubseteq f_j$ does not imply the identity $f_j = f_k$ (because generally they have different domains), but only the isomorphism $f_j \approx f_k$). That is, for any two $f_j, f_k \in \mathcal{F}_P$, from this Proposition 8 we have that

$$f_j \approx f_k \quad \text{iff} \quad f_j \sqsubseteq f_k \text{ and } f_k \sqsubseteq f_j \tag{2.12}$$

The operators $\curlywedge$ and $\curlyvee$ are monoidal tensors, i. e., commutative $f_j \curlywedge f_k \approx f_k \curlywedge f_j$, associative $f_j \curlywedge (f_k \curlywedge f_m) = (f_j \curlywedge f_k) \curlywedge f_m$, with identity element 1_t for $\curlywedge$, i. e., $(1_t \curlywedge f_j = f_j)$ and (dually) identity element 1_f for $\curlyvee$, i. e., $(1_f \curlyvee f_j \approx f_j)$.

We introduced the functional space $\mathcal{F}_P$ in order to use it as a complete lattice of "truth values" $f \in \mathcal{F}_P$ with the truth partial ordering $\sqsubseteq$, for the compressed predicates. However, in order to obtain the minimal lattice of "truth values" it is more convenient to use the quotient algebra, obtained from $\mathcal{F}_P$ and the equivalence relation $\approx$.

Corollary 7 (Skeletal functional space). *Let us define the skeletal subset of* $\mathcal{F}_P$ *by* $\mathcal{F}_S = \{\mathfrak{S}(f) \mid f \in \mathcal{F}_P\}$, *with the mapping* $\mathfrak{S} : \mathcal{F}_P \to \mathcal{F}_S$, *such that for any element* $f(\mathbf{x}) \in \mathcal{F}_P$, *i. e.,* $f : \mathfrak{D}(\mathbf{x}) \to \mathbf{2}$, *the representation element of all equivalent elements in* $\mathcal{F}_P$ *is the function* $f_j(\mathbf{V}) = \mathfrak{S}(f) : \mathfrak{D}(\mathbf{V}) \to \mathbf{2}$, *such that from* (2.12), $f_j(\mathbf{V}) \approx f(\mathbf{x})$.

Thus, for any two $f_j, f_k \in \mathcal{F}_S$ *we have that* $f_j \approx f_k$ *iff* $f_j = f_k$ *(because all functions in* $\mathcal{F}_S$ *have the same maximal domain* $\mathfrak{D}(\mathbf{V})$*), and hence* $\mathcal{F}_S$ *is a poset and complete lattice where* $\curlywedge, \curlyvee$ *are the meet and join lattice operators, respectively.*

So, we have the homomorphism $\mathrm{im} : (\mathcal{F}_S, \sqsubseteq, \curlywedge, \curlyvee, \sim) \to (\mathfrak{D}(\mathbf{V}), \subseteq, \bigcap, \bigcup, -)$, *where* $\mathrm{im} : \mathcal{F}_S \to \mathfrak{D}(\mathbf{V})$ *is a mapping such that for any* $f \in \mathcal{F}_S$, $\mathrm{im}(f) = \{\mathbf{c} \in \mathfrak{D}(\mathbf{V}) \mid f(\mathbf{c}) = t\}$.

Consequently, $(\mathcal{F}_S, \sqsubseteq, 1_f, 1_t, \curlywedge, \curlyvee, \sim, \Rrightarrow)$ *is a Boolean algebra with bottom and top elements* 1_f *and* 1_t, *respectively, such that for any two elements* $f_j, f_k \in \mathcal{F}_S$ *if* $f_j \sqsubseteq f_k$ *and* $f_k \sqsubseteq f_j$ *then* f_j *and* f_k *are* the same *elements in* $\mathcal{F}_S$.

Thus, the elements in $\mathcal{F}_S$ of this complete distributive lattice can be used as a minimal set of canonical "truth values" for the compressed predicates. So, we can define the semantics of the extended predicate logic $\mathcal{L}_E$ in Definition 24 as follows.

Definition 25 (Semantics). Let I_T^* be a Tarski's interpretation for the underlying classic predicate logic $\mathcal{L}$ with distinct proposition letters $\top$ and $\bot$ for the tautology and contradiction, respectively. Consequently, for the extension of this predicate logic $\mathcal{L}$ by hidden-quantifiers, $\mathcal{L}_E$ in Definition 24, we obtain the following syntax algebra:

$$\mathcal{A}_E = (\mathcal{L}_E, \bot, \top, \wedge, \vee, \neg, \Rightarrow, \{(\dashv x_i)_{\mathbf{x}}\}) \tag{2.13}$$

Then $I_E : \mathcal{L}_E \to \mathcal{F}_P$ is the unique extension of this Herbrand interpretation to all formulae in $\mathcal{L}_E$ and homomorphism between the syntax algebra $\mathcal{A}_E$ and truth-space algebra $\mathcal{A}_P$ in (2.10), with $I_E(\top) = 1_t$ and $I_E(\bot) = 1_f$, such that for any assignment $g \in \mathcal{D}^{\mathcal{V}}$:

[a] For any atom $p(\mathbf{x})$ with (also empty) set $\beta \subset \overline{\mathbf{x}}$ and $\mathbf{y} = \pi_{-\beta}\mathbf{x}$, we obtain the function $I_E(p[\beta/g(\beta)]) : \mathfrak{D}(\mathbf{y}) \to \mathbf{2}$ such that for any assignment $g' \in \mathcal{D}^{\mathcal{V}}$, $I_E(p[\beta/g(\beta)])(g'(\mathbf{y})) = I_T^*(p[\beta/g(\beta)]/g')$, while for the ground atoms, $I_E(p(\mathbf{x})/g) = 1_t$ if $I_T^*(p(g(\mathbf{x}))) = t$; 1_f otherwise.

[b] For any two virtual predicates $\phi(\mathbf{x})$ and $\psi(\mathbf{x}_1)$ with $\mathbf{y} = \mathbf{x} \times \mathbf{x}'_1$ where $\mathbf{x}'_1$ is the subtuple obtained from $\mathbf{x}_1$ by eliminating from it all variables which appear also in $\mathbf{x}$, we have that $I_E(\phi(\mathbf{x})/g) = 1_t : \mathfrak{D}(\mathbf{V}) \to \mathbf{2}$ if $I_T^*(\phi(g(\mathbf{x}))) = t$; $1_f : \mathfrak{D}(\mathbf{V}) \to \mathbf{2}$ otherwise.

Moreover, for $I_E(\phi(\mathbf{x})) : \mathfrak{D}(\mathbf{x}) \to \mathbf{2}$ and $I_E(\phi(\mathbf{x}_1)) : \mathfrak{D}(\mathbf{x}_1) \to \mathbf{2}$, and any assignment $g \in \mathcal{D}^{\mathcal{V}}$, we have:

1. $I_E(\phi(\mathbf{x}) \wedge \psi(\mathbf{x})_1) = I_E(\phi(\mathbf{x})) \curlywedge I_E(\psi(\mathbf{x}_1)) : \mathfrak{D}(\mathbf{y}) \to \mathbf{2}$, and $I_E((\phi \wedge \psi)/g) = I_E(\phi/g) \curlywedge I_E(\psi/g) \in \{1_f, 1_t\}$,
2. $I_E(\phi(\mathbf{x}) \vee \psi(\mathbf{x})_1) = I_E(\phi(\mathbf{x})) \curlyvee I_E(\psi(\mathbf{x}_1)) : \mathfrak{D}(\mathbf{y}) \to \mathbf{2}$, and $I_E((\phi \vee \psi)/g) = I_E(\phi/g) \curlyvee I_E(\psi/g) \in \{1_f, 1_t\}$,
3. $I_E(\phi(\mathbf{x}) \Rightarrow \psi(\mathbf{x})_1) = I_E(\phi(\mathbf{x})) \Rrightarrow I_E(\psi(\mathbf{x}_1)) : \mathfrak{D}(\mathbf{y}) \to \mathbf{2}$, and $I_E((\phi \Rightarrow \psi)/g) = I_E(\phi/g) \Rrightarrow I_E(\psi/g) \in \{1_f, 1_t\}$,
4. $I_E(\neg\phi(\mathbf{x})) =\sim I_E(\phi(\mathbf{x})) : \mathfrak{D}(\mathbf{x}) \to \mathbf{2}$, and $I_E(\neg\phi/g) =\sim I_E(\phi/g) \in \{1_f, 1_t\}$,
5. $I_E((\dashv x_i)_{\mathbf{x}}\phi_\alpha(\mathbf{x})/g) = \dashv_{x_i \in \mathbf{x}}(I_E(\phi_\alpha(\mathbf{x})/g)) \notin \{1_f, 1_t\}$ for $x_i \in \overline{\mathbf{x}} - \alpha$.

It is easy to see that the interpretation I_E is two-valued for all ground atoms and sentences, but it is not two-valued for the "ground" compressed virtual predicates (having hidden quantifiers) as shown in the point 5 above. Consequently, by extending classical two-valued predicate logic $\mathcal{L}$ into this new predicate logic $\mathcal{L}_E$ with also hidden quantifiers, from the fact that the hidden variables are not affected by variable assignments $g \in \mathcal{D}^{\mathcal{V}}$, the compressed virtual predicate cannot be transformed into a sentence by assignment, and hence its truth value is not two-valued. As a result, the predicate logic $\mathcal{L}_E$ with hidden quantifiers, having compressed virtual predicates, is a *many-valued logic*.

Corollary 8. *The extended predicate logic $\mathcal{L}_E$ with hidden-quantifier operators is a truth-functional many-valued extension of the classic 2-valued predicate logic.*

Proof. The definition of the semantics for the logic operators of this logic $\mathcal{L}_E$ in Definition 25 results in the fact that the many-valued interpretation $I_E : \mathcal{L}_E \to \mathcal{F}_P$ is an homomorphism, so that the truth-compositionality is preserved, and consequently, this logic is truth-functional. By elimination of all hidden-quantifier operators, we obtain the classic 2-valued predicate logic. Thus, $\mathcal{L}_E$ is conservative extension of the classic Boolean 2-valued predicate logic, and this property is preserved also by the P-space

$\mathcal{F}_P$ of algebraic (functional) truth values, which is also Boolean algebra extended by the set of unary algebraic operators $\dashv_{x_i \in \mathbf{x}}$ for hidden quantifiers (attribute compressions). □

It is easy to verify that $I_E(p_\alpha(\mathbf{x})/g) = I_E((\prod_{x_i \in \alpha}(\dashv x_i)_\mathbf{x})p[\beta/g(\beta)]) = f_k : \mathfrak{D}(\mathbf{y}) \to \mathbf{2}$, where $\beta = \overline{\mathbf{x}} - \alpha$ and $\mathbf{y} = \pi_{-\beta}\mathbf{x}$, such that for any assignment $g' \in \mathcal{D}^\mathcal{V}$ for all $x_i \in \beta$, $g'(x_i) = g(x_i)$, we obtain $f_k(g'(\mathbf{y})) = I_E(p(g(\mathbf{x}))) = I_H(p(g(\mathbf{x})))$. So, we can see how these higher-order logic values for compressed predicates are derivable from the values of ground atoms of the original (underlying) logic $\mathcal{L}$, in the way that compressed predicates are *knowledge invariant* transformations of the original predicates. That is, any compressed atom $p_\alpha(\mathbf{x})$ of the original two-valued atom $p(\mathbf{x})$ contains the same amount of knowledge, and we can use independently any of them: the flattened knowledge of $p(\mathbf{x})$ (the set of tuples of the original atom $p(\mathbf{x})$ for which this atom is true in the Herbrand interpretation I_H) is transformed into hidden knowledge of the compressed atom $p_\alpha(\mathbf{x})$ with visible attributes in β in the way that the truth values of this atom are characteristic functions for hidden attributes (that encapsulate the hidden knowledge). That is, compressed predicates have less visible attributes of the original predicates, but they do not lose the information of these hidden attributes. In the extreme case of compression $p_\alpha(\mathbf{x})$ when $\alpha = \overline{\mathbf{x}}$ and $\beta = \emptyset$, we obtain that $f_0 =_{\text{def}} I_E(p_\alpha(\mathbf{x})) : \mathfrak{D}(\mathbf{x}) \to \mathbf{2}$ is the *characteristic function* for the predicate $p(\mathbf{x})$ (see the last vertical arrow in the commutative diagram (2.11)) under the given Herbrand interpretation $I_H : H \to \mathbf{2}$ obtained for a given Tarski's interpretation I_T^*, so that $I_H(p(g(\mathbf{x}))) = t$ iff $g(\mathbf{x}) \in I_T^*(p(\mathbf{x}))$.

The functional P-space constitutes the complete lattice $(\mathcal{F}_P, \sqsubseteq, \curlywedge, \curlyvee)$ of logic values for the extended logic $\mathcal{L}_E$; thus, what we obtained is a kind of many-valued logic, where the set of logic values is of higher-order type (functions).

Proposition 9 (Knowledge-conservative predicate compression). *For any compressed virtual predicate $\phi_\alpha(\mathbf{x})$ in $\mathcal{L}_P$ with $\beta = \overline{\mathbf{x}} - \alpha$ and $\mathbf{y} = \pi_{-\beta}\mathbf{x}$, for any assignment $g \in \mathcal{D}^\mathcal{V}$ it holds that*

$$I_E(\phi_\alpha(\mathbf{x})/g)(g(\mathbf{y})) = I_E(\phi(\mathbf{x})/g)(g(\mathbf{V})) \in \mathbf{2} \tag{2.14}$$

where $\phi(\mathbf{x})$ is the formula obtained from the formula $\phi_\alpha(\mathbf{x})$ by eliminating all hidden-quantifier operators from it, $I_E(\phi_\alpha(\mathbf{x})/g) \in \mathbf{2}^{\mathfrak{D}(\mathbf{y})}$ is a function $f(\mathbf{y}) \in \mathcal{F}_P$ and $I_E(\phi(\mathbf{x})/g) \in \{1_f, 1_t\}$. That is, it holds

$$f(\mathbf{y}) =_{\text{def}} I_E(\phi_\alpha(\mathbf{x})/g) = I_E(\phi[\beta/g(\beta)]) : \mathfrak{D}(\mathbf{y}) \to \mathbf{2} \tag{2.15}$$

where $\mathbf{x}[\beta/g(\beta)]$ is the tuple obtained from the tuple of variables in $\mathbf{x}$ by substituting the variables in β by the values in $g(\beta)$. From the fact that the Herbrand base of $\mathcal{L}_P$ is equal to that of $\mathcal{L}$, the reduction of I_E to this Herbrand base is equal to Herbrand interpretation *of $\mathcal{L}$, $I_H : H \to \mathbf{2}$ defined for a given Tarski's interpretation I_T^* for each predicate $p \in P$ and each $g \in \mathcal{D}^{\mathcal{V}}$ with $p(\mathbf{x})/g \in H$, by*

$$I_H(p(\mathbf{x})/g) = t \quad \textit{iff} \quad g(\mathbf{x}) \in I_T^*(p(\mathbf{x})),$$

so that for compressed predicates (2.14) *reduces to*

$$I_E(p_\alpha(\mathbf{x})/g)(g(\mathbf{y})) = I_H(p(\mathbf{x})/g).$$

Proof. By structural induction, it holds for all formulae with one logic operator. Let us assume that it holds for all formulae with n logic operators. So, we can prove that it holds also for all formulae with $n+1$ operators, as for the following possible cases:
1. Let $\phi_\alpha(\mathbf{x}) = \neg\psi_\alpha(\mathbf{x})$, where $\psi_\alpha(\mathbf{x})$ is a formula with n logic operators, so for any g,

$$\begin{aligned} I_E(\phi_\alpha(\mathbf{x})/g)(g(\mathbf{y}) &= I_E(\neg\psi_\alpha(\mathbf{x})/g)(g(\mathbf{y}))\\ &=\sim I_E(\psi_\alpha(\mathbf{x})/g)(g(\mathbf{y})) \quad \text{(by homomorphic property of } I_E)\\ &=\sim I_E(\psi(\mathbf{x})/g)(g(\mathbf{V})) = \quad \text{(by inductive hypothesis)}\\ &= I_E(\neg\psi(\mathbf{x})/g)(g(\mathbf{V})) = I_E(\phi(\mathbf{x})/g)(g(\mathbf{V})). \end{aligned}$$

2. Let $\phi_\alpha(\mathbf{x}) = \psi_{\alpha_1}(\mathbf{x}_1) \wedge \varphi_{\alpha_2}(\mathbf{x}_2)$, where $\alpha = \alpha_1 \bigcup \alpha_2$, $\overline{\mathbf{x}} = \overline{\mathbf{x}}_1 \bigcup \overline{\mathbf{x}}_2$. So, for any g,

$$\begin{aligned} &I_E(\phi_\alpha(\mathbf{x})/g)(g(\mathbf{y}))\\ &= I_E(\psi_{\alpha_1}(\mathbf{x}_1)/g \wedge \varphi_{\alpha_2}(\mathbf{x}_2)/g)(g(\mathbf{y}))\\ &= (I_E(\psi_{\alpha_1}(\mathbf{x}_1)/g) \wedge I_E(\varphi_{\alpha_2}(\mathbf{x}_2)/g))(g(\mathbf{y})) = \quad \text{(by homomorphic property)}\\ &= I_E(\psi_{\alpha_1}(\mathbf{x}_1)/g)(g(\mathbf{y}_1)) \wedge I_E(\varphi_{\alpha_2}(\mathbf{x}_2)/g)(g(\mathbf{y}_2)) = \quad \text{(from point 1 in Proposition 8)}\\ &= I_E(\psi(\mathbf{x}_1)/g)(g(\mathbf{V})) \wedge I_E(\varphi(\mathbf{x}_2)/g)(g(\mathbf{V})) = \quad \text{(by inductive hypothesis)}\\ &= I_E(\psi(\mathbf{x}_1)/g \wedge \varphi(\mathbf{x}_2)/g)(g(\mathbf{V})) = I_E(\phi(\mathbf{x})/g)(g(\mathbf{V})). \end{aligned}$$

3. Than, as in 2, we obtain the same result if $\wedge$ substitute by $\vee$ or implication $\Rightarrow$.
4. Let $f(\mathbf{y}) =_{\text{def}} I_E(\phi_\alpha(\mathbf{x})/g) \in \mathcal{F}_P$ and by by inductive hypothesis $f(g(\mathbf{y})) = I_E(\phi_\alpha(\mathbf{x})/g)(g(\mathbf{y})) = I_E(\phi(\mathbf{x})/g)(g(\mathbf{V}))$. Then for $x_i \in \overline{\mathbf{x}} - \alpha$, we define the function $f_1(\mathbf{y}_1) =_{\text{def}} I_E((\exists x_i)_{\mathbf{x}}\phi_\alpha(\mathbf{x})/g) = \exists_{x_i \in \mathbf{x}} I_E(\phi_\alpha(\mathbf{x})/g) = \exists_{x_i \in \mathbf{x}}(f(\mathbf{y})) \in \mathcal{F}_P$, where $\overline{\mathbf{y}}_1 = \overline{\mathbf{y}} \bigcup \{x_i\}$. Thus,

$$\begin{aligned} I_E((\exists x_i)_{\mathbf{x}}\phi_\alpha(\mathbf{x})/g)(g(\mathbf{y}_1)) &= f_1(g(\mathbf{y}_1)) = f(g(\mathbf{y})) \quad \text{(by (2.8))}\\ &= I_E(\phi_\alpha(\mathbf{x})/g))(g(\mathbf{y}))(g(\mathbf{V})) = I_E(\phi(\mathbf{x})/g)(g(\mathbf{V}))\\ &\text{(by inductive hypothesis)} \end{aligned}$$

□

The knowledge conservation means that any adding or deleting of hidden quantifiers in a given formula we obtain a logically equivalent formula: because of such property, we call the compression and decompression *invariant* operators. It is easy to show the validity of this proposition directly from the external commutative diagram (2.11)

$$\begin{array}{ccc} \mathbf{2}^{\mathfrak{D}(\mathbf{y})} \times \mathfrak{D}(\mathbf{y}) & \xrightarrow{\text{eval}} & \mathbf{2} \\ \uparrow \Lambda(f_{g(\beta)} \circ \mathrm{is}_{\mathbf{x}/\alpha}^{-1}) \times \mathrm{id}_{\mathfrak{D}(\mathbf{y})} & & \uparrow f_{g(\beta)}(\mathbf{x}) \\ \{g(\mathbf{z})\} \times \mathfrak{D}(\mathbf{y}) & \xrightarrow{\mathrm{is}_{\mathbf{x}/\alpha}^{-1}} & \mathfrak{D}(\mathbf{x}[\beta/g(\beta)]) \\ & & \\ \phi_\alpha(\mathbf{x})/g & & \phi(\mathbf{x}[\beta/g(\beta)]) \end{array} \tag{2.16}$$

where $f(\mathbf{y}) = I_E(\phi_\alpha(\mathbf{x})/g) =_{\text{def}} \Lambda(f_{g(\beta)} \circ \mathrm{is}_{\mathbf{x}/\alpha}^{-1})(g(\mathbf{z})) \in \mathbf{2}^{\mathfrak{D}(\mathbf{y})}$ and $f_{g(\beta)}(\mathbf{x})$ is the reduction of $f_0(\mathbf{x}) =_{\text{def}} I_E(\phi(\mathbf{x})) \in \mathbf{2}^{\mathfrak{D}(\mathbf{x})}$ to subdomain $\mathfrak{D}(\mathbf{x}[\beta/g(\beta)])$. Then, from the commutativity of the diagram above, we obtain that $I_E(\phi_\alpha(\mathbf{x})/g)(g(\mathbf{y})) = f(g(\mathbf{y})) = f_0(g(\mathbf{x})) = I_E(\phi(\mathbf{x}))(g(\mathbf{x}))(g(\mathbf{V})) = I_E(\phi(g(\mathbf{x})))(g(\mathbf{V}))$, i. e., we obtained (2.14). Equation (2.15) results directly from the commutativity of this diagram. In the case when β is an empty set, then $g(\mathbf{z})$ is the empty tuple $\langle\,\rangle$, so that $\mathbf{y} = \mathbf{x}$, i. e., $f(\mathbf{x}) = \Lambda(f_{g(\beta)} \circ \mathrm{is}_{\mathbf{x}/\alpha}^{-1})(\langle\,\rangle)$, and hence (2.15) reduces to $f(\mathbf{x}) = f_0(\mathbf{x})$.

Example 8 (Continuation of Example 7). Thus, the higher-order interpretations I_E can be naturally obtained by the predicate compression of constrained atoms (of the constraint databases), and if we use this extended predicate logic language $\mathcal{L}_E$ with hidden quantifiers, we do not need to introduce ad hoc new predicates, like that for sphere $p_j^7 \in P$, and we do not need the constraint logic programming clauses (2.6),

$$p_j^7(x, a, y, b, z, c, d) \leftarrow C(\mathbf{y})$$

but it is sufficient to use the compressed virtual predicate $\phi_\alpha(\mathbf{x})$, provided by the formula (2.5), for a direct definition of these constraint database concepts.

This fact would introduce the higher-order interpretations I_E instead of standard two-valued interpretations, but in next section we will see how to overcome this side effect and to remain inside the two-valued intensional FOL.

It remains to show what kind of logical connectives are the hidden-quantifiers.

Corollary 9. *The hidden-quantifiers $(\exists x_i)_{\mathbf{x}}$ are modal logic operators. The functional space algebra $\mathcal{F}_P$ of the truth values of the many-valued modal predicate logic $\mathcal{L}_E$ is a Galois algebra (Section* A.1 *in the Appendix) where each operator (function) $\exists_{x_i \in \mathbf{x}} : \mathcal{F}_P \to \mathcal{F}_P$ is a self-adjoint modal operator.*

Proof. From point 4 of Proposition 8, we obtain that "negation" operator "$\sim$" in the complete bounded lattice $\_P$ is just the pseudo-complement, i. e., for any $f_k \in \mathcal{F}_P$, $\sim f_k = f_k \Rrightarrow 1_f$ so that $\mathcal{F}_P$ is a Heyting algebra.

For any function $\dashv_{x_i \in \mathbf{x}}$, corresponding to a logic hidden-quantifier $(\dashv x_i)_{\mathbf{x}}$ and elements of this Heyting algebra $f, f_1 \in \mathcal{F}_P$, from point 5 in Proposition 8 and $\dashv_{x_i \in \mathbf{x}} f \approx f$ in (2.9), we obtain that $f \sqsubseteq f_1$ implies that $\dashv_{x_i \in \mathbf{x}} f \sqsubseteq \dashv_{x_i \in \mathbf{x}} f_1$, and hence $\dashv_{x_i \in \mathbf{x}}$ is a monotone function. Moreover, from (2.9) it preserves the lattice meet operation,

$$\dashv_{x_i \in \mathbf{x}} 1_t \approx 1_t \quad \text{and} \quad \dashv_{x_i \in \mathbf{x}} (f \curlywedge f_1) \approx (\dashv_{x_i \in \mathbf{x}} f) \curlywedge (\dashv_{x_i \in \mathbf{x}} f_1),$$

and preserves the lattice join operation,

$$\dashv_{x_i \in \mathbf{x}} 1_f \approx 1_f \quad \text{and} \quad \dashv_{x_i \in \mathbf{x}} (f \curlyvee f_1) \approx (\dashv_{x_i \in \mathbf{x}} f) \curlyvee (\dashv_{x_i \in \mathbf{x}} f_1)$$

so that $\dashv_{x_i \in \mathbf{x}}$ is self-adjoint modal operator in Heyting algebra $\mathcal{F}_P$, and consequently, $\mathcal{F}_P$ is a Galois algebra as well. □

The Galois algebra in the functional-space $\mathcal{F}_P$ of the truth values of the many-valued predicate modal logic (with hidden quantifiers as self-adjoint, universal and existential, modal operators) $\mathcal{L}_E$ is the basis for the construction of the autoreferential Kripke where the set of explicit possible worlds $\mathcal{W}_e$ is just the set of the elements (truth values) of this Galois algebra, where each possible world $w \in \mathcal{W}_e = \mathcal{F}_P$ is a function. But we have seen that also in intensional FOL with modal operators (transformed from existential and universal logic quantifiers of FOL) has as possible worlds in W_e the Tarski's interpretations, which are the functions as well. Thus, it is not a surprise that the hidden quantifiers in predicate modal logic L_E have the similar Kripke semantics where each possible world (the truth value in many-valued $\mathcal{L}_E$) is a higher-order element (a function). The Kripke semantics for modal hidden-quantifier operators, that is for the modal many-valued predicate logic $\mathcal{L}_E$, has been provided, e. g., in [69], and for interested readers in the Appendix, Definition 107 in Section A.3.4. The example of Galois algebra with a banal self-adjoint modal operator (identity function) is provided by Proposition 41 in the Appendix, Section A.3.3.

2.1.3 Predicate compression by intensional abstract terms: application to constraint databases

In order to implement the compressed predicates into intensional FOL, we must explain what will be their intensional concept, obtained by intensional interpretation I from this compressed predicate, and consequently, what is its meaning (sense) by using Montague's definition.

Let us consider the following attributes (variables): x_1 for the name, x_2 for the forename, x_3 for the birthday and x_4 for the personal Id for the predicate student $p^4(\mathbf{x})$, which denotes a set of students. Its intensional interpretation is a concept $I(p^4(\mathbf{x})) \in$

D_4, while for its compression the intensional interpretation would be $I(p^4_\alpha(\mathbf{x})) \in D_{|\alpha|}$ which, e. g., if we hide the birthday and Id, i. e., with $\alpha = \{x_3, x_4\}$, $p^4_\alpha(\mathbf{x})/g$ is intensional concept of the "student" with individual name and forname defined by $g(x_1)$ and $g(x_2)$, relatively, we have that the intensional concept $I(p^4_\alpha(\mathbf{x})/g) \in D_2$ is different from the general concept $I(p^4(\mathbf{x})) \in D_4$. Thus, the extension of predicate logic with the compression of attributes is a natural candidate for intensional logics.

Notice that for the intensional FOL, in the case of the complete compression of variables of a predicate $p^4(\mathbf{x})$, when $\alpha = \overline{\mathbf{x}}$ and β is empty set of visible variables, we would obtain that $I(p^4_\alpha(\mathbf{x})) = I(p^4(\mathbf{x}))$ is *the same* intensional concept, also if, it is different from a noncompressed predicate $p(\mathbf{x})$; the compressed predicate $p^4_\alpha(\mathbf{x})$ has no free variables (all of them are bound by hidden quantifiers). This intensional identity, of elementary predicate $p^4(\mathbf{x})$ and its *total* compression $p^4_\alpha(\mathbf{x})$, is required from the knowledge conservation, and hence the extension of this compressed predicate in any possible world (Tarski's interpretation which is a model of Γ, $I^*_T = w \in \mathcal{W}_e = \mathfrak{I}_T(\Gamma)$, of intensional FOL as specified in Section 1.3 or, equivalently, the extensionalization function $h = \mathcal{F}(w)$ of a compressed predicate $p^4_\alpha(\mathbf{x})$) has to be equal to the set of tuples for which the original 2-valued predicate $p(\mathbf{x})$ is true for a given Tarski's interpretation I^*_T.

Because of that, by considering that the semantics of intensional FOL with modal operators for existential and universal quantifiers are based on the Kripke possible worlds that are Tarski's interpretations, we must define what is Tarski's interpretation of any compressed virtual predicate and then demonstrate that the many-valued interpretation $\mathcal{I}_E$ of the many-valued predicate logic $\mathcal{L}_E$ with modal operators for its hidden quantifiers can be well-defined from the Tarski's interpretations

Proposition 10. *For a given Tarski's interpretation I^*_T, the interpretation of compressed predicates $\phi_\alpha(\mathbf{x})$ with $\beta = \overline{\mathbf{x}} - \alpha$, for a given assignment $g \in \mathcal{D}^{\mathcal{V}}$, is defined by*

$$I^*_T(\phi_\alpha(\mathbf{x})/g) =_{\text{def}} \begin{cases} \pi_{-\beta}(I^*_T(\phi[\beta/g(\beta)])) \subseteq \mathcal{D}^{|\alpha|}, & \textit{if } \beta \textit{ is not empty} \\ I^*_T(\phi(\mathbf{x})), & \textit{otherwise} \end{cases} \tag{2.17}$$

where

$$I^*_T(\phi[\beta/g(\beta)]) = \{g'(\mathbf{x}) \mid g' \in \mathcal{D}^{\mathcal{V}} \textit{ such that } \forall x_j \in \beta.(g'(x_j) = g(x_j)) \\ \textit{and } I_T(\phi(g'(\mathbf{x}))) = t\}.$$

So, for general compressed virtual predicate $\phi_\alpha(\mathbf{x})$ and its truth value $I_E(\phi_\alpha(\mathbf{x})/g) : \mathfrak{D}(\mathbf{y}) \to \mathbf{2}$ where $\mathbf{y} = \pi_{-\beta}\mathbf{x}$ is the tuple of hidden variables, for each tuple of values $\mathbf{d} \in \mathfrak{D}(\mathbf{y})$, we obtain the following general relationship between many-valued interpretation I_E in Definition 25 and Tarski's interpretation I^*_T for the compressed predicates:

$$I_E(\phi_\alpha(\mathbf{x})/g)(\mathbf{d}) = t \quad \textit{iff} \quad \mathbf{d} \in I^*_T(\phi_\alpha(\mathbf{x})/g) \tag{2.18}$$

This equation is valid also in the case when β is empty ($\alpha = \overline{\mathbf{x}}$ and hence $\mathbf{y} = \mathbf{x}$) when we have no visible variables. For noncompressed virtual predicates $\phi(\mathbf{x})$ when α is empty (i. e., without hiddenquantifiers inside this formula), we obtain for each $\mathbf{d} \in \mathfrak{D}(\mathbf{x})$,

$$I_E(\phi(\mathbf{x}))(\mathbf{d}) = t \quad \textit{iff} \quad \mathbf{d} \in I_T^*(\phi(\mathbf{x})) \tag{2.19}$$

*such that for any assignment $g \in \mathcal{D}^{\mathcal{V}}$ the interpretation I_E of the sentence $\phi(\mathbf{x})/g = \phi(g(\mathbf{x}))$ is two-valued corresponding to its Tarski's interpretation as specified in point [**b**] of Definition 25.*

So, the many-valued interpretation I_E is completely defined for a given Tarski's interpretation I_T^*.

Proof. From (2.15), we have that for a fixed $g' \in \mathcal{D}^{\alpha}$, $I_E(\phi_\alpha(\mathbf{x})/g') = I_E(\phi[\beta/g'(\beta)]) : \mathfrak{D}(\mathbf{y}) \to \mathbf{2}$. Then for each $g \in \mathcal{D}^{\mathcal{V}}$, such that for all $x_k \in \beta.(g(x_k) = g'(x_k))$, and tuple of values $\mathbf{d} = g(\mathbf{y}) \in \mathfrak{D}(\mathbf{y})$ (which does not depend on g' from the fact that the hidden variables in $\mathbf{y}$ are disjoint from the visible variables in β), from (2.14) we obtain

$$\begin{aligned} I_E(\phi_\alpha(\mathbf{x})/g)(\mathbf{d}) &= I_E(\phi_\alpha(\mathbf{x})/g)(g(\mathbf{y})) = I_E(\phi(g(\mathbf{x})))(g(\mathbf{V})) = t \\ &\text{iff} \quad I_E(\phi(g(\mathbf{x}))) = 1_t \\ &\text{iff} \quad g(\mathbf{x}) \in I_T^*(\phi(\mathbf{x})) \quad (\text{from point } [\mathbf{b}] \text{ in Definition 25}) \\ &\text{iff} \quad \mathbf{d} = g(\mathbf{y}) \in \pi_{-\beta} I_T^*(\phi(\mathbf{x})) \\ &\text{iff} \quad \mathbf{d} \in I_T^*(\phi_\alpha(\mathbf{x})/g) \quad (\text{from (2.17)}). \end{aligned}$$

So, we obtained (2.18). □

Notice that in the simple cases when virtual predicate $\phi(\mathbf{x})$ is just a predicate $p^k \in P$, from (2.18), we obtain for each tuple of values $\mathbf{d} \in \mathfrak{D}(\mathbf{y})$, $I_E(p_\alpha^k(\mathbf{x})/g)(\mathbf{d}) = t$ iff $\mathbf{d} \in I_T^*(p_\alpha^k(\mathbf{x}))/g = I_T^*(p_\alpha^k[\beta/g(\beta)])$, which was introduced in (2.7).

Let us show now that for each compressed predicate in $\mathcal{L}_E$, Montague's meaning can be derived from the many-valued interpretation I_E of this many-valued modal predicate logic $\mathcal{L}_E$, and hence also the compressed predicates have intensional properties.

Lemma 1. *Montague's meaning $I_n : \mathcal{L}_E \to R^{\mathcal{W}_e}$, where the set of possible worlds $\mathcal{W}_e$ is the set of Tarski's interpretations of $\mathcal{L}_E$, for any compressed predicate $\phi_\alpha(\mathbf{x}) \in \mathcal{L}_E$ with $\beta = \overline{\mathbf{x}} - \alpha$ and $\mathbf{y} = \pi_{-\beta}\mathbf{x}$, assignment $g \in \mathcal{D}^{\mathcal{V}}$ and possible world $w \in \mathcal{W}_e$, is defined by*

$$I_n(\phi_\alpha(\mathbf{x})/g)(w) =_{\text{def}} \{\mathbf{d} \in \mathfrak{D}(\mathbf{y}) \mid I_E(\phi_\alpha(\mathbf{x})/g)(\mathbf{d}) = t\} \tag{2.20}$$

Proof. From Proposition 10, we have that for each possible world (Tarski's interpretation), $I_T^* = w \in \mathcal{W}_e$ of the many-valued modal predicate logic $\mathcal{L}_E$, we obtain a particular many-valued interpretation I_E of $\mathcal{L}_E$, and that from (1.10) in Section 1.3, we have that $I_n(\phi_\alpha(\mathbf{x})/g)(w) = I_T^*(\phi_\alpha(\mathbf{x})/g)$, and hence from (2.18) we obtain the result in (2.20). □

So, the truth values of a given compressed predicate determine the meaning of this compressed predicate. We also can consider that each truth value $I_E(\phi_\alpha(\mathbf{x})/g) \in \mathcal{F}_P$ of the compressed predicate $\phi_\alpha(\mathbf{x})/g$ corresponds to Montague's possible world (as in the case of autoreferential Kripke semantics of many-valued logics provided in the Appendix).

However, if we extend the intensional FOL also with compressed predicates, such that Tarski's interpretation of them is that given in (2.17), in that case we would obtain as a side effect the necessity to introduce the hidden quantifiers as well. We can avoid this side effect by using the intensional abstract operators.

Corollary 10. *Each well-defined compressed virtual predicate $\phi_\alpha(\mathbf{x})$ with $\beta = \overline{\mathbf{x}} - \alpha$ of the many-valued predicate logic $\mathcal{L}_E$ can be substituted by the atom $A(<\phi(\mathbf{x})>^{\beta}_{\alpha})$ in the intensional FOL with intensional abstraction operators.*

Proof. From the fact that from Proposition 10 each many-valued interpretation I_E of the many-valued predicate logic $\mathcal{L}_E$ can be derived from the Tarski's interpretation I_T^*, it is sufficient to demonstrate that the Tarski's interpretation of the compressed virtual predicate $\phi_\alpha(\mathbf{x})$ is identical to the Tarski's interpretation of the atom $A(<\phi(\mathbf{x})>^{\beta}_{\alpha})$, for any given Tarski's interpretation I_T^*.

So from (1.29) in Section 1.3.1 and (2.17) above, we obtain for any assignment $g \in \mathcal{D}^{\mathcal{V}}$ directly that $I_T^*(\phi_\alpha(\mathbf{x})/g) = I_T^*(A(<\phi(\mathbf{x})>^{\beta}_{\alpha})/g)$. Then generally:

1. If β is not empty, then from (2.17),

$$\begin{aligned} I_T^*(\phi_\alpha(\mathbf{x})) &= \bigcup\{I_T^*(\phi_\alpha(\mathbf{x})/g) \mid g \in \mathcal{D}^{\beta}\} \\ &= \bigcup\{I_T^*(A(<\phi(\mathbf{x})>^{\beta}_{\alpha})/g) \mid g \in \mathcal{D}^{\beta}\} \\ &= I_T^*(A(<\phi(\mathbf{x})>^{\beta}_{\alpha})) \end{aligned}$$

   from (1.30) in Section 1.3.1.
2. If β is empty, then from (2.17),

$$I_T^*(\phi_\alpha(\mathbf{x})) = I_T^*(\phi(\mathbf{x})) = I_T^*(A(<\phi(\mathbf{x})>^{\beta}_{\alpha}))$$

   from (1.29) in Section 1.3.1. □

Note that in the case of the replacement of the compressed predicates by the atoms $A(<\phi(\mathbf{x})>^{\beta}_{\alpha})$, we do not need the extension of the Tarski's interpretation for a compressed predicate given by (2.17), which was necessary for the many-valued modal predicate logic $\mathcal{L}_E$. In fact, the Tarski's interpretation of $A(<\phi(\mathbf{x})>^{\beta}_{\alpha})$ and $A(<\phi(\mathbf{x})>^{\beta}_{\alpha}/g)$ are already provided for intensional FOL in Definition 17, Section 1.3.1:

$$I_T^*(A(<\phi(\mathbf{x})>^{\beta}_{\alpha})/g) =_{\text{def}} \begin{cases} \pi_{-\beta}(I_T^*(\phi[\beta/g(\beta)])) \subseteq \mathcal{D}^{|\alpha|}, & \text{if } \beta \text{ is not empty} \\ I_T^*(\phi(\mathbf{x})), & \text{otherwise} \end{cases} \quad (2.21)$$

and when β is not empty, $I_T^*(A(<\phi(\mathbf{x})>^{\beta}_{\alpha})) = \bigcup\{I_T^*(A(<\phi(\mathbf{x})>^{\beta}_{\alpha})/g) \mid g \in \mathcal{D}^{\beta}\}$.

Example 9 (*Constraint databases* (continuation of Example 7)). The concept of "class of spheres" given by a virtual predicate $\phi(\mathbf{x})$ with the tuple of free variables $\mathbf{x} = (x, x_0, y, y_0, z, z_0, v)$ where v represents the radius, $\{x_0, y_0, z_0\}$ coordinates of center and $\{x, y, z\}$ a point inside a sphere. This virtual predicate is provided by the built-in binary predicate $\leq ((x - x_0)^2 + (y - y_0)^2 + (z - z_0)^2, v^2)$, or with a common mathematical expression, $(x - x_0)^2 + (y - y_0)^2 + (z - z_0)^2 \leq v^2$. Let us now consider a compressed virtual predicate $\phi_\alpha(\mathbf{x}) \in \mathcal{L}_E$, where the set of hidden (compressed) variables is $\alpha = \{x, y, z\}$ and the set of visible variables is $\beta = \{v, x_0, y_0, z_0\}$, with the order-preserving tuple of hidden variables $\mathbf{y} = \pi_{-\beta}\mathbf{x} = (x, y, z)$ and the order-preserving tuple of visible variables $\mathbf{z} = \pi_{-\alpha}\mathbf{x} = (x_0, y_0, z_0, v)$. The logic formula of this compressed virtual predicate, by using the hidden quantifiers, is defined in intensional FOL by $A(\lessdot\phi(\mathbf{x})\gtrdot_\alpha^\beta)$, i. e., if $p_j^2 \in P$ is the built-in binary predicate "$\leq$," by

$$A(\lessdot p_j^2((x - x_0)^2 + (y - y_0)^2 + (z - z_0)^2, v^2)\gtrdot_\alpha^\beta) \tag{2.22}$$

Then a *concrete* concept of sphere, fixed by an assignment $g \in \mathcal{D}^{\mathcal{V}}$, with a radius $d = g(v)$ and the center in $(a, b, c) = g(x_0, y_0, z_0)''$, is given by the "ground" atom

$$A(\lessdot p_j^2((x - x_0)^2 + (y - y_0)^2 + (z - z_0)^2, v^2)\gtrdot_\alpha^\beta)/g,$$

i. e., to the atom $A(\lessdot p_j^2((x-a)^2 + (y-b)^2 + (z-c)^2, d^2)\gtrdot_{x,y,z})$. Note we do not need more of the logic-program constraint (2.6) for the definition of the semantics of these atoms, because they are rigid concepts whose extension is equal for any Tarski's interpretation $I_T^* \in \mathcal{W}_e$ (and corresponding extensionalization function $h = \mathcal{F}(I_T^*)$ such that for a fixed intensional interpretation I, $h \circ I = I_T^*$), defined by (1.29) in Section 1.3.1,

$$\begin{aligned}
&I_T^*(A(\lessdot p_j^2((x - a)^2 + (y - b)^2 + (z - c)^2, d^2)\gtrdot_{x,y,z})) \\
&\quad = \pi_{-\beta}(I_T^*(p_j^2((x - a)^2 + (y - b)^2 + (z - c)^2, d^2))) \\
&\quad = \{(g(x), g(y), g(z)) \mid g \in \mathcal{D}^{\mathcal{V}}, I_T(p_j^2((g(x) - a)^2 + (g(y) - b)^2 + (g(z) - c)^2, d^2)) = t\} \\
&\quad = \{(g(x), g(y), g(z)) \mid g \in \mathcal{D}^{\mathcal{V}}, ((g(x) - a)^2 + (g(y) - b)^2 + (g(z) - c)^2) \leq d^2\},
\end{aligned}$$

which represents all (infinite) points inside this sphere with radius equal to $d = g(v)$ and with a center in $(a, b, c) = (g(x_0), g(y_0), g(z_0))$. So, the intensional concept $I(A(\lessdot p_j^2((x - a)^2 + (y - b)^2 + (z - c)^2, d^2)\gtrdot_{x,y,z})) \in D_3$ is a *rigid concept* in intensional FOL. The advantage is that any assignment g cannot have the effects to the hidden variables in the atom (2.22), which remains the concept of a sphere, different from the binary atom with two terms $p_j^2((x - x_0)^2 + (y - y_0)^2 + (z - z_0)^2, v^2)$, which can be only true or false.

The utility of such conceptual organization of compressed predicates in the intensional FOL, provided by the example above, is also that we can use these constraint database concepts $A(\lessdot\phi(\mathbf{x})\gtrdot_\alpha^\beta)$, e. g., in (2.22), also to observe the knowledge hidden by compressed attributes in α, in a very simple way by controlling the truth of the sentences $\lhd A(<\phi(\mathbf{x})>^{\beta}_{\alpha})/g$, where "$\lhd$" is the inverse logic operator (w. r. t. the intensional abstraction operators) defined by (1.39) in Section 1.3.1.

It can be realized if we fix the intensional interpretation I for such sentences $\lhd A(<\phi(\mathbf{x})>^{\beta}_{\alpha})/g$ in a different way than that used for open (without any assignment $g \in \mathcal{D}^{\mathcal{V}}$) formula $\lhd A(<\phi(\mathbf{x})>^{\beta}_{\alpha})$ for which, by using (1.39) in Section 1.3.1, $I(\lhd A(<\phi(\mathbf{x})>^{\beta}_{\alpha})) = I(\phi(\mathbf{x})) \in D_{|\mathbf{x}|}$, that is by

$$I(\lhd A(<\phi(\mathbf{x})>^{\beta}_{\alpha})/g) =_{\text{def}} \text{pred}(g(\pi_{-\beta}\mathbf{x}), I(A(<\phi(\mathbf{x})>^{\beta}_{\alpha})/g)) \tag{2.23}$$

where the new intensional operator "pred" is defined by

$$\text{pred} : \mathcal{D}^k \times D_k \to D_0, \quad k = 1, 2, 3, \ldots \tag{2.24}$$

such that for any two $u_1 \in \mathcal{D}^k$ and $u \in D_k$, and an extensionalization function h,

$$h(\text{pred}(u_1, u)) = t \quad \text{iff} \quad u_1 \in h(u) \tag{2.25}$$

so that "pred" is a predication intensional operator (i. e., the membership relation). So, in (2.23), we have that $u_1 = g(\pi_{-\beta}\mathbf{x}) \in D^k_{-1}$ where $k = |\alpha|$, and $u = I(A(<\phi(\mathbf{x})>^{\beta}_{\alpha})/g)) \in D_k$, i. e., from (1.31) in Section 1.3.1,

$$u = I(A(<\phi(\mathbf{x})>^{\beta}_{\alpha})/g) =_{\text{def}} \begin{cases} I(\phi[\beta/g(\beta)]), & \text{if } \beta \text{ is not empty} \\ I(\phi(\mathbf{x})), & \text{otherwise} \end{cases} \tag{2.26}$$

Let us now consider the case when β is not empty, so that for a given extensionalization function h, and hence the Tarski's interpretation $I^*_T = h \circ I$, we obtain from (2.26) that $h(u) = h(I(A(<\phi(\mathbf{x})>^{\beta}_{\alpha})/g)) = I^*_T(A(<\phi(\mathbf{x})>^{\beta}_{\alpha})/g)$, i. e., from (2.21),

$$h(u) = \pi_{-\beta}(I^*_T(\phi[\beta/g(\beta)])) \subseteq \mathcal{D}^{|\alpha|}, \tag{2.27}$$

which is the extension of the tuples of hidden variables in α. So, if we would like that a tuple of values $\mathbf{d} \in \mathcal{D}^{|\alpha|}$ is an element or not of $h(u)$ in (2.27), then we define an assignment $g' \in \mathcal{D}^{\alpha \bigcup \beta}$ such that $g'(\pi_{-\beta}\mathbf{x}) = \mathbf{d}$ and for each $x_j \in \beta$, $g'(x_j) = g(x_j)$, then the question if $\mathbf{d}$ is in $h(u)$, it corresponds to the truth of the membership relation:

if $u_1 = g'(\pi_{-\beta}\mathbf{x}) \in h(u) = h(I(A(<\phi(\mathbf{x})>^{\beta}_{\alpha})/g'))$,
if $h(\text{pred}(u_1, u))$ is true,
if $h(I(\lhd A(<\phi(\mathbf{x})>^{\beta}_{\alpha})/g'))$ is true, (from (2.23))
if $I^*_T(\lhd A(<\phi(\mathbf{x})>^{\beta}_{\alpha})/g')$ is true (from $I^*_T = h \circ I$, Proposition 7 in Section 1.3.1).

That is, if we consider the concrete sphere in the previous example (2.22), $A(<p^2_j((x-x_0)^2+(y-y_0)^2+(z-z_0)^2, v^2)>^{\beta}_{\alpha})/g$, with the tuple of hidden variables $\pi_{-\beta}\mathbf{x} = (x, y, z)$ corresponding to the points inside this sphere with coordinate center $(g'(x_0), g'(y_0), g'(z_0))$

and radius $g'(v)$, then the question if the point **d** is inside this particular sphere corresponds to the truth of the sentence

$$\lhd A(<p_j^2((x-x_0)^2+(y-y_0)^2+(z-z_0)^2,v^2)>_\alpha^\beta)/g' \quad (2.28)$$

in a given Tarski's interpretation I_T^* of the constraint database where this sphere (2.22) is defined. Consequently, we can observe the hidden tuples of values of a compressed predicates, by the Tarski's truth of the sentence (2.28).

In a similar way, e. g., we can define the intersection of two different spheres, defined by the sentence, where $\phi(\mathbf{x})$ is equal to atom $p_j^2((x-x_0)^2+(y-y_0)^2+(z-z_0)^2,v^2)$,

$$A(<\phi(\mathbf{x})>_\alpha^\beta)/g \wedge A(<\phi(\mathbf{x})>_\alpha^\beta)/g'$$

for two different assignments $g \neq g'$ of the class sphere, with intensional interpretation

$$I(A(<\phi(\mathbf{x})>_\alpha^\beta)/g \wedge A(<\phi(\mathbf{x})>_\alpha^\beta)/g') = \mathrm{conj}(I(A(<\phi(\mathbf{x})>_\alpha^\beta)/g), I(A(<\phi(\mathbf{x})>_\alpha^\beta)/g)).$$

Then, for the sentence,

$$\lhd (A(<\phi(\mathbf{x})>_\alpha^\beta)/g \wedge A(<\phi(\mathbf{x})>_\alpha^\beta)/g'), \quad (2.29)$$

we obtain its intensional interpretation,

$$I(\lhd (A(<\phi(\mathbf{x})>_\alpha^\beta)/g \wedge A(<\phi(\mathbf{x})>_\alpha^\beta)/g')) = \mathrm{pred}(\pi_{-\beta}\mathbf{x}, u), \quad \text{where}$$

$$u = I(A(<\phi(\mathbf{x})>_\alpha^\beta)/g \wedge A(<\phi(\mathbf{x})>_\alpha^\beta)/g') = \mathrm{conj}(I(A(<\phi(\mathbf{x})>_\alpha^\beta)/g), I(A(<\phi(\mathbf{x})>_\alpha^\beta)/g)),$$

and hence

$$h(u) = I(A(<\phi(\mathbf{x})>_\alpha^\beta)/g) \bigcap I(A(<\phi(\mathbf{x})>_\alpha^\beta)/g)$$

Consequently, the answer if the point **d** is inside the intersection of these two spheres is given by the truth value of the sentence (2.29) for a given Tarski's interpretation of the constraint database.

Thus, by using "A" atoms to define different geometrical objects (by a compression of different virtual predicates), and logic connectives $\neg$, $\wedge$ and $\vee$ we are able to obtain the sentence describing very complex geometrical objets, and to use the same method, presented previously for the intersection of two spheres, to verify if some given point is inside or outside such complex objects.

Notice that this techniques can be used also for the applications which use the nonrigid intensional concepts obtained from the compressed virtual predicates.

2.1.4 Invariances and symmetries in predicate compression transformations

The knowledge-conservative predicate compression transforms any given atom $p_j^k(\mathbf{x})$ with the tuple (sequence) of variables $\mathbf{x} = (x_1, \ldots, x_k)$ (the set of these variables is denoted by $\overline{\mathbf{x}} = \{x_1, \ldots, x_k\}$) into the compressed predicate denoted by $p_\alpha(\mathbf{x})$ where $\alpha \subseteq \overline{\mathbf{x}}$ is a non-empty subset of hidden variables, and by $\beta = \overline{\mathbf{x}} - \alpha$ we denote the remaining subset of visible (free) variables, as specified by Definition 23 in Section 2.1.1. Based on the Corollary 10 in Section 2.1.3, such a compressed predicate $p_\alpha(\mathbf{x})$ (by using hidden quantifiers for the variables in α) is represented by the atom $A(<p_j^k(\mathbf{x})>_\alpha^\beta)$ in the intensional FOL with intensional abstraction operators (1.29).

In what follows, the subtuple (preserving ordering of variables) of the tuple $\mathbf{x}$ composed by all variables in β is denoted by $\mathbf{y}$, while the subtuple composed by all variables in α is denoted by $\mathbf{z}$, with the bijective permutation mapping (in point 4 of Definition 23), $is_{\mathbf{x}/\alpha} : \mathfrak{D}(\mathbf{x}) \to \mathfrak{D}(\mathbf{z}) \times \mathfrak{D}(\mathbf{y})$, such that it divides the tuples of constants in $\mathfrak{D}(\mathbf{x}) =_{\text{def}} \{g(\mathbf{x}) \mid g \in \mathcal{D}^{\overline{\mathbf{x}}}\}$ into two order-preserving subtuples of hidden and visible attributes.

From the fact that a predicate compression regards each single predicate, we define the category $\mathbf{D} = \mathbf{Sch}(G_{p_j^k})$ for a k-ary predicate p_j^k, obtained from the graph $G_{p_j^k}$ with unique arrow $p_j^k(\mathbf{x}) : \mathbf{x} \to x_X$ representing a nonground atom of this predicate. Note that all variables in $\mathbf{x}$ are "object" variables, while x_X is distinguished "metavariable" of logic truth values.

Thus, for any given assignment of free variables in β, $g \in \mathcal{D}^\beta$, and given Tarski's interpretation I_T^* of intensional FOL with abstraction operators and the special unary predicate $A(\_)$ with semantics specified by (1.29) in Definition 18, we can express the logic equivalence of the "ground" compressed atom $A(<p_j^k(\mathbf{x})>_\alpha^\beta)/g$ with hidden variables in α with the standard (noncompressed) atom $p_j^k(\mathbf{x}[\beta/g(\beta)])$ where the variables in α remain to be free variables (exposed to logic quantification and assignments) by using functorial models in the category of functors $\mathbf{Set}^{\mathbf{D}}$ with the same method used in Definition 22.

Definition 26. Let, for a k-ary predicate $p_j^k \in P$, the category $\mathbf{D} = \mathbf{Sch}(G_{p_j^k})$ be obtained from the graph $G_{p_j^k}$ with a unique nonground atom's arrow $p_j^k(\mathbf{x}) : \mathbf{x} \to x_X$. Then given Tarski's interpretation I_T^* and assignment $g \in \mathcal{D}^\beta$, such that $\mathbf{z}$ is the subtuple of $\mathbf{x}$ composed by only variables in $\alpha = \overline{\mathbf{x}} - \beta$, we can introduce the following functors:

1. The covariant functor $F(I_T^*; g) = (F^0, F^1) : \mathbf{D} \to \mathbf{Set}$, a model of $p_j^k(\mathbf{x})[\beta/g(\beta)]$, such that $F^0(x_X) = \mathbf{2} = \{f, t\}$ and $F^0(\mathbf{x}) = \mathfrak{D}(\mathbf{x}[\beta/g(\beta)])$ is the subset of $\mathfrak{D}(\mathbf{x})$ in which all attributes in $\beta \subset \overline{\mathbf{x}}$ are fixed by assignment g. The arrow component F^1 of this functor for the unique nonidentity arrow $p_j^k(\mathbf{x}) : \mathbf{x} \to x_X$ in $\mathbf{D}$ is defined by the function $F^1(p_j^k(\mathbf{x})) = f_\emptyset : \mathfrak{D}(\mathbf{x}[\beta/g(\beta)]) \to \mathbf{2}$, such that for each assignment $g' : \alpha \to \mathcal{D}$,

$$f_\emptyset(\mathbf{x}[\beta/g(\beta), \alpha/g'(\alpha)]) = t \quad \text{iff} \quad g'(\mathbf{z}) \in I_T^*(p_j^k(\mathbf{x})[\beta/g(\beta)]) \tag{2.30}$$

2. The covariant functor $G(I_T^*; g) = (G^0, G^1) : \mathbf{D} \to \mathbf{Set}$, a model of the compressed predicate, such that $G^0(x_X) = \mathbf{2}$ and $G^0(\mathbf{x}) = \mathfrak{D}(\mathbf{z})$. The arrow component G^1 of this functor for the unique nonidentity arrow $p_j^k(\mathbf{x}) : \mathbf{x} \to x_X$ in $\mathbf{D}$ is defined by the function $G^1(p_j^k(\mathbf{x})) = l : \mathfrak{D}(\mathbf{z}) \to \mathbf{2}$, such that for each assignment $g' : \alpha \to \mathcal{D}$,

$$l(g'(\mathbf{z})) = t \quad \text{iff} \quad g'(\mathbf{z}) \in I_T^*(A(<p_j^k(\mathbf{x})>_\alpha^\beta)/g) \tag{2.31}$$

Note that the function $f_\emptyset$ in (2.30) is derived from the extension of the (standard) atom $p_j^k(\mathbf{x})[\beta/g(\beta)]$ while the function l in (2.31) is derived from the extension of the compressed atom $A(<p_j^k(\mathbf{x})>_\alpha^\beta)/g$, and that from (1.29) for any Tarski's interpretation I_T^* their extension is equal (knowledge remains invariant by predicate compression), so that for every assignment $g' \in \mathcal{D}^\alpha$, from (2.30) and (2.302) we obtain the equality

$$l(g'(\mathbf{z})) = f_\emptyset(\mathbf{x}[\beta/g(\beta), \alpha/g'(\alpha)]) \tag{2.32}$$

The knowledge invariance of the predicate compression transformation shown in all details in Section 2.1 can be formalized by the following.

Corollary 11. *The knowledge* invariance *of the predicate compression transformations is based on categorial* natural isomorphism *symmetry* $\tau : F(I_T^*; g) \xrightarrow{\bullet} G(I_T^*; g)$ *of functors (models) in Definition 26, for a given Tarski's interpretation* I_T^* *and assignment* $g \in \mathcal{D}^\beta$.

Proof. Let us consider the arrow $p_j^k(\mathbf{x}) : \mathbf{x} \to x_X$ in the category $\mathbf{D} = \mathbf{Sch}(G_{p_j^k})$. Let us show that the natural transformation τ applied to the arrow $p_j^k(\mathbf{d})$, generates the following natural transformation diagram in **Set**:

$$\begin{array}{ccc} A = F^0(\mathbf{x}) = \mathfrak{D}(\mathbf{x}[\beta/g(\beta)]) & \xrightarrow{\tau_A} & \mathfrak{D}(\mathbf{z}) = G^0(\mathbf{x}) \\ f_\emptyset = F^1(p_j^k(\mathbf{d})) \downarrow & & \downarrow l = G^1(p_j^k(\mathbf{d})) \\ B = F^0(x_X) = \mathbf{2} & \xrightarrow{\tau_B} & \mathbf{2} = G^0(x_X) \end{array} \tag{2.33}$$

where for τ_A is the isomorphism, such that for each k-ary tuple $\mathbf{d}_n \in \mathfrak{D}(\mathbf{x}[\beta/g(\beta)])$, $\tau_A(\mathbf{d}_n) = \pi_{-\beta}\mathbf{d}_n \in \mathfrak{D}(\mathbf{z})$, and τ_B is an identity arrow (thus isomorphic as well) of the object $B = \mathbf{2}$. This diagram commutes (easy to verify from (2.32) for $\mathbf{d}_n = \mathbf{x}[\beta/g(\beta), \alpha/g'(\alpha)]$ and $\pi_{-\beta}\mathbf{d}_n = g'(\mathbf{z})$ for an assignment $g' : \alpha \to \mathcal{D}$). So, all components τ_A are isomorphic arrows, and hence τ is natural isomorphism. Note that the isomorphism between objects of a category is a general case of the categorial *symmetry of the objects.* □

Consequently, as we have seen previously in Section 1.3.2 for two examples of transformation we obtained two different symmetries: for the reification transformation, we obtained the internal categorial symmetry between morphisms and objects but not the logic knowledge invariance; for the ontological encapsulation transformation, we obtained the symmetry of morphisms of categorial duality principle (between category and its opposite category) and logic knowledge invariance (symmetry) as well. Here, instead, for the compression predicate transformations we obtain the symmetry of objects (the isomorphism of objects, in our case in the category of functors).

Thus, as in the case of the laws of nature that are results of specific symmetries expressed by partial differential equations, also in the case of computer science, some laws of invariant knowledge transformations are the result of specific symmetries.

2.2 Nilsson's structures and probabilistic logics

The probability theory is a well-studied branch of mathematics, in order to carry out formal reasoning about probability. Thus, it is important to have a logic, both for computation of probabilities and for reasoning about probabilities, with a well-defined syntax and semantics. Both current approaches, based on Nilsson's probability structures/logics, and on linear inequalities in order to reason about probabilities, have some weak points.

In this section, we will present the complete revision of both approaches. We have shown that the full embedding of Nilsson's probabilistic structure into propositional logic results in a *truth-functional* many-valued logic, different from Nilsson's intuition and current considerations about propositional probabilistic logic. Then we will show that the logic for reasoning *about* probabilities can be naturally embedded into a 2-valued intensional FOL with intensional abstraction, by avoiding the current ad hoc system composed of *two different* 2-valued logics: one for the classical propositional logic at a lower-level, and a new one at a higher-level for probabilistic constraints with probabilistic variables. The obtained theoretical results are then applied to probabilistic logic programming.

The main motivation for an introduction of the intensionality in the probabilistic theory of the propositional logic is based on the desire to have the *full* logical embedding of the probability into the First-Order Logic (FOL), with a clear difference from the classic concept of truth of the logic formulae and the concept of their probabilities. In this way, we are able to replace the ad hoc syntax and semantics, used in current practice for probabilistic logic programs [14, 16, 70, 71] and probabilistic deduction [72], by the standard syntax and semantics used for the FOL where the probabilistic theory properties are expressed simply by the particular constraints on their interpretations and models.

In this section, we will consider the probabilistic semantics for the propositional logic (it can be easily extended to predicate logics as well) [62, 63] with a fixed finite set $P = \{p_1, \dots, p_n\}$ of primitive propositions, which can be thought of as corresponding to basic probabilistic events. The set $\mathcal{L}(P)$ of the propositional formulae is the closure of P under the Boolean operations for conjunction and negation, $\wedge$ and $\neg$, i. e., it is the set of all formulae of the *propositional* logic $(P, \{\wedge, \neg\})$.

In order to give the probabilistic semantics to such formulae, we first need to review briefly the probability theory (see, e. g., [73, 74]).

Definition 27. A probability space $(S, \mathcal{X}, \mu)$ consists of a set S, called the sample space, a σ-algebra $\mathcal{X}$ of subsets of S (i. e., a set of subsets of S containing S and closed under complementation and countable union, but not necessarily consisting of all subsets of S) whose elements are called measurable sets, and a probability measure $\mu : \mathcal{X} \to [0, 1]$ where $[0, 1]$ is the closed interval of reals from 0 to 1. This mapping satisfies Kolmogorov axioms [75]:
A.1 $\mu \geq 0$ for all $X \in \mathcal{X}$.
A.2 $\mu(S) = 1$.
A.3 $\mu(\bigcup_{i\geq 1} X_i) = \sum_{i\geq 1} \mu(X_i)$,

if X_i's are nonempty pairwise disjoint members of $\mathcal{X}$. We define a probability density function, $\mathrm{KI} = \mu \circ \mathrm{in}$, where $\mathrm{in} : S \hookrightarrow \mathcal{P}(S)$ is an inclusion such that $\mathrm{in}(s) = \{s\}$.

The $\mu(\{s\}) = \mathrm{KI}(s)$ is the value of probability in a single point of space s.

The property A.3 is called *countable additivity* for the probabilities in a space S. In the case when $\mathcal{X}$ is a finite set, then we can simplify property A.3 above to
A.3′ $\mu(X \bigcup Y) = \mu(X) + \mu(Y)$,

if X and Y are disjoint members of $\mathcal{X}$, or, equivalently, to the following axiom:
A.3″ $\mu(X) = \mu(X \bigcap Y) + \mu(X \bigcap \overline{Y})$,

where $\overline{Y}$ is the compliment of Y in S, so that $\mu(\overline{X}) = 1 - \mu(X)$.

In what follows, we will consider only finite sample space S, so that $\mathcal{X} = \mathcal{P}(S)$. Thus, in our case of a finite set S we obtain, form A.1 and A.2, that for any $X \in \mathcal{P}(S)$,

$$\mu(X) = \sum_{s \in X} \mu(\{s\}) = \sum_{s \in X} \mathrm{KI}(s) \tag{2.34}$$

Based on the work of Nilsson in [62], we can define for a given propositional logic with a finite set of primitive propositions P the sample space $S = \mathbf{2}^P$, where $\mathbf{2} = \{0, 1\} \subset [0, 1]$, so that the probability space is equal to the Nilsson's structure $N = (\mathbf{2}^P, \mathcal{P}(\mathbf{2}^P), \mu)$.

In his work (p. 2, lines 4–6 in [62]) Nilsson considered a probabilistic logic "in which the truth values of sentences can range between 0 and 1. The truth value of a sentence in *probabilistic logic* is taken to be the probability of that sentence in ordinary first-order logic." That is, he considered this logic as a kind of a *many-valued*, but not a compositional truth-valued logic. But in his paper he did not define the formal syntax and semantics for such a probabilistic logic, but only the matrix equations where the probability of a sentence $\phi \in \mathcal{L}(P)$ is the sum of the probabilities of the sets of possible worlds (equal to the set $S = \mathbf{2}^P$) in which that sentence is *true*. So that he assigns *two* different logic values to each sentence ϕ: one is its probability value and another is a classic 2-valued truth value in a given possible world $v \in \mathcal{W} = S = \mathbf{2}^P$.

The *logic* inadequacy of this seminal work [62] of Nilsson is also considered in [76], by extending this Nilsson's structure into a more general *probability structure* $M = (\mathbf{2}^P, \mathcal{P}(\mathbf{2}^P), \mu, \pi)$, where π associates with each $s \in S = \mathbf{2}^P$ the truth assignment $\pi(s) : P \to \mathbf{2}$. However, in our case when $S = \mathbf{2}^P$, π is just an identity, so not necessary, and we consider each s as a truth valuation $s = v : P \to \{0, 1\}$, which can be uniquely extended to the truth assignment v^* to all formulae in $\mathcal{L}(P)$, by taking the usual rules of propositional logic (the unique homomorphic extension to all formulae), and we can associate to each propositional formula $\phi \in \mathcal{L}(P)$ the set ϕ^M consisting of all states $s \in S$ where the sentence ϕ is true, so that

$$\|\phi\| = \{v \in \mathcal{W} = \mathbf{2}^P \mid v^*(\phi) = 1\}.$$

But, different from Nilsson, in [76] we did not define a many-valued propositional logic, but a kind of 2-valued logic based on probabilistic constraints. They denoted by $w_N(\phi)$ the *weight* or *probability* of ϕ in Nilsson structure N, correspondent to the value $\mu(\|\phi\|)$, so that the basic probabilistic 2-valued constraint can be defined by expressions $c_1 \leq w_N(\phi)$ and $w_N(\phi) \leq c_2$ for given constants $c_1, c_2 \in [0, 1]$. They expected their logic to be used for reasoning *about* probabilities. But, again, they did not define a unique logic, but *two different* logics: one for the classical propositional logic $\mathcal{L}(P)$, and a new one for 2-valued probabilistic constraints obtained from the basic probabilistic formulae above and Boolean operators $\wedge$ and $\neg$. They did not consider the introduced symbol w_N as a formal functional symbol for a mapping $w_N : \mathcal{L}(P) \to [0, 1]$, such that for any propositional formula $\phi \in \mathcal{L}(P)$, with $\mathcal{W} = S = \mathbf{2}^P$, the probability of sentence ϕ is

$$w_N(\phi) = \mu(\|\phi\|) = \sum_{v \in \mathcal{W}} \mathrm{KI}(s).$$

Instead of this intuitive meaning for w_N, they considered each expression $w_N(\phi)$ as a particular probabilistic term (more precisely, as a structured probabilistic *variable* over the domain of values in $[0, 1]$).

It seams that such a dichotomy and difficulty to have *a unique* 2-valued probabilistic logic, both for an original propositional formulae in $\mathcal{L}(P)$ and for the probabilistic constraints, is based on the fact that if we consider w_N as a function with one argument then it has to be formally represented as a binary predicate $w_N(\phi, a)$ (for the graph of this function) where the first argument is a formula and the second is its resulting probability value. Consequently, a constraint "the probability of ϕ is less or equal to c," has to be formally expressed by the logic formula $w_N(\phi, a) \wedge \leq (a, c)$ (here we use a symbol $\leq$ as a built-in rigid binary predicate where $\leq (a, c)$ is equivalent to $a \leq c$), which is a *second-order* syntax because ϕ is a logic *formula* in such a unified logic language. That is, the problem of obtaining the unique logical framework for probabilistic logic comes out with the necessity of a *reification* feature of this logic language, analogously to the case of the intensional semantics for RDF data structures [77] in Section 2.3.

Consequently, we need a logic, which is able to deal directly with reification of logic formulae, that transforms a propositional formulae $\phi \in \mathcal{L}(P)$ into an abstracted *term*, denoted by $<\phi>$ (Section 1.3.1). By this approach, the expression $w_N(<\phi>, a) \wedge \leq (a, c)$ remains to be an ordinary first-order formula. In fact, if $<\phi>$ is translated into a nonsentence "that ϕ," then the first-order formula above corresponds to the sentence "the probability `that` ϕ is true is less than or equal to c."

2.2.1 Probabilistic algebra for Nilsson's structure

The work of Jan Lukasiewicz was without doubt the most influential in the development of many-valued modal logics [78–81]. In Lukasiewicz's conception, the real definition of a logic must be semantic and truth-functional (the logic connectives are to be truth functions operating on these logical values): "logic is the science of objects of a specific kind, namely a science of *logical values*." Many-valued logics are nonclassical logics. They are similar to classical logic because they accept the principle of truth functionality, namely, that the truth of a compound sentence is determined by the truth values of its component sentences (and so remains unaffected when one of its component sentences is replaced by another sentence with the same truth value). But they differ from classical logic by the fundamental fact that they do not restrict the number of truth values to only two: they allow for a larger set of truth degrees. Introduction to many-valued logic and $\mathcal{O}$-matrices is provided in the dedicated chapter, Section 5.1 by Definition 54. We will use the reduction of Nielsen's many-valued logic into 2-valued logic, by reification of sentences into a particular binary predicate w_N, by ontological encapsulation, and more information is provided in Section A.4.2 in the Appendix.

Lukasiewicz's work promoted the concept of *logic matrix*, a central concept for the construction of many-valued logics, implicit in the works of C. S. Pierce and E. Post as well (see also the second, nonmatrix based method in Section 5.1.1 and also in Section A.4.4 in the Appendix). We denote by $\mathcal{L}(P)$ the set of all formulae. Lindenbaum algebra of $\mathcal{L}$ is the quotient algebra $\mathcal{L}(P)_{\equiv}$, where for any two formulae $\phi, \psi \in \mathcal{L}(P)$, holds the equivalence $\phi \equiv \psi$ iff $\phi \Vdash \psi$ and $\psi \Vdash \phi$. The standard approach to matrices uses a subset $D \subset X$ of the set of truth-values X (nullary operators, i. e., logic constants), denominated designated elements; informally a designated element represent an equivalence class of the *theorems* in $\mathcal{L}$. Given an algebra $\mathbf{A} = (X, \{o\}_{o \in \mathcal{O}})$, the $\mathcal{O}$-matrix is the pair $(\mathbf{A}, D)$, where $D \subset X$ is a subset of designated elements.

Any modal 2-valued logic can be considered as a many-valued truth-functional logic for a given set $\mathcal{W}$ of possible worlds as well, given by a complex algebra $\mathbf{A}^+ = (X^+, \subseteq, \{\bigcap, \bigcup, /, m, l\})$ of "truth-values," where $X^+ \subseteq \mathcal{P}(\mathcal{W})$ is the complete lattice of "truth values" (see, e. g., the case of the autoreferential canonic representation, with the isomorphism (5.10) in Section 5.1.2) and $\bigcap, \bigcup, /$ are algebraic operations for conjunction, disjunction and negation (i.e„ the set-intersection, set-union and set-substraction operators), respectively, while m and l are algebraic operations for universal and existential modal logic operators: in this approach the "truth value" of a given sentence ϕ is equal to the subset of possible worlds $\|\phi\|$ where this formula ϕ is satisfied, i. e., equal to $\{w \in \mathcal{W} \mid \mathcal{M} \models_w \phi\} \in \mathcal{P}(\mathcal{W})$ (the general case of Kripke semantics for many-valued logics is provided by Definition 65 and Theorem 17 in Section 5.1.2). In what follows, we set that $\mathcal{W} =_{\text{def}} S$ (sample space in Definition 27).

Notice that instead of a set-based algebra $\mathbf{A}^+ = (X^+, \subseteq, \{\bigcap, \bigcup, /, m, l\})$ we can use the functional algebra $(\widetilde{A}, \{\widetilde{\bigcap}, \widetilde{\bigcup}, \widetilde{/}, \widetilde{m}, \widetilde{l}\})$ with higher order "truth values" [82, 83] given by functions in the functional space $\widetilde{A} = \mathbf{2}^S$, where for each $Y \in \mathcal{P}(S)$ we have the correspondent functional truth-value $f \in \mathbf{2}^S$, such that for any possible world $s \in S$ it holds that $f(s) = 1$ iff $s \in Y$. For example, the function $f \widetilde{\bigcap} g : S \to \mathbf{2}$ is defined for any $s \in S$ by $(f \widetilde{\bigcap} g)(s) = \min\{f(s), g(s)\}$, while $(f \widetilde{\bigcup} g)(s) = \max\{f(s), g(s)\}$ and $(\widetilde{/} f)(s) = 1 - f(s)$.

For any function $f \in \mathbf{2}^S$, we denote its image by $\mathrm{Im}(f) = \{s \in S \mid f(s) = 1\}$, so that $\mathrm{Im}(f \widetilde{\bigcap} g) = \mathrm{Im}(f) \bigcap \mathrm{Im}(g)$ and $\mathrm{im}(\widetilde{/} f) = S / \mathrm{Im}(f)$. Hence, we define basic functional algebra $\mathbf{A}_f = (\mathbf{2}^S, \leq, \widetilde{\bigcap}, \widetilde{/})$, with $f \leq g$ iff $\mathrm{im}(f) \subseteq \mathrm{im}(g)$, so that $\widetilde{\bigcap}$ is meet lattice operation. Here we consider the possibility to have also infinite matrices for many-valued truth-functional logics, different from other approaches that consider only finite matrices [84]. In fact, based on Nilsson's probabilistic structure $N = (\mathbf{2}^P, \mathcal{P}(\mathbf{2}^P), \mu)$, we can define the following many-valued *probabilistic algebra*.

Definition 28. Let $N = (\mathbf{2}^P, \mathcal{P}(\mathbf{2}^P), \mu)$ be Nilsson's structure with a sample space $S = \mathbf{2}^P$. Then we define the probabilistic algebra $\mathbf{A} = (X, \curlywedge, \sim)$ based on the complete distributive lattice $(X, \preccurlyeq) =_{\text{def}} (\mathbf{A}_f \times [0,1], \leq)$ of truth values such that $(f, x) \preccurlyeq (g, y)$ iff $\mathrm{im}(f) \subseteq \mathrm{im}(g)$ and $x \leq y$, with the $\mathcal{O}$-matrix (A, D) where $D = \{(f, \mu(\mathrm{im}(f))) \mid f \in \mathbf{2}^S\}$ is a set of designated elements. Modal binary operator p-conjunction "$\curlywedge$" and unary operator p-negation "$\sim$" are defined as follows:

$$\curlywedge((f,x),(g,y)) = \begin{cases} (f \widetilde{\bigcap} g, \mu(\mathrm{Im}(f \widetilde{\bigcap} g))), & \text{if } x = \mu(\mathrm{im}(f)) \text{ and } y = \mu(\mathrm{im}(g)) \\ (f \widetilde{\bigcap} g, 0), & \text{otherwise} \end{cases}$$

$$\sim (f,x) = \begin{cases} (\widetilde{/} f, \mu(\mathrm{im}(\widetilde{/} f))), & \text{if } x = \mu(\mathrm{im}(f)) \\ (\widetilde{/} f, 0), & \text{otherwise} \end{cases} \tag{2.35}$$

Notice that each truth value of this algebra is a pair of elements $\mathbf{a} = (f,x) \in X = \mathbf{2}^P \times [0,1]$: first, a function $f = \pi_1(\mathbf{a}) : S \to \{0,1\}$ that defines the set of possible worlds in S where a propositional formula in $\mathcal{L}(P)$ is satisfied, while the second element $x = \pi_2(\mathbf{a})$ is the probability of this formula (here $\pi_i, i = 1,2$ are first and second Cartesian projections), so that the meet and join operators of this complete distributive lattice is defined by $(f,x)\bigwedge(g,y) = (f\widetilde{\bigcap}g, \min(x,y))$ and $(f,x)\bigvee(g,y) = (f\widetilde{\bigcup}g, \max(x,y))$, relatively.

The set of truth values in X is infinite, but its subset of designated elements is finite for the finite set of propositional variables in P. Let us show that this algebra represents a *truth-functional* many-valued semantics for the propositional Nilsson's probabilistic logic.

Proposition 11. *Let* $\mathbf{A} = (X, \curlywedge, \sim)$ *be probabilistic algebra of Nislon's structure* $N = (\mathbf{2}^P, \mathcal{P}(\mathbf{2}^P), \mu)$ *with a sample space* $S = \mathbf{2}^P$, *with the* $X = \mathbf{2}^S \times [0,1]$ *and* $\mathcal{O}$*-matrix* $(\mathbf{A}, D)$ *given by Definition 28. Each valuation* $v : P \to X$ *is a mapping that assigns the logic values to propositional variables, such that for any* $p \in P$,

$$v(p) =_{\text{def}} (f, \mu(\text{Im}(f))), \quad \textit{for } f : S \to \mathbf{2} \textit{ such that } \forall s \in S.f(s) = s(p).$$

We denote by $v^* : (\mathcal{L}(P), \wedge, \neg) \to \mathbf{A}$ *the unique homomorphic extension of* v *to all formulae of the propositional logic* $(\mathcal{L}(P), \wedge, \neg)$.

Then, for any propositional formula $\phi \in \mathcal{L}(P)$ *we have that* $(\mathbf{A}, D) \vDash_v^a \phi$ *implies that* $\pi_2(v^*(\phi))$ *is the Nilsson's probability of* ϕ. *That is, a many-valued truth-functional assignment* v^* *is a* `model` *for this propositional probabilistic logic.*

Proof. Let us demonstrate this proposition by structural induction on formulae $\phi \in \mathcal{L}(P)$:

1. For any basic propositional formula $p \in P$, we have that $(\mathbf{A}, D) \vDash_v^a p$ (it holds that $v(p) = (f, \mu(\text{Im}(f))) \in D$).

Let us suppose that $\phi_1, \phi_2 \in \mathcal{L}(P)$ satisfy this property, i. e., $v^*(\phi_1) = (f, \mu(\text{Im}(f))) \in D$ and $v^*(\phi_2) = (g, \mu(\text{Im}(g))) \in D$. Then we have the following two cases:

Case 2.1 When $\phi = \phi_1 \wedge \phi_2$. Then

$$\begin{aligned}
v^*(\phi) &= v^*(\phi_1 \wedge \phi_2)\\
&= \curlywedge(v^*(\phi_1), v^*(\phi_2)) \quad \text{(from the homomorphic property)}\\
&= \curlywedge((f, \mu(\text{Im}(f))), (g, \mu(\text{Im}(g)))) = \left(f\widetilde{\bigcap}g, \mu\left(\text{Im}(f)\bigcap\text{Im}(g)\right)\right) \quad \text{(from Def. 28)}\\
&= \left(f\widetilde{\bigcap}g, \mu\left(\text{Im}\left(f\widetilde{\bigcap}g\right)\right)\right) \in D \quad \left(\text{from } f\widetilde{\bigcap}g \in \mathbf{2}^S\right).
\end{aligned}$$

Case 2.2 When $\phi = \neg\phi_1$. Then

$$\begin{aligned}
v^*(\phi) &= v^*(\neg\phi_1)\\
&=\sim (v^*(\phi_1)) \quad \text{(from homomorphic property)}
\end{aligned}$$

$$=\sim (f,\mu(\mathrm{Im}(f))) = (\widetilde{\rceil}(f),\mu(S/\mathrm{Im}(f))) \quad \text{(from Definition 28)}$$
$$= (\widetilde{\rceil}(f),\mu(\mathrm{Im}(\widetilde{\rceil}(f)))) \in D \quad (\text{from } \widetilde{\rceil}(f) \in \mathbf{2}^S).$$

Thus, for any $\phi \in \mathcal{L}(P)$ we have that $v^*(\phi) = (f,\mu(\mathrm{Im}(f))$, where $f : S \to \mathbf{2}$ satisfies for any $s \in S = \mathbf{2}^P$ that $f(s) = 1$ if $\overline{s}(\phi) = 1$, so that $\mu(\mathrm{Im}(f)) = \pi_2(v^*(\phi))$ is the Nilsson's probability of the formula ϕ. From the fact that for any $\phi \in \mathcal{L}(P)$ holds that $(\mathbf{A},D) \vDash_v^a \phi$, we deduce that v^* is a *model* for this propositional probabilistic logic. □

Notice that for a given propositional logic $(\mathcal{L}(P),\wedge,\neg)$ and Nilsson's structure $N = (\mathbf{2}^P,\mathcal{P}(\mathbf{2}^P),\mu)$, a model $v^* : (\mathcal{L}(P),\wedge,\neg) \to \mathbf{A}$ computes the probabilities of all formulae in $\mathcal{L}(P)$. But there is no way for this many-valued propositional logic $(\mathcal{L}(P),\wedge,\neg)$ to reason *about* these probabilities. Notice that this approach to probabilistic many-valued logic demonstrate that, different from Nilsson's remark (1.3–5, p. 72 in [62]):

> "...we present a semantic generalization of ordinary first-order logic in which the truth values of sentences can range between 0 and 1. The truth value of a sentence in *probabilistic logic* is taken to be the *probability* of that sentence ..."

The truth value of a sentence *is not the probability* of that sentence but the pair (f,a) where the first element $f \in \mathbf{2}^S$ is a mapping from the sample space $S = \mathbf{2}^P$ into the set $\mathbf{2}$; only its second component $a \in [0,1]$ is the probability of that sentence. It demonstrates that his intuition was only correct but approximative one, and hence we need this complete and formal revision of his original intuition.

The second consequence is that, different from THE current opinion in the computer science community that the probabilistic logic is not truth-functionally many-valued logic, we demonstrated that indeed *it is*: the truth value of a complex sentence is functionally dependent on the truth values of its proper subsentences, as in standard many-valued logics.

2.2.2 Probabilistic logic reasoning and intensionality

In order to reason about probabilities of the logic formulae, both of propositional logic with sample space $S = \mathbf{2}^P$ or a predicate logic where P is the set of predicate symbols and $S = \mathbf{2}^{H_F}$ where H_F is Herbrand base of this logic, we need a kind of 2-valued metalogic with *reification* features [85]; thus, a kind of intensional FOL with *intensional abstraction* was presented in Section 1.3.1.

The *intensional abstract terms* are "that clauses" so that, for a logic formula $\phi(\mathbf{x})$, "that ϕ" is denoted by the ground abstracted term $<\phi(\mathbf{x})[\beta/g(\beta)]>_\alpha$ (if ϕ is a sentence then both α and β are empty). Hence, the sentence "the probability that a sentence ϕ is less then or equal to c" is expressed by the first-order logic formula $w_N(<\phi>,a) \wedge \leq (a,c)$, where $\leq$ is the binary built-in predicate with standard denotation $a \leq c$, while "the probability that ϕ is equal to a" is denoted by the ground atom $w_N(<\phi>,a)$ with the binary predicate w_N.

The intensional FOL with abstracted terms, with the intensional algebra in Definition 16, Section 1.3, $\mathrm{Alg}_{\mathrm{int}} = (\mathcal{D}, f, t, \mathrm{Id}, \mathrm{Truth}, \{\mathrm{conj}_S\}_{S\in\mathcal{P}(\mathbb{N}^2)}, \mathrm{neg}, \{\mathrm{exists}_n\}_{n\in\mathbb{N}})$, and extensionalization functions $h \in \mathcal{E}$, are provided in Section 1.2, in the form (1.4),

$$h = h_{-1} + \sum_{i\geq 0} h_i : \sum_{i\geq -1} D_i \longrightarrow D_{-1} + \sum_{i\geq 0} \mathcal{P}(\mathcal{D}^i)$$

where $h_{-1} : D_{-1} \to D_{-1}$ is the identity, $h_0 : D_0 \to \{f, t\}$ assigns the truth values in $\{f, t\}$, to all propositions, and $h_i : D_i \to \mathcal{P}(\mathcal{D}^i)$, $i \geq 1$ assigns an extension to all concepts. Thus, the intensions can be seen as *names* of an abstract or concrete entities, while the extensions correspond to various rules that these entities play in different worlds and we use the bijective mapping $\mathcal{F} : \mathcal{W} \to \mathcal{E}$ (see the two-step interpretation in Definition 10) as the Montague–Bealer's isomorphism (bijection) between explicit possible worlds and the set of extensionalization functions. The Tarski-style definitions of truth and validity for this intensional FOL language $\mathcal{L}$ is given in the customary way in Section 1.3, so we can introduce the following probabilistic logic.

Definition 29 (Syntax). The basic intensional logic language $\mathcal{L}_{\mathrm{PR}}$ for probabilistic theory is composed by formulae in $\mathcal{L}(P)$, with
1. Application dependent predicate symbols in P, where propositional symbols are 0-ary predicate symbols $p_i^0 = p_i \in P$, with $I(p_i^k) \in D_k$.
2. Binary predicate $p_3^2 \in P$ for the weight or probabilistic function w_N.
3. Binary built-in (with constant fixed extension in each $h \in \mathcal{E}$) predicate p_2^2 for $\leq$ (the binary predicate $=$ for identity is defined by $a = b$ iff $a \leq b$ and $b \leq a$).
4. Two built-in ternary predicates p_1^3, p_2^3, denoted by $\oplus$ and $\odot$, for addition and multiplication operations $+, \cdot$, respectively, as required for a logic for reasoning about probabilities [63].

The 0-ary functional symbols $a, b, c, \ldots$ in this logic language will be used as numeric constants for denotation of probabilities in $[0, 1]$.

Thus, in the case of propositional logic, the extensionalization functions will be reduced to the mappings $h = h_{-1} + h_0 + h_2 + h_3$.

We recall that in intensional FOL each n-ary functional symbol is represented by the $(n+1)$-ary predicate letter, where the last attribute is introduced for the resulting values of such a function. For example, the first attribute of the predicate letter w_N will contain the intensional abstract of a propositional formula in $\mathcal{L}(P)$, while the second place will contain the probabilistic value in the interval of reals $[0, 1] \subset D_{-1}$, so that the ground atom $w_N(<\phi>, a)$ in $\mathcal{L}_{\mathrm{PR}}$ will have the interpretation $I(w_N(<\phi>, a)) \in D_0$.

Analogously, for the ground atom $\oplus(a, b, c)$, with $a, b, c \in D_{-1}$ real numbers, we have that $I(\oplus(a, b, c)) \in D_0$ such that for any $h \in \mathcal{E}$ we have that $h(I(\oplus(a, b, c))) = t$ iff $a + b = c$. For the addition of more than two elements in this intensional logic we will use intensional abstract, e. g., for the sum of three elements we can use a ground formula $\oplus(a,b,d) \wedge \oplus(d,c,e)$, such that it holds that $h(I(\oplus(a,b,d) \wedge \oplus(d,b,c))) = \mathrm{conj}(I(\oplus(a,b,d)), I(\oplus(d,c,e))) = t$ iff $a + b = d$ and $d + c = e$, i. e., iff $a + b + c = e$.

The fixed extensions of the two built-in ternary predicates $\oplus(x,y,z)$ and $\odot(x,y,z)$ are

$$R_{\oplus} = \{(u_1, u_2, u_1 + u_2) \mid u_1, u_2 \in D_{-1} \text{ are real numbers}\},$$
$$R_{\odot} = \{(u_1, u_2, u_1 \cdot u_2) \mid u_1, u_2 \in D_{-1} \text{ are real numbers}\}$$

Notice that in the case of the intuitionistic FOL with a fixed intensional interpretation I, instead of probabilistic structure $N = (\mathbf{2}^P, \mathcal{P}(\mathbf{2}^P), \mu)$ where P in this case is the Herbrand base, we can use instead of possible worlds $v \in \mathcal{W} = \mathbf{2}^P$ the possible worlds $h \in \mathcal{W} = \mathcal{E}$, from the fact that for each extensionalization function h, the valuation $v \in \mathbf{2}^P$ is derivable from h as follows: for each ground atom in the Herbrand base $A \in P$,

$$v(A) =_{\mathrm{def}} h(I(A))$$

so in the case of intensional FOL as set of possible worlds (Nilsson's sample space) we will take the set of extensionalization functions $\mathcal{E}$, and hence we can define the satisfaction for the binary predicate w_N as follows.

Definition 30 (Semantics). Intensional FOL $\mathcal{L}_{\mathrm{PR}}$ is a probabilistic logic with a Nilsson's structure $N = (\mathcal{E}, \mathcal{P}(\mathcal{E}), \mu)$ if, for a fixed intensional interpretation I, satisfy the following property for any formula $\phi \in \mathcal{L}(P)$ and assignment g such that $\|\phi/g\| = \{h \circ I \mid h \in \mathcal{E} \text{ and } h(I(\phi/g)) = t\}$ is a subset of possible worlds $\mathcal{W}_e$ in (1.9):

$$h(I(w_N(g^*(<\phi>^{\beta}_{\alpha}), a))) = t \quad \text{iff} \quad a = \sum_{h' \circ I \in \|\phi/g\|} \mathrm{KI}(h' \circ I) \tag{2.36}$$

Thus, for the most simple linear inequality, "the probability that ϕ/g is less then or equal to c," expressed by the formula $w_N(<\phi/g>, a) \wedge \leq (a, c)$, is true iff $h(I(w_N(<\phi/g>, a) \wedge \leq (a, c))) = t$ and $a \leq c$.

Similar to the results obtained for a logic for reasoning about probabilities in [63], we obtain the following property.

Theorem 2. *The intensional FOL $\mathcal{L}_{\mathrm{PR}}$ with binary predicate w_N defined in Definition 30, the built-in binary predicate $\leq$ and ternary built-in predicates $\oplus$ and $\odot$ is sound and complete with respect to the measurable probability structures.*

Proof. We will follow the demonstration analogous to the demonstration of Theorem 2.2 in [63] for the sound and complete axiomatization of the axiomatic system $\mathrm{AX}_{\mathrm{MEAS}}$ for logic reasoning about probabilities, divided into three parts, which deal respectively with propositional reasoning, reasoning about linear inequalities and reasoning about probabilities:

1. Propositional reasoning: the set of all instances of propositional tautologies, with unique inference rule modus ponens.
2. Reasoning about linear inequalities: the set of all instances of valid formulae about linear inequalities of the form $a_1 \cdot x_1 + \cdots + a_k \cdot x_k \leq c$, where $a_1, \ldots, a_k$ and c are integers with $k \geq 1$, while $x_1, \ldots, x_k$ are probabilistic variables.
3. Reasoning about probability function w_N in [63] (here transformed into the binary predicate as it is done for all functional symbols in intensional FOL), such that $a = w_N(\phi/g)$ iff $h(I(w_N(g^*(<\phi>^{\beta}_{\alpha}), a))) = t$:
   3.1 $w_N(\phi/g) \geq 0$ (nonnegativity)
   3.2 $w_N(\text{true}) = 1$ (the probability of the event true is 1)
   3.3 $w_N((\phi \wedge \psi)/g) + w_N((\phi \wedge \neg\psi)/g) = w_N(\phi/g)$ (additivity)
   3.4 $w_N(\phi/) = w_N(\psi/g)$ if $\phi \equiv \psi$ (distributivity).

It is easy to verify that for any axiom ϕ/g, we have that for all "worlds" $h\circ I \in \mathcal{W}_e$ it holds that $h(I(\phi/g)) = t$, so that it is true in the S5 Kripke model of the minimal intensional FOL given in Definition 15 (Section 1.3) where $\mathcal{W}_e = \mathfrak{I}_T(\Gamma)$ is the set of explicit possible worlds (here is the set of Tarski's interpretation of FOL $\mathcal{L}_{\mathrm{PR}}$) have bijection with $\mathcal{E}$ (for a fixed intensional interpretation I, from the two-step interpretation, for each $h \in \mathcal{E}$ we have a unique $I^*_T = h\circ I \in \mathcal{W}_e$), because all algebraic operations in $\mathrm{Alg}_{\mathrm{int}}$ in Definition 16 (Section 1.3) are defined in order to satisfy standard propositional logic. Moreover, the modus ponens rule is satisfied in every "world" $h \circ I \in \mathcal{W}_e$. Thus, the point 1 above is satisfied by intensional logic $\mathcal{L}_{\mathrm{PR}}$.

The definition of built-in predicates $\odot, \oplus$ and $\leq$ satisfy all linear inequalities, thus the point 2 above.

The definition of binary predicate $w_N(x, y)$ is given in order to satisfy Nilsson's probability structure, thus all properties of probability function in the point 3 above are satisfied by $w_N(x, y)$ built-in predicate in every "world" $h \circ I \in \mathcal{W}_e$. Consequently, the soundness and completeness of the intensional logic $\mathcal{L}_{\mathrm{PR}}$ with respect to measurable probability structures, based on Theorem 2.2 in [63] is satisfied. □

For example, the satisfaction of the linear inequality $a_1{\cdot}x_1{+}a_2{\cdot}x_2 \leq c$, where x_1 and x_2 are the probabilities of the sentences ϕ_1 and ϕ_2 relatively, (here the list of quantifications $(\exists x_1)\ldots(\exists x_k)$ is abbreviated by $(\exists x_1, \ldots, x_k)$), expressed by the following FOL intensional formula:

$$(\exists x_1, x_2, x_3, x_4, x_5)(w_N(<\phi_1>, x_1) \wedge w_N(<\phi_2>, x_2) \wedge \odot(a_1, x_1, x_3) \wedge \odot(a_2, x_2, x_4) \\ \wedge \oplus(x_3, x_4, x_5) \wedge \leq (x_5, c)), \quad \text{is true iff}$$

$$u_1 = \sum_{h\circ I \in \|\phi_1\|} \mathrm{KI}(h \circ I), \quad u_2 = \sum_{h\circ I \in \|\phi_2\|} \mathrm{KI}(h \circ I),$$

$$(I(a_1), u_1, v_1), (I(a_2), u_2, v_2) \in R_{\odot}, (v_1, v_2, v_3) \in R_{\oplus} \text{ and } v_3 \leq I(c),$$

where $u_1, u_2, v_1, \ldots, v_3 \in D_{-1}$ are real numbers.

Analogously, the satisfaction of any linear inequality $a_1 \cdot x_1 + \cdots + a_k \cdot x_k \leq c$, where x_i are the probabilities of the propositional formulae ϕ_i for $i = 1, \ldots, k$, $k \geq 2$, can be expressed by the logic formula

$$\begin{aligned}(\exists x_1, \ldots, x_{3k})(w_N(<\phi_1>, x_1) \wedge \cdots \wedge w_N(<\phi_k>, x_k) \\ \wedge \odot(a_1, x_1, x_{k+1}) \wedge \cdots \wedge \odot(a_k, x_k, x_{2k}) \wedge \oplus(0, x_{k+1}, x_{2k+1}) \\ \wedge \oplus(x_{2k+1}, x_{k+2}, x_{2k+2}) \wedge \cdots \wedge \oplus(x_{2k-1}, x_{2k}, x_{3k}) \wedge \leq (x_{3k}, c)).\end{aligned}$$

Based on Theorem 2.9 in [63], we can conclude that the problem of deciding whether such an intensional formula in $\mathcal{L}_{\mathrm{PR}}$ is satisfiable in a measurable probability structure of Nilsson is NP-complete.

2.2.3 Application to probabilistic logic programs

The semantics of the interval-based Probabilistic Logic Programs (PLP), based on possible worlds with the fixed-point semantics for such programs [70], has been considered valid for more than 13 years. But in 2005, when I worked with Professor V. S. Subrahmanian, Director of the UMIACS Institute, I had the opportunity to consider the general problems of (temporal) probabilistic databases [15], to analyze their semantics of interval-based probabilistic logic programs and to realize that unfortunately it was not correctly defined.[3]

Because of that, I formally developed, in [68], the reduction of (temporal) probabilistic databases into constraint logic programs. Consequently, it was possible to apply the interval PSAT in order to find the models of such interval-based probabilistic programs, as presented and compared with other approaches in [16]. Moreover, in this complete revision, presented in Section A.4.1 in the Appendix, it was demonstrated that the temporal-probabilistic logic programs can be reduced into the particular case of the ordinary probabilistic logic programs, so that our application of intensional semantics can apply only to this last general case of logic programs.

In what follows, I will briefly introduce the syntax of probabilistic logic programs (see also the introduction of Section A.4 in the Appendix). More about it can be found in the original work in [70] and in its last revision in [16]. Let ground(PL) denote the set of all ground instances of rules of a probabilistic logic program PL with a given domain for object variables, and let H denote the Herbrand base of this program PL.

3 This application of intensional FOL theory provided by this book, I formalized during my J1 visa post-doc work at UMIACS. After my examination of fixpoint semantics of PLP (a background for work on TP-databases and resolution of complex algebraic problems of aggregations for such databases, that was my primary goal) and invitation to correct his for long time erroneous fixpoint semantics of PLP in order to publish this revision together, hi began to use his notorious relationships with conference's committees with requests to do not accept any my research paper. Anyway, I published two good papers with him [14, 15], before leaving UMIACS. But after his decision, obviously, I could not use any recommendation letter for my professionally successful work at College Park University.

Then each ground instance of rules in ground(PL) has the following syntax:

$$A : \gamma_0 \leftarrow \phi_1 : \gamma_1 \wedge \cdots \wedge \phi_m : \gamma_m \tag{2.37}$$

where $A \in H$ is a ground atom in a Herbrand base H, $\phi_i, i \geq 1$ are logic formulae composed by ground atoms and standard logic connectives $\wedge$ and $\neg$, while $\gamma_i = (b_i, c_i)$, $i \geq 0$, where $b_i, c_i \in [0,1]$, are the lower and upper probability boundaries.

The expression $\phi_i : \gamma_i$ is a probabilistic-annotated (p-annotated) basic formula, which is true if the probability x_i of the ground formula ϕ_i is between b_i and c_i; false otherwise. Thus, this basic p-annotated formula is the particular case of the 2-valued probabilistic formula:

$$(1 \cdot x_i \geq a_i) \wedge (1 \cdot x_i \leq b_i) \tag{2.38}$$

composed by two linear inequalities.

Consequently, the standard logic embedding of annotated interval-based logic programs can be easily obtained by the intensional logic $\mathcal{L}_{PR}$ described in Section 2.2.2 where P is equal to the Herbrand base H of the annotated interval-based probabilistic logic program PL.

Thus, based on the translation (2.38), the logic formula in intensional logic $\mathcal{L}_{PR}$ correspondent to basic annotated formula $\phi_i : \gamma_i$ of the annotated logic program ground(PL) is equal to the following first-order closed formulae with a variable x_i:

$$\exists x_i (w_N(<\phi_i>, x_i) \wedge \leq (b_i, x_i) \wedge \leq (x_i, c_i)) \tag{2.39}$$

Based on this translation, the rule (2.37) of the annotated logic program ground(PL) can be replaced by the following rule of an intensional probabilistic logic program:

$$\begin{aligned} &\exists x_0 (w_N(<A>, x_0) \wedge \leq (b_0, x_0) \wedge \leq (x_0, c_0)) \\ &\quad \leftarrow \exists x_1 (w_N(<\phi_1>, x_1) \wedge \leq (b_1, x_1) \wedge \leq (x_1, c_1)) \\ &\quad \wedge \cdots \wedge \exists x_m (w_N(<\phi_m>, x_m) \wedge \leq (b_m, x_m) \wedge \leq (x_m, c_m)), \end{aligned}$$

with the variables $x_0, x_1, \ldots, x_m$.

In this way, we obtain a grounded intensional probabilistic logic program P_{PR}, which has both the syntax and semantics different from the original annotated probabilistic logic program ground(PL).

As an alternative to this full intensional embedding of the annotated logic programs into the first-order intensional logic, we can use a partial embedding by preserving the old ad hoc annotated syntax of the probabilistic program ground(PL), by extending the standard predicate-based syntax of the intensional FOL logic with annotated formulae and by defining only the new intensional interpretation I for these annotated formulae, as follows:

$$\begin{aligned} I(\phi_i : \gamma_i) &= I((\exists x)(w_N(<\phi_i>, x)) \wedge (\leq (b_i, x) \wedge \leq (x, c_i))) \\ &= \mathrm{exist}(\mathrm{conj}_{\{(1,1)\}}(I(w_N(<\phi_i>, x)), \mathrm{conj}_{\{(1,1)\}}(I(\leq (b_i, x)), I(\leq (x, c_i))))), \end{aligned}$$

where $I(w_N(<\phi_i>, x)), I(\leq (b_i, x)), I(\leq (x, c_i)) \in D_1$.

So that $h(I(\phi_i : \gamma_i)) = t$ iff $h(\mathrm{exist}(u_1)) = t$, where

$$\begin{aligned} u_1 &= \mathrm{conj}_{\{(1,1)\}}(I(w_N(<\phi_i>, x)), \mathrm{conj}_{\{(1,1)\}}(I(\leq (b_i, x)), I(\leq (x, c_i)))) \in D_1, \\ \text{iff} \quad & \exists a(a \in h(u_1)) \text{ iff } h(I(b_i)) \leq a \leq h(I(c_i)), \end{aligned}$$

where $a \in [0, 1] \subset D_{-1}$ is a particular value (probability of ϕ_i) of the variable x.

Notice that, from the Appendix and the fact that $u_1 \in D_1$,

$$\begin{aligned} h(\mathrm{exist}(u_1)) &= f_{\langle\,\rangle}(h(I(w_N(<\phi_i>, x))) \bowtie_{\{(1,1)\}} (h(I(\leq (b_i, x))) \bowtie_{\{(1,1)\}} h(I(\leq (x, c_i))))) \\ &= f_{\langle\,\rangle}(h(I(w_N(<\phi_i>, x))) \bigcap h(I(\leq (b_i, x))) \bigcap h(I(\leq (x, c_i)))), \\ & \text{where } f_{\langle\,\rangle}(R) = f \text{ if } R = \emptyset; \quad t \text{ otherwise.} \end{aligned}$$

The advantage of this second, partial embedding is that we can preserve the old syntax for (temporal) probabilistic logic programs [16, 70], but providing to them the standard intensional FOL semantics instead of current ad hoc semantics for such a kind of logic programs.

There are two consequences of this full and natural embedding of the probability theory in a logic:

1. The full embedding of Nilsson's probabilistic structure into propositional logic results in a *truth-functional* many-valued logic, different from Nilsson's intuition and current considerations about propositional probabilistic logic.
2. The logic for reasoning *about* probabilities can be embedded into an intensional FOL that remains to be *2-valued logic*, both for propositional formulae in $\mathcal{L}(P)$ and predicate formulae for probability constraints, based on the binary built-in predicate $\leq$ and binary predicate w_N used for the probability function, where the basic propositional letters in P are formally considered as nullary predicate symbols.

The intensional FOL for reasoning about probabilities is obtained by the particular fusion of the intensional algebra (analogously to Bealer's approach) and Montague's possible-worlds modal logic for the semantics of the natural language.

In this work, we enriched such a logic framework by a number of built-in binary and ternary predicates, which can be used to define the basic set of probability inequalities and to render the probability weight function w_N an explicit object in this logic language. We conclude that this intensional FOL logic with intensional abstraction is a good candidate language for specification of probabilistic logic programs, and we apply two different approaches: the first one is obtained by the translation of the annotated syntax of current logic programs into this intensional FOL; the second one, instead, modifies only the semantics of these logic programs by preserving their current ad hoc annotated syntax.

2.2.4 Application to temporal-probabilistic databases

There are numerous applications where we have to deal with temporal uncertainty associated with events. We assume that every event occurs at a point in time. An instant (time point or chronon) **t** is specified w. r. t. a given time granularity of a linear calendar structure S_T; for example, "day/month/year." Often, however, we do not know the exact time point; instead, we only know that the instant is located sometime during a time interval. We call such an instant an *indeterminate instant* [86].

The Temporal Probabilistic (TP) database management systems should provide support for *valid-time indeterminacy* of events, by proposing the concept of an indeterminate instant, i. e., an interval of time-points (event's time-window) with an associated, lower and upper, probability distribution. In particular, users should be able to control, via query language constructs, the amount of temporal/probability approximation present in derived information.

Basic notions about TP Logic programs and concepts are provided in Section A.4.1 in the Appendix. Moreover, it has presented [68] a new, equivalent to the denotational specification, the logic specification of TP-databases as *constraint databases* (in Section 2.1 we provide more details): The TP-database can be seen as a deductive database with *incomplete* information, and consequently, with a number of possible Herbrand models.

We can see the approximate (uncertain) information as some kind of *relativization* of truth values for sentences also: Let H be a Herbrand base for a logic program, which handles the uncertain information and $r_j(\mathbf{d})$ an event (ground atom) in $\mathrm{Ev} \subset H$, which defines some particular event in time for which we have only an approximated information when it happened. Thus, this atom $r_j(\mathbf{d})$ is not longer *absolutely* true or false, but its truth depends on the approximate temporal information about this fact: in some time points, it can be true, in others, it can be false. If we consider such temporal approximation as a *context* for this ground fact $r_j(\mathbf{d}) \in H$, then we obtain that the truth of $r_j(\mathbf{d})$ is a function depending on the time. That is, they have a *higher-order type* of truth constants (as explained in Section 2.1), and such context sensitive applications, with higher-order Herbrand models, can be transformed (i. e., *flattened*) to logic theories with basic (ordinary) Herbrand interpretations, by enlarging the original predicates with new attributes for the properties of the context: in this way, the context becomes a part of the language of the logic theory, i. e., it becomes *visible*. Consequently, in this case of TP databases, the original event expressed by a ground atom $r_j(\mathbf{d}) \in \mathrm{Ev}$ (of k-ary predicate r_j) in higher-order Herbrand base H, will be flattened into new flattened atoms (with flattened Herbrand base H_F) by

$$r_j(\mathbf{d}) \mapsto r_j^T(\mathbf{d}, y, L_j \cdot z, U_j \cdot z, z_1) \tag{2.40}$$

where y is a time variable of the calendar, the real numbers $L_j, U_j \in [0,1]$ with $L_j \leq U_j$ are lower and upper boundaries for the probability and z is variable for reals in $[0,1]$, and z_1 is probability-variable. So, this new "flattened" predicate r_j^T has $k+3$ attributes where first $k = |\mathbf{d}|$ attributes are that of the original event's predicate r_j.

Note that in such a flattening, introduced in [68] (in Section 3, constraint logic programs for TP-databases), we have the probability attribute directly in the flattened event's atoms, so we are able to reason about probabilities without introducing the binary predicate w_N as in previous sections.

Consequently, by using the temporal constraints $C(y)$ of Definition 113 in Section A.4.1 in the Appendix, and the built-in function $\delta_j = \delta(r_j(\mathbf{d})) : S_\tau \to [0,1]$ (obtained from mapping $\delta : \mathrm{Ev} \to [0,1]^{S_\tau}$ for a given set of events $\mathrm{Ev} \subset H$, which is a subset of higher-order Herbrand base) associated to this event $r_j(\mathbf{d}) \in \mathrm{Ev}$, the constraint TP database uses the following constraint logic program clauses, analog to (2.6) in Example 7 in Section 2.1.1, for each event $r_j(\mathbf{d})$ and by using the exclusive existential quantifier ($\exists!$) quantifier ("there exist a unique value such that"),

$$(\exists! z_1) r_j^T(\mathbf{d}, y, L_j \cdot z, U_j \cdot z, z_1) \leftarrow C(y) \wedge \delta_j(y, z) \tag{2.41}$$

where a free variable is only the time-variable y used in constraint $C(y)$, and $\delta_j(y,z)$ is a graph representation of the built-in function δ_j (each functional symbol represented an intensional FOL as a predicate) where z is the result of function for the argument y. The exclusive existential quantifier used for the probability express the fact that, for a given Tarski's interpretation $I_T^* = h \circ I$ (for a fixed intensional interpretation I), for any assignment g such that the $C(g(y))$ is true, from this clause also the sentence $(\exists! z_1) r_j^T(\mathbf{d}, g(y), L_j \cdot g(z), U_j \cdot (z), z_1)$ must be true. Hence, there is exactly one value $a \in [0,1]$ for which the ground atom $r_j^T(\mathbf{d}, g(y), L_j \cdot g(z), U_j \cdot (z), a)$ is true for this interpretation I_T^*, corresponding to the fact that in a given time instance $\mathbf{t}_i = g(y) \in \mathrm{sol}(C(y)) = I_T^*(C(y))$ this event $r_j(\mathbf{d})$ can have exactly one value a of its probability.

We recall that this exclusive existential quantifier can be expressed by a formula with only standard logic quantifiers, that is a sentence $(\exists! x)\psi(x)$ is logically equivalent to the FOL formula $(\exists x)(\psi(x) \wedge (\forall x_1)((x_1 = x) \vee \neg\psi(x_1)))$.

Note that in the left-hand side of the logic clause (2.41) it was necessary to transform the probability argument z_1 into a bound variable in order to render impossibility to assign the value to such probability variable a value by using the logic clauses. We recall that the probabilistic value can be obtained only from Nilsson's structure, and not assigned by using the logic expression.

Remark. In the simplest case, we can assume that δ_i is a constant function such that for each $\mathbf{t}_i \in S_\tau$, $\delta_j(\mathbf{t}_i) = 1$, so that for each event $r_j(\mathbf{d}) \in \mathrm{Ev}$ the uncertainty interval is constant in time and equal to $[L_j, U_j] \subseteq [0,1]$, as it is used in TP logic programs in (2.37) in Section 2.2.3. □

Let ϕ be the formula $(\exists! z_1) r_j^T(\mathbf{x}, y, L_j \cdot z, U_j \cdot z, z_1)$ with also free variables $\mathbf{x} = (x_1, \dots, x_k)$, the tuple of variables of predicate r_j of the event, and we denote by ϕ/g

the sentence obtained with assignment $g \in \mathcal{D}^\beta$ for $\beta = \{x_1, \dots, x_k, y, z\}$, so that ϕ/g is equal to the ground atom $(\exists! z_1) r_j^T(\mathbf{d}, \mathbf{t}_i, L_t, U_t, z_1)$ with $\mathbf{d} = g^*(\mathbf{x})$, $\mathbf{t}_i = g(y)$, $L_t = L_j \cdot \delta_j(\mathbf{t}_i)$ and $U_t = U_j \cdot \delta_j(\mathbf{t}_i)$, and we define the set of worlds (for a fixed intensional interpretation I),

$$\begin{aligned}\|\phi/g\| &=_{\text{def}} \{h' \circ I \in \mathcal{W}_e \mid h'(I(\phi/g)) = t\} \\ &= \{h' \circ I \in \mathcal{W}_e \mid h'(I((\exists! z_1) r_j^T(\mathbf{d}, \mathbf{t}_i, L_t, U_t, z_1))) = t\}\end{aligned}$$

so that from the clause (2.41), we obtain that

$$\|\phi/g\| = \{h' \circ I \in \mathcal{W}_e \mid h'(I(C(\mathbf{t}_i))) = t\} \subseteq \mathcal{W}_e \tag{2.42}$$

In order to involve the probability as an argument for the probabilistic reasoning by using the Nilsson's semantics of the probabilistic logic (2.36) in Definition 30, with the introduction of binary predicate w_N, we can use the correspondence of the formula ϕ, equal to $(\exists! z_1) r_j^T(\mathbf{x}, y, L_j \cdot z, U_j \cdot z, z_1)$, with the abstracted term $\lessdot r_j^T(\mathbf{x}, y, L_j \cdot z, U_j \cdot z, z_1)\gtrdot_{z_1}^{\beta}$. So, for a given possible world $I_T^* = h \circ I \in \mathcal{W}_e$, from (2.36) we obtain

$$\begin{aligned}&h(I(w_N(\lessdot r_j^T(\mathbf{x}, y, L_j \cdot z, U_j \cdot z, z_1)\gtrdot_{z_1}^{\beta}, z_1)/g)) \\ &\quad = h(I(w_N(\lessdot r_j^T(\mathbf{d}, \mathbf{t}_i, L_t, U_t, z_1\gtrdot_{z_1}, g(z_1))))) = t \quad \text{iff} \quad a = g(z_1) = \sum_{h' \circ I \in \|\phi/g\|} \mathrm{KI}(h' \circ I)\end{aligned} \tag{2.43}$$

so that $a = g(z_1)$ is the probability of this event in the time-point $\mathbf{t}_i = g(y)$ w. r. t. the interpretation $I_T^* = h \circ I \in \|\phi/g\|$.

Thus, by introduction of the flattened predicate r_j^T for the events, we are able to reason about the probabilities of the temporal events in the TP-database. So, for the case provided previously, we are able to express the satisfaction of the constraints for the events in this TP-database by the truth of the following sentence for the assignment $g : \{x_1, \dots, x_k, y, z, z_1\} \to \mathcal{D}$:

$$(r_j^T(\mathbf{x}, y, L_j \cdot z, U_j \cdot z, z_1) \wedge (L_j \cdot z \le z_1 \le U_j \cdot z))/g, \tag{2.44}$$

which tells that the event $r_j(\mathbf{x})/g \in \mathrm{Ev}$ at time-point $\mathbf{t}_i = g(y)$ has the probability $a = g(z_1)$, in accordance with the constraints defined in the TP-database.

From the fact that $I_T^* = h \circ i \in \|\phi/g\|$ from the definition of $\|\phi/g\|$, we have that for this interpretation I_T^* the sentence $(\exists! z_1) r_j^T(\mathbf{d}, \mathbf{t}_i, L_t, U_t, z_1)$ is true, and there is a unique value a for quantified variable z_1 such that

$$I_T^*(r_j^T(\mathbf{d}, \mathbf{t}_i, L_t, U_t, a)) = h(I(r_j^T(\mathbf{d}, \mathbf{t}_i, L_t, U_t, a))) = t \tag{2.45}$$

where, from (2.43), the value a is just the probability of this event in the time-point $\mathbf{t}_i$ as we intended. Thus, the extension of flattened predicate r_j^T for Tarski's interpretation $I_T^* = h \circ I$ is the relation $R = I_T(r_j^T) \subseteq \mathcal{D}^{k+4}$ composed by all events expressed by this predicate and their probabilities in time, as it is required by the relations of PT-databases. Consequently, it is enough to materialize only the relations of the flattened predicates p_j^T in the TP-databases (without using the binary relation w_N), in order to be able, by simple standard SQL expressions, to reason about the probabilities of the events saved in relations of this TP-database. In this way, our materialized TP-database is a standard RDB, and we used intensional FOL only for the embedding of Nilsson's probabilistic structure this intensional FOL and able to compute the probabilities (2.43) of the events over possible worlds $I_T^* = h \circ I \in \mathcal{W}_e$.

Consequently, if the mathematical structure of "TP-tuples," tp $= (\mathbf{d}, \gamma)$ analyzed previously [68], can be seen as a denotational specification of events, then the constraint logic programs with clauses (2.41) defined in intensional FOL can be seen as a declarative logical specification of events: so, we move from mathematical (algebraic) toward logical semantics of databases for events, based on the classical two-valued Herbrand models.

Such logic point of view can be useful for considering reasoning capabilities of event-based databases, for data-integration semantics when we integrate two or more event-based databases into one global virtual event-based database, for the logic definition of query language (as in relational database: duality between SQL predicate-logic language and relational algebra), etc.

In [86] is presented a syntactic extension to SQL, needed to support valid time indeterminacy, and its *operational* semantic extension to ordinary SQL. In another approach [87], based on the extension of probabilistic databases with time dimension (*Probabilistic Temporal Databases*, or shortly TP-databases), is defined as a relational *algebra* extension that integrates both time and probabilities: such algebra supports also the *partial* probabilistic distribution for events. In this work, was shown how the PDM can be modified to support temporal indeterminacy, even if there might be several million elements in a set of possible chronons: it is obtained by passing from explicit (annotated) classical relations to implicit representation of events (called also TP-relations) and executing the "implicit" algebra operations directly over such representation.

The advantage of the logical point of view for a TP-database, provided in this section, is that it can be *easily integrated* with an ordinary deductive database. By adding to TP-database the set of clauses for ordinary database relations (which are not event-based relations), we obtain a unique deductive logic theory where we integrate the ordinary database relations with also temporal/probability event-based relations. Another advantage is that we can also define a logic theory for integration of different TP-mixed-databases, based on views, as in ordinary GLAV (Global and Local As View) data integration systems. Based on the set of Herbrand models for such logic programs, we can define [68] the event-based modal logic language and the set of Kripke models, which define the semantics for it. Such modal language may be seen as an *epistemic* extension of temporal logics, and can be used as basis for definition of the high-level SQL-like query language for TP-databases also.

2.3 Semantic WEB applications

The notion of ontology has become widespread in fields such as intelligent information integration, cooperative information systems, information retrieval, electronic commerce and knowledge management. Using ontologies, semantic annotations on Web resources will allow structural and semantic definitions of documents, providing completely new possibilities: Intelligent search instead of keyword matching, query answering instead of information retrieval, document exchange between departments via ontology mappings and *definition of views* on documents. The semantic web is a proposal to build an infrastructure of machine-readable semantics for the data on the web.

The semantic web [88] and ontologies play very important role in the recent explosion of interest in the world wide web. The enormous amount of data has made it difficult to find, access, present and maintain the information required by users. This is because information content is presented primarily in a natural language, and needs the formal language specification with natural language features, as, e. g., *reification*.

In semantic web languages, such as Resource Description Framework (RDF) and Web Ontology Language (OWL), a statement is a binary relation. It is used to link two individuals or an individual and a value. Applications sometimes need to describe other RDF statements, for instance, to record information like when statements were made, or who made them, which is sometimes called "provenance" information. As an example, we may want to represent properties of a relation, such as our certainty about it, severity or strength of a relation, relevance of a relation, and so on. RDF [89] follows the W3C design principles of interoperability, extensibility, evolution and decentralization. Particularly, the RDF model was designed with the following goals: simple data model and extensible URI-based vocabulary allowing anyone to make statements about any resource.

The RDF schema specification provides a machine-understandable formalism for defining schemas for descriptive vocabularies like the Dublin Core. It allows designers to specify classes of resource types and properties to convey descriptions of those classes, relationships between those properties and classes and constraints on the allowed combinations of classes, properties and values.

Basically, RDF defines a *data model* for describing machine understandable information on the web. The basic data model consists of three object types: resources, properties and statements. The modeling primitives of RDF are very basic: actually they correspond to binary predicates (RDF-properties) of ground terms (source and value), where, however the predicates may be used as terms so that RDF cannot be embedded into the standard *extensional* first-order logic (FOL). RDF has blank nodes, which are essentially globally quantified existential variables. The statements are also resources, so that statements can be applied recursively to statements, allowing their nesting (*reification*) but such most innovative feature (early versions of RDF made quite strong claims for RDF reification) is not actually supported by RDF: such problem will be explored in more detail in the following (one of the main reasons to introduce the *intensional* FOL [27], as discussed in the introductory part of Section 1.3.1). Reification is widely used in conceptual modeling. Reifying a relationship means viewing it as an entity. The purpose of reifying a relationship is to make it explicit, when additional information needs to be added to it (consider, e. g., the relationship "*isMemberOf*").

Therefore, the RDF Schema (RDFS) specification [90] enriches RDF by giving an externally specified semantics to specific resources, e. g., to rdf:subclassOf, to rdf:Class, etc. It is only because of this external semantics that RDFS is useful. RDFS is recognizable as an *ontology* representation language: it talks about classes and RDF-properties (binary relations), range and domain constraints (on RDF-properties), and subclass and subproperty (subsumption) relations.

2.3.1 Introduction to semantic web languages RDF and OWL

RDFS has a very interesting extension to natural language (e. g., reification), but at least in some logical aspects is a weakly expressive language, and such limitations of RDFS led to the development of new web ontology languages such as, e. g., DAML+OIL adopted by W3C as the basis of a new OWL web ontology language [91].

So, all attempts to integrate RDFS into some more expressive FOL sublanguage with a built-in *extensional* equality theory (as OWL, largely based on description logic, or other interesting languages as logic programming, deductive databases or modal logic languages (e. g., epistemic logic), etc.) are unsuccessful [92, 93]: these FOL sublanguages cannot embed the reification, which is a natural-language property and is a more innovative feature of the RDF w. r. t. other ontology specification languages based on the FOL sublanguages. Thus, the motivation for this work is just to valorize this very important feature of RDF, for building intelligent database systems.

The difficulty comes from the fact that all FOL sublanguages have the model theory in which individuals are interpreted as *elements* of some domain, classes are interpreted as subsets of the domain and RDF-properties are interpreted as binary relations on the domain. The semantics of RDFS, on the other hand, are given by a nonstandard model theory, where individuals, classes and RDF-properties are *all* elements in the domain, RDF-property elements have extension which are binary relations on the domain, and class extensions are only implicitly defined by the rdf:type property.

Such properties can be directly embedded into Jigher-order logics (HOL) with a built-in extensional equality theory (under standard HOL semantics, an equation between the predicate (or function) symbols is true if and only if these symbols are interpreted via the same relation (extension)), in particular, the use of predicates in a variable position. Unfortunately, extensional equality of predicates and functions is not decidable, which carries over to the *unification problem*. For genuine second-order theories (e. g., second-order predicate calculus and Church's simple theory of types, both under the standard semantics) extensional equality is not even semidecidable.

Moreover, RDFS support reflection on its own syntax: it is defined in terms of classes and RDF-properties, which are interpreted in the same way as other classes and RDF-properties, and whose meaning can be extended by statements in the language. This violates the very principles of set theory, i. e., that set membership should be a well-defined relationship, so when we try to integrate RDFS into some (extensional) FOL sublanguage we meet Russel's paradox, that result from an attempt to make sets too powerful.

For example, it is not possible in RDFS to provide defined classes, classes that give a formula that determines which resources belong to them. We can provide an even richer theory of classes and RDF-properties, allowing for defined classes and more relationships between classes.

The RDF syntax based on triples (RDF sentences) is a *graph* data structure, reminiscent of semantic networks. Such graph structure have well-known problems with scoping of quantifiers, negations and disjunctions (consequently, with logic implication). RDF solves these problems by disallowing all these constructs (anonymous nodes in RDF can be considered to be existentially quantified, but the scope of the quantifier is the entire graph).

There is an attempt [94] of embedding RDF into the F-logic or its subcomponent HiLog [24], which has the second-order syntax with intensional equality theory, but from our point of view such approach degenerates and unusefully complicates the original elegant syntax of RDF, which is one of the most important reasons for its wide and unquestionable success.

The attempt [95, 96] of embedding RDF into (S)KIF is analog to HiLog (has the second- order syntax with intensional equality theory). It is incomplete [93], and does not address reification and anonymous resources, but has the similar semantics to RDFS: it is not casual, the same author Patrick Hayes defined the semantics for RDF [97].

In the RDF model theory is formally expressed as the adoption of the *intensional semantics*, so that standard extensional FOL language is explicitly refused as a candidate for larger logic embedding framework [97]:

> "The use of the explicit extension mapping also makes it possible for two properties to have exactly the same values, or two classes to contain the same instances, and still be distinct entities. This means that RDFS classes can be considered to be rather more than simple sets; they can be thought of as "classifications" or "concepts," which have a robust notion of identity that goes beyond a simple extensional correspondence. This property of the model theory has significant consequences in more expressive languages built on top of RDF, such as OWL [91], which are

capable of expressing identity between properties and classes directly. This "intensional" nature of classes and properties is sometimes claimed to be a useful property of a descriptive language [97]."

Motivation and main contributions

This section is a formal continuation of this approach to the semantics of RDF databases, considering that RDF *is not* First-order Logic (FOL), nor in syntax nor in semantics: thus, what we will explore is the *formal* definition for a particular kind of intensional FOL language with *abstraction* operator, which we consider as a natural logic framework that uses only the minimum of the logic machinery for the formal and full embedding of RDFS into FOL language. Notice that the *abstraction operator* is a necessary prerequisite in order to avoid the second-order *syntax* as in HiLog and KIF, and the confusion between predicate forms and the (intensional) *names* of the same forms (which in our theory are *terms* of the language); as we will see this abstraction operation is based on the particular kind of natural language "subsentences," which are different from ordinary "complete" logic sentences that cannot have logic values.

Because of all points discussed in precedence, our approach is very close to these last two attempts, but we prefer to use the pure intensional FOL with an *abstraction operator* [42, 58], as a natural and well-suited logic embedding of the RDFS data structures, which provides all nice features of the FOL language, all logic connectives (RDF uses only conjunction for its triples), predicates, variables and quantifiers.

Other contribution, and a peculiarity of our approach, is that we consider RDF language and its data structures as terms of an *algebra of triples*, i. e., of RDF *graphs*, and *not* as logic theory itself: we distinguish the *triple structure* $\langle r, p, v\rangle$ from a *ground atom* $p(r, v)$ in logic: the first one, as is, e. g., a tuple of a database, can be (or not) an element of the given RDF ontology (RDF graph), and have no truth value, while the second is a logic formula, which can be true or false. The embedding of such data structures into logic is an analog of the embedding of relations and *tuples* of relational databases into a predicate logic and ground atoms of the FOL.

Basically, we will avoid the second-order syntax by transforming predicates into *intensional terms* by using an abstraction operation $<\_>$; thus, we consider each RDF triple as a term, obtained by abstraction of the predicate corresponding to the property element of this RDF triple.

Consequently, a RDF triple $\langle r, p, v\rangle$, where r, v are instances or values, is equal to the intensional abstract (term) $<p(r, v)>$ of the ground atom of binary predicate p in this intensional FOL. Thus, apart of this slight syntax difference, each RDF triple is an intensional term in the intensional FOL for RDFS, and the reification structure $\langle\langle r, p, v\rangle, p_1, v_1\rangle$ is an intensional term $<p_1(<p(r, v)>, v_1)>$, obtained by abstraction from the ground atom $p_1(<p(r, v)>, v_1)$.

As we see, this logic embedding is very close to the original RDF syntax, and as we will see in the rest of this paper, the semantics of this intensional FOL fully incorporates the nonstandard semantics of RDF [93, 97]. In this framework, individuals and data values correspond to FOL constants, classes and data types correspond to unary predicates, properties to binary predicates and subclass/property relationships correspond to logic implication.

2.3.2 General embedding of RDF data structures into intensional FOL

In this section, we will make a confrontation of the actual RDF model theory (model theory) and the proposed intensional logic embedding of RDF into minimal intensional FOL given by Definition 15 in Section 1.3 and enriched by intensional abstraction operator provided in Section 1.3.1.

RDF model theory

An interpretation I_{RDF} of the RDF vocabulary V, i. e., RDF model theory, is a triple $(\mathrm{IR}, I_{\mathrm{EXT}}, I_S)$, where:

1. A nonempty set IR is the domain (of resources), called the domain of the universe of the I_{RDF}.
2. A set IP, called the set of properties of I_{RDF}.
3. A mapping $I_{\mathrm{EXT}} : \mathrm{IP} \to \mathcal{P}(\mathrm{IR} \times \mathrm{IR})$, mapping each property in $\mathrm{IP} \subset \mathrm{IR}$ into the set of pairs, which identify the arguments for which the property is true.
4. A mapping $I_S : V \to \mathrm{IR}$ from URI references in V into IR.
5. A mapping $I_L : V \to \mathrm{IR}$ from typed literals in V into IR.
6. A distinguished subset LV (of real entities that "exist") of IR, called the set of literal values, which contains all the plain literals in V. □

For example, the denotations of ground RDF graphs are as follows:

1. if E is a plain literal "aaa" in V, then $I_{\mathrm{RDF}}(E) = aaa$;
2. if E is a plain literal "aaa"@ttt in V, then $I_{\mathrm{RDF}}(E) = \langle aaa, ttt \rangle$;
3. if E is a typed literal in V, then $I_{\mathrm{RDF}}(E) = I_L(E)$;
4. if E is a URI reference in V, then $I_{\mathrm{RDF}}(E) = I_S(E)$;
5. if E is a ground triple $\langle r, p, v \rangle$, then:

$$I_{\mathrm{RDF}}(E) = t \quad \text{if } r, p, v \in V, \quad I_{\mathrm{RDF}}(p) \in \mathrm{IP} \quad \text{and} \quad (I_{\mathrm{RDF}}(r), I_{\mathrm{RDF}}(v)) \in I_{\mathrm{EXT}}(I_{\mathrm{RDF}}(p));$$
$$f \text{ otherwise.}$$

6. if E is a ground RDF graph, then:

$$I_{\mathrm{RDF}}(E) = f \quad \text{if } I_{\mathrm{RDF}}(E') = f \text{ for some triple } E' \in E; \quad t \text{ otherwise.}$$

Embedding of RDFS into intensional FOL

In what follows, we will first show how to manage the RDF triples by the intensional FOL defined in Section 1.3, and show that it is a conservative extension of RDF.

We will consider an RDF-ontology as finite set of triples $\langle r,p,v\rangle$, where r is a *resource* name (for class, an instance or a value), p is a *property* (*InstanceOf* or *Property* in RDF, or subclass or property in RDFS), and v is a value (which could also be a resource name). We denote by $\mathcal{T}$ the set of all triples which satisfy such requirements.

Definition 31. Each RDFS ontology can be embedded into the intensional FOL $\mathcal{L}_\omega$ as follows:

1. The individuals and data values correspond to FOL constants, the classes and data types correspond to unary predicates, the properties to binary predicates and the sub-class/property relationships correspond to the implication.
2. RDF triple $\langle r,p,v\rangle$ can be represented as a formula of the intensional FOL by:
   2.1 If p is the special URI reference `rdf:type`, then $\langle r,p,v\rangle \mapsto v(r)$,
   2.2 If p is the special URI reference `rdfs:subClassOf`, then
   $$\langle r,p,v\rangle \mapsto (r(x) \Rightarrow v(x)).$$
   Otherwise:
   Case 2.4 When r and v are classes,
   $$\langle r,p,v\rangle \mapsto p(\lessdot r(x)\gtrdot_x, \lessdot v(y)\gtrdot_y),$$
   where in the right-hand side, p is a binary predicate symbol introduced for the property, while r, v are unary predicate symbols introduced for the classes, subject and object, respectively.
   Case 2.5 When r is a class and v is an instance or value, $\langle r,p,v\rangle \mapsto p(\lessdot r(x)\gtrdot_x, v)$,
   Case 2.6 When v is a class and r is an instance or value, $\langle r,p,v\rangle \mapsto p(r, \lessdot v(y)\gtrdot_y)$,
   Case 2.7 When r and v are the instances or the values (ground triple),
   $$\langle r,p,v\rangle \mapsto p(r,v).$$
3. The RDFS ontology graph $\mathcal{O} = \{\langle r_i,p_i,v_i\rangle \mid 1 \le i \le n, n \ge 2\}$ is embedded into the formula $\phi_1 \wedge \cdots \wedge \phi_n$, where ϕ_i is the embedding of a triple $\langle r_i,p_i,v_i\rangle, 1 \le i \le n$.

A blank node x in a triple $\langle x,p,v\rangle$ is embedded into the formula $\exists x.p(x, \lessdot v(y)\gtrdot_y)$ if v is a class; into the formula $\exists x.p(x,v)$ otherwise.

The reified RDF statements are embedded into the intensional terms by nidifying abstraction operator. For example, $\langle\langle r,p,v\rangle, p_1, v_1\rangle$ is represented in intensional FOL as a formula $p_1(\lessdot p(r,v)\gtrdot, v_1)$.

Notice that in this embedding of RDF triples, we consider them as intensional terms, and not as logic sentences (as in current RDF interpretation and its model theory), which identify a ground triple $\langle r, p, v\rangle$ with a logic atom $p(r, v)$. As we have explained in the Introduction, such an identification used in RDF will be epistemically equivalent to consideration of a tuple t of a relation R, as the ground atom $R(t)$, which is not acceptable: tuples of constants are considered in a logic theory as the terms from which we can build logic predicate forms and sentences. So, by the definition above of transformation of RDF triples (considered as tuples of a ternary relation) into a formal logic formulae, we obtained a correct epistemic framework as well.

Another advantage in this embedding is that we do not need to define the meaning of a predicate `rdfs:subClassOf` by the axioms for reflexivity and transitivity as in RDFS. We do not need more of the RDF axiom for the relationship between `rdfs:subClassOf` and `rdf:type` as well.

Example 10. Let us consider some of the properties of RDFS, which cannot be embedded into standard (extensional) FOL, but are perfectly accepted by intensional FOL $\mathcal{L}_\omega$:

On the one hand, *rdfs:Resource* is an instance of *rdfs:Class*; on the other hand, *rdfs:Class* is a subclass of *rdfs:Resource*. Thus, *rdfs:Resource* is an instance of its subclass.

This is a contradiction for a standard extensional FOL. But in the intensional FOL, where there is distinction between the intension and extension of a given concept (formalized as a logical predicate), we have that for these two intensional concepts (represented in intensional FOL by unary predicates $p_R(x)$ and $p_C(y)$, respectively), e. g., in the actual world with the extensionalization function h, and an intensional interpretation $I : \mathcal{L} \to \mathcal{D}$:

$I(p_R(x)) = \mathit{rdfs{:}Resource} \in D_1$ is an unary concept-instance, and hence an element of the intensional concept $I(p_C(y)) = \mathit{rdf{:}Class} \in D_1$. That is, $\mathit{rdfs{:}Resource} = I(p_R(x)) \in h(I(p_C(y))) = h(\mathit{rdf{:}Class})$, while the denotation of the intensional concept $\mathit{rdf{:}Class} = I(p_C(y))$ is a subset of a denotation of the intensional concept $\mathit{rdfs{:}Resource} = I(p_R(x))$, i. e., for the extensions of these two intensional concepts it holds that $h(\mathit{rdf{:}Class}) \subseteq h(\mathit{rdfs{:}Resource}) \subseteq \mathcal{D}$. So, we have the following fact in the intensional FOL:

$$\text{rdfs:Resource} = I(p_R(x)) \in h(\text{rdf:Class}) \subseteq h(\text{rdfs:Resource}) \tag{2.46}$$

Analysis of the embedding

Let us consider the correspondence between the RDF nonstandard model, with an interpretation $I_{\text{RDF}} : V \to \text{IR}$, where V is the RDF vocabulary (in our case it is also part of the syntax of the intensional FOL language $\mathcal{L}_\omega$), and IR is the domain of RDF resources (in our case $\text{IR} = D_{-1} \bigcup D_0 \bigcup D_1 \bigcup D_2 \subseteq \mathcal{D}$) with $\text{IP} = D_2$ (the set of RDF properties is the set of binary relation-in-intensions), and LV (the set of literal values of RDF) is a subset of D_{-1}. In Figure 2.1, the embedding of the nonstandard RFS model into the intensional FOL logic model is schematically represented: in grey color

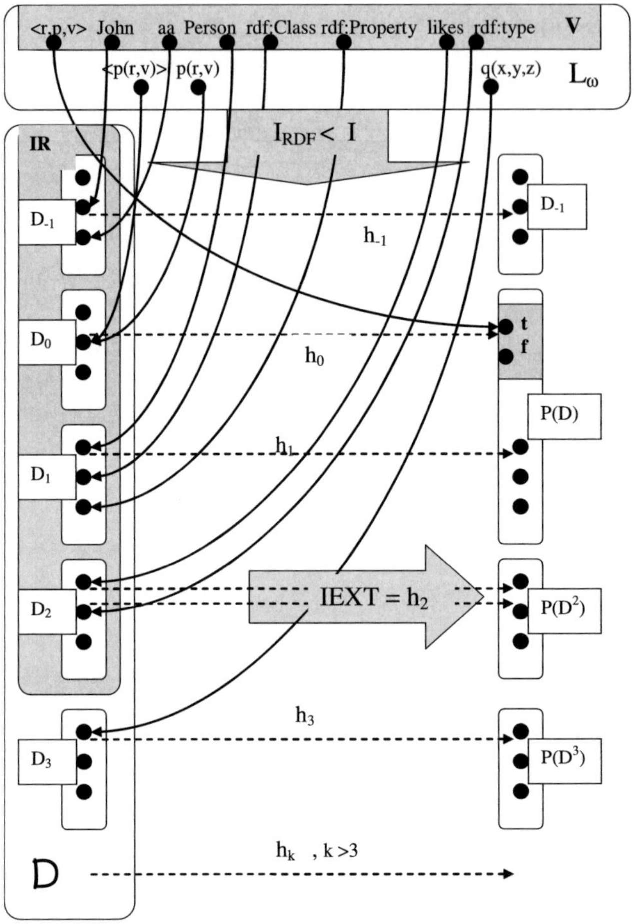

Figure 2.1: Embedding of RFS.

are represented the original RDF model components. There are the following differences:

1. The original RDF model theory has a partial intensional structure: only its properties in IP (embedded into $D_2 \subset \mathcal{D}$) are intensional entities, and for them there exists the extensionalization function I_{EXT}. In intensional FOL language, all intensional entities have an extension: thus, instead of the complex derivation of the class extension I_{CEXT} in RDF model theory, defined through the extension of $I_S(\mathit{rdf{:}type}) \in \mathrm{IP} \subset \mathrm{IR}$:

$$I_{\mathrm{CEXT}}(x) = \{y \mid (y, x) \in I_{\mathrm{EXT}}(I_S(\mathrm{rdf{:}type}))\}$$

   we can directly find the extension by the mapping component h_1 of the extensionalization function h of the intensional FOL model.

2. The other difference is that in a language $\mathcal{L}_\omega$, for any ground RDF triple $\langle r,p,v\rangle$, we have the logic atom $p(r,v)$ and its intensional abstraction, i. e., a term $<p(r,v)>$. So, the RDF interpretation of the ground triple $\langle r,p,v\rangle$, $I_{\mathrm{RDF}}(\langle r,p,v\rangle)$, where r, v are individual constants, corresponds to the following extension, in the actual world, of the intensional "name" $I(p(r,v)) \in D_0$ of the ground atom $p(r,v)$ obtained from atom with variables $p(x,y)$, where I is the intensional interpretation for $\mathcal{L}_\omega$:

$$I_{\mathrm{RDF}}(\langle r,p,v\rangle) = h(I(p(r,v))) = t \quad \text{iff} \quad (h(I(r)), h(I(v))) \in h(I(p(x,y))).$$

3. The domain IR in RDFS model theory has no any algebraic structure, different from the algebraic structure over a domain $\mathcal{D}$ where, e. g., $I(A \wedge B) = \mathrm{conj}(I(A), I(B))$, and hence the denotation of all complex formulae in $\mathcal{L}_\omega$ can be computed from the denotation of its subformulae (the denotation relation of all the complex intensional terms in $\mathcal{L}_\omega$ is recursively defined).
4. While the different extensions of the actual RDFS framework, e. g., by introducing the predicates with arity bigger than two, would modify its nonstandard model theory, in the model structure of the intensional FOL $\mathcal{L}_\omega$ we do not need any change for such extensions.
5. We do not force the RDF triples and graphs to have logic values, but consider them what they are: complex data structures.
6. With FOL language $\mathcal{L}_\omega$, we have the full logic inference, based on the intensional equality theory. We can enrich original RDFS graphs also with other n-ary predicates, which can be useful for more compact ontology representations. We can also introduce integrity constraints for such ontologies, which can use more complex logic formulae with quantifiers.

In what follows, we will show that disadvantages of the actual nonstandard RDF model theory (RDF model theory), taken from [98], does not hold in its embedding in the intensional FOL $\mathcal{L}_\omega$:

1. *Too few entailment*: Let us consider two formulae, $q(x)$ be equal to $\mathtt{Student}(x) \wedge \mathtt{Employee}(x) \wedge \mathtt{European}(x)$, and $q_1(x)$ be equal to $\mathtt{Student}(x) \wedge \mathtt{Employee}(x)$, such that holds $q(\mathtt{John})$. So, in the RDF model theory, since every concept is also an object, there is no guarantee that if "John" is an instance of the class

$$\mathtt{Student} \bigcap \mathtt{Employee} \bigcap \mathtt{European}$$

also if "John" is an instance of the class $\mathtt{Student} \bigcap \mathtt{Employee}$. But by the embedding into intensional FOL $\mathcal{L}_\omega$, we have that $q(\mathtt{John}) \Rightarrow q_1(\mathtt{John})$ is true, i. e.,

$$\begin{aligned}
h(I(q(x))) &= h(I(\mathtt{Student}(x))\,\mathrm{conj}\, I(\mathtt{Employee}(x))\,\mathrm{conj}\, I(\mathtt{European}(x))) \\
&= h(I(\mathtt{Student}(x))) \bigcap h(I(\mathtt{Employee}(x))) \bigcap h(I(\mathtt{European}(x))) \\
&\subseteq h(I(\mathtt{Student}(x))) \bigcap h(I(\mathtt{Employee}(x))) = h(I(q_1(x))).
\end{aligned}$$

2. *"Contradiction" classes*: Such problem does not exist when RDFS is embedded into the intensional FOL: we cannot define a class "eg:C" as an instance of itself and add a cardinality constraint "= 0;' on the rdf:type property of it.
3. *Size of the universe*: The semantic consequences of the RDFS thesis include that all RDF properties (predicate symbols) are elements of discourse (i. e., of IR): it is valid also in this embedding. We cannot have the situations as in RDFS with only one object in universe, and hence to have an interpretation such that "John" is a member of "Person," but not a member of "Car." In fact, in intensional FOL, all of them are intensionally different entities, and hence we must have their intensional interpretations in $\mathcal{D}$, so that the universe $\mathcal{D}$ cannot have only one object. Thus, in intensional FOL, always there exist interpretations such that Person(John), and $\neg$ Car(John) are true.

This is a characteristic *for all* kinds of logics, which distinguish the intension from the extension of its entities, and hence differentiate them from the logics with *extensional* equality theory.

2.3.3 Logic programs for data integration with RDF ontologies

The approach to use conventional first-order logic (FOL) as the semantic underpinning for RDF has many advantages: FOL is well established and well understood. There is a family of languages based on various FOL subsets offering different tradeoffs with respect to expressive power, complexity and computability, and the direct mapping of such languages into a subset of FOL provides semantic interpretability also.

This approach is not directly compatible with full RDFS, as provided in the previous Section 2.3.2 by considering a general reification by means of abstracted terms of intensional FOL, but it is compatible with the following *simplified version* of RDFS in which it is not used the reification: In what follows, we will adopt the approach used in [98] but not constrained only to description logic. Instead of that, we will consider this RDF sublanguage as Herbrand semantic bases for a world-based introduction of probabilistic information into RDF theory [14].

Data integration in RDF – motivation

The new P2P data integration systems in the semantic web [88] needs rich ontologies for the peer databases and efficient query-answering algorithms for expressive SQL-like query languages. So, the mapping between peer databases has to be based on the *views* (expressed by such SQL-like query languages), defined over peer ontologies, as in other cases of data integration systems [53, 99–101].

Thus, our attempt is to extend the database technology of data integration based on rich ontologies and view-based P2P mappings also for semantic for the data on the

Web expressed in the RDF syntax: principal motivation is that RDF is a reality in Web applications, so that P2P integration of RDF ontologies is necessarily a very important issue. Just because of that, the introduction if new intensional RDB in Chapter 4 is more important as well, because in such databases we unify classical RDB applications and these web applications written in RDF.

RDF ontology

We will consider an RDF-ontology as (only) finite set of triples $\langle r, p, v\rangle$, where r is a *resource* name (for class, an instance or a value), p is a *property* (InstanceOf or property in RDF, or subclass or property in RDFS), and v is a value (which could also be a resource name). We denote by $\mathcal{T}$ the set of all triples, which satisfy such requirements.

Definition 32 (Embedding of RDF-ontologyinto logic programs). We define the logic embedding into logic program clauses as a mapping $\mathbb{E} : \mathcal{T} \to \mathcal{L}$, where $\mathcal{L}$ is intensional FOL with a domain $\mathcal{D}$ and without an intensional abstract operator, such that for any triple $\langle r, p, v\rangle \in \mathcal{T}$ holds:

Case 1: when p = Subclass:

$$\mathbb{E}(\langle r, \text{Subclass}, v\rangle) = r'(x) \leftarrow v'(x)$$

where r', v' are unary predicates for the subject and object of a triple, respectively, and x is a variable over a domain $\mathcal{D}$.

Case 2: When p = InstanceOf:

$$\mathbb{E}(\langle r, \text{InstanceOf}, v\rangle) = r'(v) \leftarrow$$

where r' is an unary predicate for the resource of the RDF triple.

Case 3: When $p \notin$ {InstanceOf, Subclass}:

$$\begin{aligned}
\mathbb{E}(\langle r, p, v\rangle) &= (r'(x) \wedge v'(y)) \leftarrow p'(x, y), \quad \text{if } r, v \text{ are classes;}\\
&= r'(x) \leftarrow p'(x, v), \quad \text{if } r \text{ is a class and } v \text{ is an instance or value;}\\
&= v'(y) \leftarrow p'(r, y), \quad \text{if } v \text{ is a class and } r \text{ is an instance or value;}\\
&= p'(r, v) \leftarrow, \quad \text{if } r \text{ and } v \text{ are instances or values;}
\end{aligned}$$

where, in the right side of equation, p' is a binary predicate assigned by this embedding to the property name p, and r', v' are unary predicates assigned to the subject and the object classes of a triple.

Given an RDF-ontology $\mathcal{O} \subset \mathcal{T}$, we denote by $\mathbb{E}(\mathcal{O})$ its logic ontology obtained by this embedding, i. e., a logic program $\mathbb{E}(\mathcal{O}) =_{def} \{\mathbb{E}(\langle r, p, v\rangle) \mid \langle r, p, v\rangle \in \mathcal{O}\}$. Let $I_H : H \to \mathbf{2}$ be a Herbrand model of this logic program with the Herbrand base H obtained from an RDF-ontology. We define the RDF-model $\mathcal{M}(\mathcal{O})$ of an RDF-ontology

$\mathcal{O}$ recursively for any triple $\langle r,p,v\rangle \in \mathcal{O}$, and for the following cases (a,b are elements of a domain $\mathcal{D}$): $\langle a,p,b\rangle \in \mathcal{M}(\mathcal{O})$ if
1. $p'(a,b), r'(a), v'(b) \in H$ are true in I_H, when r,v are classes;
2. $p'(a,v), r'(a) \in H$ are true in I_H, when r is a class and v is an instance or value;
3. $p'(r,b), v'(b) \in H$ are true in I_H, when v is a class and r is an instance or value;
4. $p'(r,v) \in H$ is true in I_H, when r,v are instances or values.

Thus, all triples in the RDF-model of an ontology $\mathcal{O}$ are ground triples.

Remark. Notice that if $\mathcal{M}(\mathcal{O})$ is an RDF-model of an ontology $\mathcal{O}$, then for any ground RDF triple $\langle r,p,v\rangle$ holds that clause

$$\text{clause} \quad \mathbb{E}(\langle r,p,v\rangle) \quad \text{is satisfied} \quad \text{iff} \quad \langle r,p,v\rangle \in \mathcal{M}(\mathcal{O}) \tag{2.47}$$

We can also enrich the RDF-ontology language by the negation operation.

Definition 33 (Negation). We define the negation algebraic operation $\sim$ for extended algebraic RDF-ontology language, for a RDF triple $\langle r,p,v\rangle$, by

$$\mathbb{E}(\sim \langle r,p,v\rangle) =_{\text{def}} \neg\mathbb{E}(\langle r,p,v\rangle),$$

where $\neg$ is the logic negation of program's clauses such that

$$\neg(\phi \leftarrow \psi) =_{\text{def}} ((\psi \wedge \neg\phi) \leftarrow)$$
$$\neg(\phi \leftarrow) =_{\text{def}} (\neg\phi \leftarrow)$$

The triples or their negations will be called RDF-literals.

Notice that for any ground RDF triple $\langle r,p,v\rangle$ holds: $\mathbb{E}(\sim \langle r,p,v\rangle)$ is true iff $\langle r,p,v\rangle \notin \mathcal{M}(\mathcal{O})$. It is reasonable to use negation $\sim$ in order to specify complex terms for RDF ontologies. It is kind of an explicit constraint. For example, when we introduce the ground literal term $\sim \langle r,p,v\rangle$ in an ontology specification, we specify a constraint that the triple $\langle r,p,v\rangle$ *cannot* be part of any RDF-model of such ontology (like the specification of explicit negative information in a *logic* ontology language).

The Peer-to-Peer (P2P) database systems offer an alternative to traditional client-server systems for some application domains. A P2P system has no centralized schema and no central administration. Instead, each peer is an autonomous information system, and information integration is achieved by establishing P2P mappings among various peers. Queries are posed to one peer, and the role of query processing is to exploit both the data that are internal to the peer, and the mappings with other peers in the system.

In what follows, we consider an RDF ontology as a basic data strata of a peer database. In order to define the logical views over such RDF ontologies, we will use the logic theory obtained by embedding this RDF-ontology $\mathcal{O}$ into intensional FOL with abstraction, as provided previously.

It has become customary to define the notion of RDF programming via a long list of triples (binary RDF-properties), which each resource must possess. In relational language, instead, the data are conceptually grouped around n-ary predicates with a set of attributes, which together describe different properties attributed to such logical concept.

Views are an established technology for both relational and object-oriented databases. They are mainly used to provide data customization, i. e., the adaptation of content to meet the demands of specific applications and users, so that they present the key technology for integrating heterogeneous and distributed systems, facilitating interoperability by hiding the foibles of each information component and gluing individual components together to form an integrated P2P application system.

The simple idea is to see a view $\varphi(x_1, \dots, x_n)$ over an RDF-ontology, expressed as a formula in some query language for RDF databases (for example, as a SELECT-FROM-WHERE structure in [102, 103], as n-ary relation-in-intension (intensional name) whose extension in the actual world (a possible world corresponds to the possible RDF database extension) is equal to its query answer.

Example 11 (from [104]). To find all (sculpture, museum) pairs, in an RDF peer database, where the sculpture was created by Rodin, the museum houses the given sculpture, and the museum web site was not modified since January 1, 2001, and we can define the following query: rdql-query =:

```
SELECT ?sculpture, ?museum
WHERE (?sculpor, <ns1:lname>,"Rodin"),
   (?sculptor, <ns1:creates>, ?sculpture),
   (?sculpture, <ns1:exhibited>, ?museum),
   (?museum, <ns1:last-modified>, ?date),
AND ?date <2001.01.01
USING ns1 FOR <http://www.icom.com/schema1>
```

and the correspondent view, by:

$$\varphi(x_1, x_2) = \text{CREATEVIEW view-name AS rdql-query},$$

where $\varphi(x_1, x_2)$ is a virtual predicate, obtained by the following FOL translation into logic clause (Definition 32):

$$\varphi(x_1, x_2) \leftarrow \text{lname}(y, \text{“Rodin”}) \wedge \text{creates}(y, x_1) \wedge \text{exhibited}(x_1, x_2) \\ \wedge \text{last-modified}(x_2, z) \wedge (z < 2001.01.01),$$

where x_1, x_2 are free variables for `sculpture` and `museum`, respectively.

The peer database in this framework is just the logic theory, defined as union of the RDF database's FOL-embedding and a number of views defined over it (they constitute a virtual user-type interface). Such an embedding of a RDF database, together with its view-extension can be used as mean for intensional mapping with other peer databases in a web P2P networks [57, 105]. There are the following nice properties for this RDF peer database framework:

- The FOL embedding of standard RDF database together with views corresponds to the definite logic program, thus the database model of such RDF peer database has a *unique* Herbrand model, different from the standard Data Integration Systems (DIS) with *relational* schema ontology, which usually suffer incomplete information and a very high number of Herbrand models (possible completions of this withdraw): so, the query answering from peer databases with RDF database is very efficient (polynomial complexity).
- The defined views can be materialized and there are efficient algorithms [104] for maintenance of RDF views when new RDF data triples are inserted in a peer database, when some of them are deleted or modified.
- From the theoretical point of view, the possibility to transform the original RDF based peer database into the more expressive, but *decidable*, FOL sublanguages, is important if we want to add also integrity constraints over a peer database ontology (e. g., in the simplest case, the key constraints over a view). In that case, we are able to parse the original RDF structures into a deductive predicate-based database. In such way, we are able to rich the expressive power of standard relational DIS (see more in the dedicated Chapter 3).

Now we can use the new intensional equivalence relation between intensional entities (1.11), defined in intensional FOL by Corollary 3 in Section 1.3, which can be used as intensional mapping between databases: we can define the set of intensionally equivalent views over two different databases as semantic mapping between them as explained in detail in Chapter 3. Such approach to the mapping between RDF ontologies has been proposed in [54]. Such interschema mappings is not invasive w. r. t. the local epistemic knowledge of any single peer: each database-peer with a proper RDF-ontology and the number of *intensional views* defined by RDF queries is completely free to change its local RDF structure (insert, delete and modification of RDF triples). It does not import the extensional knowledge from other peer databases of a P2P system, but specify only which part of its own knowledge has the same meaning as some knowledge (intensional views) of other actors.

We consider only RDF ontologies, which can be embedded in the intensional FOL, for which the resulting logic theory corresponds to definite logic programs with a *unique* Herbrand model of a peer database: so, the query answering for such peer is very efficient and suitable for intensive Web information retrieval.

The intensional views (RDF queries) over peers present the key technology for integrating heterogeneous and distributed systems, facilitating interoperability by hiding the foibles of each information component and gluing individual components together to form an integrated P2P application system. The epistemic independence of such peers is a guarantee for development of very robust P2P database systems.

The intensional mapping semantics for peer databases with RDF ontologies, presented here, constitutes a sound basis for studying the various issues related to interschema knowledge representation and reasoning, especially for P2P database systems in the web environment where peers can be considered as complex database agents.

3 Intensional semantics for P2P database systems

3.1 Intensionality and epistemic independency of database peers

Ontologies play a prominent role on the semantic web. An ontology specifies a conceptualization of a domain in terms of concepts, attributes and relations. However, because of the semantic web distributed nature, data on it will inevitably come from many different ontologies. A key challenge in building the semantic web, one that has received relatively little attention, is finding semantic mappings among the ontologies (peers). Given the decentralized nature of the development of the semantic web, there will be an explosion in the number of ontologies. Many of these ontologies will describe similar domains, but using different terminologies, and others will have overlapping domains. To integrate data from disparate ontologies, we must know the *semantic correspondence* between their elements [106]. Recently, a number of different architecture solutions have been given [53, 101, 107–110].

Indeed, current P2P systems focus strictly on handling semantic-free, large-granularity requests for objects by identifier (typically a name), which both limits their utility and restricts the techniques that might be employed to distribute the data. These current sharing systems are largely limited to applications in which objects are large, opaque and atomic, and whose content is well described by their name. Moreover, they are limited to caching, prefetching or pushing of content at the object level, and know nothing of overlap between objects.

These limitations arise because the P2P world is lacking in the areas of semantics, data transformation and data relationships, yet these are some of the core strengths of the data management community. Queries, views and integrity constraints can be used to express relationships between existing objects.

The Peer-to-Peer (P2P) database systems offer an alternative to traditional client-server systems for some application domains. A P2P system has no centralized schema and no central administration. Instead, each peer is an autonomous information system, and information integration is achieved by establishing P2P mappings among various peers. Queries are posed to one peer, and the role of query processing is to exploit both the data that are internal to the peer, and the mappings with other peers in the system. An increasing amount of data is becoming available in the world wide web, and the data is managed under an increasing diversity of a data model and access mechanisms. Much of this data is semistructured. In what follows, we will consider the reach ontology of peer databases, formally expressed as a global schema of a data integration system (specified in Section A.6.4 in the Appendix). A Data Integration System (DIS) [21, 111] is a triple $\mathcal{I}_i = (\mathcal{G}_i, \mathcal{S}_i, \mathcal{M}_i)$, where $\mathcal{G}_i = (\mathcal{G}_{T_i}, \Sigma_{T_i})$ is a global schema (ontology), expressed in a language $\mathcal{L}_\mathcal{O}$ over an alphabet $\mathcal{A}_{\mathcal{G}_i}$, Σ_{T_i} are the integrity constraints, $\mathcal{S}_i$ is a source schema and $\mathcal{M}_i$ is a set of mappings between a global schema $\mathcal{G}_{T_i}$ and a source schema $\mathcal{S}_i$.

https://doi.org/10.1515/9783110981438-003

The main *motivation* for the introduction of intensional logic for the mappings between peers is based on the desire to have the *full* epistemic independency of peer databases: we consider that they can change their ontology and/or extension of their knowledge independently from other peers and without any communication to other peers. So, we intend to use the mappings between peers that are not controlled by any centralized system, which are not permanently correct during the evolution of a P2P system in time but express only assumptions based on their local belief about knowledge of other peers: here, there is not any transfer of local knowledge of a peer to knowledge of other peers, which can possibly generate inconsistency of other peers, but only belief based assumption that they can speak about intensionally equivalent concepts. From a practical point of view, we assume that there is no any *omniscient* query agent and able to know the whole global P2P system. So, as in human communication, based on the fact that the same concepts have the same meaning, but not extensions for any human being, query answering must be based on the weaker form of deduction of that of the omniscient deduction, which uses the modus ponens and necessity rule (for normal modal logic) to derive all possible deductions. In this way, we intend to obtain very robust P2P systems but also the possibility to map naturally P2P database systems into grid computation: if the peers are fully independent, it is enough to associate each pair (peer, query formulae) to a particular resource of grid computing, in order to obtain known answer from such peer.

The intensional logic is necessary in order to develop more intelligent query agents, which have to manage the data concepts in similar way as humans. The classical extensional logic, developed to work with *rigid* concepts (which do not change their extension in different circumstances (possible worlds)) as are mathematical concepts, natural numbers, integers, prime numbers, reals or *built-in* relations over numbers $\leq, =$, etc.), is too limited when we have to deal with *nonrigid* concepts, as for example, the relation "Car," whose extension in the same database change in time. In the classic extensional logic, any two concepts are equal if they have the same extension (any two sets with the same members are equal), so that the same concept "Car," as commonly considered by humans, in extensional logics will be divided in a number of different concepts (each one with different set of members).

When we are dealing with problems concerning only a given world (e. g., the actual world in a given time instance), as the most traditional software applications do, we can describe the data semantics by standard first-order extensional logic (whose model will determine the actual extension for any database relation). But when, as in this case, we pass to more intelligent P2P systems, when the query agent has to consider the query-rewriting algorithms over two concepts in two different and epistemically independent peers, it is the identical *meaning* of these two concepts, which has to be considered as a semantic connection between two different peers.

Similarly, as human do when they communicate: when I speak with my friend about the "Car," I know that we are speaking about the same concept also, when I do not know my whole knowledge extension about cars (and really I am not able to enumerate all instances of cars that is part of my memory), not his actual extension about cars. This observation is useful in order to understand why the meaning of nonrigid concepts cannot be defined constructively based on its possible extensions: it is the human mental process, developed in the brain of one person, able to recognize that one object is a car or is not a car that corresponds to the meaning of this concept for this person. This distinction will be useful when we will approach the two complementary approaches to intensional logics: Montague's and Bealer's.

The intensional mappings, based on intensionally equivalent views of two different peers, is considered also in [53, 55] where they used the *extensional* FOL and described the algorithm able to extract the answers to conjunctive queries. Logic theory was not defined in which the set of answers is the extension of a conjunctive query (seen as virtual predicate) in a given model of this logic. That is, was not given was the logic theory with the proof-theoretic framework where the set of answers is exactly the set of inferred ground facts from this logic theory: in [53, 55] is presented the procedural, algorithmic method for computing the answers to conjunctive queries, but they missed the logic theoretical approach to query answering. The main contributions in this chapter are:

1. We define the two-level modal logic framework: At the higher level, we define the intensional modal FOL with intensional identity for a P2P system, $\mathcal{L}_\omega$, and enrich it with the *intensional equivalence*, as provided by Example 3 in Section 1.3. It is a *predicate* modal logic (FOL quantifiers are transformed into modal operators). This logic is used by query agents, and uses only predicates of mediator schema of peer databases and views defined over them. This logic is modal logic where the set of possible worlds is the set of all possible evolutions in a time of a given P2P system (when peers modify their ontologies or their extension). We define the *weak deduction* inference for this intensional logic to be implemented by a query answering algorithm of nonomniscient query agents: this weak inference is the result of the fact that, different from all other P2P systems based on extensional mappings between peers, and there is no any dictionary, which contains the set of *all* interpeer mappings (it corresponds to a kind of global P2P schema), but the query agent, when they can access a particular peer can access only its local semantic mappings to other peers.
2. We show that the extensionalization function in the *actual world* $h = \Bbbk$ of the intensional FOL $\mathcal{L}_\omega$, which defines the extension of all intensional entities of this logic, interesting for a query answering, can be modeled by the second, lower "computational" level multimodal logic, where each peer database P_i is characterized by its "know" modal operator K_i. For the computation of the *extension* of peer's concepts in a given actual world we use the "normal" *extensional* logic. The global P2P modal logic has two-level accessibility relations: the higher level is the accessibility relation between peers, determined by the mappings between peers

defined by the developer of peer ontologies in public conciliation with other developers of web peers; This conceptual level is the workspace for query agents in the web and corresponds to the query rewriting process. The lower level is represented by the accessibility relations of the S5 epistemic models of each local peer database; this is the query computation level of the known answer for any peer database, and can be translated directly to the grid computation nodes.

3. Finally, we define an object-oriented class for query agents, which implements as the method for the query rewriting algorithm, able to reformulate the original user conjunctive query, specified over a peer P_i, in intensionally equivalent queries for other peers. We show that this algorithm is sound and complete w. r. t. the weak deduction of the intensional logic $\mathcal{L}_\omega$. This issue is much more complex than in extensional semantics of interpeers mappings ("strong" mappings) [101, 112] where is possible to use the recursive DATALOG programs for query agents: for the intensional semantics, which cannot be embedded into such extensional logic, we need a new more general recursive approach based on the mathematical coalgebras and nonwell-founded sets [113, 114]. As far as we know, this is the first *necessary* introduction of these mathematical instruments for query answering problems in databases, which is not part of the common background of the database community, and we hope that it would not be serious obstacle for the comprehension of these techniques.

3.2 Peer-to-peer database systems

In what follows, we will introduce the Peer-to-Peer (P2P) database systems, where each peer is considered as an independent two-tier architecture, of a data integration system (specified in Section A.6.4 in the Appendix), with the virtual mediated (global) schema used for posing the conjunctive queries, and the relations at the data sources, and we will introduce the basic notion about the intensional FOL logic: Montague's and Bealer's approaches.

P2P systems offer an alternative to traditional client-server systems for some application domains. A P2P system has no centralized schema and no central administration. In P2P systems, every node (peer) of the system acts as both client and server and provides part of the overall information available from an internet-scale distributed environment. In this paper, we consider a formal framework based on the following considerations [115]: what we need here is

- A mechanism that is able, given any two peer databases, to define mappings between them, without resorting to any unifying (global) conceptual structure.
- A completely decentralized network of database peers: all peers serve as entry points for search, offering their relational schema in order to formalize user queries.

- Query answering, fundamentally based on interactions, which are strictly local and guided by locally defined mappings of a considered peer w. r. t. other peers.
- Not limit a priori the topology of the mapping assertions between peers in the system: we do not impose acyclicity of assertions.
- A semantic characterization that leads to setting where query answering is decidable, and possibly, polynomially tractable.

The last two considerations, decidability and nonacyclicity enforce the reason to use an epistemic modal logic instead of FOL (see, e. g., [101]) to model P2P systems.

Epistemic multimodal logic framework for peers

We consider that a logic theory for a peer database (see, e. g., [116]) has *one or more* minimal 2-valued Herbrand models: because of *incomplete* or *inconsistent* information in the web we will usually have more than one minimal Herbrand model for a peer database, one for each possible completion of incomplete information or for each repairing of the inconsistent information. For generality, we define only a subset of *preferred* minimal Herbrand models for a query answering from a peer (e. g., we can consider only the set of "minimal" repairing for inconsistent information).

In the data integration framework [21], each peer can be seen as global schema, which integrates incomplete semistructured web sources, with integrity constraints: such integrity constraints introduce Skolem functions (constants). It is known that such global schema can have also an infinite canonical database with Skolem constants [117].

In the previous section, it was shown that *plausible* query answering, such that is true in each preferred model of a peer database, corresponds to the cumulative nonmonotonic inference [118]; in the limit case when we consider *all* minimal Herbrand models, we will have the case of *known* query answering. Anyway, if we consider the set of preferred models as the set of possible worlds for a peer database, we obtain that such query answering corresponds to the S5 modal logic, following Levesque [119] that we can consider peer P_i as a kind of *epistemic* logic with universal modal operator K_i "Peer P_i knows that ..." Thus, queries should be formulas in an epistemic modal FOL, $K_i q(\mathbf{x})$, where $q(\mathbf{x})$ is the original user that defined conjunctive query over the ontology $\mathcal{O}_i$ of a peer P_i. Consequently, we consider that each peer database P_i is an independent epistemic logic theory with *incomplete* information, such that given some conjunctive query $q(x)$ over its ontology, responds by known answers (true in all Herbrand models, and derived from them Tarski's interpretations, of such a theory). Thus, following Levesque [119], queries should be formulas in an epistemic modal FOL, with a single universal modal operator K_i (for "know"). In this chapter, we will consider S5 modal logic for peers (more details in Definition 36 of Section 3.3): we consider that if some sentence is *known* in a peer P_i it is also *true*. Thus, given a single peer database, the possible words are Herbrand models (legal databases) of this database, each one connected to all others. Thus, a modal query formula at some world $K_i q(x)$ is a believed (known) iff $q(x)$ is true with all possible words (Herbrand models). In [120], it was proven that such modal semantics lead to first-order, Prolog-like, query evaluators.

Thus, we consider that each peer database P_i is an epistemic S5 normal modal logic, where possible worlds are preferred Herbrand models of a peer database with incomplete/inconsistent information, with an epistemic operator "peer P_i knows," K_i, and with relational database schema (ontology) $\mathcal{O}_i$ for *conjunctive* query language.

Such an epistemic semantics of peers is presented in [53] based on the *hybrid mono-modal* language with a unique universal modal operator $\Box$ [121], so that where $K_i = @_i\Box$, where new modal operator, @, for this hybrid logic enables to "retrieve" worlds: A formula of the form $@_i\varphi$ is an instruction to *move* to the world labeled by the variable i and evaluate φ there.

Let $q_{P_i}(\mathbf{x})$ and $q_{P_k}(\mathbf{x})$ be two views (conjunctive queries) over P_i and P_k, respectively, with the same set of free variables $\mathbf{x}$, then we can have two scenarios:

1. The *strong (extensional)* multimodal mapping, introduced by a formula $K_i q_{P_i}(\mathbf{x}) \Rightarrow K_k q_{P_k}(\mathbf{x})$, where '$\Rightarrow$' is the logic implication, used in a single S5 modality [101, 122, 123] (and also in Piazza P2P system [112], where they do not use the autoepistemic logic formalism, but they are considering the same query answering based on *certain* (that is known) answers [124] from peers), and in K45 multi-modality [123]. It tells that the knowledge of the peer P_i contained in its view $q_{P_i}(\mathbf{x})$ *must be* contained in the view $q_{P_k}(\mathbf{x})$ of the peer P_k. In this case, this forced transfer of the local data of one peer to other peers that can render inconsistent knowledge of other peers, and from the semantic point of view, reassembles the kind of strong data integration system, with a global logic of the whole P2P system and a recursive datalog for query rewriting [101].
2. The *weak (intensional)* mapping [43, 53, 125, 126], defined by the intensional equivalences, denoted by $q_{P_i}(\mathbf{x}) \approx q_{P_k}(\mathbf{x})$. In what follows, we will consider only this intensional version for P2P mapping based on considerations presented in [43]. The more complete comparative analysis of these two different approaches can be found in [55].

What is the fundamental difference of these two approaches?

1. First of all, in the first "strong" mapping case, the instance database of any peer is *strictly dependent* of current (in a given instance of time) instance databases of other peers. That means that we cannot encapsulate a peer as an independent ADT (Abstract Data Type) and see it as a block module of data during query-answering processing. Moreover, we need a global logic for all peers in order to determine the exact extension of one peer database. Thus, also if we do not provide any "global schema" of a P2P network, semantically we must assume it: the way in which it is used for conjunctive-query answering as explained in [101], where it is used as a recursive datalog for this *whole P2P logic theory*, in order to process a given

conjunctive query over a single peer database. This global P2P datalog program returns with the union of conjunctive queries for each peer database in the considered P2P network. Such query-rewriting approach, based on a global P2P recursive datalog logic theory, *avoids to materialize* the propagations of facts between peer databases, caused by material implications, $K_i q_{P_i}(\mathbf{x}) \Rightarrow K_k q_{P_k}(\mathbf{x})$, between peers: in web applications, such dynamic (and cyclic) transfer of ground facts between peer databases practically cannot be accepted, because so high traffic of data in the internet would drastically slow down the whole web system.
In the second approach, we do not have such problems: each logic theory of a single peer database is completely independent from all other peers, and can be encapsulated in a modular P2P structure as an ADT (as will be explained in what follows), so easily implemented in a greed computation framework. Moreover, each peer is free to change not only its data extension, but also its schema representation, without invalidating the P2P mapping system.

2. The second problem is that in the first "strong" approach, the "system" has to know the whole set of peer databases in the P2P network in any time; otherwise, no one peer database can know which are other peers that maps the data toward himself: thus, there must exist some centralized control. The addition of other peer databases must be explicitly communicated to this global system controller. This information is used by the query-answering agent (consequently, every query-agent *knows the global* P2P database schema, different from the declared fact against any globalization) with above described recursive datalog program, which contains the whole logic theory of a P2P network. Otherwise, when any other peer, which was not considered in the actually P2P network, makes one mapping (by the material implication defined above) toward some existing peer database in a P2P network, if the "system" (basic part of any query-answering agent) is not aware of that, the query-answer is incomplete and can be also unsound (in the case when this new mapping introduces the mutually inconsistent information in the P2P network system).
In the second, weak approach, there is no any concept explicitly or implicitly assumed for a global P2P system. Different from the first approach where the mappings between peers are part of the underlying "system" (i. e., global logic theory of the whole P2P network system), the mappings based on intensional equivalences are a local component of a peer: each peer defines its belief set of the correspondent equivalent views of other peers, and the query agent can use these mappings only when it has access to a particular peer. When the user query is generated over a schema (ontology) of a given peer, the activated query agent has no any global knowledge about the whole P2P network system, but can only use the local mappings of the accessed peer to pass to other locally mapped peers.
3. The third problem is the *inconsistency tolerance*. When we consider a peer database as a single data integration system with GLAV (Global/local as views) mappings between the data sources and the global (virtual) peer database schema,

the problem with mutually inconsistent information from different sources can be localized and resolved inside the local peer database (its logic theory defined by the data integration system), by a kind of 2-valued, e. g., in [127, 128], or many-valued belief revision, e. g., 4-valued Belnap's bilattice based belief revision [129]. Such approach for the resolution of local inconsistency inside a particular peer database is valid, just because it is local to a peer, and there is a team of developers, which are responsible for a correct implementation of this particular peer database. This handling of local inconsistency of a peer database is common for both approaches to mapping semantics between different peers. What is problematic in the first "strong" approach is that when each peer database is consistent by himself (by handling its proper local consistency), the externally mapped data from other peers into a particular peer database can generate the inconsistency (in peer databases with integrity constraints) of this particular peer. In the first approach, such problem is addressed in [123] and does not have an easy, also from a theoretical point of view, solution: in that approach, it is only *partially* resolved by the very strong requirement to simply *eliminate* any external data coming from another *single* peer, which is potentially inconsistent with the information of this peer. But such drastic approach, which loses a part of information (instead of considering the mutually inconsistent information as "possible" versions of the same information), it does not resolve the problem: let us consider, e. g., two different data, which comes into the same peer from two different peers, and each of these data, taken singularly, is consistent with the local knowledge of a peer, but these two data are mutually inconsistent if taken together (e. g., the destination peer has a key constraint for the attribute x of a relation `Person(x,y)` where x is name of a person and y is its age, and two external data, which come from two different peers are {John, 40} and {John, 41}).

In the weak mapping semantic, instead such problem does not exist, just because there is not any correlation between *extensions* of concepts in different peers, but only intensional mapping between them, based on belief sentences of each local peer. Different from the "strong" approach, where if we adopt the possibility of materialization of consequences of material implications between peers, an interrogated peer can completely respond to the user query, in the "weak" approach it is not possible theoretically also: each peer who has the knowledge about the user query has to respond by himself only to the (appropriately rewritten for it) user query; thus, we make an *epistemic difference* between the certain answers of the peer interrogated directly by the user, from the "possible" answers obtained from all other peers. We do not eliminate any information, which comes from different peers, but the user who receives all answers will take the appropriate actions for him to verify the part of information that he considers mutually inconsistent. It is easy to understand that the complexity of the "weak" approach, in a presence of mutually inconsistent P2P information, is less than the complexity of the first-order multimodal logic for the "strong" semantic mapping. □

In what follows, we will consider only this *new intensional version* for P2P mapping better suited for fully independent peers [43]: different from the GLAV (Global-Local-as-view) strong mappings, here the deductive system of the modal S5 intensional FOL, given a user query, derives all intensionally equivalent queries over other peers, and there is *no any transfer* of data from one peer to other, which can introduce inconsistent information to other peers.

Consequently, what we argue is the *full* epistemic independency of peer databases where there is no any forced transfer of a local knowledge of one peer to other peers, but only their collaboration in order to answer to user queries. They can change their ontology and/or extension of their knowledge independently from other peers and without any communication to other peers. In this way, we intend to obtain very robust P2P systems, able to answer to user queries also when intended mappings between peers become incompatible with the modified ontologies (relational database schemas) of peers, but also to have the possibility to map naturally P2P database systems into greed computation: having fully independent peers, which as we will see can be represented as ADTs (Abstract Data Types), it is enough to associate each pair (peer, query-formulae) to a particular resource of greed computing, in order to obtain the known answer from such peer.

3.2.1 Plausible query-answering inference in a peer database with also inconsistent information

In what follows, we will consider a peer database as a Data Integration System (DIS) described in Section A.6.4. Each DIS must be robust enough in order to take in account not only the incomplete but also *inconsistent information* of its source databases, typical in web applications: the extension of source databases change in an unpredictable way so that in different time instances we pass from a consistent to inconsistent DIS and vice versa. Thus, DIS will generally have a possibly infinite number of consistent repairs in their models, and consequently, query answering in such DISs is very complex and time consuming. The current systems adopt the two extreme solutions for query answering: *certain* answers (true in all models of a given DIS) or *all possible* answers (true at any model). The first solution which uses certain answers is to much strong requirement and practically nonapplicable in real situations, and the second one is less meaningful and time/space consuming (they may be infinite also). In this section, we provide the middle solution [118] between these two extremes based on the plausible nonmonotonic query-answering inference. For the rest of this section, we will use the basic notions of the deductive logic provided in Section A.2 in the Appendix. The essential idea behind semantic modeling of nonmonotonic inference goes back to McCarthy's classical paper on *circumscription* [130]: the essential model-theoretic idea is to single out only a subset of "minimal" models. Shoham [131] generalized the concept of circumscription, or minimal entailment, to a more abstract notion: *preferential entailment*. Other approaches are used in order to generalize the semantics for nonmonotonic reasoning [132–134], based on preference structures and choice functions, and in [135] is presented the comparison between these two semantic approaches. In this section is presented a reexamination of a *choice function* approach.

In the following, we denote the fixed part of a DIS $\mathcal{I} = \langle \mathcal{G}, \mathcal{S}, \mathcal{M} \rangle$ (i. e., without the extension of its source data bases $\mathbf{D}$) by $\mathcal{I}_{\text{fix}}$, so that we denote by $\mathcal{I} = (\mathcal{I}_{\text{fix}}, \mathbf{D})$. Informally, $\mathcal{I}_{\text{fix}}$ is the set of sentences (usually universally quantified) of integrity constraints over global schema and mapping assertions (sentences). It may be the case that, for a given source data base extension $\mathbf{D}$, $\mathcal{I} = (\mathcal{I}_{\text{fix}}, \mathbf{D})$ is inconsistent. We denote with $\mathbf{D} \vDash_{\mathcal{I}} \mathcal{I}_{\text{fix}}$ the fact that for this extension of a source databases $\mathbf{D}$ all integrity constraints and mappings are satisfied. In this case, we say that $\mathbf{D}$ is consistent w. r. t. $\mathcal{I}_{\text{fix}}$; otherwise, we say that $\mathbf{D}$ is inconsistent w. r. t. $\mathcal{I}_{\text{fix}}$.

We denote by U the set of *all consistent* DISs. It is easy to verify that each model of a consistent DIS $\mathcal{I}$ is a $\mathcal{L}$-maximal set of the underlying deductive logic $\mathcal{L}$ for data integration systems. Consider that a models of Γ (the set of sentences of $\mathcal{L}$) are interpretations $f : \Gamma \to 2$, with truth values $2 = \{0, 1\}$, i. e., subset of mappings $f \in 2^{\Gamma}$, which satisfy logical connectives (i. e., $f(\neg\phi) = 1 - f(\phi)$, $f(\phi \wedge \phi') = \min(f(\phi), f(\phi'))$, etc.). Thus, each model $m = \{\phi \in \Gamma \mid f(\phi) = 1\}$ is a closed set (theory in $\mathcal{L}$, such that $m = C_n(m)$). The Herbrand model is the restriction of such closed set (i. e., model) m to only *ground atoms*.

We define the mapping $\text{Mod} : U \to 2^{\Gamma}$, such that for any consistent DIS, $\mathcal{I} \in U$, the nonempty set $\text{Mod}(\mathcal{I})$ is the set of all models for this data integration system $\mathcal{I}$.

Now, following [136], given an extension $\mathbf{D}$, possibly inconsistent with $\mathcal{I}_{\text{fix}}$, we say that, for a given extension (instance) $\mathbf{D}'$ of source databases, the DIS $\mathcal{I}' = (\mathcal{I}_{\text{fix}}, \mathbf{D}')$ is a *repair* for $\mathcal{I}$ iff $\mathbf{D}' \vDash_{\mathcal{I}} \mathcal{I}_{\text{fix}}$.

We denote by $R(\mathcal{I})$ the set of all repairs of $\mathcal{I}$; if $\mathcal{I}$ is consistent, then $R(\mathcal{I}) = \{\mathcal{I}\}$.

We say that a sentence ϕ holds in a state (i. e., DIS) $\mathcal{I} \in U$ (relative to the DIS-structure $\mathcal{I}_{\mathcal{M}}$) and write $\mathcal{I}_{\mathcal{M}} \Vdash_{\mathcal{I}} \phi$ iff for every $m \in \text{Mod}(\mathcal{I}), \phi \in m$. Intuitively, a sentence ϕ is true in the state $\mathcal{I}$ (consistent data integration system) just in case ϕ is true in all models (set $\text{Mod}(\mathcal{I})$) of this consistent DIS.

The set of consistent DISs in which ϕ holds will be written $\widehat{\phi} = \{\mathcal{I} \in U \mid \mathcal{I}_{\mathcal{M}} \Vdash_{\mathcal{I}} \phi\} = \{\mathcal{I} \in U \mid \phi \in \bigcap \text{Mod}(\mathcal{I})\}$, and for a set of sentences Γ:

$$\widehat{\Gamma} = \bigcap \{\widehat{\phi} \mid \phi \in \Gamma\} = \left\{\mathcal{I} \in U \mid \Gamma \subseteq \bigcap \text{Mod}(\mathcal{I})\right\},$$

so by monotonicity of C_n, and the fact that $\bigcap \text{Mod}(\mathcal{I})$ is a closed set, i. e., $\bigcap \text{Mod}(\mathcal{I}) = C_n(\bigcap \text{Mod}(\mathcal{I}))$, we obtain

$$\widehat{\Gamma} = \left\{\mathcal{I} \in U \mid C_n(\Gamma) \subseteq \bigcap \mathrm{Mod}(\mathcal{I})\right\},$$

i. e., $\widehat{\Gamma}$ is the set of all DISs in which all sentences in Γ are accepted.

Given a set of consistent DISs, $X \subseteq U$, we may also define the set $\mathrm{th}(X)$ of sentences that are accepted in all DISs in X, i. e., $\mathrm{th}(X) = \{\phi \mid X \subseteq \widehat{\phi}\}$.

Proposition 12. *For any set X of consistent DISs, the set of accepted sentences* $\mathrm{th}(X)$ *is a theory in* $\mathcal{L}$.

Proof 1. $\mathrm{th}(X) = \{\phi \mid X \subseteq \widehat{\phi}\} = \{\phi \mid \forall \mathcal{I} \in X.\phi \in \bigcap \mathrm{Mod}(\mathcal{I})\} = \bigcap\{\bigcap \mathrm{Mod}(\mathcal{I}) \mid \mathcal{I} \in X\}$, thus from the fact that the intersection of closed sets is a closed set, we obtain that $\mathrm{th}(X)$ is a theory. In the singleton case, we obtain the theory $\mathrm{th}(\{\mathcal{I}\}) = \bigcap \mathrm{Mod}(\mathcal{I})$, while $\mathrm{th}(\{\}) = \Gamma$. □

It is easy to verify these two mappings form a Galois connection between $\mathcal{P}(\Gamma)$ and $\mathcal{P}(U)$, that is held:
1. if $\Gamma \subseteq \Delta$, then $\widehat{\Delta} \subseteq \widehat{\Gamma}$,
2. if $X \subseteq Y$, then $\mathrm{th}(Y) \subseteq \mathrm{th}(X)$,
3. $\Gamma \subseteq \mathrm{th}(\widehat{\Gamma})$,
4. $X \subseteq \widehat{\mathrm{th}(X)}$.

Thus, the mapping $C_{\mathcal{I}} = \widehat{\_} \circ \mathrm{th} : \mathcal{P}(U) \to \mathcal{P}(U)$ is a closure operation on the set of DISs, that is held for all $X, Y \in U$:
1. $X \subseteq C_{\mathcal{I}}(X) = \widehat{\{\phi \mid X \subseteq \widehat{\phi}\}} = \bigcap\{\widehat{\phi} \mid X \subseteq \widehat{\phi}\}$,
2. if $X \subseteq Y$, then $C_{\mathcal{I}}(X) \subseteq C_{\mathcal{I}}(Y)$,
3. $C_{\mathcal{I}}(X) = C_{\mathcal{I}}(C_{\mathcal{I}}(X))$.

Proposition 13. *Each closed (sub)set* $X \subseteq U$ *is the set of all repairs of some data integration system* $\mathcal{I}$. *We denote by* U_{clo} *the set of all closed subsets of U.*

Proof 2. Let X be the set of all repairs of some DIS $\mathcal{I}_1$. Let us prove that $X = C_{\mathcal{I}}(X)$. From the property of the closure operator holds that $X \subseteq C_{\mathcal{I}}(X)$. Let $\mathcal{I} \in C_{\mathcal{I}}(X)$ and prove that $\mathcal{I} \in X$.

From $\mathcal{I} \in C_{\mathcal{I}}(X)$, we have that $\mathcal{I} \in \bigcap\{\widehat{\phi} \mid X \subseteq \widehat{\phi}\} = \bigcap\{\widehat{\phi} \mid \mathcal{I}' \in \widehat{\phi}$ for all $\mathcal{I}' \in X\}$. Suppose that $\mathcal{I} \notin X$, i. e., that $\mathcal{I}$ is not a repair of $\mathcal{I}_1$ so that does not satisfy the constraints in $\mathcal{I}_1$, but it is not possible because all members in the set $\bigcap\{\widehat{\phi} \mid \mathcal{I}' \in \widehat{\phi}$ for all $\mathcal{I}' \in X\}$ satisfy such constraints. □

Example 12. For a consistent DIS $\mathcal{I} \in U$, we have that $X = \{\mathcal{I}\} = R(\mathcal{I})$ is closed subset of U, i. e., $\{\mathcal{I}\} = C_{\mathcal{I}}(\{\mathcal{I}\})$.

Let us describe the semantics for plausible query answering in the data integration system $\mathcal{I} = \langle \mathcal{G}, \mathcal{S}, \mathcal{M} \rangle$ by the following structure.

Definition 34 (Prefered repairs). A DIS-structure based on the deductive logic $\mathcal{L}$ is a tuple $\mathcal{I}_{\mathcal{M}} = \langle U, \mathrm{Mod}, F \rangle$, where $F : U_{\mathrm{clo}} \to \mathcal{P}(U)$ is a choice function such that for any inconsistent data integration system $\mathcal{I}$ takes its preferred repairs, i. e., for any $\mathcal{I} \in U$ holds:

$$F(R(\mathcal{I})) \subseteq R(\mathcal{I}),$$

where $R(\mathcal{I})$ is a closed subset of U composed by all repairs of $\mathcal{I}$.

Example 13. For a consistent DIS $\mathcal{I} \in U$, we have that $R(\mathcal{I}) = \{\mathcal{I}\}$, thus $F(R(\mathcal{I})) = F(\{\mathcal{I}\}) \subseteq R(\{\mathcal{I}\}) = \{\mathcal{I}\}$. So, we obtain that $F(\{\mathcal{I}\}) = \{\mathcal{I}\}$.

Cumulative inference for query-answering in data integration

Instead of the monotonic deduction, presented in the Introduction, we will consider nonmonotonic inference, considering that generally the query answering in data integration is nonmonotonic (e. g., when we use a negation operator in query languages, in the case of incomplete information in sources, or in the case when we consider only a subset of preferred repairs for mutually inconsistent information coming from different source databases).

The natural way is to relax the monotonicity property by introducing the cautious monotonicity: it was introduced by Gabbay [137] for finite set of premises (Gentzen-style), and by Makinson [138] (Tarski-style) for a more general infinite set of premises. The last one is a necessary condition in the data integration framework: the incomplete information introduce Skolem functions and infinite Herbrand bases, so that together with recursive logic specification of global schema constraints, the models for databases are possibly infinite.

The following table presents the definition for a *cumulative* nonmonotonic inference relation $\vdash_C$ and operation C_C (reflexivity, cut and cautious monotonicity):

Finitistic or "Gentzen-style" (Table 3.1).

Table 3.1: Finitistic or "Gentzen-style".

$\phi \in \Gamma$ implies $\Gamma \vdash_C \phi$
$\Gamma \bigcup \Delta \vdash_C \phi, \forall \psi \in \Delta.(\Gamma \vdash_C \psi)$ implies $\Gamma \vdash_C \phi$
$\forall \psi \in \Delta.(\Gamma \vdash_C \psi), \Gamma \vdash_C \phi$ implies $\Gamma \bigcup \Delta \vdash_C \phi$

Infinitistic or "Tarski-style" (Table 3.2).

It is easy to verify that the cut and cautious monotonicity can be combined into a simple principle of *cumulation*:

$$\Gamma \subseteq \Delta \subseteq C_C(\Gamma) \quad \text{implies } C_C(\Gamma) = C_C(\Delta) \tag{3.1}$$

Table 3.2: Infinitistic or "Tarski-style".

$\Gamma \subseteq C_C(\Gamma)$
$\Delta \subseteq C_C(\Gamma)$ implies $C_C(\Gamma \bigcup \Delta) \subseteq C_C(\Gamma)$
$\Delta \subseteq C_C(\Gamma)$ implies $C_n(\Gamma) \subseteq C_C(\Gamma \bigcup \Delta)$

or to the following two conditions [132]:

- Right weakening: if $\forall\phi \in \Delta.\Gamma \vdash_C \phi$, and $\Delta \vdash \psi$, then $\Gamma \vdash_C \psi$ i. e., $C_n(C_C(\Gamma)) \subseteq C_C(\Gamma)$
- Left logic equivalence: if $\forall\phi.(\Gamma \vdash \phi$ iff $\Delta \vdash \phi)$, then $\Gamma \vdash_C \psi$ iff $\Delta \vdash_C \psi$ i. e., $C_n(\Gamma) = C_n(\Delta)$ implies $C_C(\Gamma) = C_C(\Delta)$

The common idea in the literature on nonmonotonic reasoning is the following: ϕ is a nonmonotonic consequence of Γ, i. e., $\Gamma \vdash_C \phi$, just in the case α holds in all those Γ-states (in our case Γ-DISs repairs) that are maximally plausible. Formally, we represented this idea by introducing a *choice function* F, which given a set $R(\mathcal{I})$ of all repairs of DIS $\mathcal{I}$, picks out the set $F(R(\mathcal{I}))$ of all the "best" repairs in $R(\mathcal{I})$.

For the DIS-structure $\mathcal{I}_{\mathcal{M}}$, based on the deductive logic $\mathcal{L}$, we define the following relation $\Vdash$ between sets of sentences and single sentences:

$$\Gamma \Vdash \phi \quad \text{iff} \quad F(\widehat{\Gamma}) \subseteq \widehat{\phi} \tag{3.2}$$

We have to demonstrate that this relation is a nonmonotonic consequence (or plausible inference). First, this definition will in general lead to $\Vdash$ being nonmonotonic, since there is no guarantee that $F(\widehat{\Gamma}) \subseteq \widehat{\phi}$ will imply that $F(\widehat{\Gamma \bigcup \{\phi\}}) \subseteq \widehat{\phi}$.

Clearly, one of the best preferred $\Gamma \bigcup \{\phi\}$-states may fail to be a best preferred member of the more inclusive class of Γ-states. Therefore, it need not be the case that $F(\widehat{\Gamma \bigcup \{\phi\}}) \subseteq \widehat{\Gamma}$. Neither does it follow that $F(\widehat{\Gamma \bigcup \{\phi\}}) \subseteq \widehat{\phi}$.

Different choices on the selection function F will give rise to different nonmonotonic logics.

Example 14. Let us consider the choice function, in the case of the so-called minimal repairs w. r. t. *set inclusion preference criterion* [136]: the distance between two database instances $\mathbf{D}_1$ and $\mathbf{D}_2$ is their symmetric difference $\delta(\mathbf{D}_1, \mathbf{D}_2) = (\mathbf{D}_1 - \mathbf{D}_2) \bigcup (\mathbf{D}_2 - \mathbf{D}_1)$. It is *minimal* under set inclusion in the class of instances that satisfy $\mathcal{I}_{\text{fix}}$.

Another example for the choice function is the *minimal cardinality preference criterion* [139]: used in order to minimize deletions and insertions of tuples during a repairing.

Let us now show the fundamental property of the introduced relation $\Vdash$ from data integration systems.

Proposition 14. *If $\mathcal{I}_{\mathcal{M}}$ is a DIS-structure based on the deductive logic $\mathcal{L}$, then $\Vdash$ is a cumulative inference relation based on $\mathcal{L}$. We define the cumulative operation C by*

$$\text{for any } \Gamma' \subseteq \Gamma, \quad C(\Gamma') = \{\phi \mid \Gamma' \Vdash \phi\}.$$

Proof. It is an analog to the proof of the Lemma 4.4. in [133]. □

Let now consider the problem of a plausible query-answering in data integration systems. Let $q(x) \in \mathcal{L}_Q$ be a user query over a global schema $\mathcal{G}$ of the (possibly inconsistent) data integration system $\mathcal{I} = \langle \mathcal{G}, \mathcal{S}, \mathcal{M} \rangle$. We can consider the set of sentences $\text{th}(R(\mathcal{I})) = \{\phi \mid R(\mathcal{I}) \subseteq \widehat{\phi}\}$, where $R(\mathcal{I})$ is a set of all repairs of $\mathcal{I}$, and define the relation $\vDash_I$ as follows:

$$\mathcal{I} \Vdash_I q(c) \quad \text{iff} \quad \text{th}(R(\mathcal{I})) \Vdash q(c) \tag{3.3}$$

where $q(c)$ is a (ground) sentence obtained by substitution of a variables in x by database constants in a query formula. Thus, a plausible answer to the query $q(x)$ can be defined by this cumulative nonmonotonic inference as follows:

$$q^{\mathcal{DB}} = \{q(c) \mid \mathcal{I} \Vdash_I q(c), c \text{ is a tuple of constants of a fixed DIS alphabet}\}.$$

This plausible query answering in DISs is a general one: it holds for any particular query language $\mathcal{L}_Q$, any kind of mappings between source databases and a global schema, and in presence of incomplete and inconsistent information.

Example 15. Let us see that in the case of a consistent DIS, this plausible answering corresponds to the certain (or known) answering to queries.

When DIS $\mathcal{I}$ is consistent, then $R(\mathcal{I}) = \{\mathcal{I}\}$, and $\text{th}(R(\mathcal{I})) = \text{th}(\{\mathcal{I}\}) = \bigcap \text{Mod}(\mathcal{I})$, thus, for any given query $q(x)$ we have that

$$\mathcal{I} \Vdash_I q(c) \quad \text{iff} \quad \text{th}(\{\mathcal{I}\}) \Vdash q(c) \quad \text{iff} \quad F(\widehat{\text{th}(\{\mathcal{I}\})}) \subseteq \widehat{q(c)} \tag{3.4}$$

So, from the fact that $F(\widehat{\text{th}(\{\mathcal{I}\}}) = F(C_{\mathcal{I}}(\mathcal{I})) = F(\{\mathcal{I}\})) = \{\mathcal{I}\}$, and the fact that $\widehat{q(c)} = \{\mathcal{I}' \in U \mid q(c) \in \bigcap \text{Mod}(\mathcal{I}')\}$, we obtain that must hold

$$\{\mathcal{I}\} \subseteq \left\{\mathcal{I}' \in U \mid q(c) \in \bigcap \text{Mod}(\mathcal{I}')\right\},$$

i. e., must hold $q(c) \in \bigcap \text{Mod}(\mathcal{I})$. That is, $q(c)$ must hold in all models of this consistent $\mathcal{I}$, i. e., $q(c)$ is a certain (or known) answer of this data integration system.

The algorithms for answering queries using views are already incorporated into a number of data integration systems with integrity constraints to obtain certain answers. The difficulties basically arise because of the need of dealing with incomplete information and, moreover, with mutually inconsistent information, which comes from different source databases. So, we presented such general framework for a plausible query-answering inference, based on choice functions. As a result, we obtained a cumulative nonmonotonic inference for query answering in data integration.

In what follows, we will use this theory for the definition of single database peers in a network of a given P2P system, by encapsulation in a single peer such as DIS and able to deal with incomplete information and with mutually inconsistent information, which comes from different source databases, and we will mathematically present each such peer as an abstract data object able to respond to user's queries by plausible (known) answers.

3.2.2 Abstract object types for peer databases

The current world wide web has well over billions of pages, but the vast majority of them are in human-readable format only (e. g., HTML). As a consequence, software agents cannot understand and process this information, and much of the potential of the web has so far remained untapped. In response, researchers have created the vision of the *semantic web* [88], where data has structure and *ontologies* that describe the semantics of the data. An ontology specifies a conceptualization of a domain in terms of concepts, attributes and relations [140], and thus introduce the *mediator schema* for user queries, and consequently, *data integration systems*. When data is marked up using mediator schemas (ontologies) software query agents can better understand the semantics and, therefore, more intelligently locate and integrate data for a wide variety of tasks [115, 141].

Information integration is the problem of combining the data residing at different sources, and providing the user with a unified view of these data, called *global schema*.

The global schema is therefore a reconciled view of the information, which can be queried by the user. It can be thought of as a set of virtual relations, in the sense that their extensions are not actually stored anywhere. A data integration system frees the user from having to locate the sources relevant to a query, interact with each source in isolation and manually combine the data from different sources.

Two basic approaches have been used to specify the mapping between sources and the global schema. The first approach, called query centric or global-as-view (GAV), requires that the global schema is expressed in terms of the data sources. More precisely, to every concept of the global schema, a view over the data sources is associated, so that its meaning is specified in terms of the data residing at the sources. The second approach, called source centric or local-as-view (LAV), requires the global schema to be specified independently of the sources. The relationships between the global schema and the sources are established by associating each element of the sources with a view over the global schema. Thus, in the LAV approach, we specify the meaning of the sources in terms of the concepts in the global schema.

The natural way to make more modular structure of a data-intensive internet system, and to open up the possibility of effective query answering techniques is to organize a number of application-domain data integration systems as a P2P system. The most important advantage of organizing a peer as a data integration system is that it enables users to focus on specifying *what* they want, rather then thinking about *how* to obtain the answers: so that we can see it as an *Abstract Object Type* (AOT), which hides internal integration structure with data sources, and offers to users only a mediator schema with the standard query language in order to be able to formulate the questions in a declarative way.

As result, it frees the users from the tedious tasks of finding the relevant data sources, interacting with each source in isolation using a particular interface, and combining data from multiple sources.

The main characteristic distinguishing data integration systems from distributed and parallel database systems is that data sources underlying the system are autonomous. In particular, a data integration system provides access to *preexisting* sources, which were created independently.

The aim of the encapsulation of a data integration system into an Abstract Object Type (AOT) is to hide the internal structure of such complex object and to offer to the user the rich ontology of the global (mediator) schema in order to focus on specifying *what* they want, by ordinary conjunctive queries.

The main point is that every peer can be seen as an AOT (*Abstract Object Type*), which acts at the same level, with no unifying structure above it: in order to respond to the complex user queries (union of conjunctive queries). Thus, we assume that expressive power of peers can be generally given by a single-encapsulated data integration semantic. In this way, considering the (incomplete) sources extracted by wrappers, we may enrich the peer database schema by integrity constraints in order to overcome incompleteness of heterogenous web information: we assume that each AOT peer has a unique model or otherwise a *canonical (universal)* [142, 143] global database, and that responds to user queries by *certain* (i. e., known [120]) answers.

- *Query reformulation*: A user of an AOT poses queries in terms of the mediated schema, rather than directly in the data sources, which are encapsulated and hidden by AOT. As a consequence, the AOT must contain a module that uses the source descriptions in order to reformulate a user query that refers directly to the schemas of the sources. Clearly, we would like the reformulation to be sound, (i. e., the answers to the reformulated query should all be correct answers to the input query), and complete (i. e., all the answers that can be extracted from the data sources should be in the result of applying the reformulated query): the methods of this AOT, which satisfy these requirements give to users the *known answers*.
- *Wrappers*: The other layer of an AOT that does not exist in a traditional system is the (hidden) wrapper layer. Unlike a traditional query execution engine that communicates with a local storage manager to fetch the data, the query execution plan in the AOT must obtain data from remote sources. An encapsulated AOT

wrapper is a program (method), which is specific to a data source, whose task is to translate data from the source to a form that is usable by the query processor (agent) of the system.

Dually to the theory of *algebraic specifications* where an Abstract Data Type (ADT) is specified by a set of operations (constructors), the *coagebraic specification* of a class of systems, i. e., Abstract Object Types (AOT), is characterized by a set of operations (destructors), which tell us what can be *observed* out of a system-*state* (i. e., an element of the carrier), and how can a state be transformed to successor state. Recently [144], the coalgebraic semantics are extended to the logic programming, thus to the specification of database ontologies.

We start introducing the class of coalgebras for database query-answering systems by Definition 133 in the Appendix (Section A.6.2). They are presented in an algebraic style, by providing a cosignature. In particular, sorts include one single "hidden sort," corresponding to the carrier of the coalgebra, and other "visible" sorts for inputs and outputs, which are given a fixed interpretation. Visible sorts will be interpreted as sets without any algebraic structure defined on them. Coalgebraic terms, built only over destructors, have for us a precise interpretation as the basic *observations* that one can make on the states of a coalgebra. Input sorts are considered as the set $\mathcal{L}_Q$ of modal conjunctive queries, $K_i q(\mathbf{x})$, while output sorts are "valuations," i. e., the set of a resulting views, for each query $q(\mathbf{x})$ over a database $\mathcal{A}$ (considered as a carrier of the coalgebra).

In object-oriented terminology, the coalgebras just introduced are expressive enough to specify parametric methods and attributes for a database (conjunctive) query answering systems. In what follows, we conceive a peer P_i as a AOT software module characterized by a network ontology G_i expressed in a language $\mathcal{L}_\mathcal{O}$ over an alphabet $\mathcal{A}_{\mathcal{G}_i}$. The internal structure of a peer database is hidden to the user, encapsulated in the way that only its logical relational schema $\mathcal{G}_{T_i}$ can be seen by users, and is able to respond to the union of conjunctive queries by *known* answers [111].

3.2.3 Database P2P network definition

In order to be able to share the knowledge with other peer P_j in the network $\mathcal{N}$, each peer P_i has also an export-interface module $\mathcal{M}^{ij}$ composed by groups of ordered pairs of intensionally equivalent views (conjunctive queries over peer's ontologies), denoted by (q_i, q_j), or equivalently, by $q_i(\mathbf{x}) \approx q_j(\mathbf{x})$, such that q_i is a view defined over DB schema of peer P_i and q_j over P_j. The extension of such a view $q_i(\mathbf{x})$ is usually the set of known (certain) answers to this conjunctive query, that is ground atoms $q(\mathbf{c})$, which are true in all preferred Herbrand models of a peer database P_i.

Notice that (q_i, q_j) does *not* mean that q_i logically implicates q_j or vice versa, as in *extensional* mapping definitions, based on material implication. So, the syntax [53] for the database P2P can be given as follows.

Definition 35. The P2P network system $\mathcal{N}$ is composed by $2 \le N$ independent peers, where each peer module P_i is defined as follows:

$$P_i =_{\text{def}} \left\langle \mathcal{O}_i, \bigcup_{i \neq j \in N} \mathcal{M}^{ij} \right\rangle$$

where $\mathcal{M}^{ij}$ is a (possibly empty) interface to other peer P_j in the network, defined as a group of intensionally equivalent query connections, denoted by $(q^{ij}_{1k}, q^{ij}_{2k})$ where $q^{ij}_{1k}(\mathbf{x})$ is a conjunctive query defined over $\mathcal{O}_i$, while $q^{ij}_{2k}(\mathbf{x})$ is a conjunctive query defined over the ontology $\mathcal{O}_j$ of the connected peer P_j:

$$\mathcal{M}^{ij} = \{(q^{ij}_{1k}, q^{ij}_{2k}) \mid 1 \le k \le |ij|\}$$

and $|ij|$ is the total number of query connections of the peer P_i toward a peer P_j.

Intuitively, when a user defines a conjunctive query over the ontology $\mathcal{O}_i$ of the peer P_i, the intensionally equivalent concepts between this peer and other peers will be used in order to obtain the answers from a P2P system.

They will be the "bridges," which a query agent can use to rewrite the original user query over a peer P_i into *intensionally equivalent* query over other peer P_j, which has different (and independent) ontology from the peer P_i.

The answers of other peers will be epistemically considered as *possible* answers because they are based on the *belief,* which has the peer P_i about the knowledge of a peer P_j: this belief is formally represented by supposition of a peer P_i that the pair of queries $(q^{ij}_{1k}, q^{ij}_{2k}) \in \mathcal{M}^{ij}$ is intensionally equivalent.

Example 16. Let us consider the acyclic P2P system in a Figure 3.1, with the peers: P_i, with the ontology $\mathcal{O}_i$ and the interface

$$\mathcal{M}^{ij} = \{(v_{im}, v_{jm}) \mid v_{im} \approx v_{jm}, \text{and } 1 \le m \le k\}$$

toward the peer P_j with the ontology $\mathcal{O}_j$.

The idea is the following: given a query $q_i(\mathbf{x})$ over a peer P_i, a query agent will rewrite (if it is possible) the *identical* query $\Psi(v_{i1}, \dots, v_{ik})$ over the set of views $\{v_{i1}, \dots, v_{ik}\}$ of a peer P_i, then it will use the set of intensional equivalences $v_{im} \approx v_{jm}, 1 \le m \le k$, to obtain the *intensionally equivalent* query $\Psi(v_{j1}, \dots, v_{jk})$ over the set of views $\{v_{j1}, \dots, v_{jk}\}$ of a peer P_j, and then it will rewrite this query into the *identical* query $q_j(\mathbf{x})$ over the ontology $\mathcal{O}_j$ of the peer P_j.

The *known answers* of both peers P_i, P_j to the queries $q_i(\mathbf{x})$ and $q_j(\mathbf{x})$ will constitute the subset of the global P2P answer to the original user query; other possible answers

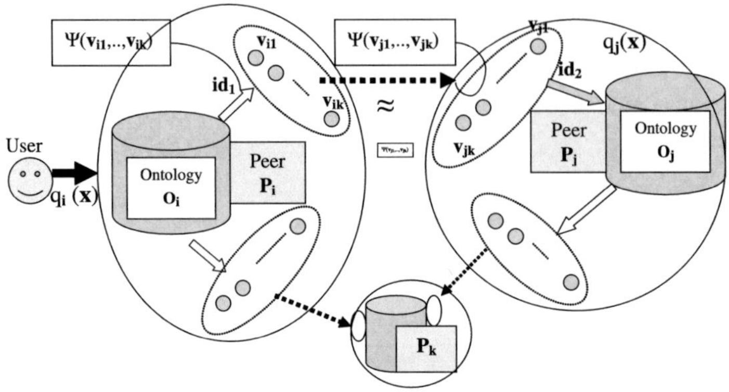

Figure 3.1: P2P database system.

to the same user query can be obtained by the similar method from the intensionally equivalent queries over a peer P_k obtained from intensional mappings from P_i to P_k and from P_j to P_k, respectively.

For example, all currently used integrity constraints (as the key and the foreign key constraints) in a global schema are valid integrity constraints in order to use also intensional semantics for the mapping between peer databases.

There is a number of different *context-dependent* scenarios for a query-answering with intensional semantics, as in human society: for example, the *confidential* scenario where an interviewer can interview a single person at time (we will denominate it as a *pure* P2P context), or a *conference* scenario where an interviewer can interact with a number of persons at a time and possibly integrate partial knowledge of them in order to obtain the answer.

Let us consider the simplest scenario: the *pure* P2P context. Informally, given a conjunctive query $\varphi(x)$ over a peer P_i, the answer to this query of the whole P2P system, w. r. t. *intensional semantics* is the union of known answers from this peer, and (known) answers of all other peers, which have intensionally equivalent to $\varphi(x)$ virtual predicates. It corresponds to the query-answering paradigm in a society of individuals: given a question $\varphi(x)$ to some person P_i, and its beliefs about the knowledge of other persons in this society, the interviewer can obtain the answer from P_i and from other persons who know something about the same concept $\varphi(x)$. In the real-world environment, the answer of other persons (in different languages) can be considered certain also, but in the virtual P2P database framework their answer is mediated by the belief of the P_i w. r. t. the knowledge of other peers, which may be imperfect, so the answers of other peers are epistemically different, i. e., they can be epistemically considered as *possible* answers.

3.3 Modal intensional FOL for P2P systems

As we have discussed in Chapter 1, the distinction between intensions and extensions is important especially because we are now able to have an *equational theory* over intensional entities, i. e., predicate and function "names," that is separate from the extensional equality of relations and functions. Thus, intensional FOL has the simple Tarski first-order semantics, with a decidable unification problem, but we need also the actual world mapping, which maps any intensional entity to its *actual world extension*. In what follows, we will identify a *possible world* by a particular mapping, which assigns to intensional entities their extensions in such possible world. We have see in Chapter 1 that the direct relationship between Bealer's nonreductionistic and Montague's possible worlds ($\mathcal{W}_e$) approach to intensional logic can be given by the bijective mapping

$$\mathcal{F} : \mathcal{W}_e \simeq \mathcal{E}$$

where $\mathcal{E}$ is a set of possible extensionalization functions corresponding to explicit possible worlds (up to the previous isomorphism). Such a correspondence, not present in original intensional theory [23], is a natural identification of intensional logics with modal Kripke based logics.

Each extensionalization function $h \in \mathcal{E}$ assigns to the intensional elements of $\mathcal{D}$ an appropriate extension as it was presented in Chapter 1. Among the possible functions in $\mathcal{E}$, there is a distinguished function $\Bbbk$, which is to be thought as the *actual* extensionalization function: it tells us the actual extension of the intensional elements in the world $w_0 = \mathcal{F}^{-1}(\Bbbk)$. The syntax and semantics of the intensional FOL algebra $\mathcal{A}_{\text{int}} = (\mathcal{D}, \text{Id}, \text{Truth}, \{\text{conj}_S\}_{S\in\mathcal{P}(\mathbb{N}^2)}, \text{neg}, \{\text{exists}_n\}_{n\in\mathbb{N}})$ of the minimal $\text{FOL}_{\mathcal{I}}(\Gamma)$ has been presented in Definition 16.

Definition 36. The intensional logic for P2P database systems is that described in Example 3 in Section 1.3, obtained as an enrichment of minimal intensional FOL by "high-level" modal operator $\widehat{\Diamond}$ of S5 modal logic such that operator $\neg\widehat{\Diamond}\neg$ is a well-known "necessity" modal operator w. r. t. the accessibility relation $\widehat{\mathcal{R}} = \mathcal{W}_e \times \mathcal{W}_e$. So, the Kripke model of this intensional logic is the extension of the $\mathcal{M}_{\text{FOL}_{\mathcal{I}}(\Gamma)}$ in Definition 15,

$$\widehat{\mathcal{M}} =_{\text{def}} (\widehat{\mathbb{W}}, \{\mathcal{R}_i\}, \widehat{\mathcal{R}}, \mathcal{D}, \widehat{I}_K)$$

with a set of (generalized) possible worlds $\widehat{\mathbb{W}} = \mathfrak{I}_T(\Gamma) \times \mathcal{D}^{\mathcal{V}}$, where $\mathcal{W}_e = \mathfrak{I}_T(\Gamma)$ is the set of explicit possible worlds (Tarski's interpretations), and for each possible world $\mathbf{w} = (I_T^*, g) \in \widehat{\mathbb{W}}$ we have also (w. r. t. the first 4 satisfaction rules in Definition 15) this fifth rule for "high-level" modal operator $\widehat{\Diamond}$,

5. $\widehat{\mathcal{M}} \vDash_{I_K, g} \widehat{\Diamond}\varphi$ iff exists $I_T^{*\prime} \in \mathcal{W}_e$ such that $(I_T^*, I_T^{*\prime}) \in \widehat{\mathcal{R}}$ and $\widehat{\mathcal{M}} \vDash_{I_T^{*\prime}, g} \varphi$.

This modal FOL for P2P database systems we will denote by $\mathcal{L}_\omega(\Gamma)$ and its syntax algebra, obtained from $\mathcal{A}_{\text{int}}$ by addition of the new modal "high-level" operator $\widehat{\Diamond}$, we will denote by $\mathcal{A}^+_{\text{int}}$.

These semantics are similar to the algebraic semantics for $\mathcal{L}_\omega$ in [27] for the case of the conception where intensional entities are considered to be *identical* if and only if they are *necessarily equivalent*. Intensional identity is much stronger that the standard *extensional equality* in the actual world, just because it requires the extensional equality in *all* possible worlds.

Example 17. Let two predicate formulae $\phi(\mathbf{x})$ and $\psi(\mathbf{x})$ be intensionally equal, i. e., $I(\phi(\mathbf{x})) = I(\psi(\mathbf{x}))$, then for any $h \in \mathcal{E}$ holds that $h(I(\phi(\mathbf{x}))) = h(I(\psi(\mathbf{x})))$, i. e., have the same extension, thus

$$\phi(\mathbf{x}) \equiv \psi(\mathbf{x}) \text{ is true} \quad \text{iff} \quad (\phi(\mathbf{x}) \Rightarrow \psi(\mathbf{x})) \wedge (\psi(\mathbf{x}) \Rightarrow \phi(\mathbf{x})) \text{ is true}$$

in each world $\mathcal{F}^{-1}(h)$.

Consequently, $\widehat{\Box}(\phi(\mathbf{x}) \equiv \psi(\mathbf{x}))$ is true (where $\widehat{\Box}$ for the S5 modal logic in Definition 36 is a universal "necessity" operator equal o $\neg\widehat{\Diamond}\neg$), and from the definition holds the intensional identity for their intensional abstracts, $< \phi(\mathbf{x}) >_{\mathbf{x}} = < \psi(\mathbf{x}) >_{\mathbf{x}}$, and finally from (1.22), $g^*(< \phi(\mathbf{x}) >_{\mathbf{x}}) = I(\phi(\mathbf{x})) = g * (< \psi(\mathbf{x}) >_{\mathbf{x}}) = I(\psi(\mathbf{x}))$.

Vice versa, if $\widehat{\Box}(\phi(\mathbf{x}) \equiv \psi(\mathbf{x}))$ then $< \phi(\mathbf{x}) >_{\mathbf{x}} = < \psi(\mathbf{x}) >_{\mathbf{x}}$, and we obtain that $I(\phi(\mathbf{x})) = I(\psi(\mathbf{x}))$, and consequently, $\phi(\mathbf{x})$ and $\psi(\mathbf{x})$ are intensionally equal. So, the modal formula $\widehat{\Box}(\phi(\mathbf{x}) \equiv \psi(\mathbf{x}))$ corresponds to the intensional equality of $\phi(\mathbf{x})$ and $\psi(\mathbf{x})$.

Consequently, from Corollary 3 in Section 1.3, any two first-order open formulae, $\phi(x_1, \dots x_n)$ and $\psi(x_1, \dots x_n)$, are intensionally *equivalent* iff $\widehat{\Diamond}\phi(x_1, \dots x_n)$ and $\widehat{\Diamond}\psi(x_1, \dots x_n)$ are intensionally *equal*, i. e., from (1.11),

$$\phi(x_1, \dots x_n) \approx \psi(x_1, \dots x_n) \quad \text{iff} \quad \widehat{\Diamond}\phi(x_1, \dots x_n) \equiv \widehat{\Diamond}\psi(x_1, \dots x_n)$$

and we have the following conjunctive extension of the intensional equivalent logic formulae with formulae with built-in predicates:

Proposition 15. *Let $C(\mathbf{x})$ be a logic formula defined from built-in predicates (ex, $\leq, \geq$, etc.), then*

$$\psi_1(\mathbf{x}) \approx \psi_2(\mathbf{x}) \quad \textit{implies } (C(\mathbf{x}) \wedge \psi_1(\mathbf{x})) \approx (C(\mathbf{x}) \wedge \psi_2(\mathbf{x}))$$

Proof. Immediately from the fact that a built-in formulae $\phi(\mathbf{x})$ has constant extension in any possible world (Tarski's interpretation I^*_T) in $\mathcal{W}_e$. □

Based on this intensional equivalence "$\approx$," we can define the following quotient algebra.

Definition 37 (Intensional quotient algebra). This intensional equivalence "$\approx$" defines the QUOTIENT algebra $\mathcal{A}^{+}_{\mathrm{int}}/_{\approx}$ for a quotient-intensional first-order logic $\mathcal{L}_{\omega}/_{\approx}$, as follows:

Given an intensional logic $\mathcal{L}_{\omega}(\Gamma)$ with a basic, user defined, set of intensional equivalences $S_{\mathrm{eq}} \subseteq \Gamma$, and its deductive inference relation $\vdash_{\mathrm{in}}$ of the S5 modal logic with intensional equality theory, then for any virtual predicate $\phi(\mathbf{x})$ with tuple of free variables $\mathbf{x} = \{x_1, \dots, x_k\}$, we obtain an intensional-equivalence class

$$\mathcal{C} = \{\psi_i(\mathbf{x}) \in \mathcal{L}_{\omega}(\Gamma) \mid \mathcal{L}_{\omega}(\Gamma) \vdash_{\mathrm{in}} \psi_i(\mathbf{x}) \approx \phi(\mathbf{x})\}.$$

For any $\phi(\mathbf{x}) \in \mathcal{A}_{\mathrm{int}}/_{\approx}$, the quotient intensional entity for this equivalence class, its extension in a world $I^*_T = w \in \mathcal{W}_e$ (with $h = F(w)$ and $h \circ I = I^*_T$) is defined by

$$\begin{aligned} F(w)(I(\phi(\mathbf{x}))) &= \{\mathbf{d} \in \mathcal{D}^k \mid \psi_i(\mathbf{d}) \text{ is true in } w, \psi_i(\mathbf{x}) \in \mathcal{C}\} \\ &= \bigcup_{\psi_i \in \mathcal{C}} \mathcal{F}(w)(I(\psi_i(\mathbf{x}))) = \bigcup_{\psi_i \in \mathcal{C}} I^*_T(\psi_i(\mathbf{x})) \end{aligned} \tag{3.5}$$

This definition of equivalence relation is the flat-accumulation case presented in [43, 53]: if the first predicate is true in some world, then the second must be true in some world also, and vice versa. Each equality is also intensional equivalence, but not vice versa. In what concerns this paper, we will consider *only* the actual world $w_0 = \mathcal{F}^{-1}(\Bbbk)$. Moreover, the set of *basic* intensional equivalences are designed by users, and we will not verify if they satisfy the modal formula used to define the intensional equivalence: the definition above is of theoretical interest but useful to understand the meaning of the intensional equivalence, and the "omniscient" inference relation $\vdash_{\mathrm{in}}$, able to deduce all other intensional equivalences from the given basic set.

The formal semantic framework for P2P database systems, presented previously in [53] as a hybrid modal logic, in this section will be defined as quotient (by intensional equivalence) intensional FOL. We will consider *only* the actual world $w_0 = \mathcal{F}^{-1}(\Bbbk)$, correspondent to the extensionalization function $h = \Bbbk$ of the intensional FOL $\mathcal{L}_{\omega}(\Gamma)$: the actual world for $\mathcal{L}_{\omega}(\Gamma)$ corresponds to the actual extension (corresponding to a current Tarski's interpretation of the modal FOL logic theory of all peers P_i) of peer databases. When a user defines a conjunctive query $q(\mathbf{x})$ over an ontology $\mathcal{O}_i$ of a peer database Pi, the answer to this query is computed in this actual world w_0, i. e., for the Tarski's interpretation $I^*_T = w_0 \in \mathcal{W}_e = \mathfrak{I}_T(\Gamma)$, and hence in the actual extension of all peer databases in a P2P network $\mathcal{N} = \{P_i \mid 1 \le i \le N\}$ where the extension of each predicate $p^k_i(x_1, \dots, x_k)$ (corresponding to a given relational table r of a peer database schema) is equal to relation $R = I^*_T(p^k_i(x_1, \dots, x_k)) = \Bbbk(I(p^k_i(x_1, \dots, x_k))) \subseteq \mathcal{D}^k$ where $I : \mathcal{L}_{\omega} \to \mathcal{D}$ is a fixed intensional interpretation of logic formulae (into the PRP domain in Definition 6, Section 1.2).

Definition 38 (Intensional embedding of P2P database systems). Let $\mathcal{W}_0 = \{P_i \mid 1 \le i \le N\}$ be a P2P database system. The intensional FOL $\mathcal{L}_{\omega}(\Gamma)$ for a P2P network $\mathcal{W}_0$ (the

FOL quantifiers are necessary for definition of the integrity constraints of each peer database), with a given intensional mapping $I : \mathcal{L}_\omega(\Gamma) \to \mathcal{D}$, is composed by:

1. The set of basic intensional concepts must contain the disjoint union of entities corresponding to the predicates (relations) of all peers $S_I = \biguplus_{1 \le i \le N}\{I(p_i^k(x_1, \ldots, x_k)) \mid r = p_i^k \in \mathcal{O}_i\}$. Other intensional concepts has to be defined for each logic formula (virtual predicate) in $\phi(x_1, \ldots, x_k) \in \mathcal{L}_w$ used to define the peer databases, so that $I(\phi(x_1, \ldots, x_k)) \in D_k$, $k \ge 1$.
2. The particulars of the domain, D_{-1}, corresponds to the disjoint union of domains of peer databases. The intension-in-proposition part, D_0, contains also the disjoint union of peer's Herbrand bases.
3. The basic set of the equivalence relation $\approx$ is defined as a disjoint union for each peer P_i as follows: if $(q_{1k}^{ij}, q_{2k}^{ij}) \in \mathcal{M}^{ij}$, then $q_{1k}^{ij}(\mathbf{x}) \approx q_{2k}^{ij}(\mathbf{x})$, where $q_{1k}^{ij}(\mathbf{x})$ is a view (query) over peer P_i ontology (DB schema) and $q_{2k}^{ij}(\mathbf{x})$ is a view over peer P_j ontology. It is considered to be an axiom in Γ of $\mathcal{L}_\omega$,

$$(\widehat{\Diamond} q_{1k}^{ij}(\mathbf{x}) \equiv \widehat{\Diamond} q_{2k}^{ij}(\mathbf{x})) \in \Gamma$$

The COMPLETE answer to a conjunctive query $q(\mathbf{x})$, over a given peer P_i, is equal to the extension of the quotient-intensional concept given by (3.5) in Definition 37, whose equivalence class $\mathcal{C}$ is determined by the deductive omniscient closure of $\vdash_{\text{in}}$, in the quotient intensional P2P logic $\mathcal{L}_\omega/_\approx$.

The quotient modal intensional FOL $\mathcal{L}_\omega/_\approx$ (its algebraic counterpart is a Lindenbaum–Tarski algebra) is fundamental for *query answering* in intensional P2P database mapping systems: given a query $q(\mathbf{x})$ over a peer P_i, the answer to this query is defined as the extension of the intensional concept $I(q(\mathbf{x}))$, in the intensional P2P logic $\mathcal{L}_\omega/_\approx$.

While this logical omniscience of the embedding of P2P database systems may be acceptable in the study of theoretically perfect query-agent reasoners, any model or belief with this property will be unacceptable for representing resource and time bounded query agents.

In real web applications, we will never have *omniscient query agents* that will contemporarily have the complete and whole knowledge about *all* ontologies of all peers. Such a supposition would generate the system with a global and centralized knowledge, in contrast with our pragmatic and completely decentralized P2P systems with completely independent peers, which can change their local ontology in any instance of time without informing any other peer or "global" systems about it. Thus, what we will consider for a query-agent reasoning system is a weaker form of deduction than $\vdash_{\text{in}}$, of this ideal omniscient intensional logic inference, more adequate for the limited and local knowledge of query agents about the peers.

What we consider is that a query agent will begin its work for a given user query $q(\mathbf{x})$ over a peer P_i, and by using only the *local* knowledge about this peer's ontology and the set of its local intensional mappings toward other peers, will be able to move to the locally-next peers to obtain answers from them also. This context-sensitive query answering is an analog to the human query answering: the interviewer will ask the indicated person and will obtain his known answer, but this person can tell also which other people, he believes are able to respond to this question also. It will be the task of the interviewer to find other people and to reformulate the question to them. It is practically impossible to have all people who know something about this question to be in a common interaction one with all others to combine the partial knowledge of each of them in order to provide the complete possible answer to such question.

This context dependent and locally-based query answering system is partially described in Example 18. In the next section, we will define the *weaker deductive inference* relation also, denoted by $\Vdash$, for the intensional FOL $\mathcal{L}_\omega(\Gamma)$ of a P2P system in Definition 36, such that the query answering algorithm used by these nonomniscient query agents, is complete w. r. t. this intensional logic deductive system.

3.3.1 Bridge rules for local contextual deduction

It is well known that the standard epistemic logics used to model the agents suffer from the omniscience problem. That is, an agent is logically omniscient if it knows all of the valid formulae, and its knowledge is closed under logical equivalence (or alternatively under logical implication). On the standard epistemic, possible worlds model, we must assume that an agent can derive all consequences of a belief in an instant, i. e., without computational effort.

We investigate why this might be a problem for real-life agents, especially when the standard possible worlds model poses a problem for agents with a big number of large databases, as we will have in semantic web applications and P2P databases. Agents may establish immediately certain logical truths or simple consequences of what they consciously assented to. However, there are highly remote dispositional states, which could only be established by complex, time-consuming reasoning. The modal framework cannot distinguish between a sentence that an agent consciously assented to and a piece of potential knowledge, which could never be made actual by the agent and is therefore not suited to model resource-bounded reasoning.

Whose aim is it to develop a usable logic in which they can reason about an agent's beliefs that commonly distinguish *semantic* from *syntax* approaches? The former expresses the agent's beliefs in a modal language with a modal operator for belief, whereas the later uses a metalanguage, containing a belief predicate, to talk about an agent's beliefs.

Instead of epistemic modal operator for belief, in this section, we will use the "belief" predicate of this intensional logic, as in the syntax approach [145, 146]. But in our case, instead of using a singular referring term *name* as in classic extensional FOL, to denote the sentence φ an agent is believing, we will use *intensional abstract* term, which contains the whole structure of the sentence in composite algebraic form (the denotation of such abstract terms is an algebraic formula with the denotations of all subcomponents of the original sentence, i. e., it has a recursive denotation definition).

We can use also the approach in [147], which takes a set of sentences in the internal language of an agent (in our case it is the language for conjunctive queries), which we can view as initial assumptions (in our case the set of intensional equivalences between views of the actual peer database toward other peers), to comprise an agent's knowledge base. We combine this approach with the *contextual reasoning* [109, 148–150], by considering, for instance, contexts as peer databases: each peer database is a (local) context for a query agent. It can access to the local knowledge of this peer, during a query-answering process, and also to the set of local *bridge rules* [150] of this peer. We can consider the whole P2P database system, composed by a number of peer databases, as a knowledge base, which contains a set of interacting contexts $P_1, \ldots P_N$ (peer databases). The kind of bridge rules, of a context (peer) P_i toward the peer P_j, is of the form:

$$\frac{v_i : P_i}{v_j : P_j}$$

where $v_i \approx v_j$ are intensionally equivalent views (conjunctive queries) of a peer database P_i and P_j, respectively. This rules allow us to bridge deductions in P_i to deductions in P_j by allowing us to derive v_j in P_j just because we have derived v_i in P_i. So, for any context, the query agent uses the subset of deduction rules $\rho(P_i)$, derived from a context P_i, in order to derive new information. We write $\Gamma \vdash_{\rho(P_i)} \phi$ to denote that ϕ is deducible from Γ using the rules assigned by $\rho(P_i)$. A formula ϕ is said to be believed by an agent, which Konolige writes $B\phi$, where B is a belief modal operator, iff it is in an agent's belief set $\mathbf{B}$, iff it is either in the agent's initial knowledge base Γ or else is derivable form the knowledge base by applying the agent's deduction rules:

$$B\phi \quad \text{iff} \quad \phi \in \mathbf{B} \quad \text{iff} \quad \phi \in \Gamma \text{ or } \Gamma \vdash_{\rho(P_i)} \phi \tag{3.6}$$

As Konolige, we assume the deductive closure of an agent's belief set $\mathbf{B}$ w. r. t. the agent's deduction rules, i. e.,

$$\text{If} \quad \mathbf{B} \vdash_{\rho(P_i)} \phi \quad \text{and} \quad \mathbf{B} \bigcup \{\phi\} \vdash_{\rho(P_i)} \psi, \quad \text{then } \mathbf{B} \vdash_{\rho(P_i)} \psi \tag{3.7}$$

The property of the deductive closure should not be confused with that of logical omniscience: if the deduction rules are logically incomplete, then there will be sentences that are logical consequences of the base set and yet not in the belief set. Thus, deductive closure is a much *weaker* notion than closure under logical consequence of the intensional FOL theory for P2P system. In what follows, we will call it "*local contextual deduction*": in general, agents modeled in the framework of the deduction model are not logically omniscient because the rules they use, to derive new sentences in their belief set, are in some respect incomplete because they are context-dependent. But if an agent has a complete set of deduction rules, then all logical consequences of an agent's base beliefs will be in the belief set.

The contextual reasoning has some similarities with the Labeled Deduction System (LDS) [151]. In the LDS approach, the basic unit of a deductive process is not just formulae but the labeled formulae, where the labels belong to a given "labeling algebra" (which represents the additional information), and are *explicitly* incorporated into the object language. In the contextual reasoning, we have no explicit labels associated with logic formulae, and even more, we have no *all* inference rules (bridges), which a deductive system can use in its deduction. We have standard logic formulae but at each context only the subset of context dependent inference rules can be used for a (nonlabeled) deduction. Also, there is not any centralized place where we can see how are partitioned rules in different contexts. Thus, the deduction process is similar to the traveling in an unknown country without any global map, by using only local indications (actual context) in order to take the next decisions, which depends on the traveler's objectives (here it is represented by a user query).

The context of a peer P_i represents the whole information contribution of other peers to the local knowledge of this peer, and consequently, can be used during the query answering: given any conjunctive query $\varphi(\mathbf{y})$ over a peer P_i in a world w, first we compute the set of *certain* answers, and after that also the set of *intensionally-possible answers* obtained from the information contribution from other peers, i. e., from the context $\mathcal{C}(P_i)$ of the considered peer P_i. Thus, the answer to a query over a given peer is *context-dependent*. By changing the context of a peer, we will obtain different set of possible answers: the syntax of the interface module of a peer is a specification for such context. For each peer, there are at least two modalities in order to obtain intensionally possible answers:

1. *Atomic* or pure P2P query answering: in this case, each peer can have a number of contexts, each one for a distinct interface toward another peer. The query agent has to try to completely reformulate the original query $\varphi(\mathbf{y})$ (specified over a peer P_i) for any other peer P_j if in $\mathcal{M}^{ij}$ are specified bridges between P_i and P_j (i. e., if $|ij| \geq 1$ in Definition 35). Then a peer P_j will be able to respond with its answers. In this case, we define the context of P_i by $\mathcal{C}(P_i) = \mathcal{M}^{ij}$.
2. *Data integration* P2P query answering: we can consider partial answers from all contextual peers for a given peer P_i, defined in its interface module. The query agent will assemble (join) the partial answers from them in order to obtain possible answers. In this case, we define the unique complete context as follows:

$$\mathcal{C}(P_i) = \{(q_{i_l}(x_l), \{q_{j_l}(x_l) \mid (q_{i_l}(x_l), q_{j_l}(x_l)) \in \mathcal{R}\}) \mid q_{i_l}(x_l) \in \pi_1(\mathcal{R})\}$$

where $\mathcal{R} = \bigcup_{1\leq j\leq N} \mathcal{M}^{ij}$, and π_1 is a first projection.

In what follows, we will consider the atomic case only.

Definition 39 (Single bridge rule). For a given context $\mathcal{C}(P_i) = \mathcal{M}^{ij}$, we define its deduction model as follows:

1. It is composed by the logic theory, $\mathcal{L}_{\omega,P_i}$ for the single peer P_i, a disjoint component of total P2P logic theory $\mathcal{L}_\omega(\Gamma)$ obtained by embedding a P2P database system into intensional FOL (from Definition 38), with only the interface $\mathcal{M}^{ij}$ to the peer P_j.
2. For any query $q(\mathbf{x})$ over a peer P_i, intensionally equivalent to the conjunctive query $C(\mathbf{x}) \wedge v_{i_1} \wedge \cdots \wedge v_{i_k}$, where $\{v_{i_1}, \dots, v_{i_k}\} = \pi_1(\{(v_{i_1}, v_{j_1}), \dots, (v_{i_k}, v_{j_k})\}) \subseteq \pi_1(\mathcal{M}^{ij})$ is a subset of views over P_i, and $C(\mathbf{x})$ is a logic formula defined from built-in predicates only (see Proposition 15) with the variables in $\mathbf{x} = (x_1, \dots, x_n)$, we introduce in ρ the following deductive bridge rule:

$$\frac{(v_{i_1} \approx v_{j_1}, \dots, v_{i_k} \approx v_{j_k}, q(\mathbf{x}) \equiv (C(\mathbf{x}) \wedge v_{i_1} \wedge \cdots \wedge v_{i_k})) : P_i}{(q(\mathbf{x}) \approx C(\mathbf{x}) \wedge v_{j_1} \wedge \cdots \wedge v_{j_k})) : P_j} \tag{3.8}$$

Intuitively, the logic theory $\mathcal{L}_{\omega,P_i} \subset \mathcal{L}_\omega(\Gamma)$, is the logic of the "pure" peer P_i with only the interface module toward a peer P_j, which for a given query $q(\mathbf{x})$ over its ontology $\mathcal{O}_i$, is able to deduce if there is an intensionally equivalent query over its views contained in the interface module $\mathcal{C}(P_i) = \mathcal{M}^{ij}$. If such deduction there exists (in practice for that we can use the perfect query-rewriting algorithms [99]), i. e., if $\mathcal{L}_{\omega,P_i} \vdash_{\text{in}} q(\mathbf{x}) \approx (C(\mathbf{x}) \wedge v_{i_1} \wedge \cdots \wedge v_{i_k})$, then it is possible to use the bridge rule in order to derive, intensionally equivalent to user query, the query $C(\mathbf{x}) \wedge v_{j_1} \wedge \cdots \wedge v_{j_k}$ overviews of the other peer P_j.

We can introduce the reasoning capabilities of the query agents, able, for a given user query $q(\mathbf{x})$ over a peer P_i, to infer other query formulae, intensionally equivalent to $q(\mathbf{x})$ over the ontologies of other peers in a given P2P database system. Let us show the way how we define the belief set $\mathbf{B}$ of the agent, composed by the intensionally equivalent queries over peer databases to user's query $q(\mathbf{x})$, by using the bridge rules in Definition 39.

Example 18 (One step local contextual deduction between two peers). Let us consider the *cyclic* P2P system in Figure 3.2, with two peers: P_i, with the ontology $\mathcal{O}_i$ and the interface $\mathcal{M}^{ij} = \{(v_{im}, v_{jm}) \mid v_{im} \approx v_{jm}, \text{and } 1 \leq m \leq k_1\}$ toward the peer P_j, and the peer P_j, with the ontology $\mathcal{O}_j$ and the interface $\mathcal{M}^{ji} = \{(w_{jm}, w_{im}) \mid v_{jm} \approx v_{im}, \text{ and } 1 \leq m \leq n_1\}$ toward the peer P_i. In what follows, the bottom index of a query identifies the peer relative to such a query.

Let $q_i(\mathbf{x})$ be the original user's conjunctive query over the ontology $\mathcal{O}_i$ of the peer database P_i, and the query agent takes its first context $\mathcal{C}(P_i) = \mathcal{M}^{ij} = \{(v_{im}, v_{jm}) \mid v_{im} \approx v_{jm}, \text{and } 1 \leq m \leq k_1\}$. If we obtain the following logic equivalence eq_1,

$$\mathcal{L}_{\omega,P_i} \vdash_{\rho(P_i)} q_i(\mathbf{x}) \equiv \Psi(v_{i1}, \dots, v_{ik}) \tag{3.9}$$

where $\Psi(v_{i1}, \dots, v_{ik})$ denotes a conjunctive formula $C(\mathbf{x}) \wedge v_{i_1} \wedge \cdots \wedge v_{i_k}$, then the agent can use the bridge rule (3.8) in order to derive, intensionally equivalent to user query, the query $\Psi(v_{j1},\dots,v_{jk})$ equal to conjunctive formula $C(\mathbf{x}) \wedge v_{j_1} \wedge \cdots \wedge v_{j_k}$ overviews of the other peer P_j, i. e.,

$$\mathcal{L}_{\omega,P_i} \vdash_{\rho(P_i)} q_i(\mathbf{x}) \approx \Psi(v_{j1},\dots,v_{jk}) \tag{3.10}$$

In the next step, the query agent will try to take the next context of the current peer P_i, but there is no other nonelaborated previously context of this peer, and hence, based on the precedent bridge rule, will pass from the peer P_i to the peer P_j, and will take its context

$$C(P_j) = \mathcal{M}^{ji} = \{(w_{jm}, w_{im}) \mid v_{jm} \approx v_{im}, \text{and } 1 \le m \le n_1\}.$$

We assume that when the agent changes the context, all intensional equivalences where at least one argument is a query formula contained in its belief set **B**, are preserved together with its belief set in **B**. If for some query formula $q_j(\mathbf{x})$ over the ontology of a peer P_J, hold the following logic equivalence eq_2:

$$\mathcal{L}_{\omega,P_j} \vdash_{\rho(P_j)} q_j(\mathbf{x}) \equiv \Psi(v_{j1},\dots,v_{jk}), \tag{3.11}$$

and hence from (3.9), (3.10) and (3.11) we obtain the intensional equivalence $q_j(\mathbf{x})q_j(\mathbf{x})$, between queries over two different peers P_i and P_j, which can be inserted into the agent's belief set **B**, i. e.,

$$(\widehat{\Diamond} q_i(\mathbf{x}) \equiv \widehat{\Diamond} q_j(\mathbf{x})) \in \mathbf{B} \tag{3.12}$$

This query-agent reasoning corresponds to the top-horizontal arrow in Figure 3.2.

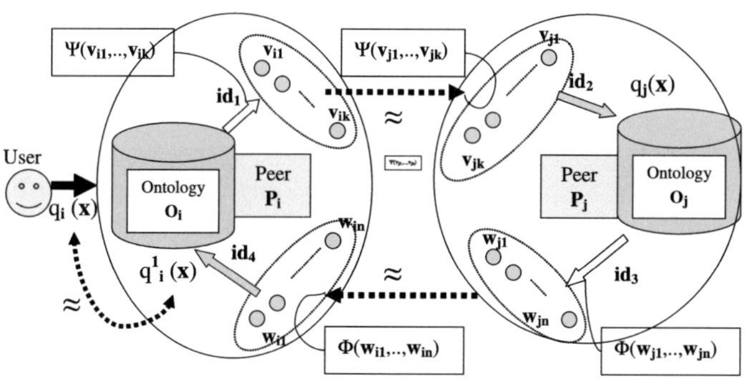

Figure 3.2: Derivation of intensionally equivalent queries.

The analog process can be described for the bottom-horizontal arrow in Figure 3.2.

At the end of deduction, the set of intensionally equivalent queries over peers in a P2P database system is equal to the set

$$S_I = \bigcup_{(\widehat{\diamond}q_i(\mathbf{x}) \equiv \widehat{\diamond}q_j(\mathbf{x})) \in \mathbf{B}} \{q_i(\mathbf{x}), q_j(\mathbf{x})\} \tag{3.13}$$

This set of queries S_I is the set of intensional queries directly over peers ontologies (database schemas) as a subset of the equivalent class C for the given initial user query, which in the intensional FOL $\mathcal{L}_\omega/_\approx$ is represented by the quotient intensional entity $Q(\mathbf{x})$, whose extension (from Definition 37) in the actual world w_0 is defined by equation (3.5).

Remark. This query-answering process is valid also for the *union* of conjunctive queries. In fact, given two intensional equivalences between conjunctive queries, $q_{i1} \approx q_{j1}$ and $q_{i2} \approx q_{j2}$, we have that $(q_{i1} \vee q_{i2}) \approx (q_{j1} \vee q_{j2})$, from the fact that the S5 modal intensional FOL is a normal modal logic where it holds that $\widehat{\diamond}(A \vee B) \equiv (\widehat{\diamond}A \vee \widehat{\diamond}B)$. □

Theorem 3. *The local contextual deductive inference of a query agent at a peer P_i, $\vdash_{\rho(P_i)}$, is a sound weakening of the omniscient deductive inference $\vdash_{\text{in}}$ of the S5 modal intensional FOL, for the P2P database system $\mathcal{L}_\omega$ with the peer databases, which does not contain the integrity constraints in the form of negative clauses $\neg A_1 \vee \cdots \vee \neg A_m$, $m \geq 2$.*

Proof. By structural induction on the number of conjuncts in the expression, it is enough to prove for expressions composed by two conjuncts.

From the definition in (1.37) for a given Tarski's interpretation $I_T^* = w \in \mathcal{W}_e$ of the intensional FOL and the commutativity $I_T^* = h \circ I$ for fixed intensional interpretation I and the extensionalization function $h = \mathcal{F}(I_T^*) = \mathcal{F}(w)$, we have that

$$\text{lub}(\phi(\mathbf{x})) =_{\text{def}} \bigcup_{w \in \mathcal{W}_e} \mathcal{F}(w)(I(\phi(\mathbf{x}))) \tag{3.14}$$

so that we have from (1.36) and (1.38),

$$\phi(\mathbf{x}) \approx \phi_1(\mathbf{x}) \quad \text{iff} \quad \widehat{\diamond}\phi(\mathbf{x}) \equiv \widehat{\diamond}\phi_1(\mathbf{x}) \quad \text{iff} \quad \text{lub}(\phi(\mathbf{x})) = \text{lub}(\phi_1(\mathbf{x})) \tag{3.15}$$

Let b_1, b_2 be any two (virtual) predicates over a peer P_i, $q_{i1}(x,y)$ and $q_{i2}(y,z)$, respectively, and c_1, c_2 (equal to $q_{j1}(x,y)$ and $q_{j2}(y,z)$, respectively) any two (virtual) predicates over a peer P_j, such that $b_i \approx c_i >, i = 1, 2$. We have to prove that $\text{lub}(\varphi(x,z)) = \text{lub}(\psi(x,z))$, where

$$\varphi(x,z) \equiv (q_{i1}(x,y) \wedge q_{i2}(y,z)) \quad \text{and} \quad \psi(x,z) \equiv (q_{j1}(x,y) \wedge q_{j2}(y,z)).$$

From the facts that $\text{lub}(q_{i1}(x,y)) = \text{lub}(q_{j1}(x,y))$ and $\text{lub}(q_{i2}(y,z)) = \text{lub}(q_{j2}(y,z))$, we define the set

$$\begin{aligned} S_L &= \{(a,c) \mid \exists b.((a,b) \in \text{lub}(q_{i1}(x,y)) \wedge (b,c) \in \text{lub}(q_{i2}(y,z)))\} \\ &= \{(a,c) \mid \exists b.((a,b) \in \text{lub}(q_{j1}(x,y)) \wedge (b,c) \in \text{lub}(q_{j2}(y,z)))\}. \end{aligned}$$

Let us prove that

$$\text{lub}(\varphi(x,z)) = \bigcup_{w \in W_e} \{(a,c) \mid \exists b.((a,b) \in \mathcal{F}(w)(I(q_{i1}(x,y))) \wedge (b,c) \in \mathcal{F}(w)(I(q_{i2}(x,y))))\}$$

is equal to S_L: First, from

$$\mathcal{F}(w)(I(q_{ik}(x,y))) \subseteq \text{lub}(q_{ik}(x,y)), \quad k = 1,2,$$

it holds that $\text{lub}(\varphi(x,z)) \subseteq S_L$.

Let us prove that also $\text{lub}(\varphi(x,z)) \supseteq S_L$, i. e., that for any $(a,b) \in S_L$ also $(a,b) \in \text{lub}(\varphi(x,z))$.

Let us suppose that there is one (a,c) such that $(a,c) \in S_L$ but $(a,c) \notin \text{lub}(\varphi(x,z))$, i. e., that for all possible worlds for this P2P system, $w \in \mathcal{W}_e$, holds that $\pi_2(\mathcal{F}(w)(I(q_{i1}(a, y)))) \bigcap \pi_1(\mathcal{F}(w)(I(q_{i2}(y,c)))) = \{\}$ (is empty), where π_1, π_2 are the first and the second projections. That is, the following logic formula must hold $\neg q_{i1}(a,y) \vee \neg q_{i2}(y',c) \vee \neg(y = y')$.

But such constraint (negative clause) cannot exist in this class of peers, and hence the supposition is false, and we conclude that $S_L = \text{lub}(\varphi(x,z))$.

By the same way, we obtain that $S_L = \text{lub}(\psi(x,z))$, thus $\varphi(x,z) \approx \psi(x,z)$, and the bridge rules of the query agents,

$$\frac{(v_{i_1} \approx v_{j_1}, \ldots, v_{i_k} \approx v_{j_k},\ q(\mathbf{x}) \approx (C(\mathbf{x}) \wedge v_{i_1} \wedge \cdots \wedge v_{i_k})) : P_i}{(q(\mathbf{x}) \approx (C(\mathbf{x}) \wedge v_{j_1} \wedge \cdots \wedge v_{j_k})) : P_j}$$

are valid deductions also for the omniscient S5 modal intensional FOL $\mathcal{L}_\omega$ of a P2P system: thus $\vdash_{\rho(P_i)}$, is a sound weakening of the omniscient deductive inference $\vdash_{\text{in}}$.

It is easy to verify, from $v_{i_1} \approx v_{j_1}, \ldots, v_{i_k} \approx v_{j_k}$ we conclude that $(v_{i_1} \wedge \cdots \wedge v_{i_k}) \approx (v_{j_1} \wedge \cdots \wedge v_{j_k})$, and from Proposition 15 we obtain that $(C(\mathbf{x}) \wedge v_{i_1} \wedge \cdots \wedge v_{i_k}) \approx (C(\mathbf{x}) \wedge v_{j_1} \wedge \cdots \wedge v_{j_k})$; from the fact that $q(\mathbf{x}) \approx (C(\mathbf{x}) \wedge v_{i_1} \wedge \cdots \wedge v_{i_k})$ and the transitivity of equivalence relation "$\approx$," we deduce that $q(\mathbf{x}) \approx (C(\mathbf{x}) \wedge v_{j_1} \wedge \cdots \wedge v_{j_k})$. □

3.3.2 Nonomniscient weak intensional inference

A query agent can use the "bridge rules," described previously, to derive from the original user query over a peer P_i, a new *intensionally-equivalent* query over another peer P_j, which has different (and independent) ontology from the peer P_i. In this section, we propose just this method presented in Example 18 to implement for the query agents the local contextual logic inference $\vdash_{\rho(P_i)}$ formalized previously by the rule bridges (3.10) and by query-rewriting methods for the logic equivalences (3.9) and (3.11).

The answers of other peers will be epistemically considered as *possible* answers because they are based on the *belief*, which has the peer P_i about the knowledge of a peer P_j. This belief is formally represented by supposition of a peer P_i that the pair of queries $(q_{1k}^{ij}, q_{2k}^{ij}) \in \mathcal{M}^{ij}$ (used for the bridge rules) is intensionally equivalent.

We discussed previously the necessity to employ *nonomniscient* query agents, which can use only some local P2P information in order to answer to user queries. In such *context-dependent* query answering, the answer to the query depends of the topology of the P2P network, with the intensional equivalences (the "bridges") between the peers, so that for equivalent queries, but formalized over different peers we will generally obtain different answers. Thus, the semantics for this weaker form of deduction of intensional equivalences, i. e., intensional equivalent queries over other "contextual" peers, w. r. t. the user interrogated peer P_i, can be formally expressed by deduction chains, which begin from a peer P_i.

However, each local contextual logic inference $\vdash_{p(P_i)}$ depends on a particular peer P_i and of only a small part of intensional FOL logic $\mathcal{L}_{\omega,P_i}$ of the total P2P database system intensional FOL logic $\mathcal{L}_\omega(\Gamma)$. We need to define the *global* nonomniscient (weak) intensional inference relation valid for the whole logic P2P theory $\mathcal{L}_\omega(\Gamma)$.

Proposition 16. *Given an intensional logic $\mathcal{L}_\omega(\Gamma)$ for a P2P system (in Definition 36), with a basic, user defined, set of intensional equivalences $S_{eq} \subseteq \Gamma$, and its deductive inference relation $\vdash_{in}$, then we define the weak intensional inference relation $\Vdash$ for $\mathcal{L}_\omega(\Gamma)$, as follows:*

- *$\mathcal{L}_\omega(\Gamma) \Vdash \varphi(\mathbf{x}) \approx \phi(\mathbf{x})$ iff there is a chain $\psi_1, \psi_2, \psi_3 \ldots, \psi_{3n+1}$ of the formulae with the same set of free variables in a tuple $\mathbf{x}$ but each of them expressed by relation symbols of only one particular peer's ontology, such that ψ_1 corresponds to φ, ψ_{3n+1} corresponds to ϕ and $\psi_i(\mathbf{x}) \cong_{i+1} \psi_{i+1}(\mathbf{x})$, for '$\cong_{3i}$' equal to intensional equivalence '$\approx$' used in local bridge deductions (3.10); to (strong) equivalence '$\equiv$' otherwise (used in query-rewriting local deductions (3.9) and (3.11)).*

  $\psi_{3i-2}(\mathbf{x})$ and $\psi_{3i+1}(\mathbf{x})$ are the queries over two different peer's ontologies, and $\psi_{3i-1}(\mathbf{x}), \psi_{3i}(\mathbf{x})$ over views of these peers, respectively, for $1 \le i \le n$.
- *Such chains for the intensional logic $\mathcal{L}_\omega(\Gamma)$ of a P2P database system are finite, and holds that*

$$\mathcal{L}_\omega(\Gamma) \Vdash \varphi(\mathbf{x}) \approx \phi(\mathbf{x}) \quad \textit{implies} \quad \mathcal{L}_\omega(\Gamma) \vdash_{in} \varphi(\mathbf{x}) \approx \phi(\mathbf{x})$$

  but not vice versa.

Proof. This proposition, as in Example 18, tells us that two formulae, over any two peer's ontologies, with the same free variables, are intensionally equivalent, if there is a chain of the formulae, identical or intensionally equivalent, and these two formulae are initial and final formulae of such a chain. From the transitive property of the equivalence, we obtain that initial and final formula in this chain are intensionally equivalent.

The finite chain property for P2P systems is the result of the fact that, also in presence of cyclic mappings between peers, the number of *different* conjunctive queries but intensionally equivalent, which can be expressed by the finite set S of views of a peer P_i, used for an intensional mapping toward the peer P_j $(i \neq j)$, is always finite: the number of subsets of this set S of view, sufficient to formalize the intensionally equivalent conjunctive formula, is finite. So, the "bridge" passage from P_i to P_j during the derivation of new intensional equivalences, can be used only a finite number of time. □

Moreover, this proposition explains the way in which this weak deduction of the intensional FOL is able to derive the intensionally equivalent formulae from the basic set (explicitly defined by a peer's developers) of intensionally equivalent formulae: in our case, from the set of intensionally equivalent views (conjunctive queries) over different peers (see point 3 of Definition 38).

Proposition 17. *Let for two queries of the same peer P_i we obtain $\mathcal{L}_\omega(\Gamma) \Vdash q_i(\mathbf{x}) \approx q_i'(\mathbf{x})$, from a finite chain $\psi_1, \psi_2, \dots, \psi_n$ (from the Proposition 16) of the formulae with the same tuple $\mathbf{x}$ of free variables, such that*

- *ψ_1 corresponds to $q_i(\mathbf{x})$,*
- *ψ_2 corresponds to conjunctive query over peer's views $\Psi(v_1, \dots, v_k)$ (obtained by a query-rewriting algorithm from $q_i(\mathbf{x})$), with $\psi_1(\mathbf{x}) \equiv \psi_2(\mathbf{x})$ (logic equivalence (3.9)),*
- *ψ_{n-1} corresponds to conjunctive query $\Phi(v_1, \dots, v_k)$*
- *ψ_n corresponds to $q_i'(\mathbf{x})$ (obtained by query-unfolding algorithm from $\Phi(v_1, \dots, v_k)$), with $\psi_{n-1}(\mathbf{x}) \equiv \psi_n(\mathbf{x})$ (logic equivalence (3.11)),*

where conjunctive queries Ψ and Φ have the same set of views $v_1, \dots, v_k$.

Then for the extensionalization function $\Bbbk$ of the actual world $w_0 \in \mathcal{W}_e$,

$$\Bbbk(I(q_i'(\mathbf{x}))) \subseteq \Bbbk(I(q_i(\mathbf{x}))) \tag{3.16}$$

Proof. It comes directly for all user conjunctive queries without built-in predicates: two conjunctive queries with the same set of predicates and the same set of variables in the query head are identical. In the case when the user query contains also a derived built-in predicate $C(\mathbf{x})$, we can take out this formula from the rest of query, and consider the intensional equivalence only for such reduct without built-in predicates, based on Proposition 15: at the end of derivation of the intensional equivalence class, w. r. t. this reduct query, we can add to each conjunctive formula of this equivalence class the formula "$\wedge C(\mathbf{x})$." The chain of derivations can only add some new conjunction of built-in predicates, thus we will obtain that $\Phi(\mathbf{x}) \equiv \Psi(\mathbf{x}) \wedge C_1(\mathbf{x})$, where $C_1(\mathbf{x})$ can be also empty. So,

$$\Bbbk(I(\Phi(v_1,\ldots,v_k))) \subseteq \Bbbk(I(\Psi(v_1,\ldots,v_k))),$$

and hence from the logic equivalence with the two queries, initial and final in a chain, we obtain (3.16). □

This proposition tells us that any two intensionally equivalent conjunctive queries, with the same set of virtual predicates (views $v_1,\ldots,v_k$ of a peer P_i) and the same set of variables in the head of these two queries, the second derived query (in a given chain of derivations) is extensionally contained in the first, so that we can stop the propagation of deductions and to discard $\Phi(v_1,\ldots,v_k)$, and hence also $q_i^!(\mathbf{x})$.

As a consequence of Propositions 16 and 17, given a query $q(\mathbf{x})$ over a peer P_i, the set of *different* conjunctive queries (such that one is not subsumed in other), but intensionally equivalent to $q(\mathbf{x})$, over any peer P_k is a finite set. This means that in principle we are able to define a complete query rewriting algorithm for finite *P2P* database systems w. r. t. the weak deduction $\Vdash$ of the intensional FOL $\mathcal{L}_\omega(\Gamma)$.

In what follows, we will consider that each single peer database (such as DIS) is able to deal with incomplete information and with mutually inconsistent information, which comes from different source databases, and we will mathematically present such query answering by using the coalgebras able to respond to the user's queries by plausible (known) answers.

3.4 Sound and complete query derivation of intensional equivalence-classes

The implementation of query answering in P2P systems needs a standard mathematical semantics based on an adequate (co)algebra, as for example, is the *relational* (co)algebra for SQL query answering in relational databases. Here, the computation is more intricate because of complex epistemic logic structures of peers and necessity of query rewriting algorithms Rew (*Minicon* for the rewriting of query in the equivalence (3.9) and *Unfolding* for the equivalence (3.11), for example).

We consider that the rule of the query agent is to start and to maintain a complete *query answering transaction*: this transaction starts when it is given a user query $q(\mathbf{x})$ over a peer P_i. The query agent provides the Rew algorithm in order to construct intensionally equivalent rewritten queries over other peers and then calls the grid computation network to calculate answers, by assigning to each grid computation node one peer with a *union* of rewritten conjunctive queries for it. The transaction ends when query agent receives the answers from all grid nodes, and presents collected (cumulative) answers to the user. Note that the query agent does not extract the answers to these rewritten queries from the peers, but for it is responsible the abstract object types with its methods formally provided by a coalgebra as presented in Section 3.2.2 and Definition 133 in the Appendix.

So, the definition of this P2P query computing system, which abstracts all not necessary implementation details, has to be given in an abstract (co)algebraic mathematical language; this abstract mathematical specification (coalgebraic abstract type) can be successively implemented in any current grid computing system.

But the query answering for intensionally based P2P mappings cannot be embedded into recursive datalog, as in the case of a standard view-based mappings based on a material implication [101], so we need a more complex and general mathematical framework for it.

3.4.1 Final coalgebra semantics for weak intensional deduction $\Vdash$

The Kripke structure of the frame $\mathcal{F} = (\widehat{\mathcal{W}}, \{\mathcal{R}_i\}, \widehat{\mathcal{R}})$, given in Definition 36, is a prerequisite in order to obtain a *coalgebraic semantics* for query answering in the P2P database framework. (Co)algebras provide a unifying view on a large variety of dynamic systems such as transition systems, automata, data structures and objects [152, 153] or Kripke models; they are especially useful for the dynamic query answering P2P systems. Consequently, for whoever is not familiar with these mathematical instruments, it will be useful to present the formal definition for coalgebras (see also Section A.5, the category **Set**).

Definition 40 (Abstract coalgebras). Let **Set** be a category with its objects all (small) sets and its arrows all functions, and T be an endofunctor $T : \mathbf{Set} \to \mathbf{Set}$. A T-coalgebra is a pair of a (small) set C and a **Set**-arrow $\alpha : C \to TC$, i. e., $(C, \alpha : C \to TC)$.

T is called a signature functor or type, and C a carrier set. Let (C, α) and (D, β) be T-coalgebras, and $f : C \to D$ a Set-arrow. f is said to be a morphism of T-coalgebras or T-morphism, if $\beta \circ f = Tf \circ \alpha$. It is an isomorphism if it is a bijective mapping.

Note that, instead, for $T : \mathbf{Set} \to \mathbf{Set}$, a *T-algebra* is a pair of a (small) set C and an arrow $\alpha : TC \to C$, i. e., $(C, \alpha : TC \to C)$. If (D, β) is a T-algebra as well, and $f : C \to D$ a Set-arrow, then f is a morphism of T-algebras, if $f \circ \alpha = \beta \circ Tf$.

Example 19. Aczel's semantics of CCS [113], is described by the coalgebra $k : \text{Prog} \to \mathcal{P}_{\text{fin}}(\text{Act} \times \text{Prog})$, of the endofunctor $T = \mathcal{P}_{\text{fin}}(\text{Act} \times \_)$ with the set of actions $a \in \text{Act}$, such that $k(P) = \{\langle a, P' \rangle \mid P \to_{a_i} P'\}$ is the set of atomic transitions, which the CCS program P can perform and pass to the new program P'. The symbol $\mathcal{P}_{\text{fin}}$ is the finite powerset operator. This semantics exploits the special final coalgebra theorem, that is a unique homomorphism $k^{@} : (\text{Prog}, k) \to (\text{gfp}(T), \simeq)$ to the *final coalgebra*, which is a isomorphic (bijective) coalgebra: $\simeq$: $\text{gfp}(T) \to \mathcal{P}_{\text{fin}}(\text{Act} \times \text{Prog})$ with $\text{gfp}(T)$, greatest fixed point of T, the set of (infinite) labeled transition systems (labeled trees), which are the greatest fixed points of the "behavioral functor" $T = \mathcal{P}_{\text{fin}}(\text{Act} \times \_)$, i. e., for every program P, $k^{@}(P) = \{\langle a, k^{@}(P') \rangle \mid P \to_{a_i} P'\}$, such that the following diagram:

$$\begin{array}{ccc}
\text{Prog} & \xrightarrow{k^{@}} & \text{gfp}(T) \\
{\scriptstyle k}\downarrow & & \downarrow{\scriptstyle \simeq} \\
T(\text{Prog}) & \xrightarrow{T(k^{@})} & T(\text{gfp}(T))
\end{array}$$

commutes. Final coalgebras are "strongly extensional," i. e., two elements of the final coalgebra are equal iff they are *T-bisimilar*.

The semantics above for the CCS and its properties can be generalized to arbitrary behaviors: in our case, for a given conjunctive query language $\mathcal{L}_Q$ over relational symbols of the P2P database system, we consider the programs as pairs $(P_i, q_i(\mathbf{x}))$ (a query over a peer $P_i \in \mathcal{W}_0$), where $\mathcal{W}_0$ is the set of peers introduced by Definition 38, can be considered as a program. The execution of this program will return the known answers to this query, so that Prog $= \mathcal{W}_0 \times \mathcal{L}_Q$, the set Act $= \{\Vdash_3\}$ as a singleton, with the only deductive action $\Vdash_3$ (restriction of $\Vdash$ for chains of length 3 only), so that $\mathcal{P}_{\text{fin}}(\text{Act} \times \text{Prog})$ can be substituted by $\mathcal{P}_{\text{fin}}(\text{Act} \times \text{Prog})$, i. e., in our case $T = \mathcal{P}_{\text{fin}}$.

In what follows, we will denote by $q_{ij}(\mathbf{x})$ the j-th query of the i-th peer P_i. Thus, we can consider the *intensional deduction* process, defined in Proposition 16, as a colalgebra $k : \mathcal{W}_0 \times \mathcal{L}_Q \to \mathcal{P}_{\text{fin}}(\mathcal{W}_0 \times \mathcal{L}_Q)$, such that, given an initial query $q_{i1}(\mathbf{x}) \in \mathcal{L}_Q$ over a peer P_i that is a pair $(P_i, q_{i1}(\mathbf{x})) \in \mathcal{W}_0 \times \mathcal{L}_Q$, the inferential step will generate the complete set $k(P_i, q_{i1}(\mathbf{x})) = \{(P_j, q_{jn}(\mathbf{x})) \mid \mathcal{M}^{ij}$ is not empty $\} \in \mathcal{P}_{\text{fin}}(\mathcal{W}_0 \times \mathcal{L}_Q)$, where $q_{jn}(\mathbf{x}) \approx q_{i1}(\mathbf{x})$ if can be derived an intensional-equivalent query $q_{jn}(\mathbf{x})$ over a peer P_j (i. e., if $\mathcal{L}_\omega(\Gamma) \Vdash_3 q_{i1}(\mathbf{x}) \approx q_{jn}(\mathbf{x})$); otherwise, $q_{jn}(\mathbf{x}) = \emptyset$ is an empty query.

We can use $\mathcal{P}_{\text{fin}}$ because the P2P system is composed by a finite number N of peers, so that for any peer P_i the number of accessible peers for it is finite.

By recursively applying the function k, equivalent to the single application of the *unique* homomorphism $k^{@}$, we obtain a possibly infinite transition relation (tree) (see Figure 3.3) with a root in the initial state (that is program): we consider the general case of cyclic mappings of the P2P system as in Figure 3.2.

This tree will have a lot of nodes with empty queries, and possibly infinite copies of nodes (with the same query over a given peer). So, we need to "normalize" this unique solution of the weak deduction, by eliminating duplicates and nodes with an empty query.

Consequently, we define the mapping, which generates for each peer P_i the *complete set* of deduced queries for it (from the set of pairs (P_i, q_{ik}) in a given tree in $\text{gfp}(\mathcal{P}_{\text{fin}})$), $\text{fl} : \text{gfp}(\mathcal{P}_{\text{fin}}) \to \mathcal{P}_{\text{fin}}(\mathcal{W}_0 \times \mathcal{P}(\mathcal{L}_Q))$, such that, given the unique solution (a tree) $k^{@}(P_i, q_{i1}(\mathbf{x}))$, and for each peer P_k the set of queries $S_k = \{q_{kn}(\mathbf{x}) \mid (P_k, q_{kn}(\mathbf{x})) \in k^{@}(P_i, q_{i1}(\mathbf{x}))\}$,

$$\text{fl}(k^{@}(P_i, q_{i1}(\mathbf{x}))) = \{(P_k, S_k) \mid 1 \le k \le N\}, \tag{3.17}$$

where $N \ge 2$ is the number of peers in $\mathcal{W}_0$.

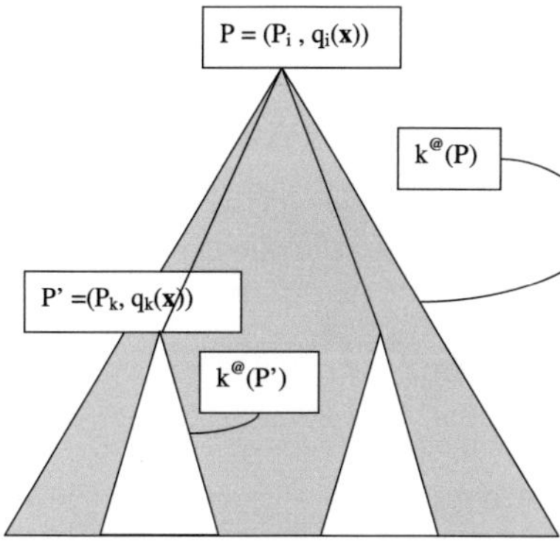

Figure 3.3: Weak deduction solution.

In this way, we will obtain for each peer the set of all conjunctive queries, intensionally equivalent to the user query $q_{i,1}(\mathbf{x})$. This set of queries for a given peer is complete (the largest equivalence relation class, i. e., the closure $C_{\Vdash}(\mathcal{L}_\omega(\Gamma), q_{i1}(\mathbf{x}))$ of the inference $\Vdash$, defined by $q(\mathbf{x}) \in C_{\Vdash}(\mathcal{L}_\omega(\Gamma), q_{i1}(\mathbf{x}))$ iff $\mathcal{L}_\omega(\Gamma) \Vdash q_{i1}(\mathbf{x}) \approx q(\mathbf{x})$) w. r. t. the intensional FOL logic $\mathcal{L}_\omega(\Gamma)$ and its weak deductive inference $\Vdash$ for intensionally equivalent formulae.

3.4.2 Sound and complete query rewriting algorithm with respect to weak deduction $\Vdash$

The P2P query one-step rewriting algorithm is defined by the following composition of the three different algorithms corresponding to the three inference steps, of the logic equivalence (3.9), which uses the algorithm "MiniCon," of the "bridge" intensional equivalence (3.10), which uses the algorithm "Subst" (the substitution of the views of a peer P_i with intensionally equivalent views of the peer P_j), and of the logic equivalence (3.11), which uses the algorithm "Unfolding" in the Example 18,

$$\text{Rew} =_{\text{def}} \text{Unfolding} \circ \text{Subst} \circ \text{MiniCon}, \tag{3.18}$$

where $\circ$ is the sequential composition for algorithms (as specified in the Appendix for the composition of arrows in a category), can be described as follows (see the Example 18):

1. Given a conjunctive query $q(\mathbf{x})$ over a peer P_i, by using the set of intensional equivalences in its interface $\mathcal{M}^{ij} = \{(v_{im}, v_{jm}) \mid v_{im} \approx v_{jm}, \text{and } 1 \leq m \leq k_1\}$ toward a peer P_j (see Definition 35), in the case when such set is not enough for the complete and *equivalent* rewriting [154], returns with the empty query $q_{jn}(\mathbf{x}) = \emptyset$ for the peer P_j. Otherwise it uses the MiniCon algorithm [154] over the set of views in $\{v_{i1}, \dots, v_{ik}\} \subseteq \pi_1\mathcal{M}^{ij}$, to rewrite equivalently a query $q(\mathbf{x})$ into a query $\Psi(v_{i1}, \dots, v_{ik})$.

2. After that, it makes the substitution of views of P_i in $\{v_{i1},\ldots,v_{ik}\}$ by an intensionally equivalent set of views of P_j in $\{v_{j1},\ldots,v_{jk}\}$, to obtain the intensionally equivalent query formula $\Psi(v_{j1},\ldots,v_{jk})$ over views of P_j.
3. Finally, it uses the unfolding algorithm [154], to unfold $\Psi(v_{j1},\ldots,v_{jk})$ and to obtain the query $q_{jn}(\mathbf{x})$ over the ontology of a peer P_j. Notice that in the case when the ontology of P_j is changed, so that the set of views $v_{i1},\ldots,v_{ik}$ in the interface $\mathcal{M}^{ij}$ of the peer P_i does not match with this new ontology of P_j, the algorithm returns with the empty query, i. e., with $q_{jn}(\mathbf{x}) = \emptyset$.

In order to have a decidable complete query answering, we need to prove that the set of all rewritten queries for each peer is finite. After that, we need to prove that it terminates, and returns with the same solution as the unique solution of the final coalgebra for the weak deduction. In what follows, we define also the following functions for a list of queries:

1. "ln" (length) denotes the function which returns with a number of elements in a list $L = \langle q_{i1}(\mathbf{x}), q_{i2}(\mathbf{x}),\ldots,q_{in}(\mathbf{x})\rangle$ of queries over a peer P_i, so that $\ln(L) = n$. For the empty list $\langle\ \rangle$, we have that $\ln(\langle\ \rangle) = 0$.
2. "push" is the function, which inserts the query ϕ over a peer P_i as the last element of this list, i. e., $\mathrm{push}(L,\phi) = \langle q_{i1}(\mathbf{x}), q_{i2}(\mathbf{x}),\ldots,q_{in}(\mathbf{x}), \phi_{i(n+1)}(\mathbf{x})\rangle$.

Our aim now is to define the query agent in an object-oriented style, as a class, by

- A coalgebra [152], $\mathrm{st} = \langle \mathfrak{fin}, \mathrm{next}\rangle : X \to B + X$, with final map $\mathfrak{fin} : X \to B$ and recursive map $\mathrm{next} : X \to X$, of a deterministic system for a polynomial functor $T = B + \_$ for a one-step query rewrite algorithm Rew in (3.18).
- The set $B = \mathcal{P}_{\mathrm{fin}}(\mathcal{W}_0 \times \mathcal{P}_{\mathrm{fin}}(\mathcal{L}_Q))$ of termination values of query rewriting algorithm, defined as the set of finite queries for each peer.
- The set of internal states $X = (Ls_Q \times \mathbb{N})^{\mathcal{W}_0}$ of this query agent class. Each state is the function $f : \mathcal{W}_0 \to Ls_Q \times \mathbb{N}$, which maps any peer $P_i \in \mathcal{W}_0$ into a list of conjunctive queries over this peer in Ls_Q (Ls_Q is the set of lists L composed by possible conjunctive queries over the alphabet of the P2P system), and to the pointer $k \in \mathbb{N}$, which defines the position of the last elaborated query for this peer. We denote by π_m, $m = 1, 2, \ldots$ the m-th projections, so that for any peer P_k, $\pi_1 f(P_k)$ is the list of its queries, and $\pi_2 f(P_k)$ is the pointer to the last elaborated query in this list.

Such a query agent class is instantiated into a query agent *object*by using the "new" operation, performed by a user when he defines a query over a peer P_i, denoted by the injective mapping in **Set** category $\mathrm{new} : \mathbf{1} \hookrightarrow X$, where $\mathbf{1} = \{*\}$ is the singleton set (the terminal[1] object in **Set**). This operation "new" specifies the initial state f_0 of the agent

1 For any object in a category, there is a unique arrow from it to terminal object. So, in category **Set**, for any set S there is a unique function from it into the terminal object **1**.

object, $f_0 = \text{new}(*) \in X$. So, it is a function $f_0 : \mathcal{W}_0 \to Ls_Q \times \mathbb{N}$, such that for a given initial user query $q_{i1}(\mathbf{x})$ over a peer P_i, for any $P_k \in \mathcal{W})0$ we have that

$$f_0(P_k) = \begin{cases} (\langle q_{i1}(\mathbf{x})\rangle, 0), & \text{if } k = i \\ (\langle\,\rangle, 0), & \text{otherwise} \end{cases} \tag{3.19}$$

where $\langle\,\rangle$ denotes an empty list, and hence every query agent object (instance of this object-oriented class) can be denoted as a couple (st, f_0).

The polynomial functor $T(X) = B + X$, where $+$ is the operation of the set union, has the final coalgebra semantics [152], with $\text{gfp}(B+\_) = \mathcal{P}_{\text{fin}}(\mathcal{W}_0 \times \mathcal{P}(\mathcal{L}_Q))$, the infinite extension of B when for each peer in W_0 we can have also infinite number of queries, so that $B + \text{gfp}(B + \_) = \text{gfp}(B + \_)$ and holds the bijection $\simeq$ for the final coalgebra of the functor $T = B + \_$ as presented in commutative diagram of Example 19.

We denote the unique solution of the deterministic system $\text{st} = \langle \mathfrak{fin}, \text{next}\rangle : X \to B + X$ (corresponding to the one-step query rewriting coalgebra), where $\text{next} : X \rightarrow X$ is a recursive operation on the states in X and $\mathfrak{fin} : X \to B$ is the final execution of the one-step rewriting mapping "st," by the unique homomorphism between this coalgebra and the final coalgebra, i. e., $\text{st}^{@} : (X, \text{st}) \to (\text{gfp}(B + \_), \simeq)$; this homomorphism corresponds to the top commutative diagram in the next diagram after the theorem.

The one-step query rewriting coalgebra

The coalgebra mapping, st, specifies the *method* of this query agent class for the one-step query rewriting algorithm Rew (3.18) as follows: given an initial state $f_0 \in X$, the st terminates with a result of query rewriting algorithm if all queries of every peer are elaborated, and are not generated new queries; otherwise st, when it elaborates a first non-elaborated query $q_{km}(\mathbf{x})$ of a peer P_k, can generate the set of *new* intensionally equivalent queries over other peers, and passes (deterministically) to the next state in $X = (Ls_Q \times \mathbb{N})^{\mathcal{W}_0}$. Formally, for any state $f : \mathcal{W}_0 \to Ls_Q \times \mathbb{N}$,

$$\text{st}(f) = \begin{cases} \mathfrak{fin}(f) = \{(P_k, \{q_{kn} \mid q_{kn} \in \pi_1 f(P_k)\}) \mid P_k \in \mathcal{W}_0\} \in B, & \text{if } N_d = 0 \\ \text{next}(f) = f_1 : \mathcal{W}_0 \to Ls_Q \times \mathbb{N}, \text{ with } f_1 \in X & \text{otherwise} \end{cases} \tag{3.20}$$

where $N_d =_{\text{def}} \sum_{P_i \in \mathcal{W}_0} \ln(\pi_1 f(P_i)) - \pi_2 f(P_i)$ corresponds to the final execution $\mathfrak{fin} : X \to B$ of the st and $\mathfrak{fin}(f)$ transform the final list into *the set* of rewritten queries. Note that in the bottom line, the function $f_1 \in X = (Ls_Q \times \mathbb{N})^{\mathcal{W}_0}$ increments only the pointer for next query to be elaborated in the list L_k of queries of P_k, i. e., if $(L_k, n) = f(P_k)$ then we obtain that $f_1(P_k) = (L_k, n + 1)$, and *for each* P_j locally (directly) "connected" by intensional "bridge" to this P_k, with $(L_j, m) = f(P_j)$ and $l = \ln(L_j)$,

$$f_1(P_j) = \begin{cases} (\text{push}(L_j, q_{j(l+1)}), m), & \text{if } \varepsilon \text{ (from Proposition 17)} \\ f(P_j), & \text{otherwise} \end{cases} \tag{3.21}$$

where $q_{j(l+1)} = \mathrm{Rew}(\pi_n(\pi_1 f(P_k)), P_j)$ is a one-step query rewriting of the n-th query of peer P_k into the intensionally equivalent query over peer P_j if it is possible, or $q_{j(l+1)}$ is empty query $\emptyset$ otherwise (if rewriting is not successful), while ε denotes the following condition:

$$q_{j(l+1)} \neq \emptyset \quad \text{and} \quad \forall_{1\leq i\leq l}\neg(q_{j(l+1)} = \pi_i(\pi_1 f(P_j))), \tag{3.22}$$

i.e., after one-step rewriting for a peer P_j, if it is successful and different from all queries previously rewritten for the same peer, then this new query is added to the set of rewritten queries for this peer. □

We have the following simple property.

Proposition 18. *The mapping* next : $X \to X$ *is monotonic w.r.t. the ordering* $\preceq$ *such that for any two internal agent's states* $f_1, f_2 \in X = (Ls_Q \times \mathbb{N})^{\mathcal{W}_0}$,

$$f_1 \preceq f_2 \quad \textit{iff} \quad \forall P_i \in \mathcal{W}_0(\pi_1(f_1(P_i)) \subseteq \pi_1(f_2(P_i))).$$

For the least fix point for this "next-consequence-operator" of $f_0 = \mathrm{new}(*)$, *denoted by* $\mathrm{lst}(f_0)$, *it holds that* $\mathrm{st}^{@}(f_0) = \mathrm{st}(\mathrm{lst}(f_0))$.

Notice that this algorithm works well also for *union* of conjunctive queries: it works well for Unfolding and MiniCon [154], while for Subst works from the fact that for a normal modal logic holds $\Diamond(A \vee B) \equiv \Diamond A \vee \Diamond B$. Instead, the Subst works for conjunctive queries and the class of peers defined as follows.[2]

Proposition 19 ([43]). *Let us consider the class of peers with the integrity constraints, which does not contain negative clauses of the form* $\neg A_1 \vee \cdots \vee \neg A_m$, $m \geq 2$. *Then the intensional equivalence is preserved by conjunction logic operation, i.e., if* $\varphi \equiv (b_1 \wedge \cdots \wedge b_k)$, $k \geq 1$, *is a conjunctive query over a peer* P_i, *and* $b_i \approx c_i$, $1 \leq i \leq k$, *the set of intensionally equivalent views toward a peer* P_j, *then* $\varphi \approx \psi$, *where* $\equiv$ *is a logic equivalence and* $\psi \equiv (c_1 \wedge \cdots \wedge c_k)$ *is the conjunctive query over a peer* P_j.

We are able to define the mapping pop : $X \to \mathcal{W}_0 \times \mathcal{L}_Q$ between domains of the query agent class coalgebra and deductive coalgebra, such that, for any $f \in X$, i.e., $f : \mathcal{W}_0 \to Ls_Q \times \mathbb{N}$, with $q_{in} = \pi_n(\pi_1(f(P_i)))$,

$$\mathrm{pop}(f) = \begin{cases} (P_i, \pi_1 f(P_i)), & \text{if } \ln(\pi_1 f(P_i)) = 1 \text{ and } \forall P_k \in \mathcal{W}_0.(\pi_2 f(P_k)) = 0 \\ (P_1, \emptyset), & \text{otherwise} \end{cases} \tag{3.23}$$

where in $(P_1, \emptyset) \in \mathcal{W}_0 \times \mathcal{L}_Q$ the symbol $\emptyset \in \mathcal{L}_Q$ denotes an empty query, such that $k(P_1, \emptyset) = (P_1, \emptyset)$, and hence also $k^{@}(P_1, \emptyset) = (P_1, \emptyset)$, so that the weak deduction diagram (see next diagram) commutes as well, and hence this prefixed choice (with

2 See also Theorem 3 in Section 3.3.1.

empty query for a given peer) in equation (3.23) works well. That is, for $(P_1, \emptyset) \in \mathcal{W}_0 \times \mathcal{L}_Q$ by weak deduction for an empty query we do not deduce any other query.

For the first case above, when f is equal to $f_0 =_{\mathrm{def}} \mathrm{new}(*)$, we obtain from (3.19) that $(P_i, \pi_1 f(P_i)) = (P_i, \pi_1 f_0(P_i)) = (P_i, q_{i1}(\mathbf{x})) \in \mathcal{W}_0 \times \mathcal{L}_Q$, i. e., to the initial user's query $q_{i1}(\mathbf{x})$ over the peer P_i, so that by equalizer we obtain that the tree of all weak deductions of intensionally equivalent formulae generated from this initial query corresponds to all queries obtained by the query-rewriting algorithm, as follows.

Theorem 4. *The query answering algorithm implemented by the query class* st : $X \to B + X$ *will terminate for any user conjunctive query* $q(\mathbf{x})$ *over a peer* P_i. *It is a sound and complete algorithm w. r. t. the weak deduction inference* $\Vdash$ *of the intensional logic* $\mathcal{L}_\omega(\Gamma)$ *for a P2P database system. That is, for any user query action* new, *holds that*

$$\mathrm{st}^{@} \circ \mathrm{new} = \mathrm{fl} \circ k^{@} \circ \mathrm{pop} \circ \mathrm{new}$$

or, equivalently, any user's action "new," such that the initial agent's state $f_0 = \mathrm{new}(*)$ *defines a conjunctive query* $q(\mathbf{x})$ *over a peer* P_i, *is an* EQUALIZER *(Section* A.5 *in the Appendix, for* Set *category with the limit* LimE *equal to terminal object* **1** *and h equal to monomorpfism (injective function) "new") of the functions* $\mathrm{st}^{@}$ *and* $\mathrm{fl} \circ k^{@} \circ \mathrm{pop}$, *i. e., graphically in the* Set *category:*

$$\mathbf{1} \overset{\mathrm{new}}{\hookrightarrow} (Ls_Q \times \mathbb{N})^{\mathcal{W}_0} \underset{\mathrm{fl} \circ k^{@} \circ \mathrm{pop}}{\overset{\mathrm{st}^{@}}{\rightrightarrows}} \mathrm{gfp}(B + \_\,)$$

The meaning of this equalizer is that for any given initial query $q_{i1}(\mathbf{x})$ *over a peer* P_i, *the set of intensionally equivalent queries for any peer in the P2P system obtained by the weak deduction* $\Vdash$ *is equal to the set of queries obtained by the query rewriting algorithm* Rew.

Proof. The query rewriting algorithm is sound, because it derives intensionally equivalent queries. From the fact that it derives the subset of the intensionally equivalent queries over peers, w. r. t. the weak deductive inference $\Vdash$, which for a given finite P2P system derives only a *finite* number of equivalent queries (from Propositions 16, 17), we conclude that it must terminate. Let us now sketch the completeness proof for a given user action new, which specifies a query q_{i1} over a peer P_i, such that $f_0 = \mathrm{new}(*)$, and $(P_i, q_{i1}) = \mathrm{pop}(f_0)$: We can focus only on nonempty queries:

1. Let (P_k, q_{kl}), with $q_{kl} \neq \emptyset$, be a node in the tree $k@(P_i, q_{i1}) \in \mathrm{gfp}(\mathcal{P}_{\mathrm{fin}})$. So, there is a chain (path) from the root of this tree (P_i, q_{i1}) to this node: the set of mutually different nodes with nonempty queries in this path must be finite number n. Thus, there is a maximal number $m \leq n$ of consecutive executions of the query rewriting method st, denoted by $\mathrm{st}^m = \mathrm{next}^m$, so that $q_{kl} \in \pi_1(f(P_k))$ for $f = \mathrm{st}^m(f_0) = \mathrm{next}^m(f_0)$. So, there exists $(P_k, S) \in \mathrm{st}^{@}(f_0)$ (a unique solution for the user query in f_0, with $f_0(P_i) = q_{i1}$) such that $q_{kl} \in S$.

2. Vice versa, let $(P_k, S) \in \mathrm{st}^@(f_0)$ (a unique solution for the user query in f_0, with $\pi_1 f_0(P_i) = \langle q_{i1} \rangle$) such that $q_{kl} \in S$ where S is a finite set of rewritten queries over P_k peer. Let us show that (P_k, q_{kl}) must be a node in the tree $k@(P_i, q_{i1}) \in \mathrm{gfp}(\mathcal{P}_{\mathrm{fin}})$.

From the fact that $(P_k, S) \in \mathrm{st}^@(f_0)$, we conclude that there exists a finite number n such that $f_n = \mathrm{st}^n(f_0) = \mathrm{next}^n(f_0)$ and $q_{kl} = \pi_l(\pi_1(f_n(P_k)))$, with $l = \ln(\pi_1(f_n(P_k)))$. Thus, there exists the following sequence-ordered subset of all recursive executions of the query algorithm method st, which begins from f_0 and ends with f_n, inductively defined in the backward direction: the immediate precedent to the step n in this subset is the step $m_1 = n - 1$ in which the method st invokes the action f_{m_1} to the increment pointer of a locally-connected peer P_j, and $f_{m_1}(P_k) = (\mathrm{push}(L_k, q), m')$, which inserts q as the query q_{kl} in the list L_k of the peer P_k; so, also for the step $m_2 = n - 2$ the method st invokes the action $\mathrm{push}(L_m, q')$ for a locally-connected peer P_m to P_j, i. e., $f_{m_2}(P_j) = (\mathrm{push}(L_j, q'), m'')$, which inserts the query q' as the query $q_{jl'}$ in the list L_j of the peer P_j, etc. In this kind of backward recursion, we will reach the beginning element f_0 for the initial query couple (P_i, q_{i1}).

The chain of nodes $C = \langle (P_i, q_{i1}), \dots, (P_j, q_{jl'}), (P_k, q_{kl}) \rangle$ is a chain of intensionally equivalent queries; thus, must be a weak deduction inference chain, and consequently, a part of the unique derivation tree $k^@(P_i, q_{i1})$ (with the root in the node (P_i, q_{i1})), and consequently, (P_k, q_{kl}) is a node in this tree. □

This theorem can be represented by the following commutative diagram: the top commutative square corresponds to the query agent with the (unique) solution for its query rewriting algorithm, while the bottom commutative square corresponds to the unique solution of the weak deduction inference. The dashed diagram in the middle corresponds to the equalizer of this theorem, and intuitively, shows that each unique solution of query answering algorithm is equal to the unique solution set obtained by the weak deductive inference $\Vdash$ of the intensional logic $\mathcal{L}_\omega(\Gamma)$ for a P2P database system:

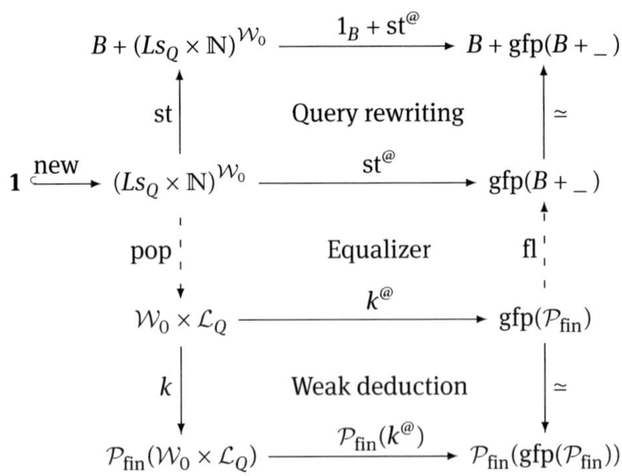

In what follows, we will consider that each single peer database (such as DIS) is able to deal with incomplete information and with mutually inconsistent information, which comes from different source databases, and we will mathematically present such query answering by using the coalgebras able to respond to user's queries by plausible (known) answers.

3.5 (Co)algebraic representation of P2P query answering

(Co)algebras provide an unifying view on a large variety of dynamic systems such as transition systems, automata, data structures and objects [152, 153] or Kripke models; they are especially useful for the dynamic query answering P2P systems.

The implementation of query answering in P2P systems by grid computing needs a standard mathematical semantics based on an adequate (co)algebra: as for example, the relational (co)algebra used for SQL query answering in relational databases. Here, the computation is more intricate because of the complex epistemic logic structures of peers and the necessity of query rewriting algorithms Rew. We consider that the rule of the query agent is to start and to maintain complete a *query answering transaction*: this transaction starts when s user query $q(\mathbf{x})$ over a peer P_i is defined. A query agent supports the Rew algorithm in order to construct intensionally equivalent rewritten queries over other peers and then calls the grid computation network to calculate answers, by assigning to each grid computation node one peer with a rewritten query for it. The transaction (agent's deduction) ends when the query agent receives the answers from all grid nodes, and presents collected answers to the user.

In the previous sections, we considered only the deduction of the intensionally equivalent queries over the P2P database system, when the user defines an initial query $q(\mathbf{x})$ over a given peer P_i. So, in order to obtain this finite set of intensionally equivalent *formulae* to this initial user's query $q(\mathbf{x})$, from all peers in a given P2P system, we embedded this P2P database system into the modal intensional FOL $\mathcal{L}_\omega(\Gamma)$ with one "high-level" existential S5 modal operator $\widehat{\Diamond}$, provided by Definition 36 in Section 3.3.

However, the execution of these query formulae over a given single peer database, which returns with a set of tuples R (a relation) extracted from a database of this peer, does not use this intensional logic $\mathcal{L}_\omega(\Gamma)$. In fact, for any peer P_i, in order to answer to any of these query formulae $q(\mathbf{x})$, we need to formulate for this peer an epistemic *extensional* modal FOL logic with universal modal operator K_i which means"Peer P_i knows that ..." in order, in the situation of an incomplete data of this peer, to obtain the meaningful subset of certain (known) tuples of data. In the rest of this section, we will consider this particular extensional epistemic modal logic (different from the "global" P2P intensional first-order modal logic $\mathcal{L}_\omega(\Gamma)$, which we used only for derivation of intensionally equivalent query-formulae for each peer in P2P system).

The definition of this P2P grid computing system, which abstracts all not necessary implementation details of a peer, and has to be given in an abstract (co)algebraic mathematical language; so, this abstract mathematical specification (coalgebraic abstract type) can be successively implemented in any current grid computing system. In fact, we defined previously in Section 3.2 only an Abstract Object Type (AOT) as an observational coalgebra (which hides the internal integration structure of the peer database, e. g., defined as a data integration system by using GLAV schema mappings) able to respond to the queries as presented in Section 3.2.2. They are functional components of the universal algebraic mathematical language, which can be used to translate the logical semantic structure of the P2P systems into (co)algebraic structures, especially useful for the dynamic query answering P2P systems. The coalgebraic definition of the Abstract Data Type (ADT) for a query answering from the single peer database is presented in [55]. It is very similar to the consideration of the relationship, that exists between the declarative (logic) SQL language and its mathematical translation into relational-algebra which can be effectively implemented in current database technology.

Because of this pragmatic, implementation point of view toward the epistemic P2P database systems, we need to pass from the epistemic model-theory for P2P systems into the (co)algebraic representation of its functional-mathematical structures (in Definition 40), which can be used for the practical grid computation implementations also. The Kripke structure of the frame $\mathcal{F}_R = (\mathcal{W}, \{\mathcal{R}_i\})$, given in the Definition 3, is a prerequisite in order to obtain a *coalgebraic semantics* for query answering in a P2P database framework.

Example 20 (Coalgebraic semantics of predicate modal logics). Let $\mathcal{M} = (\mathcal{W}, \mathcal{R}, \mathcal{D}, I_K)$ be a simple monomodal Kripke model for a set of ground predicates in P and $A_P =_{\text{def}} \{p_j^n(g(x)) \mid p_j^n \in P, g \in \mathcal{D}^{\mathcal{V}}\}$ is the set of all ground atoms obtained from the predicate letters in P.

Let us define two functions, $\text{next} : \mathcal{W} \to \mathcal{P}(\mathcal{W})$ and $\text{prop} : \mathcal{W} \to \mathcal{P}(A_P)$, where $\mathcal{P}(\_)$ is a powerset operator, such that for any $w \in \mathcal{W}$:

$$\text{next}(w) = \{w_k \mid (w, w_k) \in \mathcal{R}\}, \quad \text{(points that are potentially the next of } w)$$
$$\text{prop}(w) = \{p_j^n(\mathbf{c}) \mid p_j^n \in P, \mathcal{I}_K(w, p_j^n)(\mathbf{c}) = 1\}, \quad \text{(ground atoms true at } w).$$

Taking a Cartesian product, the coalgebraic semantics of predicate modal logic is the mapping $(\mathcal{W}, \langle \text{prop}, \text{next} \rangle : \mathcal{W} \to T(\mathcal{W}))$ with the signature functor $T = \mathcal{P}(A_P) \times \mathcal{P}(\_) : \text{Set} \to \text{Set}$, where Set is the category of all sets and functions between them.

Remark. Here, we will use the standard *extensional* multimodal logic framework of this “computational” level of query answering of each independent peer. This is very important observation. What we obtained is relatively simple modal predicate logic without quantifiers, with only a subset of predicates used in the global schema of peer databases with the set of views (virtual predicates) defined for the queries. The extension of these predicates is wrapped by ADT of each peer independently. The logic specification for these sophisticated wrappers can be obtained by using the epistemic FOL logic [55] of each single peer database. Here, a peer is considered as a data integration system with Global-As-View (GAV) mappings between its source and its global database schemas [111], and with integrity constraints over global schema also. □

So, this P2P database architecture uses the strong (extensional) semantic mapping, based on views, *inside* each peer database, as in standard data integration systems [118, 155], with the possibility to use also the logic negation [156].

This architecture takes advantage of both semantical approaches: extensional for building independent peer databases (a development of any particular peer database can be done by an independent software group, dedicated to develop and to maintain in time its functionalities), with intensional, robust and noninvasive, mapping between peers, based on the beliefs of developers of one peer about the intensionally equivalent knowledge of other peers (which are not under their control).

Different from the intensional embedding in Definition 38 for the *query rewriting*, here we need an extensional embedding of P2P database system in a multimodal epistemic logic for the *query answering* able to provide the set of certain (known) tuples for the queries obtained previously by query rewriting of the intensionally equivalent formulae.

Definition 41 (Extensional embedding of P2P database systems). For a query answering, we consider a model $\mathcal{M} = (\mathcal{W}, \{\mathcal{R}_i\}, \mathcal{D}, I_K)$, for the extensional predicate modal logic translation of a P2P database system, composed by N peers (with the set P of predicate letters (each one corresponding to some relation in peer database or to some built-in predicate) and set F of functional letters), where

- The set of possible words (points) is a union $\mathcal{W} = \bigcup_{1\leq i\leq N} \mathcal{W}_i$, with $\mathcal{W}_i = \{P_i\} \times \mathrm{Mod}(P_i)$ for $1 \leq i \leq N$, and $\mathcal{W}_0 = \{P_i \mid 1 \leq i \leq N\}$ is the finite set of peers in the P2P database system, such that:
  1. Each world, which is a peer P_i, is considered as a predicate modal logic theory with incomplete information, composed by extensional (ground atoms/facts).
  2. For each peer database P_i, the set of worlds $\mathrm{Mod}(P_i), 1 \leq i \leq N$ is a subset of preferred Herbrand models of such peer database. Each $w \in \mathrm{Mod}(P_i)$ as a Herbrand base of the predicate modal logic of peer P_i, and hence can be seen as a logical theory also, composed by only ground terms (only extensional part).
     - The Cartesian product $\mathcal{R}_i = \mathcal{W}_i \times \mathcal{W}_i \subset \mathcal{W} \times \mathcal{W}$, for each $1 \leq i \leq N$ is a binary accessibility relation, i. e., it is a reflexive, symmetric and transitive relation in $\mathcal{W}_i$, used for the "known" universal S5 modal operator K_i of the peer P_i.

- $I_K : \mathcal{W} \times (P \bigcup F) \to \bigcup_{n \in \mathcal{N}} (\mathbf{2} \bigcup \mathcal{D})^{\mathcal{D}^n}$, where $\mathbf{2} = \{f, t\}$, is a function, which assigns to each pair consisting of an n-place predicate letter $r_j^n \in P$ and of an element $w \in \mathcal{W}$ a function $I_K(w, r_j^n)$ from $\mathcal{D}^n$ to $\{f, t\}$ and for any n-ary functional letter $f_j^n \in F$ a function $I_K(w, f_j^n)$ from $\mathcal{D}^n$ to $\mathcal{D}$, such that for any n-ary relation r_j^n of peer P_i, n-ary tuple $\mathbf{d} \in \mathcal{D}^n$,

3. For any $w = (P_i, H) \in \mathcal{W}_i$, where $H \in \mathrm{Mod}(P_i)$ is a one of the preferred Herbrand models of this peer database, $I_K(w, r_j^n)(\mathbf{d}) = t$ if the ground atom $r_j^n(\mathbf{d})$ is true in the world $w = (P_i, H) \in \mathcal{W}_i$, and hence

$$\mathcal{M} \vDash_{w,g} r_j^n(\mathbf{y}) \quad \text{iff} \quad I_K(w, r_j^n)(g(\mathbf{y})) = t \tag{3.24}$$

The extension of satisfaction relation $\vDash_{w,g}$ to all formulae is standard, as that provided in Definition 3, by considering that $K_i = \neg\Diamond_i\neg$, so that for a formula $q_j(\mathbf{y})$ (a n-ary virtual predicate q_j with a tuple of variables in $\mathbf{y}$),

$$\mathcal{M} \vDash_{w,g} K_i q_j(\mathbf{y}) \quad \text{iff} \quad \text{for all } w' \in \mathcal{W} \text{ such that } (w, w') \in \mathcal{R}_i \text{ holds } \mathcal{M} \vDash_{w',g} q_j(\mathbf{y}) \tag{3.25}$$

so that the number of known tuples is defined by

$$\|K_i q_j(\mathbf{y})\|_{\mathcal{M},w} = \{g(\mathbf{y}) \in \mathcal{D}^n \mid g \in \mathcal{D}^{\mathcal{V}} \text{ and } \mathcal{M} \vDash_{P_i,H,g} K_i q_j(\mathbf{y})\} \tag{3.26}$$

So, for any virtual n-ary predicate q_j corresponding to the conjunctive query $q_j(\mathbf{y})$ of a peer P_i, $n \geq 1$, where $\mathbf{y}$ and $\mathbf{c}$ are n-tuples of variables and constants in $\mathcal{D}$, respectively, we obtain the extension (n-ary relation) in a world $w = (P_i, H) \in \mathcal{W}$, for $H \in \mathrm{Mod}(P_i)$, of this predicate (see point 2 in Definition 3) by

$$\begin{aligned}
\|K_i q_j(\mathbf{y})\|_{\mathcal{M},w} &= \{g(\mathbf{y}) \in \mathcal{D}^n \mid g \in \mathcal{D}^{\mathcal{V}} \text{ and } \mathcal{M} \vDash_{P_i,H,g} K_i q_j(\mathbf{y})\} \\
&= \bigcup_{g \in \mathcal{D}^{\mathcal{V}}} \{g(\mathbf{y}) \in \mathcal{D}^n \mid \forall (P_i, H') \in \mathcal{W}.((P_i, H), (P_i, H')) \in \mathcal{R}_i, \mathcal{M} \vDash_{P_i,H',g} q_j(\mathbf{y})\} \\
&= \bigcup_{g \in \mathcal{D}^{\mathcal{V}}} \{g(\mathbf{y}) \in \mathcal{D}^n \mid \forall H' \in \mathrm{Mod}(P_i), \mathcal{M} \vDash_{P_i,H',g} q_j(\mathbf{y})\},
\end{aligned}$$

i. e., are extracted from the peer P_i database only the tuples that are satisfied in the subset of *preferred* Herbrand models of this database, i. e., only the certain (known) answers.

In this way, the binary relation of each partition (peer database), $\mathcal{R}_i, i \geq 1$, is the S5 modal logic (reflexive, symmetric and transitive): it models the *local* universal epistemic modal operator K_i for each peer database.

3.5.1 P2P query-answering dynamics

The main *motivation* for this section is to provide the clear *semantics* for P2P database systems, based on the fact that each peer is a database with incomplete information able to provide known answers based on its epistemic S5 modal logic, and to provide the clear *mathematical* framework for its query-answering computation, which successively can be *implemented* into massive grid computing frameworks.

In the case of a P2P database system network, $\mathcal{W}_0 = \{P_i \mid 1 \le i \le N\}$, with the multimodal Kripke models defined in Definition 41, its coalgebraic semantics of the *query answering* can be given by the following definition.

Definition 42 (Coalgebraic P2P query-answering system). Let $\mathcal{M} = (\mathcal{W}, \{\mathcal{R}_i\}, \mathcal{D}, I_K)$ be the Kripke model (in Definition 41) of the finite P2P database system with $\mathcal{W}_0 = \{P_i \mid 1 \le i \le N\} \in \mathcal{W}$ with the bijective function $\mathrm{is}_0 : \mathcal{W}_0 \to \mathrm{st}^{@}(f_0)$ where $f_0 = \mathrm{new}(*) : \mathcal{W}_0 \to Ls_Q \times \mathbb{N}$ defines the initial user's query of a given peer in (3.19) and $\mathrm{st}^{@}$ the final coalgebra defined in Section 3.4.2, such that for any $P_k \in \mathcal{W}_0$, $\mathrm{is}_0(P_k) = (P_k, S_k)$ where S_k is the set of all intensionally equivalent queries over the peer database P_k obtained by the query-rewriting algorithm in Section 3.4.2.

In what follows, this initial state f_0 will be called the "*parameter*" as well.

We define two functions, $n^M : \mathcal{W} \to \mathcal{P}(\mathcal{W})$ and parameterized function $p^M_{f_0} = \langle \alpha^M_{f_0}, \mathrm{db}^M \rangle : \mathcal{W} \to \mathfrak{R} \times \mathcal{P}(\mathfrak{R})$, where $\mathfrak{R} = \bigcup_{k \in \mathbb{N}} \mathcal{P}(\mathcal{D}^k)$ is the set of all k-ary relations introduced in Definition 4, as follows: for any $w = (P_i, H) \in \mathcal{W}$:

1. $n^M(w) = \{w_k \mid w_k \in \mathcal{W}_i \text{ and } ((P_i, H), w_k) \in \mathcal{R}_i\} = \mathrm{Mod}(P_i)$,
2. the parameterized function $\alpha^M_{f_0} = \mathrm{out} \circ \pi_2 \circ \mathrm{is}_0 \circ \pi_1 : \mathcal{W}_0 \to \mathfrak{R}$, where $\mathrm{out} \circ \pi_2 : \mathrm{st}^{@}(f_0) \to \mathfrak{R}$, such that for any $(P_k, S_k) \in \mathrm{st}^{@}(f_0)$, and by using (3.26) we have that $\mathrm{out}(S_k) = \bigcup_{1 \le n \le |S_k|} \|K_k \pi_n(S_k)\|_{\mathcal{M},w}$ where $|S_k|$ denotes the number of queries in the set S_k.
3. $\mathrm{db}^M : \mathcal{W} \to \mathcal{P}(\mathfrak{R})$ such that $\mathrm{db}^M(w) = \mathrm{db}^M(P_i, H) = \{\|r^n_j(\mathbf{x})\|_{\mathcal{M},w} \mid r^n_j \in P \text{ and } r^n_j \in S_{P_i}\} = \{\mathbf{d} \in \mathcal{D}^n \mid I_K(w, r^n_j)(\mathbf{d}) = t\}$, where S_{P_i} is the set of relational symbols of P_i peer's database schema.

The coalgebra $\langle p^M_{f_0}, n^M \rangle : \mathcal{W} \to Q(\mathcal{W})$, of the endofunctor $Q = \mathfrak{R} \times \mathcal{P}(\mathfrak{R}) \times \mathcal{P}(\_) : \mathbf{Set} \to \mathbf{Set}$, defines the semantics of the P2P query-answering system.

It is easy to verify that the answers to the query are known answers: from the definition of the function p_M in the Definition 42, it holds that any tuple of the query answer has to be true in *every* preferred Herbrand model of that peer database. By the coalgebraic definition of a query answer, we obtain that for any $w = (P_i, H) \in \mathcal{W}$, the relation R_i (the set of tuples extracted from the peer database P_i):

$$\begin{aligned} R_i &=_{\mathrm{def}} \alpha^M_{f_0}(w) = \mathrm{out} \circ \pi_2 \circ \mathrm{is}_0 \circ \pi_1(P_i, H) = \mathrm{out} \circ \pi_2 \circ \mathrm{is}_0(P_i) \\ &= \mathrm{out} \circ \pi_2(P_i, S_i) = \mathrm{out}(S_i) = \bigcup_{1 \le n \le |S_i|} \|K_i \pi_n(S_i)\|_{\mathcal{M},w} \in \mathfrak{R} \end{aligned}$$

where S_i is the set of all intensionally equivalent queries rewritten over this peer $P_i \in \mathcal{W}_0$ and $|S_i|$ is the number of queries in this set S_i.

Proposition 20. *Each peer database P_i is represented by the subcoalgebra $(\{P_i\} \times \mathcal{W}_i, \langle p_i^M, n_i^M \rangle)$ of the global P2P coalgebra in Definition 42, where p_i^M and n_i^M are restrictions of $p_{f_0}^M, n^M$ on $\{P_i\} \times \mathcal{W}_i \subset \mathcal{W}$, respectively.*

Proof. It is easy to prove, from Definition 42, by simple reduction of the possible worlds only to a single peer database P_i. □

The definition of the parameterized mapping $p_{f_0}^M$ reflects the epistemic multimodal semantics for a P2P system: for a given parameter $f_0 = \text{new}(*)$ (in equation (3.19)) such that $f_0(P_i) = (\langle q_{i1}(\mathbf{x})\rangle, 0)$, the ground atoms defined by this mappings for a peer P_i (for the restriction p_i^M) with a query $q_{i1}(\mathbf{x})$ is the set of *known* facts by this peer, i. e., they must be true in all preferred Herbrand models $\mathcal{W}_i = \text{Mod}(P_i)$ of this peer. This is just the property of the epistemic multimodal P2P systems.

The union of these known answers from different peers P_i (answered to rewritten queries) is equal to $\bigcup_{P_i \in \mathcal{W}_0} R_i$. This union, collected by a query agent, of partial (but known) answers from different peers, will eliminate duplicate tuples of known answers of different peers. We assume that a query agent has a common thesauri in order to eliminate synonymous.

Now we will apply the function introduced in Definition 42 in order to define the entire categorial coalgebraic semantics for the *query answering* P2P system. Let $q_{i1}(\mathbf{x})$ be the original user query specified over the i-th peer database, such that for the parameter (state) $f_0 = \text{new}(*) : \mathcal{W}_0 \to Ls_Q \times \mathbb{N}$ with $f_0(P_i) = (\langle q_{i1}(\mathbf{x})\rangle, 0)$ (see the query-rewriting diagram after Theorem 4). This initial user's query $q_{i1}(\mathbf{x})$ is successively rewritten by a query one-step rewriting algorithm Rew (based on view-based mappings between peers and represented in the query-rewriting diagram by the arrow st, in equation (3.20)) into the set of intensionally equivalent queries over peers in the P2P system, given by the set

$$\text{st}^{@}(f_0) = \{(P_k, S_k) \mid P_k \in W_0\} \tag{3.27}$$

represented in the final coalgebraic semantics by the top commutative diagram of query rewriting (part of the equalizer in Theorem 4), where S_k is the set of all intensionally equivalent queries over the peer database P_k. Thus, we have the following.

Proposition 21. *Let $\{(P_k, S_k) \mid P_k \in W_0\} = \text{st}^{@}(f_0)$ be the final semantics of the query-rewriting algorithm where for each peer database P_k, the set S_k is the set of all intensionally equivalent queries rewritten above the database schema of this peer database P_k, for the given parameter (initial state) $f_0 = \text{new}(*) : \mathcal{W}_0 \to Ls_Q \times \mathbb{N}$ with $f_0(P_i) = (\langle q_{i1}(\mathbf{x})\rangle, 0)$ where q_{i1} is the initial user's query over peer P_i, and for all other peers P_k, $k \neq i$, $f_0(P_k) = (\langle\,\rangle, 0)$ (peers without initial user's query).*

Then, for this parameter (state) f_0*, the following diagram in* Set *category commutes*

$$\begin{array}{ccccc}
\mathbf{1} & \xrightarrow{\text{choice}} & \mathcal{W} & \xrightarrow{\langle p^M_{f_0}, n^M\rangle} & \mathfrak{R} \times \mathcal{P}(\mathfrak{R}) \times \mathcal{P}(\mathcal{W}) \\
& & \big\downarrow{\scriptstyle i_{d_W}} & & \big\downarrow{\scriptstyle \bot_R \times i_{d_{\mathcal{P}(R)}} \times i_{d_{\mathcal{P}(W)}}} \\
& & \mathcal{W} & \xrightarrow{\langle p^M_{\bot}, n^M\rangle} & \mathfrak{R} \times \mathcal{P}(\mathfrak{R}) \times \mathcal{P}(\mathcal{W})
\end{array}$$

where the mapping choice $: \mathbf{1} \to \mathcal{W}$ *form the singleton set (terminal object in Set),* $\mathbf{1} = \{*\}$*, and takes a single world* $w = (P_i, H) \in \mathcal{W}_i \subseteq \mathcal{W}$ *corresponding to the parameter* f_0 *(to the unique peer* P_i *for which user defined initial query* $q_{i1}(\mathbf{x})$ *and a chosen preferred Herbrand base* $H \in \mathrm{Mod}(P_i)$*). The functions* $p^M_{f_0}$ *and* n^M *are provided by Definition 42. The other two new functions (different from the identity functions* id*) are defined by:*

1. *The mapping* $p^M_{\bot} = \langle \bot, \mathrm{db}^M\rangle : \mathcal{W} \to \mathfrak{R} \times \mathcal{P}(\mathfrak{R})$*, where* $\mathrm{db}^M : \mathcal{W} \to \mathcal{P}(\mathfrak{R})$ *is defined in point 3 of Definition 42, and constant function* $\bot : \mathcal{W} \to \mathfrak{R}$ *such that for each* $w \in \mathcal{W}$*,* $\bot(w) = \emptyset$ *is an empty set (relation).*
2. *The constant function* $\bot_R : \mathfrak{R} \to \mathfrak{R}$*, such that for every relation* $R \in \mathfrak{R}$*, we have that* $\bot_R(R) = \emptyset$*.*

Proof. It is easy to verify because of the identity functions (the vertical arrows in this commutative diagram), so that we need to verify the commutativity for the vertical component $\bot_R$, but in that case it maps into the empty relation $\emptyset \in \mathfrak{R}$ and also the component $\bot : \mathcal{W} \to \mathfrak{R}$ of the bottom horizontal mapping $p^M_{\bot}$ is a constant function that maps to $\emptyset$ as well. □

Notice that in the diagram above, the bottom horizontal arrow corresponds to the model of the P2P system in a stable idle state, i. e., to the Q-coalgebra $(\mathcal{W}, \langle p^M_{\bot}, n^M\rangle) : \mathcal{W} \to Q(\mathcal{W})$, for the endofunctor $Q = \mathfrak{R} \times \mathcal{P}(\mathfrak{R}) \times \mathcal{P}(\_) : \mathrm{Set} \to \mathrm{Set}$.

Any parameter $f_0 = \mathrm{new}(*)$, i. e., any user's query $q_{i1}(\mathbf{x})$ over a peer P_i extends this model by known answers for rewritten queries over all peers, which are able to give a partial answer to this initial user's query. This temporary extended model of a P2P system is represented by the top horizontal arrow, i. e., to the Q-coalgebra:

$$(\mathcal{W}, \langle p^M_{f_0}, n^M\rangle) : \mathcal{W} \to Q(\mathcal{W}).$$

Consequently, we obtain the following generalized mathematical concept for the P2P query-answering.

Corollary 12. *Let us denote by* $\mathrm{CoAlg}_W(Q)$ *the full subcategory composed by only Q-coalgebras with a prefixed carrier set* $\mathcal{W}$ *for a given P2P system. Then:*

1. *The Q-coalgebra of a P2P database system,* $(\mathcal{W}, \langle p^M_{\bot}, n^M\rangle) : \mathcal{W} \to Q(\mathcal{W})$ *is the* ***terminal*** *object in* $\mathrm{CoAlg}_W(Q)$*.*

2. *Each user's query in this P2P database system determined by a parameter* $f_0 = \mathrm{new}(*)$ *can be represented by the unique coalgebra morphism in* $\mathrm{CoAlg}_W(Q)$ *from the Q-coalgebra of the query answering system* $(\mathcal{W}, \langle p^M_{f_0}, n^M\rangle) : \mathcal{W} \to Q(\mathcal{W})$ *into the terminal Q-coalgebra. This unique morphism corresponds to the vertical arrow of the diagram in Proposition* 21.

Proof. This proof comes directly from the commutative diagram in Proposition 21, where this unique coalgebra morphism is the vertical arrow $i_{d_W} \times (\bot_R \times i_{d_{\mathcal{P}(R)}} \times i_{d_{\mathcal{P}(W)}})$. □

This proposition defines the query answering of a P2P database system by the universal property of the terminal (unique) object: such object is the Kripke model of the idle P2P database system (which is unique for a given P2P system). For each given user's query, there exists a unique arrow into this terminal (idle state) object, from the extended (by rewritten intensionally equivalent queries) Kripke model, which contains all known answers to the user's given initial query.

It is interesting to observe how the coalgebraic view of query answering syntactically represents its dynamic dimension, by a simple arrow between coalgebras: the idle model of a P2P system (terminal object in $\mathrm{CoAlg}_W(Q)$), which define the Kripke's worlds (the set of preferred Herbrand models $\mathrm{Mod}(P_i)$ of each peer P_i), and by the query extended model of a P2P system, which is complementary to the standard query rewriting logic analysis. The known query answers obtained for a given parameter f_0 (given the user's query over a peer database P_i) can be seen as observations of this terminal object (idle state of a P2P system). The obtained query-answer relation does not modify the P2P system: this unique "forget" arrow into this terminal object, which represents the Kripke model of the idle P2P database system represents this fact that such observation does not produce the side effects on the P2P database system.

This coalgebraic semantics of P2P query answering can be used also as a simple mathematical instrument in order to study the behavioral equivalences between different P2P systems based on the observations (obtained results of the thuser's queries).

4 Intensional RDB manifesto: flexible big data and NewSQL

4.1 State of the art in RDBMS and NoSQL big data

This chapter is an ideal continuation of my previous "Big data integration theory" book [21], which has been dedicated to extension of RDB databases and methods of query rewriting in the data integration of traditional RDB's: In that book, I developed an abstract categorial framework and definition of categorial RDB, based on the standard FOL semantics, and topology of data integration between them. Here, instead, we will introduce the new intensional RDB (IRDB) based on the intensional FOL theory developed in this book, which are conservative but more powerful extensions of standard RDBs. Because of that, the name of this chapter is just this "Manifesto for new intensional RDBMS" [20].

This evolutive extension of the standard RDB technology can have a deep industrial impact in IT practice as well, to all current DB applications, and because of that this chapter is probably the central innovative (not only theoretically) issue of this book, and hence dedicated to a very large number of IT experts and researches.

The program of this manifesto

In what follows, we provide the method of parsing of a standard relational (RDB) instance-database A with the user-defined schema $\mathcal{A}$ into a vector relation $\vec{A}$, used in order to represent the information in a standard and simple key/value form, today in various applications of big data, and introduces the intensional concepts for the user-defined relations of the schema $\mathcal{A}$. In Tarskian semantics of the FOL, used to define the semantics of the standard RDBs, one defines what it takes for a sentence in a language to be true and relative to a model. This puts one in a position to define what it takes for a sentence in a language to be valid. Tarskian semantics often prove to be quite useful in logic. Despite this, Tarskian semantics neglects meaning, as if truth in language were autonomous. Because of that, the Tarskian theory of truth becomes inessential to the semantics for more expressive logics, or more "natural" languages.

Both Montague's and Bealer's approaches were useful for this investigation of the intensional FOL with intensional abstraction operator, but the first is not adequate and explains why we adopted two-step intensional semantics (intensional interpretation with the set of extensionalization functions). Based on this intensional extension of the FOL, we will define a new family of IRDBs. We will show that also with these extended intensional semantics we may continue to use the same SQL used for the RDBs. This new family of IRDBs extends the traditional RDBS with new features. However, it is compatible in the way how to present the data by user-defined database schemas (as in RDBs) and with SQL for management of such a relational data. The structure of

https://doi.org/10.1515/9783110981438-004

RDB is parsed into a vector key/value relation so that we obtain a column representation of data used in big data applications, covering the key/value and column-based big data applications as well, into a unifying RDB framework.

Note that the method of parsing is well suited for the migration from all existent RDB applications where the data is stored in the relational tables, so that this solution gives the possibility to pass easily from the actual RDBs into the new machine engines for the IRDB. We preserve all metadata (RDB schema definitions) without modification and only dematerialize its relational tables by transferring their stored data into the vector relation r_V (possibly in a number of disjoint partitions over a number of nodes). From the fact that we are using the query rewriting IDBMS, the current user's (legacy) applications does not need any modification and they continue to "see" the same user-defined RDB schema as before. Consequently, this IRDB solution is adequate for a massive migration from the already obsolete and slow RDBMSs into a new family of fast, NewSQL schema-flexible (with also "open schemas") and big data scalable IRDBMSs.

Moreover, in other sections of this chapter, after this basic introduction to new IRDBMS with query rewriting over its vectorial databases, we will provide other significant features of this powerful evolution of standard RDBMSs. □

First of all, let us analyze the state of the art of actual standard RDBs w. r. t. the new big data applications and NoSQL languages for them. The term NoSQL was selected in 2009 and used in the conferences for advocates of nonrelational databases. In an article of the Computerworld magazine [157], June 2009, dedicated to the NoSQL meetup in San Francisco and reported the following: "*NoSQLers came to share how they had overthrown the tyranny of slow, expensive relational databases in favor of more efficient and cheaper ways of managing data.*" In this article, Computerworld summarizes the following reasons:

- *High throughput*. The NoSQL databases provide a significantly higher data throughput than traditional RDBMSs.
- *Horizontal scalability*. In contrast to RDBMSs, most NoSQL databases are designed to scale well in the horizontal direction and not rely on highly available hardware.
- *Cost setting and complexity of database clusters*. NoSQL does not need the complexity and cost of sharing, which involves cutting up databases into multiple tables to run on large clusters or grids.
- *"One size fits all"* [158] *Database thinking is wrong*. The thinks that the realization and the search for alternatives toward traditional RDBMs can be explained by the following two major trends: the continuous growth of data volumes and the growing need to process larger amounts of data in shorter time.
- *Requirement of cloud computing*. Two major requirements are mentioned: High until almost ultimate scalability (especially in the horizontal direction) and low administration overhead. Developed cloud Amazon's SimpleDB can store large

collections of items, which themselves are hash tables containing attributes that consist of key-value pairs.
- *Avoidance of unneeded complexity*. The reach feature set and the ACID properties implemented by RDBMSs might be more than necessary for particular applications. There are different scenarios where applications would be willing to compromise reliability for better performances.

Moreover, the NoSQL movements advocate that standard relational databases fit well for data that is *rigidly structured* with relations and are designated for central deployments with single, large high-end machines, and not for distribution. Often they emphasize that SQL queries are expressed in a sophisticated language. But usually they do not tell that also the NoSQL databases often need the sophisticated languages (as object-oriented databases, or graph-based databases) as well. Moreover, they do not say that SQL and RDB are based on a sound logical framework (a subset of the first-order logic language), and hence it is not a procedural language, but a higher level declarative language able to specify "what" we need instead of "how" to obtain what we need. Thus, from the point of view of the development of computer science, instead to go in the direction of the logically higher levels of knowledge representation and query languages, more appropriated to the human understanding, they propose the old technics as key-value representations or the simpler forms of object-oriented representations and their relative procedural query languages.

They jumped into the past instead to jump in the future of the social and scientific human development. It happened because the current RDBMSs were obsolete and not ready to accept the new social-network web applications in the last 10 years, so that the isolated groups of developers of these ad hoc systems (e. g., Google, Amazon, LinkedIn, Facebook, etc.) could use only the readily old-known techniques and development instruments in order to satisfy the highly urgent business market requirements. From the academic research side, instead, most of the work has been done in the sematic web "industrial-funded" programs (e. g., the European IST projects) by considering the new knowledge and reasoning logic systems, whose impact to the existing RDB applications framework would be very hard, with difficult migration and implementation in these new semantics systems (it would need one or more decade of time). Instead, we needed more fundamental and theoretical research for the significant technological advances and evolutions of the existing RDB engine. Thus, the core RDB technology was in some way "abandoned" from both major development initiatives in the last 20 years. Nobody probably wanted to consider the most natural evolution of the RDBMSs and its FOL and SQL query framework, and the database industry tried only to cover "with pieces" and "adding" the new emergent customer's necessities, without a strong investment and the necessary efforts for the complete revision of their old System R based RDB engines of the 1970s. The world's economic crisis from 2007 did not help for such an effort.

However, from the technical point of view, it is clear that if we would come back to make the application programs in Assembler, we probably will obtain better computational performances for some algorithms than with more powerful programming languages, but it is justifiable when we write the system infrastructures and parsers, and not when we have to develop the legacy software for user's requirements. Analogously, we may provide the BD infrastructure and physical level in a form of simpler structures, adequate to support the distributive and massive big data query computations, and by preserving the logically higher level interface to customer's applications. That is, it is possible to preserve the RDB interface to data, with SQL query languages for the programmers of the software applications, with the "physical" parsing of data in more simple structures, able to deal with big data scalability in a highly distributive computation framework.

The first step to maintain the logical declarative (nonprocedural) SQL query language level, is done by the group (M. I. T. and Microsoft) and in the widely adopted paper "The end of an architectural era" (cf. [159] Michael Stonebraker et al.) where the authors come to the conclusion

> "that the current RDBMS code lines, while attempting to be a "one size fits all" solution, in fact excel at nothing."

At first, Stonebraker et al. argued that RDBMSs have been architected more than 25 years ago when the hardware characteristics, user requirements and database markets were very different from those today. The resulting revision of traditional RDBMSs is provided by developing H-store (M. I. T., Brown and Yale University), a next generation OLTP systems that operates on distributed clusters of shared-nothing machines where the data resides entirely in main memory, so that it was shown to significantly outperform (83 times) a traditional, disc-based DBMS. A more full-featured version of the system [160] that is able to execute across multiple machines within a local area cluster was presented in August 2008. The data storage in the H-store is managed by a single-thread execution engine that resides underneath the transaction manager. Each individual site executes an autonomous instance of the storage engine with a fixed amount of memory allocated from its host machine. Multi-side nodes do not share any data structures with collocated sites, and hence there is no need to use concurrent data structures (every read-only table is replicated on all nodes and other tables are divided horizontally into disjoint partitions with a k-safety factor two). Thus, H-store (at http://hstore.cs.brown.edu/documentation/architecture-overview/) was designed as a parallel, row-storage relational DBMS that runs on a cluster of shared-nothing, main memory executor nodes. The commercial version of H-store's design is VoltDB.

More recently, during 2010 and 2011, Stonebraker has been a critic of the NoSQL movement [161, 162]:

> "*Here, we argue that using MR systems to perform tasks that are best suited for DBMSs yields less than satisfactory results* [163], *concluding that MR is more like an extract-transform-load (ETL) sys-*

tem than a DBMS, as it quickly loads and processes large amounts of data in an ad hoc manner. As such, it complements DBMS technology rather than competes with it."

After a number of arguments about MR (MapReduction) w. r. t. SQL (with GROUP BY operation), the authors conclude that parallel DBMSs provide the same computing model as MR (popularized by Google and Hadoop to process key/value data pairs), with the added benefit of using a declarative SQL language. Thus, parallel DBMSs offer great scalability over the range of nodes that customers desire, where all parallel DBMSs operate (pipelining) by creating a query plan that is distributed to the appropriate nodes at execution time. When one operator in this plan sends data to next (running on the same or a different node), the data are pushed by the first to the second operator (this concept is analog to the process described in my book [21], February 2014, in Section 5.2.1 dedicated to the normalization of SQL terms (completeness of the action-relational-algebra category **RA**), so that (different from MR), the intermediate data is never written to disk. The formal theoretical framework (the database category **DB**) of the parallel DBMSs and the semantics of database mappings between them is provided in "big data integration theory" as well [21].

It is interesting that in [162], the authors conclude that parallel DBMSs excel at efficient querying of large data sets while MR key/value style systems excel at complex analytics and ETL tasks, and propose:

"The result is a much more efficient overall system than if one tries to do the entire application in either system. That is, 'smart software' is always a good idea."

The aim of this chapter is to go one step in advance in developing this NewSQL approach, and to extend the "classic" RDB systems with both features: to offer, on the user's side, the standard RDB database schema for SQL querying, and on the computational side, the "vectorial" relational database able to efficiently support the low-level key/value data structures together, in the same logical SQL framework. Moreover, this parsing of the standard RDBs into a "vectorial" database efficiently resolves also the problems of NoSQL applications with sparse-matrix and 'open schema" data models.

4.2 Intensional RDB: data integration system with a vector source database

The plan of this section is the following: we present the method of parsing of any RDB into a vector relation of the key/value structure, compatible with most big data structures, and open schema solutions, but with preserving the RDB user-defined schema for the software applications. We show that such a parsing changes the standard semantics of the RDBs based on the FOL by introducing the intensional concepts for user-defined relational tables, based on the *conservative intensional extension* of the FOL provided in the first chapter, adequate to express the semantics for the IRDBs and the SQL. Then we define a new semantics for the IRDBSs and their canonical models based on the data integration systems, where the user-defined RDB is a global schema and the source schema is composed by the unique vector relation r_V, which contains the parsed data of the whole used-defined RDB. As in GAV (Global-As-View) data integration systems (introduced in Sections A.6.3 and A.6.4 in the Appendix), we dematerialize the global schema (i. e., user-defined RDB) by providing the schema mappings (tgds) from source DB schema with vector relation r_V into global RDB user's schema (4.3). Finally, we define a *query-rewriting algorithm* to translate the original query written for the user-defined RDB schema into the source database composed by the vector relation r_V containing the parsed data.

In what follows, we denote by B^A the set of all functions from A to B, and by A^n a n-folded Cartesian product $A \times \cdots \times A$ for $n \geq 1$, we denote by $\neg, \wedge, \vee, \Rightarrow$ and $\Leftrightarrow$ the logical operators negation, conjunction, disjunction, implication and equivalence, respectively. For any two logical formulae ϕ and ψ, we define the XOR logical operator $\underline{\vee}$ by $\phi \underline{\vee} \psi$ logically equivalent to $(\phi \vee \psi) \wedge \neg(\phi \wedge \psi)$. Then we will use the following RDB definitions (more detail is provided in Section A.6 in the Appendix), based on the standard First-Order Logic (FOL) semantics:

- A *database schema* is a pair $\mathcal{A} = (S_A, \Sigma_A)$ where S_A is a countable set of relational symbols (a subset of predicates P in FOL) $r \in \mathbb{R} \subset P$ with finite arity $n = \mathrm{ar}(r) \geq 1$ ($\mathrm{ar} : \mathbb{R} \to \mathcal{N}$), disjoint from a countable infinite set **att** of attributes (a domain of $a \in$ **att** is a nonempty finite subset dom(a) of a countable set of individual symbols **dom**). For any $r \in \mathbb{R}$, the sort of r, denoted by tuple $\mathbf{a} = \mathrm{atr}(r) = \langle \mathrm{atr}_r(1), \ldots, \mathrm{atr}_r(n) \rangle$ where all $a_i = \mathrm{atr}_r(m) \in \mathbf{att}, 1 \leq m \leq n$, must be distinct: if we use two equal domains for different attributes, then we denote them by $a_i(1), \ldots, a_i(k)$ (a_i equals to $a_i(0)$). Each index ("column") i, $1 \leq i \leq \mathrm{ar}(r)$, has a distinct column name $nr_r(i) \in \mathrm{SN}$ where SN is the set of names with $nr(r) = \langle nr_r(1), \ldots, nr_r(n) \rangle$. A relation symbol $r \in \mathbb{R}$ represents the *relational name* and can be used as an atom $r(\mathbf{x})$ of FOL with variables in $\mathbf{x}$ assigned to its columns, so that Σ_A denotes a set of sentences (FOL formulae without free variables) called *integrity constraints* of the sorted FOL with sorts in **att**.
- An *instance-database* of a nonempty schema $\mathcal{A}$ is given by $A = (\mathcal{A}, I_T) = \{R = \|r\| = I_T(r) \mid r \in S_A\}$ where I_T is a Tarski's FOL interpretation, which satisfies *all* integrity constraints in Σ_A and maps a relational symbol $r \in S_A$ into an n-ary relation $R = \|r\| \in A$. Thus, an instance-database A is a set of n-ary relations, managed by relational database systems.

  Let A and $A' = (\mathcal{A}, I'_T)$ be two instances of $\mathcal{A}$, then a function $h : A \to A'$ is a *homomorphism* from A into A' if for every k-ary relational symbol $r \in S_A$ and every tuple $\langle v_1, \ldots, v_k \rangle$ of this k-ary relation in A, $\langle h(v_1), \ldots, h(v_k) \rangle$ is a tuple of the same symbol r in A'. If A is an instance-database and ϕ is a sentence, then we write $A \models \phi$ to mean that A satisfies ϕ. If Σ is a set of sentences, then we write $A \models \Sigma$ to mean that $A \models \phi$ for every sentence $\phi \in \Sigma$. Thus, the set of all instances of $\mathcal{A}$ is defined by $\mathrm{Inst}(\mathcal{A}) = \{A \mid A \models \Sigma_A\}$.

- We consider a rule-based *conjunctive query* over a database schema $\mathcal{A}$ as an expression $q(\mathbf{x}) \longleftarrow r_1(\mathbf{u}_1), \ldots, r_n(\mathbf{u}_n)$, with finite $n \geq 0$, r_i are the relational symbols (at least one) in $\mathcal{A}$ or the built-in predicates (e. g., $\leq, =$, etc.), q is a relational symbol not in $\mathcal{A}$ and $\mathbf{u}_i$ are free tuples (i. e., one may use either variables or constants). Recall that if $\mathbf{v} = (v_1, \ldots, v_m)$ then $r(\mathbf{v})$ is a shorthand for $r(v_1, \ldots, v_m)$. Finally, each variable occurring in $\mathbf{x}$ is a *distinguished* variable that must also occur at least once in $\mathbf{u}_1, \ldots, \mathbf{u}_n$. Rule-based conjunctive queries (called rules) are composed of a subexpression $r_1(\mathbf{u}_1), \ldots, r_n(\mathbf{u}_n)$ that is the *body*, and the *head* of this rule $q(\mathbf{x})$. The Yes / No conjunctive queries are the rules with an empty head. If we can find values for the variables of the rule, such that the body is logically satisfied, then we can deduce the head-fact. This concept is captured by a notion of "valuation." The deduced head-facts of a conjunctive query $q(\mathbf{x})$ defined over an instance A (for a given Tarski's interpretation I_T of schema $\mathcal{A}$) are equal to $\|q(x_1, \ldots, x_k)\|_A = \{\langle v_1, \ldots, v_k\rangle \in \mathbf{dom}^k \mid A \models \exists \mathbf{y}(r_1(\mathbf{u}_1) \wedge \ldots \wedge r_n(\mathbf{u}_n))[x_i/v_i]_{1\leq i\leq k}\} = I_T^*(\exists \mathbf{y}(r_1(\mathbf{u}_1) \wedge \ldots \wedge r_n(\mathbf{u}_n)))$, where the $\mathbf{y}$ is a set of variables, which are not in the head of query, and I_T^* is the unique extension of I_T to all formulae. We recall that the conjunctive queries are monotonic and satisfiable, and that a (Boolean) query is a class of instances that is closed under isomorphism [164]. Each conjunctive query corresponds to a "select-project-join" term $t(\mathbf{x})$ of SPRJU algebra obtained from the formula $\exists \mathbf{y}(r_1(\mathbf{u}_1) \wedge \ldots \wedge r_n(\mathbf{u}_n))$, as explained in Section 4.2.2.
- We consider a finitary *view* as a union of a finite set S of conjunctive queries with the same head $q(\mathbf{x})$ over a schema $\mathcal{A}$, and from the equivalent algebraic point of view, it is a "select-project-join-rename + union" (SPJRU) finite-length term $t(\mathbf{x})$, which corresponds to union of the terms of conjunctive queries in S. In what follows, we will use the same notation for a FOL formula $q(\mathbf{x})$ and its equivalent algebraic SPJRU expression $t(\mathbf{x})$. A materialized view of an instance-database A is an n-ary relation $R = \bigcup_{q(\mathbf{x})\in S} \|q(\mathbf{x})\|_A$. Notice that a finitary view can also have an infinite number of tuples. We denote the set of all finitary materialized views that can be obtained from an instance A by TA.

The principal idea is to use an analogy with a GAV data integration [21, 111] (specified in Section A.6.4 in the Appendix) by using the database schema $\mathcal{A} = (S_A, \Sigma_A)$ as a global relational schema, used as a user/application-program interface for the query definitions in SQL, and to represent the source database of this data integration system by parsing of the RDB instance A of the schema $\mathcal{A}$ into a single vector relation $\vec{A}$. Thus, the original SQL query $q(\mathbf{x})$ has to be equivalently rewritten over (materialized) source vector database $\vec{A}$.

Remark. The idea of a vector relation $\vec{A}$ for a given relational database instance A comes from the investigation of the topological properties of the RDB systems, presented in Chapter 8 of my Big Data Integration book [21]:

In order to analyze the algebraic lattice of all RDB database instances, each instance database A, composed by a set of finitary relations $R_i \in A$, $i = 1,\dots,n$, in Lemma 21 is defined as the transformation of the instance database A into a vector relation $\vec{A}$, with $\vec{A} = \bigcup_{R \in A} \vec{R}$ where for each relation R $\text{ar}(R) \geq 1$ is the arity (the number of its columns) of this relational table and π_i is its i-th column projection, and hence $\vec{R} = \bigcup_{1 \leq i \leq \text{ar}(R)} \pi_i(R)$. Such vectorial representation of a given database A in [21] is enough to define the lattice of RDB lattices, because we do not need the converse process (to define a database A from its vectorial representation). □

However, by considering that a database A is interfaced by users and their software applications (with the embedded SQL statements), while $\vec{A}$ is its single-table internal representation, over which a rewritten user's query is executed, the extracted information has to be converted in the RDB form w. r. t. the relational schema of the original user's model. Consequently, we need a teacher version of the vector database, such that we can obtain an equivalent inverse transformation of it into the standard user defined RDB schema.

Definition 43 (3-dim vector database coordinates). Each atomic value d_i in a tuple $\mathbf{d} = (d_1,\dots,d_i,\dots,d_{\text{ar}(r)})$ of a relation $R_k = \|r_k\|$, $r_k \in S_A$, of the instance database A, is collocated in the 3-dim data space with the following dimensional coordinates:
1. The relational name $nr(r)$ of a given relation (predicate) letter $r \in P$,
2. The tuple index Hash($\mathbf{d}$) obtained by hashing the string of the tuple $\mathbf{d}$,
3. The attribute name $nr_r(i)$ of the i-th column.

Thus, the relational schema of the vector relation r_V is composed by the four attributes, relational name, tuple-index, attribute name and value, i. e., `r-name`, `t-index`, `a-name` and `value`, respectively. The key of the relation r_V in vector database $\vec{A}$ is composed by all of its four attributes.[1]

So, if we assume r_V (the name of the database $\mathcal{A}$) for the name of this vector relation $\vec{A}$ then this relation can be expressed by the 4-ary predicate letter $r_V \in P$ of the intensional FOL,

$$r_V(\texttt{r-name}, \texttt{t-index}, \texttt{a-name}, \texttt{value}) \tag{4.1}$$

with its extension for a given Tarski's interpretation I_T, denoted by $\|r_V\| = I_T^*(r_V)$.

So, the parsing of any RDB instance A of a schema $\mathcal{A}$ can be defined as

1 The fact that we chose to use all four attributes as the key of this relation instead of three-dimensional coordinates permits us to generalize RDB with the possibility to have multivalued attributes as well; in fact, for a given multivalued attribute, we can have more than one value in the attribute `value` of this relation r_V from the fact that also this attribute composes the key of this relation.

Definition 44 (Parsing RDB instances). Given a database instance $A = \{R_1, \ldots, R_n\}$, $n \geq 1$, of a RDB schema $\mathcal{A} = (S_A, \Sigma_A)$ with $S_A = \{r_1, \ldots, r_n\}$ such that $R_k = \|r_k\|, k = 1, \ldots, n$, then the extension $\vec{A} = \|r_V\|$ of the vector relational symbol (name) r_V with the schema r_V(`r-name`, `t-index`, `a-name`, `value`), and *NOT NULL* constraints for all its four attributes, and with the primary key composed by the first three attributes, is defined by the following.

We define the operation $\underline{\text{PARSE}}$ for a tuple $\mathbf{d} = (d_1, \ldots, d_{\mathrm{ar}(r_k)})$ of the relation $r_k \in S_A$ by the transformation

$$(r_k, \mathbf{d}) \mapsto \{(nr(r_k), \mathrm{Hash}(\mathbf{d}), nr_{r_k}(i), d_i) \mid d_i \neq NULL, 1 \leq i \leq \mathrm{ar}(r_k)\},$$

so that

$$\vec{A} =_{\mathrm{def}} \bigcup_{r_k \in S_A, \mathbf{d} \in \|r_k\|} \underline{\text{PARSE}}(r_k, \mathbf{d}) \tag{4.2}$$

Based on the vector database representation $\|r_V\|$, we define a GAV data integration system $\mathcal{I} = \langle \mathcal{A}, \mathcal{S}, \mathcal{M} \rangle$ with the global schema $\mathcal{A} = (S_A, \Sigma_A)$, the source schema $\mathcal{S} = (\{r_V\}, \emptyset)$ and the set of mappings $\mathcal{M}$ expressed by the tgds (tuple generating dependencies, introduced in Section A.6.3 in the Appendix):[2]

$$\begin{aligned}
&\exists z, z_1, z_2 (r_V(nr(r_k), z, z_1, z_2)) \wedge \\
&\quad \forall y, x_1, \ldots, x_{\mathrm{ar}(r_k)} [((r_V(nr(r_k), y, nr_{r_k}(1), x_1) \underline{\vee} (x_1 = \mathrm{NULL})) \wedge \ldots \\
&\quad \ldots \wedge (r_V(nr(r_k), y, nr_{r_k}(\mathrm{ar}(r_k)), x_{\mathrm{ar}(r_k)}) \underline{\vee} (x_{\mathrm{ar}(r_k)} = \mathrm{NULL}))) \\
&\quad \Rightarrow r_k(x_1, \ldots, x_{\mathrm{ar}(r_k)})]
\end{aligned} \tag{4.3}$$

for each $r_k \in S_A$.

The operation $\underline{\text{PARSE}}$ corresponds to the parsing of the tuple $\mathbf{d}$ of the relation $r_k \in S_A$ of the user-defined database schema $\mathcal{A}$ into a number of tuples of the vector relation r_V. In fact, we can use this operation for virtual inserting/deleting of the tuples in the user- defined schema $\mathcal{A}$, and store them only in the vector relation r_V. This operation avoids to materialize the user-defined (global) schema, but only the source database $\mathcal{S}$, so that each user-defined SQL query has to be equivalently rewritten over the source database (i. e., the big table $\vec{A} = \|r_V\|$) as in standard FOL data integration systems.

Notice that this parsing defines a kind of GAV Data integration system, where the source database $\mathcal{S}$ is composed by the unique vector relation $\|r_V\| = \vec{A}$ (big data vector

---

2 The first sentence $\exists z, z_1, z_2(r_V(nr(r_k), z, z_1, z_2))$ is true if there exists at least one tuple for the relation r_k, so that the second conjunctive component can be used to generate the extension of r_k from the vector relation $\vec{A}$.

table), which does not contain NULL values, so that we do not unnecessarily save the NULL values of the user-defined relational tables $r_k \in S_A$ in the main memories of the parallel RDBMS used to horizontal partitioning of the unique big-table $\vec{A}$. Moreover, any adding of the new columns to the user-defined schema $\mathcal{A}$ does not change the table $\vec{A}$, while the deleting of a i-th column of a relation r will delete all tuples $r_V(x, y, z, v)$ where $x = nr(r)$ and $z = nr_r(i)$ in the main memory of the parallel RDBMS. Thus, we obtain very *schema-flexible* RDB model for big data.

Other obtained NoSQL systems' properties are:

- *Compatible with key/value systems*. Note that the vector big-table $\vec{A}$ is in the 6th normal form, that is with the primary key corresponding to the first three attributes (the free-dimensional coordinates) and the unique value attribute. Thus, we obtained the key/value style used for NoSQL big data systems. That is, the RDB parsing with resulting data integration system subsumes all big data key/value systems.
- *Compatible with 'open schema" systems*. Entity-attribute-value model (EAV) is a data model to describe entities where the number of attributes (properties, parameters) that can be used to describe them is potentially vast, but the number that will actually apply to a given entity is relatively modest. In mathematics, this model is known as a sparse matrix. EAV is also known as an object-attribute-value model, vertical database model and open schema. We can use the special relational symbol with name `OpenSchema` in the user database schema $\mathcal{A}$ so that its tuples in $\vec{A}$ will correspond to atoms $r_V(\texttt{OpenSchema}, \text{object}, \text{attribute}, \text{value})$. In this case, the software developed for the applications, which use the open schema data will directly access to the vector relation $\vec{A}$ and DBMS will restrict all operations only to tuples where the first attribute has the value equal to `OpenSchema` (during an insertion of a new tuple $\langle \text{object}, \text{attribute}, \text{value} \rangle$ the DBMS inserts also the value `OpenSchema` in the first column of $\vec{A}$).

But this simple and unifying framework needs more investigation for the SQL and underlying logical framework. In fact, we can easy see that the mapping tgds used from the big data vector table $\vec{A}$ (the source schema in data integration) into user-defined RDB schema $\mathcal{A}$ (the global schema of this data integration system with integrity constraints) is not a simple FOL formula. Because the same element r_k is used as a predicate symbol (on the right side of the tgds implication) and as a value (on the left side of the implication as the first value in the predicate r_V). It means that the elements of the domain of this logic are the elements of other classes and are the classes for themselves as well. Such semantics are not possible in the standard FOL, but only in the *intensional* FOL provided in Chapter 1, especially in Section 1.3, with the commutative diagram (1.14) between intensional and Tarski's (extensional) interpretations of Frede/Russell semantics of Corollary 4:

$$\begin{array}{ccccc} & & \mathcal{A}_{\mathrm{int}}\ \text{(concepts/meaning)} & & \\ & \text{intensional interpret. } I \nearrow & \dfrac{\text{Frege/Russell}}{\text{semantics}} & \searrow h\ \text{(extensionalization)} & \\ \mathcal{A}_{\mathrm{FOL}}\ \text{(syntax)} & & \xrightarrow[I_T^*\ \text{(Tarski's interpretation)}]{} & & \mathcal{A}_{\mathfrak{R}}\ \text{(denotation)} \end{array} \tag{4.4}$$

Consequently, the Data Integration $\mathcal{I}$ is not a classic FOL data integration as in [111] but an intensional data integration system. In the next sections, we will investigate what is the proper logic framework for this class of RDBs, denominated as IRDBs (intensional RDBs), and to show that the standard SQL is complete in this new logical framework.

4.2.1 Canonical models for IRDBs

The application of the intensional FOL semantics to the data integration system $\mathcal{I} = (\mathcal{A}, \mathcal{S}, \mathcal{M})$ in Definition 44 with the user-defined RDB schema $\mathcal{A} = (S_A, \Sigma_A)$ and the vector big table r_V can be summarized in the following:

- Each relational *name* $nr(r_k)$ (first data coordinate in Definition 43), of the predicate (relational) letter $r_k \in S_A = \{r_1, \dots, r_n\}$ with the arity $m = \mathrm{ar}(r_k)$, is an intensional m-ary concept $nr(r_k) = I(r_k(\mathbf{x})) \in D_m$, obtained from the atom $r_k(\mathbf{x})$ of the intensional FOL with the tuple of variables $\mathbf{x} = (x_1, \dots, x_m)$ for a given intensional interpretation I. For a given Tarski's interpretation I_T, the extensionalization function h is determined by $h(I(r_k(\mathbf{x}))) = \|r_k\| = \{\langle d_1, \dots, d_m\rangle \in \mathcal{D}^m \mid I_T^*(r_k(d_1, \dots, d_m)) = t\} = I_T^*(r_k(\mathbf{x})) \in A$, corresponding to the commutativity of diagram (4.4). The instance database A of the user-defined RDB schema $\mathcal{A}$ is a model of $\mathcal{A}$ if it satisfies all integrity constraints in Σ_A.
- The relational name $nr(r_V) = I(r_V(y_1, y_2, y_3, y_4)) \in D_4$ of the vector big table is a particular 4-ary intensional concept, such that for a given model $A = \{\|r_1\|, \dots, \|r_n\|\}$ of the user-defined RDB schema $\mathcal{A}$, correspondent to a given Tarski's interpretation I_T, its extension is determined by $\|r_V\| = h(nr(r_V)) = I_T^*(r_V(y_1, y_2, y_3, y_4)) = \vec{A}$.
- Intensional nature of the IRDB is evident in the fact that each tuple

  $$(nr(r_k), \mathrm{Hash}(d_1, \dots, d_m), nr_{r_k}(i), d_i) \in \vec{A},$$

  corresponding to the ground atom $r_V(y_1, y_2, y_3, y_4)/g$ for an assignment g with $g(y_1) = nr(r_k) \in D_m$, $g(y_3) = nr_{r_k}(i) \in D_{-1}$, $g(y_4) = d_i \in \mathcal{D}$ and $g(y_2) = \mathrm{Hash}(d_1, \dots, d_m) \in D_{-1}$, is equal to the intensional tuple $(I(r_k(\mathbf{x})), \mathrm{Hash}(d_1, \dots, d_m), nr_{r_k}(i), d_i)$. Notice that the intensional tuples are different from ordinary tuples composed by only particulars (extensional elements) in D_{-1}, what are the characteristics of the standard FOL (where the domain of values is equal to D_{-1}), while here the "value" $nr(r_k) = I(r_k(\mathbf{x})) \in D_m$ is an m-ary intensional concept, for which $h(nr(r_k))$ is a m-ary relation.

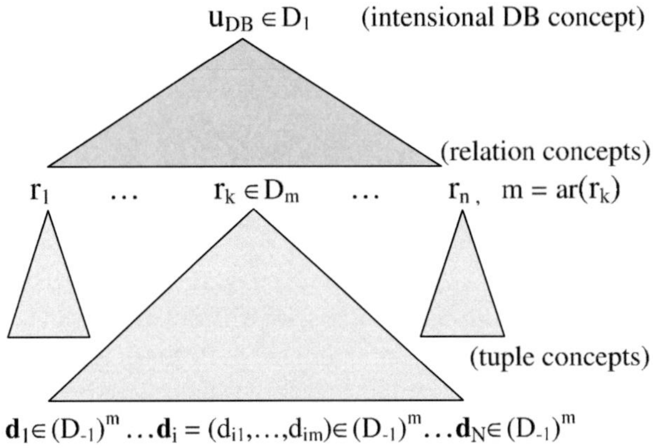

Figure 4.1: Intensional hierarchy system of concepts.

Based on the intensional interpretation above, we are able to represent any instance user-defined database A as an intensional hierarchy system of concepts, presented in the diagram, where for each tuple of data $\mathbf{d}_i = (d_{i1}, \dots, d_{im}) \in D^m_{-1}$, $1 \leq i \leq N$, of the relation $h(r_k) = \|r_k\|$, we have that $h(I(r_V(nr(r_k), \text{Hash}(\mathbf{d}_i), nr_{r_k}(j), d_{ij}))) = t$, for d_{ij} different from NULL, $j = 1, \dots, m$.

The intensional data integration system $\mathcal{I} = (\mathcal{A}, \mathcal{S}, \mathcal{M})$ in Definition 44 provides the global schema $\mathcal{A} = (S_A, \Sigma_A)$, which is only virtual (empty) database used to define the SQL user-defined query, which then has to be equivalently rewritten over the vector relation r_V in order to obtain the answer to this query. Thus, the information of the database is stored only in the big vector table $\|r_V\|$ while the materialization of the original user-defined schema $\mathcal{A}$ can be obtained by the following operation:

Definition 45 (Materialization of the RDB). Given a user-defined RDB schema $\mathcal{A} = (S_A, \Sigma_A)$ with $S_A = \{r_1, \dots, r_n\}$ and a big vector table $\|r_V\|$, the (non-SQL) operator $\underline{\text{MATTER}}$, which materializes the schema $\mathcal{A}$ into an instance database $A = \{R_1, \dots, R_n\}$ where $R_k = \|r_k\|$, for $k = 1, \dots, n$, is given by the following mapping derived from (4.3), for any $R \subseteq \|r_V\|$:

$$(r_k, R) \mapsto \{(d_1, \dots, d_{\text{ar}(r_k)}) \mid \exists y \in \pi_2(R)((r_V(nr(r_k), y, nr_{r_k}(1), d_1) \underline{\vee} (d_1 = \text{NULL})) \wedge \cdots \\ \wedge (r_V(nr(r_k), y, nr_{r_k}(\text{ar}(r_k)), d_{\text{ar}(r_k)}) \underline{\vee} (d_{\text{ar}(r_k)} = \text{NULL})))\},$$

so that the complete materialization of the schema $\mathcal{A}$ is defined for each $r_k \in S_A$ by

$$R_k = \|r_k\| =_{\text{def}} \underline{\text{MATTER}}(r_k, \|r_V\|) \tag{4.5}$$

The canonical models of the intensional data integration system $\mathcal{I} = (\mathcal{A}, \mathcal{S}, \mathcal{M})$ in Definition 44 are the database instances A of the schema $\mathcal{A}$ such that

$$\|r_k\| = \underline{\text{MATTER}}\Big(r_k, \bigcup_{\mathbf{d}\in\|r_k\|} \underline{\text{PARSE}}(r_k, \mathbf{d})\Big) \tag{4.6}$$

i. e., when

$$A = \{\underline{\text{MATTER}}(r_k, \vec{A}) \mid r_k \in S_A\}.$$

The canonical models of such intensional data integration system $\mathcal{I} = \langle \mathcal{A}, \mathcal{S}, \mathcal{M}\rangle$ can be provided in a usual logical framework as well.

Proposition 22. *Let the IRDB be given by a data integration system $\mathcal{I} = \langle \mathcal{A}, \mathcal{S}, \mathcal{M}\rangle$ for a user-defined global schema $\mathcal{A} = (S_A, \Sigma_A)$ with $S_A = \{r_1, \dots, r_n\}$, the source schema $\mathcal{S} = (\{r_V\}, \emptyset)$ with the vector big data relation r_V and the set of mapping tgds $\mathcal{M}$ from the source schema into he relations of the global schema.*

Then a canonical model of $\mathcal{I}$ is any model of the schema $\mathcal{A}^+ = (S_A \bigcup\{r_V\}, \Sigma_A \bigcup \mathcal{M} \bigcup \mathcal{M}^{\text{OP}})$, where $\mathcal{M}^{\text{OP}}$ is an opposite mapping tgds from $\mathcal{A}$ into r_V given by the following set of tgds:

$$\begin{aligned}\mathcal{M}^{\text{OP}} = \{&\forall x_1, \dots, x_{\text{ar}(r_k)}[(r_k(x_1, \dots, x_{\text{ar}(r_k)}) \wedge (x_i \neq \mathit{NULL}))\\ &\Rightarrow r_V(nr(r_k), \text{Hash}(x_1, \dots, x_{\text{ar}(r_k)}), nr_{r_k}(i), x_i)] \mid 1 \le i \le \text{ar}(r_k), r_k \in S_A\}.\end{aligned}$$

Proof. It is enough to show that for each $r_k \in S_A$, and $\mathbf{x} = (x_1, \dots, x_{\text{ar}(r_k)})$,

$$\begin{aligned}r_k(\mathbf{x}) \Leftrightarrow {} & ((r_V(nr(r_k), \text{Hash}(\mathbf{x}), nr_{r_k}(1), x_1) \underline{\vee} (x_1 = \text{NULL})) \wedge \dots\\ & \wedge (r_V(nr(r_k), \text{Hash}(\mathbf{x}), nr_{r_k}(\text{ar}(r_k)), x_{\text{ar}(r_k)}) \underline{\vee} (x_{\text{ar}(r_k)} = \text{NULL}))).\end{aligned}$$

From $\mathcal{M}^{\text{OP}}$, we have

$$\neg r_k(\mathbf{x}) \vee \neg(x_i \neq \text{NULL}) \vee r_V(nr(r_k), \text{Hash}(\mathbf{x}), nr_{r_k}(i), x_i), \quad \text{i. e.,}$$

(a) $\neg r_k(\mathbf{x}) \vee (x_i = \text{NULL} \vee r_V(nr(r_k), \text{Hash}(\mathbf{x}), nr_{r_k}(i), x_i))$.

From the other side, from the fact that we have the constraint NOT NULL for the attribute `value` (in Definition 44), then

$$\neg r_k(\mathbf{x}) \vee \neg(x_i = \text{NULL}) \vee \neg r_V(nr(r_k), \text{Hash}(\mathbf{x}), nr_{r_k}(i), x_i), \quad \text{i. e.,}$$

(b) $\neg r_k(\mathbf{x}) \vee \neg(x_i = \text{NULL} \wedge r_V(nr(r_k), \text{Hash}(\mathbf{x}), nr_{r_k}(i), x_i))$,

is true and also the conjunction of (a) and (b) has to be true, i. e.,

$$\begin{aligned}&(\neg r_k(\mathbf{x}) \vee (x_i = \text{NULL} \vee r_V(nr(r_k), \text{Hash}(\mathbf{x}), nr_{r_k}(i), x_i)))\\ &\quad \wedge (\neg r_k(\mathbf{x}) \vee \neg(x_i = \text{NULL} \wedge r_V(nr(r_k), \text{Hash}(\mathbf{x}), nr_{r_k}(i), x_i)));\end{aligned}$$

thus, by distributivity,

(c) $\neg r_k(\mathbf{x}) \vee (x_i = \text{NULL} \underline{\vee} r_V(nr(r_k), \text{Hash}(\mathbf{x}), nr_{r_k}(i), x_i))$.

If we repeat this for all $1 \leq i \leq \text{ar}(r_k)$ and make conjunction of all these true formula, by distributive property of such conjunction $\wedge$, we obtain

$$\neg r_k(\mathbf{x}) \vee ((x_1 = \text{NULL} \underline{\vee} r_V(nr(r_k), \text{Hash}(\mathbf{x}), nr_{r_k}(1), x_1)) \wedge \ldots$$
$$\wedge (x_{\text{ar}(r_k)} = \text{NULL} \underline{\vee} r_V(nr(r_k), \text{Hash}(\mathbf{x}), nr_{r_k}(\text{ar}(r_k)), x_{\text{ar}(r_k)}))), \quad \text{i.e.,}$$

(d) $r_k(\mathbf{x}) \Rightarrow ((r_V(nr(r_k), \text{Hash}(\mathbf{x}), nr_{r_k}(1), x_1) \underline{\vee} x_1 = \text{NULL}) \wedge \ldots \wedge (r_V(nr(r_k), \text{Hash}(\mathbf{x}), nr_{r_k}(\text{ar}(r_k)), x_{\text{ar}(r_k)}) \underline{\vee} x_{\text{ar}(r_k)} = \text{NULL}))$.

Moreover, from the definition we also have
(e) $r_k(\mathbf{x}) \Leftarrow ((r_V(nr(r_k), \text{Hash}(\mathbf{x}), nr_{r_k}(1), x_1) \underline{\vee} x_1 = \text{NULL}) \wedge \ldots \wedge (r_V(nr(r_k), \text{Hash}(\mathbf{x}), nr_{r_k}(\text{ar}(r_k)), x_{\text{ar}(r_k)}) \underline{\vee} x_{\text{ar}(r_k)} = \text{NULL}))$.

That is, the logical equivalence of the formula on the left-hand and on the right-hand side of the logical implication, and hence if the atom $r_k(\mathbf{x})$ is true for some assignment g to the variables so that the tuple $(g(x_1), \ldots, g(x_{\text{ar}(r_k)}))$ is in relation $r_k \in \mathcal{A}$, then for the same assignment g the every formula

$$r_V(nr(r_k), \text{Hash}(\mathbf{x}), nr_{r_k}(1), x_1) \underline{\vee} x_1 = \text{NULL},$$
$$\ldots,$$
$$r_V(nr(r_k), \text{Hash}(\mathbf{x}), nr_{r_k}(\text{ar}(r_k)), x_{\text{ar}(r_k)}) \underline{\vee} x_{\text{ar}(r_k)} = \text{NULL}$$

has to be true, and hence generates the tuples in r_V for NOT NULL values of $g(x_i)$, $1 \leq i \leq \text{ar}(r_k)$.

Notice that the implication (d) corresponds to the non-SQL operator PARSE, while the implication (e) is the logical semantics of the non-SQL operator MATTER.

Consequently, we obtain $\|r_k\| = \underline{\text{MATTER}}(r_k, \bigcup_{\mathbf{v} \in \|r_k\|} \underline{\text{PARSE}}(r_k, \mathbf{v}))$, i. e., $A = \{\underline{\text{MATTER}}(r_k, \vec{A}) \mid r_k \in S_A\}$ and the database instance A, which satisfies all integrity constraints $\Sigma_A \bigcup \mathcal{M} \bigcup \mathcal{M}^{\text{OP}}$ is the canonical model of the intensional data integration system $\mathcal{I} = (\mathcal{A}, \mathcal{S}, \mathcal{M})$. □

We are also able to render more flexible this approach and to decide only a subset of relations to be the intensional concepts whose extension has to be parsed in to the big vector table r_V. For standard legacy systems, we can chose to avoid at all to have the intensional concepts, thus to have the standard RDBs with standard FOL Tarski's semantics. By declaring any of the relational names of $r_k \in S_A$ as an intensional concept, we conservatively extend the Tarski's semantics for the FOL in order to obtain more expressive intensional FOL semantics for the IRDBs.

The fact that we assumed r_V to be used only as particular (extensional entity) and not as intensional 4-ary concept $nr(r_V) = I(r_V(x_1, x_2, x_3, x_4))$ is based on the fact that it will always be materialized (into the nonempty relational table) as standard tables in the RDBs. The other reason is that the extension $h(nr(r_V))$ has to represent the whole *set of relations* in the instance database A. That is, $nr(r_V)$ is not a significant user's concept but only a mathematical entity useful to parse the user's conceptual ER database and to contain its relations $r_k \in S_A$ in atomic vectorial form compatible with practice of big data.

Consequently, we do not use the 4-ary intensional concept $nr(r_V)$ (equal to the name of the database $\mathcal{A}$) as a value in the tuples of other relations, or in any tuple of vector relation r_V, and we do not apply the parsing to r_V different from all relations $r_k \in S_A$ (assumed to be the intensional concepts as well) in the user-defined conceptual RDB schema $\mathcal{A}$.

This vector relation, hidden to users, is only a mathematical object, which supports the virtual reality of user's defined conceptual RDB schema, and used to respond to user's queries over their RDB virtual schema by *query-rewriting methods* (transforming original user's query over his virtual RDB schema into a query over this materialized big vector relation r_v).

Example 21 (Hypothesis of a recursive parsing of vector relation into itself). If we would decide to use also r_V as an intensional concept in D_4, we would be able to parse it (as all other intensional concepts in $\mathcal{A}$) into itself, and such recursive definition will render (only theoretically) an infinite extension of the r_V, thus nonapplicable, as follows:

Let for an user-defined n-ary relational table $r_k \in S_A$, it intensional n-ary concept (name) be $I(r_k(\mathbf{x})) = nr(r_k) = \text{Person} \in D_n$, and Pname an attribute-name of this table r_k, and let ID be the t-index value obtained by Hash function from one tuple of r_k where the value of the attribute Pname is "Marco Aurelio," then we will obtain by parsing these tuples in the vector table r_V with its name (intensional concept) $nr(r_V) \in D_4$:

1.

$$(\text{Person}, \text{ID}, \text{Pname}, \text{Marco Aurelio}) \in \|r_V\|;$$

then by parsing this tuple 1, we will obtain for

$$\text{ID}_1 = \text{Hash}(\text{Person}, \text{ID}, \text{Pname}, \text{Marco Aurelio})$$

also the following new tuples in the vector relation $\|r_V\|$:

2. $(nr(r_V), \text{ID}_1, \texttt{r-name}, \text{Person})$;
3. $(nr(r_V), \text{ID}_1, \texttt{t-index}, \text{ID})$;
4. $(nr(r_V), \text{ID}_1, \texttt{a-name}, \text{Pname})$;
5. $(nr(r_V), \text{ID}_1, \texttt{value}, \text{Marco Aurelio})$; then by parsing the tuple 2 above, we will obtain for

$$\mathrm{ID}_2 = \mathrm{Hash}(nr(r_V), \mathrm{ID}_1, \texttt{r-name}, \mathrm{Person}),$$

the following new tuples in the vector relation $\|r_V\|$:

6. $(nr(r_V), \mathrm{ID}_2, \texttt{r-name}, nr(r_V))$;
7. $(nr(r_V), \mathrm{ID}_2, \texttt{t-index}, \mathrm{ID}_1)$;
8. $(nr(r_V), \mathrm{ID}_2, \texttt{a-name}, \texttt{r-name})$;
9. $(nr(r_V), \mathrm{ID}_2, \texttt{value}, \mathrm{Person})$; then by parsing this tuple 9 above, we will obtain for

$$\mathrm{ID}_3 = \mathrm{Hash}(nr(r_V), \mathrm{ID}_2, \texttt{r-name}, \mathrm{Person}),$$

the following new tuples:

10. $(nr(r_V), \mathrm{ID}_3, \texttt{r-name}, nr(r_V))$;
etc.

Thus, as we see, the tuple 10 is equal to the tuple 6, but only with new t-index (tuple index) value, so by continuing this process, theoretically (if we do not pose the limits for the values of t-indexes) we obtain an infinite process and an infinite extension of r_V. Obviously, it can not happen in real RDBs, because the length of the attribute `t-index` is finite so that at some point we will obtain the previously generated value for this attribute (we reach a fixed point), and from the fact that this attribute is a part of the primary key this tuple would not be inserted in r_V because r_V contains the same tuple already.

Notice that this process, described in the example above, is analogous to the self-referencing process, where we try to use an intensional concept *as an element of itself* that has to be avoided, and hence there is no sense to use (in software applications) r_V as an intensional concept. Consequently, the IRDB has at least one relational table, which is not used as an intensional concept, and hence will not be parsed: the big vector table r_V.

4.2.2 NewSQL property of the IRDBs

This section will be dedicated to demonstrate that the IRDBs are complete w. r. t. the standard SQL. This demonstration is based on the fact that each SQL query, defined over the user-defined schema $\mathcal{A}$, which (in its full (virtual) intensional immersion) is composed by the only intensional concepts, and hence will be executed over standard relational tables that *are not* the intensional concepts. If a query is defined over the nonintensional concepts (materialized relations with saved tuples) in $\mathcal{A}$, in this case it will be directly executed over these relational tables as in each RDB. If a query is defined over the intensional relation-concepts $nr(r_k) = I(r_k(\mathbf{x}))$, with $r_k \in \mathcal{A}$, (without their direct materialized extensions *tables* $h(nr(r_k)) = h(I(r_k(\mathbf{x}))) = I_T^*(r_k(\mathbf{x}))$ for a given Tarski model I_T of this data base), then we need to demonstrate the existence of an effective query rewriting into an equivalent SQL query over the (nonintensional concept) big vector table r_V.

In order to define this query rewriting, we will shortly introduce the abstract syntax and semantics of Codd's relational algebra, as follows. Five primitive operators of Codd's algebra are: the *selection*, the *projection*, the *Cartesian product* (also called the cross-product or cross-join), the *set union* and the *set difference*. Another operator, *rename*, was not noted by Codd, but the need for it is shown by the inventors of Information Systems Base Language (ISBL) for one of the earliest database management systems, which implemented Codd's relational model of data. These six operators are fundamental in the sense that if we omit any one of them, we will lose expressive power. Many other operators have been defined in terms of these six. Among the most important are set intersection, division and the natural join. In fact, ISBL made a compelling case for replacing the Cartesian product with the *natural join*, of which the Cartesian product is a degenerate case.

Remark. We recall the following notation conventions: for any k-ary relational table r, with $k = \text{ar}(r)$, with the injective function $nr_r : \{1, \dots, k\} \to SN$, which assigns distinct names to each column of this relation r, we denote its tuple of attributes $\text{atr}(r) = \mathbf{a} = (a_1, \dots, a_k) = (\text{atr}_r(1), \dots, \text{atr}_r(k))$, and the set of attributes denoted by $\overline{\mathbf{a}} = \overline{\text{atr}}(r)$. We recall that two relations r_1 and r_2 are union compatible iff $\overline{\text{atr}}(r_1) = \overline{\text{atr}}(r_2)$. If a relation r_2 is obtained from a given relation r_1 by permutating its columns, then we tell that they are not equal (in set theoretic sense) but that they are equivalent. Notice that in the RDB theory the two equivalent relations are considered equal as well.

In what follows, given any two lists (tuples), $\mathbf{d} = (d_1, \dots, d_k)$ and $\mathbf{b} = (b_1, \dots, b_m)$ their concatenation $(d_1, \dots, d_k, b_1, \dots, b_m)$ is denoted by $\mathbf{d}\&\mathbf{b}$, where '&' is the symbol for concatenation of the lists. By $\|r\|$, we denote the extension of a given relation (relational symbol) r; it is extended to any term t_R of Codd's algebra, so that $\|t_R\|$ is the relation obtained by computation of this term. □

Let us briefly define these basic operators, and their correspondence with the formulae of FOL:

1. Rename is a unary operation written as "_ RENAME name_1 AS name_2" where the result is identical to the input argument (relation) r except that the column i with name $nr_r(i) = \text{name}_1$ in all tuples is renamed to $nr_r(i) = \text{name}_2$.
   This operation is neutral w. r. t. the logic, where we are using the variables for the columns of relational tables and not their names.

2. The Cartesian product is a binary operation "_ TIMES _," written also as "_ $\bigotimes$ _," such that for the relations r_1 and r_2, first we do the rename normalization of r_2 (w. r. t. r_1), denoted by r_2^ρ, such that:

For each k-th copy of the attribute a_i (or, equivalently, $a_i(0)$) of the m-th column of r_2 (with $1 \leq m \leq \mathrm{ar}(r_2)$), denoted by $a_i(k) = \mathrm{atr}_{r_2}(m) \in \mathrm{atr}(r_2)$, such that the maximum index of the same attribute a_i in r_1 is $a_i(n)$, we change r_2 by:
1. $a_i(k) \mapsto a_i(k+n)$;
2. if $\mathrm{name}_1 = nr_{r_2}(m)$ is a name that exists in the set of the column names in r_1, then we change the naming function $nr_{r_2} : \{1,\dots,\mathrm{ar}(r_2)\} \to \mathrm{SN}$, by $nr_{r_2}(m) = \mathrm{name}_2$, where $\mathrm{name}_2 \in \mathrm{SN}$ is a new name distinct from all other used names, and we define the renaming normalization ρ by mapping $\mathrm{name}_1 \mapsto \mathrm{name}_2$.
   The relation obtained from r_2, after this renaming normalization, will be denoted by r_2^ρ. Then we define the new relation r (when both $\|r_1\| \neq \{\langle\,\rangle\}$ and $\|r_2\| \neq \{\langle\,\rangle\}$, i. e., when are not empty relations) by $r_1 \bigotimes r_2^\rho$, with $\|r\| =_{\mathrm{def}} \{\mathbf{d}_1\&\mathbf{d}_2 \mid \mathbf{d}_1 \in \|r_1\|, \mathbf{d}_2 \in \|r_2\|\}$, with the naming function $nr_r : \{1,\dots,\mathrm{ar}(r_1)+\mathrm{ar}(r_2)\} \to \mathrm{SN}$, such that $nr_r(i) = nr_{r_1}(i)$ for $1 \leq i \leq \mathrm{ar}(r_1)$ and $nr_r(i) = nr_{r_2}(i)$ for $1 + \mathrm{ar}(r_1) \leq i \leq \mathrm{ar}(r_1) + \mathrm{ar}(r_2)$, and $\mathrm{atr}_r : \{1,\dots,\mathrm{ar}(r_1) + \mathrm{ar}(r_2)\} \to \mathbf{att}$ function defined by $\mathrm{atr}_r(i) = \mathrm{atr}_{r_1}(i)$ for $1 \leq i \leq \mathrm{ar}(r_1)$ and $\mathrm{atr}_r(i) = \mathrm{atr}_{r_2}(i)$ for $1 + \mathrm{ar}(r_1) \leq i \leq \mathrm{ar}(r_1) + \mathrm{ar}(r_2)$.
   This Cartesian product is given by the following logical equivalence, by considering the relational symbols as predicates,

$$r(x_1,\dots,x_{\mathrm{ar}(r_1)},y_1,\dots,y_{\mathrm{ar}(r_2)}) \Leftrightarrow (r_1(x_1,\dots,x_{\mathrm{ar}(r_1)}) \wedge r_2(y_1,\dots,y_{\mathrm{ar}(r_2)})),$$
$$\text{so that } \|r\| = \|r_1(x_1,\dots,x_{\mathrm{ar}(r_1)}) \wedge r_2(y_1,\dots,y_{\mathrm{ar}(r_2)})\|$$

   (if $\|r_1\|$ is empty, then $r_1 \bigotimes r_2^\rho = r_2$; if $\|r_2\|$ is empty, then $r_1 \bigotimes r_2^\rho = r_1$).
3. Projection is a unary operation written as "_ $[S]$," where S is a tuple of column names such that for a relation r_1 and $S = \langle nr_{r_1}(i_1),\dots,nr_{r_1}(i_k)\rangle$, with $k \geq 1$ and $1 \leq i_m \leq \mathrm{ar}(r_1)$ for $1 \leq m \leq k$, and $i_m \neq i_j$ if $m \neq j$, we define the relation r by $r_1[S]$, with $\|r\| = \|r_1\|$ if $\exists\,\mathrm{name} \in S.\mathrm{name} \notin nr(r_1)$; otherwise $\|r\| = \pi_{\langle i_1,\dots,i_k\rangle}(\|r_1\|)$, where $nr_r(m) = nr_{r_1}(i_m)$, $\mathrm{atr}_r(m) = \mathrm{atr}_{r_1}(i_m)$, for $1 \leq m \leq k$.
   This projection is given by the following logical equivalence:

$$r(x_{i_1},\dots,x_{i_k}) \Leftrightarrow \exists x_{j_1}\dots x_{j_n} r_1(x_1,\dots,x_{\mathrm{ar}(r_1)}),$$

   where $n = \mathrm{ar}(r_1) - k$ and for all $1 \leq m \leq n$, $j_m \notin \{i_1,\dots,i_k\}$, so that

$$\|r\| = \|\exists x_{j_1}\dots x_{j_n} r_1(x_1,\dots,x_{\mathrm{ar}(r_1)})\|.$$

4. Selection is a unary operation written as "_ WHERE C," where a condition C is a finite-length logical formula that consists of atoms '$(\mathrm{name}_i\,\theta\,\mathrm{name}_j)$' or '$(\mathrm{name}_i\,\theta d)$', with built-in predicates $\theta \in \Sigma_\theta \supseteq \{\doteq, \rangle, \langle\}$, a constant d, and the

logical operators $\wedge$ (AND), $\vee$ (OR) and $\neg$ (NOT), such that for a relation r_1 and name_i, name_j the names of its columns, we define the relation r by

$$r_1 \text{ WHERE } C,$$

as the relation with $\mathrm{atr}(r) = \mathrm{atr}(r_1)$ and the function nr_r equal to nr_{r_1}, where $\|r\|$ is composed by the tuples in $\|r_1\|$ for which C is satisfied.
This selection is given by the following logical equivalence:

$$r(x_{i_1}, \ldots, x_{i_k}) \Leftrightarrow (r_1(x_1, \ldots, x_{\mathrm{ar}(r_1)}) \wedge C(\mathbf{x})),$$

where $C(\mathbf{x})$ is obtained by substitution of each $\mathrm{name}_i = nr_{r_1}(j)$ (of the j-th column of r_1) in the formula C by the variable x_j, so that

$$\|r\| = \left\|r_1(x_1, \ldots, x_{\mathrm{ar}(r_1)}) \wedge C(\mathbf{x})\right\|.$$

5. Union is a binary operation written as "_ UNION _," such that for two union-compatible relations r_1 and r_2, we define the relation r by: r_1 UNION r_2, where $\|r\| =_{\mathrm{def}} \|r_1\| \bigcup \|r_2\|$, with $\mathrm{atr}(r) = \mathrm{atr}(r_1)$, and the functions $\mathrm{atr}_r = \mathrm{atr}_{r_1}$, and $nr_r = nr_{r_1}$. This union is given by the following logical equivalence:

$$r(x_1, \ldots, x_n) \Leftrightarrow (r_1(x_1, \ldots, x_n) \vee r_2(x_1, \ldots, x_n)),$$

where $n = \mathrm{ar}(r) = \mathrm{ar}(r_1) = \mathrm{ar}(r_2)$, so that

$$\|r\| = \left\|r_1(x_1, \ldots, x_n) \vee r_2(x_1, \ldots, x_n)\right\|.$$

6. Set difference is a binary operation written as "_MINUS_" such that for two union-compatible relations r_1 and r_2, we define the relation r by: r_1 MINUS r_2, where $\|r\| =_{\mathrm{def}} \{\mathbf{t} \mid \mathbf{t} \in \|r_1\| \text{ such that } \mathbf{t} \notin \|r_2\|\}$, with $\mathrm{atr}(r) = \mathrm{atr}(r_1)$, and the functions $\mathrm{atr}_r = \mathrm{atr}_{r_1}$ and $nr_r = nr_{r_1}$.
Let r_1 and r_2 be the predicates (relational symbols) for these two relations. Then their difference is given by the following logical equivalence:

$$r(x_1, \ldots, x_n) \Leftrightarrow (r_1(x_1, \ldots, x_n) \wedge \neg r_2(x_1, \ldots, x_n)),$$

where $n = \mathrm{ar}(r) = \mathrm{ar}(r_1) = \mathrm{ar}(r_2)$, and hence

$$\|r\| = \|r_1(x_1, \ldots, x_n) \wedge \neg r_2(x_1, \ldots, x_n)\|.$$

Natural join $\bowtie_S$ is a binary operator, written as $(r_1 \bowtie_S r_2)$, where r_1 and r_2 are the relations. The result of the natural join is the set of all combinations of tuples in r_1 and r_2 that are equal on their common attribute names. In fact, $(r_1 \bowtie_S r_2)$ can be obtained by creating the Cartesian product $r_1 \bigotimes r_2$ and then by execution of the selection with the condition

C defined as a conjunction of atomic formulae $(nr_{r_1}(i) = nr_{r_2}(j))$ with $(nr_{r_1}(i), nr_{r_2}(j)) \in S$ (where i and j are the columns of the same attribute in r_1 and r_2, respectively, i. e., satisfying $\text{atr}_{r_1}(i) = \text{atr}_{r_2}(j)$) that represents the equality of the common attribute names of r_1 and r_2. The natural join is arguably one of the most important operators since it is the relational counterpart of logical AND. Note carefully that if the same variable appears in each of two predicates that are linked by AND, then that variable stands for the same thing and both appearances must always be substituted by the same value. In particular, natural join allows the combination of relations that are associated by a foreign key. It can also be used to define composition of binary relations.

Altogether the operators of relational algebra have identical expressive power to that of the domain relational calculus or tuple relational calculus. However, relational algebra is less expressive than first-order predicate calculus without function symbols. Relational algebra corresponds to *a subset* of FOL (denominated *relational calculus*), namely Horn clauses without recursion and negation (or union of conjunctive queries). Consequently, relational algebra is essentially equivalent in expressive power to *relational calculus* (and thus FOL and queries defined in Section 4.2); this result is known as Codd's theorem. However, the negation, applied to a formula of the calculus, constructs a formula that may be true on an infinite set of possible tuples. To overcome this difficulty, Codd restricted the operands of relational algebra to finite relations only and also proposed restricted support for negation $\neg$ (NOT) and disjunction $\vee$ (OR). Codd defined the term "relational completeness" to refer to a language that is complete with respect to first-order predicate calculus apart from the restrictions he proposed. In practice, the restrictions have no adverse effect on the applicability of his relational algebra for database purposes.

Several papers have proposed new operators of an algebraic nature as candidates for an addition to the original set. We choose the additional unary operator "EXTEND_ADD a, name AS e" denoted shortly as $\_\langle a, \text{name}, e\rangle$, where a is a new added attribute as the new column (at the end of relation) with a new fresh name name and e is an expression (in the most simple cases it can be the value NULL or a constant d, or the i-th column name $nr(i)$ of the argument (i. e., relation) of this operation), for *update* relational algebra operators, in order to cover all of the basic features of data manipulation (DML) aspects of a relation models of data, so that

- We define a unary operator $\_\langle a, \text{name}, e\rangle$, for an attribute $a \in \mathbf{att}$, its name, and expression e, as a function with a set of column names, such that for a relation r_1 and expression e composed of the names of the columns of r_1 with $n = \text{ar}(r_1)$, we obtain the $(\text{ar}(r_1) + 1)$-ary relation r by $\langle a, \text{name}, e\rangle(r_1)$, with naming function $nr_r : \{\text{ar}(r_1) + 1\} \to \text{SN}$ such that $nr_r(i) = nr_{r_1}(i)$ if $i \leq \text{ar}(r_1)$; $nr_r(\text{ar}(r_1) + 1) = \text{name}$ otherwise, being a fresh new name for this column; with the attribute function $\text{atr}_r : \{\text{ar}(r_1) + 1\} \to \mathbf{att}$ such that $\text{atr}_r(i) = \text{atr}_{r_1}(i)$ if $i \leq \text{ar}(r_1)$; $\text{atr}_r(\text{ar}(r_1) + 1) = a$ otherwise, and

$$\|r\| = \{\langle\,\rangle\}\bigcup\{\mathbf{d}\&e(\mathbf{d}) \mid \mathbf{d} \in \|r_1\|\},$$

where $e(\mathbf{d}) \in \mathrm{dom}(a)$ is a constant or the value obtained from the function e where each name $nr_r(i)$ is substituted by the value d_i of the tuple $\mathbf{d} = (d_1, \ldots, d_n) \in \|r_1\|$; in the special cases, we can use nullary functions (constants) for the expression e (e. g., for the NULL value).
(note that r is empty if e is an expression and r_1 empty as well).
Then, for a nonempty relation r_1, the EXTEND r_1 ADD a, name AS e (i. e., $r_1\langle a$, name, $e\rangle$) can be represented by the following logical equivalence:

$$r(x_1, \ldots, x_{n+1}) \Leftrightarrow (r_1(x_1, \ldots, x_n) \wedge (x_{n+1} = e(\mathbf{x})))$$

where $e(\mathbf{x})$ is obtained by substituting each name$_i$ $= nr_{r_1}(j)$ (of the j-th column of r_1) in the expression e by the variable x_j.

We are able to define a new relation with a single tuple $(d_1, \ldots, d_k), k \geq 1$ with the given list of attributes $(a_1, \ldots, a_k)$, by the following finite length expression:

$$\text{EXTEND}(\ldots(\text{EXTEND } r_\emptyset \text{ ADD } a_1, \text{name}_1 \text{ AS } d_1)\ldots) \text{ ADD } a_k, \text{name}_k \text{ AS } d_k,$$

or equivalently by

$$r_\emptyset(a_1, \text{name}_1, d_1) \bigotimes \cdots \bigotimes r_\emptyset(a_k, \text{name}_k, d_k),$$

where $r_\emptyset$ is the empty type relation with $\|r_\emptyset\| = \{\langle\,\rangle\} = \mathcal{D}^0$, $\mathrm{ar}(r_\emptyset) = 0$ introduced after Definition 6 in Section 1.2, and empty functions $\mathrm{atr}_{r_\emptyset}$ and $nr_{r_\emptyset}$. Such single tuple relations can be used for an insertion in a given relation (with the same list of attributes) in what follows.

Update operators

The three update operators, “UPDATE,” “DELETE” and “INSERT” of the relational algebra, are derived operators from these previously defined operators in the following way:

1. Each algebraic formulae “DELETE FROM r WHERE C” is equivalent to the formula “r MINUS (r WHERE C).”
2. Each algebraic expression (a term) “INSERT INTO $r[S]$ VALUES (list of values),” “INSERT INTO $r[S]$ AS SELECT...,” is equivalent to “r UNION r_1” where the union compatible relation r_1 is a one-tuple relation (defined by list) in the first, or a relation defined by “SELECT...” in the second case.
   In the case of a single tuple insertion (version with “VALUES”) into a given relation r, we can define a single tuple relation r_1 by using “EXTEND...” operations.
3. Each algebraic expression “UPDATE r SET $[nr_r(i_1) = e_{i_1}, \ldots, nr_r(i_k) = e_{i_k}]$ WHERE C,” for $n = \mathrm{ar}(r)$, where $e_{i_m}, 1 \leq i_m \leq n$ for $1 \leq m \leq k$ are the expres-

sions and C is a condition, is equal to the formula "(r WHERE $\neg C$) UNION r_1," where r_1 is a relation expressed by

$$\begin{aligned}&(\text{EXTEND}(\ldots(\text{EXTEND } (r \text{ WHERE } C) \text{ ADD } \text{att}_r(1), \text{name}_1 \text{ AS } e_1)\ldots)\\&\quad \text{ADD } \text{att}_r(n), \text{name}_n \text{ AS } e_n)[S],\end{aligned}$$

such that for each $1 \leq m \leq n$, if $m \notin \{i_1, \ldots, i_k\}$ then $e_m = nr_r(m)$, and $S = \langle \text{name}_1, \ldots, \text{name}_n \rangle$.

Consequently, all update operators of the relational algebra can be obtained by addition of these "EXTEND_ADD a, name AS e" operations.

Let us define the Σ_R-algebras sa follows ([21], Definition 31 in Section 5.1).

Definition 46. We denote the algebra of the set of operations, introduced previously in this section (points from 1 to 6 and "EXTEND_ADD a, name AS e") with additional nullary operator (empty-relation constant) $\perp$, by Σ_{RE}. Its subalgebra without "_MINUS_" operator is denoted by Σ_R^+, and without $\perp$ and unary operators 'EXTEND_ADD a, name AS e' is denoted by Σ_R (it is the "select-project-join-rename+union" (SPJRU) subalgebra).

We define the set of terms $\mathcal{T}_P X$ with variables in X of this Σ_R-algebra (and analogously for the terms $\mathcal{T}_P^+ X$ of Σ_R^+-algebra), inductively as follows:

1. Each relational symbol (a variable) $r \in X \subseteq \mathbb{R}$ and a constant (i. e., a nullary operation) is a term in $\mathcal{T}_P X$;
2. Given any term $t_R \in \mathcal{T}_P X$ and an unary operation $o_i \in \Sigma_R$, $o_i(t_R) \in \mathcal{T}_P X$;
3. Given any two terms $t_R, t_R' \in \mathcal{T}_P X$ and a binary operation $o_i \in \Sigma_R$, $o_i(t_R, t_R') \in \mathcal{T}_P X$.

We define the evaluation of terms in $\mathcal{T}_P X$, for $X = \mathbb{R}$, by extending the assignment $\|\_\| : \mathbb{R} \to \underline{\Upsilon}$, which assigns a relation to each relational symbol (a variable) to all terms by the function $\|\_\|_\# : \mathcal{T}_P\mathbb{R} \to \underline{\Upsilon}$ (with $\|r\|_\# = \|r\|$), where $\underline{\Upsilon}$ is the universal database instance (set of all relations for a given universe $\mathcal{D}$). For a given term t_R with relational symbols $r_1, \ldots, r_k \in \mathbb{R}$, $\|t_R\|_\#$ is the relational table obtained from this expression for the given set of relations $\|r_1\|, \ldots, \|r_k\| \in \underline{\Upsilon}$, with the constraint that

$$\begin{aligned}&\|t_R \text{ UNION } t_R'\|_\# = \|t_R\|_\# \bigcup \|t_R'\|_\#\\&\quad \text{if the relations } \|t_R\|_\# \text{ and } \|t_R'\|_\# \text{ are union compatible;}\\&\quad \perp = \{\langle\,\rangle\} = \|r_\emptyset\| \quad \text{(empty relation) otherwise.}\end{aligned}$$

We say that two terms $t_R, t_R' \in \mathcal{T}_P X$ are equivalent (or equal), denoted by $t_R \approx t_R'$, if for all assignments $\|t_R\|_\# = \|t_R'\|_\#$.

We say that an extension $\|t_R\|_\#$, of a term $t_R \in \mathcal{T}_P X$, is a *vector relation* of the *vector view* denoted by $\overrightarrow{t_R}$ if the type of $\|t_R\|_\#$ is equal to the type of the vector relation r_V.

Let $R = \|\overrightarrow{t_R}\|_\#$ be the relational table with the following four attributes (as in r_V) `r-name`, `t-index`, `a-name` and `value`, then its user-defined view representation can be derived as follows

Definition 47 (View materialization). Let $t_R \in \mathcal{T}_P X$ be a user-defined SPJU (Select-Project-Join-Union) view over a database schema $\mathcal{A} = (S_A, \Sigma_A)$ with the type (the tuple of the view columns) $\mathfrak{S} = \langle (r_{k_1}, \mathrm{name}_{k_1}), \dots, (r_{k_m}, \mathrm{name}_{k_m}) \rangle$, where the i-th column $(r_{k_i}, \mathrm{name}_{k_i})$ is the column with name equal to name_{k_i} of the relation $r_{k_i} \in S_A$, $1 \leq i \leq m$, and $\overrightarrow{t_R}$ be the rewritten query over vector relation r_V.

Let $R = \|\overrightarrow{t_R}\|_\#$ be the resulting relational table with the four attributes (as that of r_V) `r-name`, `t-index`, `a-name` and `value`. We define the operation $\underline{\mathrm{VIEW}}$ of the transformation of R into the user defined view representation by:

$$\underline{\mathrm{VIEW}}(\mathfrak{S}, R) = \{(d_1, \dots, d_m) \mid \exists\, \mathrm{ID} \in \pi_2(R), \forall_{1 \leq i \leq m}(nr(r_{k_i}), \mathrm{ID}, \mathrm{name}_{k_i}, d_i) \in R;$$
$$\text{otherwise set } d_i \text{ to NULL}\}.$$

Notice that we have, from (4.6), for each $r_k \in S_A$ with $R = \bigcup_{\mathbf{d} \in \|r_k\|} \underline{\mathrm{PARSE}}(r_k, \mathbf{d})$, and $\mathfrak{S} = \langle (r_k, nr_{r_k}(1)), \dots, (r_k, nr_{r_k}(\mathrm{ar}(r_k))) \rangle$,

$$\|r_k\| = \underline{\mathrm{MATTER}}\,(r_k, R) = \underline{\mathrm{VIEW}}\,(\mathfrak{S}, R) \tag{4.7}$$

and hence the non-SQL operation $\underline{\mathrm{MATTER}}$ is a special case of the operation $\underline{\mathrm{VIEW}}$.

For any original user-defined query (term) t_R over a user-defined database schema $\mathcal{A}$, by $\overrightarrow{t_R}$ we denote the equivalent (rewritten) query over the vector relation r_V. We have the following important result for the IRDBs.

Proposition 23 (SQL completeness of IRDB). *There exists a finite algorithm for the term rewriting of any user-defined SQL term t_R over a schema $\mathcal{A}$, of the full relational algebra Σ_{RE} in Definition 46, into an equivalent vector query $\overrightarrow{t_R}$ over the vector relation r_V.*

If t_R is a user-defined SPJU term (in Definition 47) of the type $\mathfrak{S}$, then

$$\|t_R\|_\# = \underline{\mathrm{VIEW}}(\mathfrak{S}, \|\overrightarrow{t_R}\|_\#).$$

Proof. In this proof, we will use the convention that two NULL values cannot be compared as equal, because their meaning is that the value is missing, and two missing values not necessarily are equal. In fact, in r_V we do not store the null values but consider them as unknown missing values. Thus, when there are null values in the columns of the user-defined tables being joined, the null values do not match each other. For simplicity, we will use for relations symbols and their names the same symbol in what follows.

Let us show that there is such a query (relation algebra term) rewriting for each basic relational operator previously described, recursively (in what follows, if $t_R = r$ then $\overrightarrow{t_R} = r_V$ WHERE `r-name` $= r$):

1. (Rename). $t'_R = r$ RENAME name$_1$ AS name$_2$ where the result is identical to input argument (relation) r except that the column i with name $nr_r(i)$ = name$_1$ in all tuples is renamed to $nr_r(i)$ = name$_2$. The rewritten vector query is

$$\overrightarrow{t'_R} = \text{UPDATE } r_V \text{ SET } [\texttt{a-name} = \text{name}_2] \text{ WHERE } (\texttt{r-name} = r) \wedge (\texttt{a-name} = \text{name}_1);$$

2. (Projection). $t'_R = t_R[S]$, where $S = \langle (r_{j_1}, nr_{r_{j_1}}(i_1)), \ldots, (r_{j_k}, nr_{r_{j_k}}(i_k))\rangle \subseteq \mathfrak{S}$, with $k \geq 1$ and $1 \leq i_m \leq \text{ar}(r_{j_m})$ for $1 \leq m \leq k$, is a subset of the type $\mathfrak{S}$ of the term t_R. We define the rewritten vector query

$$\begin{aligned}\overrightarrow{t'_R} = \overrightarrow{t_R[S]} = \overrightarrow{t_R} \text{ WHERE } &((nr_{\overrightarrow{t_R}}(1) = r_{j_1}) \wedge (nr_{\overrightarrow{t_R}}(2) = nr_{r_{j_1}}(i_1))) \vee \cdots \\ &\vee ((nr_{\overrightarrow{t_R}}(1) = r_{j_k}) \wedge (nr_{\overrightarrow{t_R}}(2) = nr_{r_{j_k}}(i_k)));\end{aligned}$$

3. (Join). $t'_R = t_{R,1} \bowtie_S t_{R,2}$, where $S = (((r_{l_1}, nr_{r_{l_1}}(i_1)), (r_{n_1}, nr_{r_{n_1}}(j_1))), \ldots, (((r_{l_m}, nr_{r_{l_m}}(i_m)), (r_{n_m}, nr_{r_{n_m}}(j_m)))))$ with $1 \leq i_k \leq |\mathfrak{S}_1|$ and $1 \leq j_k \leq |\mathfrak{S}_2|$ for $1 \leq k \leq m$, where $\mathfrak{S}_1$ and $\mathfrak{S}_2$ are the types of $t_{R,1}$ and $t_{R,2}$, respectively.

Let us define the following relational algebra terms: $r = \overbrace{\overrightarrow{t_{R,1}} \bigotimes \cdots \bigotimes \overrightarrow{t_{R,1}}}^{m} \otimes \overbrace{\overrightarrow{t_{R,2}} \bigotimes \cdots \bigotimes \overrightarrow{t_{R,2}}}^{m}$; (the first m are for the attributes of $\overrightarrow{t_{R,1}}$ in S, and the last m are for the corresponded joined attributes of $\overrightarrow{t_{R,2}}$ in S). Note that each column name of $\overrightarrow{t_{R,1}}$ will be renamed m times in order to have for each column different name in standard way as for attributes: for example, the column a-name in $\overrightarrow{t_{R,1}}$ will be repeated by a-name$(1), \ldots,$ a-name(m) (and similarly for each column name of $\overrightarrow{t_{R,2}}$), and the attribute $\text{at}_r(2)$ (of the column t-index in r_V) will be repeated by its copies $\text{at}_r(2)(1), \ldots, \text{at}_r(2)(2m)$ (in what follows will be also generated the $(2m+1)$-th copy $\text{at}_r(2)(2m+1)$ in the algebra term t_2). Thus,

$$\begin{aligned}t_1 = r \text{ WHERE } \Bigg(\bigwedge_{1 \leq k \leq m} &((nr_r(4k-3) = r_{l_k}) \wedge (nr_r(4k-1) = nr_{r_{l_k}}(i_k)) \\ &\wedge (nr_r(4(m+k)-3) = r_{n_k}) \wedge (nr_r(4(m+k)-1) = nr_{r_{n_k}}(j_k)) \\ &\wedge (nr_r(4k) = nr_r(4(m+k)+4))) \\ &\wedge ((m = 1) \vee ((nr_r(2) = nr_r(6) = \ldots = nr_r(4m-2)) \\ &\wedge (nr_r(4m+2) = nr_r(4m+6) = \ldots = nr_r(8m-2)))) \Bigg); \\ t_2 = (\text{EXTEND } t_1 \text{ ADD } &((\text{atr}_r(2))(2m+1), \text{name}_3, \text{Hash}(\text{atr}_r(1), \text{atr}_r(2), \ldots, \\ &\text{atr}_r(8m))))[nr_{t_1}(2), nr_{t_1}(4m+2), \text{name}_3];\end{aligned}$$

where name$_3$ is a fresh new name and

$$\|t_2\|_\# = \{\langle \mathrm{ID}_1, \mathrm{ID}_2, \mathrm{ID}_3\rangle \mid \mathrm{ID}_1$$

is the tuple index in $\|t_{R,1}\|_\#$ and ID_2 is the corresponding joined tuple index in $\|t_{R,2}\|_\#$, while ID_3 is the fresh new generated (by Hash function) tuple index for the tuple obtained by join operation$\}$, then for the Cartesian products $t_3 = \overrightarrow{t_{R,1}} \bigotimes t_2$ and $t_4 = \overrightarrow{t_{R,2}} \bigotimes t_2$,

$$\begin{aligned}\overrightarrow{t'_R} &= \overrightarrow{t_{R,1} \bowtie_S t_{R,2}} \\ &= ((t_3 \text{ WHERE } (nr_{t_3}(2) = nr_{t_3}(5)))[nr_{t_3}(1), \mathrm{name}_3, nr_{t_3}(3), nr_{t_3}(4)]) \\ &\quad \text{UNION } ((t_4 \text{ WHERE } (nr_{t_4}(2) = nr_{t_4}(6)))[nr_{t_4}(1), \mathrm{name}_3, nr_{t_4}(3), nr_{t_4}(4)]);\end{aligned}$$

4. (Selection). $t'_R = t_R$ WHERE C:

   4.1 When a condition C is a finite-length logical formula that consists of atoms '$((r_{i_1}, \mathrm{name}_i)\theta(r_{j_1}, \mathrm{name}_j))$' or '$(r_{i_1}, \mathrm{name}_i)\theta d$' or '$(r_{i_1}, \mathrm{name}_i)$' NOT NULL with built-in predicates $\theta \in \Sigma_\theta \supseteq \{\doteq, >, <\}$, a constant d, and the logical operators, between the columns in the type $\mathfrak{S}$ of the term t_R.
   The condition C, composed by $k \geq 1$ different columns in $\mathfrak{S}$, we denote by $C((r_{i_1}, \mathrm{name}_{i_1}), \dots, (r_{i_k}, \mathrm{name}_{i_k}))$, $k \geq 1$, and hence we define the rewritten vector query

   $$\overrightarrow{t'_R} = \overrightarrow{t_R \text{ WHERE } C} = \overrightarrow{t_R} \text{ WHERE } nr_{\overrightarrow{t_R}}(2) \text{ IN } t_1$$

   where for $r = \overbrace{\overrightarrow{t_R} \bigotimes \cdots \bigotimes \overrightarrow{t_R}}^{k}$ we define the unary relation, which contains the tuple indexes of the relation $\|t_R\|$ for its tuples, which satisfy the selection condition C, by the following selection term:

   $$\begin{aligned}t_1 = (r \text{ WHERE } &((nr_r(1) = r_{i_1} \wedge nr_r(3) = \mathrm{name}_{i_1}) \wedge \dots \wedge (nr_r(1 + 4(k-1)) \\ &= r_{i_k} \wedge nr_r(3 + 4(k-1)) = \mathrm{name}_{i_1})) \wedge C(nr_r(4), \dots, nr_r(4k)) \\ &\wedge ((k = 1) \vee (nr_r(2) = nr_r(6) = \dots = nr_r(2 + 4(k-1)))))[nr_r(2)];\end{aligned}$$

   4.2 Case when $C = (r_{i_1}, \mathrm{name}_i)$ NULL,

   $$\overrightarrow{t'_R} = \overrightarrow{t_R \text{ WHERE } (r_{i_1}, \mathrm{name}_i) \text{ NULL}} = \overrightarrow{t_R} \text{ WHERE } nr_{\overrightarrow{t_R}}(2) \text{ NOT IN } t_2,$$

   where $t_2 = (\overrightarrow{t_R} \text{ WHERE } ((nr_{\overrightarrow{t_R}}(1) = r_{i_1}) \wedge (nr_{\overrightarrow{t_R}}(3) = \mathrm{name}_i))[(nr_{\overrightarrow{t_R}}(2)]$.
   From the fact that t_R WHERE $C_1 \wedge C_2 = (t_R$ WHERE $C_1)$ WHERE C_2 and t_R WHERE $C_1 \vee C_2 = (t_R$ WHERE $C_1)$ UNION $(t_R$ WHERE $C_2)$, and De Morgan laws, $\neg(C_1 \wedge C_2) = \neg C_1 \vee \neg C_2$, $\neg(C_1 \vee C_2) = \neg C_1 \wedge \neg C_2$, we can always divide any selection in the components of the two disjoint cases above;

5. (Union). $t'_R = t_{R,1}\ \text{UNION}_R t_{R,2}$, where R is a table $\{\langle r_{l_k}, \text{name}_{l_k}, r_{n_k}, \text{name}_{n_k}\rangle \mid 1 \le k \le m\}$ such that $\mathfrak{S}_1 = \langle (r_{l_1}, \text{name}_{l_1}), \dots, (r_{l_m}, \text{name}_{l_m})\rangle$ and $\mathfrak{S}_2 = \langle (r_{n_1}, \text{name}_{n_1}), \dots, (r_{n_m}, \text{name}_{n_m})\rangle$ are the types of $t_{R,1}$ and $t_{R,1}$, respectively, with the union-compatible columns $(\langle r_{l_k}, \text{name}_{l_k})$ and $(\langle r_{n_k}, \text{name}_{n_k})$ for every $1 \le k \le m$. We define the relational algebra term $t_1 = \overrightarrow{t_{R,2}} \bigotimes R$, so that

$$\begin{aligned}\overrightarrow{t'_R} &= \overrightarrow{t_{R,1}\ \text{UNION}_R\ t_{R,2}}\\ &= \overrightarrow{t_{R,1}}\ \text{UNION}\ ((t_1\ \text{WHERE}\ ((nr_{t_1}(1) = nr_{t_1}(7))\\ &\quad \wedge (nr_{t_1}(3) = nr_{t_1}(8))))[nr_{t_1}(5), nr_{t_1}(2), nr_{t_1}(6), nr_{t_1}(4)]),\end{aligned}$$

so that the relation-column names of the union will be equal to the column names of the first term in this union;

6. (Set difference). $t'_R = t_{R,1}\ \text{MINUS}_R t_{R,2}$, where R is a table $\{\langle r_{l_k}, nr_{r_{l_k}}(i_k), r_{n_k}, nr_{r_{n_k}}(j_k)\rangle \mid 1 \le k \le m\}$ such that $\mathfrak{S}_1 = \langle (r_{l_1}, nr_{r_{l_1}}(i_1)), \dots, (r_{l_m}, nr_{r_{l_m}}(i_m))\rangle$ and $\mathfrak{S}_2 = \langle (r_{n_1}, nr_{r_{n_1}}(j_1)), \dots, (r_{n_m}, nr_{r_{n_m}}(j_m))\rangle$ are the types of $t_{R,1}$ and $t_{R,1}$, respectively, with the union-compatible columns $(\langle r_{l_k}, nr_{r_{l_k}}(i_k))$ and $(\langle r_{n_k}, nr_{r_{n_k}}(j_k))$ for every $1 \le k \le m$. Let us define the following relational algebra terms:

$$r = \overbrace{\overrightarrow{t_{R,1}} \bigotimes \cdots \bigotimes \overrightarrow{t_{R,1}}}^{m} \bigotimes \overbrace{\overrightarrow{t_{R,2}} \bigotimes \cdots \bigotimes \overrightarrow{t_{R,2}}}^{m};$$

(the first m are for the attributes of $\overrightarrow{t_{R,1}}$ in $\mathfrak{S}_1$, and the last m are for the corresponded joined attributes of $\overrightarrow{t_{R,2}}$ in $\mathfrak{S}_2$). Thus,

$$\begin{aligned}t_1 = \Bigg(r\ \text{WHERE}\ \Bigg(&\bigwedge_{1\le k\le m}((nr_r(4k-3) = r_{l_k}) \wedge (nr_r(4k-1)\\ &= nr_{r_{l_k}}(i_k)) \wedge (nr_r(4(m+k)-3) = r_{n_k}) \wedge (nr_r(4(m+k)-1)\\ &= nr_{r_{n_k}}(j_k)) \wedge (nr_r(4k) = nr_r(4(m+k)+4)))\\ &\wedge ((m=1) \vee ((nr_r(2) = nr_r(6) = \dots = nr_r(4m-2))\\ &\wedge (nr_r(4m+2) = nr_r(4m+6) = \dots = nr_r(8m-2))))\Bigg)\Bigg)[nr_{t_1}(2)];\end{aligned}$$

where $\|t_1\|_\# = \{\langle \text{ID}_1\rangle \mid \text{ID}_1$ is the tuple index of a tuple in $\|t_{R,1}\|_\#$ for which there exists an equal tuple in $\|t_{R,2}\|_\#\}$. Then

$$\overrightarrow{t'_R} = \overrightarrow{t_{R,1}\ \text{MINUS}_R t_{R,2}} = \overrightarrow{t_{R,1}}\ \text{WHERE}\ nr_{\overrightarrow{t_{R,1}}}(2)\ \text{NOT IN}\ t_1.$$

It is easy to show that for the cases from 2 to 6, we obtain that $\|t'_R\|_\# = \underline{\text{VIEW}}(\mathfrak{S}, \|\overrightarrow{t'_R}\|_\#)$, where $\mathfrak{S}$ is the type of the relational algebra term t'_R. Thus, for any SPJU term t_R obtained by the composition of these basic relational algebra operators we have that $\|t_R\|_\# = \underline{\text{VIEW}}(\mathfrak{S}, \|\overrightarrow{t_R}\|_\#)$.

The update operators are rewritten as follows:

1. (Insert). INSERT INTO $r[S]$ VALUES $(d_1, \dots, d_m)$, where $S = \langle nr_r(i_1), \dots, nr_r(i_m)\rangle$, $1 \leq m \leq \text{ar}(r)$, is the subset of mutually different attribute names of r and all d_i, $1 \leq i \leq m$ are the values different from NULL. It is rewritten into the following set of terms:

$$\{\text{INSERT INTO } r_V[\texttt{r-name}, \texttt{t-index}, \texttt{a-name}, \texttt{value}]$$
$$\text{VALUES } (r, \text{Hash}(d_1, \dots, d_m), nr_r(i_k), d_k) \mid 1 \leq k \leq m\}.$$

   Note that before the execution of this set of insertion operations in r_V, the DBMS has to control if it satisfies all user-defined integrity constraints in the user-defined database schema $\mathcal{A}$;
2. (Delete). DELETE FROM r WHERE C, is rewritten into the term:

$$\text{DELETE FROM } r_V \text{ WHERE } \texttt{t-index} \text{ IN } \overrightarrow{t_R}[nr_{\overrightarrow{t_R}}(2)],$$

   where $\overrightarrow{t_R} = \overrightarrow{r \text{ WHERE } C}$ is the selection term as described in point 4 above;
3. (Update). The existence of the rewriting of this operation is obvious from the fact that it can always be decomposed as deletion and after that the insertion of the tuples. □

This proposition demonstrates that the IRDB is a SQL database, so that each user-defined query over the used-defined RDB database schema $\mathcal{A}$ can be equivalently transformed by query rewriting into a query over the vector relation r_V. However, in the IRDBMSs we can use more powerful and efficient algorithms in order to execute each original user-defined query over the vector relation r_V.

Notice that this proposition demonstrates that the IRDB is a kind of GAV Data Integration System $\mathcal{I} = (\mathcal{A}, \mathcal{S}, \mathcal{M})$ in Definition 44 where we do not materialize the user-defined schema $\mathcal{A}$ but only the vector relation $r_V \in \mathcal{S}$ and each original query $q(\mathbf{x})$ over the empty schema $\mathcal{A}$ will be rewritten into a vector query $\overrightarrow{q(\mathbf{x})}$ of the type $\mathfrak{S}$ over the vector relation r_V, and then the resulting view $\underline{\text{VIEW}}(\mathfrak{S}, \|\overrightarrow{q(\mathbf{x})}\|_\#)$ will be returned to user's software program.

For aggregate functions, SUM, MIN, MAX, COUNT and AVG, which are not affected by null values in the column being aggregated, their definition over r_V is combined by a selection which specifies the relation-name and attribute-name for the column being aggregated. Thus, an IRDB is a member of the NewSQL, i. e., a member of a class of modern relational database management systems that seek to provide the same scalable performance of NoSQL systems for online transaction processing (read-write) workloads while still maintaining the ACID guarantees of a traditional database system.

4.2.3 Comparison with related work

The idea of having relational names as arguments goes back to [165] where the authors describe an algebraic operator called SPECIFY that converts a single relation name into its relation, but it is too far from our work by considering the Codd's normal forms with their concept of "aggregation" and their concept of "generalization" (as in Quillian's semantic networks) and trying to mix both the database and AI areas.

The version of the relational model in which relation names may appear as arguments of other relations is also provided in [166]. In such approach, an extension of the relational calculus using HiLog as logical framework rather than FOL has been proposed, and they call this extension "relational HiLog." But this is an ad hoc second-order logic where the variables may appear in predicate names, and where there is ambiguity in programming semantics because there is no distinction between the variables, function, constant and predicate symbols. Thus, it seams syntactically to be a FOL but it has the particular semantics of the second-order logic. In our approach, we remain in the FOL syntax with only new terms for the intensional elements (n-ary concepts) and with only simple intensional extension of the standard Tarski's semantics for the FOL. The extension of the relational algebra in [166] is very different from our standard SQL algebra framework: instead of this standard relational SQL algebra, in [166] are provided two relational algebra extensions:

1. "E-relational algebra," which extends standard relational algebra with a set of expansion operators (these operators expand a set of relation names into the union of their relations, with the relational name as an extra argument, and hence not to a key/value representations in big data used in our vector relation r_V);
2. The second is "T-relational algebra," which extends e-relational algebra by a set of "totality" operators (to allow the access to the names of all nonempty relations in the relational database). Thus, from the algebraical, structural and logical framework this approach is very different from our GAV Data integration model and a minimal conservative intensional extension of the Tarski's FOL semantics.

Another approach in which relation and attribute names may appear as arguments of other relations are provided in the area of integration of heterogeneous databases. In [167], a simple Prolog interpreter for a subset of F-logic was presented, but the negation in Prolog is not standard as in FOL, and such an approach is far from SQL models of data and querying of RDB databases. Also in [168] is demonstrated the power of using variables that uniformly range over data and metadata, for schema browsing and interoperability, but their languages have a syntax closer to that of logic programming languages, and far from that of SQL. The more powerful framework (where the variables can range over the following five sets:

(i) names of databases in a federation;
(ii) names of the relations in a database;
(iii) names of the attributes in the scheme of a relations;

(iv) tuples in a given relation in a database;
(v) values appearing in a column corresponding to a given attribute in a relation) is presented in SchemaSQL [169] where the SQL is extended in order to be able to query metadata.

In our case, this is not necessary because we preserve the original RDB SQL in order to be able to migrate from the RDB models into IRDB models with the big data vector relation without unnecessarily complications. In fact, the extended relational algebra in SchemaSQL would be a nondesirable complication in order to obtain the flexible schema and big data RDB features. What is interesting work in this direction is to investigate the conservative intensional extension of Tarski's FOL semantics used in our approach also to the algebraic framework used in SchemaSQL.

One of the similar approaches to the flexible and sparsely populated schemas is that of "Open Schema" EAV models, mentioned previously in Section 4.2. Such requirements for the e-commerce applications have been presented in [170]. Such a specific e-commerce software has been adopted in the IBM Websphere Commerce Server running on top of the DB2. But it needs ad hoc structures of the standard horizontal table representations, where each such table must have a special key attribute for the object identity. Thus, it cannot be applied to transform any RDB schema into vertical table representation of the EAV type, composed by the three attributes: *Oid* (object identifier), *Key* (attribute name) and *Val* (attribute value). They noted that the values of the *Key* field in the vertical format become column names in the current database systems (the metadata) and that such "*higher-order views are not supported in the current database systems*" [170]. But they do not provide the logical framework for such a new RDB model. They do not use the relation names as arguments of other relations so their logical framework remains to be standard FOL.

Different from our approach, their approach loses data typing since all values are stored as VARCHARs in the *Val* column (in our approach we store all values as VARCHARs, however, we know its data type, which is saved in the users ER database schema $\mathcal{A}$, which is a necessary user-software interface in our data integration system).

Their method is similar to that of the ShemaSQL, i. e., nonintrusive implementations without requiring changes of the database engine code and they extend the relational algebra with two operations, v2h and h2V, that can be viewed as the specializations of *unfold* and *fold* in [169], respectively. They are analog to the operations $\underline{\text{MATTER}}(r_k, \_)$ and $\bigcup_{\mathbf{v}\in\|\_\|} \underline{\text{PARSE}}(\_, \mathbf{v})$, respectively. However, the difference is not only in their syntactical and semantical compositions, but also in the fact that in their framework v2h and h2V are new DDL instructions, which extend the standard SQL RDB framework, while in our approach these operations are only internal functionalities of IRDB and not a kind of DDL instructions, which can be used by programmers. Thus, in our more general framework we intentionally *do not change the SQL language* (in order to migrate easily from RDBs to IRDBs, without any modification or addition of new SQL instructions).

Their approach is not suitable for a general parsing of any horizontal database representation into vertical representations. It is more restrictive and each horizontal table representation must have a *Oid* column (it has to be the primary key of such a table), which has to be also repeated in the vertical table representation as a part of the primary key of this table.

Finally, we mention the work presented in [171], which introduces the PIVOT and UNPIVOT operators on tabular data that exchange rows and columns, enabling data transformations useful in data modeling and data presentation (e. g., Microsoft Excel supports pivoting). These two operators can be used for the composition of our PARSE and MATTER operators for a given user-defined table with a relational name r_k and number of columns $n = \mathrm{ar}(r_k) \geq 1$, as follows (we are using the syntax introduced in [171] (un)pivoting operators):

- *Parsing a relation* r_k. Let us define the following SQL terms:

$$t_1 = \text{EXTEND } r_k \text{ ADD } \mathrm{atr}_{r_V}(2),\ \texttt{t-name} \text{ AS Hash}(S)$$

where $\mathrm{atr}_{r_V}(2)$ is the attribute for the column `t-name` in r_V and $S = (nr_{r_k}(1), \ldots, nr_{r_k}(n))$ is a list of column names (the variables) to be used by the Hash function for each tuple $\mathbf{v} \in \|r_k\|$;

$$t_2 = t_1\ \textbf{UNPIVOT}\ \texttt{value} \text{ FOR } \texttt{a-name} \text{ IN } S;$$

$$t_3 = (\text{EXTEND } t_2 \text{ ADD } \mathrm{atr}_{r_V}(1), \texttt{r-name} \text{ AS } r_k)[\texttt{r-name}, \texttt{t-name}, \texttt{a-name}, \texttt{value}]$$

where $\mathrm{atr}_{r_V}(1)$ is the attribute for the column `r-name` in r_V. Then the operation of parsing of the relation r_k into the vector table r_V, $\bigcup_{\mathbf{v}\in\|r_k\|} \underline{\text{PARSE}}\,(r_k, \mathbf{v})$, is equal to the relational algebra extended by the UNPIVOT operation,

$$\text{INSERT INTO } r_V \text{ AS SELECT * FROM } t_3.$$

- *Materialization of a relation* r_k. The operation of materialization of the relation $\|r_k\|$, given in Definition 45 by $\underline{\text{MATTER}}\,(r_k, \|r_V\|)$, can be expressed by the following relational algebra (extended with the PIVOT operation) term:

$$(((r_V \text{ WHERE } \texttt{r-name} = r_k)[\texttt{t-name}, \texttt{a-name}, \texttt{value}])$$
$$\textbf{PIVOT}\ (\texttt{value} \text{ FOR } \texttt{a-name} \text{ IN } S))[S].$$

- *Presentation of views*. The operation of presentation of an user-defined view (SQL term) t_R of the type $\mathfrak{S} = \langle (r_{k_1}, \mathrm{name}_{k_1}), \ldots, (r_{k_m}, \mathrm{name}_{k_m})\rangle$, given in Definition 47 by $\underline{\text{VIEW}}(\mathfrak{S}, \|\overrightarrow{t_R}\|_\#)$, can be expressed the following relational algebra (extended with the PIVOT operation) term:

$$(\overrightarrow{t_R}\ \textbf{PIVOT}\ (nr_{\overrightarrow{t_R}}(4)\ \text{FOR}\ (nr_{\overrightarrow{t_R}}(1), nr_{\overrightarrow{t_R}}(3))\ \text{IN}\ \mathfrak{S})[\mathfrak{S}].$$

Different from [171], we did not use these operations as an extension of the SQL relational algebra, but only as an internal operation, which has to be implemented in the IRDBMSs. The opportunity to extend the standard SQL with these two inverse operations can be considered in questions connected with optimization and execution of certain user-defined query computations.

Note that PIVOT and UNPIVOT does not introduce the intensionality in the FOL used for standard SQL semantics. While the PARSE operator introduce the intensional elements(relational names) into the vector relation r_V, and it is provided by the relational term t_3 above, applied after the UNPIVOT operation in the term t_2.

Another advantage of the parsing is that we can write the queries directly over the vector relation r_V, and hence the metadata are the "first-class" entities, so that in this framework we are able to provide the queries that manipulate data as well as their schema.

Note that the method of parsing is well suited for the migration from all existent RDB applications where the data is stored in the relational tables, so that this solution gives a possibility to pass easily from the actual RDBs into the new machine engines for the IRDB. We preserve all metadata (RDB schema definitions) without modification and only dematerialize its relational tables by transferring their stored data into the vector relation r_V (possibly in a number of disjoint partitions over a number of nodes). From the fact that we are using the query rewriting IDBMS, the current user's (legacy) applications does not need any modification and they continue to "see" the same user-defined RDB schema as before. Consequently, this IRDB solution is adequate for a massive migration from the already obsolete and slow RDBMSs into a new family of fast, NewSQL schema-flexible (with also 'open schemas") and big data scalable IRDBMSs.

4.2.4 Big data interoperability with IRDBs

The *interoperability* is the ability to share, interpret and manipulate the information across the heterogeneous database systems supported by Multidatabase systems (MDBS) in a distributed network by encompassing a heterogeneous mix of local database systems. Languages based on higher-order logic have been used for the interoperability by considering that the schematic information should be considered as part of a database's information content. The major advantage associated with such approaches, used in SchemaLog [169, 172], is the declaratively they derive from their logical foundation. The weak points of the SchemaLog is that it uses the second-order logic syntax and an ad hoc Prolog-like fixed- point semantics. However, both of them are not necessary, as we will show by using the IRDBs, just because the ordinary

RDBs have the FOL syntax and do not need fixed-point semantics but ordinary FOL semantics.

However, before the presentation of the IRDB interoperability features, it is useful to compare it in more detail with SchemaLog, and hence to provide the short introduction of the syntax and semantics of SchemaLog in what follows. It will be useful also to understand the objective difficulties for formalization of more sophisticated database systems and to avoid in the same time the ad hoc languages and semantics, as it is SchemaLog. With this in mind, readers will be able to appreciate the general intensional extension of FOL, used in this book, with well-known FOL syntax but able, with its intensional semantics, to satisfy the more complex requirements than what the standard extensional FOL is able to provide.

The SchemaLog is syntactically higher-order clausal logic, and is based on the technical benefits of soundness, completeness and compactness by a reduction to first-order predicate calculus. It has a strictly higher expressive power than first-order logic based on this syntax, different from IRDB, which has the standard FOL syntax but with intensional semantics which is conservative w. r. t. the Tarski's extensional semantics.

The vocabulary of the SchemaLog language $\mathcal{L}_S$ consists of the disjoint sets: $\mathcal{G}$ of k-ary ($k \geq 1$) functional symbols, $\mathcal{S}$ of nonfunctional symbols (language constants, i. e., nullary functional symbols), $\mathcal{V}$ of variables and usual logical connectives $\neg, \vee, \wedge, \exists$ and $\forall$.

Every symbol in $\mathcal{S}$ and $\mathcal{V}$ is a term of the language, i. e., $\mathcal{S} \bigcup \mathcal{V} \subseteq \mathcal{T}$. If $f \in \mathcal{G}$ is a n-ary function symbol and $t_1, \dots, t_n$ are terms in $\mathcal{T}$, then $f(t_1, \dots, t_n)$ is a term in $\mathcal{T}$.

An atomic formula of $\mathcal{L}_S$ is *an expression* (note that it is not a predicate-based atom of the FOL, i. e., in SchemaLog we do not use the predicate letters) of the following forms [172]:

(i) $\langle\text{db}\rangle :: \langle\text{rel}\rangle[\langle\text{tid}\rangle : \langle\text{attr}\rangle \rightarrow \langle\text{val}\rangle]$;
(ii) $\langle\text{db}\rangle :: \langle\text{rel}\rangle[\langle\text{attr}\rangle]$;
(iii) $\langle\text{db}\rangle :: \langle\text{rel}\rangle$;
(iv) $\langle\text{db}\rangle$;

where $\langle\text{db}\rangle$ (the database symbols or names), $\langle\text{rel}\rangle$ (the relational symbols or names), $\langle\text{attr}\rangle$ (the attribute symbols or names), $\langle\text{tid}\rangle$ (the tuple ids) and $\langle\text{val}\rangle$ are the sorts in $\mathcal{S}$ of $\mathcal{L}_S$.

The well-formed formulae (wff) of $\mathcal{L}_S$ are defined as usual: every atom is a wff; $\neg\phi$, $\phi \vee \psi$, $\phi \wedge \psi$, $(\exists x)\phi$ and $(\forall x)\phi$ are wffs of $\mathcal{L}_S$ whenever ϕ and ψ are wffs and $x \in \mathcal{V}$ is a variable.

A *literal* is an atom or the negation of an atom. A *clause* is a formula of the form $\forall x_1, \dots, \forall x_m(L_1 \vee \dots \vee L_n)$ where each L_i is a literal and $x_1, \dots, x_m$ are the variables occurring in $L_1 \vee \dots \vee L_n$. A *definite clause* is a clause in which one positive literal is present and represented as $A \leftarrow B_1, \dots, B_n$ where A is called the *head* and $B_1, \dots, B_n$ is called the *body* of the definite-clause. A *unit clause* is a clause of the form $A \leftarrow$, i. e., a definite clause with an empty body.

Let $\mathcal{D}$ be a nonempty set of elements (called “intensions”). A *semantic structure* [172] of the language $\mathcal{L}_S$ is a tuple $M = \langle \mathcal{D}, \mathcal{I}, \mathcal{I}_{\text{fun}}, \mathcal{F} \rangle$ where:

1. $\mathcal{I} : \mathcal{S} \to \mathcal{D}$ is a an interpretation of nonfunction symbols in $\mathcal{S}$;
2. $\mathcal{I}_{\text{fun}}(f) : \mathcal{D}^n \to \mathcal{D}$ is an interpretation of the functional symbol $f \in \mathcal{G}$ of arity n;
3. $\mathcal{F} : \mathcal{D} \rightsquigarrow [\mathcal{D} \rightsquigarrow [\mathcal{D} \rightsquigarrow [\mathcal{D} \rightsquigarrow \mathcal{D}]]]$, where $[A \rightsquigarrow B]$ denotes the set of all partial functions from A to B.

To illustrate the role of $\mathcal{F}$, consider the atom $d :: r$. For this atom to be true, $\mathcal{F}(\mathcal{I}(d))(\mathcal{I}(r))$ should be defined in M. Similarly, for the atom $d :: r[t : a \to v]$ to be true, $\mathcal{F}(\mathcal{I}(d))(\mathcal{I}(r))(\mathcal{I}(a))(\mathcal{I}(t))$ should be defined in M and $\mathcal{F}(\mathcal{I}(d))(\mathcal{I}(r))(\mathcal{I}(a))(\mathcal{I}(t)) = \mathcal{I}(v)$.

A variable assignment g is a function $g : \mathcal{V} \to \mathcal{D}$ (i. e., $g \in \mathcal{D}^{\mathcal{V}}$). We extend it to all terms in $\mathcal{T}$ as follows:

$$g(\overline{s}) = \mathcal{I}(\overline{s}) \quad \text{for every } \overline{s} \in \mathcal{S};$$

$g(f(t_1, \dots, t_n)) = \mathcal{I}_{\text{fun}}(f)(g(t_1), \dots, g(t_n))$ where $f \in \mathcal{G}$ is a functional symbol of arity n and t_i are terms.

For a given set of terms $t_i \in \mathcal{T}$, $i = 1, 2, \dots$ and the formulae ϕ and ψ, we define the satisfaction relation $\vDash_g$ for a given assignment g and the structure M as follows:

1. $M \vDash_g t_1$ iff $\mathcal{F}(g(t_1))$ is defined in M;
2. $M \vDash_g t_1 :: t_2$ iff $\mathcal{F}(g(t_1))(g(t_2))$ is defined in M;
3. $M \vDash_g t_1 :: t_2[t_3]$ iff $\mathcal{F}(g(t_1))(g(t_2))(g(t_3))$ is defined in M;
4. $M \vDash_g t_1 :: t_2[t_4 : t_3 \to t_5]$ iff $\mathcal{F}(g(t_1))(g(t_2))(g(t_3))(g(t_4))$ is defined in M and $\mathcal{F}(g(t_1))(g(t_2))(g(t_3))(g(t_4)) = g(t_5)$;
5. $M \vDash_g \phi \vee \psi$ iff $M \vDash_g \phi$ or $M \vDash_g \psi$;
6. $M \vDash_g \neg\phi$ iff not $M \vDash_g \phi$;
7. $M \vDash_g (\exists x)\phi$ iff for some valuation g', that may differ from g only on the variable x, $M \vDash_{g'} \phi$. □

The specification of an extension of a RDB in this logic framework can be done by specification of the logic program with the (high) number of unit and definite ground clauses (for each tuple in some relational table of such an RDB), which renders it nonuseful for the big data applications, because such a logic program would be enormous. Moreover, we do not need to use the fixed-point semantics of logic programming for the definition of the extension of the RDBs instead of the standard Tarski's semantics of the FOL.

Thus, the SchemaLog framework, defined for the Multidatabase interoperability, can not be used for the interoperability in big data applications, and hence we will show that SchemaLog can be reduced to intensional RDB (IRDB), which is designed for big data NewSQL applications.

The main work in this section is dedicated to the Multidatabase IRDBs and we explain how a metadata interoperability SchemaLog framework is embedded into the IRDBs big multidatabase systems.

From the introduction of SchemaLog, we can deduce that the definition of the multidatabases has to be obtained mainly by the following unit clauses (the "facts" in logic programming) of the following forms [172]:

(i) $(\langle \text{db} \rangle :: \langle \text{rel} \rangle [\langle \text{tid} \rangle : \langle \text{attr} \rangle \to \langle \text{val} \rangle]) \leftarrow;$

(ii) $(\langle \text{db} \rangle :: \langle \text{rel} \rangle [\langle \text{attr} \rangle]) \leftarrow;$

(iii) $(\langle \text{db} \rangle :: \langle \text{rel} \rangle) \leftarrow;$

(iv) $\langle \text{db} \rangle \leftarrow;$

where the clause (i) correspond to the SQL-like operation of inserting the value ⟨val⟩ into the attribute ⟨attr⟩ of the relation ⟨rel⟩ of the database ⟨db⟩ while other cases correspond to the DDL-like operations of definitions of the attributes of the relations, the relations of the databases and the databases. From the fact that we are interested in the operations over the vector relations $r_{V_1}, \ldots, r_{V_n}$, each one dedicated to a single database of the given multidatabase system, the unit clause $\langle \text{db} \rangle \leftarrow$ corresponds to the RDB DDL of the creation of the vector relation with the name $r_{V_i} = \langle \text{db} \rangle$ with the four fixed attributes `r-name`, `t-index`, `a-name` and `value`. We do not use the clauses (ii) and (iii) for vector relations, and the only interesting clause is (i).

In fact, we can use only the clause (i), which corresponds to the SQL statement

$$\text{“INSERT INTO } r_{V_i} \text{ VALUES } (\langle \text{rel} \rangle, \langle \text{tid} \rangle, \langle \text{attr} \rangle, \langle \text{val} \rangle).\text{”}$$

However, here we can see why SchemaLog cannot be used for real Multidatabase systems. Because each insertion, deletion or update must be realized by the updating of the whole Logic program P_L, which defines the extension of the databases, and then for such a modified program P_L to compute its least fixed point. It is not only a hard computational process (to rebuild the complete extension of all databases of a given multidatabase system by the fixed-point semantics), but also very complicated task of the concurrent updates of these databases by different users. This is the common problem and weak point for almost all AI logic-programming approaches to big databases, and explains why they cannot replace the concurrent RDBMSs and why we intend to translate the SchemaLog framework into the concurrent and big data IRDBMSs and then to show that IRDBMs can support the interoperability for the multidatabase systems.

Remark. (*): We will consider only the meaningful cases of the SchemaLog used for multidatabases, when each relation r of any database $\mathcal{A}$ is not empty and for each attribute of such a relation there is at least one value different from NULL, i. e., when every relation and its attributes are really *used* in such a database to contain the information. □

Implementation of SchemaLog interoperability by IRDB

Consequently, we consider the IRDB interoperability with a set of relational databases $S_{\mathrm{DB}} = \{u_{\mathrm{DB}_1}, \ldots, u_{\mathrm{DB}_n}\}$, for a given intensional interpretation (homomorphisms) $I : \mathcal{A}_{\mathrm{FOL}} \to \mathcal{A}_{\mathrm{int}}$ in commutative diagram (4.4) in Section 4.2, where each

$$u_{\mathrm{DB}_i} =_{\mathrm{def}} I(\exists y_2, y_3, y_4 r_{V_i}(y_1, y_2, y_3, y_4)) = \mathrm{exists}_{2,3,4}(u_{r_{V_i}}) \in D_1 \tag{4.8}$$

for $i = 1, \ldots, n$, is the intensional DB concept of the i-th RDB parsed into the vector relation with the name r_{V_i} (with $u_{r_{V_i}} = I(r_{V_i}(y_1, \ldots, y_4)) \in D_4$). So, the extension of the intensional DB concept u_{DB_i} is, commutative diagram (4.4) in Section 4.2,

$$h(u_{\mathrm{DB}_i}) = I_T^*(\exists y_2, y_3, y_4 r_{V_i}(y_1, y_2, y_3, y_4)) = \{nr(r_{ij}) \mid r_{ij} \in \mathcal{A}_i\}$$

is just the set of relation names of the schema of i-th RDB $\mathcal{A}_i$.

Thus, in this interoperability framework, we will have $n \geq 1$ tree-systems of concepts with the top multidatabase intensional concept $u_{\mathrm{mdb}} = I(\mathrm{call}_1(x)) \in D_1$ (where call_1 is the unary predicate letter introduced for this concept introduced for SchemaLog reduction in [172]) such that $h(u_{\mathrm{mdb}}) = S_{\mathrm{DB}}$ is the set of database names in a given tree-system of multidatabases, represented graphically in Figure 4.2.

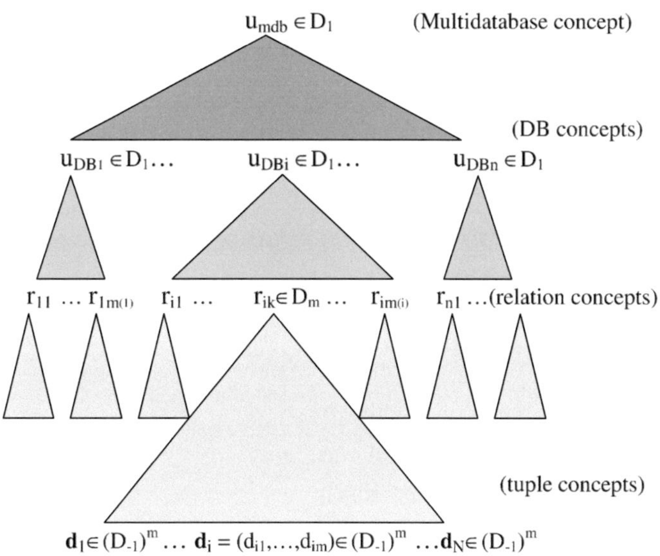

Figure 4.2: Tree-system of multidatabases.

So, we can introduce the following intensional concepts (the terms intensional algebra $\mathcal{A}_{\mathrm{int}}$ of Definition 16 in Section 1.3, for the sorts of relations, tuples, attributes and values):

1. $u_{\mathrm{rel}} = \mathrm{disj}_{S_1}(u_{\mathrm{DB}_1}, \mathrm{disj}_{S_1}(\ldots, \mathrm{disj}_{S_1}(u_{\mathrm{DB}_{n-1}}, u_{\mathrm{DB}_n})\ldots) \in D_1$;
2. $u_{\mathrm{tid}} = \mathrm{disj}_{S_2}(\mathrm{exists}_{1,3,4}(u_{r_{V_1}}), \mathrm{disj}_{S_2}(\ldots, \mathrm{disj}_{S_2}(\mathrm{exists}_{1,3,4}(u_{r_{V_{n-1}}}), \mathrm{exists}_{1,3,4}(u_{r_{V_n}}))\ldots) \in D_1$;
3. $u_{\mathrm{attr}} = \mathrm{disj}_{S_3}(\mathrm{exists}_{1,2,4}(u_{r_{V_1}}), \mathrm{disj}_{S_3}(\ldots, \mathrm{disj}_{S_3}(\mathrm{exists}_{1,2,4}(u_{r_{V_{n-1}}}), \mathrm{exists}_{1,2,4}(u_{r_{V_n}}))\ldots) \in D_1$;
4. $u_{\mathrm{val}} = \mathrm{disj}_{S_4}(\mathrm{exists}_{1,2,3}(u_{r_{V_1}}), \mathrm{disj}_{S_4}(\ldots, \mathrm{disj}_{S_4}(\mathrm{exists}_{1,2,3}(u_{r_{V_{n-1}}}), \mathrm{exists}_{1,2,3}(u_{r_{V_n}}))\ldots) \in D_1$;

where $S_i \{(i,i)\}$ for $i = 1, 2, 3, 4$. Notice that these intensional unary concepts above are derived from the FOL formulae, as follows:

$$u_{\mathrm{rel}} = I((\exists x_2, x_3, x_4)r_{V_1}(x_1, x_2, x_3, x_4) \vee (\ldots \vee (\exists x_2, x_3, x_4)r_{V_n}(x_1, x_2, x_3, x_4)\ldots));$$
$$u_{\mathrm{tid}} = I((\exists x_1, x_3, x_4)r_{V_1}(x_1, x_2, x_3, x_4) \vee (\ldots \vee (\exists x_1, x_3, x_4)r_{V_n}(x_1, x_2, x_3, x_4)\ldots));$$
$$u_{\mathrm{attr}} = I((\exists x_1, x_2, x_4)r_{V_1}(x_1, x_2, x_3, x_4) \vee (\ldots \vee (\exists x_1, x_2, x_4)r_{V_n}(x_1, x_2, x_3, x_4)\ldots));$$
$$u_{\mathrm{val}} = I((\exists x_1, x_2, x_3)r_{V_1}(x_1, x_2, x_3, x_4) \vee (\ldots \vee (\exists x_1, x_2, x_3)r_{V_n}(x_1, x_2, x_3, x_4)\ldots));$$

Then, given a SchemaLog formula ϕ, its encoding in the intensional FOL of the IRDB is determined by the recursive transformation rules given below. In this transformation, $s \in S \subseteq \mathcal{T}, f \in \mathcal{G}, t_i, t_{\mathrm{rel}}, t_{\mathrm{attr}}, t_{\mathrm{id}}, t_{\mathrm{val}} \in \mathcal{T}$, $t_{\mathrm{db}} \in \{r_{V_1}, \ldots, r_{V_n}\} \subset S \subseteq \mathcal{T}$, are the SchemaLog terms, and ϕ, ψ are any formulae:

1. $\mathrm{encode}(s) = s$, $\mathrm{encode}(f) = f$
2. $\mathrm{encode}(f(t_1, \ldots, t_m)) = \mathrm{encode}(f)(\mathrm{encode}(t_1), \ldots, \mathrm{encode}(t_m))$
3. $\mathrm{encode}(t_{\mathrm{db}} :: t_{\mathrm{rel}}[t_{\mathrm{id}} : t_{\mathrm{attr}} \rightarrow t_{\mathrm{val}}]) == \mathrm{encode}(t_{\mathrm{db}})(\mathrm{encode}(t_{\mathrm{rel}}), \mathrm{encode}(t_{\mathrm{id}}), \mathrm{encode}(t_{\mathrm{attr}}), \mathrm{encode}(t_{\mathrm{val}}))$
4. $\mathrm{encode}(t_{\mathrm{db}} :: t_{\mathrm{rel}}[t_{\mathrm{attr}}]) = (\exists x_2, x_4)\,\mathrm{encode}(t_{\mathrm{db}})(\mathrm{encode}(t_{\mathrm{rel}}), x_2, \mathrm{encode}(t_{\mathrm{attr}}), x_4)$
5. $\mathrm{encode}(t_{\mathrm{db}} :: t_{\mathrm{rel}}) = (\exists x_2, x_3, x_4)\,\mathrm{encode}(t_{\mathrm{db}})(\mathrm{encode}(t_{\mathrm{rel}}), x_2, x_3, x_4)$
6. $\mathrm{encode}(t_{\mathrm{db}}) = \mathrm{call}_1(t_{\mathrm{db}})$
7. $\mathrm{encode}(\phi \odot \psi) = \mathrm{encode}(\phi) \odot \mathrm{encode}(\psi)$, for $\odot \in \{\wedge, \vee\}$
8. $\mathrm{encode}(\neg\phi) = \neg\,\mathrm{encode}(\phi)$
9. $\mathrm{encode}(\rightarrow \phi) = \mathrm{encode}(\phi)$
10. $\mathrm{encode}(\psi \rightarrow \phi) = \neg\,\mathrm{encode}(\psi) \vee (\mathrm{encode}(\psi) \wedge \mathrm{encode}(\phi))$
11. $\mathrm{encode}((Qx)\phi) = (Qx)\,\mathrm{encode}(\phi)$, where $Q \in \{\exists, \forall\}$.

In the case of the intensional FOL defined in Definition 15 in Section 1.3, we obtain the syntax of the standard FOL but with intensional semantics. Such a FOL has a well-known Tarski's interpretation I_T^*, defined in Chapter 1. Consequently, from the intensional point of view, an interpretation of Tarski is a possible world in the Montague's intensional semantics, i. e., from Section 1.3, $w = I_T^* \in \mathcal{W}_e$, with the corresponding extensionalization function h, such that $I_T^* = h \circ I$.

Semantics

Given a SchemaLog structure $M = \langle \mathcal{D}, \mathcal{I}, \mathcal{I}_{\mathrm{fun}}, \mathcal{F} \rangle$, we construct a corresponding Tarski's interpretation $I_T = \mathrm{encode}(M)$ on the domain $\mathcal{D}$ as follows:

$$I_T(s) =_{\mathrm{def}} \mathcal{I}(s), \quad \text{for each } s \in \mathcal{S};$$

$I_T(f_i(d_1, \ldots, d_k)) =_{\mathrm{def}} \mathcal{I}_{\mathrm{fun}}(f_i)(d_1, \ldots, d_k)$, for each k-ary functional symbol $f_i \in \mathcal{G}$ and $d_1, \ldots, d_k \in \mathcal{D}$;

Note that the Hash functional symbol has to be inserted into $\mathcal{G}$, so that the built-in function on strings $\mathcal{I}_{\mathrm{fun}}(\mathrm{Hash})$ satisfies the condition, for relation names $u = nr(r_{V_i}), u' = nr(r)$ and $\mathrm{ID}, nr_r(k), d_k \in \mathcal{D}$, for $k = 1, \ldots, \mathrm{ar}(r)$:

$$\text{If } (\mathcal{F}(u)(u')(\mathrm{ID})(nr_r(1)) = d_1) \wedge \ldots \wedge (\mathcal{F}(u)(u')(\mathrm{ID})(nr_r(\mathrm{ar}(r))) = d_{\mathrm{ar}(r)}),$$
$$\text{then } \mathrm{ID} = \mathcal{I}_{\mathrm{fun}}(\mathrm{Hash})(d_1, \ldots, d_{\mathrm{ar}(r)}),$$

where some of values d_i can be equal to the value NULL $\in D_{-1}$ as well.

We recall that, for intensional FOL, each k-ary functional symbol f_i is considered as a $(k+1)$-ary relational concept, so that $I(f_i) \in D_{k+1}$ with

$$I_T(f_i) = h(I(f_i)) = \{(d_1, \ldots, d_k, \mathcal{I}_{\mathrm{fun}}(f_i)(d_1, \ldots, d_k)) \mid d_1, \ldots, d_k \in \mathcal{D}\}.$$

The unique relations that are materialized in IRDBs are the vector relations, and hence we will consider only these relations $r_{V_1}, \ldots, r_{V_n}$ (corresponding to databases $\mathcal{A}_1, \ldots, \mathcal{A}_n$ of this multidatabase interoperability system), so that the Tarski's interpretation for them is constructed in the following way:

1. For relation names $u = nr(r_{V_i}), u' = nr(r)$ and $\mathrm{ID}, a, d \in \mathcal{D}$, $(u', \mathrm{ID}, a, d) \in I_T(r_{V_i})$ iff $\mathcal{F}(u)(u')(a)(\mathrm{ID})$ is defined in M and $\mathcal{F}(u)(u')(a)(\mathrm{ID}) = d$.
2. For the unary predicate call_1, such that from the Tarski's constraints $u_{\mathrm{mdb}} = I(\mathrm{call}_1(x))$, we have that $I_T(\mathrm{call}_1) = h(I(\mathrm{call}_1(x))) = h(u_{\mathrm{mdb}}) = S_{\mathrm{DB}}$ (the set of intensional DB concepts (DB names) in the figure above). Then $nr(r_{V_i}) \in I_T(\mathrm{call}_1)$ iff $\mathcal{F}(nr(r_{V_i}))$ is defined in M.

Proposition 24. *Let ϕ be a SchemaLog formula, M be a SchemaLog structure and $g \in \mathcal{D}^{\mathcal{V}}$ an assignment. Let* $\mathrm{encode}(\phi)$ *be the first-order formula corresponding to ϕ and $I_T =$* $\mathrm{encode}(M)$ *the corresponding Tarski's interpretation. Then, for a given assignmen g, we denote by $I_T^* \vDash_g \psi$ the fact that $I_T^*(\psi/g) = t$, and hence it holds that*

$$M \vDash_g \phi \quad \textit{iff} \quad I_T^* \vDash_g \mathrm{encode}(\phi).$$

Proof. Let us show that it holds for all atoms of SchemaLog:

Case 1: When ϕ is equal to an atom $(t_1 :: t_2[t_4 : t_3 \to t_5])$, then

$$
\begin{aligned}
M \models_g\ & (t_1 :: t_2[t_4 : t_3 \to t_5]) \\
\text{iff}\ \ & \mathcal{F}(g(t_1))(g(t_2))(g(t_3))(g(t_4)) \text{ is in } M \text{ and } \mathcal{F}(g(t_1))(g(t_2))(g(t_3))(g(t_4)) = g(t_5) \\
\text{iff}\ \ & \langle g(t_2), g(t_4), g(t_3), g(t_5)\rangle \in I_T(g(t_2)) \text{ iff } I_T^* \models_g (t_1/g)(t_2, t_4, t_3, t_5) \\
\text{iff}\ \ & I_T^* \models_g (\text{encode}(t_1)/g)(\text{encode}(t_2), \text{encode}(t_4), \text{encode}(t_3), \text{encode}(t_5)) \\
\text{iff}\ \ & I_T^* \models_g \text{encode}(t_1 :: t_2[t_4 : t_2 \to t_5]).
\end{aligned}
$$

Case 2: When ϕ is equal to an atom $(t_1 :: t_2[t_3])$, then

$$
\begin{aligned}
M \models_g (t_1 :: t_2[t_3]) \quad & \text{iff} \quad \mathcal{F}(g(t_1))(g(t_2))(g(t_3)) \quad \text{is defined in } M \\
\text{iff}\ \ & I_T^* \models_g (\exists x_2, x_4)(t_1/g)(t_2, x_2, t_3, x_4) \\
\text{iff}\ \ & I_T^* \models_g (\exists x_2, x_4)(\text{encode}(t_1)/g)(\text{encode}(t_2), x_2, \text{encode}(t_3), x_4) \\
\text{iff}\ \ & I_T^* \models_g \text{encode}(t_1 :: t_2[t_3]).
\end{aligned}
$$

Case 3: When ϕ is equal to an atom $(t_1 :: t_2)$, then

$$
\begin{aligned}
M \models_g (t_1 :: t_2) \quad & \text{iff} \quad \mathcal{F}(g(t_1))(g(t_2)) \text{ is defined in } M \\
\text{iff}\ \ & I_T^* \models_g (\exists x_2, x_3, x_4)(t_1/g)(t_2, x_2, x_3, x_4) \\
\text{iff}\ \ & I_T^* \models_g (\exists x_2, x_3, x_4)(\text{encode}(t_1)/g)(\text{encode}(t_2), x_2, x_3, x_4) \\
\text{iff}\ \ & I_T^* \models_g \text{encode}(t_1 :: t_2).
\end{aligned}
$$

Case 4: When ϕ is equal to an atom t_{db}, then

$$
\begin{aligned}
M \models_g t_{\text{db}} \quad & \text{iff} \quad \mathcal{F}(g(t_{\text{db}})) \quad \text{is defined in } M \\
\text{iff}\ \ & g(t_{\text{db}}) \in I_T(\text{call}_1) \text{ iff } I_T^* \models_g \text{call}_1(t_{\text{db}}) \text{ iff } I_T^* \models_g \text{encode}(t_{\text{db}}).
\end{aligned}
$$

Case 5: For the composed formulae, we can demonstrate by induction. Let us suppose that this property holds for ϕ and for ψ. Then

$$
\begin{aligned}
M \models_g \phi \vee \psi \quad & \text{iff} \quad M \models_g \phi \text{ or } M \models_g \phi \\
\text{iff}\ \ & I_T^* \models_g \text{encode}(\phi) \text{ or } I_T^* \models_g \text{encode}(\psi) \text{ iff } I_T^* \models_g \text{encode}(\phi \vee \psi),
\end{aligned}
$$

and analogously for all other cases. □

Note that w. r. t. the remark (*) above, the relations (predicates) $\text{call}_1, \text{call}_2, \text{call}_3$ and call_4 (obtained by a similar reduction of SchemaLog in FO logic programs in [172]), can be defined by the vector relations in IRDBs as follows:

$$
\begin{aligned}
\text{call}_4 = {} & (\text{EXTEND } r_{V_1} \text{ ADD a}, \texttt{db-name}, r_{V_1}) \text{ UNION } (\ldots \text{UNION(EXTEND } r_{V_n} \text{ ADD} \\
& \text{a}, \texttt{db-name}, r_{V_n}) \ldots), \quad \text{where } a \text{ is the attribute used for the database names;} \\
\text{call}_3 = {} & \text{call}_4[\texttt{db-name}, \texttt{r-name}, \texttt{a-name}]; \\
\text{call}_2 = {} & \text{call}_3[\texttt{db-name}, \texttt{r-name}];
\end{aligned}
$$

(note that we also have $\text{call}_1 = \text{call}_2[\texttt{db-name}]$), with $h(u_{\text{rel}}) = \|\text{call}_4[\texttt{r-name}]\|_\#$, $h(u_{\text{attr}}) = \|\text{call}_4[\texttt{a-name}]\|_\#$, and $h(u_{\text{val}}) = \|\text{call}_4[\texttt{value}]\|_\#$.

Thus, based on [172], we obtain the result that *technically* SchemaLog has no more expressive power than the intensional first-order logic used for IRDBs.

However, different from the SchemaLog that needs a particular extension $\mathcal{ERA}$ of the conventional (standard) relational algebra with the new operations, δ, ρ, α and γ [172] (so that the resulting algebra is capable of accessing the database names, relational names and attribute names besides the values in a federation of database), here we can use the conventional (standard) SQL over the vector relations $r_{V_1}, \ldots, r_{V_n}$ and call_1.

These new operators β, ρ, α are defined in IRDBs by the following SQL expressions:

$$\delta() = \|\text{call}_1\|;$$
$$\rho(S) = \text{call}_2 \text{ WHERE } nr_{\text{call}_2}(1) \text{ IN } S, \text{for each } S \subseteq \|\text{call}_1\|_\#;$$
$$\alpha(S) = \text{call}_3 \text{ WHERE } (nr_{\text{call}_2}(1), nr_{\text{call}_2}(2)) \text{ IN } S, \text{for each } S \subseteq \|\text{call}_2\|_\#;$$

Only the operation γ is a more complex, defined in [172] as follows:

A *pattern* is a sequence $(p_1, \ldots, p_k)$, $k \geq 0$, where each p_i is one of the forms '$a_i \to d_i$', '$a_i \to$', '$\to d_i$' and '$\to$'. Here, a_i is called the *attribute component* and d_i is called the *value component* of p_i. Let r be any relation, then

"$a_i \to d_i$" is satisfied by a tuple tid in relation r if $\text{tid}[a_i] = d_i$;

'$a_i \to$' is satisfied by a tuple tid in relation r if a_i is an attribute name in r;

"$\to d_i$" is satisfied by a tuple tid in relation r if there exists an attribute a_i in the scheme of r such that $t[a_i] = d_i$;

'$\to$' is trivially satisfied by every tuple tid in relation r.

A pattern $(p_1, \ldots, p_k)$ is satisfied by a tuple tid in relation r if every $p_i, i = 1, \ldots, k$, is satisfied by tid.

Operator γ takes a binary relation S as input, and a pattern as a parameter and returns a relation that consists of tuples corresponding to those parts of the database where the queried pattern is satisfied. That is, let S be a binary relation and $(p_1, \ldots, p_k)$ be a pattern, then [172],

$$\gamma_{(p_1,\ldots,p_k)}(S) =_{\text{def}} \{\text{db}, r, a_1, d_1, \ldots, a_k, d_k | \langle \text{db}, r \rangle \in S$$

and db is a database in the federation, and r is a relation in db, and a_i's are attributes in r, and there exists a tuple tid in r such that $\text{tid}[a_1] = d_1, \ldots, \text{tid}[a_k] = d_k$, and tid satisfies $(p_1, \ldots, p_k)\}$.

Note that when the pattern is empty ($k = 0$), $\gamma_{()}(S)$ would return the set of all pairs $\langle \text{db}, r \rangle \in S$ such that r is a nonempty relation in the database db in the federation. □

Theorem 5. *All new relational operators introduced in SchemaLog extended relational algebra $\mathcal{ERA}$ can be equivalently expressed by standard SQL terms in IRDBs.*

Proof. The call_1 and call_2 are SQL terms (over the vector relations r_{V_i} of the federated databases) defined previously, so that the definition of the SchemaLog operators δ, ρ and α, given above, are the standard SQL terms as well. It is enough to demonstrate that each $\gamma_{(p_1,\dots,p_k)}$ operator defined above, can be equivalently represented by a standard SQL term in the IRDBs as follows:

(i) Case when $k = 0$. Then $\gamma_{()}(S) = \rho(S)$ (because from Remark (*) we are dealing with the databases with all nonempty relations);

(ii) Case when $k = 1$. Then for the SQL term $t = \text{call}_4$

$$\gamma_{(p_1)}(S) = (t \text{ WHERE } C_{p_1})[\texttt{db-name}, \texttt{r-name}, \texttt{a-name}, \texttt{value}],$$

where the condition C_{p_1} is defined by (here $\top$ is a tautology):

$$C_{p_1} = \begin{cases} (nr_t(4) = a_i) \wedge (nr_t(5) = d_i), & \text{if } p_1 = \text{`}a_i \to d_i\text{'} \\ nr_t(4) = a_i, & \text{if } p_1 = \text{`}a_i \to \text{'} \\ nr_t(5) = d_i, & \text{if } p_1 = \text{`} \to d_i\text{'} \\ \top, & \text{otherwise} \end{cases}$$

(iii) Case when $k \geq 2$. So, for the SQL Cartesian product

$$\begin{aligned} t &= \overbrace{\text{call}_4 \bigotimes \cdots \bigotimes \text{call}_4}^{k}, \\ \gamma_{(p_1,\dots,p_k)}(S) &= (t \text{ WHERE } (nr_t(1) = \ldots = nr_t(5k-4)) \\ &\quad \wedge (nr_t(2) = \ldots = nr_t(5k-3)) \wedge (nr_t(3) = \ldots = nr_t(5k-2)) \\ &\quad \wedge (C_{p_1} \wedge \ldots \wedge C_{p_k}))[nr_t(1), nr_t(2), nr_t(4), nr_t(5), nr_t(9), nr_t(10), \ldots, \\ &\quad nr_t(5k-1), nr_t(5k)], \end{aligned}$$

where the conditions C_{p_m}, for $m = 1, \ldots, k$, are defined by

$$C_{p_m} = \begin{cases} (nr_t(5m-1) = a_i) \wedge (nr_t(5m) = d_i) & \text{if } p_m = \text{`}a_i \to d_i\text{'} \\ nr_t(5m-1) = a_i & \text{if } p_m = \text{`}a_i \to \text{'} \\ nr_t(5m) = d_i & \text{if } p_m = \text{`} \to d_i\text{'} \\ \top & \text{otherwise} \end{cases}$$

□

Example 22. Let us consider the multidatabase (federated) system given in Example 2.1 in [172], consisting of RDBase `univ_A`, `univ_B` and `univ_C` corresponding to universities A, B and C. Each database maintains information on the university's departments, staff and the average salary in 1997, as follows:

1. The RDB `univ_A` has the following single relation `pay-info`, which has one tuple for each department and each category in that department:

$\|$pay-info$\|$ =

category	dept	avg-sal
Prof	CS	70,000
Assoc. Prof	CS	60,000
Secretary	CS	35,000
Prof	Math	65,000

2. The RDB univ_B has the single relation, (also pay-info), but in this case, department names appear as attribute names and the values corresponding to them are the average salaries:

$\|$pay-info$\|$ =

category	CS	Math
Prof	80,000	65,000
Assoc. Prof	65,000	55,000
Assist. Prof	45,000	42,000

3. The RDB univ_C has as many relations as there are departments, and has tuples corresponding to each category and its average salary in each of the detp$_i$ relations:

$\|$CS$\|$ =

category	avg-sal
Prof	65,000
Assist. Prof	40,000

$\|$ece$\|$ =

category	avg-sal
Secretary	30,000
Prof	70,000

By parsing of these three RDBs, we obtain the three vector relations r_{V_1} with the name $nr(r_{V_1})$ = univ_A, r_{V_2} with the name $nr(r_{V_2})$ = univ_B and r_{V_3} with the name $nr(r_{V_3})$ = univ_C. Let us consider the tuple ID_1 = Hash(Secretary CS 35,000) of the database univ_A, so that

$\|r_{V_1}\| \supset$

r-name	t-index	a-name	value
pay-info	ID_1	category	Secretary
pay-info	ID_1	dept	CS
pay-info	ID_1	avg-sal	35,000

,

and consider the tuple ID_2 = Hash(Secretary 30,000) of the relation ece of the database univ_C, so that

$\|r_{V_3}\| \supset$

r-name	t-index	a-name	value
ece	ID_2	category	Secretary
ece	ID_2	avg-sal	30,000

so that the following set of tuples are the part of the relation obtained from the SQL algebraic term call_4:

$\|\text{call}_4\|_\# \supset$

db-name	r-name	t-index	a-name	value
univ_A	pay-info	ID_1	category	Secretary
univ_A	pay-info	ID_1	dept	CS
univ_A	pay-info	ID_1	avg-sal	35,000
univ_C	ece	ID_2	category	Secretary
univ_C	ece	ID_2	avg-sal	30,000

,

Then the operation $\gamma_{(\rightarrow \text{Secretary}, \rightarrow)}(S)$ against the university databases above is equivalent to the SQL term (for $t = \text{call}_4 \otimes \text{call}_4$)

$$(t \text{ WHERE } (nr_t(1) = nr_t(6)) \wedge (nr_t(2) = nr_t(7)) \wedge (nr_t(3) = nr_t(7)) \\ \wedge (nr_t(5) = \text{Secretary}))[nr_t(1), nr_t(2), nr_t(4), nr_t(5), nr_t(9), nr_t(10)],$$

will yield for

$S =$

univ_A	pay-info
univ_B	pay-info
univ_C	CS
univ_C	ece

$= \|\text{call}_2\|_\# = \|\text{call}_4[\texttt{db-name}, \texttt{r-name}]\|_\#$

the relation

univ_A	pay-info	category	Secretary	dept	CS
univ_A	pay-info	category	Secretary	category	Secretary
univ_A	pay-info	category	Secretary	avg-sal	35,000
univ_C	ece	category	Secretary	category	Secretary
univ_C	ece	category	Secretary	avg-sal	30,000

Thus, we obtain he following completeness result for the SQL in the IRDBs w. r. t. the querying fragment ($\mathcal{L}_Q$) of SchemaLog (provided in Definition 6.6 in [172]).

Corollary 13. *Let $\mathcal{DB}$ be a relational multidatabase system with nonempty relations and attributes (in Remark (*)), $\mathcal{P}$ be a set of safe rules in the querying fragment $\mathcal{L}_Q$ of the SchemaLog and p any (virtual) predicate defined by $\mathcal{P}$.*

Then there exists a standard SQL expression t such that the computed relation $\|t\|_\#$ in the IRDB obtained by parsing of this multidatabase system is equal to the relation corresponding to p computed by SchemaLog.

Proof. From Lemma 6.1 in [172] for such a query $p \in \mathcal{L}_Q$, there is an expression E of the extended relational algebra $\mathcal{ERA}$, such that the relation corresponding to p is equal to the relation obtained by computing the relational expression E. From Theorem 5, we are able to translate this expression $E \in \mathcal{ERA}$ into an equivalent standard SQL term t whose extension $\|t\|_\#$ in the IRDB obtained by parsing of this multidatabase system is equal to the relation corresponding to p computed by SchemaLog. □

Consequently, any querying of data and metadata information (of nonempty relations and nonempty attributes, as explained in Remark (*)) of the federated relational database system $\mathcal{DB}$ provided by the interoperability framework of the SchemaLog can be done in the IRDBs framework *by the standard SQL*.

Remark. If we need to use the interoperability framework also for the empty database schemas or empty relations, in that case we need to create the relation table $call_3$ not by deriving it as a particular projections from $call_4$ (SQL term) but directly from the RDB dictionary of the multidatabase system. □

Consequently, by permitting the SQL querying over the vector relations in the IRBDs we can obtain the answers (see [172] for more useful cases), e. g.:

(Q_4) "*Find the names of all the relations in which the token 'John' appears*";

(Q_5) "*Given two relations r and s (in database db), whose schemas are unknown, compute their natural join*";

etc.

The method of parsing of a relational instance-database A with the user-defined schema $\mathcal{A}$ into a vector relation $\vec{A} = \|r_V\|$, used in order to represent the information in a standard and simple key/value form, today in various applications of big data, introduces the intensional concepts for the user-defined relations of the schema $\mathcal{A}$. Moreover, we can consider the vector relations as the concept of *mediator*, proposed by Wiederhold [173], as a means for integrating data from also nonrelational heterogeneous sources.

The expressive power of IRDB, which includes the expressive power of SchemaLog and its ability to resolve data/metadata conflicts suggests that it has the potential for being used in the interoperability frameworks for the multidatabase systems and as a platform for developing mediators. This new family of IRDBs extends the traditional RDBS with new features. However, it is compatible in the way of how to present the data by user-defined database schemas (as in RDBs) and with SQL for management of such a relational data.

The structure of RDB is parsed into a vector key/value relation so that we obtain a column representation of data used in big data applications, covering the key/value and column-based big data applications as well, into a unifying RDB framework. The standard SQL syntax of IRDB makes it possible to express powerful queries and programs in the context of component database interoperability. We are able to treat the data in the database, the schema of the individual databases in a multidatabase (a federation) system, as well as the databases and relations themselves as first class citizens, without using a higher-order syntax or semantics.

4.3 Enrichment of IRDB by multivalued attributes

MultiValue databases include commercial products from Rocket Software, TigerLogic, jBASE, Revelation, Ladybridge, InterSystems, Northgate Information Solutions and other companies. These databases differ from a relational database in that they have features that support and encourage the use of attributes, which can take a list of values, rather than all attributes being single-valued. They are often categorized with MUMPS within the category of post-relational databases, although the data model actually predates the relational model. In spite of a history of more than 40 years of implementations, starting with TRW, many in the MultiValue industry have remained current so that various MultiValue implementations now employ object-oriented versions of Data BASIC, support AJAX frameworks, and because no one needs to use SQL (but some can) they fit under the NoSQL umbrella. In fact, MultiValue developers were the first to acquire noSQL domain names, likely prior to other database products classifying their offerings as NoSQL as well. MultiValue is a seasoned data model, but with so many vendors competing in this space, it has been constantly enhanced over the years.

On the other side, the standard RDBs can only simulate the multivalued attributes, by introducing the new relational tables for the values of these attributes, and cannot use them directly as the multivalued attributes of the tables because in this case we would need to pass from the FOL to the second-order logic. Consequently, in order to pass from NoSQL multivalue databases to NewSQL relational multivalue databases we need to semantically enrich the standard RDBs.

The first step to maintain the logical declarative (nonprocedural) SQL query language level, is done by a revision of traditional RDBMSs: it was provided by developing H-store (M. I. T., Brown and Yale University), a next generation OLTP systems that operates on distributed clusters of shared-nothing machines where the data resides entirely in the main memory, so that it was shown to significantly outperform (83 times) a traditional, disc-based DBMS. A more full-featured version of the system [160] that is able to execute across multiple machines within a local area cluster has been presented in August 2008. The data storage in the H-store is managed by a single-thread execution engine that resides underneath the transaction manager. Each individual site executes an autonomous instance of the storage engine with a fixed amount of memory allocated from its host machine. The commercial version of H-store's design is VoltDB.

The parallel DBMSs offer great scalability over the range of nodes that customers desire, where all parallel DBMSs operate (pipelining) by creating a query plan that is distributed to the appropriate nodes at execution time. When one operator in this plan sends data to next (running on the same or a different node), the data are pushed by the first to the second operator (this concept is analog to the process described in my book [21] dedicated to normalization of SQL terms (completeness of the action-relational-algebra category **RA**)), so that (different from MR), the intermediate data is never written to disk. The formal theoretical framework (the database category **DB**) of the parallel DBMSs and the semantics of database mappings between them is provided in big data integration theory as well [21]. It is interesting that in [162], the authors conclude that parallel DBMSs excel at efficient querying of large data sets while MR key/value style systems excel at complex analytics and ETL tasks, and propose:

> *"The result is a much more efficient overall system than if one tries to do the entire application in either system. That is, "smart software" is always a good idea."*

In this section, we present a conceptually new version with multivalued attributes of a family of Intensional RDBs (IRDBs). However, different from the basic version described in previous sections, which are fully compatible with the standard RDBs, this is a more powerful new conceptual RDB model, which does not support the first normal form in Codd's requirements for RDBs, and hence permits the relaxation of the atomicity requirement for data. Here, we do not use the intensional semantics only for big data and to manage the queries with both data and metadata, but we are using the full power of the intensional FOL in order to support the new intensional concepts in these IRDBs able to store the multivalued attributes.

In order to preserve the standard table-based representation of query results, the multivalued attributes in the tuples of this representation do not show any value but a functional link, and hence, by activating it as the powerset function, we can obtain the corresponding set of stored values. Moreover, these functional links in the tuples (which are intensional concepts) can be used for the joins as well, because each of them represents a set of values, and two links with the same set of values are intensionally equal, and hence can be used in the joins as the standard atomic values.

We define a new query rewriting algorithm taking in consideration the multivalued attributes, based again on the GAV integration, so that each user-defined SQL query is rewritten into a SQL query over the vector relation of the IRDB and an auxiliary binary relation used to store all sets of values for the multivalued attributes. Thus, as in the basic case of IRDBs, the user-defined RDB schema is an empty global schema used only for the RDB modeling and as the standard SQL interface. However, we will also mention different SQL's enrichments in order to manage more efficiently the multivalued attributes.

4.3.1 Canonical models for IRDBs with multivalued attributes

Let us show why we are not able to implement directly the multivalued attributes in standard RDBs (without chaining the database's schema by introducing the side effects with new relations in the schema used to store the set of values of the introduced "multivalued attributes"), and why it is possible to do in IRDBs without any kind of side effects, obtaining the full joins capability over the multivalued attributes as well.

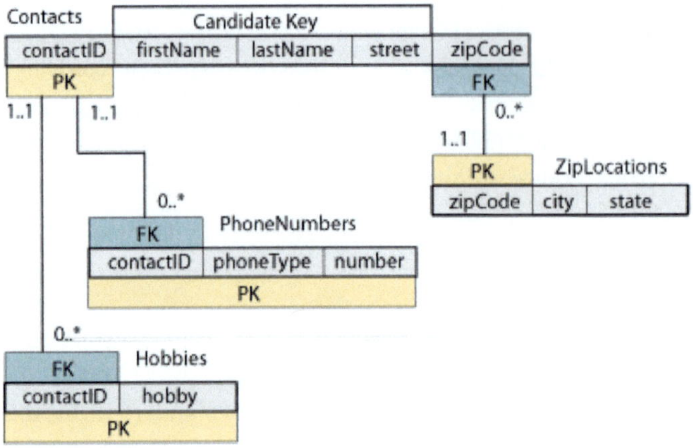

Figure 4.3: Example for multivalued attributes.

Let us consider the following simple example with three relations:

1. ZipLocations(zipCode, city, state), with primary key (PK) zipCode,
2. Contacts(contactID, firstName, lastName, street, zipCode), with PK corresponding to contactID, and foreign key (FK) to zipCode, and
3. PhoneNumbers(contactID, phoneType, number), with FK contactID, such that for each contact we can store the name and forename of the contacted person, his address and phone numbers.
   Suppose that we want to know what hobbies each person on our contact list is interested in. Introduction of such a multivalued attribute in RDB can be only done *indirectly* by introducing a new relation
4. Hobbies(contactID, hobby), with FK contactID, and hence we obtained the schema presented graphically.

We might add an attribute hobbies to relation Contacts to hold these. More likely, someone added this attribute without thinking about it, obtaining the modified relation

Contacts(contactID, firstName, lastName, street, zipCode, hobbies),

but from the fact that the attribute hobbies must contain a set of values, in FOL it corresponds to a unary predicate hobies(x), so that this modified relation would have the following second-order formulation, Contacts(x_1, x_2, x_3, x_4, x_5, hobbies(x)); consequently, this is the reason why we cannot implement directly the multivalued attributes in standard RDBs.

However, in intensional FOL, this relation can be provided by the following FOL atom, by using the intensional abstraction in order to substitute the predicate hobbies(x) by the abstracted term, so that for a given intensional interpretation I (and corresponding assignment g). In intensional FOL, as explained in detail in Example 5 in Section 1.3.1 dedicated to formal semantics of abstracted terms applied just to this case, we introduced a binary atom $p_i^2(x_1, y)$ with name of this binary predicate letter $nr(p_i^2) = \texttt{hobbies}$, where x_1 is used for the KEY attribute `ContactID` of relation `Contacts` and y used for the hobbies, and an atom for contacts $p_j^6(x_1, x_2, x_3, x_4, x_5, \lessdot p_i^2(x_1, y)\gtrdot_{\alpha_i}^{\beta_i})$ in (1.25) with $nr(p_j^6) = \texttt{Contacts}$. However, here instead of the formal predicate symbols of intensional FOL, we will use directly their names, in order to render more easy the presentation, so that these two intensional concepts are presented as follows for a given assignment $g \in \mathcal{D}^{\mathcal{V}}$:

$$\texttt{Contacts}(x_1, x_2, x_3, x_4, x_5, \lessdot\texttt{hobbies}(x_1, y)\gtrdot_y^{x_1})/g$$
$$= \texttt{Contacts}(132, \text{Zoran}, \text{Majkic}, \text{Appia}, 0187, u),$$

where from (1.22),

$$u = g^*(\lessdot\texttt{hobbies}(x_1, y)\gtrdot_y^{x_1}) = I(\texttt{hobbies}(132, y)) \in D_1 \tag{4.9}$$

is unary intensional concept (property) for the value $g(x_1) = 132$ of the attribute `contactID`. So, for example, in what follows, for this concept u we can generate automatically from the name of this relation and this value as the name $u = \texttt{hobbies\_of\_132}$. If the set of hobbies of this contact 132 is $S = \{\text{photography}, \text{travel}, \text{art}, \text{music}\}$, it must be equal to the extension of this unary concept, i. e.,

$$h(I(\lessdot\texttt{hobbies}(132, y)\gtrdot_y)) = h(u) = S.$$

The function list(S) is used to obtain a unique ordered list from a given set of strings in S (e. g., by alphabetical ordering), so that we obtain the list list(S) = (art, music, photography, travel).

Consequently, in order to save the extensions of the intensional concepts associated to each multivalued-attribute value (e. g., for the value $u \in D_1$ of a multivalued attribute `hobbies` of the relation `Contacts`), we define the new relation

$$r_{MA}(\texttt{value}, \texttt{atom-value}) \tag{4.10}$$

with FK `value` and PK is composed by both attributes `value` and `atom-value`. Thus, in this example, we have that the set of tuples

$$\{(u, \text{photography}), (u, \text{travel}), (u, \text{art}), (u, \text{music})\} \subseteq \|r_{MA}\| = I_T(r_{MA})$$

will be inserted in the table with name $nr(r_{MA})$.

The application of the intensional FOL semantics to the data integration system $\mathcal{I} = (\mathcal{A}, \mathcal{S}, \mathcal{M})$ in Definition 44 with the user defined RDB schema $\mathcal{A} = (S_A, \Sigma_A)$ and the vector big table r_V is summarized in Section 4.2.1.

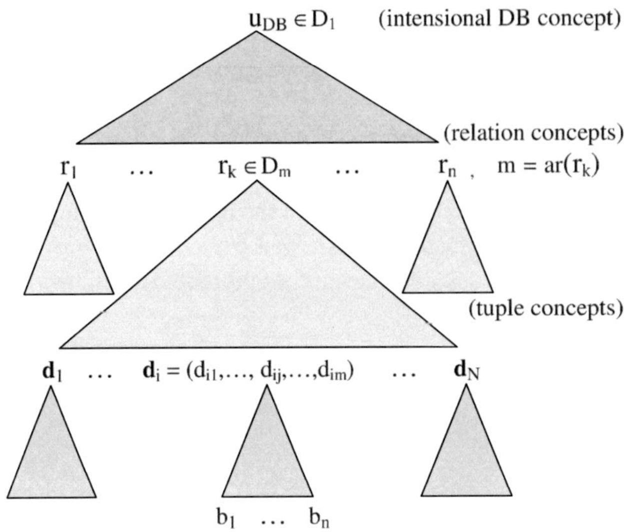

Figure 4.4: Hierarchy of concepts for IRDB with multivalued attributes.

Based on the intensional interpretation above, we are able to represent any instance user-defined database A as an intensional hierarchy system of concepts, presented in Fig. 4.4, which has one more level (last of this tree structure, for the multivalued attribute's values) than that in Section, where:

For each tuple of data $\mathbf{d}_i = (d_{i1}, \dots, d_{im})$, $1 \le i \le N$, of the relation r_k, we have that $h(I(r_V(nr(r_k), \mathrm{Hash}(\mathbf{d}_i), nr_{r_k}(j), d_{ij}))) = t$, for d_{ij} (different from NULL), $j = 1, \dots, m = \mathrm{ar}(r_k)$. If, in this example, we consider that j-th column of relation r_k is a multivalued attribute, so that for $d_{ij} \in D_1$ (equal to the name of an unary concept (property) derived from the multivalued attribute with name $nr_{r_k}(j)$), its extension $h(d_{ij}) = \{b_1, \dots, b_n\}$ is the set of values for this multivalued attribute linked to the tuple $\mathbf{d}_i$ of the relation $nr(r_k)$. Note that the bottom level of the information hierarchy is stored in the r_{MA} table for all multivalued attributes of the instance database A.

The intensional data integration system $\mathcal{I} = (\mathcal{A}, \mathcal{S}, \mathcal{M})$, in Definition 44 of Section 4.2, is used in the way that the global schema is the only virtual (empty) database with a user-defined schema $\mathcal{A} = (S_A, \mathrm{Sigma}_A)$ used to define the SQL user-defined query, which then has to be equivalently rewritten over the vector relation r_V in order to obtain the answer to this query. Thus, the information of the database is stored only in the big table $\|r_V\|$. Thus, the materialization of the original user-defined schema $\mathcal{A}$ can be obtained by the operation $\underline{\mathrm{MATTER}}$ of Definition 45 in Section 4.2.

The canonical models of the intensional data integration system $\mathcal{I} = (\mathcal{A}, \mathcal{S}, \mathcal{M})$ in Definition 44 in Section 4.2 are the instances A of the schema $\mathcal{A}$ such that

$$\|r_k\| = \underline{\mathrm{MATTER}}\Big(r_k, \bigcup_{\mathbf{v} \in \|r_k\|} \underline{\mathrm{PARSE}}(r_k, \mathbf{v})\Big), \quad \text{i. e., when}$$

$$A = \{\underline{\text{MATTER}}(r_k, \vec{A}) \mid r_k \in S_A\}.$$

Remark. Both operations, PARSE and MATTER, are equal to that of the IRDBs without multivalued attributes (provided in Section 4.2). Thus, also the data integration system holds the same. The only difference is that in the multivalued attribute version of the IRDBs we have another relation r_{MA} where all (and only) values of multivalued attributes of a given IRDB instance A are stored. Thus, if we will use the standard RDB solution, where the instance database A is materialized, we will add to it also the relational table r_{MA}, and in order to select the values of a multivalued attribute in A we would need to use a join with the first attribute `value` of r_{MA}, in order to pickup the atomic values of this multivalued attribute stored in the second attribute `atom-value`. With such a join, for the tuple $\mathbf{d}_i = \langle 132, \text{Zoran}, \text{Majkic}, \text{Appia}, 0187, u\rangle$ of the table `Contacts` (presented previously), we would obtain the following set of tuples (in our example we proposed for unary concept u to be the following name $u =$ `hobbies_of_132`):

con.ID	firstName	lastName	street	zipCode	hobbies	atom-value
132	Zoran	Majkic	Appia	0187	u	photography
132	Zoran	Majkic	Appia	0187	u	music
132	Zoran	Majkic	Appia	0187	u	art
132	Zoran	Majkic	Appia	0187	u	travel

But it has some disadvantages: we do not support *directly* the multivalued attributes, so we have to repeat the same tuple for each different value of a multivalued attribute, which is an explosive effect when we have more than one multivalued attribute in the relations (for each combination of the values of these multivalued attributes we have to repeat the same tuple). In what follows, we will provide a different "functional" solution in order to avoid such an explosive repetition of the equal tuples. □

The canonical models of such intensional data integration system $\mathcal{I} = \langle \mathcal{A}, \mathcal{S}, \mathcal{M}\rangle$ can be provided in a usual logical framework as in Section 4.2, but for the multivalued attribute features we need the following extension for the introduced relation r_{MA}:

– We introduce the multivalued attribute specification "a MULTIVALUED" (like "a NOT NULL") for an attribute a of a given relation.

Consequently, the canonical models of the IRDB with multivalued attributes are given by the following.

Proposition 25. *Let the IRDB be given by a data integration system $\mathcal{I} = \langle \mathcal{A}, \mathcal{S}, \mathcal{M}\rangle$ for a used-defined global schema $\mathcal{A} = (S_A, \Sigma_A)$ with $S_A = \{r_1, \dots, r_n\}$ and auxiliary relation r_{MA}, the source schema $\mathcal{S} = (\{r_V\}, \emptyset)$ with the vector big data relation r_V and the set of mapping tgds $\mathcal{M}$ from the source schema into the relations of the global schema.*

Then a canonical model of $\mathcal{I}$ *is any model of the schema* $\mathcal{A}^+ = (S_A \bigcup \{r_V, r_{MA}\}, \Sigma_A \bigcup \mathcal{M} \bigcup \mathcal{M}^{OP} \bigcup \{\rho_V\})$, *where* $\mathcal{M}^{OP}$ *is an opposite mapping tgds from* $\mathcal{A}$ *into* r_V *given by the following set of tgds:*

$$\mathcal{M}^{OP} = \{\forall x_1, \ldots, x_{\mathrm{ar}(r_k)}((r_k(x_1, \ldots, x_{\mathrm{ar}(r_k)}) \wedge x_i \; \mathit{NOT\ NULL}) \Rightarrow r_V(nr(r_k), \mathrm{Hash}(x_1, \ldots, x_{\mathrm{ar}(r_k)}), nr_{r_k}(i), x_i)) \mid 1 \le i \le \mathrm{ar}(r_k), r_k \in S_A\},$$

and the new mapping ρ_V *is equal to*

$$\forall x_1, \ldots, \forall x_4 \exists y((r_V(x_1, x_2, x_3, x_4) \wedge x_3 \; \mathit{MULTIVALUED}) \Rightarrow r_{MA}(x_4, y))$$

Proof. For all relations of the schema $\mathcal{A}$, the proof is equal to the case of non-multivalued-attributes IRDB version provided in Proposition 22 in Section 4.2. It is easy to verify that the canonical model of the auxiliary relation r_{MA} is well-defined: in fact, the mapping ρ_V guarantees that each nonempty multivalued attribute in RDB $\mathcal{A}$ has the corresponding set of values in r_{MA}. □

Note that the auxiliary relation r_{MA} for the values of the multivalued attributes is a part of the global schema in the data integration system $\mathcal{I}$ and we have the mapping ρ_V from the source schema into it. This auxiliary relation is necessary also in the case when we decide to materialize the schema $\mathcal{A}$, because it is a unique table where the values are stored and contained in the multivalued attributes of schema $\mathcal{A}$.

The fact that we assumed r_V and r_{MA} to be only the particulars (extensional entities) is based on the fact that they always will be materialized (thus nonempty relational tables) as standard tables of the RDB $\mathcal{A}$.

4.3.2 NewSQL property of the IRDBs with multivalued attributes

This last subsection will be dedicated to demonstrate that the IRDBs are complete w. r. t. the standard SQL and to introduce the INSERT/DELETE operations for the tuples with the multivalued attributes. As in the case of IRDB without multivalued attributed, presented in Section 4.2.2, a user query is defined over the intensional concepts in $\mathcal{A}$ (which will remain *empty tables*, i. e., nonmaterialized). Hence, we need to demonstrate the existence of an effective query rewriting into an equivalent SQL query over the (nonintensional concept) vector big table r_V and auxiliary table r_{MA} where the sets of values of the multivalued attributes are stored. In order to define this query rewriting, we will shortly introduce the abstract syntax and semantics of Codd's relational algebra, as follows.

We recall that for any k-ary relational table r, with $k = \mathrm{ar}(r)$, with the injective function $nr_r : \{1, \ldots, k\} \to SN$, which assigns distinct names to each column of this relation r, we denote its tuple of attributes $\mathrm{atr}(r) = \mathbf{a} = (a_1, \ldots, a_k) = (\mathrm{atr}_r(1), \ldots, \mathrm{atr}_r(k))$, and the set of attributes denoted by $\overline{\mathbf{a}} = \overline{\mathrm{atr}}(r)$. We recall that two relations r_1 and r_2 are union compatible iff $\overline{\mathrm{atr}}(r_1) = \overline{\mathrm{atr}}(r_2)$. Given any two lists (tuples), $\mathbf{d} = \langle d_1, \ldots, d_k \rangle$ and $\mathbf{b} = \langle b_1, \ldots, b_m \rangle$, their concatenation $\langle d_1, \ldots, d_k, b_1, \ldots, b_m \rangle$ is denoted by **d&b**, where '&' is the symbol for concatenation of the lists. By $\|r\|$, we denote the extension of a given relation (relational symbol) r; it is extended to any term t_R of Codd's algebra, so that $\|t_R\|$ is the relation obtained by computation of this term.

Five primitive operators of Codd's algebra are: the *selection*, the *projection*, the *Cartesian product* (also called the cross-product or cross-join), the *set union* and the *set difference*. Another operator, *rename*, was not noted by Codd, but the need for it is shown by the inventors of the Information Systems Base Language (ISBL) for one of the earliest database management systems, which implemented Codd's relational model of data. They are provided in Section 4.2.2. Natural join $\bowtie_S$ is a binary operator, written as $(r_1 \bowtie_S r_2)$, where r_1 and r_2 are the relations.

Remark. The multivalued attribute version of IRDBs SQL operations above differs from the ordinary version without multivariable attributes only in the case of selection operation "_WHERE C," which uses also the multivalued attributes in the condition C. In fact, for such attributes the values are not in the tuples of the original relations, but in the auxiliary relation r_{MA}. □

Update operators for multivalued attribute version of IRDB

- We define a unary operator "EXTEND_ADD a, name AS e." for an added attribute at the end of relation $a \in \mathbf{att}$, its name and expression e (in the most simple cases it can be the value NULL or a constant d, or the i-th column name $nr(i)$ of the argument (i. e., relation) of this operation), as a function with a set of column names, such that for a relation r_1 and expression e composed of the names of the columns of r_1 with $n = \mathrm{ar}(r_1)$, we obtain the $(\mathrm{ar}(r_1) + 1)$-ary relation r by $\langle a, \mathrm{name}, e \rangle (r_1)$, with naming function $nr_r : \{\mathrm{ar}(r_1) + 1\} \to \mathrm{SN}$ such that $nr_r(i) = nr_{r_1}(i)$ if $i \leq \mathrm{ar}(r_1)$; $nr_r(\mathrm{ar}(r_1) + 1) = \mathrm{name}$ otherwise, being a fresh new name for this column; with the attribute function $\mathrm{atr}_r : \{\mathrm{ar}(r_1) + 1\} \to \mathbf{att}$ such that $\mathrm{atr}_r(i) = \mathrm{atr}_{r_1}(i)$ if $i \leq \mathrm{ar}(r_1)$; $\mathrm{atr}_r(\mathrm{ar}(r_1) + 1) = a$ otherwise, and

$$\|r\| = \{\langle\,\rangle\} \bigcup \{\mathbf{d}\&e(\mathbf{d}) \mid \mathbf{d} \in \|r_1\|\},$$

  where $e(\mathbf{d}) \in \mathrm{dom}(a)$ is a constant or the value obtained from the function e where each name $nr_r(i)$ is substituted by the value d_i of the tuple $\mathbf{d} = \langle d_1, \ldots, d_n \rangle \in \|r_1\|$; in the special cases, we can use nullary functions (constants) for the expression e (e. g., for the NULL value). Note that r is empty if e is an expression and r_1 empty as well.

  Multivalued constraint: the multivalued attributes cannot be used in the expression e; if a is a multivalued attribute, then e must be equal to NULL.

We are able to define a new relation with a single tuple $(d_1, \ldots, d_k), k \geq 1$ with the given list of attributes $(a_1, \ldots, a_k)$, by using the "EXTEND" operation as explained in Section 4.2.2. The three update operators, "UPDATE," "DELETE" and "INSERT" of the relational algebra, are derived operators as explained in Section 4.2.2, with a multivalued attribute version of UPDATE as a combination of DELETE and INSERT operations, and:

1. Each algebraic expression (a term) "INSERT INTO $r[S]$ VALUES (list of values)," "INSERT INTO $r[S]$ AS SELECT...," is equivalent to "r UNION r_1" where the union compatible relation r_1 is a one-tuple relation (defined by list) in the first, or a relation defined by "SELECT..." in the second case.
   Multivalued extension: In the case of a single tuple insertion (version with "VALUES") into a given relation r with multivalued attributes, for each multivalued attribute instead of simple value has to be inserted empty set $\emptyset$ or a nonempty set of values $\{b_1, \ldots, b_n\}$.

For example, the insertion of the contact 132 in the table `Contacts` used in the previous section has to be done by the operation

$$\text{INSERT INTO } \texttt{Contacts}[\texttt{contactID}, \texttt{firstName}, \texttt{lastName}, \texttt{street}, \texttt{zipCode}, \texttt{hobbies}] \text{ VALUES } (132, \text{Zoran}, \text{Majkic}, \text{Appia}, 0187, \{\text{photography}, \text{travel}, \text{art}, \text{music}\}).$$

This operation inserts the tuple $\langle 132, \text{Zoran}, \text{Majkic}, \text{Appia}, 0187, u\rangle$ in table `Contacts` (where u, given by (4.9) is a unary concept, e. g., defined by name "`hobbies_of_132`"), and the set of tuples $S = \{\langle u, \text{photograpy}\rangle, \langle u, \text{travel}\rangle, \langle u, \text{art}\rangle, \langle u, \text{music}\rangle\}$ in r_{MA}.

Each algebraic expression "UPDATE r SET $[nr_r(i_1) = e_{i_1}, \ldots, nr_r(i_k) = e_{i_k}]$ WHERE C," for $n = \text{ar}(r)$, where $e_{i_m}, 1 \leq i_m \leq n$ for $1 \leq m \leq k$ are the expressions and C is a condition, we will consider in the multivalued attribute version as a combination of DELETE and INSERT operations.

Remark. After a number of delete operations, we can obtain the situation where we have the stored lists of values for the multivalued attributes, which are not used more, so periodically we can delete them from r_{MA} by, e. g., the following operation:

$$\text{DELETE FROM } r_{MA} \text{ WHERE } \texttt{value} \text{ NOT IN } ((r_V \text{ WHERE } \texttt{a-name} \text{ MULTIVALUED})[\texttt{value}]) \qquad \square$$

Notice that we are able to introduce also the new update operations, optimized to change only the lists of values of the multivalued attributes (e. g., the deleting of one value or inserting a new value in a list of values of a given multivalued attribute of some tuple of relational tables with the multivalued attributes).

We recall that the Σ_R-algebra of the set of operations, introduced previously, with its terms t_R, which will be used in what follows, is introduced by Definition 46 in Section 4.2.2.

Notice that the syntax and semantics of the relational algebra for IRDB with the multivalued attributes is the *same* as in the case of IRDB without the multivalued attributes. This orthogonality is obtained from the fact that in relational tables the multivalued attributes in the tuples are represented by unary concepts $u \in D_1$ provided in (4.9). Thus, each computed relation $\|t_R\|_\#$ is well-defined, and by using the joins with the auxiliary table $\|r_{\mathrm{MA}}\|$, we are able to obtain the complete list of values of each multivalued attribute in any tuple of $\|t_R\|_\#$. Hence, for any standard SQL statement (term) t_R, its evaluation must return the ordinary resulting view $\|t_R\|_\#$ with the subset of tuples in $\|r_{\mathrm{MA}}\|$, which contains all lists of values used for the multivalued attributes in the tuples of this view $\|t_R\|_\#$. This fact will be formally presented in next Definition 48 dedicated to views.

We say that an extension $\|t_R\|_\#$, of a term $t_R \in \mathcal{T}_P X$, is a *vector relation* of the *vector view* denoted by $\overrightarrow{t_R}$ if the type of $\|t_R\|_\#$ is equal to the type of the vector relation r_V.

Let $R = \|\overrightarrow{t_R}\|_\#$ be the relational table with the following four attributes (as in r_V) `r-name`, `t-index`, `a-name` and `value`, then its user-defined view representation can be derived as follows (analog to Definition 47 without multivalued attributes).

Definition 48 (View materialization with multivalued attributes). Let $t_R \in \mathcal{T}_P X$ be a user-defined SPJU (Select-Project-Join-Union) view over a database schema $\mathcal{A} = (S_A, \Sigma_A)$ with the type (the tuple of the view columns) $\mathfrak{S} = \langle (r_{k_1}, \mathrm{name}_{k_1}), \dots, (r_{k_m}, \mathrm{name}_{k_m})\rangle$, where the i-th column $(r_{k_i}, \mathrm{name}_{k_i})$ is the column with the name equal to the name_{k_i} of the relation $r_{k_i} \in S_A$, $1 \le i \le m$, and $\overrightarrow{t_R}$ be the rewritten query over r_V.

Let $R = \|\overrightarrow{t_R}\|_\#$ be the resulting relational table with the four attributes (as r_V) `r-name`, `t-index`, `a-name` and `value`. We define the operation $\underline{\mathrm{VIEW}}$ of the transformation of R into the user defined view representation by:

$$
\begin{aligned}
&\underline{\mathrm{VIEW}}(\mathfrak{S}, R) = (R_1, R_2), \quad \text{where}\\
&R_1 = \{(d_1, \dots, d_m) \mid \exists\, \mathrm{ID} \in \pi_3(R), \forall_{1\le i\le m}(\langle nr(r_{k_i}), \mathrm{ID}, \mathrm{name}_{k_i}, d_i\rangle \in R);\\
&\qquad \text{otherwise set } d_i \text{ to NULL})\}, \text{ and } R_2 = \|t'_R\|_\# \subseteq \|r_{\mathrm{MA}}\| \text{ with}\\
&t'_R = r_{\mathrm{MA}} \text{ WHERE } \mathtt{value} \text{ IN } (\overrightarrow{t_R} \text{ WHERE } \mathtt{a\text{-}name} \text{ MULTIVALUED})[\mathtt{value}]),
\end{aligned}
$$

which represents all lists of values for the multivalued attributes in the view R_1.

Notice that we have, from (4.6), for each $r_k \in S_A$ with $R = \bigcup_{\mathbf{d}\in\|r_k\|} \underline{\mathrm{PARSE}}(r_k, \mathbf{d})$, and $\mathfrak{S} = \langle (r_k, nr_{r_k}(1)), \dots, (r_k, nr_{r_k}(\mathrm{ar}(r_k)))\rangle$, as in (4.7)

$$
\|r_k\| = \underline{\mathrm{MATTER}}\,(r_k, R) = \underline{\mathrm{VIEW}}\,(\mathfrak{S}, R),
$$

and hence the non-SQL operation $\underline{\mathrm{MATTER}}$ is a special case of the operation $\underline{\mathrm{VIEW}}$.

For any original user-defined query (term) t_R over a user-defined database schema $\mathcal{A}$, by $\overrightarrow{t_R}$ we denote the equivalent (rewritten) query over the vector relation r_V. We have the following important result for the IRDBs (analog to Proposition 23 in Section 4.2.2).

Proposition 26. *There exists a complete algorithm for the term rewriting of any user-defined SQL term t_R over a schema $\mathcal{A}$, of the full relational algebra Σ_{RE} in Definition 46, into an equivalent vector query $\overrightarrow{t_R}$ over the vector relation r_V. If t_R is a SPJU term (in Definition 48) of the type $\mathfrak{S}$, then $\|t_R\|_\# = \pi_1(\underline{\text{VIEW}}(\mathfrak{S}, \|\overrightarrow{t_R}\|_\#))$.*

Proof. We will use the convention and recursive method used in the proof of Proposition 23 in Section 4.2.2. The cases for Rename, Projection, Join, Union and Set difference are equal to the transformations presented in the proof of Proposition 23 used in the IRDB without multivalued attributes. The only difference is for the Select operations in which the selection condition contains the multivalued attributes, because the values of these attributes have to be checked in the auxiliary relation r_{MA}. Thus, for the Selection without multivalued attributes the transformation is equal to point 4 in the proof of Proposition 23. So, here we will consider only the Selection with also multivalued attributes:

4. (Selection). $t_R' = t_R$ WHERE C:
   4.1 When a condition C is a finite-length logical formula that consists of atoms '$((r_{i_1}, \text{name}_i)\theta(r_{j_1}, \text{name}_j))$' or '$(r_{i_1}, \text{name}_i)\theta d$' or '$(r_{i_1}, \text{name}_i)$' NOT NULL with built-in predicates $\theta \in \Sigma_\theta \supseteq \{\doteq, >, <\}$, a constant $\overline{d}'$ and the logical operators, between the columns in the type $\mathfrak{S}$ of the term t_R. The condition C, composed by $k \geq 1$ different columns in $\mathfrak{S}$, we denote by $C((r_{i_1}, \text{name}_{i_1}), \ldots, (r_{i_k}, \text{name}_{i_k}))$, $k \geq 1$, and hence we defined the rewritten vector query

$$\overrightarrow{t_R'} = \overrightarrow{t_R \text{ WHERE } C} = \overrightarrow{t_R} \text{ WHERE } nr_{\overrightarrow{t_R}}(2) \text{ IN } t_1$$

where for $r = \overbrace{\overrightarrow{t_R} \bigotimes \cdots \bigotimes \overrightarrow{t_R}}^{k}$ we define the unary relation, which contains the tuple-indexes of the relation $\|t_R\|$ for its tuples, which satisfy the selection condition C, by the following selection term:

$$\begin{aligned} t_1 = (r \text{ WHERE } ((nr_r(1) = r_{i_1} \wedge nr_r(3) = \text{name}_{i_1}) \wedge \ldots \wedge (nr_r(1 + 4(k-1)) \\ = r_{i_k} \wedge nr_r(3 + 4(k-1)) = \text{name}_{i_1})) \wedge C'(nr_r(4), \ldots, nr_r(4k)) \wedge ((k = 1) \\ \vee (nr_r(2) = nr_r(6) = \ldots = nr_r(2 + 4(k-1)))))[nr_r(2)], \end{aligned}$$

where the transformed condition C' is obtained from the original condition C by substituting the atoms '$((r_{i_1}, \text{name}_i)\theta(r_{j_1}, \text{name}_j))$' where the left or right side is a multivalued attribute, and '$(r_{i_1}, \text{name}_i)\theta d$' where (r_{i_1}, name_i) is a multivalued attribute, by

- Case '$((r_{i_1}, \mathrm{name}_i)\theta(r_{j_1}, \mathrm{name}_j))$' where only $(r_{i_1}, \mathrm{name}_i)$ is a multivalued attribute. We substitute this expression by $\exists x(r_{\mathrm{MA}}(\mathrm{name}_i, x) \wedge (x\theta(r_{j_1}, \mathrm{name}_j)))$;
- Case '$((r_{i_1}, \mathrm{name}_i)\theta(r_{j_1}, \mathrm{name}_j))$' where both sides are the multivalued attributes. We substitute this expression by $\exists x \exists y(r_{\mathrm{MA}}(\mathrm{name}_i, x) \wedge r_{\mathrm{MA}}(\mathrm{name}_j, y) \wedge (x\theta y))$;
- Case '$(r_{i_1}, \mathrm{name}_i)\theta d$' where $(r_{i_1}, \mathrm{name}_i)$ is a multivalued attribute. We substitute this expression by $\exists x(r_{\mathrm{MA}}(\mathrm{name}_i, x) \wedge (x\theta d))$.

4.2 Case when $C = (r_{i_1}, \mathrm{name}_i)$ NULL,

$$\overrightarrow{t'_R} = \overrightarrow{t_R \text{ WHERE } (r_{i_1}, \mathrm{name}_i) \text{ NULL}} = \overrightarrow{t_R} \text{ WHERE } nr_{\overrightarrow{t_R}}(2) \text{ NOT IN } t_2,$$

where $t_2 = (\overrightarrow{t_R} \text{ WHERE } ((nr_{\overrightarrow{t_R}}(1) = r_{i_1}) \wedge (nr_{\overrightarrow{t_R}}(3) = \mathrm{name}_i)))[(nr_{\overrightarrow{t_R}}(2)]$.

From the fact that t_R WHERE $C_1 \wedge C_2 = (t_R$ WHERE $C_1)$ WHERE C_2 and t_R WHERE $C_1 \vee C_2 = (t_R$ WHERE $C_1)$ UNION $(t_R$ WHERE $C_2)$, and De Morgan laws, $\neg(C_1 \wedge C_2) = \neg C_1 \vee \neg C_2$, $\neg(C_1 \vee C_2) = \neg C_1 \wedge \neg C_2$, we can always divide any selection in the components of the two disjoint cases above.

It is easy to show that for the selection, we obtain that $\|t'_R\|_\# = \pi_1(\underline{\mathrm{VIEW}}(\mathfrak{S}, \|\overrightarrow{t'_R}\|_\#))$, where $\mathfrak{S}$ is the type of the relational algebra term t'_R, and for other operators (which are equal as in the standard nonmany-valued attribute version of IRDB) it holds as well, as it was demonstrated in Proposition 23. Thus, for any SPJU term t_R obtained by the composition of these basic relational algebra operators we have that $\|t_R\|_\# = \pi_1(\underline{\mathrm{VIEW}}(\mathfrak{S}, \|\overrightarrow{t_R}\|_\#))$. The update operators (for relation symbols we consider their names depending on context):

1. (Insert). INSERT INTO $r[S]$ VALUES $(d_1, \dots, d_m)$, where $S = \langle nr_r(i_1), \dots, nr_r(i_m)\rangle$, $1 \leq m \leq \mathrm{ar}(r)$, is the subset of mutually different attribute names of r and all d_k, $1 \leq k \leq m$ are the values different from NULL. It is rewritten into the following set of terms, for each attribute $1 \leq k \leq m$:
   (a) If the attribute $nr_r(i_k)$ is not multivalued:
   INSERT INTO r_V[`r-name`, `t-index`, `a-name`, `value`] VALUES $((nr(r), \mathrm{Hash}(c_1, \dots, c_m), nr_r(i_k), d_k)$, where for $1 \leq i \leq m$, $c_i = d_i$ if $nr_r(i)$ is not a multivalued attribute; otherwise $c_i = u_i$ for new unary intensional concept of $nr_r(i)$ for this tuple to be inserted.
   (b) If the attribute $nr_r(i_k)$ is multivalued:
   INSERT INTO r_V[`r-name`, `t-index`, `a-name`, `value`] VALUES $(nr(r), \mathrm{Hash}(c_1, \dots, c_m), nr_r(i_k), u_k))$, where for $1 \leq i \leq m$, $c_i = d_i$ if $nr_r(i)$ is not a multivalued attribute; otherwise $c_i = u_i$ (u_k is one of them) for new unary intensional concept of $nr_r(i)$ for this tuple to insert. Thus, if $\neg\exists y r_{\mathrm{MA}}(u_k, y)$ then generate the following set of terms for $d_k = \{b_1, \dots, b_n\}$:

$$\{\text{INSERT INTO } r_{\text{MA}}[\texttt{value}, \texttt{atom-value}] \text{ VALUES } (u_k, b_i) \mid 1 \le i \le n\}.$$

Note that before the execution of this set of insertion operations in r_V, the DBMS has to control if it satisfies all user-defined integrity constraints in the user-defined database schema $\mathcal{A}$;

2. (Delete). DELETE FROM r WHERE C, is rewritten into the term:

$$\text{DELETE FROM } r_V \text{ WHERE } \texttt{t-index} \text{ IN } \overrightarrow{t_R}[nr_{\overrightarrow{t_R}}(2)],$$

where $\overrightarrow{t_R} = \overrightarrow{r \text{ WHERE } C}$ is the selection term as described above;

3. (Update). The existence of the rewriting of this operation is obvious; it can always be decomposed as a deletion and after that the insertion of the tuples. □

This proposition demonstrates that the IRDB with multivalued attributes is a SQL database, so that each user-defined query over the used-defined RDB database schema $\mathcal{A}$ can be equivalently transformed by query rewriting into a query over the vector relation r_V and r_{MA}. However, in the IRDBMSs we can use more powerful and efficient algorithms in order to execute each original user-defined query over the vector relation r_V and r_{MA}.

Notice that this proposition demonstrates that the IRDB is a kind of GAV data integration system $\mathcal{I} = (\mathcal{A}, \mathcal{S}, \mathcal{M})$ in Definition 44 where we do not materialize the user-defined schema $\mathcal{A}$ but only the vector relation $r_V \in \mathcal{S}$ and auxiliary relation r_{MA} where the sets of values of the multivalued attributes are stored. So, each original query $q(\mathbf{x})$ over the empty schema $\mathcal{A}$ will be rewritten into a vector query $\overrightarrow{q(\mathbf{x})}$ of the type $\mathfrak{S}$ over the vector relation r_V, and then the resulting view $\underline{\text{VIEW}}(\mathfrak{S}, \|\overrightarrow{q(\mathbf{x})}\|_{\#})$ will be returned to user's application. Notice that this result is composed by two distinct tables: first one R_1 is the view relation and the second R_2 is a subrelation of $\|r_{\text{MA}}\|$ composed by all (and only) lists of values of the multivalued attributes for the tuples in R_1. The visualization of an obtained resulting view can be, e. g., done for the table R_1 where the multivalued attributes are the colored links, and hence if one of them is pointed, then the set of values of it will appear in a smaller window.

So, IRDB with multivalued attributes is a member of the NewSQL, i. e., a member of a class of modern relational database management systems that seek to provide the same scalable performance of NoSQL systems for online transaction processing (read-write) workloads while still maintaining the ACID guarantees of a traditional database system.

Example 23. For example, if we want to select all tuples in the table `Contacts`, such that music is one of the hobbies of the contacts, we can use the SQL expression

$$\text{“}\texttt{Contacts}\text{ WHERE } \texttt{hobbies} = \text{music,”}$$

and we will obtain the two following tables:

$R_1 =$

contactID	firstName	lastName	street	zipCode	hobbies
...	...	...	...	...	...
132	Zoran	Majkic	Appia	0187	u
...	...	...	...	...	...

$R_2 =$

value	atom-value
...	...
u	photography
u	music
u	art
u	travel
...	...

$\subseteq \|r_{MA}\|$

Remark. With the condition "hobbies = music," we extract all tuples in Contacts that in the multivalued attribute hobbies have the set of values, which contain also the value "music," and not only the tuples that have exactly the singleton set {music}.

In order to make more powerful extractions, we can enrich the standard set of SQL conditions also with multivalued features, like "hobbies CONTAINS [music, art]," so that we are able to extract only tuples, which for this attribute, have the set of values that contains the subset [music, art], or like "hobbies EQUALS [music, art]" in order to extract only the tuples which for this attribute have *exactly* the set [music, art] of values, etc.

Notice that by *direct implementation* of the multivalue attributes we are able, e. g., to extract the pairs of contacts that have the same set of hobbies by simply auto-joins of the table Contacts over its multivalued-attribute hobbies. □

So, this new family of IRDBs extends the traditional RDBS with new features, as the interoperability, i. e., ability to share, interpret and manipulate across the heterogeneous database systems supported by multidatabase systems and to query together their data and metadata. However, it is compatible in the way of how to present the data by user-defined database schemas (as in RDBs) and with SQL for the management of such a relational data.

Finally, we extend the ability of the IRDBs to support the SQL features also with the presence of the multivalued attributes. Thanks to the intensional semantics, different from ordinary RDBs, which cannot directly support the multivalued attributes, here we obtained a natural support for such a direct "reification-based" multivalued framework. It is an orthogonal extension of the ordinary IRDBs without multivalued attributes, from a semantic point of view, and hence all sets of the values of the multivalued attributes are stored in an auxiliary binary relation r_{MA}. Consequently, the computed view for any SQL query over a user-defined schema $\mathcal{A}$ returns two distinct tables: the first one R_1 is the ordinary view table with the indexed (links) values for the multivalued attributes, and the second table R_2 contains the sets of values of the multivalued attributes in the tuples of the view table R_1.

The passage from the existing RDB legacy systems into the IRDBs with multivalued attributes is easy: the structure of RDB is parsed into a vector key/value relation so that we obtain a column representation of data used in big data applications, covering the key/value and column-based big data applications as well, into a unifying RDB framework. After this step, we are able to add new multivalued attributes to the database schema, and continue to work in this new framework. Note that the method of parsing is well suited for the migration from all preexistent RDB applications where the data is stored in the relational tables, so that this solution gives the possibility to pass easily from the actual RDBs into the new machine engines for the IRDB. We preserve all metadata (RDB schema definitions) without modification and only dematerialize its relational tables by transferring their stored data into the vector relation r_V (possibly in a number of disjoint partitions over a number of nodes). From the fact that we are using the query rewriting IDBMS, the current user's (legacy) applications does not need any modification and they continue to "see" and manage the same user-defined RDB schema as before. Consequently, this IRDB solution is adequate for a massive migration from the already obsolete and slow RDBMSs into a new family of fast, NewSQL schema-flexible (with also 'open schemas") and big data scalable IRDBMSs.

We are able to return in any moment to the standard RDBMS by materialization of the user defined schema into an RDB A and adding to this obtained RDB also the auxiliary table r_{MA}, which contains the sets of values for the multivalued attributes. So, we can use the joins to link the values of the multivalued attributes in RDB A to the sets of values in r_{MA} in similar way as it is done in ad hoc indirect realization of the multivalued attributes by introduction of new entities (tables) in the original RDB schemas. Thus, the passage from RDBMs into the multivalued attribute version of the IRDBs is easy and reversible as well.

4.4 Kleisli semantics for intensional RDB with multivalued attributes

In this section, we present a denotational semantics of a new family of Intensional RDBs (IRDBs) with also multivalued attributes. The categorial logic used for this denotational semantics is based on the category **DB** where the objects are the instances of RDBs and the morphisms are the set of functions, which express the schema mappings between RDBs, provided by big data Integration theory [21] (see Section A.6 in the Appendix). It was demonstrated that the denotational semantics of database mappings is given by morphisms of the Kleisli category given by a power-view monad over the category **DB**. For the semantics of the multivalued attributes, we defined the particular "powerset" monad over **DB** and its Kleisli category. In this section, we demonstrate that **DB** is able to support the intensional extension of the FOL and that the semantics of the intensional elements, which represents the multivalued attributes can be expressed by particular saturated morphisms in **DB**. We show that these saturated morphisms are derived from the data integration mapping graph used to define the canonical models of the IRDBs with the multivalued attributes.

The parallel DBMSs offer great scalability over the range of nodes that customers desire, where all parallel DBMSs operate (pipelining) by creating a query plan that is distributed to the appropriate nodes at execution time. When one operator in this plan sends data to the next (running on the same or a different node), the data are pushed by the first to the second operator (this concept is analog to the process described in my book [21] dedicated to normalization of SQL terms (completeness of the action-relational algebra category **RA**)), so that (different from MR), the intermediate data is never written to disk.

The idea of using Kleisli categories (an introduction to category theory is given in Section A.5 in the Appendix) in databases has been introduced for the database mapping systems in [174], based on the power-view monad [175]. This approach of categorial semantics for the RDBs and their mappings is provided in [21] (an introduction is provided in Section A.6 in the Appendix). The notion of a monad is one of the most general mathematical notions. For instance, *every* algebraic theory, i. e., every set of operations satisfying equational laws, can be seen as a monad. Moggi [176, 177] stressed the computational significance of monads and explained how they may help understand programs "*as functions from values to computations*". The idea of Moggi, roughly, is to give denotational semantics to computations and it presents an alternative to the conceptual gap between the intensional (operational) and the extensional (denotational) approaches to the semantics of programming languages.

The idea of monad as a model for computations, based on an endofunctor T for a given category, is that for each set of values of type A, TA is the object of computations of "type A," introduced in Section A.6.2 in the Appendix. Let us explain the way we can use such denotational semantics, based on monads, in the case of relational databases. It is well known that the relational databases are complex structures, defined by some sets of n-ary relations. In addition, the mappings between the relational databases are based on some sets of view mappings between a source database A and a target database B, as specified in Section A.6.3 in the Appendix. We consider the views as an universal property for databases (i. e., possible observations of the information contained in some database).

We assume that *a view* of a database A as the relation (set of tuples) obtained by a "Select-Project-Join + Union" (SPJRU) query $q(\mathbf{x})$ where $\mathbf{x}$ is a list of attributes of this view. We denote by $\mathcal{L}_A$ the set of all such queries over a database A and by $\mathcal{L}_A/_\approx$ the quotient algebra obtained by introducing the equivalence relation $\approx$, such that $q(\mathbf{x}) \approx q'(\mathbf{x})$ if both queries result in the same relation (view). Thus, a view can be equivalently considered as a *term* of this quotient algebra $\mathcal{L}_A/_\approx$ with carrier set of relations in A and a finite arity of their operators, whose computation returns a set of tuples of this view.

A categorical logic (denotational semantics) for database schema mapping *based on views*, presented in [21], is a very general framework for database-integration/exchange and peer-to-peer. The base database category **DB** (instead of traditional **Set** category of sets and functions between them), with objects instance-databases and with morphisms (mappings which are not simple functions) between them, is used at an *instance level* as a proper semantic domain for a database mapping based on a set of complex query computations.

The higher logical *schema level* of mappings between databases, usually written in some high expressive logical language ([111, 143], GLAV (LAV and GAV), tuple generating dependency) can then be translated functorially into this base "computation" category. We will use such a framework also because an IRDB is formally defined as an intensional GAV data integration system, so we are able to use all mathematical tools developed in [21] in order to present a formal denotational semantics for the IRDBs with multivalued attributes.

A similar approach in using Kleisli semantics to relax the atomicity requirement for data in standard RDBs has been recently presented in [178], but in that case the level of presentation of a database schema is given by the graphs (sketch categories) composed by binary relations only and the functional dependencies between them. Consequently, in such a low level schema representation we can use the topos **Set** category as a base category and simple powerset functor as a monad, while in our higher-level abstraction we present the whole RDB schema as a node of the sketch and we represent also complex integrity constraints over schemas by schema mappings. Consequently, in our higher level presentation framework the monads have to be developed for the weak monoidal topos **DB**, which is a somewhat mathematically more complicated task.

The aim of this section is just to find the monad for **DB**, which is able to simulate the powerset monad for **Set**, and to use the new sketch representation for the IRDB schemas. So, this work is a direct continuation of the categorial semantics for standard RDB data integration provided in my previous book, Big Data Integration [21].

We consider that a *mapping* between two database schemas $\mathcal{A} = (S_A, \Sigma_A)$ and $\mathcal{B} = (S_B, \Sigma_B)$ is expressed by an union of "conjunctive queries with the same head." Such mappings are called "view-based mappings," defined by a set of FOL sentences $\{\forall \mathbf{x}_i(q_{Ai}(\mathbf{x}_i) \Rightarrow q_{Bi}(\mathbf{y}_i)) \mid \text{with } \mathbf{y}_i \subseteq \mathbf{x}_i, 1 \leq i \leq n\}$, where $\Rightarrow$ is the logical implication between these conjunctive queries $q_{Ai}(\mathbf{x}_i)$ and $q_{Bi}(\mathbf{x}_i)$, over the databases $\mathcal{A}$ and $\mathcal{B}$, respectively.

Schema mappings are often specified by the source-to-target tuple-generating dependencies (tgds), used to formalize a data exchange [143], and in the data integration scenarios under a name "GLAV assertions" [111, 142] as provided in detail with Definition 134 in Section A.6.3 in the Appendix. We use for the integrity constraints Σ_A of a database schema $\mathcal{A}$ both tgds and egds, while for the interschema mappings, between a schema $\mathcal{A} = (S_A, \Sigma_A)$ and a schema $\mathcal{B} = (S_B, \Sigma_B)$, only the tgds $\forall \mathbf{x}(q_A(\mathbf{x}) \Rightarrow q_B(\mathbf{x}))$. The so-called second-order tgds (SO tgds) has been introduced in [179] as follows.

Definition 49 ([179]). Let $\mathcal{A}$ be a source schema and $\mathcal{B}$ a target schema. A second-order tuple-generating dependency (SO tgd) is a formula of the form
$\exists\mathbf{f}((\forall\mathbf{x}_1(\phi_1 \Rightarrow \psi_1)) \wedge \ldots \wedge (\forall\mathbf{x}_n(\phi_n \Rightarrow \psi_n)))$, where:

1. Each member of the tuple $\mathbf{f}$ is a functional symbol. Each variable in $\mathbf{x}_i$ appears in some atomic formula of ϕ_i.
2. Each ϕ_i is a conjunction of:
   – atomic formulae of the form $r_A(y_1,\ldots,y_k)$, where $r_A \in S_A$ is a k-ary relational symbol of schema $\mathcal{A}$ and $y_1,\ldots,y_k$ are variables in $\mathbf{x}_i$, not necessarily distinct;
   – the formulae with conjunction and negation connectives and with built-in predicate's atoms of the form $t \odot t'$, $\odot \in \{\doteq,<,>,\ldots\}$, where t and t' are the terms based on $\mathbf{x}_i$, $\mathbf{f}$ and constants.
3. Each ψ_i is a conjunction of atomic formulae $r_B(t_1,\ldots,t_m)$ where $r_B \in S_B$ is an m-ary relational symbol of schema $\mathcal{B}$ and $t_1,\ldots,t_m$ are terms based on $\mathbf{x}_i$, $\mathbf{f}$ and constants.

Notice that each constant a in an atom on the left-hand side of implications must be substituted by new fresh variable y_i and by adding a conjunct $(y_i = a)$ in the left-hand side of this implication, so that such atoms will have only the variables (condition 2 above). For the empty set of tgds, we will use the SOtgd tautology $r_\emptyset \Rightarrow r_\emptyset$. The forth condition is a "safety" condition, analogous to that made for (first-order) tgds. It is easy to see that every tgd is equivalent to one SOtgd without equalities. For example, let σ be the tgd (consider, e. g., the mapping ρ_V in Proposition 25 in Section 4.3.1 for the data integration system of the IRDB with multivalued attributes)

$$\forall x_1 \ldots \forall x_m(\phi_A(x_1,\ldots,x_m) \Rightarrow \exists y_1 \ldots \exists y_n \psi_B(x_1,\ldots,x_m,y_1,\ldots,y_n)).$$

It is logically equivalent to the following SOtgd without equalities, which is obtained by Skolemizing existential quantifiers in σ:

$$\begin{aligned}&\exists f_1 \ldots \exists f_n(\forall x_1 \ldots \forall x_m(\phi_A(x_1,\ldots,x_m)\\&\quad \Rightarrow \psi_B(x_1,\ldots,x_m,f_1(x_1,\ldots,x_m),\ldots,f_n(x_1,\ldots,x_m)))).\end{aligned}$$

Given a finite set S of tgds of an interschema mapping (as, e. g., $\mathcal{M}$ and $\mathcal{M}^{\mathrm{OP}}$ in Proposition 25), we can find a *single* SOtgd that is equivalent to S by taking, for each tgd σ in S, a conjunct of the SOtgd to capture σ as described above (we use disjoint sets of function symbols in each conjunct, as before). Thus, the mapping ρ_V here is transformed into an equivalent SOtgd

$$\exists f_1(\forall x_1,\ldots,\forall x_4((r_V(x_1,x_2,x_3,x_4) \wedge x_3 \text{ MULTIVALUED}) \Rightarrow r_{\mathrm{MA}}(x_4,f_1(x_4)))) \tag{4.11}$$

The integrity constraints of a schema $\mathcal{A}$ are transformed into schema mappings from $\mathcal{A}$ into the particular "FOL-identity" schema $\mathcal{A}_\top = (\{r_\top\},\emptyset)$ with empty set of integrity constraints (introduced in [21], Section 4.1.1 for categorial semantics of database schemas) where its binary built-in relation $r_\top$ corresponds to FOL identity (so that the ground atom $r_\top(a,a)$ is true for each $a \in \mathcal{D}$ while, e. g., the ground atom $r_\top(0,1)$ *is false*), based on the two following lemmas [21]:

Lemma 2. *Any normalized tgd constraint of a schema $\mathcal{A} = (S_A, \Sigma_A)$, $\forall \mathbf{x}(\phi_A(\mathbf{x}) \Rightarrow r(\mathbf{t})) \in \Sigma_A^{egd} \subseteq \Sigma_A$, where $\mathbf{t}$ is a tuple of terms with variables in $\mathbf{x}$ and $r \in S_A$, is logically equivalent to the FOL sentence $\forall \mathbf{x}((\phi_A(\mathbf{x}) \wedge \neg r(\mathbf{t})) \Rightarrow r_\top(0,1))$.*

Lemma 3. *Any egd $\forall \mathbf{x}(\phi_A(\mathbf{x}) \Rightarrow (\mathbf{y} \doteq \mathbf{z})) \in \Sigma_A^{egd} \subseteq \Sigma_A$ of a given schema database $\mathcal{A} = (S_A, \Sigma_A)$ where $\mathbf{y} = \langle x_{j_1}, \ldots, x_{j_k} \rangle \subseteq \mathbf{x}$ and $\mathbf{z} = \langle x_{l_1}, \ldots, x_{l_k} \rangle \subseteq \mathbf{x}$ such that $j_i \neq l_i$ for $1 \leq i \leq k$, is logically equivalent to the FOL formula:*

$$\forall \mathbf{x}((\phi_A(\mathbf{x}) \wedge (\mathbf{y} \neq \mathbf{z})) \Rightarrow r_\top(0,1)),$$

where $\mathbf{y} \neq \mathbf{z}$ is an abbreviation for the formula $(x_{j_1} \neq x_{l_1}) \vee \ldots \vee (x_{j_k} \neq x_{l_k})$.

Consequently, for the set of integrity constraints $\Sigma_A = \Sigma_A^{tgd} \bigcup \Sigma_A^{egd}$, of a RDB schema $\mathcal{A} = (S_A, \Sigma_A)$, we construct, by conjunction the SOtgd in Σ_A denoted by a formula Φ, and the schema "truth mapping" $\mathcal{T}_{AA_\top} = \{\Phi\} : \mathcal{A} \to \mathcal{A}_\top$, as explained in [21], Section 4.1.1, Proposition 15. We recall that the "truth mapping" does not transfer any tuple of data from the source to the target object.

Introduction to schema mappings, sketches and functorial semantics into **DB** category, based on R-algebras, is provided in Section A.6.3 in the Appendix. Formal definition of an R-algebra α as a mapping interpretation of a schema mapping $\mathcal{M}_{AB} : \mathcal{A} \to \mathcal{B}$ is given in [21] (Section 2.4.1, Definition 11) as follows.

Definition 50. Let $\phi_{Ai}(\mathbf{x}) \Rightarrow r_B(\mathbf{t})$ be an implication χ in a normalized SOtgd $\exists \mathbf{f}(\Psi)$ (where Ψ is a FOL formula) of the mapping $\mathcal{M}_{AB}$, $\mathbf{t}$ be a tuple of terms with variables in $\mathbf{x} = (x_1, \ldots, x_m)$, and $q_i \in \text{MakeOperads}(\mathcal{M}_{AB})$ be the operad's operation of this implication obtained by MakeOperads algorithm, equal to the expression $(e \Rightarrow (\_)(\mathbf{t})) \in O(r_1, \ldots, r_k, r_B)$, where $q_i = v_i \cdot q_{A,i}$ with $q_{A,i} \in O(r_1, \ldots, r_k, r_q)$ and $v_i \in O(r_q, r_B)$ such that for a new relational symbol r_q, $\text{ar}(r_q) = \text{ar}(r_B) \geq 1$.

Let S be an empty set and $e[(\_)_n / r_n]_{1 \leq n \leq k}$ be the formula obtained from expression e where each place-symbol $(\_)_n$ is substituted by relational symbol r_n for $1 \leq n \leq k$. Then do the following as far as it is possible: For each two relational symbols r_j, r_n in the formula $e[(\_)_n / r_n]_{1 \leq n \leq k}$ such that j_h-th *free variable* (which is not an argument of a functional symbol) in the atom $r_j(\mathbf{t}_j)$ is equal to n_h-th free variable in the atom $r_n(\mathbf{t}_n)$ (both atoms in $e[(\_)_n / r_n]_{1 \leq n \leq k}$), we insert the set $\{(j_h, j), (n_h, n)\}$ as one element of S. At the end, S is the set of sets that contain the pairs of mutually equal free variables.

An R-algebra α is a *mapping interpretation* of $\mathcal{M}_{AB} : \mathcal{A} \to \mathcal{B}$ if it is an extension of a Tarski's interpretation I_T, of all predicate and functional symbols in FOL formula Ψ, with I_T^* being its extension to all formulae, and if for each $q_i \in \text{MakeOperads}(\mathcal{M}_{AB})$ it satisfies the following:

1. For each relational symbol, $r_i \neq r_\emptyset$ in $\mathcal{A}$ or $\mathcal{B}$, $\alpha(r_i) = I_T(r_i)$.
2. We obtain a function $f = \alpha(q_{A,i}) : R_1 \times \cdots \times R_k \to \alpha(r_q)$,

where for each $1 \leq i \leq k$, $R_i = \mathcal{D}^{ar(r_i)} \backslash \alpha(r_i)$ if the place symbol $(\_)_i \in q_i$ is preceded by negation operator $\neg$; $\alpha(r_i)$ otherwise, such that for every $\mathbf{d}_i \in R_i$:

$$f(\mathbf{d}_1, \ldots, \mathbf{d}_k) = g^*(\mathbf{t}) = (g^*(t_1), \ldots, g^*(t_{ar(r_B)}))$$

if $\bigwedge\{\pi_{j_h}(\mathbf{d}_j) = \pi_{n_h}(\mathbf{d}_n) \mid \{(j_h, j), (n_h, n)\} \in S\}$ is true and the assignment g satisfies the formula $e[(\_)_n/r_n]_{1\leq n\leq k}$; $\langle\,\rangle$ (empty tuple) otherwise, where the assignment $g : \{x_1, \ldots, x_m\} \to \mathcal{D}$ is defined by the tuple of values $(g(x_1), \ldots, g(x_m)) = \mathrm{Cmp}(S, (\mathbf{d}_1, \ldots, \mathbf{d}_k))$, and its extension g^* to all terms such that for any term $f_i(t_1, \ldots, t_n)$:

$$g^*(f_i(t_1, \ldots, t_n)) = I_T(f_i)(g^*(t_1), \ldots, g^*(t_n)) \quad \text{if } n \geq 1;\ I_T(f_i) \text{ otherwise.}$$

The algorithm Cmp (compacting the list of tuples by eliminating the duplicates defined in S) is defined as follows:

Input: a set S of joined (equal) variables defined above, and a list of tuples $(\mathbf{d}_1, \ldots, \mathbf{d}_k)$.

Initialize $\mathbf{d}$ to $\mathbf{d}_1$. Repeat consecutively the following, for $j = 2, \ldots, k$:

Let $\mathbf{d}_j$ by a tuple of values $(v_1, \ldots, v_{j_n})$, then for $i = 1, \ldots, j_n$ repeat consecutively the following:

$\mathbf{d} = \mathbf{d}\&v_i$ if there does not exist and element $\{(j_h, j), (n_h, n)\}$ in S such that $j \leq n$; $\mathbf{d}$, otherwise.

(The operation of concatenation '&' appends the value v_i at the end of tuple $\mathbf{d}$)

Output: The tuple $\mathrm{Cmp}(S, (\mathbf{d}_1, \ldots, \mathbf{d}_k)) = \mathbf{d}$.

3. $\alpha(r_q)$ is equal to the image of the function f in point 2 above.
4. The function $h = \alpha(v_i) : \alpha(r_q) \to \alpha(r_B)$ such that for each $\mathbf{b} \in \alpha(r_q)$,

$$h(\mathbf{b}) = \mathbf{b} \quad \text{if } \mathbf{b} \in \alpha(r_B);\ \text{empty tuple } \langle\,\rangle \text{ otherwise.}$$

Note that the formulae $\phi_{Ai}(\mathbf{x})$ and expression $e[(\_)_n/r_n]_{1\leq n\leq k}$ are logically equivalent, with the only difference that the atoms with characteristic functions $f_r(\mathbf{t}) = 1$ in the first formula are substituted by the atoms $r(\mathbf{t})$, based on the fact that the assignment g satisfies $r(\mathbf{t})$ iff $g^*(f_r(\mathbf{t})) = f_r(g^*(\mathbf{t})) = 1$, where $f_r : \mathcal{D}^{ar(r)} \to \{0, 1\}$ is the characteristic function of relation $\alpha(r)$ such that for each tuple $\mathbf{c} \in \mathcal{D}^{ar(r)}$, $f_r(\mathbf{c}) = 1$ if $\mathbf{c} \in \alpha(r)$; 0 otherwise.

Example 24. Let us show how we construct the set S and the compacting of tuples given by Definition 50 above.

Let us consider an operad $q_i \in \mathrm{MakeOperads}(\mathcal{M}_{AB})$, obtained from a normalized implication $\phi_{Ai}(\mathbf{x}) \Rightarrow r_B(\mathbf{t})$ in $\mathcal{M}_{AB}$, $((y = f_1(x, z)) \wedge r_1(x, y, z) \wedge r_2(v, x, w) \wedge (f_{r_3}(y, z, w', w) = 1)) \Rightarrow r_B(x, z, w, f_2(v, z))$, so that q_i is equal to the expression $(e \Rightarrow$

$(\_)(\mathbf{t})) \in O(r_1, r_2, r_3, r_B)$, where $\mathbf{x} = (x, y, z, v, w, w')$ (the ordering of variables in the atoms (with database relational symbols) from left to right), $\mathbf{t} = (x, z, w, f_2(v, z))$, and the expression e equal to $(y \doteq f_1(x, z)) \wedge (\_)_1(\mathbf{t}_1) \wedge (\_)_2(\mathbf{t}_2) \wedge (\_)_3(\mathbf{t}_3)$, with $\mathbf{t}_1 = (x, y, z)$, $\mathbf{t}_2 = (v, x, w)$ and $\mathbf{t}_3 = (y, z, w', w)$. Consequently, we obtain

$$S = \{\{(1,1),(2,2)\},\{(2,1),(1,3)\},\{(3,1),(2,3)\},\{(3,2),(4,3)\}\},$$

that are the positions of duplicates (or joined variables) of x, y, z and w, respectively.

Thus, for given tuples $\mathbf{d}_1 = (a_1, a_2, a_3) \in \alpha(r_1)$, $\mathbf{d}_2 = (b_1, b_2, b_3) \in \alpha(r_2)$ and $\mathbf{d}_3 = (c_1, c_2, c_3, c_4) \in \alpha(r_3)$, the statement $\bigwedge\{\pi_{j_h}(\mathbf{d}_j) = \pi_{n_h}(\mathbf{d}_n) \mid \{(j_h, j), (n_h, n)\} \subset S\}$ is equal to $(\pi_1(\mathbf{d}_1) = \pi_2(\mathbf{d}_2)) \wedge (\pi_2(\mathbf{d}_1) = \pi_1(\mathbf{d}_3)) \wedge (\pi_3(\mathbf{d}_1) = \pi_2(\mathbf{d}_3)) \wedge (\pi_3(\mathbf{d}_2) = \pi_4(\mathbf{d}_3))$, which is true when $a_1 = b_2$, $a_2 = c_1$, $a_3 = c_2$ and $b_3 = c_4$.

The compacting of these tuples is equal to

$$\mathbf{d} = \mathrm{Cmp}(S, (\mathbf{d}_1, \mathbf{d}_2, \mathbf{d}_3)) = (a_1, a_2, a_3, b_1, b_3, c_3),$$

with the assignment to variables $[x/a_1]$, $[y/a_2]$, $[z/a_3]$, $[v, b_1]$, $[w/b_3]$ and $[w'/c_3]$.

That is, $\mathbf{d} = \mathbf{x}[x/a_1, y/a_2, z/a_3, v/b_1, w/b_3, w'/c_3]$ is obtained by this assignment g to the tuple of variables $\mathbf{x}$, so that the sentence $e[(\_)_n/r_n]_{1 \le n \le k}/g$ is well-defined and equal to:

$$(a_2 = I_T(f_1)(a_1, a_3)) \wedge r_1(a_1, a_2, a_3) \wedge r_2(b_1, a_1, b_3) \wedge r_3(a_2, a_3, c_3, b_3), \quad \text{that is to}$$
$$(a_2 = I_T(f_1)(a_1, a_3)) \wedge r_1(\mathbf{d}_1) \wedge r_2(\mathbf{d}_2) \wedge r_3(\mathbf{d}_3),$$

and if this formula is satisfied by such an assignment g, i. e.,

$$I_T^*(e[(\_)_n/r_n]_{1 \le n \le k}/g) = 1, \quad \text{then}$$
$$f((\mathbf{d}_1, \mathbf{d}_2, \mathbf{d}_3)) = g^*(\mathbf{t}) = (g(x), g(z), g(w), g^*(f_2(v, z))) = (a_1, a_3, b_3, I_T(f_2)(b_1, a_3)),$$

for a given Tarski's interpretation I_T, where I_T^* is the extension of I_T to all FOL formulae.

If $\mathcal{M}_{AB}$ is satisfied by the mapping interpretation α, this value of $f((\mathbf{d}_1, \mathbf{d}_2, \mathbf{d}_3))$ corresponds to the truth of the normalized implication in the SOtgd of $\mathcal{M}_{AB}$, $\phi_{Ai}(\mathbf{x}) \Rightarrow r_B(\mathbf{t})$ for the assignment g derived by substitution $[\mathbf{x}/\mathbf{d}]$, when $\phi_{Ai}(\mathbf{x})/g$ is true. Hence, $r_B(\mathbf{t})/g$ is equal to $r_B(a_1, a_3, b_3, I_T(f_2)(b_1, a_3))$, i. e., to $r_B(f((\mathbf{d}_1, \mathbf{d}_2, \mathbf{d}_3)))$ and has to be true as well (i. e., $I_T^*(r_B(f((\mathbf{d}_1, \mathbf{d}_2, \mathbf{d}_3)))) = 1$ or, equivalently, $f((\mathbf{d}_1, \mathbf{d}_2, \mathbf{d}_3)) \in \alpha(r_B) = I_T(r_B)$).

Consequently, if $\mathcal{M}_{AB}$ is satisfied by a mapping interpretation α (and hence $\alpha(v_i)$ is an injection function with $\alpha(r_q) \subseteq \alpha(r_B)$) then $f((\mathbf{d}_1, \mathbf{d}_2, \mathbf{d}_3)) \in \|r_B\|$, so that the function $f = \alpha(q_{A,i})$ represents the transferring of the tuples in relations of the source instance databases into the target instance database $B = \alpha^*(\mathcal{B})$, according to the SOtgd Φ of the mapping $\mathcal{M}_{AB} = \{\Phi\} : \mathcal{A} \to \mathcal{B}$.

In this way, for a given R-algebra α which satisfies the conditions for the mapping interpretations in Definition 50, we translate a logical representation of database mappings, based on SOtgds, into an algebraic representation based on relations of the instance databases and the functions obtained from mapping operads.

It is easy to verify that for a *query mapping* $\phi_{Ai}(\mathbf{x}) \Rightarrow r_B(\mathbf{t})$, a mapping interpretation α is an R-algebra such that the relation $\alpha(r_q)$ is just equal to the image of the function $\alpha(q_{A,i})$. The mapping interpretation of v_i is the transfer of information of this computed query into the relation $\alpha(r_B)$ of the database $\mathcal{B}$.

When α satisfies this query mapping $\phi_{Ai}(\mathbf{x}) \Rightarrow r_B(\mathbf{t})$, then $\alpha(r_q) \subseteq \alpha(r_B)$ and, consequently, the function $\alpha(v_i)$ is an injection, i. e., the *inclusion* of $\alpha(r_q)$ into $\alpha(r_B)$. Moreover, each R-algebra α of a given set of mapping operads between a source schema $\mathcal{A}$ and target schema $\mathcal{B}$ determines a particular information flux from the source into the target schema.

Definition 51 (Information flux). Let α be a mapping interpretation (an R-algebra in Definition 50) of a given set $\mathbf{M}_{AB} = \{q_1, \dots, q_n, 1_{r_\emptyset}\} = \text{MakeOperads}(\mathcal{M}_{AB})$ of mapping operads, obtained from an *atomic* mapping $\mathcal{M}_{AB} : \mathcal{A} \to \mathcal{B}$, and $A = \alpha^*(S_A)$ be an instance of the schema $\mathcal{A} = (S_A, \Sigma_A)$ that satisfies all constraints in Σ_A.

For each operation $q_i \in \mathbf{M}_{AB}$, $q_i = (e \Rightarrow (\_)(\mathbf{t}_i)) \in O(r_{i,1}, \dots, r_{i,k}, r_i')$, let $\mathbf{x}_i$ be its tuple of variables which appear at least one time free (not as an argument of a function) in $\mathbf{t}_i$ and appear as variables in the atoms of relational symbol of the schema $\mathcal{A}$ in the formula $e[(\_)_j/r_{i,j}]_{1\le j\le k}$. Then we define:

(1) $\text{Var}(\mathbf{M}_{AB}) = \bigcup_{1\le i\le n}\{\{x\} \mid x \in \mathbf{x}_i\}$.

We define the kernel of the information flux of $\mathbf{M}_{AB}$, for a given mapping interpretation α, by (we denote the image of a function f by "im(f)")

(2) $\Delta(\alpha, \mathbf{M}_{AB}) = \{\pi_{\mathbf{x}_i}(\text{im}(\alpha(q_i))) \mid q_i \in \mathbf{M}_{AB}$, and $\mathbf{x}_i$ is not empty $\} \bigcup \perp^0$, if $\text{Var}(\mathbf{M}_{AB}) \neq \emptyset$; $\perp^0$ otherwise.

We define the information flux from its kernel by

$$\text{Flux}(\alpha, \mathbf{M}_{AB}) = T(\Delta(\alpha, \mathbf{M}_{AB})) \tag{4.12}$$

The flux of composition of $\mathbf{M}_{AB}$ and $\mathbf{M}_{BC}$ is defined by

$$\text{Flux}(\alpha, \mathbf{M}_{BC} \circ \mathbf{M}_{AB}) = \text{Flux}(\alpha, \mathbf{M}_{AB}) \bigcap \text{Flux}(\alpha, \mathbf{M}_{BC}) \tag{4.13}$$

We say that an information flux is *empty* if it is equal to $\perp^0 = \{\perp\}$ (and hence it is not the empty set), analogously as for an empty instance database.

The information flux of the SOtgd of the mapping $\mathcal{M}_{AB}$ for the instance-level mapping $f = \alpha^*(\mathbf{M}_{AB}) : A \to \alpha^*(\mathcal{B})$, composed of the set of functions $f = \alpha^*(\mathbf{M}_{AB}) = \{\alpha(q_1), \dots, \alpha(q_n), q_\perp\}$, is denoted by $\widetilde{f}$. Notice that $\perp \in \widetilde{f}$, and hence the information flux $\widetilde{f}$ is a instance database as well.

From this definition, each instance mapping is a set of functions whose information flux is the intersection of the information fluxes of all atomic instance mappings that compose this composed instance mapping. These basic properties of the instance mappings are used in order to define the database **DB** category where the instance mappings are the morphisms (i. e., the arrows) of this category, while the instance databases (each instance database is a set of relations of a schema also with the empty relation $\perp$) are its objects. So, we obtain the fundamental property in **DB**.

Equality of morphisms
Any two arrows $f, g : A \to B$ where A and B are the instance databases (the simple sets of the relations) in **DB** are *equal* if $\widetilde{f} = \widetilde{g}$, i. e., if they have the same information fluxes. □

4.4.1 Functorial semantics for IRDBs with multivalued attributes

In what follows, we use the algorithm MakeOperads in [21] in order to transform logical schema mappings $\mathcal{M}_{AB} = \{\Phi\} : \mathcal{A} \to \mathcal{B}$ given by the SOtgds Φ in Definition 49 into the algebraic operads $\mathbf{M}_{AB} = \text{MakeOperad}(\mathcal{M}_{AB}) = \{v_1 \cdot q_{A,1}, \ldots, v_n \cdot q_{A,1}, 1_{r_\emptyset}\} : \mathcal{A} \to \mathcal{B}$. The basic idea of the operad's operations $v_i \in O(r', r_B)$ and $q_{A,i} \in O(r_1, \ldots, r_k, r')$, where $r_i, 1 \leq i \leq k$ are relational symbols of the source schema $\mathcal{A} = (S_A, \Sigma_A)$ and r_B is a relational symbol of the target schema $\mathcal{B}$, and r' has the same type as r_B, is to formalize algebraically a mapping from the set of source relations r_i into a target relation r_B. In Section A.6.3 in the Appendix and Section 4.4, we provide an introduction to functorial semantics of schema mappings into the **DB** category, with a number of examples.

In our IRDB case, for the two logical schema mappings we obtain the following two algebraic operads:

$$\mathbf{T}_{AA_\top} = \text{MakeOperads}(\top_{AA_\top}) : \mathcal{A} \to \mathcal{A}_\top,$$
$$\mathbf{T}_{A_{\text{MA}}A_\top} = \text{MakeOperads}(\top_{A_{\text{MA}}A_\top}) : \mathcal{A}_{\text{MA}} \to \mathcal{A}_\top.$$

Remark. The schema $\mathcal{A}_{\text{MA}} = (\{r_{\text{MA}}\}, \emptyset)$ with an empty set of integrity constraints is transformed in "truth mapping" $\top_{A_{\text{MA}}A_\top} = \{\Psi\} : \mathcal{A}_{\text{MA}} \to \mathcal{A}_\top$, where Ψ is the SOtgd tautology formally denoted by implication between the nullary relation $r_\emptyset \Rightarrow r_\emptyset$ (because in the schema $\mathcal{A}_{\text{MA}}$ we have the empty set of tgds and egds). □

The R-algebra α is derived from a given Tarski's interpretation I_T of the given IRDB schema (in Section 4.4): α is equal to I_T for the relations of the data schemas, $\alpha(r_i) = I_T(r_i)$ is a relational table of the instance database $A = \alpha^*(\mathcal{A}) = \{\alpha(r_i) \mid r_i \in S_A\}$ (α^* denotes the extension of α to sets), and $\alpha(q_{A,i}) : \alpha(r_1) \times \cdots \times \alpha(r_k) \to \alpha(r')$ is a surjective function from the relations in the instance database A into its image (relation) $\alpha(r')$, with a function $\alpha(v_i) : \alpha(r') \to \alpha(r_B)$ into the relation of the instance database $B = \alpha^*(\mathcal{B})$.

From the fact that the operads can be composed, the composition of two schema mappings $\mathcal{M}_{AB}$ and $\mathcal{M}_{\text{BC}} : \mathcal{B} \to \mathcal{C}$ can be translated into the composition of operads, which is associative, so that they can be represented by the sketch categories derived from the graphs of the schema mappings. We have that for any R-algebra α, $\alpha(r_\emptyset) = \bot = \{\langle\rangle\}$ is the empty relation composed by only empty tuple $\langle\rangle \in D_{-1}$, and $1_{r_\emptyset}$ is the identity operads operation of the empty relation $r_\emptyset$, so that $q_\bot = \alpha(1_{r_\emptyset}) = \mathrm{id}_\bot : \bot \to \bot$ is the identity function. We denote by $\bot^0$ the database composed by only empty relations, i. e., $\bot^0 = \{\bot\}$.

Now we can define the mapping graph between database schemas of an IRDB.

Definition 52. For a GAV data integration system $\mathcal{I} = (\mathcal{A}, \mathcal{S}, \mathcal{M})$ of an IRDB $\mathcal{A}$, where $\mathcal{S} = (\{r_V\}, \emptyset)$, and its extended schema

$$\mathcal{A}^+ = \left(S_A \bigcup \{r_V, r_{\mathrm{MA}}\}, \Sigma_A \bigcup \mathcal{M} \bigcup \mathcal{M}^{\mathrm{OP}} \bigcup \{\rho_V\}\right)$$

in Proposition 25, we define its schema mapping noncommutative graph G,

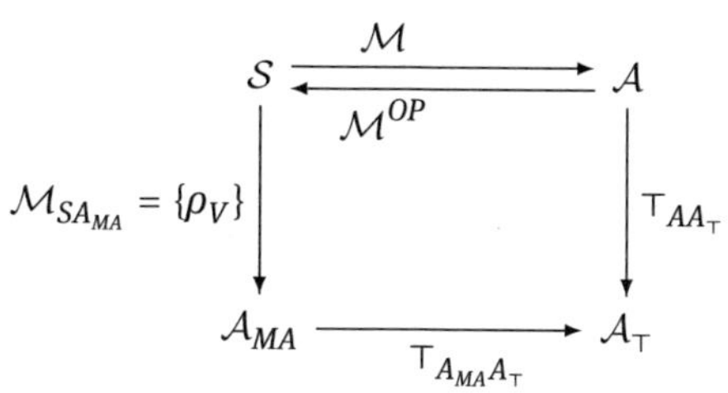

with the auxiliary schema $\mathcal{A}_{\mathrm{MA}} = (\{r_{\mathrm{MA}}\}, \emptyset)$ for the values of the multivalued attributes in schema $\mathcal{A}$.

Notice that all arrows of this graph are based on the SOtgds so that we can use the MakeOperads algorithm for all arrows of this mapping graph in order to transform the schema mapping graph G into the sketch category **Sch**(G) of the GAV data integration system $\mathcal{I}$ of a IRDB $\mathcal{A}$ above. Sketches are called graph-based logic and provide very clear and intuitive specifications of computational data and activities, as described in Section 4.4.

In what follows, we will use the database category **DB**, developed in [21] and introduce here in Section A.6 of the Appendix and in Section 4.4, with fundamental *idempotent power-view* operator $T : \mathbf{DB} \to \mathbf{DB}$, with the domain and codomain equal to the set of all instance databases such that for any instance database A, the object $\mathrm{TA} = T(A)$ denotes a database composed of the set of *all views* of A. For every object A, $A \subseteq \mathrm{TA}$ and $\mathrm{TA} = T(\mathrm{TA})$, i. e., each (element) view of database instance TA is also an element (view) of a database instance A.

In fact, we translate each database mapping logic theory based on SOtgds into an algebraic theory expressed by a sketch-category **Sch**(G) where all arrows are R-algebra terms. Then we describe R-algebraic structures using these sketch categories for theories and α functors into the base category **DB** in order to obtain the models of the database-mapping theories.

Notice that the mapping arrow $\mathcal{M}$ in a graph G is replaced by the morphism $\mathbf{M} = \text{MakeOperads}(\mathcal{M})$ in this sketch [180], while the nodes (objects) are eventually augmented by introducing another auxiliary schema $\mathcal{A}_\top$ as explained in the graph above for the integrity constraints of the nodes (RDB schemas). Each mapping interpretation α for the schema-mapping graph G is also a functor $\alpha^* : \mathbf{Sch}(G) \longrightarrow \mathbf{DB}$ such that it generates an instance database $A = \alpha^*(\mathcal{A})$ for each schema $\mathcal{A} \in \mathbf{Sch}(G)$, the unique instance of "truth" schema $A_T = \alpha^*(\mathcal{A}_\top) =_{\text{def}} \{\alpha(r_\top), \perp\}$, where $\alpha(r_\top) = R_=$ (binary identity built-in relation), and the following arrows in **DB**:

1. For each schema $\mathcal{A} \in \mathbf{Sch}(G)$, the identity morphism $\text{id}_A : A \to A$ and, eventually, its integrity-constraint morphism $f_{\Sigma_A} : A \to A_\top$ as specified in [21], Section 4.1.1, Proposition 15.
2. For each mapping-operad arrow $\mathbf{M}_{AB} : \mathcal{A} \to \mathcal{B}$ in $\mathbf{Sch}(G)$, we define the morphism $f = \alpha^*(\mathbf{M}_{AB}) : A \to B$, where $A = \alpha^*(\mathcal{A})$ and $B = \alpha^*(\mathcal{B})$.

Consequently, the set $\text{Int}(G)$ of all mapping interpretations of a given mapping system graph G is a subset of all functors from $\mathbf{Sch}(G)$ into **DB**, i. e., $\text{Int}(G) \subseteq \mathbf{DB}^{\mathbf{Sch}(G)}$, such that for each functor $\alpha^* \in \text{Int}(G)$ of an IRDB we obtain the functorial mapping (where $\alpha^*(\mathcal{S}) = \{\alpha(r_V), \perp\} = \{\|r_V\|, \perp\}$, $\alpha^*(\mathcal{A}_{\text{MA}}) = \{\alpha(r_{\text{MA}}), \perp\} = \{\|r_{\text{MA}}\|, \perp\}$, $f_M = \alpha^*(\mathbf{M})$ and $f_M^{\text{OP}} = \alpha^*(\mathbf{M}^{\text{OP}})$):

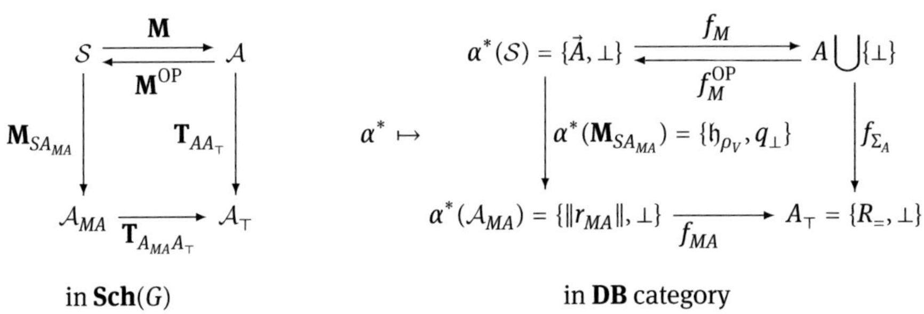

with $q_\perp : \perp \to \perp$ and the function $\mathfrak{h}_{\rho_V} : \vec{A} \to \|r_{\text{MA}}\|$, such that for any tuple

$$\mathbf{d} = \langle nr(r_k), \text{ID}, a_i, d \rangle \in \vec{A} = \|r_V\|$$

where a_i is multivalued attribute of relation r_k, we obtain that $(\pi_2 \cdot \mathfrak{h}_{\rho_V})(\mathbf{d}) = \pi_2(\mathfrak{h}_{\rho_V}(\mathbf{d}))$ is one of the values of this attribute a_i in the tuple ID of the relation r_k. The morphisms f_{Σ_A} and f_{MA} are equivalent to the empty morphism $\perp^1 =_{\text{def}} \{q_\perp\}$.

It was demonstrated in [21], Proposition 17, Section 4.1.3, that α^* is a *model* of the sketch $\mathbf{Sch}(G)$ iff for each its arrow $\mathbf{M}_{AB} = \text{MakeOperad}(\mathcal{M}_{AB}) = \{v_1 \cdot q_{A,1}, \ldots, v_n \cdot q_{A,n}, 1_{r_\emptyset}\} : \mathcal{A} \to \mathcal{B}$ we have that all $\alpha(v_i), 1 \le i \le n$ are *injective functions*. Thus, in what follows, we will consider only the subset $\text{Mod}(\mathbf{Sch}(G)) \subseteq \text{Int}(G)$ of the models of the IRDBs, i. e., $\alpha^* \in \text{Mod}(\mathbf{Sch}(G))$.

The GAV categorial semantics for standard RDBs, for the schema mapping arrows $\mathbf{M}, \mathbf{M}^{OP}$ and $\mathbf{T}_{AA_T}$, are presented in detail in [21], Section 4.2.2, and here we demonstrate the following property.

Theorem 6. *For any $\alpha \in \text{Int}(G)$ of the data integration graph G and corresponding sketch $\mathbf{Sch}(G)$, such that $\alpha(\mathcal{S}) =\perp^0 \bigcup_{r_k \in S_A, \mathbf{d} \in \alpha(r_k)} \underline{\text{PARSE}}(r_k, \mathbf{d})$ and $A = \alpha^*(\mathcal{A})$, the morphisms $f_M = \alpha^*(\mathbf{M})$ and $f_M^{OP} = \alpha^*(\mathbf{M}^{OP})$ are satisfied and $f_M \circ f_M^{OP} = \text{id}_A$.*

Conversely, if $A = \alpha^*(\mathcal{A})$ and $f_M = \alpha^*(\mathbf{M})$ and $f_M^{OP} = \alpha^*(\mathbf{M}^{OP})$ are satisfied morphisms then $f_M \circ f_M^{OP} = \text{id}_A$ and $\alpha(\mathcal{S}) =\perp^0 \bigcup_{r_k \in S_A, \mathbf{d} \in \alpha(r_k)} \underline{\text{PARSE}}(r_k, \mathbf{d})$.

Proof. We have the mapping $\mathcal{M}^{OP} = \{\forall x_{k,1}, \ldots, x_{k,\text{ar}(r_k)}((r_k(x_{k,1}, \ldots, x_{k,\text{ar}(r_k)}) \wedge x_{k,i} \text{ NOT NULL}) \Rightarrow r_V(nr(r_k), \text{Hash}(x_{k,1}, \ldots, x_{k,\text{ar}(r_k)}), nr_{r_k}(i), x_{k,i})) \mid 1 \le i \le \text{ar}(r_k), r_k \in S_A, 1 \le k \le n\}$. Thus,

$$\mathbf{M}^{OP} = \text{MakeOperads}(\mathcal{M}^{OP}) = \{1_{r_\emptyset}\} \bigcup \{q_{k,i} | r_k \in S_A \text{ and } 1 \le i \le \text{ar}(r_k)\} : \mathcal{A} \to \mathcal{S}$$

with $q_{k,i} = (((\_)(x_{k,1}, \ldots, x_{k,\text{ar}(r_k)}) \wedge x_{k,i} \text{ NOT NULL}) \Rightarrow (\_)(\mathbf{t}_{k,i})) \in O(r_k, r_V)$, where $\mathbf{t}_{k,i} = \{t_1, \ldots, t_4\}$ with the terms:

1. t_1 is the nullary built-in function, i. e., the fixed constant, which does not depend on Tarski's interpretations, equal to the relation table name r_k;
2. $t_2 = \text{Hash}(x_{k,1}, \ldots, x_{k,\text{ar}(r_k)})$ where Hash is a built in-function equal for every Tarski's interpretation;
3. t_3 is the nullary built-in function, i. e., the fixed constant, which does not depend on Tarski's interpretations, equal to the i-th column name of the relational table r_k;
4. t_4 is the variable $x_{k,i}$.

Consequently, we obtain the function $\alpha(q_{k,i}) : \alpha(r_k) \to \alpha(r_V) = \vec{A}$, such that for its image $\text{im}(\alpha(q_{k,i}))$ we obtain from the parsing that $\pi_4(\text{im}(\alpha(q_{k,i}))) = \pi_i(\alpha(r_k))$.

Thus, from Definition 13, Section 2.4.3 in [21], the kernel of the information flux of $\mathbf{M}^{OP}$, for a given mapping interpretation α, is equal to

$$\begin{aligned}\triangle(\alpha, \mathbf{M}^{OP}) &= \{\pi_4(\text{im}(\alpha(q_{k,i}))) \mid q_{k,i} \in \mathbf{M}^{OP}\} \bigcup \perp^0 \\ &= \{\pi_i(\alpha(r_k)) \mid q_{k,i} \in \mathbf{M}^{OP}\} \bigcup \perp^0 \\ &= \{\pi_i(\alpha(r_k)) \mid r_k \in S_A, 1 \le i \le \text{ar}(r_k)\} \bigcup \perp^0.\end{aligned}$$

Let us show that for the power-view operator T (which is a monotonic closure operator [21] with $TT = T$),

$$T\Big(\{\pi_i(\alpha(r_k)) \mid r_k \in S_A, 1 \le i \le \text{ar}(r_k)\} \bigcup \perp^0\Big) = T\Big(\{\alpha(r_k) \mid r_k \in S_A\} \bigcup \perp^0\Big):$$

(a) From monotonicity, $T(\{\pi_i(\alpha(r_k)) \mid r_k \in S_A, 1 \le i \le \text{ar}(r_k)\} \bigcup \perp^0) \subseteq T(\{\alpha(r_k) \mid r_k \in S_A, 1 \le i \le \text{ar}(r_k)\} \bigcup \perp^0) = T(\{\alpha(r_k) \mid r_k \in S_A\} \bigcup \perp^0) = T(A)$.

(b) We have that $\alpha(r_k) \subseteq \pi_1(\alpha(r_k)) \times \cdots \times \pi_{\mathrm{ar}(r_k)}(\alpha(r_k)) \in T(\{\pi_i(\alpha(r_k)) \mid r_k \in S_A, 1 \le i \le \mathrm{ar}(r_k)\} \bigcup \bot^0)$. Thus, $A = \{\alpha(r_k) \mid r_k \in S_A\} \bigcup \bot^0 \subseteq T(\{\pi_i(\alpha(r_k)) \mid r_k \in S_A, 1 \le i \le \mathrm{ar}(r_k)\} \bigcup \bot^0)$ and, by applying T to left and right side, we obtain from the monotonic and idempotent property of T,

$$\begin{aligned} T(A) &= T\Big(\{\alpha(r_k) \mid r_k \in S_A\} \bigcup \bot^0\Big) \\ &\subseteq T\Big(T\Big(\{\pi_i(\alpha(r_k)) \mid r_k \in S_A, 1 \le i \le \mathrm{ar}(r_k)\} \bigcup \bot^0\Big)\Big) \\ &= T\Big(\{\pi_i(\alpha(r_k)) \mid r_k \in S_A, 1 \le i \le \mathrm{ar}(r_k)\} \bigcup \bot^0\Big). \end{aligned}$$

Consequently, from (a) and (b) we obtain the equivalency above. Thus, the information flux of the morphisms $f_M^{\mathrm{OP}} = \alpha^*(\mathbf{M}^{\mathrm{OP}})$ is equal to

$$\begin{aligned} \widetilde{f_M^{\mathrm{OP}}} &= T(\triangle(\alpha, \mathbf{M}^{\mathrm{OP}})) = T\Big(\{\pi_i(\alpha(r_k)) \mid r_k \in S_A, 1 \le i \le \mathrm{ar}(r_k)\} \bigcup \bot^0\Big) \\ &= T\Big(\{\alpha(r_k) \mid r_k \in S_A\} \bigcup \bot^0\Big) = T(A) = \widetilde{\mathrm{id}_A}, \end{aligned}$$

where $\mathrm{id}_A = \{\mathrm{id}_{r_1}, \dots, \mathrm{id}_{r_n}, q_\bot\} : A \to A$ is the identity morphisms (with the identity functions $\mathrm{id}_{r_k} : \alpha(r_k) \to \alpha(r_k)$ for $k = 1, \dots, n$) of the object (database) A in **DB**.

Analogously, from Definition 44 for each $r_k \in S_A$ we have the tgd (4.3),

$$\begin{aligned} &\exists z, z_1, z_2(r_V(nr(r_k), z, z_1, z_2)) \wedge \forall y, x_1, \dots, x_{\mathrm{ar}(r_k)}(((r_V(nr(r_k), y, nr_{r_k}(1), x_1) \veebar x_{k,1}\ \mathrm{NULL}) \\ &\wedge \cdots \wedge (r_V(nr(r_k), y, nr_{r_k}(\mathrm{ar}(r_k)), x_{k,\mathrm{ar}(r_k)}) \veebar x_{\mathrm{ar}(r_k)}\ \mathrm{NULL})) \Rightarrow r_k(x_{k,1}, \dots, x_{k,\mathrm{ar}(r_k)})) \end{aligned}$$

in $\mathcal{M}$. Consequently, we obtain $\mathbf{M} = \{q_1, \dots, q_n, 1_{r_\emptyset}\} : \mathcal{S} \to A$, where $q_k = (e \Rightarrow (\_)(x_{k,1}, \dots, x_{k,\mathrm{ar}(r_k)})) \in O(r_V, r_k)$, such that for the mapping interpretation α we obtain the function $\alpha(q_k) : \vec{A} \to \alpha(r_k)$ (where $\vec{A} = \alpha(r_V)$), with $\mathrm{im}(\alpha(q_k)) = \alpha(r_k)$.

Consequently, the kernel of the information flux of **M**, for α, is equal to

$$\begin{aligned} \triangle(\alpha, \mathbf{M}) &= \{\pi_{[1,\dots,\mathrm{ar}(r_k)]}(\mathrm{im}(\alpha(q_k))) \mid q_k \in \mathbf{M}\} \bigcup \bot^0 \\ &= \{\mathrm{im}(\alpha(q_k)) \mid 1 \le k \le n\} \bigcup \bot^0 \{\alpha(r_k) \mid 1 \le k \le n\} \bigcup \bot^0 = A. \end{aligned}$$

Thus, the information flux of the morphism $f_M = \alpha^*(\mathbf{M})$ is equal to

$$\widetilde{f_M} = T(\triangle(\alpha, \mathbf{M})) = T(A).$$

Consequently, $\widetilde{f_M \circ f_M^{\mathrm{OP}}} = \widetilde{f_M} \bigcap \widetilde{f_M^{\mathrm{OP}}} = T(A) = \widetilde{\mathrm{id}_A}$, and hence

$$f_M \circ f_M^{\mathrm{OP}} = \mathrm{id}_A : A \to A. \qquad \square$$

This theorem is valid for *any* IRDB. In fact, if we have no the multivalued attributes then the graph G of the sketch $\mathbf{Sch}(G)$ is still composed by these two mappings **M** and $\mathbf{M}^{\mathrm{OP}}$ and the integrity-constraint mapping $\mathbf{T}_{AA_\top}$. The morphisms in DB category obtained from the "truth arrows," $f_{\mathrm{MA}} = \alpha^*(\mathbf{T}_{A_{\mathrm{MA}}A_\top})$ and $f_{\Sigma_A} = \alpha^*(\mathbf{T}_{AA_\top})$ have empty information flux, i. e., $\widetilde{f_{\mathrm{MA}}} = \widetilde{f_{\Sigma_A}} = \bot^0$, so the only interesting mapping, derived from the intensional nature of the IRDB and the multivalued attribute features, is $\mathbf{M}_{SA_{\mathrm{MA}}} : \mathcal{S} \to \mathcal{A}_{\mathrm{MA}}$:

$$\mathbf{M}_{SA_{\mathrm{MA}}} = \mathrm{MakeOperads}(\{\rho_V\}) = \{q_{\rho_V}, 1_{r_\emptyset}\} : \mathcal{S} \to \mathcal{A}_{\mathrm{MA}}, \quad q_{\rho_V} = v_1 \cdot q_{S,1}$$

with $v_1 = ((\_)(x,y) \Rightarrow (\_)(x,y)) \in O(r', r_{\mathrm{MA}})$ and $q_{S,1} = (((\_)(x_1,x_2,x_3,x_4) \wedge x_3$ MULTIVALUED$) \Rightarrow (_)(x_4, f_1(x_4))) \in O(r_v, r')$, so that $\alpha^*(\mathbf{M}_{SA_{\mathrm{MA}}}) = \{\mathfrak{h}_{\rho_V}, q_\bot\}$ with the composed function $\mathfrak{h}_{\rho_V} = \alpha(q_{\rho_V}) = \alpha(v_1 \cdot q_{S,1}) = \alpha(v_1)\cdot\alpha(q_{S,1})$, where $\alpha(v_1)$ is an injection and the function $\alpha(q_{S,1}) : \|r_V\| \to \alpha(r')$ is defined for each tuple $\mathbf{d} = (nr(r_k), \mathrm{ID}_t, a_i, d)$ by

$$\alpha(q_{S,1})(\mathbf{d}) = \begin{cases} (d, I_T(f_1)(d)), & \text{if } a_i \text{ is a multivalued attribute of } r_k \\ & \text{and } I_T(f_1)(d) \text{ is a value of this attribute} \\ \langle\,\rangle, & \text{empty tuple otherwise} \end{cases} \tag{4.14}$$

where α is derived from the Tarski's interpretation I_T, (with $\alpha(r_V) = I_T(r_V) = \|r_V\|$) and $I_T(f_1)$ is a Tarski's interpretation of the Skolem function f_1 introduced in SOtgd by elimination of an existentially quantified variable. Let $\alpha(r') = \mathrm{im}(\alpha(q_{S,1}))$ be the binary relation equal to image of the function $\alpha(q_{S,1})$. So, if this mapping is satisfied then the function $\alpha(v_1) : \alpha(r') \to \alpha(r_{\mathrm{MA}}) = \|r_{\mathrm{MA}}\|$ is an injection, and hence the function

$$\mathfrak{h}_{\rho_V} = \alpha(q_{\rho_V}) : \|r_V\| \to \|r_{\mathrm{MA}}\| \tag{4.15}$$

is equal to the function $\alpha(q_{S,1})$ defined above. In the next section, we will see how we can use the morphisms (4.15) above for the categorial semantics of the multivalued attributes in **DB** category, because tgd ρ_V is second-order logic where the function f is existentially quantified, and for a given (single) Tarski's interpretation I_T, $I_T(f_1)(d)$ gives only *one value* of this multivalued attribute, while we need to cover all values of this attribute. So this morphism in **DB** has to be a "powerset" mapping denominated "saturated" morphism as well, and we provide the new algorithm (nonpresent in [21]) for it in what follows.

Let $\phi_{Ai}(\mathbf{x}) \Rightarrow r_B(\mathbf{t})$, as in Definition 50 in Section 4.4, be an implication in a normalized SOtgd $\exists\mathbf{f}(\Psi)$ (where Ψ is a FOL formula) of the mapping $\mathcal{M}_{AB} : \mathcal{A} \to B$ with the sketch's arrow $\mathbf{M}_{AB} = \mathrm{MakeOperads}(\mathcal{M}_{AB}) = \{q_1, \dots, q_n, 1_{r_\emptyset}\}$, $\mathbf{t} = (t_1, \dots, t_{\mathrm{ar}(r_B)})$ be a tuple of terms with variables in $\mathbf{x} = (x_1, \dots, x_m)$, and $q_i \in \mathbf{M}_{AB}$ be the operad's operation of this implication, equal to the expression $(e \Rightarrow (\_)(\mathbf{t})) \in O(r_1, \dots, r_k, r_B)$, where $q_i = v_i \cdot q_{A,i}$ with $q_{A,i} = (e \Rightarrow (\_)(\mathbf{t})) \in O(r_1, \dots, r_k, r_q)$ and

$$v_i = ((\_)(y_1, \dots, y_{\mathrm{ar}(r_B)}) \Rightarrow (\_)(y_1, \dots, y_{\mathrm{ar}(r_B)})) \in O(r_q, r_B)$$

such that for a new relational symbol r_q, $ar(r_q) = ar(r_B) \geq 1$. It is important to underline that each term t_i is a simple variable, which appears in the tuple $\mathbf{x}$ (left-hand side of the implication) or the term $f_l(\mathbf{z})$ where the variables in the tuple $\mathbf{z}$ are a subset of the variables in $\mathbf{x}$.

Let dom, cod and graph be the operators, which for each function, return the domain, codomain and graph of this function, respectively, and $\mathcal{P}$ be the powerset operation.

For a given mapping interpretation α such that $A = \alpha^*(\mathcal{A})$ and $B = \alpha^*(\mathcal{B})$ are two models of the schemas $\mathcal{A}$ and $\mathcal{B}$, respectively, and α satisfies the schema mapping $\mathcal{M}_{AB} = \{\exists \mathbf{f}\Psi\}$, with the tuple of existentially quantified Skolem functions $\mathbf{f}$, the process of saturation of the morphism $\mathfrak{h} = \alpha^*(\mathbf{M}_{AB}) = \{\alpha(q_1), \dots, \alpha(q_n), q_\perp\}$ (such that a k-ary function $\alpha(q_i) : R_1 \times \cdots \times R_k \to \|r_B\|$ returns a single tuple (or empty tuple $\langle\,\rangle$) of $\|r_B\|$) is *relevant* only for the operads operations q_i, which have at least one functional symbol of $\mathbf{f}$ in the right-hand side of implication, as follows.

Saturation algorithm Sat($\alpha^*(\mathbf{M}_{AB})$)
Input: A mapping arrow $\mathbf{M}_{AB} = \{q_1, \dots, q_N, 1_{r_\emptyset}\} : \mathcal{A} \to \mathcal{B}$, and a mapping interpretation α such that $A = \alpha^*(\mathcal{A})$ and $B = \alpha^*(\mathcal{B})$ are two models of the schemas $\mathcal{A}$ and $\mathcal{B}$, respectively, and α obtained of a given Tarski's interpretation I_T, satisfies the schema mapping $\mathcal{M}_{AB} = \{\exists \mathbf{f}\Psi\}$, with the tuple of existentially quantified Skolem functions $\mathbf{f}$.
Output: Saturated morphism from A into B in the **DB** category.

1. Let $\mathfrak{h} = \alpha^*(\mathbf{M}_{AB}) = \{\mathfrak{h}_{1,0}, \dots, \mathfrak{h}_{N,0}, \mathrm{id}_\perp\}$, $\mathfrak{h}_{n,0} = \alpha(q_n)$, with $\mathrm{Sat}(\mathfrak{h}) = \mathfrak{h}$, $\mathrm{i} = 0$.
2. $i = i + 1$. If $i > N$, go to 8.
3. Let the mapping component $q_i \in \mathbf{M}_{AB}$ be the expression $(e \Rightarrow (\_)(\mathbf{t})) \in O(r_1, \dots, r_k, r_B)$, where $q_i = v_i \cdot q_{A,i}$ with $q_{A,i} = (e \Rightarrow (\_)(\mathbf{t})) \in O(r_1, \dots, r_k, r_q)$ and $v_i = ((\_)(y_1, \dots, y_{ar(r_B)}) \Rightarrow (\_)(y_1, \dots, y_{ar(r_B)})) \in O(r_q, r_B)$. Define the set $\mathcal{F} \subseteq \mathbf{f}$ of all functional symbols in the tuple of terms $\mathbf{t}$. If $\mathcal{F}$ is empty, then go to 2.
4. (*Fix the function of* q_i for given α) Let $\alpha(q_{A,i}) : R_1 \times \cdots \times R_k \to \alpha(r_q)$ be the function of this mapping interpretation provided in Definition 50 in Section 4.4 where $\alpha(r_q) \subseteq \|r_B\|$ is image of this function with relation $\|r_B\| = \alpha(r_B) \in B$, $\mathbf{x} = (x_1, \dots, x_m)$ be the tuple of all variables in the left-side expression e of the operad's operation q_i, and S be the set of sets that contain the pairs of mutually equal free variables in the formula $e[(\_)_n/r_n]_{1 \leq n \leq k}$ obtained from q_i (in Definition 50).
   Set $R_L = R_1 \times \cdots \times R_k$.
5. (*Expansion of* $q_{A,i}$) If R_L is empty, then go to 2.
   Take a tuple $(\mathbf{d}_1, \dots, \mathbf{d}_k) \in R_L \subseteq R_1 \times \cdots \times R_k$ and delete it from R_L. Then define the assignment $g : \overline{\mathbf{x}} \to \mathcal{D}$ such that $g(\mathbf{x}) = \mathrm{Cmp}(S, (\mathbf{d}_1, \dots, \mathbf{d}_k)$ (from Definition 50 in Section 4.4).
   If $\alpha(q_{A,i})((\mathbf{d}_1, \dots, \mathbf{d}_k)) = g^*(\mathbf{t}) = (g(t_1), \dots, g(t_{ar(r_B)})) \neq \langle\,\rangle$, then go to 6.
   Go to 5.
6. (*Definition of the extension corresponding to the tuple* $(\mathbf{d}_1, \dots, \mathbf{d}_k)$)

Let Z be the set of indexes of the terms in $\mathbf{t} = (t_1, \ldots, t_{ar(r_B)})$, which are simple variables and we denote by $nr_{r_B}(j)$ the name of the j-th column of the relation $r_B \in \mathcal{B}$. Then we define the relation:

$$R = \left\| \left(\text{SELECT } (*) \text{ FROM } \|r_B\| \text{ WHERE } \bigwedge_{j \in Z} (nr_{R_B}(j) = g(t_j)) \right) \right\|_{\#} \backslash \{g^*(\mathbf{t})\}.$$

7. If R is an empty relation, then go to 5.
   Take from R a tuple $\mathbf{b} = (b_1, \ldots, b_{ar(r_B)})$ and delete it from R. We define a new Tarski's interpretation I'_T, different from I_T only for the functional symbols $f_l \in \mathcal{F}$ of the j-th term $t_j = f_l(x_{j1}, \ldots, x_{jp}) \in \mathbf{t}$, as follows:
   1.
   $$I'_T(f_l)(g(x_{j1}), \ldots, g(x_{jp})) = b_j \neq g(t_j) = I_T(f_l)(g(x_{j1}), \ldots, g(x_{jp}));$$
   2. For all assignments $g_1 \neq g$, we have that
   $$I'_T(f_l)(g_1(x_{j1}), \ldots, g_1(x_{jp})) = I_T(f_l)(g_1(x_{j1}), \ldots, g_1(x_{jp}));$$

   so that for the R-algebra α' derived from the Tarski's interpretation I'_T:
   7.1 If $\exists \mathfrak{h}_{i,n} \in \text{Sat}(\mathfrak{h})$ such that $(\mathbf{d}_1, \ldots, \mathbf{d}_k) \notin \text{graph}(\mathfrak{h}_{i,n})$, then insert $((\mathbf{d}_1, \ldots, \mathbf{d}_k), \mathbf{b})$ into $\text{graph}(\mathfrak{h}_{i,n})$ and go to 5.
   7.2 Generate, for new index m, a new function $\mathfrak{h}_{i,m} = \alpha'(q_{A,i}) : R_1 \times \cdots \times R_k \to \|r_B\|$ with $\text{graph}(\mathfrak{h}_{i,m} =_{\text{def}} \{((\mathbf{d}_1, \ldots, \mathbf{d}_k), \mathbf{b})\}$, insert it in $\text{Sat}(\mathfrak{h})$ and go to 7.
8. **Return** the saturated morphism $\text{Sat}(\alpha^*(\mathbf{M}_{AB})) : A \to B$ after completion of each function $\mathfrak{h}_{i,n}$ in it as follows: for each $(\mathbf{d}_1, \ldots, \mathbf{d}_k)) \in (\text{dom}(\mathfrak{h}_{i,n}) \backslash \pi_1(\text{graph}(\mathfrak{h}_{i,n})))$, set $\mathfrak{h}_{i,n}(\mathbf{d}_1, \ldots, \mathbf{d}_k)) = \langle \rangle$.

By the saturation of $\mathfrak{h}$, we obtain the morphism $\text{Sat}(\mathfrak{h}) : A \to B$ from which we are able to define the set $\mathcal{F}_{q_i} = \{\mathfrak{h}_{i,j} : \text{dom}(\alpha(q_i)) \to \text{cod}(\alpha(q_i)) \mid \mathfrak{h}_{i,j} \in \text{Sat}(\mathfrak{h})\}$ and function $f_{q_i} = \bigcup \mathcal{F}_{q_i}$ with graph $(f_{q_i}) =_{\text{def}} \bigcup_{\mathfrak{h}_{i,j} \in \mathcal{F}_{q_i}} \text{graph}(\mathfrak{h}_{i,j})$, where

$$(\mho) \quad \text{graph}(\mathfrak{h}_{i,j}) = \{((\mathbf{d}_1, \ldots, \mathbf{d}_k), \mathfrak{h}_{i,j}(\mathbf{d}_1, \ldots, \mathbf{d}_k)) \mid (\mathbf{d}_1, \ldots, \mathbf{d}_k) \in \text{dom}(\mathfrak{h}_{i,j}) \text{ and } \mathfrak{h}_{i,j}(\mathbf{d}_1, \ldots, \mathbf{d}_k) \neq \langle \rangle\}$$

is the nonempty-tuple graph of this function. Thus, in this way we obtain the p-function:

$$(\wp) \quad f_{q_i} : \text{dom}(\alpha(q_i)) \to \mathcal{P}(\text{cod}(\alpha(q_i))),$$

for each operad's operation $q_i \in \mathbf{M}_{AB}$, which has the functional symbols on he right side of implication in q_i. We have the following property for these derived p-functions.

Lemma 4. *Let the mapping component $q_i \in \mathbf{M}_{AB} : \mathcal{A} \to \mathcal{B}$ be the expression $(e \Rightarrow (\_)(\mathbf{t})) \in O(r_1, \ldots, r_k, r_B)$, with the tuple $\mathbf{x} = (x_1, \ldots, x_m)$ of all variables in the left-side expression e, such that the set of functional symbols in the tuple of terms $\mathbf{t}$ is not empty.*

Let R-algebra α be a model of $\mathbf{M}_{AB}$ with $R_n = \alpha(r_n) \in A = \alpha^*(\mathcal{A})$, $n = 1, \ldots, k$, and $\|r_B\| = \alpha(r_B) \in B = \alpha^*(\mathcal{B})$, and $\mathfrak{h}_{i,0} = \alpha(q_i) : R_1 \times \cdots \times R_k \to \|r_B\|$ with $\mathfrak{h}_{i,0} \in \mathfrak{h} = \alpha^*(\mathbf{M}_{AB}) : A \to B$. So, for the component $q_i \in \mathbf{M}_{AB} : \mathcal{A} \to \mathcal{B}$, the set

$$\mathcal{F}_{q_i} = \{\mathfrak{h}_{i,j} : \mathrm{dom}(\alpha(q_i)) \to \mathrm{cod}(\alpha(q_i)) \mid \mathfrak{h}_{i,j} \in \mathrm{Sat}(\mathfrak{h})\}$$

we define the p-function:

$$f_{q_i} =_{\mathrm{def}} \bigcup \mathcal{F}_{q_i} : R_1 \times \cdots \times R_k \to \mathcal{P}(\|r_B\|), \quad \textit{with } \mathrm{graph}(f_{q_i}) = \bigcup_{\mathfrak{h}_{i,j} \in \mathcal{F}_{q_i}} \mathrm{graph}(\mathfrak{h}_{i,j}) \tag{4.16}$$

Let Z be the set of indexes of the terms in $\mathbf{t} = (t_1, \ldots, t_{\mathrm{ar}(r_B)})$, which are simple variables and we denote by $nr_{r_B}(j)$ the name of the j-th column of the relation $r_B \in \mathcal{B}$. Then, for each tuple $(\mathbf{d}_1, \ldots, \mathbf{d}_k) \in R_1 \times \cdots \times R_k$ with the assignment $g : \{x_1, \ldots, x_m\} \to \mathcal{D}$ such that $(g(x_1), \ldots, g(x_m)) = \mathrm{Cmp}(S, (\mathbf{d}_1, \ldots, \mathbf{d}_k))$ (from Definition 50 in Section 4.4), we obtain

$$f_{q_i}(\mathbf{d}_1, \ldots, \mathbf{d}_k) = \|\text{SELECT } (*) \text{ FROM } \|r_B\| \text{ WHERE } \bigwedge_{j \in Z} (nr_{R_B}(j) = g(t_j))\|_{\#} \tag{4.17}$$

and, if $\alpha(q_i)(\mathbf{d}_1, \ldots, \mathbf{d}_k) = \langle\, \rangle$ then $f_{q_i}(\mathbf{d}_1, \ldots, \mathbf{d}_k) = \emptyset \in \mathcal{P}(\|r_B\|)$.

Proof. From the steps 6 and 7 of the algorithm for saturation, we have that for every tuple in $\mathbf{b} \in R = \|\text{SELECT } (*) \text{ FROM } \|r_B\| \text{ WHERE } \bigwedge_{j \in Z}(nr_{R_B}(j) = g(t_j))\|_{\#}$, we have a function $\mathfrak{h}_{i,j} \in \mathcal{F}_{q_i}$, with $\mathbf{b} \in \pi_2(\mathrm{graph}(\mathfrak{h}_{i,j}))$, and hence (4.17) is valid. □

Corollary 14. *For every R-algebra α which is a model of a given schema mapping $\mathbf{M}_{AB} : \mathcal{A} \to \mathcal{B}$, we have that $\alpha^*(\mathbf{M}_{AB}) : \alpha^*(\mathcal{A}) \to \alpha^*(\mathcal{B})$ and $\mathrm{Sat}(\alpha^*(\mathbf{M}_{AB})) : \alpha^*(\mathcal{A}) \to \alpha^*(\mathcal{B})$ are two* equal *morphisms in the category* **DB**. *Thus, the saturation of morphisms is an invariant process in* **DB**, *so that we can replace any nonsaturated morphisms with its saturated version in any commutative diagram in* **DB**.

Proof. From the fact that the introduction of the new functions changes only the terms with nonbuilt-in functional symbols on the right sides of implications, so that they are not in $\mathrm{Var}(\mathbf{M}_{AB})$, and hence, from Definition 51 in Section 4.4, they do not change the information flux of the morphism $\alpha^*(\mathbf{M}_{AB})$. □

Example 25 (Continuation of Example 23 in Section 4.3.2). We have the schema mapping $\mathcal{M}_{AB} : \mathcal{A} \to \mathcal{B}$ by the tgd

$$\forall x_1, x_2, x_3, x_4, x_5(\mathtt{Contacts}(x_1, x_2, x_3, x_4, x_5, x_6) \Rightarrow \exists y r_{\mathrm{MA}}(x_6, y)),$$

so that by Skolemization we obtain the SOtgd Φ equal to the logic formula

$$\exists f_1(\forall \mathbf{x}(\texttt{Contacts}(\mathbf{x}) \Rightarrow r_{\mathrm{MA}}(x_6, f_1(x_6)))),$$

where $\mathbf{x} = (x_1, x_2, x_3, x_4, x_5, x_6)$. So, $\mathbf{M}_{AB} = \mathrm{MakeOperads}(\{\Phi\}) = \{q_1, 1_{r_\emptyset}\} : \mathcal{A} \to \mathcal{B}$, with $q_1 = v_1 \cdot q_{A,1} \in O(\texttt{Contacts}, r_{\mathrm{MA}})$ with $q_{A,1} = ((\_)(\mathbf{x}) \Rightarrow (\_)(\mathbf{t})) \in O(\texttt{Contacts}, r_q)$, where $\mathbf{t} = \langle t_1, t_2\rangle$ with the term t_1 equal to variable x_6 and term t_2 equal to $f_1(x_6)$, and $v_1 = ((\_)(y_1, y_2) \Rightarrow (\_)(y_1, y_2)) \in O(r_q, r_{\mathrm{MA}})$.

Let us consider a model of this schema mapping α, such that $R_1 = \alpha(\texttt{Contacts})$ and $\|r_B\| = \|r_{\mathrm{MA}}\| = \alpha(r_{\mathrm{MA}})$, with

$R_1 =$

contID	firstName	lastName	street	zipCode	hobbies
...	...	...	...	...	...
132	Zoran	Majkic	Appia	0187	hobbies_of_132
...	...	...	...	...	...

$\|r_B\| = \|r_{\mathrm{MA}}\| =$

value	atom-value
...	...
hobbies_of_132	photography
hobbies_of_132	music
hobbies_of_132	art
hobbies_of_132	travel
...	...

so that for $\mathbf{d}_1 = (132, \mathrm{Zoran}, \mathrm{Majkic}, \mathrm{Appia}, 0187, \mathrm{hobbies\_of\_132}) \in R_1$, we obtain the assignment $g : \overline{\mathbf{x}} \to \mathcal{D}$ such that $g(\mathbf{x}) = \mathrm{Cmp}(\emptyset, \mathbf{d}_1) = \mathbf{d}_1$, i. e., $g(x_1) = 132, g(x_2) = \mathrm{Zoran}, g(x_3) = \mathrm{Majkic}, g(x_4) = \mathrm{Appia}$, $g(x_5) = 0187$, and $g(x_6) = \mathrm{hobbies\_of\_132}$, and for $\mathfrak{h}_{1,0} = \alpha(q_1) : R_1 \to \|r_B\|$ such that $\mathfrak{h}_{1,0}(\mathbf{d}_1) = g^*(\mathbf{t}) = (g(x_6), f_1(g(x_6))) = (\mathrm{hobbies\_of\_132}, I_T(f_1)(\mathrm{hobbies\_of\_132})) = (\mathrm{hobbies\_of\_132}, \mathrm{art})$, i. e.,

(a) $I_T(f_1)(\mathrm{hobbies\_of\_132}) = \mathrm{art}$.

Then in step 6 of the algorithm, we have $Z = \{t_1\} = \{x_6\}$ with $nr_{r_{\mathrm{MA}}}(1) = \texttt{value}$ and

(b)

$$R = \left\| \left(\text{SELECT } (*) \text{ FROM } \|r_B\| \text{ WHERE } \bigwedge_{j \in Z} (nr_{R_B}(j) = g(t_j))\right)\right\|_{\#} \backslash \{g^*(\mathbf{t})\}$$

$$= \|(\text{SELECT } (*) \text{ FROM } \|r_B\| \text{ WHERE value} = \mathrm{hobbies\_of\_132})\|_{\#} \backslash \{g^*(\mathbf{t})\}$$

$=$

value	atom-value
hobbies_of_132	photography
hobbies_of_132	music
hobbies_of_132	travel

Consequently, in step 7 of the algorithm will be introduced the three new functions $\mathfrak{h}_{1,j} : R_1 \to \|r_B\|$, for each tuple $\mathbf{b} \in R$, into $\mathrm{Sat}(\alpha^*(\mathbf{M}_{AB}))$ so that (for $u = \mathrm{hobbies\_of\_132}$)

$$\mathfrak{h}_{1,1}(\mathbf{d}_1) = (u, \mathrm{photography}), \quad \text{with } I'_T(f_1)(u) = \mathrm{photography};$$

$$\mathfrak{h}_{1,2}(\mathbf{d}_1) = (u, \text{music}), \quad \text{with } I''_T(f_1)(u) = \text{music};$$
$$\mathfrak{h}_{1,3}(\mathbf{d}_1) = (u, \text{travel}), \quad \text{with } I'''_T(f_1)(u) = \text{travel}.$$

Thus, from the algorithm we obtain $\{\mathfrak{h}_{1,0}, \mathfrak{h}_{1,1}, \mathfrak{h}_{1,2}, \mathfrak{h}_{1,3}, \mathrm{id}_\perp\} \subseteq \mathrm{Sat}(\mathfrak{h})$ and derived p-function (4.16), $f_{q_1} = \bigcup \mathcal{F}_{q_1} : \alpha(\texttt{Contacts}) \to \mathcal{P}(\alpha(r_{\mathrm{MA}}))$, with

$$f_{q_1}(\mathbf{d}_1) = f_{q_1}(132, \text{Zoran}, \text{Majkic}, \text{Appia}, 0187, \text{hobbies\_of\_132})$$

=

value	atom-value
hobbies_of_132	art
hobbies_of_132	photography
hobbies_of_132	music
hobbies_of_132	travel

and hence, by using the second projection π_2, we obtain that, for ID = 132,

$$(\pi_2 \cdot f_{q_1})(\mathbf{d}_1) = \{\text{photography}, \text{art}, \text{music}, \text{travel}\},$$

i. e., for each contact ID, the function $\pi_2 \cdot f_{q_1}$ returns the set of hobbies of this ID.

In this way, we are able to represent also the 1:N relationships between relational tables by the morphisms in **DB** category.

It is important that the saturation can be done only for the nonbuilt-in functional symbols. In fact, we have only one prefixed interpretation of the built-in functional symbols, so that their interpretation is equal for every Tarski's interpretation.

4.4.2 Kleisli semantics in DB category

The notion of a monad is one of the most general mathematical notions [181–183]. For instance, *every* algebraic theory, i. e., every set of operations satisfying equational laws, can be seen as a monad (which is also a *monoid* in a category of endofunctors of a given category: the "operation" μ being the associative multiplication of this monoid and η its unit). Given an endofunctor $T : \mathbf{C} \to \mathbf{C}$ with a natural transformation $\eta : \mathrm{id}_{\mathbf{C}} \stackrel{\cdot}{\longrightarrow} T$ and a natural transformation $\mu : T^2 \stackrel{\cdot}{\longrightarrow} T$ (here T^2 denotes the composition TT) such that the diagrams (A.9), in Section A.5 in the Appendix, of natural transformations commute, then a triple (T, η, μ) is called a *monad*. Thus, monoid laws of the monad do subsume all possible algebraic laws. More specifically, the monads are used as a way of modeling computational/collection types [176, 177, 184, 185] as we intend to use them in this section.

Example 26. It is very easy to use the monads over **Set**. In particular, within a Kleisli instance it is permitted to relax the atomicity requirement for data (i. e., the first normal form in Codd's requirements for RDBs). For example, for the List monad, List :

Set $\to$ **Set**, which assigns to any set S (an object in **Set**) the set of all lists List(S), which can be obtained from elements in S, so that an arrow $f : X \to \text{List}(S)$ in **Set** assigns to each element a of the set X a particular list L in List(S). Similarly, the powerset endofunctor $\mathcal{P} : \textbf{Set} \to \textbf{Set}$ assigns to each set S the set of all its subsets $\mathcal{P}(S)$, and for a function $f : X \to S$ (it is a "renaming" arrow in **Set**), the arrow $\mathcal{P}(f) : \mathcal{P}(X) \to \mathcal{P}(S)$ is a function such that for each $Y \in \mathcal{P}(X)$ (i. e., $Y \subseteq X$), $\mathcal{P}(f)(Y) = \{f(a) \mid a \in Y\}$. Consequently, any arrow $g : X \to \mathcal{P}(S)$ specifies the assignment of a subset $Y \subseteq S$ of values to the elements $a \in X$, so that this mapping in **Set** can be used to assign a set of values to the multivalued attributes.

This powerset endofunctor is a monad $(\mathcal{P}, \eta, \mu)$ where μ is the set union operation and $\eta_X : X \to \mathcal{P}(X)$ is a function, which assigns to each element $a \in X$ the singleton set $\{a\}$. Thus, this assignment of values to the multivalued attributes can be equivalently done by a morphism $f_T : X \to S$ in the Kleisli category of this monad.

So, we need to define a "powerset" monad for the category **DB**. We need it to represent the p-functions (4.16), $f_{q_i} = \bigcup \mathcal{F}_{q_i} : R_1 \times \cdots \times R_k \to \mathcal{P}(\|r_B\|)$ with $\text{graph}(f_{q_i}) = \bigcup_{\mathfrak{h}_{i,j} \in \mathcal{F}_{q_i}} \text{graph}(\mathfrak{h}_{i,j})$, of saturated morphisms from Lemma 4 and Example 25.

Proposition 27. *Let us define the mapping* $\mathfrak{P} = (\mathfrak{P}^0, \mathfrak{P}^1) : \textbf{DB} \to \textbf{DB}$, *such that for any object* $A = \{R_1, \dots, R_n, \bot\}$ *in* **DB** *and a morphism* $f = \{f_1, \dots, f_m, q_\bot\} : A \to B$:
1. $\mathfrak{P}(A) = \mathfrak{P}^0(A) =_{\text{def}} \bigcup_{R_i \in A} \{R \bigcup \bot \mid R \in \mathcal{P}(R_i)\}$;
2. $\mathfrak{P}(f) = \mathfrak{P}^1(f) =_{\text{def}} \text{is}_B \circ f \circ \text{is}_A^{-1} : \mathfrak{P}(A) \to \mathfrak{P}(B)$ *where* $\text{is}_B : B \to \mathfrak{P}(B)$ *and* $\text{is}_A^{-1} : \mathfrak{P}(A) \to A$ *are two isomorphisms in* **DB**.

Then $(\mathfrak{P}, \eta, \mu)$ *is a monad, where* $\eta : \text{Id}_{\text{DB}} \stackrel{\cdot}{\longrightarrow} \mathfrak{P}$ *is natural isomorphism,* $\mathfrak{P}^2 = \mathfrak{P}$, *and* $\mu : \mathfrak{P}^2 \stackrel{\cdot}{\longrightarrow} \mathfrak{P}$ *is the identity natural transformation. Thus, for each object* A, $\eta_A : A \to \mathfrak{P}(A)$ *is an isomorphism and* $\mu_A = \eta_{\mathfrak{P}(A)} = \text{id}_{\mathfrak{P}(A)} : \mathfrak{P}(A) \to \mathfrak{P}(A)$ *is the identity morphism for the object* $\mathfrak{P}(A)$.

Proof. For any RDB (a set of relational tables) $A = \{R_1, \dots, R_n, \bot\}$, such that each relation has the empty tuple as well, $\langle\,\rangle \in R_i$ (note that $\langle\,\rangle \in D_{-1}$ is not the empty set $\emptyset$), and we have that $\mathfrak{P}(R_i)$ is the set of all subrelations $R \subseteq R_i$ such that $\langle\,\rangle \in R$ and $\mathfrak{P}(\{\bot\}) = \{\bot\}$ (where $\langle\,\rangle$ is the empty tuple and $\mathcal{P}(\bot) = \{\emptyset, \bot\}$. From the fact that each relation has the empty tuple $\langle\,\rangle \in R$, we have $\mathcal{P}(\bot) = \{\emptyset, \bot\} \subseteq \mathcal{P}(R)$), so that $\mathfrak{P}(A)$ is an object in **DB** (we recall that each object A (an instance database) in **DB** has the empty relation $\bot$ as well, so that between any two objects A and B we have at least the empty morphism $\bot^1 = \{q_\bot\} : A \to B$). Let us show that for any A we have the isomorphism $A \simeq \mathfrak{P}(A)$. In fact, $\mathfrak{P}(A)$ can be seen as the set of all relations, which can be obtained by only the selection operations of SPRJU relational algebra (SQL), while $T(A)$ is the set of all relations that can be obtained from A by using all operations in SPRJU, and consequently, we have that $\mathfrak{P}(A) \subseteq T(A)$, so that $A \subseteq \mathfrak{P}(A) \subseteq T(A)$, and consequently by applying the power-view operation T, $T(A) \subseteq T(\mathfrak{P}(A)) \subseteq T(T(A)) = T(A)$, i. e.,

$T(\mathfrak{P}(A)) = T(A)$, and from the fact that in **DB**, $A \simeq B$ iff $T(A) = T(B)$, we obtain the isomorphism

$$\eta_A : A \simeq \mathfrak{P}(A) \tag{4.18}$$

Let us represent this isomorphism [21] by the arrow $\text{is}_A = \{\text{id}_R : R \to R \mid R \in A\} : A \to \mathfrak{P}(A)$. Thus, the information flux is $\widetilde{\text{is}_A} = T(A) = T(\mathfrak{P}(A))$, and hence (from Proposition 8, [21]), this arrow is an isomorphic arrow in **DB**. Its inverse is as usual $\text{is}_A^{-1} = \{\text{id}_R : R \to R \mid R \in A\} : \mathfrak{P}(A) \to A$, so that $\text{is}_A^{-1} \circ \text{is}_A = \{\text{id}_R : R \to R \mid R \in A\} = \text{id}_A : A \to A$, and $\text{is}_A \circ \text{is}_A^{-1} = \text{id}_{\mathfrak{P}(A)} : \mathfrak{P}(A) \to \mathfrak{P}(A)$ from the fact that the information flux

$$\widetilde{\text{is}_A \circ \text{is}_A^{-1}} = \widetilde{\text{is}_A} \bigcap \widetilde{\text{is}_A^{-1}} = T(A) \bigcap T(A) = T(A) = T(\mathfrak{P}(A)) = \widetilde{\text{id}_{\mathfrak{P}(A)}},$$

and hence, (from [21], Definition 23), $\text{is}_A \circ \text{is}_A^{-1} = \text{id}_{\mathfrak{P}(A)}$.

Let us show that for each identity arrow $\text{id}_A = \{\text{id}_R : R \to R \mid R \in A\} : A \to A$, we have that $\mathfrak{P}(\text{id}_A) = \text{is}_A \circ \text{id}_A \circ \text{is}_A^{-1} = \text{is}_A \circ \text{is}_A^{-1} = \text{id}_{\mathfrak{P}(A)} = \{\text{id}_R : R \to R \mid R \in \mathfrak{P}(A)\} : \mathfrak{P}(A) \to \mathfrak{P}(A)$. In fact, $\widetilde{\text{id}_{\mathfrak{P}(A)}} = T(\mathfrak{P}(A)) = T(A)$.

For the composition of two arrows $f : A \to B$ and $g : B \to C$, we have that

$$\begin{aligned}\mathfrak{P}(g \circ f) &= \text{is}_C \circ (g \circ f) \circ \text{is}_A^{-1} = \text{is}_C \circ g \circ \text{id}_B \circ f \circ \text{is}_A^{-1} \\ &= \text{is}_C \circ g \circ (\text{is}_B^{-1} \circ \text{is}_B) \circ f \circ \text{is}_A \quad (\text{from } \text{id}_B = \text{is}_B^{-1} \circ \text{is}_B) \\ &= (\text{is}_C \circ g \circ \text{is}_B^{-1}) \circ (\text{is}_B \circ f \circ \text{is}_A) = \mathfrak{P}(g) \circ \mathfrak{P}(f).\end{aligned}$$

So, $\mathfrak{P}$ is a well-defined endofunctor. It is easy to verify that $(\mathfrak{P}, \eta, \mu)$ is a monad where $\eta : \text{Id}_{\text{DB}} \simeq \mathfrak{P}$ is a natural isomorphism. Thus for any object A, the arrow $\eta_A = \{\text{id}_R : R \to R \mid R \in A\} : A \to \mathfrak{P}(A)$ is an isomorphism in **DB**, so that its information flux is $\widetilde{\eta_A} = T(A)$, while for any $A = \{R_1, \dots, R_n, \bot\}$,

(a) $\mathfrak{P}(A) \subseteq \mathfrak{P}(\mathfrak{P}(A))$, because $\mathfrak{P}$ is monotonic operation;
(b) For any relation, $R' \bigcup \bot \in \mathfrak{P}(\mathfrak{P}(A)) = \{R' \bigcup \bot \mid R' \in \mathcal{P}(R), R \in \mathfrak{P}(A)\}$ and from $R \in \mathfrak{P}(A)$, we have that $R \in \mathcal{P}(R_i)$ for some $R_i \in A$. Thus, from $R' \in \mathcal{P}(R)$ and $R \in \mathcal{P}(R_i)$, we have $R' \in \mathcal{P}(R_i)$, and hence $R' \bigcup \bot \in \{R' \bigcup \bot \mid R' \in \mathcal{P}(R_i)\} \subseteq \bigcup_{R_i \in A}\{R' \bigcup \bot \mid R' \in \mathcal{P}(R_i)\} = \mathfrak{P}(A)$. Hence, $\mathfrak{P}(A) \supseteq \mathfrak{P}(\mathfrak{P}(A))$.

Consequently, for (a) and (b), $\mathfrak{P}(A) = \mathfrak{P}(\mathfrak{P}(A))$. Thus, $\mathfrak{P}$ is idempotent, so that $\mu_A : \mathfrak{P}(\mathfrak{P}(A)) \to \mathfrak{P}(A)$ reduces to $\mu_A : \mathfrak{P}(A) \to \mathfrak{P}(A)$ and if we take $\mu_A = \text{id}_{\mathfrak{P}(A)}$ (with the information flux $\widetilde{\mu_A} = \widetilde{\text{id}_{\mathfrak{P}(A)}} = T(\mathfrak{P}(A)) = T(A)$) the two monad diagrams (where μ is the identity natural transformation) commute. □

Notice that, for each relational database instance A (an object in **DB**), we have that the "powerset" object $\mathfrak{P}(A)$ is a database instance obtained from A by evaluation of all selection operations over the relations in A, while the power-view object $T(A)$ is a database instance obtained from A by evaluation of *all* terms of the SPRJU relational algebra over the relations in A. So, we have that $A \subseteq \mathfrak{P}(A) \subseteq T(A)$ and, from the fact that T is a monotonic and idempotent operator, $T(A) \subseteq T(\mathfrak{P}(A)) \subseteq T(T(A)) = T(A)$. Thus, $T(A) = T(\mathfrak{P}(A))$ and, from the fact that two objects in **DB** are isomorphic, $A \simeq B$ iff $T(A) = T(B)$, we obtain the isomorphism of this monad $A \simeq \mathfrak{P}(A)$ expressed by the natural isomorphism (4.18), $\eta_A = \mathrm{is}_A : A \to \mathfrak{P}(A)$.

Next, we will present the denotational semantics for the multivalued attributes based on this "powerset" monad in relational database category **DB** and its Kleisli category.

Definition 53. Given a monad (T, η, μ) over a category **C**, we have [181]:

- *Kleisli triple* is a triple $(T, \eta, -^*)$, where for $f : A \longrightarrow T(B)$ we have $f^* : T(A) \longrightarrow T(B)$, such that the following equations hold: $\eta_A^* = \mathrm{id}_{T(A)}, f^* \circ \eta_A = f, g^* \circ f^* = (g^* \circ f)^*$, for $f : A \longrightarrow T(B)$ and $g : B \longrightarrow T(C)$. A Kleisli triple satisfies the *mono requirement* provided η_A is monic for each object A.
- *Kleisli category* $\mathbf{C}_T$ has the same objects as **C** category. For any two objects A,B, there is the bijection between arrows $\theta : \bigcup_{A,B \in \mathbf{C}} \mathbf{C}(A, TB) \longrightarrow \bigcup_{A,B \in \mathbf{C}} \mathbf{C}_T(A, B)$, such that for $f : A \to TB$ in **C**, $\theta(f) : A \to B$ is the corresponding arrow in $\mathbf{C}_T$. For any two arrows $f_T : A \longrightarrow B, g_T : B \longrightarrow C$ in $\mathbf{C}_T$, their composition is defined by $g_T \circ f_T =_{\mathrm{def}} \theta(\mu_C \circ T(\theta^{-1}(g_T)) \circ \theta^{-1}(f_T))$.

A Kleisli category is a "minimal" solution to the problem of finding an adjunction, which induces the given monad (T, η, μ). This "minimal; adjunction $\mathbf{C}_T \underset{G_T}{\overset{F_T}{\rightleftarrows}} \mathbf{C}$ is defined by

- The functor G_T sends the object X to $T(X)$ and $f_T : X \to Y$ (which is $\theta^{-1}(f_T) : X \to T(Y)$ in **C**) to $\mu_Y \circ T(\theta^{-1}(f_T)) : T(X) \to T(Y)$;
- The functor F_T is the identity on objects and sends $f : X \to Y$ to $\theta(\eta_Y \circ f) : X \to Y$ in $\mathbf{C}_T$.

Lemma 5. *The Kleisli category* $\mathbf{DB}_{\mathfrak{P}}$ *of the monad* $(\mathfrak{P}, \eta, \mu)$ *satisfies the following property for any two morphisms* $f : A \to B$ *and* $g : B \to C$ *of the* **DB** *category:*

$$\theta(\eta_C \circ (g \circ f)) = \theta(\eta_C \circ g) \circ \theta(\eta_B \circ f),$$

where θ *is bijective mapping in Definition* 53.

The Kleisli triple $(\mathfrak{P}, \eta, -^*)$, *where* $-^*$ *is equal to the arrow component* $\mathfrak{P}^1$ *of the endofunctor* $\mathfrak{P} = (\mathfrak{P}^0, \mathfrak{P}^1)$, *satisfies the mono requirement.*

Proof. From the definition of composition of the arrows in the Kleisli category, we have that $\theta(\eta_C \circ g) \circ \theta(\eta_B \circ f) = \theta(\mu_C \circ \mathfrak{P}(\theta^{-1}(\theta(\eta_C \circ g))) \circ \theta^{-1}(\theta(\eta_B \circ f))) = \theta(\mu_C \circ \mathfrak{P}(\eta_C \circ g) \circ \eta_B \circ f)$.

Thus, it is enough to demonstrate the equality of two arrows in **DB**:

$$\eta_C \circ g \circ f = \mu_C \circ \mathfrak{P}(\eta_C \circ g) \circ \eta_B \circ f = \mu_C \circ \mathrm{is}_C \circ (\eta_C \circ g) \circ \mathrm{is}_B^{-1} \circ \eta_B \circ f : X \to \mathfrak{P}(C).$$

That is, they must have the same information fluxes. In fact, from $\widetilde{f} \subseteq T(A)\bigcap T(B)$, $\widetilde{g} \subseteq T(B)\bigcap T(C)$, $\widetilde{\eta_C} = \widetilde{\mathrm{is}_C} = T(C)$, $\widetilde{\eta_B} = \widetilde{\mathrm{is}_B} = \widetilde{\mathrm{is}_B^{-1}} = T(B)$ and $\widetilde{\mu_C} = \widetilde{\mathrm{id}_{\mathfrak{P}(C)}} = T(\mathfrak{P}(C)) = T(C)$, we have

(a) $\widetilde{\eta_C \circ g \circ f} = \widetilde{\eta_C}\bigcap\widetilde{g}\bigcap\widetilde{f} = \widetilde{g}\bigcap\widetilde{f}$;

(b) $\widetilde{\mu_C \circ \mathrm{is}_C \circ (\eta_C \circ g) \circ \mathrm{is}_B^{-1} \circ \eta_B \circ f} = \widetilde{\mu_C}\bigcap\widetilde{\mathrm{is}_C}\bigcap(\widetilde{\eta_C}\bigcap\widetilde{g})\bigcap\widetilde{\mathrm{is}_B^{-1}}\bigcap\widetilde{\eta_B}\bigcap\widetilde{f} = \widetilde{g}\bigcap\widetilde{f}$.

Consequently, from (a) and (b) these two arrows have the same information flux in **DB**, and hence they are equal arrows in **DB**.

The mono requirement for the monad $(\mathfrak{P},\eta,\mu)$ [177] is satisfied because, by Proposition 9 in 3.2.1 in [21], for each object A the arrow $\eta_A : A \longrightarrow \mathfrak{P}(A)$ is an isomorphism $\eta_A = \mathrm{is}_A$ (we denote its inverse by η_A^{-1}), and hence it is also monic. Moreover, the isomorphism $\eta_{\mathfrak{P}(A)} = \mathrm{is}_{\mathfrak{P}(A)} : \mathfrak{P}(A) \to \mathfrak{P}^2(A) = \mathfrak{P}(A)$ is just the identity arrow $\mathrm{id}_{\mathfrak{P}(A)}$ and $\mathfrak{P}(\eta_A) = \mathrm{is}_{\mathfrak{P}(A)} \circ \eta_A \circ \mathrm{is}_A^{-1} = \mathrm{id}_{\mathfrak{P}(A)} \circ \eta_A \circ \mathrm{is}_A^{-1} = \eta_A \circ \mathrm{is}_A^{-1} = \mathrm{is}_A \circ \mathrm{is}_A^{-1} = \mathrm{id}_{\mathfrak{P}(A)}$.

Thus if we substitute $\_^*$ with the arrow component $\mathfrak{P}^1$ of the endofunctor $\mathfrak{P}$, we have that $\eta_A^* = \mathfrak{P}(\eta_A) = \mathrm{id}_{\mathfrak{P}(A)}$ satisfies the Kleisli triple. Also, for $f : A \to \mathfrak{P}(B)$, $f^* \circ \eta_A = \mathfrak{P}(f) \circ \mathrm{is}_A = \mathrm{is}_{\mathfrak{P}(B)} \circ f \circ \mathrm{is}_A^{-1} \circ \mathrm{is}_A = \mathrm{id}_{\mathfrak{P}(B)} \circ f \circ \mathrm{id}_A = f$ is the satisfied Kleisli triple. Let us show the last condition, $(g * \circ f)^* = \mathfrak{P}(\mathfrak{P}(g) \circ f)$ = (from functorial property) = $\mathfrak{P}^2(g) \circ \mathfrak{P}(f)$ = (from idempotence of $\mathfrak{P}$) = $\mathfrak{P}(g) \circ \mathfrak{P}(f) = g^* \circ f^*$. □

Consequently, the category **DB** is a *computational model* for “powerset” computations of the sets of values for the multivalued attributes as well, with the typed operator $\mathfrak{P}$, so that:

- $\mathfrak{P}(A)$ is a *type of computations*, which are the views of the database A obtained by ony selection operations over the relations in A.
- η_A is the *inclusion* of values into computations (i. e., inclusion of relations of the DB A into the set of views in $\mathfrak{P}(A)$). It is the isomorphism $\eta_A = \mathrm{is}_A : A \longrightarrow \mathfrak{P}(A)$.

Let us see now how the Kleisli category $\mathbf{DB}_T$ is “internalized” into the **DB** category.

Theorem 7. *The Kleisli category* $\mathbf{DB}_{\mathfrak{P}}$ *of the monad* $(\mathfrak{P},\eta,\mu)$ *is isomorphic to* **DB** *category. That is, it may be “internalized” in* **DB** *by the faithful forgetful functor* $K = (K^0, K^1) : \mathbf{DB}_{\mathfrak{P}} \longrightarrow \mathbf{DB}$ *such that object-component* K^0 *is an identity function and the arrow-component* $K^1 =_{\mathrm{def}} \phi\theta^{-1}$ *where, for any two objects A and B, we have the following bijections of the hom-sets:*

θ: $\mathbf{DB}(A,\mathfrak{P}(B)) \cong \mathbf{DB}_{\mathfrak{P}}(A,B)$ *is Kleisli bijection and*

ϕ: $\mathbf{DB}(A,\mathfrak{P}(B)) \cong \mathbf{DB}(A,B)$ *such that* $\phi(\_) = \eta^{-1}_{\mathrm{cod}(\_)} \circ (\_)$ *is a* **DB** *category bijection respectively, where for any object A,* $\eta_A^{-1} : \mathfrak{P}(A) \to A$ *is the isomorphism (inverse of the isomorphism* η_A*).*

Proof. We can use the same method as in [174], or in [21] (Section 8.4, Theorem 17), but here we will use an alternative way based on the Kleisli adjunction $\mathbf{DB}_{\mathfrak{P}} \underset{G_T}{\overset{F_T}{\rightleftarrows}} \mathbf{DB}$.

In fact, in order to demonstrate the isomorphism of the Kleisli category $\mathbf{DB}_{\mathfrak{P}}$ and $\mathbf{DB}$, we have to show that there are the natural transformations $\nu : Id_{\mathbf{DB}} \stackrel{\bullet}{\longrightarrow} G_T F_T$ and $\varpi : Id_{\mathbf{DB}_{\mathfrak{P}}} \stackrel{\bullet}{\longrightarrow} F_T G_T$ whose components are all isomorphisms. In fact, from $G_T F_T = \mathfrak{P}$ we take the natural isomorphism $\nu = \eta$ of the monad $(\mathfrak{P}, \eta, \mu)$.

Let us show that for each object A, $\varpi_A = \theta(\eta_{\mathfrak{P}(A)} \circ \eta_A) : A \to \mathfrak{P}(A)$ is an isomorphic arrow in Kleisli category $\mathbf{DB}_{\mathfrak{P}}$. Let us consider a morphism $f : A \to B$, its corresponding arrow $f_T = \theta(\eta_B \circ f) : A \to B$ and the ϖ diagram in $\mathbf{DB}_{\mathfrak{P}}$:

$$\begin{array}{ccc} A & \xrightarrow{\ \varpi_A\ } & \mathfrak{P}(A) = F_T G_T(A) \\ {\scriptstyle f_T = \theta(\eta_B \circ f)} \Big\downarrow & & \Big\downarrow {\scriptstyle F_T G_T(f_T)} \\ B & \xrightarrow{\ \varpi_B\ } & \mathfrak{P}(B) = F_T G_T(B) \end{array}$$

Let us show that this diagram is commutative and that ϖ_A and ϖ_A are two isomorphisms in $\mathbf{DB}_{\mathfrak{P}}$. In fact, we have that (from Lemma 5),

(a) $F_T G_T(\theta(\eta_B \circ f)) \circ \varpi_A = \theta(\eta_{\mathfrak{P}(B)} \circ \mu_B \circ \mathfrak{P}(\eta_B \circ f)) \circ \theta(\eta_{\mathfrak{P}(A)} \circ \eta_A) = \theta(g_1)$

where $g_1 = \eta_{\mathfrak{P}(B)} \circ \mu_B \circ \mathfrak{P}(\eta_B \circ f) \circ \eta_{\mathfrak{P}(A)} \circ \eta_A$ is an arrow in $\mathbf{DB}$ with the information flux $\widetilde{g_1} = \widetilde{\eta_{\mathfrak{P}(B)} \circ \mu_B \circ \mathfrak{P}(\eta_B \circ f) \circ \eta_{\mathfrak{P}(A)} \circ \eta_A} = \widetilde{\eta_{\mathfrak{P}(B)}} \bigcap \widetilde{\mu_B} \bigcap \widetilde{\mathfrak{P}(\eta_B)} \bigcap \widetilde{\mathfrak{P}(f)} \bigcap \widetilde{\eta_{\mathfrak{P}(A)}} \bigcap \widetilde{\eta_A} = \widetilde{\mathfrak{P}(f)} = \widetilde{f}$.

(b) $\varpi_B \circ \theta(\eta_B \circ f) = \theta(\eta_{\mathfrak{P}(B)} \circ \eta_B) \circ \theta(\eta_B \circ f) = \theta(g_2)$ (from Lemma 5)

where $g_2 = \eta_{\mathfrak{P}(B)} \circ \eta_B \circ f$ is an arrow in $\mathbf{DB}$ with the information flux

$$\widetilde{g_2} = \widetilde{\eta_{\mathfrak{P}(B)} \circ \eta_B \circ f} = \widetilde{\eta_{\mathfrak{P}(B)}} \bigcap \widetilde{\eta_B} \bigcap \widetilde{f} = \widetilde{f}.$$

Thus, from (a) and (b), $g_1 = g_2 : A \to \mathfrak{P}(B)$ in $\mathbf{DB}$, so that $\theta(g_1) = \theta(g_2) : A \to \mathfrak{P}(B)$ in $\mathbf{DB}_{\mathfrak{P}}$, and hence the natural transformation diagram above commutes, so that ϖ is a natural transformation. Let us show that its components are all isomorphisms. In fact, for any object A, we have that $T(A) = T(\mathfrak{P}(A))$, i. e., $A \simeq \mathfrak{P}(A)$, and $\varpi_A = A \to \mathfrak{P}(A)$ is just this isomorphism in $\mathbf{DB}_{\mathfrak{P}}$ (notice that $\varpi_A = \theta(\eta_{\mathfrak{P}(A)} \circ \eta_A)$ and $\eta_{\mathfrak{P}(A)} \circ \eta_A = id_{\mathfrak{P}(A)} \circ \eta_A = \eta_A$ is an isomorphism in $\mathbf{DB}$). □

Remark. Each arrow $f_T : A \longrightarrow B$ in $\mathbf{DB}_{\mathfrak{P}}$ is "internalized" in $\mathbf{DB}$ by its representation $f =_{def} K^1(f_T) = \phi\theta^{-1}(f_T) = \eta_B^{OP} \circ \theta^{-1}(f_T) : A \longrightarrow B$, where $\theta^{-1}(f_T) : A \longrightarrow TB$ is a program equivalent to the database mapping $f : A \longrightarrow B$, i. e., $\theta^{-1}(f_T) \approx f$.

The functor K is faithful. In fact, for any two arrows $f_T, h_T : A \longrightarrow B$ in $\mathbf{DB}_{\mathfrak{P}}$, $K^1(f_T) = K^1(h_T)$ implies $f_T = h_T$: from $K^1(f_T) = K^1(h_T)$, we obtain $\phi\theta^{-1}(f_T) = \phi\theta^{-1}(h_T)$, and if we apply a bijection $\phi\theta^{-1}$, we obtain $\phi\theta^{-1}\phi\theta^{-1}(f_T) = \phi\theta^{-1}\phi\theta^{-1}(h_T)$, i. e., $\theta\theta^{-1}(f_T) = \theta\theta^{-1}(h_T)$, i. e., $f_T = h_T$ (the compositions $\theta\theta^{-1}$ and $\phi\phi^{-1}$ are the identity functions). □

Let us consider a model $\alpha^* \in \text{Mod}(\mathbf{Sch}(G))$, derived from the Tarski's interpretation I_T (and the extensionalization function h for the intensional entities in IRDB such that for a given intensional interpretation I, the extended Tarski's interpretation is $I_T^* = h \circ I$), of a given IRDB $\mathcal{A}$. It defines the instance database $A = \alpha^*(\mathcal{A}) = \{R_i = \|r_i\| = \alpha(r_i) =_{\text{def}} I_T(r_i) = h(I(r_i)) = h(nr(r_i)) \mid r_i \in S_A\}$ of the RDB schema $\mathcal{A} = (S_A, \Sigma_A)$ (the relations r_i in $\mathcal{A}$ are the intensional n-ary concepts (names) $nr(r_i)$, which the extension is determined by h and Tarski's constraints), and other two databases $S = \alpha^*(\mathcal{S}) = \{\vec{A}, \bot\}$ (of the vector relation of the "source" database) with $\vec{A} = \|r_V\| = \alpha(r_V) =_{\text{def}} I_T(r_V)$, and $A_{\text{MA}} = \alpha^*(\mathcal{A}_{\text{MA}}) = \{\|r_{\text{MA}}\|, \bot\}$ where $\|r_{\text{MA}}\| = \alpha(r_{\text{MA}}) =_{\text{def}} I_T(r_{\text{MA}}) = h(nr(r_{\text{MA}}))$, which contains the values for the multivalued attributes in schema $\mathcal{A}$.

Notice that the integrity-constraint arrows in $\mathbf{Sch}(G)$ do not map the information from source to target schema but only are used to verify if the given R-algebra α is a model or not. The schema mappings $\mathbf{M}$ and $\mathbf{M}^{\text{OP}}$ define the extension of the database $\mathcal{A}$ and corresponding vector relation $\vec{A}$ and contain only the built-in functions Hash and list (fixed, thus independent on various Tarski's interpretations).

Consequently, only the unary functional symbol f_1 in the SOtgd of the mapping $\mathbf{M}_{SA_{\text{MA}}} : \mathcal{S} \to \mathcal{A}_{\text{MA}}$ can have different Tarski's interpretations, with $\alpha^*(\mathbf{M}_{SA_{\text{MA}}}) = \{\mathfrak{h}_{\rho_V}, q_\bot\} : \alpha^*(\mathcal{S}) \to \alpha^*(\mathcal{A}_{\text{MA}})$, where from (4.15) we have the function $\mathfrak{h}_{\rho_V} = \alpha(q_{\rho_V}) : \|r_V\| \to \|r_{\text{MA}}\|$, such that for each $\mathbf{d} = (nr(r_k), \text{ID}, a_i, d) \in \vec{A} = \|r_V\|$ from (4.14),

$$\mathfrak{h}_{\rho_V}(\mathbf{d}) = \begin{cases} (d, I_T(f_1)(d)), & \text{if } a_i \text{ is a multivalued attribute of } r_k \\ & \text{and } I_T(f_1)(d) \text{ is a value of this attribute} \\ \langle\,\rangle, & \text{empty tuple otherwise} \end{cases}$$

We can have different Tarski's interpretations for f, which does not change the extension *of the schemas* in the mapping system in $\mathbf{Sch}(G)$ but can change the interpretation (the graph) of the existentially quantified function f. Thus, we can produce the saturation of the morphism $\mathfrak{h} = \alpha^*(\mathbf{M}_{SA_{\text{MA}}}) = \{\mathfrak{h}_{\rho_V}, q_\bot\} : \alpha^*(\mathcal{S}) \to \alpha^*(\mathcal{A}_{\text{MA}})$, with the saturation algorithm [186] provided in the previous section with Example 25 (here we have that $\mathfrak{h}_{1,0} = \mathfrak{h}_{\rho_V}$). Consequently, we are able to define the following particular saturated morphism $\text{Sat}(\alpha^*(\mathbf{M}_{SA_{\text{MA}}}))$ in $\mathbf{DB}$ for a given model $\alpha \in \text{Mod}(\mathbf{Sch}(G))$.

Corollary 15 (Kleisli semantics for MV-attributes). *Let $\alpha^* \in \text{Mod}(\mathbf{Sch}(G))$ be a model of the IRDB with schema $\mathcal{A}$ (of the graph G in Definition 52) for a given Tarski's interpretation I_T, with $A = \alpha^*(\mathcal{A})$, $S = \{\|r_V\|, \bot\} = \alpha^*(\mathcal{S})$ and $A_{\text{MA}} = \{\|r_{\text{MA}}\|, \bot\} = \alpha^*(\mathcal{A}_{\text{MA}})$. Then we define the saturated morphism $\mathcal{F}_{\rho_V} = \text{Sat}(\alpha^*(M_{SA_{\text{MA}}})) : S \to A_{\text{MA}}$ in* **DB***. Hence, the Kleisli "powerset" semantics for the multivalued attributes are given by the following arrow in the Kleisli category $\mathbf{DB}_{\mathfrak{P}}$:*

$$\theta(\eta_{A_{\text{MA}}} \circ \mathcal{F}_{\rho_V}) : S \to A_{\text{MA}},$$

which for $S_{\text{MA}} = \pi_2(\|r_{\text{MA}}\|)$ and $S_V = \|r_V$ WHERE a-name MULTIVALUED$\|_\#$ defines uniquely the extensionalization function h for the intensional elements in $\pi_4(S_V)$ associ-

ated to the multivalued attributes of any tuple in database A: for any $\mathbf{d} \in S_V$, *and unary concept obtained for multivalued attributes* $u = \pi_4(\mathbf{d}) \in D_1$,

$$h(u) =_{\mathrm{def}} \pi_2\{\mathfrak{h}_{1,i}(\mathbf{d}) \neq \langle\,\rangle \mid \mathfrak{h}_{1,i} \in \mathcal{F}_{\rho_V}, \mathfrak{h}_{1,i} \neq \mathrm{id}_\perp\} \in \mathcal{P}(S_{\mathrm{MA}}) \tag{4.19}$$

For any intensional element, $u \in \pi_4(S_V)$ is defined for a multivalued attribute a_i of some tuple ID in a given relation r_k in the database instance $A = \alpha(\mathcal{A})$, which is a model of IRDB $\mathcal{A}$ represented by mapping system in the graph G. We have:

1. The tuple $\mathbf{d} = \langle nr(r_4), \mathrm{ID}, a_i, u\rangle$ in $\|r_V\| = \alpha(r_V)$ with unary concept $u \in D_1$;
2. The set of values $h(u) = X$ with cardinality $n = |X| \geq 1$ corresponds to the set of values of this multivalued attribute for the tuple **d** above.
3. We have only to show that $h(u)$ is completely covered by the functions in $\mathcal{F}_{\rho_V}$: it is easy to verify from the generation of saturated morphism, as is shown in next Example 27. □

The derived arrows $\mathcal{F}_{\rho_V} = \{\mathfrak{h}_{1,i} \mid \mathfrak{h}_{1,i} \in \mathrm{Sat}(\alpha(\mathrm{M}_{SA_{\mathrm{MA}}}))\}$ in **DB** are *saturated* morphisms, obtained from the sketch's arrow $\mathbf{M}_{SA_{\mathrm{MA}}} = \{q_{\rho_V}, 1_{r_\emptyset}\} : \mathcal{S} \to \mathcal{A}_{\mathrm{MA}}$, because generally they are not images of any functor α^* of the schema mapping $\mathbf{M}_{SA_{\mathrm{MA}}}$.

From such a saturated morphism, we can define the p-function (4.16),

$$f_{q_{\rho_V}} =_{\mathrm{def}} \bigcup \mathcal{F}_{\rho_V} : \alpha(r_V) \to \mathcal{P}(\alpha(r_{\mathrm{MA}})), \quad \text{with } \mathrm{graph}(f_{q_{\rho_V}}) = \bigcup_{\mathfrak{h}_{i,j} \in \mathcal{F}_{\rho_V}} \mathrm{graph}(\mathfrak{h}_{i,j})$$

This p-function represents the 1:N relationship between the relation r_V and r_{MA}, and we have for the extensionalization function h that $h(u) = \pi_2(f_{q_{\rho_V}}(u)) \backslash \{\langle\,\rangle\}$.

Example 27. : Let us consider the continuation of Example 25, for a model α of the schema $\mathcal{A}$, which contains the vector relation $\vec{A} = \|r_V\| = \alpha(r_v) = I_T(r_V)$, obtained by parsing all user's relations, thus also the relation $R_1 = \alpha(\texttt{Contacts})$ in Example 25. So, by parsing the tuple $\mathbf{d}_C$ = (132, Zoran, Majkic, Appia, 0187, hobbies_of_132) $\in R_1$, we have

$\|r_V\| \supseteq$

r-name	t-index	a-name	value
...	...	...	...
Contacts	ID_{132}	hobbies	hobbies_of_132
...	...	...	...

where $\mathrm{ID}_{132} = \mathrm{Hash}(\mathbf{d}_C)$, and $\|r_{\mathrm{MA}}\| = \alpha(r_{\mathrm{MA}}) = I_T(r_{\mathrm{MA}})$ with ρ_V mapping corresponding to the SOtgd (4.11)

$$\exists f_1(\forall x_1, \ldots, \forall x_4((r_V(x_1, x_2, x_3, x_4) \wedge x_3 \text{ MULTIVALUED}) \Rightarrow r_{\mathrm{MA}}(x_4, f_1(x_4)))).$$

Let $S_V = \|r_V$ WHERE a-name MULTIVALUED $\|_\# \subseteq \|r_V\|$. The `hobbies` are a multivalued attribute of the relation `Contacts`, so we have for the tuple

$$\mathbf{d} = (\texttt{Contacts}, \mathrm{ID}_{132}, \texttt{hobbies}, \text{hobbies\_of\_132}) \in S_V \subseteq \|r_V\|,$$

and

$\|r_{MA}\| \supseteq$

value	atom-value
...	...
hobbies_of_132	photography
hobbies_of_132	music
hobbies_of_132	art
hobbies_of_132	travel
...	...

where from (4.9) in Section 4.3.1,

$$u = \texttt{hobbies\_of\_132} = g^*(\lessdot\texttt{hobbies}(x_1, y)\gtrdot^{x_1}_{y})) = I(\texttt{hobbies}(132, y)) \in D_1 \subset \mathcal{D}$$

is the intensional unary concept in the IRDB such that, from $I^*_T(\texttt{hobbies}(132, y)) =$ {photography, music, art, travel} and $I^*_T = h \circ I$, we obtain

$$h(u) = h(\texttt{hobbies\_of\_132}) = \{\text{photography, music, art, travel}\} \tag{4.20}$$

where h is the extensionalization function corresponding to the Tarski's interpretation I_T and derived functor α^*. Let for Tarski's model I_T from which α is uniquely derived, the function $I_T(f_1) : \mathcal{D} \to \mathcal{D}$ satisfies $I_T(f_1)(u) = \text{music}$, and hence

$$\mathfrak{h}_{1,0}(\mathbf{d}) = \alpha(q_{\rho_V})(\mathbf{d}) = (u, I_T(f_1)(u)) = (u, \text{music}) \in \|r_{MA}\|.$$

Consequently, from step 6 of Saturation algorithm and relation R in point (b) of Example 25, in step 7 of the algorithm will be introduced the three new functions $\mathfrak{h}_{1,j} : \|r_V\| \to \|r_{MA}\|$, for each tuple $\mathbf{b} \in R$, into $\mathrm{Sat}(\alpha^*(\mathbf{M}_{AB}))$ so that, for $u = \text{hobbies\_of\_132}$,

$$\mathfrak{h}_{1,1}(\mathbf{d}) = (u, \text{photography}), \quad \text{with } I'_T(f_1)(u) = \text{photography};$$
$$\mathfrak{h}_{1,2}(\mathbf{d}) = (u, \text{travel}), \quad \text{with } I''_T(f_1)(u) = \text{travel};$$
$$\mathfrak{h}_{1,3}\mathbf{d}) = (u, \text{art}), \quad \text{with } I'''_T(f_1)(u) = \text{art},$$

so, from the saturation algorithm we obtain

$$\mathcal{F}_{\rho_V} = \mathrm{Sat}(\alpha(\mathbf{M}_{SA_{MA}})) \supset \{\mathfrak{h}_{1,0}, \mathfrak{h}_{1,1}, \mathfrak{h}_{1,2}, \mathfrak{h}_{1,3}, \mathrm{id}_\perp\}$$

and derived p-function (4.16), $f_{q_{\rho_V}} = \bigcup \mathcal{F}_{\rho_V} : \alpha(r_V) \to \mathcal{P}(\alpha(r_{MA}))$, with

$$f_{q_{\rho_V}}(\mathbf{d}) = f_{q_{\rho_V}}(\texttt{Contacts}, \mathrm{ID}_{132}, \texttt{hobbies}, \mathrm{hobbies\_of\_132})$$

=

value	atom-value
hobbies_of_132	art
hobbies_of_132	photography
hobbies_of_132	music
hobbies_of_132	travel

and, from (4.19) in Corollary 15, we obtain

$$\pi_2\{\mathfrak{h}_{1,i}(\mathbf{d}) \neq \langle\,\rangle \mid \mathfrak{h}_{1,i} \in \mathcal{F}_{\rho_V}, \mathfrak{h}_{1,i} \neq \mathrm{id}_\perp\}$$
$$= \{\text{photography}, \text{music}, \text{art}, \text{travel}\} = h(u) \in \mathcal{P}(S_{\mathrm{MA}}), \quad \text{from (4.20)},$$

where $S_{\mathrm{MA}} = \pi_2(\|r_{\mathrm{MA}}\|)$.

Hence, the denotational semantics of database mappings are given by morphisms of the Kleisli category $\mathbf{DB}_T$, based on the fundamental (from Universal algebra) monad (power-view endofunctor) T, here instead the "powerset" endofunctor $T = \mathfrak{P} : \mathbf{DB} \to \mathbf{DB}$. The big data integration framework presented in [21] considers only the standard RDBs with Tarskian semantics of the FOL, where one defines what it takes for a sentence in a language to be true relative to a model.

Thanks to the intensional semantics, different from the ordinary RDBs multivalued framework, which cannot directly support the multivalued attributes, here we obtained a natural support for such a direct "reification-based" property. In this section, we demonstrated both facts, that **DB** is able to support the intensional extension of the FOL and that the semantics of the intensional elements, which express the multivalued attribute properties can be done by the morphisms in **DB** derived from the data integration mapping graph used to define the canonical models of the IRDBs.

We defined the particular "powerset" monad $\mathfrak{P}$ for **DB** and demonstrated that the denotational semantics of the intensional elements used for the multivalued attributes can be given by particular saturated arrows of the Kleisli category $\mathbf{DB}_{\mathfrak{P}}$, which may be "internalized" in **DB** category as multivalued attribute "computations." In this way, we obtained an algebraic denotational semantics for the data integration (defined by logic formulae with second-order logic tgds) used to support the IRDB management system.

With this, we obtained a full theoretical model for the new IRDBs, and opened the door and the opportunity for their concrete industrial developments and future implementations, which what was primary objective of the initial IRDB Manifesto in 2014 [20].

5 Theory of many-valued intensional first-order logic

5.1 Introduction to many-valued logics

Many-valued logic was conceived as a logic for uncertain, incomplete and possibly inconsistent information, which is very close to the statements containing the words "necessary" and "possible," i. e., to the statements that make an assertion about the *mode of truth* of some other statement. *Algebraic* semantics interpret modal connectives as operators, while *Relational* semantics uses relational structures, often called Kripke models, whose elements are thought of variously as being possible worlds; for example, moments of time, belief situations, states of a computer, etc. The two approaches are closely related: the subsets of relational structures from an algebra with modal operators, while conversely any modal algebra can be embedded into an algebra of subsets of a relational structure via extensions of Stone's Boolean representation theory. For example, the first (1934) and the most known *Stone's representation theorem* for Boolean algebras [187], is the duality between the category of Boolean algebras and the category of Stone spaces. Every Boolean algebra $(BA, +, \cdot, \backslash, 0, 1)$, where $+, \cdot, \backslash$ are corresponding algebraic operations (addition, multiplication and complement) for classical logic connectives $\vee, \wedge, \neg$, respectively, is isomorphic to an algebra of particular clopen (i. e., simultaneously closed and open) subsets of its Stone space. Stone's theorem has since been the model for many other similar representation theorems.

Our new representation theorem provided in next section, in the case of distributive complete lattice of truth values, is a particular Stone-like autoreferential representation based on the particular subsets of these truth values.

The representation theorems are based on Lindenbaum algebra of a logic $\mathcal{L} = (\mathrm{Var}, \mathcal{O}, \Vdash)$, where Var is a set of propositional symbols of a language $\mathcal{L}$ (denoted by $p, q, \ldots$), $\mathcal{O}$ is the set of logical connectives and $\Vdash$ is the entailment relation of this logic. We denote by $F(\mathcal{L})$ the set of all formulae denoted by $\phi, \psi, \varphi \ldots$ Notice that the truth values in $X \subset \mathrm{Var} \subseteq F(\mathcal{L})$ are the constant propositional symbols as well, and we will use the same symbols for them as those used for elements in lattice $(X, \leq)$, with the bottom and top elements $0, 1$, respectively. Lindenbaum algebra of $\mathcal{L}$ is the quotient algebra $F(\mathcal{L})/\equiv$, where for any two $\phi, \psi \in F(\mathcal{L})$, it holds that $\phi \equiv \psi$ iff $\phi \Vdash \psi$ and $\psi \Vdash \phi$.

Remark. It is necessary to have clear in mind the difference between a many-valued *logic* and its underlying *algebra* of truth values (e. g., the propositional logic and its Boolean algebra, the intuitionistic logic and its Heyting algebra), so that we can informally use the term lattice (of algebraic truth values) speaking about logics as well. Next, for a many-valued logic with standard connectives $\neg, \wedge$ and $\vee$, the corresponding algebraic operator in $(X, \leq)$ will be usually denoted by $\sim: X \to X$ and $\widetilde{\wedge}, \widetilde{\vee} : X^2 \to X$, relatively.

https://doi.org/10.1515/9783110981438-005

A *valuation* v as a mapping $v : \text{Var} \to X$ such that for any $x \in X$, $v(x) = x$. It can be uniquely extended to the homomorphism from the absolutely free syntax algebra to the many-valued algebra $v^* : (F(\mathcal{L}), \{o\}_{o\in\mathcal{O}}) \to (X, \{\widetilde{o}\}_{o\in\mathcal{O}})$ (i. e., for any $\phi, \psi \in F(\mathcal{L})$, $v^*(\phi \odot \psi) = v^*(\phi) \circledast v^*(\psi)$, where $\odot \in \{\wedge, \vee, \Rightarrow\}$ and corresponding algebraic operators $\circledast \in \{\widetilde{\wedge}, \widetilde{\vee}, \Rrightarrow\}$ relatively, $v^*(\neg\phi) =\sim v^*(\phi)$, and $v^*(\Diamond_i\phi) = \widetilde{o}_i(v^*(\phi))$, where $\wedge, \vee, \Rightarrow, \neg, \Diamond_i$ are conjunction, disjunction, implication, negation and existential logic modal operator, respectively). The set of *logic* universal modal operators will be denoted by the standard way $\Box_i \in \mathcal{O}$. We denote by $\mathbb{V}$ the set of all valuations $v : \text{Var} \to X$. □

The algebraic existential *modal* operators $o_i : X \to X, i = 1, 2, \ldots$, are monotonic, additive ($o_i(x\widetilde{\vee}y) = o_i(x)\widetilde{\vee}o_i(y)$) and $o_i(0) = 0$ (the universal modal operators are monotonic and multiplicative $\overline{o}_i(x\widetilde{\wedge}y) = \overline{o}_i(x)\widetilde{\wedge}\overline{o}_i(y)$, $\overline{o}_i(1) = 1$). They appear often in many-valued logics, e. g., as a conflation operator (knowledge negation [188]) and Moore's autoepistemic operator [189] in Belnap's 4-valued bilattice [190], or modal operators L and M of Lukasiewicz's 4-valued logic [79, 81, 191], or recently in [192–195].

A many-valued *modal* logic here is a truth-functional many-valued logic with a non-empty set of modal operators with properties defined above.

Relevant work

We will briefly present the previous work, based on algebraic *matrices*, and explain some weak points of such a matrix-based approach.

The standard approach to representation theorems uses a subset $D \subset X$ of the set of truth values X, denominated designated elements; informally the designated elements represent the equivalence class of the theorems of $\mathcal{L}$. Given an algebra $\mathbf{A} = (X, \{o\}_{o\in\mathcal{O}})$, the $\mathcal{O}$-matrix is the pair $(\mathbf{A}, D)$, where $D \subset X$ is a subset of designated elements. The *algebraic* satisfaction relation $\models^a$ ("a" stands for "algebraic") is defined as follows.

Definition 54. Let $\mathcal{L} = (\text{Var}, \mathcal{O}, \Vdash)$ be a logic, $M = (\mathbf{A}, D)$ a $\mathcal{O}$-matrix and $\phi \in F(\mathcal{L})$. Let $v : \text{Var} \to X$ be a map that assigns logic values to propositional variables, and $v^* : F(\mathcal{L}) \to X$ be its unique extension to all formulae in a language $\mathcal{L}$. Let $\mathfrak{M}$ be a class of $\mathcal{O}$-matrices. We define the relation $\models^a$ inductively as follows:

1. $(\mathbf{A}, D) \models^a_v \phi$ iff $v^*(\phi) \in D$,
2. $(\mathbf{A}, D) \models^a \phi$ iff $v^*(\phi) \in D$ for every $v : \text{Var} \to X$,
3. $\mathfrak{M} \models^a \phi$ iff $(\mathbf{A}, D) \models^a \phi$ for every $(\mathbf{A}, D) \in \mathfrak{M}$.

A logic $\mathcal{L}$ is sound w. r. t. $\mathfrak{M}$ iff for every $\phi \in F(\mathcal{L})$, if $\mathcal{L} \Vdash \phi$ then $\mathfrak{M} \models^a \phi$.

$\mathcal{L}$ is complete w. r. t. $\mathfrak{M}$ iff for every $\phi \in F(\mathcal{L})$, if $\mathfrak{M} \models^a \phi$ then $\mathcal{L} \Vdash \phi$.

Dual to algebraic semantics, based on the class $\mathfrak{M}$ of $\mathcal{O}$-matrices we also have the Kripke-style semantics based on a class $\mathcal{R}$ of relational models where the satisfiability relation $\models^r$ is defined by induction on the structure of the formulae. Substantially, each relational model $K \in \mathcal{R}$ is a Kripke frame over a set of possible worlds with additional accessibility *relations* between possible worlds associated with logical operators. The distinctive feature of this relational semantics is that the accessibility relations are used in the definition of satisfiability, which is not just a mechanical truth-functional translation of the formula structure into the model.

The definition of the algebraic/relational duality is based on the following assumption.

Definition 55 (Representation assumption [196]). Assume that there exists a class $\mathcal{R}$ of relational structures such that there exist $\mathbb{D} : \mathfrak{M} \to \mathcal{R}$, $\mathbb{E} : \mathcal{R} \to \mathfrak{M}$ such that (C):
(i) for every $K \in \mathcal{R}$, $\mathbb{E}(K) = (\mathbf{A}_K, D_K) \in \mathfrak{M}$, where $\mathbf{A}_K = (X_K, \{o_K\}_{o \in \mathcal{O}})$ is an algebra of subsets of the support 1_K (possible worlds) of K, i. e., with $X_K \subseteq \mathcal{P}(1_K)$;
(ii) for every $M = (\mathbf{A}, D) \in \mathfrak{M}$, if $\mathbb{E}(\mathbb{D}(M)) = (\mathbf{A}_{\mathbb{D}(M)}, D_{\mathbb{D}(M)})$ then there is an injective homomorphism $i_n : \mathbf{A} \to \mathbf{A}_{\mathbb{D}(M)}$ with $i_n^{-1}(D_{\mathbb{D}(M)}) \subseteq D$.

Let $m : \text{Var} \to X_K$ be a meaning function (assigns logic values to propositional variables), then (K, m) is the Kripke model for a Kripke-frame $K = (1_K, \{R_j\}_{j \le n})$ where 1_K is the set of possible worlds, $\{R_j\}_{j \le n}$ a finite set of accessibility relations between them (relational structure). Then the definition of the relation $\vDash^r$ can be given as follows.

Definition 56 ([196]). Assume that $\mathfrak{M}$ and $\mathcal{R}$ satisfy condition (C)(i). Let $\mathcal{K} \in \mathcal{R}$, $m : \text{Var} \to X_K$ with $X_K \subseteq \mathcal{P}(1_K)$, and $m^* : F(\mathcal{L}) \to X_K$ be its extended unique homomorphism of $\mathcal{O}$-algebras. Let y be an element in the support of K. Then for $y \in 1_K$:
1. $K \vDash^r_{m,y} \phi$ iff $y \in m^*(\phi)$;
2. $K \vDash^r_m \phi$ iff $m^*(\phi) \in D_K$;
3. $K \vDash^r \phi$ iff for every m, $K \vDash^r_m \phi$,

where $\|\phi\| = m^*(\phi)$ is the set of possible worlds in 1_K where ϕ is satisfied.

A logic $\mathcal{L}$ is sound w. r. t. $\mathcal{R}$ iff for every $\phi \in F(\mathcal{L})$, if $\mathcal{L} \Vdash \phi$ then $\mathcal{R} \vDash^r \phi$. $\mathcal{L}$ is complete w. r. t. $\mathcal{R}$ iff for every $\phi \in F(\mathcal{L})$, if $\mathcal{R} \vDash^r \phi$ then $\mathcal{L} \Vdash \phi$.

In [196], it is demonstrated that if $\mathcal{L} = (\text{Var}, \mathcal{O}, \Vdash)$ is sound and complete w. r. t. a class $\mathfrak{M}$ of $\mathcal{O}$-matrices, and there exists a class $\mathcal{R}$ such that the Assumption (C) holds, then $\mathcal{L}$ is sound and complete w. r. t. the class of Kripke-style models $\mathcal{K}_{\mathcal{M},\mathcal{R}} = \{(K, m) \mid K \in \mathcal{R}, m : \text{Var} \to X_K \text{ where } \mathbb{E}(K) = (\mathbf{A}_K, D_K)\}$. The strong and weak points of this approach:
- In a matrix-based many-valued logic, a formula is *satisfied* if its logic value is a designated value. Such an approach, *based on $\mathcal{O}$-matrices*, is very effective for all kinds of 2-valued logic where the set of designated elements is a singleton set composed by only true value, $D = \{1\}$, as in the case of classical, intuitionistic and 2-value modal logics (extension of Boolean algebra). It is only a partially good solution for the case when a set of truth values *cannot* be easily divided into two complementary subsets: $D \subset X$ for values for which we retain that a formula can

be considered satisfied, and its complement $X \backslash D$ for those, which we retain that a formula cannot be considered satisfied. This difficulty can be found in the case of bilattices [188, 197–202].

- The second observation is that the representation theorems define the isomorphism between a many-valued algebra and the set-based algebra that is a subalgebra of the canonical extension of the original many-valued algebra. It will be useful to define directly such an isomorphism based on the duality assumption (C).

In next section, we provide a new general representation theorem for many-valued logics with the *truth-invariance* entailment for *any* set of truth values X. It is *substantially* different w. r. t. the previous representation theorems that are all based on matrices, and is based on algebraic models of a logic.

For example, in the case of logic programs, let $v : \mathrm{Var} \to X$ be a many-valued valuation, and $(X, \leq)$ be the set X of logic values with partial truth order $\leq$. Then, given any rule $B \leftarrow B_1 \wedge \cdots \wedge B_n$ where B is a propositional letter and B_i is a ground literal (propositional letter or negation of them), we say that it is *satisfied* iff $v(B) \geq v(B_1) \wedge \cdots \wedge v(B_n)$; the valuation that satisfies all rules is a *model* for such a logic program. As we have seen in this case, instead of the subset $D \subseteq X$ of designated elements, we simply use the truth ordering between logic values.

The simple way to extend this example to any propositional logic $\mathcal{L} = (\mathrm{Var}, \mathcal{O}, \Vdash)$ is to consider equivalently this logic as a sequent system of (structural and logical) rules $\frac{s_1,\ldots,s_k}{s}$ where each s_i is a sequent $\phi_1, \ldots, \phi_n \vdash \psi$ where, accordingly to Gentzen,[1] the commas in the left are conjunctions and $\phi_i, \psi \in F(\mathcal{L})$ are logic formulae. Notice that this sequent-based approach is always possible, independently of the algebraic properties of the set of truth values in X, e. g., by transforming the original many-valued logic into 2-valued modal logic [203, 204], and defining the classical 2-valued sequent rules as presented in [205] with the truth-preserving entailment for many-valued logics.

Definition 57 (New truth-preserving entailment). Let $\Gamma = \{\phi_1, \ldots, \phi_n\}$ be a set of sentences and we define the truth-preserving entailment in two alternative cases:

1. *Sequent-based entailment* with sequents $\Gamma \vdash \psi$. We say that a valuation $v : \mathrm{Var} \to X$ *satisfies* this sequent iff $v^*(\phi_1) \bigwedge \cdots \bigwedge v^*(\phi_n) \leq v^*(\psi_1)$, where $\bigwedge$ is the meet operator in lattice $(X. \leq)$, and we denote this sequent satisfaction by $\Gamma \vDash_v \psi$. A sequent is *valid* (an axiom) in $(X, \leq)$ if it is satisfied for all valuations in $(X, \leq)$.
We denote by $\phi \preceq \psi$ iff for all homomorphisms $v \in \mathbb{V}$, $v^*(\phi) \leq v^*(\psi)$.
Valuation v satisfies a rule $\frac{s_1,\ldots,s_k}{s}$ iff v satisfies the conclusion sequent s of this rule whenever it satisfies all sequent premises $s_1, \ldots, s_k$ of this rule. Then a *model* of

1 Our attention to singular Genzen systems (the sequents with exactly one sentence on the right side) is less restrictive than it seems (compare Belnap's “Display logic”).

this logic is any valuation v, which satisfies all logic sequent rules of this logic (the structural sequent rules as Cut, Weakening, etc. are satisfied by all valuations).
2. *Model-based entailment* where Γ is the set of theses ϕ_i with associated prefixed bottom-truth values $a_i \in X$, such that their *models* are defined as a subset of all valuations:

$$\mathbb{V}_\Gamma =_{\text{def}} \{v \in \mathbb{V} \mid \forall \phi_i \in \Gamma.(v^*(\phi_i) \geq a_i)\} \tag{5.1}$$

So, we introduce the model-based truth-preserving entailment of a sentence ψ from the theses in Γ by

$$\Gamma \models \psi \quad \text{iff} \quad (\exists \phi_i \in \Gamma).(\forall v \in \mathbb{V}_\Gamma).(v^*(\psi) \geq v^*(\phi_i)) \tag{5.2}$$

Different from an arbitrary fixing of the set of designated truth-values D (with the introduction of possible errors for complex nontotally-ordered lattices), the idea of truth-preserving entailment is a deep concept *underlying many-valuedness* valid for classic 2-valued logics (with $a_i = 1$ for all thesis) as well.

So, we can replace the duality algebras (matrices)-relational structures described in the previous work, by the semantic duality algebraic models—Kripke models. The examples by using Gentzen-like sequent calculi [205] to obtain the set of models of a given logic, without using necessarily the subset of designated elements (matrices), are provided in Section A.3.1 (with Example 44 and truth-preserving entailment in Definition 102) and in Section A.4.3 by Definition 124. The example in Section A.3.1, when X is a complete distributive lattice, is used in Section A.3.2 for a concrete definition of Kripke frames based on an autoreferential assumption [69] where the set of possible worlds is fixed by a subset of algebraic truth values in X. The strict autoreferential Kripke semantics of a many-valued logic is that the set of possible worlds $\mathcal{W}$ is the set of truth values in the lattice $(X, \leq)$, and that for a given valuation v each formula is satisfied only in the world $w = v^*(\phi)$, or formally we have the following.

Definition 58 (Strict autoreferential Kripke semantics). For a given propositional many-valued logic $\mathcal{L}$ with absolutely free syntax algebra $\mathcal{A}_L = (F(\mathcal{L}), \{o_i\}_{o_i \in \mathcal{O}})$ and corresponding algebra of truth-values $\mathbf{A} = (X, \{\widetilde{o}_i\}_{o_i \in \mathcal{O}})$, we define the Kripke frame $K = (\mathcal{W}, \{R_{o_i}\}_{o_i \in \mathcal{O}})$ with $\mathcal{W} = X$ and the accessibility relations:
1. For each unary logic connective, $o_i \in \mathcal{O}$, $R_{o_i} = \{(\widetilde{o}_i x, x) \mid x \in \mathcal{W}\}$;
2. Fore each binary logic connective, $o_i \in \mathcal{O}$, $R_{o_i} = \{(x\widetilde{o}_i y, x, y) \mid x \in \mathcal{W}\}$.

A Kripke model $\mathcal{M} = (K, I_K)$ with mapping $I_K : \text{Var} \times \mathcal{W} \to \mathbf{2}$ defines the Kripke satisfaction relation $\models_w$, for a given world $w \in \mathcal{W}$ by $\mathcal{M} \models_w p$ iff $I_K(p, w) = 1$ for each $p \in \text{Var} \subseteq F(\mathcal{L})$, and for any $\phi, \psi \in F(\mathcal{L})$, for unary and binary logic connectives, respectively, by:
1. $\mathcal{M} \models_w o_i\phi$ iff $\exists y(w, y) \in R_{o_i}$ such that $\mathcal{M} \models_y \phi$;
2. $\mathcal{M} \models_w \phi o_i \psi$ iff $\exists y, z(w, y, z) \in R_{o_i}$ such that $\mathcal{M} \models_y \phi$ and $\mathcal{M} \models_z \psi$.

This Kripke semantics is strictly autoreferential if, for a given valuation $v : \mathrm{Var} \to X$, the mapping $I_K : \mathrm{Var} \times \mathcal{W} \to \mathbf{2}$, for each proposition $p \in \mathrm{Var} \subseteq F(\mathcal{L})$ and $x \in \mathcal{W}$, it holds that $I_K(p, x) = 1$ iff $x = v(p)$.

So, we obtain the following simple property of strict autoreferential semantics.

Corollary 16. *For any formula $\phi \in F(\mathcal{L})$ and possible world $x \in \mathcal{W}$ from Definition* 58, *for strict autoreferential semantics we obtain that*

$$\mathcal{M} \models_x \phi \quad \textit{iff} \quad x = v^*(\phi) \tag{5.3}$$

Proof. For each proposition p, it holds directly from Definition 58. Let it holds for any ϕ. Then by structural induction on number of connectives it holds in both cases, for unary and binary logic connectives from Definition 58. □

In what follows, we denote by $y < x$ iff ($y \leq x$ and not $x \leq y$), and we denote by $x \bowtie y$ two unrelated elements in X (so that not ($x \leq y$ or $y \leq x$)).

5.1.1 Nonmatrix based representation theorem for many-valued logics

Based on the considerations of *truth-preserving entailment* in Definition 57 in the previous section, we intend to define an algebraic/relational duality in the way that we do not need to define a subset of designated elements D of a many-valued algebra. Let $v : \mathrm{Var} \to X$ be a given many-valued model of the logic $\mathcal{L}$, extended homomorphically to $v^* : F(\mathcal{L}) \to X$ to the set of all formulae $F(\mathcal{L})$, then we can use the *algebraic* model $(\mathbf{A}, v)$, instead of o-matrices $(\mathbf{A}, D)$. Let Γ be a set of sentences (or sequents) of $\mathcal{L}$. The intuitive idea is to use the *models* $\mathbb{V}_\Gamma \subset \mathbb{V}$ of the logic $\mathcal{L}$ (notice that all $v \in \mathbb{V}_\Gamma$ satisfy each sentence (or sequent) in Γ, and that the representation theorem is interesting only for logics that have at least one model, i. e., when $\mathbb{V}_\Gamma$ is not empty).

In what follows, we will consider a bounded lattice $(X, \leq, \wedge, \vee, 0, 1)$ of truth values for this many-valued logic, and $\{o_i\}_{o_i \in \mathcal{O}}$ the set of functions $o_i : X^n \to X$ (with arity $n \geq 1$) assigned to operation names in $\mathcal{O}$ of the logic $\mathcal{L} = (\mathrm{Var}, \mathcal{O}, \Vdash)$. We assume that the carrier set of *every* algebra for a logic $\mathcal{L}$ contains also a set of propositional variables in Var, so that the terms of an algebra $\mathbf{A} = (X, \{o\}_{o \in \mathcal{O}})$ are the terms with variables in Var. Consequently, any pair $(\mathbf{A}, v)$ can be seen as a ground term algebra obtained by assigning to Var the values in a model v of $\mathcal{L}$.

Thus, the algebraic satisfaction relation $\models^a$ will be relative to a model v of the logic $\mathcal{L}$ instead of the prefixed set of elements in D. In fact, from the strict autoreferential semantics in Definition 58, we can write the satisfaction $(\mathbf{A}, v) \models^a_x \phi$ of the formula ϕ at world $x \in X$ to be an algebraic analog to the Kripke satisfaction in (5.3), $\mathcal{M} \models_x \phi$ (iff $x = v^*(\phi)$).

For example, in the case of a logic program $\mathcal{L}$ we can use the Fitting's 3-valued fixed- point operator to obtain its well-founded 3-valued model. Here, we will apply the *truth-preserving* entailment principle in Definition 57, which is a conservative extension of the definition for classic 2-valued logic, the idea originally used to define the inference closure in the bilattice based logics [203], and used to develop a new sequent system for many-valued logics presented in [205] as well.

In any case, in the representation theorem framework we are interested in establishing what is a canonical isomorphic algebra for a logic $\mathcal{L}$, and its relationship with Kripke relational structures. So, we can use models $v \in \mathbb{V}_\Gamma$ of a logic $\mathcal{L}$ only as a means to obtain these results. Now we can introduce a *new definition* of the algebraic/relational duality, where instead of a class of $\mathcal{O}$-matrices $(\mathbf{A}, D)$, we will consider a *class of models* of the same given algebra $\mathbf{A}$, as follows [206].

Definition 59 (New representation assumption). Let, for a fixed algebra $\mathbf{A} = (X, \wedge, \vee, \{o_K\}_{o \in \mathcal{O}})$, $\mathfrak{M}$ be a class of all algebraic models $(\mathbf{A}, v)$ (of all valuations v which are models for a given logic $\mathcal{L}$), and for this algebra $\mathbf{A}$ there exists corresponding fixed Kripke-frame $K = (1_K, \{R_j\}_{j \leq n})$, where 1_K is the set of possible worlds and $\{R_j\}_{j \leq n}$ a finite set of accessibility relations between them (relational structure) and we denote by $\mathcal{K}_\mathcal{M}$ a class of Kripke models of the same logic $\mathcal{L}$ for this fixed frame.

Then assume that there exists a mapping $\mathbb{D} : \mathfrak{M} \to \mathcal{K}_\mathcal{M}$, such that $(K, I_K) = \mathbb{D}(\mathbf{A}, v) \in \mathcal{K}_\mathcal{M}$, with a mining mapping $I_K : \mathrm{Var} \times 1_K \to \mathbf{2}$ and there exists a mapping $\mathbb{E} : \mathcal{K}_\mathcal{M} \to \mathfrak{M}^+$, where $\mathfrak{M}^+$ is a class of set-based algebraic models of $\mathcal{L}$ such that:

(i) for every *Kripke* model $\mathcal{M} = (K, I_K) \in \mathcal{K}_\mathcal{M}$ of $\mathcal{L}$, the $(\mathbf{A}_K, v_K) = \mathbb{E}((K, I_K)) \in \mathfrak{M}$ is an algebraic model of $\mathcal{L}$, where $\mathbf{A}_K = (X_K, \bigcap, \bigcup, \{o_K\}_{o \in \mathcal{O}})$ with $X_K \subseteq \mathcal{P}(1_K)$ is an algebra of subsets of the support 1_K of K with a set-valuation $v_K : \mathrm{Var} \to X_K$ such that for each formula ϕ in $\mathcal{L}$, $v_K^*(\phi) = \{w \in 1_K \mid I_K^*(\phi, w) = 1\}$;

(ii) for every *algebraic* model $M = (\mathbf{A}, v) \in \mathfrak{M}$ of $\mathcal{L}$, the $(K, I_K) = \mathbb{D}(M)$ is a Kripke model, so that if $\mathbb{E}(\mathbb{D}(M)) = (\mathbf{A}_K, v_K)$, then there is a injective mapping $i_n : X \hookrightarrow X_K$, such that $v_K = i_n \circ v : \mathrm{Var} \to X_K$.

A representation is *autoreferential* when $1_K \subseteq X$.

Example 28. Thus, for an original algebraic model $(\mathbf{A}, v)$ with the *strict* autoreferential Kripke model (with possible worlds $1_K = \mathcal{W} = X$) in Definition 58 when for each $x \in X$, $i_n(x) = \{x\}$, for the set-based (complex) algebra $(\mathbf{A}_K, v_K) = \mathbb{E}(\mathbb{D}(\mathbf{A}, v))$ with $X_K = \{\{x\} \mid x \in X\} \subseteq \mathcal{P}(1_K)$, for any formula ϕ, we have from (5.3) that $\|\phi\| = \{x \mid \mathcal{M} \vDash_x \phi\} = \{v(\phi)\} = v_K^*(\phi)$, which is a singleton, and hence the $\wedge$ operation in $\mathbf{A}$ cannot be represented by the set intersection operation $\bigcap$ in $\mathbf{A}_K$, and hence such Kripke models do not satisfy the new representation assumptions. Let us consider instead another examples that satisfy representation assumptions:

Case A: Let us consider the standard propositional logic $\mathcal{L} = (\mathrm{Var}, \mathcal{O}, \Vdash)$, where $\mathcal{O} = \{\wedge, \neg\}$ and its simple Boolean algebra $\mathbf{A} = (X, \leq, \widetilde{\wedge}, \sim)$, where $X = \mathbf{2} = \{0, 1\}$ with logic operators "and," $\wedge$, and logic negation $\sim$, respectively, with $0 \leq 1$. Let us take $1_K = X = \{0, 1\} = \mathbf{2}$, so that the canonical representation of the Boolean algebra $\mathbf{A}$ is the powerset algebra $\mathbf{A}_K = (X_K, \subseteq, \bigcap, \neg^+)$, with $X_K \subseteq \mathcal{P}(\{0,1\})$ and $\neg^+\emptyset = \neg^+\{0\} =_{\text{def}} \{0,1\}$ and $\neg^+\{1\} = \neg^+\{0,1\} =_{\text{def}} \{0\}$ and with injection $i_n : \{0,1\} \hookrightarrow \mathcal{P}(\{0,1\})$. We can define that $i_n(0) = \{0\}$ and $i_n(1) = \{0,1\}$, and hence, from $v_k = i_n \circ v$, for any $p \in \text{Var}$, $v(p) = 1$ iff $v_K(p) = \{0,1\}$ and $v(p) = 0$ iff $v_K(p) = \{0\}$.

Case B: Let us consider the 4-valued Belnap's distributive bilattice $X = \mathcal{B}_4 = \{f, \bot, \top, t\}$ in the next Section 5.1.3, with $\bot$ for *unknown* and $\top$ for *inconsistent* logic value, $f = 0$, $t = 1$ are bottom and top values w. r. t. the *truth* ordering $0 \leq \bot, 0 \leq \top, \bot \leq 1, \top \leq 1$ and $\bot \bowtie \top$. It is the smallest many-valued logic capable of dealing with incomplete (unknown) and inconsistent logics. In this case, we can take $1_K = \{0, \bot, \top\} \subset X$, with injection $i_n : (X, \leq, \widetilde{\wedge}, \widetilde{\vee}) \hookrightarrow (X_K, \subseteq, \bigcap, \bigcup)$ where $X_K \subseteq \mathcal{P}(X)$, such that: $i_n(0) = \{0\}, i_n(\bot) = \{0, \bot\}, i_n(\top) = \{0, \top\}, 1_K = i_n(1) = \{0, \bot, \top\}$.

In this new definition, we replaced the old duality algebras-relational structures by the semantic duality algebraic models—Kripke models of a logic $\mathcal{L}$.

Notice that in the definition above, we do not require the injection i_n to be an injective *homomorphism*, as in Definition 55, but we require that the following diagram commutes (here id_{X_K} is the identity mapping for X_K):

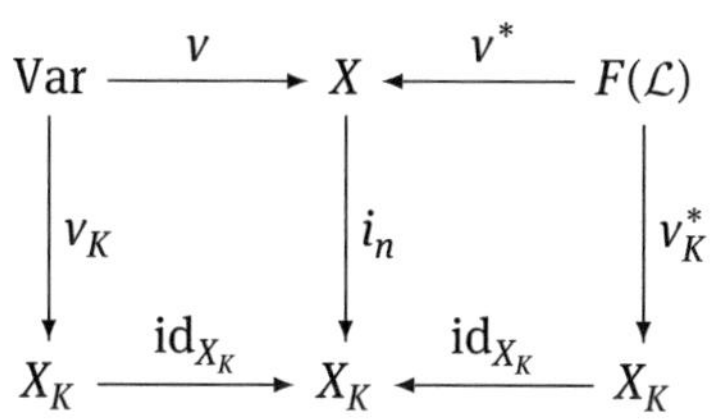

Now, from the fact that in new representation assumption in Definition 59 instead of $\mathcal{O}$-matrices with subsets of designated truth values D, we used only the models of algebras (valuations), we need also the new definition of algebraic and Kripke-frame satisfaction relations that do not use more the subsets of designated truth values. The *algebraic* satisfaction relation $\models^a$ is defined as follows.

Definition 60. Let $\mathcal{L} = (\text{Var}, \mathcal{O}, \Vdash)$ be a logic with a tautology $\top$, $M = (\mathbf{A}, v) \in \mathfrak{M}$ be an algebraic logic model of a logic $\mathcal{L}$, defined by a many-valued valuation $v : \text{Var} \to X$, and $\phi \in F(\mathcal{L})$, and $v^* : F(\mathcal{L}) \to X$ be its unique standard extension to all formulae in a language $\mathcal{L}$.

Assume that $\mathfrak{M}$ and $\mathcal{K}_{\mathcal{M}}$ satisfy the assumptions in Definition 59 with $(\mathbf{A}_K, v_K) =_{\text{def}} \mathbb{E}(\mathbb{D}(\mathbf{A}, v))$ so that $\mathbf{A}_K = (X_K, \subseteq, \{o_K\}_{o \in \mathcal{O}})$ and $v_K = i_n \circ v : \text{Var} \to X_K$. We define the algebraic satisfaction relation $\models^a$ as follows, for $x \in X$:

1. $(\mathbf{A}, v) \models^a_x \phi$ iff $x = v^*(\phi)$
2. $(\mathbf{A}, v) \models^a \phi$ iff $v^*_K(\phi) = v^*_K(\top)$
3. $\mathfrak{M} \models^a_x \phi$ iff $(\mathbf{A}, v) \models^a_x \phi$ for every $(\mathbf{A}, v) \in \mathfrak{M}$.
4. $\mathfrak{M} \models^a \phi$ iff $(\mathbf{A}, v) \models^a \phi$ for every $(\mathbf{A}, v) \in \mathfrak{M}$.

We define the entailment relation of a logic $\mathcal{L}$ by:

$$\text{for every } \phi \in F(\mathcal{L}), x \in X, \quad \mathcal{L}; x \Vdash \phi \quad \text{iff} \quad \mathfrak{M} \models^a_x \phi.$$

Analogously, for the set-based algebraic models in $\mathfrak{M}^+ =_{def} \{\mathbb{D}(\mathbb{E}(\mathbf{A}, v)) \mid (\mathbf{A}, v) \in \mathfrak{M}\}$, we define algebraic satisfaction for each set $S = i_n(x) \in X_K$, by:

1^+. $(\mathbf{A}_K, v_K) \models^a_S \phi$ iff $S = v^*_K(\phi)$

2^+. $(\mathbf{A}_K, v_K) \models^a \phi$ iff $v^*_K(\phi) = v^*_K(\top)$

3^+. $\mathfrak{M}^+ \models^a_S \phi$ iff $(\mathbf{A}_K, v_K) \models^a_S \phi$ for every $(\mathbf{A}_K, v_K) \in \mathfrak{M}^+$.

4^+. $\mathfrak{M}^+ \models^a \phi$ iff $(\mathbf{A}_K, v_K) \models^a \phi$ for every $(\mathbf{A}_K, v_K) \in \mathfrak{M}^+$.

Notice that in this definition, analogous to Definition 54, we do not use the set of designated values D, and we are able to determine which set of formulae is deduced *for each* algebraic logic value $x \in X$. It is a generalization of classical deduction, where $\mathcal{L} \Vdash \phi$ is equivalent to this new definition $\mathcal{L}; 1 \Vdash \phi$ and $\mathcal{L} \Vdash \neg\phi$ are equivalent to $\mathcal{L}; 0 \Vdash \phi$ (i. e., $\mathcal{L}; 1 \Vdash \neg\phi$). The inference of ϕ defined by Definition 54, based on set D of designated values, can be expressed from this more accurate definition above by: there exists $x \in D$ such that $\mathcal{L}; x \Vdash \phi$, i. e., "it is valid that ϕ has the truth value x." In the case when $x = 1$, this is classical validity for a formula ϕ when $\mathfrak{M} \models^a \phi$.

Thus, this new entailment relation $\Vdash$ given by Definition 60 is more powerful and more general than the entailment relation of $\mathcal{L}$ given by Definition 54. Notice that if $\mathcal{G}$ is a sequent theory for $\mathcal{L}$, then $\mathcal{L}; x \Vdash \phi$ iff $\forall v \in \mathbb{V}_\Gamma(v^*(\phi) = x)$, i. e., in the case of the sequent system, $\mathcal{G} \Vdash (\phi \vdash x)$ and $\mathcal{G} \Vdash (x \vdash \phi)$. Consequently, $\Vdash$ satisfies the truth-preserving principle, as specified in details in Definition 102 in Appendix and in Definition 57.

Definition 61. Assume that $\mathfrak{M}$ and $\mathcal{K}_\mathcal{M}$ satisfy the assumptions in Definition 59. Let $(K, I_K) \in \mathcal{K}_\mathcal{M}$, 1_K be the support of K with $I_K : \text{Var} \times 1_K \to \mathbf{2}$ and $I^*_K : F(\mathcal{L}) \times 1_K \to \mathbf{2}$ be the unique extension of I_K for all formulae in $F(\mathcal{L})$, which defines the sets $\|\phi\| =_{def} \{y \in 1_K \mid I^*_K(\phi, y) = 1\}$ for each $\phi \in F(\mathcal{L})$. Let for a possible world $w \in 1_K$ and $\phi \in F(\mathcal{L})$:
1. $(K, I_K) \models_w \phi$ iff $w \in \|\phi\|$;
2. $(K, I_K) \models \phi$ iff $\|\phi\| = 1_K$;
3. $\mathcal{K}_\mathcal{M} \models_w \phi$ iff $(K, I'_K) \in \mathcal{K}_\mathcal{M}, (\{w' \in 1_K \mid I'^*_K(\phi, w') = 1\} = \|\phi\|)$;
4. $\mathcal{K}_\mathcal{M} \models \phi$ iff $(K, I_K) \models \phi \; \forall (K, I_K) \in \mathcal{K}_\mathcal{M}$.

The following theorem is the basic result for the next representation theorem, and shows that (from Definition 59) the new relational inference $\models$ is sound and complete w. r. t. the algebraic inference $\models^a$.

Corollary 17. *Assume that $\mathfrak{M}$ and $\mathfrak{M}^+$ satisfy the assumptions in Definition 59. Then, for every $\phi \in F(\mathcal{L})$ and $x \in X$,*

$$\mathfrak{M} \models^a_x \phi \quad \textit{iff} \quad \mathfrak{M}^+ \models^a_{i_n(x)} \phi \tag{5.4}$$

Proof. Assume that $\mathfrak{M}$ and $\mathcal{K}_{\mathcal{M}}$ satisfy the assumptions in Definition 59, and show from left to right:

Let us suppose that $\mathfrak{M} \models_x^a \phi$, i. e., for each $(\mathbf{A}, v) \in \mathfrak{M}$ we have that $(\mathbf{A}, v) \models_x^a \phi$, and hence from point 1 in Definition 60, $x = v^*(\phi)$, i. e., $i_n(x) = v_K^*(\phi)$. In fact, from (C)(ii), we obtain the composition of homomorphisms $v_K^* = i_n \circ v^*$ it holds that $v_K^*(\phi) = i_n(v^*(\phi)) = i_n(x)$ with $(\mathbf{A}_K, v_K) \models_{i_n(x)}^a \phi$. Thus, we obtain the satisfaction at point 1^+ of Definition 59, and hence also the point 3^+. Notice that the general standard result

$$\mathfrak{M} \models^a \phi \quad \text{iff} \quad \mathfrak{M}^+ \models^a \phi \tag{5.5}$$

is just equal to (5.4) when $x = 1$ (equivalent to the points 2 and 2^+) from the fact that for all v, $v(\top) = 1$ is the top truth value in X. □

From this corollary, we are able to define a direct duality between algebraic and Kripke-style semantics for a logic $\mathcal{L}$

$$\mathfrak{M} \xrightarrow{\mathbb{D}} \mathcal{K}_{\mathcal{M}} \xrightarrow{\mathbb{E}} \mathfrak{M}^+$$

Theorem 8 (Representation theorem). *Assume that $\mathfrak{M}$ and $\mathcal{R}$ satisfy the assumptions in Definition 59. Injective mapping i_n can be extended to the injective homomorphism*

$$i_n : (\mathbf{A}, v) \hookrightarrow (\mathbf{A}_K, v_K).$$

Thus, the dual *representation of the algebra* $\mathbf{A}$ *is the subalgebra of* $\mathbf{A}_K$ *defined by image of the homomorphism* i_n.

We call it canonical representation when i_n *is an isomorphism.*

Proof. It follows from the fact that v and I_K are the homomorphisms between O-algebras. So, we can show it by structural induction on the formulae in $F(\mathcal{L})$.

For example, for a formula composed by conjunction, $\phi \wedge \psi$, with $x = v^*(\phi)$ and $y = v^*(\psi)$, we have that

$$\begin{aligned} i_n(x \wedge_A y) &= i_n(v^*(\phi) \wedge_A v^*(\psi)) = i_n(v^*(\phi \wedge \psi)), \quad \text{from the homomorphism of } v^* \\ &= (i_n \circ v^*)(\phi \wedge \psi) = v_K^*(\phi \wedge \psi), \quad \text{from (C)(ii)} \\ &= v_K^*(\phi) \wedge_K v_K^*(\psi) \quad \text{from the homomorphism of } v_K \\ &= i_n(v^*(\phi)) \wedge_K i_n(v^*(\psi)) \\ &= i_n(x) \wedge_K i_n(y). \end{aligned}$$

Thus, we obtained that the homomorphism holds for the restriction of i_n to the image of v, but it is generally valid for *any* v. □

Thus, in the case of the autoreferential semantics considered in next section, given an algebraic model $(\mathbf{A}, v)$ of the algebra $\mathbf{A} = (X, \leq, \{o\}_{o \in \mathcal{O}})$ with many-valued valuation

$v : \mathrm{Var} \to X$ for a logic $\mathcal{L}$, the corresponding Kripke model $\mathcal{M} = (K, I_K) = \mathbb{D}(\mathbf{A}, v)$ with the frame $K = (1_K, \{R_j\})$ with the set of possible worlds 1_K and accessibility relations R_j for the modal operators of $\mathcal{L}$ and Kripke interpretation $I_K : \mathrm{Var} \times 1_K \to \mathbf{2}$, the representation of the original algebraic model $(\mathbf{A}, v)$ is the set-based algebraic model $(\mathbf{A}_K, v_K) = \mathbb{E}(K, I_K) = \mathbb{E}(\mathbb{D}(\mathbf{A}, v))$ where $\mathbf{A}_K = (X_K, \subseteq, \{o_K\}_{o \in \mathcal{O}})$ is a *canonical representation* of the algebra $\mathbf{A}$. That is, in the autoreferential case we obtain that i_n is just an *isomorphism*.

Example 29 (The continuation of Example 28). **Case A:** Let us consider now the algebraic models for $\mathcal{L}$, based on the Boolean algebra, with $(\mathbf{A}, v) \in \mathfrak{M}$, where $v : \mathrm{Var} \to \mathbf{2}$ is the interpretation for propositional variables in Var, and on its canonical extension $(\mathbf{A}_K, v_K) = \mathbb{E}(\mathbb{D}((\mathbf{A}, v)))$, where $(K, I_K) = \mathbb{D}((\mathbf{A}, v))$, $\mathbf{A}_K = (\mathcal{P}(\{0,1\}), \subseteq, \bigcap, \neg^+)$, with $\neg^+\emptyset = \neg^+\{0\} =_{\mathrm{def}} \{0,1\}$ and $\neg^+\{1\} = \neg^+\{0,1\} =_{\mathrm{def}} \{0\}$ and with injective homomorphisms

$$i_n : (\{0,1\}, \leq, \widetilde{\wedge}, \sim) \hookrightarrow \left(\mathcal{P}(\{0,1\}), \subseteq, \bigcap, \neg^+\right).$$

We have that for any $p \in \mathrm{Var}$, $v(p) = 1$ iff $v_K(p) = \{0,1\}$ and $v(p) = 0$ iff $v_K(p) = \{0\}$. We do not have any modal operator in these algebras, thus the frame $K \in (K, I_K) = \mathbb{D}((\mathbf{A}, v))$ has the set of only two possible worlds equal to $1_K = \mathbf{2} = \{0,1\}$ and an empty accessibility relation, i. e., $K = (\{0,1\}, \{\})$. Thus, the subalgebra $(\{\{0\}, \{0,1\}\}, \subseteq, \bigcap, \neg^+)$ is *canonical* representation of Boolean algebra $\mathbf{A}$ because we obtain that i_n is just an isomorphism.

Case B: Let us consider the 4-valued Belnap's distributive bilattice $X = \mathcal{B}_4 = \{f, \bot, \top, t\}$, with $f = 0$ and $t = 1$, and in this case we can take $1_K = \{0, \bot, \top\} \subset X$, with injective homomorphism i_n in Example 28. However, if we take that $X_K = \{\{0\}, \{0,\bot\}, \{0,\top\}, \{0,\bot,\top\}\} \subset \mathcal{P}(X)$, then we obtain the isomorphism

$$i_n : (X, \leq, \widetilde{\wedge}, \widetilde{\vee}) \simeq \left(X_K, \subseteq, \bigcap, \bigcup\right),$$

i. e., canonical representation, with $X_K = \{\{0\}, \{0,\bot\}, \{0,\top\}, \{0,\bot,\top\}\} \subset \mathcal{P}(X)$, such that: $i_n(0) = \{0\}$, $i_n(\bot) = \{0,\bot\}$, $i_n(\top) = \{0,\top\}$, $1_K = i_n(1) = \{0,\bot,\top\}$.

The general canonical *autoreferential* representation for algebras defined above complete distributive lattices is given in next Section 5.1.2.

Extension to predicate logics

Note that all of this representation theory for a many-valued propositional logic can be used also for the more expressive many-valued *predicate logics*. An extension of propositional logic to corresponding predicate logics is direct and simple:

Let H be the Herbrand base (i. e., the set of all ground atoms that can be considered as propositions in propositional logic) for a given set P of n-ary predicates with variables in $\mathcal{V}$ (e. g., and atom for a predicate letter $p \in P$ with $\mathrm{ar}(p) = n \geq 1$, we have the atom $p(x_1, \ldots, x_n)$ with $x_1, \ldots, x_n \in \mathcal{V}$) and the domain $\mathcal{D}$ of values, with the set of valuations $g \in \mathfrak{G} = \mathcal{D}^{\mathcal{V}}$ that assign the values to variables of logic atoms. Then we can define an interpretation for this predicate logic as a map $v : H \to X$.

Note that in the case of the predicate logic we use the ground atoms of Herbrand base w. r. t. the propositional symbols in Var of a propositional logic. Because if that we use the same symbol used for propositional valuation $v : \mathrm{Var} \to X$ for the predicate logic as well, by considering that we use now only the set of ground atoms $p(x_1, \ldots, x_n)/g \in H$ instead of the set of propositional letters $p \in \mathrm{Var}$.

Definition 62. This Herbrand interpretation $v : H \to X$ can be inductively extended into the map v^* to all ground formulae in the standard truth-functional way, for any two ground formulae (i. e., without free variables) ϕ and ψ (if ϕ is a formula with free variables then by ϕ/g we define the ground formula obtained by the given assignment $g \in \mathfrak{G} = \mathcal{D}^{\mathcal{V}}$):

1. $v^*(p(x_1, \ldots, x_n)/g) = v(p(x_1, \ldots, x_n)/g)$, for any ground atom in H;
2. $v^*(\phi \odot \psi) = v^*(\phi) \otimes v^*(\psi)$, for any binary connective $\odot \in \{\wedge, \vee, \Rightarrow, \ldots\}$ and its algebraic operations $\otimes \in \{\widetilde{\wedge}, \widetilde{\vee}, \rightharpoonup, \ldots\}$;
3. $v^*(o_i\phi) = \widetilde{o}_i(v^*(\phi))$, for any unary modal or negation logical connective $o_i \in \{\neg, \Diamond_i, \ldots\}$;
4. $v^*(\forall x\phi) = \bigwedge_{g\in\mathfrak{G}}(v^*(\phi/g))$, where $\bigwedge$ is the extension of meet lattice binary operator $\wedge$ to the any set;
5. $v^*(\exists x\phi) = \bigvee_{g\in\mathfrak{G}}(v^*(\phi/g))$, where $\bigvee$ is the extension of join lattice binary operator $\vee$ to the any set.

We recall that the set-based (for infinite sets as well) of the operators $\bigwedge$ and $\bigvee$ is well- defined because our many-valued logics are based on the complete (and distributive) lattices $(X, \leq)$, which satisfy these requirements. Then it can be easily shown, that we can use the formulae with free variables as well (for this predicate logic with existential $\exists$ and universal $\forall$ quantifiers as well), in the axiom schemas in propositional many-valued systems: for each assignment $g : \mathcal{V} \to \mathcal{D}$, we will obtain identical propositional schemas.

5.1.2 Canonical autoreferential representation for algebras over complete distributive lattices

In Examples 28 and 29, we have shown the cases for this new definition of representation theorem, based on models of a logic $\mathcal{L}$, which define only relational structures $K \in (K, I_K) = \mathbb{D}((\mathbf{A}, v))$, with a set of possible worlds (support) equal to the set $1_K \subseteq X$.

Remark. In what follows, if the algebraic binary operations $\widetilde{\wedge}$ and $\widetilde{\vee}$ correspond to the meet and join lattice operators, we will denote them simply as corresponding logical connectives $\wedge$ and $\vee$, respectively.

Moreover, we will consider the subclass of complete latices in which each lattice of truth values $(X, \leq, \wedge, \vee)$ is *isomorphic* to the complete sublattice of the powerset lattice $(\mathcal{P}(X), \subseteq, \bigcap, \bigcup)$. Consequently, we will consider the cases when there exists the subset $S = C_L(\mathcal{P}(X)) \subseteq \mathcal{P}(X)$, closed under intersection $\bigcap$ and union $\bigcup$, with the isomorphism $i_S : (X, \leq, \wedge, \vee) \simeq (C_L(\mathcal{P}(X)), \subseteq, \bigcap, \bigcup)$, so that we obtain the inclusion map $i_n =\subseteq \circ i_S : X \hookrightarrow A_K \subseteq \mathcal{P}(1_K)$ as required in Definition 59.

For such a subclass of complete lattices $(X, \leq, \wedge, \vee)$, with $|X| \geq 3$ of truth values, we will obtain that the carrier set $1_K \subset X$, of the many-valued logic algebra $\mathbf{A}$, is the set of possible worlds for the Kripke frame in Definition 59 for the dual relational representation of the algebraic semantics: this is an *autoreferential assumption* [69]. The relational semantic of other modal operators of the algebra $\mathbf{A}$ will be obtained successively by a correct definition of the accessibility relations of the Kripke frame. □

It is well known that any complete lattice X has the following property: each (also infinite) subset S of X has the least upper bound (supremum) denoted by $\bigvee S$ (when S has only two elements, the supremum corresponds to the join operator $\vee$), and the greatest lower bound (infimum) denoted by $\bigwedge S$ (when S has only two elements the infimum corresponds to the meet operator $\wedge$). Thus, it has the bottom element $0 = \bigwedge X \in X$, and the top element $1 = \bigvee X \in X$. The cardinality of the set of hereditary subsets of X is generally greater than the cardinality of the lattice X. But in what follows we will consider the class of complete *distributive* lattices X, for which we are able to define an isomorphism [207] between the original lattice X and the particular collection X^+ of hereditary subsets of X. Thus, in each distributive lattice we are able to define the implication and negation logical operators based on relative pseudo-complement and pseudo-complement relatively, i. e.,

$$(x \rightharpoonup y) =_{\text{def}} \bigvee\{z \in X \mid z \wedge x \leq y\}, \quad \text{and} \quad {\sim} x =_{\text{def}} (x \rightharpoonup 0) \tag{5.6}$$

From the Birkhoff's representation theorem [207] for distributive lattices, every finite (thus complete) distributive lattice is isomorphic to the lattice of lower sets of the poset of *join-irreducible* elements. An element $x \neq 0$ in X is a join-irreducible element iff $x = a \vee b$ implies $x = a$ or $x = b$ for any $a, b \in X$. The lower set (down closed) is any subset Y of a given poset $(X, \leq)$ such that, for all elements x and y, if $x \leq y$ and $y \in Y$ then $x \in Y$.

More details about autoreferential semantics is provided in Section A.3.2 in the Appendix. However, here, in this section, we provide the *complete* autoreferential semantics, and Kripke semantics based on it, by using only the subset of join-irreducible elements of X instead of the complete set of truth-values in X.

Proposition 28 (0-Lifted Birkhoff isomorphism [207]). *Let X be a complete distributive lattice, then we define the following mapping $\downarrow^+: X \to \mathcal{P}(X)$: for any $x \in X$,*

$$\downarrow^+ x = \downarrow x \bigcap \widehat{X},$$

where $\widehat{X} = \{y \mid y \in X \text{ and } y \text{ is join-irreducible }\} \bigcup \{0\}$, such that for any $S \subseteq \widehat{X}$,

$$S = \downarrow^+ \vee S \tag{5.7}$$

We define the set $X^+ = \{\downarrow^+ a \mid a \in X\} \subseteq \mathcal{P}(X)$, so that $\downarrow^+ \bigvee = \mathrm{id}_{X^+} : X^+ \to X^+$ and $\bigvee \downarrow^+ = \mathrm{id}_X : X \to X$. Thus, the operator $\downarrow^+$ is inverse of the supremum operation $\bigvee : X^+ \to X$. The set $(X^+, \subseteq)$ is a complete lattice, such that there is the following 0-lifted Birkhoff isomorphism

$$\downarrow^+ : (X, \leq, \wedge, \vee, 0, 1) \simeq (X^+, \subseteq, \cap, \cup, \{0\}, \widehat{X}) \tag{5.8}$$

Proof. See the proof of Proposition 38 and more details in Section A.3.2 in the Appendix. The closure property (5.7) we can show as follows: Let $y = \bigvee S$, and hence $S \subseteq \downarrow^+ y$. Let us suppose that $S \subset \downarrow^+ y$, so that exists $z \in \widehat{X}$ such that $0 \neq z \notin S$ but $z \in \downarrow^+ y$. In this case, it has to be that $y = \bigvee(S \bigcup \{z\})$ with join-irreducible element $z \notin S$, which is in contradiction with $y = \bigvee S$ because S is composed by join-irreducible element as well. Consequently, it must hold the equation (5.7). From Birkhoff's representation theorem [207] for distributive lattices, every complete distributive lattice is isomorphic to the lattice of lower sets of the poset of join-irreducible elements, i. e., (5.8) is such an isomorphism. □

The fundamental result of this proposition is that $\downarrow^+$ is a bijection between algebraic truth values X and the set X^+ composed of subsets of joint-irreducible elements in X plus bottom element 0, that is of the set $\widehat{X}$. That is, the elements of the lattice $(X^+, \subseteq)$ *can be used for the canonical set-based algebras* of any algebra **A** with carrier set composed by elements of the lattice $(X, \leq)$. More over, each subset $S \in X^+$ is hereditary, such that if $x \in S \subset \widehat{X}$, then each $y \in \widehat{X}$ such that $y \leq x$ must belong to S.

The name lifted here is used to denote the difference from the original Birkhoff's isomorphism. That is, we have that for any $x \in X$, $0 \in \downarrow^+ x$, so that $\downarrow^+ x$ is never empty set (it is lifted by bottom element 0). It is easy to verify that $\downarrow^+ 0 = \{0\}$ is the bottom element in X^+. Notice that $(A^+, \subseteq, \bigcap, \bigcup)$ is a *subalgebra* of the powerset algebra $(\mathcal{P}(A), \subseteq, \bigcap, \bigcup)$.

Example 30. Belnap's bilattice in the Example 28 is a distributive lattice w. r. t. the $\leq_t$ ordering, with two join-irreducible elements $\bot$ and $\top$, so that $\widehat{X} = \{0, \bot, \top\}$. In this case, we have that

$$\downarrow^+ 1 = \downarrow^+(\bot \vee \top) = \downarrow^+ \bot \bigcup \downarrow^+ \top = \downarrow \bot \bigcup \downarrow \top = \{0, \bot, \top\} = \widehat{X} \neq \downarrow 1 = X.$$

Remark. For a many-valued logic with distributive complete lattice of truth values, we have that $X_K = \mathcal{P}(1_K) \subseteq \mathcal{P}(X)$, with $1_K = \widehat{X}$ and $D_K = X^+$, and the injective homomorphism $\downarrow^+ : X \to \mathcal{P}(X)$ corresponds to the injective homomorphism $i_n : (\mathbf{A}, v) \hookrightarrow (\mathbf{A}_K, v_K)$ in the representation Theorem 8. Thus, the dual representation of this algebra (in this case a distributive complete lattice) **A** is the subalgebra $(X^+, \subseteq, \bigcap, \bigcup)$ of $\mathbf{A}_K$, defined by the image of the homomorphism $i_n = \downarrow^+$. □

Based on these results, we are able to extend the complete distributive lattices with other unary algebraic operators $o_i : X \to X$ and binary operators $\otimes_i : X \times X \to X$ in order to obtain a class of algebras $((X, \leq, \wedge, \vee), \{o_i\}_{i \in N}, \{\otimes_i\}_{i \in N})$, with the following set-based canonical representation

Proposition 29 (Canonical representation). *Let* $\mathbf{A} = ((X, \leq, \wedge, \vee, \neg_c), \{o_i\}_{i \in N}, \{\otimes_i\}_{i \in N})$ *be a complete distributive lattice-based algebra. The unary operation* $\neg_c$ *corresponds to the classical negation and is defined for each* $x \in X$ *by*

$$\neg_c x =_{\text{def}} \bigvee((\widehat{X} - \downarrow^+ x) \cup \{0\}) \tag{5.9}$$

We define its canonical representation by the algebra

$$\mathbf{A}^+ = \left(\left(X^+, \subseteq, \bigcap, \bigcup, \neg_c^+\right), \{o_i^+\}_{i \in N}, \{\otimes_i^+\}_{i \in N}\right),$$

with the representation isomorphism:

$$\downarrow^+ : ((X, \leq, \wedge, \vee, 0, 1), \{o_i\}_{i \in N}, \{\otimes_i\}_{i \in N}) \simeq ((X^+, \subseteq, \cap, \cup, \{0\}, \widehat{X}), \{o_i^+\}_{i \in N}, \{\otimes_i^+\}_{i \in N}) \tag{5.10}$$

so that the operators of the canonical (set-based) algebra **A**+ *are directly defined from the operators of algebra* **A** *by*

$$o_i^+ = \downarrow^+ o_i \bigvee : X^+ \to X^+, \quad \otimes_i^+ = \downarrow^+ \otimes_i (\bigvee \times \bigvee) : X^+ \times X^+ \to X^+ \tag{5.11}$$

Proof. For any $x, y \in X$, we have for any unary algebraic operator $\downarrow^+ o_i(x) = \downarrow^+ o_i(\bigvee \downarrow^+)(x) = (\downarrow^+ o_i \bigvee) \downarrow^+ x = o_i^+(\downarrow^+ x)$ and for any binary operator $\downarrow^+ \otimes_i(x, y) = \otimes_i^+(\downarrow^+ x, \downarrow^+ y)$. Thus, $\downarrow^+$ is an isomorphism $\downarrow^+ : \mathbf{A} \simeq \mathbf{A}^+$. □

Example 31. Consider two cases:

1. Classical negation in Belnap's bilattice: In this case, $X = \{0, \bot, \top, 1\}$ and $\widehat{X} = \{0, \bot, \top\}$, so from (5.9) that $\neg_c 0 = 1$, $\neg_c 1 = 0$, $\neg_c \bot = \top$ and $\neg_c \top = \bot$. The set-based classical negation is defined by the homomorphism (5.10), $\neg_c^+(\downarrow^+ x) = \downarrow^+(\neg_c x) = \downarrow^+ \bigvee((\widehat{X} - \downarrow^+ x) \cup \{0\})$ = (from (5.7)) $= (\widehat{X} - \downarrow^+ x) \cup \{0\} \subseteq \widehat{X}$. Thus, $\neg_c^+(\downarrow^+ 0) = \widehat{X}$, $\neg_c^+(\downarrow^+ 1) = \{0\}$, $\neg_c(\downarrow^+ \bot) = \{0, \top\}$ and $\neg_c(\downarrow^+ \top) = \{0, \bot\}$.
2. For intuitionistic implication: Let us consider the binary implication operator $\otimes_i$ equal to the relative pseudo-complement $\rightharpoonup$ over a complete distributive lattice. Then we have that

$$(\downarrow^+ x) \rightharpoonup^+ (\downarrow^+ y) = \otimes_i^+(\downarrow^+ x, \downarrow^+ y) = \downarrow^+ \otimes_i (x, y) = \downarrow^+(x \rightharpoonup y) = \downarrow^+\Big(\bigvee\{z \mid z \wedge x \leq y\}\Big)$$
$$= \bigcup\{\downarrow^+ z \mid z \wedge x \leq y\}$$

(from the homomorphism $\downarrow^+$ w. r. t. the join operator of this lattice)

$$= \bigcup\{\downarrow^+ z \mid \downarrow^+(z \wedge x) \subseteq \downarrow^+ y\} \quad (\text{from } \downarrow^+ v \subseteq \downarrow^+ w \text{ iff } v \leq w)$$
$$= \bigcup\Big\{\downarrow^+ z \mid \downarrow^+ z \bigcap \downarrow^+ x) \subseteq \downarrow^+ y\Big\}$$

(from the homomorphism $\downarrow^+$ w. r. t. the meet operator of this lattice)

$$= \bigcup\Big\{S \in X^+ \mid S \bigcap (\downarrow^+ x) \subseteq \downarrow^+ y\Big\}.$$

That is, we obtain that the correspondent operator $\otimes_i^+ : X^+ \times X^+ \to X^+$ is a relative pseudo-complement for the lattice X^+.

It is well known that the standard unary *existential modal* operators are homomorphisms between join semilattices, $o_i : (X, \leq, \vee) \to (X, \leq, \vee)$, and modal negation operators $\widetilde{o_i} : (X, \leq, \vee) \to (X, \leq, \vee)^{OP}$, where the dual join semilattice $(X, \leq, \vee)^{OP}$ has $\leq^{OP} = \geq$, and $\vee^{OP} = \wedge$. For the *normal* modal logics, they are monotone ($x \leq y$ implies $o_i(x) \leq o_i(y)$, and $\widetilde{o_i}(x) \leq^{OP} \widetilde{o_i}(y)$), additive ($o_i(x \vee y) = o_i(x) \vee o_i(y)$) and ($\widetilde{o_i}(x \vee y) = \widetilde{o_i}(x) \vee^{OP} \widetilde{o_i}(y) = \widetilde{o_i}(x) \wedge \widetilde{o_i}(y)$), and normal ($o_i(0) = 0$ and $\widetilde{o_i}(0) = 0^{OP} = 1$).

Now we are able to show that for any algebraic model $M = (\mathbf{A}, I)$, of a logic $\mathcal{L}$ with relative pseudo-complement for implication and a number of unary modal operators, there exists the correspondent Kripke model $\mathcal{M}_K = \mathbb{D}(M) = (K, I_K)$. In what follows, we denote by $\Rightarrow$ the *logic* connective for implication, correspondent to the *algebraic* relative pseudo-complement $\rightharpoonup$, by $\diamondsuit_i$ the existential modal connective for the algebraic additive operator o_i, and by $\neg_i$ the logic negation modal connective for the algebraic additive negation operator $\widetilde{o_i}$, so that for the homomorphism (valuation) $v^* : F(\mathcal{L}) \to X$ holds that $v^*(\phi \Rightarrow \psi) = v^*(\phi) \rightharpoonup v^*(\psi)$, $v^*(\diamondsuit_i \phi) = o_i(v^*(\phi))$ and $v^*(\neg_i \phi) = \widetilde{o_i}(v^*(\phi))$.

Notice that if we denote by $\downarrow_X : \widehat{X} \to \mathcal{P}(\widehat{X})$ the restriction of $\downarrow : X \to \mathcal{P}(X)$ to the subset of join-irreducible elements $\widehat{X} \subseteq X$, then for any $x \in \widehat{X}$ we obtain

$$\downarrow^+ x = \downarrow_X x = \{y \in \widehat{X} \mid y \leq x\} \in X^+ \subseteq \mathcal{P}(\widehat{X}) \tag{5.12}$$

Consequently, in the next Kripke-style definition for modal many-valued logics we will use the set $\widehat{X}$, of join-irreducible elements in X, for the set of possible worlds.

Now we will define the standard accessibility relation for any given additive normal existential modal operator $\diamondsuit_i$ and negation modal operator $\neg_i$.

Definition 63 (Accessibility relations for unary operators). Let $o_i : (X, \leq, \vee) \to (X, \leq, \vee)$ and negation operator $\widetilde{o}_i : (X, \leq, \vee) \to (X, \leq, \vee)^{OP}$ be the additive normal modal operators. Then we define the accessibility relation for existential modal operator $\diamond_i$ by

$$\mathcal{R}_i =_{\text{def}} \{(x, y) \mid y \in \widehat{X}, \text{ and } x \in \downarrow^{+} o_i(y)\},$$

and the incompatibility relation for negation connective $\neg_i$ by

$$\widetilde{\mathcal{R}_i} =_{\text{def}} \bigcup_{x \in X} (\downarrow^{+} x) \times (\downarrow^{+} \widetilde{o}_i(x)) \tag{5.13}$$

Remark. More about a hierarchy of negation operators for complete lattices and their relational semantics can be found in [69] and Definition 104 in Section A.3.2 in the Appendix. This semantics is based on the Birkhoff concept of *polarity* [207]:

If (X, R) is a set with a particular relation on a set X, $R \subseteq X \times X$, with mappings $\lambda : \mathcal{P}(X) \to \mathcal{P}(X)^{OP}, \varrho : \mathcal{P}(X)^{OP} \to \mathcal{P}(X)$, such that for subsets $U, V \in \mathcal{P}(X)$,

$$\lambda U = \{x \in X \mid \forall u \in U.((u, x) \in R)\}, \quad \rho V = \{x \in X \mid \forall v \in V.((x, v) \in R)\},$$

where the powerset $\mathcal{P}(X)$ is a *poset* with bottom element empty set $\emptyset$ and top element X, and $\mathcal{P}(X)^{OP}$ is its dual (with $\subseteq^{OP}$ inverse of $\subseteq$). Then we have an induced Galois connection $\lambda \dashv \rho$, i. e., $\lambda U \subseteq^{OP} V$ iff $U \subseteq \rho V$. The additive modal operator λ is a set-based corresponding operator for the modal negation operator $\widetilde{o}_i$, when we consider the relation R as an *incompatibility* (or "perp") relation $\widetilde{\mathcal{R}_i}$ in (5.13) for this modal negation operator, and $\lambda U = \{x \in X \mid \forall u(u \in U \text{ implies } (u, x) \in \widetilde{\mathcal{R}_i})\}$, which will be used for the relational Kripke-style semantics of modal negation operators in what follows.

The following lemma is relevant for the definition of the incompatibility relation in (5.13).

Lemma 6. *For a given negation (antitonic additive modal operator) $\widetilde{o}_i$, we are able to define the hereditary-incompatibility relation by* (5.13) *in order to define the split negation λ, which satisfies the autoreferential semantics isomorphism* (5.10), *i. e., the condition*

$$\lambda = \downarrow^{+} \widetilde{o}_i \bigvee : X^{+} \to X^{+} \tag{5.14}$$

Proof. For the case when $S = \{0\} \in X^{+}$, from the fact that $\downarrow^{+} 0 = \{0\}$ and $\downarrow^{+} \widetilde{o}_i 0 = \downarrow^{+} 1 = \widehat{X}$, we obtain the banal result that $\lambda\{0\} = \widehat{X} \in X^{+}$. Thus, we are interested only for non-singleton hereditary subsets (with at least one join-irreducible element from $\widehat{X}$), $S = \downarrow^{+} x \in X^{+}$ for some $x \in X$, and hence we have that

$$\begin{aligned}\lambda S &=_{\text{def}} \{y \in X \mid \forall u \in S.(u, y) \in \widetilde{\mathcal{R}_i}\} \\ &= \{y \in X \mid \forall u \in (\downarrow^{+} x).(u, y) \in \widetilde{\mathcal{R}_i}\} \\ &\supseteq (\downarrow^{+} \widetilde{o}_i x) \quad \text{from (5.13).}\end{aligned}$$

Let us show that we obtain strictly the result $\lambda S = (\downarrow^+ \widetilde{o}_i x)$, i. e., that we have no any contribution to λS of another components $(\downarrow^+ a) \times (\downarrow^+ \widetilde{o}_i a) \subset \widetilde{\mathcal{R}}_i$ in (5.13). In order to give such a contribution to λS, from definition of λ we must have that $S \subset (\downarrow^+ a)$ and from the fact that $S = (\downarrow^+ a)$ it is possible only if $x < a$, that is $\widetilde{o}_i x \geq \widetilde{o}_i a$, and hence $(\downarrow^+ \widetilde{o}_i x) \supseteq (\downarrow^+ \widetilde{o}_i a)$. Consequently, any $y \in (\downarrow^+ \widetilde{o}_i a)$ is already in $(\downarrow^+ \widetilde{o}_i x)$ as well, and we cannot have any new contribution to λS, i. e., we obtain the strict result that for each $x \in X$, $(\downarrow^+ \widetilde{o}_i x) = \lambda S = \lambda(\downarrow^+ x)$, and hence we obtain that $\downarrow^+ \widetilde{o}_i = \lambda \downarrow^+$, so that $\lambda = \lambda(\downarrow^+ \bigvee) = (\downarrow^+ \widetilde{o}_i) \bigvee$. □

Example 32 (Continuation of Examples 28 and 30 for Belnap's bilattice $X = \mathcal{B}_4$). Notice that the knowledge negation operator—(see more in next section) is *normal* additive modal operator w. r. t. the $\leq_t$ ordering. As we will see in the next definition, its dual is truth negation $\neg$, which is a normal modal operator w. r. t. the $\leq_k$ ordering. Thus, in the case of the believe (conflation) modal operator, $o_i = -$, in Belnap's bilattice, $\widehat{X} = \{f, \bot, \top\}$, such that $-f = f = 0, -t = t = 1, -\bot = \top, -\top = \bot$, we obtain that

$$\mathcal{R}_- = \{(0,0), (0,\bot), (\top,\bot), (0,\top), (\bot,\top)\},$$

while for the autoepistemic Moore's operator [197], $o_i = \mu : X \to X$, defined by

$$\mu(x) = t = 1 \quad \text{if } x \in \{\top, t\}; \quad f = 0 \text{ otherwise, we have that}$$
$$\mathcal{R}_\mu = \{(0,0), (0,\bot), (0,\top)(\bot,\top), (\top,\top)\}.$$

Both of these modal operators are additive and normal. For the modal negation additive operator $\widetilde{o_i} = \neg$, we have the incompatibility relation:

$$\widetilde{\mathcal{R}_\neg} = \{(0,0), (0,\bot), (0,\top), (\bot,\bot), (\bot,0), (\top,\top), (\top,0)\}.$$

As we have seen, generally for the unary operators we need binary accessibility relations, and hence for the binary operators we need generally ternary accessibility relations. Only in some special cases, e. g., for relative pseudo-complement (used for intuitionistic implication), which can be expressed by using lattice ordering $\leq$ with meet and join operators, we can use simpler binary accessibility lattice ordering relation $\leq$ (reflexive and transitive) directly (see Example 31) because intuitionistic implication is a composition of universal "necessity" modal operator, which needs the reflexive and transitive accessibility relation $\leq$ and classical implication. So in next, we will not consider these singular limited cases, but only more complex cases that needs ternary accessibility relations, as follows.

Definition 64 (Accessibility relations for binary operators). Let $\otimes_i : (X, \leq, \vee)^2 \to (X, \leq, \vee)$ be a binary modal operator of an algebra $\mathbf{A}$ in Proposition 29. Then we define the accessibility relation for these operators:

$$\mathbf{R}_i =_{\text{def}} \{(z, x, y) \mid x, y \in \widehat{X}, \text{and } z \in \downarrow^+ x \otimes_i y\} \tag{5.15}$$

Now we are able to define the relational Kripke-style semantics for a propositional modal logic $\mathcal{L}$, based on the modal Heyting algebras in Proposition 29.

Definition 65. For a complete distributive lattice-based logics, the mapping $\mathbb{D} : \mathcal{M} \to \mathcal{K}_{\mathcal{M}}$ is defined as follows: Let $(\mathbf{A}, v) \in \mathcal{M}$ be an algebra model (with algebra $\mathbf{A}$ in Proposition 29), then $M_K = (K, I_K) = \mathbb{D}(\mathbf{A}, v)$ is the correspondent Kripke model, such that $K = \langle(1_K, \leq), \{\mathcal{R}_j\}_{j\in\mathcal{N}}, \{\mathbf{R}_j\}_{j\in\mathcal{N}}\rangle$ is a frame, where $1_K = \widehat{X}$, $\mathcal{R}_j$ is an accessibility relation in Definition 63 for a modal operator o_j, $\mathbf{R}_j$ is a ternary accessibility relation in Definition 64 for binary operator $\otimes_j$ (different from relative pseudo-complement), and $I_K : \mathrm{Var} \times 1_K \to \mathbf{2}$ is a canonical valuation, such that for any atomic formula (propositional variable) $p \in \mathrm{Var}$ and $w \in 1_K$, $I_K(p, w) = 1$ iff $w \in \downarrow^+(v(p))$. Then, for any world $x \in 1_K$, and formulae $\psi, \phi \in F(\mathcal{L})$:

1. $M_K \vDash_x p$ iff $I_K(p, x) = 1$
2. $M_K \vDash_x \phi \wedge \psi$ iff $M_K \vDash_x \phi$ and $M_K \vDash_x \psi$,
3. $M_K \vDash_x \phi \vee \psi$ iff $M_K \vDash_x \phi$ or $M_K \vDash_x \psi$,
4. $M_K \vDash_x \neg_c\phi$ iff $x = 0$ or not $M_K \vDash_x \phi$
5. $M_K \vDash_x \phi \Rightarrow \psi$ iff $\forall y \in 1_K((y \leq x$ and $M_K \vDash_y \phi)$ implies $M_K \vDash_y \psi)$,
6. $M_K \vDash_x \sim \phi$ iff $M_K \vDash_x \phi \Rightarrow 0$,
7. $M_K \vDash_x \Diamond_j\phi$ iff $\exists y \in 1_K((x, y) \in \mathcal{R}_j$ and $M_K \vDash_y \phi)$, for a modal operator o_j, (universal modal operators are derived by $\Box_j = \neg_c\Diamond_j\neg_c$),
8. $M_K \vDash_x \neg_j\phi$ iff $\forall y \in 1_K(M_K \vDash_y \phi$ implies $(y, x) \in \widetilde{\mathcal{R}_j})$,
$$\text{iff}\quad \forall y \in 1_K\big((x, y) \in (1_K \times 1_K - \widetilde{\mathcal{R}_j})^{-1} \text{ implies not } M_K \vDash_y \phi\big),$$
for a negation modal operator $\widetilde{o}_j$,
9. $M_K \vDash_x \phi \otimes_j \psi$ iff $\exists y, z \in 1_K((x, y, z) \in \mathbf{R}_j$ and $M_K \vDash_y \phi$ and $M_K \vDash_z \psi)$, for a binary operator $\otimes_j$ monotonic in both arguments,
10. $M_K \vDash_x \phi \otimes_j \psi$ iff $\exists y, z \in 1_K((x, y, z) \in \mathbf{R}_j$ and $M_K \vDash_y \phi$ and $M_K \vDash_z \psi$ and $\forall w \in 1_K(M_K \vDash_w \phi$ implies $w \leq y))$, for a binary operator $\otimes_j$ monotonic in second and antitonic in first argument.

The mapping $\mathbb{E} : \mathcal{K}_{\mathcal{M}} \to \mathcal{M}$ is defined as follows: for any $(K, I_K) \in \mathcal{K}_{\mathcal{M}}$,
$$\mathbb{E}(K, I_K) =_{\text{def}} (\mathcal{P}(1_K), I_K) \in \mathcal{M}.$$

Notice that in the world $x = 0$ (bottom element in X) each formula $\phi \in F(\mathcal{L})$ is satisfied: because of that we will denominate this world by inconsistent or *trivial* world. The semantics for the implication is the Kripke modal semantics for the implication of the intuitionistic logic (only with inverted ordering for the accessibility relation $\leq$).

In any modal logic, the set of worlds where a formula ϕ is satisfied is denoted by $\|\phi\| = \{x \mid M_K \vDash_x \phi\}$, so that we have $M_K \vDash_x \phi$ iff $x \in \|\phi\|$.

Theorem 9 (Soundness and completeness). *Let* $(\mathbf{A}, v) \in \mathcal{M}$ *be an algebraic model of* $\mathcal{L}$ *and* $(K, I_K) = \mathbb{D}(\mathbf{A}, v)$ *be the correspondent Kripke model, with a frame* $K = \langle (1_K, \leq), \{\mathcal{R}_j\}_{j\in\mathcal{N}}, \{\mathbf{R}_j\}_{j\in\mathcal{N}} \rangle$, *where* $1_K = \widehat{X}$, *and the canonical valuation* $I_K : \mathrm{Var} \times 1_K \to \mathbf{2}$ *given by Definition 65. Then, for any propositional formula* ϕ, *the set of worlds where* ϕ *holds is equal to*

$$\|\phi\| =_{\mathrm{def}} \{x \mid M_K \models_x \phi\} = \downarrow^+(v^*(\phi)) \in X^+ \tag{5.16}$$

so that $(\mathbf{A}^+, v_K) = \mathbb{E}((K, I_K)) = \mathbb{E}(\mathbb{D}(\mathbf{A}, v))$ *is the set-based (complex) algebra where from Definition 59,* $v_K = i_n \circ v = \downarrow^+ \circ v : \mathrm{Var} \to X^+$. *Thus, from equation above* $\|\phi\| = v_K^*(\phi)$, *i. e.,* $\|\_\| = v_K^* : F(\mathcal{L}) \to X^+$, *and hence* $\mathbf{A}^+$ *is canonical representation of the algebra* $\mathbf{A}$ *of the isomorphism* (5.10).

Proof. By structural induction (we will follow the ordering in Definition 65):

1. For any proposition variable $p \in \mathrm{Var}$, $x \in \widehat{X}$, $M_K \models_x p$ iff $x \in I_K(p, x) = 1$ iff (from Definition) $x \in \downarrow^+(v(p))$, thus $\|p\| = \downarrow^+(v(p))$.
2. From $M_K \models_x \phi \wedge \psi$ iff $M_K \models_x \phi$ and $M_K \models_x \psi$, holds that $\|\phi \wedge \psi\| = \|\phi\| \bigcap \|\psi\| = \downarrow^+ v^*(\phi) \bigcap \downarrow^+ v^*(\psi)$, (by structural induction), $= \downarrow^+ v^*(\phi \wedge \psi)$ (Proposition 28).
3. Similarly, $\|\phi \vee \psi\| = \|\phi\| \bigcup \|\psi\| = \downarrow^+ v^*(\phi) \bigcup \downarrow^+ v^*(\psi) = \downarrow^+ v^*(\phi \vee \psi)$.
4. For classical negation: let from inductive hypotheses $\|\phi\| = \downarrow^+ v^*(\phi)$, then $\|\neg_c \phi\| = \{0\} \bigcup \{x \in \widehat{X} \mid \text{not } M_K \models_x \phi\} = \{0\} \bigcup \{x \in \widehat{X} \mid x \notin \|\phi\|\} = \{0\} \bigcup (\widehat{X} - \|\phi\|) =$ (from (5.7)) $= \downarrow^+ \bigvee(\{0\} \bigcup (\widehat{X} - \|\phi\|) = \downarrow^+ \bigvee(\{0\} \bigcup (\widehat{X} - \downarrow^+ v^*(\phi)) =$ (from (5.9)) $= \downarrow^+ (\neg_c v^*(\phi)) =$ (from homomorphism of $v*$) $= \downarrow^+ v^*(\neg_c \phi)$.
5. Suppose that $\|\phi\| = \downarrow^+ v^*(\phi)$ and $\|\psi\| = \downarrow^+ v^*(\psi)$. Then for any $x \in \widehat{X}$ we have $x \in \|\phi \Rightarrow \psi\|$ iff $M_K \models_x \phi \Rightarrow \psi$ iff $\forall y \in \widehat{X}((y \leq x \text{ and } M_K \models_y \phi)$ implies $M_K \models_y \psi)$ iff $\forall y \in \widehat{X}((y \in \downarrow_X x$ and $M_K \models_y \phi)$ implies $M_K \models_y \psi)$ iff (from (5.12) holds $\downarrow^+ x = \downarrow_X x$) $\forall y (y \in \downarrow^+ x \bigcap \|\phi\|$ implies $y \in \|\psi\|)$ iff $\downarrow^+ x \bigcap \|\phi\| \subseteq \|\psi\|$. So that $S = \|\phi \Rightarrow \psi\| = \{x \mid \downarrow^+ x \bigcap \|\phi\| \subseteq \|\psi\|\}$.
   Then $S = \mathrm{id}_{X^+}(S) = \downarrow^+ \bigvee S = \bigcup \downarrow^+ S$ (from the homomorphism $\downarrow^+$) $= \bigcup_{x\in S} \downarrow^+ x = \bigcup \{\downarrow^+ x \mid \downarrow^+ x \bigcap \|\phi\| \subseteq \|\psi\|\} = \bigcup \{S' \in X^+ \mid S' \bigcap \downarrow^+ v^*(\phi) \subseteq \downarrow^+ v^*(\psi)\} = \downarrow^+(v^*(\phi) \rightharpoonup v^*(\psi))$ (as shown in the Example 5) $= \downarrow^+ v^*(\phi \Rightarrow \psi)$ (from the homomorphism of the valuation v^*). Consequently, $\|\phi \Rightarrow \psi\| = \downarrow^+ v^*(\phi \Rightarrow \psi)$.
6. For the pseudo-complement negation $\sim$, it is derived from point 5, from the fact that $\sim \phi$ is equal to $\phi \Rightarrow 0$.
7. For any additive algebraic modal operator o_i, we obtain an existential logic modal operator $\Diamond_i$, so that for any $x \in \widehat{X}$, $M_K \models_x \Diamond_i \phi$ iff $\exists y \in \widehat{X}((x, y) \in \mathcal{R}_i$ and $M_K \models_y \phi)$, iff $\exists y \in \widehat{X}((x, y) \in \mathcal{R}_i$ and $y \in \downarrow^+ \alpha)$, where $\alpha = v^*(\phi)$. Then $\|\Diamond_i \phi\| = \{x \mid \exists y((x, y) \in \mathcal{R}_i \text{ and } y \in \downarrow^+ \alpha)\} = \{x \mid \exists y (y \in \widehat{X}, x \in \downarrow^+ o_i(y) \text{ and } y \in \downarrow^+ \alpha)\} = \{x \mid y \in \downarrow^+ \alpha \text{ and } x \in \downarrow^+ o_i(y)\} = \{x \mid y \in \downarrow^+ \alpha \text{ and } x \in \downarrow^+ o_i \bigvee(\{y\})\} = \{x \mid y \in \downarrow^+ \alpha \text{ and } x \in o_i^+(\{y\})\} = \bigcup_{y \in \downarrow^+ \alpha} o_i^+(\{y\}) =$ (from the additivity of o_i) $= o_i^+(\downarrow^+ \alpha) = \downarrow^+ o_i \bigvee(\downarrow^+ \alpha) = \downarrow^+ o_i(\alpha)$.
   Thus, we have that $\|\Diamond_i \phi\| = \downarrow^+ o_i(\alpha) = \downarrow^+ o_i(v^*(\phi)) = \downarrow^+ v^*(\Diamond_i \phi)$.

8. For any additive algebraic negation operator $\widetilde{o_i}$, we obtain a logic modal negation operator $\neg_i$, so that for any $x \in \widehat{X}$, $M_K \vDash_x \neg_i\phi$ iff $\forall y(M_K \vDash_y \phi$ implies $(y,x) \in \widetilde{\mathcal{R}_i})$, iff $\forall y(y \in \downarrow^+\alpha$ implies $(y,x) \in \widetilde{\mathcal{R}_i})$, where $\alpha = v^*(\phi)$. Then $\|\neg_i\phi\| = \{x \mid \forall y(y \in \downarrow^+\alpha$ implies $(y,x) \in \widetilde{\mathcal{R}_i})\} = \downarrow^+\widetilde{o_i}\alpha$ (from definition of $\widetilde{\mathcal{R}_i}$ in (5.13) and Lemma 6). Thus, we have that $\|\neg_i\phi\| = \downarrow^+\widetilde{o_i}(\alpha) = \downarrow^+\widetilde{o_i}(v^*(\phi)) = \downarrow^+v^*(\neg_i\phi)$.
9. For the binary operators monotonic in both arguments: suppose that $\|\phi\| = \downarrow^+v^*(\phi)$ and $\|\psi\| = \downarrow^+v^*(\psi)$. Then $\|\phi \otimes_j \psi\| = \{x \mid \exists y,z \in 1_K((x,y,z) \in \mathbf{R}_j$ and $M_K \vDash_y \phi$ and $M_K \vDash_z \psi)\} = \{x \mid \exists y,z \in 1_K((x,y,z) \in \mathbf{R}_j$ and $y \in \|\phi\|$ and $z \in \|\psi\|)\} = \{x \mid \exists y,z \in 1_K((x,y,z) \in \mathbf{R}_j$ and $y \in \|\phi\|$ and $z \in \|\psi\|)\} = \bigcup_{y\in\|\phi\|,z\in\|\psi\|}\{x \mid (x,y,z) \in \mathbf{R}_j\} = \bigcup_{y\in\downarrow^+v^*(\phi),z\in\downarrow^+v^*(\psi)}\{x \mid (x,y,z) \in \mathbf{R}_j\} = \bigcup_{y\in\downarrow^+v^*(\phi),z\in\downarrow^+v^*(\psi)}\{\downarrow^+(y \otimes_j z)\} = \downarrow^+(v^*(\phi) \otimes_j v^*(\psi))$ = (by homomorphism of v^*) = $\downarrow^+ v^*(\phi \otimes_j \psi)$.
10. For the binary operators monotonic in second and antitonic in first argument: suppose that $\|\phi\| = \downarrow^+v^*(\phi)$ and $\|\psi\| = \downarrow^+v^*(\psi)$. Then $\|\phi \otimes_j \psi\| = \{x \mid \exists y,z \in 1_K((x,y,z) \in \mathbf{R}_j$ and $M_K \vDash_y \phi$ and $M_K \vDash_z \psi$ and $\forall w \in 1_K(M_K \vDash_w \phi$ implies $w \le y))\} = \{x \mid \exists y,z \in 1_K((x,y,z) \in \mathbf{R}_j$ and $y \in \downarrow^+v^*(\phi)$ and $z \in \downarrow^+v^*(\psi)$ and $\forall w(w \in \downarrow^+v^*(\phi)$ implies $w \le y))\} = \{x \mid \exists z((x,v^*(\phi),z) \in \mathbf{R}_j$ and $z \in \|\psi\|)\} = \bigcup_{z\in\|\psi\|}\{x \mid (x,v^*(\phi),z) \in \mathbf{R}_j\} = \bigcup_{z\in\downarrow^+v^*(\psi)}\{\downarrow^+ (v^*(\phi) \otimes_j z)\} = \downarrow^+(v^*(\phi) \otimes_j v^*(\psi)) =$ (by homomorphism of v^*) = $\downarrow^+ v^*(\phi \otimes_j \psi)$. □

This theorem demonstrates that the satisfaction relation in Definition 65 satisfies the general property for relational semantics given by point 1 of Definition 61, i. e., that holds $(K,m) \vDash_x \phi$ iff $x \in \|\phi\|$.

Remark. Notice that from this Theorem and (5.16), $\|\phi\| =_{\text{def}} \{x \mid M_K \vDash_x \phi\} = \downarrow^+(v^*(\phi))$, we obtain that a formula is accepted by a possible world (satisfied in it) if the truth value of the formula $v^*(\phi)$ is equal or bigger than the possible-world (truth) x.

The philosophical assumption of *canonical* autoreferential sematics is based on the consideration that each possible world represents a level of *credibility*, so that only propositions with the right logic value (i. e., level of credibility) can be accepted by this world. The canonical autoreferential relational semantics of the Kripke is based on this principle: each possible world, which has a given credibility can accept only the formulae which have equal or bigger than that level of credibility (i. e., its truth value). The bottom truth value in this complete lattice corresponds to the *trivial world* in which each formula is satisfied, i. e., to the world with explosive inconsistency (the world with zero credibility). That is, for each formula ψ holds that $M_K \vDash_0 \psi$, and hence $0 \in \|\psi\|$. □

Notice that in the case when a lattice X is a complete ordering where for any $x \in X$, $\downarrow^+ x = \downarrow x$ (e. g., in the fuzzy logic), then the minimum requirement for an unary modal operators o_i is to be monotonic. We do not require it to be surjective, by defining the accessibility relation as $\mathcal{R}_i = \{(o_i(x),x) \mid x \in X\}\bigcup\{(x,0) \mid x \in X$ and $\nexists y(x = o_i(y))\}$. In that case, we have that $M_K \vDash_x \Diamond_i\phi$ iff $\exists y \in X.((x,y) \in \mathcal{R}_i$ and $M_K \vDash_y \phi)$, iff $\exists y \in X.(x = o_i(y)$ and $M_K \vDash_y \phi)$ iff (by inductive hypothesis $\|\phi\| = \downarrow v^*(\phi)$) $\exists y \in X.(x = o_i(y)$

and $y \leq \downarrow v^*(\phi))$ iff (from the monotonicity of o_i) $\exists y \in X.(x = o_i(y) \leq o_i(v^*(\phi)))$ iff $\exists y \in X.(x = o_i(y) \in \downarrow o_i(v^*(\phi)))$ iff (such y exists, at least as 0) $x \in \downarrow o_i(v^*(\phi)) = \downarrow(v^*(\Diamond_i\phi))$. Consequently,

$$\|\Diamond_i\phi\| = \downarrow(v^*(\Diamond_i\phi)) = \downarrow^+(v^*(\Diamond_i\phi)).$$

From the canonical representation, we obtained that the isomorphism, between the original algebra $\mathbf{A}$ with unary modal operators and its canonical representation algebra $\mathbf{A}_K = \mathbf{A}^+$, corresponds to the representation of any propositional formula ϕ by the set of worlds $\|\phi\|$ where ϕ is satisfied, in the canonical Kripke model for the algebra $\mathbf{A}$. So, e. g., the term $\phi\wedge\psi$ in the original algebra $(\mathbf{A}, v)$ corresponds to the set $\|\phi\| \bigcap \|\psi\|$ in the canonical algebra $(\mathbf{A}_K, v_K)$, where $\|\phi\|$ is the set of worlds in the canonical Kripke model in Definition 65, $\langle(1_K, \leq), \{\mathcal{R}_j\}_{j\in\mathcal{N}}, \{\mathbf{R}_j\}_{j\in\mathcal{N}}, I_K\rangle$ with $1_K = \widehat{X}$, $\mathcal{R}_j$, where ϕ holds.

As a consequence, we obtained that this simple Kripke model is the model of the normal modal logic with inference relation $\psi \vdash \phi$ iff $\|\psi\| \subseteq \|\phi\|$. In fact, $\psi \vdash \phi$ iff (based on the truth ordering) $v^*(\psi) \leq v^*(\phi)$ iff (based on the monotonicity of $\downarrow^+$)

$$\|\psi\| = \downarrow^+(v^*(\psi)) \subseteq \downarrow^+(v^*(\phi)) = \|\phi\|.$$

In next section, we will present the canonical autoreferential representation for the Belnap's 4-valued logic. More examples will be provided in the next chapter dedicated to applications of many-valued intensional FOL.

5.1.3 Application to Belnap's bilattice

In this section, we will apply the results obtained in the previous section to the 4-valued Belnap's bilattice based logic $\mathcal{L}$. Such a logic is a significant extension of normal strong Kleene's 3-valued logic to the paraconsistent type of logics, where we are able to obtain a nonexplosive inconsistency.

This is a very important class of logics, which is able to deal also with mutually-inconsistent information, in typical Web data integration of different and independent source data with mutually inconsistent information [129]. That is the main reason that we applied a new representation theorem to this case instead of more complex bilattices.

Bilattice theory is a ramification of multivalued logic by considering both truth $\leq_t$ and knowledge $\leq_k$ partial orderings. Given two truth values x and y, if $x \leq_t y$ then y is at least as true as x, i. e., $x \leq_t y$ iff $x <_t y$ or $x = y$. The negation operation for these two orderings, $\neg$ and $-$, respectively, are defined as the involution operators, which satisfy De Morgan law between the join and meet operations.

Definition 66 (Ginsberg [197]). A bilattice $\mathcal{B}$ is defined as a sixtuple $(\mathcal{B}, \wedge, \vee, \otimes, \oplus, \neg)$, such that: The t-lattice $(\mathcal{B}, \leq_t, \wedge, \vee)$ and the k-lattice $(\mathcal{B}, \leq_k, \otimes, \oplus)$ are both complete lattices, and $\neg : \mathcal{B} \rightarrow \mathcal{B}$ is an involution ($\neg\neg$ is the identity) mapping such that $\neg$ is a lattice homomorphism from $(\mathcal{B}, \wedge, \vee)$ to $(\mathcal{B}, \vee, \wedge)$ and $(\mathcal{B}, \otimes, \oplus)$ to itself.

The following definition introduces the subclass of D-bilattices [208] (the Belnap's bilattice is the smallest nontrivial D-bilattice). For more information and a more compact definition of D-bilattices and their properties, as well as a number of significant examples, the reader can use [209].

Definition 67 ([209]). A D-bilattice $\mathcal{B}$ is a distributive bilattice $(\mathcal{B}, \wedge, \vee, \otimes, \oplus, \neg)$ with the isomorphism of truth-knowledge lattices $\partial : (\mathcal{B}, \leq_t) \simeq (\mathcal{B}, \leq_k)$, which is an involution. Let us define the unary operator $- =_{\text{def}} \partial\neg\partial : \mathcal{B} \rightarrow \mathcal{B}$. Then we say that a D-lattice is `perfect` if two truth negations, the intuitionistic negation $\neg_t$ (pseudocomplement), such that $\neg_t x = \bigvee\{z \mid z \wedge x = 0\}$, and the bilattice negation $\neg$, are correlated by $\neg = \neg_t -$.

In each D-bilattice $(\mathcal{B}, \wedge, \vee, \otimes, \oplus, \neg)$, the operator $-$ is self-adjoint modal operator w. r. t. the $\leq_t$, and the bilattice negation operator for k-lattice satisfy $-1_k = 0_k$, $-0_k = 1_k$, while $-1 = 1$, $-0 = 0$.

Corollary 18 ([209]). *For any D-bilattice $\mathcal{B}$, the duality operator ∂ can be extended to the following isomorphism of modal Heyting algebras*

$$\partial : (\mathcal{B}, \leq_t, \alpha_t) \simeq (\mathcal{B}, \leq_k, \alpha_k),$$

with $\alpha_t = \{\wedge, \rightharpoonup, -\}$ and $\alpha_k = \{\otimes, \rightharpoondown, \neg\}$, where $\rightharpoonup$ and $\rightharpoondown$ are the intuitionistic implications (the relative pseudo-complements) w. r. t. the $\leq_t$ and $\leq_k$, respectively.

Informally, these dual lattices are the modal extensions of Heyting algebras. The conjugate modal operators are the *belief* operators. As we will see, they correspond also to *default* negations in *dual* algebras.

The smallest *nontrivial* D-bilattice is Belnap's 4-valued bilattice [190], $X = \mathcal{B}_4 = \{t, f, \bot, \top\} = \{1, 0, \bot, \top\}$ in Figure 5.1, where $t = 1$ is *true*, $f = 0$ is *false*, $\top$ is inconsistent (both true and false) or *possible*, and $\bot$ is *unknown*. In what follows, we denote by $x \bowtie y$ two unrelated elements in X (so that not ($x \leq y$ or $y \leq x$)).

As Belnap observed, these values can be given two natural orders: *truth* order, $\leq_t$, and *knowledge* order, $\leq_k$, such that $f \leq_t \top \leq_t t$, $f \leq_t \bot \leq_t t$, $\bot \bowtie_t \top$ and $\bot \leq_k f \leq_k \top$, $\bot \leq_k t \leq_k \top$, $f \bowtie_k t$. That is, bottom element 0 for $\leq_t$ ordering is f, and for $\leq_k$ ordering is $\bot$, and top element 1 for $\leq_t$ ordering is t, and for $\leq_k$ ordering is $\top$. Meet and join operators under $\leq_t$ are denoted $\wedge$ and $\vee$; they are natural generalizations of the usual conjunction and disjunction notions. Meet and join under $\leq_k$ are denoted $\otimes$ and $\oplus$, such that hold: $f \otimes t = \bot$, $f \oplus t = \top$, $\top \wedge \bot = f$ and $\top \vee \bot = t$.

There is a natural notion of the *bilattice truth negation*, denoted $\neg$, (reverses the $\leq_t$ ordering, while preserving the $\leq_k$ ordering): switching f and t, leaving $\bot$ and $\top$ and corresponding knowledge negation (*conflation*), denoted $-$, (reverses the $\leq_k$ ordering,

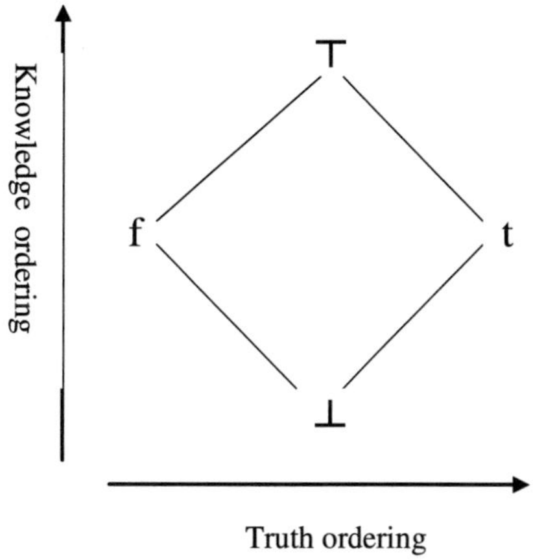

Figure 5.1: Belnap's bilattice.

while preserving the $\leq_t$ ordering), switching $\bot$ and $\top$, leaving f and t. These two kinds of negation commute: $-\neg x = \neg - x$ for every member x of a bilattice.

In what follows, we will use the *relative pseudo-complements*, defined by $x \rightharpoonup y = \bigvee\{z \mid z \wedge x \leq_t y\}$, and *pseudo-complements*, defined by $\neg_t x = \sim x = x \rightharpoonup f$ (and, analogously, for $\leq_k$ ordering, $x \rightharpoondown y$ and $\neg_k x = x \rightharpoondown \bot$).

The conflation is a monotone function that preserves all finite meets (and joins) w. r. t. the lattice $(\mathcal{B}_4, \leq_t)$, thus it is the universal (and existential, because $- = \neg - \neg$) modal many-valued operator: “it is believed that” for a bilattice (as in ordinary 2-valued logic, the epistemic negation is composition of strong negation $\neg_t$ and this belief operator, $\neg = \neg_t -$), which extends the 2-valued belief of the autoepistemic logic as follows:

1. if A is true than “it is believed that A,” i. e., $-A$, is true;
2. if A is false than “it is believed that A” is false;
3. if A is unknown than “it is believed that A” is inconsistent: it is really inconsistent to believe in something that is unknown;
4. if A is inconsistent (that is *both* true and false) than “it is believed that A” is unknown: really, we cannot tell nothing about believing in something that is inconsistent.

This belief modal operator can be used to define the *epistemic*(bilattice) negation $\neg$, as a composition of strong negation $\neg_t$ and this belief operator, i. e., $\neg = \neg_t -$. That is, the epistemic negation is negation as a modal operator [210] and as a paraconsistent negation [211][2] Such an autoepistemic intuitionistic logic, based on Belnap's bi-

2 We can introduce also Moore's *autoepistemic* operator [197], $\mu : \mathcal{B} \to \mathcal{B}$, for a Belnap's bilattice, defined by $\mu(x) = t$ if $x \in \{\top, t\}$; f otherwise. It is easy to verify that it is monotone w. r. t. the $\leq_t$, that is

lattice, $(\mathcal{B}_4, \leq_t, \wedge, \vee, \neg_t, \rightharpoonup, -, \mu, f, t)$ can be used for logic programming with incomplete and partially inconsistent information [129]: in such a logic we use only the epistemic negation $\neg = \neg_t -$.

Ginsberg [197] defined a world-based bilattices, considering a collection of words W, where by world we mean some possible way of things might be the following.

Definition 68. [197] A pair $[U, V] \in \mathcal{P}(W) \times \mathcal{P}(W)$ of subsets of W (here $\mathcal{P}(W)$ denotes the powerset of the set W) express truth of some sentence p, with $\leq_t, \leq_k$ truth and knowledge preorders relatively, as follows:

1. U is a set of worlds where p is true, V is a set of worlds where p is false, $P = U \bigcap V$ is a set where p is inconsistent (both true and false), and $W - (U \bigcup V)$ where p is unknown.
2. $[U, V] \leq_t [U_1, V_1]$ iff $U \subseteq U_1$ and $V_1 \subseteq V$
3. $[U, V] \leq_k [U_1, V_1]$ iff $U \subseteq U_1$ and $V \subseteq V_1$.
   The bilattice operations associated with $\leq_t$ and $\leq_k$ are:
4. $[U, V] \wedge [U_1, V_1] = [U \bigcap U_1, V \bigcup V_1]$, $[U, V] \vee [U_1, V_1] = [U \bigcup U_1, V \bigcap V_1]$
5. $[U, V] \otimes [U_1, V_1] = [U \bigcap U_1, V \bigcap V_1]$, $[U, V] \oplus [U_1, V_1] = [U \bigcup U_1, V \bigcup V_1]$
6. $\neg[U, V] = [V, U]$.
   Let denote by $\mathcal{B}_W$ the set $\mathcal{P}(W) \times \mathcal{P}(W)$, then $(\mathcal{B}_W, \wedge, \vee, \otimes, \oplus, \neg)$ is a bilattice.

Such definition is well suited for the 3-valued Kleene logic, but for the 4-valued logic used to overcome "localizable" inconsistencies it is not useful, mainly for two following reasons:

1. The *inconsistent* (both true and false) top knowledge value $\top$ in the Belnap's bilattice can't be assigned to sentences, otherwise we will obtain an inconsistent logic theory where *all* sentences are inconsistent [197]; because of that consistent logics in this interpretation can have only three remaining values. Thus, we interpret $\top$ as *possible* value, which will be assigned to mutually inconsistent sentences, in order to obtain the consistent 4-valued logic theories that overcome such 3-valued inconsistencies.
2. Let denote by $T = U - P, F = U - P$, where P is a set of worlds where p has a possible logic value. Then we obtain that $[U, V] \leq_t [U_1, V_1]$ also when $T \supset T_1$, which is in contrast with our intuition.

The world-based bilattice of Ginsberg, in Definition 68, is not the standard *powerset algebra* with a subset ordering relation, $\subseteq$, and set intersection $\bigcap$ as meet operation, as

multiplicative ($\mu(x \wedge y) = \mu(x) \wedge \mu(u)$ and $\mu(t) = t$) and additive ($\mu(x \vee y) = \mu(x) \vee \mu(u)$ and $\mu(f) = f$), consequently also it is a self-adjoint (contemporary universal and existential) modal operator, $\mu = \neg_t \mu \neg_t$. Notice that differently from the belief modal operator $-$, Moore's modal operator μ is not surjective.

the representation theorem requires. As the consequence of this approach, the existing representation theorem's isomorphisms for Belnap's bilattice suffer from the same kind of deficiency, that is the obtained canonical Belnap's bilattice algebras *are not* powerset algebras.

Because of that we will use the autoreferential semantics for Belnap's bilattice, provided in Example 45, Section A.3.2 in the Appendix.

The approach that we will use in order to find the representation theorem for a Belnap's billatice, based on the fact that it is a D-bilattice, is different than the standard one, based on the *natural duality theorems* [212], (a natural duality for a quasi-variety gives us a uniform method to represent each algebra in the quasi-variety as the algebra of all continuous homomorphisms over some structured Boolean space), but close in spirit to the higher-order Herbrand model types [83].

A many-valued interpretation of a logic $\mathcal{L}$ in an algebraic model $(\mathbf{A}, v) = (\mathcal{B}_4, \leq, \{o_i\}_{o_i \in \mathcal{O}}, v)$ is of the form $v : \mathrm{Var} \to \mathcal{B}_4$, while for its canonical representation algebra, provided by Proposition 29, $(\mathbf{A}_K, v_K) = \mathbb{E}(\mathbb{D}((\mathbf{A}, v)))$ and isomorphism (5.10), the interpretation is set-based $v_K : \mathrm{Var} \to A_K \subseteq \mathcal{P}(\mathcal{B}_4)$. In what follows, we will use both of these algebras for truth and knowledge ordering of Belnap's bilattice.

Both latices $(\mathcal{B}_4, \leq_t)$ and $(\mathcal{B}_4, \leq_k)$ are distributive latices, thus, from the Proposition 28 we obtain that:

1. For the truth-ordered lattice $(\mathcal{B}_4, \leq_t)$:

$$\mathcal{B}_t^+ = \{\downarrow^+ a \mid a \in \mathcal{B}_4\} = \{\{0\}, \{0, \bot\}, \{0, \top\}, \{0, \bot, \top\}\} \subseteq \mathcal{P}(\{0, \bot, \top\}),$$

   with bottom $0_t = \downarrow^+ 0 = \{0\}$, and top element $1_t = \downarrow^+ 1 = \{0, \bot, \top\}$.
   So, we have the isomorphism (5.10), $i_t = \downarrow^+ : (\mathcal{B}_4, \leq_t) \simeq (\mathcal{B}_t^+, \subseteq) \subset (\mathcal{P}(1_t), \subseteq)$, such that $i_t(0) = \{0\}, i_t(\bot) = \{0, \bot\}, i_t(\top) = \{0, \top\}$ and $i_t(1) = \{0, \bot, \top\}$, which satisfies the requirement (C)(ii) in Definition 59 for inclusion $i_n \equiv i_t$.
2. For the knowledge-ordered lattice $(\mathcal{B}_4, \leq_k)$:

$$\mathcal{B}_k^+ = \{\downarrow^+ a \mid a \in \mathcal{B}_4\} = \{\{\bot\}, \{\bot, 0\}, \{\bot, 1\}, \{\bot, 0, 1\}\} \subseteq \mathcal{P}(\{\bot, 0, 1\}),$$

   with bottom $0_k = \downarrow^+ \bot = \{\bot\}$, and top element $1_k = \downarrow^+ \top = \{\bot, 0, 1\}$.
   That is, we have the isomorphism (5.10), $i_k = \downarrow^+ : (\mathcal{B}_4, \leq_k) \simeq (\mathcal{B}_k^+, \subseteq) \subset (\mathcal{P}(1_k), \subseteq)$, such that $i_k(\bot) = \{\bot\}, i_k(f) = \{\bot, 0\}, i_k(t) = \{\bot, 1\}$ and $i_k(\top) = \{\bot, 0, 1\}$.

These two lattices $(\mathcal{B}_t^+, \subseteq)$ and $(\mathcal{B}_k^+, \subseteq)$ satisfy the closure property [213] for elements of these lattices (from Proposition 28), and we are able to define the relative-pseudocomplements for them (from Example 31) based on the algebra representation isomorphism (5.10) and from (5.11), $\otimes_i^+ =_{\mathrm{def}} \downarrow^+ \otimes_i (\bigvee \times \bigvee) : X^+ \times X^+ \to X^+$,

$$\rightharpoonup^+ = \downarrow^+ \rightharpoonup \left(\bigvee \times \bigvee\right) \quad \text{for } \mathcal{B}_t^+, \quad \text{and} \quad \rightharpoonup^+ = \downarrow^+ \rightharpoonup \left(\bigvee \times \bigvee\right) \quad \text{for } \mathcal{B}_k^+.$$

Thus, $(\mathcal{B}_t^+, \subseteq, \{\bigcap, \rightharpoonup^+\})$ and $(\mathcal{B}_k^+, \subseteq, \{\bigcap, \rightharpoonup^+\})$ are Heyting algebras. The negation is defined by $\neg_t Y = Y \rightharpoonup^+ 0_t$ for any $Y \in \mathcal{B}_t^+$, and by $\neg_k Y = Y \rightharpoonup^+ 0_k$ for any $Y \in \mathcal{B}_k^+$, respectively. But as Halmos has shown [37], in the structures as $(\mathcal{B}_t^+, \subseteq)$ (and also $(\mathcal{B}_k^+, \subseteq)$) each closed element is also open and can support also the *modal* operator $\diamond$ conjugate to itself. This is exactly our case.

Proposition 30. *Let $\diamond_t$ and $\diamond_k$ be two operators on sets such that for a given set $Y \in \mathcal{P}(1_t)$,*

$$\diamond_t Y = \{-x \mid x \in Y\}, \quad \text{and for } Y \in \mathcal{P}(1_k), \quad \diamond_k Y = \{\neg y \mid y \in Y\}.$$

Then $(\mathcal{P}(1_t), \subseteq, \{\bigcap, \rightharpoonup^+, \diamond_t\})$ and $(\mathcal{P}(1_k), \subseteq, \{\bigcap, \rightharpoonup^+, \diamond_k\})$ are modal extensions of Heyting algebras. Their restriction on $\mathcal{B}_t^+$ and $\mathcal{B}_k^+$ are $\diamond_t = \downarrow^+ - \bigvee$, $\diamond_k = \downarrow^+ \neg \bigvee$, and $(\mathcal{B}_t^+, \subseteq, \{\bigcap, \rightharpoonup^+, \diamond_t\})$ and $(\mathcal{B}_k^+, \subseteq, \{\bigcap, \rightharpoonup^+, \diamond_k\})$ are modal Heyting algebras.

Proof. We have that $\diamond_t(\{0\}) = \{-0\} = \{0\}$, so $\diamond_t$ is normal modal operator, and for any two sets $Z, Y \in \mathcal{P}(1_t)$, $\diamond_t(Z \bigcup Y) = \{-x \mid x \in Z \bigcup Y\} = \{-x \mid x \in Z \text{ or } x \in Y\} = \{-x \mid x \in Z\} \bigcup \{-x \mid x \in Y\} = \diamond_t(Z) \bigcup \diamond_t(Y)$, i. e., $\diamond_t$ is additive.

It is easy to show that for any $Y \in \mathcal{B}_t^+$, $\diamond_t Y = \neg_t \diamond_t \neg_t Y = \Box_t Y \in \mathcal{B}_t^+$, thus $\diamond_t \equiv \Box_t$, i. e., it is conjugate to yourself. The same holds for $\diamond_k$ w. r. t. $\mathcal{B}_k^+$, thus $(\mathcal{B}_t^+, \subseteq, \{\bigcap, \rightharpoonup^+, \diamond_t\})$ and $(\mathcal{B}_t^+, \subseteq, \{\bigcap, \rightharpoonup^+, \diamond_k\})$ are modal Heyting subalgebras of $(\mathcal{P}(1_t), \subseteq, \{\bigcap, \rightharpoonup^+, \diamond_t\})$ and $(\mathcal{P}(1_k), \subseteq, \{\bigcap, \rightharpoonup^+, \diamond_k\})$, respectively. □

From Definition 63, we can define the accessibility relations for these two modal operators used in truth and knowledge algebras in proposition above, for autoreferential Kripke semantics. Thus, for Kripke frames of these modal Heyting algebras we have that $K_t = (1_t, \leq_t, R_-)$, where for the modal operator $\diamond_t$ the accessibility relation is

$$\mathcal{R}_- = \{(x, y) \mid y \in 1_t, \text{ and } x \in \downarrow^+ - (y)\} = \{(0,0), (0,\bot), (\top,\bot), (0,\top), (\bot,\top)\}.$$

Dually, for knowledge ordering we obtain the Kripke frame $K_k = (1_k, \leq_k, R_\neg)$, where for a modal operator $\diamond_k$ the accessibility relation is

$$\mathcal{R}_\neg = \{(x, y) \mid y \in 1_k, \text{ and } x \in \downarrow^+ \neg(y)\} = \{(\bot,\bot), (\bot,0), (1,0), (\bot,1), (0,1)\}.$$

It is easy to verify that these two Kripke frames are dual, i. e., $\partial_P : K_t \simeq K_k$.

Notice that we do not represent the bilattice negation $\neg$ as an independent modal negation operator (in the truth-ordering lattice) with an incompatibility relation (5.13) $\mathcal{R}_\neg$, because in Belnap's bilattice it is derived as the composition $\neg = -\neg_t = \neg_t -$ of the selfadjoint (existential and universal) operator $-$ (conflation) and pseudo-complement $\neg_t$. It is represented as self-adjoint modal operator in dual (knowledge ordering) lattice instead.

Thus, for an intuitionistic autoepistemic 4-valued logic $\mathcal{L} = (\mathrm{Var}, \{\wedge, \Rightarrow, \flat\}, \Vdash)$, where $\Rightarrow$ is the intuitionistic implication and $\flat$ the belief modal operator, we have the following.

Theorem 10 (Canonical representation for dual Heyting algebras of Belnap's bilattice). *Let $\partial : (\mathcal{B}_4, \leq_t, \alpha_t) \cong (\mathcal{B}_4, \leq_k, \alpha_k)$ be a D-bilattice isomorphism for Belnap's bilattice $\mathcal{B}$, with $\alpha_t = \{\wedge, \rightharpoonup, -\}$ and $\alpha_k = \{\otimes, \rightharpoonup, \neg\}$, and $v : \mathrm{Var} \to \mathcal{B}$ be a many-valued interpretation of intuitionistic autoepistemic logic $\mathcal{L} = (\mathrm{Var}, \{\wedge, \Rightarrow, \flat\}, \Vdash)$.*

Let the isomorphism $\partial_{\mathcal{P}}$ be the extension of the isomorphism ∂ to sets, i. e., for any set $Y \in \mathcal{P}(1_t)$, $\partial_{\mathcal{P}} Y = \{\partial x \mid x \in Y\} \in \mathcal{P}(1_k)$, while $\partial^*_{\mathcal{P}}$ be its reduction to $\mathcal{B}^+_t$ and $\mathcal{B}^+_k$ respectively. Then the following commutative diagram, where $v' = \partial v$, $v_K = {\downarrow^+}_t v$, $v'_K = {\downarrow^+}_k v'$, $\mathcal{B}^+_k = \partial^*_{\mathcal{P}}(\mathcal{B}^+_t)$, $1_k = \partial_{\mathcal{P}}(1_t)$, for algebraic models of $\mathcal{L}$ holds

$$
\begin{array}{ccc}
((\mathcal{B}_4, \leq_t, \alpha_t), v) & \xrightarrow{\quad \partial \quad} & ((\mathcal{B}_4, \leq_k, \alpha_k), v') \\
\Big\downarrow {\scriptstyle \downarrow^+_t} & & \Big\downarrow {\scriptstyle \downarrow^+_k} \\
((\mathcal{B}^+_t, \{\bigcap, \rightharpoonup^+, \diamond_t\}), v_K) & \xrightarrow{\quad \partial^*_{\mathcal{P}} \quad} & ((\mathcal{B}^+_k, \{\bigcap, \rightharpoonup^+, \diamond_k\}), v'_K) \\
\Big\downarrow {\scriptstyle \mathrm{in}_t} & & \Big\downarrow {\scriptstyle \mathrm{in}_k} \\
((\mathcal{P}(1_t), \{\bigcap, \rightharpoonup^+, \diamond_t\}), v_K) & \xrightarrow{\quad \partial_{\mathcal{P}} \quad} & ((\mathcal{P}(1_k), \{\bigcap, \rightharpoonup^+, \diamond_k\}), v'_K) \\
\Big\downarrow {\scriptstyle =} & & \Big\downarrow {\scriptstyle =} \\
(\mathbb{E} \circ \mathbb{D})((\mathcal{B}_4, \leq_t, \alpha_t), v) & \xrightarrow{\quad \partial_{\mathcal{P}} \quad} & (\mathbb{E} \circ \mathbb{D})((\mathcal{B}_4, \leq_k, \alpha_k), v')
\end{array}
$$

where in_t, in_k are injective homomorphisms, and $\downarrow^+_t, {\downarrow^+}_k$ are the isomorphisms of $\downarrow^+$ w. r. t. the truth and knowledge ordering, respectively.

Proof. It is easy to verify, based on Propositions 28, 29, 30 and Definition 67. Let us consider a simple case, for the term $\bot \wedge \top \in (\mathcal{B}_4, \leq_t, \{\wedge, \rightharpoonup, -\})$. Then $(\partial^*_{\mathcal{P}} \downarrow^+_t)(\bot \wedge \top) = \partial^*_{\mathcal{P}}(\{0, \bot\} \bigcap \{0, \top\}) = \{\bot, 0\} \bigcap \{\bot, 1\} = \{\bot\} = {\downarrow^+}_k(0 \otimes 1) = (\downarrow^+_k \partial)(\bot \wedge \top)$. □

In this diagram, we have to consider the *horizontal arrows* as a D-bilattice, from up to down: Belnap's original D-bilattice, its set-based *isomorphic representation*, and its powerset *extension*. Notice that all arrows (homomorphism between modal Heyting algebras) of the commutative diagram on the top are *isomorphisms*. The lower part of the commutative diagram represents the fact that the modal Heyting algebras of isomorphic representations are the *subalgebras* of the powerset extensions.

5.2 General many-valued intensional first-order logic with abstraction operator

In this section, we will consider the many-valued logic directly, instead by using method of ontological encapsulation of many-valued logic provided by Section A.4.2 in the Appendix.[3] So, the basic issue of the work in this section is a definition of such a many-valued logic by generalization of the standard FOL, able to distinguish the intensional and extensional aspects of the semantics and adopting only a trivial equality theory of intensions for many-valued logics. The distinction between intensions and extensions is important, considering that extensions can be notoriously difficult to handle in an efficient manner. The extensional equality theory of predicates and functions under higher-order semantics (e. g., for two predicates with the same set of attributes $p = q$ is true iff these symbols are interpreted by the same relation), i. e., the strong equational theory of intensions, is not decidable, in general. However, different from 2-valued logic where extension of a given predicate is composed by only *true* atoms, here for MV-logics the ground atoms of extension of this predicate can have all truth values *except the false value*. Thus, separating intensions from extensions makes it possible to have an equational theory over predicate and function names (intensions) that is separate from the extensional equality of relations and functions.

The intensional predicate logic described in Section 1.2 is developed in the classic 2-valued framework. Consequently, we need to generalize such a framework and the theory of the PRP intensionality for the case of predicate many-valued logics, based on the *complete* (important for the semantics of many-valued existential and universal quantifiers) lattice $(X, \leq, \widetilde{\wedge}, \widetilde{\vee})$ of algebraic truth values, with f, t the bottom and top value, respectively, and with other many-valued logic connectives (e. g., $\sim, \Rightarrow$, negation and implication respectively). We denote by $\mathbf{2} = \{f, t\} \subseteq X$ the classic 2-valued logic lattice. The smallest paraconsistent many-valued extension can be, e. g., an extension of the strong Kleene's 3-valued logic [214, 215], able to deal with Lear paradoxes.

5.2.1 Many-valued algebra of concepts and extensions: embedding of DL

Concept languages steam from semantic networks [45–47], which for a large group of graphical languages used in the 1970s to represent and reason with conceptual knowl-

3 Moreover, in Section 2.2 we used an ad hoc solution for representation of the multivalued logic for logic formulae by introducing a particular binary predicate $w_N(<\phi_i>, x)$ that express the fact "the sentence ϕ_i has a probability value x," so that we remain in the framework of the classical two valued logics (the ground atoms of this binary predicate w_N can be only true o false). In fact, such a logic is not really many-valued but indirectly speaks about values of the formulae, and was a good solution to reason about the probabilities.

edge. But they did not have a rigorously defined statement as emphasized by Brachman and Levesque [48, 49]. After that, different versions of description logics [50] with formal semantics appeared, as a family of knowledge representation formalisms that represent the knowledge of an application domain by first defining the relevant *concepts* and *roles* as a terminology (TBox) and then the *assertions* (ABox) about named individuals in terms of this terminology. The concepts denote sets of individuals, and roles denote binary relationships between individuals.

Example 33 (Description Logic (DL)). In what follows, we will consider the attribute language with complements, $\mathcal{ALC}$, with a set of atomic concepts and roles denoted by at and r, respectively. Concept descriptions, denoted by $u, v, \ldots$, in $\mathcal{ALC}$, introduced in [216], are formed according to the following current form variable-free *DL syntax*:

$$u := \text{at} \mid \top \mid \bot \mid \neg u \mid u_1 \sqcap u_2 \mid \forall r.u \mid \exists r.u$$

An *extensional* interpretation $\mathcal{I}_e$ for $\mathcal{ALC}$ concepts consist of a nonempty set $\mathcal{D}$ (domain of interpretation) and an interpretation function, which assigns to every atomic (basic) concept at its extension $\mathcal{I}_e(\text{at})$, denoted as a set $\text{at}^{\mathcal{I}_e} \subseteq \mathcal{D}$, and to every atomic role r a binary relation $r^{\mathcal{I}_e} = \mathcal{I}_e(r) \subseteq \mathcal{D} \times \mathcal{D}$. If we consider concepts as *intensional* entities, then $\mathcal{I}_e$ can be considered as a possible extensionalization mapping, which for a given context (or "possible world") determines the extension of this concept in that context. The extensional interpretation is extended to concepts descriptions by the following inductive definitions.

Definition 69 (DL semantics).

$$\begin{aligned}
\top^{\mathcal{I}_e} &= \mathcal{D}, \quad \text{for universal concept,}\\
\bot^{\mathcal{I}_e} &= \emptyset, \quad \text{empty set for bottom (inconsistent) concept,}\\
(\neg u)^{\mathcal{I}_e} &= \mathcal{D} \backslash u^{\mathcal{I}_e}, \quad \text{where } \backslash \text{ is a set difference,}\\
(u_1 \sqcap u_2)^{\mathcal{I}_e} &= u_1^{\mathcal{I}_e} \bigcap u_2^{\mathcal{I}_e},\\
(\forall r.u)^{\mathcal{I}_e} &= \{a \in \mathcal{D} \mid \forall b.(a,b) \in r^{\mathcal{I}_e} \text{ implies } b \in u^{\mathcal{I}_e}\}, \quad \text{for value restriction,}\\
(\exists r.u)^{\mathcal{I}_e} &= \{a \in \mathcal{D} \mid \exists b.(a,b) \in r^{\mathcal{I}_e} \text{ and } b \in u^{\mathcal{I}_e}\}, \quad \text{for full existential quantification.}
\end{aligned}$$

It is easy to verify that $\bot$ stands for $\neg\top$, $\exists r.u$ stands for $\neg(\forall r.(\neg u))$, and we can introduce concept disjunction $u \sqcup v$ as abbreviation for $\neg(\neg u \sqcap \neg v)$. In fact, for this special variable-free syntax (differently from predicate *logics* with variables) without any reference to logic truth values, is more appropriate the name 'concept *algebra*" then description *logic*, analogously to the difference between relation *algebra* and predicate *logic*.

Two concepts u_1, u_2 are *equivalent*, $u_1 \equiv u_2$, if $u_1^{\mathcal{I}_e} = u_2^{\mathcal{I}_e}$ for all interpretations; a concept u is subsumed by a concept u_1, $u \sqsubseteq u_1$, if $u^{\mathcal{I}_e} \subseteq u_1^{\mathcal{I}_e}$ for all interpretations.

A TBox, or terminology, $\mathcal{T}$ is a set of axioms: concept descriptions $u \equiv \phi$ and subsumptions $u \sqsubseteq \phi$, where ϕ is an expression of the concept language $\mathcal{ALC}$. A *base interpretation* of $\mathcal{T}$ is an interpretation for atomic concepts only. If this interpretation can be extended to all derived concepts in $\mathcal{T}$ in a unique way then it is a *model* of a terminology $\mathcal{T}$. A concept u is satisfiable w. r. t. the TBox $\mathcal{T}$ if there exists a model $\mathcal{I}_e$ of $\mathcal{T}$ such that $u^{\mathcal{I}_e}$ is nonempty.

Using concepts u and roles r, one can make assertions of the following two kinds in an ABox: $u(a)$, $r(a,b)$, where a,b are any two individuals. In a simplified view, an ABox can be seen as an instance of a relational database with only unary or binary relations. However, contrary to the "closed-world assumption" (CWA) semantics of relational databases, the semantics of ABoxes is an "open-world semantics" (OWA): it means that we cannot assume that the knowledge is complete, different from a relational database where a missed information is considered as false. That is, we have 3-valued logic with third "unknown" truth value as well (as Kleene's 3-valued logic).

An interpretation $\mathcal{I}_e$ *satisfies* the concept assertion $u(a)$ if $a^{\mathcal{I}_e} \in u^{\mathcal{I}_e}$, and *satisfies* the role assertion $r(a,b)$ if $(a^{\mathcal{I}_e}, b^{\mathcal{I}_e}) \in r^{\mathcal{I}_e}$. It is a *model* of an ABox $\mathcal{A}$ if it satisfies each assertion in $\mathcal{A}$. Finally, $\mathcal{I}_e$ satisfies an assertion α or an ABox $\mathcal{A}$ *with respect to* a TBox $\mathcal{T}$ if in addition to being a model of α or of $\mathcal{A}$, it is a model of $\mathcal{T}$.

Different from standard 2-valued logics where we are using the logic concepts of truth and falsity, in DL we are using only the concept of satisfaction: indeed it is an *algebra for concepts* and relationships between them. Its logic translation into predicate logic demonstrates that it is a 2-variable sublogic of FOL, where the concepts are unary predicates, and roles are binary predicates. In this paper, we will see how this DL algebra of concepts can be embedded into the algebra of concepts of many-valued intensional predicate logic.

The description logic for databases $\mathcal{DLR}$ [50] extends the basic DL with n-ary relations, $n \geq 3$, with also two new syntax expressions, $(\$i/n : u)$ and $\exists(\$i)r$, with the following semantics:

1. $(\$i/n : u)$ denotes all tuples of arity n in which the i-th component is an instance of concept u, and thus represents a unary selection. It can be used in order to define n-ary concept u from given set of unary (standard DL) concepts u_k, $1 \leq k \leq n$, by description
$$u \equiv (\$1/n : u_1) \sqcap \cdots \sqcap (\$n/n : u_n),$$
which can be used to represent a Database n-ary relation.
2. $\exists(\$i)r$ denotes all objects that participate as i-th component in an tuple of relation r, and thus represents a unary projection. Consequently, it is inverse to the first operator and transforms n-ary roles into standard DL unary concepts, so that the following description is an axiom: $r \equiv (\$1/n : \exists(\$1)r) \sqcap \cdots \sqcap (\$n/n : \exists(\$n)r)$, for any n-ary role r.

There are many aspects of description logics, which we have not considered here, because they are not important for the present work. For example, we recall the expressive description logics $\mathcal{SHIF}(D)$ and $\mathcal{SHOIN}(D)$, which stand behind the Web ontology languages OWL Lite and OWL DL [93, 217], respectively.

What we need here is a generalization of the extension for predicates in standard 2-valued logics, into an *m-extension* for predicates in the framework of *many-valued* logics. In standard predicate logic with a set of predicate symbols in P, the extension of any k-ary, $k \geq 1$, predicate $r_i^k \in P$ is determined by a given Herbrand interpretation $v : H \to \mathbf{2}$, where H is a Herbrand base and $\mathbf{2} = \{f, t\}$ set of classic truth values, by

$$\|r_i^k\| = \{(t_1, \ldots, t_k) \mid r_i^k(t_1, \ldots, t_k) \in H \text{ and } v(r_i^k(t_1, \ldots, t_k)) = t\}$$

vice versa, given the extensions of all predicates, then the Herbrand interpretation $v : H \to \mathbf{2}$ is determined by, for any $r_i^k(t_1, \ldots, t_k) \in H$,

$$v(r_i^k(t_1, \ldots, t_k)) = t \quad \text{if } (t_1, \ldots, t_k) \in \|r_i^k\|; \quad f, \text{ otherwise.}$$

In what follows, we will consider only conservative homomorphic many-valued extensions of the classic 2-valued logic with logical connectives $\wedge, \vee, \neg, \Rightarrow, \equiv$ (conjunction, disjunction, negation, implication and equivalence, respectively) and their corresponding operators $\widetilde{\wedge}, \widetilde{\vee}, \sim, \Rrightarrow$ and $\Leftrightarrow$ of the algebra of truth values in the lattice $(X, \leq)$.

Definition 70. For a given many-valued predicate logic, by $\mathcal{A}_{\text{mv}} = (X, \leq, \sim \widetilde{\wedge}, \widetilde{\vee}, \Rrightarrow, \Leftrightarrow)$ we denote the algebra of the truth values in the complete lattice $(X, \leq)$. The conjunction "$\widetilde{\wedge}$" and disjunction "$\widetilde{\vee}$" operators of this MV truth-algebra may be different from the meet and join operator of the complete lattice X of truth values as well.[4]

We assume that there exist an element $\kappa \in X$ such that $\sim \kappa = \kappa$, where "$\sim$" is the unary antitonic negation operator, and the many-valued equivalence operator is defined for any two $a, b \in X$ by

$$a \Leftrightarrow b = \begin{cases} t, & \text{if } a = b \\ f, & \text{otherwise} \end{cases} \tag{5.17}$$

Note that differently from the 2-valued intensional logic introduced in Chapter 1, here the bottom value f and top value t are not represented by $\mathcal{P}(D^0) = \mathcal{P}(\{\langle\rangle\})$, i. e., $f \neq \emptyset$ and $t \neq \langle\rangle$.

The fact that classic 2-valued algebra is the subalgebra of this many-valued algebra X, means that X is a conservative extension of the classic logic operators, and

4 The classic 2-valued algebra $\mathcal{A}_2$ is particular case with lattice $\mathbf{2} = \{f, t\}$ and if $\mathbf{2} \subset X$ (the top and bottom elements in X).

consequently, we have that for every $a \in X, f \leq a \leq t$ and $\sim f = t, \sim t = f$. This extension has to preserve the antitonic property for the negation operator $\sim$ as well: for example, from the fact that $f < \kappa < t$ we obtain that $t =\sim f >\sim \kappa = \kappa >\sim t = f$.

For example, the minimal 3-valued extension of the classic 2-valued logic is the strong Kleene's 3-valued logic with $X = \mathcal{B}_3 = \{f < \kappa < t\}$ where κ is considered as "unknown" truth value, or its extension to Belnap's 4-valued bilattice $\mathcal{B}_4$ described in Section 5.1.3. We define a m-extension (many-valued extension), denoted by $\| \_ \|_m$, which takes the logic values in its representation explicitly, as follows:

$$\|r_i^k\|_m = \{(t_1, \dots, t_k, a) \mid r_i^k(t_1, \dots, t_k) \in H \text{ and } a = v(r_i^k(t_1, \dots, t_k)) \neq f\} \tag{5.18}$$

It is easy to verify that for the classic 2-valued predicate logic these two representations of an extension, are equivalent, i. e., given standard extension $\|r_i^k\|$ we derive that its m-extension is equal to $\|r_i^k\|_m = \{(t_1, \dots, t_k, t) \mid (t_1, \dots, t_k) \in \|r_i^k\|\}$. Otherwise, given an m-extension $\|r_i^k\|_m$, we derive a standard extension by $\|r_i^k\| = \{(t_1, \dots, t_k) \mid (t_1, \dots, t_k, t) \in \|r_i^k\|_m\} = \pi_{-k-1}(\|r_i^k\|_m)$, where $\pi_{-i}, i \geq 1$ is the operation that eliminates i-th column of a relation, while π_i denotes i-th projection.

In any given m-valued predicate logic, where $m \geq 3$ is a set of algebraic truth values in X, we can use only m-extensions which is an alternative specification of many-valued Herbrand interpretation $v : H \to X$, as we have shown above. That is, for any $r_i^k(t_1, \dots, t_k) \in H$,

$$v(r_i^k(t_1, \dots, t_k)) = \begin{cases} a, & \text{if } (t_1, \dots, t_k, a) \in \|r_i^k\|_m \\ f, & \text{otherwise} \end{cases} \tag{5.19}$$

So that a many-valued extension is just the extension of an ontologically encapsuled meta 2-valued logic, as presented in [218].

We assume that a concept algebra has a nonempty domain $\mathcal{D} = D_0 + D_I$, (here $+$ is a disjoint union) where a subdomain D_0 is made of particulars or individuals (we denote by ® the non-meaning individuals, for interpretation of language entities that are no meaningful, as "Unicorn" for example) with $X \subseteq D_0$.

The rest $D_I = D_1 + D_2 \dots + D_n \dots$ is made of universals (concepts): D_1 for many-valued logic concepts, or `L-concepts` (their extension corresponds to some logic value), and $D_n, n \geq 2$, for `concepts` (their m-extension is an n-ary relation); we consider the property (for an unary predicate) as a concept in D_2. The concepts in $\mathcal{D}_I$ are denoted by $u, v, \dots$, while the values (individuals) in D_0 by $a, b, \dots$.

Remark. Notice that all concepts in D_i, $i \geq 2$ corresponds to the *ontologically encapsuled* virtual predicates (as in the case of the ontological encapsulation of many-valued atoms $p_i^{n-1}(x_1, \dots, x_{n-1})$ by extending them with another attribute to obtain extended 2-valued "flattened" atom $p_F(x_1, \dots, x_{n-1}, y)$ where domain of y is the set of logic-values in X, in Section A.4.2).

So, for a given assignment $g \in \mathcal{D}^{\mathcal{V}}$, and valuation (from Definition 62, Section 5.1.1) $v^* : \mathcal{L}^G_{\mathrm{mv}} \to X$, where $\mathcal{L}^G_{\mathrm{mv}}$ is the set of sentences of the many-valued *predicate* logic $\mathcal{L}_{\mathrm{mv}}$, the ground many-valued atom $p_i^{n-1}(g(x_1), \dots, g(x_{n-1}))$ is substituted by the true "flattened" atom $p_F(g(x_1), \dots, g(x_{n-1}), a)$ where $a \in X$. If $a = v(p_i^{n-1}(g(x_1), \dots, g(x_{n-1})))$ then this flattened atom $p_F(g(x_1), \dots, g(x_{n-1}), a)$ is true; false otherwise (as explained in Section A.4.2 in the Appendix).

In this way, the last $(k+1)$th attribute of the extension of any concept in D_{k+1}, $k \geq 1$, will have the assigned logic value to the original many-valued k-ary concept of the many-valued predicate logic $\mathcal{L}_{\mathrm{mv}}$ for a given valuation v. □

Sort S is a subset of a domain $\mathcal{D}$. For example, $X \subset D_0$ is a many-valued-logic sort, $\mathbf{2} \subseteq X$ is a classic-logic sort, $[0,1] \subset D_0$ is closed-interval-of-reals sort, $\mathbb{N} = \{1,2,3,\dots\} \subset D_0$ is a sort of positive integers, etc. These sorts are used for sorted variables in many-sorted predicate logics so that the assigned values for each sorted variable must belong to its sort. The unsorted variables are the variables with a top sort equal to $\mathcal{D}$.

Definition 71 (m-sorted extensions). We define the set of all m-extensions in the many-sorted framework of universals,

$$\mathfrak{Rm} = \widetilde{X} \bigcup \left\{ R \in \bigcup_{n \geq 1} \mathcal{P}(\mathcal{D}^n \times (X \backslash \{f\})) \mid (u_1, \dots, u_n, a), (u_1, \dots, u_n, b) \in R \text{ implies } b = a \right\} \tag{5.20}$$

so that each $(n+1)$-ary relation is a graph of a function, and by $\mathfrak{Rm}_k, k \geq 1$, we will denote the subset of all k-ary relations in $\mathfrak{Rm}$, and by $\emptyset$ each empty relation in $\mathfrak{Rm}$, with

$$\widetilde{X} = \{\{a\} \mid a \in X \text{ and } a \neq f\} \bigcup \{\emptyset\} \tag{5.21}$$

and hence, $\emptyset \in \widetilde{X} \subset \mathcal{P}(X) \subseteq \mathcal{P}(D_0)$, with $\mathfrak{Rm}_1 = \widetilde{X}$. So, $(\widetilde{X}, \preceq)$ is complete lattice with $\emptyset$ bottom element and $\{a\} \preceq \{b\}$ iff $a \leq b$, with the isomorphism of two lattices

$$\mathrm{in}_X : (X, \leq) \to (\widetilde{X}, \preceq),$$

such that $\mathrm{in}_X(f) = \emptyset$, and for all $a \neq f, \mathrm{in}_X(a) = \{a\}$

Note that for an open formula $\phi(x_1, \dots, x_k)$ and any many-valued interpretation $v : H \to X$ the relation $R = I^*_{\mathrm{mv}}(\phi(x_1, \dots, x_k)) =_{\mathrm{def}} \{(g(x_1), \dots, g(x_k), a) \mid g \in \mathcal{D}^{\mathcal{V}}$ and $a = v^*(\phi/g) \neq f\}$ (see equation (5.31) and Theorem 11) is just one particular relation in $\mathfrak{Rm}$.

We introduce for the concepts in D_I an *extensional interpretation h*, which assigns the *m-extension* to each intensional element in $\mathcal{D}$, and can be considered as an *interpretation of concepts* in $\mathcal{D}$. Thus, each concept in D_I represents a set of tuples in $\mathcal{D}$, and can be also an element of the extension of another concept and of itself also. Each extensional interpretation h assigns to the intensional elements of $\mathcal{D}$ (with image of intensional interpretation I) an appropriate extension: in the case of particulars $u \in D_0$, $h_0(u) \in D_0$, such that for each logic value $a \in X \subset D_0$, $h_0(a) = a$. Thus, we have the particular's mapping $h_0 : D_0 \to D_0$ and more generally (here $+$ is considered as disjoint union),

$$h = \sum_{i \in \mathbb{N}} h_i : \mathcal{D} \longrightarrow D_0 + \sum_{i \geq 1} \mathfrak{Rm}_i \tag{5.22}$$

where $h_1 : D_1 \to \widetilde{X}$ assigns to each sentence $u \in D_1$ a relation (composed by the single tuple $h_1(u) = \{a\}$ with a truth value $a \in X$ if $a \neq f$), $\emptyset$ otherwise, and $h_i : D_i \to \mathfrak{Rm}_i$, $i \geq 2$, assigns a m-extension to all concepts.

Definition 72 (Built-in concepts). Let $\mathcal{E}_{\text{in}}$ be a fixed subset of extensionalization functions (in what follows, we will consider the set of all well-defined extensionalization functions for the many-valued intensional FOL $\mathcal{L}_{\text{in}}$, specified by Definitions 76 and 77).

We say that a given concept $u \in D_I$ is a *built-in concept* if its extension is invariant w. r. t. extensionalization functions. It is the case of elementary datatypes or data values (used also in DL) as the "Natural-number," "Real-number," "Truth-value" that are concepts in D_2 such that for $\mathbb{N} \subset D_0$ and $X \subset D_0$,

$$h_2(\text{Natural number}) = \{(n, t) \mid n \in \mathbb{N}\}, \quad h_2(\text{Truth value}) = \{(a, t) \mid a \in X\}.$$

We define a number of another most used built-in concepts:
1. We introduce the following many-valuedness assumptions for intensional elements in $\mathcal{D}$ and their extensionalization functions: for any algebraic truth value $a \in X$, we introduce a built-in truth-concept $u_a \in D_1$ such that if $a \neq f$,

$$\forall h \in \mathcal{E}_{\text{in}}(h(u_a) = \{a\}) \quad \text{and} \quad \forall h \in \mathcal{E}_{\text{in}}(h(u_f) = \emptyset).$$

2. The universal and bottom (inconsistent) unary DL concept $\top, \bot \in D_2$, respectively, satisfy that for every $h \in \mathcal{E}_{\text{in}}$, $h(\top) = \mathcal{D} \times \{t\}$ and $h(\bot) = \emptyset$.
3. The corresponding concept to the binary identity predicate $=$ used in FOL is denoted by the symbol $\text{Id} \in D_3$. We have that for this "concept of identity" Id, its m-extension is constant and 2-valued in every extensionalization function $h\mathcal{E}_{\text{in}}$, i. e.,

$$h(\text{Id}) = R_= = \{(u, v, t) \mid u, v \in D_k, k \geq 0 \text{ such that } u = v \text{ in FOL}\}.$$

4. The corresponding concept to the binary weak-intensional-equivalence predicate $=_{\text{in}}$ is denoted by the symbol $\text{Eq} \in D_3$. We have that for this "concept of weak-

intensional-equivalence" Eq, its m-extension is constant and 2-valued in every extensionalization function h, i. e.,[5]

$$h(\mathrm{Eq}) = R_{=_{\mathrm{in}}} = \Big\{(u, v, t) \mid u, v \in D_k, k \geq 2 \text{ and } \bigcup_{h \in \mathcal{E}_{\mathrm{in}}} h(u) = \bigcup_{h \in \mathcal{E}_{\mathrm{in}}} h(v)\Big\}$$

Another important concept that has a specific semantics, but *is not* built-in concepts is the *self-reference* truth-concept $u_T \in D_2$, such that for any particular extensionalization function h we have that $h(u_T) = \{(u, a) \mid u \in D_1, \emptyset \neq h(u) = \{a\}\}$. This concept represents the truth of all logic-concepts in D_1, in the way that for any logic-concept $u \in D_1$ we have that $h(u) = \{a\}$ iff $(u, a) \in h(u_T)$.

We define the following partial ordering $\preceq$ for the m-extensions in $\mathfrak{Rm}$.

Definition 73 (Extensional partial order in $\mathfrak{Rm}$). For any two m-relations $R_1, R_2 \in \mathfrak{Rm}$ with arity $k_1 = \mathrm{ar}(R_1), k_2 = \mathrm{ar}(R_2)$ and $m = \max(k_1, k_2)$, $R_1 \preceq R_2$ iff

$$\text{for each } (u_1, \ldots, u_m, a) \in \mathrm{Ex}(R_1, m), \quad \exists (u_1, \ldots, u_m, b) \in \mathrm{Ex}(R_2, m) \quad \text{with } a \leq b,$$

where this expansion-mapping $\mathrm{Ex} : \mathfrak{Rm} \to \mathfrak{Rm}$ is defined as follows for any $R \in \mathfrak{Rm}$:

$$\mathrm{Ex}(R, m) = \begin{cases} \bigcup\{\{(u_1, \ldots, u_k)\} \times \mathcal{D}^{m-k} \times \{a\} \mid (u_1, \ldots, u_k, a) \in R\}, & \text{if } m > k \\ R, & \text{otherwise} \end{cases} \tag{5.23}$$

We denote by $R_1 \simeq R_2$ iff $R_1 \preceq R_2$ and $R_2 \preceq R_1$, the equivalence relation between m-extensions. We define the completion of $R \in \mathfrak{Rm}$ with $i = \mathrm{ar}(R) \geq 1$ by

$$\mathrm{Com}(R) = \begin{cases} R \bigcup\{(v_1, \ldots, v_{i-1}, f) \mid (v_1, \ldots, v_{i-1}) \notin \pi_{-i}(R) \text{ or } R = \emptyset\}, & \text{if } i \geq 2 \\ \{f\}, & \text{if } R = \emptyset \\ R, & \text{otherwise} \end{cases} \tag{5.24}$$

It is easy to verify that Ex is monotonic operation w. r. t. to the ordering $\preceq$, i. e., if $R_1 \preceq R_2$ then $\mathrm{Ex}(R_1, m) \preceq \mathrm{Ex}(R_2, m)$ for every $m \in \mathbb{N}$.

We chose $\emptyset, \{t\} \in \mathfrak{Rm}$ to be the representative elements of the bottom and top equivalence classes in $\mathfrak{Rm}$ relatively (determined by $\simeq$), so that $(\forall R \in \mathfrak{Rm})(\emptyset \preceq R \preceq \{t\})$. Consequently, the *extensional* ordering $\preceq$ in $\mathfrak{Rm}$ is the resulting consequence of the *logic* truth ordering $\leq$ in X where we have the analog result $(\forall a \in X)(f \leq a \leq t)$.

5 This definition is a many-valued generalization of the flat-accumulation case presented in [43, 53, 105] for the 2-valued FOL: if the first predicate is true in some interpretation (or "possible world") $h \in \mathcal{E}_{\mathrm{in}}$ then the second must be true in some interpretation $h' \in \mathcal{E}_{\mathrm{in}}$ as well, and vice versa. It has been used successively in the intensional 2-valued FOL [42, 58, 219] for the semantic Web and P2P data integration, but differently, by introducing a new existential modal S5 operator in that logical language (here we avoided the introduction of this modal operator).

In what follows, for each set of couples of indexes $S \in \mathcal{P}(\mathbb{N}^2)$, the binary operation $\bowtie_S$ is the natural join from relational database algebra if S is a nonempty set of pairs of joined columns of respective relations (where the first argument is the column index of the relation R_1 while the second argument is the column index of the joined column of the relation R_2); `otherwise` it is equal to the cartesian product $\times$. We can define an m-extensional algebra over the poset $(\mathfrak{Rm}, \preceq)$ as follows.

Definition 74. Let us define the m-extensional relational algebra for a given truth-values algebra $\mathcal{A}_{mv} = (X, \leq, \sim, \widetilde{\wedge}, \widetilde{\vee}, \Rrightarrow)$ of Definition 70 by

$$\mathcal{A}_{\mathfrak{Rm}} = ((\mathfrak{Rm}, \preceq, \emptyset, \{t\}), R_{=}, \oslash, \{\otimes_S, \oplus_S, \ominus_S\}_{S \in \mathcal{P}(\mathbb{N}^2)}, \{\boxplus_i, \boxtimes_i, \preccurlyeq_i, \succcurlyeq_i\}_{i \in \mathbb{N}}, \text{Inc}, \{\rhd_{i,a}, \lhd_{i,a}^{k}\}_{i \leq k \in \mathbb{N} \& f \neq a \in X}),$$

where $R_{=}$ is the binary relation for extensionally equal elements. We will use "=" for the extensional identity for relations in $\mathfrak{Rm}$, and relation-completion mapping $\text{Com} : \mathfrak{Rm} \to \mathfrak{Rm}$ in (5.24). The unary operators $\oslash, \boxplus_i, \boxtimes_i, \preccurlyeq_i, \succcurlyeq_i : \mathfrak{Rm} \to \mathfrak{Rm}$, and binary operators $\otimes_S, \oplus_S, \ominus_S, \text{Inc} : \mathfrak{Rm}^2 \to \mathfrak{Rm}$, and particular DL-unary operators $\rhd_{i,a}: (\mathfrak{Rm} \backslash \mathfrak{Rm}_1) \to \mathfrak{Rm}_2$ and $\lhd_{i,a}^{k}: \mathfrak{Rm}_2 \to \mathfrak{Rm}$, are defined as follows:

1. For negation $\oslash$:
   1.1 $\oslash(R) = \{\sim a \mid \{a\} = R, \sim a \neq f\}$, for $\text{ar}(R) = 1$.
   1.2 $\oslash(R) = \{(v_1, \ldots, v_{i-1}, \sim a) \mid (v_1, \ldots, v_{i-1}, a) \in \text{Com}(R), \sim a \neq f\}$, for $i = \text{ar}(R) \geq 2$.
2. For any pair $(\odot, \circ) \in \{(\otimes_S, \widetilde{\wedge}), (\oplus_S, \widetilde{\vee}), (\ominus_S, \Rrightarrow)\}$:
   2.1 $R_1 \odot R_2 = \{a \circ b \mid \{a\} = \text{Com}(R_1), \{b\} = \text{Com}(R_2) \text{ and } a \circ b \neq f\}$, for $\text{ar}(R_1) = \text{ar}(R_2) = 1$ and S is the empty set.
   2.2 $R_1 \odot R_2 = \{(v_1, \ldots, v_{i-1}, a \circ b) \mid (v_1, \ldots, v_{i-1}, a) \in \text{Com}(R_1), \{b\} \in \text{Com}(R_2)$ and $a \circ b \neq f\}$, for $\text{ar}(R_1) = i \geq 2, \text{ar}(R_2) = 1$ and S is the empty set.
   2.3 $R_1 \odot R_2 = \{(v_1, \ldots, v_{i-1}, a \circ b) \mid \{a\} \in \text{Com}(R_1), (v_1, \ldots, v_{i-1}, b) \in \text{Com}(R_2)$ and $a \circ b \neq f\}$, for $\text{ar}(R_1) = 1, \text{ar}(R_2) = i \geq 2$ and S is the empty set.
   2.4 Otherwise, let $i = \text{ar}(R_1) \geq 2, \text{ar}(R_2) \geq 2$, and from Definition 9, binary operator $\bowtie_S : \mathfrak{Rm} \times \mathfrak{Rm} \to \mathfrak{Rm}$, such that for any two relations $R_1, R_2 \in \mathfrak{Rm}$, the $R_1 \bowtie_S R_2$ is equal to the relation obtained by natural join of these two relations `if` S is a nonempty set of pairs of joined columns of respective relations (where the first argument is the column index of the relation R_1 while the second argument is the column index of the joined column of the relation R_2); `otherwise` it is equal to the Cartesian product $R_1 \times R_2$. Then $R_1 \odot R_2 = \{(v_1, \ldots, v_k, a \circ b) \mid ((v_1, \ldots, v_{i-1}, a, v_i, \ldots, v_k, b) \in \text{Com}(R_1) \bowtie_S \text{Com}(R_2)$ with $(v_1, \ldots, v_{i-1}, a) \in R_1$ and $(v_i, \ldots, v_k, b)$ is a (also empty) subtuple of R_2 without elements in $\pi_2(S))$ and $a \circ b \neq f\}$.[6]
3. For quantifiers $\boxplus_i$ and $\boxtimes_i$, (here "$\bigwedge$" and "$\bigvee$" are the meet and join operators in lattice of truth values X, respectively):

6 Note that in the case of the two-valued logic, we obtain that $R_1 \odot R_2 = (R_1 \bowtie_S R_2) \times \{t\}$.

3.1 $\boxplus_i(R) = \boxtimes_i(R) = R$, for $ar(R) = 1$.

3.2 $\boxplus_i(R) = \{b \mid \text{ if } b = \bigvee\{a \mid (v,a) \in Com(R)\} \neq f\}$ if $i = 1$; R otherwise, $\boxtimes_i(R) = \{b \mid \text{ if } b = \bigwedge\{a \mid (v,a) \in Com(R)\} \neq f\}$ if $i = 1$; R otherwise, for $ar(R) = 2$.

3.3 $\boxplus_i(R) = \{(v_1,\dots,v_{i-1},v_{i+1},\dots,v_k,b) \mid \text{ if } b = \bigvee\{a \mid (v_1,\dots,v_k,a) \in Com(R)\} \neq f\}$ if $1 \leq i \leq k$; R otherwise, $\boxtimes_i(R) = \{(v_1,\dots,v_{i-1},v_{i+1},\dots,v_k,b) \mid \text{ if } b = \bigwedge\{a \mid (v_1,\dots,v_k,a) \in Com(R)\} \neq f\}$ if $1 \leq i \leq k$; R otherwise, for $ar(R) \geq 3$.

4. Control cardinality, where $|R|$ denote the cardinality of R:

$$\lessdot_i (R) = \{t\} \quad \text{if } |R| \leq i; \quad \emptyset \text{ otherwise},$$

$$\gtrdot_i (R) = \{t\} \quad \text{if } |R| \geq i; \quad \emptyset \text{ otherwise}.$$

5. Inclusion $Inc(R_1, R_2) = \{t\}$ if $ar(R_1) = ar(R_2)$ and there is a relation R_2' obtained by a permutation of columns in R_2 such that $R_1 \subseteq R_2'$; $\emptyset$ otherwise.
6. $\triangleright_{i,a} (R) = \{(v_i, t) \mid (v_1,\dots,v_i,\dots,v_k,a) \in R\}$ if $i \leq k$; empty binary m-relation otherwise.
7. $\triangleleft^k_{i,a} (R) = \{(v_1,\dots,v_i,\dots,v_k,t) \mid (v_i,a) \in R \text{ and } v_m \in \mathcal{D}, m \neq i, 1 \leq m \leq k\}$.

Notice that definition of operators $\boxplus_i, \boxtimes_i$ are valid because X is *complete* lattice.

We define the following binary derived operator $\circledast = \otimes(Inc(\_), Inc((\_)^{-1})) : \mathfrak{Rm}^2 \to \mathfrak{Rm}$, so that $\circledast(R_1, R_2) = \otimes(Inc(\_), Inc((\_)^{-1}))(R_1, R_2) = \otimes(Inc(R_1, R_2), Inc((R_1, R_2)^{-1})) = \otimes(Inc(R_1, R_2), Inc(R_2, R_1)) \in \{\emptyset, \{t\}\}$.

Moreover, we define the many-valued-ISA relationship for concepts in $u, v \in D_I$ by $u \sqsubseteq v$ iff for all h, $(h(u) \preceq h(v))$, which is a generalization of the ISA relationship in DL. The strong intensional equality, denoted by $u \triangleq v$ (i. e., $(u,v) \in \triangleq$), holds if $(u \sqsubseteq v)$ and $(v \sqsubseteq u)$. We introduce the following algebra for concepts, that is conservative extension of Concept language used in DL, and able to support the intensional semantics for the FOL.

Definition 75. Algebra for concepts is a structure

$$\mathcal{A}m_{int} = \langle (\mathcal{D}, \sqsubseteq, u_f, u_t), Id, \neg, \{\sqcap_S, \sqcup_S, \Rightarrow_S\}_{S \in \mathcal{P}(\mathbb{N}^2)}, \leftrightarrow, \{\exists_i, \forall_i, \leq_i, \geq_i, pred_i\}_{i \in \mathbb{N}}, \{\exists(\$i, a), k(\$i, a)\}_{i \leq k \in \mathbb{N} \& f \neq a \in X} \rangle,$$

with unary negation, exists, for all and cardinality restriction operations $\neg, \exists_i, \forall_i, \leq_i, \geq_i$: $D_I \to D_I$, binary operation for the intersection, union and implication of concepts $\sqcap_S, \sqcup_S, \Rightarrow_S$: $D_I \times D_I \to D_I$, binary operation for the equivalence of concepts $\leftrightarrow$: $D_I \times D_I \to D_1$, and $pred_i : \mathcal{D}^{i-1} \times X \times D_i \to D_1$; while $\exists(\$i, a) : D_I \to D_2$, $k(\$i, a) : D_2 \to D_{k+1}$ are particular generalized DL operations.

The semantics of these intensional algebraic operations for any given extensionalization function $h : D_I \to \mathfrak{Rm}$ is given as follows:

1. $h(\neg u) = \oslash(h(u))$.
2. For any pair, $(\odot, \circ) \in \{(\sqcap_S, \otimes_S), (\sqcup_S, \oplus_S), (\Rightarrow_S, \ominus_S)\}$, $h(u \odot v) = h(u) \circ h(v)$.

3. $h(u \leftrightarrow v) = \circledast(h(u), h(v)) = \otimes(\mathrm{Inc}(h(u), h(v)), \mathrm{Inc}(h(v), h(u)))$.
4. $h(\exists_i u) = \boxplus_i(h(u)), h(\forall_i u) = \boxtimes_i(h(u))$.
5. $h(\leq_i u) = \preccurlyeq_i (h(u)), h(\geq_i u) = \succcurlyeq_i (h(u))$.
6. $h(\mathrm{pred}_k(v_1, \ldots, v_k, u)) = \mathrm{Inc}(\{(v_1, \ldots, v_k)\}, \mathrm{Com}(h(u)))$, where $u \in D_k$, i. e., the predication that the tuple $(v_1, \ldots, v_k)$ is an element of the extension of the k-ary concept u.
7. $h(\exists(\$i, a)u) = \rhd_{i,a} (h(u)), h(k(\$i, a)u) = \lhd^k_{i,a} (h(u))$.

Notice that if for all h, $h(u \leftrightarrow v) = \{t\}$ then $u \equiv v$.

Example 34 (Embedding of DL into the concept algebra $\mathcal{A}\mathfrak{m}_{\mathrm{int}}$). It is easy to verify that the algebraic operators $\sqcap_{(1,1)}$ and $\neg$ are a generalization of the analog operators in (algebraic) description logic used for composition of unary concepts. The "predication" operation pred_i can be used to define the DL-assertions in this concept algebra, e. g., the *satisfied* DL-assertion $r(u_1, u_2)$ (i. e., when $(u_1, u_2) \in r^{\mathcal{I}_e}$) here will be defined by the algebraic expression $\mathrm{pred}_3(u_1, u_2, t, r) \in D_1$ with $r \in D_3$, such that $h(\mathrm{pred}_3(u_1, u_2, t, r)) = \{t\}$, i. e., if the tuple (u_1, u_2, t) is an element of relation $h(r)$. Indeed, it is possible to make embedding also for other expressions of description logic, which use atomic rules also.

For example, the value restriction $(\forall r.u)$ with $r \in D_3, u \in \mathcal{D}$ here is expressed by the algebraic concept expression $\forall_2(r \Rightarrow_{(2,1)} u) \in D_2$, while the full DL existential quantification $(\exists r.u)$ is expressed by the algebraic concept expression $\exists_2(r \sqcap_{(2,1)} u) \in D_2$. In the case of 2-valued DL, we have that each m-relation $R \in \mathfrak{Rm}$ with $k = \mathrm{ar}(R) - 1$ is an element in $\mathcal{P}(\mathcal{D}^k) \times \{t\}$, thus for $h(r) \in \mathcal{P}(\mathcal{D}^2) \times \{t\}, h(u) \in \mathcal{P}(\mathcal{D}^1) \times \{t\}$, we obtain

$$\begin{aligned} h(\exists_2(r \sqcap_{(2,1)} u)) &= \boxplus_2(h(r) \otimes_{(2,1)} h(u)) \\ &= \boxplus_2(\{(v_1, v_2, t) \mid (v_1, v_2, t, t) \in h(r) \bowtie_{(2,1)} h(u)\}) \\ &= \boxplus_2(\{(v_1, v_2, t) \mid (v_1, v_2, t) \in h(r) \text{ and } (v_2, t) \in h(u)\}) \\ &= \{(v_1, t) \mid (v_1, v_2) \in \pi_{-3}(h(r)) \text{ and } v_2 \in \pi_{-2}(h(u))\} \\ &= \{(v_1, t) \mid v_1 \in (\exists \pi_{-3} r.\pi_{-2} u)^{\mathcal{I}_e}\}. \end{aligned}$$

That is, $\pi_{-2} h(\exists_2(r \sqcap_{(2,1)} u)) = (\exists \pi_{-3} r.\pi_{-2} u)^{\mathcal{I}_e}$, by considering that the relations in DL are m-relations without the last column, so that the concepts r, u in $\mathcal{A}_{\mathrm{int}}$ correspond to the concepts $\pi_{-3} r, \pi_{-2} u$ in DL relatively, and each h defines the correspondent DL interpretation $\mathcal{I}_e$. The expressions $\leq_n r$, $\geq_n r$ for $r \in D_I$ are the DL cardinality restrictions.

It is easy to verify that for any $u \in D_k$ where $k \geq 2$, we have that

$$h(u) = \bigcup_{f \neq a \in \mathcal{B}} h(\sqcap_S\{(k(\$i, a)(\exists(\$i, a)u)) \mid 1 \leq i \leq k\}),$$

where $S = \{(1, 1,), \ldots, (k-1, k-1)\}$ and $\sqcap_S\{u_1, \ldots u_k\}$ denotes the expression $u_1 \sqcap_S (u_2 \sqcap_S (\ldots \sqcap_S u_k) \ldots)$.

As we have seen previously, in DL there is no explicit use of the truth and falsehood as in classic 2-valued logics, but instead they are using the *satisfaction* as means for the definition of semantics for concepts and assertions. But, as we noted, the consequence of Open World Assumption (OWA) is that, in contrast with standard databases, is some relationship is not known to hold, it is not assumed to be false. One consequence of this is that any question about the membership of an individual in a concept, or its relationship to another individual, has *three* possible answers: "yes," "no" or "unknown."

It is a sign that from the truth-functional way of point, the DL has to be a kind of 3-valued logic, as for example, Kleene's 3-valued logic.

Remark. This point which was not formally investigated is the one of the important reasons to consider a possible embedding of DL into the many-valued algebra of concepts $\mathcal{A}_{\text{int}}$, which is target object in the intensional interpretation of the predicate many-valued intensional logic with abstraction $\mathcal{L}_{\text{in}}$, defined in Definition 76.

The relationships between the *identity* of u and v (i. e., when $h(\text{pred}_3(u, v, t, \text{Id})) = \{t\}$) and (strong) *equivalence* $u \equiv v$ is the standard relationship: if u is identical to v, then $u \equiv v$ but not vice versa: let us consider two different concepts $u, v \in D_2$ for "has been sold" and "has been bought," respectively, we have that u is not identical to v (i. e., $h(\text{pred}_3(u, v, t, \text{Id})) = \emptyset$), while $u \equiv v$ from the fact that for all h, $h(u) = h(v)$.

Remark. By these operators, it is possible also to make metasentences about sentences, i. e., if a is a algebraic value for the sentence $u \in D_1$ (i. e., if $h(u) = \{a\}$) then the metalogic sentence "it is true that u has an algebraic truth value a" corresponds to the fact $h(\text{pred}_1(a, u)) = \{t\}$. So, it holds that for the *self-reference truth-concept* $u_T \in D_2$, $h(\text{pred}_2(u, a, u_T)) = h(\text{pred}_1(a, u))$. □

The following important homomorphism between intensional and extensional algebras, provided by Definition 75 and Definition 74, there exists the following.

Corollary 19. *The semantics of the algebra for concepts in Definition 75 extends an extensionalization function h given by (5.22) into the homomorphism from intensional into the m-extensional algebra (in Definition 74):*

$$h : \mathcal{A}\mathrm{m}_{\text{int}} \to \mathcal{A}_{\mathfrak{R}\mathrm{m}} \tag{5.25}$$

We denote by $\mathcal{E}$ the set of all homomorphisms between these two algebras, represented by the following set-mapping:

$$\mathcal{A}\mathrm{m}_{\text{int}} \Longrightarrow_{h \in \mathcal{E}} \mathcal{A}_{\mathfrak{R}\mathrm{m}} \tag{5.26}$$

Proof. Directly from Definition 75, it preserves the ordering, i. e., if $u \sqsubseteq v$ then $h(u) \preceq h(v)$, with $h(u_f) = \emptyset, h(u_t) = \{t\}$ for bottom/top elements, and $h(\text{Id}) = R_=$.

For algebraic operations, we have that $h(\bar{\neg}) = \oslash$, $h(\sqcap_S) = \otimes_S, h(\sqcup_S) = \oplus_S, h(\Rightarrow_S) = \ominus_S$, $h(\leftrightarrow) = \circledast$, $h(\exists_i) = \boxplus_i, h(\forall_i) = \boxtimes_i$, $h(\leq_i) = \preccurlyeq_i, h(\geq_i) = \succcurlyeq_i$, $h(\text{pred}_i(v_1, \ldots, v_i, \_)) = \text{Inc}(\{(v_1, \ldots, v_i)\}, \text{Com}(\_))$, $h(\exists(\$i, a)) = \rhd_{i,a}$, $h(k(\$i, a)) = \lhd^k_{i,a}$. □

5.2.2 Syntax and interpretation of many-valued intensional FOL with abstraction operator

The syntax of the many-valued intensional first-order logic extends the syntax of the standard two-valued First-order Logic (FOL) with identity, introduced in Section 1.1.1, enriched by abstraction operator $< \_ >$ provided in Section 1.3.1, and hence with extended set of terms obtained by the abstraction of logic formulae. However, different from previous section where is presented an example the embedding of a many-valued logic (in our case DL), here we will consider the embedding of *any kind* of many-valued predicate logic $\mathcal{L}_{\text{mv}}$ (with examples given in the next chapter).

Definition 76 (Syntax of many-valued intensional FOL $\mathcal{L}_{\text{in}}$). We define the syntax of $\mathcal{L}_{\text{in}}$, obtained by embedding of a many-valued predicate logic $\mathcal{L}_{\text{mv}}$ over a bounded complete lattice of truth-values $(X, \leq)$, by:

- Variables $x, y, z, \ldots$ in $\mathcal{V}$;
- Language constants $c, d, \ldots$ are considered as nullary functional letters (all non-nullary functional letters are represented as the predicate letters for graphs of these functions);
- Predicate letters in P, denoted by $p_1^{k_1}, p_2^{k_2}, \ldots$ with a given arity $k_i \geq 1$, $i = 1, 2, \ldots$ Nullary predicate letters are considered as propositional letters, as for example, the built-in predicate letters $\{p_a \mid a \in X\}$;
- The many-valued logic connectives: a negation $\neg$, logic conjunction $\wedge$, disjunction $\vee$, implication $\Rightarrow$ and equivalence $\equiv$, with additional set Σ of another specific connectives of $\mathcal{L}_{\text{mv}}$, and many-valued quantifiers $\exists_i, \forall_i$; By $\mathcal{A}_X$, we denote the extension of the "minimal" many-valued algebra $\mathcal{A}_{\text{mv}}$ in Definition 70 for the connectives in Σ. We consider also that the extensional algebra $\mathcal{A}_{\mathfrak{Rm}}$ in Definition 74 and intensional algebra $\mathcal{A}m_{\text{int}}$ in Definition 75 are extended by new operators in Σ, by preserving the homomorphisms of Corollary 19.
- Abstraction operator $< \_ >$, and punctuation symbols (comma, parenthesis).

With the following simultaneous inductive definition of *terms* and *formulae*:

1. All variables and constants (0-ary functional letters in P) are terms. We denote by p_a a logic constant (built-in 0-ary predicate symbol) for each truth value $a \in X$, so that a set of constants is a not empty set.
2. If $t_1, \ldots, t_k$ are terms, then $p_i^k(t_1, \ldots, t_k)$ is a formula ($p_i^k \in P$ is a k-ary predicate letter).

3. In what follows, any open-formula $\phi(\mathbf{x})$ with nonempty tuple of free variables $\mathbf{x} = (x_1, \ldots, x_m)$, will be called a m-ary *virtual predicate*, denoted also by $\phi(x_1, \ldots, x_m)$ and provided in Definition 8 in Section 1.2.
   If ϕ and ψ are formulae, then $\neg\phi$, $(\forall_k x)\phi$, $(\exists_k x)\phi$ and, for each connective $\odot$, if binary $\phi \odot \psi$ or if unary $\odot\phi$, are the formulae. In a formula $(\exists_k)\phi(\mathbf{x})$ (or $(\forall_k)\phi(\mathbf{x})$), the virtual predicate $\phi(\mathbf{x})$ is called "action field" for the quantifier $(\exists_k)$ (or $(\forall_k)$) of the k-th free variable in the tuple $\mathbf{x}$. A variable y in a formula ϕ is called bounded variable iff it is the variable quantified by $(\exists_k)$ (or $(\forall_k)$). A variable x is free in $\psi(\mathbf{x})$ if it is not bounded. A *sentence* is a closed-formula having no free variables.
4. If $\phi(\mathbf{x})$ is a formula and, from Definition 23 in Section 2.1.1, $\alpha \subseteq \overline{\mathbf{x}}$ is a possibly empty subset of *hidden* (compressed) variables, then $<\phi(\mathbf{x})>^{\beta}_{\alpha}$ is an abstracted term, as provided in Definition 17 in Section 1.3.1, where β is remained subset of free visible variables in ϕ. So, the subtuples of hidden and visible variables (preserving the ordering of the tuple $\mathbf{x}$ are $\pi_{-\beta}\mathbf{x}$ and $\pi_{-\alpha}\mathbf{x}$, respectively). If α or β is an empty sequence, than it can be omitted (e. g., if ϕ is closed formula, then this term is denoted by $<\phi>$).

An occurrence of a variable x_i in a term $<\phi(\mathbf{x})>^{\beta}_{\alpha}$ is *bound* if $x_i \in \alpha$, free if $x_i \in \beta$, so that the variables in α are not subjects of assignment $g \in \mathcal{D}^{\mathcal{V}}$ and cannot be quantified by existential and universal FOL quantifiers.

In particular, we introduce the following distinguished predicates:

(a) The binary predicate letter $p_1^2 \in P$ is singled out as a distinguished logical predicate and formulae of the form $p_1^2(t_1, t_2)$ are to be rewritten in the form $t_1 = t_2$. It is a 2-valued built-in predicate for the identity.
(b) The binary predicate letter $p_2^2 \in P$ is singled out as a distinguished logical predicate and formulae of the form $p_2^2(t_1, t_2)$ are to be rewritten in the form $t_1 =_{\text{in}} t_2$. It is a 2-valued built-in predicate for the weak-intensional-equivalence.
(c) The unary predicate letter $p_1^1 \in P$ is singled out as distinguished truth-predicate for sentences and formulae of the form $p_1^1(t_1)$ are to be rewritten in the form $T(t_1)$.

Notice that "built-in" is used for predicate letters that have fixed invariant interpretation, and consequently fixed invariant extension: each possible interpretation of $\mathcal{L}_{\text{in}}$ has to satisfy this constraint for built-in predicates, so that different interpretations can be used only for the remaining set of predicate letters in P. The T is the many-valued version of the truth-predicate in the standard 2-valued logic where a formula $T(<\phi>)$ is true iff the (closed) sentence ϕ is true.

We can introduce the sorts in order to be able to assign each variable x_i to a sort $S_i \subseteq \mathcal{D}$. An assignment $g : \mathcal{V} \to \mathcal{D}$ for variables in $\mathcal{V}$ is applied only to free variables in terms and formulae. If we use sorts for variables, then for each sorted variable $x_i \in \mathcal{V}$ an assignment g must satisfy the auxiliary condition $g(x_i) \in S_i$. We denote by t_1/g (or ϕ/g) the ground term (or formula), without free variables, obtained by assignment g from a term t_1 (or a formula ϕ). We denote by $\mathcal{L}$ and $\mathcal{T}$ the set of all formulae and terms in his logic $\mathcal{L}_{in}$, respectively. The assignment $g : \mathcal{V} \to \mathcal{D}$ can be extended to all terms $g^* : \mathcal{T} \to \mathcal{D}$ as specified in Definition 17 of Section 1.3.1.

A Herbrand base of the logic $\mathcal{L}_{in}$ is defined by $H = \{p_i^k(g(x_1), \ldots, g(x_k)) \mid p_i^k \in P$ and $g \in \mathcal{D}^{\mathcal{V}}\} \subset \mathcal{L}$.

The main difference with standard FOL syntax is that here we can use abstracted terms obtained from logic formulae, as provided in Section 1.3.1: for example, "x believes that A" is given by formula $p_i^2(x, \lessdot\phi\gtrdot)$ (where p_i^2 is binary "believe" predicate).

Let $\phi(\mathbf{x})$ be any well-formed virtual predicate in $\mathcal{L}_{in}$, then $\lessdot\phi(\mathbf{x})\gtrdot_\alpha^\beta/g$ with the set of hidden variables $\alpha = (x_1, \ldots, x_m)$, $m \geq 1$, is the ground term (the assignment g is applied only to free visible variables in $\beta = \overline{\mathbf{x}} - \alpha$ as explained in Section 1.3.1) whose semantics correlate is an intensional entity (concept) of degree m. If $m = 0$, the intensional correlate of this singular ground term is the proposition (sentence) "that ϕ"; if $m = 1$, the intensional correlate is the property of "being something x_1 such that ϕ"; if $m > 1$, then the intensional correlate is the concept "the relation among $x_1, \ldots, x_m$ such that ϕ".

Certain complex nominative expressions (namely, gerundive and infinitive phrases) are best represented as singular terms of the sort provided by our generalized bracket notation $\lessdot\phi(\mathbf{x})\gtrdot_{x_1,\ldots,x_m}^\beta$, where $m \geq 1$. This MV-intensional logic $\mathcal{L}_{in}$ differs from two-valued intensional FOL in Chapter 1 in heaving these singular terms $\lessdot\phi(\mathbf{x})\gtrdot_{x_1,\ldots,x_m}^\beta$ where the virtual predicate $\phi(\mathbf{x})$ is *many-valued*. Such abstracted terms obtained not from the sentences but from the virtual predicates $\phi(\mathbf{x})$ can be embedded also into a particular unary predicate $A(\lessdot\phi(\mathbf{x})\gtrdot_{x_1,\ldots,x_m}^\beta)$, as explained in Section 1.3.1 with its "ground" (for a given assignment $g \in \mathcal{D}^{\mathcal{V}}$) intensional interpretation (1.31), which for a given extensionalization function h can have a many-valued extension of the formula $\phi[\beta/g(\beta)]$. More about intensional abstract operators is provided in Section 1.3.1.

As in the case of two-valued intensional FOL, in this many-valued case we will use the *virtual predicates* provided by Definition 8 in Section 1.2, useful for intensional mapping into concepts in $\mathcal{D}_I$, i. e., into intensional algebra $\mathcal{A}m_{int}$ provided by Definition 75.

Now we can consider the intensional semantics of $\mathcal{L}_{in}$, based on the translation of this logic into the intensional algebra of concepts $\mathcal{A}m_{int}$, given by Definition 75. It is an algebraic two-step semantics based on the two consecutive interpretations: intensional interpretation of logic formulae into intensional entities (concepts) and extensional semantics of concepts given by Corollary 19 in previous section.

The *intensional interpretation* I maps each nullary predicate symbol into D_1, and for each logic constant p_a, $a \in X$, we have that $I(p_a) = u_a \in D_1$. The language constants (nullary functional symbols in P) are mapped in concepts in $\mathcal{D}$. Notice that for any non-meaningful language constant (as "Unicorn" for example) we have that $I(c) = ® \in D_0$.

Consequently, each atom $p_i^k(t_1, \ldots, t_k)$, $p_i^k \in P$, is mapped into the concept $u \in D_{m+1}$, where m is a number of the free variables of the virtual predicate obtained from this atom. Consequently, each ground atom $p_i^k(t_1, \ldots, t_k)$ is mapped into D_1, and if there is any t_i, $1 \le i \le k$, such that $I(t_i) = ®$, then $I(p_i^k(t_1,\dots,t_k)) = u_\kappa$, where $\kappa \in X$ such that $\sim \kappa = \kappa$ is the "unknown" logic value. In this way, we guarantee that unmeaningful sentences as blu(Unicorn) will always have the "unknown" logic value. This intensional interpretation can be given also to all contradictory formulae that cannot be nor true nor false, as the Liars paradoxes.

We have that $I(p_1^2(x,y)) = I(x = y) = \mathrm{Id} \in D_3$, while $I(p_1^2(x,y)/g) = I((x = y)/g) = \mathrm{pred}_3(g(x),g(y),t,\mathrm{Id}) \in D_1$. Analogously, we have that $I(p_2^2(x,y)) = I(x =_{\mathrm{in}} y) = \mathrm{Eq} \in D_3$, while $I(p_2^2(x,y)/g) = I((x =_{\mathrm{in}} y)/g) = \mathrm{pred}_3(g(x),g(y),t,\mathrm{Eq}) \in D_1$. The atom $T(x)$ is mapped into self-reference concept, i. e., $I(T(x)) = I(p_1^1(x)) = u_T \in D_2$ (notice that from footnotes in Definition 78 we have that for any assignment g, the ground atom $T(t_i)/g$ is equivalent to the ground formula ϕ/g if t_i in this predicate T represents the term $<\phi/g>$; to built-in predicate letter p_f otherwise).

For example, given two virtual predicates with the same set of free variables, $\phi(x_1,\dots,x_k)$ and $\psi(y_1,\dots,y_k)$, with $\psi(y_1,\dots,y_k)_\lambda$ virtual predicate obtained by a permutation λ with the same sequence of variables as in virtual predicate $\phi(x_1,\dots,x_k)$, then we are able to establish the weak-intensional equivalence (1.35) between them, $<\phi(x_1,\dots,x_k)>_\alpha \approx <\psi(x_1,\dots,x_k)_\lambda>_\alpha$, where $\alpha = (x_1,\dots,x_k)$. Consequently, from the fact that intensionally equivalent concepts are rigid concepts (with extension equal in each possible world $w \in \mathcal{W}$, introduced in next Definition 79 and used in the Kripke semantics for many-valued intensional FOL in Section 5.2.3, corresponding to the extensionalization function $h = \mathrm{is}_{\mathrm{in}}(w)$ in Theorem 11) we can use the definition of the intensional equivalence given by modal formula in (1.35), and extend the Kripke semantics, provided in next Definitions 81 and 82 in Section 5.2.3, by this new existential modal operator in Proposition 33 in Section 6.3.

This kind of intensional equivalence has been used in the 2-valued intensional FOL for P2P intensional view-based data-integration in a number of papers [42, 54, 55, 58, 105, 219], where RDB views can be considered as particular virtual predicates. This equivalence, both with embedding of description logic in $\mathcal{L}_{\mathrm{in}}$ (explained previously), is a main point for pragmatic considerations about many-valued intensional FOL in order to be used as more advanced logic layer in semantic web.

Corollary 20. *The intensional interpretation defines the homomorphism between free syntax FOL language algebra* $\mathcal{A}m_{\mathrm{FOL}} = (\mathcal{L}, \wedge, \vee, \neg, \Rightarrow, \equiv, \{\exists_i, \forall_i\}_{i\in\mathbb{N}})$, *representing the many-valued intensional FOL* $\mathcal{L}_{\mathrm{in}}$ *in Definition 76, into the intensional algebra* $\mathcal{A}m_{\mathrm{int}}$,

$$I : \mathcal{A}m_{\mathrm{FOL}} \to \mathcal{A}m_{\mathrm{int}} \tag{5.27}$$

Proof. We define the following extension of the intensional interpretation from atoms to all formulae $I : \mathcal{L} \to \mathcal{D}$ (notice that in this recursive definition we are using virtual predicates obtained from open formulae in $\mathcal{L}$):

1. The logic formula $\phi(x_i,x_j,x_k,x_l,x_m) \wedge \psi(x_l,y_i,x_j,y_j)$ will be intensionally interpreted by the concept $u_1 \in D_8$, obtained by the algebraic expression $u \sqcap_S v$ where $u =$

$I(\phi(x_i, x_j, x_k, x_l, x_m)) \in D_6, v = I(\psi(x_l, y_i, x_j, y_j)) \in D_5$ are the concepts of the virtual predicates ϕ, ψ, relatively, and $S = \{(4,1),(2,3)\}$. Consequently, we have that for any two formulae $\phi, \psi \in \mathcal{L}$ and a particular operator uniquely determined by tuples of free variables in these two formulae, $I(\phi \wedge \psi) = I(\phi) \sqcap_S I(\psi)$, and, analogously,

$$I(\phi \vee \psi) = I(\phi) \sqcup_S I(\psi), \quad I(\phi \Rightarrow \psi) = I(\phi) \Rightarrow_S I(\psi), \quad I(\phi \Leftrightarrow \psi) = I(\phi) \leftrightarrow I(\psi).$$

2. The logic formula $\neg\phi(x_i, x_j, x_k, x_l, x_m)$ will be intensionally interpreted by the concept $u_1 \in D_6$, obtained by the algebraic expression $\bar{\neg} u$ where $u = I(\phi(x_i, x_j, x_k, x_l, x_m)) \in D_6$ is the concept of the virtual predicate ϕ. Consequently, we have that for any formula $\phi \in \mathcal{L}$, $I(\neg\phi) = \bar{\neg}(I(\phi))$.
3. The logic formula ψ equal to the formula $(\exists_i)\phi(\mathbf{x})$ where $\phi(\mathbf{x})$ is a virtual predicate with $\mathbf{x} = (x_1, \ldots, x_m)$, and $x_i \in (x_1, \ldots, x_m)$ is i-th variable in ϕ. Then we obtain the virtual predicate $\psi(x_1, \ldots, x_{i-1}, x_{i+1}, \ldots, x_m)$, so that $I(\psi) = I((\exists_i)\phi) = \exists_i u \in D_m$ where $u = I(\phi) \in D_{m+1}$. For example, the logic formula $(\exists_3)\phi(x_i, x_j, x_k, x_l, x_m)$ will be intensionally interpreted by the concept $u_1 \in D_5$, obtained by the algebraic expression $\exists_3 u$ where $u = I(\phi(x_i, x_j, x_k, x_l, x_m)) \in D_6$ is the concept of the virtual predicate ϕ. Thus, we have that for any formula $(\exists_n)\phi \in \mathcal{L}$, the operator $\exists_n$ is uniquely determined by the n-th position of the existentially quantified variable in the tuple of free variables in the virtual predicate ϕ,

$$I((\exists_n)\phi) = \exists_n(I(\phi)), \quad \text{and, analogously,} \quad I((\forall_n)\phi) = \forall_n(I(\phi)). \qquad \square$$

For the set of additional many-valued connectives in Σ for any concrete many-valued logic $\mathcal{L}_{\mathrm{mv}}$, we consider that this homomorphism is valid also for them. Now we are able to define formally the intensional semantics of this logic.

Definition 77 (Two-step algebraic intensional semantics). The intensional semantics of the logic $\mathcal{L}_{\mathrm{in}}$ with the set of formulae $\mathcal{L}$ can be represented by the mapping

$$\mathcal{L} \longrightarrow_I \mathcal{D} \Longrightarrow_{h \in \mathcal{E}_{\mathrm{in}} \subseteq \mathcal{E}} \mathfrak{Rm} \tag{5.28}$$

where $\longrightarrow_I$ is a *fixed intensional* interpretation (homomorphism in Corollary 20) $I : \mathcal{L} \to \mathcal{D}$ and $\Longrightarrow_{h \in \mathcal{E}_{\mathrm{in}}}$ is *the subset* of all homomorphisms $h \in \mathcal{E}$ in Corollary 19, such that respect all built-in concepts in Definition 72, and for any virtual predicate $\phi(x_1, \ldots, x_n) \in \mathcal{L}$, the following many-valued generalization of Tarski's FOL constraint is valid:

$$h(I(\phi(x_1, \ldots, x_n))) =_{\mathrm{def}} \{(g(x_1), \ldots, g(x_n), a) \mid g \in \mathcal{D}^{\mathcal{V}}, h(I(\phi(x_1, \ldots, x_n)/g)) = \{a\}, a \neq f\} \tag{5.29}$$

with $h(I(\phi(x_1, \ldots, x_n)/g)) = \emptyset$ iff $(g(x_1), \ldots, g(x_n)) \notin \pi_{-n-1}(h(I(\phi(x_1, \ldots, x_n))))$.

This set $\mathcal{E}_{in}$ of homomorphisms $h : \mathcal{A}m_{int} \to \mathcal{A}_{\mathfrak{R}m}$ will be called as possible worlds as well.

Notice that for any $h \in \mathcal{E}_{in}$ and a permutation λ, $\text{Inc}(h(\phi(x_1,\ldots,x_m)_\lambda), h(\phi(x_1,\ldots,x_m))) = \text{Inc}(h(\phi(x_1,\ldots,x_m)), h(\phi(x_1,\ldots,x_m)_\lambda)) = \{t\}$. We are able to define the many-valued algebraic semantics of $\mathcal{L}_{in}$, based on the standard extension of Herbrand interpretations to all sentences $\mathcal{L}_0$ of $\mathcal{L}_{in}$.

Definition 78 (Semantics of many-valued intensional FOL). The algebraic semantics of the many valued intensional FOL $\mathcal{L}_{in}$ given in Definition 76 and its syntax-algebra $\mathcal{A}m_{FOL}$ in Corollary 20, can be obtained by the unique extension of a given Herbrand interpretation $v : H \to X$, into the valuation $v^* : \mathcal{L}_0 \to X$ (from Definition 62, Section 5.1.1), where $\mathcal{L}_0 \subset \mathcal{L}$ is the strict subset of all sentences (formulae without free variables), inductively as follows:

for any formula $\phi, \psi \in \mathcal{L}$ and a given assignment $g : \mathcal{V} \to \mathcal{D}$, we have that (here $\bigwedge$ and $\bigvee$ are the meet and joint operators of the lattice X, respectively)

1. $v^*(\neg\phi/g) = \sim v^*(\phi/g)$,
2. $v^*(\phi/g \odot \psi/g) = v^*(\phi/g)\widetilde{\odot}v^*(\psi/g)$, for each logic connective $\odot \in \{\wedge, \vee, \Rightarrow, \equiv\}$ into $\mathcal{A}_{mv}$-operators $\widetilde{\odot} \in \{\widetilde{\wedge}, \widetilde{\vee}, \widetilde{\Rightarrow}, \Leftrightarrow\}$,
3. $v^*(((\exists_i)\phi)/g) = v^*(\phi/g)$ if i-th variable x is not a free in ϕ; $= \bigvee\{v^*(\phi/g_1) \mid g_1 \in \mathcal{D}^{\mathcal{V}}$ such that for all $y \in \mathcal{V}\backslash\{x\}, g_1(y) = g(y)\}$ otherwise,
4. $v^*(((\forall_i)\phi)/g) = v^*(\phi/g)$ if i-th variable x is not a free in ϕ; $= \bigwedge\{v^*(\phi/g_1) \mid g_1 \in \mathcal{D}^{\mathcal{V}}$ such that for all $y \in \mathcal{V}\backslash\{x\}, g_1(y) = g(y)\}$ otherwise.

We denote by $\mathcal{I}_{MV} \subseteq X^{\mathcal{L}_0}$ the set of all many-valued valuations of $\mathcal{L}_{in}$ that have fixed (invariant) interpretation for each built-in predicate.[7]

Clearly, the many-valued quantifiers defined in definition above does not satisfy the standard FOL property that $\forall = \sim \exists \sim$, but in the case of the 2-valued logic when $X = \mathbf{2}$, then this requirement is satisfied by Definition 78 and points 3 and 4 corresponds to the standard semantics of quantifiers of the FOL.

Notice that this many-valued extended interpretation $v^* : \mathcal{L}_0 \to X$ defined above *is not a homomorphism*, because of the point 3 (and 4 as well), where the truth of the closed formula $(\forall x_i)\phi(x_i)$ cannot be obtained from the logic value of $\phi(x_i)$ from the fact that to any formula with free variables we cannot associate any logic value. Because of that, we define a new version of many-valued interpretation, denominated "MV-interpretation."

---

7 As, for example, the identity predicate $p_1^2 \in P$ or nullary predicate letters $\{p_a \mid a \in X\}$ for which it must be satisfied that for any $v^* \in \mathcal{I}_{MV}, v^*(p_a) = a$, $v^*(p_1^2(u_1,u_2)) = t$ iff $(u_1,u_2,t) \in R_=$, and $v^*(p_2^2(u_1,u_2)) = t$ iff $(u_1,u_2,t) \in R_{=_{in}}$, and for any assignment g, $v^*(p_1^1(t_i)) = v^*(T(t_i)) =_{def} v^*(\phi/g)$ if term $t_i = <\phi/g>$; f otherwise. The difference between $\mathcal{I}_{MV}$ and the total set of Herbrand interpretations X^H is caused by the presence of the built-in predicates.

Definition 79 (MV-interpretations). We define, for a valuation $v^* : \mathcal{L}_0 \to X$ of the sentences in $\mathcal{L}_0 \subset \mathcal{L}$ of the many-valued intensional FOL $\mathcal{L}_{in}$ in Definition 76, the MV-interpretation $I^*_{mv} : \mathcal{L}_0 \to \mathfrak{Rm}$, such that for any sentence $\phi/g \in \mathcal{L}_0$,

$$I^*_{mv}(\phi/g) = \begin{cases} \{v^*(\phi/g)\} \in \widetilde{X} \subset \mathfrak{Rm}, & \text{if } v^*(\phi/g) \neq f \\ \emptyset, & \text{otherwise} \end{cases} \tag{5.30}$$

and we define also the unique extension of I^*_{mv} to all open formulae $\mathcal{L}$ in $\mathcal{L}_{in}$ as well, such that for any open formula (virtual predicate) $\phi(x_1, \ldots, x_k) \in \mathcal{L}$,

$$I^*_{mv}(\phi(x_1, \ldots, x_k)) = \{(g(x_1), \ldots, g(x_k), a) \mid g \in \mathcal{D}^{\mathcal{V}} \text{ and } a = v^*(\phi/g) \neq f\} \in \mathfrak{Rm} \tag{5.31}$$

We denote by $\mathcal{W}$ the set of all MV-interpretations derived from the set of many-valued interpretations $v^* \in \mathcal{I}_{MV}$ specified in Definition 78, with bijection $\mathrm{is}_{MV} : \mathcal{I}_{MV} \simeq \mathcal{W}$ such that for any $v^* \in \mathcal{I}_{MV}$ we have that $I^*_{mv} = \mathrm{is}_{MV}(v^*) : \mathcal{L} \to \mathfrak{Rm}$.

Now we can demonstrate that the many-valued semantics given by Definition 78 of the logic $\mathcal{L}_{in}$ is corresponds to the two-step concept-algebra semantics given by Definition 77.

Theorem 11 (Many-valuedness and concept-algebra semantics). *For any fixed intensional interpretation I of $\mathcal{L}_{in}$ into algebra of concepts $\mathcal{A}\mathfrak{m}_{int}$, there is a bijection $\mathrm{is}_{in} : \mathcal{W} \simeq \mathcal{E}_{in}$, so that for any many-valued interpretation $v^* \in \mathcal{I}_{MV}$, i. e., MV-interpretation $I^*_{mv} = \mathrm{is}_{MV}(v^*) \in \mathcal{W}$ (in Definition 79) the correspondent equivalent extensionalization functions is $h = \mathrm{is}_{in}(I^*_{mv}) \in \mathcal{E}_{in}$ (by T-constraint (5.29) and Definition 72), and vice versa, given any extensionalization homomorphism $h : \mathcal{A}\mathfrak{m}_{int} \to \mathcal{A}_{\mathfrak{Rm}}$ the correspondent equivalent MV-interpretation of $\mathcal{L}_{in}$ is $I^*_{mv} = \mathrm{is}^{-1}_{in}(h) \in \mathcal{W}$, so that the following truth-diagram:*

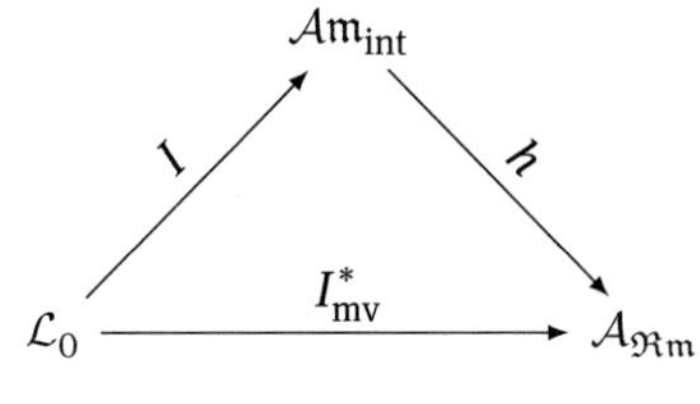

commutes, as a consequence of the basic Herbrand base correspondence

$$I^*_{mv}(p^k_i(u_1, \ldots, u_k)) = h(I(p^k_i(u_1, \ldots, u_k))) \tag{5.32}$$

for each ground atom $p^k_i(u_1, \ldots, u_k)$ in Herbrand base $H \subset \mathcal{L}_0$.

The arrow $I^*_{mv} : \mathcal{L}_0 \to \widetilde{X} = \mathfrak{Rm}_1 \subset \mathfrak{Rm}$ is the "standard" many-valued semantics, while the arrow $h \circ I : \mathcal{L}_0 \to \mathcal{A}_{m\mathfrak{R}}$ corresponds to the two-step concept-algebra semantics.

Proof. Notice that only the arrow h in the diagram above is a homomorphism (5.25), while I is a nonhomomorphic restriction of the homomorphism $I : \mathcal{A}m_{FOL} \to \mathcal{A}m_{int}$ given by (5.27) in Corollary 20 to the subset $\mathcal{L}_0$ of closed formulae of the free syntax algebra $\mathcal{A}m_{FOL}$ of the $\mathcal{L}_{in}$. Thus, this diagram is not homomorphic. In what follows, we consider that the intensional interpretation is fixed one. We have to show that for any given extensionalization function h the MV-interpretation $I^*_{mv} = h \circ I$ is uniquely determined by the commutative diagram above, i. e., from the fact that for any $\phi \in \mathcal{L}$ and assignment $g \in \mathcal{D}^{\mathcal{V}}$ it holds that $v^*(\phi/g) = is^{-1}_{MV}(I^*_{mv})(\phi/g)$, i. e., $is^{-1}_{in}(is_{MV}(v^*))(\phi/g) = h(I(\phi/g))$.

First, from the correspondence (5.32), this diagram commutes for each ground atom in Herbrand base, and we need only to show that it is valid for any other composed sentence in $\mathcal{L}_0$. Notice that it is satisfied for the unary self-reference predicate p^1_1 and for the binary identity predicate p^2_1 as well. We will use the structural induction on number of logic operators of the sentences in $\mathcal{L}_0$. Suppose that it holds for every closed formula $\psi_1/g \in \mathcal{L}_0$ (with $R_1 = \mathrm{Com}(h(I(\psi/g))) = \{a_1\}$ and $a_1 = v^*(\psi_1/g)$) with $n-1$ connectives, and $\psi_2/g \in \mathcal{L}_0$ (with $R_2 = \mathrm{Com}(h(I(\psi/g))) = \{a_2\}$ and $a_2 = v^*(\psi_2/g)$ with less than n logic connectives, and let us demonstrate that it holds for any formula ϕ with n or more connectives. There are the following cases:

1. $\phi = \neg\psi_1$. Then $h(I(\neg\psi_1/g)) = h(\bar{\neg} I(\psi_1/g)) =$ (by Definition 75) $= \oslash h(I(\psi_1/g)) =$ (by Definition 74)

$$= \begin{cases} \{\sim a_1\}, & \text{if} \sim a_1 \neq f \\ \emptyset, & \text{otherwise,} \end{cases}$$

while $I^*_{mv}(\neg\psi_1/g) =$ (from (5.30))

$$= \begin{cases} \{\neg v^*(\psi_1/g)\} = \{\sim a_1\}, & \text{if} \sim a_1 \neq f \\ \emptyset, & \text{otherwise.} \end{cases}$$

2. $\phi = (\psi_1 \wedge \psi_2)$. Then, $h(I(\phi/g)) = h(I(\psi_1/g) \sqcap I(\psi_2/g)) =$ (by Definition 75) $= h(I(\psi_1/g)) \otimes h(I(\psi_2/g))) = R_1 \otimes R_2 =$ (by Def. 74)

$$= \begin{cases} \{a_1 \tilde{\wedge} a_2\}, & \text{if } a_1 \tilde{\wedge} a_2 \neq f \\ \emptyset, & \text{otherwise,} \end{cases}$$

while $I^*_{mv}(\psi_1/g \wedge \psi_2/g) =$ (from Definition 78 and (5.30))

$$= \begin{cases} \{v^*(\psi_1/g) \tilde{\wedge} v^*(\psi_2/g)\} = \{a_1 \tilde{\wedge} a_2\}, & \text{if } a_1 \wedge a_2 \neq f \\ \emptyset, & \text{otherwise} \end{cases}$$

Analogously, we obtain for cases when ϕ is $\psi_1 \vee \psi_2$ or $\psi_1 \Rightarrow \psi_2$, or $\psi_1 \equiv \psi_2$.

3. $\phi = (\exists x_1)\psi(x_1)$, with $h(I(\psi(x_1))) = I_{mv}(\psi(x_1))$, in accordance with (5.29) and (5.31), and $R = h(I(\psi(x_1)))$.

Then $h(I(\phi/g)) = h(I((\exists x_1)\psi(x_1))) = h(\exists_1 I(\psi(x_1))) =$ (by Definition 75)

$$= \boxplus_1(h(I(\psi(x_1)))) = \quad \text{(by Defintion 74)}$$

$$= \begin{cases} b = \bigvee\{a \mid (u,a) \in R\}, & \text{if } b \neq f \\ \emptyset, & \text{otherwise,} \end{cases}$$

while $I^*_{\mathrm{mv}}(\phi/g) = I^*_{\mathrm{mv}}((\exists x_1)\psi(x_1)) =$ (from Definition 78 and (5.30))

$$= \begin{cases} b = \bigvee\{a \mid (u,a) \in R\}, & \text{if } b \neq f \\ \emptyset, & \text{otherwise} \end{cases}$$

where $\bigvee$ is the join operator in lattice X. Analogously, we obtain for cases when $\phi = (\forall x_i)\psi(x_1,\ldots,x_i,\ldots,x_k)$. Thus, for any fixed intensional interpretation I of $\mathcal{L}_{\mathrm{in}}$, the diagram commutes and the bijection $\mathrm{is}_{\mathrm{in}}$ is well-defined. □

This truth diagram explains the equivalence of many-valued interpretations of the logic $\mathcal{L}_{\mathrm{in}}$, and the two-step semantics for concept algebras. But it is given only for the set of ground (without free variables) formulae, and its nucleus composed by ground atoms of the Herbrand base H: the truth of (closed) sentences with quantifiers is uniquely determined by the truth of atoms of this Herbrand base. Now we will extend this correspondence to open formulae in $\mathcal{L}$ as well. The following Intensional/extensional many-valued FOL semantics is a generalization of the Intensional/extensional semantics of the standard FOL, presented in Corollary 4, Section 1.3.

Corollary 21 (Intensional/extensional many-valued FOL semantics). *For a given fixed intensional interpretation I and any many-valued interpretation* $v^* : \mathcal{L}_0 \to X$ *of the* $\mathcal{L}_{\mathrm{in}}$*, with MV-interpretation* $I^*_{\mathrm{mv}} = \mathrm{is}_{\mathrm{MV}}(v^*)$*, the following diagram, as a homomorphic extension of the diagram in Theorem 11, commutes*

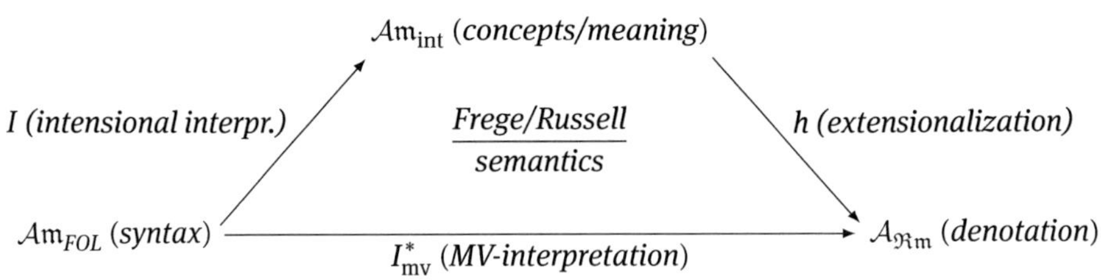

where $h = \mathrm{is}_{\mathrm{in}}(I^*_{\mathrm{mv}})$ *represents the bijective semantic equivalence given by Theorem 11 and the set of sentences* $\mathcal{L}_0 \subset \mathcal{L}$ *is substituted by the free syntax algebra* $\mathcal{A}\mathfrak{m}_{\mathrm{FOL}}$ *of the many-valued intensional FOL* $\mathcal{L}_{\mathrm{in}}$*, introduced in Corollary 20, with the carrier set of all formulae* $\mathcal{L}$*.*

Proof. The homomorphism of intensional mapping I is defined by Corollary 20. Let us show that also for a given many-valued valuation $v^* \in \mathcal{I}_{MV}$, which determines the

MV-interpretation $I^*_{mv} = \mathrm{is}_{MV}(I_{mv})$ from Definition 79 and, from Theorem 11, the extensionalization $h = \mathrm{is}_{in}(I^*_{mv})$, the diagram above commutes.

In fact, for any closed formula $\phi/g \in \mathcal{L}_0 \subset \mathcal{L}$, by definition of I^*_{mv} we have that $I^*_{mv}(\phi) =$ (from the commutative diagram in Theorem 11) $= (h \circ I)(\phi) = h(I(\phi))$, and the set of different "possible worlds"

$$\mathcal{W} = \{I^*_{mv} = \mathrm{is}_{MV}(v^*) \mid v^* \in \mathcal{I}_{MV} \subset X^H\} \simeq \mathcal{I}_{MV} \tag{5.33}$$

For any open formula (virtual predicate) $\phi(x_1,\ldots,x_k) \in \mathcal{L}$, from definition of I^*_{mv} we have that $I^*_{mv}(\phi(x_1,\ldots,x_k)) = \{(g(x_1),\ldots,g(x_k),a) \mid g \in \mathcal{D}^{\mathcal{V}}$ and $a = v^*(\phi/g) \neq f\}$ $=$ (from Theorem 11) $= \{(g(x_1),\ldots,g(x_k),a) \mid g \in \mathcal{D}^{\mathcal{V}}$ and $a = h(I(\phi/g)) \neq f\} =$ (from many-valued generalization of Tarski's constraint for the algebraic two-step semantics in Definition 77) $= h(I(\phi(x_1,\ldots,x_k)))$.

Thus, the diagram above commutes for every formula in $\mathcal{L}$, and we obtain that $I^*_{mv} = I \circ h$ is a *many-valued homomorphism* between the free syntax algebra of the logic $\mathcal{L}_{in}$ and the extensional algebra $\mathcal{A}_{\mathfrak{R}m}$ of m-extensions. □

Remark. Notice that for $X = \mathbf{2}$ we obtain a m-version of the 2-valued intensional FOL presented in Corollary 4, Section 1.3. The only difference is that in this more general many-valued representation each virtual predicate $\phi(x_1,\ldots,x_k)$ is ontologically encapsuled into $(k+1)$-arity virtual predicate by adding at the end of list of variables also the logic-value attribute, so that

$$\begin{aligned} &I^*_{mv}(\phi(x_1,\ldots,x_k)) = I^*_T(\phi(x_1,\ldots,x_k)) \times \{t\}, \quad \text{and} \\ &I^*_T(\phi(x_1,\ldots,x_k)) = \pi_{-(k+1)} I^*_{mv}(\phi(x_1,\ldots,x_k)) \end{aligned} \tag{5.34}$$

□

This homomorphic diagram formally express the fusion of Frege's and Russell's semantics [25, 51, 52] of meaning and denotation of the FOL language, and renders mathematically correct the definition of what we call an "intuitive notion of intensionality," in terms of which a language is intensional if denotation is distinguished from sense: that is, if both a denotation and sense is ascribed to its expressions. This notion is simply adopted from Frege's contribution (without its infinite sense-hierarchy, avoided by Russell's approach where there is only one meaning relation, one fundamental relation between words and things, here represented by one fixed intensional interpretation I), where the sense contains mode of presentation here described algebraically as an algebra of concepts (intensions) $\mathcal{A}m_{int}$, and where sense determines denotation for any given extensionalization function h (corresponding to a given many-valued interpretation v^*). More about the relationships between Frege's and Russell's theories of meaning may be found in the Chapter 7, "Extensionality and Meaning," in [12].

As noted by Gottlob Frege and Rudolf Carnap (he uses terms intension/extension in the place of Frege's terms sense/denotation [31]), the two logic formulae with the same denotation (i. e., the same m-extension for a given many-valued interpretation v^*) need not have the same sense (intension), thus such co-denotational expressions are not *substitutable* in general.

In fact, there is exactly *one* sense (meaning) of a given logic formula in $\mathcal{L}$, defined by the uniquely fixed intensional interpretation I, and *a set* of possible denotations (extensions) each determined by a given many-valued interpretation of the FOL as follows from Definition 77 and Theorem 11:

$$\mathcal{L} \longrightarrow_I \mathcal{D} \Longrightarrow_{h=is_{in}(I^*_{mv})\&I^*_{mv}\in\mathcal{W}} \mathfrak{Rm} \tag{5.35}$$

Often "intension" has been used exclusively in connection with possible worlds semantics, however, here we use (as many others; as Bealer for example) "intension" in a more wide sense, that is as an *algebraic expression* in the intensional algebra of meanings (concepts) $\mathcal{A}m_{int}$, which represents the structural composition of more complex concepts (meanings) from the given set of atomic meanings.

Consequently, not only the denotation (extension) is compositional, but also the meaning (intension) is compositional. So, the Montague's intension given by Definition 4, can be generalized fir the many-valued intensional FOL as well.

Definition 80 (MV-Montague's intension). For a given many-valued intensional FOL language $\mathcal{L}_{in}$ with the set of logic formulae $\mathcal{L}$, the MV-Montague *intension* as a mapping (higher-order function)

$$I_n : \mathcal{L} \to \mathfrak{Rm}^{\mathcal{W}}$$

where the set of possible worlds $\mathcal{W}$ is the set of MV-interpretations given by (5.33). Thus, for any virtual predicate $\phi(x_1,\dots,x_k) \in \mathcal{L}$ we obtain the mapping $f_k = I_n(\phi(x_1,\dots,x_k)) : \mathcal{W} \to \mathfrak{Rm}$, such that for each $I^*_{mv} \in \mathcal{W}$, $R = I_n(\phi(x_1,\dots,x_k))(I^*_{mv}) \in \mathfrak{Rm}$ is equal to the relation $I^*_{mv}(\phi(x_1,\dots,x_k))$ obtained from the MV-interpretation I^*_{mv} (derived from many-valued interpretation $v^* = is^{-1}_{MV}(I^*_{mv}) : \mathcal{L}_0 \to X$ where the bijection is_{MV} is defined in Definition 79). That is, for each virtual predicate $\phi(x_1,\dots,x_k) \in \mathcal{L}$ and "world" $h \in \mathcal{W}$, from the commutative diagram of Corollary 21, the equation

$$I_n(\phi(x_1,\dots,x_k))(I^*_{mv}) = I^*_{mv}(\phi(x_1,\dots,x_k)) \tag{5.36}$$

is analog to (1.10) and explains how works the idea of MV-Montague's intension.

It is easy to verify that in the case of the two-valued intensional FOL, when $X = \mathbf{2}$, the MV-Montague's intension is equal to the standard Montague's intension given by Definition 4 in Section 1.1.3. Just from this fact that the many-valued intensional FOL, developed previously in this chapter, is a *conservative extension* of the standard two-valued intensional FOL, the complex theoretical work presented previously has important impact to practical applications of any kind of intensional logics.

A number of *new relevant* many-valued logics, improved by the modification of classic logic connectives of some significant examples of many-valued logics, which can be embedded in this intensional many-valued FOL $\mathcal{L}_{\text{in}}$, is developed as examples in a dedicated next chapter.

5.2.3 Model-based entailment and Kripke semantics for many-valued intensional FOL

The distinction between intensions and extensions is important especially because we are now able to have an *equational theory* over intensional entities (as $<A>$), that is predicate and function "names," that is separate from the extensional equality of relations and functions. Thus, intensional predicate many-valued logic has the simple Tarski first-order semantics, with a decidable unification problem, but we need also the actual world mapping which maps any intensional entity to its *actual world extension*. As we have seen previously for the Montague's representation of the intension in Definition 80 for a many-valued intensional FOL, we identified the *possible worlds* $\mathcal{W}$ as a particular set of MV-interpretations and by a particular mapping I_n, which assigns to intensional entities (virtual predicates $\phi(x_1, \dots, x_k) \in \mathcal{L}$) their extensions in such possible world $w = I^*_{\text{mv}} \in \mathcal{W}$, such that is satisfied the equation (5.36). It is the direct bridge between intensional and the possible worlds representation [7–11], where intension of a proposition is a *function* from a set of possible worlds $\mathcal{W}$ to truth values, and properties and functions (in predicate intensional logics each functional k-ary symbol f_i^k is substituted by a $(k+1)$-ary predicate) from $\mathcal{W}$ to sets of possible (usually not-actual) objects.

The *Model-based entailment*: For any embedding of a predicate many-valued logic $\mathcal{L}_{\text{mv}}$ with a lattice $(X, \leq)$ of truth values, into intensional FOL $\mathcal{L}_{\text{in}}$, and the given set of thesis $\phi_i \in \Gamma$, $\phi_i \in \mathcal{L}_0$, with associated prefixed bottom-truth values $a_i \in X$ different from f, the many-valued *models* of $\mathcal{L}_{\text{in}}$ is defined, from (5.1), as a subset of all valuations:

$$\mathbb{V}_\Gamma =_{\text{def}} \{I^*_{\text{mv}} \in \mathcal{W} \mid \forall \phi_i \in \Gamma.(I^*_{\text{mv}}(\phi_i) \succeq \{a_i\})\} \tag{5.37}$$

So, we introduce the model-based truth-preserving entailment of a formula ψ of intensional many-valued FOL $\mathcal{L}_{\text{in}}$, for a given assignment g, from the theses of $\mathcal{L}_{\text{in}}$ in Γ and from (5.38), by

$$\Gamma \vDash \psi/g \quad \text{iff} \quad (\exists \phi_i \in \Gamma).(\forall I^*_{\text{mv}} \in \mathbb{V}_\Gamma).(I^*_{\text{mv}}(\psi/g) \succeq I^*_{\text{mv}}(\phi_i)) \tag{5.38}$$

In propositional modal logics, the possible worlds are entities where a given propositional symbol can be true or false. Thus, from *logical* point of view the possible worlds in Kripke's relational semantics are characterized by property to determine the truth of logic sentences. The important question relative to the syntax of the many-valued

FOL is if there is a kind of basic set of possible worlds that have such properties. The answer is affirmative as in the case of the standard two-valued FOL, and we can use the analog results provided in Section 1.3, by adapting them to the many-valued approach.

In fact, if we consider a k-ary many-valued predicate letter p_i^k as a new kind of "propositional letter," then an assignment $g : \mathcal{V}_X \to \mathcal{D}$ can be considered as an *intrinsic* (par excellence) possible world, where the truth of this "propositional letter" p_i^k is equal to the truth of the ground atom $p_i^k(g(x_1), \dots, g(x_k)) \in \mathcal{L}_0$ of the many-valued intensional FOL $\mathcal{L}_{\text{in}}$. Here, $\mathcal{V}_X = \mathcal{V} \bigcup \{x_X\}$ where x_X is the new typed "logic" variable (whose domain is the set of truth values in $X \subset D_0$) not used in the intensional many-valued FOL $\mathcal{L}_{\text{in}}$ whose syntax is given in Definition 76, so that for any assignment $g \in \mathcal{D}^{\mathcal{V}_X}, g(x_X) \in X$.

Consequently, in what follows, analogously to the two-valued framework of the generalized Kripke semantics for predicate modal logics, given by Definition 12 in Section 1.2.1, we will denote by $\mathcal{W}$ the set of *explicit* possible worlds (defined explicitly for each particular case of modal logics, and in Definition 77 for this logic $\mathcal{L}_{\text{in}}$), while the set $\mathcal{D}^{\mathcal{V}_X}$ we will be called as the set of *intrinsic* possible worlds (which is invariant and common for every *predicate* modal logic). By $\mathbb{W} \subseteq \{(w, g) \mid w \in \mathcal{W}, g \in \mathcal{D}^{\mathcal{V}_X}\}$, we will denote the set of (generalized) possible worlds. In this way, as in the case of propositional modal logic, we will have that a formula φ is *true* in a Kripke's interpretation $\mathcal{M}$ if for each (generalized) possible world $u = (w, g) \in \mathbb{W}$, $\mathcal{M} \vDash_u \varphi$.

We denote by $\|\phi\| = \{(w, g) \in \mathbb{W} \mid \mathcal{M} \vDash_{w,g} \phi\}$ the set of all worlds where the formula ϕ is satisfied by interpretation $\mathcal{M}$. Thus, as in the case of propositional modal logics, also in the case of predicate modal logics we have that a formula ϕ is true iff it is satisfied in all (generalized) possible worlds, i. e., iff $\|\phi\| = \mathbb{W}$.

With this new arrangement, we can reformulate the generalized Kripke semantics for two-valued modal predicate logic in Definition 12 in Section 1.2.1 (as usual, π_1 and π_2 denote the first and the second projections, and we recall that we replaced each functional symbol by corresponding predicate symbol, so the set F of functional letters is empty).

Definition 81 (Generalized Kripke semantics for many-valued logics). We denote by $\mathcal{M} = (\mathbb{W}, \{\mathcal{R}_i\}, \mathcal{D}, I_K)$ a multimodal Kripke's interpretation with a set of (generalized) possible worlds $\mathbb{W} = \mathcal{W} \times \mathcal{D}^{\mathcal{V}_X}$, a set of explicit possible worlds $\mathcal{W} = \pi_1(\mathbb{W})$ and $\pi_2(\mathbb{W}) = \mathcal{D}^{\mathcal{V}_X}$, the accessibility relations $\mathcal{R}_i \subseteq \mathbb{W} \times \mathcal{P}(\mathbb{W})$, $i = 1, 2, \dots$, nonempty domain $\mathcal{D}$, and a function $I_K : \mathcal{W} \times P \to \bigcup_{n \in \mathcal{N}} \mathbf{2}^{\mathcal{D}^n}$, such that for any explicit world $w \in \mathcal{W}$: For any predicate letter $p_i^k \in P$, the function $I_K(w, p_i^k) : \mathcal{D}^k \to \mathbf{2}$ defines the m-extension of p_i^k in an explicit world w,

$$\|p_i^k(x_1, \dots, x_k)\|_{\mathcal{M},w} =_{\text{def}} \{(d_1, \dots, d_{k+1}) \in \mathcal{D}^k \times X \mid I_K(w, p_i^k)(d_1, \dots, d_{k+1}) = t \text{ and } d_{k+1} \neq f\}.$$

Based on this generalized Kripke semantics for many-valued logics, we can reformulate the standard Kripke semantics for two-valued minimal intensional FOL logic in

Definition 15 in Section 1.3, and hence we can present the Kripke semantics for many-valued intensional FOL logic $\mathcal{L}_{in}$.

Definition 82 (Kripke semantics for $\mathcal{L}_{in}$). Let $(I, \mathcal{W})$ be the two-step intensional semantics in (5.35) for many-valued intensional FOL $\mathcal{L}_{in}$ (where the functional letters with arity greater than zero are substituted by predicate letters) given in Definition 77 with $I^*_{mv} \in \mathcal{W}$ possible worlds in (5.33).

By $\mathcal{M} = (\mathbb{W}, \mathcal{R}_{\sim}, \mathcal{R}_{\widetilde{\wedge}}, \mathcal{R}_{\widetilde{\vee}}, \mathcal{R}_{\Rightarrow}, \{\mathcal{R}_{\exists x_i}, \mathcal{R}_{\forall x_i}\}_{i \in \mathbb{N}}, \{\mathcal{R}_{\odot}\}_{\odot \in \Sigma}, \mathcal{D}, I_K)$, we denote a multimodal Kripke's interpretation with a set of (generalized) possible worlds $\mathbb{W}$, a set of explicit possible worlds $\mathcal{W} = \pi_1(\mathbb{W})$ and $\pi_2(\mathbb{W}) = \mathcal{D}^{\mathcal{V}_X}$, nonempty domain $\mathcal{D}$, the accessibility relations:

a. $\mathcal{R}_{\odot} = \{(g, g_1) \mid g, g_1 \in \mathcal{D}^{\mathcal{V}_X}$, such that for all $x \in \mathcal{V}, g_1(x) = g(x)$ and $g(x_X) = \odot g_1(x_X)\}$, for each unary operator different from the quantifiers, $\odot \in \{\sim, \dots\}$,
b. $\mathcal{R}_{\odot} = \{(g, g_1, g_2) \mid g, g_1, g_2 \in \mathcal{D}^{\mathcal{V}_X}$, such that for all $x \in \mathcal{V}, g_1(x) = g_2(x) = g(x)$ and $g(x_X) = g_1(x_X) \odot g_2(x_X)\}$, for each $\odot \in \{\widetilde{\wedge}, \widetilde{\vee}, \Rightarrow, \Leftrightarrow, \dots\}$,
c. $\mathcal{R}_{\odot} \subseteq \mathcal{D}^{\mathcal{V}_X} \times \mathcal{P}(\mathcal{D}^{\mathcal{V}_X})$, such that

$$(g, G) \in \mathcal{R}_{\odot} \quad \text{iff} \quad g(x_X) = \diamond\{g'(x_X) \mid g' \in G \text{ and for all } x \in \mathcal{V} \backslash \{x_i\}, g'(x) = g(x)\},$$

for each pair $(\odot, \diamond) \in \{(\exists x_i, \bigvee), (\forall x_i, \bigwedge)\}$, where $\bigwedge$ and $\bigvee$ are the meet and join operator of lattice X, respectively,

with mapping $I_K : \mathcal{W} \times P \to \bigcup_{n \in \mathcal{N}} \mathbf{2}^{\mathcal{D}^n \times X}$, such that for any explicit world $w = I^*_{mv} \in \mathcal{W}$, i. e., many-valued interpretation $v^* = \mathrm{is}^{-1}_{MV}(I^*_{mv})$, $p^k_i \in P$ and $(u_1, \dots, u_{k+1}) \in \mathcal{D}^k \times X$,

$$I_K(I^*_{mv}, p^k_i)(u_1, \dots, u_{k+1}) = t \quad \text{iff} \quad u_{k+1} = v^*(p^k_i(u_1, \dots, u_k)).$$

Then, for any world $(w, g) \in \mathbb{W}$ with $w = I^*_{mv} \in \mathcal{W}$, we define the many-valued satisfaction, denoted by $\vDash_{w,g}$, as follows:

1. $\mathcal{M} \vDash_{w,g} p^k_i(x_1, \dots, x_k)$ iff $I_K(w, p^k_i)(g(x_1), \dots, g(x_k), g(x_X)) = t$,
2. $\mathcal{M} \vDash_{w,g} \odot\phi$ iff $\exists g_1 \in \mathcal{D}^{\mathcal{V}_X}.((g, g_1) \in \mathcal{R}_{\odot}$ and $\mathcal{M} \vDash_{w,g_1} \phi)$, for each unary logic connective different from the quantifiers $\odot \in \{\neg, \dots\}$,
3. $\mathcal{M} \vDash_{w,g} \phi \circledast \psi$ iff $\exists g_1, g_2 \in \mathcal{D}^{\mathcal{V}_X}.((g, g_1, g_2) \in \mathcal{R}_{\odot}$ and $\mathcal{M} \vDash_{w,g_1} \phi$ and $\mathcal{M} \vDash_{w,g_2} \psi)$, for each $\circledast \in \{\wedge, \vee, \Rightarrow, \dots\}$ and $\odot \in \{\widetilde{\wedge}, \widetilde{\vee}, \Rightarrow, \dots\}$, relatively,
4. $\mathcal{M} \vDash_{w,g} (\exists x_i)\phi(x_1, \dots, x_i, \dots, x_k)$ iff exists $(g, G) \in \mathcal{R}_{\exists x_i}$ such that $G = \{g_1 \in \mathcal{D}^{\mathcal{V}_X} \mid \forall_{1 \le j \le k} j \neq i.(g_1(x_j) = g(x_j))$ and $g_1(x_X) \in \mathrm{Com}(w(\phi/g_1))\}$, and ($g_1 \in G$ iff $\mathcal{M} \vDash_{w,g_1} \phi$),
5. $\mathcal{M} \vDash_{w,g} (\forall x_i)\phi(x_1, \dots, x_i, \dots, x_k)$ iff exists $(g, G) \in \mathcal{R}_{\forall x_i}$ such that $G = \{g_1 \in \mathcal{D}^{\mathcal{V}_X} \mid \forall_{1 \le j \le k} j \neq i.(g_1(x_j) = g(x_j))$ and $g_1(x_X) \in \mathrm{Com}(w(\phi/g_1))\}$, and ($g_1 \in G$ iff $\mathcal{M} \vDash_{w,g_1} \phi$),
6. $\mathcal{M} \vDash_{w,g} \phi \equiv \psi$ iff $\mathcal{M} \vDash_{w,g} \phi$ and $\mathcal{M} \vDash_{w,g} \psi$.

Note that we used ternary Kripke accessibility relations as in Definition 119 in Section A.4.2 in the Appendix, used for the two-valued reduction (ontological encapsulation) of the many-valued logics. Let us show that this multimodal Kripke semantics of

$\mathcal{L}_{in}$ is correct semantics, able to support the Montague's approach to the intensional semantics.

Theorem 12. *For any given multimodal Kripke interpretation $\mathcal{M}$ of $\mathcal{L}_{in}$, it is valid that for any formula $\phi(x_1,\ldots,x_k) \in \mathcal{L}, k \geq 0$, and world $(w,g) \in \mathbb{W}$ where $w = I^*_{mv}$ with many-valued interpretation $v^* = \mathrm{is}^{-1}_{MV}(w)$:*

$$\mathcal{M} \models_{w,g} \phi(x_1,\ldots,x_k) \quad \textit{iff} \quad g(x_X) = v^*(\phi(x_1,\ldots,x_k)/g) \tag{5.39}$$

that is, by Theorem 11, iff ($g(x_X) \neq f$ and $w(\phi(x_1,\ldots,x_k)/g) = \{g(x_X)\}$, or $g(x_X) = f$ and $w(\phi(x_1,\ldots,x_k)/g) = \emptyset$). So,

$$\mathcal{M} \models_{w,g} \phi \equiv \psi \quad \textit{iff} \quad v^*(\phi/g) = v^*(\psi/g).$$

Consequently, the m-extension of $\phi(x_1,\ldots,x_k)$ computed by the multimodal Kripke's interpretaion $\mathcal{M}$ in a given explicit world $w = I^*_{mv} \in \mathcal{W}$ is equal to m-extension of the same formula computed by the intensional semantics of the $\mathcal{L}_{in}$, i. e.,

$$\|\phi(x_1,\ldots,x_k)\|_{\mathcal{M},w} = w(\phi(x_1,\ldots,x_k)) \tag{5.40}$$

Thus, from the Montague's approach to the intension (meaning) of the logic formulae given by the mapping $I_n : \mathcal{L} \to \mathfrak{Rm}^{\mathcal{W}}$ in Definition 80, it holds that $I_n(\phi(x_1,\ldots,x_k))(w) = \|\phi(x_1,\ldots,x_k)\|_{\mathcal{M},w}$ is the m-extension of this formula in this possible world. Consequently, this multimodal Kripke semantics for $\mathcal{L}_{in}$ is adequate to support Montague's intensional semantics.

Proof. Let us prove (5.39) by structural induction on number of logic operators in a virtual predicate (open formula) $\phi(x_1,\ldots,x_k)$:

1. Let $\phi(x_1,\ldots,x_k)$ be an atom $p_i^k(x_1,\ldots,x_k)$ (with zero logic operators). Consequently, if $\mathcal{M} \models_{w,g} p_i^k(x_1,\ldots,x_k)$ then, from point 1 of Definition 82 we have that $I_K(w,p_i^k)(g(x_1),\ldots,g(x_k),g(x_X)) = t$, that is $g(x_X) = v^*(p_i^k(x_1,\ldots,x_k)/g)$. And vice versa.
2. Let us suppose that this theorem holds for each open formula with less than $n \geq 1$ logic operators, and consider any formula $\phi(x_1,\ldots,x_k)$ with n operators. There are the following cases:
   2.1. $\phi(x_1,\ldots,x_k) = \neg\psi(x_1,\ldots,x_k)$ where $\psi(x_1,\ldots,x_k)$ has less than n operators. Let $\mathcal{M} \models_{w,g} \phi(x_1,\ldots,x_k)$, so that from the point 2 of Definition 82 we obtain that $\mathcal{M} \models_{w,g_1} \psi(x_1,\ldots,x_k)$ with $g_1(x_X) = a, g(x_X) =\sim a$, and consequently, by inductive hypothesis $v^*(\psi(x_1,\ldots,x_k)/g_1) = v^*(\psi(x_1,\ldots,x_k)/g) = a$. Then $g(x_X) =\sim a =\sim v^*(\psi(x_1,\ldots,x_k)/g) =$ (from point 1 of Definition 78) $= v^*(\neg\psi(x_1,\ldots,x_k)/g) = v^*(\phi(x_1,\ldots,x_k)/g)$, and vice versa, analogously, for another unary logic connectives different from the quantifiers.
   2.2. $\phi(x_1,\ldots,x_k) = \psi_1 \wedge \psi_2$ where ψ_1, ψ_2 have less than n operators.

Let $\mathcal{M} \models_{w,g} \phi(x_1,\ldots,x_k)$, so that from the point 3 of Definition 82 we obtain that $\mathcal{M} \models_{w,g_1} \psi_1$ and $\mathcal{M} \models_{w,g_2} \psi_2$ with $g(x_X) = g_1(x_X)\widetilde{\wedge}g_2(x_X)$. Consequently, by inductive hypothesis $g_1(x_X) = v^*(\psi_1/g_1) = v^*(\psi_1/g)$ and $g_2(x_X) = v^*(\psi_2/g_2) = v^*(\psi_2/g)$. Then $g(x_X) = g_1(x_X)\widetilde{\wedge}g_2(x_X) = v^*(\psi_1/g)\widetilde{\wedge}v^*(\psi_1/g) =$ (from point 2 of Definition 78) $= v^*(\psi_1/g \wedge \psi_2/g) = v^*(\phi(x_1,\ldots,x_k)/g))$, and vice versa. Analogously, we can show that it holds for the cases when $\phi(x_1,\ldots,x_k)$ is $\psi_1 \odot \psi_2$ for other binary connectives as well.

2.3. $\phi(x_1,\ldots,x_k) = (\exists x_i)\psi$ where ψ has less than n operators.
Let $\mathcal{M} \models_{w,g} \phi(x_1,\ldots,x_k)$, so that from the point 4 of Definition 82 we obtain that $\mathcal{M} \models_{w,g} (\exists x_i)\psi$ with $g(x_X) = \bigvee G = \bigvee\{g_i(x_X) \mid \mathcal{M} \models_{w,g_i} \psi, g_i \in \mathcal{D}^{\mathcal{V}}$ such that for all $x \in \mathcal{V}\backslash\{x_i\}, g_i(x) = g(x)\}$, so that from the inductive hypothesis $g(x_X) = \bigvee\{g_i(x_X) \mid g_i(x_X) = v^*(\psi/g_i), g_i \in \mathcal{D}^{\mathcal{V}}$ such that for all $x \in \mathcal{V}\backslash\{x_i\}, g_i(x) = g(x)\} = \bigvee\{v^*(\psi/g_i) \mid g_i \in \mathcal{D}^{\mathcal{V}}$ such that for all $x \in \mathcal{V}\backslash\{x_i\}, g_i(x) = g(x)\} =$ (from point 3 of Definition 78) $= v^*((\exists x_i)\psi)$, and vice versa.

Analogously, we can show that it holds for the case when $\phi(x_1,\ldots,x_k) = (\forall x_i)\psi$ as well.

Consequently, we obtain (5.40),

$$\begin{aligned}
\|\phi(x_1,\ldots,x_k)\|_{\mathcal{M},w} &=_{\text{def}} \{(g(x_1),\ldots,g(x_k),g(x_X)) \mid g \in \mathcal{D}^{\mathcal{V}} \text{ and } \mathcal{M} \models_{w,g} \phi(x_1,\ldots,x_k)\} \\
&= w(\phi(x_1,\ldots,x_k)) \\
&= I^*_{\text{mv}}(\phi(x_1,\ldots,x_k)) \\
&= I_n(\phi(x_1,\ldots,x_k))(I^*_{\text{mv}}), \quad \text{from (5.36)},
\end{aligned}$$

and hence correspondence with Montague's approach to the intension (meaning). □

Notice that the meaning of the logic formulae is given by mapping $I_n : \mathcal{L} \to \mathfrak{Rm}^{\mathcal{W}}$, such that for any formula $\phi(x_1,\ldots,x_k) \in \mathcal{L}$ its Montague's meaning is a function $I_n(\phi(x_1,\ldots,x_k)) : \mathcal{W} \to R$ that maps each explicit possible world into the m-extension of this formula in each given possible world, given by

$$I_n(\phi(x_1,\ldots,x_k))(w) = \|\phi(x_1,\ldots,x_k)\|_{\mathcal{M},w}.$$

This meaning is *compositional*. That is, the meaning of a complex logic formula (or the complex concept obtained by applying the intensional interpretation I to this formula), is functionally dependent on meanings of its subformulae. It is result of the fact that for any formula,

$$I_n(\phi(x_1,\ldots,x_k))(w) = \|\phi(x_1,\ldots,x_k)\|_{\mathcal{M},w} = w(\phi(x_1,\ldots,x_k)) = I^*_{\text{mv}}(\phi(x_1,\ldots,x_k)),$$

from the fact that $w = I^*_{\text{mv}}$ and is a *homomorphism* between free syntax algebra $\mathcal{A}m_{\text{FOL}}$ and algebra of m-extensions $\mathcal{A}_{\mathfrak{Rm}}$ given in Corollary 21. For example,

$$I_n(\phi \wedge \psi)(w) = I^*_{\mathrm{mv}}(\phi \wedge \psi) = I^*_{\mathrm{mv}}(\phi) \otimes_S I^*_{\mathrm{mv}}(\phi) = I_n(\phi)(w) \otimes_S I_n(\psi)(w),$$

where S is uniquely determined by the common subset of free variables in ϕ and in ψ.

Consequently, the Kripke semantics of $\mathcal{L}_{\mathrm{in}}$ given by Definition 82, based on possible worlds and accessibility relations, represents this intensional aspect of the logic $\mathcal{L}_{\mathrm{in}}$.

The meaning, concept-algebra semantics and the many-valuedness of any logic formulae $\phi(x_1, \dots, x_k)$ in $\mathcal{L}_{\mathrm{in}}$, can be represented synthetically by the following equalities:

$$\begin{aligned} & I_n(\phi(x_1,\dots,x_k))(w) \quad \text{(Montague's "meaning" semantics)} \\ & \quad = \|\phi(x_1,\dots,x_k)\|_{\mathcal{M},w} \quad \text{(Kripke semantics)} \\ & \quad = I^*_{\mathrm{mv}}(\phi(x_1,\dots,x_k)) \quad \text{(concept-algebra semantics)} \\ & \quad = \{(g(x_1),\dots,g(x_k), v^*(\phi(x_1,\dots,x_k)/g)) \mid g \in \mathcal{D}^{\mathcal{V}}\} \quad \text{(many-valued semantics),} \end{aligned}$$

where $I^*_{\mathrm{mv}} = \mathrm{is}^{-1}_{\mathrm{in}}(h)$ (from Corollary 21) is a MV-interpretation of $\mathcal{L}_{\mathrm{in}}$, equivalent to the Bealer's concept-extensionalization function h for a given fixed intensional homomorphic interpretation $I : \mathcal{A}m_{\mathrm{FOL}} \to \mathcal{A}m_{\mathrm{int}}$.

5.3 Resolution of Liar formula in many-valued intensional FOL

Let us introduce the Liar paradox in the standard 2-valued FOL of arithmetic (standard *2-valued* first-order Peano arithmetic), extended by a primitive satisfaction binary predicate (Gödel) $\mathrm{Sat}(x, y)$, governed by Tarskian axioms. This system of axioms governing $\mathrm{Sat}(x, y)$ was given in [220].

The philosophical significance of such FOL logic is discussed in [221], compared with minimalistic extensions generated by adding just the "T-schema" (the set of formulae $T(\ulcorner\phi\urcorner) \Leftrightarrow \phi$ where $\ulcorner\phi\urcorner$ is the code (positive integer) obtained by Gödel's codification of logic formula ϕ, and T is a unary truth predicate introduced in Definition 76). Similar constructions are considered in [222].

The idea is then $\mathrm{Sat}(x, y)$ expresses the satisfaction relation between (codes of) formulae and (codes of) sequences of the formulae. Then $T(x)$ expresses the *concept of truth* for such formulae and sequences. In fact, it can be shown that this theory satisfies Tarski's convention (T): i. e., that

$$T(\ulcorner\phi\urcorner) \Leftrightarrow \phi \tag{5.41}$$

is a theorem in this 2-valued Peano arithmetic FOL.

If ϕ is any formula with one free variable x, then the *diagonalization* of ϕ, can be defined by mapping $d : \mathcal{L} \to \mathcal{L}$, such that $d(\phi(x)) = \phi(\ulcorner\phi(x)\urcorner)$, equivalent to the formula $(\exists y)(y = \ulcorner\phi(x)\urcorner \wedge \phi(y))$.

Based on this mapping, we can define the mapping diag : $N \to N$, such that for any non-negative integer $n \in N$, $\text{diag}(n) = \ulcorner d(\phi(x))\urcorner$ if $n = \ulcorner \phi(x)\urcorner$; 0 otherwise.

Now we can introduce the binary predicate $\text{Diag}(x,y)$ such that for any two $n, k \in N$, $\text{Diag}(k,n)$ is true iff $n = \text{diag}(k) \neq 0$, i. e., if n is the code of the formula obtained by diagonalization of the formula $\phi(x)$ whose code is equal to k.

From the diagonalization lemma (or fixed-point theorem) in Peano arithmetic FOL, there must be a fixed-point formula λ such that, the following formula is a theorem in this logic:

$$\lambda \Leftrightarrow \sim T(\ulcorner\lambda\urcorner), \quad \text{for } \lambda \text{ equal to } d(\sim T(\text{diag}(x))) \tag{5.42}$$

It is easy to show that $\sim T(\text{diag}(x))$ is equal to the formula $(\exists y)(\text{Diag}(x,y) \wedge \sim T(y))$ with the free variable x. Thus,

$$\begin{aligned} &\lambda \text{ is equal to the formula } d((\exists y)(\text{Diag}(x,y) \wedge \sim T(y))), \\ &\quad \text{that is, to } (\exists z)(\text{Diag}((\ulcorner \exists y)(\text{Diag}(x,y) \wedge \sim T(y))\urcorner, z) \wedge \sim T(z)) \end{aligned} \tag{5.43}$$

The analysis of the proof of this diagonalization lemma [223, 224] shows that this formula λ must contain the predicate $T(x)$. This formula is the formal analogue of the so-called "*strengthened liar*" for this system. It is a formula that "*says of itself that it is not true.*"

In fact, it expresses the Liar paradox. If we assume that λ is true than $\sim T(\ulcorner\lambda\urcorner)$ must be true, i. e., $T(\ulcorner\lambda\urcorner)$ must be false and, consequently, from (5.41) we obtain that λ is false: the contradiction. This is the same contradiction that we obtain if we assume that λ is false.

Let us consider now this problem inside the intensional many-valued FOL $\mathcal{L}_{in}$ defined previously. In fact, instead of the formula $\lambda \Leftrightarrow \sim T(\ulcorner\lambda\urcorner)$ in (5.42) for the sentence λ defined in (5.43), we can use the intensional abstraction operator $<\_>$ and obtain equivalent to it formula

$$\lambda \Leftrightarrow \sim T(<\lambda>) \tag{5.44}$$

where the ground atom $T(<\lambda>)$ has the natural language meaning "it is true *that* λ," so that in the classic 2-valued logic again we obtained famous Liar contradiction.

Let us show that the unary truth-predicate T in $\mathcal{L}_{in}$ (with $\mathcal{L}_0$ the subset of closed formulae) used to represent the concept of truth defined by the equivalence (5.41) *cannot* be 2-valued as in the case of the standard 2-valued FOL. In fact, if we try to define it as a 2-valued built-in predicate, such that for each $I^*_{mv} \in \mathcal{W}$,

$$I^*_{mv}(T(x)) =_{def} \{(<\psi>, t) \mid \psi \in \mathcal{L}_0 \text{ and } I^*_{mv}(\psi) = \{t\}\}$$

then for any sentence ϕ from (5.44) we would have that $I^*_{mv}(\phi) \in \{\emptyset, \{t\}\}$, thus $I^*_{mv}(\lambda) \in \{\emptyset, \{t\}\}$, but in that case for the Liar formula (5.42) we will have that $I^*_{mv}(\lambda) = I^*_{mv}(\sim$

$T(<\lambda>)) = \oslash I^*_{mv}(T(<\lambda>)) = \oslash I^*_{mv}(\lambda)$ what is impossible for any $I^*_{mv} \in \mathcal{W}$, because $\oslash\emptyset = \{t\} \neq \emptyset$ and $\oslash\{t\} = \emptyset \neq \{t\}$.

Consequently, the built-in unary predicate T has to be many-valued as well and to satisfy the condition (5.44), as we defined for the many-valued semantics of T in the logic $\mathcal{L}_{in}$.

From the considerations above, in $\mathcal{L}_{in}$ there is no any MV-interpretation $I^*_{mv} \in \mathcal{W}$ such that $I^*_{mv}(\lambda) \in \{\emptyset, \{t\}\}$. But for each MV-interpretation I^*_{mv} of $\mathcal{L}_{in}$, we may fix $I^*_{mv}(\lambda) = \{\kappa\}$ in the way that the fixed-point Liar formula λ satisfy (5.44), with the many-valued unary predicate T, such that

$$(<\lambda>, \kappa) \in I^*_{mv}(T(x)), \tag{5.45}$$

and hence to avoid the "Liar paradox" in the many-valued intensional FOL $\mathcal{L}_{in}$.

Corollary 22. *The Liar self-reference sentence is not a paradox in $\mathcal{L}_{in}$, thus, does not create the contradictions.*

Proof. For any MV-interpretation I^*_{mv}, such that $I^*_{mv}(\lambda) = \{\kappa\}$ (or an equivalent many-valued interpretation v^* such that $v^*(\lambda) = \kappa$), such that $\sim \kappa = \kappa$ in the lattice of truth values X we have that $I^*_{mv}(\sim T(<\lambda>)) = \oslash I^*_{mv}(\lambda) = \oslash(\{\kappa\}) = \{\kappa\} = I^*_{mv}(\lambda)$ so that (5.42) is satisfied. Thus, in $\mathcal{L}_{in}$ the value to λ is assigned without any contradiction. □

Remark. The minimal many-valued logic that resolve this problem can be the Kleene three-valued logic (where κ is "unknown" value). However, for this case better solution would be to use the 4-valued Belnap's bilattice $X = \mathcal{B}_4$ (more about it can be found in Section 5.1.3), by assigning the $\top$ ("inconsistent value") to κ. In effect, Belnap's bilattice $\mathcal{B}_4$ is the best candidate to use the many-valued intensional FOL $\mathcal{L}_{in}$ for data integration systems where we can have both unknown and mutually inconsistent information coming from different sources. □

Analogously, the Gödel's contradictory formulae obtained by diagonalization of the formula $\sim$ Prov(diag(x)), where Prov(x) is a formula representing provability in the Peano arithmetic FOL can be resolved in $\mathcal{L}_{in}$ by interpreting these formulae with the value $\kappa = \bot$ ("unknown value") of Belnap's bilattice.

Moreover, in Section 6.3 we will consider the P2P database systems, such that each peer database is a single data integration system (adopting, however, the Belnap's multivalued logic for each peer in order to consider directly the incomplete and inconsistent data), with inter-peer mappings defined by intensionally equivalent *many-valued views*, in the way as described the query-answering in the P2P database systems (see Sections 3.2 and 3.2.3) by classic two-valued FOL in Chapter 3.

All these examples, and much more provided in [209], explain how the Belnap's based intensional FOL $\mathcal{L}_I$ can have very important rule in the mathematical logics theory and practice.

6 Applications of many-valued intensional first-order logic

6.1 Relevant Lukasiewicz–Tarski logics

As far as I know, the study of the relevant implication dates back at least to 1928 with I. E. Orlov's axiomatization of propositional logic weaker than classical logic [225], shown by my colleague from Belgrade, Kosta Dosen [226]: we worked independently and at different times on the possible weakening of negation logical connective [210], but different from him, I worked for the weakening of the negation for the da Costa paraconsistent logic [227, 228] presented with some new advances here in Section 6.2.

In Orlov's system, the only rule is modus ponens, and he axiomatized this logic in order to "represent relevance between propositions in symbolic form," as follows:

$$\phi \Rightarrow \neg\neg\phi \quad \text{double negation introduction}$$
$$\neg\neg\phi \Rightarrow \phi \quad \text{double negation elimination}$$
$$\phi \Rightarrow (\neg\phi \Rightarrow \neg\phi) \quad \text{contraposed reduction}$$
$$(\phi \Rightarrow \psi) \Rightarrow (\neg\psi \Rightarrow \neg\phi) \quad \text{contraposition}$$
$$(\phi \Rightarrow (\psi \Rightarrow \varphi)) \Rightarrow (\psi \Rightarrow (\phi \Rightarrow \varphi)) \quad \text{permutation}$$
$$(\phi \Rightarrow \psi) \Rightarrow ((\varphi \Rightarrow \phi) \Rightarrow (\varphi \Rightarrow \psi)) \quad \text{prefixing}$$
$$\phi, \phi \Rightarrow \psi \vdash \psi \quad \text{modus ponens rule}$$

The axioms and rules here form a traditional Hilbert system. Neither of the following formulae are provable in Orlov's system:

$$\phi \Rightarrow (\psi \Rightarrow \psi), \quad \neg(\psi \Rightarrow \psi) \Rightarrow \phi$$

These axioms and the rule do not explicitly represent any notion of relevance. Instead, we have an axiomatic system governing the behavior of implication and negation. The system tells us about relevances in virtue of what it leaves out, rather than what it includes. In Orlov's system, a formula $\phi \Rightarrow \psi$ is provable only when ϕ and ψ *share a propositional atom*. There is no way to prove a condition in which the antecedent and the consequent have nothing to do with one another! The effect, as was demonstrated more than 30 years later, Orlov axiomatized the implication and negation fragment of the now well-known relevant logic R.

In 1958, Anderson and Belnap took up ideas from Church and Ackermann, and started a research program into what in time became relevance (now often called relevant) logic. Their chosen name picked up an informal use before that time of the epithet "relevant" to characterize a consequence relation, and an implication, which was not paradoxical in the way material and strict implications were. For example, the truth-functional material implication $\phi \Rightarrow \psi$ is true whenever ϕ is false or ψ

https://doi.org/10.1515/9783110981438-006

is true, i. e., equivalent to $(\neg\phi \vee \psi)$ for the truth-functional disjunction $\vee$ and negation $\neg$. Among the paradoxes of material implication are the following: $\phi \Rightarrow (\psi \Rightarrow \phi)$, $\neg\phi \Rightarrow (\phi \Rightarrow \psi)$ and $(\phi \Rightarrow \psi) \vee (\psi \Rightarrow \varphi)$. The first asserts that every proposition implies a true one; the second suggests that a false proposition implies every proposition, and the third, that for any three propositions, either the first implies the second or the second implies the third.

Also, the strict implication defined by $\neg\Diamond(\phi \wedge \neg\psi)$, where $\Diamond$ is an existential "possible" modal operator, so that it is true whenever it is *not possible* that ϕ is true and ψ false has a number of paradoxes.

Relevance logicians have attempted to construct logics that reject theses and arguments that commit "fallacies of relevance." For example, they do not admit the classical valid inference such as, "*The moon is made of green cheese. Therefore, either it is raining in Ecuador now or it is not.*"

I believe that are the correct philosophical reasons for rejecting classical logic and adopting a relevant logic as a correct description of the basis of inference. These are not, in general, the reasons which led historically to the development of the subject, and are not those emphasized in the writings of Anderson, Belnap and Dunn.

In relevance logic, it is admitted that "if ϕ then ψ" can be false without ϕ being true or ψ false, so that 'if" is not truth-functional material implication but a binary modal operator. From the realization that "if" is not truth-functional, we can draw three morals. The first is that ex falso quodlibet is invalid.

The Lewis arguments

We can return to the famous derivation of ψ from ϕ and "not-ϕ," which Lewis gave. The derivation was not original to Lewis. The earliest presentation I know was given by Alexander Neckam in his De Naturis Rerum [229], written around 1200. Neckam retails many of the logical subtleties and included among these is the following derivation. The derivation proceeds rapidly by two applications of simplification, one of addition, and the notorious final step of disjunctive syllogism:

> *"I am amazed also at those criticising the claim that from the impossible in itself anything whatever follows. This may be established in many ways, but few will show more clearly. Is it not the case that if Socrates is a man and Socrates is not a man, then Socrates is a man? But if Socrates is a man, Socrates is a man or a stone. So if Socrates is a man and Socrates is not a man, Socrates is a man or a stone. But if Socrates is a man and Socrates is not a man, Socrates is not a man. So if Socrates is a man and Socrates is not a man, Socrates is a stone. By a similar deduction, it may be proved that if Socrates is a man and Socrates is not a man, Socrates is a goat, and so on for any other thing, such as a rose, a lily and so on. Don"t you therefore see that in this way from this impossibility, that Socrates is a man and Socrates is not a man, anything follows?"*

The structure of the argument is as follows:
(1) Suppose ϕ and not-ϕ
(2) Then ϕ (by Simplification of (1)),

(3) whence ϕ or ψ (by Addition),
(4) not-ϕ (by Simplification of (1) again),
(5) and finally ψ (by Disjunctive syllogism from (3) and (4)).

However, I will not consider the relevant implication, studied so long time, but other logic connectives. So, I would chose initially the logics, which do not use the implication as logic connective, and hence the first candidate to analyze is the De Morgan logic, which uses three other classical logic connectives. From the fact that the negation connective is often used as an epistemic modal operator, I think that it is a more original approach to consider the relevance of other two binary (extensional) connectives, disjunction and conjunction, which are algebraically defined as join and meet operations in a given lattice $(X, \leq)$ of truth values (also in the case of the classical two-valued logics), and to replace them with the new intensional disjunction and conjunction. Such intensional disjunction and conjunction are introduced in the well-known infinite-valued Lukasiewicz–Tarski logic called fusion and fission connectives as well. With this approach, I will try to give some original new contributions for the relevance logics.

Orlov's work looked at the behavior of other connectives definable in terms of conjunction and negation. He showed that defining a conjunction connective

$$\phi \wedge \psi =_{\text{def}} \neg(\phi \Rightarrow \neg\psi) \tag{6.1}$$

gives you a connective that can be shown to be commutative and associative

$$\phi \wedge \psi \Rightarrow \psi \wedge \phi, \quad (\phi \wedge \psi) \wedge \varphi \Rightarrow \phi \wedge (\psi \wedge \varphi), \quad \phi \wedge (\psi \wedge \varphi) \Rightarrow (\phi \wedge \psi) \wedge \varphi, \tag{6.2}$$

and *square increasing*

$$\phi \Rightarrow \phi \wedge \phi \tag{6.3}$$

In the same way, Orlov defined disjunction connective

$$\phi \vee \psi =_{\text{def}} \neg\phi \Rightarrow \psi, \tag{6.4}$$

which can be shown to be associative, commutative and *square decreasing*,

$$\phi \vee \phi \Rightarrow \phi \tag{6.5}$$

It follows that these defined connectives for conjunction and disjunction do not have the full force of the lattice meet and join operations present in classical and intuitionistic logic. In effect, his conjunction and disjunction are *intensional* notions, while that based on lattice operations are *extensional* ones. At the very first example of the study of substructural logics, we are at the doorstep of one of the profound insights made clear in this area: the splitting of notions identified in stronger logical systems. In the literature of relevant logic, the intensional notions of conjunction and disjunction (6.2) and (6.4), and call them *fusion* and *fission*.

Remark. My aim is just to define a new semantics of conjunction and disjunction connectives (fusion and fission) as *intensional* notions, but different from Orlov, such that they *do not satisfy* the associativity. The same approach will be in detail applied to infinite-valued Lukasiewicz–Tarski logics where square increasing and decreasing are opposite of this Orlov's system.

Moreover, I would like to render the relevant implication independent from these two basis connectives, I will not define the conjunction and disjunction from the implication connective, and will leave the implication outside of this investigation and will work only with these basic logical connectives and with negation, and hence will consider the De Morgan logics.

From the fact that I will try to remain also after transformation of these two binary logic connectives in De Morgan logics, where the conjunction operator is derivable from the negation and disjunction, i. e., $\phi \wedge \psi$ is logically equivalent to the formula $\neg(\neg\phi \vee \neg\psi)$, the only logical connective considered for the relevance "weakening" in this methodological approach is the *disjunction* connective, i. e., its corresponding algebraic operation denoted by $\widetilde{\vee}$ (derived from it, by De Morgan law, intensional conjunction (fission) will be denoted by $\widetilde{\wedge}$). □

Consequently, the most work will be dedicated to the De Morgan algebras of truth values in a lattice $(X, \leq)$, where the relevant disjunction will be a binary modal operation. The semantics that is presented here for this binary modal operator for disjunction is the ternary relation semantics, due to Richard Routley and Robert K. Meyer. These semantics are a development of Alasdair Urquhart's "semilattice semantics" [230]. There is a similar semantics, due to Kit Fine, that was developed at the same time as the Routley–Meyer theory [231]. And there is an algebraic semantics due to J. Michael Dunn. The idea behind the ternary relation semantics is rather simple. Consider C. I. Lewis' attempt to avoid the paradoxes of material implication. He added a new connective to classical logic, that of strict implication. Unfortunately, from a relevant point of view, the theory of strict implication is still irrelevant. One interpretation is suggested in Jon Barwise [232] and developed in Restall [233]. On this view, worlds are taken to be information-theoretic "sites" and "channels." A site is a context in which information is received and a channel is a conduit through which information is transferred. Another interpretation is developed in Mares [234]. This interpretation takes the Routley–Meyer semantics to be a formalization of the notion of "situated implication." This interpretation takes the "worlds" of the Routley–Meyer semantics to be situations. A situation is a perhaps partial representation of the universe. The information contained in two situations, *a* and *b* might allow us to infer further information about the universe that is contained in neither situation. Another informational interpretation is in Dunn [235].

Note that we cannot use Dunn's Gaggle theory [236] as a general method for obtaining Kripke-style semantics for our algebraic logics, where n-ary logical connective is associated with $n + 1$-ary relation over a set of possible worlds, because in our case does not hold more square increasingness $x \leq x \widetilde{\wedge} x$ for the modal conjunctive operation $\widetilde{\wedge}$ for our intensional (modal) logical conjunction. In fact, in our relevant De Morgan sublogics of the infinite-valued Lukasiewicz's logic, we will have that $x \widetilde{\vee} x \geq x$; so that from fact that $\sim\sim x = x$ we obtain $x \widetilde{\wedge} x =\sim (\sim x \widetilde{\vee} \sim x) \leq\sim\sim x = x$, for the De Morgan negation $\sim$. So, in order to dedicate our attention to the definition of relevant Lukasiewicz's logic based on the lattice of reals $X = [0, 1]$ with fusion defined as a t-norm, we will begin to consider the substructural properties of t-norm fuzzy logics in the next section.

Moreover, we cannot use the Routley–Meyer Kripke-style frames with ternary accessibility relations for the binary conjunction operation $\widetilde{\wedge}$, which has to be used in De Morgan monoids and its Routley–Meyer representation. The fact is that our conjunction operation *is not associative* (it is only commutative), so a lattice-ordered groupoid $(X, \leq, \bigwedge, \bigvee, \widetilde{\wedge})$, where $\bigwedge$ and $\bigvee$ are the lattice's meet and join operations, respectively, cannot be a lattice-ordered semigroup (see Definition 1 in [237]). So with this binary modal operation $\widetilde{\wedge}$, we cannot obtain the Pierce grupoid, and hence Pierce monoid. Moreover, we cannot obtain also the De Morgan monoid, which requires the square increasingness $x \leq x \widetilde{\wedge} x$ [237] as in the case of the Dunn's Gaggle theory.

So, I followed a new approach used also for the definition of the autoreferential Kripke semantics for many-valued logics, in different context, from the strict autoreferential semantics (provided in Definition 58 in Section 5.1) to a more general canonical semantics case in Section A.3, and a new philosophical interpretation in order to give a real meaning on this autoreferential semantics where the set of possible worlds is just the (sub)set of truth values of the many-valued logic.

6.1.1 Introduction to substructural properties of T-norm fuzzy logics

In the application of fuzzy logic to expert systems, fuzzy control and the like, it is not a single logic that is used, but a plethora of distinct logics. The choice used in a specific application is often ad hoc decided on the basis of empirical factors or mere whim. There is a technical commonality to these logics in that they all arise in the same manner through the specification of an algebra of truth values, i. e., a set of truth values equipped with algebraic operations corresponding to each of the logical connectives in question.

The difference and the logical meaning are introduced when an algebra of truth values is given. This is just an algebra with the same number of basic operations as there are connective symbols and with matching arities. In many cases, the operations corresponding to conjunction and disjunction are taken to be idempotent or to have other special properties. However, we wish to stress that we are not placing any such restrictions on the algebra, as for instance in [238].

We apply our methods to the study of fuzzy logics arising from truth value algebras on the unit interval that are strict De Morgan systems. This class of logics includes also, e. g., the ones in which the fuzzy conjunction is given by the usual multiplication of real numbers, a common choice in applications.

However, here we mainly consider applications to the t-norm fuzzy logic (t-norm fuzzy logics impose certain natural constraints on the truth function of intensional (strong) conjunction in Definition 83) as members of the family of fuzzy logics, and then we will modify the disjunction and conjunction connectives to obtain a kind of relevant fuzzy logics. The standard set of truth degrees for fuzzy logics is the real unit interval $X = [0, 1]$ with its natural ordering $\leq$, ranging from total falsity (represented by 0) to total truth (represented by 1) through a continuum of intermediate truth degrees. The most fundamental assumption of (mainstream) mathematical fuzzy logic is that connectives are to be interpreted truth-functionally over the set of truth degrees. Such truth functions are assumed to behave classically on the extremal values 0 and 1. A very natural behavior of conjunction and disjunction is achieved by imposing $x \bigwedge y = \min\{x, y\}$ and $x \bigvee y = \max\{x, y\}$ for each $x, y \in X$, so that $\bigwedge$ and $\bigvee$ are the meet and join operations of the lattice $(X, \leq)$.

Another, nonidempotent, binary conjunction $\otimes$ is typically added to account for the intuition that by applying a partially true hypothesis twice might lead to a different degree of truth than using it only once. That is, for $x \in X$,

$$x \otimes x \neq x \tag{6.6}$$

So, it is not necessarily idempotent, but still commutative and nondecreasing in both arguments, associative and has 1 as a neutral element (see point 4 of Definition 83 where T is this binary conjunction). These operations are called t-norms (triangular norms) and their mathematical properties have been thoroughly studied. Prominent examples of t-norms are the already mentioned function min (meet lattice operation), the standard product of real numbers and the Lukasiewicz t-norm: $x \otimes y = \max\{x + y - 1, 0\}$.

Definition 83. A binary function $T : [0, 1]^2 \to [0, 1]$ is called a triangular norm (simply a t-norm) in the theory of probabilistic metric spaces, if the following holds for x, y, z:
1. $T(x, y) = T(y, x)$,
2. $x \leq y$ implies $T(x, z) \leq T(y, z)$.
3. $T(x, T(y, z)) = T(T(x, y), z)$,
4. $T(x, 1) = x$.

Continuity of the function T (the previous conditions reduce this requirement to the continuity in either argument) informally expresses the assumption that microscopic changes of the truth degrees of conjuncts should not result in a macroscopic change of the truth degree of their conjunction.

Thus, $([0,1], \otimes, 1)$ forms a commutative monoid if we define $\otimes$ by $x \otimes y = T(x,y)$.

Formulae that always evaluate to 1 are called tautologies with respect to the given left-continuous t-norm $\otimes$ or $\otimes$-tautologies. The set of all $\otimes$-tautologies is called the logic of the t-norm $\otimes$, as these formulae represent the laws of fuzzy logic (determined by the t-norm), which hold (to degree 1) regardless of the truth degrees of atomic formulae. Some formulae are tautologies with respect to a larger class of left-continuous t-norms; the set of such formulae is called the logic of the class. Important t-norm logics are the logics of particular t-norms or classes of t-norms, e. g.:

1. Basic fuzzy logic **BL** is the logic of (the class of) all continuous t-norms,
2. Lukasiewicz logic is the logic of the Lukasiewicz t-norm $x \otimes y = \max\{x + y - 1, 0\}$,
3. Gödel–Dummett logic of the minimum t-norm $x \otimes y = \min\{x, y\}$ was implicit in Gödel's 1932 proof of infinite-valuedness of intuitionistic logic,
4. Product fuzzy logic is the logic of the product t-norm $x \otimes y = x \cdot y$.

Basic fuzzy Logic (or shortly **BL**), the logic of the continuous t-norms is one of the t-norm fuzzy logics. It belongs to the broader class of substructural logics, or logics of residuated lattices. Basic fuzzy logic and its corresponding **BL**-algebras were introduced by Hájek (see [239] and the references given there) with the purpose of formalizing the many-valued semantics induced by the continuous t-norms on the real unitary interval $X = [0,1]$.

Definition 84. A generalized **BL** is an algebra $(X, \bigwedge, \bigvee, \otimes, \to, 1)$ such that:

1. $(X, \bigwedge, \bigvee)$ is a lattice with greatest element 1,
2. $(X, \otimes, 1)$ is an abelian monoid (commutative and associative monoid with the unit element 1), with equations:
3. $x \to x = 1$
4. $(x \otimes y) \to z = x \to (y \to z)$
5. $x \bigwedge y = x \otimes (x \to y)$
6. $(x \to y) \bigvee (y \to x) = 1$

A **BL**-algebra $(X, \bigwedge, \bigvee, \otimes, \to, 1, 0)$ is bounded generalized **BL** algebra with 0 the lower bound.

Hájek showed that a propositional formula is provable in **BL** if and only if it is a tautology in any linearly ordered **BL**-algebra.

Definition 85. An algebra $(X, \bigwedge, \bigvee, \otimes, \to, 1)$ is a commutative residuated lattice if:

1. $(X, \bigwedge, \bigvee)$ is a lattice,
2. $(X, \otimes, 1)$ is an Abelian monoid (commutative and associative monoid with the unit element 1),
3. for $x, y \in X$, $x \otimes y \leq z$ iff $x \leq y \to z$ (the law of residuation).

A commutative residuated lattice $(X, \bigwedge, \bigvee, \otimes, \rightarrow, 1)$ is a $\mathrm{FL}_{\mathrm{ew}}$ algebra if 1 is the greatest element and 0 is least element in the lattice.

The residuum of a left-continuous t-norm can explicitly be defined as $(x \rightarrow y) = \bigvee\{z \mid z \otimes x \leq y\}$. This ensures that the residuum is the pointwise largest function such that for all $x, y \in X$, $x \otimes (x \rightarrow y) \leq y$. The latter can be interpreted as a fuzzy version of the modus ponens rule of inference.

Truth functions of further propositional connectives can be defined by means of the t-norm and its residuum, for instance the residual negation $\sim x = (x \rightarrow 0)$.

Remark. The sequent calculus $\mathrm{FL}_{\mathrm{ew}}$ is obtained from Gentzen's sequent system **LJ** for intuitionistic logic by *deleting the contraction rule* [240] and adding rules for the logical connective *fusion* $\otimes$. The algebraic condition which corresponds to the contraction rule is $x \otimes x \geq x$ (square-increasingness), from which the inequality $x \otimes y \geq x \bigwedge y$ holds. For each $\mathrm{FL}_{\mathrm{ew}}$-algebra M, the monoid operation $\otimes$ is square-increasing in M iff it is equal to the meet operation $\bigwedge$, iff M is Heyting algebra where $x \otimes x = x \bigwedge x = x$. □

In fact, the Gentzen's sequent system for $\mathrm{FL}_{\mathrm{ew}}$ consists of the following two axioms[1] (here $\bot$ denotes the falsity nullary logical constant, such that for each many-valued valuation v, $v(\bot) = 0$, while $\top$ denotes the tautology nullary logic constant such that for all valuations $v(\top) = 1$), from [240][2]:

1. $\phi \vdash \phi$
2. $\Gamma, \bot \vdash \phi, \Gamma \vdash \top$

and the following rules of inference:

$$\frac{\Gamma \vdash \phi, \quad \Gamma_1, \phi \vdash \psi}{\Gamma, \Gamma_1 \vdash \psi} \quad \text{(cut/transitivity rule)}$$

$$\frac{\Gamma, \phi, \psi, \Gamma_1 \vdash \varphi}{\Gamma, \psi, \phi, \Gamma_1 \vdash \varphi} \quad \text{(exchange)}, \qquad \frac{\Gamma \vdash \psi}{\Gamma, \phi \vdash \psi} \quad \text{(weak)}$$

Rules for logical connectives:

$$\frac{\Gamma, \phi \vdash \psi}{\Gamma \vdash \phi \Rightarrow \psi} \quad (\rightarrow\Rightarrow), \qquad \frac{\Gamma \vdash \phi, \quad \Gamma_1, \psi \vdash \varphi}{\Gamma, \phi \Rightarrow \psi \vdash \varphi} \quad (\Rightarrow\rightarrow)$$

$$\frac{\Gamma \vdash \phi}{\Gamma \vdash \phi \vee \psi} \quad (\rightarrow \vee)_1, \qquad \frac{\Gamma \vdash \psi}{\Gamma \vdash \phi \vee \psi} \quad (\rightarrow \vee)_2$$

$$\frac{\Gamma, \phi \vdash \varphi, \quad \Gamma, \psi \vdash \varphi}{\Gamma, \phi \vee \psi \vdash \varphi} \quad (\vee \rightarrow)$$

1 We recall that, for a $\Gamma = \{\phi_1, \ldots, \phi_n\}$, the sequent $\Gamma \vdash \psi$ is an axiom iff it is *valid*, i. e., when for all valuations v, $v^*(\Gamma) =_{\mathrm{def}} v^*(\phi_1) \bigwedge \ldots \bigwedge v^*(\phi_n) \leq v^*(\psi)$.

2 From my opinion, this sequent system is not complete because the "residuation property" between implication and fusion is not provided. Because of that, I explicitly added these two rules in (6.8).

$$\frac{\Gamma \vdash \phi, \quad \Gamma \vdash \psi}{\Gamma \vdash \phi \wedge \psi} \quad (\to \wedge)$$

$$\frac{\Gamma, \phi \vdash \varphi}{\Gamma, \phi \wedge \psi \vdash \varphi} \quad (\wedge \to)_1, \quad \frac{\Gamma, \psi \vdash \varphi}{\Gamma, \phi \wedge \psi \vdash \varphi} \quad (\wedge \to)_2$$

$$\frac{\Gamma \vdash \phi, \quad \Gamma_1 \vdash \psi}{\Gamma, \Gamma_1 \vdash \phi \otimes \psi} \quad (\to \otimes), \quad \frac{\Gamma, \phi, \psi \vdash \varphi}{\Gamma, \phi \otimes \psi \vdash \varphi} \quad (\otimes \to) \tag{6.7}$$

and, added by me, for the "residuation property" between implication and fusion

$$\frac{\phi \otimes \psi \vdash \varphi}{\phi \vdash \psi \Rightarrow \varphi} \quad (\text{res } 1), \quad \frac{\phi \vdash \psi \Rightarrow \varphi}{\phi \otimes \psi \vdash \varphi} \quad (\text{res } 2) \tag{6.8}$$

where (6.7) are the insertion and elimination rules for the t-norm strong conjunction logical connective.

Example 35. Let us show that the monoidal Abelian properties of the fusion $\otimes$ can be obtained from two axioms and rules in (6.7):

1. Commutativity: from axioms and $(\to \otimes)$, $\frac{\phi \vdash \phi, \quad \psi \vdash \psi}{\phi, \psi \vdash \phi \otimes \psi}$. Then by the exchange rule $\phi, \psi \mapsto \psi, \phi$ and with φ equal to $\phi \otimes \psi$, from $(\otimes \to)$, we obtain $\psi \otimes \phi \vdash \phi \otimes \psi$. We derive analogously also $\phi \otimes \psi \vdash \psi \otimes \phi$.
2. Monoidal unit property: From axioms and $(\to \otimes)$, $\frac{\phi \vdash \top, \quad \phi \vdash \phi}{\phi \vdash \phi \otimes \top}$, and from $(\otimes \to)$, $\frac{\phi, \top \vdash \phi}{\phi \otimes \top \vdash \phi}$.
3. Associativity: from axioms and $(\to \otimes)$, $\frac{\psi \vdash \psi, \quad \varphi \vdash \varphi}{\psi, \varphi \vdash \psi \otimes \varphi}$. Then again from $(\to \otimes)$, $\frac{\phi \vdash \phi, \quad \psi, \varphi \vdash \psi \otimes \varphi}{\phi, \psi, \varphi \vdash \phi \otimes (\psi \otimes \phi)}$ and from exchange and $(\otimes \to)$, we obtain $\frac{\varphi, \phi, \psi \vdash \phi \otimes (\psi \otimes \varphi)}{\varphi, \phi \otimes \psi \vdash \phi \otimes (\psi \otimes \varphi)}$. And again from exchange and $(\otimes \to)$, we obtain $\frac{\phi \otimes \psi, \varphi \vdash \phi \otimes (\psi \otimes \varphi)}{(\phi \otimes \psi) \otimes \varphi \vdash \phi \otimes (\psi \otimes \varphi)}$, i. e., $(\phi \otimes \psi) \otimes \varphi \vdash \phi \otimes (\psi \otimes \varphi)$.

Sometimes we call substructural logics over FL_{ew}, or logics without contraction rule, although the contraction rule holds in some of them. The class of logics without the contraction rule contains intermediate logics, BCK-logics, Lukasiewicz's many-valued logics and fuzzy logics (in the sense of [239]).

It has been shown that Hájek's basic logic **BL** is an extension of the substructural logic FL_{ew}, or equivalently, Höhle's monoidal logic. Thus, fuzzy logics can be viewed as a special subclass of substructural logics. On the other hand, their close connections are often overlooked, since these two classes of logics have been motivated by different aims, and so introduced and studied separately. So, we start to give a definition of commutative residuated lattices and then give a definition of FL_{ew}-algebras. MV-algebras, the algebras of Lukasiewicz infinite-valued logic (Lukasiewicz-Tarski logic [241]), form a subvariety of **BL**, which is characterized by the De Morgan equation $\sim\sim x = x$ (see [239]), and hence we can naturally view fuzzy logics and Lukasiewicz"s many-valued logics as extensions of the substructural logic FL_{ew}. The variety of MV-algebras is denoted by $\mathbb{MV}$. Relations between **BL** and Lukasiewicz infinite valued logic are similar to the ones existing between intuitionistic and classical logics [242].

Propositional infinite-valued Lukasiewicz logic can also be axiomatized by adding the following axioms to the axiomatic system of monoidal t-norm logic FL_{ew}.

Divisibility

$(\phi \wedge \psi) \Rightarrow (\phi \otimes (\phi \Rightarrow \psi))$ (see equation (6.10) of the MV-algebras). With this axiom, extending FL_{ew} algebra by equation $x \bigwedge y = x \otimes (x \rightarrow y)$, we obtain fuzzy logic with **BL**-algebra (point 5 in Definition 84).

Double negation

$\neg\neg\phi \Rightarrow \phi$. By adding the equation $\sim\sim x = x$ to **BL**-algebra, we obtain MV-algebra (see poit 4 in Definition 87).

That is, infinite-valued Lukasiewicz logic arises by adding the axiom of double negation to basic t-norm logic **BL**. The axioms of the infinite-valued Lukasiewicz logic are the following:

(A1) $\phi \Rightarrow (\psi \Rightarrow \phi)$

(A2) $(\phi \Rightarrow \psi) \Rightarrow ((\psi \Rightarrow \varphi) \Rightarrow (\phi \Rightarrow \varphi))$

(A3) $((\phi \Rightarrow \psi) \Rightarrow \psi) \Rightarrow ((\psi \Rightarrow \phi) \Rightarrow \phi)$

(A4) $(\neg\phi \Rightarrow \neg\psi) \Rightarrow (\psi \Rightarrow \phi)$

and with modus ponens as the only primitive rule: $\phi, \phi \Rightarrow \psi \vdash \psi$.

Thus, Lukasiewicz''s infinite-valued logic is commonly defined as the set of formulae that take the value 1 under all evaluations in the Lukasiewicz algebra on the unit real interval. In the literature, a deductive system axiomatized in a Hilbert style was associated to it, and was later shown to be semantically defined from Lukasiewicz algebra by using a truth-preserving scheme. However, there exists no Gentzen calculus fully adequate for it.

Here, instead, we use the framework of abstract algebraic logic to study a different deductive system, which uses the aforementioned algebra under a scheme of "preservation of degrees of truth" used in this book and provided in Section 5.1 by Definition 57. This deductive system is algebraizable, nonself-extensional and does not satisfy the deduction theorem [243]. The resulting deductive system is defined in a natural way by using the lattice filters of Wajsberg algebras $(X, \rightarrow, \sim)$ (equivalent to **DL** algebras by defining all other operations as presented below, and by adding the equation $\sim\sim x = x$) and also by using a structural Gentzen calculus, which is shown to be fully adequate for it.

Definition 86. Wajsberg algebras $(X, \rightarrow, \sim)$ are defined by the following set of equations:

(W1) $y = (x \rightarrow x) \rightarrow y$

(W2) $x \rightarrow x = (x \rightarrow y) \rightarrow ((y \rightarrow x) \rightarrow (x \rightarrow z))$

(W3) $(x \rightarrow y) \rightarrow y = (y \rightarrow x) \rightarrow x$

(W4) $(x \rightarrow x) = (\sim x \rightarrow \sim y) \rightarrow (y \rightarrow x)$

These algebras are polynomially equivalent [243] to Wajsberg algebras as originally defined by Rodriguez in [244]. The variety of all Wajsberg algebras, denoted by **W**, is generated by the lattice on the unit real interval $(X, \bigwedge, \bigvee)$ with the well-known Lukasiewicz operations $\sim x = 1 - x$ and $x \rightarrow y = \min\{1, 1 - x + y\}$.

This logic is an interesting example for the general theory: it is self-extensional, non-protoalgebraic, and satisfies a "graded" deduction theorem. Moreover, the Gentzen system is algebraizable following Blok and Pigozzi's theory in [245]. The first mentioned deductive system turns out to be the extension of the second by the rule of modus ponens.

By considering the logical language $\mathcal{L}$ with only two connectives $(\neg, \Rightarrow)$ of type $(1, 2)$ with also defined connectives $\wedge, \vee, \otimes$ and $\oplus$ given by
$\phi \vee \psi$ defined by $(\phi \Rightarrow \psi) \Rightarrow \psi$
$\phi \wedge \psi$ defined by $\neg(\neg\phi \vee \neg\psi)$
$\phi \otimes \psi$ defined by $\neg(\phi \Rightarrow \neg\psi)$
$\phi \oplus \psi$ defined by $\neg\phi \Rightarrow \psi$

the Gentzen's sequent system $\mathfrak{G}_\infty$ for Lukasiewicz's logic [243], consists of the following axioms and rules:
(1) $\phi \vdash \phi$
(2) $\vdash \phi \Rightarrow \phi$
(3) $\phi \Rightarrow (\psi \Rightarrow \varphi) \vdash (\psi \Rightarrow \phi) \Rightarrow \varphi$

and the following rules of inference:

$$\frac{\Gamma \vdash \phi, \quad \Gamma_1, \phi \vdash \psi}{\Gamma, \Gamma_1 \vdash \psi}\ (\text{cut}) \qquad \frac{\Gamma \vdash \varphi}{\Gamma, \phi \vdash \varphi}\ (\text{weak})$$

rules for logical connectives:

$$\frac{\Gamma \vdash \phi}{\Gamma \vdash \phi \vee \psi}\ (\rightarrow \vee)_1, \qquad \frac{\Gamma \vdash \psi}{\Gamma \vdash \phi \vee \psi}\ (\rightarrow \vee)_2 \qquad \frac{\Gamma, \phi \vdash \varphi, \quad \Gamma, \psi \vdash \varphi}{\Gamma, \phi \vee \psi \vdash \varphi}\ (\vee \rightarrow)$$

$$\frac{\Gamma \vdash \phi, \quad \Gamma \vdash \psi}{\Gamma \vdash \phi \wedge \psi}\ (\rightarrow \wedge) \qquad \frac{\Gamma, \phi \vdash \varphi}{\Gamma, \phi \wedge \psi \vdash \varphi}\ (\wedge \rightarrow)_1, \qquad \frac{\Gamma, \psi \vdash \varphi}{\Gamma, \phi \wedge \psi \vdash \varphi}\ (\wedge \rightarrow)_2$$

$$\frac{\phi \vdash \psi}{\neg\psi \vdash \neg\phi}\ (\neg)$$

$$\frac{\Gamma \vdash \phi}{\Gamma \vdash \neg\neg\phi}\ (\rightarrow \neg\neg), \qquad \frac{\Gamma, \phi \vdash \varphi}{\Gamma, \neg\neg\phi \vdash \varphi}\ (\neg\neg \rightarrow),$$

residuation property rules,[3]

3 They are identical to that given by (6.8), and from the fact that $\otimes$ is a defined (derived) operation, we simply substituted $\phi \otimes \psi$ by $\neg(\phi \Rightarrow \neg\psi)$, without changing in any way the Gentzen's sequent sys-

$$\frac{\neg(\phi \Rightarrow \neg\psi) \vdash \varphi}{\phi \vdash \psi \Rightarrow \varphi} \quad (\text{res 1}), \qquad \frac{\phi \vdash \psi \Rightarrow \varphi}{\neg(\phi \Rightarrow \neg\psi) \vdash \varphi} \quad (\text{res 2}) \tag{6.9}$$

Notice that it is not necessary to put the structural rules of exchange and contraction explicitly, because the left-hand side of our sequents are finite sets of formulae. Thus, this Gentzen system satisfies all structural rules. Notice also that from defined connectives, both $(\wedge, \vee, \neg)$ and $(\otimes, \oplus, \neg)$ satisfy De Morgan laws.

Example 36. We obtain the following deductions:

1. By weakening the axiom (2) in $\phi \vdash \phi \Rightarrow \phi$, from (res2), we obtain $\phi \otimes \phi \vdash \phi$, i. e., $\phi \otimes \phi \preceq \phi$ (for all valuations $v^*(\phi \otimes \phi) \leq v^*(\phi)$ from Definition 57 in Section 5.1, or algebraically $x \otimes x \leq x$ for all $x \in X = [0,1]$), that is the result that fusion is square-decreasing in Lukasiewicz logic.
2. The rule $(\neg)$ means algebraically that if $x \leq y$ then $\sim y \leq \sim x$, while from axiom (1) and two rules $(\rightarrow \neg\neg)$ and $(\neg\neg \rightarrow)$, we obtain $\phi \vdash \neg\neg\phi$ and $\neg\neg\phi \vdash \phi$, this the idempotent negation, algebraically $\sim\sim x = x$ for all $x \in X$.
3. By rule (weak) for every ψ, it holds from axiom (2), $\psi \vdash \phi \Rightarrow \phi$, so for all valuations $v^*(\phi \Rightarrow \phi) = 1$, or algebraically $x \rightarrow x = 1$ for each $x \in X$.

However, if we take the negation $\sim$ and the monoid $(X, \oplus, 0)$ with intensional disjunction (fission) as two basic binary operations from which derived operations are fusion $x \otimes y =_{\text{def}} \sim(\sim x \oplus \sim y)$ and implication $x \rightarrow y =_{\text{def}} \sim x \oplus y$, such that the join and meet lattice operations can be derived by the following two equations:

$$x \bigvee y = (x \otimes \sim y) \oplus y, \quad x \bigwedge y = x \otimes (x \rightarrow y), \tag{6.10}$$

and hence the algebraic structure $(X, \oplus, \sim, 0)$ represents completely the algebraic structure of infinite-valued Lukasiewicz logic (and its dual algebraic structure $(X, \otimes, \sim, 1)$ as well). That is, we obtain an MV-algebra.

Definition 87. An MV-algebra is an algebraic structure $(X, \oplus, \sim, 0)$, which satisfies the following equations for each $x, y, z \in X$:

1. $x \oplus (y \oplus z) = (x \oplus y) \oplus z$,
2. $x \oplus 0 = x$,
3. $x \oplus y = y \oplus x$,
4. $\sim\sim x = x$,
5. $x \oplus \sim 0 = \sim 0$,
6. $\sim(\sim x \oplus y) \oplus y = \sim(\sim y \oplus x) \oplus x$.

---

tem $\mathfrak{G}_\infty$ for Lukasiewicz's logic [243]. In this way, we can change the semantics of fusion $\otimes$ without elimination of any axiom or inference rule from this given by [243], but only to provide some new axioms/rules for the introduction of these different fusion operations *nonderivable* more from the implication and negation operations of Lukasiewicz's algebra/logic.

A *standard MV-algebra* with operations $x \oplus y = \min\{1, x + y\}$ and $\sim x = 1 - x$, in mathematical fuzzy logic, forms the standard real-valued semantics of Lukasiewicz logic.

If we take out the last two equations (5) and (6), then we obtain a generalized De Morgan algebra.

By virtue of the first three axioms, $(X, \oplus, 0)$ is an Abelian commutative monoid. Being defined by equations, MV-algebras form a variety of algebras. The variety of MV-algebras is a subvariety of the variety of **BL**-algebras, which is characterized by equation $\sim\sim x = x$, and contains all Boolean algebras. An MV-algebra can equivalently be defined (Hájek [239]) as a prelinear commutative bounded integral residuated lattice $(X, \bigwedge, \bigvee, \otimes, \rightarrow, 0, 1)$ satisfying the additional equation $x \bigvee y = (x \rightarrow y) \rightarrow y$ (the first equation in (6.10)).

6.1.2 Weakening of fission and fusion operations of Lukasiewicz algebra

We have explained that the relations between residuated-based **BL** and Lukasiewicz infinite valued logic similar to the ones existing between intuitionistic and classical logics [242]. Thus, the fact that in Lukasiewics'z logic the fusion $\otimes$ is a t-norm in our weakening of it and it will not be more t-norm, but the subalgebra $(X, \oplus, \otimes, \sim)$ will still remain a De Morgan algebra. Consequently, for the wider family of relevant Lukasievicz-based logics in the first position come their classical logic property based on De Morgan subalgebras. In order to underline this more general point of view, the relationship with **BL** algebras is not fundamental, but the classical logic properties based on the two basic De Morgan subalgebras of the Lukasiewicz's algebras.

The unique two equations of the De Morgan algebras are that they fix the semantics of negation $\sim$ in the following particular way:
1. $\sim\sim x = x$;
2. DeMorgan laws between conjunction and disjunction, mediated by such a negation operation, $\sim (x \wedge y) =\sim x \vee \sim y$, so that the minimal requirement for the conjunction and negation operations is to be mutually *commutative*.

In the De Morgan algebras, the law of excluded middle $\sim x \vee x = 1$ and the law of noncontradiction $\neg x \wedge x = 0$ do not always hold (in fact for the meet $\bigwedge$ and join $\bigvee$ connectives in Lukasiewicz's algebra they do not hold, while for the fusion $\otimes$ and $\oplus$ intensional connectives they hold).

De Morgan algebras are important for the study of the mathematical aspects of fuzzy logic. The standard fuzzy algebra is an example of a De Morgan algebra [246, 247] where the laws of excluded middle and noncontradiction do not hold. De Morgan algebras are not the only plausible way to generalize Boolean algebras. Another way is to keep $\sim x \wedge x = 0$ (i. e., the law of noncontradiction) but to drop the law of the excluded middle and the law of double negation. This approach (called semicomplementation) is well-defined even for a (meet) semilattice; if the set of semicomplements has a greatest element, it is usually called a pseudo-complement. If the pseudo-complement satisfies the law of the excluded middle, the resulting algebra is also Boolean. However, if only the weaker law $\sim x \vee \sim\sim x = 1$ is required, this results in Stone algebras. More generally, both De Morgan and Stone algebras are proper subclasses of Ockham algebras [248].

De Morgan algebras (called quasi-Boolean algebras as well), which are (not necessarily bounded) distributive lattices with a De Morgan negation, has been introduced by Bialynicki-Birula and Rasiowa [249]. This type of algebras was investigated by Moisil [250] under the term De Morgan lattices, and by Kalman under the term distributive i-lattices (cf. [251], pp. 44–48). They have been widely discussed in the literature on universal algebra [251–253], relevance logic [254], Belnap's four-valued logic and the logic of bilattices [255, 256], rough set theory and prerough algebras [257], etc., from algebraic and logical perspectives.

The connection between Belnap's 4-valued logic and the class of De Morgan lattices (or algebras)was also recognized from the very beginning, and has been shown that the class of De Morgan lattices is the algebraic counterpart of Belnap's logic [258]. The Belnap's logic is in fact considered in this book in Section 6.3 for the application of the Intensional FOL for the important application of a P2P data integration system in order to manage mutually-inconsistent and incomplete information as well.

Based on this classical logic point of view, founded on the De Morgan algebras, it is easy to verify that we can define the underlying algebra of infinite-valued Lukasiewicz logic as follows.

Definition 88 (Infinite-valued Lukasiewicz algebra operations). It is defined on the lattice of reals $X = [0,1]$ with $\bigwedge$ and $\bigvee$ meet and join operations in the lattice $(X, \leq)$, relatively, such that for $x, y \in X$, $x \bigvee y = \min\{x, y\}$, $x \bigvee y = \max\{x, y\}$, and:

1. Implication

$$x \rightarrow y =_{\mathrm{def}} \min\{1, 1 - x + y\} \tag{6.11}$$

2. De Morgan subalgebra $(X, \bigwedge, \bigvee, \sim)$ with negation

$$\sim x =_{\mathrm{def}} 1 - x \tag{6.12}$$

so that $\sim x = x \rightarrow 0$, with two *derived* operations:

[a]. Intensional disjunction (fission) of the Abelian monoid $(X, \oplus, 0)$, defined classically

$$x \oplus y =_{\mathrm{def}} \sim x \rightarrow y \tag{6.13}$$

[**b**]. Intensional conjunction (fusion) ⊕, which defines its second De Morgan subalgebra $(X, \otimes, \oplus, \sim)$, i. e.,

$$x \otimes y =\sim (\sim x \oplus \sim y) =\sim (x \rightarrow \neg y) \tag{6.14}$$

We will denote by $\mathbf{A} = (X, \leq, \bigwedge, \bigvee, \rightarrow, 0, 1)$ the "minimal" Lukasiewicz algebra, by considering $\sim$, $\oplus$ and $\otimes$ derived algebraic operators. Analogously, we denote by $\mathcal{A}_L = (\mathcal{L}, \wedge, \vee, \Rightarrow, \top, \bot)$ where $\top$ is "tautology" and $\bot$ the 'contradiction," such that for any given valuation $v : \text{Var} \rightarrow X$, $v(\top) = 1$ and $v(\bot) = 0$. Such a valuation can be uniquely extended to all formulae in $\mathcal{L}$ to homomorphism from the syntax algebra $\mathcal{A}_L$ into **A**:

$$v^* : (\mathcal{L}, \wedge, \vee, \Rightarrow, \top, \bot) \rightarrow \left(X, \leq, \bigwedge, \bigvee, \rightarrow, 0, 1\right) \tag{6.15}$$

An advantage of such presentation of Lukasiewicz's algebra is that its basic lattice-based operations are defined as De Morgan subalgebra in points 1 and 2, while the other two "nonstandard" operations fission and fusion, derived from the two basic operations, define a second De Morgan subalgebra, such that we obtain well-known operations: from [**a**] the fission ⊕, and from [**b**] the fusion ⊗:

$$x \oplus y = \min\{1, x + y\}$$
$$x \otimes y = \max\{0, x + y - 1\}$$

Consequently, from a particular definition of fission and fusion operations, given by [**a**] and [**b**], we obtain the famous residuation property

$$x \rightarrow y = \bigvee\{z \mid x \otimes z \leq y\},$$

and hence it is satisfied for the law of residuation in point 3 of Definition 85, so that ⊗ is really a t-norm (satisfies Definition 83), and hence its subalgebra $(X, \bigwedge, \bigvee, \otimes, \rightarrow, 1)$ is a FL_{ew} algebra.

As anticipated, we would like to generate a *relevant* Lukasiewicz logic, by the weakening of the intensional disjunction and conjunctions ⊕ and ⊗ in the way that they preserve their De Morgan properties, but are not more definable from the basic two connectives, negation and implication. In this way, such relevant Lukasiewicz algebras will be separated from the Hájek's residuated lattices, and will generate a new class of algebras.

This can be done by elimination of the Abelian monoidal properties of fission and fusion operations, and hence also the law of residuation between fusion and implication is specified in Definition 85. By this proposed weakening, only the commutative property for the fission and fusion operations will be preserved and the new relevant Lukasiewicz's logic will not be more a t-norm logic. Consequently, we can define a class of bi-Morgan algebras $\mathbf{BDM} = (X, \bigvee, \bigwedge, \sim, \rightarrow, \oplus, \otimes, 0, 1)$ that cover a number of preexistent algebras from classical propositional to Lukasievicz–Tarski and new *relevant* Lukasiewicz algebras.

Definition 89 (Bi-Morgan algebras). We define a class of bi-Morgan algebras **BDM** = $(X, \bigvee, \bigwedge, \sim, \rightarrow, \oplus, \otimes, 0, 1)$ over a bounded lattice $(X, \bigvee, \bigwedge, 0, 1)$ with bottom and top elements 0 and 1, relatively, such that for each $x, y \in X$:

1. Implication operation $\rightarrow$, antitonic for the first and monotonic for the second argument, satisfies the classical propositional implication in the sublattice $\mathbf{2} = \{0, 1\} \subseteq X$, conservatively extended to all $x, y \in X$ by, if $x \leq y$ then $x \rightarrow y = 1$.
2. $(X, \bigvee, \bigwedge, \sim)$ is the (extensional) De Morgan algebra with the negation operation $\sim$; i. e., satisfying $x \bigwedge y =\sim (\sim x \bigvee \sim y)$ and $\sim\sim x = x$.
3. Let $\oplus$ be the fission (intensional disjunction), then $(X, \oplus, \otimes, \sim)$ is an intensional De Morgan algebra such that the fusion (intensional conjunction) is defined by $x \otimes y =_{\text{def}} \sim (\sim x \oplus \sim y)$. We have two alternative cases.
   3.1 Lukasiewicz's relevance logic: with the square-increasing property for fission for each $x \in X$, $x \oplus x \geq x$, and the square-decreasing property for fusion, $x \otimes x \leq x$, i. e., by equations

$$x \rightarrow (x \oplus x) = 1 \quad \text{and} \quad (x \otimes x) \rightarrow x = 1 \tag{6.16}$$

   3.2 Orlov's relevance logic (see (6.2) and (6.4)): with the square-decreasing property for fission for each $x \in X$, $x \oplus x \leq x$, and the square-increasing property for fusion, $x \otimes x \geq x$, i. e., by equations

$$(x \oplus x) \rightarrow x = 1 \quad \text{and} \quad x \rightarrow (x \otimes x) = 1 \tag{6.17}$$

Thus, **BDM**-algebras are fundamentally composed by an extensional and an intensional De Morgan subalgebras. The relationship between intensional De Morgan subalgebra with the remaining part of the algebra is provided by the common negation operation of these two De Morgan subalgebras and by the relationship of implication and intensional connectives given by two equations (6.16) and (6.17).

Example 37. Let us consider the following examples of **BDM**-algebras:

1. Standard propositional logic: for $X = \mathbf{2}$, from point 1, the implication is that of standard propositional logic, and negation defined by $\sim x =_{\text{def}} x \rightarrow 0$. In this case, the intensional operations coincide with extensional (lattice) operations, and two De Morgan subalgebras are identical with $x \oplus x = x \otimes x = x$ for (6.16) and (6.17).
2. Lukasiewicz–Tarski infinitary logic: $X = [0, 1]$ and the rest is provided in Definition 88. Note that in this case the intensional connectives, fission and fusion, are *derivable* operations from implication and negation operations. It is easy to verify that (6.16) is satisfied as well.

3. Relevant Lukasiewicz logics: In this case, the implication and negation operations are that provided by points 1 and 2 of Definition 88. However, in this case the intensional connectives, fission and fusion, *are not* more derivable from lattice connectives, implication and negation. Thus, they can be weakened by reducing some of their properties that they have in original Lukasiewicz logic, and this will be considered in what follows.

In effect, we can see that the original fission operation $\oplus$, such that $x \oplus y = \min\{1, x + y\}$, of the original Lukasiewicz's algebra in Definition 88 is given as a composition of the arithmetic operation $+ : X^2 \to [0, 2]$, which generates Abelian monoid $(X^2, +, 0)$ commutative and associative as well, and a unary *monotone and linear* function $f : [0, 2] \to X$, by $\oplus = f \circ +$, with

$$f = 1 \bigwedge \_ : [0, 2] \to X \tag{6.18}$$

where $\bigwedge$ is the meet operation of the lattice of reals $([0, 2], \leq)$. Note that this characteristic function $f(z)$, such that $f(0) = 0$, $f(2) = 1$ and $f(z) \geq \frac{z}{2}$, used in original Lukasiewicz's algebra is a continuous linear function with $f(z) = z$ if $z \leq 1$; 1 otherwise. So, its first derivative is antitonic but *not continuous*, in the value $z = 1$.

Let us now define a class of functions that can be used for the relevant Lukasiewicz algebras, that preserve the properties of $f(z)$ above, but their first derivative is continuous as well

Definition 90. We define the following class $\mathbf{F}_{dm}$ of monotone and continuous nonlinear functions $f_L, f_O : [0, 2] \to X$, which first derivatives are continuous as well, such that satisfy the following requirements:
(**a**) Min and max values are $f_L(0) = f_O(0) = 0$, $f_L(2) = f_O(2) = 1$;
(**b**) Lukasiewicz's function $f_L(z) \geq \frac{z}{2}$ for all $z \in (0, 2)$ and its derivative is antitonic. By f_S, we denote the subset of *strong* Lukasiewicz's functions that satisfy also: $f_S(1) = 1$, and for its derivative $f'_S(z) = \frac{df_S}{dz}$, $f'_S(0) \geq 1$ and $f'_S(1) = 0$ as well.
(**c**) Orlov's function $f_O(z) \leq \frac{z}{2}$ for all $z \in (0, 2)$ and its derivative is monotonic.

Now we can define the first class of relevant De Morgan algebras with square-decreasing intensional conjunction (Case 3.1 in Definition 89) for the relevant Lukasiewicz's logics (we will denote these new weakened fusion and fission operations by $\widetilde{\wedge}$ and $\widetilde{\vee}$ instead of nonweakened $\otimes$ and $\oplus$, relatively).

Corollary 23 (Fusion and fission for relevant Lukasiewicz's logic). *If we define the weakening of the t-norm $\otimes$ of the Lukasiewicz–Tarski logic such that for any $x, y \in X$, and a nonlinear continuous function $f_L \in \mathbf{F}_{dm}$ specified by points (**a**) and (**b**) in Definition* 90,

$$x \widetilde{\wedge} y =_{\text{def}} 1 - f_L(2 - x - y), \tag{6.19}$$

and hence with the intensional disjunction $\widetilde{\vee}$, derived by De Morgan's law, $x \widetilde{\vee} y =_{def} \sim (\sim x \widetilde{\wedge} \sim y)$,

$$x \widetilde{\vee} y = f_L \circ +(x,y) = f_L(x+y) \tag{6.20}$$

They satisfy the bi-Morgan algebras in Definition 89 *with point* 3.1, *such that for these weakened fusion and fission operations:*
1. *Will not be satisfied the associativity property;*
2. *Top value* 1 *will not be the unit for the fusion operation, i. e., $x \widetilde{\wedge} 1 \neq x$ and* 0 *will not be the unit for the fission operation, i. e., $x \widetilde{\vee} 0 \neq x$.*

Consequently, the weakened fusion operation is not a t-norm, and the following properties are satisfied: $x \widetilde{\wedge} y \leq x \bigvee y$, $x \widetilde{\wedge} y \leq x \widetilde{\vee} y$, i. e., the following equations in the bi-Morgan ***BDM****-algebra are satisfied:*

$$(x \widetilde{\wedge} y) \rightarrow \left(x \bigvee y\right) = 1 \quad \textit{and} \quad (x \widetilde{\wedge} y) \rightarrow (x \widetilde{\vee} y) = 1 \tag{6.21}$$

However, $x \widetilde{\wedge} y \leq x \bigwedge y$ and $x \widetilde{\vee} y \geq x \bigvee y$ are not generally valid (they are valid only for $x = y$ as specified in (6.16)*).*

If in (6.19) *and* (6.20) *we substitute f_L with a strong Lukasiewicz's function f_S, then we obtain the strong fusion and fission operations (as that used in original Lukasiewicz's algebra), such that for each $x, y \in X$,*

$$x \widetilde{\wedge} y \leq x \bigwedge y \leq x \bigvee y \leq x \widetilde{\vee} y$$

so that, instead of equations (6.21)*, we obtain stronger equations:*

$$(x \widetilde{\wedge} y) \rightarrow \left(x \bigwedge y\right) = 1 \quad \textit{and} \quad \left(x \bigvee y\right) \rightarrow (x \widetilde{\vee} y) = 1 \tag{6.22}$$

Proof. It is easy to verify that the first two t-norm properties in Definition 83 of derived intensional conjunction $\widetilde{\wedge}$ are preserved, from the fact that $f_L(2-x-y)$ is commutative $(-x-y = -y-x)$ and is monotone as well. We have that, from the fact that f_L is a non-linear function, $(x \widetilde{\wedge} y) \widetilde{\wedge} z = 1 - f_L(1 + f(2-x-y) - z) \neq 1 - f_L(1 - x - f_L(2-y-z)) = x \widetilde{\wedge} (y \widetilde{\wedge} z)$, and hence the point 1 is satisfied.

Point 2: it will be shown by contradiction. We have that there exists $x \in X$ such that $x \widetilde{\wedge} 1 = 1 - f_L(1-x) \neq x$. Suppose that $1 - f_L(1-x) = x$, i. e., for $z = 1-x$, $f_L(z) = z$ for all $0 \leq z \leq 1$. But in that case for $z = 1$ we would have $f_L(1) = 1$, and hence for all other $1 < z \geq 2$ from the monotonic property we must have that for this interval $f_L(z) = 1$ (maximum value of this function). Let $0 < z_0 \leq 1$ (from (**a**), $f_L(0) = 0$) be the first point in which this monotone and continuous function reaches the maximal value 1, and hence in this point will not be satisfied the continuity of the first derivative of this function in contradiction with the requirements.

Square-decreasing property (6.16): let us suppose that there exists $x \in X$ such that $x \otimes x = 1 - f_L(2 - 2x) > x$. But, if we substitute $2 - 2x$ by z, then we obtain $f_L(z) < \frac{z}{2}$, which is in contrast with requirement (**b**) for the Lukasiewicz's functions.

Consequently, the semantics of intensional conjunction (fusion) is well-defined. So, also the definition of the intensional disjunction (fission) $\widetilde{\vee}$ by the De Morgan law is correct and we obtain from (6.19), for any $x, y \in X$, $x \widetilde{\vee} y = f_L(x + y)$, which is square-increasing, i. e., $x \widetilde{\vee} x = f_L(2x) \geq x$. In fact, by substitution $z = 2x$, we obtain $f_L(z) \geq \frac{z}{2}$, as it was specified by requirement (**b**) in Definition 90.

Let us show (6.21): in fact, $x \widetilde{\wedge} y = 1 - f_L(2 - x - y) \leq 1 - \frac{2-x-y}{2} = \frac{x+y}{2} \leq \max\{x, y\} = x \bigvee y$. To show that $x \widetilde{\wedge} y \leq x \widetilde{\vee} y$, we have to show that $1 - f_L(2-x-y) \leq f_L(x+y)$, i. e., that $f_L(x+y) + f_L(2-x-y) \geq 1$, which is true because $f_L(x+y) \geq \frac{x+y}{2}$ and $f_L(2-x-y) \geq \frac{2-x-y}{2}$. So, we have from (**b**) in Definition 90 that

$$x \widetilde{\wedge} y \leq \frac{x+y}{2} \leq x \widetilde{\vee} y \tag{6.23}$$

and hence, for $x = y$, we obtain square-increasing and square decreasing properties of the fission and fusion, respectively, with $0 = 0 \widetilde{\wedge} 0 \leq 0 \widetilde{\vee} 0 = 0$ and $1 = 1 \widetilde{\wedge} 1 \leq 1 \widetilde{\vee} 1 = 1$, all result obtained from original Lukasiewicz's logic.

Let us show that if we use the strong Lukasiewicz's functions $f_S(z) : [0, 2] \to X$ instead of f_L, then stronger equations (6.22) are valid. Let us show for the second, an suppose that $x \geq y$. Then, from the fact that f_S is monotonic with first derivative at $z = 0$ greater than one and decreasing we have that in the interval $[0, 1]$, $f_S(z) \geq z$, so that $x \widetilde{\vee} y = f_S(x + y) \geq x + y \geq x = x \bigvee y$. Note that in the rest of interval $z \in [1, 2]$, $f_S(z) = 1$, and that in $z = 1$ also the first derivative of $f_S(z)$ is continuous as required generally for all functions in $\mathbf{F}_{dm}$ by Definition 90. That is, the fission operation is a strong disjunction. Analogously, it can be shown that in this case the fusion operation is a strong conjunction. □

Consequently, the De Morgan algebra with intensional conjunction and disjunction, obtained from Lukasiewicz's functions f_L or stronger f_S, $\mathbf{DM} = (X, \leq, \widetilde{\wedge}, \widetilde{\vee}, \sim)$ is well-defined, such that for any $x \in X$,

$$\sim x = 1 - x, \quad x \widetilde{\wedge} x \leq x, \quad x \widetilde{\vee} x \geq x \tag{6.24}$$

Notice that our weakening preserves square-decreasingness for Lukasiewicz's t-norm conjunction $\otimes$, but does not preserve its associative property and its monoidal property ($x \otimes 1 = x$), and hence *it is not* satisfied the monoidal property of intensional conjunction in point 1 of Definition 88 for the infinite-valued Lukasiewicz logic (while all other points from 2 to 4 are satisfied).

Consequently, the logic obtained by replacing Lukasiewicz's t-norm conjunction and disjunction with these new intensional connectives $\widetilde{\wedge}$ and $\widetilde{\vee}$ *deduces less sentences* than the original Lukasiewicz's infinite-valued logic.

Example 38. In this example, we will consider the Lukasiewicz's functions f_L and L_S, used to define the new fusion as a fission operation. First, we will consider the strong functions f_S from which we obtain the strong conjunction $\widetilde{\wedge}$ and disjunction operations $\widetilde{\vee}$ of intensional De Morgan algebras $(X, \widetilde{\vee}, \widetilde{\wedge}, \sim)$, and after that, their weakened versions that use the functions f_L:

1. Strong fusion and fission: Let us consider the family of functions, for each $\alpha = \frac{m}{n}$, where $m \leq n$ are positive integers:

$$f_S(z) =_{\text{def}} \begin{cases} (2z - z^2)^{\alpha}, & \text{if } z \in X \\ 1, & \text{if } z \in [1, 2] \end{cases} \tag{6.25}$$

   with first derivative $f_S'(z) = 2\alpha(1 - z)/(2z - z^2)^{1-\alpha}$ so that $f_S'(0) \geq 1$ and $f_S'(1) = 0$, as required. It is easy to show that $f_S(z) \geq z$ for $z \in [0, 1]$, and that with decreasing of α we obtain stronger intensional conjunction and disjunction. From the fact that in the interval $z \in X$, $1 \geq z^{\alpha-1}$, we obtain $2 \geq z + z^{\alpha-1}$, i. e., $(2z - z^2)^{\alpha} \geq z$, and hence it holds that for each $x, y \in X$, and $z = x + y \leq 1$, $x \widetilde{\vee} y = f_S(z) \geq z = x + y \geq x \bigvee y$. Otherwise, if $x + y > 1$, then $f_S(x + y) = 1 \geq x \bigvee y$. Thus, $\widetilde{\vee}$ is a strong intensional disjunction and square-increasing (analogously we obtain that $x \widetilde{\wedge} y \leq x \bigwedge y$, and hence $\widetilde{\wedge}$ is a strong intensional conjunction and square-decreasing).
2. Nonstrong fusion and fission: in this case, we are using the functions f_L, and we can consider two extremal cases:

   2.1 The family of functions for quasistrong fusion/fission:

$$f_L(z) = \sqrt[n]{\sin\left(\frac{\pi}{4}z\right)}, \quad n = 1, 2, 3, \ldots \tag{6.26}$$

   with the strongest cases when $n \gg 1$ (extremely nonlinear functions). These functions are monotone in the interval [0.2] and their first derivative is antitonic and continuous as well, with $f_L(0) = 0$, $f_L(2) = 1$ and $f_L(z) \geq \frac{z}{2}$ for all $z \in (0, 2)$, so that they satisfy all requirements in Definition 90. Hence, for any small positive value $\delta \ll 1$, there exist enough big value $n \gg 1$, such that for a function (6.26), we obtain that practically $f_L(z) \approx 0$ if $z \leq \delta$; 1 otherwise. So, we obtain $x \widetilde{\vee} y =\sim (x \widetilde{\wedge} y) \geq x \bigvee y$ if $\delta < x + y < 2 -$ delta; $x \widetilde{\wedge} y$ otherwise. That is, almost always we obtain the strong fusion and fission operations (6.22), when $x \widetilde{\wedge} y \leq x \bigwedge y \leq x \bigvee y \leq x \widetilde{\vee} y$ (only for infinitesimal intervals $0 \leq x + y \leq \delta$ and $2 - \delta \leq x + y \leq 2$ this strong intensional connectives property does not hold).

   2.2 The family of quasilinear functions for weakest fusion/fission for infinitely-small positive values δ:

$$f_L(z) = \frac{z}{2} + \mathcal{O}(z), \quad \mathcal{O}(z) < \delta \tag{6.27}$$

with infinitesimal monotonic functions $\mathcal{O}(z)$ such that $\mathcal{O}(0) = \mathcal{O}(2) = 0$. Thus, these are the smallest Lukasiewicz's function satisfying all requirements in Definition 90. In this case, we obtain that $x \tilde{\wedge} y \approx \frac{x+y}{2} \approx x \tilde{\vee} y$, and almost always the fusion and fission connectives are very weak, i. e., $x \bigwedge y \leq x \tilde{\wedge} y$ but $\tilde{\wedge}$ is still square-decreasing ($x \bigwedge x \geq x \tilde{\wedge} x = x$) and $x \tilde{\vee} y \leq x \bigvee y$, but still square-increasing ($x \tilde{\vee} x \geq x \bigvee x = x$).

Consequently, we obtained a different relevant logic from the Orlov's logic where the conjunction is square-increasing, and for which we cannot use the Kripke-style semantics and Dunn's Gaggle theory (as explained at the end of Section 6.1). The relevant Orlov's logic is obtained by defining fission by $x \tilde{\vee} y =_{\mathrm{def}} f_O \circ +(x, y) = f_o(x + y)$ and fusion derived by the De Morgan law.

The Gentzen's sequent system $\mathfrak{G}_\infty^{\circledS}$ for the relevant Lukasiezic's logic, obtained by the weakening of fusion and fission intensional connectives by using strong Lukasiewicz's functions $f_S(z) : [0, 2] \to X$, which satisfied the equations (6.22), must be obtained by an extension of the original Gentzen's system $\mathfrak{G}_\infty$ provided previously (where we eliminated the t-norm fusion $\otimes$ in (6.9) because it is derived operation from implication and negation operations of the original Lukasiewicz's algebra). We need new axioms and rules for these new fusion/fission logical connectives, which are now completely independent of the rest of logical connectives ($\vee, \wedge$ and implication $\Rightarrow$), and only have the relationship with negation $\neg$ in their inter-De Morgan law relationship. Thus, in order to consider these new axioms and rules of inference, it is useful to analyze the Gentzen's system for the sequent calculus for FL_{em}, especially for the rules (6.7) and (6.8) for the fusion t-norm $\otimes$, and Example 35 where we have shown how the commutative and associative properties of the fusion $\otimes$ are direct consequences of the rules for introduction and elimination of fusion in (6.7). If we eliminate one of these two rules, then it would not be possible to obtain the commutativity and associativity of $\otimes$.

In effect, this is just the case, because the rule for the introduction of $\otimes$ is not more valid for its substitution by weaker connective $\tilde{\wedge}$. From the truth-preserving semantics of satisfaction of a sequent, in Definition 54 in Section 5.1, there exists a valuation v, which satisfies the upper sequents of the rule (6.7), $v^*(\Gamma) \leq v^*(\phi)$ and $v^*(\Gamma_1) \leq v^*(\psi)$, but not $v^*(\Gamma, \Gamma_1) = v^*(\Gamma) \bigwedge v^*(\Gamma_1) \leq v^*(\phi \tilde{\wedge} \psi)$, because it holds that $v^*(\phi \tilde{\wedge} \psi) \leq v^*(\phi \wedge \psi) = v^*(\phi) \bigwedge v^*(\psi)$. Analogously, the rule for elimination of intensional disjunction (fission) does not hold more. Hence, from the fact that we must exclude the rule for introduction of intensional conjunction $\tilde{\wedge}$ and the rule for elimination of intensional disjunction $\tilde{\vee}$, and hence without the possibility to derive from the inference rules the commutativity of these two logical connectives, we need to specify their commutativity by two new axioms. In an analog way, from the fact that we cannot obtain the De Morgan relationship between these two logical connectives by the rules of inference, also for the De Morgan relationship we must introduce two new rules, as follows.

Corollary 24. *The Gentzen's sequent system $\mathfrak{G}_{\infty}^{\textcircled{s}}$ for the relevant Lukasiezic's logic, obtained by the weakening of fusion and fission intensional connectives by using strong Lukasiewicz's functions $f_S(z) : [0,2] \to X$, which satisfies the equations (6.22), is obtained by the extension of the original Gentzen's system $\mathfrak{G}_{\infty}$ provided previously (where we eliminated the t-norm fusion ⊗ in (6.9), by the following new axioms:*
(4) $\phi \,\widetilde{\wedge}\, \psi \vdash \psi \,\widetilde{\wedge}\, \phi$ *commutativity*
(5) $\neg(\neg\phi \,\widetilde{\wedge}\, \neg\psi) \vdash \phi \,\widetilde{\vee}\, \psi$ *De Morgan 1*
(6) $\phi \,\widetilde{\vee}\, \psi \vdash \neg(\neg\phi \,\widetilde{\wedge}\, \neg\psi)$ *De Morgan 2*

and the following new rules for relevant fusion and fission connectives:

$$\frac{\Gamma \vdash \phi}{\Gamma \vdash \phi \,\widetilde{\vee}\, \psi} \; (\to \widetilde{\vee})_1, \qquad \frac{\Gamma \vdash \psi}{\Gamma \vdash \phi \,\widetilde{\vee}\, \psi} \; (\to \widetilde{\vee})_2 \tag{6.28}$$

$$\frac{\Gamma, \phi \vdash \varphi}{\Gamma, \phi \,\widetilde{\wedge}\, \psi \vdash \varphi} \; (\widetilde{\wedge} \to)_1, \qquad \frac{\Gamma, \psi \vdash \varphi}{\Gamma, \phi \,\widetilde{\wedge}\, \psi \vdash \varphi} \; (\widetilde{\wedge} \to)_2 \tag{6.29}$$

Proof. We obtain the following results:
1. From the axiom (4) of the commutativity of fusion connective $\widehat{\wedge}$, the rules for negation in $\mathfrak{G}_{\infty}$, and two De Morgan axioms, we obtain the commutativity of fission as well:
   (a) $\phi \,\widetilde{\vee}\, \psi \vdash \psi \,\widetilde{\vee}\, \phi$
2. From the rule $(\widetilde{\wedge} \to)_1$, in the case when Γ is empty and φ equal to ϕ, so that in the upper level we obtain the axiom $\phi \vdash \phi$, as consequence we obtain:
   (b) $\phi \,\widetilde{\wedge}\, \psi \vdash \phi$,
   and hence when ψ is equal to ϕ we derived that square-decreasing property of the fusion, $\phi \,\widetilde{\wedge}\, \phi \vdash \phi$.
3. from the rule $(\to \widetilde{\vee})_1$, in the case when $\Gamma = \{\phi\}$, again the upper sequent is an axiom, and as a consequence we obtain:
   (c) $\phi \vdash \phi \,\widetilde{\vee}\, \psi$,
   and hence when ψ is equal to ϕ we derived that square-increasing property of the fission, $\phi \vdash \phi \,\widetilde{\vee}\, \phi$.
4. From (b) and from the axiom (4) of the commutativity, we obtain also $\phi \,\widetilde{\wedge}\, \psi \vdash \psi$, and by using the rule $(\to \wedge)$ of $\mathfrak{G}_{\infty}$ for $\Gamma = \{\phi \,\widetilde{\wedge}\, \psi\}$, as a consequence we obtain:
   (d) $\phi \,\widetilde{\wedge}\, \psi \vdash \phi \wedge \psi$
5. From (c), and analogously derived $\psi \vdash \phi \,\widetilde{\vee}\, \psi$, and by using the $(\vee \to)$ of $\mathfrak{G}_{\infty}$ for Γ empty and φ equal to $\phi \,\widetilde{\vee}\, \psi$, as a consequence we obtain:
   (e) $\phi \vee \psi \vdash \phi \,\widetilde{\vee}\, \psi$
   Consequently, from (d) and (e), and from the sequant $\vdash \phi \wedge \psi \vdash \phi \,\widetilde{\vee}\, \psi$ derived from $\mathfrak{G}_{\infty}$, we obtain the chain of sequents:

$$\phi \,\widetilde{\wedge}\, \psi \vdash \phi \wedge \psi \vdash \phi \vee \psi \vdash \phi \,\widetilde{\vee}\, \psi$$

i. e., from the truth-preserving semantics of satisfaction of sequent in Definition 54 in Section 5.1,

$$\phi \widetilde{\wedge} \psi \preceq \phi \wedge \psi \preceq \phi \vee \psi \preceq \phi \widetilde{\vee} \psi,$$

i. e., strong fusion and fission property corresponding to algebraic equations in (6.22). □

Remark. Note that if instead of strong Lukasiewic'z functions $f_S(z)$ we use weaker versions $f_L(z)$, and define fusion and fission operations by (6.19) and (6.20), we have to eliminate the inference rules in (6.28) and (6.29) and insert another two axioms, corresponding to algebraic equations in (6.21), respectively,

(7) $\phi \widetilde{\wedge} \psi \vdash \phi \bigvee \psi$

(8) $\phi \widetilde{\wedge} \psi \vdash \phi \widetilde{\vee} \psi$

so that from axiom (5) in the case when ψ is equal to ϕ and from a derived sequent $\phi \bigvee \phi \vdash \phi$ in $\mathfrak{G}_\infty$, by rule (cut) in $\mathfrak{G}_\infty$, we obtain the square decreasing property of fusion

$$\phi \widetilde{\wedge} \phi \vdash \phi$$

which in the case when ϕ is equal to $\neg\psi$ (where ψ is equivalent to $\neg\phi$), we obtain by substitution the sequent $\neg\psi \widetilde{\wedge} \neg\psi \vdash \neg\psi$, and from the rule $(\neg)$ in $\mathfrak{G}_\infty$, we obtain the sequent $\neg\neg\psi \vdash \neg(\neg\psi \widetilde{\wedge} \neg\psi)$ and from the axiom (5), by using the cut rule in $\mathfrak{G}_\infty$, we obtain the sequent $\neg\neg\psi \vdash \psi \widetilde{\vee} \psi$. Hence, from this sequent and from the derivable sequent $\psi \vdash \neg\neg\psi$ in $\mathfrak{G}_\infty$, by applying the cut rule, we obtain the square-increasing property for the fission:

$$\psi \vdash \psi \widetilde{\vee} \psi.$$ □

Now we can define the relevant Lukasiewicz's algebra and its canonical representation algebra.

Definition 91 (Relevant Lukasiewicz algebra). From Corollary 23 for the weakened fusion $\widetilde{\wedge}$ in (6.19) and weakened fission $\widetilde{\vee}$ in (6.20), which now are not more derivable from the another Lukasiewicz's algebra operations, and from the fact that the negation $\sim$ is derived from the implication (which is not relative pseudo-complement) by $\sim x =_{def} (x \to 0)$, we obtain the following relevant Lukasiewicz's algebra:

$$\mathbf{A} = (X, \leq, \wedge, \vee, \to, \widetilde{\wedge}, \widetilde{\vee}), \tag{6.30}$$

and hence by Proposition 29 in Section 5.1.2, from the fact for the total ordering in X, $\widehat{X} = X = [0,1]$ we obtain a canonical representation isomorphism (5.10),

$$\downarrow^+ : ((X, \leq, \wedge, \vee, 0, 1), \to, \widetilde{\wedge}, \widetilde{\vee}) \simeq ((X^+, \subseteq, \cap, \cup, \{0\}, X), \to^+, \widetilde{\wedge}^+, \widetilde{\vee}^+) \tag{6.31}$$

with set-based canonical relevant Lukasiewicz's algebra $\mathbf{A}^+ = ((X^+, \subseteq, \cap, \cup, \{0\}, X), \rightarrow^+, \widetilde{\wedge}^+, \widetilde{\vee}^+)$, with, from general definitions in (5.11), new set-based operations:

1. $\rightarrow^+ = \downarrow^+ \rightarrow (\bigvee \times \bigvee) = \downarrow^+ \min\{1, 1 - \bigvee\_ + \bigvee\_\} : X^+ \times X^+ \rightarrow X^+$,
2. $\widetilde{\wedge}^+ = \downarrow^+ \widetilde{\wedge} (\bigvee \times \bigvee) = \downarrow^+(1 - f_L(2 - \bigvee\_ - \bigvee\_)) : X^+ \times X^+ \rightarrow X^+$,
3. $\widetilde{\vee}^+ = \downarrow^+ \widetilde{\vee} (\bigvee \times \bigvee) = \downarrow^+ f_L(\bigvee\_ + \bigvee\_) : X^+ \times X^+ \rightarrow X^+$,

where, for each $x \in X$, $\downarrow^+ x = [0, x] \in X^+$.

Consequently, based on the canonical representation Theorem 17 in Section 5.1.2, the relational Kripke semantics of this relevant Lukasiewicz's logic is a following particular case of Definition 65 in Section 5.1.2.

Definition 92. The Kripke semantics of relevant Lukasiewicz's logic given by its algebra **A** provided by Definition 91 is given by a Kripke model $M_K = (K, I_K)$ with the frame $K = \langle (X, \leq), \mathbf{R}_{\rightarrow}, \mathbf{R}_{\wedge}, \mathbf{R}_{\vee} \rangle$, where these three ternary accessibility relations are provided in Definition 63 in Section 5.1.2, for implication $\rightarrow$ in (6.11), weakened fusion $\widetilde{\wedge}$ in (6.19) and weakened fission $\widetilde{\vee}$ in (6.20) relatively. Mapping $I_K : \mathrm{Var} \times 1_K \rightarrow \mathbf{2}$ is a canonical valuation, such that for any atomic formula (propositional variable) $p \in \mathrm{Var}$, formulae $\psi, \phi \in F(\mathcal{L})$, and possible world $x \in X$:

1. $M_K \vDash_x p$ iff $I_K(p, x) = 1$
2. $M_K \vDash_x \phi \wedge \psi$ iff $M_K \vDash_x \phi$ and $M_K \vDash_x \psi$,
3. $M_K \vDash_x \phi \vee \psi$ iff $M_K \vDash_x \phi$ or $M_K \vDash_x \psi$,
4. $M_K \vDash_x \phi \widetilde{\wedge} \psi$ iff $\exists y, z \in X((x, y, z) \in \mathbf{R}_{\wedge}$ and $M_K \vDash_y \phi$ and $M_K \vDash_z \psi)$,
5. $M_K \vDash_x \phi \widetilde{\vee} \psi$ iff $\exists y, z \in X((x, y, z) \in \mathbf{R}_{\vee}$ and $M_K \vDash_y \phi$ and $M_K \vDash_z \psi)$,
6. $M_K \vDash_x \phi \Rightarrow \psi$ iff $\exists y, z \in X((x, y, z) \in \mathbf{R}_{\rightarrow}$ and $M_K \vDash_y \phi$ and $M_K \vDash_z \psi$ and $\forall w \in X(M_K \vDash_w \phi$ implies $w \leq y))$.

Notice that in this definition of Kripke semantics we considered the fact that the fusion $\widetilde{\wedge}$ and fission $\widetilde{\vee}$ are monotonic in both arguments, while implication $\Rightarrow$ (which is not intuitionistic, and hence representable algebraically by a relative pseudo-complement) is monotonic for second and antimonotonic for the first argument.

Now, based on this Kripke models $M_K = (K, I_K)$, we are able for such a model to define the mapping $v : \mathrm{Var} \rightarrow X$, such that for each atomic formula $p \in \mathrm{Var}$, $v(p) = w$ iff $I_K(p, w) = 1$, and to extend this mapping to the unique homomorphism $v^* : F(\mathcal{L}) \rightarrow X$ for the formulae $\phi \in F(\mathcal{L})$ of this relevant Lukasiewicz's logic. So, from Theorem 17 in Section 5.1.2, it holds that

$$\|\phi\| = \downarrow^+ v^*(\phi) = [0, v^*(\phi)] \in X^+ \tag{6.32}$$

where $v^*(\phi) \in X$ is the truth value of the formula ϕ in this Kripke model $M_K = (K, I_K)$.

Thus, by this division of the fusion and fission logical connectives from the lattice conjunction, disjunction and implication connectives, we can also consider independently the weakening of the implication to obtain a more relevant implication. For example, instead of original Lukasiewicz's implication (6.11), defined algebraically by $x \to y =_{\text{def}} \min\{1, 1-x+y\}$, we can use an intuitionistic implication (with residuation property w. r. t. lattice meet operation $\bigwedge$) such that

$$x \to y =_{\text{def}} \bigvee \left\{ z \mid x \bigwedge z \le y \right\} \tag{6.33}$$

and to obtain still more relevant Lukasiewicz's logics.

6.2 Relevant mZ-logic: paraconsistent intuitionistic logic with Da Costa weakening of intuitionistic negation

In what follows, we will try to summarize, by a short introduction, the previous historic approach to two important concepts in the logics: paraconsistency and constructivism.

A *paraconsistent* logic is a logical system that attempts to deal with contradictions in a discriminating way. Alternatively, paraconsistent logic is the subfield of logic that is concerned with studying and developing paraconsistent (or inconsistency-tolerant) systems of logic. Paraconsistent logics are propositionally weaker than classical logic; that is, they deem fewer propositional inferences valid. The point is that a paraconsistent logic can never be a propositional extension of classical logic, i. e., propositionally validate everything that classical logic does. In that sense, then paraconsistent logic is more conservative or cautious than classical logic.

The recent history of the development of substructural relevant logics has an important example of reduction of Classical Propositional Calculus (CPC) in a number of its substructural logics, called intermediate propositional logics as well, as we presented in Section 6.1. In this framework of progressively weakening of CPC, we obtained a lattice of the intermediate logics, where the top element of this lattice was CPC and the bottom element the Intuitionistic Propositional Calculus (IPC). This "weakening" from CPC into IPC can be seen as weakening of the interdependence of the basic for logic connectives: negation $\neg$ (unary operation) and binary operations, conjunction $\wedge$, disjunction $\vee$ and implication $\Rightarrow$. In order to distinguish these connectives ($\neg$ and $\Rightarrow$ only) in this hierarchy of different propositional logics, we will label them by a kind of logics: by a label C for the CPC and label I for the IPC, while the logic connectives of mZ will remain unlabeled.

The fundamental distinguishing characteristic of *intuitionism* is its interpretation of what it means for a mathematical statement to be *true*. In Brouwer's original intuitionism, the truth of a mathematical statement is a subjective claim: a mathematical statement corresponds to a mental construction, and a mathematician can assert the truth of a statement only by verifying the validity of that construction by intuition. To an intuitionist, the claim that an object with certain properties exists is a claim that an object with those properties can be constructed. Any mathematical object is considered to be a product of a construction of a mind and, therefore, the existence of an object is equivalent to the possibility of its construction. This contrasts with the classical approach, which states that the existence of an entity can be proved by refuting its nonexistence. For the intuitionist, this is not valid; the refutation of the nonexistence does not mean that it is possible to find a construction for the putative object, as is required in order to assert its existence.

The interpretation of negation is different in intuitionist logic than in classical logic. In classical logic, the negation of a statement asserts that the statement is false; to an intuitionist, it means the statement is refutable (e. g., that there is a counterexample). There is thus an asymmetry between a positive and negative statement in intuitionism. If a statement ϕ is provable, then it is certainly impossible to prove that there is no proof of ϕ. But even if it can be shown that no disproof of ϕ is possible, we cannot conclude from this absence that there is a proof of ϕ. Thus, ϕ is a stronger statement than $\neg\neg\phi$. As such, intuitionism is a variety of mathematical constructivism; but it is not the only kind. Regardless of how it is interpreted, intuitionism does not equate the truth of a mathematical statement with its provability. However, because the intuitionistic notion of truth is more restrictive than that of classical mathematics, the intuitionist must reject some assumptions of classical logic to ensure that everything he/she proves is in fact intuitionistically true. This gives rise to intuitionistic logic.

Intuitionistic logic allows $\phi \vee \neg\phi$ not to be equivalent to true, while paraconsistent logic allows $\phi \wedge \neg\phi$ not to be equivalent to false. Thus, it seems natural to regard paraconsistent logic as the *dual* of intuitionistic logic. However, intuitionistic logic is a specific logical system whereas paraconsistent logic encompasses a large class of systems. Accordingly, to this historic approach, the dual notion to paraconsistency is called paracompleteness, and the "dual" of intuitionistic logic (a specific paracomplete logic) is a specific paraconsistent system called antiintuitionistic or dual-intuitionistic logic (sometimes referred to as Brazilian logic, for historical reasons) [211, 259–261]. The duality between the two systems is best seen within a sequent calculus framework.

The intuitionistic implication operator cannot be treated like "$(\neg_C\phi \vee \psi)$," but as a modal formula $\Box(\neg_C\phi \vee \psi)$ where $\neg_C$ is the classic negation and $\Box$ universal modal S4 operator with reflexive and transitive accessibility relation R in Kripke semantics. Dual-intuitionistic logic [262] contains a connective $\multimapdotbothA$ known as pseudo-difference, which is the dual of intuitionistic implication. Very loosely, $\phi \multimapdotbothA \psi$ can be read as "ϕ but not ψ" and is equivalent to a modal formula $\Diamond(\phi \wedge \neg_C\psi)$, where $\Diamond$ is the existential modal operator with inverse accessibility relation R^{-1} in a Kripke-like semantics [263].

Dual of intuitionistic logic has been investigated to varying degrees of success using algebraic, relational, axiomatic and sequent-based perspectives. The concept of anti-intuitionism, proposed through the concept of a dual intuitionistic logic, was already mentioned in the 1940s by K. Popper (without any formalism), but he disapproved such a logic as "too weak to be useless." In fact, K. Popper puts in the Logic of Scientific Discovery [264]:

> *"The falsifying mode of inference here referred to—the way in which the falsification of conclusion entails the falsification of the system from which it is derived—is the modus tollens of classic logic."*

Consequently, dual intuitionistic logic can be labeled as "falsification logic." In the falsification, logic truth is essentially nonconstructive as opposed to falsity that is conceived constructively. In intuitionistic logic, instead, falsity is essentially nonconstructive as opposed to truth that is conceived constructively. Thus, historically, the main research about the relationships between intuitionistic and paraconsistent logic was directed toward an exploration of their dual and opposite properties instead of investigation of their possible common properties. Such common properties are interesting in order to obtain the logics that may have a reasonable balance of both opposite (dual) properties: the logics where both $\neg(\phi \wedge \neg\psi)$ is not false and $\neg(\phi \vee \neg\psi)$ is not true.

This consideration was the basic motivation at the beginning of my investigation of intuitionism and paraconsistency, in order to obtain an useful logic for significant practical applications as well. In fact, after a meeting with Walter Carnielli, M. Coniglio and J. Y. Béziau at IICAI-2007 (Pune, India), I decided to dedicate much more time to these problems. My first result was the publication of an autoreferential semantics for modal logics based on a complete distributive lattice [69]. In this research, I dedicated the last section exclusively to the paraconsistency of this new semantics w. r. t. the formal LFI system [261], which I obtained in preprint personally from Walter.

My decisive advances in this direction of research was published in [227] and then upgraded in [228] by considering the paraconsistent properties of newly introduced mZ_n logics. Consequently, in this paper, we will consider in a more detailed way, the dual quasi-intuitionistic properties of this mZ_n logic.

There are different approaches to paraconsistent logics. The first one is the nonconstructive approach, based on abstract logic (as LFI [261]), where logic connectives and their particular semantics are not considered. The second one is the constructive approach and is divided in two parts: an axiomatic proof theoretic (in Da Costa [265] and [254, 266, 267]), and a many-valued model theoretic [69] based on truth-functional valuations (i. e., it satisfies the truth-compositionality principle). The best scenario is when we obtain both, the proof and the model theoretic definition, which are mutually sound and complete.

One of the main founders with Stanislav Jaskowski [268], Da Costa, built his propositional paraconsistent system C_ω in [265] by weakening the logic negation operator $\neg$, in order to avoid the explosive inconsistency [261, 269] of the classic propositional logic, where the ex falso quodlibet proof rule $\frac{\phi, \neg\phi}{\psi}$ is valid. In fact, in order to avoid this classic logic rule, he changed the semantics for the negation operator, so that:

- NdC1: in these calculi, the principle of noncontradiction, in the form $\neg(\phi \wedge \neg\phi)$, should not be a generally valid schema, but if it does hold for formula ϕ, it is a well-behaved formula and is denoted by ϕ°;
- NdC2: from two contradictory formulae, ϕ and $\neg\phi$, it would not in general be possible to deduce an arbitrary formula ψ. That is, it does not hold the ex falso quodlibet proof rule $\frac{\phi, \neg\phi}{\psi}$;
- NdC3: it should be simple to extend these calculi to corresponding predicate calculi (with or without equality);
- NdC4: they should contain most parts of the schemata and rules of classical propositional calculus, which do not infer with the first conditions

In fact, Da Costa's paraconsistent propositional logic is made up of the unique modus ponens inferential rule
(MP)$\phi, \phi \Rightarrow \psi \vdash \psi$,

and two axiom subsets. But before stating them, we need the following definition as it is done in Da Costa's systems (cf. [265, p. 500]), which uses three binary connectives, $\wedge$ for conjunction, $\vee$ for disjunction and $\Rightarrow$ for implication.

Definition 93. Let ϕ be a formula and $1 \leq n < \omega$. Then we define $\phi^\circ, \phi^{\mathrm{n}}, \phi^{(\mathrm{n})}$ as follows:

$$\phi^\circ =_{\mathrm{def}} \neg(\phi \wedge \neg\phi), \quad \phi^{\mathrm{n}} =_{\mathrm{def}} \phi^{\overbrace{\circ\circ\cdots\circ}^{n}}, \quad \text{and} \quad \phi^{(\mathrm{n})} =_{\mathrm{def}} \phi^1 \wedge \phi^2 \wedge \cdots \wedge \phi^{\mathrm{n}}.$$

The first one is for the positive propositional logic (without negation), composed by the following eight axioms, borrowed from the classic propositional logic of the Kleene L_4 system, and also from the more general propositional *intuitionistic* system IPC (these two systems differ only regarding axioms with the negation operator),

(IPC$^+$) positive logic axioms

(1) $\phi \Rightarrow (\psi \Rightarrow \phi)$
(2) $(\phi \Rightarrow \psi) \Rightarrow ((\phi \Rightarrow (\psi \Rightarrow \varphi)) \Rightarrow (\phi \Rightarrow \varphi))$
(3) $\phi \Rightarrow (\psi \Rightarrow (\phi \wedge \psi))$
(4) $(\phi \wedge \psi) \Rightarrow \phi$
(5) $(\phi \wedge \psi) \Rightarrow \psi$
(6) $\phi \Rightarrow (\phi \vee \psi)$
(7) $\psi \Rightarrow (\phi \vee \psi)$
(8) $(\phi \Rightarrow \varphi) \Rightarrow ((\psi \Rightarrow \varphi) \Rightarrow ((\phi \vee \psi) \Rightarrow \varphi))$

We change the original axioms for negation operator of the classic propositional logic (CPL in Section A.1 in the Appendix), by defining the semantics of negation operator by the following subset of axioms:

(NLA) logic axioms for negation

(9) $\phi \vee \neg\phi$

(10) $\neg\neg\phi \Rightarrow \phi$

(11) $\psi^{(n)} \Rightarrow ((\phi \Rightarrow \psi) \Rightarrow ((\phi \Rightarrow \neg\psi) \Rightarrow \neg\phi))$ (Reductio relativization axiom)

(12) $(\phi^{(n)} \wedge \psi^{(n)}) \Rightarrow ((\phi \wedge \psi)^{(n)} \wedge (\phi \vee \psi)^{(n)} \wedge (\phi \Rightarrow \psi)^{(n)})$ □

It is easy to see that the axiom (11) relativizes the classic *reduction* axiom

$$(\phi \Rightarrow \psi) \Rightarrow ((\phi \Rightarrow \neg\psi) \Rightarrow \neg\phi)$$

which is equivalent to the contraposition axiom $(\phi \Rightarrow \neg\psi) \Rightarrow (\psi \Rightarrow \neg\phi)$ and the trivialization axiom $\neg(\phi \Rightarrow \phi) \Rightarrow \psi$, *only* for propositions ψ such that $\psi^{(n)}$ is valid, and in this way avoids the validity of the classic ex falso quodlibet proof rule. It provides a qualified form of reduction, helping to prevent general validity of $\psi^{(n)}$ in the paraconsistent logic C_n. The axiom (12) regulates only the propagation of n-consistency. It is easy to verify that n-consistency also propagates through negation, i. e., $\phi^{(n)} \Rightarrow (\neg\phi)^{(n)}$ is provable in C_n. So that for any fixed n (from 0 to ω) we obtain a particular Da Costa paraconsistent logic C_n. Each C_n is strictly weaker than any of its predecessors, i. e., denoting by Th(S) the set of theorems of calculus S, we have

$$\text{Th}(\text{CPL}) \supset \text{Th}(C_1) \supset \cdots \supset \text{Th}(C_n) \supset \cdots \supset \text{Th}(C_\omega).$$

Thus, we are fundamentally interested in the C_1 system, which is a paraconsistent logic closer to the CPL (Classical propositional logic), i. e., C_1 is the paraconsistent logic of Da Costa's hierarchy obtained by minimal change of CPL.

It is well known that the classic propositional logic based on the classic 2-valued complete distributive lattice $(\mathbf{2}, \leq)$ with the set $\mathbf{2} = \{0, 1\}$ of truth values, has a truth-compositional model theoretic semantics. For this, Da Costa calculi is not given any truth-compositional model theoretic semantics instead.

Based on these observations, in [227] are explained some weak properties of the Da Costa weakening for a negation operator and it was shown that negation is not antitonic, different from the negations in the classic and intuitionistic propositional logics (that have the truth-compositional model theoretic semantics).

The negation in the classic and intuitionistic logics are not paraconsistent (see, e. g., Proposition 30, p. 118, in [69]), so that basic idea in [227] was to make a weakening of the intuitionistic negation by considering only its general antitonic property. In fact, the formula $(\phi \Rightarrow \psi) \Rightarrow (\neg\psi \Rightarrow \neg\phi)$ is a thesis in both classic and intuitionistic logics. Consequently, our idea was to use the Da Costa weakening of the *intuitionistic* negation [227, 228], e. g., from [228] where it has been shown than such obtained mZ_n logic does not depend on n, because is satisfies Da Costa axioms for all $n \geq 1$. Because of that, we will denote mZ_n in [228] simply by mZ-logic in what follows.

Definition 94 (Relevant paraconsistent intuitionistic mZ logic). We define the mZ logic by adding the following axioms to eight axioms of the system IPC^+:

(9b) $(\phi \Rightarrow \psi) \Rightarrow (\neg\psi \Rightarrow \neg\phi)$

(10b) $1 \Rightarrow \neg 0$

(11b) $\phi \Rightarrow 1, 0 \Rightarrow \phi$

(12b) $(\neg\phi \wedge \neg\psi) \Rightarrow \neg(\phi \vee \psi)$

This mZ logic is a *relevant intuitionistic* logic obtained by weakening negation by the Da Costa paraconsistent method. Another mCZ logic can be formulated by adding the axiom

(13b) $\neg(\phi \wedge \psi) \Rightarrow (\neg\phi \vee \neg\psi)$

to these formulae.

The following formulae are derivable in mZ logic (since mZ contains IPC^+):

$$((\phi \Rightarrow \psi) \wedge (\phi \Rightarrow \varphi)) \Rightarrow (\phi \Rightarrow (\psi \wedge \varphi)) \tag{T0}$$

$$(\phi \Rightarrow (\psi \Rightarrow \varphi)) \Rightarrow (\psi \Rightarrow (\phi \Rightarrow \varphi)) \tag{T1}$$

$$(\phi \Rightarrow \psi) \Rightarrow ((\psi \Rightarrow \varphi) \Rightarrow (\phi \Rightarrow \varphi)) \tag{T2}$$

$$(\phi \Rightarrow (\psi \Rightarrow \varphi)) \equiv ((\phi \wedge \psi) \Rightarrow \varphi) \tag{T3}$$

where we denote by $\phi \equiv \psi$ the formulae $(\phi \Rightarrow \psi) \wedge (\psi \Rightarrow \phi)$.

Theorem 13. *The* mZ *and* mCZ *logics are paraconsistent.*

Proof. We interpret the negation as a function always giving the truth value 1, whereas other connectives are interpreted in a standard way done in two valued for classical propositional calculus. □

Lemma 7 ([228]). *The following formulae are derivable in mZ logic:*

$$(\phi \wedge \neg\phi) \Rightarrow \neg\psi \tag{NEFQ}$$

$$\neg\neg(\phi \wedge \psi) \Rightarrow (\neg\neg\phi \wedge \neg\neg\psi) \tag{$\heartsuit$}$$

$$\neg((\phi * \psi)^n) \Rightarrow (\neg(\phi^n) \vee \neg(\psi^n)) \tag{$\clubsuit$}$$

where $* \in \{\Rightarrow, \wedge, \vee\}$.

Proof. Let us derive NEFQ:

1 $\phi \Rightarrow (\psi \Rightarrow \phi)$ [(1)]

2 $(\psi \Rightarrow \phi) \Rightarrow (\neg\phi \Rightarrow \neg\psi)$ [(9b)]

3 $\phi \Rightarrow (\neg\phi \Rightarrow \neg\psi)$ [1, 2, (T2)]

4 $(\phi \wedge \neg\phi) \Rightarrow \neg\psi$ [3, (T3), (MP)]

Notice that NEFQ is not desirable for some logicians of paraconsistent systems.

Let us derive ~ now. We will only prove the following, since the case in which $\neg\neg\phi$ is replaced by $\neg\neg\psi$ can be proved analogously: $\neg\neg(\phi \wedge \psi) \Rightarrow \neg\neg\phi$.

This can be proved easily by making use of axioms (3) and (9b).

Let us derive | now. The proof runs as follows:

1 $\neg((\phi * \psi)^n) \equiv \neg\neg((\phi * \psi)^{n-1} \wedge \neg(\phi * \psi)^{n-1})$ [Definition of ϕ^n]
2 $\neg\neg((\phi * \psi)^{n-1} \wedge \neg(\phi * \psi)^{n-1}) \Rightarrow (\neg\neg(\phi * \psi)^{n-1} \wedge \neg\neg\neg(\phi * \psi)^{n-1})$ [(♡)]
3 $(\neg\neg(\phi * \psi)^{n-1} \wedge \neg\neg\neg(\phi * \psi)^{n-1}) \Rightarrow \neg(\phi^n)$ [(NEFQ)]
4 $\neg(\phi^n) \Rightarrow (\neg(\phi^n) \vee \neg(\psi^n))$ [(6)]
5 $\neg((\phi * \psi)^n) \Rightarrow (\neg(\phi^n) \vee \neg(\psi^n))$ [1, 2, 3, 4, (T2), (MP)] □

Let us show now that the axioms (11) and (12) are redundant in the mZ logic.

Theorem 14 ([228]). *The axioms (11) and (12) are redundant in* mZ *logic in the sense that they can be proved by another axioms.*

Proof. The redundance of the axiom (11) can be proved as follows:

1 $(\phi \Rightarrow (\psi \wedge \neg\psi)) \Rightarrow (\neg(\psi \wedge \neg\psi) \Rightarrow \neg\phi)$ [(9b)]
2 $\neg(\psi \wedge \neg\psi) \Rightarrow ((\phi \Rightarrow (\psi \wedge \neg\psi)) \Rightarrow \neg\phi)$ [1, (T1), (MP)]
3 $\psi^{(n)} \Rightarrow \psi^1$ [Definition of $\psi^{(n)}$]
4 $\psi^{(n)} \Rightarrow \neg(\psi \wedge \neg\psi)$ [Definition of ψ^1]
5 $\psi^{(n)} \Rightarrow ((\phi \Rightarrow (\psi \wedge \neg\psi)) \Rightarrow \neg\phi)$ [2, 4, (T2), (MP)]

Let us prove the redundance of the axiom (12). It would be sufficient to prove the following in order to prove the desired result:

$$(\phi^{(n)} \wedge \psi^{(n)}) \Rightarrow (\phi * \psi)^n \qquad (\diamond)$$

Indeed, if we have $(\diamond)$ at hand then we can prove $(\phi^{(n)} \wedge \psi^{(n)}) \Rightarrow (\phi * \psi)^m$ for any $1 \leq m \leq n$ and combining all these cases, we obtain $(\phi^{(n)} \wedge \psi^{(n)}) \Rightarrow (\phi * \psi)^{(n)}$ which is axiom (12). So, we now prove $(\diamond)$, which runs as follows:

1 $(\phi^{(n)} \wedge \psi^{(n)}) \Rightarrow (((\phi * \psi)^{n-1} \wedge \neg(\phi * \psi)^{n-1}) \Rightarrow (\neg(\phi^{n-1}) \vee \neg(\psi^{n-1})))$ [(♣)]
2 $(\phi^{(n)} \wedge \psi^{(n)}) \Rightarrow (((\phi * \psi)^{n-1} \wedge \neg(\phi * \psi)^{n-1}) \Rightarrow ((\phi^{n-1} \wedge \neg(\phi^{n-1})) \vee (\psi^{n-1} \wedge \neg(\psi^{n-1}))))$ [1, Definition 93]
3 $(((\phi * \psi)^{n-1} \wedge \neg(\phi * \psi)^{n-1}) \Rightarrow ((\phi^{n-1} \wedge \neg(\phi^{n-1})) \vee (\psi^{n-1} \wedge \neg(\psi^{n-1})))) \Rightarrow (\neg((\phi^{n-1} \wedge \neg(\phi^{n-1})) \vee (\psi^{n-1} \wedge \neg(\psi^{n-1}))) \Rightarrow \neg((\phi * \psi)^{n-1} \wedge \neg(\phi * \psi)^{n-1}))$ [(9b)]
4 $(\phi^{(n)} \wedge \psi^{(n)}) \Rightarrow (\neg((\phi^{n-1} \wedge \neg(\phi^{n-1})) \vee (\psi^{n-1} \wedge \neg(\psi^{n-1}))) \Rightarrow \neg((\phi * \psi)^{n-1} \wedge \neg(\phi * \psi)^{n-1}))$ [2, 3, (T2), (MP)]
5 $(\neg(\phi^{n-1} \wedge \neg(\phi^{n-1})) \wedge \neg(\psi^{n-1} \wedge \neg(\psi^{n-1}))) \Rightarrow \neg((\phi^{n-1} \wedge \neg(\phi^{n-1})) \vee (\psi^{n-1} \wedge \neg(\psi^{n-1})))$ [(12b)]
6 $(\phi^{(n)} \wedge \psi^{(n)}) \Rightarrow ((\phi^n \wedge \psi^n) \Rightarrow (\phi * \psi)^n)$ [4, (T1), 5, (T2), Definition 93, (MP)]
7 $(\phi^{(n)} \wedge \psi^{(n)}) \Rightarrow (\phi^n \wedge \psi^n)$ [Definition 93]
8 $(\phi^{(n)} \wedge \psi^{(n)}) \Rightarrow (\phi * \psi)^n$ [6, 7, (2), (MP)] □

Although it is not directly connected to the story of mZ and mCZ, it should be noted that the propagation axiom for negation, i. e., the following formula can be derived in an analogous manner: $\phi^{(n)} \Rightarrow (\neg\phi)^{(n)}$.

Therefore, the propagation axioms can be fully *proved* in systems mZ and mCZ.

Remark. After all, we now know that systems mZ do not form a hierarchy but are equivalent to a single system, which consists of IPC$^+$ together with axioms (9b), (10b), (11b), (12b).

6.2.1 Intuitionistic constructivism and Birkhoff's polarity of negation in mZ-logic

It was demonstrated in [227] (Proposition 3) that the positive fragment of mZ system corresponds to the complete distributive lattice $(X, \leq, \wedge, \vee, 0, 1)$ (the positive fragment of the Heyting algebra), where the logic implication corresponds to the relative pseudo-complement, $(x \rightharpoonup y) =_{\text{def}} \bigvee\{z \mid z \wedge x \leq y\}$ and 0 and 1 are the bottom and top elements in X, respectively.

The autoreferential representation of such truth-values lattice is provided in Section 5.1.2. From Proposition 28, we have that $X^+ = \{\downarrow^+ x \mid x \in X\}$ is a hereditary set of join-irreducible elements of truth values in X, and $(X^+, \subseteq)$ is a complete lattice with meet operator $\bigcap$ (set intersection), and join operator $\bigcup$ (set union).

For the positive intuitionistic logic fragment IPC$^+$ of mZ logic, the following autoreferential representation isomorphism holds for the Heyting algebras (from Proposition 29 in Section 5.1.2, where we use only the relative pesudo-complement $\rightharpoonup$ for the binary operators $\otimes_i$ in algebras $\mathbf{A}$ for its representation isomorphism (5.10)):

$$\downarrow^+ : (X, \leq, \wedge, \vee, \rightharpoonup, 0, 1) \simeq (X^+, \subseteq, \cap, \cup, \rightarrowtail, \{0\}, \widehat{X}) \tag{6.34}$$

such that for any two $\downarrow^+ x, \downarrow^+ y \in X^+$, $(\downarrow^+ x) \rightarrowtail (\downarrow^+ y) = \downarrow^+(x \rightharpoonup y)$ (from Example 31 in Section 5.1.2).

A hierarchy of negation operators [69] for many-valued logics based on complete lattices of truth values $(X, \leq)$, w. r. t. their homomorphic properties is introduced in Definition 104, Section A.3.2 in the Appendix. The negation with the lowest requirements (antitonic) denominated "general" negation can be defined in any complete lattice (e. g., see [227]) as a monotone mapping between posets ($\leq^{\text{OP}}$ is inverse of $\leq$),

$$\neg : (X, \leq) \to (X, \leq)^{\text{OP}}, \quad \text{such that } 1 \in \{\neg x \mid x \in X\}$$

such that (see Lemma 14 in Section A.3.2 in the Appendix) for any $x, y \in X$,

$$\neg(x \vee y) \leq \neg x \wedge \neg y, \quad \neg(x \wedge y) \geq \neg x \vee \neg y, \quad \text{with } \neg 0 = 1$$

Remark. We can see (as demonstrated in [227]) that the negation in the system mZ without axiom (12b) is a particular case of *general* negation, that the negation in the whole system mZ is a *split* negation, as specified in Definition 104, Section A.3.2 in the Appendix, while the negation in the system mCZ [227] is a *constructive* negation.

Thus, from Section 5.1.2, the set-based semantics for the split negations (with Galois connections) can be given by the Bikhoff polarity operator

$$\lambda : (\mathcal{P}(X), \subseteq) \to (\mathcal{P}(X), \subseteq)^{\mathrm{OP}}, \quad \text{such that for any } U \in \mathcal{P}(X),$$
$$\lambda U = \{x \in X \mid \forall u \in U.((u,x) \in \mathcal{R})\} = \{x \in X \mid \forall u.(u \in U \text{ implies } (u,x) \in \mathcal{R})\},$$

which in a modal logic can be represented (the relation $\mathcal{R}$ is an incompatibility relation) by,

$$\text{“}\mathcal{M} \vDash_x \neg\phi \text{ iff } \forall u.(\mathcal{M} \vDash_u \phi \text{ implies } (u,x) \in \mathcal{R})\text{.”}$$

The construction of the incompatibility (“perp”) relation $\mathcal{R}$ for a given split negation $\neg$ is provided by (5.13) in Section 5.1.2 (where is denoted by operation $\widetilde{o}_i : (X, \leq) \to (X, \leq)^{\mathrm{OP}}$). The set-based semantics for the constructive negation is obtained in the case where the incompatibility relation $\mathcal{R}$ is symmetric.

Hence, what we have to do is only to extend the Heyting algebras in (6.34) by algebraic negation operation λ, corresponding to the logical negation $\neg$ of the mZ logic (different from the intuitionistic negation), and to obtain from the following representation algebra for many-valued mZ logics:

$$\downarrow^{+}: (X, \leq, \wedge, \vee, \rightharpoonup, \neg, 0, 1) \simeq (X^{+}, \subseteq, \cap, \cup, \rightarrowtail, \lambda, \{0\}, \widehat{X}) \tag{6.35}$$

from Proposition 29 in Section 5.1.2, where for negative operator $\widetilde{o}_i$ we use the symbol $\neg$ in the algebra **A** for its representation isomorphism (5.10), with homomorphic property (5.14), $\lambda = \downarrow^{+}\widetilde{o}_i \bigvee : X^{+} \to X^{+}$, for λ, so that for each $\downarrow^{*} x \in X^{+}$, $\lambda(\downarrow^{+} x) = \downarrow^{+}(\neg x) \in X^{+}$.

It is easy to see that, as in the demonstration given in [227], for any given incompatibility relation $\mathcal{R}$, the additive algebraic operator λ can be used as a split negation for mZ logic.

Corollary 25 ([228]). *Each split negation (modal negation), based on the hereditary incompatible relation of Birkhoff polarity, satisfies the Da Costa weakening axioms (11) and (12).*

Proof. To prove the Birkhoff polarity, we note that the following additivity property holds for any hereditary subsets $U, V \in X^{+}$: $\lambda(U \bigcup V) = \lambda U \bigcup^{\mathrm{OP}} \lambda V = \lambda U \bigcap \lambda V$, with $\lambda\emptyset = \emptyset^{\mathrm{OP}} = X$. It is well known that Heyting algebra operators are closed for hereditary subsets, so that λ applied to a hereditary subset $U \in X^{+}$ has to result in a hereditary subset $\lambda(U) \in X^{+}$ as well (from homomorphic property (5.14), $\lambda = \downarrow^{+}\widetilde{o}_i \bigvee : X^{+} \to X^{+}$), and the Lemma 6 in Section 5.1.2 demonstrates that it is satisfied if the relation $\mathcal{R}$ is hereditary as provided by (5.13). It is enough now to prove that in mZ logic the following formulae are valid (the logic negation operator $\neg$ corresponds to the algebraic operator λ):

$$\neg(\phi \vee \psi) \equiv (\neg\phi \wedge \neg\psi), \quad \text{and} \quad \neg 0 \equiv 1.$$

Indeed, we can derive this as follows:

1	$(1 \Rightarrow \neg 0) \Rightarrow ((\neg 0 \Rightarrow 1) \Rightarrow ((0 \Rightarrow \neg 1) \wedge (\neg 1 \Rightarrow 0)))$	[(3)]
2	$(\neg 0 \Rightarrow 1) \Rightarrow ((0 \Rightarrow \neg 1) \wedge (\neg 1 \Rightarrow 0))$	[1, (10b), (MP)]
3	$(0 \Rightarrow \neg 1) \wedge (\neg 1 \Rightarrow 0)$	[2, (11b), (MP)]
4	$\neg 0 \equiv 1,$	[3, definition of $\equiv$]

and,

1	$(\phi \Rightarrow (\phi \vee \psi)) \Rightarrow (\neg(\phi \vee \psi) \Rightarrow \neg\phi)$	[(9b)]
2	$(\psi \Rightarrow (\phi \vee \psi)) \Rightarrow (\neg(\phi \vee \psi) \Rightarrow \neg\psi)$	[(9b)]
3	$\neg(\phi \vee \psi) \Rightarrow \neg\phi$	[1, (6), (MP)]
4	$\neg(\phi \vee \psi) \Rightarrow \neg\psi$	[2, (7), (MP)]
5	$(\neg(\phi \vee \psi) \Rightarrow \neg\phi) \wedge (\neg(\phi \vee \psi) \Rightarrow \neg\psi)$	[3, 4, (3), (MP)]
6	$((\neg(\phi \vee \psi) \Rightarrow \neg\phi) \wedge (\neg(\phi \vee \psi) \Rightarrow \neg\psi)) \Rightarrow (\neg(\phi \vee \psi) \Rightarrow (\neg\phi \wedge \neg\psi))$	[(TO)]
7	$\neg(\phi \vee \psi) \Rightarrow (\neg\phi \wedge \neg\psi)$	[5, 6, (MP)]
8	$\neg(\phi \vee \psi) \equiv (\neg\phi \wedge \neg\psi)$	[7, (12b), definition of $\equiv$]

□

This property holds for the constructive negation as well, thus for the systems mCZ. Thus, for these two paraconsistent systems we can define the Kripke semantics in the similar way as for the intuitionistic logic. Let us show that in this weak intuitionistic negation, modeled by Birkhoff polarity, the Da Costa principle NdC1 of noncontradiction is generally valid.

Lemma 8 ([228]). *In these mZ calculi, the principle of noncontradiction, in the form, $\neg(\phi \wedge \neg\phi)$, should not be a generally valid schema.*

Proof. In order to show that $\neg(\phi \wedge \neg\phi)$ is not valid in mZ calculi, it is enough to find an example for a system mZ calculi, where this schema $\neg(\phi \wedge \neg\phi)$ is not valid. Consider, e. g., the mZ logic in Lemma 9, with the minimal cardinality is represented by the 3-valued logic $X = \{0, \frac{1}{2}, 1\}$ (a Belnap's sublattice obtained by elimination of the value $\top$) but with negation different from the well-known 3-valued Kleene logic. In the proof of this lemma is demonstrated that $\neg(\frac{1}{2} \wedge \neg\frac{1}{2}) \neq 1$.

Consequently, in the system mZ calculi, the schema $\neg(\phi \wedge \neg\phi)$ is not valid. □

Consequently, this system mZ satisfies Da Costa's requirements, NdC1 and NdC2, and NdC4 as well, because the positive fragment of this logics is equal to the positive part of propositional logic, and hence it is conservative extension of positive propositional logic.

The mZ logic is many-valued propositional logic with a set X of logic truth values, with autoreferential representation in (6.35). That is, different from the original Da Costa weakening of the classical negation that results in a nontruth-functional logics, mZ is a system of many-valued truth-functional logics with a lattice $(X, \leq)$ of truth values. Consequently, we are able to obtain an embedding of mZ logics into the MV intensional FOL presented in a dedicated chapter of this book.

The intuitionistic interpretation of negation and logic constructivism

The fundamental characteristic of the IPC is that negation is a derived operation from the constructive implication, i. e., $\neg_I \phi$ is defined by $\phi \Rightarrow 0$. Thus, in order to analyze the intuitionistic negation $\neg_I$ we have to consider the intuitionistic implication $\Rightarrow$. In Kolmogorov [270], he took care to lay down the meaning of constructive implication:

> *"The meaning of the symbol $\phi \Rightarrow \psi$ is exhausted by the fact that, once convinced of the truth of ϕ, we have to accept the truth of ϕ, too."*

From this point of view, the ex falso (quodlibet) principle (EF) $\neg\phi \Rightarrow (\phi \Rightarrow \psi)$ was questionable, to say the least. In fact, he decided to reject it (in the sense of paraconsistent logic). He argued that axiom now considered does not have and cannot have any intuitive foundation, since it asserts something about the consequence of something impossible. In 1932, Kolmogorov published [271] a full version of this "problematic interpretation," by considering a proposition ϕ as a problems and constructive truth of ϕ comes to "*we have a solution of A.*" Thus, a problem (proposition) $\phi \Rightarrow \psi$ is formulated as "*given a solution of ϕ, find solution of ψ.*" The ex falso axiom $\neg_I \phi \Rightarrow (\phi \Rightarrow \psi)$ was accepted by Kolmogorov on the strength of the following *convention*:

> *"As far as problem $\neg_I \phi \Rightarrow (\phi \Rightarrow \psi)$ is concerned, as soon as $\neg_I \phi$ is solved, the solution of ϕ is impossible, and the problem $\phi \Rightarrow \psi$ has no content. In what follows, the proof that a problem is without content will always be considered as its solution."*

Thus, this *convention* about negation is highly nonconstructive. The modern formulation of intuitionistic implication appears first time in 1934 in Heyting [272], page 14:

> *"A proof of a proposition consists of the realization of the construction demanded by it. $\phi \Rightarrow \psi$ means the intension on a construction, which leads from any proof of ϕ to a proof of ψ."*

Kolmogorov never returned to intuitionistic logic and the matter of EF rule, Heyting on the other hand returned to this principle in his intuitionism where he recognized that in the case of a false antecedent the construction interpretation is problematic:

> *"Now suppose that $\neg_I \phi$ is true, i. e., we have deduced a contradiction from supposition that ϕ were carried out. Then, in sense, this can be considered as a construction, which, joined to a prof of ϕ (which cannot exist) leads to a proof of ψ. I shall interpret the implication in this wider sense."*

Thus, Heyting's justification of the intuitionistic negation is, albeit hesitant, the standard argument of today. We recall that the current intuitionistic meaning of logic connectives:

- A proof of $\phi \wedge \psi$ consists of a proof of ϕ and a proof of ψ plus the conclusion $\phi \wedge \psi$, or in Kripke semantics, for any possible world $w \in \mathcal{W}$,

$$\mathcal{M} \models_w \phi \wedge \psi \quad \text{iff} \quad \mathcal{M} \models_w \phi \text{ and } \mathcal{M} \models_w \psi.$$

- A proof of $\phi \vee \psi$ consists of a proof of ϕ or a proof of ψ plus the conclusion $\phi \vee \psi$, or in Kripke semantics, for any possible world $w \in \mathcal{W}$,

$$\mathcal{M} \models_w \phi \vee \psi \quad \text{iff} \quad \mathcal{M} \models_w \phi \text{ or } \mathcal{M} \models_w \psi.$$

- A proof of $\phi \Rightarrow \psi$ consists of a method (or algorithm) of converting any proof of ϕ into a proof of ψ, or in Kripke semantics, for any possible world $w \in \mathcal{W}$,

$$\mathcal{M} \models_w \phi \Rightarrow \psi \quad \text{iff} \quad (\forall w' \in \mathcal{W})((w, w') \in R_\Box \text{ implies } (\mathcal{M} \models_{w'} \phi \text{ implies } \mathcal{M} \models_{w'} \psi)),$$

  where $R_\Box$ is a reflexive and transitive relation, so that $\phi \Rightarrow \psi$ is equivalent to a modal formula $\Box(\phi \Rightarrow_c \psi) \equiv \Box(\neg_c \phi \vee \psi)$, where $\Box$ is the universal modal "necessary" operator of S4 modal logic and $\Rightarrow_c, \neg_c$ the classical implication and negation, respectively.

  Notice that $\neg_I \phi$ is obtained when ψ is the falsum 0, so that $\neg_I \phi \equiv \Box\neg_c \phi$.
- No proof of 0 (falsum) exists, i. e., for each $w \in \mathcal{W}$, $\mathcal{M} \not\models_w 0$, i. e., "not $\mathcal{M} \models_w 0$."

These historical considerations give more justifications in our attempt to modify this intuitionistic unconstructive negation into another more constructive and paraconsistent.

Proposition 31. *A paraconsistent negation in mZ logic is paraconsistently-constructive, i. e., $\neg = \Box_P \neg_c$ where $\neg_c$ is the classical negation and $\Box_P$ is new universal paraconsistent modal operator.*

Proof. Let us consider the standard Kripke semantics of the intuitionistic negation $\neg_I \phi$ (equivalent to $\phi \Rightarrow 0$) with the set of possible worlds $\mathcal{W}$ for intuitionistic negation (pseudocomplement), where $\neg_c$ is the classic negation and $\Box$ is the universal modal "necessity" (S4) operator, with the reflexive+transitive accessibility relation $R_\Box \subseteq \mathcal{W} \times \mathcal{W}$ between theoretical constructions (from the Brower's constructive point of view). So that $(w, w') \in R_\Box$ means that a theoretical construction (proof) w' is a result of positive development of a theoretical construction w. So that,

$$\begin{aligned} \mathcal{M} \models_w \neg_I \phi \quad & \text{iff} \quad \mathcal{M} \models_w \phi \Rightarrow 0 \\ & \text{iff} \quad \forall w' \in \mathcal{W}((w, w') \in R_\Box \text{ implies } (\mathcal{M} \models_{w'} \phi \text{ implies } \mathcal{M} \models_{w'} 0)) \end{aligned}$$

$$\begin{aligned}&\text{iff} \quad \forall w' \in \mathcal{W}((w,w') \in R_{\Box} \text{ implies (not } \mathcal{M} \vDash_{w'} \phi \text{ or } \mathcal{M} \vDash_{w'} 0))\\ &\text{iff} \quad \forall w' \in \mathcal{W}((w,w') \in R_{\Box} \text{ implies not } \mathcal{M} \vDash_{w'} \phi) \text{ iff } \mathcal{M} \vDash_{w} \Box\neg_c\phi,\end{aligned}$$

So, from this constructive point of view, an informal Kripke semantics is as follows:

> "$\neg_I\phi$ *is proved in the framework* w *iff in the framework of every possible construction* w' *(which is the result of some development of the construction* w*)* ϕ *is not proved.*"

The Kripike semantics for a paraconsistent negation $\neg$ in mZ is, instead, based on an incompatibility relation $\mathcal{R}$ (from Birkhoff's polarity), defined by

$$\|\neg\phi\| = \lambda(\|\phi\|) = \{w \in \mathcal{W} \mid \forall w' \in \|\phi\|.(w',w) \in \mathcal{R}\}, \quad \text{i.e.,}$$

$$\begin{aligned}\mathcal{M} \vDash_w \neg\phi \quad &\text{iff} \quad \forall w'(\mathcal{M} \vDash_{w'} \phi \text{ implies } (w',w) \in \mathcal{R})\\ &\text{iff} \quad \forall w' \text{ (not } \mathcal{M} \vDash_{w'} \phi \text{ or } (w',w) \in \mathcal{R})\\ &\text{iff} \quad \forall w'((w',w) \notin \mathcal{R} \text{ implies not } \mathcal{M} \vDash_{w'} \phi)\\ &\text{iff} \quad \forall w'((w,w') \in R_{\Box_P} \text{ implies not } \mathcal{M} \vDash_{w'} \phi) \text{ iff } \mathcal{M} \vDash_w \Box_P\neg_c\phi,\end{aligned}$$

where $R_{\Box_P} = ((\mathcal{W}\times\mathcal{W})-\mathcal{R})^{-1}$ is the paraconsistently-constructive accessibility relation for the universal *paraconsistent* modal operator $\Box_P$. □

However, our working framework is based on the canonical autoreferential representation and Kripke semantics provided by Definition 65 in Section 5.1.2, and hence we will use the set of possible worlds $\mathcal{W} = \widehat{X}$ in what follows.

What we obtain for the mZ logic is that it is a bimodal logic with two universal modal operators, the necessity universal modal operator $\Box$ (with accessibility binary relation equal to a poset $(\widehat{X}, \leq)$) used for the intuitionistic implication $\Rightarrow$ equal to $\Box \Rightarrow_S$ where $\Rightarrow_S$ is standard (classical) implication, and the universal paraconsistent modal operator $\Box_P$ (with the accessibility binary relation $R_{\Box_P} = ((\widehat{X} \times \widehat{X}) - \mathcal{R})^{-1}$ derived from the *hereditary* incompatibility relation $\mathcal{R}$ defined by (5.13) in Section 5.1.2) used for the modal paraconsistent operator $\neg$ equal to $\Box_P\neg_c$ where $\neg_c$ is classical negation.

Thus, here we will provide a Kripke semantics for the mZ logic, as a particular case of Definition 65 in Section 5.1.2.

Definition 95. We define the Kripke model $\mathcal{M} = (\widehat{X}, \leq, \mathcal{R}, I_K)$ for the mZ logic, where the set of possible worlds is $\widehat{X}$ (join-irreducible elements plus bottom value 0), for a many-valued algebra represented by (6.35), $\mathcal{R}$ is an hereditary incompatibility binary accessibility relation (5.13) for weakened paraconsistent negation, with $R_{\Box_P} = ((\widehat{X} \times \widehat{X}) - \mathcal{R})^{-1}$, and $I_K : \text{Var} \times \widehat{X} \to \mathbf{1}$ is a Kripke interpretation. Then, for any world $x \in \widehat{X}$, and formulae ψ and ϕ,
1. $\mathcal{M} \vDash_x p$ iff $I_K(p,x) = 1$, for any $p \in \text{Var}$.
2. $\mathcal{M} \vDash_x \phi \wedge \psi$ iff $\mathcal{M} \vDash_x \phi$ and $\mathcal{M} \vDash_x \psi$,
3. $\mathcal{M} \vDash_x \phi \vee \psi$ iff $\mathcal{M} \vDash_x \phi$ or $\mathcal{M} \vDash_x \psi$,
4. $\mathcal{M} \vDash_x \phi \Rightarrow \psi$ iff $\forall y \in \widehat{X}((y \leq x$ and $\mathcal{M} \vDash_y \phi)$ implies $\mathcal{M} \vDash_y \psi)$,

5. $\mathcal{M} \models_x \neg\phi$ iff $\forall y \in \widehat{X}(\mathcal{M} \models_y \phi$ implies $(y,x) \in \mathcal{R})$, iff $\forall y \in \widehat{X}((x,y) \in R_{\square_P}$ implies not $\mathcal{M} \models_y \phi)$,

for a negation modal operator $\neg$.

Consequently, from Theorem 17 in Section 5.1.2, we obtain that for any mZ formula ψ, $\|\psi\| \in X^+ =_{def} \{\downarrow^+ x \mid x \in X\}$. is a hereditary subset of join-irreducible truth values of the complete distributive lattice $(X, \leq)$ as represented by the isomorphism (6.35).

Let us show that the intuitionistic negation $\neg_I$ may be obtained as a special case of the Birkhoff's polarity as well (as is our paraconsistent negation).

Corollary 26. *For the incompatibility relation defined by* $\mathcal{R} = (\widehat{X}\times\widehat{X}) - R_\square^{-1}$, *where* $R_\square$ *is a reflexive and transitive accessibility relation of the intuitionistic logic, from the Birkhoff's polarity method we obtain exactly the intuitionistic negation.*

Proof. We have that $R_\square = ((\widehat{X}\times\widehat{X}) - \mathcal{R})^{-1}$, and from Birkhoff's polarity,

$$\|\neg\phi\| = \lambda(\|\phi\|) = \{x \in \widehat{X} \mid \forall y \in \|\phi\|.(y,x) \in \mathcal{R}\}, \quad \text{i.e.,}$$

$$\begin{aligned} \mathcal{M} \models_x \neg\phi \quad &\text{iff} \quad \forall y(\mathcal{M} \models_y \phi \text{ implies } (y,x) \in \mathcal{R}) \\ &\text{iff} \quad \forall y((x,y) \in R_\square \text{ implies not } \mathcal{M} \models_y \phi) \text{ iff } \mathcal{M} \models_x \square\neg_c\phi \text{ iff } \mathcal{M} \models_x \neg_I\phi. \quad \square \end{aligned}$$

Proposition 31 and Corollary 26 demonstrate the general constructive approach to the paraconsistent negations based on the construction of an incompatibility relation with Birkhoff's polarity, and show that in this very general framework, the non-paraconsistent intuitionistic logic is only a special particular case.

Consequently, if we consider these three logics (the intermediate logics between IPC and CPC are well understood and studied already), this weakening of logic connectives can be summarized as follows:

- CPC: here we have only to independent operators: the negation $\neg_c$ and one (usually taken implication) of the three binary operators. Another two operators are only derived operators.
- IPC: here we have the three mutually independent operators, $\wedge, \vee$ and $\Rightarrow$, while negation operator $\neg_I$ is derived one such that $\neg_I\phi$ is logically equivalent to the formula $\phi \Rightarrow 0$, where 0 is a contradiction (falsum) constant.
- mZ: here, we have generally all four operators mutually independent, where the negation $\neg$ is obtained as a weakening of the intuitionistic negation $\neg_I$ by preserving its two fundamental properties: antitonicity and modal additivity.

This kind of weakening of the interdependence of the logic operators is a kind of obtaining of more powerful and relevant logics, by progressively extending classical logic with more powerful semantics: IPC can be seen as a means of extending classical logic with constructive semantics, so that IPC $\prec$ CPC, where $\preceq$ is the ordering in the current lattice of intermediate logics.

In what follows, we will see that mZ logic can be seen as means of extending IPC with paraconsistent semantics as well. So, from the philosophical point of view, mZ will become a new bottom element of the lattice of intermediate logics, that is mZ $\prec$ IPC.

Consequently, mZ extends a constructive logic IPC with Da Costa paraconsistent semantics. In this hierarchy, we obtain more and more relevant logics (where the number of derivable theorems is progressively diminished), in the way that mZ is more relevant logic than IPC, and IPC is more relevant logic than all intermediate logics, while CPC is not relevant at all.

In this new point of view, the relationship between intuitionistic and paraconsistent logics is rather new one and in apparent opposition with the previous historical approach, where these two approaches are considered "dual," and are seen as two opposite extremes.

Theorem 15. *All negative axioms in* mZ *logic are the theorems in IPC.*

Consequently, mZ $\prec$ IPC *is a strict constructive paraconsistent weakening of the intuitionistic logic.*

Proof. 1. From definition of the intutitionistic negation, $(\phi \Rightarrow 0) \equiv \neg_I\phi$, it holds that $(\phi \Rightarrow 0) \Rightarrow \neg_I\phi$ and by substituting ϕ with 0 (denoted by $\phi \mapsto 0$) we obtain

1.1 $(0 \Rightarrow 0) \Rightarrow \neg_I 0$,
1.2 $\phi \Rightarrow \phi$, [theorem in IPC]
1.3 $0 \Rightarrow 0$, [1.2, and substitution $\phi \mapsto 0$]
1.4 $\neg_I 0$, [1.1, 1.3, (MP)]
1.5 $\neg_I 0 \Rightarrow (1 \Rightarrow \neg_I 0)$, [axiom (1) IPC$^+$, with $\phi \mapsto \neg_I 0, \psi \mapsto 1$]
(10.b) $1 \Rightarrow \neg_I 0$, [1.4, 1.5, (MP)]
1.6 $(1 \Rightarrow (\phi \Rightarrow 1))$, [axiom (1) IPC$^+$, with $\phi \mapsto 1, \psi \mapsto \phi$]
1.7 theorem 1, [theorem in IPC]
(11.b) $\phi \Rightarrow 1$, [1.6, 1.7, (MP)]

2. (11.b) $0 \Rightarrow \phi$ is an axiom in IPC.
3. Let us show that the weak contraposition (9.b), $(\phi \Rightarrow \psi) \Rightarrow (\neg_I\psi \Rightarrow \neg_I\phi)$, is a theorem in IPC:
   3.1. The formula (T2), $(\phi \Rightarrow \psi) \Rightarrow ((\psi \Rightarrow \varphi) \Rightarrow (\phi \Rightarrow \varphi))$, is a theorem in IPC.
   3.2. By substitution of φ with 0 in (T2), we obtain $(\phi \Rightarrow \psi) \Rightarrow ((\psi \Rightarrow 0) \Rightarrow (\phi \Rightarrow 0))$, that is, from the fact that $\neg_I\psi$ in IPC is defined by $\psi \Rightarrow 0$, we obtain that (9.b) is a theorem in IPC.
4. From the IPC+ theorem $((\phi \vee \psi) \Rightarrow \varphi) \equiv ((\phi \Rightarrow \varphi) \wedge (\psi \Rightarrow \varphi))$, by substitution of φ by 0 and by definition of intuitionistic negation $\neg_I$, we obtain $\neg_I(\phi \vee \psi) \equiv (\neg_I\phi \wedge \neg_I\psi)$ (modal additive property for intuitionistic negation), thus the theorem (12.b) $\neg_I(\phi \vee \psi) \Rightarrow (\neg_I\phi \wedge \neg_I\psi)$.

Notice that, as in mZ logic, also in IPC, the intuitionistic negation $\neg_I$ is an additive modal operator with Birkhoff's polarity semantics given in Corollary 26.

Corollary 27. *The relationship between the intuitionistic negation $\neg_I$ and the weakened paraconsistent negation $\neg$ in* mZ *logic is: $\neg_I \leq \neg$.*

Proof. The meaning of $\neg_I \leq \neg$ in the Heyting algebra $(X, \leq, \wedge, \vee, \rightharpoonup)$, extended by the modal paraconsistent negation $\neg : X \to X$, is expressed by the sentence $(\forall x \in X)(\neg_I x \leq \neg x)$ or, equivalently, in mZ logic, by the theorem $\neg_I\phi \Rightarrow \neg\phi$ for any ϕ. By considering that $\neg_I\phi$ is a formula $\phi \Rightarrow 0$, it means that we have to show that a formula $(\phi \Rightarrow 0) \Rightarrow \neg\phi$ is a theorem as follows:

1	$(\phi \Rightarrow 1) \Rightarrow ((\phi \Rightarrow (1 \Rightarrow \varphi)) \Rightarrow (\phi \Rightarrow \varphi))$,	[axiom (2) IPC$^+$, where $\psi \mapsto 1$]
2	$(\phi \Rightarrow (1 \Rightarrow \varphi)) \Rightarrow (\phi \Rightarrow \varphi)$,	[1, (11,b), (MP)]
3	$((1 \Rightarrow \varphi) \Rightarrow (1 \Rightarrow \varphi)) \Rightarrow ((1 \Rightarrow \varphi) \Rightarrow \varphi)$,	[2, where $\phi \mapsto 1 \Rightarrow \varphi$]
4	$(1 \Rightarrow \varphi) \Rightarrow \varphi$,	[3, $(1 \Rightarrow \varphi) \Rightarrow (1 \Rightarrow \varphi)$, (MP)]
5	$(1 \Rightarrow \neg\phi) \Rightarrow \neg\phi$,	[4, where $\varphi \mapsto \neg\phi$]
6	$\neg\phi \equiv (1 \Rightarrow \neg\phi)$,	[5, axiom (1) IPC$^+$ with $\psi \mapsto 1$]
7	$(\phi \Rightarrow 0) \Rightarrow (\neg 0 \Rightarrow \neg\phi)$,	[from axiom (9.b), where $\psi \mapsto 0$]
8	$(\phi \Rightarrow 0) \Rightarrow (1 \Rightarrow \neg\phi)$,	[$\neg 0 \equiv 1$, from (10.b) and (11.b) with $\phi \mapsto \neg 0$]
9	$(\phi \Rightarrow 0) \Rightarrow \neg\phi$,	[from 8 and 5]

i. e., $\neg_I\phi \Rightarrow \neg\phi$. □

Now we will show which axioms are necessary to add to mZ logic in order to obtain the intuitionistic logic.

Proposition 32. *The intuitionistic logic IPC is equal to* mZ *plus axiom $(\neg\phi \Rightarrow (\phi \Rightarrow 0))$.*

Consequently, both formulae, $\phi \vee \neg\phi$ and $\neg(\phi \wedge \neg\phi)$, excluded middle and paraconsistent noncontradiction relatively, are not valid schemas in mZ.

Proof. The IPC is defined by eight positive axioms in IPC$^+$, plus:

(11.b) $0 \Rightarrow \phi$, falsity axiom, plus two axioms for the intuitionistic negation,

(N1) $\neg\phi \Rightarrow (\phi \Rightarrow 0)$,

(N2) $(\phi \Rightarrow 0) \Rightarrow \neg\phi$.

Consequently, it is enough only to show that $(\phi \Rightarrow 0) \Rightarrow \neg\phi$ is a theorem in mZ.

From the weak contraposition axiom schemata (9.b) in the case when ψ is substituted by 0, we obtain that $(\phi \Rightarrow 0) \Rightarrow (\neg 0 \Rightarrow \neg\phi)$ and from the fact that $\neg 0 \equiv 1$ (from (11.b) when ϕ is substituted by $\neg 0$ and (10.b)), we obtain $(\phi \Rightarrow 0) \Rightarrow (1 \Rightarrow \neg\phi)$.

It is enough to show that $(1 \Rightarrow \neg\phi) \equiv \neg\phi$ is a theorem in mZ, and it is demonstrated in point 6 of the proof of Corollary 27.

Thus, we have that the noncontradiction schema is not a valid schema in mZ (from previous Lemma 8). Moreover, if we denote the set of theorems of IPC by $\mathcal{L}_{\mathrm{ICP}}$ and the set of theorems of mZ by $\mathcal{L}_{\mathrm{mZ}}$, from the fact that $\mathcal{L}_{\mathrm{mZ}} \subset \mathcal{L}_{\mathrm{ICP}}$ and from the fact that the excluded-middle schema does not hold in IPC, i. e., $\phi \vee \neg\phi \notin \mathcal{L}_{\mathrm{ICP}}$, we also obtain $\phi \vee \neg\phi \notin \mathcal{L}_{\mathrm{mZ}}$. □

Consequently, based on Theorem 15 and Proposition 32, we obtain that mZ is constructive logic as IPC (they have the same set of theorems for their positive fragment), but the set of theorems with negation operator $\neg$ in mZ is a strict paraconsistent *subset* of theorems with intuitionistic negation $\neg_I$ in IPC.

Consequently, mZ is a *subintuitionistic* logic, and hence mZ is a more useful logic than IPC, i. e., more relevant w. r. t. the IPC, because it avoids explosive inconsistency. From the point of Da Costa paraconsistency of the mZ logic, it was demonstrated (by Theorem 14) that the Da Costa axioms (11) and (12) are theorems in mZ, so that in mZ all hierarchy of Da Costa's systems are present in this single mZ logic; thus, mZ logic is by itself Da Costa paraconsistent and its axioms implicitly cover the Da Costa's reductio relativization property (and its propagation) and combines it with the constructive property of the intuitionistic logics.

These results demonstrate that the paraconsistency is not simply dual to the constructivism, as it was historically supposed and investigated. In fact, mZ logic combines both constructive and paraconsistent properties, where both excluded middle and the non-contradiction schemas are not valid.

We have demonstrated that the paraconsistency is based on a very constructive approach, and we will show it in next sections by the construction of incompatibility relations for the paraconsistent negations: we will present a number of useful subintuitionistic mZ logics for practical applications as well.

6.2.2 Subintuitionistic paraconsistent mZ-logics derived from Kleene, Belnap, fuzzy and Gödel–Dummett logics

In what follows, we will present a number of examples of many-valued logics that are members of the mZ system. We will use the Kripke-style models of the mZ logics in Definition 95, where the set of possible worlds $\mathcal{W} = \widehat{X}$ used for the Birkhof-polarity semantics of its algebraic split negation λ, used for negation connective $\neg$ in mZ logic, with the algebra on hereditary subsets $(X^+, \subseteq, \bigcap, \bigcup, \rightarrowtail, \lambda)$ as provided by representation isomorphism (6.35) between many-valued Heyting algebra of truth values in X (with implication defined as pseudo-complement $x \rightharpoonup y = \bigvee\{z \in X \mid z \wedge x \leq y\}$ and negation by $\neg x = x \rightharpoonup 0$) and its set-based representation algebra (6.34),

$$\downarrow^+ : (X, \leq, \wedge, \vee, \rightharpoonup, \neg, 0, 1) \simeq \left(X^+, \subseteq, \cap, \cup, \rightarrowtail, \lambda, \{0\}, \widehat{X}\right)$$

in Section 6.2.1, where the set-based implication operator is defined by

$$(\downarrow^+ x) \rightarrowtail (\downarrow^+ y) = \downarrow^+(x \rightharpoonup y)$$

Thus, what we need is only to replace the intuitionistic negation used in Heyting algebras by their paraconsistent weakening (substitute $\widehat{\neg}$ by λ in the isomorphism above), and hence to find the incompatibility relation $\mathcal{R}$ used in Birkhoff-polarity for the split negation λ, in order to preserve this representation-isomorphism above.

Now we will apply this definition of autoreferential semantics to a number of examples of the logics to be transformed into the mZ intuitionistic paraconsistent systems. In particular, we will consider the logics with a minimal cardinality (three and four-valued logics) and then of also infinite-valued logics.

In [190], Belnap introduced a logic intended to deal in a useful way with inconsistent or incomplete information, as we explained in Section 5.1.3, but here we will represent slightly different its four truth values in accordance with representation of truth values in mZ logic. So, we denote the four logic values as $X = \mathcal{B}_4 = \{0, \frac{1}{2}, 1, \top\}$, where 1 is *true*, 0 is *false*, $\top$ is inconsistent (both true and false) or *possible*, and $\frac{1}{2}$ is *unknown*. As Belnap observed, these values can be given two natural orders: *truth* order, $\leq$, and *knowledge* order, $\leq_k$, such that $0 \leq \top \leq 1$, $0 \leq \frac{1}{2} \leq 1$, and $\frac{1}{2} \leq_k 0 \leq_k \top$, $\frac{1}{2} \leq_k 1 \leq_k \top$.

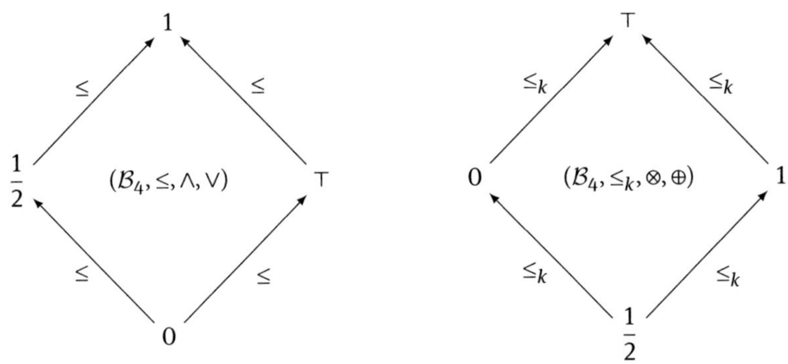

Meet and join operators under $\leq$ are denoted $\wedge$ and $\vee$; they are natural generalizations of the usual conjunction and disjunction notions. Meet and join under $\leq_k$ are denoted $\otimes$ (*consensus*, because it produces the most information that two truth values can agree on) and $\oplus$ (*gullibility*, it accepts anything it's told). We have that:

$$0 \otimes 1 = \frac{1}{2}, \quad 0 \oplus 1 = \top, \quad \top \wedge \frac{1}{2} = 0 \text{ and } \top \vee \frac{1}{2} = 1.$$

There is an epistemic notion of truth negation, denoted by $\sim$, (reverses the truth $\leq$ ordering, while preserving the knowledge $\leq_k$ ordering): switching 0 and 1, leaving $\frac{1}{2}$ and $\top$. Let us consider the minimal cardinality for such one many-valued logic of the system mZ.

Lemma 9. *In the* mZ *logic, the minimal cardinality is represented by the 3-valued logic $X = \{0, \frac{1}{2}, 1\}$ (a Belnap's sublattice obtained by elimination of the value $\top$) but with negation different from the well-known 3-valued Kleene logic. We obtain a weakening of the Kleene-negation by the fact that, instead of $\neg 1 = 0$, we have that $\neg 1 = \frac{1}{2}$.*

Proof. The set of join-irreducible elements is $\mathcal{W} = \{\frac{1}{2}, 1\}$ and $\widehat{X} = \mathcal{W} \bigcup \{0\}$, with the isomorphism (6.34) such that $\downarrow^+ 0 = \{0\}$, $\downarrow^+ \frac{1}{2} = \{0, \frac{1}{2}\}$ and $\downarrow^+ 1 = \{0, \frac{1}{2}, 1\} = \widehat{X}$, and hence $X^+ = \{\{0\}, \{0, \frac{1}{2}\}, \widehat{X}\}$ and hereditary relation, from (5.13), $\mathcal{R} = \{(0,0), (0, \frac{1}{2}), (0,1), (\frac{1}{2}, 0), (\frac{1}{2}, \frac{1}{2}), (1,0), (1, \frac{1}{2})\}$ for the split negation λ.

It is easy to verify that $\lambda(\widehat{X}) = \{0, \frac{1}{2}\} \neq \{0\}$ (i. e., from the algebra isomorphism (6.34), $\neg 1 = \frac{1}{2} \neq 0$) and that for $V = \{0, \frac{1}{2}\}$, $\lambda(V \bigcap \lambda(V)) = \{0, \frac{1}{2}\} \neq \widehat{X}$ (i. e., $\neg(\frac{1}{2} \wedge \neg \frac{1}{2}) = \frac{1}{2} \neq 1$), so that the principle of noncontradiction is valid.

It is different from the Kleene logic where $\neg 1 = 0$, while in our 3-valued paraconsistent mZ logic we have by the weakening of negation that $\neg 1 = \frac{1}{2}$ (i. e., $\neg 1 = \neg \frac{1}{2} = \frac{1}{2}, \neg 0 = 1$), but $\neg$ is monotonic w. r. t. the knowledge ordering $\leq_k$ so that this logic can be used for logic programming with Fitting's fixed-point semantics and stable models. □

Note that this paraconistent 3-valued logic satisfy all axioms of the mCZ logics as well.

Let us show that in mZ system there is a Belnap's bilattice based logic with weakened negation that is monotonic w. r. t. the knowledge ordering $\leq_k$. Consequently, we can use this 4-valued paraconsistent mZ logic for a logic programming for the standard bilattice negation $\sim$.

Lemma 10. *In the* mZ *systems, the bilattice based logic is represented by the 4-valued Belnap's bilattice* $X = \mathcal{B}_4 = \{0, \frac{1}{2}, 1, \top\}$, *but with negation* $\neg$ *different from the original bilattice negation* $\sim$. *We obtain a weakening of the negation* $\sim$ *by the fact that, instead of* $\sim 1 = 0$ *and* $\sim \top = \top$, *we define* $\neg 1 = \frac{1}{2}$ *and* $\neg \top = 1$, *respectively.*

Proof. The set of join-irreducible elements is $\mathcal{W} = \{\frac{1}{2}, \top\}$ and $\widehat{X} = \mathcal{W} \bigcup \{0\}$, with the isomorphism (6.34) such that $\downarrow^+ 0 = \{0\}$, $\downarrow^+ \frac{1}{2} = \{0, \frac{1}{2}\}$, $\downarrow^+ \top = \{0, \top\}$ and $\downarrow^+ 1 = \{0, \frac{1}{2}, \top\} = \widehat{X}$, and hence $X^+ = \{\{0\}, \{0, \frac{1}{2}\}, \{0, \top\}, \widehat{X}\}$ and hereditary relation, from (5.13), $\mathcal{R} = \{(0,0), (0, \frac{1}{2}), (0, \top), (\frac{1}{2}, 0), (\frac{1}{2}, \frac{1}{2}), (\top, 0), (\top, \frac{1}{2}), (\top, \top)\}$ for the split negation λ. It is easy to verify that $\lambda(\widehat{X}) = \{0, \frac{1}{2}\} \neq \{0\}$ and for $V = \{0, \frac{1}{2}\}$, $\lambda(V \bigcap \lambda(V)) = \{0, \frac{1}{2}\} \neq \widehat{X}$, so that the principle of noncontradiction is valid.

We have that $\lambda(\{0, \frac{1}{2}\}) = \{0, \frac{1}{2}\}$ and $\lambda(\{0, \top\}) = \widehat{X} = \{0, \frac{1}{2}, \top\}$.

Consequently, we obtain that $\neg 1 = \neg \frac{1}{2} = \frac{1}{2}$ and $\neg 0 = 1$ and $\neg \top = 1$. Consequently, it is easy to verify that the obtained weakened negation $\neg$ is monotonic w. r. t. the knowledge ordering $\leq_k$ and we are able to use Fitting's fixed-point semantics and stable models, in the same way as the Belnap's logic with the standard negation $\sim$. □

Note that if we omit the 4-th value $\top$ from the paraconsistent Belnap's logic in Lemma 10, i. e., replace it by $\frac{1}{2}$, we obtain, as reduction, the paraconsistent Kleene's logic in Lemma 9, as my be seen from their truth-value tables:

	IPC	mZ
0	1	1
$\frac{1}{2}$	$\top$	$\frac{1}{2}$
1	0	$\frac{1}{2}$
$\top$	$\frac{1}{2}$	1

$\mapsto$

	IPC	mZ
0	1	1
$\frac{1}{2}$	$\frac{1}{2}$	$\frac{1}{2}$
1	0	$\frac{1}{2}$

In both cases of these two lemmas for mZ-logics obtained from intuitionistic Kleene's and Belnap's logics, the split negation λ is modeled by the incompatibility relation $\mathcal{R} = \bigcup_{x \in X}(\downarrow^+ x) \times (\downarrow^+ \neg x)$ in (5.13) in Section 5.1.2.

Now we will apply this method to an important infinitary many valued logic: Zadeh's fuzzy logic.

Da Costa paraconsistent Zadeh-fuzzy logic

Let us consider the original set of Zadeh fuzzy operators on the closed interval $X = [0,1]$ of reals, with negation $\neg$, conjunction $\wedge$ and disjunction $\vee$, defined as follows:

1. $\neg x = 1 - x$;
2. $x \wedge y = \min(x, y)$;
3. $x \vee y = \max(x, y)$;

so that the conjunction and disjunction are the meet and join operators of the complete distributive lattice $([0,1], \leq)$.

The closed interval of reals $[0,1]$ is a total ordering, i. e., a complete distributive lattice, so that we can enrich the original fuzzy logic with intuitionistic implication (as in t-norm logics), that is with a relative pseudo-complement. Thus, for any $x, y \in [0,1]$ we define $x \rightharpoonup y$ by $\bigvee\{z \mid x \wedge z \leq y\} = \max\{z \mid \min(x,z) \leq y\}$.

It is easy to verify that the fuzzy logic is not Da Costa paraconsistent, because of the fact that $\neg 1 = 0$. In the standard fuzzy logic, the sentences are considered true if their truth value x satisfy $0 < \varepsilon_1 \leq x \leq 1$ for a prefixed value ϵ_1, so that the set of designated truth values is $D = [\varepsilon_1, 1]$ (each sentence with the truth value in D is considered as true sentence).

Consequently, as in the case of the 3-valued Kleene logic and 4-valued Belnap's bilattice logic, we need to change the original negation, where $\neg x = 1 - x$, in the way that $\neg 1 = \varepsilon_0 > 0$, where $\varepsilon_0 > 0$ is a prefixed positive infinitesimal value. In this way, with this very slightly changed fuzzy logic, we obtain a paraconsistent fuzzy mZ logic.

We recall that in any many-valued mZ logic the set of designated elements is exactly the singleton $\{1\}$ (this fact comes out from the Kripke-like semantics of the mZ system, where a sentence (proposition) is true only and only if it is true in *all* possible worlds $\widehat{X}$). Thus the set of truth values in the paraconsistent fuzzy logic that is a member of mZ system has to be changed from $[0,1]$ for the set D of designated elements in the fuzzy logic, as follows.

Lemma 11. *Let us consider a fuzzy logic with a matrix defined by a set of designated elements* $D = [\varepsilon_1, 1]$, *with* $0.5 < \varepsilon_1 \leq 1$, *and let us fix an infinitesimal positive value* ε_0 *such that* $0 < \varepsilon_0 \ll \varepsilon_1$. *We define the intuitionistic implication by the relative-pseudo-complement* $\rightharpoonup$ *in* $X = [0,1]$, *and the negation operator for any* $x \in X$,

$$\neg x = \max(\varepsilon_0, 1 - x) \tag{6.36}$$

Then the logic $(X, \leq, \wedge, \vee, \rightharpoonup, \neg)$ *is a paraconsistent mZ fuzzy logic.*

Proof. First of all, let us show that $\neg$ is an antitonic additive operator, thus a split negation that can be modeled by Birkhof polarity and its incompatibility relation.

In fact, for any two $x, y \in X$ if $x \geq y$ then $\neg x = \max(\varepsilon_0, 1 - x) \leq \max(\varepsilon_0, 1 - y) = \neg y$. Thus, it is antitonic. The antitonicity is preserved in the cases when $\neg x = 1$ as well. Let us show that it is also additive:

1. For the bottom element $0 \in X$, we have that $\neg 0 = \max(\varepsilon_0, 1) = 1$.
2. For $x, y \in X$, $\neg(x \vee y) = \neg(\max(x, y)) = \max(\varepsilon_0, 1 - \max(x, y)) = \max(\varepsilon_0, \min(1 - x, 1 - y)) = \max(\varepsilon_0, (1 - x) \wedge (1 - y)) = \varepsilon_0 \vee ((1 - x) \wedge (1 - y)) = (\varepsilon_0 \vee (1 - x)) \wedge (\varepsilon_0 \vee (1 - x)) = \neg x \wedge \neg y$.

Thus, $\neg$ is an additive antitonic operation, and consequently, it is a split negation.

Let us define the hereditary incompatible relation for this split negation. The subset of join-irreducible elements of X is the set $\mathcal{W} = [0, 1] - \{0\}$.

So, the set of all hereditary subsets of the complete distributive lattice $\mathcal{W}$ is $X^+ = \{\downarrow^+ x \mid x \in X\} = \{[0, x] \mid x \in X\}$. Thus, based on (5.13) in Section 5.1.2 the incompatibility relation for λ is

$$\mathcal{R} = \bigcup_{x \in X} [0, x] \times [0, \max(\varepsilon_0, 1 - x)],$$

Consequently, for each $x \in X$, $\lambda([0, x]) = [0, \max(\varepsilon_0, 1 - x)]$, and it corresponds to $\neg x = \max(\varepsilon_0, 1 - x)$.

Thus, this is a well-defined paraconsistent fuzzy logic, which belongs to the mZ logics. □

It is easy to verify, that in the limit case for the set of designated elements $D = \{1\}$, i. e., when $\varepsilon_1 = 1$, we obtain that $\neg x \in D$ (i. e., it is true) if and only if $x = 0$.

Notice that for each $\max\{\varepsilon_0, 1 - \varepsilon_1\} < x < \varepsilon_1$, we have that $\neg(x \wedge \neg x) \notin D$ (i. e., it is not true), which satisfies the principle of noncontradiction Nd1 of Da Costa negation weakening (consider, e. g., the limit case when $\varepsilon_1 = 1$).

Paraconsistent subintuitionistic Gödel–Dummett logic

Gödel–Dummett logic (the logic of the minimum t-norm) was implicit in Gödel's 1932 proof of infinite-valuedness of intuitionistic logic [273]. Later (1959), it was explicitly studied by Dummett who proved a completeness theorem for the logic [274].

Definition 96. Gödel–Dummett logics, $LC_n = (X_n, \wedge, \vee, \rightharpoonup, \neg, 0, 1)$, where for finite $n \geq 2$, $X_n = \{0, \frac{1}{n-1}, \ldots, \frac{n-2}{n-1}, 1\}$ and for infinite n, $X_\infty = [0,1]$ (closed interval of reals) are both total orders, where $\wedge, \vee$ are the meet and join operators of these distributive complete lattices and $\rightharpoonup$ and $\neg$ are defined as in the IPC.

Thus, they are intermediate logics, i. e., IPC + $(\phi \Rightarrow \psi) \vee (\psi \Rightarrow \phi)$.

From the fact that this (added to IPC) axiom $(\phi \Rightarrow \psi) \vee (\psi \Rightarrow \phi)$ does not contain negation symbols, we conclude that the logic obtained by addition of this axiom to mZ axiom system would not change the paraconsistent weakening of the intuitionistic negation. Consequently, we are able to make the paraconsistent weakening of Gödel–Dummett logic in the same way as for IPC.

Lemma 12. *The paraconsistent Gödel–Dummett logic is obtained by addition the axiom $(\phi \Rightarrow \psi) \vee (\psi \Rightarrow \phi)$ to mZ system.*

In this case, we do not change X_n and we define $X_\infty = \{0\} \bigcup [a, 1]$ for an enough big value $n \gg 2$ and atom $a = \frac{1}{n-1}$, and the paraconsistent negation for any x in X_n:

$$\neg x = 1 \quad \text{if } x = 0; \quad a \text{ otherwise.}$$

Proof. It is easy to verify that $\neg$ is an antitonic operator. Let us show that it is an additive modal operator as well:

1. $\neg 0 = 1$.
2. Let us show that for each $x, y \in X$, $\neg(x \vee y) = \neg x \wedge \neg y$:
   2.1 when $x = 0$ (or $y = 0$), we have $\neg(0 \vee y) = \neg y = 1 \wedge \neg y = \neg 0 \wedge \neg y$.
   2.2 when both x and y are different from 0: $\neg(x \vee y) = a = a \wedge a = \neg x \wedge \neg y$. □

Notice that the set of join-irreducible elements is $\mathcal{W} = X \backslash \{0\}$, so that the incompatibility relation, based on (5.13) in Section 5.1.2, is

$$\begin{aligned}\mathcal{R} &= \bigcup_{x \in X_n} (\downarrow^+ x) \times (\downarrow^+ \neg x) = \{\{0\} \times X_n\} \bigcup_{x \in X_n - \{0\}} (\downarrow^+ x) \times \left\{0, \frac{1}{n-1}\right\} \\ &= \left(\bigcup_{x \in X_n} \left\{(0,x), (x,0), \left(x, \frac{1}{n-1}\right)\right\}\right) - \left\{\left(0, \frac{1}{n-1}\right)\right\}\end{aligned}$$

so that for each $x \in X$,

$$\lambda(\downarrow^+ x) = X_n \quad \text{if } x = 0; \quad \left\{0, \frac{1}{n-1}\right\} \text{ otherwise.}$$

It is easy to verify that $\neg_I \preceq \neg$, as demonstrated by Corollary 27 for mZ logic, and $\neg_I \neq \neg$. It is interesting to note that

$$\neg x \neq \neg_I x =_{\text{def}} (x \rightharpoonup a) = 1 \quad \text{if } x \in \{0, a\}; \quad a \text{ otherwise.}$$

Both formulae, $\phi \vee \neg\phi$ and $\neg(\phi \wedge \neg\phi)$, are not theorems. In fact for each $x \in X_n$ such that $x \neq 0$, we have that $\neg(x \wedge \neg x) = a < 1$, and for every $x \notin \{0,1\}, \neg x \vee x = x < 1$.

Notice that by the paraconsistent weakening of the minimal cardinality Gödel–Dummett logic (when $n = 3$), we obtain the paraconsistent Kleene logic in Lemma 9.

6.3 Belnap's 4-valued P2P data integration with incomplete and inconsistent data

Data quality in Cooperative Information Systems (CISs), which integrate a number of local heterogeneous database systems is an increasingly important issue. Current in-practice developed CISs are based on different software and architectural paradigms, and are specified a number of ad hoc algorithms for quality query answering, without an unifying logic framework (different from well-defined semantics in DIS (Data Integration Systems), introduced in Section A.6.4). The consequence is that each software system responds in some way to user queries with record for which is not often clear if it is really a logic answer from CISs database, if it is certain or only possible answer, or, in some way, a new created information nonlogically deducible from a database. Sometimes it is not also clear if the records obtained are complete answers w. r. t. the logically derivable answers from the system. Because of such considerations, in this section we present a general framework for a query answering in a logic theory in Data Quality Cooperative Information Systems (DaQuinCIS) [275], by an epistemic extension of the standard data integration systems, and we introduce also a 4-valued logic based on the Belnap's bilattice (introduced in Section 5.1.3) and applied also in Section 5.3, in order to deal with incomplete and inconsistent information.

The Cooperative Information Systems (CISs) is distributed and heterogeneous information systems that cooperate by sharing information, constraints, and goals [276]. CISs *include* data integration systems as well as systems that share common information while not explicitly integrating data. It is well known that quality of data is a *necessary* requirement for a CIS, i. e., CISs *need data quality*. First, a system in the CIS will not easily exchange data with another system without a knowledge on their quality, and cooperation becomes difficult without data exchanges. Second, when poor quality data are exchanged, there is a progressive deterioration of data stored in the whole CIS.

Quality of data is not simply their correctness. Let us consider the case of an `address` to delivery some mail: it can be correct, as having a `street name` and a `street number` specified, but if not having a `city` included, it is useless for most applications. The example shows that quality of data also means completeness. In a similar way, we could show that data quality means many other things, such as currency, interpretability, consistency and other "dimensions," often depending from the context where data are used and also from specific users within a given context. It follows that data of good quality are not easy to be obtained: data quality itself is a complex concept defined by multiple dimensions, depending from many variables, often very subjective.

The Data Quality in CIS (DaQuinCIS) is a platform for exchanging and improving data quality in cooperative information systems, such that includes a data integration system that allows to access data and quality "dimensions" (metadata): a *data integration system* $\mathcal{I}$ [111] is a triple $\mathcal{I} = \langle \mathcal{G}, \mathcal{S}, \mathcal{M} \rangle$, where $\mathcal{G}$ is the *global schema*, $\mathcal{S}$ is the *source schema*, and $\mathcal{M}$ is the *mapping* between $\mathcal{G}$ and $\mathcal{S}$ (see Section A.6.4).

Organizations export data and quality data according to a common model, referred to as the *Data and Data Quality* (D^2Q) *model*. It includes the definitions of constructs to represent data, a common set of data quality properties, constructs to represent them and the association between data and quality data. More details on the model can be found in [277].

Thus, in DaQuinCIS, the Data integration system of an application is extended by a number of auxiliary concepts used to support quality "dimensions" for correspondent concepts of application: the structure of such auxiliary information is expressed in the same definition language of the ordinary data integration system. We restrict the consideration of D^2Q models to those models where both ordinary "application-oriented" data and their metadata (quality "dimensions") are embedded into the same definition language: we refer such D^2Q models as *flattened* models. The characteristic of flattened D^2Q models is that metadata concern only data values: they do not deal with aspects concerning quality of logical schema and data format. Also the query language for such D^2Q models is able to elaborate these metadata as ordinary data, so that we are able to formulate complex queries over both data and their metadata.

Thus, *formal framework* for DaQuinCIS is that of data integration system, $\mathcal{I}_Q$, is a triple $\mathcal{I}_Q = \langle \mathcal{G}_Q, \mathcal{S}_Q, \mathcal{M}_Q \rangle$, where $\mathcal{G}_Q$ is the *global schema*, an extension of $\mathcal{G}$ by quality "dimensions" concepts, $\mathcal{S}_Q$ is the *source schema*, an extension of $\mathcal{S}$ by quality "dimensions" concepts, and $\mathcal{M}_Q$ is the *mapping* between $\mathcal{G}_Q$ and $\mathcal{S}_Q$, an extension of $\mathcal{M}$ by mappings between "dimension" concepts. We will refer to $\mathcal{I}_Q$ by: *logic theory*, which define this quality-data integration system.

Generally speaking, when data are considered locally, they must satisfy only the integrity constraints specified in the source to which they belong, but they are not required to satisfy the fundamental integrity constraint for the global schema: the *real world entity* must be represented by the unique record of the corresponding concept in the global schema. In CIS, such requirement is often unsatisfied: different records from local (source) databases (each one of them can have a particular quality), which corresponds to the same real world entity are mapped to the concept in global schema. Thus, while integrating data coming from different sources, it often happens that the global database, which is constructed in the integration process, is *inconsistent* with such fundamental integrity constraint. Because of that in CIS we do not impose any integrity constraint over global schema, but we need to distinguish the *true* records in the global schema (which uniquely represents some real world entity) from *possible* records (the case when more than two records represent the same real world entity, and there is not any system-provided inference able to choose some of them as *true*). Notice that also in the presence of quality filtering, such as the best quality principle, can happen that two different records of the same real world entity have the same best quality value.

Another aspect is that the set of available sources might not store exactly the data needed to answer a query posed to the system, so that the mapping cannot be considered exact. Hence, query processing in a data integration system is, in general, a form of reasoning with *incomplete* information. In the context of data integration, the incomplete information is introduced by existentially quantified integration rules: such quantifiers are eliminated by introducing Skolem functions in the place of existentially quantified attributes of concepts in a global schema.

Example 39. For example, a set of public administrations, which need to exchange information about citizens and their health state in order to provide social aids, is a cooperative business system derived from the Italian *e*-Government scenario [278]. In order to improve the quality of the data, and thus to improve the service level offered to businesses and enterprises, the agencies can deploy a cooperative information system according to the architecture; therefore, each agency exports its data according to a local schema (see Figure 6.1).

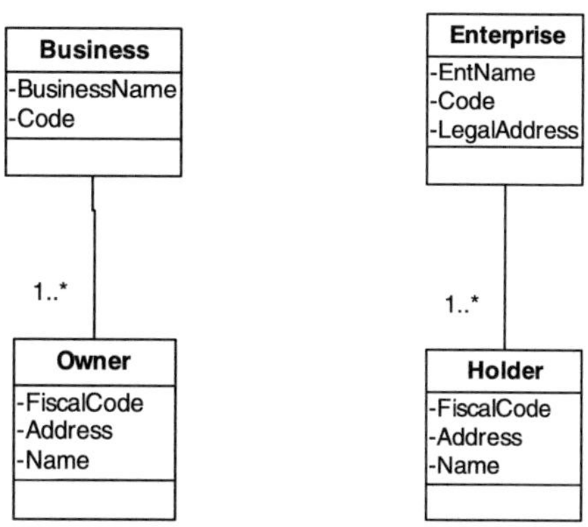

Figure 6.1: Conceptual representation of local schemas.

In the shown figure, two simplified versions of the local schemas are shown: two agencies, namely the Social Security Agency, referred to as INPS (Istituto Nazionale Previdenza Sociale) at the left-hand side and the Chambers of Commerce, referred to as CoC (Camere di Commercio) at the right-hand side.

Let us assume that the global schema derived from INPS and CoC local schemas is composed by two analog concepts:

1. Business: with Name, ID and Legal/Address attributes, denoted by $P_G(x_n, x_{\mathrm{ID}}, x_a)$
2. Holder: with, FiscalCode, Address and Name attributes.

Let $P_{\mathrm{INPS}}(x_n, x_{\mathrm{ID}})$ and $P_{\mathrm{CoC}}(x_n, x_{\mathrm{ID}}, x_a)$ denote the local concepts in local schemas respectively, then the following mapping $\mathcal{M}_Q$, between global and local schemas, can be given in the first-order logic:

$$\exists x_a P_G(x_n, x_{\mathrm{ID}}, x_a) \leftarrow P_{\mathrm{INPS}}(x_n, x_{\mathrm{ID}})$$
$$P_G(x_n, x_{\mathrm{ID}}, x_a) \leftarrow P_{\mathrm{CoC}}(x_n, x_{\mathrm{ID}}, x_a)$$

Thus, the first of these two mapping formulae introduce incomplete information in the attribute Legal/Address of Business in the global schema. Consequently, also for global schemas without any integration constraint, we can have incomplete information in the database of the global schema. The records in global schema with Skolem constants, introduced for existentially quantified attributes, may be considered an *unknown* facts, which is not possible to support directly in the classical two-valued FOL, and hence we can assign to them the logic value $\bot$ of the Belnap's bilattice by working with many-valued intensional FOL, introduced in Section 5.2.

Once one has made the transition from classical 2-valued to partial models, or three-valued logic models, allowing *incomplete* information, it is a small step toward allowing models admitting *inconsistent* information: introducing 4-th "possible" logic value, and consequently the minimal 4-valued Belnap's bilattice.

It is obvious that data integration over different local source databases make inconsistent the database system also in the case of the more *fundamental* database constraint based on the principle that each real world entity has to be represented by at most one record in a database. If we consider the Example 39, we can for instance suppose that the attribute FiscalCode is right identification for persons (real world instances) in each local database, and that such identification constraint on local databases is *explicitly* expressed in the local schema definition. But if we now define explicitly such identity constraint over global schema, we would (possibly) obtain an *inconsistent* database, i. e., a database with empty set of models.

Usually, during the design phase of an application database we try to render explicit all user constraint by means of integrity constraints over a database. Here, we consciously reject such a method: we do not impose any constraint over the global schema, thus the explicit (formal, or system) constrains are always satisfied but the implicit (user) constraints are not satisfied. Just because of such problems, in Cooperative Information Systems (CIS) it has been introduced auxiliary quality "dimensions" information. Such added information would be used during query-answering process, in order to satisfy this implicit user requirement also: in the case when more than one tuple of data, for the same real world entity, are returned by the certain answer, the *record matching algorithm* has to provide the unique record (with the best quality) to the user. Thus, this matching algorithm, is an alternative "external-to-DBtheory" way (w. r. t. the explicit "internal" integrity constraint over database) to guarantee the satisfaction of this fundamental user implicit requirement.

In the rest of this section, we will show that also in such setting, the obtained database system, while formally (explicitly) consistent, remains again implicitly "inconsistent" (more than one records for the same real world entity may happen in the query answering). There are two questions in order to resolve such impasse:

- The first is to consider all records of the cluster not as *true* but as *possible* answers. In this case, we abandon the strict 2-valued logic and assume the more flexible 4-valued Belnap's logic.
- The second is to abandon the query-answering semantics and to accept other different principle: "creating the best-answering" principle. Shortly, the cluster of records in the certain answer to the query, related to the same real world entity, is used to create a new, in some way best-quality, or more-true, record. In this case, we must consider the databases with partial orders (e. g., the truth ordering of the lattice of truth values) and develop a query language for such databases.

Because of this problem it is necessary to give a formal definitions in order to distinguish these two query-answering approaches: the *query answering* from the best-answer *creation*. This approach is reasonable if CIS is composed by different epistemically independent peer-databases (as two independent databases of INPS and CoC in Example 39), so that we obtain the P2P where each of them is a single Data integration system with the Belnap's multivalued logic. The interpeer mappings can be defined by intensionally equivalent views, in the way as described the query-answering in the P2P database systems (see Sections 3.2 and 3.2.3) by classic two-valued FOL in Chapter 3. So, we need to define the intensional equivalence "≈" between P2P databases (see Corollary 3 in Section 1.3) *but in the many-valued logic framework.*

Because of that we can enrich the many-valued intensional FOL $\mathcal{L}_{\text{in}}$ by an existential modal operator "$\Diamond$," and hence its Kripke semantics in Definition 82 will be enlarged by the new accessibility relation $\mathcal{R}_\Diamond$ and many-valued satisfaction as follows.

Proposition 33 (MV intensional equivalence). *We enrich the many-valued intensional logic $\mathcal{L}_{\text{in}}$ by the existential modal operator $\Diamond$, by enlarging its Kripke's interpretation $\mathcal{M}$ in Definition* 82 *by new accessibility relation $\mathcal{R}_\Diamond =_{\text{def}} \mathcal{W} \times \mathcal{W}$, such that for any world $(w,g) \in \mathbb{W} = \mathcal{W} \times \mathcal{D}^{\mathcal{V}_\mathcal{B}}$ with $w = I^*_{\text{mv}} \in \mathcal{W}$,*

$$\mathcal{M} \vDash_{w,g} \Diamond\phi \quad \textit{iff} \quad \textit{exists } w' \in \mathcal{W}, (w,w') \in \mathcal{R}_\Diamond \textit{ and } \mathcal{M} \vDash_{w',g} \phi, \tag{6.37}$$

and hence we define the many-valued intensional equivalence "≈" between two virtual predicates ϕ and ψ with the same tuple of free variables $\mathbf{x} = (x_1, \dots, x_n)$, analogously to (1.11),

$$\phi(x_1, \dots x_n) \approx \psi(x_1, \dots x_n) \quad \textit{iff} \quad \Diamond\phi(x_1, \dots x_n) \Leftrightarrow \Diamond\psi(x_1, \dots x_n) \tag{6.38}$$

So, any two first-order open formulae, $\phi(x_1, \dots x_n)$ and $\psi(x_1, \dots x_n)$, are intensionally equivalent *iff $\widehat{\Diamond\phi}(x_1, \dots x_n)$ and $\widehat{\Diamond\psi}(x_1, \dots x_n)$ are intensionally* equal.

Proof. We have that for any explicit possible world (MV-interpretation) $w' = I^*_{mv} \in \mathcal{W}$, corresponding to the many-valued interpretation I'_{mv},

$$\begin{aligned}
&I_n(\widehat{\Diamond}\phi(x_1,\dots,x_k))(w') \\
&\quad = \|\Diamond\phi(x_1,\dots,x_k)\|_{\mathcal{M},w'} \quad \text{(from (5.36) and (5.40))} \\
&\quad = \{(g(x_1),\dots,g(x_k),g(x_B)) \mid g \in \mathcal{D}^{\mathcal{V}_B} \text{ and } g(x_B) = I'_{mv}(\Diamond\phi/g) \neq f\} \quad \text{(from (5.31))} \\
&\quad = \{(g(x_1),\dots,g(x_k),g(x_B)) \mid g \in \mathcal{D}^{\mathcal{V}_B}, g(x_B) \neq f \text{ and } \mathcal{M} \vDash_{w',g} \widehat{\Diamond}\phi(x_1,\dots,x_k)\} \\
&\quad \text{(from (5.39))} \\
&\quad = \{(g(x_1),\dots,g(x_k),g(x_B)) \mid g \in \mathcal{D}^{\mathcal{V}_B}, g(x_B) \neq f \text{ and exists } w \in \mathcal{W} \\
&\quad \text{such that } (w',w) \in \mathcal{R}_\Diamond = \mathcal{W}\times\mathcal{W} \text{ and } \mathcal{M} \vDash_{w,g} \phi(x_1,\dots,x_k)\} \\
&\quad \text{(from (6.37))} \\
&\quad = \{(g(x_1),\dots,g(x_k),g(x_B)) \mid g \in \mathcal{D}^{\mathcal{V}_B}, g(x_B) \neq f \text{ and exists } w \in \mathcal{W} \\
&\quad \text{with } \mathcal{M} \vDash_{w,g} \phi(x_1,\dots,x_k)\} \\
&\quad = \bigcup_{w\in\mathcal{W}} \{(g(x_1),\dots,g(x_k),g(x_B)) \mid g \in \mathcal{D}^{\mathcal{V}_B}, g(x_B) \neq f \text{ and } \mathcal{M} \vDash_{w,g} \phi(x_1,\dots,x_k)\} \\
&\quad = \bigcup_{w\in\mathcal{W}} \|\phi(x_1,\dots,x_k)\|_{\mathcal{M},w'} \\
&\quad = \bigcup_{w\in\mathcal{W}} I_n(\phi(x_1,\dots,x_k))(w).
\end{aligned}$$

That is, the intension of $\Diamond\phi(x_1,\dots x_n)$, i. e., $I_n(\phi(x_1,\dots,x_k)) : \mathcal{W} \to \mathfrak{R}\mathrm{m}$, is a *constant* function (which does not depend on explicit possible world $w \in \mathcal{W}$).

Thus, $\phi(x_1,\dots x_n)$ and $\psi(x_1,\dots x_n)$ are intensionally *equivalent* if

$$\bigcup_{w\in\mathcal{W}} I_n(\phi(x_1,\dots,x_k))(w) = \bigcup_{w\in\mathcal{W}} I_n(\psi(x_1,\dots,x_k))(w), \quad \text{i. e.,}$$
$$\text{if } I_n(\Diamond\phi(x_1,\dots,x_k))(w) = I_n(\Diamond\phi(x_1,\dots,x_k))(w) \quad \text{for every world } w \in \mathcal{W}, \quad \text{i. e.,}$$
$$\text{if } \Diamond\phi(x_1,\dots x_n) \text{ and } \Diamond\psi(x_1,\dots x_n) \quad \text{are intensionally } \textit{equal}.$$

□

It is easy to verify that the definition of the many-valued intensional equivalence (6.38) is just a generalization of the two-valued intensional equivalence (1.11), where the two-valued logic equality "≡" is substituted by the many-valued "⇔" version. Moreover, it is easy to show that

$$\begin{aligned}
&\mathcal{M} \vDash_{w,g} \Diamond\phi(x_1,\dots x_n) \Leftrightarrow \Diamond\psi(x_1,\dots x_n) \\
&\text{iff} \quad \exists w,w' \in \mathcal{W}, \quad \mathcal{M} \vDash_{w,g} \phi(x_1,\dots x_n) \text{ and } \mathcal{M} \vDash_{w',g} \psi(x_1,\dots x_n), \quad \text{that is,} \\
&\text{iff} \quad \mathcal{M} \vDash_{w,g} \phi(x_1,\dots x_n) \quad \text{implies } \exists w' \in \mathcal{W} \text{ such that } \mathcal{M} \vDash_{w',g} \psi(x_1,\dots x_n).
\end{aligned}$$

So, we are able to use the query-answering in the P2P database systems in this many-valued framework based on Belnap's bilattice $\mathcal{B}_4$, based on the query-rewriting algorithms used in Chapter 3 for the two-valued FOL.

A more general information of the meaning of possible logic value in the framework of logic programming for databases with inconsistent information is given in [279]. In this way, we consider the *possible* value as weak true value and *not as inconsistent* (that is both true and false). We have more knowledge for record with such value, w. r. t. the true record, because we know also that there are other records in database, which are different from this one but are referred to the same real world entity, and the user query which extracts such real world entity from a database must also retrieve *all* records referred to it, in order to obtain complete answer.

In effect, by using the many-valued logic based on the Belnap's bilattice, each peer database in a network of P2P databases used in CIS will respond by a set of records, so the union of the records obtained from all these peer databases will not be only many-valued but also we will have two records obtained from two different peer databases refer to the same real world entity. Because of that, this union of records obtained as query-answer from different peer databases will be called *the preanswers*, and in CIS we will need also some kind of filtering of them, in order to chose the best candidate record from the cluster of record that refer the same real world entity. By such a post-query-answering process of filtering we will obtain the desired result in which we will have that for any real world entity there is only one and the best quality record in the query answer. This post query filtering of the query preanswer will be analyzed in the next sections.

6.3.1 Filtering query preanswers: real world identity constraint

As we have explained, the preanswer obtained as a union of records (obtained as the simple union of query answers to given user query from different peer databases in a given CIS P2P system, by using the MV-intensional equivalences between views of different peers) needs, as counterpart, the *record matching* algorithms during the query answering processing, in order to select (for each cluster of many-valued answers to a query from different peer databases in a given P2P system) at maximum one record for a real world entity underlined in the query.

We recall (see Section A.6.4) that each peer database is a DIS $(\mathcal{I}, \mathcal{D})$ where $\mathcal{I} = \langle \mathcal{G}, \mathcal{S}, \mathcal{M} \rangle$ is a data integration system with global schema $\mathcal{M}$, source schema $\mathcal{S}$ and GLAV mapping $\mathcal{M}$ between them, and $\mathcal{D}$ be a source database for $\mathcal{I}$. Given a user query $q(\mathbf{x})$ the answered records will be many-valued: an answered record will be "possible" answer (with logic value $\top \in \mathcal{B}_4$) if from two different source data of $\mathcal{S}$ we obtain mutually inconsistent answers; will be "unknown" answer (with logic value $\bot \in \mathcal{B}_4$) if we have Skolem constants in this record; otherwise the true record (with logic value $t \in \mathcal{B}_4$).

The preanswers $q(\mathbf{x})^{\mathcal{I},\mathcal{D}}$ defined in precedence will has to be successively filtered in order to avoid to have more records associated *by user* to the same real world entity. Thus, all DaQuinCIS database systems hidden some part of preanswers, $q(\mathbf{x})^{\mathcal{I},\mathcal{D}}$, in order to satisfy the implicit (user's) real world identity constraint. If we consider such constraint at epistemic (user's) meta-level, the following two logic principles must be satisfied:

1. *Epistemic consistency*: at maximum one record for a real world entity can be contained in the answer.
2. *Epistemic completeness*: the filtered answers has to contain a record for every real world entity referred by model-theoretic answers.

The first principle is clear and discussed in precedence. The second is more complex to understand: roughly, it has to guarantee to users that *every* real world entity, which *satisfies* the user query, in a given *logic theory* of DaQuinCIS, must be represented at the answer by one record. For instance, such logic principle is not satisfied by the algorithm for querying for best quality data in a LAV (Local as view) integration system, [280], thus, it *is not* a query-answering system: it is based on data integration system but needs some other formal logic semantics in order to define what is the meaning of their answers to user queries.

Let us try now to give a general logical/mathematical framework for the semantics of query answering, which satisfy also epistemic principles defined in precedence.

Let $|\mathbf{x}|$ denote the number of variables (attributes) of the query $q(\mathbf{x})$, and the set $S_k = \{i \mid 1 \leq i \leq k\}$, so that $S_{|\mathbf{x}|} = \{1, 2, \ldots, |\mathbf{x}|\}$. Thus, we introduce the functional space, $2_{\text{space}} = \{\{0,1\}^{S_k} \mid k = 1, 2, \ldots\}$, such that each element $f_k \in 2_{\text{space}}$ is a function $f_k : S_k \to \{0,1\}$ for some $k \geq 1$. Thus, we can define the choice of the matching key algorithm, Ω_{mkey}, such that for any given preanswer $q(\mathbf{x})^{\mathcal{I},\mathcal{D}}$ returns with the *matching key* set of attributes $\mathbf{x}_{\text{ID}}$, as follows.

Definition 97. Let $\mathcal{L}_Q$ denote the set of all queries, $\mathcal{D}_I^Q$ the set of all DaQuinCIS P2P systems, and $\mathcal{P}(V)$ the powerset of all variables in $\mathcal{L}_Q$. Then the choice of the matching key algorithm can be defined as the function $\Omega_{\text{mkey}} : \mathcal{L}_Q \times \mathcal{D}_I^Q \to \mathcal{P}(V)$, such that for any query $q(\mathbf{x}) \in \mathcal{L}_Q$ and DaQuinCIS system $(\mathcal{I}, \mathcal{D}) \in \mathcal{D}_I^Q$,

$$\mathbf{x}_{\text{ID}} = \Omega_{\text{mkey}}(q(\mathbf{x}), (\mathcal{I}, \mathcal{D})) \subseteq \mathbf{x},$$

where $\mathbf{x}_{\text{ID}}$ is the obtained matching key, thus a subset of all attributes $\mathbf{x}$ of the query.

Notice that in the case when in a data integration systems $\mathcal{I}$ are defined ID-attributes for their concepts in global and local schemas (e. g., when global schema is defined as the universal relation [281]), the function Ω_{mkey} does not depend by the second argument, i. e., its λ-abstraction, function $\Lambda(\Omega_{\text{mkey}}) : \mathcal{D}_I^Q \to \mathcal{P}(V)^{\mathcal{L}_Q}$ is a constant mapping, where Λ is the currying operator from lambda calculus used in diagram A.10 in Section A.5. In this case, the matching key is defined directly from ID-attributes used in the query $q(\mathbf{x})$.

Example 40. In [282], it is proposed to exploit quality data exported by each cooperating organization in order to automatically choose the matching key. The idea is to choose a high "quality" key. Let us consider as an example the choice of a key with a low completeness value; after a sorting on the basis of such a key, the potential matching records can be not close to each other, due to null values. Similar considerations can be made also in the case of low accuracy or low consistency of the chosen key; a low accurate or low consistent key does not allow to have potential matching records close to each other. Therefore, we evaluate the quality of the matching key in terms of accuracy, consistency and completeness. Besides quality of data, the other element influencing the choice of the key is the *identification power*.

The Identification Power IP_j of the field j is defined as

$$\frac{\text{Number of } \mathrm{eq}_j \text{ Classes}}{\text{Total Number of Records}}$$

where eq_j Classes are the equivalence classes originated by the relation eq_j applied to the totality of records: given two records (tuples) $\mathbf{r}_1$ and $\mathbf{r}_2$, and given a field j of the two records, we define the equivalence relation eq_j such that

$$\mathbf{r}_1 \,\mathrm{eq}_j\, \mathbf{r}_1 \quad \text{iff} \quad \pi_j(\mathbf{r}_1) = \pi_j(\mathbf{r}_2),$$

i. e., the values of the field j of the records $\mathbf{r}_1$ and $\mathbf{r}_2$ are equal.

The data quality parameter called "Data Quality of the field j" (DQ_j) represents an overall quality value for the field j and can be calculated in different ways. As an example, in [282], we calculate (DQ_j) as a linear combination of accuracy, consistency and completeness values for the field j, where the coefficients were experimentally determined.

Given the overall quality value DQ_j and the identification power IP_j, we introduce the parameter K_j equal to multiplication of DQ_j and IP_j.

Let us consider all the fields j of records, different from the last field containing the logic value of this record, the steps to calculate the matching key are the following ones:

- Computation of the Data Quality DQ_j of the field j.
- Computation of the Identification Power IP_j of the field j.
- Computation of the parameter $K_j = \mathrm{DQ}_j \cdot \mathrm{IP}_j$.
- Selection of the matching key as $\max\{K_j\}$.

The selection of a set of fields to construct the key is also possible and the computation of the data quality and the identification power can be easily extended to such cases. In this way, the algorithm for function Ω_{mkey} is well-defined.

When we obtain matching key for a given query $q(\mathbf{x})$ over DaQuinCIS database system, we are ready to consider matching method in order to obtain a partition of records (set of *clusters*), each one consisting of records referring to the same world entity.

Example 41. Usually a matching decision is based on a specific edit distance function; string or edit distance functions consider the amount of difference between strings of symbols. We can chose the Levenshtein distance [283], which is a well-known early edit distance where the difference between two text strings is simply the number of insertions, deletions or substitutions of letters to transform one string into another.

The function we use for deciding if two strings S_1 and S_2 are the same is also dependent from the lengths of the two strings as follows:

$$f(S_1, S_2) = \frac{\max(\mathrm{length}(S_1), \mathrm{length}(S_2)) - \mathrm{LD}(S_1, S_2)}{\max(\mathrm{length}(S_1), \mathrm{length}(S_2))}$$

According to such a function, we normalize the value of the Levenshtein distance $\mathrm{LD}(S_1, S_2)$ by the maximum between the lengths of the two strings, i. e., the function f is 0 if the strings are completely different, 1 if the strings are completely equal.

The procedure we propose to decide if two records match each other is the following:

- the function f is applied to the values of a same field in the two records. If the result is greater than a fixed threshold T_1, the two values are considered equal; we call T_1 *field the similarity threshold.* It is fixed experimentally.
- If the number of equal pairs of values in the two records is greater than a threshold T_2, then the two records are considered as match; we call T_2 *record the similarity threshold.* It is fixed experimentally.

Let now try to give an abstract definition for matching algorithm.

Definition 98 (Matching algorithm for partition of preanswers). The matching algorithm for a DaQuinCIS system $(\mathcal{I}, \mathcal{D}) \in \mathcal{D}_I^Q$ with the set of queries $\mathcal{L}_Q$ over it (with the set V of all free variables in $\mathcal{L}_Q$) can be given by the following function: Match : $\mathcal{L}_Q \times \mathcal{P}(V) \times \mathfrak{Rm} \times \mathfrak{Rm} \to \{0, 1\}$, such that for a query $q(\mathbf{x}) \in \mathcal{L}_Q$, tuple of variables $\mathbf{y} \in \mathcal{P}(V)$ and records $\mathbf{r}_1, \mathbf{r}_2 \in \mathfrak{Rm}$, we have that

$$\mathrm{Match}(q(\mathbf{x}), \mathbf{y}, \mathbf{r}_1, \mathbf{r}_2) = \begin{cases} 1, & \text{if } \mathbf{y} = \mathbf{x}_{\mathrm{ID}}, \mathbf{r}_1, \mathbf{r}_2 \in q(\mathbf{x})^{\mathcal{I},\mathcal{D}} \text{ and } \mathbf{r}_1 \approx \mathbf{r}_2 \\ 0, & \text{otherwise} \end{cases} \tag{6.39}$$

where $\mathbf{x}_{\mathrm{ID}} = \Omega_{\mathrm{mkey}}(q(\mathbf{x}), (\mathcal{I}, \mathcal{D})) \subseteq \mathbf{x}$, $q(\mathbf{x})^{\mathcal{I},\mathcal{D}}$ is the query preanswer in the DaQuinCIS system $(\mathcal{I}, \mathcal{D})$ and $\mathbf{r}_1 \approx \mathbf{r}_2$ means that they refer the same real world entity (are in the same cluster).

By λ-abstraction, we obtain the function $\Lambda(\mathrm{Match}) : \mathcal{L}_Q \times \mathcal{P}(V) \to \{0, 1\}^{\mathfrak{Rm} \times \mathfrak{Rm}}$, so that for a given query $q(\mathbf{x})$ we obtain the derived matching function

$$\mathrm{Match}_{q(\mathbf{x})} = \Lambda(\mathrm{Match})(q(\mathbf{x}), \Omega_{\mathrm{mkey}}(q(\mathbf{x}), (\mathcal{I}, \mathcal{D}))) : q(\mathbf{x})^{\mathcal{I},\mathcal{D}} \times q(\mathbf{x})^{\mathcal{I},\mathcal{D}} \to \{0, 1\}.$$

The meaning of this abstraction is that the reduced function $\mathrm{Match}_{q(\mathbf{x})}$ contains implicitly all data quality "dimensions" (metadata), necessary to compare any two records $\mathbf{r}_1, \mathbf{r}_2 \in q(\mathbf{x})^{\mathcal{I},\mathcal{D}}$ in order to decide if they are referred to the same real-world entity. Formally, only this functional abstractions deal with metadata knowledge of DaQuinCIS database systems, their *semantics* represent the metadata of DaQuinCIS, i. e., we may consider that *metadata are encapsulated* into such functional abstractions. So, for any given query $q(\mathbf{x})$ over DaQuinCIS database system $(\mathcal{I}, \mathcal{D})$, and for any two records in the pre-answer, $\mathbf{r}_1, \mathbf{r}_2 \in q(\mathbf{x})^{\mathcal{I},\mathcal{D}} \subseteq \mathfrak{Rm}$, they are in the same cluster,

$$\mathbf{t}_1 \approx \mathbf{t}_2 \quad \text{if } \mathrm{Match}_{q(\mathbf{x})}(\mathbf{r}_1, \mathbf{r}_2) = 1.$$

In the simplest case when the functional abstraction $\mathrm{Match}_{q(\mathbf{x})}$ does not depend of the metadata (quality dimensions), then it is the characteristic function of the equality $|\mathbf{r}_1|_{\mathbf{x}_{\mathrm{ID}}} = |\mathbf{r}_2|_{\mathbf{x}_{\mathrm{ID}}}$, $\mathbf{r}_1, \mathbf{r}_2 \in q(\mathbf{x})^{\mathcal{I},\mathcal{D}}$, where $|\mathbf{r}|_{\mathbf{x}_{\mathrm{ID}}}$ denotes a projection of the record $\mathbf{r}$ on attributes in $\mathbf{x}_{\mathrm{ID}}$. Now we will introduce the following quality preorders, different from that in [275] in the 2-valued framework, for the many-valued logic framework of database peers in the CIS based on the Belnap's bilattice $\mathcal{B}_4$.

Definition 99 (Quality preorder between tuples in query preanswers). We define the quality function by $\mathrm{Qual} : \mathcal{L}_Q \times \mathcal{D}_I^Q \times \mathfrak{Rm} \to \mathbb{R}$, where $\mathbb{R}$ is a set of real numbers, such that for a given query $q(\mathbf{x}) \in \mathcal{L}_Q$, a DaQuinCIS system $(\mathcal{I}, \mathcal{D}) \in \mathcal{D}_I^Q$, and any two records $\mathbf{r}_1, \mathbf{r}_2 \in \mathfrak{Rm}$, with $k = |\mathbf{x}| + 1$,

$$\begin{aligned} &\mathrm{Qual}(q(\mathbf{x}), (\mathcal{I}, \mathcal{D}), \mathbf{r}_1) < \mathrm{Qual}((\mathcal{I}, \mathcal{D}), \mathbf{r}_2) \quad \text{iff} \quad \mathbf{r}_1, \mathbf{r}_2 \in q(\mathbf{x})^{\mathcal{I},\mathcal{D}} \quad \text{with} \\ &\quad \pi_k(\mathbf{r}_1) = \pi_k(\mathbf{r}_2), \quad \mathrm{Match}_{q(\mathbf{x})}(\mathbf{r}_1, \mathbf{r}_2) = 1 \text{ and } \mathbf{r}_2 \text{ has better computed quality than } \mathbf{r}_1. \end{aligned}$$

So, we are able to define the total quality preorder between the tuples in any cluster of the query preanswer $q(\mathbf{x})^{\mathcal{I},\mathcal{D}}$ with number $k = |\mathbf{x}| + 1$ of query free variables, for any two $\mathbf{r}_1, \mathbf{r}_2 \in q(\mathbf{x})^{\mathcal{I},\mathcal{D}}$ with $\mathrm{Match}_{q(\mathbf{x})}(\mathbf{r}_1, \mathbf{r}_2) = 1$, by

$$\mathbf{r}_1 \preceq \mathbf{r}_2 \quad \text{iff} \quad \begin{cases} \pi_k(\mathbf{r}_1) <_t \pi_k(\mathbf{r}_2), \text{ or} \\ \pi_k(\mathbf{r}_1) = \bot \text{ and } \pi_k(\mathbf{r}_2) = \top, \text{ or} \\ \pi_k(\mathbf{r}_1) = \pi_k(\mathbf{r}_2) \text{ and } \mathrm{Qual}(q(\mathbf{x}), (\mathcal{I}, \mathcal{D}), \mathbf{r}_1) \leq \mathrm{Qual}((\mathcal{I}, \mathcal{D}), \mathbf{r}_2) \end{cases} \tag{6.40}$$

where "$<_t$" is the truth-order in the Belnap's bilattice $\mathcal{B}_4$.

Note that for each record in query preanswer, $\mathbf{r} \in q(\mathbf{x})^{\mathcal{I},\mathcal{D}}$, with $k = |\mathbf{x}| + 1$, we have that its last field contains a logic value of this record, with $\pi_k(\mathbf{r}) \in \{t, \bot, \top\} \subset \mathcal{B}_4$, so that quality preorder "$\preceq$" in the clusters of this preanswer is generated by the truth and knowledge orders in Belnap's billatice, and only when both record have the same truth value we need also the computation of the quality $\mathrm{Qual}(q(\mathbf{x}), (\mathcal{I}, \mathcal{D}), \mathbf{r})$ in order to define "$\preceq$." The most simple way to compute this quality is to assign to any peer database the unique level of its data quality w. r. t. all other peers, because if we have in any cluster two records with the same truth value these two records are obtained as query answers from two different peers.

Now we are ready to give the formal definition for the semantics of a query answering in DaQuinCIS database systems.

Corollary 28 (Filtering preanswers by their quality preorders). *For any query $q(\mathbf{x}) \in \mathcal{L}_Q$ and DaQuinCIS system $(\mathcal{I}, \mathcal{D}) \in \mathcal{D}_I^Q$, the quality preorder "$\preceq$" in each cluster of the query preanswer $q(\mathbf{x})^{\mathcal{I},\mathcal{D}}$ is a total preorder.*

Consequently, by using this quality preorders in each cluster, we can extract the best quality record, and hence we obtain a perfectly filtered answers that satisfy both epistemic constraints: consistency and completeness.

We will denote this filtering algorithm by a mapping $m_{\text{alg}} : \mathfrak{Rm} \to \mathfrak{Rm}$, such that for a query preanswer $q(\mathbf{x})^{\mathcal{I},\mathcal{D}}$, the perfectly filtered answer is equal to $m_{\text{alg}}(q(\mathbf{x})^{\mathcal{I},\mathcal{D}})$.

Proof. It is easy to verify that "$\preceq$" is really a preorder, so that for any $\mathbf{r} \in q(\mathbf{x})^{\mathcal{I},\mathcal{D}}$, from the third line in (6.40), we obtain that $\mathbf{r} \preceq \mathbf{r}$. Moreover, for each cluster from the fact that $\pi_k(\mathbf{r}) \in \{t, \perp, \top\} \subset \mathcal{B}_4$ with $\perp <_t t$ and $\top <_t t$, for each two record of a given cluster at least one of the three conditions in (6.40) is satisfied.

Thus, at each cluster we have a uniquely determined best quality record, and hence at maximum one record for a real world entity (corresponding to a given cluster in $q(\mathbf{x})^{\mathcal{I},\mathcal{D}}$) we will have for the user, after this filtering of the query preanswer. From the fact that each real world entity corresponds to some cluster in the query preanswer and that by filtering we obtain the best record for each cluster, and also the epistemic completeness is satisfied. □

In next section, we will provide for this filtering process, based on the quality preorder "$\preceq$," over a query preanswer, the equivalent logic form of the user's query, such that filtered query answer corresponds to the satisfaction of this new logic formulae (obtained by an epistemic modification of the original user's query).

6.3.2 Modal query language for databases with a partial order

The Abstract Object Type (AOT) for a query-answering system of a CIS for a computation of query preanswers from the P2P many-valued database system, can be represented by the coalgebra provided in Definition 133 in Section A.6.2 in the Appendix, by substitution $\mathcal{L}_A \mapsto \mathcal{L}_Q$, $\Upsilon \mapsto \mathfrak{Rm}$ and X_A is a hidden sort (a set of internal states of the CIS).

So, the AOT for a query-answering system of a CIS together with the *external algorithm* $m_{\text{alg}} : \mathfrak{Rm} \to \mathfrak{Rm}$ for the query preanswers in Corollary 28, can be represented by the following filter-process coalgebra:

$$\alpha = \langle \Lambda(\text{Next}_Q), m_{\text{alg}} \circ \Lambda(\text{Out}_Q) \rangle : X_A \to X_A^{\mathcal{L}_Q} \times \mathfrak{Rm}^{\mathcal{L}_Q} \tag{6.41}$$

where Λ is the currying operator from lambda calculus used in diagram A.10 in Section A.5.

Such database with external software (algorithm m_{alg}) can be equivalently represented as an AOT for a *database with a partial order* $\preceq$ (obtained by *embedding* of the algorithm m_{alg} into a database logic theory), denoted by "$A+\preceq$," and given by a following logically query-modified coalgebra:

$$\beta = \langle \Lambda(\mathrm{Next}_{mQ}), \Lambda(\mathrm{Out}_{mQ})\rangle : X_{A+\preceq} \to X_{A+\preceq}^{\mathcal{L}_{mQ}} \times \mathfrak{Rm}^{\mathcal{L}_{mQ}} \tag{6.42}$$

of the polynomial endofunctor $(\_)^{\mathcal{L}_{mQ}} \times \mathfrak{Rm}^{\mathcal{L}_{mQ}} : \mathbf{Set} \to \mathbf{Set}$, where $\mathcal{L}_{mQ}$ is the set of all *modified* conjunctive queries, $\mathcal{L}_{mQ} = \{\triangledown q(\mathbf{x}) \mid q(\mathbf{x}) \in \mathcal{L}_Q\}$, so that $\triangledown q(\mathbf{x})^{\mathcal{I},\mathcal{D}}$ denotes the set of filtered answers equal to $m_{\mathrm{alg}}(q(\mathbf{x})^{\mathcal{I},\mathcal{D}})$. The set of internal states of this AOT is defined by $X_{A+\preceq} = \{s \bigcup R_{\preceq} \mid s \in W_A\}$, where $R_{\preceq}$ denotes the partial ordered set with, $(\mathbf{r}_1, \mathbf{r}_2) \in R_{\preceq}$ iff $\mathbf{r}_2 \preceq \mathbf{r}_1$, which is an *invariance* (i. e., it holds in all internal states of AOT system).

We denote by $\simeq_A : X_A \to X_{A+\preceq}$ this bijection between these two sets of states.

The idea is to obtain the behavioral equivalence of these two AOT's: that is, the original CIS P2P database, for a given conjunctive query $q(\mathbf{x})$ in the first step computes the query preanswer $q(\mathbf{x})^{\mathcal{I},\mathcal{D}}$, and successively filtered answer $m_{\mathrm{alg}}(q(\mathbf{x})^{\mathcal{I},\mathcal{D}})$, while the AOT of a database with hidden internal states $A+\preceq$ computes the (equivalent) answer to the modified logic formula $\triangledown q(\mathbf{x})$.

Example 42. It is easy to verify [275] that, for the Example 59 in Section A.5.2 in the Appendix, $\triangledown q(\mathbf{x})$ is equivalent to the modified query formula $q(\mathbf{x}) \wedge \forall \mathbf{x}'.((q(\mathbf{x}') \wedge \mathbf{x} \preceq \mathbf{x}') \Rightarrow \mathbf{x}' \preceq \mathbf{x})$, so that the semantics of the operator $\triangledown$ corresponds to the mapping m_{alg}, i. e.,

$$[\triangledown] = m_{\mathrm{alg}}.$$

Proposition 34. *The following commutative diagrams represent the behavioral equivalence for AOT's of a CIS P2P database system with external and embedded algorithm m_{alg} of Corollary 28, respectively,*

$$\begin{array}{ccc}
X_A \times \mathcal{L}_Q & \xrightarrow{\langle \mathrm{Next}_Q, \mathrm{Out}_Q\rangle} & X_A \times \mathfrak{Rm} \\
\Big\downarrow {\simeq_A \times \triangledown} & & \Big\downarrow {\simeq_A \times m_{\mathrm{alg}}} \\
X_{A+\preceq} \times \mathcal{L}_{mQ} & \xrightarrow{\langle \mathrm{Next}_{mQ}, \mathrm{Out}_{mQ}\rangle} & X_{A+\preceq} \times \mathfrak{Rm}
\end{array}
\qquad
\begin{array}{ccc}
(X_A & \xrightarrow{\alpha} & X_A^{\mathcal{L}_Q} \times \mathfrak{Rm}^{\mathcal{L}_Q}) \\
\Big\uparrow {\simeq_A^{-1}} & & \Big\downarrow {\gamma = \gamma_1 \times \gamma_2} \\
(X_{A+\preceq} & \xrightarrow{\beta} & X_{A+\preceq}^{\mathcal{L}_{mQ}} \times \mathfrak{Rm}^{\mathcal{L}_{mQ}})
\end{array}$$

where the coalgebras α and β are given by (6.41) and (6.42), respectively, and:

- $\gamma_1 : X_A^{\mathcal{L}_Q} \to X_{A+\preceq}^{\mathcal{L}_{mQ}}$ *is defined for each $f : \mathcal{L}_Q \to X_A$, we take function $\gamma_1(f) = f_1 : \mathcal{L}_{mQ} \to X_{A+\preceq}$ such that for each $\triangledown q(\mathbf{x}) \in L_{mQ}$, $f_1(\triangledown q(\mathbf{x})) == \simeq_A (f(q(\mathbf{x})))$;*

– $\gamma_2 : \mathfrak{Rm}^{\mathcal{L}_Q} \to \mathfrak{Rm}^{\mathcal{L}_{mQ}}$ *is defined for each function* $l : \mathcal{L}_Q \to \mathfrak{Rm}$, *we take function* $\gamma_2(l) = l_1 : \mathcal{L}_{mQ} \to \mathfrak{Rm}$ *such that for each* $\triangledown q(\mathbf{x}) \in L_{mQ}$, $l_1(\triangledown q(\mathbf{x})) = l(q(\mathbf{x}))$;

So, for any filter-processing coalgebra α, *its behaviorally-equivalent query-modified coalgebra (generated by different functor) is* $\beta = \gamma \circ \alpha \circ \simeq_A^{-1}$ *determined by the second commutative diagram.*

This behavior-equivalence can be also represented by the isomorphism between coalgebras $\simeq_A$: $(X_A, \alpha) \simeq (X_{A+\preceq}, \delta)$, *where* $\delta = \theta \circ \beta$, *of the polynomial functor* $T_c = (\_)^{\mathcal{L}_Q} \times \mathfrak{Rm}^{\mathcal{L}_Q} : \mathrm{Set} \to \mathrm{Set}$ *for the language of conjunctive queries* $\mathcal{L}_Q$, *and the mapping* $\theta = \theta_1 \times \theta_2 : X_{A+\preceq}^{\mathcal{L}_{mQ}} \times \mathfrak{Rm}^{\mathcal{L}_{mQ}} \to T_c(X_{A+\preceq})$ *where:*

– $\theta_1 : X_{A+\preceq}^{\mathcal{L}_{mQ}} \to X_{A+\preceq}^{\mathcal{L}_Q}$ *is defined for each* $f : \mathcal{L}_{mQ} \to X_{A+\preceq}$, *we take function* $\theta_1(f) = f_1 : \mathcal{L}_Q \to X_{A+\preceq}$ *such that for each* $q(\mathbf{x}) \in L_Q$, $f_1(q(\mathbf{x})) = f(\triangledown q(\mathbf{x}))$;
– $\theta_2 : \mathfrak{Rm}^{\mathcal{L}_{mQ}} \to \mathfrak{Rm}^{\mathcal{L}_Q}$ *is defined for each function* $l : \mathcal{L}_{mQ} \to \mathfrak{Rm}$, *we take function* $\theta_2(l) = l_1 : \mathcal{L}_Q \to \mathfrak{Rm}$, *such that for each* $q(\mathbf{x}) \in L_Q$, $l_1(q(\mathbf{x})) = l(\triangledown q(\mathbf{x}))$.

Proof. Notice that in the right commutative diagram, the horizontal arrows α and β represents these two equivalent AOT's, for database with external algorithm and the "encapsulated" database with embedded algorithm, respectively, such that for any state of database $s \in X_A$, and the conjunctive query $q(\mathbf{x}) \in \mathcal{L}_Q$, we obtain that for a two bisimilar states (s, s_1), i. e., $s_1 = \simeq_A (s) \in X_{A+\preceq}$:

$$\begin{aligned} & s_1' = \simeq_A (s'), \quad \text{where} \\ & s' = \mathrm{Next}_Q(s, q(\mathbf{x})) = \Lambda(\mathrm{Next}_Q)(s)(q(\mathbf{x})) \quad \text{and} \\ & s_1' = \mathrm{Next}_{mQ}(s_1, \triangledown q(\mathbf{x})) = \Lambda(\mathrm{Next}_{mQ})(s_1)(\triangledown q(\mathbf{x})) \end{aligned}$$

are two next (bisimilar) states of these two AOTs, and

$$\begin{aligned} m_{\mathrm{alg}}(\mathrm{Out}_Q(s, q(\mathbf{x}))) &= m_{\mathrm{alg}}(\Lambda(\mathrm{Out}_Q)(s)(q(\mathbf{x}))) = \mathrm{Out}_{mQ}(s_1, \triangledown q(\mathbf{x})) \\ &= \Lambda(\mathrm{Out}_{mQ})(s_1)(\triangledown q(\mathbf{x})) \end{aligned}$$

are identical observations (i. e., answers to user queries).

Let verify the second part of the proposition. The first commutative diagram can be equivalently represented by the following commutative diagram:

$$\begin{array}{ccccc} X_A \times \mathcal{L}_Q & \xrightarrow{\langle \mathrm{Next}_Q, \mathrm{Out}_Q \rangle} & X_A \times \mathfrak{Rm} & \xrightarrow{\mathrm{id} \times m_{\mathrm{alg}}} & X_A \times \mathfrak{Rm} \\ \downarrow{\scriptstyle \simeq_A \times \triangledown} & & & & \downarrow{\scriptstyle \simeq_A \times \mathrm{id}} \\ X_{A+\preceq} \times \mathcal{L}_{mQ} & & \xrightarrow{\langle \mathrm{Next}_{mQ}, \mathrm{Out}_{mQ} \rangle} & & X_{A+\preceq} \times \mathfrak{Rm} \end{array}$$

The horizontal arrow above corresponds to the AOT of the original CIS P2P database system and represents the two-step query computation: the first step computes query preanswer to the conjunctive query and then is applied the filtering algorithm m_{alg} (external to the logic theory of CIS); while the horizontal arrow below corresponds to the AOT of query answering of the CIS based on the query-modification taking in consideration the quality preorder $\preceq$ in Definition 99. From this diagram, by λ-abstraction (currying) we obtain the following commutative diagram:

$$\begin{array}{ccccc}
X_A & \xrightarrow{\alpha} & X_A^{\mathcal{L}_Q} \times \mathfrak{Rm}^{\mathcal{L}_Q} = T_c(X_A) & \qquad & (X_A, \alpha) \\
\Big\downarrow{\scriptstyle \simeq_A} & & \Big\downarrow{\scriptstyle T_c(\simeq_A)} & & \Big\downarrow{\scriptstyle \simeq_A} \\
X_{A+\preceq} & \xrightarrow{\delta} & X_{A+\preceq}^{\mathcal{L}_Q} \times \mathfrak{Rm}^{\mathcal{L}_Q} = T_c(X_{A+\preceq}) & & (X_{A+\preceq}, \delta)
\end{array}$$

where $\delta = \theta \circ \beta = \langle \Lambda(\text{Next}_{mQ} \circ (\text{id} \times \triangledown)), \Lambda(\text{Out}_{mQ} \circ (\text{id} \times \triangledown)) \rangle$ and $T_c(\simeq_A) = (\simeq_A \circ \_) \times \text{id}$.

This diagram is the isomorphism (bijective homomorphism) $\simeq_A$: $(X_A, \alpha) \to (X_{A+\preceq}, \delta)$ between two coalgebras of the polynomial functor $T_c = (\_)^{\mathcal{L}_Q} \times \mathfrak{Rm}^{\mathcal{L}_Q}$: Set $\to$ Set. □

We need that for the "best answering," w. r. t. the given partial order $\preceq$ and user defined conjunctive query $q(\mathbf{x})$, is satisfied the following condition:

$$\triangledown q(\mathbf{x})^{\mathcal{I},\mathcal{D}} = m_{\text{alg}}(q(\mathbf{x})^{\mathcal{I},\mathcal{D}}).$$

Now we will show that the semantics of the syntax symbol $\triangledown$ corresponds to the modal logic operator, so that $\mathcal{L}_{mQ}$ is the modal query language. We begin from the fact that for any given CIS $(\mathcal{I}, \mathcal{D})$ with set of records $X \subset \mathfrak{Rm}$, the couple $(X, R_{\preceq})$, with $R_{\preceq} \subseteq X^2$, corresponds to the frame with X the set of worlds, and partial order $R_{\preceq}$ its accessibility relation.

Definition 100. We define the set of all views (preanswers) Υ of given CIS $(\mathcal{I}, \mathcal{D})$, and the set of all tuples (records) X, which can be obtained from a CIS P2P database $(\mathcal{I}, \mathcal{D})$, as follows:

$$\Upsilon = \{q(\mathbf{x})^{\mathcal{I},\mathcal{D}} \mid q(\mathbf{x}) \in \mathcal{L}_Q\}, \quad X = \bigcup_{w \in \Upsilon_{\mathcal{DB}}} w.$$

The frame $(X, R_{\preceq})$, with $R_{\preceq} \subset X^2$, can be represented by the coalgebra $y : X \to \mathcal{P}(X)$, where $\mathcal{P}$ is a powerset operation (moreover, it is powerset functor $\mathcal{P}$: Set $\to$ Set) and for any $\mathbf{r} \in X \subset \mathfrak{Rm}$, $y(\mathbf{r})$ is the set of all successors of the world (record) $\mathbf{r}$ (i. e., the set of all $\mathbf{r}'$ such that $(\mathbf{r}, \mathbf{r}') \in R_{\preceq}$, or, equivalently, $\mathbf{r}' \preceq \mathbf{r}$).

For any subset $Y \subseteq X$ of the partially ordered set (poset) X, we denote by $\bigvee Y$ the subset *of all* Least Upper Bounds (lub's) in Y.

Example 43. It is easy to verify that for any conjunctive query $q(\mathbf{x})$ for its preanswer $w = q(\mathbf{x})^{\mathcal{I},\mathcal{D}} \in \Upsilon$, we have that $\bigvee w = \bigvee q(\mathbf{x})^{\mathcal{I},\mathcal{D}} = m_{\text{alg}}(q(\mathbf{x})^{\mathcal{I},\mathcal{D}})$.

That is, in our framework the "best answers" filtering algorithm m_{alg} is an operation, which extracts only lub's of the conjunctive-query preanswer.

The idea that the functor of a coalgebra determines a certain modal logic was first put forward by Moss [284]. He developed it for very general functors, namely those which admit the existence of the initial algebra, however, it is lack of abstract syntax. Here, we will use the other approach [285, 286] based on Kripke polynomial functors: Multimodal logic for coalgebras, which utilize *predicate lifting* to interpret modalities (interested reader can find a short overview in Section A.5.2 of the Appendix).

Definition 101. Based on Definition 100, we define a *partial-bounded* set of successors for a frame $(X, R_{\preceq})$ by the following mapping: $l : X \times \Upsilon \to \mathcal{P}(X)$ such that for any point (record) $\mathbf{r} \in X$ and the query preanswer $w \in \Upsilon \subseteq \mathcal{P}(X)$, (thus $w \subseteq X$), holds that

$$l(\mathbf{r}, w) = \begin{cases} y(\mathbf{r}) \bigcap w, & \text{if } \mathbf{r} \in \bigvee w \\ X, & \text{otherwise} \end{cases} \tag{6.43}$$

We denote by $\Lambda(l)$ its λ-abstraction (curring), $\Lambda(l) : X \to \mathcal{P}(X)^{\Upsilon}$. It is a coalgebra $(X, \Lambda(l))$ with a carrier set X, of the functor $T = \mathcal{P}(\_)^{\Upsilon} : \mathbf{Set} \to \mathbf{Set}$.

Based on this definition, and point 4 of Definition 131 in Section A.5.2 in the Appendix, we have the following property.

Proposition 35 (Modal operator for filtering). *The operator $\triangledown$ is a next time modal operator defined for any conjunctive query $q(\mathbf{x})$, and $w = q(\mathbf{x})^{\mathcal{I},\mathcal{D}} \in \Upsilon$ by the path $p = \text{eval}(w) \cdot \mathcal{P} : \mathcal{P}(\_)^{\Upsilon} \rightsquigarrow \text{Id}$, so that*

$$[\text{eval}(w) \cdot \mathcal{P}](w) = (\Lambda(l))^{-1} \circ (\_)^{\text{eval}(w) \cdot \mathcal{P}}(w) = m_{\text{alg}}(w) \tag{6.44}$$

Thus, by generalization, we obtain the interpretation of the modal operator $\triangledown$, restricted to a subset $\Upsilon \subseteq \mathcal{P}(X)$, given by

$$[\triangledown] = (\Lambda(l))^{-1} \circ (\_)^{\text{eval}(\_) \cdot \mathcal{P}} : \Upsilon \to \mathcal{P}(X) \tag{6.45}$$

Proof. For any preanswer $w \in \Upsilon$, thus, $w \subset X$, we have that

$$\begin{aligned} &[\text{eval}(w) \cdot \mathcal{P}](w) \\ &= (\Lambda(l))^{-1} \circ (\_)^{\text{eval}(w) \cdot \mathcal{P}}(w) \quad \text{from (A.11) in Definition 132 in the Appendix:} \\ &= (\Lambda(l))^{-1}((w)^{\text{eval}(w) \cdot \mathcal{P}}) = (\Lambda(l))^{-1}(\mathcal{P}(w))^{\text{eval}(w)} \\ &= (\Lambda(l))^{-1}(\{f \mid f(w) \in \mathcal{P}(w)\}) \end{aligned}$$

from point 4 in Definition 132, Section A.5.2 in the Appendix:

$$= \{x \mid \Lambda(l)(x) \in \{f \mid f(w) \in \mathcal{P}(w)\}\}$$
$$= \bigvee w, \quad \text{from the fact that } x \notin \bigvee w \text{ iff } \Lambda(l)(x)(w) = l(x,w) = X \notin \mathcal{P}(w)$$
$$= m_{\text{alg}}(w).$$

□

Corollary 29. *The query formulae for a databases enriched with partial order (by an embedded best-answer filtering algorithm) are the modal logic formulae obtained by predicate lifting of original conjunctive queries. The answer to such lifted query is equal to the (by algorithm) filtered answer to the original conjunctive query.*

Now, from the fact that $\triangledown$ is the syntax of the (surjective) modal operation $\triangledown : \mathcal{L}_Q \to \mathcal{L}_{mQ}$, where the set of modified conjunctive queries, $\mathcal{L}_{mQ}$ is the image of this mapping, we can introduce its inverse mapping, denoted by $\triangledown^{-1}$, such that for any $\triangledown q(\mathbf{x}) \in \mathcal{L}_{mQ}$, we obtain that $\triangledown^{-1}(\triangledown q(\mathbf{x})) = q(\mathbf{x}) \in \mathcal{L}_Q$. Thus, the T_c-coalgebra isomorphism $\simeq_A: (X_A, \alpha) \to (X_{A+\preceq}, \delta)$, of the polynomial functor $T_c = (\_)^{\mathcal{L}_Q} \times \Upsilon^{\mathcal{L}_Q} : \mathbf{Set} \to \mathbf{Set}$ for the language $\mathcal{L}_Q$ of finite conjunctive queries, can be equivalently, represented by the coalgebra isomorphism $\simeq_A^{-1}: (X_{A+\preceq}, \beta) \to (X_A, \delta_1)$, of the "modal" endofunctor $T_m = (\_)^{\mathcal{L}_{mQ}} \times \mathfrak{Rm}^{\mathcal{L}_{mQ}} : \mathbf{Set} \to \mathbf{Set}$ for the modal language $\mathcal{L}_{mQ}$.

That is, the following commutative diagram holds:

$$\begin{array}{ccccc}
X_A \times \mathcal{L}_{mQ} & \xrightarrow{\ \mathrm{id} \times \triangledown^{-1}\ } & X_A \times \mathcal{L}_Q & \xrightarrow{\ \langle \mathrm{Next}_Q,\, m_{\text{alg}} \circ \mathrm{Out}_Q \rangle\ } & X_A \times \mathfrak{Rm} \\
\uparrow {\scriptstyle \simeq_A^{-1} \times \mathrm{id}} & & & & \uparrow {\scriptstyle \simeq_A^{-1} \times \mathrm{id}} \\
X_{A+\preceq} \times \mathcal{L}_{mQ} & & \xrightarrow{\ \langle \mathrm{Next}_{mQ},\, \mathrm{Out}_{mQ} \rangle\ } & & X_{A+\preceq} \times \mathfrak{Rm}
\end{array}$$

where the horizontal arrow above corresponds to the three steps computation: for a given modal formula first step, reduce it to the conjunctive query, after that is computed a certain answer for this query on a database A, and it is filtered by the algorithm m_{alg}. From this diagram, by λ-abstraction (curring) we obtain the following commutative diagram:

$$\begin{array}{ccccc}
X_A & \xrightarrow{\ \delta_1\ } & X_A^{\mathcal{L}_{mQ}} \times \mathfrak{Rm}^{\mathcal{L}_{mQ}} = T_m(X_A) & \qquad & (X_A, \delta_1) \\
\uparrow {\scriptstyle \simeq_A^{-1}} & & \uparrow {\scriptstyle T_m(\simeq_A^{-1})} & & \uparrow {\scriptstyle \simeq_A^{-1}} \\
X_{A+\preceq} & \xrightarrow{\ \beta\ } & X_{A+\preceq}^{\mathcal{L}_{mQ}} \times \mathfrak{Rm}^{\mathcal{L}_{mQ}} = T_m(X_{A+\preceq}) & & (X_{A+\preceq}, \beta)
\end{array}$$

where $T_m(\simeq_A) = \mathrm{id}$ is the identity and $\delta_1 = \simeq_A \circ \beta = \langle \Lambda(\mathrm{Next}_Q \circ (\mathrm{id} \times \triangledown^{-1})), \Lambda(m_{\text{alg}} \circ \mathrm{Out}_Q \circ (\mathrm{id} \times \triangledown^{-1}))\rangle$.

These two isomorphisms, $\simeq_A: (X_A, \alpha) \to (X_{A+\preceq}, \delta)$, and $\simeq_A^{-1}: (X_{A+\preceq}, \beta) \to (X_A, \delta_1)$, represent the behavioral equivalence of these two AOTs: AOT for a original CIS P2P database system with the external-to-database algorithm m_{alg} w. r. t. the conjunctive query language $\mathcal{L}_Q$, and the AOT for CIS P2P database system with these modal queries in $\mathcal{L}_{mQ}$, respectively.

So, we have proposed a novel formal logic method to the well known and important, yet frequently ignored problem of considering the query-answering semantics in information integration with also filtering algorithms, which restricts the answers to conjunctive queries in a subset of "best consistent" answers. This problem has not, to our best knowledge, been adequately addressed before: the developed in practice software systems are mainly focused in formalization and implementation of their filtering algorithms, considering that such software systems implicitly support their particular *operational* semantics, by a particular developed algorithm, for a query answering of the whole system.

But such discrepancy in the formal logic theory of the database and, external to it, the software which implements filtering algorithm needs to be improved by the logic: theoretical considerations in order to provide a model theoretic (denotational) semantics for the query answering.

The formalization of query-answering database systems by mean of abstract object types is useful for embedding other procedural database features also. Such abstraction, together with the concept of behavior equivalence for query answering is a good framework to analyze the model theoretic properties of the whole system, but also to define the specification for mappings, based on views, between different database systems, as for example, in complex P2P database systems, where each peer can be considered as an AOT which possibly encapsulate a database system (thus all internal structure and application embedded algorithms, of a database peer, are hidden).

A Appendix

A.1 Introduction to lattices, algebras and propositional logics

Lattices are the posets (partially ordered sets) such that for all their elements a and b, the set $\{a, b\}$ has both a join ((lub) least upper bound and a meet (glb) greatest lower bound) with a partial order $\leq$ (reflexive, transitive and antisymmetric). A *bounded* lattice has the greatest (top) and least (bottom) element, denoted by convention as 1 and 0. Finite meets in a poset will be written as $1, \wedge$ and finite joins as $0, \vee$. By $(W, \leq, \wedge, \vee, 0, 1)$, we denote a bounded lattice iff for every $a, b, c \in W$ and the following equations are valid:

1. $a \vee a = a$, $a \wedge a = a$ (idempotency laws)
2. $a \vee b = b \vee a$, $a \wedge b = b \wedge a$ (commutativity laws)
3. $a \vee (b \vee c) = (a \vee b) \vee c$, $a \wedge (b \wedge c) = (a \vee b) \wedge c$ (associativity laws)
4. $a \vee 0 = a$, $a \wedge 1 = a$
5. $a \vee (b \wedge a) = a$, $a \wedge (b \vee a) = a$ (absorption laws).

It is distributive if it satisfies the distributivity laws:

6. $a \vee (b \wedge c) = (a \vee b) \wedge (a \vee c)$, $a \wedge (b \vee c) = (a \wedge b) \vee (a \wedge c)$.

A lattice W is *complete* if each (also infinite) subset $S \subseteq W$ (or $S \in \mathcal{P}(W)$ where $\mathcal{P}$ is the powerset symbol, with empty set $\emptyset \in \mathcal{P}(W)$) has the least upper bound (lub, supremum) denoted by $\bigvee S \in W$. When S has only two elements, the supremum corresponds to the join operator "$\vee$." Each finite bounded lattice is a complete lattice. Each subset S has the greatest lower bound (glb, infimum) denoted by $\bigwedge S \in W$, given as $\bigvee\{a \in W \mid \forall b \in S.a \leq b\}$. A complete lattice is bounded and has the bottom element $0 = \bigvee \emptyset = \bigwedge W \in W$ and the top element $1 = \bigwedge \emptyset = \bigvee W \in W$. An element $a \in W$ is *compact* iff whenever $\bigwedge S$ exists and $a \leq \bigwedge S$ for $S \subseteq W$, then $a \leq \bigwedge S'$ for some finite $S' \subseteq W$. W is *compactly generated* iff every element in W is a supremum of compact elements. A lattice W is *algebraic* if it is complete and compactly generated.

A function $l : W \to Y$ between the posets W, Y is *monotone* if $a \leq a'$ implies $l(a) \leq l(a')$ for all $a, a' \in W$. Such a function $l : W \to Y$ is said to have a right (or upper) adjoint if there is a function $r : Y \to W$ in the reverse direction such that $l(a) \leq b$ iff $a \leq r(b)$ for all $a \in W, b \in Y$. Such a situation forms a Galois connection and will often be denoted by $l \dashv r$. Then l is called a left (or lover) adjoint of r. If W, Y are complete lattices (posets), then $l : W \to Y$ has a right adjoint iff l preserves all joins (it is *additive*, i. e., $l(a \vee b) = l(a) \vee l(b)$ and $l(0_W) = 0_Y$ where $0_W, 0_Y$ are bottom elements in complete lattices W and Y, respectively). The right adjoint is then $r(b) = \bigvee\{c \in W \mid l(c) \leq b\}$. Similarly, a monotone function $r : Y \to W$ is a right adjoint (it is *multiplicative*, i. e., has a left adjoint) iff r preserves all meets; the left adjoint is then $l(a) = \bigwedge\{c \in Y \mid a \leq r(c)\}$.

https://doi.org/10.1515/9783110981438-007

Each monotone function $l : W \to Y$ on a complete lattice (poset) W has both a *least* fixed-point (Knaster–Tarski) $\mu l \in W$ and *greatest* fixed-point $\nu l \in W$. These can be described explicitly as $\mu l = \bigwedge\{a \in W \mid l(a) \leq a\}$ and $\nu l = \bigvee\{a \in W \mid a \leq l(a)\}$.

In what follows, we write $b < a$ iff ($b \leq a$ and not $a \leq b$) and we denote by $a \bowtie b$ two unrelated elements in W (so that not ($a \leq b$ or $b \leq a$)). An element in a lattice $c \neq 0$ is a *join-irreducible* element iff $c = a \vee b$ implies $c = a$ or $c = b$ for any $a, b \in W$. An element in a lattice $a \in W$ is an *atom* iff $a > 0$ and $\nexists b.(a > b > 0)$.

A lower set (down closed) is any subset Y of a given poset $(W, \leq)$ such that, for all elements a and b, if $a \leq b$ and $b \in Y$ then $a \in Y$.

A *Heyting algebra* is a distributive bounded lattice W with finite meets and joins such that for each element $a \in W$, the function $(\_) \wedge a : W \to W$ has a right adjoint $a \rightharpoonup (\_)$, also called an algebraic implication. An equivalent definition can be given by considering a bonded distributive lattice such that for all a and b in W there is a greatest element c in W, denoted by $a \rightharpoonup b$, such that $c \wedge a \leq b$, i. e., $a \rightharpoonup b = \bigvee\{c \in W \mid c \wedge a \leq b\}$ (relative pseudo-complement). We say that a lattice is *relatively pseudo-complemented* (r. p. c.) lattice if $a \rightharpoonup b$ exists for every a and b in W. Thus, a Heyting algebra is, by definition, an r. p. c. lattice that has 0.

Formally, a distributive bounded lattice $(W, \leq, \wedge, \vee, 0, 1)$ is a Heyting algebra iff there is a binary operation $\rightharpoonup$ on W such that for every $a, b, c \in W$:

7. $a \rightharpoonup a = 1$,
8. $a \wedge (a \rightharpoonup b) = a \wedge b$, $b \wedge (a \rightharpoonup b) = b$,
9. $a \rightharpoonup (b \wedge c) = (a \rightharpoonup b) \wedge (a \rightharpoonup c)$.

In a Heyting algebra, we can define the negation $\neg a$ as a pseudo-complement $a \rightharpoonup 0$. Then $a \leq \neg\neg a$. Each *finite distributive* lattice is a Heyting algebra. A complete Heyting algebra is a Heyting algebra $\mathbf{H} = (W, \leq, \wedge, \vee, \rightharpoonup, \neg, 0, 1)$, which is complete as a poset. A complete distributive lattice is thus a complete Heyting algebra iff the following *infinite distributivity* holds [287]:

10. $a \wedge \bigvee_{i \in I} b_i = \bigvee_{i \in I}(a \wedge b_i)$, for every $a, b_i \in W, i \in I$.

The negation and implication operators can be represented as the following monotone functions: $\neg : W \to W^{OP}$ and $\rightharpoonup: W \times W^{OP} \to W^{OP}$, where W^{OP} is the lattice with inverse partial ordering and $\wedge^{OP} = \vee$, $\vee^{OP} = \wedge$.

The following facts are valid in any $\mathbf{H}$:

(H1) $a \leq b$ iff $a \rightharpoonup b = 1$, $(a \rightharpoonup b) \wedge (a \rightharpoonup \neg b) = \neg a$

(H2) $\neg 0 = 0^{OP} = 1$, $\neg(a \vee b) = \neg a \vee^{OP} \neg b = \neg a \wedge \neg b$ (additive negation), with the following weakening of classical propositional logic:

(H3) $\neg a \vee b \leq a \rightharpoonup b$, $a \leq \neg\neg a$, $\neg a = \neg\neg\neg a$

(H4) $a \wedge \neg a = 0$, $a \vee \neg a \leq \neg\neg(a \vee \neg a) = 1$ (weakening excluded middle)

(H5) $\neg a \vee \neg b \leq \neg(a \wedge b)$ (weakening of De Morgan laws)

Notice that since negation $\neg : W \to W^{OP}$ is a monotonic and additive operator, it is also a *modal* algebraic negation operator. The smallest complete distributive lattice is denoted by $\mathbf{2} = \{0,1\}$ with twp classic values, false and true, respectively. It is also a complemented Heyting algebra, and hence it is Boolean.

From the point of view of universal algebra, given a signature Σ with a set of functional symbols $o_i \in \Sigma$ with arity ar $: \Sigma \to \mathcal{N}$, an algebra (or algebraic structure) $\mathbf{A} = (W, \Sigma_{\mathbf{A}})$ is a carrier set W together with a collection $\Sigma_{\mathbf{A}}$ of operations on W with an arity $n \geq 0$. An n-ary operator (functional symbol) $o_i \in \Sigma$, $\mathrm{ar}(o_i) = n$ on W will be named an n-ary operation (a function) $\widehat{o_i} : W^n \to W$ in $\Sigma_{\mathbf{A}}$ that takes n elements of W and returns a single element of W. Thus, a 0-ary operator (or nullary operation) can be simply represented as an element of W, or a constant, often denoted by a letter like a (thus, all 0-ary operations are included as constants into the carrier set of algebra). An algebra $\mathbf{A}$ is *finite* if the carrier set W is finite; it is *finitary* if each operator in $\Sigma_{\mathbf{A}}$ has a finite arity. For example, a lattice is an algebra with signature $\Sigma_L = \{\wedge, \vee, 0, 1\}$, where $\wedge$ and $\vee$ are binary operations (meet and join operations, respectively), while $0, 1$ are two nullary operators (the constants). The equational semantics of a given algebra is a set of equations E between the terms (or expressions) of this algebra (e. g., a distributive lattice is defined by the first six equations above).

Given two algebras $\mathbf{A} = (W, \Sigma_{\mathbf{A}})$, $\mathbf{A}' = (W', \Sigma_{\mathbf{A}})$ of the same *type* (with the same signature Σ and set of equations), a map $h : W \to W'$ is called a *homomorphism* if for each n-ary operation $\widehat{o_i} \in \Sigma_{\mathbf{A}}$ and $a_1, \ldots, a_n \in W$, $h(\widehat{o_i}(a_1, \ldots, a_n)) = \widehat{o_i'}(h(a_1), \ldots, h(a_n))$. A homomorphism h is called an *isomorphism* if h is a bijection between respective carrier sets; it is called a monomorphism (or embedding) if h is injective function from W into W'. An algebra $\mathbf{A}'$ is called a homomorphic image of $\mathbf{A}$ if there exists a homomorphism from $\mathbf{A}$ onto $\mathbf{A}'$. An algebra $\mathbf{A}'$ is a *subalgebra* of $\mathbf{A}$ if $W' \subseteq W$, the nullary operators are equal and the other operators of $\mathbf{A}'$ are the restrictions of operators of $\mathbf{A}$ to W'.

A *subuniverse* of $\mathbf{A}$ is a subset W' of W, which is closed under operators of $\mathbf{A}$, i. e., for any n-ary operation $\widehat{o}_i \in \Sigma_{\mathbf{A}}$ and $a_1, \ldots, a_n \in W'$, $\widehat{o}_i(a_1, \ldots, a_n) \in W'$. Thus, if **A'** is a subalgebra of $\mathbf{A}$, then W' is a subuniverse of $\mathbf{A}$. The empty set may be subuniverse, but it is not the underlying carrier set of any subalgebra. If $\mathbf{A}$ has nullary operators (constants), then every subuniverse contains them as well.

Given an algebra $\mathbf{A}$, $\mathrm{Sub}(\mathbf{A})$ denotes the set of subuniverses of $\mathbf{A}$, which is an algebraic lattice. For $Y \subseteq W$, we say that Y *generates* $\mathbf{A}$ (or Y is a set of generators of $\mathbf{A}$) if $W = \mathrm{Sg}(Y) =_{\mathrm{def}} \bigcap\{Z \mid Y \subseteq Z$ and Z is a subuniverse of $\mathbf{A}\}$. Sg is an algebraic closure operator on W: for any $Y \subseteq W$, let $F(Y) = Y \bigcup \{\widehat{o}_i(b_1, \ldots, b_k) | o_i \in \Sigma_{\mathbf{A}}$ and $b_1, \ldots, b_k \in Y\}$, with $F^0(Y) = Y$, $F^{n+1}(Y) = F(F^n(Y)), n \geq 0$, so that for finitary $\mathbf{A}$, $Y \subseteq F(Y) \subseteq F^2(Y) \subseteq \ldots$, and consequently, $\mathrm{Sg}(Y) = Y \bigcup F(Y) \bigcup F^2(Y) \bigcup \ldots$, and from this it follows that if $a \in \mathrm{Sg}(Y)$, then $a \in F^n(Y)$ for some $n < \omega$; hence, for some *finite* $Z \subseteq Y$, $a \in F^n(Z)$, thus $a \in \mathrm{Sg}(Z)$, i. e., Sg is an algebraic closure operator.

The algebra $\mathbf{A}$ is *finitely generated* if it has a finite set of generators.

Let X be a set of variables. We denote by $\mathcal{T}X$ the set of terms with variables $x_1, x_2, \ldots$ in X of a type Σ of algebras, defined recursively by
- all variables and constants (nullary functional symbols) are in $\mathcal{T}X$;
- if $o_i \in \Sigma$, $n = \mathrm{ar}(o_i) \geq 1$, and $t_1, \ldots, t_n \in \mathcal{T}X$, then $o_i(t_1, \ldots, t_n) \in \mathcal{T}X$.

If $X = \emptyset$, then $\mathcal{T}\emptyset$ denotes the set of ground terms. Given a class K of algebras of the same type (signature Σ), the term algebra $(\mathcal{T}X, \Sigma)$ is a free algebra with universal (initial algebra) property: for every algebra $\mathbf{A} = (W, \Sigma) \in K$ and map $f : X \to W$, there is a unique homomorphism $f_\# : \mathcal{T}X \to W$ that extends f to all terms. Given a term $t(x_1, \ldots, x_n)$ over X and given an algebra $\mathbf{A} = (W, \Sigma_\mathbf{A})$ of type Σ, we define a mapping $\hat{t} : W^n \to W$ by: (1) if t is a variable x_i then $\hat{t}(a_1, \ldots, a_n) = a_i$ is the i-th projection map; (2) if t is of the form $o_i(t_1(x_1, \ldots, x_n), \ldots, t_k(x_1, \ldots, x_n))$, where $o_i \in \Sigma$, then $\hat{t}(a_1, \ldots, a_n) = \hat{o}_i(\hat{t}_1(a_1, \ldots, a_n), \ldots, \hat{t}_k(a_1, \ldots, a_n))$. Thus, $\hat{t}$ is the *term function* on $\mathbf{A}$ corresponding to term t. For any subset $Y \subseteq W$,

$$\mathrm{Sg}(Y) = \{\hat{t}(a_1, \ldots, a_n) \mid t \text{ is } n\text{-ary term of type } \Sigma, n < \omega, \text{ and } a_1, \ldots, a_n \in Y\}.$$

The product of two algebras of the same type $\mathbf{A}$ and $\mathbf{A}'$ is the algebra $\mathbf{A} \times \mathbf{A}' = (W \times W', \Sigma_\times)$ such that for any n-ary operator $\widehat{o_{i,2}} \in \Sigma_\times$ and $(a_1, b_1), \ldots, (a_n, b_n) \in W \times W'$, $n \geq 1$, $\widehat{o_{i,2}}((a_1, b_1), \ldots, (a_n, b_n)) = (\widehat{o_i}(a_1, \ldots, a_n), \widehat{o'_i}(b_1, \ldots, b_n))$. In what follows, where there is no ambiguity, we will write $o_i(a_1, \ldots, a_n)$ for $\widehat{o_i}(a_1, \ldots, a_n)$ as well and Σ for $\Sigma_\mathbf{A}$ of any algebra $\mathbf{A}$ of this type Σ.

Given a Σ-algebra $\mathbf{A}$ with the carrier W, we say that an equivalence relation Q on W agrees with the n-ary operation $o_i \in \Sigma$ when for n-tuples $(a_1, \ldots, a_n), (b_1, \ldots, b_n) \in W^n$ we have $(o_i(a_1, \ldots, a_n), o_i(b_1, \ldots, b_n)) \in Q$ if $(a_i, b_i) \in Q$ for $i = 1, \ldots, n$. We say that equivalence relation Q on a Σ-algebra $\mathbf{A}$ is a *congruence* on $\mathbf{A}$ if it agrees with every operation in Σ. If $\mathbf{A}$ is a Σ-algebra and Q a congruence on $\mathbf{A}$, then there exists a unique Σ-algebra on the quotient set W/Q of the carrier W of $\mathbf{A}$ such that the natural mapping $W \to W/Q$ (which maps each element $a \in W$ into its equivalence class $[a] \in W/Q$) is a homomorphism. We will denote such an algebra as $\mathbf{A}/Q = (W/Q, \Sigma)$ and will call it a *quotient algebra* of an algebra $\mathbf{A}$ by the congruence Q, such that for each its k-ary operation $\hat{o}'_i$, we have $\hat{o}'_i([a_1], \ldots, [a_k]) = [\hat{o}_i(a_1, \ldots, a_k)]$.

Let K be a class of algebras of the same type. We say that K is a *variety* if K is closed under homomorphic images, subalgebras and products. Each variety can be seen as a *category* with objects being the algebras and arrows the homomorphisms between them.

The fundamental Birkhoff's theorem in universal algebra demonstrates that a class of algebras forms a variety iff it is equationally definable. For example, the class of all Heyting algebras (which are definable by the set E of nine equations above), denoted by $\mathcal{HA} = (\Sigma_H, E)$, is a variety. Arend Heyting produced an axiomatic system of propositional logic, which was claimed to generate as theorems, precisely those sentences that are valid according to the *intuitionistic* conception of truth. Its axioms are all axioms of the Classic Propositional Logic (CPL) heaving a set of propositional symbols $p, q, \ldots \in$ PR and the following axioms (ϕ, ψ, φ denotes arbitrary propositional formulae):

(1) $\phi \Rightarrow (\phi \wedge \phi)$
(2) $(\phi \wedge \psi) \Rightarrow (\psi \wedge \phi)$
(3) $(\phi \Rightarrow \psi) \Rightarrow ((\phi \wedge \varphi) \Rightarrow (\psi \wedge \varphi))$
(4) $((\phi \Rightarrow \psi) \wedge (\psi \Rightarrow \varphi)) \Rightarrow (\phi \Rightarrow \varphi)$
(5) $\psi \Rightarrow (\phi \Rightarrow \psi)$
(6) $(\phi \wedge (\phi \Rightarrow \psi)) \Rightarrow \psi$
(7) $\phi \Rightarrow (\phi \vee \psi)$
(8) $(\phi \vee \psi) \Rightarrow (\psi \vee \phi)$
(9) $((\phi \Rightarrow \varphi) \wedge (\psi \Rightarrow \varphi)) \Rightarrow ((\phi \vee \psi) \Rightarrow \varphi)$ and for negation in CPL:
(10) $\phi \Rightarrow (\neg\phi \Rightarrow \psi)$
(11) $((\phi \Rightarrow \psi) \wedge (\phi \Rightarrow \neg\psi)) \Rightarrow \neg\phi$
(12) $\phi \vee \neg\phi$

except for the 12th axiom of "excluded middle," which according to constructivist attitude (L. E. J. Brouwer) has to be replaced by "*either I have constructively demonstrated* ϕ, *or I have constructively demonstrated that* ϕ *is false*," equivalent to modal formula $\Box\phi \vee \Box\neg\phi$, where $\Box$ is a "necessity" universal modal operator in S4 modal logic (with transitive and symmetric accessibility relation between the possible worlds in Kripke semantics, i. e., where this relation is partial ordering $\leq$). In the same constructivist attitude, $\neg\neg\phi \Rightarrow \phi$ is not valid (different from CLP). According to Brouwer, to say that ϕ is not true means only that I have not at this time constructed ϕ, which is not the same as saying ϕ is false.

In fact in Intuitionistic Logic (IL), $\phi \Rightarrow \psi$ is equivalent to $\Box(\phi \Rightarrow_c \psi)$, i. e., to $\Box(\neg_c\phi \vee \psi)$ where "$\Rightarrow_c$" is a classical logical implication and "$\neg_c$" is classical negation and $\neg\phi$ is equivalent to $\Box\neg_c\phi$. Thus, in IL, the conjunction and disjunction are that of CPL and only the implication and negation are modal versions of classical versions of the implication and negation, respectively.

A.2 Introduction to deductive logic and binary sequent calculus

The concepts introduced here, based on the work of Tarski, are basic to the development of nonmonotonic logic in the rest of the paper.

We assume that a fixed 2-valued (f, false and t, true) object language $\mathcal{L}$ is given. The details of $\mathcal{L}$ are left open, except that it contains the standard connectives, $\Rightarrow, \wedge, \vee$ (material implication, conjunction and disjunction, respectively). Hence, the set $\mathcal{L}_0$ of *sentences* of $\mathcal{L}$ is closed under the rules: $f \in \mathcal{L}_0$; if $\phi, \psi \in \mathcal{L}_0$, then $\phi \Rightarrow \psi, \phi \wedge \psi, \phi \vee \psi \in \mathcal{L}_0$. $\neg\phi$ is taken as an abbreviation of $\phi \Rightarrow f$. We use $\forall$ symbol for the "for all" quantifier, and $\exists$ for the existential quantifier.

A *consequence relation* is a binary relation $\vdash$, which takes a set of sentences $\Gamma \subseteq \mathcal{L}_0$ as its first argument and a single sentences $\phi \in \mathcal{L}_0$ as its second, denoted by $\Gamma \vdash \phi$. Equivalently, we can define a *consequence operation* (infinitary) mapping $C : \mathcal{P}(\mathcal{L}_0) \to \mathcal{P}(\mathcal{L}_0)$ (here $\mathcal{P}(\mathcal{L}_0)$ denotes the set of *all* subsets of $\mathcal{L}_0$), such that $C(\Gamma) = \{\phi \mid \Gamma \vdash \phi\}$, and vice versa, $\Gamma \vdash \phi$ iff $\phi \in C(\Gamma)$. The finitary version of this operator is a mapping $C_{\text{fin}} : \mathcal{P}_{\text{fin}}(\mathcal{L}_0) \to \mathcal{P}(\mathcal{L}_0)$, where $\mathcal{P}_{\text{fin}}$ is a finitary powerset operator. We write $C(\Gamma, \Delta)$ instead of $C(\Gamma \bigcup \Delta)$, and $C(\phi)$ instead of $C(\{\phi\})$. The following table define properties of the *deductive* monotonic consequence relation (reflexivity, cut, monotonicity and compactness):

The finitistic or "Gentzen-style" (Table A.1):

Table A.1: The finitistic or "Gentzen-style".

$\phi \in \Gamma$ implies $\Gamma \vdash \phi$
$\Gamma \bigcup \Delta \vdash \phi, \forall \psi \in \Delta.(\Gamma \vdash \psi)$ implies $\Gamma \vdash \phi$
$\Gamma \vdash \phi, \Gamma \subseteq \Delta$ implies $\Delta \vdash \phi$
if $\Gamma \vdash \phi$ then for some finite $\Delta \subseteq \Gamma, \Delta \vdash \phi$

The infinitistic or "Tarski-style" (Table A.2):

Table A.2: The infinitistic or "Tarski-style".

$\Gamma \subseteq C(\Gamma)$
$\Delta \subseteq C(\Gamma)$ implies $C(\Gamma \bigcup \Delta) \subseteq C(\Gamma)$
$\Gamma \subseteq \Delta$ implies $C(\Gamma) \subseteq C(\Delta)$
$C(\Gamma) \subseteq \bigcup\{C(\Delta) \mid \Delta \subseteq \Gamma$ and Δ is finite$\}$

For example, the classical propositional logic is a deductive logic.

It is easy to verify that C is a closure idempotent operator: for any Γ, we obtain the closet set, called *theory* $T = C(\Gamma) = C(C(\Gamma))$.

For $\Gamma, \Delta \subseteq \mathcal{L}_0$ we shall say that Γ is *consistent* iff $C(\Gamma) \neq \mathcal{L}_0$ and that Γ is *consistent with* Δ iff $C(\Gamma, \Delta) \neq \mathcal{L}_0$. A set is *inconsistent* iff it is not consistent.

A set Γ is $\mathcal{L}$-maximal iff is consistent and for every Δ, if $\Gamma \subseteq \Delta$ and Δ consistent, then $\Gamma = \Delta$.

We denote by $\mathcal{M}_L$ the set of all $\mathcal{L}$-maximal sets, and by $\mathcal{T}_L$ the set of all theories in $\mathcal{P}(\mathcal{L}_0)$, and by $|\Gamma| = \{M \in \mathcal{M}_L \mid \Gamma \subseteq M\}$ the set of all maximal extensions of Γ.

For any deductive logic, the following properties hold:

1. Every $\mathcal{L}$-maximal set Γ is a theory (i. e., $\Gamma = C(\Gamma)$).
2. (Lindenbaum) Every consistent set is included in some $\mathcal{L}$-maximal theory.
3. If $\phi \notin C(\Gamma)$, then there exists a $\mathcal{L}$-maximal theory M such that $C(\Gamma) \subseteq M$ and $\phi \notin M$.

4. $C(\Gamma) = \bigcap \|\Gamma\|$, i. e., ϕ is a consequence of Γ iff ϕ belongs to every maximal extension of Γ.

So far, our discussion has been purely syntactical and proof-theoretic. We shall also suppose that, with the language $\mathcal{L}$ and the consequence operator C comes a suitable *semantics* in the form of a set $\mathcal{W}$ (the universe), the elements of which we shall call worlds, and the relation $\models \subseteq \mathcal{W} \times \mathcal{P}(\mathcal{L}_0)$ of *satisfaction* between worlds and formulae: $\phi \in C(\Gamma)$ iff $\forall w \in \mathcal{W}.(w \models \Gamma$ implies $w \models \phi)$.

We will use a deductive logics as underlying logic in order to define the inference operator for (generally nonmonotonic) query-answering in general data integration framework in Section 3.2.1.

Binary sequent calculus

It has been developed by Gentzen [288], inspired on ideas of Paul Hertz [289]. Given a propositional logic language $\mathcal{L}_A$ (a set of logic formulae), a binary sequent is a consequence pair of formulae, $s = (\phi; \psi) \in \mathcal{L}_A \times \mathcal{L}_A$, denoted also by $\phi \vdash \psi$.

A Gentzen system, denoted by a pair $\mathcal{G} = \langle \mathbb{L}, \Vdash \rangle$, where $\Vdash$ is a consequence relation on a set of sequents in $\mathbb{L} \subseteq \mathcal{L}_A \times \mathcal{L}_A$, is said to be *normal* if it satisfies the following conditions: for any sequent $s = \phi \vdash \psi \in \mathbb{L}$ and a set of sequents $\Gamma = \{s_i = \phi_i \vdash \psi_i \in \mathbb{L} \mid i \in I\}$,

1. reflexivity: if $s \in \Gamma$, then $\Gamma \Vdash s$
2. transitivity: if $\Gamma \Vdash s$ and for every $s' \in \Gamma$, $\Theta \Vdash s'$, then $\Theta \Vdash s$
3. finiteness: if $\Gamma \Vdash s$, then there is finite $\Theta \subseteq \Gamma$ such that $\Theta \Vdash s$.
4. for any homomorphism σ from $\mathbb{L}$ into itself (i. e., a substitution), if $\Gamma \Vdash s$ then $\sigma[\Gamma] \Vdash \sigma(s)$, i. e., $\{\sigma(\phi_i) \vdash \sigma(\psi_i) \mid i \in I\} \Vdash (\sigma(\phi) \vdash \sigma(\psi))$.

Notice that from (1) and (2) we obtain this monotonic property:

5. if $\Gamma \Vdash s$ and $\Gamma \subseteq \Theta$, then $\Theta \Vdash s$.

We denote the Tarskian closure operator by $C : \mathcal{P}(\mathbb{L}) \to \mathcal{P}(\mathbb{L})$, such that $C(\Gamma) =_{def} \{s \in \mathbb{L} \mid \Gamma \Vdash s\}$, with the properties: $\Gamma \subseteq C(\Gamma)$ (from reflexivity (1)); it is monotonic, i. e., $\Gamma \subseteq \Gamma_1$ implies $C(\Gamma) \subseteq C(\Gamma_1)$ (from (5)), and an involution $C(C(\Gamma)) = C(\Gamma)$ as well. Thus, we obtain:

6. $\Gamma \Vdash s$ iff $s \in C(\Gamma)$.

Any sequent theory $\Gamma \subseteq \mathbb{L}$ is said to be a *closed* theory iff $\Gamma = C(\Gamma)$. This closure property corresponds to the fact that $\Gamma \Vdash s$ iff $s \in \Gamma$.

Each sequent theory Γ can be considered as a bivaluation (a characteristic function) $\beta : \mathbb{L} \to \mathbf{2}$ such that for any sequent $s \in \mathbb{L}$, $\beta(s) = 1$ iff $s \in \Gamma$.

A.3 Autoreferential semantics for many-valued modal logics

In this section, we consider the class of truth-functional modal many-valued logics with the complete lattice of truth values. The conjunction and disjunction logic operators correspond to the meet and join operators of the lattices, while the negation is independently introduced as a hierarchy of antitonic operators, which invert bottom and top elements. The nonconstructive logic implication will be defined for a subclass of modular lattices, while the constructive implication for distributive lattices (Heyting algebras) is based on relative pseudo-complements as in intuitionistic logic. We show that the complete lattices are intrinsically modal, with a banal identity modal operator. We define the autoreferential set-based representation for the class of modal algebras, and show that the autoreferential Kripke-style semantics for this class of modal algebras is based on the set of possible worlds equal to the complete lattice of algebraic truth values.

Remark. For many-valued logics, we tell that has an *autoreferential* Kripke semantics if the set of possible worlds is the (sub)set of truth values of this MV-logic. We tell that it is *canonical* if it is the result of the representation theorem (see Section 5.1 and Section 5.1.1 for more details). □

The philosophical assumption of *canonical* autoreferential sematics is based on the consideration that each possible world represents a level of *credibility*, so that only propositions with the right logic value (i. e., level of credibility) can be accepted by this world. Then we connect it with paraconsistent properties and LFI logics. The bottom truth value in this complete lattice corresponds to the *trivial world* in which each formula is satisfied, i. e., to the world with explosive inconsistency. The top truth value corresponds to the world with classical logics, while all intermediate possible worlds represent the different levels of paraconsistent logics.

The main result of this section is a general way of establishing links between algebraic and Kripke-style semantics for the class of many-valued modal logics based on a complete lattice of truth values, by introducing autoreferential duality: it means that we will use as a set of possible worlds in Kripke-style semantics for these modal logics exactly the lattice of its truth values.

A significant number of real-world applications in artificial intelligence has to deal with partial, imprecise and uncertain information, and that is the principal reason for introducing nonclassic truth-functional many-valued logics, as for example, fuzzy, bilattice-based and paraconsistent logics, etc. All of these logics use the conjunction and disjunction logic operators as meet and join lattice operators with truth partial ordering between the set of truth values. The class of complete lattices of truth values is the most significant for logics, just because each finite set of truth values, or totally ordering in infinite set of values (as in fuzzy logic) is a *complete* lattice.

Thus, the many-valued modal logics we consider have a natural algebraic semantics based on a complete lattice of truth values, extended by other algebraic operators: negation, implication for a subclass of modular lattices, relative pseudocomplement (for distributive lattices) [290] for intuitionistic many-valued implication, and unary normal modal operators (the first formal semantics for modal logic was based on many-valuedness, proposed by Lukasiewicz in 1918–1920, and consolidated in 1953 in a 4-valued system of modal logic [79]).

There are strong links between the structural rules the logics satisfy and the properties of their *algebraic* models (which are, in the case of predicate based logic, the many-valued Herbrand models). The distinctive feature of algebraic semantics is that it is truth-functional. Besides algebraic models also Kripke-style or *relational* models exist. The distinctive feature of Kripke-style semantics is that accessibility relations over possible worlds are used in the definition of satisfiability, which is not just a mechanical truth-functional translation of the logic formula into the model.

There is a lot of work dedicated to this duality for lattices [291] with operators. A good recent overview can be found in [196, 212, 292, 293].

Differently from their general approach, we introduce the *autoreferential duality* for complete lattices: we use (autoreferentially) as a set of possible worlds for a Kripke frame the underlying complete lattice of truth values. This is a particular case where the frame is a partial order, as for example, in [294]. Consequently, the main contribution of this section is a general way of establishing links between algebraic and Kripke-style semantics for the class of many-valued modal logics, based on this autoreferential duality, and the consequent paraconsistent properties.

An introduction of multimodal predicate logic with their Kripke semantics, based on the set $\mathcal{W}$ of possible worlds, is given in Section 1.1.2. More about complete lattice is provided in Section A.1.

Remark. Here, as in the section dedicated to lattices and their algebraic extensions, we will use the values $0, 1 \in \mathbf{2}$ instead of corresponding values f, t respectively, used for intensional FOL. In what follows, we will use the algebraic meet and join symbols of a complete lattice $(X, \leq)$, where X is a set of algebraic truth values and $\leq$ a partial order in X (an extension of the complete lattice $\mathbf{2}$), also as symbols for corresponding *logic* connectives, conjunction and disjunction, while for other connectives we will maintain the formal distinction. □

Generally, normal 2-valued modal logics are not truth-valued (there is no homomorphism between the syntactical structure of the logic language and the Boolean algebra (i. e., distributive lattices with complements) of truth functions $(\mathbf{2}, \leq)$, because we have only four unary functions in $\mathbf{2}^\mathbf{2}$: identity, negation, tautology and contradiction. Thus, the existential unary modal operator $\diamond_i$, and its dual universal modal operator $\Box_i$, cannot be represented as the function from $\mathbf{2}$ into $\mathbf{2}$, and it was the reason why Jan Lukasiewicz introduced, around 1918, more truth values than the ordinary two.

In fact, there is always the equivalent *truth-functional* many-valued logic, with the set of higher-order truth values [82] in the Boolean-lattice functional space $(\mathbf{2}^{\mathcal{W}}, \leq,$

$\wedge, \vee, \neg)$, isomorphic to the powerset Boolean algebra $(\mathcal{P}(\mathcal{W}), \subseteq, \bigcap, \bigcup, -)$, i. e., there is the isomorphism of Boolean algebras im : $(\mathbf{2}^{\mathcal{W}}, \leq, \wedge, \vee, \neg) \simeq (\mathcal{P}(\mathcal{W}), \subseteq, \bigcap, \bigcup, -)$, such that for any two functional algebraic values $f_1, f_2 \in \mathbf{2}^{\mathcal{W}}$, $f_1 \leq f_2$ iff $\mathrm{im}(f_1) \subseteq \mathrm{im}(f_2)$, where $\mathrm{im}(f) = \{w \in \mathcal{W} \mid f(w) = 1\}$ is the image of f.

The meet, join and negation operations in the Boolean algebra $(\mathbf{2}^{\mathcal{W}}, \leq, \wedge, \vee, \neg)$ are defined by this isomorphism as:

$$f = f_1 \wedge f_2 : \mathcal{W} \to \mathbf{2}, \quad \text{such that } \mathrm{im}(f) = \mathrm{im}(f_1) \bigcap \mathrm{im}(f_2),$$
$$f = f_1 \vee f_2 : \mathcal{W} \to \mathbf{2}, \quad \text{such that } \mathrm{im}(f) = \mathrm{im}(f_1) \bigcup \mathrm{im}(f_2),$$
$$f = \neg f_1 : \mathcal{W} \to \mathbf{2}, \quad \text{such that } \mathrm{im}(f) = \mathcal{W} - \mathrm{im}(f_1), \quad \text{where } - \text{ is the set substriction.}$$

The logic implication in this Boolean algebra is defined classically by $f_1 \Rightarrow f_2 =_{\mathrm{def}} \neg f_1 \vee f_2$. The truth-functional universal (multiplicative) modal operator $\Box_i : \mathbf{2}^{\mathcal{W}} \to \mathbf{2}^{\mathcal{W}}$ for normal Kripke logic with the binary accessibility relation $\mathcal{R}_i$ is defined by

$$f = \Box_i f_1 : \mathcal{W} \to \mathbf{2}, \quad \text{such that } \mathrm{im}(f) = \{w \mid \forall w'((w, w') \in \mathcal{R}_i \text{ implies } w' \in \mathrm{im}(f_1))\}.$$

So that, a *non*truth-functional 2-valued modal logic is equivalently represented by a *many-valued truth-functional* algebraic logic based on Boolean algebra extended by normal modal algebraic operators $(X, 0, 1, \leq, \wedge, \vee, \neg, \Box_i)$, where $X = \mathbf{2}^{\mathcal{W}}$ and $0, 1 \in X$ are the bottom and top value in X, with also an infinite number of algebraic truth values [295]. The same approach can be applied to any many-valued *non*truth-functional modal logic, thus it is enough to analyze only the *algebraic truth-functional* many-valued modal logics, as is done in what follows. Vice versa, any algebraic many-valued logic logic program, based on the complete lattice of truth values, can be equivalently represented by a nontruth-functional 2-valued multimodal logic [204] with ternary accessibility relations.

Given a modal algebra $(X, 0, 1, \leq, \wedge, \vee, \neg, \Box_i)$, the standard relational semantics based on Stone's representation theorem, is represented by a descriptive general frame introduced by Goldblat [296, 297], where a possible world is an ultrafilter F defined as a subset of X, which satisfies the following conditions:

$1 \in F$ and not $0 \in F$
if $x, y \in F$, then $x \wedge y \in F$
if $x \in F$ and $x \leq y$ then $y \in F$
for each $x \in X$, either $x \in F$ or $\neg x \in F$.

Instead of this standard relational semantics for modal logic, where a possible world is a *subset* of elements in X (an ultrafilter), in this section we will use a more simple *autoreferential* semantics where a possible world is an *element* in X.

A.3.1 Many-valued model-theoretic autoreferential semantics

A short introduction to binary sequent calculus is provided in Section A.2. The theory presented here is more general than that used in Section A.4.3 for *finite* many-valued predicate logic and its reduction into 2-valued logics.

Let $\mathcal{L}_{mv}$ be a propositional logic language obtained as free algebra, from the connectives in Σ of an algebra based on a complete lattice $(X, \leq)$ of algebraic truth values (e. g., meet and join $\{\wedge, \vee\} \subseteq \Sigma$ are binary operators, negation $\neg \in \Sigma$ and other modal operators are unary operators, while each $a \in X \subseteq \Sigma$ is a constant (nullary operator)) and a set Var of propositional letters (Herbrand base H for predicate logic) denoted by $p, r, q, \ldots$. We will use letters $\phi, \psi, \ldots$ for the formulae of $\mathcal{L}_{mv}$. We define for (many-valued) *valuation* $v : \text{Var} \rightarrow X$ a unique extension $v^* : \mathcal{L}_{mv} \rightarrow X$ (notice that $X \subseteq \mathcal{L}_{mv}$ are the constants of this language and we will use the same symbols as for elements of the lattice X), which is an homomorphism (e. g., for any $p, q \in \text{Var}$, $v^*(p \odot q) = v(p) \odot v(q), \odot \in \{\wedge, \vee, \Rightarrow\}$ and $v^*(\neg p) = \neg v(p)$, where $\wedge, \vee, \Rightarrow, \neg$ are conjunction, disjunction, implication and negation, respectively) and is an identity for elements in X, i. e., for any $x \in X$, $v(x) = x$. We denote by $\mathbb{V}$ the set X^{Var} of all *many-valued valuations*. So, we define the lattice-based consequence binary relation $\vdash \subseteq \mathcal{L}_{mv} \times \mathcal{L}_{mv}$ between the formulae (it is analog to the binary consequence system from [193] for the distributive lattice logic DLL), where each consequence pair $\phi \vdash \psi$ is a *sequent* also.

Example 44. Let us consider the Distributive modal logic [193] (with $\Box$ universal modal operator, and its left-adjoint existential modal operator $\diamond$, with $\diamond \dashv \Box$) and with a negative modal operator $\neg$. The Gentzen-like system $\mathcal{G}$ of this logic language $\mathcal{L}_{mv}$ contains the following axioms (sequents) and rules:
(AXIOMS) $\mathcal{G}$ contains the following sequents:
1. $\phi \vdash \phi$ (reflexive)
2. $\phi \vdash 1$, $0 \vdash \phi$ (top/bottom axioms)
3. $\phi \wedge \psi \vdash \phi$, $\phi \wedge \psi \vdash \psi$ (product projections: axioms for meet)
4. $\phi \vdash \phi \vee \psi$, $\psi \vdash \phi \vee \psi$ (coproduct injections: axioms for join)
5. $\phi \wedge (\psi \vee \varphi) \vdash (\phi \wedge \psi) \vee (\phi \wedge \varphi)$ (distributivity axiom)
6. $\Box(\phi \wedge \psi) \vdash \Box\phi \wedge \Box\psi$, $1 \vdash \Box 1$ (multiplicative modal property axioms)
7. $\diamond(\phi \vee \psi) \vdash \diamond\phi \vee \diamond\psi$, $\diamond 0 \vdash 0$ (additive modal property axioms)
8. $\neg\phi \wedge \neg\psi \vdash \neg(\phi \vee \psi)$, $1 \vdash \neg 0$ (additive modal negation axiom)
9. The set of sequents, which define the poset of the lattice of truth values $(X, \leq)$: for any two $x, y \in X$, if $x \leq y$ then $x \vdash y \in \mathcal{G}$.

(INFERENCE RULES) $\mathcal{G}$ is closed under the following inference rules:
1. $\frac{\phi \vdash \psi, \psi \vdash \varphi}{\phi \vdash \varphi}$ (cut/transitivity rule)
2. $\frac{\phi \vdash \psi, \phi \vdash \varphi}{\phi \vdash \psi \wedge \varphi}$, $\frac{\phi \vdash \psi, \varphi \vdash \psi}{\phi \vee \varphi \vdash \psi}$ (lower/upper lattice bound rules)
3. $\frac{\phi \vdash \psi}{\Box\phi \vdash \Box\psi}$, $\frac{\phi \vdash \psi}{\diamond\phi \vdash \diamond\psi}$ (monotonicity of modal operators rules)

4. $\frac{\phi \vdash \psi}{\neg\psi \vdash \neg\phi}$ (antitonicity of modal negation rule)
5. $\frac{\phi \vdash \psi}{\sigma(\phi) \vdash \sigma(\psi)}$ (substitution rule: σ is substitution (y/p)).

The rules in point 2 are the consequences of diagonal mapping $\triangle : X \to Y$, where $Y = X \times X$ and $\triangle x = (x, x)$, (which is both additive and multiplicative modal operator), and its Galois adjunctions with the meet (multiplicative) and join (additive) operators $\wedge, \vee : Y \to X$, i. e., with $\triangle \dashv \wedge$ and $\vee \dashv \triangle$; that is, $\triangle x \leq_Y (y, z)$ (i. e., $x \leq y$ and $x \leq z$) iff $x \leq \wedge(y, z) = y \wedge z$, and $x \vee y = \vee(x, y) \leq z$ iff $(x, y) \leq_Y \triangle z$ (i. e., $x \leq z$ and $y \leq z$).

The axioms from 1 to 5 and the rules 1 and 2 are taken from [193] for the DLL and it was shown that this sequent based Genzen-like system is sound and complete. If we omit the distributivity axiom 5, we obtain the system $\mathcal{G}$ for complete lattice logics. Thus, for a lattice based modal many-valued logics we obtain a *normal* modal Gentzen-like deductive system, where each sequent is a valid truth-preserving consequence pair defined by the poset of the complete lattice $(X, \leq)$ of truth values (which are also the constants of this modal propositional language $\mathcal{L}_{mv}$), so that each occurrence of the symbol $\vdash$ can be substituted by the partial order $\leq$ of this complete lattice.

In according with the truth-preserving entailment for general sequents provided by Definition 57 in Section 5.1, here we introduce its simpler case for binary sequent.

Definition 102 (Binary-sequent truth-preserving entailment). For any two sentences $\phi, \psi \in \mathcal{L}_{mv}$, the truth-preserving consequence pair (sequent), denoted by $\phi \vdash \psi$ is satisfied by a given valuation $v^* : \mathcal{L}_{mv} \to X$ if $v^*(\phi) \leq v^*(\psi)$. This sequent is a tautology if it is satisfied by all valuations, i. e., when $\forall v \in \mathbb{V}.(v^*(\phi) \leq v^*(\psi))$.

For a normal Gentzen-like sequent system $\mathcal{G}$ of the many-valued logic $\mathcal{L}_{mv}$, with the set of sequents $\mathrm{Seq}_{\mathcal{G}} \subseteq \mathcal{L}_{mv} \times \mathcal{L}_{mv}$ and a set of inference rules in $\mathrm{Rul}_{\mathcal{G}}$, we tell that a many-valued valuation v is its `model` if it satisfies all sequents in $\mathcal{G}$. The set of all models of a given set of sequents (theory) Γ is denoted by

$$\mathbb{V}_\Gamma =_{def} \{v \in \mathbb{V} \mid \forall(\phi \vdash \psi) \in \Gamma(v^*(\phi) \leq v^*(\psi))\} \subseteq \mathbb{V}.$$

Proposition 36 (Soundness). *All axioms of the Gentzen-like sequent system $\mathcal{G}$, of a many-valued logic $\mathcal{L}_{mv}$ based on complete lattice $(X, \leq)$ of algebraic truth values, are the tautologies, and all its rules are sound for model satisfiability and preserve the tautologies.*

Proof. It is straightforward to check (see Example 44) that all axioms are tautologies (all constant sequents specify the poset of the complete lattice $(X, \leq)$, thus are tautologies) and that all rules preserve the tautologies. Moreover, if all premises of any rule in $\mathcal{G}$ are satisfied by given many-valued valuation $v^* : \mathcal{L}_{mv} \to X$, then also the deduced sequent of this rule is satisfied by the same valuation, i. e., the rules are sound for the model satisfiability. □

It is easy to verify that for any two $x, y \in X$ we have that $x \leq y$ iff $x \vdash y$, i. e., the truth-preserving entailment coincides with the partial truth-ordering in a lattice $(X, \leq)$. Notice that it is compatible with lattice operators, i. e., for any two formulae $\phi, \psi \in \mathcal{L}_{mv}$, $\phi \wedge \psi \vdash \psi$ and $\phi \vdash \psi \vee \phi$. This entailment imposes the following restrictions to the logic implication: in order to satisfy the "deduction theorem "$z \vdash x \Rightarrow y$ iff $z \wedge x \vdash y$" (i. e., inference rules for elimination and introduction of the logic connective $\Rightarrow$, $\frac{z \vdash x \Rightarrow y}{z \wedge x \vdash y}$ and $\frac{z \wedge x \vdash y}{z \vdash x \Rightarrow y}$) by this entailment, the logic implication must satisfy (the case when $z = 1$) the requirement that for any $x, y \in X$, $x \Rightarrow y = 1$ iff $x \leq y$, while it must satisfy $x \wedge (x \Rightarrow y) \leq y$ in order to satisfy the modus ponens inference rule.

The particularity of this entailment is that any consequence pair (sequent) $\phi \vdash \psi$ is algebraically an equation $\phi \wedge \psi = \phi$ (or, $\phi \vee \psi = \psi$).

It is easy to verify, that in the case of the classic 2-valued propositional logic this entailment is equal to the classic propositional entailment, so that the truth-preserving entailment is only a generalization of the classic entailment for a many-valued propositional logics.

Remark. It is easy to observe that each sequent is, from the logic point of view, a *2-valued object* so that all inference rules are embedded into the classic 2-valued framework, i. e., given a bivaluation $\beta : \mathcal{L}_{mv} \times \mathcal{L}_{mv} \to \mathbf{2}$, we have that a sequent $s = \phi \vdash \psi$ is satisfied when $\beta(s) = 1$, so that we have the relationship between sequent bivaluations and many-valued valuations v used in Definition 102. This sequent feature, which is only an alternative formulation for the 2-valued classic logic, is *fundamental* in the framework of many-valued logics, where often the semantics for the entailment, based on algebraic matrices (X, D) is arbitrary: consider, e. g., fuzzy logic, where the subset of designated elements $D \subseteq X$ is an closed interval $[a, 1]$, where $0 < a \leq 1$ is an arbitrary value, so difficult to fix. □

Thus, this correct definition of the 2-valued entailment in the sequent system $\mathcal{G}$, based only on the lattice ordering, can replace the current entailment based on the algebraic matrices (X, D), where $D \subseteq X$ is the subset of designated elements, which is upward closed, i. e., if $x \in D$ and $x \leq y$, then $y \in D$ (thus $1 \in D$), and where the matrix-entailment, defined by $\phi \vdash_D \psi$, is valid iff $\forall v \in \mathbb{V}.(v^*(\phi) \in D$ implies $v^*(\psi) \in D)$. It is easy to verify also that $\phi \vdash \psi$ implies $\phi \vdash_D \psi$.

This opinion is based also on the consideration that all many-valued, *implication based* (IF), logic program languages, are based on clauses $A \leftarrow B_1 \wedge \cdots \wedge B_n$ where A is a ground atom and B_i are ground literals (ground atoms or negation of ground atoms), we tell that it is *satisfied* by a valuation v^* iff $v^*(A) \leq v^*(B_1) \wedge \cdots \wedge v^*(B_n)$; Thus, this clause is the sequent $(B_1 \wedge \cdots \wedge B_n) \vdash A$, so that a logic program is in fact a set of sequents; the valuation v^* which satisfies all clauses (sequents) is a *model* for such a logic program, and demonstrates how we are able to define the models of many-valued logics without the necessity to define the algebraic matrices (X, D). The other class of many valued logic programs, Signed logic programs [298, 299] and its subclass of *annotation based* (AB) programs [300, 301] a clause is of the form A :

$f(\delta_1,\dots,\delta_n) \leftarrow B_1 : \delta_1,\dots,B_n : \delta_n$, which asserts "the certainty of the atom A is least (or is in) $f(\delta_1,\dots,\delta_n)$, whenever the certainty of the atom B_i is at least (or is in) δ_i, $1 \le i \le n$," where f is an n-ary computable function and δ_i is either a constant or a variable ranging over many-valued logic values. But they are not really many-valued logics, but a kind of meta many-valued logics, because all annotated literals $B_n : \delta_n$ are classic 2-valued objects (a valuation v is a model of the literal $B_n : \delta_n$ if $v^*(B_n) \ge \delta_n$ (or $v^*(B_n) \in \delta_n$)), and all connectives in the clauses are also classic 2-valued. In fact, in [204] it is shown that the annotated elements are 2-valued modal formulae, so that an annotated logic is a kind of 2-valued multimodal logics; the same result can be proven also in the more general case of Signed logic programming. Thus, we are able now to introduce the many-valued valuation-based (i. e., model-theoretic) semantics for many-valued logics.

Definition 103. A `many-valued` model-theoretic semantics of a given many-valued logic $\mathcal{L}_{mv}$, with a Gentzen system $\mathcal{G} = \langle \mathbb{L}, \Vdash \rangle$, is the semantic deducibility relation $\vDash_m$, defined for any set $\Gamma = \{s_i = (\phi_i \vdash \psi_i)\}$ and sequent $s = (\phi \vdash \psi) \in \mathbb{L} \subseteq \mathcal{L}_{mv} \times \mathcal{L}_{mv}$ by $\Gamma \vDash_m s$ iff all many-valued models of Γ are the models of s. That is,

$$\begin{aligned}\Gamma \vDash_m s \quad &\text{iff} \quad \forall v \in \mathbb{V}(\forall(\phi_i \vdash \psi_i) \in \Gamma(v^*(\phi_i) \le v^*(\psi_i)) \text{ implies } v^*(\phi) \le v^*(\psi))\\ &\text{iff} \quad \forall v \in \mathbb{V}_\Gamma(\forall(\phi_i \vdash \psi_i) \in \Gamma(v^*(\phi_i) \le v^*(\psi_i)) \text{ implies } v^*(\phi) \le v^*(\psi))\\ &\text{iff} \quad \forall v \in \mathbb{V}_\Gamma(v^*(\phi) \le v^*(\psi)).\end{aligned}$$

It is easy to verify that any complete-lattice based many-valued logic has the Gentzen-like system $\mathcal{G} = \langle \mathbb{L}, \Vdash \rangle$ (see the example above), which is *normal* logic.

Theorem 16. *The many-valued model theoretic semantics is an adequate semantics for a many-valued logic $\mathcal{L}_{mv}$ specified by a Gentzen-like logic system $\mathcal{G} = \langle \mathbb{L}, \Vdash \rangle$, i. e., it is sound and complete. Consequently, $\Gamma \vDash_m s$ iff $\Gamma \Vdash s$.*

Proof. Let us prove that for any many valued model $v \in \mathbb{V}_\Gamma$, the obtained sequent bivaluation $\beta = \text{eq} \circ \langle \pi_1, \wedge \rangle \circ (v^* \times v^*) : \mathcal{L}_{mv} \times \mathcal{L}_{mv} \to \mathbf{2}$ is the characteristic function of the closed theory $\Gamma_v = C(T)$ with $T = \{\phi \vdash x, x \vdash \phi \mid \phi \in \mathcal{L}_{mv}, x = v^*(\phi)\}$.

From the definition of β, we have that $\beta(\phi \vdash \psi) = \beta(\phi;\psi) = \text{eq} \circ \langle \pi_1, \wedge \rangle \circ (v^* \times v^*)(\phi;\psi) = \text{eq} \circ \langle \pi_1, \wedge \rangle (v^*(\phi), v^*(\psi)) = \text{eq}\langle \pi_1(v^*(\phi), v^*(\psi)), \wedge(v^*(\phi), v^*(\psi))\rangle = \text{eq}(v^*(\phi), \wedge(v^*(\phi), v^*(\psi))) = \text{eq}(v^*(\phi), v^*(\phi) \wedge v^*(\psi))$, where π_1 is the first projection, $\text{eq} : X \times X \to \mathbf{2} \subseteq X$ is the equality characteristic function such that $\text{eq}(x,y) = 1$ if $x = y$. Thus, $\beta(\phi \vdash \psi) = 1$ iff $v^*(\phi) \le v^*(\psi)$, i. e., when this sequent is satisfied by v^*.

1. Let us show that for any sequent s, $s \in \Gamma_v$ implies $\beta(s) = 1$: First of all, any sequent $s \in T$ is of the form $\varphi \vdash x$ or $x \vdash \varphi$, where $x = v^*(\varphi)$, so that it is satisfied by v^* (holds that $v^*(\varphi) \le v^*(\varphi)$ in both cases). So, *all* sequents in T are satisfied by v^*.

By the Proposition 36, we have that all inference rules in $\mathcal{G}$ are sound w. r. t. the model satisfiability, thus for any deduction $T \Vdash s$ (i. e., $s \in \Gamma_v$) where all sequents in premises are satisfied by the many-valued valuation (model) v^*, also the deduced sequent $s = (\phi \vdash \psi)$ must be satisfied, that is it must hold $v^*(\phi) \leq v^*(\psi)$, i. e., $\beta(s) = 1$.

2. Let us show that for any sequent s, $\beta(s) = 1$ implies $s \in \Gamma_v$:

For *any* sequent $s = (\phi \vdash \psi) \in \mathcal{L}_{mv} \times \mathcal{L}_{mv}$ if $\beta(s) = 1$, then $x = v^*(\phi) \leq v^*(\psi) = y$ (i. e., s is satisfied by v). From the definition of T, we have that $\phi \vdash x, y \vdash \psi \in T$, and from $x \leq y$ we have $x \vdash y \in Ax_{\mathcal{G}}$ (where $Ax_{\mathcal{G}}$ are axioms (sequents) in $\mathcal{G}$, with $\{x \vdash y \mid x, y \in X, x \leq y\} \subseteq Ax_{\mathcal{G}}$, thus satisfied by every valuation) by the transitivity rule, from $\phi \vdash x, x \vdash y, y \vdash \psi$, we obtain that $T \Vdash (\phi \vdash \psi)$, i. e., $s = (\phi \vdash \psi) \in C(T) = \Gamma_v$.

So, from (1) and (2) we obtain that $\beta(s) = 1$ iff $s \in \Gamma_v$, i. e., the sequent bivaluation β is the characteristic function of a closed set. Thus, any many-valued *model* v^* of this many-valued logic $\mathcal{L}_{mv}$ corresponds to the *closed* bivaluation β, which is a characteristic function of a closed theory of sequents: we define the set of all closed bivaluations obtained from the set of many-valued models $v \in \mathbb{V}_\Gamma$: $\mathrm{Biv}_\Gamma = \{\Gamma_v \mid v \in \mathbb{V}_\Gamma\}$. From the fact that Γ is satisfied by every $v \in \mathbb{V}_\Gamma$, we have that for every $\Gamma_v \in \mathrm{Biv}_\Gamma$, $\Gamma \subseteq \Gamma_v$, so that $C(\Gamma) = \bigcap \mathrm{Biv}_\Gamma$ (intersection of closed sets is a closed set also). So, for $s = (\phi \vdash \psi)$,

$$\begin{aligned}
\Gamma \vDash_m s \quad & \text{iff} \quad \forall v \in \mathbb{V}_\Gamma(\forall(\phi_i \vdash \psi_i) \in \Gamma(v^*(\phi_i) \leq v^*(\psi_i)) \text{ implies } v^*(\phi) \leq v^*(\psi)) \\
& \text{iff} \quad \forall v \in \mathbb{V}_\Gamma(\forall(\phi_i \vdash \psi_i) \in \Gamma(\beta(\phi_i \vdash \psi_i) = 1) \text{ implies } \beta(\phi \vdash \psi) = 1) \\
& \text{iff} \quad \forall v \in \mathbb{V}_\Gamma(\forall(\phi_i \vdash \psi_i) \in \Gamma((\phi_i \vdash \psi_i) \in \Gamma_v) \text{ implies } s \in \Gamma_v) \\
& \text{iff} \quad \forall \Gamma_v \in \mathrm{Biv}_\Gamma(\Gamma \subseteq \Gamma_v \text{ implies } s \in \Gamma_v) \\
& \text{iff} \quad \forall \Gamma_v \in \mathrm{Biv}_\Gamma(s \in \Gamma_v), \text{ because } \Gamma \subseteq \Gamma_v \text{ for each } \Gamma_v \in \mathrm{Biv}_\Gamma \\
& \text{iff} \quad s \in \bigcap \mathrm{Biv}_\Gamma = C(\Gamma), \text{ that is, iff } \Gamma \Vdash s.
\end{aligned}$$

□

Thus, in order to define the model-theoretic semantics for a many-valued logics we do not need to define the problematic matrices: we are able to use only the many-valued valuations, and *many-valued models* (i. e., valuations, which satisfy all sequents in Γ of a given many-valued logic $\mathcal{L}_{mv}$). This point of view is used also for definition of a new representation theorem for many-valued logics in [206].

Different from the classic logic where a formula is a theorem if it is true in all models of the logic, here in a many-valued logic $\mathcal{L}_{mv}$, but specified by a set of sequents in Γ, for a formula $\phi \in \mathcal{L}_{mv}$, which has the same value $x \in X$ (for *any* algebraic truth-value x) for all many-valued models $v \in \mathbb{V}_\Gamma$, we have that its sequent-based version $\phi \vdash x$ and $x \vdash \phi$ are theorems; that is, $\forall v \in \mathbb{V}_\Gamma(v^*(\phi) = x)$ iff $(\Gamma \Vdash (\phi \vdash x)$ and $\Gamma \Vdash (x \vdash \phi))$.

But such a value $x \in A$ does not need to be a designated element $x \in D$, as in matrix semantics for a many-valued logic, and it explains why we do not need the rigid semantic specification by matrix designated elements. Thus, by a translation of a many-valued logic $\mathcal{L}_{mv}$ into its "meta" sequent-based 2-valued logic, we obtain an unambiguous theory of inference without the introduction of problematic matrices.

There are also two other ways, alternative to 2-valued sequent systems, to reduce the many-valued logics into "meta" 2-valued logics as provided in Section A.4.

Based on this Genzen-like sequent deductive system $\mathcal{G}$, we are able to define the equivalence relation $\approx_L$ between the formulae of any modal propositional logic based on a complete lattice in order to define the Lindenbaum algebra for this logic, $(\mathcal{L}_{\mathrm{mv}}/\approx_L, \sqsubseteq)$, where for any two formulae $\phi, \psi \in \mathcal{L}_{\mathrm{mv}}$:

(a) $\phi \approx_L \psi$ iff $\phi \vdash \psi$ and $\psi \vdash \phi$, i. e., iff $\forall v^*.(v^*(\phi) \leq v^*(\psi))$ and $\forall v^*.(v^*(\phi) \geq v^*(\psi))$. So, the quotient algebra $\mathcal{L}_{\mathrm{mv}}/\approx_L$ has as elements equivalence classes, denoted by $[\phi]$, and the partial ordering $\sqsubseteq$, defined by

(b) $[\phi] \sqsubseteq [\psi]$ iff $\phi \vdash \psi$ (i. e., if $\phi \leq \psi$).

It is easy to verify that each equivalence class (set of all equivalent formulae w. r. t. $\approx_L$) $[\phi]$ has exactly one constant $x \in X$, which is an element of this equivalence class, and we can use it as the representation element for this equivalence class: so that every formula in this equivalence class has the same truth value as this constant.

Thus, we have the bijection $\mathrm{is} : \mathcal{L}_{\mathrm{mv}}/\approx_L \to X$ between elements in the complete lattice $(X, \leq)$ and elements in the Lindenbaum algebra, such that for any equivalence class $[\phi] \in \mathcal{L}_{\mathrm{mv}}/\approx_L$, the constant $\mathrm{is}([\phi]) \in X$ is the representation element for this equivalence class. It is easy to extend this bijection into an isomorphism between the original algebra and this Lindenbaum algebra, by definition of correspondent connectives in the Lindenbaum algebra, e. g.,

$$[\phi] \wedge_L [\psi] =_{\mathrm{def}} \mathrm{is}^{-1}(\mathrm{is}([\phi]) \wedge \mathrm{is}([\phi])), \quad [\phi] \vee_L [\psi] =_{\mathrm{def}} \mathrm{is}^{-1}(\mathrm{is}([\phi]) \vee \mathrm{is}([\phi])),$$
$$\neg_L[\phi] =_{\mathrm{def}} \mathrm{is}^{-1}(\neg(\mathrm{is}([\phi]))), \quad \text{etc.}$$

In the autoreferential semantics, we will assume that each equivalence class of formulae $[\phi]$ in this Lindenbaum algebra corresponds to one "state-description," that is to one possible world in the Kripke-style semantics for the original many-valued modal logic. But, from the isomorphism is, we can take, instead of equivalence class $[\phi]$, only its representation element $x = \mathrm{is}([\phi]) \in X$. Consequently, the set of possible worlds in this autoreferential semantics corresponds to the set of truth values in the complete lattice $(X, \leq)$.

A.3.2 Hierarchy of negation operators for complete lattices

Generally, lattices arise concretely as the substructures of closure systems (intersection systems) where a closure system is a family $\mathcal{F}(X)$ of subsets of a set X such that $X \in \mathcal{F}(X)$ and if $A_i \in \mathcal{F}(X), i \in I$, then $\bigcap_{i\in I} A_i \in \mathcal{F}(X)$. Then the representation problem for general lattices is to establish that every lattice can be viewed, up to an isomorphism, as a collection of subsets in a closure system (on some set X), closed under the operations of the system.

Closure operators are canonically obtained by the composition of two maps of Galois connections. The Galois connections can be obtained from any binary relation on a set X [207] (Birkhoff *polarity*) in a canonical way:

If (X, R) is a set with a particular relation on a set X, $R \subseteq X \times X$, with mappings

$$\lambda : \mathcal{P}(X) \to \mathcal{P}(X)^{\mathrm{OP}}, \varrho : \mathcal{P}(X)^{\mathrm{OP}} \to \mathcal{P}(X), \quad \text{such that for any } U, V \in \mathcal{P}(X),$$
$$\lambda U = \{x \in X \mid \forall u \in U.((u,x) \in R)\}, \quad \rho V = \{x \in X \mid \forall v \in V.((x,v) \in R)\},$$

where $\mathcal{P}(X)$ is the *powerset poset* with the bottom element empty set $\emptyset$ and top element X, and $\mathcal{P}(X)^{\mathrm{OP}}$ its dual (with $\subseteq^{\mathrm{OP}}$ inverse of $\subseteq$), then we obtain the induced Galois connection

$$\lambda \dashv \rho, \quad \text{i.e.,} \quad \lambda U \subseteq^{\mathrm{OP}} V \text{ iff } U \subseteq \rho V.$$

The following lemma is useful for the relationship of these set-based operators with the operation of negation in the complete lattices.

Lemma 13 (Incompatibility relation). *Let $(X, \leq)$ be a complete lattice. Then we can use a binary relation $R \subseteq X \times X$ as an* `incompatibility` *relation for set-based negation operators λ and ρ, with the following properties: for any $U, V \subseteq X$,*

1. $\lambda(U \bigcup V) = \lambda U \bigcup^{\mathrm{OP}} \lambda V = \lambda U \bigcap \lambda V$, *with* $\lambda\emptyset = \emptyset^{\mathrm{OP}} = X$ *(additivity),*
2. $\rho(U \bigcap^{\mathrm{OP}} V) = \rho(U \bigcup V) = \rho U \bigcap \rho V$, *with* $\rho X^{\mathrm{OP}} = \rho\emptyset = X$ *(multiplicativity),*
3. *while* $\lambda(U \bigcap V) \geq \lambda U \bigcup \lambda V$, $\rho(U \bigcap V) \geq \rho U \bigcup \rho V$ *and* $\lambda\rho V \geq V$, $\rho\lambda U \geq U$.

We will consider the case when (X, R) is a complete lattice with the binary relation R equal to the partial order $\leq$ in the lattice X. The resulting Galois connection on this partial order is the familiar Dedekind–McNeile Galois connection of antitonic mappings λ and ρ (We denote by $\downarrow x$ the ideal $\{y \in X \mid y\mathcal{L}_{\mathrm{mv}}\,\mathrm{eq}\, x\}$):

$$\lambda U = \{x \in X \mid \forall u \in U.(u \leq x)\}, \quad \rho V = \{x \in X \mid \forall v \in V.(x \leq v)\},$$

Setting $\boxdot = \rho\lambda : \mathcal{P}(X) \to \mathcal{P}(X)$, the operator $\boxdot$ is a monotone mapping and a closure operator, such that for any $U, V \in \mathcal{P}(X)$:

1. $U \subseteq V$ implies $\boxdot(U) \subseteq \boxdot(V)$,
2. $U \subseteq \boxdot(U)$, for any $U \in \mathcal{P}(X)$,
3. $\boxdot\boxdot(U) = \boxdot(U)$

The set $\{U \in \mathcal{P}(X) \mid U = \boxdot(U)\}$ is called the set of *stable* (closed) sets.

It is easy to verify that for every subset $S \subseteq X$, we obtain $\boxdot(S) = \downarrow \bigvee(S)$, which is a multiplicative monotone operator: the closure operator $\boxdot$ satisfies the multiplicative property $\boxdot(U \bigcap V) = \boxdot(U) \bigcap \boxdot(V)$, and $\boxdot(X) = X$, which is the top element in $\mathcal{P}(X)$.

Thus, $\boxdot = \downarrow\bigvee$ is a *universal modal operator* for the complete lattice $(\mathcal{P}(X), \subseteq)$ (which is a Boolean algebra, i. e., a *complemented distributive* lattice), so that we obtain the modal algebra $(\mathcal{P}(X), \subseteq, \bigcap, \bigcup, \boxdot)$ for the complete lattice $(X, \leq)$.

Notice that $\boxdot(\emptyset) = \boxdot(\{0\}) = \{0\}$. Thus, from the monotone property of $\boxdot$ and from $\emptyset \subseteq U$ (for any $U \in \mathcal{P}(X)$) we obtain that $\{0\} = \boxdot(\emptyset) \subseteq \boxdot(U)$. That is, any stable (closed) set contains the bottom element $0 \in X$, and that the minimal stable set is $\{0\}$ and not an empty set $\emptyset$, while naturally the maximal stable set is X.

Moreover, each stable set is a down-closed ideal and there is the bijection between the set of stable sets and the set of algebraic truth-values in X, so that we can define the *first (noncanonical) representation theorem* for a complete lattice $(X, \leq)$ as follows.

Proposition 37 (Autoreferential representation theorem for complete lattices). *Let $(X, \leq)$ be a complete lattice. We define the Dedekind–McNeile coalgebra $\downarrow: X \to \mathcal{P}(X)$, where $\downarrow = \boxdot\mathrm{in}$, $\boxdot = \rho\lambda$ is a Dedekind–McNeile closure operator and* in $: X \to \mathcal{P}(X)$ *the inclusion map $x \mapsto \{x\}$, such that for any two $x, y \in X$ holds (we denote by—the set substraction)*

(1) $\bigcup\{S \in \mathcal{P}(X) \mid S \bigcap \downarrow x \subseteq \downarrow y\} = (X - \downarrow x) \bigcup \downarrow y$.

We denote by $\mathcal{F}(X) = \{\downarrow x \mid x \in X\}$ the closure system because for each $x \in X$, $\downarrow x$ is a stable set. Then the $(\mathcal{F}(X), \subseteq)$ is a complete lattice with meet operator $\bigcap$ (set intersection), and join operator $\uplus = \boxdot\bigcup = \downarrow\bigvee\bigcup$ different *from the set union $\bigcup$, such that the* noncanonical *autoreferential representation isomorphism holds:*

(2) $\downarrow: (X, \leq, \wedge, \vee, 0, 1) \simeq (\mathcal{F}(X), \subseteq, \bigcap, \uplus, \{0\}, X)$.

Proof. We will show that each stable set $U \in \mathcal{F}(X)$ is an ideal in $(X, \leq)$. In fact, it holds that for any $x \in X$, $\downarrow x = \boxdot\mathrm{in}(x) = \rho\lambda(\{x\}) = \{x' \in X \mid x' \leq x\}$ is an ideal. Thus, for any two $x, y \in X$ we have that:

1. If $x \leq y$, then $\downarrow x \subseteq \downarrow y$,
2. $\downarrow x \bigcap \downarrow y = \{x' \in X \mid x' \leq x\} \bigcap \{y' \in X \mid y' \leq y\} = \{z \in X \mid z \leq x \wedge y\} \downarrow (x \wedge y) \in \mathcal{F}(X)$,
3. $\downarrow x \uplus \downarrow y = \downarrow\bigvee\bigcup(\downarrow x, \downarrow y) = \downarrow\bigvee(\downarrow x \bigcup \downarrow y) = \downarrow\bigvee(\{x' \in X \mid x' \leq x\} \bigcup \{y' \in X \mid y' \leq y\}) = \downarrow(x \vee y) \in \mathcal{F}(X)$.

The operator $\uplus$ is the join operator in $\mathcal{F}(X)$, that is it holds $\downarrow x \subseteq \downarrow y$ iff $\downarrow x \uplus \downarrow y = \downarrow y$.

Thus, the original lattice $(X, \leq)$ is isomorphic to the lattice $(\mathcal{F}(X), \subseteq)$ via map $x \mapsto \downarrow x$. It is easy to verify that the inverse of $\downarrow$, i. e., $\downarrow^{-1} = (\boxdot\mathrm{in})^{-1} = \mathrm{in}^{-1}\boxdot^{-1} : \mathcal{P}(X) \to X$ is equal to supremum $\bigvee$, i. e., $\downarrow^{-1}(U) = \bigvee\{x \in U\}$, with $\bigvee \downarrow x = x$, i. e., $\bigvee \downarrow = \mathrm{id}_X$ and $\downarrow \bigvee = \mathrm{id}_{\mathcal{F}(X)}$ are the identity functions for x and $\mathcal{F}(X)$, respectively. It is easy to verify that $\mathcal{F}(X)$ is a complete lattice with bottom element $\downarrow 0 = \{0\}$ and top element $\downarrow 1 = X$, and for any $U = \downarrow x, V = \downarrow y \in \mathcal{F}(X)$, $U \bigcap V = \downarrow(x \wedge y) \in \mathcal{F}(X)$ and $U \uplus V = \downarrow(x \vee y) \in \mathcal{F}(X)$. □

Remark. What is important to notice is that the autoreferential representation, based only on the lattice ordering of truth values, naturally introduce the modality in this logic. In fact, the universal modal operator $\boxdot : \mathcal{P}(X) \to \mathcal{F}(X) \subset \mathcal{P}(X)$, based on the partial order of the complete lattice $(X, \leq)$, plays the fundamental role for the modal disjunction $\uplus$ in the canonical autoreferential algebra $\mathcal{F}(X)$. We need it because generally for any two $x, y \in X$, we have that $\downarrow x \bigcup \downarrow y \notin \mathcal{F}(X)$. Its restriction on $\mathcal{F}(X)$ is an *identity* function $\mathrm{id}_{\mathcal{F}(X)}$, which is a self-adjoint (universal and existential) modal operator. If we denote by $\Box$ the *logic* modal operator correspondent to the algebraic modal operator $\boxdot$, we can define the join operator $\vee$ (many-valued disjunction) from the *classic* disjunction $\vee_c$ (for which holds $\downarrow \vee_c = \bigcup \downarrow$, i. e., $\downarrow (x \vee_c y) = \downarrow x \bigcup \downarrow y$) and this modal operator, as follows: for any two logic formulae ϕ and ψ: $\phi \vee \psi = \Box(\phi \vee_c \psi)$. This property will be used when we will define the Kripke-style semantics for this many-valued logic. □

Notice also that in Lewis's approach he distinguishes the standard or *extensional* disjunction $\vee_c$, from the *intensional* disjunction $\vee$ "*in such that at least one of the disjoined propositions is* necessarily *true*" [302] (1912, p. 523). In the same way, he defined also the "strict" logic implication $\phi \Rightarrow \psi = \Box(\phi \Rightarrow_c \psi)$ where $\Rightarrow_c$ is the classic extensional implication such that $\phi \Rightarrow_c \psi = \neg_c \phi \vee_c \psi$ (here $\neg_c$ denotes the classic logic negation). In what follows, we will see that this property holds also for a many-valued implication defined as relative pseudo-complement in a complete distributive lattice X, i. e., for the *intuitionistic* logic implication.

Thus, the noncanonical autoreferential semantics for many-valued logic, based on the partial order of the lattice, defines the *intensional* disjunction[1] and implication as a many-valued generalization of Lewis's 2-valued logic.

It remains to explain what an *algebraic* universal modal operator for a lattice X is, corresponding to the universal algebraic modal operator $\boxdot$ in $\mathcal{P}(X)$. The answer is simple: it is an identity operator $\mathrm{id} : X \to X$. In fact, we have that the homomorphism $\downarrow$ between the many-valued algebra over X and the powerset algebra over $\mathcal{P}(X)$ is extended by $\downarrow \mathrm{id} = \boxdot \downarrow$. Then we obtain that $\downarrow x = \downarrow \mathrm{id}(x) = \boxdot \downarrow x = \downarrow \bigvee \downarrow x = \downarrow x$, and that $\downarrow (x \vee y) = \downarrow (\mathrm{id} \vee_c(x, y)) =$ (from $\downarrow \mathrm{id} = \boxdot \downarrow$) $= \boxdot \downarrow \vee_c(x, y) =$ (from $\downarrow \vee_c = \bigcup \downarrow$) $= \boxdot \bigcup \downarrow (x, y) = \boxdot \bigcup (\downarrow x, \downarrow y) = \boxdot(\downarrow x \bigcup \downarrow y)$.

While, $\downarrow (x \wedge y) = \downarrow (\mathrm{id} \wedge_c(x, y)) =$ (from $\downarrow \mathrm{id} = \boxdot \downarrow$) $= \boxdot \downarrow \wedge_c(x, y) =$ (from $\downarrow \wedge_c = \bigcap \downarrow$) $= \boxdot \bigcap \downarrow (x, y) = \boxdot \bigcap (\downarrow x, \downarrow y) = \boxdot(\downarrow x \bigcap \downarrow y) =$ (the operator $\boxdot$ is an identity for stable sets) $= \downarrow x \bigcap \downarrow y = \downarrow (x \wedge y)$.

That is, the modal operator id has no effect on the conjunction, because $\downarrow x \bigcap \downarrow y \in \mathcal{F}(X)$ is a stable set, different from $\downarrow x \bigcup \downarrow y \notin \mathcal{F}(X)$, which is not.

Thus, we obtain the following modal version of the noncanonical autoreferential representation for many-valued algebras based on a complete lattice X:

$$\begin{aligned}\downarrow : (X, \leq, \wedge, \vee, \mathrm{id}, 0, 1) &\simeq \left(\mathcal{F}(X), \subseteq, \bigcap, \boxdot\bigcup, \mathrm{id}_{\mathcal{F}(X)}, \{0\}, X\right) \\ &\notin \left(\mathcal{P}(X), \subseteq, \bigcap, \bigcup, \boxdot, \emptyset, X\right),\end{aligned}$$

1 In the canonical autoreferential semantics, in what follows, we will preserve the classical disjunction, represented by standard union on sets.

i. e., $\mathcal{F}(X)$ *is not a subalgebra* of the powerset Boolean distributive algebra $\mathcal{P}(X)$ with a modal operator $\boxdot$, as in the standard representation theorems for algebras. In fact, here we do not impose that X (or $\mathcal{F}(X)$) has to be distributive, as it holds for any Boolean sublattice.

Example 45. The smallest *nontrivial* bilattice is Belnap's 4-valued bilattice [188, 190, 209], analyzed in Section 5.1.3, $\mathcal{B} = \{t, f, \bot, \top\}$ where t is *true*, f is *false*, $\top$ is inconsistent (both true and false) or *possible*, and $\bot$ is *unknown*. As Belnap observed, these values can be given two natural orders: *truth* order, $\leq_t$ and *knowledge* order, $\leq_k$, such that $f \leq_t \top \leq_t t, f \leq_t \bot \leq_t t, \bot \bowtie_t \top$ and $\bot \leq_k f \leq_k \top, \bot \leq_k t \leq_k \top, f \bowtie_k t$. That is, the bottom element 0 for $\leq_t$ ordering is f, and for $\leq_k$ ordering is $\bot$, and the top element 1 for $\leq_t$ ordering is t, and for $\leq_k$ ordering is $\top$.

Meet and join operators under $\leq_t$ are denoted $\wedge$ and $\vee$; they are natural generalizations of the usual conjunction and disjunction notions. Meet and join under $\leq_k$ are denoted $\otimes$ and $\oplus$, such that hold: $f \otimes t = \bot, f \oplus t = \top, \top \wedge \bot = f$ and $\top \vee \bot = t$.

The *bilattice negation* [197] is given by $\neg f = t, \neg t = f, \neg\bot = \bot$ and $\neg\top = \top$, In what follows, we will use the *relative pseudo-complements* for implication (Belnap's 4-valued lattice is distributive), defined by $x \rightharpoonup y = \bigvee\{z \mid z \wedge x \leq_t y\}$, and the *pseudo-complements* for negation, defined by $\neg_t x = x \rightharpoonup f$ (which is different from the bilattice negation $\neg$). It is easy to see that it holds the De Morgan law $\neg_t(x \wedge y) = \neg_t x \vee \neg_t y$. We have that, w. r. t. the truth ordering $\leq_t$, $\downarrow f = \{f\}$, $\downarrow \bot = \{f, \bot\}$, $\downarrow \top = \{f, \top\}$ and $\downarrow t = \mathcal{B}$. Thus, $\downarrow \bot \uplus \downarrow \top = \downarrow\bigvee(\downarrow\bot \bigcup \downarrow\top) = \downarrow\bigvee\{f, \bot, \top\} = \downarrow t = \mathcal{B} \neq \downarrow\bot\bigcup\downarrow\top$, i. e., $\uplus \neq \bigcup$.

It is easy to verify that the join operator $\uplus$ in the compact set-based representation $\mathcal{F}(X)$ reduces to the standard set union $\bigcup$ when the complete lattice $(X, \leq)$ is a total ordering (as, e. g., the fuzzy logic with the closed interval of reals $X = [0, 1]$ for the set of truth values). It can be extended to all *distributive* lattices, such that for any $x \in X$ and $Y \subseteq X$, $x \wedge (\bigvee Y) = \bigvee\{x \wedge y \mid y \in Y\}$. Let us consider how to obtain this reduction in a general case. From Birkhoff's representation theorem [207] for distributive lattices, every finite (thus complete) distributive lattice is isomorphic to the lattice of lower sets of the poset of join-irreducible elements.

Proposition 38 (0-Lifted Birkhoff isomorphism [207]). *Let X be a complete distributive lattice, then we define the following mapping $\downarrow^+ : X \to \mathcal{P}(X)$: for any $x \in X$,*

$$\downarrow^+ x = \downarrow x \bigcap \widehat{X}, \quad \text{where } \widehat{X} = \{y \mid y \in X \text{ and } y \text{ is join-irreducible}\} \bigcup \{0\}.$$

We define the set $X^+ = \{\downarrow^+ a \mid a \in X\} \subseteq \mathcal{P}(X)$, so that $\downarrow^+ \bigvee = \mathrm{id}_{X^+} : X^+ \to X^+$ and $\bigvee \downarrow^+ = \mathrm{id}_X : X \to X$. Thus, the operator $\downarrow^+$ is the inverse of the supremum operation $\bigvee : X^+ \to X$. The set $(X^+, \subseteq)$ is a complete lattice, such that there is the following 0-lifted Birkhoff isomorphism $\downarrow^+ : (X, \leq, \wedge, \vee) \simeq (X^+, \subseteq, \bigcap, \bigcup)$.

Proof. Let us show the homomorphic property of $\downarrow^+$:

$$\begin{aligned}\downarrow^+(x\wedge y) &= \downarrow(x\wedge y)\bigcap\widehat{X} = \left(\downarrow x\bigcap\downarrow y\right)\bigcap\widehat{X} = \left(\downarrow x\bigcap\widehat{X}\right)\bigcap\left(\downarrow y\bigcap\widehat{X}\right)\\ &= \downarrow^+ x\bigcap\downarrow^+ y, \quad \text{and}\\ \downarrow^+(x\vee y) &= \downarrow(x\vee y)\bigcap\widehat{X} = \left(\downarrow x\bigcup\downarrow y\right)\bigcap\widehat{X} = \left(\downarrow x\bigcap\widehat{X}\right)\bigcup\left(\downarrow y\bigcap\widehat{X}\right)\\ &=\downarrow^+ x\bigcup\downarrow^+ y.\end{aligned}$$

The isomorphic property holds from Bikhoff's theorem. □

The name "lifted" is used to denote the difference from the original Birkhoff's isomorphism: that is, we have that for any $x\in X$, $0\in\downarrow^+ x$, so that $\downarrow^+ x$ is never an empty set (it is lifted by the bottom element 0).

Notice that when X is a distributive lattice then $(X^+,\subseteq,\bigcap,\bigcup)$ is a *subalgebra* of the powerset Boolean algebra $(\mathcal{P}(X),\subseteq,\bigcap,\bigcup)$, different from the case when X is not distributive. Thus, we obtain *canonical* representation:

$$\downarrow^+ : (X,\leq,\wedge,\vee,\mathrm{id}_X)\simeq\left(X^+,\subseteq,\bigcap,\bigcup,\mathrm{id}_{X^+}\right)\subseteq\left(\mathcal{P}(X),\subseteq,\bigcap,\bigcup,\boxdot^+\right),$$

where $\boxdot^+ = \downarrow^+\bigvee : \mathcal{P}(X)\to\mathcal{P}(X)$ is a modal algebraic monotone multiplicative operator. Its reduction to the subset of join-irreducible elements $\widehat{X}\subseteq X$ is equal to

$$\boxdot^+ = \boxdot : \mathcal{P}(\widehat{X})\to\mathcal{P}(\widehat{X}).$$

Example 46. Belnap's bilattice in Example 45 is a distributive lattice w. r. t. the $\leq_t$ ordering with two join-irreducible elements $\bot$ and $\top$. In that case, we have that $\downarrow^+ t = \downarrow^+(\bot\vee\top) = \downarrow^+\bot\bigcup\downarrow^+\top = \downarrow\bot\bigcup\downarrow\top = \{f,\bot,\top\}\neq\downarrow t = \mathcal{B}$.

Now we will introduce a hierarchy of negation operators for complete lattices, based on their homomorphic properties: the negation with the lowest requirements (such that it inverts the truth ordering of the lattice of truth values and is able to produce falsity and truth, i. e., the bottom and top elements of the lattice), denominated "general" negation, can be defined in any complete lattice (see the example below).

Definition 104 (Hierarchy of negation operators). Let $(X,\leq,\wedge,\vee)$ be a complete lattice. Then we define the following hierarchy of negation operators on it:

1. A `general` negation is a monotone mapping between posets ($\leq^{\mathrm{OP}}$ is inverse of $\leq$), $\neg : (X,\leq)\to(X,\leq)^{\mathrm{OP}}$, such that $\{0,1\}\subseteq\{y=\neg x\mid x\in X\}$.
2. A `split` negation is a general negation extended into the join-semilattice homomorphism, $\neg : (X,\leq,\vee)\to(X,\leq,\vee)^{\mathrm{OP}}$, with $(X,\leq,\vee)^{\mathrm{OP}} = (X,\leq^{\mathrm{OP}},\vee^{\mathrm{OP}})$, $\vee^{\mathrm{OP}}=\wedge$.
3. A `constructive` negation is a general negation extended into full lattice homomorphism, $\neg : (X,\leq,\wedge,\vee)\to(X,\leq,\wedge,\vee)^{\mathrm{OP}}$, with $(X,\leq,\wedge,\vee)^{\mathrm{OP}} = (X,\leq^{\mathrm{OP}},\wedge^{\mathrm{OP}}\vee^{\mathrm{OP}})$, and $\wedge^{\mathrm{OP}}=\vee$.

4. A De Morgan negation is a constructive negation when the lattice homomorphism is an involution ($\neg\neg x = x$).

The names given to these different kinds of negations follow from the fact that a split negation introduces the second right-adjoint negation, a constructive negation satisfies the constructive requirement (as in Heyting algebras) $\neg\neg x \geq x$, while a De Morgan negation satisfies the well-known De Morgan laws.

Lemma 14 (Negation properties). *Let $(X, \leq)$ be a complete lattice. Then the following properties for negation operators hold: for any $x, y \in X$,*

1. *for general negation: $\neg(x \vee y) \leq \neg x \wedge \neg y$, $\neg(x \wedge y) \geq \neg x \vee \neg y$, with $\neg 0 = 1$, $\neg 1 = 0$.*
2. *for split negation: $\neg(x \vee y) = \neg x \wedge \neg y$, $\neg(x \wedge y) \geq \neg x \vee \neg y$. It is an additive modal operator with right-adjoint (multiplicative) negation $\sim: (X, \leq)^{OP} \to (X, \leq)$, and the Galois connection $\neg x \leq^{OP} y$ iff $x \leq\sim y$, such that $\sim\neg x \geq x$ and $\neg\sim x \geq x$.*
3. *for constructive negation: $\neg(x \vee y) = \neg x \wedge \neg y$, $\neg(x \wedge y) = \neg x \vee \neg y$. It is a self-adjoint operator, $\neg =\sim$, with $\neg\neg x \geq x$ satisfying the proto De Morgan inequalities $\neg(\neg x \vee \neg y) \geq x \wedge y$ and $\neg(\neg x \wedge \neg y) \geq x \vee y$.*
4. *for De Morgan negation ($\neg\neg x = x$): it satisfies also De Morgan laws $\neg(\neg x \vee \neg y) = x \wedge y$ and $\neg(\neg x \wedge \neg y) = x \vee y$, and is contrapositive, i. e., $x \leq y$ iff $\neg x \geq \neg y$.*

Proof. 1. From the definition of a *general* negation as *monotonic* mapping between posets, $\neg : (X, \leq) \to (X, \leq)^{OP}$, we have that $x \leq y$ implies $\neg x \leq^{OP} \neg y$, i. e., it inverts the ordering, $\neg x \geq \neg y$. Thus, $x \wedge y \leq x$ and $x \wedge y \leq y$ implies $\neg(x \wedge y) \geq \neg x$ and $\neg(x \wedge y) \geq \neg y$, consequently $\neg(x \wedge y) \geq \neg x \vee \neg y$. Analogously, $x \vee y \geq x$ and $x \vee y \geq y$ implies $\neg(x \vee y) \leq \neg x$ and $\neg(x \vee y) \leq \neg y$, consequently $\neg(x \vee y) \leq \neg x \wedge \neg y$. From the property $\forall y(0 \leq y$ implies $\neg 0 \geq \neg y)$, and the fact that $1 \in \{z = \neg y \mid y \in X\}$ must hold $\neg 0 \geq 1$, i. e., $\neg 0 = 1$. Analogously, we can show also that $\neg 1 = 0$.

2. From the homomorphic definition of the *split* negation (which is also general, thus with $\neg(x \wedge y) \geq \neg x \vee \neg y$) we have that $\neg(x \vee y) = \neg x \vee^{OP} \neg y = \neg x \wedge \neg y$, and from $\neg 0 = 1 = 0^{OP}$ we conclude that it is a monotone additive mapping, thus it has the right multiplicative adjoint $\sim: (X, \leq)^{OP} \to (X, \leq)$ with the Galois connection $\neg \dashv \sim$, i. e., $\neg x \leq^{OP} y$ iff $x \leq\sim y$, i. e., $\neg x \geq y$ iff $x \leq\sim y$. The operators $\neg\sim$ and $\sim\neg$ are the closure operators in $\mathcal{P}(X)$; it thus holds that $\neg\sim x \geq x$ and $\sim\neg x \geq x$.

3. The *constructive* negation is also a split negation, thus it is an additive modal operator. Let us show that it is also multiplicative; consequently, self-adjoint, i. e., $\sim= \neg$: it holds from the lattice homomorphism for meet operators, $\neg(x \wedge y) = \neg x \wedge^{OP} \neg y$ (i. e., $= \neg x \vee \neg y$), and from $\neg 1 = 0 = 1^{OP}$. Thus, $\neg\neg x = \neg\sim x \geq x$ is its constructive property. From this constructive property and the additive and multiplicative properties, we obtain that $\neg(\neg x \wedge \neg y) = \neg\neg x \vee \neg\neg y \geq x \vee y$ (because $\vee$ is monotone for both arguments). Analogously, $\neg(\neg x \vee \neg y) = \neg\neg x \wedge \neg\neg y \geq x \wedge y$ (because also $\wedge$ is monotone for both arguments), i. e., we obtained the proto De Morgan inequalities.

4. The De Morgan negation is the split negation, which is an evolution, thus we have that $\neg(\neg x \wedge \neg y) = \neg\neg x \vee \neg\neg y = x \vee y$ and $\neg(\neg x \vee \neg y) = \neg\neg x \wedge \neg\neg y = x \wedge y$. We

have that $\neg x \geq \neg y$ implies $\neg\neg x \leq \neg\neg y$. So from $\neg\neg x = x$, we obtain also that $\neg x \geq \neg y$ implies $x \leq y$, thus the contraposition $x \leq y$ iff $\neg x \geq \neg y$. □

Notice the naturality of this hierarchy, where from the general negation (the most weak negation) we reach from the antitonicity $x \leq y$ implies $\neg x \geq \neg y$ the stronger requirement of the contraposition ($x \leq y$ iff $\neg x \geq \neg y$) for De Morgan (the most strong) negation. Notice also how we pass from inequalities to stronger equality requirements. This is valid for any complete lattice where these negations exist (general negations always exist). If we impose the stronger requirements on complete lattices, as for example, distributivity, then De Morgan negations coincide with the strongest classic Boolean negation (where for all $x \in X$, $\neg x \wedge x = 0$ and $\neg x \vee x = 1$).

The set-based semantics for the split negations (with Galois connections) can be given by the Bikhoff polarity operator $\lambda : (\mathcal{P}(X), \subseteq) \to (\mathcal{P}(X), \subseteq)^{\mathrm{OP}}$, such that for any $U \in \mathcal{P}(X)$, $\lambda U = \{x \in X \mid \forall u \in U.((u,x) \in R)\} = \{x \in X \mid \forall u.(u \in U \text{ implies } (u,x) \in R)\}$, which in a modal logic can be represented by

$$\mathcal{M} \vDash_x \neg\phi \quad \text{iff} \quad \forall u.(\mathcal{M} \vDash_u \phi \text{ implies } (u,x) \in R)$$

(the relation R is an incompatibility relation in Lemma 13). The set-based semantics for the constructive negation is obtained in the case where the incompatibility relation R is symmetric.

Example 47. The example for any complete lattice $(X, \leq)$ is a *general* negation given by $\neg x = \bigvee S_x$ where $S = \{z \in X \mid z \wedge x = 0\}$. It is well-defined for complete lattices also when S_x is an *infinite* set as, e. g., in fuzzy logic where $X = [0,1]$ is the closed interval of reals between 0 and 1, where for $\neg 0$ we have that $S_0 = \{z \in X \mid z \wedge 0 = 0\} = [0,1]$. Notice that differently from distributive lattices, generally we have that in nondistributive lattices $\neg x \notin S_x$, and $\neg x \wedge x \neq 0$ (we have that $\neg x \wedge x \in \{0, x\}$, i. e., $\neg x \wedge x = x$ if $x \leq \neg x$ (it cannot be $x > \neg x$), and $\neg x \wedge x = 0$ where x and $\neg x$ are not comparable; thus, $\neg x \wedge x \leq x$). This negation in *distributive* lattices corresponds to the pseudo-complement negation where for any $x \in X$, $x \wedge \neg x = 0$ (thus it cannot be used as paraconsistent negation) and is “constructive” $x \leq \neg\neg x$ but $\neg\neg x \nleq x$. This negation in distributive algebras, where $x \vee \neg x = 1$ for any $x \in X$ is also valid, corresponds to the classic Boolean negation.

We are able to define also “nonconstructive” general negation in any complete lattice by $\overline{\neg} = \bigvee - \downarrow : X \to X$ where $-$ is the set complement in X, such that $\overline{\neg} x = 0$ if $x = 1$; 1 otherwise. It is easy to verify that for any $x \in X$, $\neg x \leq \overline{\neg} x$, $\overline{\neg} x \vee x = 1$ and $\overline{\neg}\overline{\neg} x \leq x$. One example for distributive complete lattice with *paraconsistent* De Morgan negation is the fuzzy negation $\neg x = 1 - x$ for $x \in X = [0,1]$ (where $x \wedge \neg x = \min(x, 1-x) \neq 0$). In fact, it is additive and multiplicative ($\neg(x \wedge y) = 1 - \min(x,y) = \max(1-x, 1-y) = \neg x \vee \neg y$ and $\neg(x \vee y) = 1 - \max(x,y) = \min(1-x, 1-y) = \neg x \vee \neg y$); thus, it is self-adjoint with $\neg\neg x = x$.

Another paraconsistent De Morgan negation is the *bilattice negation* [197]: in Belnap's 4-valued bilattice, it corresponds to the epistemic negation, such that $\neg f = t$,

$\neg t = f$, $\neg\bot = \bot$ and $\neg\top = \top$, with $x \wedge \neg x \neq 0$ (while the pseudo-complement negation $\neg_t$ given in Example 45 (which is not a bilattice negation) is not paraconsistent).

The most simple definition for implication for bounded lattices, which satisfies the modus ponens ($y \Rightarrow x, y \vdash x$) and deduction theorem ($z, y \vdash x$ iff $z \vdash y \Rightarrow x$) inference rules where $\vdash$ relation is equal to the $\leq$ partial order in the lattice (as in Definition 102, and where the logic entailment "preserves the truth," i. e., $x \vdash y$ iff $x \leq y$), is given by, $y \Rightarrow x = 1$ if $y \leq x$; x otherwise. But as we can see in this definition the value of y does not appear in the resulting value of the implication.

Both values x and y appear in the resulting value of the implication in the case when the lattice is modular (Dedekind's lattices) and satisfies $\neg x \wedge x = 0$ for every $x \in X$, when the deduction theorem from left to right does not hold.

The lattice is called *modular* when $x \leq z$ implies $x \vee (y \wedge z) = (x \vee y) \wedge z$.

Proposition 39. *Let X be a complete* modular *lattice where $\neg x = \bigvee\{z \mid z \wedge x = 0\}$ and $\neg x \wedge x = 0$ for every $x \in X$, then we define the implication $\Rightarrow: X \times X \to X$ for any two elements $x, y \in X$ as follows:*

$$y \Rightarrow x =_{\text{def}} \begin{cases} 1, & \text{if } y \leq x \\ \neg y \vee x, & \text{if } y > x \\ \neg y \vee (x \wedge y), & \text{otherwise} \end{cases} \tag{A.1}$$

Then $y \Rightarrow x = 1$ iff $y \leq x$, and holds the modus ponens "rule," $y \wedge (y \Rightarrow x) \leq x$ and half of the Galois connection, i. e., "$z \leq y \Rightarrow x$ implies $z \wedge y \leq x$."

If we assume that the consequence pair relation $\vdash$ of this logic coincides with the partial order $\leq$ of this complete modular lattice (in Definition 102), then in this logic holds the modus ponens rule $y \wedge (y \Rightarrow x) \vdash x$ and the partial deduction theorem, i. e., "$z \vdash y \Rightarrow x$ implies $z, y \vdash x$."

Proof. The definition of the implication is correct, i. e., it is monotonic w. r. t. the first argument and antitonic w. r. t. the second argument. Moreover, it is similar to the definition of the classic material implication.

Let us show that holds the modus ponens "rule," i. e., $(y \Rightarrow x) \wedge y \leq x$.

1.1 case when $y \leq x$: then $(y \Rightarrow x) \wedge y = 1 \wedge y = y \leq x$.
1.2 case when $y > x$: then $(y \Rightarrow x) \wedge y = (\neg y \vee x) \wedge y$ =(by modular property) = $(\neg y \wedge y) \vee x = 0 \vee x = x$.
1.3 case when x and y are not comparable: then $(y \Rightarrow x) \wedge y = (\neg y \vee (x \wedge y)) \wedge y$ =(by the modular property and $x \wedge y \leq y$) = $(\neg y \wedge y) \vee (x \wedge y) = 0 \vee (x \wedge y) = x \wedge y \leq x$.

For the deduction theorem, we have that if $z \leq y \Rightarrow x$, then:

2.1 case when $y \leq x$: then from $z \leq y \Rightarrow x = 1$, we have $z = 1$, so that $z \wedge y = 1 \wedge y = y \leq x$.
2.2 case when $y > x$: then from $z \leq y \Rightarrow x = \neg y \vee x$, we have (by the monotonicity of $\wedge$), $z \wedge y \leq y \wedge (\neg y \vee x)$ = (by the modular property) = $(\neg y \wedge y) \vee x = 0 \vee x = x$.

2.3 case when x and y are not comparable: then from $z \leq y \Rightarrow x = \neg y \vee (x \wedge y)$, we have (by the monotonicity of $\wedge$) that $z \wedge y \leq y \wedge (\neg y \vee (x \wedge y))$ = (by the modular property) $= (\neg y \wedge y) \vee (x \wedge y) = 0 \vee (x \wedge y) = x \wedge y \leq x$.

Now for $y \Rightarrow x = 1$ and $z = 1$, and ($z \leq y \Rightarrow x$ implies $z \wedge y \leq x$), we obtain that ($y \Rightarrow x = 1$ implies $z \wedge y = 1 \wedge y = y \leq x$), and from the definition of $\Rightarrow$ we have that $y \leq x$ implies $y \Rightarrow x = 1$. Consequently, in this modular lattice we have $y \Rightarrow x = 1$ (or alternatively $\vdash y \Rightarrow x$) iff $y \leq x$.

Thus, if we assume that $\vdash$ is equal to $\leq$, then the MP "rule" $y \wedge (y \Rightarrow x) \leq x$ coincides with the modus ponens rule of inference and we obtain $\vdash (y \wedge (y \Rightarrow x)) \Rightarrow x$, i. e., that $(y \wedge (y \Rightarrow x)) \Rightarrow x$ is an axiom. Analogously, the Galois implication becomes half of the deduction theorem. □

This class of modular lattices is strictly more general than the class of orthomodular lattices [303], where it is also required that $\neg\neg x = x$ and $x \vee \neg x = 1$ for every x.

In any distributive lattice, where $\neg x \wedge x = 0$ is always satisfied for every $x \in X$, which is also modular; the definition of the implication given in Proposition 39 is always possible. But as we will see in what follows, in any distributive lattice the modus ponens and deduction theorem inference rules can be completely satisfied, and the logic implication can be defined precisely by this requirement.

A.3.3 Heyting's and multimodal extensions of distributive lattices

The meet and join operators correspond to the logic conjunction and disjunction. In order to have a full logic language, we need also logic implication and logic negation. For the class of distributive lattices, we can introduce the negation operator as the pseudo-complement $\neg x = \bigvee\{z \mid z \wedge x = 0\}$, with $\neg x = 1$ iff $x = 0$, used in intuitionistic logics. In this section, we will extend this distributive lattice with other unary modal operators, and based on them, two dual logic operators: the *implication* $\rightharpoonup: X \times X \to X$, and its dual *coimplication* operator $\rightsquigarrow: X \times X \to X$. As we will see, the natural choice for the implication in complete lattices is the intuitionistic implication, based on the relative pseudo-complement, which always exists in complete distributive lattices. It is well known that the relative pseudo-complement $x \rightharpoonup y = \bigvee\{z \mid z \wedge x \leq y\}$ and classic implication satisfy the following left exponential commutative diagram:

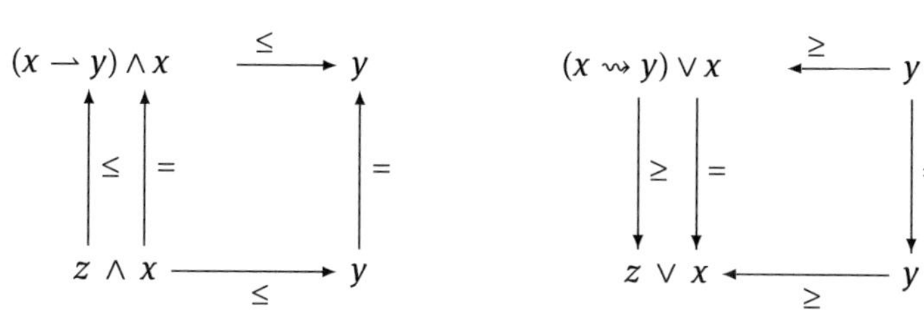

where the arrow $(x \rightharpoonup y) \wedge x \leq y$ is the modus ponens inference rule $(x \rightharpoonup y), x \vdash y$, while for any $x \in X$ the additive modal operator $l_x = \_\wedge x : X \to X$ and its right-adjoint multiplicative operator $r_x = x \rightharpoonup \_ : X \to X$ define the Galois connection $l_x \dashv r_x$, i. e., $l_x(z) = z \wedge x \leq y$ iff $z \leq x \rightharpoonup y = r_x(y)$, corresponding to the deduction theorem, $z, x \vdash y$ iff $z \vdash x \rightharpoonup y$, (where the consequence relation $\vdash$ is equal to $\leq$, based on the "truth preservation" principle for valid logic derivations in Definition 102).

The family of operators $\{l_x = \_\wedge x \mid x \in X\}$ may be considered as the family of existential modal operators, derived from the basic lattice meet operator $\wedge$, while r_x acts as its dual universal modal operator, but with $r_x \neq \neg l_x \neg$ and $l_x \neq \neg r_x \neg$.

The fundamental property (from the Galois connection when $z = 1$) of relative pseudo-complement is that $x \leq y$ iff $x \rightharpoonup y = 1$ (i. e., $x \vdash y$ iff $\vdash x \rightharpoonup y$). The right-hand coexponential commutative diagram is dual (the arrows, i. e., the partial ordering, are inverted), where the conjunction is replaced by disjunction (coconjunction) and the implication by its dual coimplication. The dual modal operators, for any $x \in X$ are the multiplicative modal operator $r_x^c = \_\vee x : X \to X$ and its left-adjoint additive operator $l_x^c = x \rightsquigarrow \_ : X \to X$ define the Galois connection $l_x^c \dashv r_x^c$, i. e., $l_x^c(y) = x \rightsquigarrow y \leq z$ iff $y \leq z \vee x = r_x^c(z)$, corresponding to the codeduction theorem, $y \vdash z \vee x$ iff $x \rightsquigarrow y \vdash z$. The arrow $(x \rightsquigarrow y) \vee x \geq y$ corresponds to the comodus ponens inference rule $y \vdash (x \rightsquigarrow y) \vee x$. Thus, the coimplication is defined by $x \rightsquigarrow y = l_x^c(y) = \bigwedge\{z \mid y \leq z \vee x = r_x^c(z)\}$, such that, $x \leq y$ iff $\neg(y \rightsquigarrow x) = 1$ (i. e., $x \vdash y$ iff $\vdash \neg(y \rightsquigarrow x)$).

Thus, $x \rightharpoonup y$ is an axiom iff $\neg(y \rightsquigarrow x)$ is an axiom, i. e., $\vdash x \rightharpoonup y$ iff $\vdash \neg(y \rightsquigarrow x)$.

Notice that in Boolean algebras (distributive lattices with $\neg x \vee x = 1$ for any $x \in X$) we have that $x \rightharpoonup y = \neg x \vee y$ and $x \rightsquigarrow y = \neg x \wedge y$.

Proposition 40. *Each complete distributive lattice $(X, \leq)$ with bottom and top element $0, 1$, respectively, can be extended into Heyting algebra $B = (X, \leq, \wedge, \vee, \neg, \rightharpoonup, 0, 1)$ with implication $\rightharpoonup$ defined by $x \rightharpoonup y = \bigvee\{z \in X \mid z \wedge x \leq y\}$ and negation $\neg : X \to X$ defined by $\neg x = x \rightharpoonup 0$. The corresponding complete distributive lattice $(\mathcal{F}(X), \subseteq, \bigcap, \biguplus, \widehat{\neg}, \rightarrowtail, \{0\}, X)$ is the Heyting algebra with implication defined, for any $U, V \in \mathcal{F}(X)$, by $U \rightarrowtail V = \biguplus\{Z \in \mathcal{F}(X) \mid Z \bigcap U \subseteq V\}$ and the negation operator (pseudo-complement) $\widehat{\neg}$, $\widehat{\neg} U = U \rightarrowtail \{0\}$.*

Then for any $x, y \in X$, $\widehat{\neg} \downarrow x = \downarrow(\neg x)$ and $\downarrow x \rightarrowtail \downarrow y = \downarrow(x \rightharpoonup y)$, i. e., the following representation for any complete Heyting algebra is valid:

(1) $\downarrow: (X, \leq, \wedge, \vee, \neg, \rightharpoonup, 0, 1) \simeq (\mathcal{F}(X), \subseteq, \bigcap, \biguplus, \widehat{\neg}, \rightarrowtail, \{0\}, X)$,

and canonical case.

(2) $\downarrow^+: (X, \leq, \wedge, \vee, \neg, \rightharpoonup, 0, 1) \simeq (X^+, \subseteq, \bigcap, \bigcup, \widehat{\neg}, \rightarrowtail, \{0\}, \widehat{X})$,

where the operations $\widehat{\neg}, \rightarrowtail$ are obtained in the same way as in (1) by substituting $\mathcal{F}(X)$ by X^+, $\biguplus$ by $\bigcup$, and $\downarrow$ by $\downarrow^+$.

Proof. We obtain $\downarrow x \rightarrowtail \downarrow y = \biguplus\{\downarrow z \in \mathcal{F}(X) \mid \downarrow z \bigcap \downarrow x \subseteq \downarrow y\} = \biguplus\{\downarrow z \in \mathcal{F}(X) \mid \downarrow (z \wedge x) \subseteq \downarrow y\} = \biguplus\{\downarrow z \in \mathcal{F}(X) \mid z \wedge x \leq y\} = \downarrow \vee \{z \in X \mid z \wedge x \leq y\} = \downarrow(x \rightharpoonup y) \in \mathcal{F}(X)$, i. e., it is a stable set. Analogously, $\widehat{\neg} \downarrow x = \downarrow(\neg x) \in \mathcal{F}(X)$ is a stable set. □

Now we are able to introduce also the unary modal operators for these Heyting algebras, based on complete distributive lattices.

Proposition 41. *Each Heyting algebra* $A = (X, \leq, \wedge, \vee, \neg, \rightharpoonup, 0, 1)$ *has an invariant modal extension denominated banal Galois algebra* $G = (X, \leq, \wedge, \vee, \mathrm{id}, \neg, \rightharpoonup, 0, 1)$, *isomorphic to* $(\mathcal{F}(X), \subseteq, \bigcap, \uplus, \mathrm{id}_{\mathcal{F}(X)}, \widehat{\neg}, \rightarrowtail, \{0\}, X)$, *where* $\uplus = \boxdot\bigcup$ *and the identity function* $\mathrm{id} : X \to X$ *is a self-adjoint* $\mathrm{id} \dashv \mathrm{id}$ *modal operator correspondent to the universal modal operator* $\boxdot : \mathcal{P}(X) \to \mathcal{P}(X)$, *whose reduction to the set of stable elements in* $\mathcal{F}(X) \subset \mathcal{P}(X)$ *is the identity operator* $\mathrm{id}_{\mathcal{F}(X)} = \downarrow\bigvee : \mathcal{F}(X) \to \mathcal{F}(X)$.

We can extend a Heyting algebra A by any other unary additive modal operator $m : X \to X$ *or* $m : X \to X^{OP}$ *(for modal negations in Lemma 14) so that we obtain the extended representation isomorphism for obtained Galois algebras:*

1. $\downarrow$: $(X, \leq, \wedge, \vee, \mathrm{id}, \neg, \rightharpoonup, m, 0, 1) \simeq (\mathcal{F}(X), \subseteq, \bigcap, \uplus, \mathrm{id}_{\mathcal{F}(X)}, \widehat{\neg}, \rightarrowtail, \widehat{m}, \{0\}, X)$ *where* $\widehat{m} = \downarrow m \downarrow^{-1}: \mathcal{F}(X) \to \mathcal{F}(X)$, *and* $\downarrow^{-1} = \bigvee$ *is inverse homomorphism of* $\downarrow$.
2. $\downarrow^{+}$: $(X, \leq, \wedge, \vee, \mathrm{id}, \neg, \rightharpoonup, m, 0, 1) \simeq (X^{+}, \subseteq, \bigcap, \bigcup, \mathrm{id}_{X^{+}}, \widehat{\neg}, \rightarrowtail, \widehat{m}, \{0\}, \widehat{X})$, *obtained in the same way as in point 1, by substituting* $\mathcal{F}(X)$ *by* X^{+}, $\uplus$ *by* $\bigcup$ *and* $\downarrow$ *by* $\downarrow^{+}$.

Proof. Let $A = (X, \leq, \wedge, \vee, \neg, \rightharpoonup, 0, 1)$ be a Heyting algebra. Then the identity function $\mathrm{id} : X \to X$ is monotone, i. e., $x \leq x'$ implies $\mathrm{id}(x) = x \leq y = \mathrm{id}(y)$, and preserves the meets: for any $x, y \in X$, $\mathrm{id}(x \wedge y) = x \wedge y = \mathrm{id}(x) \wedge \mathrm{id}(y)$. Thus, it is equivalent to the banal Galois algebra $G = (X, \leq, \wedge, \vee, \mathrm{id}, \neg, \rightharpoonup, 0, 1)$. The left adjoint to id is the operator $m : X \to X$, such that $m(x) = \bigwedge\{z \in Y \mid \mathrm{id}(z) \geq x\} = x$, i. e., $m = \mathrm{id}$, so that id is self-adjoint.

By introducing this identity modal operator, we obtain the Galois banal algebra *identical* to the original Heyting algebra, so this is an *invariant* modal extension for Heyting algebras, and can be considered as minimal modal extension for Heyting algebras. This fact explains that modal logic is intrinsic in any complete lattice $(X, \leq)$, and is based on the partial ordering $\leq$ of the poset X.

Let $m : X \to X$ be an additive modal operator (monotone which preserves all meets), then it has left adjoint $g : X \to X$, such that $g(x) \leq y$ iff $x \leq m(y)$. Then $x \leq y$ implies $m(x) \leq m(y)$, and $\downarrow m(x) \leq \downarrow m(y)$, i. e., $\downarrow m \downarrow^{-1} (\downarrow x) \leq \downarrow m \downarrow^{-1} (\downarrow y)$ with $\downarrow x \subseteq \downarrow y \in \mathcal{F}(X)$, i. e., the monotone operator $\downarrow m \downarrow^{-1}: \mathcal{F}(X) \to \mathcal{F}(X)$ exists.

Thus, for any $U, V \in \mathcal{F}(X)$, $\downarrow m \downarrow^{-1} (U \bigcap V) = \downarrow m \downarrow^{-1} (\downarrow (x \wedge y)) = \downarrow m(x \wedge y) = \downarrow m(x) \bigcap \downarrow m(y) = \downarrow m \downarrow^{-1} (\downarrow x) \bigcap \downarrow m \downarrow^{-1} (\downarrow x)$. Consequently, $\downarrow m \downarrow^{-1}$ preserves the meets, and both with a monotone property, which means that it is an additive unary modal operator in a canonical Heyting algebra. Moreover, from $g(x) \leq y$ iff $x \leq m(y)$ we obtain $\downarrow g \downarrow^{-1} (\downarrow x) \leq \downarrow y$ iff $\downarrow x \leq \downarrow m \downarrow^{-1}$, i. e., $\downarrow g \downarrow^{-1}$ is the left adjoint of the $\downarrow m \downarrow^{-1}$, with $\downarrow g \downarrow^{-1} = \widehat{\neg} \downarrow g \downarrow^{-1} \widehat{\neg}$. Consequently, $\downarrow m \downarrow^{-1}$ is the universal while $\downarrow g \downarrow^{-1}$ is the existential modal operator in the canonical Heyting (i. e., Galois) algebra $\mathcal{F}(X)$. □

Example 48. In Belnap's bilattice, the conflation—is a monotone function, which preserves all finite meets (and joins) w. r. t. the lattice $(\mathcal{B}_4, \leq_t)$; thus, it is a universal (and

existential, i. e., $m = g = -$, because $- = \neg_t - \neg_t$) modal many-valued operator: “it is believed that,” which extends the 2-valued belief of the autoepistemic logic as follows:
1. if ϕ is true, then “it is believed that ϕ,” i. e., $-\phi$, is true;
2. if ϕ is false, then “it is believed that ϕ” is false;
3. if ϕ is unknown, then “it is believed that ϕ” is inconsistent: it is really inconsistent to believe in something that is unknown;
4. if ϕ is inconsistent (that is *both* true and false), then “it is believed that ϕ” is unknown: really, we cannot tell anything about believing in something that is inconsistent.

This belief modal operator can be used to define the *epistemic*(bilattice) negation $\neg$, as a composition of strong negation $\neg_t$ and this belief operator, i. e., $\neg = \neg_t -$. That is, the epistemic negation is negation as a modal operator [210] and as a paraconsistent negation [211]. We can introduce also Moore's *autoepistemic* operator [197], $\mu : \mathcal{B}_4 \to \mathcal{B}_4$, for a Belnap's bilattice, defined by $\mu(x) = t$ if $x \in \{\top, t\}$; f otherwise.

It is easy to verify that it is monotone w. r. t. the $\leq_t$, that is multiplicative ($\mu(x \wedge y) = \mu(x) \wedge \mu(y)$ and $\mu(t) = t$) and additive ($\mu(x \vee y) = \mu(x) \vee \mu(y)$ and $\mu(f) = f$), consequently also it is a self-adjoint (contemporary universal and existential) modal operator, $\mu = \neg_t \mu \neg_t$. Notice that differently from the belief modal operator $-$, Moore's modal operator μ is not surjective.

Such an autoepistemic intuitionistic logic, based on Belnap's bilattice, $(\mathcal{B}_4, \leq_t, \wedge, \vee, \neg_t, \rightharpoonup, -, \mu, f, t)$ can be used for logic programming with incomplete and partially inconsistent information [129]: in such a logic, we use only the epistemic negation $\neg = \neg_t -$.

We have seen that the for distributive lattices we can define the “strict” implication (relative pseudo-complement), such that for any two logic formulae ϕ and ψ holds that $\phi \rightharpoonup \psi = \Box(\phi \Rightarrow_c \psi)$, where $\Rightarrow_c$ is the classical extensional implication such that $\phi \Rightarrow_c \psi = \neg_c \phi \vee_c \psi$ (here, $\neg_c$ and $\vee_c$ denote the classic logic negation and disjunction, respectively) and $\Box$ is not necessarily truth-functional in this distributive lattice. This “strict” implication is the *intuitionistic* logic implication, where all axioms of the classic propositional logic are satisfied, except the axiom for disjunction $\neg x \vee x = (x \rightharpoonup 0) \vee x$.

Now we will investigate the subclass of distributive complete lattices, where there exists the *algebraic truth-functional* counterpart $r_\Box : X \to X$, of the logic modal necessary operator $\Box$, and is an identity, so that $\neg x \vee y$ (i. e., $(x \rightharpoonup 0) \vee y$) can be used as implication $x \Rightarrow y$. In what follows, we will show that this “or-implication” satisfies the modus ponens, but generally does not satisfy the deduction theorem.

Proposition 42. *The or-implication $x \Rightarrow y =_{def} \neg x \vee y$ satisfies the modus ponens but not the deduction theorem w. r. t. the entailment in Definition* 102, *i. e., for any $x \in X$, $r = \neg x \vee \_ : X \to X$ is a monotone multiplicative operator; thus, right adjoint of the operator $l : X \to X$, with $l \neq \_ \wedge x$.*

Proof. For the or-implication, we have that, from the distributivity, $(x \Rightarrow y) \wedge x = (\neg x \vee y) \wedge x = (\neg x \wedge x) \vee (y \wedge x) = 0 \vee (y \wedge x) = y \wedge x \leq y$, i. e., the modus ponens rule holds. The operator $r = \neg x \vee \_$ is monotone because $\vee$ is monotone for both arguments. And, from the distributivity, $r(y \wedge z) = \neg x \vee (y \wedge z) = (\neg x \vee y) \wedge (\neg x \vee z) = r(y) \wedge r(z)$, and $r(1) = \neg x \vee 1 = 1$; thus, r is multiplicative, so that its left-adjoint operator l is defined for any $y \in X$, by $l(y) = \bigwedge\{z \mid y \leq r(z) = \neg x \vee z\}$, with $l(y) \neq y \wedge x$. □

The deduction theorem cannot be satisfied because there exist $x, y \in X$ such that $\neg x \vee y < x \rightharpoonup y = \bigvee\{z \mid z \wedge x \leq y\}$, and if we substitute the relative pseudo-complement $x \rightharpoonup y$ by the "or-implication" $\neg x \vee y$ we are not able to obtain the commutative exponential diagram as in the case of a relative pseudo-complement.

Thus, in order to satisfy the deduction theorem, the or-implication $r(y) = \neg x \vee y$ must be a right adjoint to $l = \_ \wedge x$, i. e., must be equal to the relative pseudo-complement $x \rightharpoonup y$. In the next proposition, we will define the subclass of complete distributive lattices where such a condition is satisfied.

Proposition 43. *Each complete distributive lattice $(X, \leq)$ with the set of join-irreducible elements $\widehat{X} - \{0\}$ equal to the set of atoms $\underline{X}$, is a complete distributive lattice, where for every $x, y \in X$, $x \rightharpoonup y = \neg x \vee y$ and vice versa.*

Proof. First of all, we will show that $\underline{X} = \widehat{X} - \{0\}$ is a sufficient condition for $x \rightharpoonup y = \neg x \vee y$. Each atom is join-irreducible, thus $\underline{X} \subseteq \widehat{X} - \{0\}$. Suppose that $\underline{X} \subset \widehat{X} - \{0\}$. Then, from the Birkhoff theorem for distributive lattices, $\bigvee \underline{X} < \bigvee(\widehat{X} - \{0\}) = 1$, and for any atom $a \in \underline{X}, \neg a < \bigvee \underline{X}$ (because $a < \bigvee \underline{X}$), so that $\neg a \vee a \leq \bigvee \underline{X} \vee a = \bigvee \underline{X} < 1$, while $a \rightharpoonup a = 1$, i. e., we obtain that $\neg a \vee a \neq a \rightharpoonup a$, which is a contradiction. Thus, $\underline{X} = \widehat{X} - \{0\}$ must be correct.

Let us assume that $\underline{X} = \widehat{X} - \{0\}$, and show that for every $x, y \in X$, $x \rightharpoonup y = \neg x \vee y$ must hold. We consider the following cases:

Case 1: When $x \leq y$: in that case $x \rightharpoonup y = 1$, and from the Birkhoff isomorphism (Proposition 38), we have that for unique subsets $S_x, S_y \subseteq \underline{X}$ such that $x = \bigvee S_x$, $y = \bigvee S_y$, must hold $S_x \subseteq S_y$, i. e., $S_y = S_x \bigcup \triangle$ and $-S_x \bigcup S_y = -S_x \bigcup (S_x \bigcup \triangle) = \underline{X} \bigcup \triangle = \underline{X}$. Thus, $x \rightharpoonup y = 1 = \bigvee \underline{X} = \bigvee(-S_x \bigcup S_y) = \bigvee(-S_x) \vee (\bigvee S_y) = \neg x \vee y$.

Case 2: When $x \nleq y$ and $\neg x = 0$: Let us show that in this case $x = 1$ must be correct. Suppose that $\exists x \neq 1. \neg x = 0$, then $\nexists y \bowtie x.(y \neq 0$ and $y = \neg x)$, i. e., $x = \bigvee \underline{X}$ but $1 = \bigvee \underline{X}$, and from the Birkhoff bijection (isomorphism) must be $x = 1$, so that $x \rightharpoonup y = 1 \rightharpoonup y = \bigvee\{z \mid z \wedge 1 = z \leq y\} = y = \neg x \vee y$.

This case holds when $x > y$. In fact, $\neg x = 0$ must be correct, otherwise the sublattice $0 < \neg x < \neg x \vee x$, $0 < y < x < \neg x \vee x$ is a N5 diagram, which cannot be a sublattice of modular (thus distributive) lattice $(X, \leq)$.

Case 3: When $x \bowtie y$ and $\neg x \neq 0$: it is enough to consider only $x, y \notin \{0, 1\}$, which are particular subcases of the cases above. It is easy to verify that for any distributive lattice it holds that

(**) $x \rightharpoonup y \geq \neg x \vee y$ (because $x \rightharpoonup y \geq \neg x$ and $x \rightharpoonup y \geq y$, from $y \in \{z \mid z \wedge x \leq y\}$).

Suppose that $x \rightharpoonup y > \neg x \vee y$, then there are the following subcases:

3.1 When $y > \neg x = \bigvee\{z \mid z \wedge x = 0\}$: then $\neg x \vee y = y$, so that $y \geq x$ (otherwise, $\neg x = y$), which is in contradiction with $x \bowtie y$.

3.2 When $y < \neg x$: then we obtain the following N5 sublattice, $0 < x < x \vee \neg x$, $0 < y < \neg x < x \vee \neg x$, which cannot hold for modular (thus distributive) lattices.

3.3 When $y = \neg x$: then $x \rightharpoonup y < 1$ (because $x \nleq y$) and cannot be $x \leq x \rightharpoonup y$. If so, then $x \wedge (x \rightharpoonup y) = x$ (modus ponens in distributive lattices), i. e., $y = \neg x \geq x$, which is in contradiction with $x \bowtie y$. It cannot be $x > x \rightharpoonup y$ (if so, then $\neg x \vee y = y \geq x \wedge (x \rightharpoonup y) = x \rightharpoonup y$, which is in contradiction with hypothesis $x \rightharpoonup y > \neg x \vee y$). Thus, we obtain the N5 sublattice $0 < x < x \vee (x \rightharpoonup y)$, $0 < \neg x \vee y < x \rightharpoonup y < x \vee (x \rightharpoonup y)$, which cannot hold for modular (thus distributive) lattices.

3.4 When $y \bowtie \neg x$: then cannot be $x \leq x \rightharpoonup y$ (if so, then $x = x \wedge (x \rightharpoonup y) \leq y$ (from definition of $x \rightharpoonup y$), which is in contradiction with $x \bowtie y$. Suppose that $x \geq x \rightharpoonup y$, then $x \rightharpoonup y = x \wedge (x \rightharpoonup y) \leq y$ (from definition of $x \rightharpoonup y$), and from $x \rightharpoonup y \geq y$ we obtain that $x \rightharpoonup y = y$. Thus, $\neg x \vee y \geq y = x \rightharpoonup y$, which is in contrast with (**) $x \rightharpoonup y \geq \neg x \vee y$. Consequently, $x \bowtie (x \rightharpoonup y)$, and $x \vee (x \rightharpoonup y) > x \rightharpoonup y$ and $x \vee (x \rightharpoonup y) > x$ (notice that from $x \bowtie y$ we have that $x \wedge y < x$ and $\neg x \vee y > x \wedge (\neg x \vee y) = (x \wedge \neg x) \vee (x \wedge y) = 0 \vee (x \wedge y) = x \wedge y$).

Thus, we obtain the N5 sublattice $x \wedge y < x < x \vee (x \rightharpoonup y)$, $x \wedge y < \neg x \vee y < x \rightharpoonup y < x \vee (x \rightharpoonup y)$, which cannot hold for modular (thus distributive) lattices. □

Remark. If for every $x, y \in X$, $x \rightharpoonup y = \neg x \vee y$, then $\neg x \vee x = x \rightharpoonup x = 1$, and from the general property for distributive lattices, $\neg x \wedge x = 0$, we obtain that the distributive lattices with the property defined in Proposition 43 are Boolean algebras. □

Example 49. The classic logic with 2-valued lattice ($\mathbf{2} = \{0, 1\}, \leq$) is a Boolean algebra: the set of atoms is equal to the set of join-irreducible elements $\{1\}$. The Cartesian product $X = \mathbf{2}^2 = \mathbf{2} \times \mathbf{2} = \{(0,0), (0,1), (1,0), (1,1)\}$, with $(x,y) \leq (v,w)$ iff $x \leq v$ and $y \leq w$, is a Boolean algebra with the set of atoms (i. e., join-irreducible elements) $\underline{X} = \{(0,1), (1,0)\}$ and the negation is defined by $\neg(x,y) = (\neg x, \neg y)$. It is isomorphic to the Belnap's 4-valued lattice $\mathcal{B}_4$ where $f \mapsto (0,0)$, $t \mapsto (1,1)$, $\bot \mapsto (0,1)$ and $\top \mapsto (1,0)$.

It is easy to verify that every lattice $X_n = (\mathbf{2}^K, \leq)$, where $K \geq 2$ and $(x_1, \dots, x_k) \leq (y_1, \dots, y_k)$ if for all $1 \leq i \leq K$, $x_i \leq y_i$, is a Boolean algebra where negation is defined by $\neg(x_1, \dots, x_k) = (\neg x_1, \dots, \neg x_k)$. But we have also that in each Boolean algebra $(\mathcal{P}(S), \subseteq, \bigcap, \bigcup, -)$ where $-$ is the set complement, the set S is exactly the set of atoms. Thus, we have the following isomorphisms of latices: $(\mathbf{2}, \leq) \simeq (\mathcal{P}(\{a_1\}), \subseteq)$, $(\mathcal{B}_4, \leq) \simeq (\mathbf{2}^2, \leq) \simeq (\mathcal{P}(\{a_1, a_2\}), \subseteq), \dots, (\mathbf{2}^K, \leq) \simeq (\mathcal{P}(\{a_1, \dots, a_K\}), \subseteq)$, $K \geq 2$.

A.3.4 Direct autoreferential Kripke semantics for many-valued predicate logics

In Section 5.1.2, we provided the canonical autoreferential Kripke semantics for the possible worlds given by the subset of join-irreducible truth values. Here, instead, we will consider the direct autoreferential Kripke semantics, where the set of possible worlds is equal to the complete set of truth values. We will use the invariant and intrinsic modal properties of complete lattices and Heyting algebras in order to obtain a basic Kripke structure for any such algebra in a general way. By $\mathbf{2} = \{0, 1\} \subseteq X$, we denote the set of classic logic values (false and true, respectively), and by H the Herbrand base, i. e., the set of all ground atoms in a many-valued predicate logic with subset of sentences $\mathcal{L}_{\mathrm{mv}}^G$, with $H \subseteq \mathcal{L}_{\mathrm{mv}}^G$.

Given a many-valued interpretation $I_H : H \to X$, we denote by $I_H^* : \mathcal{L}_{\mathrm{mv}}^G \to X$ its unique extension to all formulae, obtained inductively as follows: for any ground atom, $r(c_1, \ldots, c_n) \in H$, $I_H^*(r(c_1, \ldots, c_n)) = I_H(r(c_1, \ldots, c_n))$; for any two sentences, $\phi, \psi \in \mathcal{L}_{\mathrm{mv}}^G$, $I_H^*(\phi \wedge \psi) = I_H^*(\phi) \wedge I_H^*(\psi)$; $I_H^*(\phi \vee \psi) = I_H^*(\phi) \vee I_H^*(\psi)$; $I_H^*(\phi \Rightarrow \psi) = I_H^*(\phi) \rightharpoonup I_H^*(\psi)$; $I_H^*(\neg\phi) = \neg I_H^*(\phi)$, and for any algebraic additive modal operator o_i, $I_H^*(\Diamond_i \phi) = o_i \bar{I}(\phi)$, where $\Diamond_i$ is a logic symbol for an existential modal operator (and $\Box_i$ is its correspondent universal logic modal operator).

Based on the general representation theorem for many-valued logic in [206], and the *autoreferential assumption*, we assume that the set of possible worlds of relational Kripke frames is the set of algebraic truth values in a complete lattice X of this many-valued logic, or alternatively, the set of join-irreducible elements $\widehat{X}$ [206] for distributive complete lattices with normal additive modal operators only. In what follows, we will present the first approach, which is valid also for *nondistributive* lattices (for logics where the implication cannot be a relative pseudo-complement).

From the formal mathematical point of view, we can consider the stable sets in $\mathcal{F}(X)$ as "stable characteristic functions" in $\mathbf{2}^X$ ($\mathbf{2}^X$ denotes the set of all functions from X to $\mathbf{2}$), i. e., the functions whose image is a stable set (element in $\mathcal{F}(X)$). Let $\mathcal{F}_X \simeq \mathcal{F}(X)$ denote such a set of stable functions, bijective to $\mathcal{F}(X)$, whose elements are functions (i. e., higher-order algebraic truth values [83]). Than any many-valued valuation v, of a propositional logic with a set of propositional letters in P, based on this set of higher-order truth values is a mapping $v : P \to \mathcal{F}_X \subset \mathbf{2}^X$. So that we are able to define the valuation $I_K : P \times X \to \mathbf{2}$, such that for any $p \in P, x \in X$, $I_K(p, x) = v(p)(x) \in \mathbf{2}$, which is identical to Kripke valuations used for standard 2-valued Kripke models of propositional modal logics, if we accept (by autoreferential assumption) for the set of *possible worlds* the set of algebraic truth-values X.

Now we will define the accessibility relation for any given modal operator o_i.

Definition 105. Let $o_i : X \to X$ be a monotonic operator with $S = \{(o_i(x), x) \mid x \in X\}$, and the set $S_m \subseteq S$ obtained by elimination of each element $(x, y) \in S$ if there exists another element $(x, z) \in S$ such that $z \leq y$.

Then we define the accessibility relation for o_i by $\mathcal{R}_i = S_m \bigcup \{(x, y) \mid \nexists (x, v) \in S_m\}$, where

$$y = \begin{cases} 0, & \text{if } x = 0 \\ z, & \text{if } \exists (v, z) \in S_m.(x \leq v)\} \end{cases} \tag{A.2}$$

Notice that if $x \neq 0$ and $\nexists y \in X.(x \leq o_i(y))$ then $x \notin \pi_1(\mathcal{R}_i)$, where π_1 is the first projection.

Example 50. In the case of the believe (conflation) modal operator—in Belnap's bilattice, we obtain that $\mathcal{R}_- = S_m = S = \{(f,f),(\top,\bot),(\bot,\top),(t,t)\}$, while for the autoepistemic Moore's operator μ, $S = \{(f,f),(f,\bot),(t,\top),(t,t)\}$, $S_m = \{(f,f),(t,\top)\} \subset S$ and $\mathcal{R}_\mu = \{(f,f),(t,\top),(\top,\top),(\top,t),(\bot,\top),(\bot,t)\}$.

Definition 106. Let $\widetilde{o_i} : (X,\leq) \to (X,\leq)^{OP}$ be a split negation operator. We define the binary relation S as follows:
(a) Set initially $S = \{(x,\widetilde{o_i}(x)) \mid x \in X\}$, then
(b) For every $y \in X$ substitute S by the relation $(S - S_y)\bigcup\{(\bigvee \pi_1 S_y, y)\}$, where $S_y = \{(x,y) \mid (x,y) \in S\} \subset S$ and π_1 is the first projection.

Then we define the relation $\widetilde{\mathcal{R}_i}$ for $\widetilde{o_i}$ by downward completion of S:

$$S \subseteq \widetilde{\mathcal{R}_i} \quad \text{and if } (x,y) \in \widetilde{\mathcal{R}_i} \text{ and } x' \leq x, y' \leq y \text{ then } (x',y') \in \widetilde{\mathcal{R}_i}.$$

The split negation operators $\widetilde{o_i}$ correspond to the monotone additive operators $\widetilde{o_i} : X \to X^{OP}$, and the correspondent relations $\widetilde{\mathcal{R}_i}$ are "perp" (*Perpendicular* or *incompatibility*) relations, introduced by Goldblatt in [304].

Notice that the point (**b**) for each $y \in X$ substitutes the equivalence class S_y (of all $x \in X$ such that $y = \widetilde{o_i}(x)$) by the single pair (x,y) where $x = \bigvee \pi_1 S_y = \bigvee\{z \mid (z,y) \in S_y\}$, so that the following lemma holds (by π_2 we denote the second projection).

Lemma 15. *Let S be a binary relation in Definition 106 for a split negation operator $\widetilde{o_i} = \neg : (X,\leq) \to (X,\leq)^{OP}$. Then $\neg_r : (S_1,\leq) \to (S_2,\leq)^{OP}$, where $S_1 = \pi_1 S \subseteq X$, $S_2 = \pi_2 S \subseteq X$ is the bijective domain reduction of the split operator $\neg$ (i. e., for each $x \in S_1$, $\neg_r x = \neg x$), with its inverse $\neg_r^{-1} : (S_2,\leq)^{OP} \to (S_1,\leq)$, such that:*
1. *for any two $x, x' \in S_1$, $x < x'$ iff $\neg x > \neg x'$,*
2. *for any $x \in X$, we have that $x' = \neg_r^{-1}\neg x \in S_1$, and such that $\neg x = \neg_r x'$ with $x \leq x'$.*

Proof. Let us show that $\neg_r$ is a domain reduction of $\neg$. In fact, after the actions defined in point (b) of Definition 106, we have that the cardinalities of S_1 and S_2 are equal, and for any $y \in S_2$ we have the unique pair $(x,y) \in S$ where $x = \bigvee \pi_1 S_y = \bigvee\{z \mid (z,y) \in S_y\}$. Let us show that $\neg_r x = y$: in fact, by definition $\neg_r x =_{def} \neg x = \neg \bigvee\{z \mid (z,y) \in S_y\} = \bigwedge\{\neg z \mid (z,y) \in S_y\}$ (from the act that $\neg$ is a split negation, thus an additive operator) $= y$ (because from the definition of the equivalence class S_y in Definition 106 we have that for each $(z,y) \in S_y$, $\neg z = y$). Thus, the definition of $\neg_r$ as the domain reduction of $\neg$ is correct. We have also that for any two $(x,y),(x',y') \in S$ we have that $x \neq x'$ iff $y \neq y'$; thus, $\neg_r$ is a bijection, with inverse mapping $\neg_r^{-1} : S_2 \to S_1$ defined by, for any $y \in S_2$, $\neg_r^{-1}(y) = x$, where $(x,y) \in S$. Thus, $\neg_r^{-1}\neg_r = id_{S_1}$ and $\neg_r\neg_r^{-1} = id_{S_2}$. Consequently, also $\neg_r^{-1}$ is monotone, i. e., for any two $\neg_r x, \neg_r x' \in S_2$, if $\neg_r x >^{OP} \neg_r x'$ (i. e., $\neg_r x < \neg_r x'$), then $\neg_r^{-1}(\neg_r x) = x > \neg_r^{-1}(\neg_r x') = x'$, and from the monotonicity of $\neg$ (and its domain reduction $\neg_r$) we obtain that the point (1) of this lemma holds.

Point (2): from the definition of S, x' is the join of all elements in $\pi_1 S_y$ in an equivalence class S_y, where $y = \neg x$, with $x \in \pi_1 S_y$, so that $x \leq x'$. □

Example 51. Finite cases: In the case of the bilattice (epistemic) negation operator $\neg$ in Belnap's bilattice, which is a paraconsistent De Morgan negation (thus split negation also), we obtain

$$S = \{(f,t),(\top,\top),(\bot,\bot),(t,f)\}, \quad \text{with } S_1 = S_2 = X = \mathcal{B}_4, \neg_r = \neg_r^{-1} = \neg, \quad \text{and}$$
$$\widetilde{\mathcal{R}_\neg} = \{(f,f),(f,\bot),(f,\top),(f,t)(\bot,\bot),(\bot,f),(\top,\top),(\top,f),(t,f)\}.$$

Infinite cases: In the case of the fuzzy logic, $\neg x = 1 - x$, it is a paraconsistent De Morgan negation, thus also split negation, with $S = \{(x, 1-x) \mid x \in X = [0,1]\}$. Thus, from Definition 106, we obtain a symmetric *infinite* incompatibility relation $\widetilde{\mathcal{R}_\neg}$ as in the example above: it must be so because both negations are self-adjoint, so that this incompatibility relation must be symmetric. Other cases for paraconsistent split negations are given in belief and confidence level logics and their fuzzy extensions [202].

Now we are able to define the *many-valued relational* Kripke-style semantics (the 2-valued Kripke-style semantics is presented in [204]) for a predicate modal logic $\mathcal{L}_{\text{mv}}$ based on the modal Heyting algebras in Proposition 41.

Definition 107. Given a predicate modal logic $\mathcal{L}_{\text{mv}}$, based on the modal Heyting algebra in Proposition 41, we define the Kripke model for this logic $\mathcal{M} = (K, \mathcal{D}, I_K)$ with the frame $K = \langle (X, \leq), \{\mathcal{R}_i, \widetilde{\mathcal{R}_i}\}\rangle$, where each $\mathcal{R}_i, \widetilde{\mathcal{R}_i}, i = 1, 2, \ldots$, is the accessibility relation for existential (additive) modal operators o_i and negation modal operator $\widetilde{o_i}$, respectively, given in Definition 105, with a decreasing valuation $I_K : X \times P \to \bigcup_{n<\omega} \mathbf{2}^{S^n}$, such that for any predicate symbol $r \in P$ with arity n, and tuple of constants $(c_1, \ldots, c_n) \in \mathcal{D}^n$ (i. e., ground atom $r(c_1, \ldots, c_n) \in H$), there exists a particular value $y \in X$, such that $\forall x \in X(I_K(x,r)(c_1,\ldots,c_n) = 1$ iff $x \leq y)$.

Then, for any world $x \in X$ and assignment g, we define the many-valued satisfaction relation for a formula $\phi \in \mathcal{L}_{\text{mv}}$, denoted by $\mathcal{M} \vDash_{x,g} \phi$, as follows:

1. $\mathcal{M} \vDash_{x,g} r(x_1, \ldots, x_n)$ iff $I_K(x,r)(g(x_1), \ldots, g(x_n)) = 1$,
2. $\mathcal{M} \vDash_{x,g} \phi \wedge \psi$ iff $\mathcal{M} \vDash_{x,g} \phi$ and $\mathcal{M} \vDash_{x,g} \psi$,
3. $\mathcal{M} \vDash_{x,g} \phi \vee \psi$ iff $\forall y((y \leq x$ and not $\mathcal{M} \vDash_{y,g} \phi)$ implies $\mathcal{M} \vDash_{y,g} \psi)$,
4. $\mathcal{M} \vDash_{x,g} \phi \Rightarrow \psi$ iff $\forall y((y \leq x$ and $\mathcal{M} \vDash_{y,g} \phi)$ implies $\mathcal{M} \vDash_{y,g} \psi)$,
5. $\mathcal{M} \vDash_{x,g} \neg\phi$ iff $\mathcal{M} \vDash_{x,g} \phi \Rightarrow \bot$, where $\bot$ is a contradiction formula,
6. $\mathcal{M} \vDash_{x} \Diamond_i \phi$ iff $\exists y((x,y) \in \mathcal{R}_i$ and $\mathcal{M} \vDash_y \phi)$, for any monotone modal operator $\Diamond_i$.
7. $\mathcal{M} \vDash_x \sim_i \phi$ iff $\forall y(\mathcal{M} \vDash_y \phi$ implies $(y,x) \in \widetilde{\mathcal{R}_i})$, for any modal negation operator $\sim_i$, so that $\| \sim_i \phi \| = \lambda \|\phi\| = \{x \mid \forall y \in \|\phi\|.(y,x) \in \widetilde{\mathcal{R}_i})\}$.

By definition, $\mathcal{M}$ is a Kripke-style model of a logic $\mathcal{L}_{mv}$ if it satisfies all formulae in $\mathcal{L}_{mv}$.

The reason that we use both negations, the pseudo-complement $\neg$ and modal (weak) negations $\sim_i$ is justified by necessity to consider also the *paraconsistent* many-valued logics in which $\neg$ cannot be used as paraconsistent negation (in Proposition 45).

Notice that in the world $x = 0$ (the bottom element in X) every sentence ϕ is satisfied: because of that we will denominate this world by a *trivial world*. The semantics for implication is similar (but different) to the Kripke style definition for intuitionistic implication (where the time sequence for the accessibility relation is used, upward (in the future) closed and based on the principle "persistence of truth in time" [305]). Otherwise, the definition for disjunction is not standard. In fact, it holds that ($\mathcal{M} \vDash_{x,g} \phi$ or $\mathcal{M} \vDash_{x,g} \psi$) implies $\mathcal{M} \vDash_{x,g} \phi \vee \psi$, but *not vice versa*. It results from the fact that the disjunction in the canonical representation is the set operator $\biguplus$, (generally) different from the standard set union $\bigcup$. The satisfaction for disjunction can be given alternatively by

3.(a) $\mathcal{M} \vDash_{x,g} \phi \vee \psi$ iff $\exists y, z(x \leq y \vee z$ and $\mathcal{M} \vDash_{y,g} \phi$ and $\mathcal{M} \vDash_{z,g} \psi)$.

So, the conjunction disjunction and implication are defined independently as in intuitionistic logic [306]. In fact, the Definition 107 for a Kripke model of many-valued modal logics is similar but *not equal* (downward closed instead of upward closed hereditary subsets, and the worlds are not the time-points as in Kripke interpretation but the autoreferential *truth-levels of credibility*) to that of Kripke-style intuitionistic logic because not only the implication (as in [306]) but also the *disjunction is intensional*: it is based on Lewis's approach, as discussed in Remark after Proposition 37, where he distinguishes the standard or *extensional* logic connectives $\wedge_c, \vee_c, \Rightarrow_c$, from the *intensional* logic connectives $\wedge, \vee, \Rightarrow$, such that $x \odot y = \Box(x \odot_c y)$, for $\odot \in \{\wedge, \vee, \Rightarrow\}$ where $\Box$ is "necessarily" a universal logic modal operator corresponding to the algebraic modal operator $\boxdot : \mathcal{P}(X) \to \mathcal{P}(X)$.

The accessibility relation for the multiplicative modal operator "necessary" $\Box$ is the partial order $\geq = \leq^{-1}$ in Definition 107. For its left-adjoint (additive) dual modal operator $\Diamond$, $\Diamond \dashv \Box$, such that the Galois connection $\Diamond x \leq y$ iff $x \leq \Box y$ holds, the accessibility relation can be obtained by the gaggle theory of Dunn [236, 307], for this simple Galois connection with the following traces and tonicities:

function	tonicity	trace
$\Box$	$+$	$+ \mapsto +$
$\Diamond$	$+$	$- \mapsto -$

From [307], it holds that the binary accessibility relations of these two unary adjoint operators are mutually inverse, i. e., $\mathcal{R}_\Diamond = (\overline{\mathcal{R}_\Box})^{-1} = (X \times X - \mathcal{R}_\Box)^{-1} = X \times X - \leq$.

It is intuitive also because these two operators are usually given as two mappings $\Diamond : (X, \leq) \to (X, \leq)$ and $\Box : (X, \leq)^{OP} \to (X, \leq)^{OP}$, where $(X, \leq)^{OP}$ is a poset with inverted arrows (ordering).

We will consider that the downward closure for the satisfaction holds for each ground formula ϕ/g, i. e., if $\mathcal{M} \vDash_{x,g} \phi$ than for every $y \leq x$ holds $\mathcal{M} \vDash_{y,g} \phi$: it is satisfied for all ground atoms, directly from the definition of the mapping I_K in Definition 107, and will be proven in Theorem 17 below. Thus, we can use the standard Kripke definition for the satisfaction relation for these intensional connectives, i. e.:

1. For the principal modal operator $\Box$:

$$\begin{aligned} \mathcal{M} \vDash_{x,g} \Box r(x_1, \dots, x_n) \quad &\text{iff} \quad \forall y (y \leq x \text{ implies } \mathcal{M} \vDash_{y,g} r(x_1, \dots, x_n)) \\ &\text{iff} \quad \mathcal{M} \vDash_{x,g} r(x_1, \dots, x_n). \end{aligned}$$

   Thus, it is invariant for ground atoms. Moreover, for any ground formula ϕ/g such that $\|\phi/g\| = \{x \mid \mathcal{M} \vDash_{x,g} \phi\} \in \mathcal{F}(X)$, i. e., $\|\phi/g\| = \downarrow\alpha$ for some $\alpha \in X$, we have that $\mathcal{M} \vDash_{x,g} \Box\phi$ iff $\forall y(y \leq x$ implies $\mathcal{M} \vDash_{y,g} \phi)$ iff $\forall y(y \leq x$ implies $y \in\downarrow \alpha)$ iff $x \leq \alpha$ iff $\mathcal{M} \vDash_{x,g} \phi$. That is, $\Box$ is an identity.
   But if $\|\phi/g\| \notin \mathcal{F}(X)$, then $\Box$ is not an identity, but $\|\Box\phi/g\| = \boxdot\|\phi/g\| \in \mathcal{F}(X)$.
   Also, in the case of the dual, existential, modal operator $\Diamond$, we have for that any ground formula ϕ/g such that $\|\phi/g\| = \{x \mid \mathcal{M} \vDash_{x,g} \phi\} \in \mathcal{F}(X)$, i. e., $\|\phi/g\| = \downarrow\alpha$ for some $\alpha \in X$ holds $\mathcal{M} \vDash_{x,g} \Diamond\phi$ iff $\exists y(x \leq y$ and $\mathcal{M} \vDash_{y,g} \phi)$ iff $\exists y(x \leq y$ and $y \in\downarrow \alpha)$ iff $x \leq \alpha$ iff $\mathcal{M} \vDash_{x,g} \phi$. That is, $\Diamond$ is an identity.
2. For the intensional conjunction:

$$\begin{aligned} \mathcal{M} \vDash_{x,g} \phi \wedge \psi \quad &\text{iff} \quad \mathcal{M} \vDash_{x,g} \Box(\phi \wedge_c \psi) \\ &\text{iff} \quad \forall y(y \leq x \text{ implies } \mathcal{M} \vDash_{y,g} \phi \wedge_c \psi) \\ &\text{iff} \quad \forall y(y \leq x \text{ implies } (\mathcal{M} \vDash_{y,g} \phi \text{ and } \mathcal{M} \vDash_{y,g} \psi)) \\ &\text{iff} \quad \mathcal{M} \vDash_{x,g} \phi \text{ and } \mathcal{M} \vDash_{x,g} \psi. \end{aligned}$$

   Thus, the intensional conjunction has the same semantics as the extensional conjunction.
3. For the intensional implication:

$$\begin{aligned} \mathcal{M} \vDash_{x,g} \phi \Rightarrow \psi \quad &\text{iff} \quad \mathcal{M} \vDash_{x,g} \Box(\phi \Rightarrow_c \psi) \\ &\text{iff} \quad \forall y(y \leq x \text{ implies } \mathcal{M} \vDash_{y,g} \phi \Rightarrow_c \psi) \\ &\text{iff} \quad \forall y(y \leq x \text{ implies } (\mathcal{M} \vDash_{y,g} \phi \text{ implies } \mathcal{M} \vDash_{y,g} \psi)) \\ &\text{iff} \quad \forall y((y \leq x \text{ and } \mathcal{M} \vDash_{y,g} \phi) \text{ implies } \mathcal{M} \vDash_{y,g} \psi). \end{aligned}$$

   Here, $\|(\phi \Rightarrow_c \psi)/g\| = \{y \mid \mathcal{M} \vDash_{y,g} \phi \text{ implies } \mathcal{M} \vDash_{y,g} \psi\} \notin \mathcal{F}(X)$, but we have

$$\|\Box(\phi \Rightarrow_c \psi)/g\| = \boxdot\|(\phi \Rightarrow_c \psi)/g\| = \boxdot\Big(\bigcup\Big\{Z \mid Z \bigcap \|\phi/g\| \subseteq \|\psi/g\|\Big\}\Big) \in \mathcal{F}(X).$$

   If $\|\phi/g\|, \|\psi/g\| \in \mathcal{F}(X)$, then $\|\Box(\phi \Rightarrow_c \psi)/g\| = \|\phi/g\| \rightarrowtail \|\psi/g\| \in \mathcal{F}(X)$.

4. For the intensional disjunction:

$$\begin{aligned}\mathcal{M} \models_{x,g} \phi \vee \psi \quad &\text{iff} \quad \mathcal{M} \models_{x,g} \square(\phi \vee_c \psi)\\ &\text{iff} \quad \forall y(y \leq x \text{ implies } \mathcal{M} \models_{y,g} \phi \vee_c \psi)\\ &\text{iff} \quad \forall y(y \leq x \text{ implies } (\mathcal{M} \models_{y,g} \phi \text{ or } \mathcal{M} \models_{y,g} \psi))\\ &\text{iff} \quad \forall y(y \leq x \text{ implies } (\text{not } \mathcal{M} \models_{y,g} \phi \text{ implies } \mathcal{M} \models_{y,g} \psi))\\ &\text{iff} \quad \forall y((y \leq x \text{ and not } \mathcal{M} \models_{y,g} \phi) \text{ implies } \mathcal{M} \models_{y,g} \psi).\end{aligned}$$

Here, $\|(\phi \vee_c \psi)/g\| = \{y \mid \mathcal{M} \models_{y,g} \phi \text{ or } \mathcal{M} \models_{y,g} \psi\} = \|\phi/g\| \bigcup \|\psi/g\| \notin \mathcal{F}(X)$; thus, $\square$ is not an identity, but holds that $\|\square(\phi \vee_c \psi)/g\| = \boxdot\|(\phi \vee_c \psi)/g\| = \boxdot(\|\phi/g\| \bigcup \|\psi/g\|) = \|\phi/g\| \uplus \|\psi/g\| \in \mathcal{F}(X)$.

Notice that in the case when $(X, \leq)$ is a distributive lattice (when we are using also logic implication and negation defined as in Heyting algebras) and we are using for the set of worlds the set $\widehat{X}$ of join-irreducible elements in X (the canonical alternative for autoreferential assumption, based on the representation isomorphisms in point 2 of Propositions 40 and 41), we obtain the standard semantics for extensional disjunction, i. e., $\mathcal{M} \models_{x,g} \phi \vee \psi$ iff $\mathcal{M} \models_{x,g} \phi$ or $\mathcal{M} \models_{x,g} \psi$. In this particular case when the set of worlds is the set $\widehat{X} \subset X$, for the logic connectives $\wedge, \vee, \neg, \Rightarrow$, we obtain Kripke-style semantics of intuitionistic logic, but with inverted accessibility relation, of complete distributive lattice for the operator $\square$. This version is presented in [206] for the complete distributive lattices with additive normal modal operators.

Based on all these considerations, we can see how important a role the closure operator and universal "necessity" operator $\boxdot$ have, based on the Dedekind–McNeile Galois connection over partial order of a complete lattice $(X, \leq)$ of algebraic truth values. The next proposition shows that there is a bijective correspondence (see also in [206]) between the *algebraic* many-valued Herbrand models of a modal logic $\mathcal{L}_{\text{mv}}$, based on the complete lattice of truth values $(X, \leq)$, and the *relational* (or *Kripke-style*) models (based on the set of possible worlds equal to the set of truth values X) of the same logic $\mathcal{L}_{\text{mv}}$.

Proposition 44. *For any given Kripke model of a modal predicate logic $\mathcal{L}_{\text{mv}}$, based on a complete lattice $(X, \leq)$ of truth values, which satisfies Definition* 107*, we are able to obtain the algebraic many-valued Herbrand model $I_H : H \to X$ of the same logic $\mathcal{L}_{\text{mv}}$, such that for any ground atom $r(c_1, \ldots, c_n) \in H$ holds:*
(a) $I_H(r(c_1, \ldots, c_n)) = \bigvee\{x \in X \mid \mathcal{M} \models_x r(c_1, \ldots, c_n)\}$.

Vice versa, for any given algebraic many-valued Herbrand model $I_H : H \to X$ of a logic $\mathcal{L}_{\text{mv}}$, we are able to obtain the Kripke model of $\mathcal{L}_{\text{mv}}$, which satisfies Definition 107*, such that for any world $x \in X$, a predicate symbol $r \in P$ with arity n, and a tuple of constants $(c_1, \ldots, c_n) \in S^n$ holds:*
(b) $I_K(x, r)(c_1, \ldots, c_n) = 1$ *iff* $x \leq I_H(r(c_1, \ldots, c_n))$.

Easy to verify, directly from Definition 107, the next theorem shows the clear relationships between the *representation algebra* based on the complete lattice $(\mathcal{F}(X), \subseteq)$ and the Kripke-style model of a many-valued modal logic $\mathcal{L}_{mv}$.

Theorem 17. *Let $K = \langle (X, \leq), \{\mathcal{R}_i\} \rangle$ be a frame and $I_H : H \to X$ be a Herbrand valuation of a many-valued logic $\mathcal{L}_{mv}$, given by Definition 107. Then, for a given assignment g and for any formula ϕ, the set of worlds where ϕ/g (a formula ϕ where all variables are substituted by the assignment g) holds is*

$$\|\phi/g\| = \downarrow(I_H^*(\phi/g)) \in \mathcal{F}(X).$$

Proof. By structural induction: We have that $x \in \|\phi/g\|$ iff $\mathcal{M} \vDash_x \phi/g$ iff $\mathcal{M} \vDash_{x,g} \phi$.

1. For any ground atom $r(c_1, \dots, c_n) \in H$, $x \in X$, $\mathcal{M} \vDash_{x,g} r(c_1, \dots, c_n)$ iff $x \leq I(r(c_1, \dots, c_n))$, thus $\|r(c_1, \dots, c_n)\| = \downarrow I_H(r(c_1, \dots, c_n))$. Notice that it can be obtained directly from the equation (a) of Proposition 44, i.e., by applying the operator $\downarrow$ to both sides of this equation (a) we obtain $\downarrow I_H(r(c_1, \dots, c_n)) = \downarrow \bigvee\{x \in X \mid \mathcal{M} \vDash_x r(c_1, \dots, c_n)\} = \{x \in X \mid \mathcal{M} \vDash_x r(c_1, \dots, c_n)\} = \|r(c_1, \dots, c_n)\|$.

Suppose by hypothesis that $\|\phi/g\| = \downarrow(I_H^*(\phi/g))$ and $\|\psi/g\| = \downarrow(I_H^*(\psi/g))$, then:

2. From $\mathcal{M} \vDash_x \phi/g \wedge \psi/g$, iff $\mathcal{M} \vDash_x \phi/g$ and $\mathcal{M} \vDash_x \psi/g$, holds that $x \in \|\phi/g \wedge \psi/g\|$ iff $x \in \|\phi/g\| \bigcap \|\psi/g\|$, (and by structural induction hypothesis) iff $x \in \downarrow I_H^*(\phi/g) \bigcap \downarrow I_H^*(\psi/g) = \downarrow I_H^*(\phi/g \wedge \psi/g)$. Thus, $\|\phi/g \wedge \psi/g\| = \downarrow I_H^*(\phi/g \wedge \psi/g)$.
3. From $\mathcal{M} \vDash_{x,g} \phi \vee \psi$ iff $\forall y((y \leq x$ and not $\mathcal{M} \vDash_{y,g} \phi)$ implies $\mathcal{M} \vDash_{y,g} \psi)$ iff $\forall y(y \leq x$ and not $y \leq I_H^*(\phi/g)$ implies $y \leq I_H^*(\psi/g)$ iff $\forall y((y \in \downarrow x \bigcap (X - \|\phi/g\|)$ implies $y \in \|\psi/g\|))$ iff $\downarrow x \bigcap (X - \|\phi/g\|) \subseteq \|\psi/g\|$, so that $S = \|\phi/g \vee \psi/g\| = \{x \mid \downarrow x \bigcap (X - \|\phi/g\|) \subseteq \|\psi/g\|\}$.

Then $S = id_{\mathcal{F}(X)}(S) = \downarrow \bigvee S = \biguplus \downarrow S$ (from the homomorphism $\downarrow$) $= \biguplus_{x \in S} \downarrow x = \biguplus\{\downarrow x \mid \downarrow x \bigcap (X - \|\phi/g\|) \subseteq \|\psi/g\|\} = \downarrow \bigvee \bigcup\{\downarrow x \mid \downarrow x \bigcap (X - \|\phi/g\|) \subseteq \|\psi/g\|\} =$ (from (1) in Proposition 37) $= \downarrow \bigvee((X - (X - \|\phi/g\|)) \bigcup \|\psi/g\|) = \downarrow \bigvee(\|\phi/g\| \bigcup \|\psi/g\|) =$ (from inductive hypothesis) $= \downarrow \bigvee(\downarrow I_H^*(\phi/g) \bigcup \downarrow I_H^*(\psi/g)) =$ (from the homomorphism $\downarrow$) $= \downarrow \bigvee \downarrow (I_H^*(\phi/g) \vee I_H^*(\psi/g)) = \downarrow(I_H^*(\phi/g) \vee I_H^*(\psi/g))$.

That is, $\|\phi/g \vee \psi/g\| = \downarrow I_H^*(\phi/g \vee \psi/g)$.

The proof for the alternative Definition 3(a) is as follows:

From $\mathcal{M} \vDash_{x,g} \phi \vee \psi$, iff $\exists y, z(x \leq y \vee z$ and $\mathcal{M} \vDash_{y,g} \phi$ and $\mathcal{M} \vDash_{z,g} \psi)$, holds that $x \in \|\phi/g \vee \psi/g\|$ iff (by structural induction hypothesis) $\exists y, z(x \leq y \vee z$ and $y \leq I_H^*(\phi/g)$ and $z \leq I_H^*(\psi/g))$ iff $x \leq \bigvee\{y \vee z \mid y \leq I_H^*(\phi/g)$ and $z \leq I_H^*(\psi/g)\} = I_H^*(\phi/g) \vee I_H^*(\psi/g) = I_H^*(\phi/g \vee \psi/g)$. Thus, $\|\phi/g \vee \psi/g\| = \downarrow I_H^*(\phi/g \vee \psi/g)$.

4. From $x \in \|\phi/g \Rightarrow \psi/g\|$ iff $\mathcal{M} \vDash_x \phi/g \Rightarrow \psi/g$ iff $\forall y(((x \leq y$ and $\mathcal{M} \vDash_y \phi/g)$ implies $\mathcal{M} \vDash_y \psi/g))$ iff $\forall y(y \leq x$ and $y \leq I_H^*(\phi/g)$ implies $y \leq I_H^*(\psi/g))$ iff $\forall y(y \in \downarrow x \bigcap \|\phi/g\|$ implies $y \in \|\psi/g\|)$ iff $\downarrow x \bigcap \|\phi/g\| \subseteq \|\psi/g\|$, so that $S = \|\phi/g \Rightarrow \psi/g\| = \{x \mid \downarrow x \bigcap \|\phi/g\| \subseteq \|\psi/g\|\}$.

Then $S = \mathrm{id}_{\mathcal{F}(X)}(S) = \downarrow\bigvee S = \bigcup \downarrow S$ (from the homomorphism $\downarrow$) $= \bigcup_{x \in S} \downarrow x = \bigcup\{\downarrow x \mid \downarrow x \bigcap \|\phi/g\| \subseteq \|\psi/g\|\} = \bigcup\{S' \in \mathcal{F}(X) \mid S' \bigcap \downarrow I^*_H(\phi/g) \subseteq \downarrow I^*_H(\psi/g)\} == \downarrow I^*_H(\phi/g) \rightarrowtail \downarrow I^*_H(\psi/g) = \downarrow(I^*_H(\phi/g) \rightharpoonup I^*_H(\psi/g)) = \downarrow I^*_H(\phi/g \Rightarrow \psi/g)$ (from the homomorphism of the valuation I^*_H). Consequently, $\|\phi/g \Rightarrow \psi/g\| = \downarrow I^*_H(\phi/g \Rightarrow \psi/g)$.

5. For any additive algebraic modal operator o_i, we obtain the existential logic modal operator $\Diamond_i$, so that $\mathcal{M} \vDash_x \Diamond_i\phi/g$ iff $\exists y \in X((x,y) \in \mathcal{R}_i$ and $\mathcal{M} \vDash_y \phi/g)$, iff $\exists y((x,y) \in \mathcal{R}_i$ and $y \leq I^*_H(\phi/g))$.

Let us denote it by $\alpha = I^*_H(\phi/g)$, then the condition above, $(*)\exists y((x,y) \in \mathcal{R}_i$ and $y \leq \alpha)$, is satisfied in one of the following possible cases:

Case 5.1.1 when $x \in \pi_1(S_m)$. Then $(*)$ corresponds to $x = o_i(y)$ and $o_i(y) \leq o_i(\alpha)$, (because o_i is monotone), i. e., $x \leq o_i(\alpha)$, i. e., $x \in\downarrow o_i(\alpha)$;

Case 5.1.2 when $x \notin \pi_1(S_m)$, but $(x,y) \in \mathcal{R}_i$. Then $\exists(v,y) \in S_m.(x \leq v)$, i. e., $x \leq v = o_i(y)$, and from $(*)$, $y \leq \alpha$, and from the monotonicity of o_i, $o_i(y) \leq o_i(\alpha)$, we obtain $x \leq o_i(\alpha)$, i. e., $x \in\downarrow o_i(\alpha)$.

Vice versa, let us show that for any $x \in\downarrow o_i(\alpha)$, the condition $(*)$ is satisfied:

Case 5.2.1 when $x = o_i(\alpha)$. We have $(o_i(\alpha),\alpha) \in S_m \subseteq \mathcal{R}_i$; thus, $y = \alpha$ and $(*)$ is satisfied;

Case 5.2.2 when $x < o_i(\alpha)$ and $\exists y.x = o_i(y)$. Then $(x,y) \in S_m \subseteq \mathcal{R}_i$. Suppose that $y > \alpha$, then from the monotonicity of o_i it will hold that $o_i(y) > o_i(\alpha) > x$, which is in contrast with $x = o_i(y)$. So, it must hold that $y \leq \alpha$, and $(*)$ is satisfied;

Case 5.2.3 when $x < o_i(\alpha)$ and $\nexists y.x = o_i(y)$. Then $(z,y) \in S_m \subseteq \mathcal{R}_i$ such that $z = o_i(y) \geq x$, and consequently, $o_i(\alpha) \in \{o_i(y_1) \mid (x,y_1) \in \mathcal{R}_i \backslash S_m\}$, and $(x,y) \in \mathcal{R}_i \backslash S_m$ for $y = \alpha$ (from the fact that $x \leq o_i(y) = o_i(\alpha)$), so that $(*)$ is satisfied.

Thus, we have $\|\Diamond_i\phi/g\| = \downarrow o_i(\alpha) = \downarrow o_i(I^*_H(\phi/g)) = \downarrow I^*_H(\Diamond_i\phi/g)$.

6. For any negation operator $\tilde{o}_i$, we obtain the modal operator $\sim_i$, and we have $\mathcal{M} \vDash_x \sim_i \phi$ iff $\forall y(\mathcal{M} \vDash_y \phi$ implies $(y,x) \in \widetilde{\mathcal{R}_i})$ iff $\forall y(y \in \|\phi\|$ implies $(y,x) \in \widetilde{\mathcal{R}_i})$ iff (by inductive hypothesis $\|\phi\| = \downarrow\alpha$ where $\alpha = I^*_H(\phi/g)$)$\forall y(y \leq \alpha$ implies $(y,x) \in \widetilde{\mathcal{R}_i})$, i. e., $\| \sim_i \phi\| = \{x \mid \forall y(y \leq \alpha$ implies $(y,x) \in \widetilde{\mathcal{R}_i})\}$.

It is easy to verify that for each $x \leq \neg\alpha$ and $y \leq \alpha$, $(y,x) \in \widetilde{\mathcal{R}_i}$ (from Definition 106 and the point 2 of Lemma 15), we have that $x \in \| \sim_i \phi\|$. Thus, $\| \sim_i \phi\| \supseteq\downarrow \alpha$.

Suppose that there exists $x > \neg\alpha$ such that $x \in \| \sim_i \phi\|$. In that case, there are two possible cases (here S is the binary relation in Lemma 15 of this negation operator):

6.1 There exists $\beta \in \pi_1 S \subseteq \pi_1\widetilde{\mathcal{R}_i}$ such that $x = \neg\beta > \neg\alpha$: then (from the point 1 of Lemma 15) $\beta < \alpha$, and $(\beta,\neg\beta) \in S \subseteq \widetilde{\mathcal{R}_i}$, but $(\alpha,\neg\beta) \notin \widetilde{\mathcal{R}_i}$ (from Definition 106) so that $\forall y(y \leq \alpha$ implies $(y,\neg\beta) \in \widetilde{\mathcal{R}_i})$ is false (the case when $y = \alpha$ cannot be satisfied), in contradiction with the hypothesis.

6.2 Does not exist β such that $x = \neg\beta > \neg\alpha$: thus $(\alpha,x) \in \widetilde{\mathcal{R}_i}$ only if $\exists\alpha_1.\neg\alpha_1 > x$ with $(\alpha_1,\neg\alpha_1) \in S \subseteq \widetilde{\mathcal{R}_i}$ (from Definition 106), but from $\neg\alpha_1 > x > \neg\alpha$ we have (from the point 1 of Lemma 15) that $\alpha_1 < \alpha$, so that $(\alpha,\alpha_1) \notin \widetilde{\mathcal{R}_i}$, and consequently, $(\alpha,x) \notin \widetilde{\mathcal{R}_i}$.

Thus, $\forall y(y \leq \alpha$ implies $(y,x) \in \widetilde{\mathcal{R}_i})$ is false, in contradiction with the hypothesis. Consequently, $\| \sim_i \phi\| = \downarrow\alpha$. □

Remark. Notice that in the proof for existential modal operators, we used only the *monotonic* property for these operators and not its additive property. That means that the definition of the satisfaction for existential modal operators (point 6 in Definition 107) can be extended to *any monotonic operator*, and particularly to *universal* modal operators also. In this case, we are able to have *the same* existential definition for both joined modal operators, but with each one based on its proper specific accessibility relation. This is important if we consider that the satisfaction for universal modal operators $\mathcal{M} \models_x \Box_i\phi/g$ *is not* given by the classic definition, i. e., by $\forall y \in X((x,y) \in \mathcal{R}_{\Diamond_i}$ implies $\mathcal{M} \models_y \phi/g)$, where $\mathcal{R}_{\Diamond_i}$ is the accessibility relation given by Definition 105 for the existential modal operator. It can not be defined by $\mathcal{M} \models_x \neg\Diamond_i\neg\phi/g$ because in distributive lattices, for two adjoint modal operators $\Diamond_i \dashv \Box_i$ generally does not hold $\Diamond_i = \neg\Box_i\neg$ and $\Box_i = \neg\Diamond_i\neg$. Thus, we can define the semantics for the satisfaction of universal modal operator by this new way,
7(a) $\mathcal{M} \models_x \Box_i\phi/g$ iff $\exists y \in X((x,y) \in \mathcal{R}_{\Box_i}$ and $\mathcal{M} \models_y \phi/g)$,

where $\mathcal{R}_{\Box_i}$ is an accessibility relation obtained by Definition 105 applied to the universal modal operator $\Box_i$, such that $\mathcal{R}_{\Box_i} \neq \mathcal{R}_{\Diamond_i}$, or by dual result, when $\Diamond_i$ is an additive modal operator, obtained for accessibility relations of adjoint unary modal operators and for the "gaggle" theory of Dunn (here $\overline{A}$ denotes the set complement of A).
7(b) $\mathcal{M} \models_x \Box_i\phi/g$ iff $\forall y \in X((x,y) \in (\overline{\mathcal{R}_{\Diamond_i}})^{-1}$ implies $\mathcal{M} \models_y \phi/g)$. □

This is really *a new result*, which generalizes the relational semantics for *normal* Kripke modal logic: for any couple of adjoint modal operators $l \vdash r$ (Galois connection), which results in a normal Kripke modal logic, we are able to define the satisfaction relation of these two (universal versus existential) operators based on two accessibility relations but in the same standard way used only for existential modal operators.

This result is particularly important when we are dealing with *positive modal logic* [193, 294] (without negation) for which Definition 105 holds also if we substitute point 7, with this new definition for universal modal operator, based on its proper accessibility relation, which is different from the relation used for a existential modal operator.

Example 52. In the case of Belnaps' 4-valued logic, we can verify that $\mathcal{M} \models_{\bot,g} \neg_t\top$ iff $\mathcal{M} \models_{\bot,g} (\top \Rightarrow \emptyset)$ iff $\forall y((y \leq \bot$ and $\mathcal{M} \models_{y,g} \top)$ implies $\mathcal{M} \models_{y,g} \emptyset)$, which is true (consider that $\mathcal{M} \models_{y,g} \emptyset$ is true only if $y = f$, and false otherwise); thus, $\|\neg_t\top\| = \downarrow I_H(\neg_t\top) = \downarrow I_H(\bot) = \downarrow\bot = \{f,\bot\}$. While $\mathcal{M} \models_{\top,g} \neg_t\top$ iff $\mathcal{M} \models_{\top,g} \top \Rightarrow \emptyset$ iff $\forall y((y \leq \top$ and $\mathcal{M} \models_{y,g} \top)$ implies $\mathcal{M} \models_{y,g} \emptyset)$ is false (consider the case when $y = \top$, then $y \leq \top$ and $\mathcal{M} \models_{y,g} \top$ is true, while $\mathcal{M} \models_{\top,g} \emptyset$ is false), consequently $\top \notin \|\neg_t\top\|$. The Kripke frame for autoepistemic intuitionistic logic based on Belnap's 4-valued logic is very simple, with two accessibility relations:

$$\mathcal{R}_{-} = \{(f,f),(\top,\bot),(\bot,\top),(t,t)\},$$

for the belief (conflation) modal operator, and

$$\mathcal{R}_{\mu} = \{(f,f),(t,\top),(\top,\top),(\top,t),(\bot,\top),(\bot,t)\},$$

for the Moore's autoepistemic modal operator μ. Both of them can be obtained from Definition 105 by applying it independently to the existential or universal operator, just because in these two cases they are self-adjoint (equal). Let us consider a more general case:

	M	L
t	t	$\top$
$\top$	t	$\top$
$\bot$	$\bot$	f
f	$\bot$	f

It is easy to verify that the operator M is the multiplicative monotone operator (i. e., $M(\alpha \wedge \beta) = M(\alpha) \wedge M(\beta)$ and $M(t) = t$), used for universal modal logic operator $\Box$. The operator L is its correspondent (by Galois connection $L \dashv M$) additive operator (i. e., $L(\alpha \vee \beta) = L(\alpha) \vee L(\beta)$ and $L(f) = f$), used for an existential modal logic operator $\Diamond$, such that $M = \neg_t L \neg_t$ (because the Belnap's lattice $\mathcal{B}_4$ is a Boolean algebra) with $\neg_t \neg_t = \mathrm{id}$ an identity. The accessibility relations for these two monotone operators, obtained from Definition 105 are $\mathcal{R}_{\Diamond} = \{(\top,\top),(f,f)\}$ and $\mathcal{R}_{\Box} = \{(t,\top),(\top,\top),(\top,t),(\bot,f),(f,f)\}$, and we will denominate them as *joint accessibility relations*. Thus, for the existential modal operator

$$\mathcal{M} \models_x \Diamond\phi/g \quad \text{iff} \quad \exists y \in X((x,y) \in \mathcal{R}_{\Diamond} \text{ and } \mathcal{M} \models_y \phi/g),$$

while for the universal modal operator we have two alternative definitions:

$$\mathcal{M} \models_x \Box\phi/g \quad \text{iff} \quad \mathcal{M} \models_x \neg\Diamond\neg\phi/g \text{ iff } \forall y \in X((x,y) \in \mathcal{R}_{\Diamond} \text{ implies } \mathcal{M} \models_y \phi/g),$$

based on the relation $\mathcal{R}_{\Diamond}$, or independently, based on accessibility relation $\mathcal{R}_{\Box}$,

$$\mathcal{M} \models_x \Box\phi/g \quad \text{iff} \quad \exists y \in X((x,y) \in \mathcal{R}_{\Box} \text{ and } \mathcal{M} \models_y \phi/g).$$

Finally, from the canonical representation for a complete distributive lattice based modal intuitionistic logics in Proposition 41, we obtained that the isomorphism, between the original Galois algebra $G = (X, \leq, \wedge, \vee, \neg, \rightharpoonup, \{o_i\}_{i\leq\omega}, 0, 1)$ with unary modal operators in $\{o_i\}_{i\leq\omega}$ and its *canonical* representation algebra $\mathbf{G}_K = (\mathcal{F}(X), \subseteq, \bigcap, \biguplus, \widehat{\neg}, \rightarrowtail,$

$\{\widehat{o}_i\}_{i\leq\omega}, 0, 1)$, where $\widehat{o}_i = \downarrow o_i \downarrow^{-1}$, $i = 1, 2, \ldots$, corresponds to the representation of any ground formula ϕ/g by the set of worlds $\|\phi/g\|$ in the canonical Kripke model for the modal algebra G. So, e. g., a ground term $\phi/g \wedge \psi/g$ in a predicate modal logic $\mathcal{L}$ (based on the Galois algebra G) with a many-valued Herbrand model $I_H : H \to X$, corresponds to the set $\|\phi/g\| \bigcap \|\psi/g\|$ in the canonical algebra $\mathbf{G}_K \simeq G$, where $\|\phi/g\| = \downarrow y$ (y is an algebraic truth value in a Herbrand model I for the ground formula ϕ/g) *is equal* to the set of worlds in the canonical Kripke model $\mathcal{M} = (K, S, V)$ (given by Definition 107) where ϕ/g holds.

A.3.5 Autoreference, many-valuedness and paraconsistency

The *paraconsistent* logic goes beyond consistency but prevents triviality, i. e., the explosive inconsistency of classic logic described above. In paraconsistent logics, we can have a kind of local inconsistency, which has no total explosive feature as in 2-valued classical logic. Thus, in the presence of these local inconsistencies paraconsistent logic still separates propositions into two nonempty classes, derivable and nonderivable ones.

The most important criteria for choosing paraconsistent logics, as suggested in [227, 265, 308], and recently formalized into the Logic of Formal Inconsistencies (LFI) [261], is their abstract degree of nontriviality, rather than the mere absence of contradiction.

The LFI internalizes the very notions of consistency and inconsistency at the object-language level, instead of the usual metalogic level. It designs an expressive logic language, able of recovering both consistent reasoning and allowing for some inconsistency.

In what follows, the set of standard logic connectives $\{\wedge, \vee, \Rightarrow, \neg\}$ correspond to the Heyting algebra in Proposition 40, and the *finite* number of unary modal (normal and *non*normal) operators. We will denote by A_X the extended many-valued Heyting algebra by a finite set of modal operators $\{o_i : X \to X\}_{i<\omega}$, i. e., $A_X = (X, \leq, \wedge, \vee, \rightharpoonup, \neg, \{o_i : X \to X\}_{i<\omega})$. Any many-valued valuation $v : H \to X$, i. e., the Herbrand interpretation, can be uniquely extended to all formulae in $\mathcal{L}^G_{\mathrm{mv}}$ (the set of all sentences in $\mathcal{L}_{\mathrm{mv}}$) by the homomorphism $v^* : \mathcal{L}^G_{\mathrm{mv}} \to A_X$. By (A_X, D), we will denote the matrix where $D \subseteq X$ is any subset of designated algebraic values.

We will formally define the multimodal many-valued logic as a pair $(\mathcal{L}^G_{\mathrm{mv}}, \Vdash)$ where $\Vdash \subseteq \mathcal{P}(\mathcal{L}^G_{\mathrm{mv}}) \times \mathcal{L}^G_{\mathrm{mv}}$ is a *consequence relation* for a logic $\mathcal{L}^G_{\mathrm{mv}}$, generally defined as follows: for any *theory* Δ (a subset of sentences of $\mathcal{L}^G_{\mathrm{mv}}$), the sentence $\phi \in \mathcal{L}^G_{\mathrm{mv}}$ is a logical consequence of Δ, denoted by $\Delta \Vdash \phi$, iff $\forall v (\forall \psi \in \Delta. v^*(\psi) \in D$ implies $v^*(\phi) \in D)$. It is said that a theory Δ is *closed* iff $\{\phi \in \mathcal{L}^G_{\mathrm{mv}} \mid \Delta \Vdash \phi\} = \Delta$.

In what follows, we will briefly present basic concepts in LFI, and invite the readers to use [261, 269] for more information. The logic $(\mathcal{L}^G_{\mathrm{mv}}, \Vdash)$ with a *paraconsistent negation* $\sim$, which has to be antitonic and must satisfy $\sim 1 = 0$ and $\sim 0 = 1$ but different from strong *supplementary negation* [261] based on the pseudo-complement, $\neg\alpha = \alpha \rightharpoonup 0$, where $\rightharpoonup$, defined as a relative pseudo-complement, is a *deductive implication* [261], which satisfies the modus ponens and deduction theorem [208] (notice that w. r. t. [261] here we inverted the symbols for these two negations) is:

1. contradictory, if $\forall\Delta\exists\phi(\Delta \Vdash \phi$, and $\Delta \Vdash\sim \phi)$.
2. trivial, if $\forall\Delta\forall\phi(\Delta \Vdash \phi)$.
3. explosive, if $\forall\Delta\forall\phi\forall\psi(\Delta, \phi, \sim \phi \Vdash \psi)$.
4. *gently explosive*, if $\forall\Delta\forall\phi\forall\psi(\Delta, \phi, \sim \phi, O(\phi) \Vdash \psi)$,

where $O(\phi)$ is a possibly empty set of formulae, which depends only on ϕ, satisfying the following: there are formulae α, β such that $O(\alpha), \alpha \nVdash \beta$ and $O(\alpha), \sim \alpha \nVdash \beta$.

5. consistent, if it is both explosive and nontrivial.
6. *paraconsistent*, if it is inconsistent yet not trivial.

In [261], it was shown that for Tarskian (monotonic) logic hold:

1. if logic is trivial, then it is both contradictory and explosive,
2. an explosive logic fails nontriviality iff it fails noncontradiction.

Finally, in [261] a Logic of Formal Inconsistency (LFI) is defined as a logic, which is not explosive but is *gently explosive*. Different from LFI, we consider all kinds of many-valued logics (also nonmonotonic where the property ($\Delta \Vdash \phi$ and $\Delta \subseteq \Lambda$) implies $\Lambda \Vdash \phi$) based on a complete distributive lattice of algebraic truth values does not hold.

In what follows, we will demonstrate that all many-valued logics based on a complete *distributive* lattice of truth values (MVCL logics) are gently explosive, i. e., they are LFIs. Now we will define the paraconsistent negation $\sim$ for MVCL logics. Given an unary operator $\odot : X \to X$, we will denote its image by $\mathrm{im}\odot = \{y = \odot(x) \mid x \in X\}$. For a paraconsistent negation, we need the condition $\exists x \in X.(x \wedge \sim x \neq 0)$ (in that case we take that $x \wedge \neg x \in D$ is a designated element), so it must hold $\mathbf{2} \subset \mathrm{im} \sim$.

Proposition 45. *Strong negation* $\neg$, *defined by the pseudo-complement* $\neg\alpha = \alpha \rightharpoonup 0$ *in a complete distributive lattice* $(X, \leq)$, *cannot be used as a paraconsistent negation.*

Proof. In fact, for any $x \in X$ we have that $x \wedge \neg x = x \wedge (\bigvee\{y \mid x \wedge y = 0\}) = \bigvee\{x \wedge y \mid x \wedge y = 0\} = 0$. Thus, $\nexists x \in X.x \wedge \neg x \neq 0$, and $\neg$ is the supplementary negation. □

An *atom* in a lattice $(X, \leq)$ is an element $x \in X$ different from 0, such that $\nexists y \neq 0.(y < x)$. Now we will show how we are able to define the paraconsistent negation for any complete distributive lattice $(X, \leq)$.

Proposition 46. *Any bounded lattice* $(X, \leq)$, *with cardinality bigger than 2, can have a paraconsistent negation* $\sim$.

Proof. For any fixed $\alpha \in X$, such that $\alpha \notin \{0,1\}$, we define

$$\sim x = 1 \quad \text{if } x = 0;\ 0 \text{ if } x = 1;\ \alpha \text{ otherwise.}$$

It is easy to show that for any two $x, y \in X$, if $x \leq y$ then $\neg x \geq \neg y$. So that $\sim$ is a general negation given by Definition 104. It is easy to verify that $\alpha \wedge \neg\alpha = \alpha \neq 0$.

But in some cases there are also other kinds of paraconsistent negations:

1. When X is an infinite set and there exists the isomorphism with the closed interval of reals $[a,b]$, $\omega : (X, \leq, \wedge, \vee) \simeq ([a,b], \leq, \min, \max)$, then we define for any $x \in X$, $\sim x = \omega^{-1}(b + a - \omega(x))$, where ω^{-1} is the inverse of ω.
2. When X is finite with the cardinality $n = |X| \geq 3$. We define the following isomorphism $\sigma : (X, \leq, \wedge, \vee) \simeq (\{\frac{i}{n} \mid 1 \leq i \leq n\}, \leq, \min, \max)$, and we define for any $x \in X$, $\sim x = \sigma^{-1}(\frac{1+n}{n} - \sigma(x))$, where σ^{-1} is the inverse of σ. □

Example 53. Let us consider the following cases:

1. In the case of fuzzy logic, where the complete lattice is a closed interval of reals, $X = [0,1]$, we have Case 1.1 where ω is defined by $\omega(x) = a + (b-a) * x$ for any $x \in X$, and $\omega^{-1}(y) = (y-a)/(b-a)$ for any $y \in [a,b]$. Thus, $\sim x = \omega^{-1}(b+a-\omega(x)) = (b+a-\omega(x)-a)/(b-a) = 1-(\omega(x)-a)/(b-a) = 1-\omega^{-1}(\omega(x)) = 1-x$ is a standard negation of fuzzy logic.

The set of designated elements is $D = \{y \mid y \in X \text{ and } a \leq y\}$ for some $0 < a \leq 1$.

2. In the case of the 3-valued logic where $X = \{0, \frac{1}{2}, 1\}$, and $\sigma(x) = \frac{1+2x}{3}$, we obtain $\sim(0) = 1$, $\sim(\frac{1}{2}) = \frac{1}{2}$ and $\sim(1) = 0$. The set of designated elements is $D = \{\frac{1}{2}, 1\}$.
3. In the case of Belnap's 4-valued logic, $X = \{f, \top, \bot, t\}$, where 0 corresponds to f and 1 to t, we have two atoms, $\top$ and $\bot$, and we obtain that $\sim = \neg_t -$ is standard epistemic bilattice negation, where $\neg_t$ is a pseudo-complement (supplementary negation) and $-$ the belief modal operator (conflation). The set of designated elements is $D = \{\top, t\}$.

Now we will introduce the particular nonnormal modal operators (they are not monotone functions), used in [204] for the reduction of any MVCL logic into 2-valued modal logic, and based on them the paraconsistent negation $\sim$. Then we will define the consistency operator $\circ : X \to X$ as follows.

Definition 108. Given a complete lattice $(X, \leq)$, we define the family of unary modal operators $[x] : X \to X$, for each $x \in X$, as follows: for any $\alpha \in X$,

$$[x]\alpha = 1 \quad \text{if } \alpha = x;\ 0 \text{ otherwise.}$$

Based on them, we define the following global modal CONSISTENCY operator $\circ : X \to X$ for a lattice $(X, \leq)$: for any $\alpha \in X$,

$$\circ\alpha =_{\text{def}} \bigwedge\{\sim [x]\alpha \mid x \in X \backslash \mathbf{2}\}, \quad \text{where } \backslash \text{ is the set substraction.}$$

Notice that in the case of the classic 2-valued logic we obtain for any formula ϕ, $\circ\phi = 1$, because the meet of the empty set is equal to 1.

Otherwise, for a n-valued logic, $\circ\alpha = 1$ for $\alpha \in \mathbf{2}$ and is otherwise equal to 0.

Theorem 18 (Many-valuedness and paraconsistency). *Any many-valued logic based on a complete lattice* $(X, \leq)$ *with* $|X| \geq 3$ *is a LFI with the consistency operator defined in Definition* 108.

Proof. It is easy to verify that the following matrix holds:

	$\sim$	$[x_1]$	$[x_2]$	$\dots$	$[x_i]$	$\dots$	$[x_n]$	$\circ$
1	0	0	0	$\dots$	0	$\dots$	0	1
x_1	y_1	1	0	$\dots$	0	$\dots$	0	0
x_2	y_2	0	1	$\dots$	0	$\dots$	0	0
.	.	.	.	$\dots$	.	$\dots$	.	.
.	.	.	.	$\dots$	.	$\dots$	.	.
x_i	y_i	0	0	$\dots$	1	$\dots$	0	0
.	.	.	.	$\dots$	.	$\dots$	.	.
.	.	.	.	$\dots$	.	$\dots$	.	.
x_n	y_n	0	0	$\dots$	0	$\dots$	1	0
0	1	0	0	$\dots$	0	$\dots$	0	1

where for all $1 \leq i \leq n$, $x_i \in X \backslash \mathbf{2}$ and $y_i \in X \backslash \mathbf{2}$, and $n \geq 1$.

It is easy to verify that $\forall x \in X.(x \wedge \sim x \wedge \circ x = 0)$; consequently, $\forall \Delta \forall \phi \forall \psi (\Delta, \phi, \sim \phi, O(\phi) \Vdash \psi)$, while $\circ 1, 1 \nVdash 0$ and $\circ 0, \sim 0 \nVdash 0$. Thus, a many-valued logic based on a complete lattice $(X, \leq)$ of algebraic truth values is gently explosive, i. e., it is a LFI. □

So, for any finite many-valued logic (each finite lattice is a complete lattice) we are able to define the paraconsistent negation in Proposition 46 in order to obtain a LFI. It is possible also in the case of infinite set of algebraic truth values, when this set is a complete lattice (as, e. g., in the case of the fuzzy logic in Example 53). The relationship between the many-valuedness and the autoreferential assumption is given in precedent sections by representation theorems and dual Kripke-style semantics for many-valued logics based on complete lattices of truth values (Proposition 41 and Definitions 105 and 107).

All that remains is to explain the last relationship in the triangle many-valuedness-autoreference-paraconsistency: the relationship between the *autoreference* assumption for Kripke-style semantics of many-valued logics and *paraconsistency*.

Let us consider the multimodal many-valued logic $(\mathcal{L}_{mv}, \Vdash)$ based on the extended many-valued Heyting algebra $A_X = (X, \leq, \wedge, \vee, \rightharpoonup, \neg, \{o_i : X \to X\}_{i<\omega})$, and a particular set of formulae (theory) $\Delta \subset \mathcal{L}_{mv}$, with the Herbrand base H, for which the Kripke-style semantics is given by Definitions 105 and 107.

Let $v : H \to X$ be a many-valued Herbrand model of this theory Δ, and $v^* : \mathcal{L}^G_{mv} \to A_X$ its unique homomorphic extension to all ground formulae. Then from Theorem 17 we have that the set of ground formulae, which are satisfied in a world $x \in X$ is

$$S(x) =_{\text{def}} \{\phi \in \mathcal{L}^G_{\text{mv}} \mid v^*(\phi) \geq x\}.$$

If we consider a world x as the matrix $(A_X, D(x))$ where $D(x) = \{y \in X \mid y \geq x\}$ is the set of designated elements of this matrix, then the set $S(x)$ is the set of formulae, which are satisfied w. r. t. this matrix. That is, $\forall\phi \in S(x)(v^*(\phi) \in D(x))$, so that v is a model for all formulae in $S(x)$. Thus, we can introduce the following preorder between matrices:

$$(A_X, D(x)) \preceq (A_X, D(y)) \quad \text{iff} \quad S(x) \supseteq S(y) \quad \text{iff} \quad x \leq y.$$

So, the bottom matrix is $(A_X, D(0)) = (A_X, X)$. It corresponds to the bottom world 0, where the set $S(0) = \mathcal{L}^G_{\text{mv}}$ is the set of all sentences: this world is *trivial*, and corresponds to classic explosive inconsistency, so that this world cannot be paraconsistent.

The top world 1 corresponds to the matrix $(A_X, D(1)) = (A_X, \{1\})$, with the smallest set of formulae $S(1)$. In this world, we cannot have any true formula $\phi \wedge \neg\phi$, because if $v^*(\phi) \in D(1) = \{1\}$, i. e., $v^*(\phi) = 1$, then $v^*(\neg\phi) = 0$, i. e., $v^*(\neg\phi) \notin D(1) = \{1\}$, and consequently, $v^*(\phi \wedge \neg\phi) \notin D(1) = \{1\}$. That is, this world also cannot be paraconsistent. Thus, to be able to permit paraconsistent reasoning we need at least three different worlds, i. e., n-valued logic with $n \geq 3$.

In that case, for the world $0 < x < 1$ we are able to have the formulae $\phi \wedge \neg\phi$ such that $v^*(\phi\wedge\neg\phi) = x$, i. e., $v^*(\phi\wedge\neg\phi) \in D(x)$. Consequently, this world is paraconsistent.

An interesting point is how the hierarchy between the possible worlds (lattice ordering of truth values) corresponds to the hierarchy of matrices for the same theory, and consequently, to the hierarchy of paraconsistent logics. The level of paraconsistency is inverse to the truth level of the possible world: the higher truth level of the possible world corresponds to a lower paraconsistent logic (with a smaller number of paraconsistent formulae).

A.4 Reduction of many-valued into two-valued modal logics

Large databases obtained by the data integration of different source databases can be incomplete and inconsistent in many ways. The classical logic is not the appropriate formalism for reasoning about inconsistent databases. Certain local inconsistencies should not be allowed to significantly alter the intended meaning of such logic programs. The variety of semantical approaches that have been invented for logic programs is quite broad. In particular, we are interested for many-valued logics with negation, based on bilattices.

Semantics of logic programs are generally based on a classical 2-valued logic by means of stable models [116, 309]. Under these circumstances, not every program has a stable model. Three-valued or partial model semantics had an extensive development for logic programs generally [310, 311]. Przymusinski extended the notion of a stable model to allow 3-valued or partial, stable models, [312], and showed every program has at least one partial stable model, and the well-founded model is the smallest among them [313]. Once one has made the transition from classical to partial models allowing *incomplete* information, it is a small step to also allow models admitting *inconsistent* information. Doing so provides a natural framework for the semantic understanding of logic programs that are distributed over several sites, with possibly conflicting information coming from different places.

So far, research in many-valued logic programming has proceeded along different directions: *Signed* logics [298, 299] and *annotated* logic programming [300, 301, 314], which can be embedded into the first, *bilattice-based* logics, [188, 197], and *quantitative rule sets* [315, 316]. Earlier studies of these approaches quickly identified various distinctions between these frameworks. For example, one of the key insights behind bilattices was the interplay between the truth values assigned to sentences and the (nonclassic) notion of *implication* in the language under considerations. Thus, rules (implications) had weights (or truth values) associated with them as a whole. The problem was to study how truth values should be propagated "across" implications. Annotated logics, on the other hand, appeared to associate truth values with each component of an implication rather than the implication as a whole. Roughly, based on the way in which uncertainty is associated with facts and rules of a program, these frameworks can be classified into *implication based* (IB) and *annotation based* (AB).

In the IB approach, a rule is of the form $A \leftarrow^{\alpha} B_1, \ldots, B_n$, which says that the certainty associated with the implication is α. Computationally, given an assignment I of logical values to the B_is, the logical value of A is computed by taking the conjunction of logical values $I(B_i)$ and then somehow propagating it to the rule head A.

In the AB approach, a rule is of the form $A : f(\beta_1, \ldots, \beta_n) \leftarrow B_1 : \beta_1, \ldots, B_n : \beta_n$, which asserts "*the certainty of the atom A is least (or is in)* $f(\beta_1, \ldots, \beta_n)$, *whenever the certainty of the atom* B_i *is at least (or is in)* β_i, $1 \leq i \leq n$," where f is an n-ary computable function and β_i is either constant or a variable ranging over many-valued logic values.

The comparison in [317] shows:

1. While the way implication is treated on the AB approach is closer to the classical logic, the way rules are fired in the IB approach has definite intuitive appeal.
2. The AB approach is strictly more expressive than IB. The down side is that query processing in the AB approach is more complicated, e. g., the fix-point operator is not continuous in general, while it is in the IB approaches.

From the above points, it is believed that IB approach is easier to use and is more amenable for efficient implementations. In [301], it is shown how Fitting's 3-valued bilattice logic can be embedded into annotated logic programming.

The higher-order types of Herbrand interpretations for many-valued logic programs, where we are not able to associate a fixed logic value to a given ground atom of a Herbrand base but a function in a given functional space, often arise in practice when we have to deal with uncertain information. In such cases, we associate some *degree of belief* to ground atoms, which can be simple probability, probability interval or other more complex data structures, as for example, in Bayesian logic programs where for a different kind of atoms we may associate different kinds of *measures* as well.

But we can see approximate (uncertain) information as a kind of *relativization* of truth values for sentences as follows. Let H be a Herbrand base for a logic program, with predicate and proposition letters in P, that handles the uncertain information, and for k-ary predicate $p_i^k \in P$, $p_i^k(\mathbf{d})$ a ground atom in H that logically defines a particular fact for which we have only an approximated information about when it happened. Thus, this atom $p_i^k(\mathbf{d})$ is no longer *absolutely* true or false, but rather its truth depends on the approximate temporal information about this fact: in some time points it can be true, in others it can be false. If we consider such a temporal approximation as a *context* for this ground fact $p_i^k(\mathbf{d}) \in H$, then we obtain that the truth of $p_i^k(\mathbf{d})$ is a function from the time to the ordinary set of truth values $\mathbf{2} = \{0, 1\}$. Consequently, the truth values of ground atoms in this Herbrand base are the functions, i. e., they have a *higher-order type* (this term is taken from the typed lambda calculus) with respect to the set $\mathbf{2}$ of truth constants. Intuitively, the approximated information is relativized to its context, and such a context further specifies the semantics for this uncertain information.

The *contextualization* is a kind of *premodal* Kripke modeling: in fact, if we consider a context as a Kripke possible world, then the relativization of the truth to particular contexts is equivalent to Kripke semantics for a modal logic where the truth (or falsity) of the formulae is relativized to possible worlds. In fact, as we will see in what follows, the higher-order Herbrand models obtained by contextualization are precursors for an introduction of 2-valued epistemic concepts, i. e., for a development of (absolute) 2-valued logics, and it explains their role in a 2-valued reduction of many-valued logics.

Definition 109 (Higher-order Herbrand interpretation types [83]). Let H be a Herbrand base, then the higher-order Herbrand interpretations are defined by $I_H : H \to T$, where T is a functional space $W_1 \Rightarrow (\ldots(W_n \Rightarrow \mathbf{2})\ldots)$, denoted also as $(\ldots((\mathbf{2}^{W_n})^{W_{n-1}})\ldots)^{W_1}$, and $W_i, i \in [1, n], n \geq 1$ are the sets of parameters (the values of given domains). In the case $n = 1, \mathcal{W} = W_1$, $T = (\mathcal{W} \Rightarrow \mathbf{2})$, we will denote this interpretation by $I_H : H \to \mathbf{2}^{\mathcal{W}}$.

In [318], a general method has been developed of constructing 2-valued autoepistemic language concepts for each many-valued ground atom with higher-order Herbrand interpretation given in Definition 109, for which we would like to have a correspondent 2-valued logic language concept. The number of such atomic concepts to be used in the applications is always a *finite* subset H_M of M elements of the Herbrand base H.

Definition 110 (Epistemic concepts). [318] Let $\overline{H}_M$ be a finite sequence of N ground atoms in H, H_M a set of elements in $\overline{H}_M$ and $i_N : H_M \hookrightarrow H$ be an inclusion mapping for this finite subset of ground atoms. We define the bijection $i_C : H_M \simeq C_M$, with the set of derived concepts $C_M = \{\Box_i A \mid A = \pi_i(\overline{H}_M), 1 \leq i \leq M\}$, where π_i is i-th projection, such that for any ground atom $A = \pi_i(\overline{H}_M)$, $i_C(A) = \Box_i A$.

The idea of how to pass to the possible world Kripke semantics for universal modal operators $\Box_i$, used above for an epistemic definition of concepts, is as follows: for a given $\mathcal{W} = W_1 \times \cdots \times W_n$, we define the set

$$Q_i = \{\mathbf{w} \in \mathcal{W} \mid p_i^k(\mathbf{d}) = \pi_i(\overline{H}_M) \in H \text{ and } I(p_i^k(\mathbf{d}))(\mathbf{w}) = 1\}.$$

It is easy to verify that Q_i is the set of all points $\mathbf{w} \in \mathcal{W} = W_1 \times \cdots \times W_n$ where the ground atom $p_i^k(\mathbf{d}) = \pi_i(\overline{H}_M)$, for a given higher-order Herbrand model, is *true*. As a consequence, we may consider $\mathcal{W}$ as a set of possible worlds and define this higher-order Herbrand model for $I_H : H \to T$ as a *Kripke model*. It follows that a higher-order language concept $\Box_i A$ is false if and only if there is not any possible world where the ground atom $A = \pi_i(\overline{H}_M) \in H$ is satisfied, and true if it is satisfied exactly in the set of possible worlds that defines the *meaning* of this ground atom. We will show, in the following definition, how to define the accessibility relations for *modal* operators, used to extend an original many-valued logic by a finite set of higher-order language concepts. For example, for any ground modal atom ("concept") $\Box_i A$, where $A = \pi_i(\overline{H}_M)$, we will obtain that $|\Box_i A| \in \{\emptyset, \mathcal{W}\}$, i. e., it is a *2-valued* modal logic formula (here $\emptyset$ is the empty set).

Definition 111 (Kripke semantics for epistemic concepts). Let $I_H : H \to T$ be a higher-order Herbrand interpretation type, where T denotes a functional space $W_1 \Rightarrow (\ldots(W_n \Rightarrow \mathbf{2})\ldots)$, with $\mathcal{W} = W_1 \times \cdots \times W_n$, and P is the set of predicates. Then, for a given sequence of language concepts $\overline{H}_M$, a quadruple $\mathcal{M}_I = (\mathcal{W}, \{\mathcal{R}_i\}, \mathcal{D}, I_K)$ is a Kripke model for this interpretation I_H, such that:

1. A mapping (see Definition 3) $I_K : \mathcal{W} \times P \to \bigcup_{n \in \mathcal{N}} \mathbf{2}^{\mathcal{D}^n}$, such that for any $\mathbf{w} = (w_1, \ldots, w_n) \in \mathcal{W}$, $p_j^n \in P$ and $\mathbf{d} \in \mathcal{D}^n$ it holds that
$$I_K(\mathbf{w}, p_j^n)(\mathbf{d}) = I_H(p_j^n(\mathbf{d}))(w_1)\ldots(w_n),$$
where $\mathcal{D}^n$ denotes the set of all n-tuples of domain $\mathcal{D}$, and $\mathbf{2}^{\mathcal{D}^n}$ the set of all functions from the set $\mathcal{D}^n$ to the set $\mathbf{2}$.
2. Finite set of accessibility relations: for any $p_j^n(\mathbf{d}) = \pi_i(\overline{H}_M)$, $\mathcal{R}_i = \mathcal{W} \times Q_i$ if $Q_i \neq \emptyset$; $\mathcal{W} \times \mathcal{W}$ otherwise, where $Q_i = \{\mathbf{w} \in \mathcal{W} \mid I_K(\mathbf{w}, p_j^n)(\mathbf{d}) = 1\}$.

Then, for any world $\mathbf{w} \in \mathcal{W}$ and assignment g, we define the many-valued satisfaction relation, denoted by $\mathcal{M}_I \models_{g,\mathbf{w}}$, as follows:

A1. $\mathcal{M}_I \models_{g,\mathbf{w}} p_j^n(x_1,\ldots,x_n)$ iff $I_K(\mathbf{w},p_j^n)(g(x_1),\ldots,g(x_n)) = 1$, for any atom,
A2. $\mathcal{M}_I \models_{g,\mathbf{w}} \Box_i p_j^n(x_1,\ldots,x_n)$ iff $\forall \mathbf{w}'((\mathbf{w},\mathbf{w}') \in \mathcal{R}_i$ implies $\mathcal{M} \models_{g,\mathbf{w}'} p_j^n(x_1,\ldots,x_n))$.

Notice that we obtained the multimodal Kripke models with universal modal operators $\Box_i$, i. e., a kind of *2-valued reduction* for a many-valued atom $p_j^n(\mathbf{d})$. Obviously, this technique can only be used if the number of introduced universal modal operators is *finite*. The encapsulated information in this Kripke frame can be rendered explicit by flattening a Kripke model of this more abstract vision of data, into an ordinary Herbrand model where the original predicates are extended by set of new attributes for the hidden information.

Definition 112 (Flattening [83]). Let $I_H : H \to T$ be a higher-order Herbrand interpretation, where T denotes a functional space $W_1 \Rightarrow (\ldots(W_n \Rightarrow \mathbf{2})\ldots)$ and $\mathcal{W} = W_1 \times \cdots \times W_n$ is a Cartesian product. We define its flattening into the Herbrand interpretation $I_F : H_F \to \mathbf{2}$, where $H_F = \{r_F(\mathbf{d},\mathbf{w}) \mid p_j^n(\mathbf{d}) \in H$ and $\mathbf{w} \in \mathcal{W}\}$ is the Herbrand base of new predicates r_F, obtained by an extension of original predicates p_j^n by a tuple of parameters $\mathbf{w} = (w_1,\ldots,w_n)$, such that for any $r_F(\mathbf{d},\mathbf{w}) \in H_F$, it holds that $I_F(r_F(\mathbf{d},\mathbf{w})) = I_H(p_j^n(\mathbf{d}))(w_1)\ldots(w_n)$.

By this flattening of the higher-order Herbrand models, we again obtain a *2-valued logic*, but with a changed Herbrand base H_F. We will apply the general results obtained previously to a more specific case of many-valued logics. This is a case of many-valued logics with uncertain, approximated or context-dependent information. We consider only the class of many-valued logics $\mathcal{L}_{\text{mv}}$ based on a bounded lattice $X = \mathcal{W}$ of algebraic truth values, with $\mathbf{2} \subset \mathcal{W}$. Then the ordering relations and operations in a bounded lattice $\mathcal{W}$ are propagated to the function space $\mathcal{W}^H$, which is bounded lattice as well [319]. A many-valued Herbrand interpretation $v \in \mathcal{W}^H$, a mapping $v : H \to \mathcal{W}$, can be extended to all formulae as a homomorphism $v^* : \mathcal{L}_{\text{mv}}^G \to \mathcal{W}$, also called a many-valued valuation, where $\mathcal{L}_{\text{mv}}^G$ is the subset of all ground formulae in $\mathcal{L}_{\text{mv}}$.

Example 54. Let us, with Belnap's bilattice, consider also the following bounded lattices:

1. Fuzzy data [239, 320, 321]: then $\mathcal{W} = [0,1]$ is the *infinite* set of real numbers from 0 to 1. For any ground atom $p_j^n(\mathbf{d}) \in H$, the $I(p_j^n(\mathbf{d}))$ represents its *plausibility*. For any two $x,y \in \mathcal{W}$, we have that $x \wedge y = \min\{x,y\}$, $x \vee y = \max\{x,y\}$, and negation connective $\sim$ is determined by $\sim x = 1 - x$.
2. Belief quantified data [70, 322, 323]: then $\mathcal{W} = \mathcal{C}[0,1]$ is the set of all closed subintervals over $[0,1]$. For any ground atom $p_j^n(\mathbf{d}) \in H$, the $(L,U) = v(p_j^n(\mathbf{d}))$ represents the lower and upper bounds for expert's *belief* in $p_j^n(\mathbf{d})$. For any two $[x,y],[x_1,y_1] \in \mathcal{W}$, we have that $[x,y] \wedge [x_1,y_1] = [\min\{x,x_1\},\min\{y,y_1\}]$, $[x,y] \vee [x_1,y_1] = [\max\{x,x_1\},\max\{y,y_1\}]$.The *belief* (or truth) ordering is defined as follows: $[x,y] \leq [x_1,y_1]$ iff ($x \leq x_1$ and $y \leq y_1$). We define the epistemic negation [197] of a *belief* $[x,y]$ as the *doubt* $\sim [x,y]$, such that $\sim [x,y] = [\sim y, \sim x] =$

$[1-y, 1-x]$. The bottom value of this lattice is $0 = [0,0]$, while the top value is $1 = [1,1]$.
3. Confidence level quantified data [200, 324]: then $\mathcal{W} = \mathcal{C}[0,1] \times \mathcal{C}[0,1]$. For any ground atom $p_j^n(\mathbf{d}) \in H$, we have $((L_1, U_1), (L_2, U_2)) = v(p_j^n(\mathbf{d}))$, where (L_1, U_1) represents the lower and upper bounds for expert's *belief* in $p_j^n(\mathbf{d})$, while (L_2, U_2) represents the lower and upper bounds for the expert's *doubt* in $p_j^n(\mathbf{d})$, respectively.

Let $\alpha = ([x,y],[z,v]), \beta = ([x_1,y_1],[z_1,v_1]) \in \mathcal{W}$, then

$$\alpha \wedge \beta = ([\min\{x,x_1\}, \min\{y,y_1\}], [\max\{z,z_1\}, \max\{v,v_1\}]),$$
$$\alpha \vee \beta = ([\max\{x,x_1\}, \max\{y,y_1\}], [\min\{z,z_1\}, \min\{v,v_1\}]).$$

We are interested in the ordering $\leq$ that increases the belief and decreases the doubt of facts, $([x,y],[z,v]) \leq ([x_1,y_1],[z_1,v_1])$ iff $[x,y] \leq [x_1,y_1]$ and $[z_1,v_1] \leq [z,v]$.

The negation $\sim$, which reverses this truth ordering, of this lattice is defined by Ginsberg [197], with $\sim ([x,y],[z,v]) = ([z,v],[x,y])$. The bottom value of this lattice is $0 = ([0,0],[1,1])$, while the top value is $1 = ([1,1],[0,0])$.

All examples above are more than bounded lattices: they are complete distributive lattices [208, 209]. Thus, we consider also that for any two elements $a, b \in \mathcal{W}$ the many-valued implication $a \to b$ for complete lattices can be defined as a reduct (the relative pseudo-complement), $a \to b = \vee\{c \in \mathcal{W} \mid c \wedge a \leq b\}$, so that $a \to b = 1$ iff $a \leq b$.

For any ground atom $p_j^n(\mathbf{d}) \in H$ with a logic value $\mathbf{w} = v(p_j^n(\mathbf{d}))$, we can generate a *contextual atom*, a couple $(p_j^n(\mathbf{d}), \mathbf{w}) \in H \times \mathcal{W}$, which tell us that "the atom $p_j^n(\mathbf{d})$ in the context $\mathbf{w}$ is true." So, we obtain that the bijection is $: H_F \to H \times \mathcal{W}$, such that for any extended (or flattened) ground atom $r_F(\mathbf{d}, \mathbf{w}) \in H_F$ it holds that $\text{is}(r_F(\mathbf{d}, \mathbf{w})) = (p_j^n(\mathbf{d}), \mathbf{w})$. This *contextualization* of a many-valued logic can be represented by this commutative diagram

$$\begin{array}{lcccc}
 & \mathbf{2}^{\mathcal{W}} \times \mathcal{W} & \xrightarrow{\quad\text{eval}\quad} & & \mathbf{2} \\
\text{Higher-order} & I_H \uparrow \;\; \uparrow \text{id}_{\mathcal{W}} & & & \uparrow \text{id}_{\mathbf{2}} \\
 & H \times \mathcal{W} & \xleftarrow{\text{is}} & H_F & \xrightarrow{I_F} \mathbf{2} \\
\text{Many-valued} & v \downarrow \;\; \downarrow \text{id}_{\mathcal{W}} & & & \uparrow \text{id}_{\mathbf{2}} \\
 & \mathcal{W} \times \mathcal{W} & \xrightarrow{\quad\triangle\quad} & & \mathbf{2}
\end{array} \tag{A.3}$$

where eval is the application of the first argument (function) to the second argument, id's are the identities, and $\triangle$ is the "diagonal" function, such that $\triangle(\mathbf{w}, \mathbf{w}') = 1$ iff

$\mathbf{w} = \mathbf{w}'$, so that the higher-order Herbrand interpretation is obtained from a many-valued Herbrand interpretation by $I_H = \Lambda(\triangle \circ (v \times \mathrm{id}_W))$, where Λ is the currying (λ abstraction) operator for functions used in diagram (A.10) in Section A.5. The flattened Herbrand interpretation (of a "meta" logic obtained by an ontological encapsulation of original many-valued logic), is equal to $I_F = \mathrm{eval} \circ (\Lambda(\triangle \circ (v \times \mathrm{id}_W)) \times \mathrm{id}_W) \circ \mathrm{is}$.

Intuitively, the diagram above shows that for any many-valued interpretation v, we obtain the correspondent 2-valued interpretation I_F (but with modified Herbrand base H_F), and equivalent to it the higher-order Herbrand interpretation I_H.

By this contextualization of a many-valued logic, we obtain the simplest case of the higher-order Herbrand interpretation given by Definition 109, $I_H : H \to \mathbf{2}^{\mathcal{W}}$, such that for any atom $p_j^n(\mathbf{d}) \in H$ and $\mathbf{w} \in \mathcal{W}$ holds that:

$$I_H(p_j^n(\mathbf{d}))(\mathbf{w}) = 1 \quad \text{iff} \quad \mathbf{w} = v(r(\mathbf{d})).$$

The accessibility relations $\mathcal{R}_i = \mathcal{W} \times Q_i$, for any $p_j^n(\mathbf{d}) = \pi_i(\overline{H}_M) \in H$, in Definition 111 for many-valued logic does not depend on the number of ground atoms in a Herbrand base, but only on the number of logic values in $\mathcal{W}$: it results from the fact that to any ground atom in a *consistent* many-valued logic we can assign only *one* logic value, so that $Q_i = \{\mathbf{w} \in \mathcal{W} \mid p_j^n(\mathbf{d}) = \pi_i(\overline{H}_M) \in H \text{ and } I_H(p_j^n(\mathbf{d}))(\mathbf{w}) = 1\} = \{\mathbf{w}\}$ is a singleton, with $\mathbf{w} = v(p_j^n(\mathbf{d}))$. As we can see from the examples above, we assume the autoreferential semantics, i. e., that the set of possible worlds of the relational Kripke frames, used for the transformation of many-valued into multimodal 2-valued logic, is the set of logic values of this many-valued logic [69].

A.4.1 Higher-order Herbrand interpretations: revision of temporal-probabilistic logics

In this subsection, we will provide the theory of flattening of higher-order Herbrand interpretation shown by diagram (A.3) in the previous section, and its intensional FOL representation by diagram (1.33) in Section 1.3.1 dedicated to intensional abstraction operator.

The reasoning with probabilistic information based on PSAT (Probabilistic Satisfiability) is the problem of determining wether a set of assignments of probabilities to a collection of Boolean formulas of atomic events is consistent has a long history [325–327], and is proven that is NP-complete. But the probabilities derived from any sources may have tolerances associated with them, and Fenstad [328] has shown that when enough information is not available about the interaction between events, the probability of compound events cannot be determined precisely: one can only give bounds, lower and upper probability bounds. Consequently, the probability intervals used for uncertain information, as for interval bounded lattices for belief quantified data in Point 2 of the previous section, are the simplest extension of the traditional probability modes [329–331] and are used also as belief measure for uncertainty in fuzzy logics. Such metric for nontemporal logic programming (p-programs), of the AB approach (annotation based, as explained in the previous section) is used in a number of papers [70, 200, 323, 332, 333].

We assume that every event occurs at a point in time with a probability interval of reals $[a, b] \subseteq [0, 1]$ An instant (time point or chronon) **t** is specified w. r. t. a given time granularity of a linear calendar structure $\mathcal{T}$; for example, "day/month/year." Often, however, we do not know the exact time point; instead, we only know that the instant is located sometime during a time interval. We call such an instant an *indeterminate instant* [86]. Dyreson and Snodgrass have drawn attention to the fact that, in many temporal database applications, there is often uncertainty about the start time of events, the end time of events and the duration of events. The indeterminacy refers to the *time* when an event occurred, not whether the event occurred or not. An indeterminate instant is described by lower and upper time bound, and a probability distribution (mass) function (PDF) [87] which, for every time point in this interval, returns with a lower and upper probability value assigned to a chronons. Generally, for the interval-based lattice the first introduction of interval-based Temporal Probabilistic Logic Programs (TP-programs) is presented in [334], and is extended to TP-databases [87], so that the semantic of interval-based probabilistic logic programs based on possible worlds and the fix-point semantics for such programs [70] is considered valid for more than 13 years. But in 2005, during my one year visiting stage at College Park, I had the possibility to approach the general problems with such TP databases [15], to consider the semantics of TP-logic programs and to realize that it is not correctly defined. The reason for the fact that more than dozen papers published in very important conferences and journals from 1992 to 2005 are passed with this drawback is probably because of the complexity of the issue and the fact that the fix-point semantics were not used in practical applications.

Main drawback of V. S. Subrahmaninan's theory of TP-logic programs

The initial suspect for the validity of the fix-point semantics w. r. t. the model theory of the p-programs (probabilistic programs), defined in the seminal paper [70] and successively repeated in all other papers, was based on the two observations: on an unnatural semantics for the probability interval-based bilattice used for computation of the fix point, and on the intuition that would be possible to convert the p-programs with interval-based annotated atoms into the probabilistic constraint programs, and for them there is no guarantee that the solution will contain only simple probabilistic intervals for atoms [16].

The first consideration was analyzed and presented in [202]. In [70], it is used for the knowledge (precision) ordering for a computation of the least fix-point semantics for interval-based logic programs, but the disjunction can produce as a result of inconsistent values $[x, y]$ such that $x > y$; moreover, while the bottom solution is reasonably assigned the whole interval $0_K = [0, 1]$ (bottom value of the lattice), to the "best solution" is assigned the top value of the lattice $[0, 1]$ (denominated empty interval $\emptyset$ in [70]), which is *inconsistent* (i. e., the best solutions result inconsistently).[2]

Also, the second observation was investigated by the author and the result is presented in [68] with the reduction of TP-databases into constraint logic programs: consequently, we are able to apply interval PSAT in order to find the models of such interval-based probabilistic programs, but such models cannot, in the general case, be described by single intervals associated with atoms of a program. In fact, there are the cases when the least fix point of a p-program P *is not* a model of P: it happens always when there is a rule with an atom in the body with the probability interval more thin then the interval for this atom assigned by the least fix point (so that this rule could not be satisfied during the least fix-point computation) and with the atom in the head of this rule with the probability interval more thin that the interval for this atom computed by the least fix point.

The main drawbacks of the work in [334] can be summarized as follows: its fix-point semantics is incorrect w. r. t. its model theory in the analog way described above in the case of more simple p-programs; the second is based on the fact that its semantics for probability, based on possible worlds, is apparently taken without any plausible connection with the *standard semantics* for p-programs based on Herbrand interpretations, principally because they did not explore the possible reductions of TP-programs into p-programs (similarly as in the case when in [70] was not considered the possible reduction into constraint logic programs, and the price was the incorrect fix-point semantics).

In order to obtain a serious revision for TP-programs and their semantics, we needed some additional mathematical tools also, based on the concepts of the predicate compression and higher-order Herbrand model types [83] (used also for "abstracted" databases in [68] and presented here in the previous section) as follows:

1. The definition of the new syntax and the model theory for temporal probabilistic programs, denominated PT-programs (probabilistic temporal programs), where is considered the full temporal property of events by including the attribute for time points inside of all atoms (basic events): such atoms will be denominated t-atoms

---

2 Independently from this, my investigation about the validity of the given semantics for interval-based p-programs, and presumably in the same time (such coincidence is astounding), also the two coauthors, which previously worked on this issue for more than 5 years [332, 334], discovered the incorrectness of their previous definition of fixed-point semantics for interval-based p-programs. So that in the first paper [71] they presented the counterexamples, and proved that the fix-point semantics of p-programs is *unsound* (their Proposition 1 shows that the fix-point semantics derives the interpretations, which are not models of a p-program) and *incomplete* (their Proposition 3 shows that there are models of a p-program, which are not interval-based, so that the fix-point operator is unable to find any solution). The correct semantics for probabilistic programs (p-programs), based on interval PSAT, is presented recently [335] and shows that the entailment problem for p-programs is co-NP-complete.

in what follows. By this intuitive and simple operation, we obtain t-Herbrand models and indirectly the reduction of PT-programs into the p-programs with t-atoms, so that the possible world semantics for the PT-programs with this new syntax is based on standard Herbrand models.
2. Such new PT-programs has the same possible world semantics for p-programs [335], which can be solved, in the general case, by interval PSAT as discussed in precedence.
3. PT-programs can be transformed in the previous version of TP-programs described in [334], by means of predicate compression for the temporal attribute: thus, the possible worlds of old TP-programs is is the set of higher-order Herbrand interpretations, which are result of this predicate compression. The TP-programs obtained by this transformation (which is knowledge invariant) do not suffer the semantics drawback as in [334], and can be considered as the minimal revision of the work presented in [334].

We will use the same terminology as in [334]. The main difference is that our event atoms, different from event atoms [334], have also the temporal attribute y with a domain represented by $S_\mathcal{T}$, the set of all valid time points $\mathbf{t}_i \in S_\mathcal{T}$ of a calendar of a type $\mathcal{T}$. For example, let $p(\mathbf{d})$ be an ordinary atom with an n-ary predicate symbol p and a tuple of n constants or variables $\mathbf{d}$. Then $A = r_F(\mathbf{d}, y)$, where r_F is $n+1$-ary predicate symbol obtained from p by enlarging it with a new temporal attribute, is an event's t-atom (temporal atom). When the tuple $\mathbf{d}$ is composed by only constants and y is a time point in $S_\mathcal{T}$, then A is said to be a ground t-atom. If $A_1, \dots, A_k$ are the (simple) t-atoms, then $A_1 \wedge \cdots \wedge A_k$ and $A_1 \vee \cdots \vee A_k$ are called compound t-atoms.

Let L be a language generated for compound events by a given set of constants (Herbrand universe) and temporal predicate symbols. We assume that all variable symbols from L are partitioned into three classes: the *object variables* (contains the regular first-order logic variable symbols: variables in a tuple $\mathbf{d}$ of the example above), the *probabilistic* variables (range over the interval of reals in $[0, 1]$) and *temporal* variables (range over the set of time points $S_\mathcal{T}$ of a given calendar: in the examples, we will use integer numbers for time points): the temporal variable y in t-atoms will be called `principal` variable y and all other temporal variables will be called independent. We define two types of terms: the temporal terms, with constants in $S_\mathcal{T}$ and probabilistic terms with constants in $[0, 1]$.

Definition 113 (Temporal constraint). A temporal constraint $C = c(y, y_1, \dots, y_k)$ with principal t-variable y and other variables $y_1, \dots, y_k$ is defined inductively:
1. let λ be a temporal term with the set of variables $y_1, \dots, y_k$, then $(y \,\mathrm{op}\, \lambda)$, where $\mathrm{op} \in \{\leq, <, =, \neq, >, \geq\}$, is a temporal constraint. The $y : \lambda_1 \sim \lambda_1$ is a short denotation for $y \geq \lambda_1 \wedge y \leq \lambda_1$.
2. if C_1 and C_2 are temporal constraints with the same principal variable y, then $C_1 \wedge C_2$, $C_1 \vee C_2$ and $\neg C_1$ are temporal constraints.

A temporal constraint is called normal if it does not contain variables different from the principal variable.

Let $C = c(y)$ be a normal temporal constraint, the *solution set* of time points of C is equal to $\mathrm{sol}(C) = \{\mathbf{t} \mid \mathbf{t} \in S_\tau \text{ and } c(\mathbf{t}) \text{ is true}\}$, with the cardinality $|\,\mathrm{sol}(C)|$.

Probabilistic weight function

For any given temporal constraint $C = c(y, y_1, \dots, y_k)$, we define the function $\omega_C : S_\tau^{k+1} \to [0,1]$, such that for any tuple of time-points $(\mathbf{t}, \mathbf{t}_1, \dots, \mathbf{t}_k) \in S_\tau^{k+1}$, if $\omega_C(\mathbf{t}, \mathbf{t}_1, \dots, \mathbf{t}_k) \neq 0$ then $\mathbf{t} \in \mathrm{sol}(C)$.

Alternatively, in the case when $|\,\mathrm{sol}(C)| = m$ is a finite number, we will specify the weight function in the form of the time-ordered set of values $\{d_1, \dots, d_m\}$: For example, if $\mathrm{sol}(c(y)) = \{\mathbf{t}_1, \dots, \mathbf{t}_3\}$, a weight function ω_C can be represented as $\{0.4, 1, 0.5\}$, and it will mean that $\omega_C(\mathbf{t}_1) = 0.4, \omega_C(\mathbf{t}_2) = 1, \omega_C(\mathbf{t}_3) = 0.5$. We will denote by $\sharp$ the constant weight function (equal to 1) for the constraints with $|\,\mathrm{sol}(C)| = 1$.

The intuition underlying the above definition is that a probabilistic weight function ω_C, of a given temporal constraint C, assigns a probability $p \geq 0$ to each time point in the solution set of this temporal constraint (for all other time points it must be equal to zero).

Temporal probabilistic annotation

A tp-annotation γ_i is a triple $\langle C, \omega_{C_L}, \omega_{C_U} \rangle$ where C is temporal constraint, ω_{C_L} and ω_{C_U} are probabilistic weight functions for lower and upper boundary, respectively.

Remark. This is a more general definition than in [334], but gives us the possibility to model lower and upper probability boundaries independently.

Definition 114 (Probabilistic temporal program). Let $\psi = A_1 \odot \cdots \odot A_k$ be a compound event t-formula, where $\odot \in \{\wedge, \vee\}$, and $\gamma = \langle C, \omega_{C_L}, \omega_{C_U} \rangle$ be a tp-annotation, then $\psi : \gamma$ is a tp-annotated basic formula.

Let $A : \gamma$ and $\psi_1 : \gamma_1, \dots, \psi_m : \gamma_m$ be tp-annotated basic formulae and A a t-atom. Then

$$A : \gamma \leftarrow \psi_1 : \gamma_1 \wedge \cdots \wedge \psi_m : \gamma_m \quad \text{is a tp-clause.}$$

A PT-program is a finite set of tp-clauses. If P is a PT-program, we let ground(P) denote the set of all ground instances of rules of P. By H_F, we denote the Herbrand base of a program P for a given set of constants for object variables.

As we can see, this syntax is a simile to the syntax for TP-programs presented in [334]. The main difference is that all atoms in our definition of PT-programs are *t-atoms*: thus, we will have that the temporal constraint in tp-basic formulae is an "internal" annotation for the t-atoms (the temporal attribute of any t-atom corresponds to the dependent variable of the temporal constraint), while the probabilistic annotation remains an external (standard) annotation for t-atoms.

We will show that each PT-program PR has the standard probabilistic model theory based on the Herbrand base H_F of PR, with the set of possible worlds (equal to sample space S of the probability space in Definition 27 in Sections 2.2 and 2.2.2) is the set of Herbrand interpretations $\mathcal{W} = \mathbf{2}^{H_F}$, (see diagram (A.3) in the previous section). Each model theory assumes that in the real world each t-atom in H_F is either true or false. In our case, the set of possible worlds (equal to sample space S of the probability space in Definition 27 in Sections 2.2 and 2.2.2) is the set of Herbrand interpretations $\mathcal{W} = \mathbf{2}^{H_F}$, so that for any in any possible world $I_F \in \mathbf{2}^{H_F}$, for any t-predicate symbol r_F and the tuple of constants $\mathbf{d}$ of its object variables, the set of time points $\{\mathbf{t}_i \mid r_F(\mathbf{d}, \mathbf{t}_i) \in H_F \text{ and } I_F(r_F(\mathbf{d}, \mathbf{t}_i)) = 1\}$ corresponds to the temporal uncertainty of this event: in each time point of this set, the event's uncertainty is bounded in a form of a probability interval.

A variable assignment $g \in \mathcal{D}^{\mathcal{V}}$ maps each object variable to an object constant and each temporal variable to the set $S_\tau \subset \mathcal{D}$ of time points of the calendar. The truth of the events, expressed by the formulae $\phi \in \mathcal{L}(P)$, where P is the set of predicate letters, for a valuation $v = I_F \in \mathcal{W}$ under g, denoted by Kripke-like satisfaction $\mathcal{M} \vDash_{v,g} \phi$, is inductively defined for every t-atom $r_F(a_1, \dots, a_k, y)$ and for all formulae ϕ as follows:

1. $\mathcal{M} \vDash_{v,g} r_F(a_1, \dots, a_k, y)$ iff $v(r_F(g(a_1), \dots, g(y))) = 1$,
2. $\mathcal{M} \vDash_{v,g} \phi \wedge \psi$ iff $\mathcal{M} \vDash_{v,g} \phi$ and $\mathcal{M} \vDash_{v,g} \psi$,
3. $\mathcal{M} \vDash_{v,g} \phi \vee \psi$ iff $\mathcal{M} \vDash_{v,g} \phi$ or $\mathcal{M} \vDash_{v,g} \psi$.

An event ϕ is true in a possible world v, or v is a model of ϕ, denoted $\mathcal{M} \vDash_v \phi$, iff $\mathcal{M} \vDash_{v,g} \phi$ for all variable assignments g. In order to be able to apply the results of the standard possible world semantics for PT-programs, we have to show that each PT-program corresponds to *standard probabilistic* program (p-program).

Proposition 47. *Each PT-program is a pure probabilistic logic program.*

Proof. It can be shown by simply unfolding of the temporal constraints in tp-annotated basic formulae, that is, by partial grounding of the temporal attributes of t-atoms in a given PT-program. That is, given a tp-clause, $A : \gamma_0 \leftarrow \bigwedge_{1 \le k \le m} \psi_k : \gamma_k$, with the t-atom $A = r_F(\mathbf{x}, y)$ with a tuple of object variables e/o constants in $\mathbf{x}$ and $\gamma_k = \langle C_k, \omega_{C_{L_k}}, \omega_{C_{U_k}} \rangle$, for $0 \le k \le m$, we can unfold this tp-clause in the following finite set (because the calendar is finite) of p-clauses, for each $\mathbf{t}_i \in \mathrm{sol}(C_0)$:

$$r_F(\mathbf{x}, \mathbf{t}_i) : [\omega_{C_{L_0}}(\mathbf{t}_i), \omega_{C_{U_0}}(\mathbf{t}_i)] \leftarrow \bigwedge_{1 \le k \le m} \Big(\bigwedge_{\mathbf{t}_j \in \mathrm{sol}(C_k)} \Phi_k(\mathbf{t}_j) \Big)$$

where $\Phi_k(\mathbf{t}_j) = \psi_k(\mathbf{t}_j) : [\omega_{C_{L_k}}(\mathbf{t}_j), \omega_{C_{U_k}}(\mathbf{t}_j)]$, and $\psi_k(\mathbf{t}_j)$ is obtained from the ψ_k by substitution of the temporal variable in t-atoms of ψ_k by the constant (time point) $\mathbf{t}_j$.

So, we obtain a p-program where all annotations of basic p-formulae are constant probabilistic intervals. □

Thus, given Herbrand base H_F of a PT-program PR (equal to the Herbrand base of the p-program obtained by the unfolding described above), a world probability density function KI is defined as $\mathrm{KI} : \mathbf{2}^{H_F} \to [0,1]$ (from Kolmogorov axioms in Definition 27 in Section 2.2), so that for all $v \in \mathcal{W} = \mathbf{2}^{H_F}$, $\mathrm{KI}(v) \geq 0$ and $\sum_{v \in \mathcal{W}} \mathrm{KI}(v) = 1$.

A *probabilistic interpretation* (p-interpretation) $I_p : H_F \to [0,1]$ of a PT-program P is defined as follows for the set of possible worlds $\mathcal{W} = \mathbf{2}^{H_F}$:

$$\text{if } \|A/g\| = \{v \in \mathcal{W} \mid \mathcal{M} \models_{v,g} A\} \subseteq \mathcal{W}, \quad \text{then } I_p(A) =_{\text{def}} \sum_{v \in \|A/g\|} \mathrm{KI}(v),$$

for any ground t-atom $A \in H_F$. That is, p-interpretation assigns probabilities to individual ground t-atoms of H_F by adding up the probabilities of all worlds $v \in \mathcal{W}$ in which a given t-atom is true (i. e., $v(A/g) = 1$).

Given a p-interpretation I_p, it can be extended to all compound events in $\mathcal{L}(P)$ by the mapping $I_p^* : \mathcal{L}(P) \to [0,1]$, such that the probability of an event ψ in the probabilistic interpretation I_p^* under a variable assignment g, denoted $I_p^*(\psi/g)$, is the sum of all $\mathrm{KI}(v)$ such that $\mathcal{M} \models_{v,g} \phi$. That is, for $\|\psi/g\| = \{v \in \mathcal{W} \mid \mathcal{M} \models_{v,g} \psi\} \in \mathcal{P}(\mathcal{W})$,

$$I_p^*(\psi/g) =_{\text{def}} \sum_{v \in \|\psi/g\|} \mathrm{KI}(v) \tag{A.4}$$

p-interpretations specify the model-theoretic semantics of p-programs, as follows:

1. $I_p \models_g \psi : [a,b]$ iff $I_p^*(\psi/g) \in [a,b]$, i. e., iff $a \leq I_p^*(\psi) \leq b$;
2. $I_p \models_g (\psi_1 : [a_1,b_1] \wedge \cdots \wedge \psi_n : [a_n,b_n])$ iff $(\forall 1 \leq i \leq n)(I_p \models_g \psi_i : [a_i,b_i])$;
3. $I_p \models_g (A : [a,b] \leftarrow \psi_1 : [a_1,b_1] \wedge \cdots \wedge \psi_n : [a_n,b_n])$ iff $I_p \models_g \psi : [a,b]$ or $I_p \not\models_g (\psi_1 : [a_1,b_1] \wedge \cdots \wedge \psi_n : [a_n,b_n])$.

As we can see, from the point 1 above, the satisfaction of p-programs is based on the interval PSAT for the system of inequalities: any assignment by I_p of point probabilities to the atoms that satisfies these *constraints* is a model of PT-program PR.

Now we are ready to specify the model-theoretic semantics for PT-programs, as follows.

Definition 115 (Satisfaction). Let g be an assignment only for object variables, then for any open formula $\phi \in \mathcal{L}(P)$ with principal t-variable y :

1. $I_p \models_\sigma \psi : y$ iff $(\forall \mathbf{t} \in \mathrm{sol}(C))(I_p \models_\sigma \psi[y/\mathbf{t}] : [\omega_{C_L}(\mathbf{t}), \omega_{C_U}(\mathbf{t})])$,

where $y = \langle C, \omega_{C_L}, \omega_{C_U} \rangle$ and $\psi[y/\mathbf{t}]$ is obtained from ψ by substitution of the temporal variable in t-atoms of ψ by the constant (time-point) $\mathbf{t}$;

2. $I_p \models_g (\psi_1 : y_1 \wedge \cdots \wedge \psi_n : y_n)$ iff $(\forall 1 \leq i \leq n)(I_p \models_g \psi_i : y_i)$;
3. $I_p \models_g (A : \mu \leftarrow \psi_1 : y_1 \wedge \cdots \wedge \psi_n : y_n)$ iff $I_p \models_g A : y$ or $I_p \not\models_g (\psi_1 : y_1 \wedge \cdots \wedge \psi_n : y_n)$.

A tp-clause Cl is true in a probabilistic interpretation I_p (i. e., in its extension I_p^*), or I_p is a model of Cl, denoted $I_p \models$ Cl, iff $I_p \models_g$ Cl for all object variable assignments g. I_p is a model of a PT-program PR if it is a model for all tp-clauses in PR.

Let Mod(PP) denote the set of all models of a PT-program PR; PR is called *consistent* iff Mod(P) $\neq \emptyset$, otherwise PR is called *inconsistent*.

A PT-program PR is *satisfiable* iff a model of PR exists.

A tp-annotated basic formula $\psi : \gamma$ is a *logical consequence* of a PT-program PR, or PR entails $\psi : \gamma$, denoted PR $\models \psi : \gamma$, iff each model of PR is also model of $\psi : \gamma$.

Proposition 48. *The consistency problem for PT-programs is NP-complete, while the entailment problem for PT-programs is co-NP-complete.*

It derives from the reduction of PT-programs into ordinary p-programs, and from the complexity of interval PSAT for linear inequalities (see Theorem 4.11 in [63] and Theorem 3 in [335]).

The examples and the comparison of TP and PT model theories can be found in [16]. TP-programs and PT-programs have the same solution for their models based on the interval PSAT.

A.4.2 Mathematics via symmetry: many-valued knowledge invariance in ontological encapsulation by semantic reflection

In this section, we will use again the mathematical concept of symmetry (categorial symmetry in Section 1.3.2) for the transformation of many-valued into 2-valued logic programs by ontological encapsulation of predicates using *semantic reflection transformation*, analog to that used for predicate (de)compression in Section 2.1. The approach based on the contextualization of many-valued logics with the introduction of higher-order Herbrand interpretation types, provided in Section A.4, introduces explicitly the coexistence of a set of algebraic truth values of original many-valued logic, transformed as parameters (or possible worlds), and the set of classic two logic values. This approach offers the possibility of using the standard semantics based on Herbrand interpretations. Moreover, it uses the properties of the higher-order Herbrand types, as their fundamental nature is based on autoreferential Kripke semantics [69] where the possible worlds are algebraic truth values of original many-valued logic.

This autoreferential Kripke semantics, which has the possibility of flattening higher-order Herbrand interpretations into ordinary 2-valued Herbrand interpretations, gives us a clearer insight into the relationship between many-valued and 2-valued multimodal logics. Following this, we generalize the reduction to general structural many-valued logics, in an abstract way, based on Suszko's informal nonconstructive idea. In all cases, by using developed 2-valued reductions we obtain a kind of nontruth-valued modal metalogic, where two-valued formulae are modal sentences obtained by application of particular modal operators to original many-valued formulae.

In what follows, we will consider a general case of a many-valued logics based on bounded lattice $(X, 0, 1, \leq .\wedge, \vee)$ with antitonic negation "∼" (such that hold De Morgan rules) top value 1 and bottom value 0. The reduction of many-valued logics into the standard 2-valued logic was considered by Suszko [336], where he illustrated how Lukasiewicz's 3-valued logic could be given a 2-valued, nontruth-functional semantics. The main point, according to Suszko, is to make a distinction between the *algebraic truth values* in X of many-valued logics, which were supposed to play a merely referential role, while only two *logical truth values* in $\mathbf{2} = \{0, 1\}$ (0 for false and 1 for true value) would really exist. It is also based on the fact that the abstract logic is based on a *consequence relation* that is bivalent: given a set of logic formulae S, a formula ϕ can be inferred from S or not, i. e., the answer to the question "*if* ϕ *is inferred from* S" can only be "Yes" or "No."

This point of view for "logic values" is also considered correct by other authors, and it is also applied in our case of an ontological encapsulation of many-valued algebraic logic programs into 2-valued logic programs. Moreover, in a 2-valued reduction, for any propositional formula ϕ that has an "algebraic truth-value" α, we can consider a 2-valued meta-sentence "*the truth-value of* ϕ *is* α."

Suszko's thesis for the reduction of every Tarskian (monotonic) n-valued logic into a 2-valued logic is based on this division of a set of logic values into a subset of designated and undesignated elements, but it is quite a nonconstructive result. In fact, he does not explain how he obtained a 2-valued semantics, or how such a procedure could be effectively applied.

In the paper by D.Batens [337], the author proposes a sort of binary print of the algebraic truth values for the 2-valued reduction, where each truth value is to be put into one-to-one correspondence with one element of a set of conveniently long "equivalent" sequences of 0's and 1's. This method is similar to what had been proposed by D. Scott, a decade before [338]. But this method is not universally applicable, and thus cannot be effectively used. Some other authors argued against Suszko's thesis [339] using examples of paraconsistent logic and Malinowski's inferential many-valuedness. But recently in [340], based on Suszko's observations on complementarity of designated and undesignated elements, a method was exhibited for the effective implementation of Suszko's reduction to a subclass of finite-valued truth-functional logics, whose truth values satisfy the particular assumption of separability, where the "algebraic truth values" can be individualized by means of the linguistic resources of the logic. What is important for the present work is that they show that a reduction of truth-functional many-valued logic into 2-valued logic will simply make it lose truth-functionality: in fact, my transformation will result in *modal* logics.

Consequently, the main contribution of this section is to use *a constructive* approach to Suszko's method, and to exhibit a method for the effective implementation of

2-valued reduction *for all kinds* of many-valued logics. It avoids the necessity of dividing (in problematic way based on subjective opinions) a set of algebraic truth values into designated and undesignated disjoint subsets in order to define the satisfaction relation (i. e., entailment), by using the valuations (model-theoretic semantics): the entailment $S \models \phi$ means that every model (valuation) of S is a model of ϕ.

Let us consider an epistemic logic program P_G composed by a set of predicate and function symbols, P, F, respectively, with the Herbrand base H, composed the set of all ground atoms over the Herbrand universe $\Gamma_U = \mathcal{D} \bigcup \Omega$, where $\mathcal{D}$ is ordinary domain and Ω is an infinite enumerable set of marked null values (Skolem constants), $\Omega = \{\omega_0, \omega_1, \ldots\}$. We denote the set of all terms by $\mathcal{T}_S$, and its subset of ground terms by $\mathcal{T}_0$.

For example, any rule in a many-valued logic program $A \leftarrow B_1, \ldots, B_n$ is *satisfied* if, for a given valuation v, the algebraic truth value of the head is greater than the value of the body, i. e., if $v(A) \geq v^*(B_1 \wedge \cdots \wedge B_n)$ for a given Herbrand interpretation $v : H \to X$. More discussion about this approach can be found in in Sections 5.1 and 5.1.1.

Example 55. Let us consider the example $X = \mathcal{B}_4$ of Belnap's 4-valued epistemic logic program P_G. The truth and knowledge ordering relations and operations in a bilattice $\mathcal{B}_4$ propagates to the function space $\mathcal{B}_4^H$ of all Herbrand interpretations $v : H \to \mathcal{B}_4$. This makes a function space $\mathcal{B}_4^H$ itself a complete infinitary distributive bilattice [319].

One of the key insights behind bilattices [188, 197] was the interplay between the truth values assigned to sentences and the (nonclassic) notion of *implication*. The problem was to study how truth values should be propagated "across" implications. In [341] is proposed the following IB based approach to the "object" 4-valued logic programming, which extends the definition given for a 3-valued logic programming [312]: Let P_B be the subset of built-in predicates. The valuation, $v : H \to \mathcal{B}_4$, is extended to logic implication of a ground clause $p(\mathbf{c}) \leftarrow \phi$, where $\phi = B_1 \wedge \cdots \wedge B_n$, with $B_i \in H$, for $1 \leq i \leq n$, by

$$v^*(\phi \to p_j^n(\mathbf{c})) = t \quad \text{iff} \quad v(p_j^n(\mathbf{c})) \geq_t v^*(\phi) \quad \text{or} \quad (p_j^n \in P_B \text{ and } v(\phi) = \top).$$

We assumed the *inconsistency acceptance* principle: if $p_j^n \in P_B$ is a built-in predicate, this clause is satisfied also when $v(p_j^n(\mathbf{c})) = f$ and $v^*(\phi) = \top$.

The *built-in predicates* (ex, $=, \leq, \geq, \ldots$) may be used for integrity constraints: let $p(x, y)$ be a predicate and we define the key-constraint for attributes in x by $(y = z) \leftarrow p(x, y), p(x, z)$, where the atom $y = z$ is based on the built-in predicate $' ='$. Let consider a program : $p(x, y) \leftarrow r(x, y)$, $(y = z) \leftarrow p(x, y), p(x, z)$ where r is a source database relation with two tuples, $(a, b), (a, c)$, p is a virtual relation of this database with key constraint, and x, y, z are variables. The built-in predicates have the same prefixed extension in *each* model of a logic program, and their ground atoms are *true or false*. If we assume that $r(a, b), r(a, c)$ are true, then such facts are mutually inconsistent for p because of key constraint ($b = c$ is false). Thus, only one of them may be true in any model of this logic program, e. g., $r(a, b)$. So, if we assign the "possible" value $\top$ to $r(a, c)$ (or to both of them), we obtain that the clause $(b = c) \leftarrow p(a, b), p(a, c)$, thanks to the *inconsistency acceptance*, is satisfied.

The many-valued definition for implication, which generalize the 2-valued definition of clause satisfaction for Lukasiewicz's and Kleene's strong 3-valued matrices [218], $f_{\leftarrow} : \mathcal{B}_4 \times \mathcal{B}_4 \to \mathcal{B}_4$, can be defined (with $\alpha = t$ and $\alpha = \bot$ for Lukasiewicz's and Kleene's case, respectively) by

$\to$	t	$\bot$	$\top$	f
t	t	$\bot$	$\top$	f
$\bot$	t	α	$\top$	$\bot$
$\top$	t	t	t	t
f	t	t	t	t

For our purposes, we assume the Lukasiewicz's extension, i. e., $\alpha = t$, in order to have a tautology $a \leftarrow a$ for any formula a, and also to guarantee the truth of a clause (implication) $p(\mathbf{c}) \leftarrow \phi$, whenever $v(p(\mathbf{c})) \geq_t v^*(\phi)$, as used in fix-point semantics for "immediate consequence operators." Such conservative extensions are based on the following observation: the problem to study how the truth values should be propagated "across" implications can be restricted only to *true* implications (in fact we do not use implications when they are not true, because the "immediate consequence operator" derives new facts only for *true* clauses, i. e., when the implication used in the clauses is true).

I considered [204] two approaches for *predicate* many-valued logics (the propositional version can be considered as a special case, when all predicate symbols have a zero arity): the first one introduces the *unary* modal operator for each truth value of original many-valued logic; the second approach introduces the *binary* modal operator for each binary truth-valued logic operator (conjunction, disjunction, implication) of original many-valued logic. Both of them transform an original truth-functional many-valued logic into *nontruth-functional* 2-valued modal logic, and here we will consider only the second one, based on the ontological embedding into the syntax of new 2-valued encapsulated many-valued logic.

The "object" many-valued logic is based on the lattice X of truth values, which are *epistemic*. Sentences are to be marked with some of these lattice logic values, according as to what the computer has been told; or, with only a slight metaphor, according to what it *believes or knows*. Of course, these sentences *have* also Frege's ontological truth values (true and false), independently of what the computer has been told: we want that the computer can use also these ontological "meta" knowledge. Let, e. g., the computer believes that the sentence ϕ has a value $a \in X$; then the "meta" sentence,"*I (computer) believe that ϕ has a value* "*a*" is *ontologically true*. The many-valued encapsulation is just the way to pass from the epistemic ("object") many-valued logic into ontological ("meta") 2-valued logic.

It can be seen as a flattening of a many-valued logic, where an algebraic truth value $\beta \in X$ of an original ground atom $p_j^k(c_1,\dots,c_k)$ is deposited into the logic attribute of a new predicate r_F, obtained by an extension of the old predicate p_j^k, so that we obtain the "flattened" 2-valued ground atom $r_F(c_1,\dots,c_k,\beta)$. In that case, we will obtain the positive multimodal logic programs with binary modal operators for conjunction, disjunction and implication and unary modal operator for negation.

The flattening of an original many-valued lattice-based program into a modal metalogic is a kind of *ontological-encapsulation*, where the encapsulation of an original many-valued logic program into the 2-valued modal metalogic program corresponds to a flattening process described in Definition 112. This approach is developed in a number of papers, and more information can be found in [83, 203, 218, 342]. Here, we will present a slightly modified version. Such an encapsulation is characterized by having capability for *semantic reflection*: intuitively, for each predicate symbol we need some function, which *reflects* its logic semantic over a domain Γ_U. We introduce also the set of functional symbols κ_p over a domain Γ_U in our logical language in order to obtain an enriched logical language [218] where we can encapsulate the "object" (ordinary) many-valued logic programming. Such set of functional symbols will be derived from the lattice-semantic mapping $\mathcal{K}$. We will also introduce a new symbol $\mathbf{e}$ (for "error condition"), necessary in order to render *complete* the functions for a generalized interpretation and a semantic reflection.

Definition 116. Let P_G be a many-valued logic program with a set of predicate and functional symbols P and F, respectively, with a Herbrand model $v : H \to X$ where H is a Herbrand base, with a set $\mathcal{T}_0$ of all ground terms and a set $\mathcal{T} = \bigcup_{k\in\mathcal{N}} \mathcal{T}_0^k$ with $\mathcal{N} = \{1,2,\dots,n\}$ where n is the maximal arity of symbols in $P\bigcup F$.

1. A *generalized interpretation* is a mapping $\mathcal{I} : P \times \mathcal{T} \to X\bigcup\{\mathbf{e}\}$, such that for any $\mathbf{c} = (c_1,\dots,c_n) \in \mathcal{T}$, $\mathcal{I}(p,\mathbf{c}) = v(p(\mathbf{c}))$ if $\mathrm{ar}(p) = n$; $\mathbf{e}$ otherwise.
2. A *semantic reflection* is defined by a mapping $\mathcal{K} = \Lambda(\mathcal{I}) : P \to (X\bigcup\{\mathbf{e}\})^{\mathcal{T}}$, where Λ is the currying operator from lambda calculus used in diagram A.10 in Section A.5.

For each $p \in P$ that is not a built-in 2-valued predicate, we define a new functional symbol κ_p for a mapping $\mathcal{K}(p) : \mathcal{T} \to X\bigcup\{\mathbf{e}\}$.

3. If p is a 2-valued built-in predicate, then the mapping κ_p is defined uniquely and independently of v, by: for any $\mathbf{c} \in \mathcal{T}_0^{\mathrm{ar}(p)}$, $\kappa_p(\mathbf{c}) = 1$ if $p(\mathbf{c})$ is true; 0 otherwise.

We recall the well-known fact that 2-valued *built-in* predicates (as $\leq$, $=$, etc.) have constant extensions in any Herbrand interpretation (they preserve *the same meaning* for any logic interpretation, different from ordinary predicates).

A semantic reflection $\mathcal{K}$, obtained from a generalized interpretation $\mathcal{I}$, introduces a function symbol $\kappa_p = \mathcal{K}(p)$ for each predicate $p \in P$ of the original logic program P_G, such that for any $\mathbf{c} = (c_1,\dots,c_n) \in \mathcal{T}$, it holds that $\kappa_p(\mathbf{c}) = v(p(\mathbf{c}))$ if $\mathrm{ar}(p) = n$; $\{\mathbf{e}\}$ otherwise. These new function symbols will be used in a new metalogic language, used to transform each original many-valued atom p in P into a new atom p_F obtained as an extension of the original atom p by one "logic" attribute with the domain of values in X. The interpretation of κ_p in this new metalogic program has to reflect the meaning of the original many-valued predicate p in the original many-valued logic program P_G.

Consequently, we are able to introduce a program encapsulation (flattening) transformation $\mathcal{E}$. The many-valued ground atoms of a many-valued logical language $\mathcal{L}_{\mathrm{mv}}$ can be transformed in "encapsulated" atoms of a 2-valued logic in the following simple way [218]: the original (many-valued) fact that the ground atom $A = p_j^n(c_1, \dots, c_n)$, of the n-ary predicate $p_j^n \in P$, has an epistemic value $\alpha = \kappa_p(c_1, \dots, c_n)$ in $\mathcal{B}_4$, we transform in encapsulated atom $p_F(c_1, \dots, c_n, \alpha)$ with meaning "*A has a value* α." Indeed, what we do is to *replace* the original n-ary predicate $p_j^n(x_1, \dots, x_n)$ with $n+1$-ary predicate $p_F(x_1, \dots, x_n, \alpha)$ (flattening), with the added logic-attribute α. It is easy to verify that for any given many-valued valuation $v \in X^H$, each ground atom $p_F(c_1, \dots, c_n, \alpha)$ is ontologically true (when $\alpha = v(p_j^n(c_1, \dots, c_n))$) or false. Let EMV denote this new 2-valued encapsulation of many-valued logic *for logic programming*.

Syntax

We distinguish between what the reasoner believes in (at the *object* (epistemic many-valued sublanguage) level), and what is actually true or false in the real world (at the EMV ontological "meta" level); thus, roughly, the "meta" level is an (classic) encapsulation of the object-level.

Definition 117. Let P_G be an "object" many-valued logic program with the set of predicate symbols P. The translation in the syntax of encapsulated program P_F is as follows:

1. Each positive literal $p_j^n \in P$, $\mathcal{E}(p_j^n(x_1, \dots, x_n)) = p_F(x_1, \dots, x_n, \kappa_p(x_1, \dots, x_n))$;

Each negative literal in P, $\mathcal{E}(\sim p_j^n(x_1, \dots, x_n)) = p_F(x_1, \dots, x_n, \sim \kappa_p(x_1, \dots, x_n))$;and we denote by P_E the set of new obtained predicates p_F.

2. $\mathcal{E}(\sim \phi) =\sim_F \mathcal{E}(\phi)$;
3. $\mathcal{E}(\phi \odot \varphi) = \mathcal{E}(\phi) \odot_F \mathcal{E}(\varphi)$; for $\odot \in \{\wedge, \vee, \leftarrow\}$,

where $\sim_F, \wedge_F, \vee_F$ and $\leftarrow_F$ are new syntax symbols for the negation, conjunction, disjunction and implication at the encapsulated 2-valued "meta" level.

Thus, the obtained "meta" program is equal to $P_F = \{\mathcal{E}(\phi) \mid \phi \text{ is a clause in } P_G\}$, with the 2-valued Herbrand base $H_F = \{p_F(c_1, \dots, c_n, \alpha) \mid p_j^n(c_1, \dots, c_n) \in H \text{ and } \alpha \in X\}$.

We denote by $\mathcal{L}_F$ the set of formulae obtained from the set of predicate letters in P_E and new operators $\sim_F, \wedge_F, \vee_F$ and $\leftarrow_F$.

This embedding of the many-valued "object" logic program P_G into a 2-valued "meta" logic program P_F is an *ontological* embedding [218]: we consider the formulae of P_G as beliefs and interpret negation $\sim p_j^n(x_1, \dots, x_n)$ in rather restricted sense—as belief in the falsehood of $p_j^n(x_1, \dots, x_n)$, rather as not believing that $p_j^n(x_1, \dots, x_n)$ is true (like in an ontological embedding for classical negation), as in Moore's autoepistemic operator, for the encapsulation modal operator $\mathcal{E}$, $\mathcal{E}\phi$ is intended to capture the notion of, *"I know that ϕ has a value $v(\phi)$,"* for a given valuation v of the "object" logic program.

Let $\mathcal{L}_{\text{mv}}^G$ be the set of all sentences defined by this Herbrand base H and lattice operations (included many-valued implication $\leftarrow$ also), with $X \subseteq \mathcal{L}_{\text{mv}}^G$. So, we have the following.

Corollary 30. *The encapsulation operator $\mathcal{E}$ is:*
1. *Modal operator, such that, for any $\alpha \in X$, $\mathcal{E}(\alpha) = t$ if $\alpha = t$; f otherwise.*
2. *Homomorphism between the "object" algebra $(\mathcal{L}_{\text{mv}}, \wedge, \vee, \leftarrow)$ with carrier set of (positive and negative) literals, and "meta" algebra $(\mathcal{L}_F, \wedge_F, \vee_F, \leftarrow_F)$, where $\wedge_F, \vee_F$ and $\leftarrow_F$ are 2-valued operators corresponding to lattice's meet and join, respectively (denoted by $\wedge, \vee$ as well).*

Semantics

With the transformation of the original "object" logic program P_G into its annotated "meta" version program P_F we obtain *always positive* consistent logic program.

A Herbrand interpretation of P_F is a 2-valued mapping $I_F : H_F \to \mathbf{2}$. We denote by $\mathbf{2}^{H_F}$ the set of all interpretations from H_F into $\mathbf{2}$, and by X^H the set of all Herbrand many-valued interpretations, from H to the lattice X. The meaning of the *encapsulation* of this "object" logic program P_G into this "meta" logic program P_F is fixed into the kind of interpretation to give to such new introduced functional symbols $\kappa_p = \mathcal{K}(p)$: in fact, *we want* [341] that they reflect the semantics of the "object" level logic program P_G.

Definition 118 (Satisfaction). The encapsulation of an epistemic "object" logic program P_G into the "meta" program P_F means that, for any many-valued Herbrand interpretation $v \in X^H$, the function $\kappa_p = \mathcal{K}(p), p \in P$ reflects this semantics, i. e., for any tuple $\mathbf{c} \in \mathcal{T}_0^{\text{arity}(p)}$,

$$\kappa_p(\mathbf{c}) = v(p(\mathbf{c})).$$

So, we obtain a mapping, $\Theta : X^H \to \mathbf{2}^{H_F}$, such that $I_F = \Theta(v) \in \mathbf{2}^{H_F}$ with: for any ground atom $p(\mathbf{c})$, $I_F(\mathcal{E}(p(\mathbf{c}))) = t$, if $\kappa_p(\mathbf{c}) = v(p(\mathbf{c}))$; f otherwise.

Let $g : \mathcal{V} \to \Gamma_U$ be an assignment to variables in $\mathcal{V}$ such that $g(\mathcal{E}(p_j^n(x_1, \dots, x_n))) = \mathcal{E}(p_j^n(g(x_1), \dots, g(x_n)))$, and
1. $I_F \vDash_g \mathcal{E}(p_j^n(x_1, \dots, x_n))$ iff $\kappa_p((g(x_1), \dots, g(x_n))) = v(p_j^n(g(x_1), \dots, g(x_n)))$.
2. $I_F \vDash_g \mathcal{E}(\sim p_j^n(x_1, \dots, x_n))$ iff $\kappa_p((g(x_1), \dots, g(x_n))) =\sim v(p_j^n(g(x_1), \dots, g(x_n)))$.

Notice that in this semantics the "meta" implication used in logic program clauses $\leftarrow_F$ between two sentences ϕ and ψ, in $\mathcal{E}(\phi) \leftarrow_F \mathcal{E}(\psi) = \mathcal{E}(\phi \leftarrow \psi)$, is based on the "object" epistemic many-valued implication $\leftarrow$ (which *is not classical*, i. e., $\phi \leftarrow \psi \neq \phi \vee \sim \psi$) and determines how the logical value of a body of clause "propagates" to its head. That is, $\mathcal{E}(\phi) \leftarrow_F \mathcal{E}(\psi)$ is true if $v(\phi/g \leftarrow \psi/g)$ is true. So, the semantics of the logic operators in this "meta" (encapsuled) level are modal operators.

Corollary 31. *The semantics of encapsulation $\mathcal{E}$ is obtained by identifying the semantic reflection with the λ-abstraction of generalized Herbrand interpretation, $\mathcal{K} = \Lambda(\mathcal{I})$, so that the semantics of many-valued logic programs can be determined by $\mathcal{I}$ (at "object" level) or, equivalently, by its reflection $\mathcal{K}$ (at encapsulated or "meta" level).*

Proof. From $\mathcal{K} = \Lambda(\mathcal{I})$, where Λ is the currying operator from lambda calculus used in diagram A.10 in Section A.5, we obtain that for any $p(\mathbf{c}) \in H$ holds $v(p(\mathbf{c})) = \mathcal{I}(p, \mathbf{c}) = \Lambda(\mathcal{I})(p)(\mathbf{c}) = \mathcal{K}(p)(\mathbf{c}) = \kappa_p(\mathbf{c})$, which is the semantic of encapsulation. □

We can consider the λ-abstraction of generalized Herbrand interpretation as an epistemic semantics, because given a Herbrand many-valued (epistemic) interpretation $v : H \to X$, for any predicate p and constant $\mathbf{c} \in \mathcal{T}_0^{\mathrm{arity}(p)}$, it holds that $\Lambda(\mathcal{I})(p)(\mathbf{c}) = v(p(\mathbf{c}))$. So, the semantic of encapsulation may be expressed by the following knowledge invariance:

"ontological semantic reflection $\equiv$ epistemic semantics," i. e., $\mathcal{K} = \Lambda(\mathcal{I})$.

These semantics have been used to provide coalgebraic semantics for logic programs [144].

Remark. The new introduced logic symbols $\sim_F, \wedge_F, \vee_F$ and $\leftarrow_F$ for the metalogic connectives are not truth-functional as are original many-valued operators but modal. Hence, by this transformation of P_R we obtain a modal logic program P_F that is a *positive* logic program (without negation). Different from a sentence $\phi \in \mathcal{L}_{\mathrm{mv}}^G$, the transformed meta-formula $\Phi = \mathcal{E}(\phi) \in \mathcal{L}_F$ can be only *true or false* in a given possible world $w \in \mathcal{W} = X$ for this metamodal logic (in a given Kripke model $\mathcal{M}$ of obtained metalogic program P_F).

In this definition of a metalogic program P_F, the set of mappings $\{\kappa_p = \mathcal{K}(p) \mid p \in P\}$ is considered as a set of *built-in functions*, determined by a given semantic reflection $\mathcal{K}$, that extends a given set of functional symbols in F. □

The encapsulation operator $\mathcal{E}$ is intended to have the following property for a valuation $v^* : \mathcal{L}_{\mathrm{mv}}^G \to X$ (a homomorphic extension of Herbrand interpretation v to all formulae in $\mathcal{L}_{\mathrm{mv}}^G$) of a many-valued logic program P_G: for any sentence ϕ, the encapsulated metaformula $\mathcal{E}(\phi)$ intends to capture the notion of ϕ with its value $v(\phi)$ as well, in the way that

"*$\mathcal{E}(\phi)$ is true exactly in the possible world $w = v^*(\phi) \in \mathcal{W} = X$.*"

In order to introduce a concept of *absolute truth or falsity* (not relative to a single possible world in $\mathcal{W} = X$) for the sentences in $\mathcal{L}_F$, we need a new autoepistemic modal operator $\Diamond$. Consequently, for any given sentence $\Phi \in \mathcal{L}_F$, similar to Moore's autoepistemic operator, a formula $\Diamond\Phi$ is able to capture the 2-valued notion of

"*Φ is a semantic reflection of a many-valued logic program model v.*"

Notice that in this encapsulation, e. g., the metaimplication $\leftarrow_F$ derived from the many-valued implication, $\mathcal{E}(\phi) \leftarrow_F \mathcal{E}(\psi) = \mathcal{E}(\phi \leftarrow \psi)$, specifies how, for a given clause in P_G, a logic value of the body "propagates" to the head of this clause. It is not functionally dependent on the truth values of its arguments, thus it must be a binary *modal* operator. The idea to use ternary relations to model binary modal operators comes from relevance logic [226, 230, 236, 343]. So, based on the autoreferential semantics in Definition 58 in Section 5.1, we can define the following Kripke models.

Definition 119. Let P_G be a many-valued logic program with a set of predicate symbols P, a many-valued Herbrand model $v : H \to X$ and its semantic reflection $\mathcal{K}$.

Then the model of the flattened program P_F in Definition 117 is defined as the Kripke-style model $\mathcal{M} = (\mathcal{W}, \{\mathcal{R}_\sim, \mathcal{R}_\wedge, \mathcal{R}_\vee, \mathcal{R}_\rightarrow, \mathcal{R}_\times = \mathcal{W} \times \mathcal{W}\}, \mathcal{D}, I_K)$ with $\mathcal{W} = X$, where

$$\mathcal{R}_\wedge = \{(x \wedge y, x, y) \mid x, y \in \mathcal{W}\}, \quad \mathcal{R}_\vee = \{(x \vee y, x, y) \mid x, y \in \mathcal{W}\},$$
$$\mathcal{R}_\rightarrow = \{(x \rightarrow y, x, y) \mid x, y \in \mathcal{W} \text{ and } x \leq y\}, \quad \mathcal{R}_\sim = \{(\sim x, x) \mid x \in \mathcal{W}\},$$

and $I_K : \mathcal{W} \times P_E \to \bigcup_{n \in \mathcal{N}} \mathbf{2}^{\mathcal{D}^n \times \mathcal{W}}$ (from Definition 3), such that for any $p_j^n \in P$ with arity n (i. e., $p_F \in P_F$ with arity $n+1$), a tuple of constants $(c_1, \ldots, c_n) \in \mathcal{D}^n$ and a world $w \in \mathcal{W}$, $I_K(w, p_F)(c_1, \ldots, c_n, \alpha) = 1$ iff $w = \alpha = \kappa_p(c_1, \ldots, c_n)$, such that, for any formula $\Phi, \Psi \in \mathcal{L}_F$, the satisfaction relation $\vDash_{w,g}$, for a given assignment g and a world $w \in \mathcal{W}$, is defined as follows:
1. $\mathcal{M} \vDash_{w,g} p_F(x_1, \ldots x_n, \alpha)$ iff $I_K(w, p_F)(g(x_1), \ldots, g(x_n), \alpha) = 1$.
2. $\mathcal{M} \vDash_{w,g} \sim_F \Phi$ iff $\exists y((w, y) \in \mathcal{R}_\sim$ and $\mathcal{M} \vDash_{y,g} \Phi)$.
3. $\mathcal{M} \vDash_{w,g} \wedge_F(\Phi, \Psi)$ iff $\exists y, z((w, y, z) \in \mathcal{R}_\wedge$ and $\mathcal{M} \vDash_{z,g} \Phi$ and $\mathcal{M} \vDash_{y,g} \Psi)$.
4. $\mathcal{M} \vDash_{w,g} \vee_F(\Phi, \Psi)$ iff $\exists y, z((w, y, z) \in \mathcal{R}_\vee$ and $\mathcal{M} \vDash_{z,g} \Phi$ and $\mathcal{M} \vDash_{y,g} \Psi)$.
5. $\mathcal{M} \vDash_{w,g} \leftarrow_F (\Phi, \Psi)$ iff $\exists y, z((w, y, z) \in \mathcal{R}_\rightarrow$ and $\mathcal{M} \vDash_{z,g} \Phi$ and $\mathcal{M} \vDash_{y,g} \Psi)$.
6. $\mathcal{M} \vDash_{w,g} \Diamond\Phi$ iff $\exists y((w, y) \in \mathcal{R}_\times$ and $\mathcal{M} \vDash_{y,g} \Phi)$.

The binary operators $\wedge_F, \vee_F$ and $\leftarrow_F$ for this multimodal logic are the existential modal operators w. r. t. the ternary relation $\mathcal{R}_\wedge, \mathcal{R}_\vee$ and $\mathcal{R}_\rightarrow$, respectively, while $\sim_F$ and $\Diamond$ are the existential unary modal operator w. r. t. the binary relation $\mathcal{R}_\sim$ and $\mathcal{R}_\times$, respectively.

Proposition 49. *For any assignment g and a formula $\Phi \in \mathcal{L}_F$, we have that $\|\Diamond\Phi/g\| \in \{\emptyset, \mathcal{W}\}$, where $\emptyset$ is the empty set and $\mathcal{W} = X$ is the set of truth values. That is, for any* *many-valued formula $\phi \in \mathcal{L}_{mv}$ the formula $\Diamond\mathcal{E}(\phi/g)$ is true in the Kripke-style relational model $\mathcal{M}$ given by Definition 119, so that a Kripke-style model $\mathcal{M}$ of P_F corresponds to the many-valued algebraic model v of the original program P_G.*

Proof. In what follows, we denote by v^* the (homomorphic) extension of a Herbrand model v to all sentences. Let us demonstrate that for any $\phi \in \mathcal{L}$, i. e., $\mathcal{E}(\phi) \in \mathcal{L}_F$, holds that $\mathcal{M} \vDash_{w,g} \mathcal{E}(\phi)$ iff $w = v^*(\phi/g)$.

1. For any atomic formula $p(x_1, \ldots, x_n)$, we have that $\mathcal{M} \vDash_{w,g} \mathcal{E}(p(x_1, \ldots, x_n))$ iff $V(w, p_F)(g(x_1), \ldots, g(x_n), \kappa_p(g(x_1), \ldots, g(x_n))) = 1$ iff $w = \kappa_p(g(x_1), \ldots, g(x_n)) = \Lambda(\mathcal{I})(p)(g(x_1), \ldots, g(x_n)) = v(p(g(x_1), \ldots, g(x_n))) = v(p(x_1, \ldots, x_n)/g)$. Vice versa, if $w = v(p(x_1, \ldots, x_n)/g)$, i. e., $w = v(p(x_1, \ldots, x_n)/g) = \kappa_p(g(x_1), \ldots, g(x_n))$, then $V(w, p_F)(g(x_1), \ldots, g(x_n), \kappa_p(g(x_1), \ldots, g(x_n))) = 1$, and consequently, from point 1 of definition above, $\mathcal{M} \vDash_{w,g} \mathcal{E}(p(x_1, \ldots, x_n))$.

Suppose, by the inductive hypothesis that $\mathcal{M} \vDash_{z,g} \mathcal{E}(\phi)$ iff $z = v^*(\phi/g)$, and $\mathcal{M} \vDash_{y,g} \mathcal{E}(\psi)$ iff $y = v^*(\psi/g)$, then:

2. For any formula $\varphi =\sim \phi$, we have that $\mathcal{M} \vDash_{w,g} \mathcal{E}(\varphi)$ iff $\mathcal{M} \vDash_{w,g} \mathcal{E}(\sim \phi)$ iff $\mathcal{M} \vDash_{w,g} \sim_F \mathcal{E}(\phi)$ iff $(\exists z((w,z) \in \mathcal{R}_\sim$ and $\mathcal{M} \vDash_{z,g} \mathcal{E}(\phi)))$, i. e., if $w =\sim z$ (from the definition of accessibility relation $\mathcal{R}_\sim$)$=\sim v^*(\phi/g) = v^*(\sim \phi/g)$ (from a homomorphic property of v^*)$= v^*(\varphi/g)$. Vice versa, if $w = v^*(\varphi/g) = v^*(\sim \phi)/g =\sim v^*(\phi/g) =\sim z$ then, from the inductive hypothesis, $\mathcal{M} \vDash_{w,g} \sim_F \mathcal{E}(\phi)$, i. e., $\mathcal{M} \vDash_{w,g} \mathcal{E}(\varphi)$.
3. For any formula $\varphi = \phi \odot \psi$, where $\odot \in \{\wedge, \vee, \rightarrow\}$, we have that $\mathcal{M} \vDash_{w,g} \mathcal{E}(\varphi)$ iff $\mathcal{M} \vDash_{w,g} \mathcal{E}(\phi \odot \psi)$ iff $\mathcal{M} \vDash_{w,g} \mathcal{E}(\phi) \odot_F \mathcal{E}(\psi)$ iff $(\exists y, z((w, y, z) \in \mathcal{R}_\odot$ and $\mathcal{M} \vDash_{z,g} \mathcal{E}(\phi)$ and $\mathcal{M} \vDash_{y,g} \mathcal{E}(\psi)))$, i. e., if $w = z \odot y$ (from a definition of relation $\mathcal{R}_\odot$)$= v^*(\phi/g) \odot v^*(\psi/g) = v^*(\phi/g \odot \psi/g)$ (from a homomorphic property of v^*)$= v^*((\phi \odot \psi)/g) = v^*(\varphi/g)$. Vice versa, if $w = v^*(\varphi/g) = v^*(\phi \odot \psi)/g = v^*(\phi/g) \odot v^*(\psi/g) = z \odot y$ then, from the inductive hypothesis, $\mathcal{M} \vDash_{w,g} \mathcal{E}(\phi) \wedge_F \mathcal{E}(\psi)$, i. e., $\mathcal{M} \vDash_{w,g} \mathcal{E}(\varphi)$.

Thus, for any $\Phi \in \mathcal{L}_F$ we have that $\|\Phi/g\| = \{w\}$ for some $w \in \mathcal{W}$, if $\Phi/g = \mathcal{E}(\phi/g)$; otherwise $\|\Phi/g\| = \emptyset$. Consequently, we have that $\|\Diamond\Phi/g\| = \{w \mid \exists y((w, y) \in \mathcal{R}_\times$ and $\mathcal{M} \vDash_{y,g} \Phi)\} = \mathcal{W}$ if $\Phi/g = \mathcal{E}(\phi/g)$; otherwise $\|\Diamond\Phi/g\| = \emptyset$. That is, each sentence $\Diamond\Phi/g$ for any $\Phi \in \mathcal{L}_F$ is a *2-valued formula*.

From Definition 119, we have seen how a many-valued model v of a logic program P_G uniquely determines a Kripke model $\mathcal{M}$ of its metalogic modal program P_F. Let us now show the opposite direction, i. e., how a Kripke model $\mathcal{M}$ of a modal logic program P_F obtained by ontological encapsulation of the original many-valued logic program P_G, determines uniquely a many-valued model v of the logic program P_G. In fact, we define uniquely the mapping $v : H \rightarrow X$, as follows: for any modal atomic formula $\Diamond p_F(c_1, \ldots, c_n, \alpha)$, *true* in the Kripke model $\mathcal{M}$, we set $v(p(c_1, \ldots, c_n)) = \alpha$. It is easy to verify that such a definition of $v : H \rightarrow X$ is a Herbrand model of a many-valued logic program P_G. □

This transformation of multivalued logic programs into 2-valued multimodal logic programs can be briefly explained as follows: we transform the original multivalued atoms into the meta 2-valued atoms by enlarging the original atoms with a new logic attribute with the domain of truth values in X. This ontological encapsulation also eliminates the negation (in this case the negation $\sim$) by introducing a unary modal operator $\sim_F$. The remained binary multivalued lattice operations are substituted by the 2-valued binary modal operators with ternary accessibility relations.

Remark. In addition, this ontological encapsulation of logic programs into the *positive* (without the negation) modal programs can be used, with some opportune modifications of the definitions above where a ground atom $p_F(c_1, \dots c_n, \alpha) \in H_F$ is true only for exactly one value $\alpha \in X$, to deal with the *inconsistency* of 2-valued logic programs: the resulting positive modal program is a *paraconsistent* logic program, i. e., for any given ground atom $p(c_1, \dots c_n)$ of the original 2-valued logic program that is inconsistent (both true and false), in the transformed *consistent* positive modal program we can (consistently) have two true ground atoms, $p_F(c_1, \dots c_n, 1)$ and $p_F(c_1, \dots c_n, 0)$.

A.4.3 Binary sequent calculi for finite many-valued predicate logics

A short introduction to binary sequent calculus is provided in Section A.2. We are able to reduce [204] the multivalued predicate logic $\mathcal{L}_{mv}$, with finite set of logic *values* $a_j \in X$, to the multimodal 2-valued algebraic logic language $\mathcal{L}_M^*$, by introducing the *finite* number of modal nonstandard (nonmonotonic) algebraic truth-functional operators $[a_i] : Y \to \mathbf{2}$, where $Y = X \bigcup \mathbf{2}$ such that for any $a_i, a_j \in Y$, $[a_i](a_j) = 1$ if $a_i = a_j$; 0 otherwise.

Definition 120 (Syntax). Let $\mathcal{L}_{mv}$ be a predicate many-valued logic language with Herbrand base H, the set of valuations $\mathbb{V} = X^H$, such that each $v \in \mathbb{V}$. v^* is homomorphically extended to all sentences $\mathcal{L}_{mv}^G \subset \mathcal{L}_{mv}$, a finite set of truth values X (of a many-valued logic with a set of logic operators in Σ) and the complete distributive two-valued lattice $(\mathbf{2}, \wedge, \vee)$. The multimodal 2-valued logic language $\mathcal{L}_M^*$ is the set of all modal formulae (we will use letters Φ, Ψ for the formulae of $\mathcal{L}_M^*$) defined as follows:
1. $\mathbf{2} \subseteq \mathcal{L}_M^*$.
2. $[a_i]\phi \in \mathcal{L}_M^*$, for any $a_i \in X, \phi \in \mathcal{L}_{mv}$.
3. $[a_i]\Phi \in \mathcal{L}_M^*$, for any $a_i \in \mathbf{2}, \Phi \in \mathcal{L}_M^*$.
4. $\Phi, \Psi \in \mathcal{L}_M^*$ implies $\Phi \wedge \Psi, \Phi \vee \Psi \in \mathcal{L}_M^*$.

We denote the sublanguage of $\mathcal{L}_M^*$ without free variables by $\mathcal{L}_M$ (the ground atoms in $\mathcal{L}_M$ are considered as propositional letters).

The constants $0, 1 \in \mathbf{2}$ correspond to the tautology and contradiction proposition, respectively, and they can be considered as nullary operators in $\mathcal{L}_M$. We can use this

2-valued multimodal logic language $\mathcal{L}_M$ in order to define the sequents as elements of the Cartesian product $\mathcal{L}_M \times \mathcal{L}_M$, i. e., each sequent s is denoted by $\Phi \vdash \Psi$, where $\Phi, \Psi \in \mathcal{L}_M$.

Definition 121 (Algebraic semantics). For any many-valued valuation $v \in \mathbb{V} = X^H$ extended to all formulae in $\mathcal{L}^G_{\mathrm{mv}}$, we define the "modal valuation" $\alpha : \mathcal{L}_M \to \mathbf{2}$, for any $\phi \in \mathcal{L}^G_{\mathrm{mv}}$, $\Phi, \Psi \in \mathcal{L}_M$, $a_i \in X$ and $a_k \in \mathbf{2}$, as follows:
1. $\alpha(0) = 0$, $\alpha(1) = 1$.
2. $\alpha([a_i]\phi) = 1$ iff $a_i = v^*(\phi)$.
3. $\alpha([a_k]\Phi) = 1$ iff $a_k = \alpha(\Phi)$.
4. $\alpha(\Phi \wedge \Psi) = \alpha(\Phi) \wedge \alpha(\Psi)$, $\alpha(\Phi \vee \Psi) = \alpha(\Phi) \vee \alpha(\Psi)$.

This transformation from many-valued into modal valuations can be expressed by the mapping $\mathfrak{F} : \mathbb{V} \to \mathbb{V}_M$, where $\mathbb{V}_M$ is the set of modal valuations $\alpha : \mathcal{L}_M \to \mathbf{2}$.

It is easy to verify that the mapping $\mathfrak{F}$ is a bijection, with its inverse $\mathfrak{F}^{-1}$ defined as follows: for any modal valuation $\alpha \in \mathbb{V}_M$, for the many-valued valuation $v = \mathfrak{F}^{-1}(\alpha) : H \to X$, its unique extension for any sentence $\phi \in \mathcal{L}^G_{\mathrm{mv}}$ is defined by $v^*(\phi) = a_i \in X$ iff $\alpha([a_i]\phi) = 1$. A many-valued valuation $v : H \to X$ satisfies a 2-valued multimodal formula $\Phi \in \mathcal{L}_M$ iff $\mathfrak{F}(v)(\Phi) = 1$.

Given two $\Phi, \Psi \in \mathcal{L}_M$, the sequent $\Phi \vdash \Psi$ is satisfied by v if $\mathfrak{F}(v)(\Phi) \leq \mathfrak{F}(v)(\Psi)$.

A sequent $\Phi \vdash \Psi$ is an axiom if it is satisfied by every valuation $\alpha \in \mathbb{V}_M$.

From this definition of satisfaction for sequents, we obtain the reflexivity (axiom) $\Phi \vdash \Phi$ and transitivity (cut) inference rule, i. e., from $\Phi \vdash \Psi$ and $\Psi \vdash \Upsilon$, we deduce $\Phi \vdash \Upsilon$.

Let us define the set of 2-valued multimodal literals (or modal atoms) as

$$P_{mm} = \{[a_1]\ldots[a_k]A \in \mathcal{L}_M \mid A \in H \text{ and } k \geq 1\}.$$

For example, if $v^*(\phi) = a_i$ then $\mathfrak{F}(v)([1][a_i]\phi) = 1$, while if $v^*(\phi) \neq a_i$ then $\mathfrak{F}(v)([0][a_i]\phi) = 1$. Notice that the number of nested modal operators can be reduced from the fact that $[0][0]$ and $[1][1]$ are identities for the formulae in $\mathcal{L}_M$. For $[a_i]\phi \in \mathcal{L}_M$, we have $[0][1][1][0][a_i]\phi \equiv [0][0][a_i]\phi \equiv [a_i]\phi$, where $\equiv$ is a logic equivalence.

Then, given a formula $\phi \in \mathcal{L}^G_{\mathrm{mv}}$, the modal formula $[a_i]\phi \in \mathcal{L}_M$ can be naturally reduced to an equivalent formula, denoted by $\widehat{[a_i]\phi}$, where the modal operators $[a_i]$ are applied *only to atoms* in Herbrand base H (considered as propositional letters). Moreover, for any formula $\Phi \in \mathcal{L}_M$, there is an equivalent formula $\widehat{\Phi}$ composed by logical connectives $\wedge$, $\vee$, and by multimodal literals in P_{mm}. So, we obtain the canonical reduction.

Definition 122 (Canonical reduction). Let us define the following reduction rules, for $\phi, \psi \in \mathcal{L}^G_{\mathrm{mv}}$, $a_i \in X$, $\Phi, \Psi \in \mathcal{L}_M$ and $a_j \in \mathbf{2}$:

1. For any unary operator $\sim \in \Sigma$, $[a_i](\sim \phi) \mapsto \bigvee_{a_k \in X. a_i = \sim a_k} [a_k]\phi$,
2. For any binary operator $\odot \in \Sigma$, $[a_i](\phi \odot \psi) \mapsto \bigvee_{a_k, a_n \in X. a_i = a_k \odot a_n} ([a_k]\phi \wedge [a_n]\psi)$.
3. For $\odot \in \{\wedge, \vee\}$, $[a_j](\Phi \odot \Psi) \mapsto \bigvee_{a_k, a_n \in \mathbf{2}. a_j = a_k \odot a_n} ([a_k]\Phi \wedge [a_n]\Psi)$.

The canonic formula obtained by applying recursively these reduction rules to the formula $[a_i]\Phi$ is denoted by $\widehat{[a_i]\Phi}$.

The next tree propositions for this canonical reduction has been proved in [344].

Proposition 50. *Canonical reductions are truth preserving. That is, for any $a_i \in X$ and $\phi \in \mathcal{L}^G_{\mathrm{mv}}$ we have that $[a_i]\phi$ is logically equivalent to $\widehat{[a_i]\phi}$. Analogously, for any $a_i \in \mathbf{2}$ and $\Phi \in \mathcal{L}_M$, we have that $[a_i]\Phi$ is logically equivalent to $\widehat{[a_i]\Phi}$.*

The following proposition shows that the result of the canonical reduction of a formula $\Phi \in \mathcal{L}_M$ is a disjunction of modal conjunctions, which in the case of the formulae without nested modal operators is a simple disjunctive modal formula.

Proposition 51. *Any 2-valued logic formulae $\Phi \in \mathcal{L}_M$ is logically equivalent to a disjunctive modal formula $\bigvee_{1 \le i \le m} (\bigwedge_{1 \le j \le m_i} ([a_{ij1}] \dots [a_{ijk_{ij}}]) A_{ij})$, where for all $1 \le i \le m$, and $1 \le j \le m_i$, we have that $1 \le k_{ij}$, $a_{ijk_{ij}} \in X$, and $A_{ij} \in H$.*

In the case when we have no nested modal operators, then $k_{ij} = 1$ for all ij. Thus, $\Phi \in \mathcal{L}_M$ is logically equivalent to a disjunctive modal formula $\bigvee_{1 \le i \le m} [a_i]\phi_i$, where for all $1 \le i \le m$, $a_i \in X$, $\phi_i \in \mathcal{L}^G_{\mathrm{mv}}$.

With this normal reduction, by using truth-value tables of many-valued logical connectives, we introduced the structural compositionality and truth preserving for the 2-valued modal encapsulation of a many-valued logic $\mathcal{L}_{\mathrm{mv}}$ as well. In fact, the following property is valid:

Proposition 52. *Given a many-valued valuation $v : H \to X$ and a formula $\phi \in \mathcal{L}^G_{\mathrm{mv}}$, the normal reduct formula $\widehat{[a_i]\phi} \in \mathcal{L}_M$ is satisfied by v iff $a_i = v^*(\phi)$.*

Thus, as a consequence, for any $\phi \in \mathcal{L}^G_{\mathrm{mv}}$ and a many-valued valuation $v \in \mathbb{V}$, we have that $\mathfrak{F}(v)(\widehat{[a_i]\phi}) = 1$ iff $a_i = v^*(\phi)$.

We are able to define an equivalence relation $\approx_L$ between the formulae of any many-valued logic based on the set of truth values X, in order to define the Lindenbaum algebra for this logic ($\mathcal{L}/ \approx_L$), where for any two formulae $\phi, \psi \in \mathcal{L}^G_{\mathrm{mv}}$, $\phi \approx_L \psi$ iff $\forall v \in \mathbb{V}(v^*(\phi) = v^*(\psi))$. Thus, the elements of this quotient algebra $\mathcal{L}/ \approx_L$ are the equivalence classes, denoted by $\langle \phi \rangle$.

In an autoreferential semantics [69, 81, 227], we assume that each equivalence class of formulae $\langle \phi \rangle$ in this Lindenbaum algebra corresponds to one "state description." In particular, we are interested in the subset of "state descriptions" that are *invariant* w. r. t. many-valued interpretations v, so that can be used as the possible worlds in the Kripke-style semantics for the original many-valued modal logic.

Let us now consider the Kripke model for the 2-valued multimodal logic language $\mathcal{L}_M$.

Definition 123 (Kripke semantics). Let $\mathcal{L}_{\mathrm{mv}}$ be a many-valued predicate logic language, based on a set X of truth values, with a set of predicate letters P and Herbrand base H. Let $\mathcal{M}_v = (F, \mathcal{D}, I_K)$ be a Kripke model of its correspondent 2-valued multimodal logic language $\mathcal{L}^*_M$ with the frame $F = (\mathcal{W}, \{\mathcal{R}_w = \mathcal{W} \times \{w\} \mid w \in \mathcal{W}\})$ with the set of possible worlds $\mathcal{W} = X \bigcup \mathbf{2}$ and with mapping $I_K : \mathcal{W} \times P \to \bigcup_{n<\omega} \mathbf{2}^{\mathcal{D}^n}$ such that for any n-ary predicate $p^n_j \in P$ and tuple $(c_1, \ldots, c_n) \in \mathcal{D}^n$, there exists a unique $w \in \mathcal{W}$ such that $I_K(w, p^n_j)(c_1, \ldots, c_n) = 1$.

It defines the Herbrand interpretation $v : H \to X$ such that $v(p^n_j(c_1, \ldots, c_n)) = w$ iff $I_K(w, p^n_j)(c_1, \ldots, c_n) = 1$, and its unique homomorphic extension $v^* : \mathcal{L}^G_{\mathrm{mv}} \to X$.

For any many-valued formula $\phi \in L_{\mathrm{mv}}$, the assignment $g : \mathcal{V} \to \mathcal{D}$ and $w \in \mathcal{W}$, the satisfaction relation $\vDash_{w,g}$ is defined by $\mathcal{M}_v \vDash_{w,g} \phi$ iff $v^*(\phi/g) = w$.

It is extended to all modal formulae in $\mathcal{L}^*_M$ as follows:

1. $\mathcal{M}_v \vDash_{w,g} 1$ and $\mathcal{M}_v \nvDash_{w,g} 0$ for tautology and contradiction, respectively.
2. $\mathcal{M}_v \vDash_{w,g} [a_i]\Phi$ iff $\forall w'((w, w') \in \mathcal{R}_{a_i}$ implies $\mathcal{M}_v \vDash_{w',g} \Phi)$, for any $\Phi \in \mathcal{L}^*_M$ or $\Phi \in \mathcal{L}_{\mathrm{mv}}$.
3. $\mathcal{M}_v \vDash_{w,g} \Phi \wedge \Psi$ iff $\mathcal{M}_v \vDash_{w,g} \Phi$ and $\mathcal{M}_v \vDash_{w,g} \Psi$, for $\Phi, \Psi \in \mathcal{L}^*_M$.
4. $\mathcal{M}_v \vDash_{w,g} \Phi \vee \Psi$ iff $\mathcal{M}_v \vDash_{w,g} \Phi$ or $\mathcal{M}_v \vDash_{w,g} \Psi$, for $\Phi, \Psi \in \mathcal{L}^*_M$.

Let $\Psi/g \in \mathcal{L}_M$ be a sentence obtained from $\Psi \in \mathcal{L}^*_M$ by assignment g. So, we denote the set of worlds where the sentence $\Psi/g \in \mathcal{L}_M$ is satisfied by $\|\Psi/g\|$, with

$$\|p^n_j(x_1, \ldots, x_n)/g\| = \{v(p^n_j(g(x_1), \ldots, g(x_n))\} \quad \text{and} \quad \|\phi/g\| = \{v^*(\phi/g))\}, \quad \phi \in \mathcal{L}_{\mathrm{mv}}.$$

Different from the many-valued ground atoms in $\mathcal{L}_{\mathrm{mv}}$, the modal atoms in $\mathcal{L}_M$ have the standard 2-valued property: they are true or false in these Kripke models. So, this positive multimodal logic with modal atoms $\mathcal{L}_M$ satisfies the classic 2-valued properties.

Proposition 53. *For any sentence Φ/g of the positive multimodal logic $\mathcal{L}_M$ defined in Definition* 120, *$\|\Phi/g\| \in \{\emptyset, \mathcal{W}\}$, where $\emptyset$ is the empty set.*

Proof. By structural induction:

1. $\|1\| = \mathcal{W}$ and $\|0\| = \emptyset$, and $\|[a_i]\phi/g\| = \mathcal{W}$ if $a_i = v(\phi/g)$; $\emptyset$ otherwise.

Let Φ, Ψ be the two atomic modal formulae such that, by inductive hypothesis $\|\Phi/g\|, \|\Psi/g\| \in \{\emptyset, \mathcal{W}\}$. Then,

2. $\|[a_i]\Phi\| = \{w \in \mathcal{W} \mid a_i \in \|\Phi/g\|\} = \mathcal{W}$ if $\|\Phi/g\| = \mathcal{W}$; $\emptyset$ otherwise.
3. $\|(\Phi \wedge \Psi)/g\| = \|\Phi/g\| \bigcap \|\Psi/g\| \in \{\emptyset, \mathcal{W}\}$.
4. $\|(\Phi \vee \Psi)/g\| = \|\Phi/g\| \bigcup \|\Psi/g\| \in \{\emptyset, \mathcal{W}\}$.

Thus, from the fact that any formula $\Phi \in \mathcal{L}_M^*$ is logically equivalent to disjunctive modal formula $\bigvee_{1\le i\le m}(\bigwedge_{1\le j\le m_i}([a_{ij1}]\dots[a_{ijk_{ij}}])A_{ij})$ (from Proposition 51), where each $A_{ij} \in H$ is a ground atom (such that by inductive hypothesis for any modal atom it is true that $\|([a_{ij1}]\dots[a_{ijk_{ij}}])A_{ij}/g\| \in \{\emptyset, \mathcal{W}\}$), and from points 3 and 4 above, we obtain that

$$\|\Phi/g\| = \left\| \bigvee_{1\le i\le m}\left(\bigwedge_{1\le j\le m_i}([a_{ij1}]\dots[a_{ijk_{ij}}])A_{ij}/g\right)\right\| \in \{\emptyset, \mathcal{W}\}. \qquad \square$$

The following proposition demonstrates the existence of a one-to-one correspondence between the unique many-valued model of a many-valued logic $\mathcal{L}_{\text{mv}}$ and the Kripke model of a multimodal positive logic $\mathcal{L}_M$. The proof is provided in [344] by structural recursion and by Propositions 53 and 32.

Corollary 32. *For any many-valued formula $\phi/g \in \mathcal{L}_{\text{mv}}$ and $v : H \to X$,*

$$v(\phi/g) = a_i \quad \textit{iff} \quad \mathfrak{F}(v)([a_i]\phi/g) = 1 \textit{ iff } \|[a_i]\phi/g\| = \mathcal{W},$$

and for any sentence $\Phi/g \in \mathcal{L}_M$, $\mathfrak{F}(v)(\Phi/g) = 1$ iff $\|\Phi/g\| = \mathcal{W}$, (i. e., Φ/g is true in the Kripke model in Definition 123*).*

From this corollary, we obtain that any true formula $\Phi \in \mathcal{L}_M$ is also true in the Kripke model, and vice versa. That is, the autoreferential Kripke-style semantics for the multi-modal logic $\mathcal{L}_M$, in Definition 123, is *sound* and *complete*.

Binary sequent calculi

The Gentzen-like system $\mathcal{G}$ of the 2-valued propositional logic $\mathcal{L}_M$ (where the set of propositional letters corresponds to the set $P_{mm} = \{[a_1]\dots[a_k]A \in \mathcal{L}_M \mid k \ge 1 \text{ and } A \in H\}$) is a 2-valued distributive logic (DLL in [193]), i. e., $\mathbf{2} \subseteq \mathcal{L}_M$, extended by the set of sequent axioms, defined for each many-valued logic connective in Σ of the logic $\mathcal{L}_{\text{mv}}$, by:

(AXIOMS) The Gentzen-like system $\mathcal{G} = \langle \mathbb{L}, \Vdash \rangle$ contains the following sequents in $\mathbb{L}$ for any $\Phi, \Psi, \Upsilon \in \mathcal{L}_M$ and many-valued sentences $\phi, \psi \in \mathcal{L}_{\text{mv}}^G$:

1. $\Phi \vdash \Phi$ (reflexive)
2. $\Phi \vdash 1$, $0 \vdash \Phi$ (top/bottom axioms)
3. $\Phi \wedge \Psi \vdash \Phi$, $\Phi \wedge \Psi \vdash \Psi$ (product projections: axioms for meet)
4. $\Phi \vdash \Phi \vee \Psi$, $\Phi \vdash \Psi \vee \Phi$ (coproduct injections: axioms for join)
5. $\Phi \wedge (\Psi \vee \Upsilon) \vdash (\Phi \wedge \Psi) \vee (\Phi \wedge \Upsilon)$ (distributivity axiom)
6. The set of introduction axioms for many-valued connectives:
   6.1 $\bigvee_{a_k,a_n \in \mathbf{2}. a_i = a_k \odot a_n}([a_k]\Phi \wedge [a_n]\Psi) \vdash [a_i](\Phi \odot \Psi)$, for any $\odot \in \{\wedge, \vee\}$.
   6.2 $\bigvee_{a_k \in X. a_i = \sim a_k}[a_k]\phi \vdash [a_i](\sim \phi)$, for any unary operator $\sim \in \Sigma$.
   6.3 $\bigvee_{a_k,a_n \in X. a_i = a_k \odot a_n}([a_k]\phi \wedge [a_n]\psi) \vdash [a_i](\phi \odot \psi)$, for any binary operator $\odot \in \Sigma$.
7. The set of elimination axioms for many-valued connectives:

7.1 $[a_i](\Phi \odot \Psi) \vdash \bigvee_{a_k,a_n \in \mathbf{2}. a_i = a_k \odot a_n}([a_k]\Phi \wedge [a_n]\Psi)$, for any $\odot \in \{\wedge, \vee\}$.
7.2 $[a_i](\sim \phi) \vdash \bigvee_{a_k \in X. a_i = \sim a_k}[a_k]\phi$, for any unary operator $\sim \in \Sigma$.
7.3 $[a_i](\phi \odot \psi) \vdash \bigvee_{a_k,a_n \in X. a_i = a_k \odot a_n}([a_k]\phi \wedge [a_n]\psi)$ f,or any binary operator $\odot \in \Sigma$.

(INFERENCE RULES) $\mathcal{G}$ is closed under the following inference rules:
1. $\frac{\Phi \vdash \Psi, \Psi \vdash \Upsilon}{\Phi \vdash \Upsilon}$ (cut/transitivity rule)
2. $\frac{\Phi \vdash \Psi, \Phi \vdash \Upsilon}{\Phi \vdash \Psi \wedge \Upsilon}$, $\frac{\Phi \vdash \Psi, \Upsilon \vdash \Psi}{\Phi \vee \Upsilon \vdash \Psi}$ (lower/upper lattice bound rules)
3. $\frac{\Phi \vdash \Psi}{\sigma(\Phi) \vdash \sigma(\Psi)}$ (substitution rule: σ is substitution (y/p)). □

The axioms from 1 to 5 and the rules 1 and 2 are taken from [193] for the DLL and it was shown that this sequent based Gentzen-like system is sound and complete. The new axioms 6 and 7 correspond to the canonical (equivalent) reductions in Definition 122. The set of sequents that define the poset of the classic 2-valued lattice of truth values $(\mathbf{2}, \leq)$ is a consequence of the top/bottom axioms: for any two $a_i, a_k \in \mathbf{2}$, if $a_i \leq a_k$ then $a_i \vdash a_k \in \mathcal{G}$.

Thus, for many-valued logics, we obtain a *normal* modal Gentzen-like deductive system, where each sequent is a valid truth-preserving consequence-pair defined by the poset of the complete lattice $(\mathbf{2}, \leq)$ of classic truth values (which are also the constants of this positive propositional language $\mathcal{L}_M$), so that each occurrence of the symbol $\vdash$ can be substituted by the partial order $\leq$ of this complete lattice $(\mathbf{2}, \leq)$.

Example 56. Let us consider the Gödel's 3-valued logic $X = \{0, \frac{1}{2}, 1\}$ with implication:

$\Rightarrow$	0	$\frac{1}{2}$	1
0	1	1	1
$\frac{1}{2}$	0	1	1
1	0	$\frac{1}{2}$	1

One of the possible m-sequents for introduction *rules* for this connective, taken from [345], (each rule corresponds to the conjunction of disjunctive forms, where each disjunctive form is one m-sequent in the premise), is

$$\frac{\langle \Gamma | \Delta, \phi | \Pi, \phi \rangle \langle \Gamma_1, \psi | \Delta_1 | \Pi_1 \rangle}{\langle \Gamma, \Gamma_1, \phi \Rightarrow \psi | \Delta, \Delta_1 | \Pi, \Pi_1 \rangle} \Rightarrow: 0, \qquad \frac{\langle \Gamma | \Delta | \Pi, \phi \rangle \langle \Gamma_1 | \Delta_1, \psi | \Pi_1 \rangle}{\langle \Gamma, \Gamma_1, | \Delta, \Delta_1, \phi \Rightarrow \psi | \Pi, \Pi_1 \rangle} \Rightarrow: \frac{1}{2}$$

$$\frac{\langle \Gamma, \phi | \Delta, \phi | \Pi, \psi \rangle \langle \Gamma_1, \phi | \Delta_1, \psi | \Pi_1, \psi \rangle}{\langle \Gamma, \Gamma_1, | \Delta, \Delta_1 | \Pi, \Pi_1, \phi \Rightarrow \psi \rangle} \Rightarrow: 1$$

but in our approach, we obtain the *unique* set of binary sequent introduction *axioms*:

$$\left(\left[\frac{1}{2}\right]\phi \wedge [0]\psi\right) \vee ([1]\phi \wedge [0]\psi) \vdash [0](\phi \Rightarrow \psi)$$

$$[1]\phi \wedge \left[\frac{1}{2}\right]\psi \vdash \left[\frac{1}{2}\right](\phi \Rightarrow \psi)$$

$$\bigvee_{a_i,a_k \in X \& (a_i,a_k) \notin S} ([a_i]\phi \wedge [a_k]\psi) \vdash [1](\phi \Rightarrow \psi)$$

where $S = \{(\frac{1}{2}, 0), (1, 0), (1, \frac{1}{2})\}$, and elimination axioms:

$$[0](\phi \Rightarrow \psi) \vdash \left(\left[\frac{1}{2}\right]\phi \wedge [0]\psi\right) \vee ([1]\phi \wedge [0]\psi)$$

$$\left[\frac{1}{2}\right](\phi \Rightarrow \psi) \vdash [1]\phi \wedge \left[\frac{1}{2}\right]\psi$$

$$[1](\phi \Rightarrow \psi) \vdash \bigvee_{a_i,a_k \in X \& (a_i,a_k) \notin S} ([a_i]\phi \wedge [a_k]\psi).$$

Definition 124. For any two formulae $\Phi, \Psi \in \mathcal{L}_M$ when the sequent $\Phi \vdash \Psi$ is satisfied by a 2-valued modal valuation $\alpha : \mathcal{L}_M \to \mathbf{2}$ from Definition 121 (i. e., when $\alpha(\Phi) \leq \alpha(\Psi)$ as in standard 2-valued logics), we say that it is satisfied by the many-valued valuation $v = \mathfrak{F}^{-1}(\alpha) : H \to X$. This sequent is a tautology if it is satisfied by all modal valuations $\alpha = \mathfrak{F}(v) \in \mathbb{V}_M$, i. e., when $\forall v \in \mathbb{V}.(\mathfrak{F}(v)(\Phi) \leq \mathfrak{F}(v)(\Psi))$.

For a normal Gentzen-like sequent system $\mathcal{G} = \langle \mathbb{L}, \Vdash \rangle$ of a many-valued logic language $\mathcal{L}_{\mathrm{mv}}$, with the set of sequents $\mathbb{L} \subseteq \mathcal{L}_M \times \mathcal{L}_M$, we tell that a many-valued valuation v is its *model* if it satisfies all sequents in $\mathcal{G}$. The set of all models of a given set of sequents Γ is

$$\mathbb{V}_\Gamma = \{v \in \mathbb{V} \mid \forall (\Phi \vdash \Psi) \in \Gamma(\mathfrak{F}(v)(\Phi) \leq \mathfrak{F}(v)(\Psi))\} \subseteq \mathbb{V}.$$

The following proposition has been proven in [344].

Proposition 54 (Sequent's bivaluations and soundness). *Let us define the mapping $\mathfrak{B} : \mathbb{V} \to \mathbf{2}^{\mathcal{L}_M \times \mathcal{L}_M}$ from valuations into sequent bivaluations such that for any valuation $v \in \mathbb{V}$, we obtain the sequent bivaluation $\beta = \mathfrak{B}(v) = \mathrm{eq} \circ \langle \pi_1, \wedge \rangle \circ (\mathfrak{F}(v) \times \mathfrak{F}(v)) : \mathcal{L}_M \times \mathcal{L}_M \to \mathbf{2}$, where π_1 is the first projection, $\circ$ is the functional composition and* $\mathrm{eq} : \mathbf{2} \times \mathbf{2} \to \mathbf{2}$ *is the equality mapping such that* $\mathrm{eq}(a_i, a_k) = 1$ *iff $a_i = a_k$.*

Then a sequent $s = (\Phi \vdash \Psi)$ is satisfied by v iff $\beta(s) = \mathfrak{B}(v)(s) = 1$.

All axioms of the Gentzen-like sequent system $\mathcal{G}$, of a many-valued logic language $\mathcal{L}_{\mathrm{mv}}$ based on a set X of truth values are tautologies, and all of its rules are sound for model satisfiability and preserve the tautologies.

It is easy to verify that this entailment is equal to the classic propositional entailment.

Remark. It is easy to observe that each sequent is, from the logic point of view, a *2-valued object* so that all inference rules are embedded into the classic 2-valued framework, i. e., given a bivaluation $\beta = \mathfrak{B}(v) : \mathcal{L}_M \times \mathcal{L}_M \to \mathbf{2}$, we have that a sequent $s = \Phi \vdash \Psi$ is satisfied, $\beta(s) = 1$ iff $\mathfrak{F}(v)(\Phi) \leq \mathfrak{F}(v)(\Psi)$, so that we have a direct relationship between sequent bivaluations β and many-valued valuations v.

The definition of the 2-valued entailment in the sequent system $\mathcal{G}$, given in Definition 124, can replace the current entailment based on algebraic matrices (X, D) where $D \subseteq X$ is a subset of designated elements. Thus, we are now able to introduce the many-valued valuation-based (i. e., model-theoretic) semantics for many-valued logics [227].

Definition 125. A many-valued model-theoretic semantics of a given many-valued logic $\mathcal{L}$, with a Gentzen system $\mathcal{G} = \langle \mathbb{L}, \Vdash \rangle$, is the semantic deducibility relation $\vDash_m$, defined for any set $\Gamma = \{s_i = (\Phi_i \vdash \Psi_i)\}$ and a sequent $s = (\Phi \vdash \Psi) \in \mathbb{L} \subseteq \mathcal{L}_M \times \mathcal{L}_M$, by

$$\begin{aligned} \Gamma \vDash_m s \quad &\text{iff} \quad \text{all many-valued models of } \Gamma \text{ are the models of } s, \\ &\text{iff} \quad \forall v \in \mathbb{V}(\forall(\Phi_i \vdash \Psi_i) \in \Gamma)(\mathfrak{F}(v)(\Phi_i) \leq \mathfrak{F}(v)(\Psi_i) \text{ implies } \mathfrak{F}(v)(\Phi) \leq \mathfrak{F}(v)(\Psi)). \end{aligned}$$

Lemma 16 ([344]). *For any set $\Gamma = \{s_i = (\Phi_i \vdash \Psi_i)\}$ and a sequent $s = (\Phi \vdash \Psi)$, we have that $\Gamma \vDash_m s$ iff $\forall v \in \mathbb{V}_\Gamma(\mathfrak{B}(v)(s) = 1)$.*

So, any many-valued logic has a Gentzen-like system $\mathcal{G} = \langle \mathbb{L}, \Vdash \rangle$ (see the definition at the beginning of this section) is a *normal* logic. Many-valued model theoretic semantics is an adequate semantics for a many-valued logic $\mathcal{L}_{\mathrm{mv}}$ specified by a Gentzen-like logic system $\mathcal{G} = \langle \mathbb{L}, \Vdash \rangle$, i. e., it is sound and complete [344]. It is shown by Theorem 16 in Section A.3.1 that $\Gamma \vDash_m s$ iff $\Gamma \Vdash s$.

Thus, in order to define the model-theoretic semantics for finite many-valued logics, we do not need to use the matrices: we are able to use only the many-valued valuations and *many-valued models* (i. e., the valuations which satisfy all sequents in Γ of a given many-valued logic $\mathcal{L}_{\mathrm{mv}}$).

Example 57. Let us show that given an assumption $\Gamma = \{1 \vdash [a_i]\phi, 1 \vdash [a_k]\psi\}$ then $[a_n](\phi \odot \psi)$ for $a_n = a_i \odot a_k$ is deduced from Γ, i. e., $\Gamma \Vdash ([a_n](\phi \odot \psi))$; or equivalently if $[a_i]\phi$ and $[a_k]\psi$ are valid (i. e., for every valuation $v \in \mathbb{V}$, $v : H \to X$, the values of ϕ and ψ are equal to a_i and a_k, respectively, i. e., $\forall v \in \mathbb{V}.(v^*(\phi) = a_i \text{ and } v^*(\psi) = a_k)$) then $[a_n](\phi \odot \psi)$ is valid as well.

As a first step, we introduce the equivalence relation $\equiv$ such that $\Phi \equiv \Psi$ iff $\Phi \vdash \Psi$ and $\Psi \vdash \Phi$ (i. e., Φ iff Ψ). Consequently, from the reflexivity axiom in $\mathcal{G}$, $\Phi \equiv \Phi$, as for example, $1 \equiv 1$. The equivalent formulae can be used in the substitution inference rule: if $\Phi \equiv \Psi$, then we can use the substitution of Φ by Ψ, i. e., the substitution $\sigma : \Phi \mapsto \Psi$.

Let us show the simple equivalence $\Phi \vee \Phi \equiv \Phi$: from the reflexivity axiom $\Phi \vdash \Phi$, by using the upper bound inference rule (when $\Psi = \Phi$), we deduce $\Phi \vee \Phi \vdash \Phi$. Then, from the axioms for join $\Phi \vdash \Phi \vee \Phi$, we obtain $\Phi \vee \Phi \equiv \Phi$.

Now, from the assumptions $1 \vdash [a_i]\phi, 1 \vdash [a_k]\psi \in \Gamma$, by the lower bound inference rule in $\mathcal{G}$, we obtain (a) $1 \vdash [a_i]\phi \wedge [a_k]\psi$, i. e., $\Gamma \Vdash (1 \vdash [a_i]\phi \wedge [a_k]\psi)$. Let $a_n = a_i \odot a_k$ and let us denote $[a_i]\phi \wedge [a_k]\psi$ by Φ, so that (a) becomes (a′) $1 \vdash \Phi$. Now we can take the axiom for join, (b) $\Phi \vdash \Phi \vee \bigvee_{a_j, a_m \in X. a_j \odot a_m = a_n}([a_j]\phi \wedge [a_m]\psi)$, so from (a′) and (b) and the transitivity rule, we obtain $1 \vdash \Phi \vee \bigvee_{a_j, a_m \in X. a_j \odot a_m = a_n}([a_j]\phi \wedge [a_m]\psi)$, i. e.,

(c) $1 \vdash \Phi \vee \Phi \vee \Psi$, where $\Psi = \bigvee_{a_j,a_m \in X(a_j \neq a_i, a_m \neq a_k, a_j \odot a_m = a_n)}([a_j]\phi \wedge [a_m]\psi)$. Thus, by substitution $\sigma : \{1 \mapsto 1, \Phi \vee \Phi \mapsto \Phi\}$ and by applying the substitution rule to (c), we deduce the sequent $1 \vdash \Phi \vee \Psi$. That is, (d) $1 \vdash \bigvee_{a_j,a_m \in X.a_j \odot a_m = a_n}([a_j]\phi \wedge [a_m]\psi)$ (from $\Phi \vee \Psi = \bigvee_{a_j,a_m \in X, a_j \odot a_m = a_n}([a_j]\phi \wedge [a_m]\psi)$). Consequently, by applying the transitivity rule to the sequent (d) and the introduction axiom $\bigvee_{a_j,a_m \in X, a_j \odot a_m = a_n}([a_j]\phi \wedge [a_m]\psi) \vdash [a_n](\phi \odot \psi)$, we deduce $1 \vdash [a_n](\phi \odot \psi)$, i. e.,

$$\Gamma \Vdash (1 \vdash [a_n](\phi \odot \psi)).$$

Notice that in such deductions, no value of a_i, a_k, a_n need to be a designated value. We do not make any distinction for the truth values in X.

Based on Suszko's thesis, with a nonconstructive approach based on a distinction between designated and undesignated algebraic truth values, in these sections we analyzed a different possibility of reducing these many-valued logics into 2-valued logics in a constructive way. The reduction of a many-valued logic with finite set X into 2-valued logic, results in a nontruth-functional modal metalogic, which obviously is not an original "reference" many-valued logic. This process is explained by the fact that this reduction is based on new sentences about the original many-valued sentences, and that, by avoiding the second-order syntax of these metasentences, what is required is the introduction of new *modal* operators in this equivalent but 2-valued metalogic.

A.4.4 General abstract reductions of many-valued into 2-valued logics

The term "abstract" used for this general many-valued reduction means that we do not consider any further the specific reduction of particular functional logic operators in Σ of a many-valued logic into correspondent modal operators, but rather a general reduction independent of them, based on structural consequence operations or matrices.

In what follows, we will provide a reduction of a many-valued *predicate* logic $\mathcal{L}_{\mathrm{mv}}$, with a Herbrand base H and subset of sentences $\mathcal{L}^G_{\mathrm{mv}}$, into a 2-valued logic. For a given set of thesis (sentences) Γ of a many-valued logic $\mathcal{L}_{\mathrm{mv}}$, by $\Gamma \vDash \phi$ we denote the *2-valued* structural consequence relation (entailment), which means that a sentence ϕ is a structural consequence of the set of sentences in Γ, i. e., that $\phi \in C(\Gamma)$ where $C : \mathcal{P}(\mathcal{L}^G_{\mathrm{mv}}) \to \mathcal{P}(\mathcal{L}^G_{\mathrm{mv}})$ is a structural consequence (closure) operation conforming Tarski's conditions for a logic.

We denote by $\mathbb{V} = X^H$ the set of Herbrand many-valued interpretations $v : H \to X$, $v \in \mathbb{V}$, for a many-valued logic $\mathcal{L}_{\mathrm{mv}}$ with a Herbrand base H and a set of *algebraic* truth values in X. Let $\mathbb{V}_\Gamma \subset \mathbb{V}$ be a nonempty subset of *models* of Γ, i. e., valuations $v \in \mathbb{V}_\Gamma$ that satisfy every sentence in Γ. Then the truth of $\Gamma \vDash \phi$ is equivalent to the fact that every valuation $v \in \mathbb{V}_\Gamma$ is a model of ϕ (i. e., satisfies a sentence ϕ) as well.

In the case when we consider a many-valued logic with a given matrix (X, D), where $D \subset X$ is a subset of *designated* algebraic truth values (see also Section 2.2.1 for a short introduction, based on the work of Jan Lukasiewicz [78–81]), the well-known matrix-based inference is specified by (extension of v to $\phi \in \mathcal{L}_{mv}^{G}$ is denoted by v^*):

$$\Gamma \vDash \phi \quad \text{iff} \quad (\forall v \in \mathbb{V}_{\Gamma}).(v^*(\phi) \in D) \tag{A.5}$$

with the set of models $\mathbb{V}_{\Gamma}$ of Γ defined as the set of valuations v such that $(\forall \psi \in \Gamma).(v^*(\psi) \in \mathcal{D})$. In the classic 2-valued truth-invariance semantics of logic entailment, we have
(CL) $\Gamma \vDash \phi$ iff $(\forall v \in \mathbb{V}_{\Gamma}).(v^*(\phi) = 1)$.

Thus, classic 2-valued entailment deduces both true and false sentences if they have the same truth value in all models of Γ with $D = \{1\} \subset \mathbf{2}$. The consequence relation $\vDash_1$ defines the Tarskian closure operator $C : \mathcal{P}(\mathcal{L}_{mv}^{G}) \to \mathcal{P}(\mathcal{L}_{mv}^{G})$ such that $C(\Gamma) = \{\phi \mid \phi \in \mathcal{L}_{mv}^{G}$ and $\Gamma \vDash_1 \phi\}$. In the 2-valued logics, we do not need to use the consequence relation $\vDash_0$ because the set of false sentences deduced from Γ is equal to the set $\{\neg\phi \mid \phi \in \mathcal{L}_{mv}^{G}$ and $\Gamma \vDash_1 \phi\} = \{\neg\phi \mid \phi \in C(\Gamma)\}$. This particular property explains why, in the classic 2-valued logic, it is enough to consider only the consequence relation for deduction of true sentences, or alternatively the Tarskian closure operator C.

In the case of many-valued logics, it is not generally the case and we need the consequence relations for the derivation of sentences that are not true as well. Consequently, we will extend this classic 2-valued model-theoretic truth-invariance semantics of logic entailment (5.2) in Definition 57, Section 5.1, to many-valued logics as well. It is easy to verify that both semantics, the truth-invariance (5.2) and the matrix-based (A.5), in the case of classic 2-valued logics, where $D = \{1\}$, coincide. As we will see, both abstract reductions will result in a kind of 2-valued modal logic that are not truth-functional, as we obtained in the specific case for logic programs in Section A.4.2.

First case

In [346], Suszko's thesis was presented. This paper is extremely dense and very short, and thus it is not easy to understand; it is a kind of synthesis, in four pages, of some deep reflections carried out by Suszko over 40 years. Only 15 years after this publication, Malinowski's book [347] has thrown some light on it (see especially Chapter 10, Section 10.1). Unfortunately, neither the quoted paper by Suszko nor Malinowski's book explicitly state Suszko's thesis, but in another paper [348] Malinowski has written:

> "Suszko's thesis ... states that each logic, i. e., a *structural consequence operation* conforming Tarski's conditions, is logically two-valued," and (p. 73)

> "each (structural) *propositional logic* (L, C) can be determined by a class of logical valuations of the language $\mathcal{L}$ or, in other words, it is logically *two-valued*."

In what follows, for a fixed set of (initial) thesis $\Gamma \subset \mathcal{L}_{\mathrm{mv}}^G$ that defines a structural many-valued logic (Γ, C), we will transform the left-side construct $\Gamma \vDash (\_)$ in a composed *modal operator* $\Box_\Gamma$ ("Γ-deductive"), so that a metasentence $\Gamma \vDash \phi$ can be replaced by an equivalent modal formula $\Box_\Gamma \phi$ in this 2-valued metalogic.

Thus, analogously to the more specific cases for logic programs, also in this general abstract 2-valued reduction we are not speaking about the two-valuedness of an original *many-valued formula*, but about a *modal formula* of a 2-valued metalogic obtained by this transformation. What remains now is to define a Kripke semantics for this modal meta-logic, denoted by $\mathcal{L}_{\mathcal{F}}$, obtained from a set of sentences $\mathcal{F} = \{\Box_\Gamma \phi \mid \phi \in \mathcal{L}_{\mathrm{mv}}^G\}$ and the standard 2-valued logic connectives (conjunction, disjunction, implication and negation).

Definition 126. Given a structural many-valued logic (Γ, C), where $\Gamma \subset \mathcal{L}_{\mathrm{mv}}^G$ is a subset of theses, with Herbrand base H, let $\mathbb{V}_\Gamma \subset X^H$ be a nonempty subset of *models* of Γ, i. e., the set of valuations $v : H \to X$ that satisfy every sentence in Γ.

We define a Kripke-style model for sentences of modal metalogic $\mathcal{L}_{\mathcal{F}}$, based on Suszko's reduction $\mathcal{F} = \{\Box_\Gamma \phi \mid \phi \in \mathcal{L}_{\mathrm{mv}}^G\}$ where $\Box_\Gamma = \Diamond\Box$, by $\mathcal{M} = (\mathcal{W}, \mathcal{R}_\Diamond, \mathcal{R}_\Box, \mathcal{D}, I_K)$, with the set of possible worlds $\mathcal{W} = \Gamma \times \mathbb{V}_\Gamma$, $\mathcal{R}_\Diamond = \{((\phi_i, v), (\phi_k, v)) \mid (\phi_i, v) \in \mathcal{W}, \phi_k \in \Gamma\}$, $\mathcal{R}_\Box = \{((\phi_i, v), (\phi_i, v_1)) \mid (\phi_i, v) \in \mathcal{W}, v_1 \in \mathbb{V}_\Gamma\}$ and $I_K : \mathcal{W} \times \mathcal{L}_{\mathrm{mv}}^G \to \mathbf{2}$, such that for any many-valued sentence $\psi \in \mathcal{L}_{\mathrm{mv}}^G$ and a world $w = (\phi_i, v) \in \mathcal{W}$:

$$I_K(w, \psi) = I_K((\phi_i, v), \psi) = 1 \quad \text{iff} \quad v^*(\psi) \geq v^*(\phi_i) \tag{A.6}$$

where v^* is unique extension of Herbrand interpretation $v : H \to X$ to all sentences in $\mathcal{L}_{\mathrm{mv}}^G$. The satisfaction relation $\vDash_w$, for a world $w = (\phi_i, v) \in \mathcal{W}$, for any many-valued sentence $\psi, \phi \in \mathcal{L}_{\mathrm{mv}}^G$, is defined as follows:

1. $\mathcal{M} \vDash_w \psi$ iff $I_K(w, \psi) = 1$.
2. $\mathcal{M} \vDash_w \Box_\Gamma \psi$ iff $\mathcal{M} \vDash_w \Diamond\Box\psi$ iff $\exists w_1((w, w_1) \in \mathcal{R}_\Diamond$ and $\mathcal{M} \vDash_{w_1} \Box\psi)$ iff $\exists w_1((w, w_1) \in \mathcal{R}_\Diamond$ and $(\forall w_2((w_1, w_2) \in \mathcal{R}_\Box$ implies $\mathcal{M} \vDash_{w_2} \psi))$,
3. $\mathcal{M} \vDash_w \neg\Box_\Gamma \psi$ iff not $\mathcal{M} \vDash_w \Box_\Gamma \psi$,
4. $\mathcal{M} \vDash_w \Box_\Gamma \phi \wedge \Box_\Gamma \psi$ iff $\mathcal{M} \vDash_w \Box_\Gamma \phi$ and $\mathcal{M} \vDash_w \Box_\Gamma \psi$,
5. $\mathcal{M} \vDash_w \Box_\Gamma \phi \vee \Box_\Gamma \psi$ iff $\mathcal{M} \vDash_w \Box_\Gamma \phi$ or $\mathcal{M} \vDash_w \Box_\Gamma \psi$,
6. $\mathcal{M} \vDash_w \Box_\Gamma \phi \to \Box_\Gamma \psi$ iff $\mathcal{M} \vDash_w \Box_\Gamma \phi$ implies $\mathcal{M} \vDash_w \Box_\Gamma \psi$,

where the logic connectives $\wedge, \vee, \to$ and $\neg$ are the classic 2-valued conjunction, disjunction, implication and negation, respectively.

Notice that a satisfaction of the 2-valued formulae of this metalogic $\mathcal{L}_{\mathcal{F}}$, obtained by Suszko's reduction of the original many-valued logic, is relative to points from 2 to 6 in the definition above. Consequently, the two-valuedness is a property not of the original many-valued formulae, but of the modal formulae in this nontruth-functional modal meta-logic. Let us show that this reduction is sound and complete.

Lemma 17. *Given a Kripke model $\mathcal{M} = (\mathcal{W}, \mathcal{R}_{\Diamond}, \mathcal{R}_{\Box}, \mathcal{D}, I_K)$ in Definition 126, for a given many-valued logic (Γ, C), where $\Gamma \subset \mathcal{L}_{\mathrm{mv}}^{G}$ is a subset of sentences, then for any formula $\phi \in \mathcal{L}_{\mathrm{mv}}$ and assignment g we have that*

$$\Gamma \vDash \phi/g \quad \textit{iff} \quad \Box_{\Gamma}\phi/g \textit{ is true in } \mathcal{M}.$$

Proof. From point 2 in Definition 126, from the fact that $\exists w_1(w, w_1) \in \mathcal{R}_{\Diamond}$ for $w_1 = (\phi_k, v)$ is equivalent to $\exists \phi_k \in \Gamma$ and $\forall w_2((w_1, w_2) \in \mathcal{R}_{\Box}$ from $w_2 = (\phi_k, v_1)$ is equivalent to $\forall v_1 \in \mathbb{V}_{\Gamma}$, we obtain that

$$\mathcal{M} \vDash_w \Box_{\Gamma}\phi/g \quad \text{iff} \quad (\exists \phi_k \in \Gamma).(\forall v_1 \in \mathbb{V}_{\Gamma}).(v_1^*(\phi/g) \geq v_1^*(\phi_k))$$

i. e., from definition (5.2), $\mathcal{M} \vDash_w \Box_{\Gamma}\phi/g$ iff $\Gamma \vDash \phi/g$, and from the fact that it holds for any $w \in \mathcal{W}$, we obtain that $\Gamma \vDash \phi/g$ iff $\|\Box_{\Gamma}\phi/g\| = \mathcal{W}$, i. e., $\Box_{\Gamma}\phi/g$ is true in $\mathcal{M}$. □

These results confirm da Costa's idea [349] that a reduction to 2-valuedness can be done at an abstract level, without taking into account the underlying structure of the set of many-valued formulae (different from the particular case of logic programs given in Section A.4.2).

Second case

It is not necessary to make a detour *by matrices* in order to get this reduction. But in the case where we have a many-valued logic with a given matrix (X, D), where $D \subset X$ is a subset of *designated* algebraic truth values, then we are able to define a new modal 2-valued reduction for such a many-valued logic, based on the *universal* modal operator $\Box_D$ ("matrix-deductive"). What remains now is to define a Kripke semantics for this matrix-based reduction to a modal metalogic, denoted by $\mathcal{L}_{\mathcal{E}}$, obtained from a set of formulae $\{\Box_D\phi \mid \phi \in \mathcal{L}_{\mathrm{mv}}^{G}\}$ and standard 2-valued logic connectives (conjunction, disjunction, implication and negation).

Definition 127. Given a many-valued logic $\mathcal{L}_{\mathrm{mv}}$ with a given matrix (X, D) and a Herbrand base H, let $\mathbb{V}_{\Gamma} \subset \mathbb{V} = X^H$ be a nonempty subset of *models* of Γ, i. e., the set of valuations $v : H \to X$ that satisfy every sentence in Γ.

We define a Kripke-style model of modal metalogic $\mathcal{L}_{\mathcal{E}}$, based on Suszko's matrix-based reduction $\{\Box_D\phi \mid \phi \in \mathcal{L}_{\mathrm{mv}}^{G}\}$, by $\mathcal{M} = (\mathcal{W}, \mathcal{R}_D, \mathcal{D}, I_K)$, with the set of possible worlds $\mathcal{W} = \mathbb{V}$, accessibility relation $\mathcal{R}_D = \mathcal{W} \times \mathbb{V}_{\Gamma}$ for universal modal operator $\Box_D$, and $I_K : \mathcal{W} \times \mathcal{L}_{\mathrm{mv}}^{G} \to \mathbf{2}$, such that for any many-valued sentence $\psi \in \mathcal{L}_{\mathrm{mv}}^{G}$ and a world $w \in \mathcal{W}$,

$$I_K(w, \psi) = 1 \quad \text{iff} \quad w^*(\psi) \in D \tag{A.7}$$

where w^* is unique extension of Herbrand interpretation $w : H \to X$ to all sentences in $\mathcal{L}_{\mathrm{mv}}^{G}$. The satisfaction relation $\vDash_w$, for a world $w \in \mathcal{W}$, for any many-valued sentence $\psi, \phi \in \mathcal{L}_{\mathrm{mv}}^{G}$, is defined as follows:

1. $\mathcal{M} \models_w \psi$ iff $I_K(w, \psi) = 1$.
2. $\mathcal{M} \models_w \Box_D \psi$ iff $\forall w_1((w, w_1) \in \mathcal{R}_D$ implies $\mathcal{M} \models_{w_1} \psi)$,
3. $\mathcal{M} \models_w \neg \Box_D \phi$ iff not $\mathcal{M} \models_w \Box_D \phi$
4. $\mathcal{M} \models_w \Box_D \phi \wedge \Box_D \psi$ iff $\mathcal{M} \models_w \Box_D \phi$ and $\mathcal{M} \models_w \Box_D \psi$
5. $\mathcal{M} \models_w \Box_D \phi \vee \Box_D \psi$ iff $\mathcal{M} \models_w \Box_D \phi$ or $\mathcal{M} \models_w \Box_D \psi$
6. $\mathcal{M} \models_w \Box_D \phi \rightarrow \Box_D \psi$ iff $\mathcal{M} \models_w \Box_D \phi$ implies $\mathcal{M} \models_w \Box_D \psi$,

where the logic connectives $\wedge, \vee, \rightarrow$ and $\neg$ are the classic 2-valued conjunction, disjunction, implication and negation, respectively.

Notice that a satisfaction of the 2-valued formulae of this metalogic $\mathcal{L}_{\mathcal{E}}$, obtained by the matrix-based reduction of original many-valued logic, is relative to points 2 to 6 in the definition above.

Let us show that this matrix-based reduction is sound and complete.

Lemma 18. *Let $\mathcal{M} = (\mathcal{W}, \mathcal{R}_D, \mathcal{D}, I_K)$ be a Kripke model, given in Definition 127, for a many-valued logic (Γ, C) with a matrix (X, D), where $\Gamma \subset \mathcal{L}^G_{\mathrm{mv}}$ is a subset of sentences, then for any formula $\phi \in \mathcal{L}_{\mathrm{mv}}$ and assignment g, from definition (A.5), we have that*

$$\Gamma \models \phi/g \quad \textit{iff} \quad \Box_D \phi/g \textit{ is true in } \mathcal{M}.$$

Proof. From point 2 in Definition 127, from the fact that $\forall w_1((w, w_1) \in \mathcal{R}_D)$ is equivalent to $\forall w_1 \in \mathbb{V}_\Gamma$, we obtain that $\mathcal{M} \models_w \Box_D \phi/g$ iff $(\forall w_1 \in \mathbb{V}_\Gamma).(w_1^*(\phi/g) \in D)$, i. e., from definition (A.5), $\mathcal{M} \models_w \Box_D \phi/g$ iff $\Gamma \models \phi/g$, and from the fact that it holds for any $w \in \mathcal{W}$, we obtain that $\Gamma \models \phi/g$ iff $\|\Box_D \phi/g\| = \mathcal{W}$, i. e., $\Box_D \phi/g$ is true in $\mathcal{M}$. □

A.5 Basic category theory

Category theory is an area of mathematics that examines in an abstract way the properties of particular mathematical concepts, by formalizing them as collections of objects and arrows (also called morphisms, although this term also has a specific, noncategory-theoretic sense), where these collections satisfy certain basic conditions. Many significant areas of mathematics can be formalized as categories, and the use of category theory allows many intricate and subtle mathematical results in these fields to be stated and proved, in a much simpler way than without the use of categories.

The most accessible example of a category is the category **Set** of sets, where the objects are sets and the arrows are functions between them. However, it is important to note that the objects of a category need not be sets or the arrows functions; any way of formalizing a mathematical concept such that it meets the basic conditions on the behavior of objects and arrows is a valid category, and all the results of category theory will apply to it.

Categories were first introduced by Samuel Eilenberg and Saunders Mac Lane in 1942–1945 [181], in connection with algebraic topology. The study of categories is an attempt to axiomatically capture what is commonly found in various classes of related mathematical structures by relating them to the structure-preserving functions between them. A systematic study of category theory then allows us to prove general results about any of these types of mathematical structures from the axioms of a category.

A category $\mathbf{C}$ consists of the following three mathematical entities:

- A class $\mathrm{Ob}_{\mathbf{C}}$ whose elements are called objects;
- A class $\mathrm{Mor}_{\mathbf{C}}$ whose elements are called morphisms or maps or arrows. Each morphism f has a unique source object A and target object B. The expression (arrow) $f : A \to B$ would be verbally stated as "f is a morphism from A to B." The expression $\mathrm{hom}(A, B)$ — alternatively expressed as $\mathrm{hom}_{\mathbf{C}}(A, B)$, or $mor(A, B)$, or $\mathbf{C}(A, B)$ — denotes the hom-class of all morphisms from A to B. If for all A, B this hom-class is a set, this category $\mathbf{C}$ is called *locally small.*
- A binary operation $\circ$, called composition of morphisms, such that for any three objects A, B and C, we have a function $\circ : \mathrm{hom}(A, B) \times \mathrm{hom}(B, C) \to \mathrm{hom}(A, C)$. Each morphism $f \in \mathrm{hom}(A, B)$ has a domain $A = \mathrm{dom}(f)$ and codomain $B = \mathrm{cod}(f)$, which are objects.

  The composition of $f : A \to B$ and $g : B \to C$ is written as $g \circ f$, with two axioms:
  Associativity: If $f : A \to B, g : B \to C$ and $h : C \to D$, then $h \circ (g \circ f) = (h \circ g) \circ f$,
  Identity: For every object A, there exists a morphism $\mathrm{id}_A : A \to A$ called the identity morphism for A, such that for every morphism $f : A \to B$, we have $\mathrm{id}_B \circ f = f \circ \mathrm{id}_A = f$.

From these axioms, it can be proved that there is exactly one identity morphism for every object. Because of that we can identify each object with its identity morphism. Relations among morphisms are often depicted using commutative diagrams, with nodes representing objects and arrows representing morphisms, e. g., $g \circ f = h$ is graphically represented by the following commutative diagram:

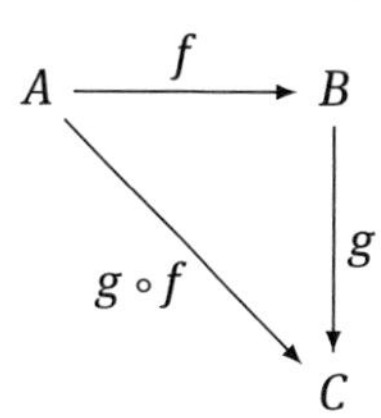

Examples:

1. Category **Set**, where the objects are sets and the arrows are functions from one set to another.
2. A preorder is a set X together with a binary relation $\leq$, which is reflexive (i. e., $x \leq x$ for all $x \in X$), and transitive (i. e., $x \leq y$ and $y \leq z$ imply $x \leq z$ for all $x, y, z \in X$).

This can be seen as a category, with set of objects X and for every pair of objects (x, y) such that $x \leq y$, exactly one arrow $x \to y$.
3. Any set X can be seen as a discrete category, with a set of objects X and only with the identity morphisms.

A morphism $f : A \to B$ can have any of the following properties:
1. *Monomorphism* (or monic) if $f \circ g_1 = f \circ g_2$ implies $g_1 = g_2$ for all morphisms $g_1, g_2 : X \to A$. It is denoted by $f : A \hookrightarrow B$.
2. *Epimorphism* (or epic) if $g_1 \circ f = g_2 \circ f$ implies $g_1 = g_2$ for all morphisms $g_1, g_2 : B \to X$. It is denoted by $f : A \twoheadrightarrow B$. This epic is called *split* if there is $g : B \to A$ such that $f \circ g = \mathrm{id}_B$ (then f is a *retraction* of g).
3. *Isomorphism* if there exists a morphism $g : B \to A$ such that $f \circ g = \mathrm{id}_B$ and $g \circ f = \mathrm{id}_A$. It is denoted by $f : A \simeq B$. Often we denote simply by $A \simeq B$ the isomorphism of two objects. If f is split epic and monic, f is an isomorphism.

For example, in **Set** the epimorphisms are surjective functions, the monomorphisms are injective functions, the isomorphisms are bijective functions.

Duality principle

The definition of epic is *dual* to the definition of monic. Given a category $\mathbf{C} = (\mathrm{Ob}_C, \mathrm{Mor}_C, \mathrm{id}, \circ)$, by $\mathbf{C}^{\mathrm{OP}} = (\mathrm{Ob}_C, \mathrm{Mor}_{C^{\mathrm{OP}}}, \mathrm{id}, \circ^{C^{\mathrm{OP}}})$ we denote the opposite category that have the same objects and where all arrows are reversed: $f^{C^{\mathrm{OP}}} \circ^{C^{\mathrm{OP}}} g^{C^{\mathrm{OP}}} = (g \circ f)^{C^{\mathrm{OP}}}$ (see diagram (A.8)), with bijection $\mathbf{C}(A, B) \simeq \mathbf{C}^{\mathrm{OP}}(B, A)$. Thus, f is monic in the category $\mathbf{C}$ iff f^{OP} is epic in $\mathbf{C}^{\mathrm{OP}}$, and vice versa. In general, given a property P of an object, arrow, diagram, etc., we can associate with P the dual property P^{OP}. The object or arrow has a property P in $\mathbf{C}$ iff it has P^{OP} in $\mathbf{C}^{\mathrm{OP}}$. For example, if $g \circ f$ is monic then f is monic. From this, by duality, if $f^{\mathrm{OP}} \circ g^{\mathrm{OP}}$ is epic then f^{OP} is epic.

An object X is called *terminal* if for any object Y there is exactly one morphism from it into X in the category. Dually, one object X is called *initial* if for any object Y there is exactly one morphism from X to Y in the category. An object X is called the *zero* object if it is both terminal and initial. For example, in **Set** the empty set is initial, while any singleton set is (up to isomorphism) the terminal object.

Given two categories $\mathbf{C}$ and $\mathbf{D}$, we can define the *product category* $\mathbf{C} \times \mathbf{D}$, which has as objects pairs $(X, Y) \in \mathrm{Ob}_C \times \mathrm{Ob}_D$ and as arrows: $(X, Y) \to (X', Y')$ pairs (f, g) with $f : X \to X'$ in $\mathbf{C}$, and $g : Y \to Y'$ in $\mathbf{D}$.

Functors are structure-preserving maps between categories. They can be thought of as morphisms in the category **Cat** of all (small) categories as objects, and all functors as morphisms. A (covariant) functor F from a category $\mathbf{C}$ to a category $\mathbf{D}$, written $F : \mathbf{C} \to \mathbf{D}$, consists of a pair of functions $F = (F^0, F^1)$, $F^0 : \mathrm{Ob}_{\mathbf{C}} \to \mathrm{Ob}_{\mathbf{D}}$ and $F^1 : \mathrm{Mor}_{\mathbf{C}} \to \mathrm{Mor}_{\mathbf{D}}$ (in what follows, we will simply use F for both functions as well):

1. For each object X in $\mathbf{C}$, an object $F^0(X)$ in $\mathbf{D}$; and
2. For each morphism $f : X \to Y$ in $\mathbf{C}$, a morphism $F^1(f) : F^0(X) \to F^0(Y)$, such that the following two properties hold:
3. For every object X in $\mathbf{C}$, $F^1(\mathrm{id}_X) = \mathrm{id}_{F(X)}$;
4. For all morphisms $f : X \to Y$ and $g : Y \to Z$, $F^1(g \circ f) = F^1(g) \circ F^1(f)$.

A contravariant functor $F : \mathbf{C} \to \mathbf{D}$, is like a covariant functor, except that it "turns morphisms around" ("reverses all the arrows"). More specifically, every morphism $f : X \to Y$ in $\mathbf{C}$ must be assigned to a morphism $F^1(f) : F^0(Y) \to F^0(X)$ in $\mathbf{D}$. In other words, a contravariant functor is a covariant functor from the opposite category $\mathbf{C}^{\mathrm{op}}$ to $\mathbf{D}$. Opposite category $\mathbf{C}^{\mathrm{op}}$ has the same objects as the category $\mathbf{C}$. Given a composition of arrows $f \circ g$ in $\mathbf{C}$ its opposite arrow in $\mathbf{C}^{\mathrm{op}}$ is $(f \circ g)^{\mathrm{OP}} = g^{\mathrm{OP}} \circ f^{\mathrm{OP}}$.

Every functor preserves epi, mono and isomorphisms.

A locally small category $\mathbf{C}$, for any object X, has a *representable functor* $F_X = \mathbf{C}(X, \_) : \mathbf{C} \to \mathbf{Set}$, such that for any object Y, $F_X(Y) = \mathbf{C}(X, Y)$, and any arrow $f : Y \to Y'$ gives by composition a function $F_X(f) : \mathbf{C}(X, Y) \to \mathbf{C}(X, Y')$.

A functor $F : \mathbf{C} \to \mathbf{D}$ is called *full* if for every two objects A and B of $\mathbf{C}$, $F : \mathbf{C}(A, B) \to \mathbf{D}(F(A), F(B))$ is a surjection. A functor F is called *faithful* if this map is always injective. A functor F is called an *endofunctor* if $\mathbf{D} = \mathbf{C}$.

A functor F *reflects* a property P if whenever the F-image of something (object, arrow, etc.) has P, then that that something has P. For example, the faithful functor reflects epimorphisms and monomorphisms. Each endofunctor $F : \mathbf{C} \to \mathbf{C}$ defines the algebras and coalgebras (the left and right commutative diagrams)

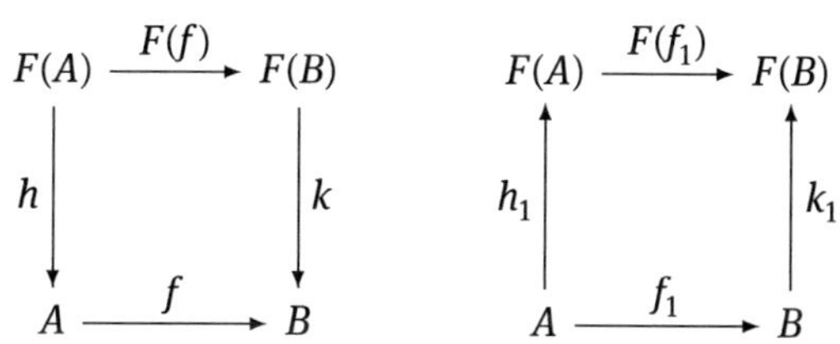

so that the morphism $f : (A, h) \to (B, k)$, which represents the commutative diagram on the left, is a morphism between F-algebras (A, h) and (B, k). For example, let $F : \mathbf{Set} \to \mathbf{Set}$ be the polynomial endofunctor, such that for the set A of all reals, $F(A) = A + A + A^2 + A^2$ (where $+$ is a disjoint union) we can represent the algebra for operators $\{\exp : A \to A, \log : A \to A, \max : A^2 \to A, \min : A^2 \to A\}$, where A^2 is the Cartesian product $A \times A$, by the morphism $h = [\exp, \log, \max, \min] : (A + A + A^2 + A^2) \to A$ in $\mathbf{Set}$, i. e., by the F-algebra (A, h).

Analogously, the morphism $f_1 : (A, h_1) \to (B, k_1)$, which represents the commutative diagram on the right, is a morphism between F-coalgebras (A, h_1) and (B, k_1).

Let $G : \mathbf{D} \to \mathbf{C}$ be a functor, and C an object of $\mathbf{C}$. A *universal arrow from C to G* is a pair (D, g) where D is an object of $\mathbf{D}$ and $g : C \to G(D)$ a morphism in $\mathbf{C}$ such that, for any object D' of $\mathbf{D}$ and morphism $f : C \to G(D')$, there exists a unique morphism $\widehat{f} : D \to D'$ in $\mathbf{D}$ such that $f = G(\widehat{f}) \circ g$. Diagrammatically,

$$\begin{array}{ccccc} C & \xrightarrow{g} & G(D) & \qquad & D \\ & \searrow^{f} & \downarrow{\scriptstyle G(\widehat{f})} & & \vdots{\scriptstyle \widehat{f}} \\ & & G(D') & & D' \end{array}$$

A *natural transformation* is a relation between two functors. Functors often describe "natural constructions" and natural transformations then describe "natural homomorphisms" between two such constructions. Sometimes two quite different constructions yield "the same" result; this is expressed by a natural isomorphism between the two functors.

If F and G are (covariant) functors between the categories $\mathbf{C}$ and $\mathbf{D}$, then a natural transformation η from F to G associates to every object X in $\mathbf{C}$ a morphism $\eta_X : F(X) \to G(X)$ in $\mathbf{D}$ such that for every morphism $f : X \to Y$ in $\mathbf{C}$, we have $\eta_Y \circ F(f) = G(f) \circ \eta_X$.

This means that the following diagram is commutative:

$$\begin{array}{ccc} F(X) & \xrightarrow{F(f)} & F(Y) \\ {\scriptstyle \eta_X}\downarrow & & \downarrow{\scriptstyle \eta_Y} \\ G(X) & \xrightarrow{G(f)} & G(Y) \end{array}$$

Example. Let P and Q be two preorders, regarded as categories. A functor F from P to Q is a monotone function, and there exists a unique natural transformation between two such, $\eta : F \overset{\cdot}{\longrightarrow} G$, exactly if $F(X) \leq G(X)$ for all X in P. □

If $\eta : F \overset{\cdot}{\longrightarrow} G$ and $\varepsilon : G \overset{\cdot}{\longrightarrow} H$ are natural transformations between functors $F, G, H : \mathbf{C} \to \mathbf{D}$, then we can compose them to get a natural transformation $\varepsilon \bullet \eta : F \overset{\cdot}{\longrightarrow} H$.

This is done componentwise: $(\varepsilon \bullet \eta)_X = \varepsilon_X \circ \eta_X : F(X) \to H(X)$.

This *vertical composition* of natural transformation is associative and has an identity, and allows one to consider the collection of all functors $\mathbf{C} \to \mathbf{D}$ itself as a category $\mathbf{D}^{\mathbf{C}}$ of all functors from $\mathbf{C}$ to $\mathbf{D}$.

There is also a *horizontal composition* of natural transformations, given the functors $F, G : \mathbf{B} \to \mathbf{C}$, $F', G' : \mathbf{C} \to \mathbf{D}$, and two natural transformations $\eta : F \overset{\cdot}{\longrightarrow} G$ and $\varepsilon : F' \overset{\cdot}{\longrightarrow} G'$, defined by $\varepsilon \circ \eta : F' \circ F \overset{\cdot}{\longrightarrow} G' \circ G$, between the composed functors $F' \circ F, G' \circ G : \mathbf{B} \to \mathbf{D}$.

The two functors F and G are called naturally isomorphic if there exists a natural transformation η from F to G such that η_X is an isomorphism for every object X in $\mathbf{C}$.

The Yoneda lemma is one of the most famous basic results of category theory. It describes representable functors in functor categories. The Yoneda embedding for any given category $\mathbf{C}$ is given by the covariant functor $H : \mathbf{C} \to \mathbf{Set}^{\mathbf{C}^{OP}}$ such that, for any object X in $\mathbf{C}$, we obtain the contravariant hom-functor $h_X = \mathbf{C}^{OP}(X, \_) : \mathbf{C}^{OP} \to \mathbf{Set}$.

Consequently, for any object Y' in $\mathbf{C}^{OP}$, $h_X(Y_1) = \mathbf{C}^{OP}(X, Y_1)$, while for any arrow $f^{OP} : Y_1 \to Y_2$ in $\mathbf{C}^{OP}$, we obtain the arrow (function) in $\mathbf{Set}$, $h_X(f^{OP}) : \mathbf{C}^{OP}(X, Y_1) \to \mathbf{C}^{OP}(X, Y_2)$ is a composition with f^{OP}, i. e., for any $g^{OP} : X \to Y_1$ in $\mathbf{C}^{OP}(X, Y_1)$ we obtain the arrow $h_X(f^{OP})(g^{OP}) = f^{OP} \circ g^{OP} = (g \circ f)^{OP} : X \to Y_2$, such that the following diagram commutes in $\mathbf{C}^{OP}$ (or, dually in $\mathbf{C}$):

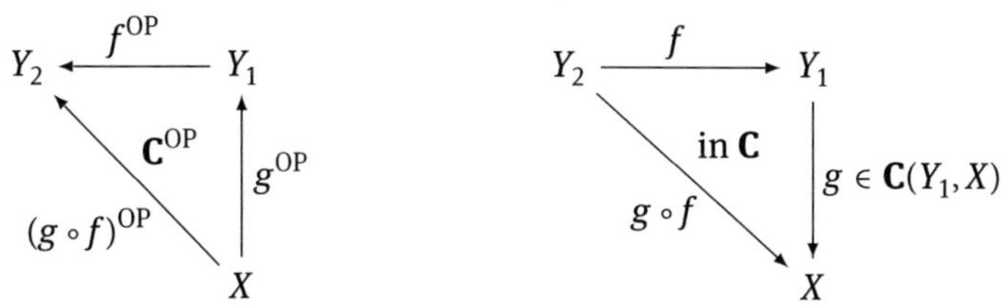

(A.8)

In the case when $f^{OP} : Y_1 \to Y_2$ in $\mathbf{C}^{OP}$ is a *universal arrow*, the function $h_X(f^{OP}) : \mathbf{C}^{OP}(X, Y_1) \to \mathbf{C}^{OP}(X, Y_2)$ (an arrow in $\mathbf{Set}$) is a bijection.

Let us consider two significant cases of Yoneda embedding for categorial *products* and *coproducts* (without the necessity to introduce the more general case of limits and colimits):

1. The universal arrows for the *products* $f^{OP} = (\pi_1, \pi_2) : (A \times B, A \times B) \twoheadrightarrow (A, B)$ in $\mathbf{C}^{OP} = \mathbf{D} \times \mathbf{D}$, and a given object $X = (C, C) \in \mathbf{C}^{OP}$, where $\pi_1 : A \times B \twoheadrightarrow A$, $\pi_2 : A \times B \twoheadrightarrow B$ are two epimorphisms in $\mathbf{D}$ corresponding to the first and second projections, respectively. Thus, we obtain the following case for the commutative diagram above in $\mathbf{C}^{OP} = \mathbf{D} \times \mathbf{D}$ (and its corresponding commutative diagram in $\mathbf{D}$ on the right), where $Y_2 = (A, B)$ and $Y_1 = (A \times B, A \times B)$, $g^{OP} = (\langle k, l \rangle, \langle k, l \rangle) : (C, C) \to (A \times B, A \times B)$, with $k : C \to A$, $l : C \to B$ two arrows in $\mathbf{D}$:

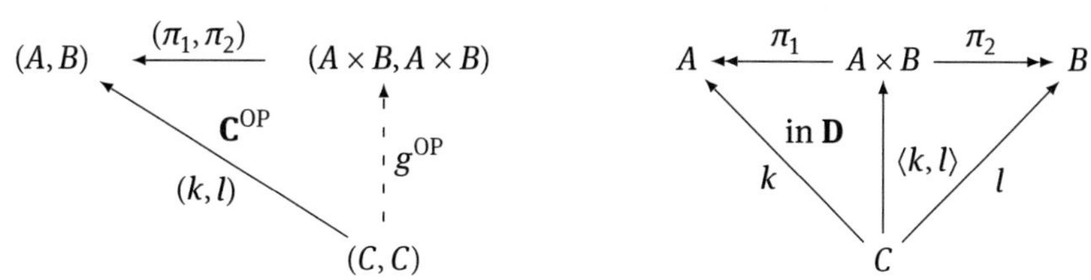

The bijective function $h_X(f^{OP}) : \mathbf{C}^{OP}(X, Y_1) \to \mathbf{C}^{OP}(X, Y_2)$ in this case means that for any arrow $(k, l) : (C, C) \to (A, B)$ in $\mathbf{C}^{OP}(X, Y_2)$ (i. e., the couple of arrows $k : C \to A$, $l : C \to B$ in $\mathbf{D}$) there is the unique arrow $(\langle k, l \rangle, \langle k, l \rangle) : (C, C) \to (A \times B, A \times B)$ in $\mathbf{C}^{OP}(X, Y_1)$ (i. e., the unique arrow $\langle k, l \rangle : C \to A \times B$ in $\mathbf{D}$).

2. Universal arrows for the *coproducts* $f = (\mathrm{in}_1, \mathrm{in}_2) : (A, B) \hookrightarrow (A + B, A + B)$ in $\mathbf{C} = \mathbf{D} \times \mathbf{D}$, and a given object $X = (C, C) \in \mathbf{C}$, where $\mathrm{in}_1 : A \hookrightarrow A + B$, $\mathrm{in}_2 : B \hookrightarrow$

$A + B$ are two monomorphisms in $\mathbf{D}$ corresponding to the first and second injections, respectively. Thus, we obtain the following case for the commutative diagram above in $\mathbf{C} = \mathbf{D} \times \mathbf{D}$ (and its corresponding commutative diagram in $\mathbf{D}$ on the right), where $Y_2 = (A, B)$ and $Y_1 = (A + B, A + B)$, $g = ([k, l], [k, l]) : (A + B, A + B) \to (C, C)$, with $k : A \to C, l : B \to C$ two arrows in $\mathbf{D}$:

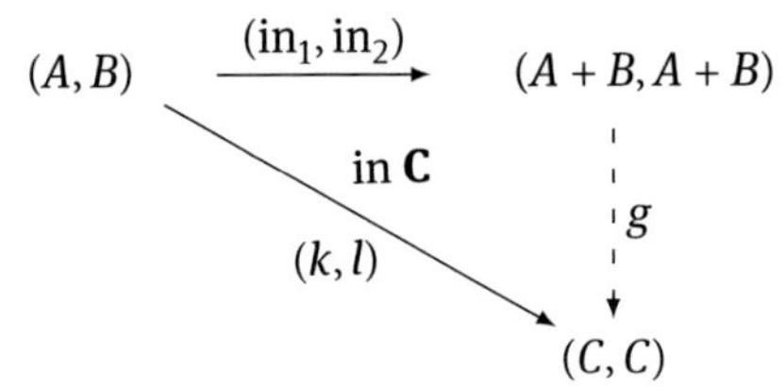

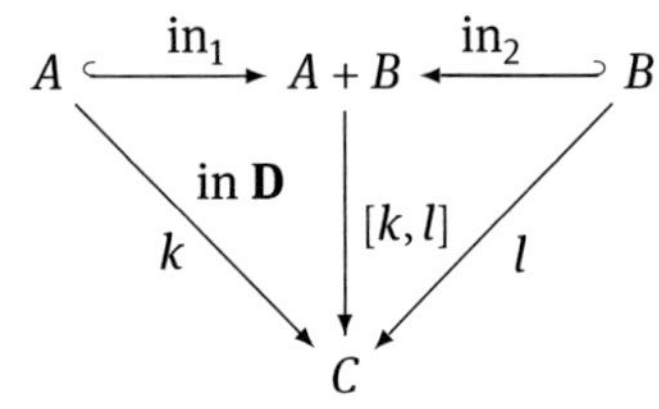

The bijective function $h_X(f^{\mathrm{OP}}) : \mathbf{C}(Y_1, X) \to \mathbf{C}(Y_2, X)$ in this case means that for any arrow $(k, l) : (A, B) \to (C, C)$ in $\mathbf{C}(Y_2, X)$ (i. e., the couple of arrows $k : A \to C, l : B \to C$ in $\mathbf{D}$) there is the unique arrow $([k, l], [k, l]) : (A + B, A + B) \to (C, C)$ in $\mathbf{C}(Y_1, X)$ (i. e., the unique arrow $[k, l] : A + B \to C$ in $\mathbf{D}$).

For example, in **Set** the object $A \times B$ is the Cartesian product of the set A and set B, while $A + B$ is the disjoint union of the set A and set B.

Products and coproducts are the particular cases of adjunctions. Given two functors $F : \mathbf{C} \to \mathbf{D}$, $G : \mathbf{D} \to \mathbf{C}$, we say that F is *left adjoint* to G, or G is *right adjoint* to F, is there are the natural isomorphism: $\theta : \mathbf{C}(\_, G(\_)) \stackrel{\cdot}{\longrightarrow} \mathbf{D}(F(\_), \_)$, where $\mathbf{C}(\_, G(\_)) : \mathbf{C}^{\mathrm{OP}} \times \mathbf{D} \to \mathbf{Set}$ is the result of composing the bivariant hom-functor $\mathbf{C}(\_, \_)$ with $\mathrm{Id}_{C^{\mathrm{OP}}} \times G$, and $\mathbf{D}(F(\_), \_)$ is similar.

Equivalently, they are adjoint if there are two natural transformations, *counit* $\varepsilon : FG \stackrel{\cdot}{\longrightarrow} \mathrm{Id}_D$ and *unit* $\eta : \mathrm{Id}_C \stackrel{\cdot}{\longrightarrow} GF$, such that the following diagrams of natural transformations commute:

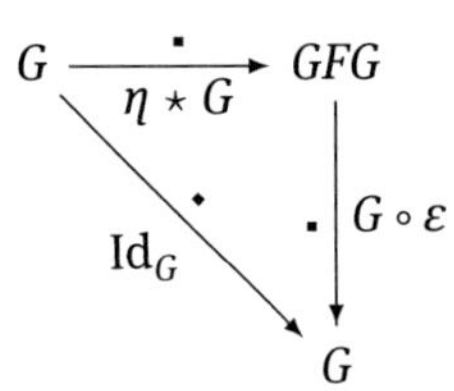

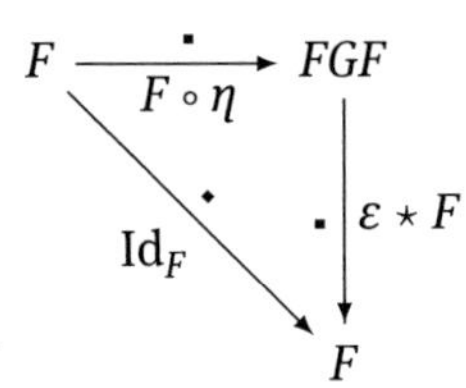

where $\eta \star G$ denotes the natural transformation with components (functions) $\eta_{G(X)} : G(X) \to GFG(X)$ and $G \circ \varepsilon$ denotes the natural transformation with components $G(\varepsilon_X) : GFG(X) \to G(X)$, for each object X in $\mathbf{D}$.

This adjunction is denoted by tuple $(F, G, \varepsilon, \eta)$, with $\eta_C : C \to G(F(C))$ a universal arrow for each object C. In fact, for any object D' in $\mathbf{D}$ and morphism $f : C \to G(D')$ there exists a unique morphism $\widehat{f} : D \to D'$, where $D = F(C)$, such that the following two adjoint diagrams commute:

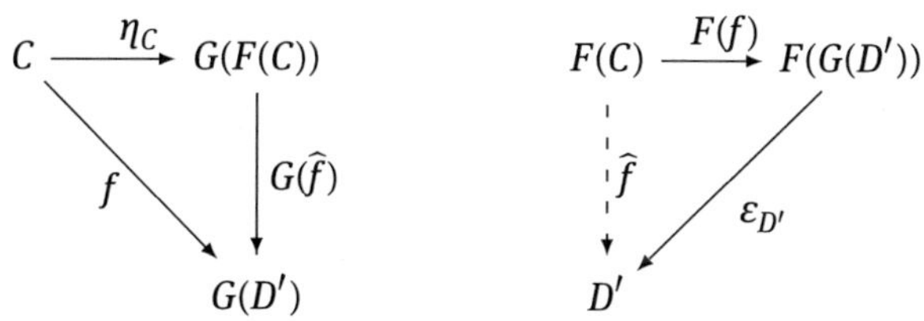

so that η_C is a universal arrow from C into G and, dually, $\varepsilon_{D'}$ is a couniversal arrow from F into D'. Consequently, in a given adjunction, the unit η generates a universal arrow for each object in **C** and counit ε generates a couniversal arrow for each object in **D**. In the case when **C** and **D** are poset categories, f and $\widehat{f}$ define this adjunction as a Galois connection, denoted by $F \dashv G$.

In category theory, the abstract notion of a *limit* captures the essential properties of universal constructions such as products, pullbacks and inverse limits. The dual notion of a *colimit* generalizes constructions such as disjoint unions, direct sums, coproducts, pushouts and direct limits. Limits and colimits, like the strongly related notions of universal properties and adjoint functors, exist at a high level of abstraction. Limits and colimits in a category C are defined by means of diagrams in C.

For example, the *equalizers* are a particular case of limits (of pullbacks). For each pair of simple morphisms $f, g : A \to B$, the Lim$E$ is a limit object (up to isomorphism) of the diagram $B \overset{f}{\underset{g}{\leftleftarrows}} A$, so that the following diagram is an equalizer:

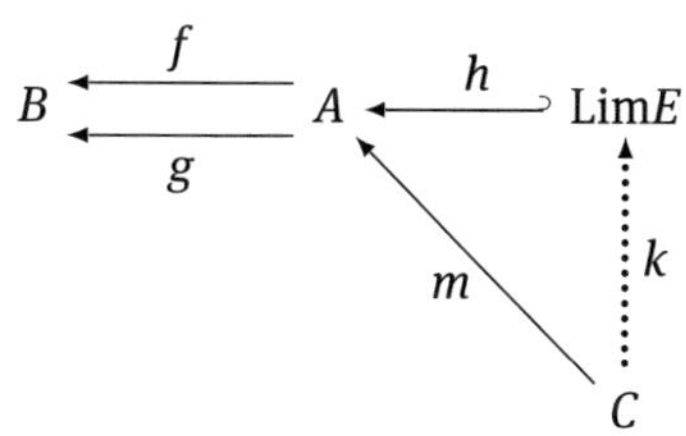

with $f \circ h = g \circ h$ where h is a monomorphism (every equalizer is monic), and for any arrow m such that $f \circ m = g \circ m$, there is a unique arrow k such that $m = h \circ k$.

Two categories **C** and **D** are *equivalent* if they are adjoint with the unit and counit whose components are all isomorphisms.

Given an adjunction $(F, G, \varepsilon, \eta)$, let us look at the endofunctor $T = GF : \mathbf{C} \to \mathbf{C}$. We have a natural transformation $\eta : \mathrm{id}_{\mathbf{C}} \stackrel{\cdot}{\longrightarrow} T$ and a natural transformation $\mu : T^2 \stackrel{\cdot}{\longrightarrow} T$ with components for each object C, $\mu_C = G(\varepsilon_{F(C)}) : T^2C \to TC$ (here T^2 denotes the composition TT and T^3 the composition TTT). Furthermore, the equalities (commutative diagrams of natural transformations)

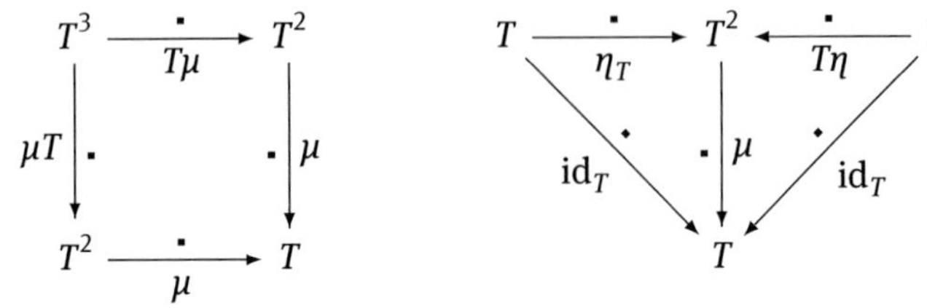

(A.9)

hold. Here, $(T\mu)_C = T(\mu_C) : T^3C \to TC$ and $(\mu T)_C = \mu_{TC} : T^3C \to TC$ (similarly for ηT and $T\eta$).

A triple (T, η, μ) satisfying these equalities is called a *monad*.

The notion of a monad is one of the most general mathematical notions. For instance, *every* algebraic theory, i. e., every set of operations satisfying equational laws, can be seen as a monad (which is also a *monoid* in a category of endofunctors of a given category: the "operation" μ being the associative multiplication of this monoid and η its unit).

Thus, monoid laws of the monad do subsume all possible algebraic laws.

We will use monads [181–183] for giving *denotational semantics to database mappings*, and more specifically as a way of modeling computational/collection types [176, 177, 184, 185].

A dual structure to a monad is a comonad (T, η^C, μ^C) such that all arrows in the commutative monad's diagrams above are inverted, so that we obtain

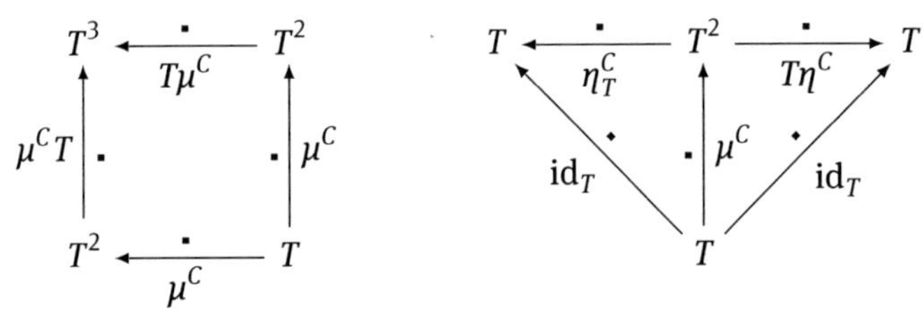

A *monoidal category* is a structure $(\mathbf{C}, \otimes, I, \alpha, \beta, \gamma)$ where $\mathbf{C}$ is a category, $\otimes : \mathbf{C} \times \mathbf{C} \to \mathbf{C}$ is a functor (*tensor*), I is a distinguished object of $\mathbf{C}$ (unit), α, β, γ are natural transformations (*structural isos* for associativity, left and right identity) with components: $\alpha_{A,B,C} : (A \otimes B) \otimes C \simeq A \otimes (B \otimes C)$, $\beta_A : I \otimes A \simeq A$, $\gamma_A : A \otimes I \simeq A$, such that the following diagrams commute (coherence conditions):

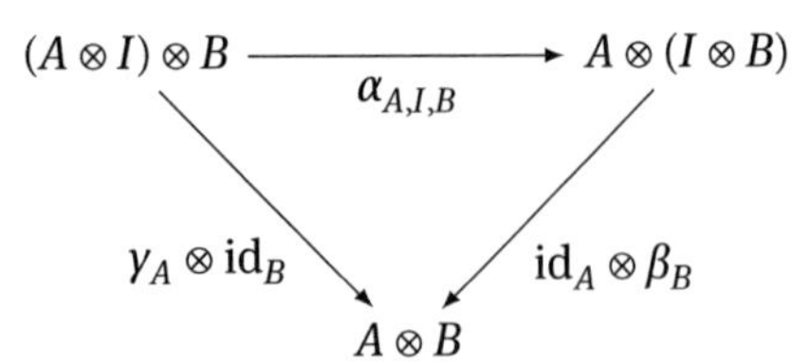

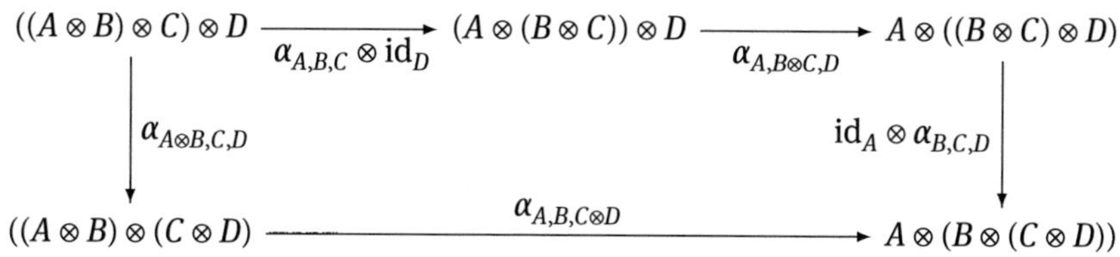

A *strict* monoidal category is one for which all of these natural transformations are identities.

If the category is finitely complete and has the *exponentiation* as well, then it is a Cartesian Closed Category (CCC). We say that a category has exponentiation if it has a product for any two objects, and if for any given objects B and C there is an object C^B and an arrow $\mathrm{eval}_{B,C} : C^B \times B \to C$, called an *evolution* arrow, such that for any object A and arrow $f : A \times B \to C$, there is a unique arrow $\Lambda(f) : A \to C^B$ making the following diagram commute:

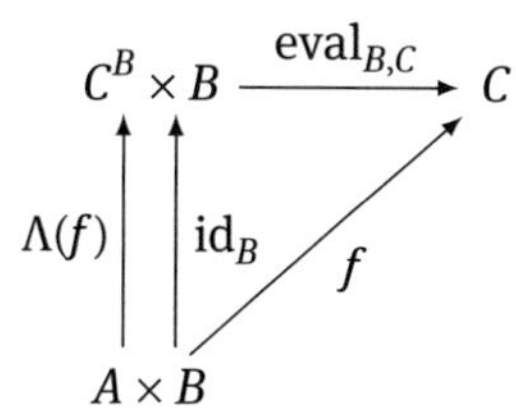

(A.10)

such that $\mathrm{eval}_{B,C} \circ (\Lambda(f) \times \mathrm{id}_B) = f$. The assignment of the curried[3] function $\Lambda(f)$ to f establishes a bijection Λ from the arrows from $A \times B$ to C and the arrows from A to C^B. The most known CCC is the category **Set**, and the meaning of the diagram above is simple:

For each pair of elements $a \in A$ and $b \in B$, we obtain a function $h =_{\mathrm{def}} \Lambda(f)(a) : B \to C$, such that by applying the function $\mathrm{eval}_{B,C}$ we obtain that it applies the function h to the element b, so that $\mathrm{eval}_{B,C}(h, b) =_{\mathrm{def}} h(b) = f(a, b)$.

This very short introduction to category theory is dedicated to experts in DB theory, which did not work previously with the concepts of the category theory.

A.5.1 Categorial symmetry

The concept of categorial symmetry was introduced in my PhD thesis [59] with a number of its applications. Here, I will only introduce some of the fundamental properties

---

3 Currying provides a way for working with functions that take multiple arguments, and using them in frameworks where functions might take only one argument. This property is inherited from lambda calculus, where multiargument functions are usually represented in curried form. A curried function is a function, which takes multiple parameters one at a time, by taking the first argument, and returning a series of functions, which each take the next argument until all the parameters have been fixed, and the function application can complete, at which point, the resulting value is returned.

of this particular class of categories, which has been considered in the database category **DB**. It is well known that all categories can be defined by only their morphisms (arrows) because each object is equivalently represented by its identity morphism. Fundamentally, a symmetric category has a nice property of a kind of (incomplete) duality between objects and arrows. In fact, there is an operator $'*'$ for the composition of objects, analogous to the standard composition of arrows $'\circ'$. However, differently from $\circ$ that is not commutative (preserves the sequential composition of the arrows), the composition $*$ of objects can be a (not necessarily) commutative binary operator as well, because the objects have no directionality.

The objects obtained from arrows will be called *conceptualized* objects. For example, let us consider the polynomial function $f(x) = (x^2 - 3x + 1)$, with the domain being the closed interval of reals from 0 to 1, and codomain $\mathbb{R}$ of all reals. It is an arrow $f : [0,1] \to \mathbb{R}$ in the category **Set**. The conceptualized object obtained from this arrow, denoted by $\widetilde{f}$, is the *set* (hence an object in **Set**) equal to the graph of this polynomial function. That is, $\widetilde{f} = \{(x, f(x)) \mid x \in [0,1]\} \in Ob_{Set}$. Let us now formally introduce the following definitions [59] for the categorial symmetry.

Definition 128 (Categorial symmetry). Let **C** be a category with a function $B_T : Mor_C \longrightarrow Ob_C$ such that for each identity arrow $id_A : A \to A$, $B_T(id_A) \simeq A$ (the "representability" principle), and with an associative composition operator for objects $*$ such that, for any composition $g \circ f \in Mor_C$ of arrows, $B_T(g) * B_T(f) = B_T(g \circ f)$.

The *conceptualized* object $B_T(f)$ of an arrow $f : A \longrightarrow B$ in **C** will be denoted by $\widetilde{f}$.

Remark. This symmetry property allows us to consider all properties of an arrow as properties of objects and their compositions. For a given category **C**, its "arrow category" is denoted by $\mathbf{C} \downarrow \mathbf{C}$. Objects of this arrow category are the triples $\langle A, B, f\rangle$ where $f : A \to B$ is a morphism in **C**, and each morphism in this arrow category is a couple of two morphisms $(k_1; k_2) : \langle A, B, f\rangle \to \langle C, D, g\rangle$ such that $k_2 \circ f = g \circ k_1 : A \to D$.

Let us introduce, for a category **C** and its arrow category $\mathbf{C} \downarrow \mathbf{C}$, an encapsulation operator $J : Mor_C \longrightarrow Ob_{C\downarrow C}$ and its inverse ψ, such that for any arrow $f : A \longrightarrow B$, $J(f) = \langle A, B, f\rangle$ is its corresponding object in $\mathbf{C} \downarrow \mathbf{C}$ and $\psi(\langle A, B, f\rangle) = f$.

We denote the first and the second comma functorial projections by $F_{st}, S_{nd} : (\mathbf{C} \downarrow \mathbf{C}) \longrightarrow \mathbf{C}$ such that for any arrow $(k_1; k_2) : \langle A, B, f\rangle \to \langle A', B', g\rangle$ in $\mathbf{C} \downarrow \mathbf{C}$ (i. e., when $k_2 \circ f = g \circ k_1$ in C) we have that $F^0_{st}(\langle A, B, f\rangle) = A$, $F^1_{st}(k_1; k_2) = k_1$, $S^0_{nd}(\langle A, B, f\rangle) = B$ and $S^1_{nd}(k_1; k_2) = k_2$. It is easy to extend the operator ψ into a natural transformation $\psi : F_{st} \stackrel{\bullet}{\longrightarrow} S_{nd}$ such that its component for an object $J(f)$ in $\mathbf{C} \downarrow \mathbf{C}$ is the arrow $\psi_{J(f)} = \psi(J(f)) = f$. We denote the diagonal functor by $\blacktriangle : \mathbf{C} \longrightarrow (\mathbf{C} \downarrow \mathbf{C})$ such that, for any object A in a category **C**, $\blacktriangle^0(A) = \langle A, A, id_A\rangle$.

An important subset of symmetric categories are the conceptually closed and extended symmetric categories, as follows.

Definition 129. [59] *A conceptually closed* category is a symmetric category **C** with a functor $T_e = (T_e^0, T_e^1) : (\mathbf{C} \downarrow \mathbf{C}) \longrightarrow \mathbf{C}$, such that $T_e^0 = B_T \psi$, i. e., $B_T = T_e^0 J$, with a natural isomorphism $\varphi : T_e \circ \blacktriangle \simeq I_C$, where I_C is an identity functor for **C**.

C is an *extended symmetric* category if $\tau^{-1} \bullet \tau = \psi : F_{\mathrm{st}} \stackrel{\bullet}{\longrightarrow} S_{\mathrm{nd}}$, for vertical composition of natural transformations $\tau : F_{\mathrm{st}} \stackrel{\bullet}{\longrightarrow} T_e$ and $\tau^{-1} : T_e \stackrel{\bullet}{\longrightarrow} S_{\mathrm{nd}}$.

It is easy to verify also that in extended symmetric categories the following is valid:

$$\tau = (T_e^1(\tau_I F_{\mathrm{st}}^0; \psi)) \bullet (\varphi^{-1} F_{\mathrm{st}}^0), \quad \tau^{-1} = (\varphi^{-1} S_{\mathrm{nd}}^0) \bullet (T_e^1(\psi; \tau_I S_{\mathrm{nd}}^0)),$$

where $\tau_I : I_C \longrightarrow I_C$ is an identity natural transformation (for any object A in **C**, $\tau_I(A) = \mathrm{id}_A$).

Example 58. The **Set** is an extended symmetric category: given any function $f : A \longrightarrow B$, the conceptualized object of this function is the graph of this function (which is a set),

$$\widetilde{f} = B_T(f) =_{\mathrm{def}} \{(x, f(x)) \mid x \in A\}.$$

The composition of objects $*$ is defined as an associative composition of binary relations (graphs of functions), $B_T(g \circ f) = \{(x, (g \circ f)(x)) \mid x \in A\} = \{(y, g(y)) \mid y \in B\} \circ \{(x, f(x)) \mid x \in A\} = B_T(g) * B_T(f)$.

Set is also conceptually closed by the functor T_e, such that for any object $J(f) = \langle A, B, f\rangle$, $T_e^0(J(f)) =_{\mathrm{def}} B_T(f) = \{(x, f(x)) \mid x \in A\}$, and for any arrow $(k_1; k_2) : J(f) \to J(g)$, the component T_e^1 is defined by,

$$\text{for any } (x, f(x)) \in T_e^0(J(f)), \quad T_e^1(k_1; k_2)(x, f(x)) = (k_1(x), k_2(f(x))).$$

It is easy to verify the compositional property for T_e^1, and that $T_e^1(\mathrm{id}_A; \mathrm{id}_B) = \mathrm{id}_{T_e^0(J(f))}$. For example, **Set** is also an extended symmetric category, such that for any object $J(f) = \langle A, B, f\rangle$ in **Set** $\downarrow$ **Set**, $\tau(J(f)) : A \twoheadrightarrow B_T(f)$ is an epimorphism, such that for any $x \in A$, $\tau(J(f))(x) = (x, f(x))$, while $\tau^{-1}(J(f)) : B_T(f) \hookrightarrow B$ is the second projection, such that for any $(x, f(x)) \in B_T(f)$,

$$\tau^{-1}(J(f))(x, f(x)) = f(x).$$

Thus, each arrow in **Set** is a composition of an epimorphism (surjective function) and a monomorphism (injective function).

The categorial symmetry can be better understood by considering a category **C** as a two-sorted algebra $\mathrm{Alg}_{\mathbf{C}} = ((\mathrm{Ob}_C, \mathrm{Mor}_C), \Sigma_{\mathbf{C}})$ (two-sorted carrier set is composed of its objects and its morphisms) with the signature $\Sigma_{\mathbf{C}} = \{\mathrm{dom}, \mathrm{cod}, \mathrm{id}, \circ\} \bigcup \{o_i \mid 0 \leq i \leq n\}$, where:

1. $\mathrm{dom}, \mathrm{cod} : \mathrm{Mor}_C \to \mathrm{Ob}_C$ are two operations such that for any morphism $f : A \to B$, $\mathrm{dom}(f) = A, \mathrm{cod}(f) = B$;
2. $\mathrm{id} : \mathrm{Ob}_C \to \mathrm{Mor}_C$ is the operation such that for any object A, $\mathrm{id}(A) = \mathrm{id}_A : A \to A$ is the identity arrow for this object;
3. $\circ : \mathrm{Mor}_C^2 \to \mathrm{Mor}_C$ is a *partial* function, such that for any two morphisms $f, g, f \circ g$ is defined if $\mathrm{dom}(f) = \mathrm{cod}(g)$, with the following set of equations:
   - associativity: $(f \circ g) \circ h = f \circ (g \circ h)$, if $\mathrm{dom}(g) = \mathrm{cod}(h)$ and $\mathrm{dom}(f) = \mathrm{cod}(g)$,
   - identity: $f \circ \mathrm{id}(\mathrm{dom}(f)) = f$ and $\mathrm{id}(\mathrm{cod}(f)) \circ f = f$;
4. For each operator $o_i \in \Sigma_{\mathbf{C}}$, the composition of objects $o_i : \mathrm{Ob}_C^{\mathrm{ar}(o_i)} \to \mathrm{Ob}_C$ (as, e. g., the product, coproduct, etc.), or the composition of morphisms $o_i : \mathrm{Mor}_C^{\mathrm{ar}(o_i)} \to \mathrm{Mor}_C$ (as, e. g., the product, coproduct, the various pairings (structural operations) $(\_,\_)$, $\langle\_,\_\rangle$, $[\_,\_]$, etc.).

Consequently, the categorial symmetry can be done by following corollary:

Corollary 33. *A category* $\mathbf{C}$ *is symmetric if for its algebra* $\mathrm{Alg}_{\mathbf{C}} = ((\mathrm{Ob}_C, \mathrm{Mor}_C), \Sigma_{\mathbf{C}})$ *we have the additional binary partial operator* $* : \mathrm{Ob}_C^2 \to \mathrm{Ob}_C$ *and unary operator* $B_T \in \Sigma_{\mathbf{C}}$ *which is a homomorphism* $B_T : (\mathrm{Mor}_C, \circ) \to (\mathrm{Ob}_C, *)$*, such that for every object* $A \in \mathrm{Ob}_C$ *there exists the isomorphism,* $B_T(\mathrm{id}(A)) \simeq A$ *(representability principle).*

Notice that the partial operations can be equivalently represented by a set of standard (total) operations. For example, the partial operation "$\circ$" can be equivalently represented by the set of total operations, $\{\circ_{A,B,C} : \mathbf{C}(A, B) \times \mathbf{C}(B, C) \to \mathbf{C}(A, C) \mid A, B, C \in OB_C\}$.

A significant example of such categorial symmetry, here applied to database mapping, is the **DB** category, as introduced in Section A.6 and developed in [21].

A.5.2 Kripke polynomial functors and predicate lifting

We shall be using a particular collection of functors (on a category Set with sets as objects and functions between them as arrows), $T : \mathrm{Set} \to \mathrm{Set}$, as interfaces of coalgebras. These so-called Kripke polynomial functors are built up inductively from the identity and constants, using products, coproducts (disjoint unions), exponents (with constants) and powersets. Products of sets S_1, S_2, written as $S_1 \times S_2$, have two projections $\pi_i : S_1 \times S_2 \to S_i$ (for $i = 1, 2$). Coproducts, $S_1 + S_2$, come with injective functions $\kappa_i : S_i \to S_1 + S_2$ (for $i = 1, 2$). The collection of functions from a set X to Y is denoted by Y^X with the evaluation mapping $\mathrm{eval}_{X,Y} : Y^X \times X \to Y$.

For a function $f : Y \to Z$, there is an associated function $f^X : Y^X \to Z^X$ by $g \mapsto f \circ g$, where $\circ$ is a composition of functions. The covariant powerset functor $\mathcal{P} : \mathrm{Set} \to \mathrm{Set}$ sends a set Y to the set of its subsets $\mathcal{P}(Y) = \{S \mid S \subseteq Y\}$, and a function $f : Y \to Z$ to the function $\mathcal{P}(f) : \mathcal{P}(Y) \to \mathcal{P}(Z)$ given by image: $S \mapsto f(S) = \{f(y) \mid y \in S\}$.

Definition 130. The collection of Kripke polynomial functors (KPFs) is defined as follows:
1. The identity functor I_d : Set $\rightarrow$ Set is a KPF.
2. For each nonempty finite set D, the constant functor D : Set $\rightarrow$ Set, given by $X \mapsto D$ and $(f : Y \rightarrow Z) \mapsto \mathrm{id}_D$, is a KPF.
3. The product $X \mapsto T_1(X) \times T_2(X)$ of two KPFs T_1, T_2 is a KPF.
4. The coproduct $X \mapsto T_1(X) + T_2(X)$ of two KPFs T_1, T_2 is a KPF.
5. For a KPF T, and an arbitrary nonempty set D the exponent functor $X \mapsto T(X)^D$ is a KPF.
6. For a KPF T, the functor $X \mapsto \mathcal{P}(T(X))$ is a KPF.

The collection of finite KPFs is constructed in the same way, except that in the last point the finite powerset $\mathcal{P}_{\text{fin}}$ is used, instead of the ordinary one.

A *coalgebra* of a KPF, T : Set $\rightarrow$ Set, consists of a set X, usually called the state space or set of states, together with a function $c : X \rightarrow T(X)$, giving the operations of the coalgebra. A homomorphism of coalgebras from $c : X \rightarrow T(X)$ to $d : Y \rightarrow T(Y)$ is a function $f : X \rightarrow Y$ between the underlying state spaces, which commutes with operations: $d \circ f = T(f) \circ c$.

Now we will consider [285, 286] the unfolding and structural properties of Kripke Polynomial Functors (KPFs), T : Set $\rightarrow$ Set, such that $T = \ldots S \ldots$ is a composition of its KPFs subcomponents S. We shall make such occurrences explicit by defining how such an S can be reached via a path p inside T, denoted by a relation $p : T \rightsquigarrow S$. The path p is a finite set of symbols (see the paragraph for KPF) $\pi_1, \pi_2, \kappa_1, \kappa_2, ev(d)$, for elements $d \in D$ of sets D occurring as exponents in T.

Definition 131. The relation $p : T \rightsquigarrow S$, for any two KPFs, is the least relation defined as follows:
1. $\langle\rangle : T \rightsquigarrow T$, where $\langle\rangle$ is the empty list.
2. $\pi_1 \cdot p : T_1 \times T_2 \rightsquigarrow T$ for $p : T_1 \rightsquigarrow S$, and $\pi_2 \cdot p : T_1 \times T_2 \rightsquigarrow T$ for $p : T_2 \rightsquigarrow S$.
3. $\kappa_1 \cdot p : T_1 + T_2 \rightsquigarrow T$ for $p : T_1 \rightsquigarrow S$, and $\kappa_2 \cdot p : T_1 + T_2 \rightsquigarrow T$ for $p : T_2 \rightsquigarrow S$.
4. $\mathrm{eval}(d) \cdot p : T^D \rightsquigarrow S$ for all $d \in D$ and $p : T \rightsquigarrow S$.
5. $\mathcal{P} \cdot p : \mathcal{P}(T) \rightsquigarrow S$ for all $p : T \rightsquigarrow S$.

We define the set of (global) nextime-modal operators $\mathrm{Op}(T)$ of the KPF T as $\mathrm{Op}(T) = \{p \mid p : T \rightsquigarrow \mathrm{Id}\}$.

It is easy to see that these paths can be composed (via concatenation of lists): if $p : T_1 \rightsquigarrow T_2$ and $q : T_2 \rightsquigarrow T_3$, then $p \cdot q : T_1 \rightsquigarrow T_3$.

Basically, we are only interested in the paths having identity functors as targets, but for a generality we introduce the following general concept of a "predicate lifting" [285, 286].

Definition 132. For a path $p : T \rightsquigarrow S$ and an arbitrary set X, there is a "predicate lifting" function $(\_)^p : \mathcal{P}(S(X)) \to \mathcal{P}(T(X))$, defined on $Y \subseteq S(X)$ by induction on p:

1. $Y^{\langle\rangle} = Y$.
2. $Y^{\pi_i \cdot p} = \{z \mid \pi_i(z) \in Y^p\}$, for $i = 1, 2$.
3. $Y^{\kappa_i \cdot p} = \{z \mid \forall y.z = \kappa_i(y) \Rightarrow y \in Y^p\}$, for $i = 1, 2$.
4. $Y^{\mathrm{eval}(d) \cdot p} = \{f \mid f(d) \in Y^p\}$.
5. $Y^{\mathcal{P} \cdot p} = \{Z \mid Z \subseteq Y^p\}$.

For a coalgebra $c : X \to T(X)$, we define for a modal operator $(p : T \rightsquigarrow \mathrm{Id}) \in \mathrm{Ob}(\mathbf{T})$ and interpretation function $[p] : \mathcal{P}(X) \to \mathcal{P}(X)$, for any $Y \in \mathcal{P}(X)$,

$$[p](Y) = c^{-1}(Y^p) = \{x \in X \mid c(x) \in Y^p\}; \tag{A.11}$$

thus, $[p] = c^{-1} \circ (\_)^p$.

Example 59. The frame $(X, R_\preceq)$, for $R_\preceq \subseteq X^2$, can be represented by the coalgebra $y : X \to \mathcal{P}(X)$, and for any $x \in X$, $y(x)$ is the set of all successors of the point x (i. e., the set of all x' such that $(x, x') \in R_\preceq$, or, equivalently, $x' \preceq x$).

Let us consider the unique modal operator $p = \mathcal{P} : T \rightsquigarrow \mathrm{Id}$ for the functor $T = \mathcal{P}$. Thus, we obtain its interpretation function $[\mathcal{P}]$ such that for any $Y \subseteq X$,

$$\begin{aligned}[\mathcal{P}](Y) &= y^{-1}((Y)^{\mathcal{P}}) = y^{-1}(\{Z \mid Z \subseteq Y\}) = \{x \in X \mid y(x) \in \{Z \mid Z \subseteq Y\}\} \\ &= \{x \in X \mid y(x) \subseteq Y\},\end{aligned}$$

i. e., this modal operator is the standard universal modal operator $\Box$.

A.6 Introduction to RDB, database mappings and DB category

Database schema mappings are so important in information integration that many mapping formalisms have been proposed for different tasks. A schema mapping is a high-level *declarative specification* of the relationship between two schemas; it specifies how data structured under one schema, called source schema, is to be converted into data structured under possibly different schema, called the target schema. It the last decade, schema mappings have been fundamental components for both data exchange and data integration. In this work, we will consider the declarative schema mappings between relational databases. A widely used formalism for specifying relational-to-relational schema mappings is that of tuple generating dependencies (tgds). In the terminology of data integration, tgds are equivalent to global-and-local-as-view (GLAV) assertions. Using a language that is based on tgds for specifying (or "programming") database schema mappings has several advantages over lower-level languages, such as XSLT scripts of Java programs in that it is declarative and it has been widely used in the formal study of the semantics of data exchange and data integration. Declarative schema mapping formalisms have been used to provide formal semantics for data exchange [143], data integration [111], peer data management [350, 351], pay-as-you-go integration systems [352] and model management operators [353].

Most of the work in the data integration/exchange and peer-to-peer (P2P) framework is based on a logical point of view (particularly for the integrity constraints, in order to define the right models for certain answers) in a "local" mode (source-to-target database) where proper attention to the general "global" problem of the *compositions* of complex partial mappings, which possibly involve a high number of databases has not been given. Today, this "global" approach cannot be avoided because of the necessity of P2P open-ended networks of heterogenous databases. Recently [21], we provided a *definition of a* **DB** *category for the database mappings,* which has to be more suitable than a generic **Set** domain category since the databases are more complex structures w. r. t. the sets and the mappings between them are so complex that they cannot be represented by a *single* function (which is one arrow in **Set**). In such an enriched categorical semantic domain for the databases, it is possible:

- To give a proper solution for a general problem of complex database-mappings and for the high-level algebra operators of the databases (merging, matching, etc.), by preserving the traditional common practice logical language for schema database mapping definitions.
- The schema mapping specifications are not the integral parts of the standard relational-database theory (used to define a database schema with its integrity constraints); they are the *programs* and we need an enriched denotational semantics context that is able to formally express these programs (derived by the mappings between the databases).
- Let us consider, e. g., the P2P systems or the mappings in a complex data warehouse. We would like to have a synthetic graphical representations of the database mappings and queries and to be able to develop a graphical tool for the metamapping descriptions of complex (and partial) mappings in various contexts, with a formal mathematical background.

Hence, we need a framework of interdatabase mappings. The main difference between the previous categorial approaches to databases and that presented in [21] is the *level* of abstraction used for the prime objects of the theory.

Another difference is methodological. In fact, the logics for relational databases are based on different kinds of First-Order Logic (FOL) sublanguages as, e. g., description logic, relational database logic, DATALOG, etc. So, the previous work on categorical semantics for the DB theory strictly follows an earlier research for categorial many-sorted FOL on the predicates with types where each attribute of a predicate has a particular sort with a given set of values. Thus, the *fibred semantics* for predicates is assumed for such a typed logic, where other basic operations as negation, conjunction and FOL quantifiers (that are algebraically connected with the Galois connection of their types, traduced by left and right adjunction of their functors in categorical translation) are defined *algebraically* in such a fibrational formulation. This algebraic method, of translation the FOL in a categorical language, is successively and directly applied to the DB theory seen as a sublanguage of the FOL. So, there are no the new results, from the previous developed for the FOL, in this translation of DB-theory into a categorical framework. No new particular *base category* is defined for databases (different from **Set**), as it happened in the cases, e. g., of the Cartesian Closed Categories (CCC) for typed λ-calculus, Bicartesian closed poset categories for Heyting algebras, or the elementary topos (with the subobject classifier diagrams) for the intuitionistic logic [354, 355]. Basically, all previously works use the **Set** category as the base denotational semantics category, without considering the question if such a topos is also *necessary* requirement for the database-mapping theory.

In our case, we are working with Relational Databases (RDB), and consequently, with Structured Query Language (SQL), which is an extension of Codd's "Select-Project-Join + Union" (SPJRU) relational algebra [29, 356]. We assume *a view* of a database A as an observation on this database, presented as a relation (a set of tuples) obtained by a query $q(\mathbf{x})$ (SPJRU term with a list of free variables in $\mathbf{x}$), where $\mathbf{x}$ is a list of attributes of this view. Let $\mathcal{L}_A$ be the set of all such queries over A and $\mathcal{L}_A/_\approx$ be the quotient term algebra obtained by introducing the equivalence relation $\approx$, such that $q(\mathbf{x}) \approx q'(\mathbf{x})$ if both queries return with the same relation (view). Thus, a view can be equivalently considered as a *term* of this quotient-term algebra $\mathcal{L}_A/_\approx$ with carrier set of relations in A and a finite arity of their SPRJU operators whose computation returns a set of tuples of this view. If this query is a finite term of this algebra, then it is called a "finitary view" (a finitary view can have an infinite number of tuples as well).

In this coalgebraic methodological approach to databases, we consider a database instance A of a given database schema $\mathcal{A}$ (i. e., the set of relations that satisfy all integrity constraints of a given database schema) as a black box and any view (the response to a given query) is considered as an *observation*. Thus, in this framework we do not consider a categorical semantic for the free syntax algebra of a given query language, but only the resulting observations and the query-answering system of this database (an Abstract Object Type (AOT)), i. e., the *coalgebra*. Consequently, all algebraic aspects of the query language are encapsulated in the single power-view operator T, such that for a given database instance A (first object in our base database category) the object TA is the set of all possible views of this database A that can be obtained from a given query language $\mathcal{L}_A/_\approx$.

A functorial translation of database schema intermappings (a small graph category) into the database category **DB** is fundamentally based on a functor that represents a given *model* of this database schema intermappings theory. This functor maps a data schema of a given database into an single object of the **DB** category, i. e., a database instance A of this database schema $\mathcal{A}$ (a *model* of this database schema, composed of a set of relations that satisfy the schema's integrity constraints). The morphisms in the **DB** category are not simple functions as in the **Set** category. Thus, the category **DB** is not an elementary (standard) topos. In fact, it was shown in [357] that if we want to progress to more expressive sketches w. r. t. the original Ehresmann's sketches for diagrams with limits and coproducts, by eliminating nondatabase objects as, e. g., Cartesian products of attributes or powerset objects, we need *more expressive arrows* for sketch categories (diagram predicates in [357] that are analog to the approach of Makkai in [358]). As we progress to a more abstract vision in which objects are the whole databases, following the approach of Makkai, in [21] we obtained more complex arrows in this new basic **DB** category for databases in which objects are just the database instances (each object is a set of relations that compose this database instance). Such arrows are not just simple functions as in the case of the **Set** category but complex trees (i. e., operads) of view-based mappings: each arrow is equivalent to the *sets of functions*. In this way, while Ehresmann's approach prefers to deal with a few fixed diagram properties (commutativity, (co)limitness), we enjoy the possibility of setting a full relational-algebra signature of diagram properties.

Different properties of this **DB** category were presented in a number of previously published papers, in initial versions, [175, 359–362] as well, and it has been demonstrated that this category is a *weak monoidal topos*. The fundamental power view-operator T has been defined in [363]. For the database applications, the powerview-monad $T : \mathbf{DB} \to \mathbf{DB}$ is used to provide *denotational semantics to database mappings* [21, 175]: in order to interpret a database mappings (morphisms) in the category **DB**, we distinguish the object $A \in \mathrm{Ob}_{\mathbf{DB}}$ (a database instance of type $\mathcal{A}$) from the object TA of observations (computations of type $\mathcal{A}$ without side-effects) and take as a denotation of (view) mappings the elements of TA (which are the views of type $\mathcal{A}$). In particular, we identify A with the object of values (of type $\mathcal{A}$) and we obtain the object of observations by applying the unary type-constructor T (power-view operator) to A, and hence in **DB** we have the isomorphism $A \simeq TA$ (for this monad η is a natural isomorphism, i. e., for each object A, $\eta_A : A \simeq TA$, and μ generates the identity morphisms, i. e., $\mu_A : T^2A \to TA$ is the identity morphism id_{TA} with $T^2A = TA$). In fact, each query (the union of conjunctive queries), expressed by FOL formulae, has an equivalent finite-length *algebraic term* of the SPJRU algebra, and hence the power view-operator T can be defined by the initial SPRJU algebra of ground terms. We define this fundamental *idempotent power-view* operator T, in Section A.6.2, with the domain and codomain equal to the set of all instance-databases such that for any instance-database A, the object $TA = T(A)$ denotes a database composed of the set of *all views* of A. For every object A, $A \subseteq TA$ and $TA = T(TA)$, i. e., each (element) view of database instance TA is also an element (view) of a database instance A.

The Kleisli category and the semantics of morphisms in the **DB** category, based on the monad (endofunctor T) have been presented in [174]. The semantics for merging and matching database operators based on complete database lattice, as in [364], were defined as well and presented in a number of papers cited above. This section is useful for better understanding of the applications of the Intensional FOL for the intensional mapping between the P2P databases and for the extension of the standard RDB theory to the more powerful Intensional Relational Databases (IRDB) defined in this book.

A.6.1 Basic database concepts

The database mappings, for a logic language (we assume the FOL language in Definition 1) with a set of predicate letters P, are usually defined at a schema level by:

1. A *database schema* is a pair $\mathcal{A} = (S_A, \Sigma_A)$ where S_A is a countable set of relational symbols (predicates in FOL) $r \in P$ with finite arity $n = \mathrm{ar}(r) \geq 1$ ($\mathrm{ar} : P \to \mathcal{N}$), disjoint from a countable infinite set **att** of attributes (a domain of $a \in \mathbf{att}$ is a nonempty finite subset $\mathrm{dom}(a)$ of a countable set of individual symbols **dom**, with $\mathcal{D} = \mathbf{dom} \bigcup SK$). For any $r \in P$, the sort of r, denoted by tuple $\mathbf{a} = \mathrm{atr}(r) = \langle \mathrm{atr}_r(1), \dots, \mathrm{atr}_r(n)\rangle$ where all $a_i = \mathrm{atr}_r(m) \in \mathbf{att}, 1 \leq m \leq n$, must be distinct: if we use two equal domains for different attributes, then we denote them by $a_i(1), \dots, a_i(k)$ (a_i equals to $a_i(0)$). Each index ("column") i, $1 \leq i \leq \mathrm{ar}(r)$, has a distinct column name $nr_r(i) \in \mathrm{SN}$ where SN is the set of names with $nr(r) = \langle nr_r(1), \dots, nr_r(n)\rangle$. A relation $r \in P$ can be used as an atom $r(\mathbf{x})$ of FOL with variables in $\mathbf{x}$ assigned to its columns, so that Σ_A denotes a set of sentences (FOL formulae without free variables) called *integrity constraints* of the sorted FOL with sorts in **att**. We denote the empty schema by $\mathcal{A}_\emptyset = (\{r_\emptyset\}, \emptyset)$, where $r_\emptyset$ is the relation with empty set of attributes (*truth* propositional letter in FOL, Definition 1), and we denote the set of all database schemas for a given (also infinite) set P by $\mathbb{S}$.
2. An *instance-database* of a nonempty schema $\mathcal{A}$ is given by $A = (\mathcal{A}, I_T) = \{R = \|r\| = I_T(r) \mid r \in S_A\}$ where I_T is a Tarski's FOL interpretation in Definition 1, which satisfies *all* integrity constraints in Σ_A and maps a relational symbol $r \in S_A$ into an n-ary relation $R = \|r\| \in A$. Thus, an instance-database A is a set of n-ary relations, managed by relational database systems (DBMSs). Let A and $A' = (\mathcal{A}, I'_T)$ be two instances of $\mathcal{A}$, then a function $h : A \to A'$ is a *homomorphism* from A into A' if for every k-ary relational symbol $r \in S_A$ and every tuple $\langle v_1, \dots, v_k\rangle$ of this k-ary relation in A, $\langle h(v_1), \dots, h(v_k)\rangle$ is a tuple of the same symbol r in A'. If A is an instance-database and ϕ is a sentence, then we write $A \models \phi$ to mean that A satisfies ϕ. If Σ is a set of sentences, then we write $A \models \Sigma$ to mean that $A \models \phi$ for every sentence $\phi \in \Sigma$. Thus, the set of all instances of $\mathcal{A}$ is defined by $\mathrm{Inst}(\mathcal{A}) = \{A \mid A \models \Sigma_A\}$. We denote the set of all values in A by $\mathrm{val}(A) \subseteq \mathcal{D}$. Then the "atomic database" $\mathfrak{J}_A = \{\{\langle v_i\rangle\} \mid v_i \in \mathrm{val}(A)\}$ is infinite iff $SK \subseteq \mathrm{val}(A)$. Note that for each $a \in \mathrm{atr}(r)$, a subset $\mathrm{dom}(a) \subseteq \mathbf{dom}$ is finite, and any introduction of Skolem constants is ordered $\omega_0, \omega_1, \dots$.
3. We consider a rule-based *conjunctive query* over a database schema $\mathcal{A}$ as an expression $q(\mathbf{x}) \longleftarrow r_1(\mathbf{u}_1), \dots, r_n(\mathbf{u}_n)$, with finite $n \geq 0$, r_i are the relational symbols (at least one) in $\mathcal{A}$ or the built-in predicates (e. g., $\leq, =$, etc.) q is a relational

symbol not in $\mathcal{A}$ and $\mathbf{u}_i$ are free tuples (i. e., one may use either variables or constants). Recall that if $\mathbf{v} = (v_1, \dots, v_m)$, then $r(\mathbf{v})$ is a shorthand for $r(v_1, \dots, v_m)$. Finally, each variable occurring in $\mathbf{x}$ is a *distinguished* variable that must also occur at least once in $\mathbf{u}_1, \dots, \mathbf{u}_n$. Rule-based conjunctive queries (called rules) are composed of a subexpression $r_1(\mathbf{u}_1), \dots, r_n(\mathbf{u}_n)$ that is the *body*, and the *head* of this rule $q(\mathbf{x})$. The *Yes/No* conjunctive queries are the rules with an empty head. If we can find values for the variables of the rule, such that the body is logically satisfied, then we can deduce the head-fact. This concept is captured by a notion of "valuation." The deduced head-facts of a conjunctive query $q(\mathbf{x})$ defined over an instance A (for a given Tarski's interpretation I_T of schema $\mathcal{A}$) are equal to $\|q(x_1, \dots, x_k)\|_A = \{\langle v_1, \dots, v_k\rangle \in \mathcal{D}^k \mid A \models \exists \mathbf{y}(r_1(\mathbf{u}_1) \wedge \dots \wedge r_n(\mathbf{u}_n))[x_i/v_i]_{1 \le i \le k}\} = I_T^*(\exists \mathbf{y}(r_1(\mathbf{u}_1) \wedge \dots \wedge r_n(\mathbf{u}_n)))$, where the $\mathbf{y}$ is a set of variables, which are not in the head of a query. We recall that the conjunctive queries are monotonic and satisfiable, and that a (Boolean) query is a class of instances that is closed under the isomorphism [164]. Each conjunctive query corresponds to a "select-project-join" term $t(\mathbf{x})$ of SPRJU algebra obtained from the formula $\exists \mathbf{y}(r_1(\mathbf{u}_1) \wedge \dots \wedge r_n(\mathbf{u}_n))$.

4. We consider a finitary *view* as a union of a finite set S of conjunctive queries with the same head $q(\mathbf{x})$ over a schema $\mathcal{A}$, and from the equivalent algebraic point of view, it is a "select-project-join + union" (SPJRU) finite-length term $t(\mathbf{x})$, which corresponds to the union of the terms of conjunctive queries in S. In what follows, we will use the same notation for a FOL formula $q(\mathbf{x})$ and its equivalent algebraic SPJRU expression $t(\mathbf{x})$. A materialized view of an instance-database A is an n-ary relation $R = \bigcup_{q(\mathbf{x}) \in S} \|q(\mathbf{x})\|_A$. Notice that a finitary view can also have an infinite number of tuples. We denote the set of all finitary materialized views that can be obtained from an instance A by TA.

We consider the views as a universal property for databases: they are the possible observations of the information contained in an instance database. We can use them in order to establish an equivalence relation between databases. Database category **DB**, defined in [21], is at the *instance level*, i. e., any object in **DB** is an instance database.

Interesting extensions of FOL by a number of second-order features are *monadic* second-order quantifiers (MSO). Such quantifiers can range over particular *subsets* of the universe (in monadic extensions we can use the quantification $\exists X$ where X is a subset of the universe, differently from FOL where X is an element of the universe). We can consider two particular restrictions:

1. An $\exists$MSO formula starts with a sequence of existential second-order quantifiers, which is followed by an FOL formula.
2. An $\forall$MSO formula starts with a sequence of universal second-order quantifiers, which is followed by an FOL formula. For example, $\exists$MSO and $\forall$MSO are different for graphs. For strings, MSO collapses to $\exists$MSO and captures exactly the *regular languages* [365]. If we restrict attention to FOL over strings, then it captures exactly the star-free languages.

MSO can be used over *trees* (for XML documents as trees, such queries choose certain nodes from trees) and tree automata, e. g., for monadic DATALOG, which can be evaluated in time linear both in the size of the program and the size of the string [366].

A.6.2 Database observations: idempotent power-view operator

We consider the views as a universal property for the databases: they are the possible observations of the information contained in an instance-database and we can use them in order to establish an equivalence relation between databases.

In the theory of algebraic specifications, an Abstract Data Type (ADT) is specified by a set of operations (constructors) that determine how the values of the carrier set are built up and by a set of formulae (in the simplest case, the equations) stating which values should be identified. In the standard initial algebra semantics, the defining equations impose a congruence on the initial algebra. Dually, a coagebraic specification of a class of systems, i. e., Abstract Object Types (AOT), is characterized by a set of operations (destructors) that specify what can be observed out of a system-state (i. e., an element of the carrier) and how a state can be transformed to a successor state.

We will introduce a class of coalgebras for database query-answering systems for a given instance-database A of a schema $\mathcal{A}$ by Definition 133. They will be presented in an algebraic style by providing a cosignature. In particular, the sorts include a single "hidden sort," corresponding to the carrier of a coalgebra, and other "visible" sorts for the inputs and outputs with a given fixed interpretation. Visible sorts will be interpreted as the sets without any algebraic structure defined on them. For us, the coalgebraic terms, built by operations (destructors), are interpreted by the basic *observations,* which one can make on the states of a coalgebra.

Input sorts for a given instance-database A is a countable set $\mathcal{L}_A$ of the union of a finite set S of conjunctive *finite-length* queries $q(\mathbf{x})$ (with the same head with a finite tuple of variables $\mathbf{x}$) so that $R = ev_A(q(\mathbf{x})) = \bigcup_{q(\mathbf{x})\in S} \|q(\mathbf{x})\|_A$ is the relation (a materialized view) obtained by applying this query to A.

Each query (FOL formula introduced in Definition 1) has an equivalent finite-length *algebraic term* of the SPJRU algebra (or equivalent to it, SPCU algebra, Chapter 4.5, 5.4 in [356]) as shortly introduced in the previous section, and hence the power view-operator T can be defined by the initial SPRJU algebra of ground terms. We define this fundamental *idempotent power-view* operator T, with the domain and codomain equal to the set of all instance databases such that for any instance-database A, the object $TA = T(A)$ denotes a database composed of the set of *all views* of A. The object TA, for a given instance-database A, corresponds to the carrier of the quotient-term Lindenbaum algebra $\mathcal{L}_A/_{\approx}$, i. e., the set of the *equivalence classes* of queries (such a query is equivalent to a term in $\mathcal{T}_P X$ of an SRRJU relational algebra Σ_R, with the select, project, join and union operators, with relational symbols of a database schema $\mathcal{A}$). More precisely, TA is "generated" from A by this quotient-term algebra $\mathcal{L}_A/_{\approx}$ and a given evaluation of queries in $\mathcal{L}_A$, $ev_A : \mathcal{L}_A \twoheadrightarrow TA$, which is surjective function. From the factorization theorem, there is a unique bijection $\mathrm{is}_A : \mathcal{L}_A/_{\approx} \to TA$ such that

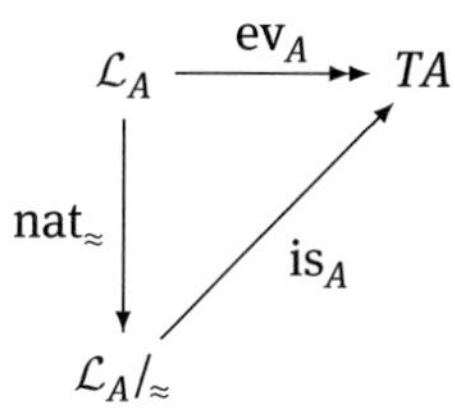

commutes, where the surjective function $nat_{\approx} : \mathcal{L}_A \to \mathcal{L}_A/_{\approx}$ is a natural representation for the equivalence of the queries $\approx$. For every object A, $A \subseteq TA$ and $TA = T(TA)$, i. e., each (element) view of database instance TA is also an element (view) of a database instance A. It is easy to verify that T corresponds to the closure operator Sg on A (introduced in Section A.1) for the Σ_R relational (SPJRU) algebra, but with relations instead of variables (i. e., relational symbols). Notice that when A has a finite number of relations, but at least one relation with an infinite number of tuples, then TA has an infinite number of relations (i. e., views of A), and hence can be an infinite object.

Based on the theory of database observations and its power-view operator T, defined in Section A.6.2, the output sort of this database AOT is the set TA of all resulting views (i. e., resulting n-ary relations) obtained by computation of queries $q(\mathbf{x}) \in \mathcal{L}_A$. It is considered as the carrier of a coalgebra as well.

Definition 133. AOT for a Database query-answering system, for a given instance-database A, is a pair $(S, \Sigma_{\mathrm{AOT}})$ such that:

1. The carrier set $S = (X_A, \mathcal{L}_A, \underline{\Upsilon})$ of the sorts where X_A is a hidden sort (a set of states of this database system), $\mathcal{L}_A$ is an input sort (a set of the unions of conjunctive queries over A), and $\underline{\Upsilon}$ is the set of all finitary relations for a given universe $\mathcal{D}$.
2. The following mappings:
   2.1 A `method` Next : $X_A \times \mathcal{L}_A \to X_A$ that corresponds to an execution of a next query $q(\mathbf{x}) \in \mathcal{L}_A$ in a current state $s \in X_A$ of a database A, such that a database A passes to the next state; so, we introduce the destructor $\Lambda(\mathrm{Next}) : X_A \to X_A^{\mathcal{L}_A}$, where Λ is the currying operator from lambda calculus used in diagram A.10 in Section A.5.
   2.2 An `attribute` Out : $X_A \times \mathcal{L}_A \to \underline{\Upsilon}$ such that for each $s \in X_A$, $q(\mathbf{x}) \in \mathcal{L}_A$, $\mathrm{Out}(s, q(\mathbf{x}))$ is a relation computed by a query $q(\mathbf{x})$; analogously, we introduce the second destructor $\Lambda(\mathrm{Out}) : X_A \to \underline{\Upsilon}^{\mathcal{L}_A}$.

Then the abstract object type for a query-answering system is given by a coalgebra with the signature $\Sigma_{\mathrm{AOT}} = \{\Lambda(\mathrm{Next}), \Lambda(\mathrm{Out})\}$:

$$\langle \Lambda(\mathrm{Next}), \Lambda(\mathrm{Out}) \rangle : X_A \to FX_A$$

of the polynomial endofunctor $F =_{\mathrm{def}} (\_)^{\mathcal{L}_A} \times \underline{\Upsilon}^{\mathcal{L}_A} : \mathbf{Set} \to \mathbf{Set}$.

In an object-oriented terminology, the coalgebras are expressive enough in order to specify the parametric methods and the attributes for a database (conjunctive) query answering systems. In a transition system terminology, such coalgebras can model a deterministic, nonterminating, transition system with inputs and outputs. In [367], a complete equational calculus for such coalgebras of restricted class of polynomial functors has been defined.

Here, we will consider only the database query-answering systems without the side effects. That is, the obtained results (views) *will not be materialized* as a new relation of this database A but only visualized. Thus, when a database answers to a query, it remains in the same initial state. Thus, the set X_A is a singleton $\{A\}$ for a given database A, and consequently, it is isomorphic to the terminal object 1 in the **Set** category. As a consequence, from $1^{\mathcal{L}_A} \simeq 1$, we obtain that a method Next is just an identity function $\mathrm{id} : 1 \to 1$. Thus, the only interesting part of this AOT is the attribute part $\mathrm{Out} : X_A \times \mathcal{L}_A \to \underline{\Upsilon}$, with the fact that $X_A \times \mathcal{L}_A = \{A\} \times \mathcal{L}_A \simeq \mathcal{L}_A$.

Consequently, we obtain an attribute mapping $\mathrm{Out} : \mathcal{L}_A \to \underline{\Upsilon}$, whose graph is equal to the query-evaluation surjective mapping $ev_A : \mathcal{L}_A \twoheadrightarrow TA$, introduced in the previous diagram.

Corollary 34. *A canonical method for the construction of the power-view database TA can be obtained by an abstract data-object type* $(S, \Sigma_{\mathrm{AOT}})$ *for a query-answering system without side effects as follows:*

$$TA =_{\mathrm{def}} \{\mathrm{Out}(q_i(\mathbf{x})) \mid q_i(\mathbf{x}) \in \mathcal{L}_A\}.$$

This corollary is a direct proof that the power-view database operator T, introduced previously, represents the *observational* point of view for the instance-databases. This mapping $ev_A : \mathcal{L}_A \twoheadrightarrow TA$ can be used as a semantic foundation for the database mappings.

A.6.3 Schema mappings, sketches and functors into the DB category

The problem of sharing data from multiple sources has recently received significant attention, and a succession of different architectures has been proposed, beginning with federated databases [368, 369], followed by data integration systems [111, 142, 370], data exchange systems [143, 351, 371] and Peer-to-Peer (P2P) data management systems [53, 122, 123, 125, 350, 372]. A lot of research has been focused on the development of logic languages for semantic mapping between data sources and mediated schemas [111, 112, 364, 373–375], and algorithms that use mappings to answer queries in data sharing systems [105, 115, 117, 141, 219, 370, 376–378].

We consider that a *mapping* between two database schemas $\mathcal{A} = (S_A, \Sigma_A)$ and $\mathcal{B} = (S_B, \Sigma_B)$ is expressed by an union of "conjunctive queries with the same head." Such mappings are called "view-based mappings," defined by a set of FOL sentences $\{\forall \mathbf{x}_i(q_{Ai}(\mathbf{x}_i) \Rightarrow q_{Bi}(\mathbf{y}_i)) |$ with $\mathbf{y}_i \subseteq \mathbf{x}_i, 1 \leq i \leq n\}$, where $\Rightarrow$ is the logical implication between these conjunctive queries $q_{Ai}(\mathbf{x}_i)$ and $q_{Bi}(\mathbf{x}_i)$, over the databases $\mathcal{A}$ and $\mathcal{B}$, respectively.

Schema mappings are often specified by the source-to-target tuple-generating dependencies (tgds), used to formalize a data exchange [143], and in the data integration scenarios under a name "GLAV assertions" [111, 142]. A tgd is a logical sentence (FOL formula without free variables), which says that if some tuples satisfying certain equalities exist in the relation, then some other tuples (possibly with some unknown values) must also exist in another specified relation.

An equality-generating dependency (egd) is a logical sentence, which says that if some tuples satisfying certain equalities exist in the relation, then some values in these tuples must be equal. Functional dependencies are egds of a special form, e. g., primary-key integrity constraints. Thus, egds are only used for the specification of integrity constraints of a single database schema, which define the set of possible models of this database. They are not used for interschema database mappings.

These two classes of dependencies together comprise the *embedded implication dependencies* (EID) [379], which seem to include essentially all of the naturally-occurring constraints on relational databases (we recall that the bold symbols $\mathbf{x}, \mathbf{y}, \ldots$ denote a nonempty list of variables).

Definition 134. We introduce the following two kinds of EIDs [379]:

1. A *tuple-generating dependency (tgd)*

$$\forall \mathbf{x}(q_A(\mathbf{x}) \Rightarrow q_B(\mathbf{x})),$$

   where $q_A(\mathbf{x})$ is an existentially quantified formula $\exists \mathbf{y} \phi_A(\mathbf{x}, \mathbf{y})$ and $q_B(\mathbf{x})$ is an existentially quantified formula $\exists \mathbf{z} \psi_A(\mathbf{x}, \mathbf{z})$, and where the formulae $\phi_A(\mathbf{x}, \mathbf{y})$ and $\psi_A(\mathbf{x}, \mathbf{z})$ are conjunctions of atomic formulae (conjunctive queries) over the given database schemas. We assume the safety condition, i. e., that every *distinguished* variable in $\mathbf{x}$ appears in q_A.
   We will consider also the class of *weakly-full* tgds for which query answering is decidable, i. e., when $q_B(\mathbf{x})$ has no existentially quantified variables, and if each $y_i \in \mathbf{y}$ appears at most once in $\phi_A(\mathbf{x}, \mathbf{y})$.
2. An *equality-generating dependency* (egd)

$$\forall \mathbf{x}(q_A(\mathbf{x}) \Rightarrow (\mathbf{y} \doteq \mathbf{z})),$$

   where $q_A(\mathbf{x})$ is a conjunction of atomic formulae over a given database schema, and $\mathbf{y} = \langle y_1, \ldots, y_k \rangle, \mathbf{z} = \langle z_1, \ldots, z_k \rangle$ are among the variables in $\mathbf{x}$, and $\mathbf{y} \doteq \mathbf{z}$ is a shorthand for the formula $(y_1 \doteq z_1) \wedge \cdots \wedge (y_k \doteq z_k)$ with the built-in binary identity predicate $\doteq$ of the FOL.

Note that a tgd $\forall\mathbf{x}(\exists\mathbf{y}\phi_A(\mathbf{x},\mathbf{y}) \Rightarrow \exists\mathbf{z}\psi_A(\mathbf{x},\mathbf{z}))$ is logically equivalent to the formula $\forall\mathbf{x}\forall\mathbf{y}(\phi_A(\mathbf{x},\mathbf{y}) \Rightarrow \exists\mathbf{z}\psi_A(\mathbf{x},\mathbf{z}))$, i. e., to $\forall\mathbf{x}_1(\phi_A(\mathbf{x}_1) \Rightarrow \exists\mathbf{z}\psi_A(\mathbf{x},\mathbf{z}))$ with the set of distinguished variables $\mathbf{x} \subseteq \mathbf{x}_1$. We will use for the integrity constraints Σ_A of a database schema $\mathcal{A}$ both tgds and egds, while for the interschema mappings, between a schema $\mathcal{A} = (S_A, \Sigma_A)$ and a schema $\mathcal{B} = (S_B, \Sigma_B)$, only the tgds $\forall\mathbf{x}(q_A(\mathbf{x}) \Rightarrow q_B(\mathbf{x}))$, as follows.

Definition 135. An elementary schema mapping is a triple $(\mathcal{A}, \mathcal{B}, \mathcal{M})$ where $\mathcal{A}$ and $\mathcal{B}$ are schemas with no relational symbol in common and $\mathcal{M}$ is a set of tgds $\forall\mathbf{x}(q_A(\mathbf{x}) \Rightarrow q_B(\mathbf{x}))$, such that $q_A(\mathbf{x})$ is a conjunctive query with conjuncts equal to relational symbols in S_A or to a formula with built-in relational symbols, $\doteq, <, >$, etc.), while $q_B(\mathbf{x})$ is a conjunctive query with relational symbols in S_B.

An instance of $\mathcal{M}$ is an instance pair (A, B) (where A is an instance of $\mathcal{A}$ and B is an instance of $\mathcal{B}$) that satisfies every tgds in $\mathcal{M}$, denoted by $(A, B) \models \mathcal{M}_{AB}$. We write $\mathrm{Inst}(\mathcal{M})$ to denote all instances (A, B) of $\mathcal{M}$.

Notice that the formula with built-in predicates, in the left side of implication of a tgd, can be expressed by only two logical connectives, conjunction and negation, from the fact that implication and disjunction can be reduced to equivalent formulae with these two logical connectives. Recall that in data exchange terminology, B is a solution for A under $\mathcal{M}$ if $(A, B) \in \mathrm{Inst}(\mathcal{M})$, and that an instance of $\mathcal{M}$ satisfies all FOL formulae in $\Sigma_A \bigcup \Sigma_B \bigcup \mathcal{M}$. For a given set of FOL formulas S, we denote by $\bigwedge S$ the conjunction of all formulae in the set S.

Lemma 19. *For any given Tarski's interpretation I_T that is a model of the schemas $\mathcal{A} = (S_A, \Sigma_A)$ and $\mathcal{B} = (S_B, \Sigma_B)$ and of the set of tgds in the mapping $\mathcal{M}$, i. e., when $I_T^*(\bigwedge \Sigma_A) = I_T^*(\bigwedge \Sigma_B) = I_T^*(\bigwedge \mathcal{M}) = t$, one has $(\{I_T(r) \mid r \in S_A\}, \{I_T(r) \mid r \in S_B\}) \in \mathrm{Inst}(\mathcal{M})$.*

Proof. Due to the fact that $I_T^*(\bigwedge \Sigma_A) = t$ means that all integrity constraints of $\mathcal{A}$ are satisfied, one has that $A = \{I_T(r) \mid r \in S_A\}$ is an instance (model) of $\mathcal{A}$. The same holds for the schema $\mathcal{B}$, so that $B = \{I_T(r) \mid r \in S_B\}$ is an instance of $\mathcal{B}$.

From the fact that $I_T^*(\bigwedge \mathcal{M}) = t$, each tgd $\phi \in \mathcal{M}_{AB}$ is satisfied, i. e., $I_T^*(\phi) = t$, and hence $(A, B) \models \mathcal{M}$, i. e., $(A, B) \in \mathrm{Inst}(\mathcal{M})$. □

The formulae (tgds) in the set $\mathcal{M}$ express the constraints that an instance (A, B) over the schemas $\mathcal{A}$ and $\mathcal{B}$ must satisfy. We assume that the satisfaction relation between formulae and instances is preserved under isomorphism, which means that if an instance satisfies a formula then every isomorphic instance also satisfies that formula.

This is a mild condition that is true for all standard logical formalisms, such as first-order logic, second-order logic, fixed-point logics and infinitary logics.

Thus, such formulae represent the queries in the sense of Chandra and Harel [164]. An immediate consequence of this property is that $\mathrm{Inst}(\mathcal{M})$ is closed under isomorphism.

Remark. Different from [179, 374, 380], each formula in $\mathcal{M}$ contains the relational symbols of both source and target schema (the integrity constraints are contained in their schemas), in order to represent an interschema mapping graphically as a graph edge $\mathcal{M}_{AB} : \mathcal{A} \to \mathcal{B}$ as in standard mathematical denotation of a mapping. □

The problem of computing semantic mappings [179, 353, 380–383], given a semantic mapping $\mathcal{M}_{AB}$ between data schemas $\mathcal{A}$ and $\mathcal{B}$, and $\mathcal{M}_{BC}$ between $\mathcal{B}$ and $\mathcal{C}$, generally was to answer if it is possible to generate a direct semantic mapping $\mathcal{M}_{AC}$ (possibly in the same logic language formalism) between $\mathcal{A}$ and $\mathcal{C}$ that is "equivalent" to the original mappings. Here, "equivalent" means that for any query in a given class of queries Q and for any instance of data sources, using the direct mapping yields exactly the same answer that would be obtained by the two original mappings [380].

The semantics of the composition of the schema mappings proposed by Madhavan and Halevy [380] was a significant first step. However, it suffers from certain drawbacks that are caused by the fact that this semantics is given relative to a class of queries. In this setting, the set of formulae specifying a composition $\mathcal{M}_{AC}$ of $\mathcal{M}_{AB}$ and $\mathcal{M}_{BC}$ relative to a class Q of queries need not be unique up to logical equivalence, even when the class Q of queries is held fixed. It was shown [179] that this semantics is rather fragile, because a schema mapping $\mathcal{M}_{AC}$ may be a composition of $\mathcal{M}_{AB}$ and $\mathcal{M}_{BC}$ when Q is the class of conjunctive queries, but may fail to be composition of these two (inter)schema mappings when Q is the class of conjunctive queries with inequalities.

We use the algorithm MakeOperads in [21] in order to transform logical schema mappings $\mathcal{M}_{AB} = \{\Phi\} : \mathcal{A} \to \mathcal{B}$ given by the SOtgds Φ in Definition 49 into the algebraic operads $\mathbf{M}_{AB} = \mathit{MakeOperad}(\mathcal{M}_{AB}) = \{v_1 \cdot q_{A,1}, \dots, v_n \cdot q_{A,1}, 1_{r_\emptyset}\} : \mathcal{A} \to \mathcal{B}$. The basic idea of the operad's operations $v_i \in O(r', r_B)$ and $q_{A,i} \in O(r_1, \dots, r_k, r')$, where $r_i, 1 \le i \le k$ are relational symbols of the source schema $\mathcal{A} = (S_A, \Sigma_A)$ and r_B is a relational symbol of the target schema $\mathcal{B}$, and r' has the same type as r_B, is to formalize algebraically a mapping from the set of source relations r_i into a target relation r_B.

Example 60. Schema $\mathcal{A} = (S_A, \emptyset)$ consists of a unary relation EmpAcme that represents the employees of Acme, a unary relation EmpAjax that represents the employees of Ajax, and unary relation Local that represents employees that work in the local office of their company. Schema $\mathcal{B} = (S_B, \emptyset)$ consists of a unary relation Emp that represents all employees, a unary relation Local1 that is intended to be a copy of Local, and unary relation Over65 that is intended to represent people over age 65. Schema $\mathcal{C} = (S_C, \emptyset)$ consists of a binary relation Office that associates employees with office numbers and unary relation CanRetire that represents employees eligible for retirement. Consider now the following schema mappings:

$$\begin{aligned}\mathcal{M}_{AB} = \{&\forall x_e(\texttt{EmpAcme}(x_e) \Rightarrow \texttt{Emp}(x_e)) \wedge \forall x_e(\texttt{EmpAjax}(x_e) \\ &\Rightarrow \texttt{Emp}(x_e)) \wedge \forall x_p(\texttt{Local}(x_p) \Rightarrow \texttt{Local1}(x_p))\}, \quad \text{and}\end{aligned}$$

$$\mathcal{M}_{BC} = \{\exists f_1(\forall x_e((\texttt{Emp}(x_e) \wedge \texttt{Local1}(x_e)) \Rightarrow \texttt{Office}(x_e, f_1(x_e))) \wedge \forall x_e((\texttt{Emp}(x_e) \wedge \texttt{Over65}(x_e)) \Rightarrow \texttt{CanRetire}(x_e)))\}.$$

Then, by their composition, we obtain the composed mapping $\mathcal{M}_{AC} : \mathcal{A} \to \mathcal{C}$ equal to

$$\begin{aligned}\mathcal{M}_{AC} = \{\exists f_1 \exists f_2 \exists f_{\text{Over65}}(&\forall x_e((\texttt{EmpAcme}(x_e) \wedge \texttt{Local}(x_e)) \Rightarrow \texttt{Office}(x_e, f_1(x_e)))\\ &\wedge \forall x_e((\texttt{EmpAjax}(x_e) \wedge \texttt{Local}(x_e)) \Rightarrow \texttt{Office}(x_e, f_2(x_e)))\\ &\wedge \forall x_e((\texttt{EmpAcme}(x_e) \wedge (f_{\text{Over65}}(x_e) \doteq \bar{1})) \Rightarrow \texttt{CanRetire}(x_e))\\ &\wedge \forall x_e((\texttt{EmpAjax}(x_e) \wedge (f_{\text{Over65}}(x_e) \doteq \bar{1})) \Rightarrow \texttt{CanRetire}(x_e)))\},\end{aligned}$$

where f_{Over65} is the characteristic function of the relation (predicate) $\texttt{Over65}$ which is not part of schema $\mathcal{A}$. Then, by transformation into abstract operad's operations, we obtain $\mathbf{M}_{AC} = \text{MakeOperads}(\mathcal{M}_{AC}) = \{q_1^A, q_2^A, q_3^A, q_4^A, 1_{r_\emptyset}\}$, $q_i^A = v_i \cdot q_{A,i}$, where:

1. The operations $q_1^A \in O(\texttt{EmpAcme}, \texttt{Local}, \texttt{Office})$ and $q_{A,1} \in O(\texttt{EmpAcme}, \texttt{Local}, r_1')$ correspond to the expression $((\_)_1(x_e) \wedge (\_)_2(x_e)) \Rightarrow (\_)(x_e, f_1(x_e))$ and $v_1 \in O(r_1', \texttt{Office})$ to $(\_)_1(x_e, x_p) \Rightarrow (\_)(x_e, x_p)$;
2. The operations $q_2^A \in O(\texttt{EmpAjax}, \texttt{Local}, \texttt{Office})$ and $q_{A,2} \in O(\texttt{EmpAjax}, \texttt{Local}, r_2')$ correspond to the expression $((\_)_1(x_e) \wedge (\_)_2(x_e)) \Rightarrow (\_)(x_e, f_2(x_e))$ and $v_2 \in O(r_2', \texttt{Office})$ to $(\_)_1(x_e, x_p) \Rightarrow (\_)(x_e, x_p)$;
3. The operations $q_3^A \in O(\texttt{EmpAcme}, \texttt{Over65}, \texttt{CanRetire})$ and $q_{A,3} \in O(\texttt{EmpAcme}, \texttt{Over65}, r_3')$ correspond to the expression $((\_)_1(x_e) \wedge (\_)_2(x_e)) \Rightarrow (\_)(x_e)$ and $v_3 \in O(r_3', \texttt{CanRetire})$ to $(\_)_1(x_e) \Rightarrow (\_)(x_e)$;
4. The operations $q_4^A \in O(\texttt{EmpAjax}, \texttt{Over65}, \texttt{CanRetire})$ and $q_{A,4} \in O(\texttt{EmpAjax}, \texttt{Over65}, r_4')$ correspond to the expression $((\_)_1(x_e) \wedge (\_)_2(x_e)) \Rightarrow (\_)(x_e)$ and $v_4 \in O(r_4', \texttt{CanRetire})$ to $(\_)_1(x_e) \Rightarrow (\_)(x_e)$.

These three arrows $\mathbf{M}_{AB} : \mathcal{A} \to \mathcal{B}$, $\mathbf{M}_{BC} : \mathcal{B} \to \mathcal{C}$ and $\mathbf{M}_{AC} : \mathcal{A} \to \mathcal{C}$ compose a graph G of this database mapping system. From the fact that the operads can be composed, the composition of two schema mappings $\mathbf{M}_{AB}$ and $\mathbf{M}_{BC}$ can be translated into composition of operads, which is associative, so that they can be represented by the sketch category $\mathbf{Sch}(G)$ derived from the graph G of the schema mappings.

Sketches are called graph-based logic and provide very clear and intuitive specification of computational data and activities. For any small sketch $\mathbf{E}$, the category of models Mod($\mathbf{E}$) is an accessible category by Lair's theorem and reflexive subcategory of $\mathbf{Set}^{\mathbf{E}}$ by the Ehresmann–Kennison theorem. A generalization to base categories other than **Set** was proved by Freyd and Kelly (1972) [384]. The generalization to **DB** category is exhaustively provided in [21], so that the functorial semantics of a database mapping system expressed by a graph G is defined by a functor (R-algebra) $\alpha^* : \mathbf{Sch}(G) \to \mathbf{DB}$.

The R-algebra α is derived from a given Tarski's interpretation I_T of the given database schema mapping graph G and represented by a sketch category $\mathbf{Sch}(G)$

(with arrows $M_{AB} : \mathcal{A} \to \mathcal{B}$, as in Example 60). R-algebra α is equal to I_T for the relations of the data schemas, $\alpha(r_i) = I_T(r_i)$ is a relational table of the instance database $A = \alpha^*(\mathcal{A}) = \{\alpha(r_i) \mid r_i \in S_A\}$ (α^* denotes the extension of α to sets), and $\alpha(q_{A,i}) : \alpha(r_1) \times \cdots \times \alpha(r_k) \to \alpha(r')$ is a surjective function from the relations in the instance database A into its image (relation) $\alpha(r')$, with a function $\alpha(v_i) : \alpha(r') \to \alpha(r_B)$ into the relation of the instance database $B = \alpha^*(\mathcal{B})$. Formal definition of an R-algebra α as a mapping-interpretation of a schema mapping $\mathcal{M}_{AB} : \mathcal{A} \to \mathcal{B}$ is given in [21] (Section 2.4.1, Definition 11) also when we have the negation in the left sides of the implications in a SOtgd of such a mapping.

We have that for any R-algebra α, $\alpha(r_\emptyset) = \perp = \{\langle\rangle\}$ is the empty relation composed by only empty tuple $\langle\rangle \in D_{-1}$, and $1_{r_\emptyset}$ is the identity operads operation of the empty relation $r_\emptyset$, so that $q_\perp = \alpha(1_{r_\emptyset}) = \mathrm{id}_\perp : \perp \to \perp$ is the identity function.

Example 61. For the operads defined in Example 60, let a mapping-interpretation (an R-algebra) α be an extension of Tarski's interpretation I_T of the source schema $\mathcal{A} = (S_A, \Sigma_A)$ that satisfies all constraints in Σ_A and defines its database instance $A = \alpha^*(S_A) = \{\alpha(r_i) \mid r_i \in S_A\}$ and, analogously, an interpretation of $\mathcal{C}$.

Let α satisfy the SOtgd of the mapping $\mathcal{M}_{AC}$ by the Tarski's interpretation for the functional symbols f_i, for $1 \le i \le 2$, in this SOtgd (denoted by $I_T(f_i)$).

Then we obtain the relations $\alpha(\texttt{EmpAcme})$, $\alpha(\texttt{EmpAjax})$, $\alpha(\texttt{Local})$, $\alpha(\texttt{Office})$ and $\alpha(\texttt{CanRetire})$. The interpretation of f_{Over65} is the characteristic function of the relation $\alpha(\texttt{Over65}$ in the instance $B = \alpha^*(S_B)$ of the database $\mathcal{B} = (S_B, \Sigma_B)$, so that $\overline{f}_{\text{Over65}}(a) = 1$ if $\langle a\rangle \in \alpha(\texttt{Over65}))$.

Then this mapping interpretation α defines the following functions:

1. The function $\alpha(q_{A,1}) : \alpha(\texttt{EmpAcme}) \times \alpha(\texttt{Local}) \to \alpha(r_1')$, such that for any tuple $\langle a\rangle \in \alpha(\texttt{EmpAcme})$ and $\langle b\rangle \in \alpha(\texttt{Local})$,
$$\alpha(q_{A,1})(\langle a\rangle, \langle b\rangle) = \langle a, I_T(f_1(a))\rangle \quad \text{if } a = b; \quad \langle\rangle \text{ otherwise.}$$
And for any $\langle a, b\rangle \in \alpha(r_1')$, $\alpha(v_1)(\langle a, b\rangle) = \langle a, b\rangle$ if $\langle a, b\rangle \in \alpha(\texttt{Office})$; $\langle\rangle$ otherwise.
2. The function $\alpha(q_{A,2}) : \alpha(\texttt{EmpAjax}) \times \alpha(\texttt{Local}) \to \alpha(r_2')$, such that for any tuple $\langle a\rangle \in \alpha(\texttt{EmpAjax})$ and $\langle b\rangle \in \alpha(\texttt{Local})$,
$$\alpha(q_{A,2})(\langle a\rangle, \langle b\rangle) = \langle a, I_T(f_2(a))\rangle \quad \text{if } a = b; \quad \langle\rangle \text{ otherwise.}$$
And for any $\langle a, b\rangle \in \alpha(r_2')$, $\alpha(v_2)(\langle a, b\rangle) = \langle a, b\rangle$ if $\langle a, b\rangle \in \alpha(\texttt{Office})$; $\langle\rangle$ otherwise.
3. The function $\alpha(q_{A,3}) : \alpha(\texttt{EmpAcme}) \times \alpha(\texttt{Over65}) \to \alpha(r_3')$, such that for any tuple $\langle a\rangle \in \alpha(\texttt{EmpAcme})$ and $\langle b\rangle \in \alpha(\texttt{Over65})$,
$$\alpha(q_{A,3})(\langle a\rangle, \langle b\rangle) = \langle a\rangle, \quad \text{if } a = b; \quad \langle\rangle \text{ otherwise.}$$
And for any $\langle a\rangle \in \alpha(r_3')$, $\alpha(v_3)(\langle a\rangle) = \langle a\rangle$ if $\langle a\rangle \in \alpha(\texttt{CanRetire})$; $\langle\rangle$ otherwise.

4. The function $\alpha(q_{A,4}) : \alpha(\texttt{EmpAjax}) \times \alpha(\texttt{Over65}) \rightarrow \alpha(r'_4)$, such that for any tuple $\langle a\rangle \in \alpha(\texttt{EmpAjax})$ and $\langle b\rangle \in \alpha(\texttt{Over65})$

$$\alpha(q_{A,4})(\langle a\rangle, \langle b\rangle) = \langle a\rangle, \quad \text{if } a = b; \quad \langle\rangle \text{ otherwise.}$$

   And for any $\langle a\rangle \in \alpha(r'_4)$, $\alpha(v_4)(\langle a\rangle) = \langle a\rangle$ if $\langle a\rangle \in \alpha(\texttt{CanRetire})$; $\langle\rangle$ otherwise.

From the fact that the mapping-interpretation satisfies the schema mappings, based on Corollary 4 in Section 2.4.1 [21], all functions $\alpha(v_i)$, for $1 \leq i \leq 4$, are the injections.

A.6.4 Data integration system

In this section, we illustrate the formalization of a data integration system (DIS) [142] that is based on the relational model with integrity constraints.

In the relational model, predicate symbols are used to denote the relations in the database, whereas constant symbols denote the values stored in the relations. We assume to have a fixed (infinite) alphabet $D_\Gamma \subset \mathcal{D}$ of constants. Unless specified otherwise, we consider only the databases defined over such an alphabet. In such a setting, the Unique Name Assumption (UNA) is implicit (i. e., different constants denote different objects).

A *relational schema* (or simply a *schema*) consists of the following:

1. An *alphabet* $\mathcal{A}$ of predicate (or relation) symbols, each one with an associated arity. Arity represents the number of arguments of a given predicate or the number of attributes of a given relation.
2. A set Σ_G of *integrity constraints*. That is, assertions on the symbols of the alphabet $\mathcal{A}$. The assertions express the conditions that are intended to be satisfied in every database that is coherent with the schema. In the proposed framework, we consider two kinds of constraints:
   2.1 *Key constraints* (we assume that, in the global schema, there is exactly one key constraint for each relation).
   2.2 *Foreign key constraints*: a foreign key constraint is a statement of the form $r_1[\mathbf{A}] \subseteq r_2[\mathbf{B}]$, where r_1 and r_2 are relations and $\mathbf{A}$ is a sequence of distinct attributes of r_1 and $\mathbf{B}$ is key(r_2). Such a constraint is satisfied in a database $\mathcal{DB}$ if for each tuple t_1 in $r_1^{\mathcal{DB}}$ there exists a tuple t_2 in $r_2^{\mathcal{DB}}$ such that $t_1[\mathbf{A}] = t_2[\mathbf{B}]$ where $t_1[\mathbf{A}]$ is the projection of the tuple t_1 over $\mathbf{A}$.

A *relational database* (or simply a *database*) $\mathcal{DB}$ for a schema $\mathcal{C}$ is a set of relations in which the constants are atomic values and in addition, there is one relation $r^{\mathcal{DB}}$ of arity n for each predicate symbol r of arity n in the alphabet $\mathcal{A}$. The relation $r^{\mathcal{DB}}$ is the interpretation in $\mathcal{DB}$ of the predicate symbol r, in the sense that it contains the set of tuples that satisfies the predicate r in $\mathcal{DB}$.

A *relational query* is a formula that specifies a set of tuples that needs to be retrieved from a database. We consider the class of *safe conjunctive queries* in which the answer to a query q of arity n over a database $\mathcal{DB}$ for $\mathcal{G}$, denoted $q^{\mathcal{DB}}$, is the set of n-tuples of constants $(c_1, \ldots, c_n)$ such that when each x_i is replaced with c_i then the formula $\exists(y_1, \ldots, y_n).\mathrm{conj}(x_1, \ldots, x_n, y_1, \ldots, y_m)$ evaluates to true in $\mathcal{DB}$. When $n = 1$ and all variables y_i, $1 \le i \le m$ are replaced by the constants in D_Γ, then the queries become Yes/No type.

A *data integration system* $\mathcal{I}$ is a triple $\mathcal{I} = \langle \mathcal{G}, \mathcal{S}, \mathcal{M} \rangle$, where:

- The *global schema* is expressed in the relational model with constraints $\Sigma_\mathcal{G}$.
- The *source schema* is expressed without integrity constraints.
- The *mapping* $\mathcal{M}$ is defined following the GAV approach. That is, to each relation r of the global schema $\mathcal{G}$ we associate a query $\rho(r)$ over the source schema $\mathcal{S}$. Logically, such mapping is *standard material implication* $\rho(r)(X) \Rightarrow r(Y)$ where $X \subseteq Y$ are the sets of attributes of these (virtual) predicates (in the case when $X \subset Y$ we have *incomplete* information).

We call any database for $\mathcal{G}$ as *global database* for $\mathcal{I}$ or simply *database* for $\mathcal{I}$.

Let **D** be a finite *source database instance* for $\mathcal{I} = \langle \mathcal{G}, \mathcal{S}, \mathcal{M} \rangle$ that is constituted by one relation $r^\mathcal{D}$ for each source r in $\mathcal{S}$. A database $\mathcal{B}$ for $\mathcal{I}$ is said to be *legal* with respect to **D** if:

- $\mathcal{B}$ satisfies the integrity constraints $\Sigma_\mathcal{G}$ of $\mathcal{G}$.
- $\mathcal{B}$ satisfies $\mathcal{M}$ with respect to $\mathcal{D}$. That is, for each relation r in $\mathcal{G}$, the set of tuples $r^\mathcal{B}$ that $\mathcal{B}$ assigns to r is a superset of the set of tuples $\rho(r)^\mathcal{D}$ computed by the associated query $\rho(r)$ over **D**, i. e., $\rho(r)^\mathcal{D} \subseteq r^\mathcal{B}$.
- we denote by $\mathrm{sem}^\mathcal{D}(\mathcal{I})$ the set of databases for $\mathcal{I}$ that are legal w. r. t. $\mathcal{D}$, i. e., that satisfies both the constraints of $\mathcal{G}$ as well as the mapping $\mathcal{M}$ with respect to **D**. If $\mathrm{sem}^\mathcal{D}(\mathcal{I}) \neq \emptyset$, then $\mathcal{I}$ is said to be *consistent* w. r. t. **D**.

Note that the above definition amounts to consider any view $\rho(r)$ as *sound* [111, 154]. It means that the data provided by the sources is only an (incomplete) subset (can be a proper subset) of the data that would satisfy the relations of the global schema.

By the definition above, it is clear that the semantics of a data integration system is formulated in terms of a *set* of databases, rather than a single one.

Retrieved global database

$\mathrm{ret}(\mathcal{I}, \mathbf{D})$ for a given finite *source database instance* **D** is defined as follows. For each relation r of the global schema, we compute the relation $r^\mathcal{D}$ by evaluating the query $\rho(r)$ over the source database **D**. We assume that for each relation r of the global schema, the query $\rho(r)$ over the source schema $\mathcal{S}$ that the mapping $\mathcal{M}$ associates to r preserves the key constraint of r (this may require that $\rho(r)$ implements a suitable duplicate record elimination strategy). This assumption is to make sure that the retrieved global database satisfies all the key constraints in $\mathcal{G}$.

Query-answering

in the data integration system: Let q be a conjunctive query to a data integration system $\mathcal{I}$ (atoms in q have symbols in $\mathcal{G}$ as predicates). The *set of certain answers* $q^{\mathcal{I},\mathcal{D}}$ to q w. r. t. $\mathcal{I}$ and $\mathbf{D}$ is the set of tuples t of constants of the same arity as q, and $t \in q^{\mathcal{B}}$, for each $\mathcal{B} \in \text{sem}^{\mathcal{D}}(\mathcal{I})$.

Let $\Delta_{\mathcal{I}}$ be a set of formulas belongs to a language $\mathcal{L}$ used to define the data integration system $\mathcal{I} = \langle \mathcal{G}, \mathcal{S}, \mathcal{M} \rangle$ and a formula A belongs to $\mathcal{L}$. We denote a *model-theoretic consequence* relation (logical entailment) with $\vDash$, defined as follows: $\Delta_{\mathcal{I}} \vDash A$ when all models of the formulas contained in $\Delta_{\mathcal{I}}$ are models of A; $\vDash_{\mathcal{B}} A$ when a formula A is true in a particular model $\mathcal{B}$. Then the certain answer to $q(\mathbf{x})$ is given in the following way:

$$q^{\mathcal{I},\mathcal{D}} = \{t \mid t \in D_{\Gamma}^{\text{arity}(q)} \text{ and } \vDash_{\mathcal{B}} q(t) \text{ for each } \mathcal{B} \in \text{sem}^{\mathcal{D}}(\mathcal{I})\}.$$

As a result, in this framework with key and foreign key constraints, we can visualize a data integration system $\mathcal{I} = \langle \mathcal{G}, \mathcal{S}, \mathcal{M} \rangle$ as a logical theory $\mathcal{P}_{\mathcal{G}}$ (a definite logic program is provided by Cali et al. [142]) that is composed by: (1) a retrieved global database $\text{ret}(\mathcal{I}, \mathbf{D})$ as an extensional part of a database theory, and (2) the integrity constraints for a global schema as its intensional part. The existential quantifiers in the foreign key constraints are eliminated by introducing the appropriate Skolem functions:

$$\text{HT}(\mathcal{G}) = \{f_{r,i} \mid r \in \mathcal{G} \text{ and } i \leq \text{arity}(r) \text{ and } i \notin \text{key}(r)\}.$$

Each $f_{r,i}$ is a function symbol with the same arity as the number of attributes of $\text{key}(r)$, i. e., $\text{arity}(f_{r,i}) = \text{arity}(\text{key}(r))$.

Intuitively, the role of the term $f_{r,i}(\alpha_1, \dots, \alpha_k)$ is to denote the value in the i-th column of the tuple of r having $\alpha_1, \dots, \alpha_k$ in the key columns. The domain of such functions is the alphabet D_{Γ}.

The construction of the canonical *model* for a global schema of this logical theory $\mathcal{P}_{\mathcal{G}}$ is presented by Cali et al. [142]. This model is an universal (canonical) one. That is, it is an *initial* minimal Herbrand model [356] such that for every other legal database model $\mathcal{B}$ of the global schema, there is a unique homomorphism [142] $\psi : \text{can}(\mathcal{I}, \mathbf{D}) \longrightarrow \mathcal{B}$ and defines the following sound and complete query rewriting algorithms:

- $\text{exp}_{\mathcal{G}}(\_)$ that expands the original conjunctive query $q(\mathbf{x})$ over a global schema into $\text{exp}_{\mathcal{G}}(q(\mathbf{x}))$ query over $\text{ret}(\mathcal{I}, \mathbf{D})$.
- $\text{unf}_{\mathcal{M}}(\_)$ algorithm which unfolds the resulting query over $\text{ret}(\mathcal{I}, \mathbf{D})$ and returns with the query $\text{unf}_{\mathcal{M}}(\text{exp}_{\mathcal{G}}(q(\mathbf{x})))$ over a source data base $\mathbf{D}$, such that for each tuple $t \in D_{\Gamma}^{\text{arity}(q)}$, $t \in q(\mathbf{x})^{\mathcal{I},\mathcal{D}}$ iff $t \in [\text{unf}_{\mathcal{M}}(\text{exp}_{\mathcal{G}}(q(\mathbf{x})))]^{\mathcal{D}}$

so that the certain answer to a conjunctive query $q(\mathbf{x})$ is equal to

$$q(\mathbf{x})^{\mathcal{I},\mathcal{D}} =_{\text{def}} \{t \mid t \in D_\Gamma^{\text{arity}(q)} \text{ and } \vDash_{M_\mathcal{D}} \text{unf}_\mathcal{M}(\exp_\mathcal{G}(q(t)))\},$$

where $M_\mathcal{D}$ is the unique minimal Herbrand model of a source database **D**.

Finite canonical database for DIS with incomplete information

Here, we introduce a new approach to canonical model and this approach is more close to the data exchange approach presented by Fagin et al. [143]. The approach is not restricted to the existence of query-rewriting algorithms. As a result, it can be used to define coherent closed world assumption [156] for data integration systems in the absence of query-rewriting algorithms also. The construction of the canonical *model* for a global schema of the logical theory $\mathcal{P}_\mathcal{G}$ for data integration system is similar to the construction of the canonical *database* $\text{can}(\mathcal{I}, \mathbf{D})$ described by Cali et al. [142]. The *difference* lies in the fact that in the construction of this revisited canonical model denoted by $\text{can}_M(\mathcal{I}, \mathbf{D})$, for a global schema, fresh *marked null values* (set Ω of Skolem constants [356]) are used instead of the terms involving Skolem functions. This follows the idea of the construction of the restricted chase of a database described by David et al. [385]. Thus, we enlarge a set of constants of our language by $U_\Gamma = D_\Gamma \bigcup \Omega$.

Topor and Sonenberg [356] informally proposed the term *canonical model* to describe a model that is selected (often from many incomparable minimal Herbrand models) to represent the "meaning" of logical programs. Another motivation for concentrating on canonical models is the view [386] that many logic programs are appropriately thought of as having two components: an *intensional* database (IDB) that represents the reasoning component and the *extensional* database (EDB) that represents a collection of facts. Over the course of time, we can "apply" the same IDB to many quite different EDBs. In this context, it makes sense to think of the IDB as if it is implicitly defining a transformation from an EDB to a set of derived facts. We would like the set of derived facts to be the canonical model.

Now, we inductively construct the revisited canonical database model $\text{can}_M(\mathcal{I}, \mathbf{D})$ over the domain U_Γ by starting from $\text{ret}(\mathcal{I}, \mathbf{D})$ (here is an EDB) and repeatedly applying the following rule based on IDB:

if $(x_1, \dots, x_h) \in r_1^{\text{can}_M(\mathcal{I},\mathbf{D})}[\mathbf{A}]$, $(x_1, \dots, x_h) \notin r_2^{\text{can}_M(\mathcal{I},\mathbf{D})}[\mathbf{B}]$, and the foreign key constraint $r_1[\mathbf{A}] \subseteq r_2[\mathbf{B}]$ is in $\mathcal{G}$, then insert in $r_2^{\text{can}_M(\mathcal{I},\mathcal{D})}$ the tuple t such that

- $t[\mathbf{B}] = (x_1, \dots, x_h)$, and
- for each i such that $1 \le i \le \text{arity}(r_2)$, and i not in $\mathbf{B}$, $t[i] = \omega_k$, where ω_k is a fresh marked null value.

Note that the above rule does enforce the satisfaction of the foreign key constraint $r_1[\mathbf{A}] \subseteq r_2[\mathbf{B}]$ (which is a part of IDB), by adding a suitable tuple in r_2: the key of the new tuple is determined by the values in $r_1[\mathbf{A}]$, and the values of the nonkey attributes are formed by means of the fresh marked values ω_k during the application of the rule above.

The above rule defines the "immediate consequence" monotonic operator T_B defined by

$$T_B(I) = I \bigcup \{A \mid A \in B_{\mathcal{G}}, A \leftarrow A_1 \wedge \cdots \wedge A_n \text{ is a ground instance of a rule in } \Sigma_{\mathcal{G}} \text{ and } \{A_1, \ldots, A_n\} \in I\}$$

where, at beginning $I = \text{ret}(\mathcal{I}, \mathbf{D})$, and $B_{\mathcal{G}}$ is a Herbrand base for a global schema. Thus, $\text{can}_M(\mathcal{I}, \mathbf{D})$ is a least a fixed point of this immediate consequence operator.

Example 62. Suppose that we have two relations r and s in $\mathcal{G}$, both of arity 2 and having the first attribute as the key and that the following dependencies hold on $\mathcal{G}$:

$$r[2] \subseteq s[1], \quad s[1] \subseteq r[1].$$

Suppose that the retrieved global database (EDB) stores a single tuple (a, b) in r. Then, by applying the above rule, we insert the tuple (b, ω_1) in s; successively we add (b, ω_2) in r, then (ω_2, ω_3) in s and so on. Observe that the two dependencies are cyclic. In this case, the construction of the canonical database requires an *infinite* sequence of applications of the rules. The following table represents the correspondence between old and revisited canonical database:

$r^{\text{can}(\mathcal{I},\mathbf{D})}$	$s^{\text{can}(\mathcal{I},\mathbf{D})}$	$r^{\text{can}_M(\mathcal{I},\mathbf{D})}$	$s^{\text{can}_M(\mathcal{I},\mathbf{D})}$
a, b	$b, f_{s2}(b)$	a, b	b, ω_1
$b, f_{r2}(b)$	$f_{r2}(b), f_{s2}f_{r2}(b)$	b, ω_2	ω_2, ω_3
$f_{r2}(b), f_{r2}^2(b)$	$f_{r2}^2(b), f_{s2}f_{r2}^2(b)$	ω_2, ω_4	ω_4, ω_5
$f_{r2}^2(b), f_{r2}^3(b)$	$f_{r2}^3(b), f_{s2}f_{r2}^3(b)$	ω_4, ω_6	ω_6, ω_7
...	...	...	...

Thus, the canonical model $\text{can}_M(\mathcal{I}, \mathbf{D})$ is a legal database model for the global schema.

Let us also introduce an unary predicate $\text{Val}(x)$, such that for any constant $c \in U_\Gamma$, $\text{Val}(c)$ is true if $c \in D_\Gamma$, false otherwise. Each certain answer of the original user query $q(\mathbf{x})$, $\mathbf{x} = \{x_1, , x_k\}$ over a global schema is equal to the answer $q_L(\mathbf{x})^{\text{can}_M(\mathcal{I},\mathbf{D})}$ of the *lifted* query $q_L(\mathbf{x}) \equiv q(\mathbf{x}) \wedge \text{Val}(x_1) \wedge \cdots \wedge \text{Val}(x_k)$ over this canonical model. Thus, in the cases when it is possible to materialize this canonical model, certain answers could be obtained over such a database. Usually, it is not possible because (as in the example above) this canonical model is *infinite*. In that case, we can use the revisited fix-point semantics described in [117]. This is based on the fact that after some point, the new tuples added into a canonical model insert only new Skolem constants that are not useful in order to obtain *certain* answers. In fact, Skolem constants are not part of any certain answer to conjunctive query. Consequently, we are able to obtain a *finite subset* of a canonical *database*, which is big enough to obtain certain answers.

Example 63. If we consider Example 62, the finite database $r = \{(a,b),(b,\omega_2),(\omega_2,\omega_4)\}$, $s = \{(b,\omega_1),(\omega_2,\omega_3)\}$ is such a finite least fixed point, which can be used in order to obtain certain answers to the lifted queries.

In fact, we introduced marked null values (instead of Skolem functions) in order to define and materialize such *finite* database. It *is not* a model of the data integration system (which is infinite) but has all necessary query-answering properties. It is able to give all certain answers to conjunctive queries over a global schema. Thus, it can be materialized and used for query answering, instead of query-rewriting algorithms. Let us denote such finite database by $C_M(\mathcal{I},\mathbf{D})$. So, we can prove the following property.

Proposition 55. *Yes/No query* $q(\mathbf{c}), \mathbf{c} = \{c_1,, c_n\} \in D_\Gamma^n, n = \mathrm{arity}(q)$ *over a canonical database* $C_M(\mathcal{I},\mathbf{D}) \subseteq \mathrm{can}_M(\mathcal{I},\mathbf{D})$ *and the rewritten query* $\mathrm{unf}_{\mathcal{M}}(\exp_{\mathcal{G}}(q(\mathbf{c})))$ *over a source database* $\mathbf{D}$*, return the same logical true/false value.*

There is a unique homomorphism $\eta : \mathrm{can}_M(\mathcal{I},\mathbf{D}) \longrightarrow \mathrm{can}(\mathcal{I},\mathbf{D})$.

Proof. The first part of this proposition is a direct consequence of the query rewriting algorithms and it is also based on the fact that each Yes/No query over a source database $\mathcal{D}$ and over a canonical database $\mathrm{can}_M(\mathcal{I},\mathbf{D})$ returns with the true/false value. Proof of the second part: from a definition of certain answers (i. e., answers which are true in all models of a database with incomplete information. Each possible completion of this incomplete information will provide a possible model), we have that $q^{\mathcal{I},\mathcal{D}} = \{t \mid t \in D_\Gamma^{\mathrm{arity}(q)}$ and $\vDash_{\mathcal{B}} q(t)$ for each $\mathcal{B} \in \mathrm{sem}^{\mathcal{D}}(\mathcal{I})\}$. Thus, $t \in q^{\mathcal{I},\mathcal{D}}$ (or, equivalently, $\vDash_{\mathrm{can}_M(\mathcal{I},\mathbf{D})} q(t)$) iff $\vDash_{\mathcal{B}} q(t)$ for each $\mathcal{B} \in \mathrm{sem}^{\mathcal{D}}(\mathcal{I})$, but, $\vDash_{\mathrm{can}_M(\mathcal{I},\mathbf{D})} q(t)$ iff $\vDash_{M_{\mathcal{D}}} \mathrm{unf}_{\mathcal{M}}(\exp_{\mathcal{G}}(q(t)))$. □

Example 64. If we consider Example 62, we define φ homomorphism as follows: for any constant in D_Γ, it is an identity function (this is an intrinsic homomorphism property). For Skolem constants, we have that $\eta(\omega_1) = f_{s2}(b)$, $\omega_{2i} = f_{r,2}^{2i-1}(b)$ and $\omega_{2i+1} = f_{s,2}(\omega_{2i}) = f_{s,2}f_{r,2}^{2i-1}(b)$, for $i = 1, 2, \ldots$.

In order to define a peer database with relational view-based logic schemata (peer ontology), the previous example on the application of data integration in web applications will be used as the building blocks for the P2P systems defined in the next section. The possibility of using the negation logic operator also for querying such data integration systems with generalized closed-world assumption was elaborated in [156]. By abstracting the internal structure of such peers, we will obtain ADTs for peers, while their relational view-based external interface (for the users) will be used for intensional mappings between the peers based on relational views.

The universal (canonical) database $\mathrm{can}(\mathcal{I},\mathbf{D})$, of the encapsulated Data integration system with the source database $\mathbf{D}$, has the interesting property of faithfully representing all legal databases (the construction of the canonical database is similar to the construction of the *restricted chase* of a database described in [385]).

Thus, theoretically, the lifted query will filter only known answers from can($\mathcal{I}$, $\mathbf{D}$). In practice, we do not use this canonical database in order to give the answer to the query, and we use a *query rewriting technics under constraints* in data integration systems (e. g., a data integration systems with key and inclusion integrity constraints [142]) to submit the rewritten query directly to source databases, extracted by wrappers from the world wide web.

Bibliography

[1] J. Pustejovsky and B. Boguraev, “Lexical knowledge representation and natural language processing,” *Artif. Intell., 63*, pp. 193–223, 1993.

[2] M.C. Fitting, “First-Order Intensional Logic,” *Ann. Pure Appl. Log., 127*, pp. 171–193, 2004.

[3] M. Orgun and W. Wadge, “Towards a unified theory of intensional logic programming,” *J. Log. Program., 13(4)*, pp. 413–440, 1992.

[4] T. Braüner, “Adding intensional machinery to hybrid logic,” *J. Log. Comput., 18(4)*, 2008.

[5] T. Braüner and S. Ghilardi, “First-order modal logic,” In *Handbook of Modal Logic, Elsevier*, pp. 549–620, 2007.

[6] S. Bond and M. Denecker, “I-logic:an intensional logic of informations,” In *Proceedings of the 19th Belgian-Dutch Conference on Artificial Intelligence, Utreht, Nederlands*, pp. 49–56, 2007.

[7] D.K. Lewis, “On the plurality of worlds,” *Oxford: Blackwell*, 1986.

[8] R. Stalnaker, “Inquiry,” *Cambridge, MA: MIT Press*, 1984.

[9] R. Montague, “Universal grammar,” *Theoria, 36*, pp. 373–398, 1970.

[10] R. Montague, “The proper treatment of quantification in ordinary English,” In *Approaches to Natural Language, J. Hintikka et al. (Eds.), Dordrecht: Reidel*, pp. 221–242, 1973.

[11] R. Montague, In *Formal philosophy. selected papers of Richard Montague R. Thomason (Ed.), New Haven, London: Yale University Press*, pp. 108–221, 1974.

[12] G. Bealer, “Quality and concept,” *USA: Oxford University Press*, 1982.

[13] A. Thayse, “From modal logic to deductive dtatabases: Introducing a logic cased approach to artificial intelligence,” *John Wiley & Sons Press*, 1988.

[14] O. Udrea, V.S. Subrahmanian, and Z. Majkić, “Probabilistic RDF,” In *IEEE Conference on Information Reuse and Integration (IEEE IRI 2006), September 16–18, Waikoloa, Hawaii, USA*, 2006.

[15] Z. Majkić, O. Udrea, and V.S. Subrahmanian, “Aggregates in generalized temporally indeterminate databases,” In *Int. Conference on Scalable Uncertainty Management (SUM 2007), October 10–12, Washington DC, USA, LNCS 4772*, pp. 171–186, 2007.

[16] Z. Majkić, “Temporal Probabilistic logic programs: State and revision,” In *International Conference in Artificial Intelligence and Pattern Recognition (AIPR-07), July 9–12, 2007, Orlando, FL, USA*, 2007.

[17] J. Minker, “Logic-based artificial intelligence,” *Springer*, 2000.

[18] Z. Majkić, “Conservative intensional extension of Tarski’s semantics,” In *Advances in Artificial Intelligence, Hindawi Publishing Corporation, 23 October*, pp. 1–17, 2012. ISSN: 1687-7470.

[19] Z. Majkić, “Intensionality and two-steps interpretations,” *arXiv:1103.0967*, pp. 1–15, 2011.

[20] Z. Majkić, “Intensional RDB manifesto: a unifying NewSQL model for flexible Big Data,” *arXiv:1403.0017*, pp. 1–29, 2014.

[21] Z. Majkić, In *Big Data Integration Theory, Spinger-Verlag, Texts in Computer Science, New York*, pp. 516, 2014.

[22] P. Blackburn, J.F. Benthem, and F. Wolter, “Handbook of modal logic,” In *Studies in Logic and Practical Reasoning 3. Elsevier Science Inc.*, 2006.

[23] G. Bealer, “Universals,” *J. Philos., 90*, pp. 5–32, 1993.

[24] W. Chen, M. Kifer, and D.S. Warren, “HiLog: A foundation for higher-order logic programming,” *J. Log. Program., 15*, pp. 187–230, 1993.

[25] G. Frege, “‘Uber Sinn und Bedeutung,” In *Zeitschrift für Philosophie und Philosophische Kritik*, pp. 22–50, 1892.

[26] G. Bealer, “A solution to Frege’s puzzle,” In *Philosophical Perspectives 7, J. Tomberlin (Ed.), Atascadero, CA: Ridgeview Press*, pp. 17–61, 1993.

[27] G. Bealer, “Theories of properties, relations, and propositions,” *J. Philos., 76*, pp. 634–648, 1979.

https://doi.org/10.1515/9783110981438-008

[28] L. Henkin, J.D. Monk, and A. Tarski, "Cylindic algebras I," *North-Holland*, 1971.

[29] E.F. Codd, "A relational model of data for large shared data banks," *Commun. ACM, 13(6)*, pp. 377–387, 1970.

[30] A. Pirotte, "A precise definition of basic relational notions and of the relational algebra," *SIGMOD Rec., 13(1)*, pp. 30–45, 1982.

[31] R. Carnap, "Meaning and Necessity," Chicago, 1947.

[32] M.C. Fitting, "Intensional Logic – Beyond First Order," In *Trends in Logic: 50 Years of Studia Logica, Kluwer Academic Publishers*, pp. 87–108, 2003.

[33] M.C. Fitting and R. Mendelsohn, "First-Order Modal Logic," *Kluwer*, 1998.

[34] H. Wansing, "A general possible worlds framework for reasoning about knowledge and belief," *Stud. Log., 49*, pp. 523–539, 1990.

[35] H. Wansing and D. Pearce, "On the methodology of possible worlds semantics, II: Nonnormal worlds and propositional attitudes," *Report 2/1989, Gruppe für Logik, Wissenstheorie und Information, Freie Universität Berlin*, 1989.

[36] Z. Majkić, "First-order logic: Modality and intensionality," *arXiv:1103.0680v1*, pp. 1–33, 2011.

[37] P.R. Halmos, "Algebraic logic," *New York: Chelsea*, 1962.

[38] C. Davis, "Modal operators, equivalence relations, and projective algebras," *Am. J. Math., 76*, pp. 746–762, 1954.

[39] J. Van Benthem, "Correspondence Theory," In *Handbook of Philosophical Logic, Vol. II, D. Gabbay and F. Guenthner (Eds.), D. Reidel Publishing Company, Holand*, pp. 167–247, 1984.

[40] H. Wansing and D. Pearce, "On the methodology of possible worlds semantics, I: Correspondence theory," *Notre Damme J. Forma Logic, 29*, pp. 482–496, 1988.

[41] Z. Majkić, "Sound and complete query-answering in intensional P2P data integration," *arXiv:1103.0490v1*, pp. 1–27, 2011.

[42] Z. Majkić, "Intensional first-order logic for P2P database systems," In *Journal of Data Semantics (JoDS XII), LNCS 5480, Berlin Heidelberg: Springer*, pp. 131–152, 2009.

[43] Z. Majkić, "Intensional logic and epistemic independency of intelligent database agents," In *2nd International Workshop on Philosophy and Informatics (WSPI 2005), April 10–13, Kaiserslautern, Germany*, 2005.

[44] Z. Majkić, "Weak deduction for queries in intensional P2P database systems," In *International Conference on Enterprise Information Systems and Web Technologies (EISWT-09), Orlando FL, USA, July 13–16*, 2009.

[45] P.J. Hayes, "Some problems and non-problems in representation theory," In *Proc. AISB Summer Conference, University of Sussex*, pp. 63–79, 1974.

[46] W.A. Woods, "What's in a link: Foundations for semantic networks," In *Representation and Understanding: Studies in Cognitive Science, D.G. Bobrow and A.M. Collins (Eds.)*, pp. 35–82, 1975.

[47] P.J. Hayes, "The logic of frames," In *Frame Conceptions and Text Understanding, D. Metzing (Ed.), Walter de Gruyter and Co.*, pp. 46–61, 1979. Republished in [387].

[48] H.J. Levesque and R.J. Brachman, "A fundamental tradeoff in knowledge representation and reasoning," In *Readings in Knowledge Representation, R.J. Brachman and H.J. Levesque (Eds.)*, pp. 41–70, 1985.

[49] H.J. Levesque and R.J. Brachman, "Expressiveness and tractability in knowledge representation and reasoning," *Comput. Intell., 3*, pp. 78–93, 1987.

[50] F. Baader, D. Calvanese, D.L. Mc Guiness, D. Nardi, and P.F. Patel-Schneider, "Description Logic Handbook," *Cambridge University Press*, 2002.

[51] B. Russell, "On Denoting," In *Mind, XIV, Reprinted in Russell, Logic and Knowledge*, pp. 479–493, 1905.

[52] A.N. Whitehead and B. Russell, "Principia Mathematica, Vol. I," *Cambridge*, 1910.

[53] Z. Majkić, "Weakly-coupled ontology integration of P2P database systems," In *1st Int. Workshop on Peer-to-Peer Knowledge Management (P2PKM), August 22, Boston, USA*, 2004.
[54] Z. Majkić, "Intensional P2P mapping between RDF ontologies," In *6th International Conference on Web Information Systems (WISE-05), November 20–22, New York, M. Kitsuregawa (Ed.), LNCS 3806*, pp. 592–594, 2005.
[55] Z. Majkić, "Intensional semantics for P2P data integration," In *Journal on Data Semantics (JoDS) VI, Special Issue on 'Emergent Semantics', LNCS 4090*, pp. 47–66, 2006.
[56] Z. Majkić, "Non omniscient intensional contextual reasoning for query-agents in P2P systems," In *3rd Indian International Conference on Artificial Intelligence (IICAI-07), December 17–19, Pune, India*, 2007.
[57] Z. Majkić, "Coalgebraic specification of query computation in intensional P2P database systems," In *Int. Conference on Theoretical and Mathematical Foundations of Computer Science (TMFCS-08), Orlando FL, USA, July 7–9*, 2008.
[58] Z. Majkić, "RDF view-based interoperability in intensional FOL for Peer-to-Peer database systems," In *International Conference on Enterprise Information Systems and Web Technologies (EISWT-08), Orlando FL, USA, July 9–11*, 2008.
[59] Z. Majkić, "Categories: symmetry, *n*-dimensional levels and applications", *PhD Thesis, University "La Sapienza", Roma, Italy*, 1998.
[60] Z. Majkić, "Completion and Unification of Quantum Mechanics with Einstein's GR Ideas, Part I: Completion of QM," *New York: Nova Science Publishers, ISBN 978-1-53611-946-6*, 2017.
[61] Z. Majkić, "Completion and Unification of Quantum Mechanics with Einstein's GR Ideas, Part III: Advances, Revisions and Conclusions," *New York: Nova Science Publishers, ISBN 978-1-53617-200-3*, 2020.
[62] N.J. Nilsson, "Probabilistic logic," *Artif. Intell., 28*, pp. 71–88, 1986.
[63] R. Fagin, J. Halpern, and N. Megiddo, "A logic for reasoning about probabilities," *Inf. Comput., 87*, pp. 78–128, 1990.
[64] J.Y. Halpern, "An analysis of first-order logics of probability," *Artif. Intell., 46*, pp. 311–350, 1990.
[65] G. Kuper, L. Libkin, and J. Paredaens, "Constraint Databases," *Springer*, 2000.
[66] K. Marriot and H. Sondergaard, "Bottom-up abstract interpretation of logic programs," In *Proc. 5th Int. Conf. and Symposium on Logic Programming, Washington, Seatle*, 1988.
[67] P. Cousot and R. Cousot, "Abstract interpretation: A unified lattice model for static analysis of programs by construction or approximation of fixpoints," In *Int. Conf. 4th ACM Symposium on Principles of Programming Languages (POPL77)*, pp. 238–252, 1977.
[68] Z. Majkić, "Constraint logic programming and logic modality for event's valid-time approximation," In *2nd Indian International Conference on Artificial Intelligence (IICAI-05), December 20-22, Pune, India*, 2005.
[69] Z. Majkić, "Autoreferential semantics for many-valued modal logics," *J. Appl. Non-Class. Log., 18(1)*, pp. 79–125, 2008.
[70] R.T. Ng and V.S. Subrahmanian, "Probabilistic logic programming," *Inf. Comput., 101(2)*, pp. 150–201, 1992.
[71] A. Dekhtyar and M.I. Dekhtyar, "Possible worlds semantics for probabilistic logic programs," In *ICLP 2004*, pp. 137–148, 2004.
[72] Z. Majkić, "Probabilistic deduction and pattern recognition of complex events," In *International Conference on Information Security and Privacy (ISP-09), Orlando FL, USA, July 13–16*, 2009.
[73] W. Feller, "An introduction to Probability Theory and its applications, Vol. I," *2nd edition, New York: Wiley*, 1957.
[74] P. Halmos, "Measure theory," *Van Nostrand*, 1950.

[75] A.N. Kolmogorov, In A.N. Shiryayev, editor, "Selected works of A.N. Kolmogorov: vol. 2 Probability theory and mathematical statistics," *Moscow: Nauka*, 1986.
[76] R. Fagin and J.Y. Halpern, "Uncertainty, belief, and probability," In *IJCAI 89*, pp. 1161–1167, 1989.
[77] Z. Majkić, "Intensional semantics for RDF data structures," In *12th International Database Engineering & Applications Systems (IDEAS08), Coimbra, Portugal, 10–13 September*, 2008.
[78] J. Lukasiewicz, "Comptes rendus des seances de la societe des sciences et des letters de Varsovie, cl. III 23," *J. Philos. Bemerk. Syst. Aussagenlogik*, pp. 51–77, 1930.
[79] J. Lukasiewicz, "A system of modal logic," *J. Comp. Syst., 1*, pp. 111–149, 1953.
[80] J. Lukasiewicz, "Selected Works," In *Studies in Logic and the Foundations of Mathematics, L. Borkowski (Ed.) Amsterdam: North-Holland*, 1970.
[81] Z. Majkić and B. Prasad, "Lukasiewicz's 4-valued logic and normal modal logics," In *4th Indian International Conference on Artificial Intelligence (IICAI-09), December 16–18, Tumkur, India*, 2009.
[82] Z. Majkić, "Functional many-valued logic and global predicate compression," In *MVLPA Multivalued Logic Programming and Applications (with ICLP), 17–20 August, Seatle, WA*, 2006.
[83] Z. Majkić, "Many-valued logic programming and fixpoint semantics for higher-order Herbrand models," In *20th Workshop on (Constraint) Logic Programming (WLP 2006), February 22–24, Vienna, Austria*, 2006.
[84] J.Y. Béziau, "Non truth-functional many-valued semantics," In *Aspects of Universal Logic, J.-Y. Béziau, A. Costa-Leite and A. Facchini (Eds.), Neuchâtel: Université de Neuchâtel*, pp. 199–218, 2004.
[85] Z. Majkić, "Probabilistic logic: Many-valuedness and intensionality," *arXiv:1103.0676v1*, pp. 1–15, 2011.
[86] C. Dyreson and R. Snodgrass, "Supporting valid-time indeterminacy," *ACM Trans. Database Syst., 23*, pp. 1–57, 1998.
[87] A. Dekhtyar, R. Ross, and V.S. Subrahmanian, "Probabilistic temporal databases, I:Algebra," *ACM Trans. Database Syst., 26*, pp. 41–95, 2001.
[88] T. Berners-Lee, J. Hendlar, and O. Lassila, "The semantic web," *Sci. Am., 279*, 2001.
[89] O. Lassila and R.R. Swick, "Resource description framework (RDF): Model and syntax specification," *World Wide Web Consortium, http://www.w3.org/TR/REC-rdf-syntax*, 1999.
[90] D. Brickley and R. Guha, "Resource description framework (RDF) schema specification 1.0," *World Wide Web Consortium, http://www.w3.org/TR/2000/CR-rdf-schema-20000327*, 2000.
[91] F. van Harmelen, J. Handler, I. Horrocks, D.L. McGuinnes, P.F. Patel-Schneider, M. Dean, D. Connolly, and L.A. Stein, "OWL Web ontology language 1.0 reference," *http://www.w3.org/TR/owl-ref/*, 2002.
[92] P.F. Patel-Schneider and D. Fensel, "Layering the semantic Web: Problems and directions," In *2002 International Sematic Web Conference*, 2002.
[93] I. Horrocks and P.F. Patel-Schneider, "Three thesis of representation in the semantic web," In *Proc. of the 12th International World Wide Web Conference (WWW2003)*, pp. 39–47, 2003.
[94] G. Yang and M. Kifer, "On the semantics of anonimous identity and reification," In *Lecture Notes in Comp. Science (ODBASE2002) 2519*, pp. 1047–1066, 2002.
[95] M.R. Genesereth, "Knowledge interchange format," *T.Report NCITS. T2/98-004, Stanford University*, 1998.
[96] P. Hayes and C. Menzel, "A semantics for the knowledge interchange format," In *Workshop on the IEEE Standard Upper Ontology (in IJCAI)*, 2001.
[97] P. Hayes, "RDF Model theory," *T.Report W3C, http:/www.w3.org/TR/rdf-mt*, 2002.
[98] J.Z. Pan and I. Horrocks, "RDFS(FA): A DL-ised sub-language of RDFS," In *Proc. of the 2003 Description Logic Workshop, (DL 2003), CEUR 81*, pp. 95–102, 2003.

[99] A. Levy, A. Mendelzon, and Y. Sagiv, "Answering queries using views," In *Proc. 14th ACM Symp. on Principles of Database Systems*, pp. 95–104, 1995.

[100] K. Aberer, M. Punceva, M. Hauswirth, and R. Schmidt, "Improving data access in P2P systems," In *IEEE Internet Computing*, 2002.

[101] D. Calvanese, G. De Giacomo, M. Lenzerini, and R. Rosati, "Logical foundations of Peer-to-Peer data integration," In *PODS 2004, June 14–16, Paris, France*, 2004.

[102] Hewlett-Packard, "RDQL-RDF data query language," *http://www.hpl.hp.com/semweb/rdql.html*.

[103] S. Alexaki, V. Christophides, D. Plexousakis, M. Scholl, G. Karvounarakis, A. Magnaraki, and K. Tolle, "Quering the semantic web with RQL," *Comput. Netw. ISDN Syst. J., 42*, 2003.

[104] Y. Deng, E. Hung, and V.S. Subrahmanian, "Maintaining RDF views," *Tech. Rep. CS-TR-4612 (UMIACS-TR-2004-54)*, 2004.

[105] Z. Majkić, "Flexible intentional query-answering for RDF Peer-to-Peer systems," In *7th International Conference on Flexible Query Answering Systems (FQAS 2006), 7–10 June, Milano, Italy*, 2006.

[106] M. Ushold, "Where is the semantics in the semantic web," In *Workshop on Ontologies in Agent Systems (OAS) at the 5th International Conference on Autonomous Agents*, 2001.

[107] S. Gribble, A. Halevy, Z. Ives, M. Rodrig, and D. Suciu, "What can databases do for Peer-to-Peer?," In *WebDB Workshop on Databases and the Web*, 2001.

[108] L. Serafini, F. Giunchiglia, J. Mylopoulos, and P.A. Bernstein, "The local relational model: Model and proof theory," *Technical Report 0112-23, ITC-IRST*, 2001.

[109] C. Ghidini and F. Giunchiglia, "Local models semantics or contextual reasoning = locality + compatibility," *Artif. Intell., 127*, pp. 221–259, 2001.

[110] R. Reiter, "Towards a logical reconstruction of relational database theory," In *On Conceptual Modeling: Perspectives from Artificial Intelligence Databases and Programming Languages, M.L. Brodie, J. Mylopoulos and J.W. Schmidt (Eds.)*, 1984.

[111] M. Lenzerini, "Data integration: a theoretical perspective," 2002, pp. 233–246.

[112] A.Y. Halevy, D. Suiu, Z.G. Ives, and I. Tatarinov, "Schema mediation for large-scale semantic data sharing," *VLDB J., 14(1)*, pp. 68–83, 2005.

[113] P. Aczel, *Non-well-founded sets*, Number 14 in Lecture Notes CSLI, 1988.

[114] P. Aczel, J. Adamek, S. Milius, and J. Velebil, "Infinite trees and completely iterative theories: a coalgebraic view," *Theor. Comput. Sci., 300*, pp. 1–45, 2003.

[115] M. Lenzerini and Z. Majkić, "General framework for query reformulation," In *Semantic Webs and Agents in Integrated Economies, D3.1, IST-2001-34825, February*, 2003.

[116] M. Gelfond and V. Lifshitz, "The stable model semantics for logic programming," In *Proc. of the Fifth Logic Programming Symposium, Cambridge, MA: MIT Press*, pp. 1070–1080, 1988.

[117] Z. Majkić, "Fixpoint semantics for query answering in data integration systems," In *AGP03 – 8th Joint Conference on Declarative Programming, Reggio Calabria*, pp. 135–146, 2003.

[118] Z. Majkić, "Plausible query-answering inference in data integration," In *18th International Florida Artificial Intelligence Conference (FLAIRS 2005), May 15–17, Clearwater Beach, USA*, 2005.

[119] H.J. Levesque, "All I know: a study in autoepistemic logic," *Artif. Intell., 42*, pp. 263–310, 1990.

[120] R. Reiter, "What should a database know?," *J. Log. Program., 14*, pp. 127–153, 1992.

[121] P. Blackburn, "Representation, reasoning, and relational structures: a hybrid logic manifesto. Methods for Modalities 1," *Log. J. IGPL, 8*, pp. 339–365, 2000.

[122] E. Franconi, G. Kuper, A. Lopatenko, and L. Serafini, "A robust logical and computational characterization of Peer-to-Peer data systems," *Technical Report DIT-03-051, University of Trento, Italy*, 2003.

[123] D. Calvanese, G. De Giacomo, D. Lembo, M. Lenzerini, and R. Rosati, "Inconsistency tollerance in P2P data integration: an epistemic approach," In *Proc. 10th Int. Workshop on Database Programming Language*, 2005.
[124] S. Abitebul and O. Duschka, "Complexity of answering queries using materialized views," In *Proc. of PODS, Seattle, WA*, pp. 254–263, 1998.
[125] Z. Majkić, "Weakly-coupled P2P system with a network repository," In *6th Workshop on Distributed Data and Structures (WDAS'04), July 5–7, Lausanne, Switzerland*, 2004.
[126] Z. Majkić, "Massive parallelism for query answering in weakly integrated P2P systems," In *Workshop GLOBE 04, August 30–September 3, Zaragoza, Spain*, 2004.
[127] M. Arenas, L.E. Bertossi, and J. Chomicki, "Consistent query answers in inconsistent databases," In *Proc. of the 18th ACM Symp. on Principles of Database Systems*, pp. 68–79, 1999.
[128] G. Greco, S. Greco, and E. Zampano, "A logic programming approach to the integration, repairing and querying of inconsistent databases," In *Proc. of the 17th Int. Conf. on Logic Programming 2237*, pp. 348–364, 2001.
[129] Z. Majkić, "Autoepistemic logic programming for reasoning with inconsistency," In *International Symposium on Logic-based Program Synthesis and Transformation (LOPSTR), September 7–9, 2005, Imperial College, London, UK*, 2005.
[130] J. McCarthy, "Circumscription – a form of non-monotonic reasoning," *Artif. Intell., 13*, 1980.
[131] Y. Shoham, "A semantical approach to nonmonotonic logics," In *Proc. 2nd IEEE Symp. on Logic in Computer Science*, pp. 275–279, 1987.
[132] S. Kraus, D. Lehmann, and M. Magidor, "Non-monotonic reasoning, preferential models and cumulative logics," *Artif. Intell., 44*, pp. 167–207, 1990.
[133] S. Lindstrom, "A semantical approach to nonmonotonic reasoning: Inference operations and choice," *Tech. Rep. Upsala Prints and Preprints in Philosophy, 1994:10, University of Upsala*, 1994.
[134] N. Friedman and J.Y. Halpern, "Plausibility measures and default reasoning," In *Proc. AAAI'96*, pp. 1297–1304, 1996.
[135] D. Lehman, "Non monotonic logics and semantics," *Tech. Rep. TR-98-6, Institute of Comp. Science, Hebrew University, Jerusalem*, 1998.
[136] M. Arenas, L. Bertossi, and J. Chomicki, "Consistent query answers in inconsistent databases," In *Proc. ACM Symp. on Principles of Database Systems*, pp. 68–79, 1999.
[137] D. Gabbay, "Theoretical foundations for non-monotonic reasoning in expert systems," In *Logics and Models of Concurrent Systems, NATO ASI Series F13, Springer*, 1985.
[138] D. Makinson, "General theory of cumulative inference," In *Non-Monotonic Reasoning, Lecture Notes on Artificial Intelligence 346, Spinger Verlag*, 1989.
[139] M. Dalal, "Investigations into a theory of knowledge base revision," In *Proc. National Conference on Artificial Intelligence*, pp. 475–479, 1988.
[140] D. Fensel, *Ontologies: A Silver Bullet for Knowledge Management and Electronic Commerce*, 2001.
[141] M. Lenzerini and Z. Majkić, "First release of the system prototype for query management," In *Semantic Webs and Agents in Integrated Economies, D3.3, IST-2001-34825*, 2003.
[142] A. Calì, D. Calvanese, G. De Giacomo, and M. Lenzerini, "Data integration under integrity constraints," pp. 262–279, 2002.
[143] R. Fagin, P.G. Kolaitis, R.J. Miller, and L. Popa, In *DATA Exchange: Semantics and query answering*, pp. 207–224, 2003.
[144] Z. Majkić, "Coalgebraic semantics for logic programming," In *18th Worshop on (Constraint) Logic Programming, W(C)LP 2004, March 04–06, Berlin, Germany*, 2004.
[145] J. de Riviers and H. Levesque, "The consistency of syntactical treatments of knowledge," *Comput. Intell., 4*, pp. 31–41, 1988.

[146] M. Morreau and S. Kraus, "Syntactical treatments of propositional attitudes," In *Artificial Intelligence*, 1998.
[147] K. Konolige, "A deduction model of belief," *Morgan Kaufman*, 1986.
[148] D. Lewis, "Index, Context, and Content," In *Philosophy and Grammar, S. Kranger and S. Ohman (Eds.), D. Reidel Publishing Company*, pp. 79–100, 1980.
[149] J. McCarthy, "Notes on formalizing context," In *Proc. of the 13th International Joint Conference on Artificial Intelligence, Chambery, France*, pp. 555–560, 1993.
[150] F. Giunchiglia, "Contextual reasoning," In *Epistemologia, special issue on I Linguaggi e le Macchine, XVI*, pp. 345–364, 1993.
[151] D.M. Gabbay, "Labelled Deductive Systems," *Volume 1 – Founrations. Tech. Report MPI-I-94-223, Max-Planc-Institut Für Informatik*, 1994.
[152] B. Jacobs, "Objects and classes, co-algebrically," In *Object-Orientation with Parallelism and Persistence, Kluwer Acad. Publ.*, pp. 83–103, 1996.
[153] J. Rutten, "Universal coalgebra: A theory of systems," *Theor. Comput. Sci., 249*, pp. 3–90, 2000.
[154] A.Y. Halevy, "Answering queries using views: A survey," *VLDB J., 10(4)*, pp. 270–294, 2001.
[155] D. Lembo, M. Lenzerini, and R. Rosati, "Source inconsistency and incompleteness in data integration," In *Proc. of the 9th Int. Workshop on Knowledge Representation meets Databases (KRDB 2002) CEUR*, 2002.
[156] Z. Majkić, "Querying with negation in data integration systems," In *9th International Database Engineering and Application Symposium (IDEAS), July 25–27, 2005, Montreal, Canada, IEEE Computer Society*, pp. 58–70, 2005.
[157] COMPUTERWORLD, "No to SQL? Anti-database movement gains steam," , *https://www.computerworld.com/article/2526317/no-to-sql--anti-database-movement-gains-steam.html*, 2009.
[158] M. Stonebraker and C. Ugur, "One size fits all," In *ICDE 05 Proceedings, Washington, DC, USA: IEEE Computer Society*, pp. 2–11, 2005.
[159] M. Stonebraker, S. Madden, D. Abadi, S. Harizopoulos, N. Hachem, and P. Helland, "The end of and architectural era: (it's time for a complete rewrite)," In *VLDB 07 Proceedings, VLDB Endowment*, pp. 1150–1160, 2007.
[160] R. Kallman, H. Kimura, J. Natkins, A. Pavio, S. Zdonik, D.J. Abadi, E.P. C. Jones, S. Madden, A. Rasin, M. Stonebraker, Y. Zhang, and J. Hugg, "H-store: a high-performance, distributed main memory transaction processing system," In *Proceedings of the VLDB 08, VLDB Endowment*, pp. 1496–1499, 2008.
[161] M. Stonebraker, "SQL databases v. NoSQL databases," *Commun. ACM, 53*, pp. 4, 2010.
[162] M. Stonebraker, D.J. Abadi, D.J. Dewitt, S. Madden, E. Paulson, A. Pavio, and A. Rasin, "MapReduce and parallel DBMSs: Friends or Foes?," *Commun. ACM, 53*, pp. 64, 2010. https://doi.org/10.1145/1629175.1629197.
[163] A. Pavio, E. Paulson, D.J. Abadi, D.J. Dewitt, S. Madden, A. Rasin, and M. Stonebraker, "A comparison of approaches to large-scale data analysis," In *Proceedings of the 35th SIGMOD Conference, New York: ACM Press*, pp. 165–178, 2009.
[164] A.K. Chandra and D. Harel, "Structure and complexity of relational queries," *J. Comput. Syst. Sci., 25(1)*, pp. 99–128, 1982.
[165] J.M. Smith and D.C. P. Smith, "Database abstractions: Aggregation and generalization," *ACM Trans. Database Syst., 2(2)*, pp. 105–133, 1977.
[166] K.A. Ross, "Relations with relation names as arguments: Algebra and calculus," In *Proceedings of the 11th ACM Symposium on Principles of Database Systems, San Diego, California*, pp. 346–353, 1992.
[167] A. Lefebvre, P. Brnus, and R. Topor, "Query transformation for accesing heterogeneous databases," In *Workshop on Deductive Databases in conjunction with JICSLP*, pp. 31–40, 1992.

[168] R. Krishnamurthy, W. Litwin, and W. Kent, "Language features for interoperability of databases with schematic discrepancies," In *Proceedings of the ACM SIGMOD, New York*, pp. 40–49, 1991.

[169] L.V. S. Lakshmanan, F. Sadri, and I.N. Subramanian, "SchemaSQL-an extension to SQL for multidatabase interoperability," *ACM Trans. Database Syst., 26(4)*, pp. 476–519, 2001.

[170] R. Agrawal, A. Somani, and Y. Xu, "Storage and querying of E-commerce data," In *Proceedings of the VLDB 01, 27th VLDB Conference, Roma, Italy*, 2001.

[171] C. Cunningham, C.A. Galindo-Legaria, and G. Graefe, "PIVOT and UNPIVOT: Optimization and execution strategies in an RDBMS," In *Proceedings of the 30th VLDB Conference, Toronto*, pp. 998–1009, 2004.

[172] L.V. S. Lakshmanan, F. Sadri, and I.N. Subramanian, "Logic and algebraic languages for interoperability in multidatabase systems," *J. Log. Program., 33(2)*, pp. 101–149, 1997.

[173] G. Wiederhold, "Mediators in the architecture of future information systems," In *IEEE Computer*, 1992.

[174] Z. Majkić and B. Prasad, "Kleisli category for database mappings," *Int. J. Intell. Inf. Database Syst., 4(5)*, pp. 509–527, 2010.

[175] Z. Majkić, "Data base mappings and monads: (co)induction," *arXiv:1102.4769v1*, pp. 1–31, 2011.

[176] E. Moggi, "Computational lambda-calculus and monads," In *Proceedings. Fourth Annual Symposium on Logic in Computer Science*, pp. 14–23, 1989.

[177] E. Moggi, "Notions of computation and monads," *Inf. Comput., 93(1)*, pp. 55–92, 1991.

[178] D.I. Spivak, "Kleisli database instances," *arXiv:1209.1011*, pp. 1–23, 2012.

[179] R. Fagin, P.G. Kolaitis, L. Popa, and W. Tan, "Composing schema mappings: second-order dependencies to the rescue," *ACM TODS, 30(4)*, pp. 994–1055, 2005.

[180] Z. Majkić, "Data base mappings and theory of sketches," *arXiv:1104.4899v1*, pp. 1–21, 2011.

[181] S. Mac Lane, "Categories for the Working Mathematician," *Springer*, 1971.

[182] J. Lambek and P. Scott, "Introduction to higher order categorial logic," *Cambidge University Press*, 1986.

[183] G.M. Kelly and A.J. Power, "Adjuntions whose counits are coequalizers, and presentations of finitary enriched monads," *J. Pure Appl. Algebra, 89*, pp. 163–179, 1993.

[184] P. Buneman, S. Naqui, V. Tanen, and L. Wong, "Principles of programming with complex objects and collection types," *Theor. Comput. Sci., 149(1)*, 1995.

[185] G.D. Plotkin and A.J. Power, "Adequacy for algebraic effects," In *Proc. FOSSACS 2001, LNCS 2030*, pp. 1–24, 2001.

[186] Z. Majkić, "Saturation of the morphisms in the database category," *arXiv:1405.3955*, pp. 1–17, 2014.

[187] P.T. Johnstone, "Stone spaces," *Cambridge: Cambridge University Press, ISBN 0-521-23893-5*, 1982.

[188] M.C. Fitting, "Bilattices and the semantics of logic programming," *J. Log. Program., 11*, pp. 91–116, 1991.

[189] M.L. Ginsberg, "Bilattices and modal operators," *Tech. Rep. N. 94305, Comp. Science Dept. Stanford University, California*, 1990.

[190] N.D. Belnap, "A useful four-valued logic," In *Modern Uses of Multiple-Valued Logic, J-M. Dunn and G. Epstein (Eds.), D. Reidel*, 1977.

[191] J. Lukasiewicz, "Aristotele's syllogistic from the standpoint of modern formal logic," *(2nd enlaged edition), Oxford: Clarendon Press*, 1957.

[192] M. Gehrke and B. Jonsson, "Bounded distributive lattices with operators," *Math. Jpn., 40(2)*, pp. 207–215, 1994.

[193] J.M. Dunn, "Positive Modal Logic," *Stud. Log., 55*, pp. 301–317, 1995.

[194] J. Dunn and C. Zhou, "Negation in the context of gaggle theory," *Stud. Log., 80(2–3)*, pp. 235–264, 2005.
[195] G. Restall, "Constant domain quantified modal logics without boolean negation," *Aust. J. Logic, 3*, pp. 45–62, 2005.
[196] V. Sofronie-Stokkermans, In *Representation theorems and the semantics of non-classical logics, and applications to automated theorem proving, M. Fitting and E. Orlowska (Eds.), Springer Verlag series Studies in Fuzziness and Soft Computing*, pp. 59–100, 2003.
[197] M. Ginsberg, "Multivalued logics: A uniform approach to reasoning in artificial intelligence," *Comput. Intell., 4*, pp. 265–316, 1988.
[198] O. Arieli and A. Avron, "Logical bilattices and inconsistent data," In *Proc. 9th IEEE Annual Symp. on Ligic in Computer Science*, pp. 468–476, IEEE Press, 1994.
[199] P. Ruet and F. Fages, "Combining explicit negation and negation by failure via Belnap's logic," In *Workshop on Uncertainty in Databases and Deductive Systems (ILPS-94)*, 1994.
[200] V.S. Lakshmanan and F. Sadri, "Probabilistic deductive databases," In *Proc. Intl. Logic Programming Symposium, Ithaca, NY: MIT Press*, pp. 254–268, 1994.
[201] K.M. Sim, "Bilattices and reasoning in artificial intelligence: Concepts and foundations," In *Artificial Intelligence Review 15, Kluwer Ac. Publishers*, pp. 219–240, 2001.
[202] Z. Majkić, "Beyond fuzzy: Parameterized approximations of Heyting algebras for uncertain knowledge," In *2nd Indian International Conference on Artificial Intelligence (IICAI-05), December 20–22, Pune, India*, 2005.
[203] Z. Majkić, "Many-valued intuitionistic implication and inference closure in a bilattice based logic," In *35th International Symposium on Multiple-Valued Logic (ISMVL 2005), May 18–21, Calgary, Canada*, 2005.
[204] Z. Majkić, "Reduction of many-valued logic programs into two-valued modal logics," In *Intellectual Archive Bulletin, Shiny World Corp., Toronto, ID:493, ISSN 1929-1329 (arXiv:1103.0920), 21 June*, pp. 1–27, 2012.
[205] Z. Majkić, "Binary sequent calculi for truth-invariance entailment of finite many-valued logics," *arXiv:1103.1334*, 2011.
[206] Z. Majkić, "A new representation theorem for many-valued modal logics," *arXiv:1103.0248v1*, pp. 1–19, 2011.
[207] G. Birkhoff, "Lattice theory," *reprinted 1979, Amer. Math. Soc. Colloquium Publications XXV*, 1940.
[208] Z. Majkić, "Intuitionistic truth-knowledge symmetric bilattices for uncertainty in intelligent systems," In *3rd Int. IEEE Conf. on Intelligent Systems (IS06), 4–6 Sept., London, UK*, pp. 703–710, 2006.
[209] Z. Majkić, "Bilattices, intuitionism and truth-knowledge duality: Concepts and foundations," *J. Mult.-Valued Log. Soft Comput., 14(6)*, pp. 525–564, 2008.
[210] K. Došen, "Negation as a modal operator," *Rep. Math. Log., 20*, pp. 15–28, 1986.
[211] J.Y. Béziau, "Are paraconsistent negations negations?," In *Paraconsistency: the logical way to the inconsistent, W. Carnielli (Ed.), New York: Marcel Dekker*, pp. 465–486, 2002.
[212] D.M. Clark and B.A. Davey, "Natural dualities for the working algebraist," In *Cambridge studies in advanced mathematics 57, 1st edition, Cambridge University Press*, 1998.
[213] J.C. C. McKinsey and A. Tarski, "On closed elements in closure algebras," *Ann. Math., 47*, pp. 122–162, 1946.
[214] M.C. Fitting, "Kleene's logic, generalized," *J. Log. Comput., 1*, pp. 797–810, 1992.
[215] M.C. Fitting, "Kleene's three valued logics and their children," *Fundam. Inform., 20*, pp. 113–131, 1994.
[216] M. Schmidt-Schauß and G. Smolka, "Attributive concept descriptions with complements," *Artif. Intell., 48(1)*, pp. 1–26, 1991.

[217] I. Horrocks and P.F. Patel-Schneider, "Reducing OWL entailment to description logic satisfiability," In *ISWC 2003, LNCS 2870, Heidelberg: Springer*, pp. 17–29, 2003.
[218] Z. Majkić, "Ontological encapsulation of many-valued logic," In *19th Italian Symposium of Computational Logic (CILC04), June 16–17, Parma, Italy*, 2004.
[219] Z. Majkić and B. Prasad, "Soft query-answering computing in P2P systems with epistemically independent peers," In *Book on Soft Computing Applications in Industry, STUDFUZZ 226, Berlin: Springer*, pp. 331–356, 2008.
[220] A. Tarski, "Der wahrheitsbegriff in den formalisierten sprachen," *Studia Philos., 1*, pp. 261–405, 1936. *English translation, 'The concepts of truth in formalized langiuges', appeared in A. Tarski 1956, Logic, Semantics and Metamathematics: Papers by Alfred Tarski from 1923 to 1938, Oxford: Clarendon Press.*
[221] J. Ketland, "Deflationism and tarski's paradise," *Mind, 108*, pp. 69–94, 1999.
[222] S. Shapiro, "Truth and proof – through thick and thin," *J. Philos., 95*, pp. 493–522, 1998.
[223] G. Boolos and R. Jeffrey, "Computability and Logic," *3rd edition, Cambridge University Press*, 1989.
[224] J. Ketland, "A proof of the (strethened) liar formula in a semantic extension of Peano arithmetic," *Analysis, 60*, pp. 1–4, 2000.
[225] I.E. Orlov, "The calculus of compatibility of propositions," *Mat. Sb., 35*, pp. 263–286, 1928 (in Russian).
[226] K. Došen, "A brief survey of frames for the Lambek calculus," *Z. Math. Log. Grundl. Math., 38*, pp. 179–187, 1992.
[227] Z. Majkić, "Weakening of intuitionistic negation for many-valued paraconsistent da Costa system," *Notre Dame J. Form. Log., 49(4)*, pp. 401–424, 2008.
[228] Z. Majkić, "Paraconsistent logic and weakening of intuitionistic negation," *Int. J. Intell. Syst., 3*, pp. 255–270, 2012.
[229] A. Neckam, "De naturis rerum," T. Wright, editor, London, 1863.
[230] A. Urquhart, "Semantics for relevant logics," *J. Symb. Log., 37(1)*, pp. 159–169, 1972.
[231] K. Fine, "Models for entailment," *J. Philos. Log., 3*, pp. 347–372, 1974.
[232] J. Barwise, "Constraints, channels and the flow of information," In *Situation Theory and Its Applications 3, P. Aczel and et al. (Eds.), Stanford: CSLI Publications*, pp. 3–27, 1993.
[233] G. Restall, "Information flow and relevant logics," In *Logic, Language and Computation (Volume 1), J. Seligman and D. Westerstahl (Eds.), Stanford: CSLI Publications*, pp. 463–478, 1996.
[234] E.D. Mares, "Four-valued semantics for the relevant logic R," *J. Philos. Log., 33*, pp. 327–341, 2004.
[235] J.M. Dunn, "The relevance of relevance to relevance logic," In *Logic and its Applications: 6th Indian Conference, ICLA 2015, Mumbai, India, M. Banerjee and S.N. Krishna (Eds.)*, 2015.
[236] J.M. Dunn, "Partial gaggles applied to logics with restricted structural rules," In *Substructural logics, in Logic and Computation 2, P. Schröeder-Heister and K. Došen (Eds.), Oxford University Press*, pp. 63–108, 1993.
[237] J.M. Dunn, "A representation of relation algebras using routley-meyer frames," In *Logic, Meaning and Computation C.A. Anderson and M. Zeleny, (Eds.), Synthese Library (Studies in Epistemology, Logic, Methodology, and Philosophy of Science) 305, Dordrecht: Springer*, 2001.
[238] M. Gehrke, C. Walker, and E. Walker, "A mathematical setting for fuzzy logics," *Int. J. Uncertain. Fuzziness Knowl.-Based Syst., 5(3)*, pp. 223–238, 1997.
[239] P. Hájek, "Metamathematics of fuzzy logic," *Trends in Logic 4. Dodrecht: Kluwer Academic Publishers*, 1998.
[240] H. Ono, "Logics without the contraction rule and residuated lattices," *Australas. J. Log., 8*, pp. 50–81, 2010.

[241] J. Lukasiewicz and A. Tarski, "Untersuchungen über den aussagenkalkül," *Comp. Rend. Soc. Sci. Lett. Varsovie Cl. III, 23*, pp. 30–50, 1930.

[242] R. Cignoli and A. Torrens, "Hájek basic fuzzy logic and Lukasiewicz infinite-valued logic," *Arch. Math. Log., 42*, pp. 361–370, 2003.

[243] J.M. Font, A.J. Gil, A. Torrens, and V. Verdu, "On the infinite-valued Lukasiewicz logic that preserves degrees of truth," *Arch. Math. Log., 45(7)*, pp. 839–868, 2006.

[244] A.J. Rodriguez, "Un estudio algebraico del calculo proposicional de lukasiewicz," *Ph.D. Dissertation, Universitat de Barcelona*, 1980.

[245] W. Blok and D. Pigozzi, "Algebraizable logics," *Mem. Amer. Math. Soc. 396. Providence: A.M.S*, 1989.

[246] M. Gehrke, C. Walker, and E. Walker, "De morgan systems on the unit interval," *Int. J. Intell. Syst., 11*, pp. 733–750, 1996.

[247] M. Gehrke, C. Walker, and E. Walker, "Fuzzy logics arising from strict De Morgan systems," In *Topological and Algebraic Structures in Fuzzy Sets: A Handbook of Recent Developments in the Mathematics of Fuzzy Sets, S.E. Rodabaugh and E.P. Klement (Eds.), Springer*, pp. 280–281, 2003.

[248] T.S. Blyth and J.C. Varlet, "Ockham algebras," *Oxford University Press*, 1994.

[249] A. Bialynicki-Birula and H. Rasiowa, "On the representation of quasi-Boolean algebras," *Bull. Polish Acad. Sci., Cl. III, 5*, pp. 159–261, 1957.

[250] J.Y. Béziau, "A history of truth-values," In *Logic: A History of its Central Concepts, D.M. Gabbay, F.J. Pelletier and J. Woods (Eds.), North Holland*, pp. 280–281, 2012.

[251] H. Rasiowa, "An algebraic approach to non-classical logics," *Amsterdam: North-Holland Co.*, 1974.

[252] M. Dunn, "A relational representation of quasi-Boolean algebras," *Notre Dame J. Form. Log., 23(4)*, pp. 353–357, 1982.

[253] R. Balbes and P. Dwinger, "Distributive lattices," *Abstract Space Publishing*, 2011.

[254] A. Anderson and N. Belnap, "Entailment: the logic of relevance and necessity," *Princeton, NY: Princeton University Press*, 1975.

[255] O. Arieli and A. Avron, "Reasoning with logical bilattices," *J. Log. Lang. Inf., 5*, pp. 25–63, 1996.

[256] F. Bou and U. Rivieccio, "The logic of distributive bilattices," *Log. J. IGPL, 19(1)*, pp. 183–216, 2011.

[257] A. Saha, J. Sen, and M.K. Chakraborty, "Algebraic structures in the vicinity of pre-rough algebra and their logics," *Inf. Sci., 282*, pp. 296–320, 2014.

[258] J.M. Font, "Belnap's four-valued logic and De Morgan lattices," *Log. J. IGPL, 5(3)*, pp. 413–440, 1997.

[259] H. Aoyama, "LK, LJ, dual intuitionistic logic, and quantum logic," *Notre Dame J. Form. Log., 45(4)*, pp. 193–213, 2004.

[260] A. Brunner and W. Carnielli, "Anti-intuitionism and paraconsistency," *J. Appl. Log., 3(1)*, pp. 161–184, 2005.

[261] W. Carnielli, M.E. Coniglio, and J. Marcos, "Logics of Formal Inconsistency," In *Handbook of Philosophical Logic 14, 2nd edition, D. Gabbay and F. Guenthner (Eds.), Kluwer Academic Publishers*, pp. 1–93, 2006. Available at http://wslc.math.ist.utl.pt/ftp/pub/MarcosJ/03-CCM-lfi.pdf.

[262] I. Urbas, "Dual-intuitionistic logic," *Notre Dame J. Form. Log., 37(3)*, pp. 440–451, 1996.

[263] C. Rauszer, "Applications of Kripke models to Hayting-Brouwer logic," *Stud. Log., 34*, pp. 61–71, 1977.

[264] K. Popper, "The logic of scientific discovery," *English translation of Logik der Forschung, Vienna: Julius Springer Verlag*, 1936.

[265] N.C. A. da Costa, "On the theory of inconsistent formal systems," *Notre Dame J. Form. Log., 15*, pp. 497–510, 1974.

[266] D. Batens, "Dialectical dynamics within formal logics," *Log. Anal., 114*, pp. 161–173, 1980.

[267] D. Batens, "A survey of inconsistency-adaptive logics," In *Frontiers in Paraconsistent Logic, Proc. I World Congress on Paraconsistency, Ghent*, pp. 49–73, 2000.

[268] S. Jaskowski, "A propositional calculus for inconsistent deductive systems," *Stud. Soc. Sci. Torun., Sect. A, 5*, pp. 57–71, 1948.

[269] W. Carnielli and J. Marcos, "A Taxonomy of C-Systems," In *Paraconsistency – the Logical Way to the Inconsistent, W.A. Carnielli, M.E. Coniglio and I.M.L. D'Ottaviano (Eds.), Lecture Notes in Pure and Applied Mathematics 228. New York: Marcel Dekker*, pp. 1–94 2002.

[270] A. Kolmogorov, "On the principle of tertium non datur," *Mat. Sb., 32*, 1925. *(Traduced in van Heijenoort, From Frege to Gödel, C.U.P., 414–437, 1967).*

[271] A. Kolmogorov, "Zur dentung der intuitionistischen logik," *Math. Z., 35*, pp. 58–65, 1932.

[272] A. Heyting, "Mathematische grundlagenforschung. Intuitionismus, beweistheorie," *Berlin: Springer*, 1934.

[273] K. Gödel, "Zum intuitionistischen aussagenkalkül," *Anz. Akad. Wiss. Wien, 69*, pp. 65–66, 1932.

[274] M. Dummett, "A propositional calculus with denumerable matrix," *J. Symb. Log., 27*, pp. 97–106, 1959.

[275] Z. Majkić, "General framework for query answering in Data Quality Cooperative Information Systems," In *International Workshop on Information Quality in Information Systems (IQIS), June 18, Paris, France*, 2004.

[276] J. Mylopoulos and M.P. Papazoglou, "Cooperative Information Systems (Special Issue)," *IEEE Intell. Syst. Appl., 12(5)*, 1997.

[277] M. Mecella, M. Scannapieco, A. Virgillito, R. Baldoni, T. Catarci, and C. Batini, "Managing Data Quality in Cooperative Information Systems," In *Proceedings, Lecture Notes in Computer Science 2519, Springer*, pp. 486–502, 2002.

[278] C. Batini and M. Mecella, "Enabling Italian e-Government Through a Cooperative Architecture," *IEEE Comput., 34(2)*, 2001.

[279] Z. Majkić, "From inconsistency to possibility: A unique minimal Herbrand model," *Notes in http://www.dis.uniroma1.it/~majkic/*, 2004.

[280] F. Naumann, U. Leser, and J.C. Freytag, "Quality-driven Integration of Heterogenous Information Systems," In *Proceedings of 25th International Conference on Very Large Data Bases (VLDB'99), Edinburgh, Scotland, UK*, 1999.

[281] D. Maier, J.D. Ullman, and M.Y. Vardi, "On the foundations of the universal relation model," *ACM Trans. Database Syst., 9*, pp. 283–308, 1984.

[282] P. Bertolazzi, L. De Santis, and M. Scannapieco, "Automatic Record Matching in Cooperative Information Systems," In *Proceedings of the ICDT'03 International Workshop on Data Quality in Cooperative Information Systems (DQCIS'03), Siena, Italy*, 2003.

[283] V.I. Levenshtein, "Binary codes capable of correcting deletions, insertions and reversals," *Dokl. Akad. Nauk SSSR, 10(8)*, 1966.

[284] L.S. Moss, "Coalgebraic logic," *Ann. Pure Appl. Log., 96*, pp. 277–317, 1999.

[285] B. Jacobs, "Towards a duality result in coalgebraic modal logic," In *Coalgebraic Methods in computer science, H. Reichel (Ed.), Elec. Notes in Theor. Comp. Sci. 33*, 2000.

[286] B. Jacobs, "Many-sorted coalgebraic modal logic: a model-theoretic study," *Theor. Inform. Appl., 35(1)*, pp. 31–59, 2001.

[287] H. Rasiowa and R. Sikorski, "The mathematics of metamathematics," *(3rd edition), Warsaw: PWN - Polisch Scientific Publishers*, 1970.

[288] G. Gentzen, "Über die Existenz unabhängiger Axiomensysteme zu unendlichen Satzsystemen," *Math. Ann., 107*, pp. 329–350, 1932.

[289] P. Hertz, "Über Axiomensysteme für beliebige Satzsysteme," *Math. Ann., 101*, pp. 457–514, 1929.
[290] J. Jipsen and C. Tsinakis, "A survey of residuated lattices," In *Ordered Algebraic Structures, J. Martinez (Ed.), Kluwer Academic Publishers*, pp. 19–56, 2002.
[291] A. Urquhart, "A topological representation theory for lattices," *Algebra Univers., 8*, pp. 45–58, 1978.
[292] C. Brink, D. Gabbay, and H.H. Olhbach, "Towards automating duality," *Technical Repotr MPI-I-93-220, Max-Planck-Institut fur Informatic, Saarbrucken, Germany*, 1993.
[293] M. Haim, "Duality for lattices with operators: a modal logic approach," *http://citeseer.ist.psu.edu/haim00duality.html*, 2000.
[294] S. Celani and R. Jansana, "A new semantics for positive modal logic," *Notre Dame J. Form. Log., 38*, 1997.
[295] J. Dugundji, "Note on a property of matrices for Lewis and Langford's calculi of propositions," *J. Symb. Log., 5*, pp. 150–151, 1940.
[296] R. Goldblatt, "Metamathematics of modal logic," *Rep. Math. Log., 6*, pp. 41–78, *7*, pp. 21–52, 1976.
[297] R.A. Bull and K. Segerberg, "Basic modal logic," In *Handbook of Philosophical Logic II, D. Gabbay and F. Guenther (Eds.), Dodrecht: Reidel*, pp. 1–88, 1984.
[298] B. Beckert, R. Hanhle, and F. Manyá, "Transformations between signed and classical clause logic," In *Proc. 29th Int. Symposium on Multiple-Valued Logics*, pp. 248–255, Freiburg, Germany, 1999.
[299] G. Escalada Imaz and F. Manyá, "The satisfiability problem for multiple-valued Horn formulae," In *Proc. International Symposium on Multiple-Valued Logics (ISMVL), Boston, Los Alamitos: IEEE Press*, pp. 250–256, 1994.
[300] H.A. Blair and V.S. Subrahmanian, "Paraconsistent logic programming," *Theor. Comput. Sci., 68*, pp. 135–154, 1989.
[301] M. Kifer and V.S. Subrahmanian, "Theory of generalized annotated logic programming and its applications," *J. Log. Program., 12(4)*, pp. 335–368, 1992.
[302] C.I. Lewis, "Implication and the algebra of logic," *Mind (New Ser.), 21*, pp. 522–531, 1912.
[303] G. Kalmbach, "Orthomodular lattices," *London: Academic Press*, 1983.
[304] R. Goldblatt, "Semantic analysis of Orthologic," *J. Philos. Log.*, pp. 19–35, 1974.
[305] S.A. Kripke, "Semantical analysis of Intuitionistic logic I," In *Formal Systems and Recursive Functions, J.N. Crossley and M.A. E. Dummett (Eds.), North Holland*, pp. 92–130, 1965.
[306] J.C. C. McKinsey and A. Tarski, "Some theorems about the sentential calculi of Lewis and Langford," *J. Symb. Log., 13*, pp. 1–15, 1948.
[307] J.M. Dunn, "Gaggle theory: An abstraction of Galois connections and residuation with applications to negation and various logical operations," In *JELIA 1990, European Workshop on Logics and Artificial Intelligence, LNCS 478, Springer*, 1991.
[308] D. Nelson, "Negation and separation of concepts in construtive systems," In *Studies in Logic and the Foundations of Mathematics, Amsterdam: North Holland*, pp. 208–225, 1959.
[309] K. Fine, "The justification of negation as failure," In *Logic, Methodology and Philosophy of Science VIII, Amsterdam: North Holland*, pp. 263–301, 1989.
[310] M.C. Fitting, "A Kripke/Kleene semantics for logic programs," *J. Log. Program., 2*, pp. 295–312, 1985.
[311] K. Kunen, "Negation in logic programming," *J. Log. Program., 4*, pp. 289–308, 1987.
[312] T. Przymusinski, "Every logic program has a natural stratification and an iterated fixed point model," In *Eighth ACM Symposium on Principles of Databases Systems*, pp. 11–21, 1989.
[313] T. Przymusinski, "Well-founded semantics coincides with thre-valued stable-semantics," *Fundam. Inform., 13*, pp. 445–463, 1990.

[314] M. Kifer and E.L. Lozinskii, "A logic for reasoning with inconsistency," *J. Autom. Reason., 9(2)*, pp. 179–215, 1992.

[315] M.H. van Emden, "Quantitative deduction and its fixpoint theory," *J. Log. Program., 4(1)*, pp. 37–53, 1986.

[316] S. Morishita, "A unified approach to semantics of multi-valued logic programs," *Tech. Report RT 5006, IBM Tokyo*, 1990.

[317] V.S. Laksmanan and N. Shiri, "A parametric approach to deductive databases with uncertainty," *IEEE Trans. Knowl. Data Eng., 13(4)*, pp. 554–570, 2001.

[318] Z. Majkić, "Logic methods for many-valued logics: Higher-order autoepistemic language concepts," In *4th Indian International Conference on Artificial Intelligence (IICAI-09), Bangalore, India, December*, 2009.

[319] M.C. Fitting, "Bilattices are nice things," In *Proceedings of Conference on Self-Reference, Copenhagen, Denmark*, 2002.

[320] M. Zemankova and A. Kandel, "Implementing imprecision in information systems," *Inf. Sci., 37*, pp. 107–141, 1985.

[321] D. Dubois and H. Prade, "Handling incomplete of uncertain data and vague queries in database applications," In *Possibility Theory: An Approach to Computerized Processing of Uncertainty 6, New York and London: Plenum Press*, pp. 217–257, 1989.

[322] M. Kifer and A. Li, "On the semantics of rule-based expert systems with uncertainty," In *2nd Intl. Conference on Database Theory, LNCS 326, Bruges, Belgium: Spinger Verlag*, pp. 102–117, 1988.

[323] V.S. Lakshmanan, N. Leone, R. Ross, and V.S. Subrahmanian, "A flexible probabilistic database system," *ACM Trans. Database Syst.*, pp. 419–469, 1997.

[324] V.S. Lakshmanan and F. Sadri, "On a theory of probabilistic deductive databases," *CoRR cs. DB/0312043*, 2003.

[325] G. Boole, "The laws of thought," *London: Macmillan*, 1884.

[326] T. Hailperin, "Best possible inequalities for the probability of a logical function of events," *Am. Math. Mon., 72*, pp. 343–359, 1965.

[327] G. Georgakopoulos, D. Kavvadias, and C.H. Papadimitriou, "Probabilistic satisfiability," *J. Complex., 4*, pp. 1–11, 1988.

[328] J.E. Fenstad, "The structure of probabilities defined on first-order languages," In *Studies in inductive logic and probabilities 2, University of California Press*, pp. 251–262, 1980.

[329] P. Walley, "Statistical reasoning with imprecise probabilities," *Chapman and Hall*, 1991.

[330] L.M. de Campos, J.F. Huete, and S. Moral, "Probability intervals: A tool for uncertain reasoning," *Int. J. Uncertain. Fuzziness Knowl.-Based Syst., 2(2)*, pp. 167–196, 1994.

[331] K. Weichselberger, "The theory of interval-probability as a unifying concept for uncertainty," In *Proc. 1st Int. Symp. on Imprecise Probabilities and Their Applications*, 1999.

[332] M. Dekhtyar, A. Dekhtyar, and V.S. Subrahmanian, "Hybrid probabilistic programs: Algorithms and complexity," In *UAI 1999*, pp. 160–169, 1999.

[333] A. Dekhtyar and V.S. Subrahmanian, "Hybrid probabilistic programs," *J. Log. Program., 43(3)*, pp. 187–250, 2000.

[334] M. Dekhtyar, A. Dekhtyar, and V.S. Subrahmanian, "Temporal probabilistic logic programs," In *ICLP 99, Las Cruces, USA*, pp. 109–123, 1999.

[335] M. Dekhtyar and A. Dekhtyar, "Revisiting the semantics of interval probabilistic logic programs," In *LPNMR 2005, September 5–8, Diamante, Cosenza, Italy*, pp. 330–342, 2005.

[336] R. Suszko, "Remarks on Lukasiewicz's three-valued logic," *Bull. Sect. Log., 4*, pp. 87–90, 1975.

[337] D. Batens, "A bridge between two-valued and many-valued semantic systems: n-tuple semantics," In *Proc. of the XII ISMVL*, pp. 318–322, 1982.

[338] D. Scott, "Completeness and axiomatizability in many-valued logic," In *Proc. of Tarski Symposium, Proc. of Symposia in Pure Mathematics 25*, pp. 411–436, 1974.
[339] N.C. A. da Costa, J.Y. Béziau, and O.A. S. Bueno, "Malinowski and Suszko on many-valuedness: on the reduction of many-valuedness to two-valuedness," *Mod. Log., 6*, pp. 272–299, 1996.
[340] C. Caleiro, W.A. Carnielli, M.E. Coniglio, and J. Marcos, "Two's company: The humbug of many logical values," In *Logica Universalis, J.Y. Béziau (Ed.), Birkhauser Verlag*, pp. 169–189, 2005.
[341] Z. Majkić, "Two-valued encapsulation of many-valued logic programming," *Technical Report, University 'La Sapienza', Roma, http://www.dis.uniroma1.it/~majkic/*, 2003.
[342] Z. Majkić, "Truth and knowledge fixpoint semantics for many-valued logic programming," In *19th Workshop on (Constraint) Logic Programming (W(C)LP 2005), February 21–25, Ulm, Germany*, 2005.
[343] R. Routley and R.K. Meyer, "Semantics of entailment I," In *Truth Syntax and Modality, H. Leblanc (Ed.), Amsterdam: North-Holland*, pp. 199–243, 1973.
[344] Z. Majkić and B. Prasad, "Binary sequent calculi for finite many-valued logics," In *5th Indian International Conference on Artificial Intelligence (IICAI-11), India, December*, 2011.
[345] M. Baaz, C.G. Fermüller, and R. Zach, "Systematic construction of natural deduction systems for many-valued logics," In *23rd Int. Syp. on Multiple Valued Logic*, pp. 208–213, 1993.
[346] R. Suszko, "The Fregean axiom and polish mathematical logic in the 1920s," *Stud. Log., 36*, pp. 377–380, 1977.
[347] G. Malinowski, "Many-valued logics," *Oxford Logic Guides 25. Oxford: Clarendon Press*, 1993.
[348] G. Malinowski, "Inferential many-valuedness," In *Philosophical Logic in Poland, J. Wolenski (Ed.), Dodrecht: Kluwer Academic Publishers*, pp. 75–84, 1994.
[349] J. Kotas and N.C. A. da Costa, "Some problems on logical matrices and valorizations," In *Proc. of the 3rd Brazilian Conference on Mathematical Logic*, pp. 131–145, 1980.
[350] A.Y. Halevy, Z.G. Ives, J. Madhavan, P. Mork, D. Suciu, and I. Tatarinov, "The Piazza peer data management system," *IEEE Trans. Knowl. Data Eng., 16(7)*, pp. 787–798, 2004.
[351] A. Fuxman, P.G. Kolaitis, R. Miller, and W.C. Tan, "Peer data exchange," *ACM TODS, 31(4)*, pp. 1454–1498, 2006.
[352] M.A. V. Salles, J.P. Dittrich, S.K. Karakashian, O.R. Girard, and L. Blunschi, "iTrial: Pay-as-you-go information integration in dataspaces," In *Proc. of VLDB, Vienna, Austria*, pp. 663–674, 2007.
[353] P. Bernstein, A. Halevy, and R. Pottinger, "A vision for management of complx models," *SIGMOD Rec., 29(4)*, pp. 55–63, 2000.
[354] R. Goldblat, "Topoi: the categorial analysis of logic," *Amsterdam: North-Holland*, 1979.
[355] G. Rosolini, "Continuity and effectiveness in Topoi," *Ph.D. dissertation, Oxford University, Also preprint, Department of Computer Science, Carnegie-Mellon University*, 1986.
[356] S. Abiteboul, R. Hull, and V. Vianu, "Foundations of Databases," *Reading, Massachusetts: Addison Wesley Publ. Co.*, 1995.
[357] Z. Diskin, "Generalized sketches as an algebraic graph-based framework for semantic modeling and database design," *Laboratory for Database Design, FIS/LDBD-97-03*, 1997.
[358] M. Makkai, "Generalized sketches as a framework for completeness theorems," *Technical report, McGill University*, 1994.
[359] Z. Majkić, "Algebraic operators for matching and merging of relational databases," In *International Conference in Artificial Intelligence and Pattern Recognition (AIPR-09), Orlando FL, USA, July 13–16*, 2009.
[360] Z. Majkić, "Induction principle in relational database category," In *Int. Conference on Theoretical and Mathematical Foundations of Computer Science (TMFCS-09), Orlando FL, USA, July 13–16*, 2009.

[361] Z. Majkić, "DB category: Denotational semantics for view-based database mappings," *arXiv:1103.0217v1*, pp. 1–40, 2011.
[362] Z. Majkić, "Matching, merging and structural properties of data base category," *arXiv:1102.2395v1*, pp. 1–27, 2011.
[363] Z. Majkić, "Abstract database category based on relational-query observations," In *International Conference on Theoretical and Mathematical Foundations of Computer Science (TMFCS-08), Orlando FL, USA, July 7–9*, 2008.
[364] P. Buneman, S. Davidson, and A. Kosky, "Theoretical aspects of schema merging," In *EDBT 1992*, pp. 152–167, 1992.
[365] J.R. Büchi, "Weak second-order arithmetic and finite automata," *Z. Math. Logic Grundl. Math., 6*, pp. 66–92, 1960.
[366] G. Gotlob and C. Koch, "Monadic datalog and the expressive power of languages for web information extraction," *J. ACM, 51*, pp. 74–113, 2004.
[367] A. Corradini, "A complete calculus for equational deduction in coalgebraic specification," *Report SEN-R9723, National Research Institute for Mathematics and Computer Science, Amsterdam*, 1997.
[368] D. McLeod and D. Heimbigner, "A Federated architecture for information management," *ACM Trans. Inf. Syst., 3(3)*, pp. 253–278, 1985.
[369] A. Sheth and J. Larsen, "Federated database systems for managing distributed, heterogenuous and autonomous databases," *ACM Comput. Surv., 22(3)*, pp. 183–236, 1990.
[370] A. Calì, D. Calvanese, G. De Giacomo, and M. Lenzerini, "Reasoning in data integration systems: why LAV and GAV are siblings," In *Proceedings of the 14th International Symposium on Methodologies for Intelligent Systems, ISMIS 2003 2871, Springer*, pp. 282–289, 2003.
[371] R. Fagin, "Inverting schema mappings," *ACM TODS, 32(4)*, pp. 25–78, 2005.
[372] A. Kementsietsidis, M. Arenas, and R.J. Miller, "Mapping data in peer-to-peer systems: Semantics and alghotitmic issues," In *Proc. of SIGMOD*, 2003.
[373] S. Davidson, P. Buneman, and A. Kosky, "Semantics of database transformations," In *Semantics in Databases, B. Thalheim and L. Libkin (Eds.), LNCS 1358*, pp. 55–91, 1998.
[374] R. Miller, L. Haas, and M. Hernandez, "Schema mapping as query discovery," In *Proc. VLDB*, pp. 77–88, 2000.
[375] Z. Majkić, "The category-theoretic semantics for database mappings," *Technical Report 14-03, University 'La Sapienza', Roma, Italy*, 2003.
[376] J. Madhavan, P.A. Bernstein, P. Domingos, and A.Y. Halevy, "Representing and reasoning about mappings between domain models," In *AAAI/IAAI*, pp. 80–86, 2002.
[377] D. Beneventano, M. Lenzerini, F. Mandreoli, and Z. Majkić, "Techniques for query reformulation, query merging, and information reconciliation-part A," In *Semantic Webs and Agents in Integrated Economies, D3.2.A, IST-2001-34825*, 2003.
[378] I. Zaihrayeu, "Query answering in peer-to-peer database networks," *Technical Report DIT-03-012, University of Trento, Italy*, 2003.
[379] R. Fagin, "Horn clauses and database dependencies," *J. ACM, 29*, pp. 952–985, 1982.
[380] J. Madhavn and A. Halevy, "Composing mappings among data sources," In *Proc. of VLDB*, pp. 572–583, 2003.
[381] S. Melnik, P.A. Bernstein, A. Halevy, and E. Rahm, "Supporting executable mapping in model management," In *SIGMOD*, pp. 167–178, 2005.
[382] A. Nash, P. Bernstein, and S. Melnik, "Composition of mappings given by embedded dependencies," In *Proc. of PODS*, pp. 172–183, 2005.
[383] R. Fagin, P.G. Kolaitis, L. Popa, and W. Tan, "Quasy-inverses of schema mappings," *ACM TODS, 33(2)*, pp. 1–52, 2008.
[384] P.J. Freyd and G.M. Kelly, "Categories of continuous functors, I," *J. Pure Appl. Algebra, 2*, pp. 169–191, 1972.

[385] D.S. Johnson and A.C. Klug, "Testing containment of conjunctive queries under functional and inclusion dependencies," *J. Comput. Syst. Sci., 28*, pp. 167–189, 1984.

[386] R. Reiter, "On closed world databases," In *Logic and Databases, H. Gallaire and J. Minker (Eds.), New York: Plenul Press*, pp. 55–76, 1978.

[387] R.J. Brachman and H.J. Levesque, editors. "Readings in Knowledge Representation," 1985.

Index

https://doi.org/10.1515/9783110981438-009

Bei Fragen zur Produktsicherheit wenden Sie sich bitte an:
If you have any questions regarding product safety,
please contact:

Walter de Gruyter GmbH
Genthiner Straße 13
10785 Berlin
productsafety@degruyterbrill.com